BUTTERWORTHS PLANNING LAW HANDBOOK

Fourth Edition

Edited by

BRIAN GREENWOOD, LLB, *Solicitor*
Partner, Norton Rose

BUTTERWORTHS
LONDON, DUBLIN AND EDINBURGH
1995

United Kingdom	Butterworths a Division of Reed Elsevier (UK) Ltd, Halsbury House, 35 Chancery Lane, LONDON WC2A 1EL and 4 Hill Street, EDINBURGH EH2 3JZ
Australia	Butterworths, SYDNEY, MELBOURNE, BRISBANE, ADELAIDE, PERTH, CANBERRA and HOBART
Canada	Butterworths Canada Ltd, TORONTO and VANCOUVER
Ireland	Butterworth (Ireland) Ltd, DUBLIN
Malaysia	Malayan Law Journal Sdn Bhd, KUALA LUMPUR
New Zealand	Butterworths of New Zealand Ltd, WELLINGTON and AUCKLAND
Puerto Rico	Butterworths of Puerto Rico, Inc, SAN JUAN
Singapore	Reed Elsevier (Singapore) Pte Ltd, SINGAPORE
South Africa	Butterworth Publishers (Pty) Ltd, DURBAN
USA	Butterworth Legal Publishers, CARLSBAD, California and SALEM, New Hampshire

A CIP Catalogue record for this book is available from the British Library.

ISBN 0 406 08128 X

Typeset, printed and bound in Great Britain by
William Clowes Limited, Beccles and London

PREFACE

This work has now entered its fourth edition. Some three years have passed since the Planning and Compensation Act 1991 reached the statute book, requiring the planning practitioner to come to terms with *planning obligations* (still doggedly known by many as planning agreements), *certificates of lawfulness of proposed use or development* (how reassuring to see that the decidedly ugly abbreviation CLOPUD does not appear to be gaining universal acceptance) and the much misunderstood *section 54A* which did not so much introduce a radical amendment to the planning code (as claimed by many) but rather merely helped to clarify and in so doing confirm the proper status of the development plan.

It is of course always difficult to identify with confidence when is the right time to produce another edition of what happily seems to be a successful formula. The stimulus has on this occasion been provided by the so-called "consolidation" of the General Development Order 1988 by two new orders, the TCP (General Permitted Development Order) 1995 and the TCP (General Development Procedure) Order 1995, known hereafter as the "Permitted Development Order" and the "Procedure Order". In addition the government has radically amended the Town and Country Planning (Use Classes) Order 1987, while at the same time implementing the European Union's Habitat Directive by way of the Conservation (Natural Habitats etc) Regulations 1994. Further, even as my ever patient publishers were finalising the proofs, the Environment Act 1995 received the Royal Assent. In the context of town and country planning this Act has revised and extended the statutory provisions relating to National Parks (ss 61–79), and introduced an inevitably complex procedure for the review of old mineral planning permissions.

A new edition was inevitable, yet the purpose of the Handbook remains as before. It is designed first and foremost as a compact, portable, single volume comprising all the primary and secondary legislation to which the practitioner or student is likely to wish to refer on a day-to-day basis.

To a certain extent, the Handbook also acts as a supplement to the *Butterworths Planning Law Service*, providing an easy compendium of relevant legislation to accompany the looseleaf format of the *Service*. This means that we will be able to update the Handbook by adding copies of the relevant primary and secondary legislation to the Noter-up section of the *Service* as and when required. The intention is that the *Service* will then act as a temporary resting place until publication of the next edition of the Handbook.

As in any such work, the editor must take full responsibility for the contents. The material that has been included is my choice and I must therefore accept the blame for any omissions. It is impossible to satisfy the needs of all planning practitioners all of the time, but I hope that the choice of primary legislation together with a selection of what I believe to be the most important statutory instruments and regulations will be of use to both practitioner and student.

Inevitably, such a work is the result of the efforts of many. I must acknowledge with considerable thanks (and awe) my learned colleagues at Halsbury's Statutes who have worked on the text, produced the annotations and updated the myriad of statutory instruments with frightening efficiency.

In addition, I am pleased to have the opportunity to recognise with thanks the assistance of the contributors to the *Butterworths Planning Law Service* whose work I have freely borrowed in writing the "Basic Summary of Planning Law" which appears as an introduction to this handbook. My special thanks in this regard go to Paul Shadarevian my partner at Norton Rose for his support, Michael Brainsby of English Heritage for his work on the division in the Service on listed buildings and conservation areas, Dick Hamilton, one of the few people in my acquaintance who actually understands the complex area of planning compensation, and Jenny Treleaven, formerly of the College of Law, who cared for the section in the *Planning Law Service* on Enforcement, and who sadly died before this fourth edition was published. I and many others owe her a great debt.

Brian Greenwood   September 1995
Norton Rose
Kempson House
Camomile Street
London EC3A 7AN

CONTENTS

INTRODUCTION
A BASIC SUMMARY OF PLANNING LAW

A   PLANNING AUTHORITIES, POLICY AND PLANS

1. Planning authorities

The Secretary of State   The administration of the planning system operates on two levels. On the strategic level, the Secretary of State for the Environment represents central government and has overall responsibility for the English planning system and the planning process. Supported by his Department, he exercises supervisory and appellate functions over the local level which comprises essentially the local authorities. He provides specialist advice on the operation of the planning system generally, and acts as the source of central government planning policy. The Secretary of State for Wales and the Welsh Office exercise comparable functions in Wales, whilst the Secretary of State for National Heritage also enjoys certain planning functions, for example the listing of buildings.

Local government   The wishes of central government are given practical effect by local authorities. It is at this local tier of government that the majority of the day-to-day operational control—plan making, development control and enforcement—is exercised. This tier consists essentially of county, district and London borough councils, but there are also a number of specialised non-elected bodies that have been created in an attempt to simplify and speed the planning process—eg urban development corporations and the Urban Regeneration Agency.

The bodies at the local level have development control responsibility within the confines of their administrative area. Such control encompasses not just the granting of planning permission for proposed development or enforcement in the case of unauthorised development, but also what are best described as special planning regimes, for example conservation areas, listed buildings, advertisement control, etc, all of which comprise other (although not lesser) elements in modern town planning.

The two-tier system   The two-tier system seeks to deal with the conflicting needs of democratic control and efficiency. Inevitably there are in-built conflicts between the local authorities at one level and the Secretary of State at central government level. These are an inherent feature of a system of dual democratic control. The ultimate power of decision on all but a few matters rests with central government. The Secretary of State can therefore wield enormous influence on a day-to-day basis through policy statements, circulars and planning policy guidance notes.

2. Planning policy—central government

The integration of national and regional policy with policy at local level is a pre-requisite to the proper functioning of the planning system. Decisions at national level or regional level will more often than not impact on planning policy at local level. For example, the identification of a need at regional level for industrial and commercial activity can have serious implications for housing provision and other social infrastructure at the local level. Even where the tone of national and regional policy is 'laissez-faire' in approach, specific land use issues will remain to be dealt with locally.

At regional or national level, policy guidance and analysis will be couched inevitably in strategic and general terms. For the Secretary of State, policy pronouncements are embodied in circulars and their policy successors, planning

vii

policy guidance notes (PPGs), regional policy guidance notes (RPGs) and mineral policy guidance notes (MPGs).

3. Planning policy—local government

The planning system inaugurated in 1947 termed the document that comprised the local planning policies for an area the 'Development Plan'. That term is still in use despite the fact that a detailed single development plan, the child of the 1947 regime, was replaced in 1968 by a two-tier system of development plans: structure plans (dealing with the general strategic and long-term issues) and local plans (dealing in effect with local detail). By virtue of the Local Government Act 1985, a futher variation has now appeared, namely the 'unitary development plan'.

Structure plans, with their regional as opposed to local bias, are prepared by the county planning authorities. As a general rule, local plans are prepared by the district councils. Unitary development plans are produced by the metropolitan district councils and the 32 London boroughs and the Corporation of the City of London. The unitary development plan is designed to combine the strategic elements of the structure plan with the detailed planning guidance of the local plan. It should be noted that a radical upheaval in the development plan process is probably unavoidable with the imminent reorganisation of local government outside London and the metropolitan conurbations.

Reference: (i) TCPA 1990, Pt I and Pt II;
(ii) Planing Law Service, Division A.

B   THE NEED FOR PLANNING PERMISSION

1. The meaning of development

The concept of 'development' is the foundation of the statutory system of planning control. The underlying principle is that if a proposal involves 'development' (as defined by statute) it will require planning permission. Such permission, depending upon the nature of the development, may either be granted expressly by a local planning authority or the Secretary of State, or be deemed to be granted by statute or order.

Development is defined in the TCPA 1990, s 55 as 'the carrying out of building, engineering, mining or other operations in, on, over or under land, or the making of any material change in the use of any buildings or other land'. The definition has two main components commonly referred to as the 'operational limb' and the 'use limb'.

'Operations' and 'use'   The essence of operational development is that the operation will result in a physical change in the character of the land. 'Use' in the planning context refers basically to the use to which the land or building is put—but although simple in concept, it is not always so simple in practical application. It must be remembered that it is the *change* of use that amounts to development, not the mere fact that a use is continuing on the land. If a change in the use of land is not considered to be 'material', that change may not constitute 'development' as defined by the TCPA 1990. A material change of use may, however, occur if the character of the use changes, even if it remains the same in kind—for example if it can be said that the use has been so intensified that it has altered in character.

In an attempt to ease the practical day-to-day application of these two basic but nevertheless complicated concepts of planning law, the government has issued secondary legislation which has an important bearing on both operational development and change of use.

2. The Town and Country Planning (Use Classes) Order 1987

One of the basic purposes of the TCPA 1990 is to regulate the 'development' of land which includes both the carrying out of 'operations' in, on, over or under land and the change in use of land or buildings, if that change is 'material'. The TCPA 1990, s 55(2)(f), however, provides that a change of use will not amount to development and therefore will not require planning permission where the former use and the new use are both within the same class specified in the relevant order made under the provisions of the Act. The present order is the Town and Country Planning (Use Classes Order) 1987, as amended.

The Order is divided into four parts, namely:

Part A shopping area uses (essentially the type of use that one would expect to find in a typical high street);

Part B other business and industrial uses which include office, high technology uses and storage;

Part C residential uses which encompass hotels, hostels as well as dwelling-houses; and

Part D social and community uses of a non-residential kind, and assembly and leisure.

The operation of the Use Classes Order may be restricted by means of a planning condition or by means of a legal agreement. The order is not exhaustive and not every use falls within a particular class. In addition, the order expressly provides that some uses are 'sui generis'—effectively, in a class of their own.

Reference: (i) TCP (Use Classes Order) 1987 (SI 1987/764) as amended;
  (ii) Planning Law Service, Division B2.

3. Town and Country Planning (General Permitted Development) Order 1995

The general rule is that planning permission is required for the development of land. The TCP (General Permitted Development) Order 1995 (the 'Permitted Development Order'), however, specifies certain categories of development for which permission is 'deemed' to be granted, thus making a formal application for planning permission unnecessary. If it is not clear whether the development proposed is permitted under the Order, then an application may be made to the local planning authority for a Certificate of Lawfulness of Proposed Use or Development under the provisions of the TCPA 1990, s 192. The Permitted Development Order, together with the TCP (General Development Procedure) Order 1995 (the 'Procedure Order') consolidate the TCP General Development Order 1988. To all practical intents and purposes, planning procedure ie matters relating to planning applications, publicity, formal notices etc are now located in the Procedure Order, whilst the Permitted Development Order comprises those classes of development for which, subject to specified conditions, caveats and qualifications etc, planning permission will not be required.

The principal Act and the Permitted Development Order, have also clarified previous uncertainty as to whether demolition constitutes development requiring planning permission. The TCPA 1990, s 55(1A) provides that a 'building operation' includes demolition and rebuilding. By virtue of the Permitted Development Order and a direction made by the Secretary of State, however, demolition of most buildings is deemed to constitute permitted development, subject to certain specific exceptions, essentially residential dwellings.

A Special Development Order may restrict the general operation of the Permitted Development Order or, alternatively, may extend its ambit. Categories of permitted development include, for example, certain defined development within the curtilage of a dwellinghouse (Part 1), minor operations (Part 2), industrial and warehouse development (Part 8), development by local authorities (Part 12), development by statutory undertakers (Part 17), and demolition of buildings (Part 31). By its very nature, the type of development deemed to be permitted by the Permitted Development Order is usually of a minor or insubstantial kind and is, in any case, only granted subject to numerous conditions, exceptions and limitations. In addition, the development rights bestowed by the Order do not apply to land which is being used unlawfully ie in contravention of the TCPA 1990 or in contravention of previous planning control.

Permitted development rights may be excluded by a condition imposed by the local planning authority on the grant of planning permission, a planning obligation made under the provisions of the TCPA 1990, s 106 or a direction made under Art 4 of the Permitted Development Order, in which case compensation may become payable.

Reference: (i) TCPA 1990, s 55 and s 59;
            (ii) TCP (General Permitted Development) Order 1995 (SI 1995/418);
           (iii) TCP (General Development Procedure) Order 1995 (SI 1995/419);
            (iv) Planning Law Service, Division B4.

C   OBTAINING PLANNING PERMISSION

1. The nature of the grant of planning permission

Subject to the important exceptions discussed in the preceding paragraphs, the general rule is that planning permission is required for the carrying out of any development of land (TCPA 1990, s 57).

Unless the permission provides otherwise, planning permission benefits and runs with the land to which the permission relates and is not personal to the applicant (s 75). The permission must, however, be implemented within specific time limits (s 91), may be granted subject to conditions, for example as to duration, size of development, identity of occupier, etc (s 70), and may be revoked or modified in which case compensation may become payable (s 97).

The formal grant of planning permission only authorises development for the purposes of the TCPA 1990, Pt III. Consequently, other approvals such as listed building consent, conservation area consent or building regulation approval must still be obtained in the appropriate circumstances. The grant of planning permission will not override any restrictive covenants affecting the development of the land, nor will the grant of permission override any restrictions contained in a planning obligation made under the TCPA 1990, s 106.

2. Applications for planning permission

An application for planning permission is made on a form obtainable from the local planning authority. The applicant must provide the information required by the form, together with sufficient plans and drawings to describe the development. The application must be accompanied by a certificate complying with the provisions of the Procedure Order 1995 to the effect that, either the applicant owns the land, or the necessary notices have been served on the owner or published locally. In some cases, notice of the application will also have to be advertised in a local newspaper and/or by way of site notice, the responsibility for such publicity falling to the local planning authority.

A fee is payable for most types of applications. Reduced fees are payable for certain categories of applications and certain developments are exempt.

Outline application   A planning application may be made in outline. This enables the local authority to approve the development in principle leaving 'reserved matters' for subsequent approval. The reserved matters comprise 'siting, design, means of access, external appearance and landscaping'. The applicant may seek to reserve all or any of the reserved matters. An application for the approval of reserved matters must be made within three years of the date of the permission or such other period as may be provided. Approval of reserved matters may be granted in phases.

Detailed application In the alternative, an applicant may submit an application for detailed or full planning permission. Such an application will include all the details and information necessary for the local planning authority to determine the application—no matters being reserved for further consideration.

The planning authority In Greater London, applications for planning permission are made to the appropriate London borough council. Elsewhere, applications are normally made to the district planning authority. Certain categories of applications, however, fall for determination by other bodies, for example, county councils in relation to defined mineral applications.

Obligation to determine The local planning authority are required to determine an application for planning permission within eight weeks of submission, or where an environmental statement is submitted, within sixteen weeks. In determining the application the authority must have regard to the development plan and all other material considerations.

Power to decline to determine an application By virtue of the TCPA 1990, s 70A, the local planning authority may decline to determine an application for planning permission if within the previous two years a similar application has been submitted and refused by the Secretary of State, there having been in that period no significant change in either the development plan or any other material consideration.

Reference: (i) TCPA 1990, Pt III;
(ii) Planning Law Service, Division C1 to 3.

3. An environmental statement

An applicant must produce an environmental statement describing the likely environmental effects of the proposed development if the application falls within Sch 1 or Sch 2 of the TCP (Assessment of Environmental Effects) Regulations 1988. The local authority will then be required to take into account all environmental information, including the applicant's statement, before reaching a decision. An applicant may effectively appeal against a local authority's requirement that an environmental statement be submitted, by applying to the Secretary of State for a direction. Conversely, the Secretary of State may himself require an environmental statement in the context of an appeal or call-in.

Reference: (i) TCPA 1990, s 71A (inserted by PCA 1991, s 15);
(ii) TCP (Assessment of Environmental Effects) Regulations 1988 (SI 1988/965);
(iii) Planning Law Service, Division C4.

4. The Secretary of State

In the context of applications for planning permission (as opposed to appeals), local planning authorities are obliged to notify the Secretary of State if they propose to grant planning permission for development that falls within certain categories defined by government direction. In such cases permission may not be granted by the local authority during the prescribed period. The Secretary of State may also call in any application for his own decision at any time prior to its formal determination, by virtue of a direction issued under the TCPA 1990, s 77. The Secretary of State's policy, however, is only to do so where a development gives rise to issues of more than local importance.

5. The determination of the application

Local planning authorities are given a discretion as to how planning applications are to be determined. This essentially means that their eventual judgment cannot be challenged in the courts unless it can be proved that they have failed to take into account relevant considerations, have taken into account irrelevant considerations, have based their decision on improper motives or have acted entirely irrationally. The TCPA 1990 directs local planning authorities to have regard to certain prescribed matters. These are the provisions of the development plan, any other material considerations and the representations which have been made as a result of the various statutory provisions requiring consultation and publicity.

In addition, the status of the development plan has been considerably enhanced by virtue of the TCPA 1990, s 54A (introduced by the PCA 1991, s 26) which provides that where 'in making any determination under the planning Acts, regard is to be had to the development plan, the determination shall be made in accordance with the Plan unless material considerations indicate otherwise.'

'*Material considerations*' basically encompass any planning considerations which are relevant to the particular application. This means that strictly any representations which are not about planning, or are not relevant, should not be considered and the same principle could apply to the policies in the development plan. It also seems that there is no hierarchy or weighting which applies to the specified matters. The weight to be given to each matter is left to the judgment of the local planning authority. The overriding principle is that no one factor is conclusive as a matter of law, provided the decision is neither perverse nor irrational.

Reference: (i) TCPA 1990, Pt III;
            (ii) Planning Law Service, Division C8.

6. Conditions

The TCPA 1990, s 70 empowers the local planning authority to grant planning permission 'either unconditionally or subject to such conditions as they think fit'. Conditions may regulate the development or use of any land under the control of the applicant—even if that land does not form part of the application site; require the carrying-out of works on such land if expedient in connection with the development authorised; or require the removal of any buildings or works authorised by the permission or the discontinuance of use and the carrying-out of works at the end of a specified period.

Circular 11/95 (WO 35/95) (which is about to be updated—Summer 1995) advises that conditions should only be imposed where they are:

    (i) necessary;
   (ii) relevant to planning;
  (iii) relevant to the development to be permitted;
  (iv) enforceable;
   (v) precise; and
  (vi) reasonable in all other respects.

In this context it should be noted that conditions may be challenged in the courts on the grounds of their 'validity'.

Reference: (i) TCPA 1990, ss 70 and 72;
            (ii) Planning Law Service, Division C9.

7. Revocation or modification of planning permission or of existing use rights

A planning permission may be revoked or modified by order made by a local planning authority or the Secretary of State. Where such an order is opposed, the

Secretary of State's confirmation must first be obtained before the order can become effective. Different procedures apply to revocation or modification orders depending on whether objections are submitted. In addition, the making of a revocation or modification order gives rise to a claim for compensation, except where the consent of those affected by the order is obtained. Where a permission has been implemented or where no permission has been granted, the local planning authority may make an order (a discontinuance order) to require the discontinuance of a use or to impose conditions on the continuation of a use or to require the alteration or removal of any buildings or works. A discontinuance order will only take effect when confirmed by the Secretary of State. Such an order will also give rise to a claim for compensation.

Reference: (i) TCPA 1990, s 100;
(ii) Planning Law Service, Division C12.

8. Planning obligations

The legal instrument known as a *planning obligation* was introduced by the PCA 1990, s 12 and is now embodied in the TCPA 1990, s 106. It is a concept that comprises both the *obligation by agreement*, previously known by virtue of the TCPA 1971 as a 'section 52 agreement', and the *'obligation by [unilateral] undertaking'*.

Obligation by agreement   Prior to 1991 the use of planning agreements had become widespread. They provided a means whereby anyone with a legal interest in land could enter into an agreement with a local planning authority which restricted or regulated the use of land. In cases where the Local Government (Miscellaneous Provisions) Act 1982, s 33 had been cited as an enabling statute, positive obligations could also be imposed. Such agreements were usually prepared in connection with the grant of planning permission, although their use was not limited to just those circumstances.

The concept of the planning obligation introduced by the PCA 1991 has changed neither the philosophy nor the practice of planning agreements. Although the enabling legislation in the TCPA 1990, s 106 has been completely revised by the PCA 1991, s 12, the theory and practical implications remain the same. A person who wishes to enter into a planning obligation by way of agreement must have a 'transferable' interest in the land. The obligation may restrict or regulate the use of land and may now also include positive obligations, without the need to cite the Local Government (Miscellaneous Provisions) Act 1982, s 33—which is in any case now statutorily excluded. An obligation by agreement may be enforced by the local planning authority against both the original party and successors in title. Local planning authorities have the power to enter upon premises themselves to carry out works contemplated by the obligation and to recover the money due for such works.

Obligation by undertaking: the unilateral undertaking   Unilateral undertakings are not a substitute for agreements, but rather afford the landowner/developer an additional negotiating weapon. For example, if it is considered that discussions with the local planning authority designed to secure a planning permission are being unnecessarily protracted, it is now possible for the applicant to enter into a planning obligation by means of a unilateral undertaking. The undertaking will be couched in conditional terms, the applicant undertaking perhaps to carry out off-site infrastructure works or not to use the land for a particular purpose subject to the grant of planning permission etc. An undertaking can be offered in connection with an appeal against refusal of planning permission. In such circumstances it will be treated by the Secretary of State as part of the appeal 'package' and may be a reason for allowing the appeal. If accepted by the Secretary of State, the developer will be legally bound to comply with the terms of that undertaking and the local planning authority will be able to enforce the undertaking against him.

Both types of planning obligation must be entered into as a legal instrument executed as a deed.

Modification or discharge   Under the old provisions, a planning agreement could only be discharged or varied by way of negotiation with the local planning authority or, in the case of restrictive covenants, by application to the Lands Tribunal, on specific legal grounds. This was notwithstanding that the planning purpose of the agreement may have been fulfilled.

The new provisions relating to planning obligations introduced by the PCA 1991 are not retrospective. They were brought into effect on the 25th October 1991. As a consequence, any planning agreements entered into before that date may still only be varied or discharged by negotiation or by application to the Lands Tribunal.

The amended provisions have introduced an entirely new procedure for the modification or discharge of planning obligations entered into after the 25th October 1991. It will still be open for an applicant to negotiate modification or discharge with a local planning authority. If this does not prove possible, however, the applicant may, after the expiry of a specified period, formally submit an application to the local planning authority for the modification or discharge of the obligation. On receipt of the application, the test to be considered by the local planning authority is whether the obligation still 'serves a useful purpose'. If the application is refused, the applicant may appeal to the Secretary of State for the Environment and in the appropriate circumstances, a public inquiry may be held.

Planning gain/planning benefit   Planning obligations are not uncontroversial, particularly in relation to the concept of planning gain. The term 'planning gain' has no statutory significance and is not now used in policy guidance. In practice, however, planning gain remains a vital instrument in the hands of applicant and local planning authority alike when negotiating a planning permission. Government guidance, Circular 16/91, lays down specific tests for the reasonableness of any benefit sought by way of planning obligation, the circumstances being essentially those where 'the benefit sought is related to the development and necessary to the grant of permission'.

Reference: (i) TCPA 1990, s 106;
             (ii) Planning Law Service, Division C13.

9. Development by local authorities

Local planning authorities wishing to obtain planning permission for their own purposes are obliged to comply with the procedures set out in the TCP General Regulations 1992, SI 1992/1492.

Reference: Planning Law Service, Division C15.

10. Development by statutory undertakers

Statutory undertakers, like local planning authorities, are subject to the controls imposed by the planning legislation. In many cases, however, they enjoy a privileged position within the planning system. Under the TCPA 1990, s 55(2)(c) certain activities undertaken by statutory undertakers are excluded from the definition of development. Further, although statutory undertakers enjoy the benefit of the general provisions of the Use Classes Order 1987, they also benefit from specific grants of planning permission for defined operations contained in the latter parts of the second Schedule to the Permitted Development Order 1995, most of which are confined to their operational land or the relevant undertaking.

Reference: Planning Law Service, Division C16.

11. Development by the Crown

The TCPA 1990, s 299 provides that in circumstances where Crown land is to be disposed of, it is possible for planning permission to be granted on a contingent basis whereby planning permission takes effect upon disposal to a third party. In respect of Crown development on Crown land, informal procedures have evolved. The most recent is set out in the Department of the Environment's Circular 18/84. Generally, the Crown, which includes government departments, is not subject to the provisions of the TCPA 1990, in respect of development carried out by it or its agencies on Crown land. It should be noted, however, that the Crown may enter into planning obligations under the TCPA 1990, s 106, the provisions of which may be enforced by the relevant local planning authority, subject to certain exceptions.

Reference: Planning Law Service, Division C17.

D ADDITIONAL CONTROLS AND POWERS

1. Listed buildings

Buildings are listed for their protection and preservation. The Secretary of State for National Heritage is under a statutory duty to prepare a list of buildings which he considers to be of 'special architectural or historic interest'.

Once listed, the building receives special protection and no works of demolition or works for its alteration or extension which will affect its character are permitted without listed building consent. The requirement to obtain listed building consent is entirely separate from the requirement to obtain planning permission under the TCPA 1990, s 57. If development requiring planning permission is involved, then it will be necessary to obtain both listed building consent and planning permission.

The local planning authority and the Secretary of State for the Environment, where appropriate, have the power to:

(i) serve a building preservation notice, the effect of which will be to render the building subject to immediate, albeit temporary, listed building status;

(ii) grant listed building consent, with or without conditions;

(iii) refuse listed building consent—appeal lies to the Secretary of State;

(iv) commence enforcement action if works have been carried out without authorisation;

(v) compulsorily acquire a listed building that is not properly being preserved;

(vi) carry out works urgently necessary for the preservation of a listed building;

(vii) contribute by way of a grant to the preservation of listed buildings.

There is no right to object per se to the listing of a building. Further, it is an offence of strict liability for any person to do or permit any action which causes or is likely to cause damage to a listed building.

Reference: (i) LBCA 1990, Pt I;
(ii) PPG15 'Planning and the Historic Environment' (England);
(iii) Planning Law Service, Division D1.

2. Conservation areas

Although the listed building regime could be used to achieve a degree of protection for a group of buildings, the process of listing is really only designed to protect individual buildings. It is the area-based protection provided by the concept of conservation areas which gives statutory protection to a locality whose appearance or character (based on its special architectural or historic interest) merits protection. The provisions of the LBCA 1990 encompass the demolition of unlisted buildings (conservation area consent), the creation of conservation areas and the special considerations to be applied when, inter alia, determining planning applications for the development of land within conservation areas.

Reference: (i) LBCA 1990, Pt II;
            (ii) PPG15 'Planning and the Historic Environment' (England);
            (iii) Planning Law Service, Division D1.

3. Ancient monuments

An ancient monument will enjoy protected status if it is included in the 'Schedule' maintained by the Secretary of State for the National Heritage by virtue of the powers granted by the Ancient Monuments and Archaeological Areas Act 1979. There are various categories of monument as defined by statute.

Scheduled Monument Consent must be obtained before any works are carried out that might affect a scheduled monument. There are limited exemptions to this rule set out in delegated legislation. Applications for consent are submitted to the Secretary of State for the National Heritage, who may hold a public inquiry or convene a hearing.

Reference: (i) Ancient Monuments and Archaeological Areas Act 1979;
            (ii) Planning Law Service, Division D4.

4. Archaeological areas

Areas of archaeological importance may be designated as such by the Secretary of State for National Heritage, English Heritage, the relevant local planning authority, or in the broads, the Broads Authority.

Once designated, it is an offence to carry out certain specified operations in an area of archaeological importance without express consent. By virtue of the Ancient Monuments and Archaeological Areas Act 1979 provision may be made for the temporary protection of archaeological sites to enable the fact of their existence to be recorded. The Secretary of State's policy on archaeological remains on land, including presentation, recording finds and the treatment of discoveries within the development control system is found in PPG16.

Reference: (i) Ancient Monuments and Archaeological Areas Act 1979;
            (ii) PPG16 'Archaeology and Planning';
            (iii) Planning Law Service, Division D5.

5. Advertisements

The general rule is that the display of advertisements requires express consent. To this rule must be added two broad categories of exception:

(i) those advertisements totally excluded from the TCP (Control of Advertisements) Regulations 1992; and

(ii) those advertisements that may be displayed with consent deemed to be granted.

Applications for express consent are submitted to the relevant local planning authority which has the power to:

(i) grant or refuse consent to display advertisements;

(ii) revoke or modify such consent;

(iii) discontinue the display of advertisements that are displayed with deemed consent; or

(iv) prosecute in the case of advertisements displayed without consent.

Once granted, consent runs with the land and is not affected by a change of ownership. Appeal lies to the Secretary of State. It should be noted that the law of advertisements is designed to control the display of advertisements—not their subject matter nor their content.

Reference: (i) TCPA 1990, ss 220–225;
             (ii) TCP (Control of Advertisements) Regulations 1992 (SI 1992/666);
             (iii) Planning Law Service, Division D8.

6. Trees

The felling and cutting of trees does not involve 'development' and therefore does not require planning permission, unless it can be argued that the extent of the works amount to an engineering or other operation. The contribution made by trees to the rural and urban landscape is recognised and provided for by the planning legislation. The TCPA 1990 imposes a general duty upon the local planning authority to consider the amenity value of trees in the exercise of their development control functions, and provides separate machinery for the protection of selected trees and woodlands through the making of orders for their preservation and protection in the interests of amenity. Development plans may also contain special policies for the planting and protection of trees.

The principal powers available to the local planning authority for the protection of trees are planning conditions imposed upon the grant of planning permission and the making of tree preservation orders. Planning conditions may be used to protect existing trees during development or to provide for additional planting to ensure adequate landscaping when planning permission is granted. They may also be used in conjunction with tree preservation orders if appropriate.

A tree preservation order prohibits the cutting or destruction of a tree without consent granted under the order, or where those acts are otherwise authorised by exemptions included in the order itself or provided for by statute. Tree preservation orders may be made at any time and not only in connection with the grant of planning permission. A breach of the order gives rise to criminal liability.

Reference: (i) TCPA 1990, ss 197–214;
             (ii) TCP (Tree Preservation Order) Regulations 1969 (SI 1969/17, as amended);
             (iii) Planning Law Service, Division D7.

7. Caravans and caravan sites

The development of land for use as a caravan site is controlled by the TCPA 1990, Pt III. There is, however, a complementary regime dealing with the management of such sites—covered by the Caravan Sites and Control of Development Act 1960, Pt I. These controls deal with the subsequent operation of a caravan site. Section 3 of the 1960 Act requires that an application for a site licence may only be made if the applicant (at the time when the site licence is issued) is entitled to the benefit of a permission granted under the TCPA 1990. Thus, before a caravan site can be set up the operator must ensure that he has the benefit of an express planning permission for such a purpose.

Problems with a different sort of caravan may also arise in the context of the statutory duty imposed on authorities to provide sites for the stationing of gypsy caravans: a duty imposed by the Caravan Sites Act 1968, s 6.

Reference: Planning Law Service, Division D10.

8. Local authorities' powers to facilitate urban regeneration

Local authorities have various powers to facilitate urban regeneration. Principal among these is the direct power to incur expenditure under the Local Government

Act 1972, s 137. The power under this section has been amended several times, most recently by the Local Government and Housing Act 1989, ss 36 and 37. This Act also grants express new powers for local authorities to promote economic development in their area (ss 33–35). Local authorities have powers to make substantial loans for the purchase or improvement of property, provided that these are secured by way of mortgage. They have additional powers to assist in industrial growth and to make loans within special designated districts and special areas under the provisions of the Inner Urban Areas Act 1978.

Reference: Planning Law Service, Division E1.

9. Control over hazardous substances

The Planning (Hazardous Substances) Act 1990 derives from statutory provisions within the TCPA 1971 which were never in fact brought into effect. Although those provisions had originally been placed within the principal planning Act of the time in recognition of the close relationship between the planning and hazardous substances regime, there are, in practice, a number of fundamental differences between the two. As a consequence, hazardous substances control has now been given its own Act. The PHSA 1990 came into force on the 1st June 1992 together with the Planning (Hazardous Substances) Regulations 1992.

By virtue of the provisions of the PHSA 1990, the presence on, over or under land of any hazardous substance in excess of the prescribed 'controlled quantity' requires consent from the hazardous substances authority.

Reference: (i) Planning (Hazardous Substances) Act 1990;
            (ii) Planning (Hazardous Substances) Regulations 1992 SI 1992/656;
            (iii) Planning Law Service, Division D11.

10. Local authority powers to acquire and/or develop land for planning purposes

Local planning authorities may compulsorily acquire land for planning purposes by virtue of the TCPA 1990, s 226. This power is in addition to other specified statutory powers for compulsory purchase which may nonetheless still be appropriate to the planning of the area, for example, powers of compulsory acquisition in connection with highways and education functions.

Reference: Planning Law Service, Division E2.

11. Urban Development Corporations

Urban Development Corporations are creatures of statute created specifically to restore or improve the economic fortunes of an area or areas of land. To this end, they are given wide statutory powers designed to enable them to bring land and buildings into effective use, to encourage the development of existing and new industry and commerce and to assist in creating an attractive environment, ensuring that housing and social facilities are available within the area. They have the power to acquire, hold, manage, reclaim and dispose of land and other property. They may also seek to ensure the provision of utilities and services within the area.

Reference: (i) LGPLA 1980, ss 134–167 and Schs 26–29;
            (ii) TCPA 1990, s 7 (urban development areas);
            (iii) Planning Law Service, Division E3.

12. Urban Regeneration Agency (URA)

The Agency was brought into being by the Leasehold Reform, Housing and Urban Development Act 1993. It has become known as 'English Partnerships'. It is essentially a Government initiative to encourage the regeneration of derelict and under-used areas and land reclamation in rural areas acting in partnership with local authorities, the private sector and other bodies. The powers of the URA are broad and mirror those powers conferred on urban development corporations. They are, however, more extensive, particularly in the giving of financial assistance and the administration of grant aid. The objects and powers of the URA are clearly defined by the 1993 Act, although there is within the statutory framework, a broad autonomy in the exercise of its functions, subject to the overriding control of the Secretary of State, who is empowered to make directions in relation to the carrying out of the URA's functions. The URA incorporates within its responsibilities, the control and administration of derelict land grant, city grant and subsumes the role of the now defunct English Estates.

The Secretary of State is also empowered to designate areas of land as urban regeneration areas and to provide the URA with attendant powers and functions in respect of them, where necessary, supplanting the power of the local planning authority in the carrying out of its development control functions.

Reference: Planning Law Service, Division E4.

13. Enterprise zones

Enterprise zones were an experimental measure introduced by the government in an attempt to increase economic activity in selected areas by the reduction of bureaucratic and administrative controls within those areas. They enjoy a significant relaxation in the application of the planning code.

A zone is designated as an enterprise zone by the local planning authority or a new town corporation or an Urban Development Corporation, in each case at the invitation of the Secretary of State for the Environment (or Wales if appropriate).

An enterprise zone designation normally lasts for ten years. During that period a prospective developer will not need to apply for planning permission, provided the development proposed falls within one of the categories designated in the enterprise zone order, whereupon planning permission will be automatically granted, in some cases subject to standard conditions.

Reference: (i) LGPLA 1980, Sch 32;
            (ii) TCPA 1990, s 6;
           (iii) Planning Law Service, Division E5.

14. Simplified planning zones

Simplified planning zones are a variant on the enterprise zone scheme. They were introduced by the government in an attempt to assist economic activity in specified areas by reducing planning controls over those areas. They do not include the very wide range of ancillary benefits enjoyed by enterprise zones.

Simplified planning zones also last for a ten-year period and a scheme designating the zone automatically grants planning permission for the range of developments specified in the scheme. Unlike enterprise zones, SPZs are designated by the relevant local planning authority and the Secretary of State need only be involved if there is an objection to the scheme prepared by the authority. Amendments introduced by the PCA 1991 are aimed at speeding the designation process, by reducing the publicity and consultation stages, and the need for the Secretary of State to intervene and hold an inquiry.

Reference: (i) TCPA 1990, ss 82–87 and Sch 7;
            (ii) TCP (Simplified Planning Zones) Regulations 1992 (SI 1992/2414) as amended;

(iii) PPG5 'Simplified Planning Zones';
(iv) Planning Law Service, Division E6.

E   THE ENFORCEMENT OF PLANNING CONTROL

1. Enforcement: criminal liability

The breach of planning control will not necessarily constitute a criminal offence. Although a breach will give rise to criminal liability where it affects some of the more important, or critical areas of the planning code, for example, listed buildings, specially protected trees, etc, on most occasions it is for the local planning authority first to issue an enforcement notice or a breach of condition notice requiring the necessary action to be taken to remedy the breach. Criminal sanctions will then only come into play if there is non-compliance with the notice.

2. Obtaining information

Planning authorities have various powers to investigate a suspected breach prior to the service of an enforcement notice or a breach of condition notice. These include a power of entry, the service of notice with a view to obtaining information (TCPA 1990, s 330) and the planning contravention notice introduced by the PCA 1991 which is designed to enable the authority to obtain information and/or to persuade the recipient to remedy a breach of planning control voluntarily.

3. Stop notices

In cases where the breach of control involves a continuing activity that the local planning authority consider should cease immediately, they may also serve a stop notice. Criminal prosecution may follow if this notice is ignored, although conversely the local planning authority may in certain circumstances be liable for the payment of compensation if service of the notice is not ultimately sanctioned by the Secretary of State for the Environment.

4. Appeals

An appeal may be submitted against the service of an enforcement notice but not against a breach of condition notice. The appeal 'freezes' the notice and, provided no stop notice has been served, the contravening use or the building operation the subject of the notice may continue, in that the notice will not take effect unless and until it is upheld on appeal. This general principle is now subject to the court's power to direct otherwise if the appeal reaches the stage of court proceedings.

5. Injunctions

An injunction may be available if necessary to restrain a particularly damaging breach of control, but the standard of proof required by the courts is high and the outcome far from certain.

6. Effect of breach

Failure to comply with a notice which has taken effect constitutes a criminal offence. In such a situation local planning authorities are empowered to carry out the steps required by the notice to rectify the breach and may charge the owner for so doing.

Reference: (i) TCPA 1990, Part VII;
             (ii) TCP (Enforcement Notices and Appeals) Regulations 1991 (SI 1981/2084) as amended by SI 1992/1904;

(iii) TCP (Enforcement) (Inquiries Procedure) Rules 1992 (SI 1992/ 1903);
(iv) TCP (Special Enforcement Notices) Regulations 1992 (SI 1992/ 1562);
(v) PPG18: Enforcing Planning Control;
(vi) Planning Law Service, Division F.

F APPEALS AGAINST THE REFUSAL OF PLANNING PERMISSION

1. The right to appeal

Following the refusal or non-determination by a local planning authority of an application for:

(i) planning permission;
(ii) consent required in compliance with a condition;
(iii) approval under a development order

an aggrieved applicant may, by virtue of the TCPA 1990, s 78, appeal to the Secretary of State for the Environment.

Type of appeal An appeal must be submitted within the period stipulated by the General Development Order, which is at present six months. Appeals may be brought before the Secretary of State for the Environment in one of three ways:

(i) at a hearing;
(ii) by the submission of written representations;
(iii) at a local inquiry.

The Secretary of State The appeal will be determined by either the Secretary of State himself, or on his behalf by an Inspector appointed by him. Both are empowered to allow or dismiss the appeal, or to reverse or vary any part of the decision of the local planning authority.

Costs Parties may apply for costs in the context of appeal proceedings involving a public inquiry or hearing. Although provision has been made for costs to be awarded in written representations appeals, the relevant statutory provisions are not yet in effect. A claim for costs must be made at the appropriate stage in the proceedings. The party against whom costs are sought must have *behaved unreasonably* and the unreasonable conduct must have caused the other party to incur cost or waste expense unnecessarily, for example by reason of the manner in which the appeal has been progressed by the other side, late cancellation of the inquiry, etc. Government guidance is provided in Circular 8/93 (WO 23/93)

Reference: (i) TCPA 1990, ss 77 to 79 and Sch 6;
(ii) TCP (Inquiries Procedure) Rules 1992 (SI 1992/2038);
(iii) TCP Appeals (Determination by Inspector) (Inquiries Procedure) Rules 1992 (SI 1992/2039);
(iv) Planning Law Service, Division S1.

2. Judicial supervision

An action taken or a decision made by a local planning authority or the Secretary of State which goes beyond the powers granted by the planning legislation may be challenged by one of two methods:

(i) an application or appeal (as the case may be) to the High Court under the

statutory provisions of the TCPA 1990 or the provisions of the P(LBCA)A
1990;

(ii) an application for judicial review to the High Court by way of RSC Ord 53.

Certain specified matters may not be challenged in any court in any proceedings
including judicial review, other than by way of statutory application or appeal made
in accordance with the provisions of the planning Acts.

In order to qualify for relief, an applicant must be able to show, inter alia:

(i) in respect of statutory applications, appeals and applications for judicial
review, that he has sufficient interest (locus standi) in the proceedings
brought;

(ii) in relation to procedural errors challenged under the statutory provisions,
that he has been substantially prejudiced by the error alleged;

(iii) in the case of local authorities in relation to applications to which the
TCPA 1990, s 288 applies, that they are an authority 'directly concerned'
in the matter.

Relief in respect of statutory applications or appeals may be interim in nature,
suspending the operation of a development plan or its alteration, repeal or
replacement, or suspending the effect of an order or action coming within the TCPA
1990. Final relief may be obtained, but there is no express requirement that the court
should exercise its powers to quash. However, if the power is exercised the court
will normally remit the matter to the Secretary of State for redetermination.

In respect of judicial review the applicant may claim all or one of several remedies
as follows:

(i) the prerogative orders of certiorari, mandamus and prohibition;

(ii) the common law remedies of declaration, injunction and in limited
circumstances, damages.

Reference: (i) TCPA 1990, Pt XII;
            (ii) Planning Law Service, Division G3.

G   COMPENSATION

One effect of the planning regime is to prevent development in some areas whilst
permitting it in others. This has produced a consequential problem of compensation
and betterment which has beset planning for many years. How to compensate those
owners whose applications were refused and secure betterment for the public purse
from those who gained?

The TCPA 1947 sought a permanent solution to the problem by transferring the
development value in all land to the State in return for a global payment to owners
of £300m. This formed a fund from which owners of interests in land who claimed
to have lost development value to the State could seek payment. The development
value in land thus having passed to the State, there would in future be no question of
a planning authority having to pay compensation if planning permission to carry out
development was refused.

Thereafter under the Act, in order to develop his land, an owner had not only to
obtain planning permission but also, as it were, buy back the development value.
This he did by paying to the State a development charge fixed at 100% of the
development value of the land attributable to the development. In due course the
development charge was abolished and was replaced after an interval by betterment
levy, and that in turn was replaced after another interval by development land tax.
That too has gone, with the result that today if an owner can obtain planning

permission he 'receives back' the development value with the permitted development for nothing, subject only to the ordinary income, capital and corporation taxes.

However, while there is now no question of having to buy permission from the State to carry out development, the other principle of the 1947 Act, namely, that development value having passed to the State in exchange for the £300m fund, no compensation should be payable for refusal of planning permission or for the imposition of burdensome conditions on a permission, still remains, and seems to be generally regarded as acceptable. This general principle still left room, however, for instances where compensation was payable for planning restrictions on an owner's use and enjoyment of his land.

First, the £300m fund was never paid out but was converted into what is termed as 'unexpended balances of established development value'. Such a balance was attached to the land of any owner who claimed against the fund and proved the loss of development value. Some balances were still attached to parcels of land in 1990 and, where planning permission was refused or granted subject to burdensome conditions, the owner might be entitled to claim payment of up to the amount of the outstanding balance. This entitlement was, however, repealed from 25 September 1991 (PCA 1991, s 31(1)).

Second, once an owner has obtained planning permission for a particular development he automatically receives back, as has been noted, the development value for that development from the State. If thereafter, owing to a change of planning policy, that permission is taken away or modified to his disadvantage before he has been able to carry out the development, so that he loses the development value, he will be entitled to full compensation for his loss. If, however, the permission expires before implementation, he receives no compensation.

Third, it was only development value which was transferred to the State; the value of the land for its existing use remained with the owner. For any restriction on its existing use caused by a planning decision he is entitled to full compensation.

Between development and existing use there was a marginal area. This contained the right to rebuild an existing building and comparatively minor forms of development, such as limited extensions of existing buildings, which the authors of the 1947 Act thought it would be reasonable to include in the existing use of land. Accordingly development value for such development, known as Schedule 3 development, was not transferred to the State although planning permission was still required. If permission was refused, or made subject to burdensome conditions, then because the development value was left with the owner, compensation would be payable (though, in the case of development in Part I of the Schedule, it could only be recovered if the owner could force an authority to purchase his land, when it would be included in the compulsory purchase compensation). The entitlement to compensation in respect of Schedule 3, Part II development has now been repealed where the relevant application for planning permission was made on or after 16th November 1990. Compensation in respect of Part I development can still be obtained in compulsory purchase compensation if compulsory purchase can be enforced through the purchase notice procedure.

Purchase notices It should be noted that there are provisions in the TCPA 1990 whereby an owner can force an authority to purchase his land if it is of no practical value to him and he cannot obtain a permission to make it of practical value. He can also force the purchase of his property if some plan contemplates its acquisition for public purposes and so makes it unsaleable at its real market value. There are further provisions in other Acts whereby an owner who is disturbed in the enjoyment of his land by public works on neighbouring land can obtain compensation in limited circumstances for his 'injurious affection' or depreciation in the value of his land.

Reference: (i) TCPA 1990, Pts V and VI;
          (ii) Planning Law Service, Division H.

PART I
PRIMARY LEGISLATION

LOCAL GOVERNMENT ACT 1972
(1972 c 70)

An Act to make provision with respect to local government and the functions of local authorities in England and Wales; to amend Part II of the Transport Act 1968; to confer rights of appeal in respect of decisions relating to licences under the Home Counties (Music and Dancing) Licensing Act 1926; to make further provision with respect to magistrates' courts committees; to abolish certain inferior courts of record; and for connected purposes [26 October 1972]

PART VI
DISCHARGE OF FUNCTIONS

101. Arrangements for discharge of functions by local authorities

(1) Subject to any express provision contained in this Act or any Act passed after this Act, a local authority may arrange for the discharge of any of their functions—

    (a) by a committee, a sub-committee or an officer of the authority; or

    (b) by any other local authority.

(2) Where by virtue of this section any functions of a local authority may be discharged by a committee of theirs, then, unless the local authority otherwise direct, the committee may arrange for the discharge of any of those functions by a sub-committee or an officer of the authority and where by virtue of this section any functions of a local authority may be discharged by a sub-committee of the authority, then, unless the local authority or the committee otherwise direct, the sub-committee may arrange for the discharge of any of those functions by an officer of the authority.

(3) Where arrangements are in force under this section for the discharge of any functions of a local authority by another local authority, then, subject to the terms of the arrangements, that other authority may arrange for the discharge of those functions by a committee, sub-committee or officer of theirs and subsection (2) above shall apply in relation to those functions as it applies in relation to the functions of that other authority.

(4) Any arrangements made by a local authority or committee under this section for the discharge of any functions by a committee, sub-committee, officer or local authority shall not prevent the authority or committee by whom the arrangements are made from exercising those functions.

(5) Two or more local authorities may discharge any of their functions jointly and, where arrangements are in force for them to do so,—

    (a) they may also arrange for the discharge of those functions by a joint committee of theirs or by an officer of one of them and subsection (2) above shall apply in relation to those functions as it applies in relation to the functions of the individual authorities; and

    (b) any enactment relating to those functions or the authorities by whom or the areas in respect of which they are to be discharged shall have effect subject to all necessary modifications in its application in relation to those functions and the authorities by whom and the areas in respect of which (whether in pursuance of the arrangements or otherwise) they are to be discharged.

(6) A local authority's functions with respect to levying, or issuing a precept for, a rate . . . shall be discharged only by the authority.

(7) A local authority shall not make arrangements under this section for the discharge of any of their functions under the Diseases of Animals Act 1950 by any other local authority.

[(7A) Subsection (7) above does not apply to arrangements as between principal councils in Wales.]

(8) Any enactment, except one mentioned in subsection (9) below, which contains any provision—

    (a) which empowers or requires local authorities or any class of local authorities to establish committees (including joint committees) for any purpose or enables a Minister to make an instrument establishing committees of local authorities for any purpose or empowering or requiring a local authority or any class of local authorities to establish committees for any purpose; or

    (b) which empowers or requires local authorities or any class of local authorities to arrange or to join with other authorities in arranging for the exercise by committees so established or by officers of theirs of any of their functions, or provides that any specified functions of theirs shall be discharged by such committees or officers, or enables any Minister to make an instrument conferring such a power, imposing such a requirement or containing such a provision;

shall, to the extent that it makes any such provision, cease to have effect.

(9) The following enactments, that is to say—

    (a) . . .
    (b) . . .
    (c) . . .
    (d) section 1 of the Sea Fisheries Regulation Act 1966;
    (e) . . .
    (f) section 2 of the Local Authority Social Services Act 1970 (social services committees);
    (g) . . .; and
    (h) *Part I of Schedule 17 to this Act;*

are exempted from subsection (8) above.

(10) This section shall not authorise a local authority to arrange for the discharge by any committee, sub-committee or local authority of any functions which by any enactment mentioned in subsection (9) above are required or authorised to be discharged by a specified committee, but the foregoing provision shall not prevent a local authority who are required by or under any such enactment to establish, or delegate functions to, a committee established by or under any such enactment from arranging under this section for the discharge of their functions by an officer of the local authority or committee, as the case may be.

[(10A) In determining what arrangements to make for the discharge of any functions, a principal council in Wales may act as if paragraph (f) were omitted from subsection (9) above.]

(11) . . .

(12) References in this section and section 102 below to the discharge of any of the functions of a local authority include references to the doing of anything which is calculated to facilitate, or is conducive or incidental to, the discharge of any of those functions.

(13) In this Part of this Act "local authority" includes the Common Council, the Sub-Treasurer of the Inner Temple, the Under Treasurer of the Middle Temple, [any joint authority except a police authority, . . .] a joint board on which a local authority within the meaning of this Act or any of the foregoing authorities are represented and, without prejudice to the foregoing, any port health authority.

(14) Nothing in this section affects the operation of section 5 of the 1963 Act or the Local Authorities (Goods and Services) Act 1970. [1]

NOTES
Words omitted from sub-s (6) repealed by the Local Government and Housing Act 1989, s 45(5).
Sub-ss (7A), (10A) inserted by the Local Government (Wales) Act 1994, s 66(5), Sch 15, paras 1, 26.
Sub-s (9)(a) repealed by the Education Act 1993, s 307(1), (3), Sch 19, para 49, Sch 21, Pt II; sub-ss (9)(b), (11) repealed by the Local Government Act 1985, s 102(2), Sch 17, and words in square brackets in sub-s (13) inserted by s 84 of, and Sch 14, Pt I, para 15 to, the 1985 Act; sub-s (9)(c) repealed by the Police and Magistrates' Courts Act 1994, s 93, Sch 9, Pt I; sub-s (9)(e) repealed by the Health and Social Services and Social Security Adjudications Act 1983, s 30(1), Sch 10, Pt I; sub-s (9)(g) repealed by the SL(R) Act 1986. Sub-s (9)(h) repealed by the Environment Act 1995, s 120(3), Sch 24, as from a day to be appointed under s 125(3).
Words omitted from sub-s (13) repealed by the Education Reform Act 1988, s 237(2), Sch 13, Pt I.
1963 Act: London Government Act 1963.

PART VII

MISCELLANEOUS POWERS OF LOCAL AUTHORITIES

Subsidiary powers

111. Subsidiary powers of local authorities

(1) Without prejudice to any powers exercisable apart from this section but subject to the provisions of this Act and any other enactment passed before or after this Act, a local authority shall have power to do any thing (whether or not involving the expenditure, borrowing or lending of money or the acquisition or disposal of any property or rights) which is calculated to facilitate, or is conducive or incidental to, the discharge of any of their functions.

(2) For the purposes of this section, transacting the business of a parish or community meeting or any other parish or community business shall be treated as a function of the parish or community council.

(3) A local authority shall not by virtue of this section raise money, whether by means of rates, precepts or borrowing, or lend money except in accordance with the enactments relating to those matters respectively.

(4) In this section "local authority" includes the Common Council. [1A]

LOCAL GOVERNMENT, PLANNING AND LAND ACT 1980
(1980 c 65)

ARRANGEMENT OF SECTIONS

PART XVI
URBAN DEVELOPMENT

Urban development areas

An Act to relax controls over local and certain other authorities; to amend the law relating to the publication of information, the undertaking of works and the payment of allowances by local authorities and other bodies; to make further provision with respect to rates and to grants for local authorities and other persons and for controlling the expenditure of local authorities; to amend the law relating to planning; to make provision for a register of public land and the disposal of land on it; to repeal the Community Land Act 1975; to continue the Land Authority for Wales; to make further provision in relation to land compensation, development land, derelict land and public bodies' acquisitions and disposals of land; to amend the law relating to town development and new towns; to provide for the establishment of corporations to regenerate urban areas; to make further provision in relation to gipsies and their caravan sites; to abolish the Clean Air Councils and certain restrictions on the Greater London Council; to empower certain further authorities to confer honorary distinctions; and for connected purposes [13 November 1980]

PART XVI
URBAN DEVELOPMENT
Urban development areas

134. Urban development areas

(1) ... if the Secretary of State is of opinion that it is expedient in the national interest to do so, he may by order made by statutory instrument designate any area of land as an urban development area.

(2) ...

(3) Separate parcels of land may be designated as one urban development area.

[(3A) The Secretary of State may by order alter the boundaries of any urban development area so as to exclude any area of land.

(3B) Before making an order under subsection (3A) above, the Secretary of

State shall consult any local authority the whole or any part of whose area is included in the area of land to be excluded by the order.]

(4) No order under [subsection (1) above] shall have effect until approved by a resolution of each House of Parliament.

[(5) The power to make an order under subsection (3A) above—

    (a) shall be exercisable by statutory instrument subject to annulment in pursuance of a resolution of either House of Parliament; and

    (b) shall include power to make such incidental consequential, transitional or supplementary provision as the Secretary of State thinks fit.]   **[2]**

NOTES
    Words omitted from sub-s (1) and whole of sub-s (2) repealed by the Housing and Planning Act 1986, ss 47, 49(2), 53(2), Sch 12, Parts III, IV.
    Sub-ss (3A), (3B) inserted, words in square brackets in sub-s (4) substituted and sub-s (5) added by the Leasehold Reform, Housing and Urban Development Act 1993, s 179(1)–(3).

Urban development corporations

135. Urban development corporations

(1) For the purposes of regenerating an urban development area, the Secretary of State shall by order made by statutory instrument establish a corporation (an urban development corporation) for the area.

(2) An order under this section may be made at the same time as an order under [section 134(1)] above.

(3) No order under this section shall have effect until approved by a resolution of each House of Parliament.

(4) An urban development corporation shall be a body corporate by such name as may be prescribed by the order establishing it.

(5) Schedule 26 below shall have effect with respect to urban development corporations.

(6) It is hereby declared that an urban development corporation is not to be regarded as the servant or agent of the Crown or as enjoying any status, immunity or privilege of the Crown and that the corporation's property is not to be regarded as the property of, or property held on behalf of, the Crown.   **[2A]**

NOTES
    Words in square brackets in sub-s (2) substituted by the Leasehold Reform, Housing and Urban Development Act 1993, s 179(4).

136. Objects and general powers

(1) The object of an urban development corporation shall be to secure the regeneration of its area.

(2) The object is to be achieved in particular by the following means (or by such of them as seem to the corporation to be appropriate in the case of its area), namely, by bringing land and buildings into effective use, encouraging the development of existing and new industry and commerce, creating an attractive environment and ensuring that housing and social facilities are available to encourage people to live and work in the area.

(3) Subject to sections 137 and 138 below, for the purpose of achieving the object an urban development corporation may—

(a) acquire, hold, manage, reclaim and dispose of land and other property;
(b) carry out building and other operations;
(c) seek to ensure the provision of water, electricity, gas, sewerage and other services;
(d) carry on any business or undertaking for the purposes of the object; and
(e) generally do anything necessary or expedient for the purposes of the object or for purposes incidental to those purposes.

(4) No provision of this Part of this Act by virtue of which any power is exercisable by an urban development corporation shall be construed as limiting the effect of subsection (3) above.

(5) Without prejudice to the generality of the powers conferred on urban development corporations by this Act, such a corporation, for the purpose of achieving the object,—

(a) may, with the consent of the Secretary of State, contribute such sums as he with the Treasury's concurrence may determine towards expenditure incurred or to be incurred by any local authority or statutory undertakers in the performance of any statutory functions of the authority or undertakers, including expenditure so incurred in the acquisition of land; and
(b) may, with the like consent, contribute such sums as the Secretary of State with the like concurrence may determine by way of assistance towards the provision of amenities.

(6) To avoid doubt it is declared that subsection (3) above relates only to the capacity of an urban development corporation as a statutory corporation; and nothing in this section authorises such a corporation to disregard any enactment or rule of law.

(7) A transaction between a person and an urban development corporation shall not be invalidated by reason of any failure by the corporation to observe the object in subsection (1) above or the requirement in subsection (3) above that the corporation shall exercise the powers conferred by that subsection for the purpose of achieving that object.   **[3]**

137. Exclusion of functions

(1) An order under section 135 above may provide that any functions which may be exercisable by an urban development corporation by virtue of this Part of this Act and which are specified in the order are not to be exercised by the corporation established by the order, either as regards the whole of its area or as regards a portion of that area; and this Part of this Act shall apply to the corporation accordingly.

(2) An order under section 135 above may amend any provision of a previous order under that section which was included in that order by virtue of subsection (1) above.

(3) Nothing in subsection (2) above shall prejudice the operation of section 14 of the Interpretation Act 1978 (power to amend orders etc.).   **[4]**

138. Restrictions on powers

(1) Without prejudice to any provision of this Act requiring the consent of the Secretary of State to be obtained for anything to be done by an urban development

corporation, he may give directions to such a corporation for restricting the exercise by it of any of its powers under this Act or for requiring it to exercise those powers in any manner specified in the directions.

(2) Before giving a direction under subsection (1) above, the Secretary of State shall consult the corporation, unless he is satisfied that because of urgency consultation is impracticable.

(3) A transaction between a person and an urban development corporation acting in purported exercise of its powers under this Act shall not be void by reason only that it was carried out in contravention of a direction given under subsection (1) above, and such a person shall not be concerned to see or enquire whether a direction under that subsection has been given or complied with.   **[5]**

139. Allocation or transfer of functions

(1) If it appears to the Secretary of State, in the case of an urban development area, that there are exceptional circumstances which render it expedient that the functions of an urban development corporation under this Part of this Act should be performed by the urban development corporation established for the purposes of any other area instead of by a separate corporation established for the purpose, he may, instead of establishing such a separate corporation, by order direct that those functions shall be performed by the urban development corporation established for the other area.

(2) If it appears to the Secretary of State that there are exceptional circumstances which render it expedient that the functions of an urban development corporation established for one area should be transferred to the urban development corporation established for the purposes of another area, or to a new urban development corporation to be established for the first-mentioned area, he may, by order, provide for the dissolution of the first-mentioned corporation and for the transfer of its functions, property, rights and liabilities to the urban development corporation established for the purposes of the other area or (as the case may be) to a new corporation established for the purposes of the first-mentioned area by the order.

(3) Without prejudice to section 14 of the Interpretation Act 1978, an order under this section providing for the exercise of functions in relation to an area by the urban development corporation established for the purposes of another area, or for the transfer of such functions to such a corporation, may modify the name and constitution of that corporation in such manner as appears to the Secretary of State to be expedient, and for the purposes of this Act that corporation shall be treated as having been established for the purposes of each of those areas.

(4) Before making an order under this section providing for the transfer of functions from or to an urban development corporation or for the exercise of any functions by such a corporation, the Secretary of State shall consult that corporation.

(5) An order under this section shall make, with regard to a corporation on which functions are conferred by the order, the same provision as that which may be made with regard to a corporation under section 137 above.

(6) An order under this section shall be made by statutory instrument.

(7) No order under this section shall have effect until approved by a resolution of each House of Parliament.   **[6]**

140. Consultation with local authorities

(1) An urban development corporation shall prepare a code of practice as to consultation with the relevant local authorities about the exercise of its powers.

(2) In this section "the relevant local authorities" means local authorities the whole or any part of whose area is included in the urban development area.

(3) Preparation of the code shall be completed not later than the expiration of the period of 12 months from the date of the establishment of the corporation.

(4) A corporation may from time to time revise the whole or any part of its code.

(5) A corporation shall prepare and revise its code in consultation with the rele vant local authorities.   [7]

LOCAL GOVERNMENT (MISCELLANEOUS PROVISIONS) ACT 1982
(1982 c 30)

An Act to make amendments for England and Wales of provisions of that part of the law relating to local authorities or highways which is commonly amended by local Acts; to make provision for the control of sex establishments; to make further provision for the control of refreshment premises and for consultation between local authorities in England and Wales and fire authorities with regard to fire precautions for buildings and caravan sites; to repeal the Theatrical Employers Registration Acts 1925 and 1928; to make further provision as to the enforcement of section 8 of the Public Utilities Street Works Act 1950 and sections 171 and 174 of the Highways Act 1980; to make provision in connection with the computerisation of local land charges registers; to make further provision in connection with the acquisition of land and rights over land by boards constituted in pursuance of section 1 of the Town and Country Planning Act 1971 or reconstituted in pursuance of Schedule 17 to the Local Government Act 1972; to exclude from the definition of "construction or maintenance work" in section 20 of the Local Government, Planning and Land Act 1980 work undertaken by local authorities and development bodies pursuant to certain agreements with the Manpower Services Commission which specify the work to be undertaken and under which the Commission agrees to pay the whole or part of the cost of the work so specified; to define "year" for the purposes of Part III of the said Act of 1980; to amend section 140 of the Local Government Act 1972 and to provide for the insurance by local authorities of persons voluntarily assisting probation committees; to make provision for controlling nuisance and disturbance on educational premises; to amend section 137 of the Local Government Act 1972; to make further provision as to arrangements made by local authorities under the Employment and Training Act 1973; to extend the duration of certain powers to assist industry or employment conferred by local Acts; to make corrections and minor improvements in certain enactments relating to the local administration of health and planning functions; and for connected purposes   [13 July 1982]

PART XII
MISCELLANEOUS

33. Enforceability by local authorities of certain covenants relating to land

(1) The provisions of this section shall apply if a principal council (in the exercise of their powers under section 111 of the Local Government Act 1972 or otherwise) and any other person are parties to an instrument under seal which—

[(a) is executed for the purpose of securing the carrying out of works on land in the council's area in which the other person has an interest, or

(b) is executed for the purpose of regulating the use of or is otherwise connected with land in or outside the council's area in which the other person has an interest,

and which is neither executed for the purpose of facilitating nor connected with the development of the land in question].

(2) If, in a case where this section applies,—

(a) the instrument contains a covenant on the part of any person having an interest in land, being a covenant to carry out any works or do any other thing on or in relation to that land, and

(b) the instrument defines the land to which the covenant relates, being land in which that person has an interest at the time the instrument is executed, and

(c) the covenant is expressed to be one to which this section or section 126 of the Housing Act 1974 (which is superseded by this section) applies,

the covenant shall be enforceable (without any limit of time) against any person deriving title from the original covenantor in respect of his interest in any of the land defined as mentioned in paragraph (b) above and any person deriving title under him in respect of any lesser interest in that land as if that person had also been an original covenanting party in respect of the interest for the time being held by him.

(3) Without prejudice to any other method of enforcement of a covenant falling within subsection (2) above, if there is a breach of the covenant in relation to any of the land to which the covenant relates, then, subject to subsection (4) below, the principal council who are a party to the instrument in which the covenant is contained may—

(a) enter on the land concerned and carry out the works or do anything which the covenant requires to be carried out or done or remedy anything which has been done and which the covenant required not to be done; and

(b) recover from any person against whom the covenant is enforceable (whether by virtue of subsection (2) above or otherwise) any expenses incurred by the council in exercise of their powers under this subsection.

(4) Before a principal council exercise their powers under subsection (3)(a) above they shall give not less than 21 days notice of their intention to do so to any person—

(a) who has for the time being an interest in the land on or in relation to which the works are to be carried out or other thing is to be done; and

(b) against whom the covenant is enforceable (whether by virtue of subsection (2) above or otherwise).

(5) If a person against whom a covenant is enforceable by virtue of subsection (2) above requests the principal council to supply him with a copy of the covenant, it shall be their duty to do so free of charge.

(6) The Public Health Act 1936 shall have effect as if any reference to that Act in—

(a) section 283 of that Act (notices to be in writing; forms of notices, etc.),

(b) section 288 of that Act (penalty for obstructing execution of Act), and

(c) section 291 of that Act (certain expenses recoverable from owners to be a charge on the premises; power to order payment by instalments), included a reference to subsections (1) to (4) above and as if any reference in those sections of that Act—

    (i) to a local authority were a reference to a principal council; and

    (ii) to the owner of the premises were a reference to the holder of an interest in land.

(7) Section 16 of the Local Government (Miscellaneous Provisions) Act 1976 shall have effect as if references to a local authority and to functions conferred on a local authority by any enactment included respectively references to such a board as is mentioned in subsection (9) below and to functions of such a board under this section.

(8) In its application to a notice or other document authorised to be given or served under subsection (4) above or by virtue of any provision of the Public Health Act 1936 specified in subsection (6) above, section 233 of the Local Government Act 1972 (service of notices by local authorities) shall have effect as if any reference in that section to a local authority included a reference to the Common Council of the City of London and such a board as is mentioned in the following subsection.

(9) In this section—

    (a) "principal council" means the council of a county, district or London borough, [the Broads Authority] a board constituted in pursuance of [section 2 of the Town and Country Planning Act 1990] *or reconstituted in pursuance of Schedule 17 to the Local Government Act 1972*, the Common Council of the City of London [, the London Residuary Body] [the Residuary Body for Wales (Corff Gweddilliol Cymru)] [, a police authority established under section 3 of the Police Act 1964] . . . [. . . or a joint authority established by Part IV of the Local Government Act 1985]; and

    (b) "area" in relation to such a board means the district for which the board is constituted *or reconstituted* [in relation to the London Residuary Body means Greater London] [, [in relation to the Residuary Body for Wales (Corff Gweddilliol Cymru) means Wales] . . . and in relation to such a joint authority means the area for which the authority was established].

(10) Section 126 of the Housing Act 1974 (which is superseded by this section) shall cease to have effect; but in relation to a covenant falling within subsection (2) of that section, section 1(1)(d) of the Local Land Charges Act 1975 shall continue to have effect as if the reference to the commencement of that Act had been a reference to the coming into operation of the said section 126.   **[7A]**

NOTES

    Sub-s (1)(a), (b) substituted for the original sub-s (1)(a)–(c) by the Planning and Compensation Act 1991, s 32, Sch 7, para 6.

    Words in square brackets in sub-s (9)(a), (b) inserted or substituted by the Norfolk and Suffolk Broads Act 1988, s 21, Sch 6, para 23(1), the Planning (Consequential Provisions) Act 1990, s 4, Sch 2, para 56(1), the Local Government Reorganisation (Miscellaneous Provisions) Order 1990, SI 1990/1765, art 4(6), the Local Government (Wales) Act 1994, s 39(2), Sch 13, para 29, the Police and Magistrates' Courts Act 1994, s 43, Sch 4, Pt I, para 23 and the Local Government Act 1985, s 84, Sch 14, Pt II, para 61(a); words omitted from sub-s (9)(a), (b) repealed by s 102(2) of, and Sch 17 to, the 1985 Act, and by the Education Reform Act 1988, s 237(2), Sch 13, Pt I. Words in italics in sub-s (9)(a), (b) repealed by the Environment Act 1995, s 120(3), Sch 24, as from a day to be appointed.

    Modification: by virtue of the Environment Act 1995, s 65(7), Sch 8, para 1(3), this section has effect as if references to a principal council included references to a National Park authority and as if the relevant Park were that authority's area; and for these purposes the reference in sub-s (1) to s 111 of the 1972 Act is to have effect as a reference to s 65 of the 1995 Act.

TOWN AND COUNTRY PLANNING ACT 1990
(c 8)

ARRANGEMENT OF SECTIONS

PART VII

ENFORCEMENT

Introductory

Planning contravention notices

Enforcement notices

Breach of condition

Injunctions

Registers

Enforcement of orders for discontinuance of use, etc

Certificate of lawful use or development

Part XIII

Application of Act to Crown Land

Preliminary

Application of Act as respects Crown land

Provisions relating to anticipated disposal of Crown land

Enforcement in respect of war-time breaches of planning control by Crown

Part XIV

Financial Provisions

Part XV

Miscellaneous and General Provisions

Application of Act in special cases

Local inquiries and other hearings

An Act to consolidate certain enactments relating to town and country planning (excluding special controls in respect of buildings and areas of special architectural or historic interest and in respect of hazardous substances) with amendments to give effect to recommendations of the Law Commission

[24 May 1990]

PART I

PLANNING AUTHORITIES

1. Local planning authorities: general

(1) In a non-metropolitan county—

(a) the council of a county is the county planning authority for the county, and

(b) the council of a district is the district planning authority for the district,

and references in the planning Acts to a local planning authority in relation to a non-metropolitan county shall be construed, subject to any express provision to the contrary, as references to both the county planning authority and the district planning authorities.

[(1A) Subsection (1) does not apply in relation to Wales.

(1B) In Wales—

(a) the local planning authority for a county is the county council; and

(b) the local planning authority for a county borough is the county borough council.]

(2) The council of a metropolitan district is the local planning authority for the district and the council of a London borough is the local planning authority for the borough.

(3) In England (exclusive of the metropolitan counties, Greater London and the Isles of Scilly) . . . all functions conferred on local planning authorities by or under the planning Acts shall be exercisable both by county planning authorities and district planning authorities.

(4) In this Act "mineral planning authority" means—

(a) in respect of a site in a non-metropolitan county, the county planning authority; and

(b) in respect of a site in a metropolitan district or London borough, the local planning authority.

[(4A) Subsection (4) does not apply in relation to Wales.

(4B) As to any site in Wales, the local planning authority is also the mineral planning authority.]

(5) This section has effect subject to any express provision to the contrary in the planning Acts and, in particular—

(a) [this section has] effect subject to *sections 5 to* [8A] of this Act *and Part I of Schedule 17 to the Local Government Act 1972 (National Parks)* [and];

(b) subsections [(1) to (2)] have effect subject to sections 2 and 9; and

(c) subsection (3) has effect subject to *section 4 and* Schedule 1 (which contains provisions as to the exercise of certain functions under this Act by particular authorities and liaison between them).

[(6) The exercise, in relation to Wales, of functions conferred on local planning authorities is subject to *section 4(3) and* Schedule 1A.]   **[8]**

NOTES

Commencement: 24 August 1990 (sub-ss (1), (2), (3), (4), (5)); 3 April 1995 (sub-ss (1A), (1B), (4A), (4B)).

Sub-ss (1A), (1B), (4A), (4B) inserted, words omitted from sub-s (3) repealed, first words in square brackets in sub-s (5)(a) and words in square brackets in sub-s (5)(b) substituted and sub-s (6) added by the Local Government (Wales) Act 1994, ss 18(2)–(6), 66(8), Sch 18, partly as from 1 April 1996.

Figure in square brackets in sub-s (5)(a) substituted by the Leasehold Reform, Housing and Urban Development Act 1993, s 187(1), Sch 21, para 28; first words in italics in sub-s (5)(a) substituted by the words "sections 4A to", second words in italics repealed and final word "and" in square brackets inserted, and words in italics in sub-ss (5)(b), (6), repealed, by the Environment Act 1995, ss 78, 120(3), Sch 10, para 32(1), Sch 24, as from a day to be appointed under s 125(3).

Planning Acts: Town and Country Planning Act 1990, Planning (Listed Buildings and Conservation Areas) Act 1990, Planning (Hazardous Substances) Act 1990, Planning (Consequential Provisions) Act 1990.

2. Joint planning boards

(1) If it appears to the Secretary of State that it is expedient that a joint board should be established as the county planning authority for the areas or parts of the areas of any two or more county councils or as the district planning authority for the areas or parts of the areas of any two or more district councils, he may by order—

    (a) constitute those areas or parts as a united district for the purposes of this Act; and

    (b) constitute a joint board . . . as the county planning authority or, as the case may be, the district planning authority for that united district.

[(1A) Subsection (1) does not apply in relation to Wales.

(1B) If it appears to the Secretary of State that it is expedient that a joint board should be established as the local planning authority for two or more areas, each of which is the whole or part of a Welsh county or county borough, he may by order—

    (a) constitute those areas or parts as a united district for the purposes of this Act; and

    (b) constitute a joint board as the local planning authority for that united district.

(1C) A joint board constituted under subsection (1) or (1B) shall be known as a "joint planning board".]

[(1D) The areas that may be constituted as a united district for the purposes of this section shall not include the whole or any part of an area which is comprised in a National Park for which there is a National Park authority.]

(2) The Secretary of State shall not make [an order under subsection (1) or (1B)] except after holding a local inquiry unless all the councils concerned have consented to the making of the order.

(3) Where a joint planning board is constituted for a united district, references in the planning Acts to the area of a local planning authority—

    (a) in relation to the board, shall be construed as references to that district; and

    (b) in relation to any local planning authority being the council of a county [or county borough] or district of which part (but not the whole) is included in the united district, shall be construed as references to so much of the county or [or county borough] district as is not so included.

(4) A joint planning board constituted by an order under subsection (1) [or (1B)] shall consist of such number of members as may be determined by the order, to be appointed by the constituent councils.

(5) A joint planning board so constituted shall be a body corporate, with perpetual succession and a common seal.

(6) An order constituting a joint planning board and any order amending or revoking any order constituting a joint planning board—

    (a) may, without prejudice to the provisions of section 241 of the Local Government Act 1972 (which authorises the application of the provisions of that Act to joint boards), provide for regulating the appointment, tenure of office and vacation of office of members of the board, for regulating the meetings and proceedings of the board, and for the payment of the expenses of the board by the constituent councils;

    (b) may provide for the transfer and compensation of officers, the transfer of property and liabilities, and the adjustment of accounts and apportionment of liabilities;

    (c) may contain such other provisions as appear to the Secretary of State to be expedient for enabling the board to exercise their functions; and

(d) may apply to the board, with any necessary modifications and adaptations, any of the provisions of sections 102 and 103 of the Local Government Act 1972.

[(6A) Section 241 of the Local Government Act 1972 shall be taken to authorise the application to a joint planning board, subject to any necessary modifications, of any provisions of Part III (accounts and audit) of the Local Government Finance Act 1982 (as well as of any provisions of the Local Government Act 1972) by such an order as is mentioned in subsection (6) above.]

(7) This section shall have effect subject to sections 5 to 9 of this Act *and Part I of Schedule 17 to the Local Government Act 1972 (joint planning boards and special planning boards for National Parks).*   **[9]**

NOTES

Commencement: 24 August 1990 (sub-ss (1), (2)–(7)); 3 April 1995 (sub-ss (1A)–(1C)); to be appointed (sub-ss (1D), (6A)).

Words omitted from sub-s (1) repealed, sub-ss (1A)–(1C) inserted, words in square brackets in sub-s (2) substituted and words in square brackets in sub-ss (3), (4) inserted by the Local Government (Wales) Act 1994, ss 19(1), (4), 66(8), Sch 18.

Sub-ss (1D), (6A) inserted, and words in italics in sub-s (7) repealed, by the Environment Act 1995, ss 78, 120(1), (3), Sch 10, para 32(2), Sch 22, para 42, Sch 24, as from a day to be appointed under s 125(3).

Planning Acts: Town and Country Planning Act 1990, Planning (Listed Buildings and Conservation Areas) Act 1990, Planning (Hazardous Substances) Act 1990, Planning (Consequential Provisions) Act 1990.

---

3. Joint planning committee for Greater London

(1) The joint planning committee for Greater London established under section 5 of the Local Government Act 1985 shall continue to discharge the functions mentioned in subsection (2).

(2) The joint planning committee shall—

(a) consider and advise the local planning authorities in Greater London on matters of common interest relating to the planning and development of Greater London;

(b) inform the Secretary of State of the views of those authorities concerning such matters including any such matters as to which he has requested their advice;

(c) inform the local planning authorities for areas in the vicinity of Greater London, or any body on which those authorities and the local planning authorities in Greater London are represented, of the views of the local planning authorities in Greater London concerning any matters of common interest relating to the planning and development of Greater London and those areas;

and the committee may, if it thinks fit, contribute towards the expenses of any such body as is mentioned in paragraph (c).

(3) The expenses of the joint planning committee which have been incurred with the approval of at least two-thirds of the local planning authorities in Greater London shall be defrayed by those authorities in such proportions as they may decide or, in default of a decision by them, as the Secretary of State may determine.

(4) References in this section to the local planning authorities in Greater London are to the authorities which are local planning authorities for the purposes of Part II.

                                                                                    [10]

NOTES
Commencement: 24 August 1990.

4. National Parks

(1) As respects an area in a National Park [in England] outside a metropolitan county all functions conferred by or under the planning Acts on a local planning authority or district planning authority shall, subject to subsections (2) and (3), be functions of the county planning authority and no other authority, and references in those Acts in their application to a National Park outside a metropolitan county to a local planning authority or district planning authority shall be construed accordingly.

(2) The functions conferred on a local planning authority by sections 198 to 201, 206 to 209 and 211 to 215 shall as respects any part of a National Park [in England] outside a metropolitan county be exercisable concurrently with the county planning authority by the district planning authority whose area includes that part of the Park.

(3) Where an order is made under section 7 of the National Parks and Access to the Countryside Act 1949 designating or extending the area of a National Park, the functions exercisable by a local planning authority immediately before the coming into force of the order for any area which under the order becomes part of the Park shall continue to be exercisable by that authority as respects that area unless and until a joint planning board is constituted under section 2 [, a special planning board is constituted under paragraph 3A of Schedule 17 to the Local Government Act 1972] or a National Park Committee is appointed under Part I of [that Schedule] for an area co-terminous with or including that area or, as the case may be, is authorised to exercise those functions.

(4) Where a joint planning board for a National Park situated partly in one or more metropolitan counties is the local planning authority as respects the part of the Park situated in that county or those counties, it shall continue to be so.

[(5) This section shall have effect subject to section 4A below.]   **[11]**

NOTES
Commencement: 24 August 1990 (sub-ss (1)–(4)); to be appointed (sub-s (5)).
Words in square brackets in sub-ss (1), (2) inserted by the Local Government (Wales) Act 1994, s 20(4)(b), Sch 6, Pt II, para 24(1)(a), as from a day to be appointed.
Words in square brackets in sub-s (3) inserted and substituted respectively by the Local Government (Wales) Act 1994, s 20(4)(b), Sch 6, Pt II, para 24(1)(b).
Sub-s (5) inserted by the Environment Act 1995, s 78, Sch 10, para 32(3), and whole section repealed by s 120(3) of, and Sch 24 to, that Act, both as from a day or days to be appointed under s 125(3).
Planning Acts: Town and Country Planning Act 1990, Planning (Listed Buildings and Conservation Areas) Act 1990, Planning (Hazardous Substances) Act 1990, Planning (Consequential Provisions) Act 1990.

[4A. National Parks with National Park authorities

(1) Where a National Park authority has been established for any area, this section, *instead of section 4(1) to (4)*, shall apply, as from such time as may be specified for the purposes of this section in the order establishing that authority, in relation to the Park for which it is the authority.

(2) Subject to subsections (4) and (5) below, the National Park authority for the Park shall be the sole local planning authority for the area of the Park and, accordingly—

    (a) functions conferred by or under the planning Acts on a planning authority of any description (including the functions of a mineral planning authority under those Acts and under the Planning and Compensation Act 1991) shall, in relation to the Park, be functions of the National Park authority, and not of any other authority; and

(b) so much of the area of any other authority as is included in the Park shall be treated as excluded from any area for which that other authority is a planning authority of any description.

(3) For the purposes of subsection (2) above functions under the planning Acts which (apart from this section) are conferred—

(a) in relation to some areas on the county or district planning authorities for those areas, and

(b) in relation to other areas on the councils for those areas,

shall be treated, in relation to those other areas, as conferred on each of those councils as the local planning authority for their area.

(4) The functions of a local planning authority by virtue of sections 198 to 201, 206 to 209 and 211 to 215, so far as they are functions of a National Park authority by virtue of this section, shall be exercisable as respects any area which is or is included in an area for which there is a district council, concurrently with the National Park authority, by that council.

(5) For the purposes of any enactment relating to the functions of a district planning authority, the functions of a district council by virtue of subsection (4) above shall be deemed to be conferred on them as a district planning authority and as if the district were the area for which they are such an authority.]   **[11A]**

NOTES
  Commencement: 19 September 1995.
  Inserted by the Environment Act 1995, s 67(1); words in italics in sub-s (1) repealed by s 120(3) of, and Sch 24 to, that Act, as from a day to be appointed under s 125(3).

5. The Broads

(1) For the purposes of Chapter I of Part VIII and sections 249, 250, [and 300] and any other provision of this Act so far as it has effect for the purposes of those provisions, "local planning authority", in relation to land in the Broads, includes the Broads Authority.

(2) For the purposes of the provisions mentioned in subsection (3) the Broads Authority shall be the sole district planning authority for the Broads.

(3) The provisions referred to in subsection (2) are [Part II, sections] 62, [65, 69 to 72], 76 to [79], 91 to 95, 97 to 99, 102, 103, 106 [to 106B] [, 171C], 172, 173, [173A,] 178, 183, 184, [187A, 187B] 188, 191 to 197, 211 to [214, 215], 219 to 221, 224, 294, 295, 297, 299, [299A,] 301, [316 and 324(1) and (7)].   **[12]**

NOTES
  Commencement: 24 August 1990.
  Words in square brackets in sub-ss (1), (3) substituted or inserted by the Planning and Compensation Act 1991, s 32, Sch 7, paras 8, 9.

6. Enterprise zones

(1) An order under paragraph 5 of Schedule 32 to the Local Government, Planning and Land Act 1980 (designation of enterprise zone) may provide that the enterprise zone authority shall be the local planning authority for the zone for such purposes of the planning Acts and in relation to such kinds of development as may be specified in the order.

(2) Without prejudice to the generality of paragraph 15(1) of that Schedule (modification of orders by the Secretary of State), an order under that paragraph may provide that the enterprise zone authority shall be the local planning authority for the zone for different purposes of the planning Acts or in relation to different kinds of development.

(3) Where such provision as is mentioned in subsection (1) or (2) is made by an order designating an enterprise zone or, as the case may be, an order modifying such an order, while the zone subsists the enterprise zone authority shall be, to the extent mentioned in the order (as it has effect subject to any such modifications) and to the extent that it is not already, the local planning authority for the zone in place of any authority who would otherwise be the local planning authority for the zone.

(4) The Secretary of State may by regulations make transitional and supplementary provision in relation to a provision of an order under paragraph 5 of that Schedule made by virtue of subsection (1).

(5) Such regulations may modify any provision of the planning Acts or any instrument made under any of them or may apply any such enactment or instrument (with or without modification) in making such transitional or supplementary provision. **[13]**

NOTES
Commencement: 24 August 1990.
Planning Acts: Town and Country Planning Act 1990, Planning (Listed Buildings and Conservation Areas) Act 1990, Planning (Hazardous Substances) Act 1990, Planning (Consequential Provisions) Act 1990.

7. Urban development areas

(1) Where an order is made under subsection (1) of section 149 of the Local Government, Planning and Land Act 1980 (urban development corporation as planning authority), the urban development corporation specified in the order shall be the local planning authority for such area as may be so specified in place of any authority who would otherwise be the local planning authority for that area for such purposes and in relation to such kinds of development as may be so specified.

(2) Where an order under subsection (3)(a) of that section confers any functions on an urban development corporation in relation to any area the corporation shall have those functions in place of any authority (except the Secretary of State) who would otherwise have them in that area. **[14]**

NOTES
Commencement: 24 August 1990.

8. Housing action areas

(1) Where an order is made under subsection (1) of section 67 of the Housing Act 1988 (housing action trust as planning authority), the housing action trust specified in the order shall be the local planning authority for such area as may be so specified in place of any authority who would otherwise be the local planning authority for that area for such purposes and in relation to such kinds of development as may be so specified.

(2) Where an order under subsection (3)(a) of that section confers any functions on a housing action trust in relation to any area the trust shall have those functions in place of any authority (except the Secretary of State) who would otherwise have them in that area. **[15]**

NOTES
  Commencement: 24 August 1990.

[8A. The Urban Regeneration Agency

(1) Where a designation order under section 170 of the Leasehold Reform, Housing and Urban Development Act 1993 (power to make designation orders) makes such provision as is mentioned in subsection (1) of section 171 of that Act (Agency as local planning authority), the Urban Regeneration Agency shall be the local planning authority for such area as may be specified in the order in place of any authority who would otherwise be the local planning authority for that area for such purposes and in relation to such kinds of development as may be so specified.

(2) Where such an order makes such provision as is mentioned in subsection (3)(a) of section 171 of that Act, the Urban Regeneration Agency shall have the functions specified in the order for such area as may be so specified in place of any authority (except the Secretary of State) who would otherwise have them in that area.]   **[15A]**

NOTES
  Commencement: 10 November 1993.
  Inserted by the Leasehold Reform, Housing and Urban Development Act 1993, s 187(1), Sch 21, para 29.

9. Power to make consequential and supplementary provision about authorities

Regulations under this Act may make such provision consequential upon or supplementary to the provisions of sections 1 and 2 as appears to the Secretary of State to be necessary or expedient.   **[16]**

NOTES
  Commencement: 24 August 1990.

PART II

DEVELOPMENT PLANS

CHAPTER I

UNITARY DEVELOPMENT PLANS: METROPOLITAN AREAS INCLUDING LONDON

Preliminary

10. Application of Chapter I to Greater London and metropolitan counties

This Chapter applies, subject to section 28, to the area of any local planning authority in Greater London or a metropolitan county (other than any area in such a county which is part of a National Park).   **[17]**

NOTES
  Commencement: this Chapter (ss 10–28) comes into force in accordance with s 28 at **[35]**. By s 28(2), in any area in relation to which an order has been made before the commencement of this Act under the Local Government Act 1985, s 4(1) (repealed by the Planning (Consequential Provisions) Act 1990, s 3, Sch 1, Pt I at **[516]**) the provisions of this Chapter come into force at the commencement of this Act or, if later, on the day appointed by the order. Otherwise, this Chapter comes into force on such day as may be appointed in relation to the area concerned by the Secretary of State under s 28(1). Until a unitary development plan becomes wholly operative under this Chapter for an area mentioned in s 28(1), the provisions of Sch 2 at **[346]**–**[348]** apply in relation to it. Pt I of that Schedule makes provision as to metropolitan counties. Pt II makes provision as to Greater London.
  The following table lists the orders made under s 4(1) of the 1985 Act, the date on which the

provisions of the 1985 Act replaced by this Chapter came into operation in relation thereto, and the areas of the local planning authorities affected.

Order	Area	Date
1988/140	County of West Midlands other than metropolitan district of Dudley	29 February 1988
1988/1179	County of Merseyside	4 August 1988
1989/637	County of Tyne and Wear other than metropolitan district of Sunderland	8 May 1989
1989/1065	County of West Yorkshire other than metropolitan district of Bradford	25 September 1989
1989/1089	Great London other than London Boroughs of Hackney, Hammersmith and Fulham, Hillingdon, Hounslow and Lewisham; metropolitan borough of Dudley	11 August 1989
1989/1979	County of South Yorkshire other than metropolitan districts of Barnsley and Rotherham; London borough of Hounslow	28 November 1989
1989/2114	County of Greater Manchester; metropolitan district of Sunderland	19 December 1989
1990/652	London Boroughs of Hackney, Hammersmith and Fulham, Hillingdon and Lewisham; city of Bradford; metropolitan borough of Barnsley	13 April 1990
1990/1183	Metropolitan borough of Rotherham	3 July 1990

[10A. Application of Chapter I in relation to Wales

(1) This Chapter also applies to the area of any local planning authority in Wales.

(2) Subsections (3) and (4) apply where the area of a local planning authority in Wales includes—

(a) the whole or any part of an area prescribed under section 23B(2) in relation to a National Park, and

(b) other land.

(3) The provisions of this Chapter apply separately in relation to—

(a) the Park area or, if there is more than one, each Park area, and

(b) the remaining area.

(4) Any reference in any of the following sections of this Chapter to the area of the local planning authority (including any reference which falls to be so construed) shall be construed—

(a) in its application in relation to any Park area, as a reference to that Park area, and

(b) in its application in relation to the remaining area, as a reference to that area.

(5) In this section—

"the Park area", in relation to a National Park, means the part of the local planning authority's area which is within the area prescribed under section 23B(2) in relation to that Park or, where there is more than one such part, those parts taken as a whole;

"the remaining area" means the part of the local planning authority's area which is not within the area so prescribed in relation to any National Park.]

[17A]

NOTES

Inserted by the Local Government (Wales) Act 1994, s 20(1), as from a day to be appointed.

Surveys etc

11. Survey of planning areas

(1) The local planning authority—

    (a) shall keep under review the matters which may be expected to affect the development of their area or the planning of its development; and

    (b) may, if they think fit, institute a survey or surveys of their area or any part of their area for examining those matters.

(2) Without prejudice to the generality of subsection (1), the matters to be kept under review or examined under that subsection shall include—

    (a) the principal physical and economic characteristics of the area of the authority (including the principal purposes for which land is used) and, so far as they may be expected to affect that area, of any neighbouring areas;

    (b) the size, composition and distribution of the population of that area (whether resident or otherwise);

    (c) without prejudice to paragraph (a), the communications, transport system and traffic of that area and, so far as they may be expected to affect that area, of any neighbouring areas;

    (d) any considerations not mentioned in paragraphs (a), (b) and (c) which may be expected to affect any matters mentioned in them;

    (e) such other matters as may be prescribed or as the Secretary of State may in a particular case direct;

    (f) any changes already projected in any of the matters mentioned in any of paragraphs (a) to (e) and the effect which those changes are likely to have on the development of that area or the planning of such development.

(3) A local planning authority shall, for the purpose of discharging their functions under this section of keeping under review and examining any matters relating to the area of another such authority, consult with that other authority about those matters.

[18]

NOTES

Commencement: see the note to s 10 at **[17]**.

Preparation and adoption of unitary development plans

12. Preparation of unitary development plan

(1) The local planning authority shall, within such period (if any) as the Secretary of State may direct, prepare for their area a plan to be known as a unitary development plan.

(2) A unitary development plan shall comprise two parts.

(3) Part I of a unitary development plan shall consist of a written statement formulating the authority's general policies in respect of the development and [use of land in their area].

[(3A) The policies shall, subject to subsection (3B), include policies in respect of—

    (a) the conservation of the natural beauty and amenity of the land;

    (b) the improvement of the physical environment; and

    (c) the management of traffic.

(3B) Regulations under this section may prescribe the aspects of such development and use with which the general policies in Part I of a unitary development plan are to be concerned, in which case the policies shall be concerned with those aspects and no others.]

(4) Part II of a unitary development plan shall consist of—

 (a) a written statement formulating in such detail as the authority think appropriate (and so as to be readily distinguishable from the other contents of the plan) their proposals for the development and ... use of land in their area ...;

 (b) a map showing those proposals on a geographical basis;

 (c) a reasoned justification of the general policies in Part I of the plan and of the proposals in Part II of it; and

 (d) such diagrams, illustrations or other descriptive or explanatory matter in respect of the general policies in Part I of the plan or the proposals in Part II of it as the authority think appropriate or as may be prescribed.

(5) A unitary development plan shall also contain such other matters as may be prescribed or as the Secretary of State may in any particular case direct.

[(6) In formulating the general policies in Part I of a unitary development plan the authority shall have regard to—

 (a) any regional or strategic planning guidance given by the Secretary of State to assist them in the preparation of the plan;

 (b) current national policies;

 (c) the resources likely to be available; and

 (d) to such other matters as the Secretary of State may prescribe or, in a particular case, direct.]

(7) The proposals in Part II of a unitary development plan shall be in general conformity with Part I.

[(7A) In formulating their proposals in Part II of a unitary development plan, the authority shall have regard to such information and other considerations as the Secretary of State may prescribe or, in a particular case, direct.]

(8) Part II of a unitary development plan may designate any part of the authority's area as an action area, that is to say, an area which they have selected for the commencement during a prescribed period of comprehensive treatment by development, redevelopment or improvement (or partly by one and partly by another method) and if an area is so designated that Part of the plan shall contain a description of the treatment proposed by the authority.

(9) In preparing a unitary development plan the authority shall take into account the provisions of any scheme under paragraph 3 of Schedule 32 to the Local Government, Planning and Land Act 1980 relating to land in their area which has been designated under that Schedule as an enterprise zone.

[(10) Regulations under this section may make different provision for different cases and shall be subject to any direction given, in a particular case, by the Secretary of State.]

[(11) Any provision made by regulations under this section in its application by virtue of section 10 may differ from that made under this section in its application by virtue of section 10A.]   **[19]**

NOTES

Commencement: as to sub-ss (1)–(3), (4), (5), (7), (9), see the note to s 10 at **[17]**; 25 November 1991 (sub-ss (3A), (6), (7A), (10) for certain purposes); 10 February 1992 (sub-ss (3A), (6), (7A), (10) for remaining purposes).

Words in square brackets in sub-s (3) and the whole of sub-s (6) substituted, sub-ss (3A), (3B), (7A) inserted, words omitted from sub-s (4)(a) repealed, and sub-s (10) added, by the Planning and Compensation Act 1991, ss 27, 84(6), Sch 4, Pt I, paras 1, 2, Sch 19, Pt I.

Sub-s (11) added by the Local Government (Wales) Act 1994, s 20(3)(a), Sch 5, Pt I, paras 1, 2, as from a day to be appointed.

Modification: sub-s (3A) (and ss 31(3), 36(3)) modified by the Waste Management Licensing Regulations 1994, SI 1994/1056, regs 1(3), 19, Sch 4, Pt I, para 7(1), (2), so as to have effect as if the policies referred to in those sections included policies in respect of suitable waste disposal sites or installations, subject, in the case of the policies referred to in s 36(3), to the provisions of s 36(5).

[12A. Urban development corporations

(1) The Secretary of State may direct that a unitary development plan—

    (a) shall not be prepared; or

    (b) shall not operate,

in relation to the area of an urban development corporation.

(2) The Secretary of State may direct that proposals for the alteration or replacement of a unitary development plan shall not be prepared in relation to the area of an urban development corporation.] **[19A]**

NOTES

Commencement: 10 February 1992.

Inserted by the Planning and Compensation Act 1991, s 27, Sch 4, Pt I, paras 1, 3.

[13. Public participation

(1) When preparing a unitary development plan for their area and before finally determining its contents the local planning authority shall—

    (a) comply with—

        (i) any requirements imposed by regulations made under section 26; and

        (ii) any particular direction given to them by the Secretary of State with respect to a matter falling within any of paragraphs (a) to (c) or (e) of subsection (2) of that section; and

    (b) consider any representations made in accordance with those regulations.

(2) Where the local planning authority have prepared a unitary development plan, before adopting it they shall—

    (a) makes copies of it available for inspection at such places as may be prescribed by those regulations;

    (b) send a copy to the Secretary of State; and

    (c) comply with any requirements imposed by those regulations.

(3) Each copy made available for inspection or sent under subsection (2) shall be accompanied by a statement of the prescribed period within which objections may be made to the authority.

(4) In this section "the prescribed period" means such period as may be prescribed by or determined in accordance with regulations made under section 26 and in this Chapter "objections made in accordance with the regulations" means objections made—

    (a) in accordance with regulations made under that section; and

(b) within the prescribed period.

(5) The persons who may make objections in accordance with the regulations include, in particular, the Secretary of State.

(6) A unitary development plan shall not be adopted by the authority under section 15 until—

(a) after they have considered any objections made in accordance with the regulations; or

(b) if no such objections are made, after the expiry of the prescribed period.]

[20]

NOTES
  Commencement: 25 November 1991 (certain purposes); 10 February 1992 (remainder).
  Substituted by the Planning and Compensation Act 1991, s 27, Sch 4, Pt I, paras 1, 4. For transitional provisions, see Sch 4, Pt III, para 41(1) to the 1991 Act at **[547]**.

14. Withdrawal of unitary development plan

(1) A unitary development plan may be withdrawn by the local planning authority at any time before it is adopted by the authority or approved by the Secretary of State and shall be withdrawn by the authority if the Secretary of State so directs.

(2) Where a unitary development plan is withdrawn the authority shall—

(a) withdraw the copies made available for inspection and sent to the Secretary of State under section [13(2)]; and

(b) give notice that the plan has been withdrawn to every person who has made an objection to it.

(3) . . .

(4) Where a unitary development plan is withdrawn the copies of the plan shall be treated as never having been made available under section [13(2)].   **[21]**

NOTES
  Commencement: see the note to s 10 at **[17]**.
  Words in square brackets in sub-ss (2), (4) substituted, and the whole of sub-s (3) repealed, by the Planning and Compensation Act 1991, ss 27, 84(6), Sch 4, Pt I, paras 1, 5, Sch 19, Pt I.

15. Adoption of unitary development plan by local planning authority

[(1) Subject to the following provisions of this section and sections [17 and 18, the local planning authority may be resolution adopt the unitary development plan, either as originally prepared or as modified so as to take account of—

(a) any objections made to the plan; or

(b) any other considerations which appear to the them to be material.]

(2) A unitary development plan shall not be adopted unless Part II of the plan is in general conformity with Part I.

(3) Where an objection to a unitary development plan [for an area in England] has been made by the Minister of Agriculture, Fisheries and Food and the local planning authority do not propose to modify the plan to take account of the objection, the authority—

(a) shall send the Secretary of State particulars of the objection and a statement of their reasons for not modifying the plan to take account of it; and

(b) shall not adopt the plan unless the Secretary of State authorises them to do so.

(4) Subject to the following provisions of this Chapter and to section 287, a unitary development plan shall become operative on the date on which it is adopted.

[22]

NOTES

Commencement: as to sub-ss (2)–(4), see the note to s 10 at **[17]**; 25 November 1991 (sub-s (1) for certain purposes); 10 February 1991 (sub-s (1) for remaining purposes).

Sub-s (1) substituted by the Planning and Compensation Act 1991, s 27, Sch 4, Pt I, paras 1, 6.

Words in square brackets in sub-s (3) inserted by the Local Government (Wales) Act 1994, s 20(3)(a), Sch 5, Pt I, paras 1, 3, as from a day to be appointed.

16. Local inquiries

[(1) Where any objections have been made, in accordance with the regulations, to proposals for a unitary development plan copies of which have been made available for inspection under section 13(2), the local planning authority shall cause a local inquiry or other hearing to be held for the purpose of considering the objections.

(1A) The local planning authority may cause a local inquiry or other hearing to be held for the purpose of considering any other objections to the proposals.

(1B) The local inquiry or other hearing shall be held by a person appointed by the Secretary of State or, in such cases as may be prescribed, by the authority themselves.]

(2) Subsections (2) and (3) of section 250 of the Local Government Act 1972 (power to summon and examine witnesses) shall apply to an inquiry held under this section as they apply to an inquiry under that section.

(3) The Tribunals and Inquiries Act [1992] shall apply to a local inquiry or other hearing held under this section as it applies to a statutory inquiry held by the Secretary of State, but as if in [section 10(1)] of that Act (statement of reasons for decisions) the reference to any decision taken by the Secretary of State were a reference to a decision taken by a local planning authority.

(4) Regulations made for the purposes of this section may—

(a) make provision with respect to the appointment and qualifications for appointment of persons to hold a local inquiry or other hearing under this section, including provision enabling the Secretary of State to direct a local planning authority to appoint a particular person or one of a specified list or class of persons;

(b) make provision with respect to the remuneration and allowances of a person appointed for that purpose.

(5) No local inquiry or other hearing need be held under this section if all persons who have made objections have indicated in writing that they do not wish to appear.   **[23]**

NOTES

Commencement: as to sub-ss (2)–(5), see the note to s 10 at **[17]**; 25 November 1991 (sub-ss (1)–(1B) for certain purposes); 10 February 1992 (sub-ss (1)–(1B) for remaining purposes).

Sub-ss (1), (1A), (1B) substituted for original sub-s (1) by the Planning and Compensation Act 1991, s 27, Sch 4, Pt I, paras 1, 7.

Words in square brackets in sub-s (3) substituted by the Tribunals and Inquiries Act 1992, s 18(1), Sch 3, para 22.

Secretary of State's powers concerning plans

17. Direction to reconsider proposals

(1) After a copy of a unitary development plan has been sent to the Secretary of State under section [13(2)] and before it is adopted by the local planning authority, the Secretary of State may, if it appears to him that the plan is unsatisfactory, direct the authority to [modify] the proposals in such respects as are indicated in the direction.

(2) An authority to whom a direction is given shall not adopt the plan unless they satisfy the Secretary of State that they have made the modifications necessary to conform with the direction or the direction is withdrawn.   **[24]**

NOTES

Commencement: See the note to s 10 at **[17]**.

Words in square brackets in sub-s (1) substituted by the Planning and Compensation Act 1991, s 27, Sch 4, Pt I, paras 1, 8, 9.

18. Calling in of unitary development plan for approval by Secretary of State

(1) After a copy of a unitary development plan has been sent to the Secretary of State under section [13(2)] and before it is adopted by the local planning authority, the Secretary of State may direct that the whole or part of the plan shall be submitted to him for his approval.

(2) If such a direction is given—

    (a) the authority shall not take any further steps for the adoption of the plan until the Secretary of State has given his decision on the plan or the relevant part of it; and

    (b) the plan or the relevant part of it shall not have effect unless approved by him and shall not require adoption under the previous provisions of this Chapter.

(3) Where particulars of an objection to a unitary development plan [for an area in England] have been sent to the Secretary of State under section 15(3), then, unless he is satisfied that the Minister of Agriculture, Fisheries and Food no longer objects to the plan, the Secretary of State must give a direction in respect of it under subsection (1).

(4) Subsection (2)(a) applies in particular to holding or proceeding with a local inquiry or other hearing in respect of the plan under section 16; and at any such inquiry or hearing which is subsequently held or resumed a local planning authority need not give any person an opportunity of being heard in respect of any objection which has been heard at an examination, local inquiry or other hearing under section 20 or which the Secretary of State states that he has considered in making his decision.   **[25]**

NOTES

Commencement: see the note to s 10 at **[17]**.

Words in square brackets in sub-s (1) substituted by the Planning and Compensation Act 1991, s 27, Sch 4, Pt I, paras 1, 9.

Words in square brackets in sub-s (3) inserted by the Local Government (Wales) Act 1994, s 20(3)(a), Sch 5, Pt I, paras 1, 3, as from a day to be appointed.

19. Approval of unitary development plan by Secretary of State

(1) Subject to section 20, the Secretary of State may after considering a plan or part of a plan submitted to him under section 18(1) either approve it (in whole or in part and with or without modifications or reservations) or reject it.

(2) In considering a plan or part of a plan submitted to him under that section the Secretary of State may take into account any matters which he thinks relevant, whether or not they were taken into account in [preparing] the plan or that part of it.

(3) The Secretary of State shall give a local planning authority such statement as he considers appropriate of the reasons governing his decision on any plan or part of a plan submitted to him.

(4) Where the whole or part of Part I of a unitary development plan is approved by the Secretary of State with modifications, the local planning authority shall, before adopting the remainder of the plan, make such modifications in Part II as may be directed by the Secretary of State for bringing it into general conformity with Part I and, in the absence of any such direction, shall make such modifications for that purpose in Part II as appear to the authority to be required.

(5) Subject to section 287, a plan or part of a plan which is approved by the Secretary of State under this section shall become operative on such day as he may appoint.   **[26]**

NOTES
Commencement: see the note to s 10 at **[17]**.
Words in square brackets in sub-s (2) inserted by the Planning and Compensation Act 1991, s 27, Sch 4, Pt I, paras 1, 10.

20. Local inquiry, public examination and consultation by Secretary of State

(1) Before deciding whether or not to approve a plan or part of a plan submitted to him under section 18(1), the Secretary of State shall consider any objection to it so far as made in accordance with [the regulations].

(2) Where the whole or part of Part II of a unitary development plan is submitted to the Secretary of State under section 18(1) (whether or not the whole or part of Part I is also submitted), then, if any objections have been made to the plan or the relevant part of it as mentioned in subsection (1), before deciding whether to approve it he shall cause a local inquiry or other hearing to be held for the purpose of considering those objections.

(3) The Secretary of State need not under subsection (1) consider any objections which have already been considered by the local planning authority and need not cause a local inquiry or other hearing to be held under subsection (2) if that authority have already held a local inquiry or other hearing into the objections under section 16 or the Secretary of State, on taking the plan or the relevant part of it into consideration, decides to reject it.

(4) Where the whole or part of Part I of a unitary development plan (but not the whole or any part of Part II) is submitted to the Secretary of State under section 18(1) he may cause a person or persons appointed by him for the purpose to hold an examination in public of such matters affecting the Secretary of State's consideration of the part of the plan submitted to him as he considers ought to be so examined.

(5) The Secretary of State may, after consultation with the Lord Chancellor, make regulations with respect to the procedure to be followed at any examination under subsection (4).

(6) The Secretary of State shall not be required to secure to any local planning authority or other person a right to be heard at an examination under subsection (4), and the bodies and persons who may take part shall be such only as he may, whether before or during the course of the examination, in his discretion invite to do so; but the person or persons holding the examination shall have power, exercisable either

before or during the course of the examination, to invite additional bodies or persons to take part if it appears to him or them desirable to do so.

(7) An examination under subsection (4) shall constitute a statutory inquiry for the purposes of section 1(1)(c) of the Tribunals and Inquiries Act [1992] but shall not constitute such an inquiry for any other purpose of that Act.

(8) On considering a plan or part of a plan submitted to him under section 18(1) the Secretary of State may consult with or consider the views of any local planning authority or other person but he need not do so except as provided by this section.

[27]

NOTES
    Commencement: see the note to s 10 at [17].
    Words in square brackets in sub-s (1) substituted by the Planning and Compensation Act 1991, s 27, Sch 4, Pt I, paras 1, 11.
    Figure in square brackets in sub-s (7) substituted by the Tribunals and Inquiries Act 1992, s 18(1), Sch 3, para 23.

Alteration of plans

21. Alteration or replacement of unitary development plan

[(1) A local planning authority may at any time prepare proposals—

  (a) for alterations to the unitary development plan for their area; or
  (b) for its replacement.

(1A) If the Secretary of State directs them to do so, the authority shall prepare, within such time as he may direct, proposals for—

  (a) such alterations to the unitary development plan as he directs; or
  (b) its replacement.

(1B) An authority shall not, without the consent of the Secretary of State, prepare proposals in respect of a unitary development plan if the plan or any part of it has been approved by the Secretary of State.]

(2) . . . sections 12 to 20 (other than subsection (1) of section 12) shall apply in relation to the making of proposals under this section and to any alteration or replacement so proposed as they apply to the preparation of a unitary development plan under section 12 and to a plan prepared under that section.

(3) As soon as practicable after—

  (a) an order has been made under paragraph 5 of Schedule 32 to the Local Government, Planning and Land Act 1980 (designation of enterprise zone); or
  (b) a notification has been given under paragraph 11(1) of that Schedule (approval of modification of enterprise zone scheme),

the local planning authority for an area in which the zone is wholly or partly situated shall review any unitary development plan for that area in the light of the provisions of the scheme or modified scheme under that Schedule and prepare proposals under this section for any consequential alterations to the plan which they consider necessary.   [28–29]

NOTES
    Commencement: as to sub-ss (2), (3), see the note to s 10 at [17]; 25 November 1991 (sub-ss (1)–(1B) for certain purposes); 10 February 1992 (sub-s (1)–(1B) for remaining purposes).
    Sub-ss (1), (1A), (1B) substituted for original sub-s (1), and the words omitted from sub-s (2) repealed, by the Planning and Compensation Act 1991, ss 27, 84(6), Sch 4, Pt I, paras 1, 12, Sch 19, Pt I.

22. (*Repealed by the Planning and Compensation Act 1991, ss 27, 84(6), Sch 4, Pt I, paras 1, 13, Sch 19, Pt I.*)

Joint plans

23. Joint unitary development plans

(1) A joint unitary development plan or joint proposals for the alteration or replacement of such a plan may be prepared by two or more local planning authorities in Greater London or by two or more local planning authorities in a metropolitan county; and the previous provisions of this Chapter shall, in relation to any such joint plan or proposals, have effect subject to the following provisions of this section.

(2)–(4) ...

(5) Each of the local planning authorities by whom a joint unitary development plan is prepared shall have the duty imposed by subsection [(2)] of section 13 of making copies of the plan available for inspection.

(6) Objections to such a plan may be made to any of those authorities and the statement required by subsection [(3)] of section 13 to accompany copies of the plan shall state that objections may be so made.

(7) It shall be for each of the local planning authorities by whom a joint unitary development plan is prepared to adopt the plan under section 15(1) and they may do so as respects any part of their area to which the plan relates, but any modifications subject to which the plan is adopted must have the agreement of all those authorities.

(8) Where a unitary development plan has been prepared jointly, the power of [preparing] proposals in respect of the plan under section 21 may be exercised as respects their respective areas by any of the authorities by whom it was prepared and the Secretary of State may under that section direct any of them to [prepare] proposals as respects their respective areas.

(9), (10) ...

(11) The date of the coming into operation of a unitary development plan prepared jointly by two or more local planning authorities or for the alteration or replacement of such a plan in pursuance of proposals so prepared shall be a date jointly agreed by those authorities.   **[30]**

NOTES
   Commencement: see the note to s 10 at **[17]**.
   Sub-ss (2)–(4), (9), (10) repealed, and words in square brackets in sub-ss (5), (6), (8) substituted, by the Planning and Compensation Act 1991, ss 27, 84(6), Sch 4, Pt I, paras 1, 14, Sch 19, Pt I.

[23A. Joint unitary development plans: Wales

(1) A joint unitary development plan or joint proposals for the alteration or replacement of such a plan may be prepared by two or more local planning authorities in Wales for their areas if—

   (a) each of those areas adjoins each of the others; or

(b) the Secretary of State has given his approval.

(2) Subsection (1) does not apply in relation to a joint plan for any area which consists of or includes a National Park.

(3) The previous provisions of this Chapter shall, in relation to any joint plan or proposals of a kind mentioned in subsection (1), have effect subject to the following provisions of this section.

(4) Each of the local planning authorities by whom a joint unitary development plan is prepared shall have the duty imposed under section 13(2) of making copies of the plan available for inspection.

(5) Objections to such a plan may be made to any of those authorities and the statement required by section 13(3) to accompany copies of the plan shall state that objections may be so made.

(6) It shall be for each of the local planning authorities by whom a joint unitary development plan is prepared to adopt the plan under section 15(1) and, subject to the provisions of this Chapter, they may do so as respects the part of their area to which the plan relates, but any modifications subject to which the plan is adopted must have the agreement of all those authorities.

(7) Where a unitary development plan has been prepared jointly, the power of preparing proposals in respect of the plan under section 21 may be exercised as respects their respective areas by any of the authorities by whom it was prepared and the Secretary of State may under that section direct any of them to prepare proposals as respects their respective areas.

(8) The date of the coming into operation of a unitary development plan prepared jointly by two or more local planning authorities or for the alteration or replacement of such a plan in pursuance of proposals so prepared shall be a date jointly agreed by those authorities.]   **[30A]**

NOTES
    Inserted, with ss 23B, 23C at **[30B]**, **[30C]**, by the Local Government (Wales) Act 1994, s 20(3)(a), Sch 5, Pt I, paras 1, 4, as from a day to be appointed.

[National Parks in Wales

23B. Unitary development plans for National Parks in Wales

(1) A unitary development plan shall be prepared for each National Park in Wales.

(2) A Welsh National Park development plan shall relate to an area prescribed in relation to the National Park in question by order made by the Secretary of State.

(3) The prescribed area in relation to a National Park which falls wholly within, but does not comprise the whole of, the area of a single local planning authority shall be—

   (a) where the local planning authority have so elected, the whole of the area of the local planning authority; and
   (b) in any other case—
      (i) the whole of the area of the National Park; or
      (ii) a composite area.

(4) The prescribed area in relation to any other Welsh National Park shall be—

   (a) the whole of the area of the National Park; or

(b) a composite area.

(5) For the purposes of this section and section 23C, "composite area", in relation to a National Park, means an area which consists of the whole of the Park together with any one or more other areas in Wales.

(6) The Secretary of State shall not under subsection (2) prescribe an area which is a composite area except with the consent of every local planning authority in whose area the prescribed area or any part of it would fall.

(7) Any order made by the Secretary of State under subsection (2) may make such saving or transitional provision as he considers appropriate.

(8) Where, by an order under subsection (2), the Secretary of State prescribes a composite area which comprises or includes part only of the area of a local planning authority, the provisions of this Chapter shall apply in relation to—

(a) the Welsh National Park development plan in question, or
(b) any proposals for its alteration or replacement,

subject to such modifications, if any, as may be prescribed by the order.

(9) Subsections (3) and (4) of section 10A do not apply for the purposes of—

(a) subsection (3) or (8) of this section, or
(b) section 23C(1), (2) or (4).

(10) For the purposes of this Act, "Welsh National Park development plan" means a unitary development plan prepared for a National Park in Wales.]   **[30B]**

NOTES
   See the notes to s 23A at **[30A]**.

[23C. Joint unitary development plans for National Parks in Wales

(1) A Welsh National Park development plan for a National Park which neither coincides with nor falls wholly within the area of a single local planning authority shall be a joint unitary development plan.

(2) A Welsh National Park development plan for any other National Park shall be a joint unitary development plan if it relates to a composite area unless the composite area coincides with or falls wholly within the area of a single local planning authority.

(3) Any Welsh National Park development plan which is required to be a joint plan shall be prepared by the authorities who will be the appropriate authorities in relation to the plan.

(4) For the purposes of this section, an authority are an appropriate authority in relation to a joint plan if—

(a) they are a local planning authority; and
(b) their area or any part of their area falls within the area to which the plan relates.

(5) Any proposals prepared under section 21 for the alteration or replacement of a joint plan of a kind mentioned in subsection (1) or (2) shall be joint proposals prepared by the appropriate authorities in relation to that plan, and any direction given by the Secretary of State under that section in relation to that plan shall be given jointly to those authorities.

(6) Subsections (3) to (6) and (8) of section 23A apply in relation to any joint

plan or proposals of a kind mentioned in subsection (1), (2) or (5) as they apply in relation to any joint plan or proposals of a kind mentioned in section 23A(1).] **[30C]**

Supplementary

24. Disregard of certain representations

Notwithstanding anything in the previous provisions of this Chapter, neither the Secretary of State nor a local planning authority shall be required to consider representations or objections with respect to a unitary development plan or any proposals for the alteration or replacement of such a plan if it appears to the Secretary of State or, as the case may be, the authority that those representations or objections are in substance representations or objections with respect to things done or proposed to be done in pursuance of—

(a) an order or scheme under section 10, 14, 16, 18, 106(1) or (3) or 108(1) of the Highways Act 1980;

(b) an order or scheme under any provision replaced by the provisions mentioned in paragraph (a), namely, an order or scheme under section 7, 9, 11, 13 or 20 of the Highways Act 1959, section 3 of the Highways (Miscellaneous Provisions) Act 1961 or section 1 or 10 of the Highways Act 1971; or

(c) an order under section 1 of the New Towns Act 1981.   **[31]**

25. Default powers

(1) Where, by virtue of any of the previous provisions of this Chapter, any unitary development plan or proposals for the alteration or replacement of such a plan are required to be prepared, or steps are required to be taken for the adoption of any such plan or proposals, then—

(a) if at any time the Secretary of State is satisfied, after holding a local inquiry or other hearing, that the local planning authority are not taking the steps necessary to enable them to prepare or adopt such a plan or proposals within a reasonable period; or

(b) in a case where a period is specified for the preparation or adoption of any such plan or proposals, if no such plan or proposals have been prepared or adopted by the local planning authority within that period,

the Secretary of State may prepare and make the plan or any part of it or, as the case may be, alter or replace it, as he thinks fit.

(2) The previous provisions of this Chapter shall, so far as practicable, apply with any necessary modifications in relation to the doing of anything under this section by the Secretary of State and the thing so done.

(3) The authority mentioned in subsection (1) shall on demand repay to the Secretary of State so much of any expenses incurred by him in connection with the doing of anything which should have been done by them as he certifies to have been incurred in the performance of their functions.   **[32]**

26. Regulations and directions

(1) Without prejudice to the previous provisions of this Chapter, the Secretary of State may make regulations with respect to the form and content of unitary development plans and the procedure to be followed in connection with their preparation, withdrawal, adoption, submission, approval, making, alteration or replacement.

(2) Such regulations may in particular—

(a) provide for publicity to be given to the results of any review or survey carried out under section 11;

(b) provide for the notice to be given of or the publicity to be given to—

(i) matters included or proposed to be included in any unitary development plan,

(ii) the approval, adoption or making of any such plan or any alteration or replacement of it, or

(iii) any other prescribed procedural step,

and for publicity to be given to the procedure to be followed as mentioned in subsection (1);

(c) make provision with respect to the making and consideration of representations with respect to matters to be included in, or objections to, any such plan or proposals for its alteration or replacement;

[(cc) make provision with respect to the circumstances in which representations with respect to the matters to be included in a plan or proposals are to be treated, for any of the purposes of this Chapter, as being objections made in accordance with the regulations;]

(d) without prejudice to paragraph (b), provide for notice to be given to particular persons of the approval, adoption, alteration or replacement of any plan if they have objected to the plan and have notified the local planning authority of their wish to receive notice, subject (if the regulations so provide) to the payment of a reasonable charge;

(e) require or authorise a local planning authority to consult with, or consider the views of, other persons before taking any prescribed procedural step;

(f) require a local planning authority, in such cases as may be prescribed or in such particular cases as the Secretary of State may direct, to provide persons making a request in that behalf with copies of any plan or document which has been made public [in compliance with the regulations or available for inspection under section 13(2)] subject (if the regulations so provide) to the payment of a reasonable charge;

(ff) make provision for steps taken in compliance with the regulations in respect of a unitary development plan which has been withdrawn to be taken into account in prescribed circumstances for the purposes of complying with the regulations in respect of a subsequent unitary development plan;]

(g) provide for the publication and inspection of any unitary development plan which has been adopted, approved or made or any document approved, adopted or made altering or replacing any such plan, and for copies of any such plan or document to be made available on sale.

(3) Regulations under this section may make different provision for different cases.

[(3A) Any provision made by regulations under this section in its application by virtue of section 10 may differ from that made under this section in its application by virtue of section 10A.]

(4) Subject to the previous provisions of this Chapter and to any regulations under this section, the Secretary of State may give directions to any local planning authority or to local planning authorities generally—

(a) for formulating the procedure for the carrying out of their functions under this Chapter;

(b) for requiring them to give him such information as he may require for carrying out any of his functions under this Chapter. **[33]**

NOTES

Commencement: see the note to s 10 at **[17]**.

Sub-s (2)(cc), (ff) inserted, and words in square brackets in sub-s (2)(f) substituted, by the Planning and Compensation Act 1991, s 27, Sch 4, Pt I, paras 1, 15.

Sub-s (3A) inserted by the Local Government (Wales) Act 1994, s 20(3)(a), Sch 5, Pt I, paras 1, 5, as from a day to be appointed.

27. Meaning of "development plan" in Greater London and metropolitan counties

For the purposes of this Act and any other enactment relating to town and country planning, the Land Compensation Act 1961 and the Highways Act 1980, the development plan for any district in Greater London or a metropolitan county (whether the whole or part of the area of a local planning authority) shall be taken as consisting of—

(a) the provisions of the unitary development plan for the time being in force for that area or the relevant part of it, together with a copy of the local planning authority's resolution of adoption or the Secretary of State's notice of approval or, where part of the plan has been adopted and the remainder approved, copies of the resolution and the notice; and

(b) any alteration to that plan, together with a copy of the authority's resolution of adoption, or the Secretary of State's notice of approval, of the alteration or, where part of the alteration has been adopted and the remainder approved, copies of the resolution and the notice. **[34]**

NOTES

Commencement: see the note to s 10 at **[17]**.

[27A. Meaning of "development plan" in relation to Wales

For the purposes of the enactments mentioned in section 27, the development plan for any area in Wales shall be taken as consisting of—

(a) the provisions of the unitary development plan for the time being in force for that area, together with a copy of the relevant local planning authority's resolution of adoption or of the Secretary of State's notice of approval or, where part of the plan has been adopted and the remainder approved, copies of the resolution and the notice; and

(b) any alteration to that plan, together with a copy of the relevant local planning authority's resolution of adoption, or the Secretary of State's notice of approval, of the alteration or, where part of the alteration has been adopted and the remainder approved, copies of the resolution and the notice.] **[34A]**

NOTES

Inserted by the Local Government (Wales) Act 1994, s 20(3)(a), Sch 5, Pt I, paras 1, 6, as from a day to be appointed.

28. Commencement of Chapter I: transitional provisions

(1) Subject to subsection (2), the provisions of this Chapter shall come into force in the area of any local planning authority in Greater London or a metropolitan county (other than any area in that county which is part of a National Park) on such day as may be appointed in relation to that area by an order made by the Secretary of State.

(2) Subsection (1) does not apply in any area in relation to which an order has been made before the commencement of this Act under section 4(1) of the Local Government Act 1985 (commencement of Part I of Schedule 1 to that Act) and in any such area the provisions of this Chapter shall come into force at the commencement of this Act or, if later, on the day appointed by the order.

(3) Until a unitary development plan becomes operative under this Chapter for such an area as is mentioned in subsection (1) (or where parts of such a plan become operative on different dates until every part has become operative)—

   (a) if it is the area of a local planning authority in a metropolitan county, Part I of Schedule 2 (which provides for existing plans to continue in force and applies some of the provisions of Chapter II) shall apply in relation to it;
   (b) if it is the area of a local planning authority in Greater London, Part II of that Schedule (which makes similar provision) shall apply in relation to it; and
   (c) Part III of that Schedule shall apply in relation to it for the purpose of making continuing provision for the transitional matters for which provision was made immediately before the commencement of this Act by Schedule 7 to the 1971 Act (old development plans etc.).

(4) The power to make orders under this section may be exercised so as to make different provision for different cases, including different provision for different areas.   **[35]**

NOTES
   Commencement: as to the areas in respect of which ss 10–28 were in force on 24 August 1990, see the note to s 10 at **[17]**. Sub-ss (1), (2) above make provision as to when ss 10–28 came into force in respect of the remaining areas.
   1971 Act: Town and Country Planning Act 1971.

[28A. Application of Chapter I in relation to Wales: transitional provisions

(1) Until a unitary development plan becomes fully operative for the area of any local planning authority in Wales—

   (a) Part IA of Schedule 2, and
   (b) Part III of Schedule 5 to the Local Government (Wales) Act 1994 (transitional provisions in relation to structure and local plans),

shall apply in relation to that area.

(2) For the purposes of this Chapter, a unitary development plan for the area of a local planning authority in Wales has become fully operative when—

   (a) it has become operative under this Chapter; or
   (b) where different parts have become operative at different times, when all parts of it have become so operative.]   **[35A]**

NOTES
   Inserted by the Local Government (Wales) Act 1994, s 20(2), as from a day to be appointed.

CHAPTER II

STRUCTURE AND LOCAL PLANS: NON-METROPOLITAN AREAS

Preliminary

29. Application of Chapter II to non-metropolitan areas

Subject to the transitional provisions in Schedule 2, this Chapter applies only to the area of any local planning authority outside Greater London and the metropolitan counties and to any part of a National Park in such a county.   [36]

NOTES

Commencement: 24 August 1990.

Substituted by the Local Government (Wales) Act 1994, s 20(3)(a), Sch 5, Pt I, paras 1, 7, as from a day to be appointed, as follows:

"**29 Application of Chapter II to non-metropolitan areas in England**

(1) This Chapter applies only to—

(a) the area of any local planning authority in England outside Greater London and the metropolitan counties; and

(b) any part of a National Park in a metropolitan county in England.

(2) Subsection (1) is subject to the transitional provisions in—

(a) Schedule 2; and

(b) Part III of Schedule 5 to the Local Government (Wales) Act 1994.".

Surveys etc

30. Survey of planning areas

(1) The local planning authority—

(a) shall keep under review the matters which may be expected to affect the development of their area or the planning of its development; and

(b) may, if they think fit, at any time institute a fresh survey of their area examining those matters.

(2) Without prejudice to the generality of subsection (1), the matters to be kept under review and examined under that subsection shall include—

(a) the principal physical and economic characteristics of the area of the authority (including the principal purposes for which land is used) and, so far as they may be expected to affect that area, of any neighbouring areas;

(b) the size, composition and distribution of the population of that area (whether resident or otherwise);

(c) without prejudice to paragraph (a), the communications, transport system and traffic of that area and, so far as they may be expected to affect that area, of any neighbouring areas;

(d) any considerations not mentioned in paragraph (a), (b) or (c) which may be expected to affect any matters so mentioned;

(e) such other matters as may be prescribed or as the Secretary of State may in a particular case direct;

(f) any changes already projected in any of the matters mentioned in any of the previous paragraphs and the effect which those changes are likely to have on the development of that area or the planning of such development.

(3) A survey under subsection (1)(b) may relate to only part of the area of an authority; and references in subsection (2) to the area of an authority or any neighbouring areas shall be construed accordingly.

(4) A local planning authority shall, for the purpose of discharging their functions

under this section of examining and keeping under review any matters relating to the area of another such authority, consult with that other authority about those matters.

[37]

NOTES
　　Commencement: 24 August 1990.

Structure plans

31. Structure plans: continuity, form and content

(1) Each structure plan approved by the Secretary of State under the 1971 Act with respect to the area of a local planning authority which is in operation immediately before the commencement of this Act shall continue in force after its commencement (subject to any alterations then in operation and to the following provisions of this Part).

[(2) A structure plan shall contain a written statement formulating the authority's general policies in respect of the development and use of land in their area.

(3) The policies shall, subject to subsection (4), include policies in respect of—

　(a) the conservation of the natural beauty and amenity of the land;
　(b) the improvement of the physical environment; and
　(c) the management of traffic.

(4) Regulations under this section may prescribe the aspects of such development and use with which the general policies in a structure plan are to be concerned, in which case the policies shall be concerned with those aspects and no others.

(5) A structure plan shall also contain—

　(a) such diagrams, illustrations or other descriptive or explanatory matter in respect of the general policies as may be prescribed; and
　(b) such other matters as the Secretary of State may, in any particular case, direct.

(6) In formulating their general policies the authority shall have regard to—

　(a) any regional or strategic planning guidance given by the Secretary of State to assist them in the preparation of the plan;
　(b) current national policies;
　(c) the resources likely to be available; and
　(d) such other matters as the Secretary of State may prescribe or, in a particular case, direct.

(7) Where there is in operation, by virtue of section 7(7) of the 1971 Act, a structure plan relating to part of the area of a local planning authority, the authority shall, within such period (if any) as the Secretary of State may direct, prepare proposals for replacing the structure plans for the time being in operation with a single structure plan relating to the whole of their area.

(8) The following provisions of this Chapter apply to such replacement as they apply to replacement in exercise of the power in section 32(1)(b).

(9) Regulations under this section may make different provision for different cases and shall be subject to any direction given, in a particular case, by the Secretary of State.

(10) For the purposes of this section, except subsection (6)(b), ''policies'' includes proposals.]

[38]

NOTES
Commencement: 24 August 1990 (sub-s (1)); 25 November 1991 (sub-ss (2)–10) for certain purposes);
10 February 1992 (sub-ss (2)–(10) for remaining purposes).
Modification: sub-s (3) modified by the Waste Management Licensing Regulations 1994, SI 1994/
1056, regs 1(3), 19, Sch 4, Pt I, para 7(1), (2); see the notes to s 12 at **[19]**.
1971 Act: Town and Country Planning Act 1971.

[32. Alteration and replacement of structure plans

(1) A local planning authority may at any time prepare proposals—

(a) for alterations to the structure plan for their area; or
(b) for its replacement.

(2) If the Secretary of State directs them to do so, the authority shall prepare, within such time as he may direct, proposals for—

(a) such alterations to the structure plan as he directs; or
(b) its replacement.

(3) An authority shall not, without the consent of the Secretary of State, prepare proposals in respect of a structure plan if the plan or any part of it has been approved by the Secretary of State under section 35A.

(4) Proposals for the alteration of a structure plan may relate to the whole or part of the area to which the plan relates.

(5) Proposals prepared under this section shall be accompanied by an explanatory memorandum.

(6) The explanatory memorandum shall state—

(a) the reasons which in the opinion of the authority justify each of their proposals;
(b) any information on which the proposals are based;
(c) the relationship of the proposals to general policies for the development and use of land in neighbouring areas which may be expected to affect the area to which the proposals relate,

and may contain such illustrative material as the authority think appropriate.

(7) Proposals for the alteration or replacement of a structure plan shall not become operative unless they are—

(a) adopted by the authority (under section 35); or
(b) approved by the Secretary of State (under section 35A).]   **[39]**

NOTES
Commencement: 25 November 1991 (certain purposes); 10 February 1992 (remaining purposes).
This section and ss 33–35, 35A–35C, 36–40 substituted for ss 33–41 by the Planning and Compensation
Act 1991, s 27, Sch 4, Pt I, paras 1, 17. For transitional provisions, see Sch 4, Pt III, paras 42–47 to that
Act at **[547]**.

[33. Public participation

(1) When preparing proposals for the alteration or replacement of a structure plan for their area and before finally determining their contents the local planning authority shall—

(a) comply with—

(i) any requirements imposed by regulations made under section 53; and
(ii) any particular direction given to them by the Secretary of State with respect to a matter falling within any of paragraphs (a) to (c) or (e) of subsection (2) of that section; and

(b) consider any representations made in accordance with those regulations.

(2) Where the authority have prepared proposals for the alteration or replacement of a structure plan they shall—

(a) make copies of the proposals and the explanatory memorandum available for inspection at such places as may be prescribed by those regulations;

(b) send a copy of the proposals and the explanatory memorandum to the Secretary of State; and

(c) comply with any requirements imposed by those regulations.

(3) Each copy made available for inspection or sent under subsection (2) shall be accompanied by a statement of the prescribed period within which objections may be made to the authority.

(4) In this section "the prescribed period" means such period as may be prescribed by or determined in accordance with regulations made under section 53 and in this Chapter "objections made in accordance with the regulations" means objections made—

(a) in accordance with regulations made under that section; and

(b) within the prescribed period.

(5) The persons who may make objections in accordance with the regulations include, in particular, the Secretary of State.

(6) The proposals shall not be adopted by the authority under section 35 until—

(a) after they have considered any objections made in accordance with the regulations; or

(b) if no such objections are made, after the expiry of the prescribed period.]

[40]

NOTES

Commencement: 25 November 1991 (certain purposes); 10 February 1992 (remaining purposes).
Substituted as noted to s 32 at **[39]**.

[34. Withdrawal of proposals for alteration and replacement of structure plans

(1) Proposals for the alteration or replacement of a structure plan may be withdrawn by the local planning authority at any time before they have adopted them or the Secretary of State has approved them.

(2) On the withdrawal of such proposals, the authority shall—

(a) withdraw the copies made available for inspection in accordance with section 33(2); and

(b) give notice that the proposals have been withdrawn to every person who has made an objection to them.]

[41]

NOTES

Commencement: 25 November 1991 (certain purposes); 10 February 1992 (remaining purposes).
Substituted as noted to s 32 at **[39]**.

[35. Adoption of proposals

(1) Subject to subsection (3) and sections 35A and 35B, the local planning authority may by resolution adopt proposals for the alteration or replacement of a structure plan, either as originally prepared or as modified so as to take account of—

(a) any objections to the proposals; or

(b) any other considerations which appear to them to be material.

(2) If it appears to the Secretary of State that the proposals are unsatisfactory he may, at any time before the local planning authority have adopted the proposals, direct the authority to modify the proposals in such respects as are indicated in the direction.

(3) An authority to whom such a direction is given shall not adopt the proposals unless—

    (a) they satisfy the Secretary of State that they have made the modifications necessary to conform with the direction; or

    (b) the direction is withdrawn.

(4) Subject to the following provisions of this Chapter and to section 287, proposals for the alteration or replacement of a structure plan shall become operative on the date on which they are adopted.]   **[42]**

NOTES
Commencement: 25 November 1991 (certain purposes); 10 February 1992 (remaining purposes).
Substituted as noted to s 32 at **[39]**.

[35A. Calling in of proposals for approval by Secretary of State

(1) The Secretary of State may, at any time before the local planning authority have adopted proposals for the alteration or replacement of a structure plan, direct that all or any part of the proposals shall be submitted to him for his approval.

(2) If he gives such a direction—

    (a) the local planning authority shall not take any further steps for the adoption of any of the proposals until the Secretary of State has given his decision on the proposals or the relevant part of the proposals; and

    (b) the proposals or the relevant part of the proposals shall not have effect unless approved by him and shall not require adoption by the authority under section 35.

(3) Subsection (2)(a) applies in particular to holding or proceeding with an examination in public under section 35B(1).

(4) The Secretary of State may, after considering proposals submitted to him in compliance with a direction under subsection (1)—

    (a) approve them, in whole or in part and with or without modifications or reservations; or

    (b) reject them.

(5) In considering proposals so submitted to him the Secretary of State—

    (a) shall take into account any objections made in accordance with the regulations; and

    (b) may take into account any matters which he thinks relevant, whether or not they were taken into account in preparing the proposals.

(6) For the purpose of taking into account any objection or matter, the Secretary of State may, but need not, consult with any local planning authority or other person.

(7) The Secretary of State shall give the authority such statement as he considers appropriate of the reasons governing his decision on any proposals submitted to him.

(8) Subject to section 287, proposals approved by the Secretary of State under this section shall become operative on such day as he may appoint.]   **[42A]**

NOTES
Commencement: 25 November 1991 (certain purposes); 10 February 1992 (remaining purposes).
Substituted as noted to s 32 at **[39]**.

[35B. Examination in public

(1) Before adopting proposals for the alteration or replacement of a structure plan, the local planning authority shall, unless the Secretary of State otherwise directs, cause an examination in public to be held of such matters affecting the consideration of the proposals as—

    (a) they consider ought to be so examined; or
    (b) the Secretary of State directs.

(2) Where proposals are submitted to the Secretary of State in compliance with a direction under section 35A(1), he may cause an examination in public to be held of any matter specified by him.

(3) An examination in public shall be conducted by a person or persons appointed by the Secretary of State for the purpose.

(4) No person shall have a right to be heard at an examination in public.

(5) The following may take part in an examination in public—

    (a) in the case of an examination held under subsection (1), the local planning authority; and
    (b) in any case, any person invited to do so by the person or persons holding the examination or the person causing the examination to be held.

(6) The Secretary of State may, after consultation with the Lord Chancellor, make regulations with respect to the procedure to be followed at any examination in public.

(7) An examination in public shall constitute a Statutory Inquiry for the purposes of section 1(1)(c) of the Tribunals and Inquiries Act 1971 but shall not constitute such an inquiry for any other purpose of that Act.]   **[42B]**

NOTES
Commencement: 25 November 1991 (certain purposes); 10 February 1992 (remaining purposes).
Substituted as noted to s 32 at **[39]**.

[35C. Duties to notify authorities responsible for local plans

(1) An authority responsible for a structure plan shall, where any proposals of theirs for the alteration or replacement of a structure plan are adopted or approved—

    (a) notify any authority responsible for a local plan in their area that the proposals have been adopted or approved; and
    (b) supply that authority with a statement that the local plan is or, as the case may be, is not in general conformity with the altered or new structure plan.

(2) A statement that a local plan is not in general conformity with a structure plan shall specify the respects in which it is not in such conformity.

(3) An authority responsible for a structure plan shall, where any proposals of theirs for the alteration or replacement of a structure plan are withdrawn, notify any authority responsible for a local plan in their area that the proposals have been withdrawn.

(4) Nothing in this section requires an authority to notify or supply a statement to themselves.

(5) For the purposes of this section an authority shall be regarded as responsible—

(a) for a structure plan, if they are entitled to prepare proposals for its alteration or replacement; and

(b) for a local plan, if they are under a duty to prepare a local plan or are entitled to prepare proposals for its alteration or replacement.]   **[42C]**

NOTES

Commencement: 25 November 1991 (certain purposes); 10 February 1992 (remaining purposes).
Substituted as noted to s 32 at **[39]**.

[Local plans

36. Local plans

(1) The local planning authority shall, within such period (if any) as the Secretary of State may direct, prepare for their area a plan to be known as a local plan.

(2) A local plan shall contain a written statement formulating the authority's detailed policies for the development and use of land in their area.

(3) The policies shall include policies in respect of—

(a) the conservation of the natural beauty and amenity of the land;
(b) the improvement of the physical environment; and
(c) the management of traffic.

(4) A local plan shall be in general conformity with the structure plan.

(5) A local plan shall not contain—

(a) any policies in respect of the winning and working of minerals or the depositing of mineral waste, unless it is a plan for a National Park;
(b) any policies in respect of the depositing of refuse or waste materials other than mineral waste, unless it is a plan for a National Park or for an area where such depositing is not a county matter for the purposes of Schedule 1.

(6) A local plan shall also contain—

(a) a map illustrating each of the detailed policies; and
(b) such diagrams, illustrations or other descriptive or explanatory matter in respect of the policies as may be prescribed,

and may contain such descriptive or explanatory matter as the authority think appropriate.

(7) A local plan may designate any part of the authority's area as an action area, that is to say, an area which they have selected for the commencement during a prescribed period of comprehensive treatment by development, redevelopment or improvement (or partly by one and partly by another method).

(8) If an area is so designated the plan shall contain a description of the treatment proposed by the authority.

(9) In formulating their detailed policies, the authority shall have regard to—

(a) such information and other considerations as the Secretary of State may prescribe or, in a particular case, direct; and
(b) the provisions of any scheme under paragraph 3 of Schedule 32 to the Local Government, Planning and Land Act 1980 relating to land in their area which has been designated under that Schedule as an enterprise zone.

(10) Subject to the following provisions of this Chapter and section 287, a local plan shall become operative on the date on which it is adopted.

(11) For the purposes of this section "policies" includes proposals.]   **[43]**

NOTES
   Commencement: 25 November 1991 (certain purposes); 10 February 1992 (remaining purposes).
   Substituted as noted to s 32 at **[39]**.
   Modification: sub-s (3) modified by the Waste Management Licensing Regulations 1994, SI 1994/1056, regs 1(3), 19, Sch 4, Pt I, paras 7(1), (2); see the notes to s 12 at **[19]**.

[37. Minerals local plans

(1) A mineral planning authority for an area other than a National Park shall, within such period (if any) as the Secretary of State may direct, prepare for their area a plan to be known as a minerals local plan.

(2) A minerals local plan shall contain a written statement formulating the authority's detailed policies for their area in respect of development consisting of the winning and working of minerals or involving the depositing of mineral waste.

(3) The local planning authority for a National Park shall, within such period (if any) as the Secretary of State may direct—

    (a) prepare for their area a plan to be known as a minerals local plan; or
    (b) include in their local plan their detailed policies in respect of development consisting of the winning and working of minerals or involving the depositing of mineral waste.

(4) In formulating the policies in a minerals local plan, the authority shall have regard to such information and other considerations as the Secretary of State may prescribe or, in a particular case, direct.

(5) Subsections (4), (6), (10) and (11) of section 36 apply with respect to minerals local plans as they apply with respect to local plans.

(6) The following provisions of this Chapter apply with respect to minerals local plans as they apply with respect to local plans, but as if references to a local planning authority were, in relation to an area other than a National Park, references to a mineral planning authority.]   **[44]**

NOTES
   Commencement: 25 November 1991 (certain purposes); 10 February 1992 (remaining purposes).
   Substituted as noted to s 32 at **[39]**.

[38. Waste policies

(1) In this section—

    "waste policies" means detailed policies in respect of development which involves the depositing of refuse or waste materials other than mineral waste; and
    "waste local plan" means a plan containing waste policies.

(2) A local planning authority other than an excluded authority shall, within such period (if any) as the Secretary of State may direct—

    (a) prepare a waste local plan for their area; or
    (b) include their waste policies in their minerals local plan.

(3) A local planning authority are an excluded authority for the purposes of subsection (2) if they are an authority—

(a) for a National Park;

(b) for an area where waste policies are not a county matter for the purposes of Schedule 1.

(4) A local planning authority for a National Park shall within such period (if any) as the Secretary of State may direct—

(a) prepare a waste local plan for their area; or

(b) include their waste policies in—

(i) their minerals local plan; or

(ii) their local plan.

(5) In formulating their waste policies, the authority shall have regard to such information and other considerations as the Secretary of State may prescribe or, in a particular case, direct.

(6) Subsections (4), (6), (10) and (11) of section 36 apply with respect to waste local plans as they apply with respect to local plans.

(7) The following provisions of this Chapter apply with respect to waste local plans as they apply with respect to local plans, but as if references to a local planning authority were references to the authority who are entitled to prepare a waste local plan.]   **[45]**

NOTES

Commencement: 25 November 1991 (certain purposes); 10 February 1992 (remaining purposes).
Substituted as noted to s 32 at **[39]**.
Modification: sub-s (1) modified by the Waste Management Licensing Regulations 1994, SI 1994/1056, regs 1(3), 19, Sch 4, Pt I, para 7(3), so as to have effect as if the definition of waste policies included detailed policies in respect of suitable disposal sites or installations for the carrying on of such development as is referred to in that definition.

[39. Alteration and replacement of local plans

(1) A local planning authority may at any time prepare proposals—

(a) for alterations to the local plan for their area; or

(b) for its replacement.

(2) A local planning authority shall—

(a) consider whether they need to prepare such proposals, if they have been supplied with a statement under section 35C that the local plan is not in general conformity with the structure plan; and

(b) prepare such proposals, if they are directed to do so by the Secretary of State, within such period (if any) as he may direct.

(3) An authority shall not, without the consent of the Secretary of State, prepare such proposals if the plan or any part of it has been approved by the Secretary of State.

(4) Proposals for the alteration of a local plan may relate to the whole or part of the area to which the plan relates.

(5) Subject to the following provisions of this Chapter and section 287, proposals for the alteration or replacement of a local plan shall become operative on the date on which they are adopted.]   **[46]**

NOTES

Commencement: 25 November 1991 (certain purposes); 10 February 1992 (remaining purposes).
Substituted as noted to s 32 at **[39]**.

[40. Public participation

(1) When preparing a local plan for their area or proposals for its alteration or replacement and before finally determining the contents of the plan or the proposals the local planning authority shall—

    (a) comply with—

        (i) any requirements imposed by regulations made under section 53; and

        (ii) any particular direction given to them by the Secretary of State with respect to a matter falling within any of paragraphs (a) to (c) or (e) of subsection (2) of that section; and

    (b) consider any representations made in accordance with those regulations.

(2) Subject to section 46(1), where the authority have prepared a local plan or proposals for its alteration or replacement they shall—

    (a) make copies of the relevant documents available for inspection at such places as may be prescribed by those regulations;

    (b) send a copy of the relevant documents to the Secretary of State; and

    (c) comply with any requirements imposed by those regulations.

(3) In subsection (2) ''the relevant documents'' means—

    (a) the plan or the proposals; and

    (b) any statement supplied under section 46(2).

(4) Each copy made available for inspection or sent under subsection (2) shall be accompanied by a statement of the prescribed period within which objections may be made to the authority.

(5) In this section ''the prescribed period'' means such period as may be prescribed by or determined in accordance with regulations made under section 53 and in this Chapter ''objections made in accordance with the regulations'' means objections made—

    (a) in accordance with regulations made under that section; and

    (b) within the prescribed period.

(6) The persons who may make objections in accordance with the regulations include, in particular, the Secretary of State.

(7) A local plan or proposals for its alteration or replacement shall not be adopted by the authority under section 43 until—

    (a) after they have considered any objections made in accordance with the regulations; or

    (b) if no such objections are made, after the expiry of the prescribed period.]

[47–48]

NOTES
    Commencement: 25 November 1991 (certain purposes); 10 February 1992 (remaining purposes).
    Substituted as noted to s 32 at **[39]**.

41. (*Substituted as noted to s 32 at* **[39]**.)

42. Objections: local inquiry or other hearing

[(1) Where any objections have been made, in accordance with the regulations, to proposals for a local plan or for its alteration or replacement copies of which have been made available for inspection under section 40(2), the local planning authority shall cause a local inquiry or other hearing to be held for the purpose of considering the objections.

(2) The local planning authority may cause a local inquiry or other hearing to be held for the purpose of considering any other objections to the proposals.

(2A) No local inquiry or other hearing need be held under this section if all persons who have made objections have indicated in writing that they do not wish to appear.]

(3) A local inquiry or other hearing shall be held by a person appointed by the Secretary of State or, in such cases as may be prescribed, by the authority themselves.

(4) Regulations may—
    (a) make provision with respect to the appointment, and qualifications for appointment, of persons to hold a local inquiry or other hearing;
    (b) include provision enabling the Secretary of State to direct a local planning authority to appoint a particular person, or one of a specified list or class of persons;
    (c) make provision with respect to the remuneration and allowances of the person appointed.

(5) Subsections (2) and (3) of section 250 of the Local Government Act 1972 (power to summon and examine witnesses) apply to an inquiry held under this section.

(6) The Tribunals and Inquiries Act [1992] shall apply to a local inquiry or other hearing held under this section as it applies to a statutory inquiry held by the Secretary of State, but as if in [section 10(1)] of that Act (statement of reasons for decisions) the reference to any decision taken by the Secretary of State were a reference to a decision taken by a local authority. **[49]**

NOTES
    Commencement: 24 August 1990 (sub-ss (3)–(6)); 25 November 1991 (sub-ss (1)–(2A) for certain purposes); 10 February 1992 (sub-ss (1)–(2A) for remaining purposes).
    Sub-ss (1), (2), (2A) substituted for original sub-ss (1), (2) by the Planning and Compensation Act 1991, s 27, Sch 4, Pt I, paras 1, 18.
    Words in square brackets in sub-s (6) substituted by the Tribunals and Inquiries Act 1992, s 18(1), Sch 3, para 24.

---

43. Adoption of proposals

[(1) Subject to the following provisions of this section and section 44, the local planning authority may by resolution adopt proposals for a local plan or for its alteration or replacement, either as originally prepared or as modified so as to take account of—

    (a) any objections to the plan; or
    (b) any other considerations which appear to them to be material.]

(3) The authority shall not adopt any proposals which do not conform generally to the structure plan.

(4) After copies of the proposals have been sent to the Secretary of State and before they have been adopted by the local planning authority, the Secretary of State may, if it appears to him that the proposals are unsatisfactory, direct the authority to [modify] the proposals in such respects as are indicated in the direction.

(5) An authority to whom a direction is given shall not adopt the proposals

unless they satisfy the Secretary of State that they have made the modifications necessary to conform with the direction or the direction is withdrawn.

(6) Where an objection to the proposals has been made by the Minister of Agriculture, Fisheries and Food and the local planning authority do not propose to modify their proposals to take account of the objection—

(a) the authority shall send particulars of the objection to the Secretary of State, together with a statement of their reasons for not modifying their proposals to take account of it, and

(b) they shall not adopt the proposals unless the Secretary of State authorises them to do so.   **[50]**

NOTES

Commencement: 24 August 1990 (sub-ss (3)–(6)); 25 November 1991 (sub-s (1) for certain purposes); 10 February 1992 (sub-s (1) for remaining purposes).

Sub-s (1) substituted for original sub-ss (1), (2), and word in square brackets in sub-s (4) substituted, by the Planning and Compensation Act 1991, s 27, Sch 4, Pt I, paras 1, 19.

44. Calling in of proposals for approval by Secretary of State

(1) After copies of proposals have been sent to the Secretary of State and before they have been adopted by the local planning authority, the Secretary of State may direct that the proposals [or any part of them] shall be submitted to him for his approval.

[(2) If he gives such a direction—

(a) the authority shall not take any further steps for the adoption of any of the proposals until the Secretary of State has given his decision on the proposals or the relevant part of the proposals; and

(b) the proposals or the relevant part of the proposals shall not have effect unless approved by him and shall not require adoption by the authority under section 43.]

(3) Where particulars of an objection made by the Minister of Agriculture, Fisheries and Food have been sent to the Secretary of State under section 43(6), then, unless the Secretary of State is satisfied that that Minister no longer objects to the proposals, he shall give a direction in respect of the proposals under this section.

[51]

NOTES

Commencement: 24 August 1990 (sub-ss (1), (3)); 25 November 1991 (sub-s (2) for certain purposes); 10 February 1992 (sub-s (2) for remaining purposes).

Words in square brackets in sub-s (1), and the whole of sub-s (2), substituted by the Planning and Compensation Act 1991, s 27, Sch 4, Pt I, paras 1, 20.

45. Approval of proposals by Secretary of State

(1) The Secretary of State may after considering proposals submitted to him under section 44 either approve them (in whole or in part and with or without modifications or reservations) or reject them.

(2) In considering the proposals he may take into account any matters he thinks are relevant, whether or not they were taken into account in the proposals as submitted.

(3) Where on taking the proposals into consideration the Secretary of State does not determine then to reject them, he shall before determining whether or not to approve them—

(a) consider any objections to them made in accordance with [the] regulations,

    (b) give any person who made such an objection which has not been withdrawn an opportunity of appearing before and being heard by a person appointed by him for the purpose, and

    (c) if a local inquiry or other hearing is held, also give such an opportunity to the authority and such other persons as he thinks fit,

except so far as the objections have already been considered, or a local inquiry or other hearing into the objections has already been held, by the authority.

(4) In considering the proposals the Secretary of State may consult with or consider the views of any local planning authority or any other person; but he need not do so, or give an opportunity for the making of representations or objections, or cause a local inquiry or other hearing to be held, except as provided by subsection (3).

[(5) Subject to section 287, proposals approved by the Secretary of State under this section shall become operative on such day as he may appoint.]   **[52]**

NOTES
    Commencement: 24 August 1990 (sub-ss (1)–(4)); 25 November 1991 (sub-s (5) for certain purposes); 10 February 1992 (sub-s (5) for remaining purposes).
    Words in square brackets in sub-s (3)(a) inserted, and sub-s (5) added, by the Planning and Compensation Act 1991, s 27, Sch 4, Pt I, paras 1, 21.

Conformity between plans

[46. Conformity between plans

(1) An authority responsible for a local plan shall not make copies available as mentioned in section 40(2) unless—

    (a) they have served on the authority responsible for the structure plan in their area a copy of the plan or the proposals; and

    (b) such period as may be prescribed has elapsed since they served the copy of the plan or proposals.

(2) Where a local planning authority have been served with a copy as mentioned in subsection (1) they shall, before the end of any period prescribed for the purposes of that subsection, supply the authority responsible for the local plan with—

    (a) a statement that the plan or the proposals are in general conformity with the structure plan; or

    (b) a statement that the plan or the proposals are not in such conformity.

(3) A statement that a plan or proposals are not in such conformity shall specify the respects in which the plan or proposals are not in such conformity.

(4) Any such statement shall be treated for the purposes of this Chapter as an objection made in accordance with the regulations.

(5) Nothing in this section requires an authority to serve a copy on or supply a statement to themselves.

(6) Where—

    (a) a local planning authority propose to make, alter or replace a local plan;

    (b) copies of proposals for the alteration or replacement of the structure plan for their area have been made available for inspection under section 33(2); and

    (c) the authority mentioned in paragraph (a) include in any relevant copy of the plan or proposals a statement that they are making the permitted assumption,

the permitted assumption shall, subject to subsection (9), be made for all purposes (including in particular any question as to conformity between plans).

    (7) In this section ''the permitted assumption'' means the assumption that—

    (a) the proposals mentioned in subsection (6)(b); or
    (b) if any proposed modifications to those proposals are published in accordance with regulations made under section 53, the proposals as so modified,

have been adopted.

    (8) For the purposes of subsection (6)(c) a copy is a relevant copy of a plan or proposals if it is—

    (a) served under subsection (1)(a); or
    (b) made available or sent under section 40(2).

    (9) The permitted assumption shall not be made at any time after the authority mentioned in subsection (6)(a) know that the proposals mentioned in subsection (6)(b) have been withdrawn.

    (10) The provisions of a local plan prevail for all purposes over any conflicting provisions in the relevant structure plan unless the local plan is one—

    (a) stated under section 35C not to be in general conformity with the structure plan; and
    (b) neither altered nor replaced after the statement was supplied.

    (11) The Secretary of State may make regulations with respect to cases where—

    (a) provisions in a structure plan or a local plan conflict with provisions in—

        (i) a minerals local plan; or
        (ii) a waste local plan;

    (b) a structure plan and a local plan are made by the same authority and the provisions of the two plans conflict.

    (12) Subsection (5) of section 35C applies for the purposes of this section as it applies for the purposes of that.]   **[53–55]**

NOTES

    Commencement: 25 November 1991 (certain purposes); 10 February 1992 (remaining purposes).
    Substituted for original ss 46–48 by the Planning and Compensation Act 1991, s 27, Sch 4, Pt I, paras 1, 22.

47, 48. (*Substituted as noted to s 46 at* **[53–55]**.)

Supplementary

49. Disregarding of representations with respect to development authorised by or under other enactments

Notwithstanding anything in the previous provisions of this Chapter, neither the Secretary of State nor a local planning authority need consider representations or objections with respect to a local plan or any proposal to alter, . . . or replace a structure plan or a local plan if it appears to the Secretary of State or, as the case may be, the authority that those representations or objections are in substance representations or objections with respect to things done or proposed to be done in pursuance of—

    (a) an order or scheme under section 10, 14, 16, 18, 106(1) or (3) or 108(1) of the Highways Act 1980;

    (b) an order or scheme under any provision replaced by the provisions of the Highways Act 1980 mentioned in paragraph (a) (namely, an order or scheme under section 7, 9, 11, 13 or 20 of the Highways Act 1959, section 3 of the Highways (Miscellaneous Provisions) Act 1961 or section 1 or 10 of the Highways Act 1971);

    (c) an order under section 1 of the New Towns Act 1981.   **[56]**

NOTES

    Commencement: 24 August 1990.

    Word omitted repealed by the Planning and Compensation Act 1991, s 27, Sch 4, Pt I, paras 1, 23.

50. Joint structure and local plans

(1) Where a structure plan has been prepared by two or more local planning authorities jointly, the power of making proposals under section 32 for the alteration or . . . replacement of the plan may be exercised as respects their respective areas by any of the authorities by whom it was prepared, and the Secretary of State may under that section direct any of them to submit such proposals as respects their respective areas.

(2), (3) . . .

(4) Each of the authorities by whom proposals for the alteration or . . . replacement of a joint structure plan have been prepared shall have the duty imposed by section [33(2)] of making copies of the proposals and explanatory memorandum available for inspection.

(5) Where two or more local planning authorities jointly prepare proposals for the alteration or . . . replacement of a structure plan under this section, all or any of them may withdraw them under section 34(1) and on their doing so all the authorities shall comply with subsection [(2)] of that section.

(6) Where two or more local planning authorities jointly prepare proposals for the making, alteration, . . . or replacement of a local plan—

    (a) . . . they each have the duty imposed by section [40(2)] . . . of making copies of the relevant documents available for inspection and objections to the proposals may be made to any of those authorities and the statement required by section [40(4)] . . . to accompany the relevant documents shall state that objections may be so made;

    (b) it shall be for each of the local planning authorities to adopt the proposals under section 43(1) . . . but any modifications subject to which the proposals are adopted must have the agreement of all those authorities.

[(7) Where a structure plan has been jointly prepared by two or more local planning authorities, the duty—

    (a) to notify and supply a statement under section 35C; and

    (b) to supply a statement under section 46,

shall apply to each of those authorities.

(7A) Where a local plan, or proposals for its alteration or replacement have been jointly prepared by two or more local planning authorities—

    (a) the requirement to serve a copy under subsection (1) of section 46; and

(b) the right to be supplied with a statement under subsection (2) of that section,

shall apply to each of those authorities.]

(8) Where a local plan has been made jointly, the power of making proposals for its alteration, . . . or replacement may be exercised as respects their respective areas by any of the authorities by whom it was made, . . . and the Secretary of State may under section [39] direct any of them to make proposals as respects their respective areas.

[(9) The date of the coming into operation—

(a) of proposals for the alteration or replacement of a structure plan prepared jointly by two or more local planning authorities; and

(b) of a local plan or proposals for its alteration or replacement so prepared,

shall be a date jointly agreed by those authorities.]   [57]

NOTES
Commencement: 24 August 1990 (sub-ss (1), (4)–(6), (8)); 25 November 1991 (sub-ss (7), (7A), (9) for certain purposes); 10 February 1992 (sub-ss (7), (7A), (9) for remaining purposes).
Words omitted from sub-ss (1), (4)–(6), (8) and the whole of sub-ss (2), (3) repealed, and words in square brackets in sub-ss (4)–(6), (8) and the whole of sub-ss (7), (7A), (9) substituted, by the Planning and Compensation Act 1991, ss 27, 84(6), Sch 4, Pt I, paras 1, 24, Sch 19, Pt I.

51. Default powers

(1) Where, by virtue of any of the previous provisions of this Chapter, any survey is required to be carried out, or any local plan or proposals for the alteration, . . . or replacement of such a plan or of a structure plan are required to be prepared or submitted to the Secretary of State, or steps are required to be taken for the adoption of any local plan or any such proposals, then—

(a) if at any time the Secretary of State is satisfied, after holding a local inquiry or other hearing, that the relevant local planning authority are not carrying out the survey or are not taking the steps necessary to enable them to submit or adopt a local plan or such proposals within a reasonable period; or

(b) in a case where a period is specified for the submission or adoption of a local plan or any such proposals, if no such plan or proposals have been submitted or adopted within that period,

the Secretary of State may carry out the survey or prepare and make a local plan or, as the case may be, alter, . . . or replace such a plan or a structure plan, as he thinks fit.

(2) Where under subsection (1) the Secretary of State may do anything which should have been done by a local planning authority (''the defaulting authority'') he may, if he thinks fit, authorise any other local planning authority who appear to him to have an interest in the proper planning of the area of the defaulting authority to do it.

(3) The previous provisions of this Chapter shall, so far as applicable, apply with any necessary modifications in relation to the doing of anything under this section by the Secretary of State or an authority other than the defaulting authority and the thing so done.

(4) The defaulting authority—

(a) shall on demand repay to the Secretary of State so much of any expenses incurred by him in connection with the doing of anything which should have been done by them as he certifies to have been incurred in the performance of their functions; and

(b) shall repay to any other authority who do under this section anything which should have been done by the defaulting authority any expenses certified by the Secretary of State to have been reasonably incurred by that other authority in connection with the doing of that thing.   **[58]**

NOTES
Commencement: 24 August 1990.
Words omitted from sub-s (1) repealed by the Planning and Compensation Act 1991, ss 27, 84(6), Sch 4, Pt I, paras 1, 25, Sch 19, Pt I.

[51A. Urban development corporations

(1) The Secretary of State may direct—

(a) that a structure plan shall not operate; or

(b) that a local plan shall not be prepared or operate,

in relation to the area of an urban development corporation.

(2) The Secretary of State may direct that proposals for the alteration or replacement of a structure plan or a local plan shall not be prepared in relation to the area of an urban development corporation.]   **[58A]**

NOTES
Commencement: 10 February 1992.
Inserted by the Planning and Compensation Act 1991, s 27, Sch 4, Pt I, paras 1, 26.

52. Reviews of plans in enterprise zones

(1) As soon as practicable after an order has been made under paragraph 5 of Schedule 32 to the Local Government, Planning and Land Act 1980 (adoption of enterprise zone scheme) or a notification has been given under paragraph 11 of that Schedule (modification of such a scheme) [any local planning authority for an area in which the enterprise zone is wholly or partly situated shall consider whether they need, in the light of the provisions in the scheme or modified scheme, to prepare proposals for the alteration or replacement of any structure or local plan in relation to which they have power to prepare such proposals.]

(2), (3) . . .   **[59]**

NOTES
Commencement: 24 August 1990.
Words in square brackets in sub-s (1) substituted, and sub-ss (2), (3) repealed, by the Planning and Compensation Act 1991, ss 27, 84(6), Sch 4, Pt I, paras 1, 27, Sch 19, Pt I.

53. Supplementary provisions as to structure and local plans

(1) Without prejudice to the previous provisions of this Chapter, the Secretary of State may make regulations with respect to the form and content of structure and local plans and the procedure to be followed in connection with their preparation, withdrawal, adoption, submission, approval, making, alteration, . . . and replacement.

(2) In particular any such regulations may—

(a) provide for publicity to be given to the report of any survey carried out by a local planning authority under section 30;

(b) provide for the notice to be given of or the publicity to be given to—

(i) matters included or proposed to be included in any such plan,

    (ii) the approval, adoption or making of any such plan or any alteration, . . . or replacement of it, or

    (iii) any other prescribed procedural step,

and for publicity to be given to the procedure to be followed as mentioned in subsection (1);

(c) make provision with respect to the making and consideration of representations with respect to matters to be included in, or objections to, any such plan or proposals for its alteration, repeal or replacement;

[(cc) make provision with respect to the circumstances in which representations with respect to the matters to be included in a plan or proposals are to be treated, for any of the purposes of this Chapter, as being objections made in accordance with the regulations;]

(d) without prejudice to paragraph (b), provide for notice to be given to particular persons of the approval, adoption or alteration of any plan, if they have objected to the plan and have notified the relevant local planning authority of their wish to receive notice, subject (if the regulations so provide) to the payment of a reasonable charge for receiving it;

(e) require or authorise a local planning authority to consult with, or consider the views of, other persons before taking any prescribed procedural step;

(f) require a local planning authority, in such cases as may be prescribed or in such particular cases as the Secretary of State may direct, to provide persons making a request with copies of any plan or document which has been made public [in compliance with the regulations or available for inspection under section 33(2) or 40(2)], subject (if the regulations so provide) to the payment of a reasonable charge;

[(ff) make provision for steps taken in compliance with the regulations in respect of a plan or proposal which has been withdrawn to be taken into account in prescribed circumstances for the purposes of complying with the regulations in respect of a subsequent plan or proposal;]

(g) provide for the publication and inspection of any structure plan or local plan which has been approved, adopted or made, or any document approved, adopted or made altering, . . . or replacing any such plan, and for copies of any such plan or document to be made available on sale.

(3) Regulations under this section may extend throughout England and Wales or to specified areas only and may make different provision for different cases.

(4) Subject to the previous provisions of this Chapter and to any regulations under this section, the Secretary of State may give directions to any local planning authority, or to local planning authorities generally—

(a) for formulating the procedure for the carrying out of their functions under this Chapter;

(b) for requiring them to give him such information as he may require for carrying out any of his functions under this Chapter.

(5) . . .   **[60]**

NOTES

    Commencement: 24 August 1990.

    Words omitted from sub-ss (1), (2)(b)(ii), (g) and the whole of sub-s (5) repealed, sub-s (2)(cc), (ff) inserted, and words in square brackets in sub-s (2)(f) substituted, by the Planning and Compensation Act 1991, ss 27, 84(6), Sch 4, Pt I, paras 1, 28, Sch 19, Pt I.

54. Meaning of "development plan" outside Greater London and the metropolitan counties

(1) Subject to subsection (4), for the purposes of this Act and any other enactment relating to town and country planning, the Land Compensation Act 1961 and the Highways Act 1980, the development plan for any district outside Greater London and the metropolitan counties (whether the whole or part of the area of a local planning authority) shall be taken as consisting of—

[(a) the provisions of the structure plan for the time being in operation in the area;

(b) any alterations to that structure plan;

(c) the provisions of the local plan and any minerals local plan or waste local plan for the time being in operation in the area;

(d) any alterations to that local plan or minerals local plan or waste local plan,

together with the resolutions of the authority who made or altered the plan or, as the case may be the Secretary of State's notice of approval.]

(2) References in subsection (1) to the provisions of any plan, notices of approval, alterations and resolutions of adoption shall, in relation to a district forming part of the area to which they are applicable, be respectively construed as references to so much of those provisions, notices, alterations and resolutions as is applicable to the district.

(3) References in subsection (1) to notices of approval shall, in relation to any plan or alteration made by the Secretary of State under section 51, be construed as references to notices of the making of the plan or alteration.

(4) This section has effect subject to Part III of Schedule 2 (old development plans) [and Part III of Schedule 4 to the Planning and Compensation Act 1991].

(5) Any reference in the Land Compensation Act 1961 to an area defined in the current development plan as an area of comprehensive development shall be construed as a reference to an action area for which a local plan is in force.   **[61]**

NOTES
    Commencement: 24 August 1990.
    Sub-s (1)(a)–(d) substituted and words in square brackets in sub-s (4) added by the Planning and Compensation Act 1991, s 27, Sch 4, Pt I, paras 1, 29.

[Chapter III

General

54A. Status of development plans

Where, in making any determination under the planning Acts, regard is to be had to the development plan, the determination shall be made in accordance with the plan unless material considerations indicate otherwise]   **[61A]**

NOTES
    Commencement: 25 November 1991 (certain purposes); 10 February 1992 (remaining purposes).
    This section and the cross-headings immediately preceding it inserted by Planning and Compensation Act 1991, s 26.

PART III

CONTROL OVER DEVELOPMENT

Meaning of development

55. Meaning of "development" and "new development"

(1) Subject to the following provisions of this section, in this Act, except where the context otherwise requires, "development," means the carrying out of building, engineering, mining or other operations in, on, over or under land, or the making of any material change in the use of any buildings or other land.

[(1A) For the purposes of this Act "building operations" includes—

    (a) demolition of buildings;
    (b) rebuilding;
    (c) structural alterations of or additions to buildings; and
    (d) other operations normally undertaken by a person carrying on business as a builder.]

(2) The following operations or uses of land shall not be taken for the purposes of this Act to involve development of the land—

    (a) the carrying out for the maintenance, improvement or other alteration of any building of works which—

        (i) affect only the interior of the building, or
        (ii) do not materially affect the external appearance of the building,
        and are not works for making good war damage or works begun after 5th December 1968 for the alteration of a building by providing additional space in it underground;

    (b) the carrying out on land within the boundaries of a road by a local highway authority of any works required for the maintenance or improvement of the road;

    (c) the carrying out by a local authority or statutory undertakers of any works for the purpose of inspecting, repairing or renewing any sewers, mains, pipes, cables or other apparatus, including the breaking open of any street or other land for that purpose;

    (d) the use of any buildings or other land within the curtilage of a dwellinghouse for any purpose incidental to the enjoyment of the dwellinghouse as such;

    (e) the use of any land for the purposes of agriculture or forestry (including afforestation) and the use for any of those purposes of any building occupied together with land so used;

    (f) in the case of buildings or other land which are used for a purpose of any class specified in an order made by the Secretary of State under this section, the use of the buildings or other land or, subject to the provisions of the order, of any part of the buildings or the other land, for any other purpose of the same class;

    [(g) the demolition of any description of building specified in a direction given by the Secretary of State to local planning authorities generally or to a particular local planning authority.]

(3) For the avoidance of doubt it is hereby declared that for the purposes of this section—

    (a) the use as two or more separate dwellinghouses of any building previously used as a single dwellinghouse involves a material change in the use of the building and of each part of it which is so used;

(b) the deposit of refuse or waste materials on land involves a material change in its use, notwithstanding that the land is comprised in a site already used for that purpose, if—

   (i) the superficial area of the deposit is extended, or
   (ii) the height of the deposit is extended and exceeds the level of the land adjoining the site.

(4) For the purposes of this Act mining operations include—

   (a) the removal of material of any description—

      (i) from a mineral-working deposit;
      (ii) from a deposit of pulverised fuel ash or other furnace ash or clinker; or
      (iii) from a deposit of iron, steel or other metallic slags; and

   (b) the extraction of minerals from a disused railway embankment.

[(4A) Where the placing or assembly of any tank in any part of any inland waters for the purpose of fish farming there would not, apart from this subsection, involve development of the land below, this Act shall have effect as if the tank resulted from carrying out engineering operations over that land; and in this subsection—

   "fish farming" means the breeding, rearing or keeping of fish or shellfish (which includes any kind of crustacean and mollusc);
   "inland waters" means waters which do not form part of the sea or of any creek, bay or estuary or of any river as far as the tide flows; and
   "tank" includes any cage and any other structure for use in fish farming.]

(5) Without prejudice to any regulations made under the provisions of this Act relating to the control of advertisements, the use for the display of advertisements of any external part of a building which is not normally used for that purpose shall be treated for the purposes of this section as involving a material change in the use of that part of the building.

(6) ...   [62]

NOTES

   Commencement: 24 August 1990 (sub-ss (1), (2)–(4), (5)); 2 January 1992 (sub-s (4A)); 27 July 1992 (sub-s (1A)).

   Sub-ss (1A), (4A) inserted, sub-s (2)(g) added, and sub-s (6) repealed, by the Planning and Compensation Act 1991, ss 13(1), (2), 14(1), 31(4), 84(6), Sch 6, paras 8, 9, Sch 19, Pts I, II. Note that insertion of sub-s (4A) does not apply to the placing or assembly of any structure before 2 January 1992 (s 14(2) of the 1991 Act).

---

56. Time when development begun

(1) Subject to the following provisions of this section, for the purposes of this Act development of land shall be taken to be initiated—

   (a) if the development consists of the carrying out of operations, at the time when those operations are begun;
   (b) if the development consists of a change in use, at the time when the new use is instituted;
   (c) if the development consists both of the carrying out of operations and of a change in use, at the earlier of the times mentioned in paragraphs (a) and (b).

(2) For the purposes of the provisions of this Part mentioned in subsection (3)

development shall be taken to be begun on the earliest date on which any material operation comprised in the development begins to be carried out.

(3) The provisions referred to in subsection (2) are sections 85(2), 86(6), 87(4), [89], 91, 92 and 94.

(4) In subsection (2) "material operation" means—

(a) any work of construction in the course of the erection of a building;

[(aa) any work of demolition of a building;]

(b) the digging of a trench which is to contain the foundations, or part of the foundations, of a building;

(c) the laying of any underground main or pipe to the foundations, or part of the foundations, of a building or to any such trench as is mentioned in paragraph (b);

(d) any operation in the course of laying out or constructing a road or part of a road;

(e) any change in the use of any land which constitutes material development.

(5) In subsection (4)(e) "material development" means any development other than—

(a) development for which planning permission is granted by a general development order for the time being in force and which is carried out so as to comply with any condition or limitation subject to which planning permission is so granted;

[(b) development of a class specified in paragraph 1 or 2 of Schedule 3;]

(c) development of any class prescribed for the purposes of this subsection.

(6) In subsection (5) "general development order" means a development order (within the meaning of section 59) made as a general order applicable (subject to such exceptions as may be specified in it) to all land in England and Wales.   **[63]**

NOTES
   Commencement: 24 August 1990.
   Words in square brackets in sub-s (3) and the whole of sub-s (4)(aa) inserted, and sub-s (5)(b) substituted, by the Planning and Compensation Act 1991, ss 31(4), 32, Sch 6, paras 8, 10, Sch 7, paras 8, 10.

Requirement for planning permission

57. Planning permission required for development

(1) Subject to the following provisions of this section, planning permission is required for the carrying out of any development of land.

(2) Where planning permission to develop land has been granted for a limited period, planning permission is not required for the resumption, at the end of that period, of its use for the purpose for which it was normally used before the permission was granted.

(3) Where by a development order planning permission to develop land has been granted subject to limitations, planning permission is not required for the use of that land which (apart from its use in accordance with that permission) is its normal use.

(4) Where an enforcement notice has been issued in respect of any development of land, planning permission is not required for its use for the purpose for which (in accordance with the provisions of this Part of this Act) it could lawfully have been used if that development had not been carried out.

(5) In determining for the purposes of subsections (2) and (3) what is or was the normal use of land, no account shall be taken of any use begun in contravention of this Part or of previous planning control.

(6) For the purposes of this section a use of land shall be taken to have been begun in contravention of previous planning control if it was begun in contravention of Part III of the 1947 Act, Part III of the 1962 Act or Part III of the 1971 Act.

(7) Subsection (1) has effect subject to Schedule 4 (which makes special provision about use of land on 1st July 1948). **[64]**

NOTES
Commencement: 24 August 1990.
1947 Act: Town and Country Planning Act 1947.
1962 Act: Town and Country Planning Act 1962.
1971 Act: Town and Country Planning Act 1971.

58. Granting of planning permission: general

(1) Planning permission may be granted—

(a) by a development order;
(b) by the local planning authority (or, in the cases provided in this Part, by the Secretary of State) on application to the authority in accordance with a development order;
(c) on the adoption or approval of a simplified planning zone scheme or alterations to such a scheme in accordance with section 82 or, as the case may be, section 86; or
(d) on the designation of an enterprise zone or the approval of a modified scheme under Schedule 32 to the Local Government, Planning and Land Act 1980 in accordance with section 88 of this Act.

(2) Planning permission may also be deemed to be granted under section 90 (development with government authorisation).

(3) This section is without prejudice to any other provisions of this Act providing for the granting of permission. **[65]**

NOTES
Commencement: 24 August 1990.

Development orders

59. Development orders: general

(1) The Secretary of State shall by order (in this Act referred to as a "development order") provide for the granting of planning permission.

(2) A development order may either—

(a) itself grant planning permission for development specified in the order or for development of any class specified; or
(b) in respect of development for which planning permission is not granted by the order itself, provide for the granting of planning permission by the local planning authority (or, in the cases provided in the following provisions, by the Secretary of State) on application to the authority in accordance with the provisions of the order.

(3) A development order may be made either—

(a) as a general order applicable, except so far as the order otherwise provides, to all land, or

(b) as a special order applicable only to such land or descriptions of land as may be specified in the order.   **[66]**

NOTES
    Commencement: 24 August 1990.

60. Permission granted by development order

(1) Planning permission granted by a development order may be granted either unconditionally or subject to such conditions or limitations as may be specified in the order.

(2) Without prejudice to the generality of subsection (1), where planning permission is granted by a development order for the erection, extension or alteration of any buildings, the order may require the approval of the local planning authority to be obtained with respect to the design or external appearance of the buildings.

(3) Without prejudice to the generality of subsection (1), where planning permission is granted by a development order for development of a specified class, the order may enable the Secretary of State or the local planning authority to direct that the permission shall not apply either—

(a) in relation to development in a particular area, or

(b) in relation to any particular development.

(4) Any provision of a development order by which permission is granted for the use of land for any purpose on a limited number of days in a period specified in that provision shall (without prejudice to the generality of references in this Act to limitations) be taken to be a provision granting permission for the use of land for any purpose subject to the limitation that the land shall not be used for any one purpose in pursuance of that provision on more than that number of days in that period. **[67]**

NOTES
    Commencement: 24 August 1990.

61. Development orders: supplementary provisions

(1) A general development order may make different provision with respect to different descriptions of land.

(2) For the purpose of enabling development to be carried out in accordance with planning permission, or otherwise for the purpose of promoting proper development in accordance with the development plan, a development order may direct that any pre 1947 Act, enactment, or any regulations, orders or byelaws made at any time under any such enactment—

(a) shall not apply to any development specified in the order, or

(b) shall apply to it subject to such modifications as may be so specified.

(3) In subsection (2) "pre 1947 Act enactment" means—

(a) any enactment passed before 6th August 1947 (the date of the passing of the 1947 Act), and

(b) any enactment contained in the Highways Act 1980 which—

(i) is an enactment derived from the Highways Act 1959, and

(ii) re-enacts (with or without modifications) any such enactment as is mentioned in paragraph (a).   **[68]**

NOTES
Commencement: 24 August 1990.
1947 Act: Town and Country Planning Act 1947.

Applications for planning permission

62. Form and content of applications for planning permission

Any application to a local planning authority for planning permission—

    (a) shall be made in such manner as may be prescribed by regulations under this Act; and

    (b) shall include such particulars and be verified by such evidence as may be required by the regulations or by directions given by the local planning authority under them.   **[69–71]**

NOTES
Commencement: 24 August 1990.
Modification: section modified by the Town and Country Planning General Regulations 1992, SI 1992/1492, reg 5(1)(c), Sch 1 at **[829]**.

63, 64. *(Repealed by Planning and Compensation Act 1991, ss 32, 84(6), Sch 7, paras 8, 11, 12, Sch 19, Pt I.)*

Publicity for applications

[65. Notice etc of applications for planning permission

(1) A development order may make provision requiring—

    (a) notice to be given of any application for planning permission, and

    (b) any applicant for such permission to issue a certificate as to the interests in the land to which the application relates or the purpose for which it is used,

and provide for publicising such applications and for the form, content and service of such notices and certificates.

(2) Provision shall be made by a development order for the purpose of securing that, in the case of any application for planning permission, any person (other than the applicant) who on such date as may be prescribed by the order is an owner of the land to which the application relates, or [an agricultural tenant of that land], is given notice of the application in such manner as may be required by the order.

(3) A development order may require an applicant for planning permission to certify, in such form as may be prescribed by the order, or to provide evidence, that any requirements of the order have been satisfied.

(4) A development order making any provision by virtue of this section may make different provision for different cases or different classes of development.

(5) A local planning authority shall not entertain an application for planning permission unless any requirements imposed by virtue of this section have been satisfied.

(6) If any person—

    (a) issues a certificate which purports to comply with any requirement imposed by virtue of this section and contains a statement which he knows to be false or misleading in a material particular; or

(b) recklessly issues a certificate which purports to comply with any such requirement and contains a statement which is false or misleading in a material particular,

he shall be guilty of an offence.

(7) A person guilty of an offence under this section shall be liable on summary conviction to a fine not exceeding level 5 on the standard scale.

(8) In this section—

["agricultural tenant", in relation to any land, means any person who—

(a) is the tenant, under a tenancy in relation to which the Agricultural Holdings Act 1986 applies, of an agricultural holding within the meaning of that Act any part of which is comprised in that land; or

(b) is the tenant, under a farm business tenancy (within the meaning of the Agricultural Tenancies Act 1995), of land any part of which is comprised in that land;] and

"owner" in relation to any land means any person who—

(a) is the estate owner in respect of the fee simple;

(b) is entitled to a tenancy granted or extended for a term of years certain of which not less than seven years remain unexpired; or

(c) in the case of such applications as may be prescribed by a development order, is entitled to an interest in any mineral so prescribed,

and the reference to the interests in the land to which an application for planning permission relates includes any interest in any mineral in, on or under the land.

(9) Notwithstanding section 127 of the Magistrates' Courts Act 1980, a magistrates' court may try an information in respect of an offence under this section whenever laid.]   [72–75]

NOTES

Commencement: 25 November 1991 (certain purposes); 17 July 1992 (remaining purposes).
Substituted for ss 65–68 by the Planning and Compensation Act 1991, s 16(1).
Words in square brackets in sub-s (2) and definition of "agricultural tenant" in sub-s (8) substituted by the Agricultural Tenancies Act 1995, s 40, Schedule, para 35.

66–68. (*Substituted as noted to s 65 at* **[72–75]**.)

69. Registers of applications, etc

(1) Every local planning authority shall keep, in such manner as may be prescribed by a development order, a register containing such information as may be so prescribed with respect to applications for planning permission . . .

(2) The register shall contain—

(a) information as to the manner in which such applications have been dealt with, and

(b) such information as may be prescribed by a development order with respect to simplified planning zone schemes relating to zones in the authority's area.

(3) A development order may make provision for the register to be kept in two or more parts, each part containing such information relating to applications for planning permission . . . as may be prescribed by the order.

(4) A development order may also make provision—

(a) for a specified part of the register to contain copies of applications and of any plans or drawings submitted with them; and

(b) for the entry relating to any application, and everything relating to it, to be removed from that part of the register when the application (including any appeal arising out of it) has been finally disposed of (without prejudice to the inclusion of any different entry relating to it in another part of the register).

(5) Every register kept under this section shall be available for inspection by the public at all reasonable hours.   **[76]**

NOTES
Commencement: 24 August 1990.
Words omitted from sub-ss (1), (3) repealed by the Planning and Compensation Act 1991, ss 32, 84(6), Sch 7, paras 8, 13, Sch 19, Pt I.

Determination of applications

70. Determination of applications: general considerations

(1) Where an application is made to a local planning authority for planning permission—

(a) subject to sections 91 and 92, they may grant planning permission, either unconditionally or subject to such conditions as they think fit; or

(b) they may refuse planning permission.

(2) In dealing with such an application the authority shall have regard to the provisions of the development plan, so far as material to the application, and to any other material considerations.

(3) Subsection (1) has effect subject to [section 65] and to the following provisions of this Act, to sections 66, 67, 72 and 73 of the Planning (Listed Buildings and Conservation Areas) Act 1990 and to section 15 of the Health Services Act 1976.   **[77]**

NOTES
Commencement: 24 August 1990.
Words in square brackets in sub-s (3) substituted by the Planning and Compensation Act 1991, s 32, Sch 7, paras 8, 14.

[70A. Power of local planning authority to decline to determine applications

(1) A local planning authority may decline to determine an application for planning permission for the development of any land if—

(a) within the period of two years ending with the date on which the application is received, the Secretary of State has refused a similar application referred to him under section 77 or has dismissed an appeal against the refusal of a similar application; and

(b) in the opinion of the authority there has been no significant change since the refusal or, as the case may be, dismissal mentioned in paragraph (a) in the development plan, so far as material to the application, or in any other material considerations.

(2) For the purposes of this section an application for planning permission for the development of any land shall only be taken to be similar to a later application if the development and the land to which the applications relate are in the opinion of the local planning authority the same or substantially the same.

(3) The reference in subsection (1)(a) to an appeal against the refusal of an application includes an appeal under section 78(2) in respect of an application.]

[77A]

NOTES
Commencement: 25 September 1991.
Inserted by the Planning and Compensation Act 1991, s 17(1).

71. Consultations in connection with determinations under s 70

[(1) A development order may provide that a local planning authority shall not determine an application for planning permission before the end of such period as may be prescribed.

(2) A development order may require a local planning authority—

    (a) to take into account in determining such an application such representations, made within such period, as may be prescribed; and

    (b) to give to any person whose representations have been taken into account such notice as may be prescribed of their decision.

(2A) A development order making any provision by virtue of this section may make different provision for different cases or different classes of development].

(3) Before a local planning authority grant planning permission for the use of land as a caravan site, they shall, unless they are also the authority with power to issue a site licence for that land, consult the local authority with that power.

(4) In this section—

    ["prescribed" means prescribed by a development order]; and
    "site licence" means a licence under Part 1 of the Caravan Sites and Control
      of Development Act 1960 authorising the use of land as a caravan site. [78]

NOTES
Commencement: 24 August 1990 (sub-ss (3), (4)); 17 July 1992 (sub-ss (1), (2), (2A)).
Sub-ss (1), (2), (2A) substituted for sub-ss (1), (2), and words in square brackets in sub-s (4) substituted, by the Planning and Compensation Act 1991, ss 16(2), 32, Sch 7, paras 8, 15.

[71A. Assessment of environmental effects

(1) The Secretary of State may by regulations make provision about the consideration to be given, before planning permission for development of any class specified in the regulations is granted, to the likely environmental effects of the proposed development.

(2) The regulations—

    (a) may make the same provision as, or provision similar or corresponding to, any provision made, for the purposes of any Community obligation of the United Kingdom about the assessment of the likely effects of development on the environment, under section 2(2) of the European Communities Act 1972; and

    (b) may make different provision for different classes of development.

(3) Where a draft of regulations made in exercise both of the power conferred by this section and the power conferred by section 2(2) of the European Communities Act 1972 is approved by resolution of each House of Parliament, section 333(3) shall not apply.]   [78A]

NOTES
Commencement: 25 September 1991.
Inserted by the Planning and Compensation Act 1991, s 15.

72. Conditional grant of planning permission

(1) Without prejudice to the generality of section 70(1), conditions may be imposed on the grant of planning permission under that section—

    (a) for regulating the development or use of any land under the control of the applicant (whether or not it is land in respect of which the application was made) or requiring the carrying out of works on any such land, so far as appears to the local planning authority to be expedient for the purposes of or in connection with the development authorised by the permission;

    (b) for requiring the removal of any buildings or works authorised by the permission, or the discontinuance of any use of land so authorised, at the end of a specified period, and the carrying out of any works required for the reinstatement of land at the end of that period.

(2) A planning permission granted subject to such a condition as is mentioned in subsection (1)(b) is in this Act referred to as "planning permission granted for a limited period".

(3) Where—

    (a) planning permission is granted for development consisting of or including the carrying out of building or other operations subject to a condition that the operations shall be commenced not later than a time specified in the condition; and

    (b) any building or other operations are commenced after the time so specified,

the commencement and carrying out of those operations do not constitute development for which that permission was granted.

(4) Subsection (3)(a) does not apply to a condition attached to the planning permission by or under section 91 or 92.

(5) Part I of Schedule 5 shall have effect for the purpose of making special provision with respect to the conditions which may be imposed on the grant of planning permission for development consisting of the winning and working of minerals [or involving the depositing of refuse or waste materials], and subsection (2) has effect subject to paragraph 1(6)(a) of that Schedule. **[79]**

NOTES
Commencement: 24 August 1990.
Words in square brackets in sub-s (5) inserted by the Planning and Compensation Act 1991, s 21, Sch 1, paras 1, 2.
Modification: sub-s (1)(a) modified by the Town and Country Planning (Crown Land Applications) Regulations 1995, SI 1995/1139, reg 2, Schedule, para 1 at **[1134]**.

73. Determination of applications to develop land without compliance with conditions previously attached

(1) This section applies, subject to subsection (4), to applications for planning permission for the development of land without complying with conditions subject to which a previous planning permission was granted.

(2) On such an application the local planning authority shall consider only the question of the conditions subject to which planning permission should be granted, and—

(a) if they decide that planning permission should be granted subject to conditions differing from those subject to which the previous permission was granted, or that it should be granted unconditionally, they shall grant planning permission accordingly, and

(b) if they decide that planning permission should be granted subject to the same conditions as those subject to which the previous permission was granted, they shall refuse the application.

(3) Special provision may be made with respect to such applications—

(a) by regulations under section 62 as regards the form and content of the application, and

(b) by a development order as regards the procedure to be followed in connection with the application.

(4) This section does not apply if the previous planning permission was granted subject to a condition as to the time within which the development to which it related was to be begun and that time has expired without the development having been begun. **[80]**

NOTES
Commencement: 24 August 1990.

[73A. Planning permission for development already carried out

(1) On an application made to a local planning authority, the planning permission which may be granted includes planning permission for development carried out before the date of the application.

(2) Subsection (1) applies to development carried out—

(a) without planning permission;

(b) in accordance with planning permission granted for a limited period; or

(c) without complying with some condition subject to which planning permission was granted.

(3) Planning permission for such development may be granted so as to have effect from—

(a) the date on which the development was carried out; or

(b) if it was carried out in accordance with planning permission granted for a limited period, the end of that period.] **[80A]**

NOTES
Commencement: 2 January 1992.
Inserted by the Planning and Compensation Act 1991, s 32, Sch 7, paras 8, 16.

Determination of applications

74. Directions etc. as to method of dealing with applications

(1) Provision may be made by a development order for regulating the manner in which applications for planning permission to develop land are to be dealt with by local planning authorities, and in particular—

(a) for enabling the Secretary of State to give directions restricting the grant of planning permission by the local planning authority, either indefinitely or during such period as may be specified in the directions, in respect of any such development, or in respect of development of any such class, as may be so specified;

(b) for authorising the local planning authority, in such cases and subject to such conditions as may be prescribed by the order or by directions given by the Secretary of State under it, to grant planning permission for development which does not accord with the provisions of the development plan;

(c) for requiring that, before planning permission for any development is granted or refused, local planning authorities prescribed by the order or by directions given by the Secretary of State under it shall consult with such authorities or persons as may be so prescribed;

(d) for requiring the local planning authority to give to any applicant for planning permission, within such time as may be prescribed by the order, such notice as may be so prescribed as to the manner in which his application has been dealt with;

(e) for requiring the local planning authority to give any applicant for any consent, agreement or approval required by a condition imposed on a grant of planning permission notice of their decision on his application, within such time as may be so prescribed;

(f) for requiring the local planning authority to give to the Secretary of State, and to such other persons as may be prescribed by or under the order, such information as may be so prescribed with respect to applications for planning permission made to the authority, including information as to the manner in which any such application has been dealt with.

[(1A) Provision may be made by a development order—

(a) for determining the persons to whom applications under this Act are to be sent; and

(b) for requiring persons to whom such applications are sent to send copies to other interested persons.]

(2) Subsection (1) is subject to the provisions of . . . sections 67(7) and 73(1) of the Planning (Listed Buildings and Conservation Areas) Act 1990.   **[81]**

NOTES
    Commencement: 24 August 1990 (sub-ss (1), (2)); 25 November 1991 (sub-s (1A) for certain purposes); 2 January 1992 (sub-s (1A) for remaining purposes).
    Sub-s (1A) inserted, and words omitted from sub-s (2) repealed, by the Planning and Compensation Act 1991, ss 19(1), 32, 84(6), Sch 7, paras 8, 17, Sch 19, Pt I.

Determination of applications

75. Effect of planning permission

(1) Without prejudice to the provisions of this Part as to the duration, revocation or modification of planning permission, any grant of planning permission to develop land shall (except in so far as the permission otherwise provides) enure for the benefit of the land and of all persons for the time being interested in it.

(2) Where planning permission is granted for the erection of a building, the grant of permission may specify the purposes for which the building may be used.

(3) If no purpose is so specified, the permission shall be construed as including permission to use the building for the purpose for which it is designed.   **[82]**

NOTES
    Commencement: 24 August 1990.

76. Duty to draw attention to certain provisions for benefit of disabled

(1) This section applies when planning permission is granted for any development which will result in the provision—

(a) of a building or premises to which section 4 of the Chronically Sick and Disabled Persons Act 1970 applies (buildings or premises to which the public are to be admitted whether on payment or otherwise);

(b) of any of the following (being in each case, premises in which persons are employed to work)—

(i) office premises, shop premises and railway premises to which the Offices, Shops and Railway Premises Act 1963 applies;

(ii) premises which are deemed to be such premises for the purposes of that Act; or

(iii) factories as defined by section 175 of the Factories Act 1961;

(c) of a building intended for the purposes of a university, university college or college, or of a school or hall of a university;

(d) of a building intended for the purposes of an institution within the PCFC funding sector; or

(e) of a building intended for the purposes of a school or an institution which provides higher education or further education (or both) and is maintained or assisted by a local education authority.

(2) The local planning authority granting the planning permission shall draw the attention of the person to whom the permission is granted—

(a) in the case of such a building or premises as are mentioned in subsection (1)(a)—

(i) to sections 4 and 7 of the Chronically Sick and Disabled Persons Act 1970; and

(ii) to the Code of Practice for Access of the Disabled to Buildings (British Standards Institution code of practice BS 5810:1979) or any prescribed document replacing that code;

(b) in the case of such premises as are mentioned in subsection (1)(b), to sections 7 and 8A of that Act and to that code or any such prescribed document replacing it;

(c) in the case of such a building as is mentioned in subsection (1)(c), (d) or (e), to sections 7 and 8 of that Act and to Design Note 18 ''Access for Disabled People to Educational Buildings'' published in 1984 on behalf of the Secretary of State, or any prescribed document replacing that note.

(3) Expressions used in subsection (1)(d) and (e) and in the Education Act 1944 have the same meanings as in that Act.   **[83]**

NOTES
Commencement: 24 August 1990.

Secretary of State's powers as respects planning applications and decisions

77. Reference of applications to Secretary of State

(1) The Secretary of State may give directions requiring applications for planning permission, or for the approval of any local planning authority required under a development order, to be referred to him instead of being dealt with by local planning authorities.

(2) A direction under this section—

(a) may be given either to a particular local planning authority or to local planning authorities generally; and

(b) may relate either to a particular application or to applications of a class specified in the direction.

(3) Any application in respect of which a direction under this section has effect shall be referred to the Secretary of State accordingly.

(4) Subject to subsection (5), where an application for planning permission is referred to the Secretary of State under this section, sections [70, 72(1) and (5), 73 and 73A] shall apply, with any necessary modifications, as they apply to such an application which falls to be determined by the local planning authority [and a development order may apply, with or without modifications, to an application so referred any requirements imposed by such an order by virtue of section 65 or 71].

(5) Before determining an application referred to him under this section, the Secretary of State shall, if either the applicant or the local planning authority wish, give each of them an opportunity of appearing before, and being heard by, a person appointed by the Secretary of State for the purpose.

(6) Subsection (5) does not apply to an application for planning permission referred to a Planning Inquiry Commission under section 101.

(7) The decision of the Secretary of State on any application referred to him under this section shall be final.   **[84]**

NOTES
    Commencement: 24 August 1990.
    Words in square brackets in sub-s (4) substituted or added by the Planning and Compensation Act 1991, s 32, Sch 7, paras 8, 18.

78. Right to appeal against planning decisions and failure to take such decisions

(1) Where a local planning authority—

(a) refuse an application for planning permission or grant it subject to conditions;

(b) refuse an application for any consent, agreement or approval of that authority required by a condition imposed on a grant of planning permission or grant it subject to conditions; or

(c) refuse an application for any approval of that authority required under a development order or grant it subject to conditions,

the applicant may by notice appeal to the Secretary of State.

(2) A person who has made such an application may also appeal to the Secretary of State if the local planning authority have [done none of the following]—

(a) given notice to the applicant of their decision on the application; . . .

[(aa) given notice to the applicant that they have exercised their power under section 70A to decline to determine the application;]

(b) given notice to him that the application has been referred to the Secretary of State in accordance with directions given under section 77,

within such period as may be prescribed by the development order or within such extended period as may at any time be agreed upon in writing between the applicant and the authority.

(3) Any appeal under this section shall be made by notice served within such time and in such manner as may be prescribed by a development order.

(4) The time prescribed for the service of such a notice must not be less than—

(a) 28 days from the date of notification of the decision; or

(b) in the case of an appeal under subsection (2), 28 days from the end of the period prescribed as mentioned in subsection (2) or, as the case may be, the extended period mentioned in that subsection.

(5) For the purposes of the application of sections 79(1), 253(2)(c), 266(1)(b) and 288(10)(b) in relation to an appeal under subsection (2), it shall be assumed that the authority decided to refuse the application in question. **[85]**

NOTES

Commencement: 24 August 1990.

Words in square brackets in sub-s (2) substituted by the Planning and Compensation Act 1991, s 17(2).

79. Determination of appeals

(1) On an appeal under section 78 the Secretary of State may—

(a) allow or dismiss the appeal, or

(b) reverse or vary any part of the decision of the local planning authority (whether the appeal relates to that part of it or not),

and may deal with the application as if it had been made to him in the first instance.

(2) Before determining an appeal under section 78 the Secretary of State shall, if either the appellant or the local planning authority so wish, give each of them an opportunity of appearing before and being heard by a person appointed by the Secretary of State for the purpose.

(3) Subsection (2) does not apply to an appeal referred to a Planning Inquiry Commission under section 101.

(4) Subject to subsection (2), the provisions of sections [70, 72(1) and (5), 73 and 73A] and Part I of Schedule 5 shall apply, with any necessary modifications, in relation to an appeal to the Secretary of State under section 78 as they apply in relation to an application for planning permission which falls to be determined by the local planning authority [and a development order may apply, with or without modifications, to such an appeal any requirements imposed by a development order by virtue of section 65 or 71].

(5) The decision of the Secretary of State on such an appeal shall be final.

(6) If, before or during the determination of such an appeal in respect of an application for planning permission to develop land, the Secretary of State forms the opinion that, having regard to the provisions of sections 70 and 72(1), the development order and any directions given under that order, planning permission for that development—

(a) could not have been granted by the local planning authority; or

(b) could not have been granted otherwise than subject to the conditions imposed,

he may decline to determine the appeal or to proceed with the determination.

[(6A) If at any time before or during the determination of such an appeal it appears to the Secretary of State that the appellant is responsible for undue delay in the progress of the appeal, he may—

(a) give the appellant notice that the appeal will be dismissed unless the appellant takes, within the period specified in the notice, such steps as are specified in the notice for the expedition of the appeal; and

(b) if the appellant fails to take those steps within that period, dismiss the appeal accordingly.]

(7) Schedule 6 applies to appeals under section 78, including appeals under that section as applied by or under any other provision of this Act.   **[86–88]**

NOTES
Commencement: 24 August 1990 (sub-ss (1)–(6), (7)); 25 September 1991 (sub-s (6A)).
Words in square brackets in sub-s (4) substituted or added and sub-s (6A) inserted by the Planning and Compensation Act 1991, ss 18, 32, Sch 7, paras 8, 19.

80, 81. (*Repealed by the Planning and Compensation Act 1991, ss 31(4), 84(6), Sch 6, paras 8, 11, Sch 19, Pt II.*)

Simplified planning zones

82. Simplified planning zones

(1) A simplified planning zone is an area in respect of which a simplified planning zone scheme is in force.

(2) The adoption or approval of a simplified planning zone scheme has effect to grant in relation to the zone, or any part of it specified in the scheme, planning permission—

(a) for development specified in the scheme, or
(b) for development of any class so specified.

(3) Planning permission under a simplified planning zone scheme may be unconditional or subject to such conditions, limitations or exceptions as may be specified in the scheme.   **[89]**

NOTES
Commencement: 24 August 1990.

83. Making of simplified planning zone schemes

(1) Every local planning authority shall consider, as soon as practicable after 2nd November 1987, the question for which part or parts of their area a simplified planning zone scheme is desirable, and then shall keep that question under review.

(2) If as a result of their original consideration or of any such review a local planning authority decide that it is desirable to prepare a scheme for any part of their area they shall do so; and a local planning authority may at any time decide—

(a) to make a simplified planning zone scheme, or
(b) to alter a scheme adopted by them, or
(c) with the consent of the Secretary of State, to alter a scheme approved by him.

(3) Schedule 7 has effect with respect to the making and alteration of simplified planning zone schemes and other related matters.   **[90]**

NOTES
Commencement: 24 August 1990.

84. Simplified planning zone schemes: conditions and limitations on planning permission

(1) The conditions and limitations on planning permission which may be specified in a simplified planning zone scheme may include—

(a) conditions or limitations in respect of all development permitted by the scheme or in respect of particular descriptions of development so permitted, and

(b) conditions or limitations requiring the consent, agreement or approval of the local planning authority in relation to particular descriptions of permitted development.

(2) Different conditions or limitations may be specified in a simplified planning zone scheme for different cases or classes of case.

(3) Nothing in a simplified planning zone scheme shall affect the right of any person—

(a) to do anything not amounting to development, or

(b) to carry out development for which planning permission is not required or for which permission has been granted otherwise than by the scheme.

(4) No limitation or restriction subject to which permission has been granted otherwise than under the scheme shall affect the right of any person to carry out development for which permission has been granted under the scheme.   **[91]**

NOTES
Commencement: 24 August 1990.

85. Duration of simplified planning zone scheme

(1) A simplified planning zone scheme shall take effect on the date of its adoption or approval and shall cease to have effect at the end of the period of 10 years beginning with that date.

(2) When the scheme ceases to have effect planning permission under it shall also cease to have effect except in a case where the development authorised by it has been begun.   **[92]**

NOTES
Commencement: 24 August 1990.

86. Alteration of simplified planning zone scheme

(1) This section applies where alterations to a simplified planning zone scheme are adopted or approved.

(2) The adoption or approval of alterations providing for the inclusion of land in the simplified planning zone has effect to grant in relation to that land, or such part of it as is specified in the scheme, planning permission for development so specified or of any class so specified.

(3) The adoption or approval of alterations providing for the grant of planning permission has effect to grant such permission in relation to the simplified planning zone, or such part of it as is specified in the scheme, for development so specified or development of any class so specified.

(4) The adoption or approval of alterations providing for the withdrawal or relaxation of conditions, limitations or restrictions to which planning permission under the scheme is subject has effect to withdraw or relax the conditions, limitations or restrictions immediately.

(5) The adoption or approval of alterations providing for—

(a) the exclusion of land from the simplified planning zone,

(b) the withdrawal of planning permission, or

(c) the imposition of new or more stringent conditions, limitations or restrictions to which planning permission under the scheme is subject,

has effect to withdraw permission, or to impose the conditions, limitations or restrictions, with effect from the end of the period of 12 months beginning with the date of the adoption or approval.

(6) The adoption or approval of alterations to a scheme does not affect planning permission under the scheme in any case where the development authorised by it has been begun.   **[93]**

NOTES
Commencement: 24 August 1990.

87. Exclusion of certain descriptions of land or development

(1) The following descriptions of land may not be included in a simplified planning zone—

(a) land in a National Park;
(b) land in a conservation area;
(c) land within the Broads;
(d) land in an area designated under section 87 of the National Parks and Access to the Countryside Act 1949 as an area of outstanding natural beauty;
(e) land identified in the development plan for the district as part of a green belt;
(f) land in respect of which a notification or order is in force under section 28 or 29 of the Wildlife and Countryside Act 1981 (areas of special scientific interest).

(2) Where land included in a simplified planning zone becomes land of a description mentioned in subsection (1), that subsection does not operate to exclude it from the zone.

(3) The Secretary of State may by order provide that no simplified planning zone scheme shall have effect to grant planning permission—

(a) in relation to an area of land specified in the order or to areas of land of a description so specified, or
(b) for development of a description specified in the order.

(4) An order under subsection (3) has effect to withdraw such planning permission under a simplified planning zone scheme already in force with effect from the date on which the order comes into force, except in a case where the development authorised by the permission has been begun.   **[94]**

NOTES
Commencement: 24 August 1990.

Enterprise zone schemes

88. Planning permission for development in enterprise zones

(1) An order designating an enterprise zone under Schedule 32 to the Local Government, Planning and Land Act 1980 shall (without more) have effect on the date on which the order designating the zone takes effect to grant planning permission for development specified in the scheme or for development of any class so specified.

(2) The approval of a modified scheme under paragraph 11 of that Schedule

shall (without more) have effect on the date on which the modifications take effect to grant planning permission for development specified in the modified scheme or for development of any class so specified.

(3) Planning permission so granted shall be subject to such conditions or limitations as may be specified in the scheme or modified scheme or, if none is specified, shall be unconditional.

(4) Subject to subsection (5), where planning permission is so granted for any development or class of development the enterprise zone authority may direct that the permission shall not apply in relation—

    (a) to a specified development; or

    (b) to a specified class of development; or

    (c) to a specified class of development in a specified area within the enterprise zone.

(5) An enterprise zone authority shall not give a direction under subsection (4) unless—

    (a) they have submitted it to the Secretary of State, and

    (b) he has notified them that he approves of their giving it.

(6) If the scheme or the modified scheme specifies, in relation to any development it permits, matters which will require approval by the enterprise zone authority, the permission shall have effect accordingly.

(7) The Secretary of State may by regulations make provision as to—

    (a) the procedure for giving a direction under subsection (4); and

    (b) the method and procedure relating to the approval of matters specified in a scheme or modified scheme as mentioned in subsection (6).

(8) Such regulations may modify any provision of the planning Acts or any instrument made under them or may apply any such provision or instrument (with or without modification) in making any such provision as is mentioned in subsection (7).

(9) Nothing in this section prevents planning permission being granted in relation to land in an enterprise zone otherwise than by virtue of this section (whether the permission is granted in pursuance of an application made under this Part or by a development order).

(10) Nothing in this section prejudices the right of any person to carry out development apart from this section.   **[95]**

NOTES

    Commencement: 24 August 1990.

    Planning Acts: Town and Country Planning Act 1990, Planning (Listed Buildings and Conservation Areas) Act 1990, Planning (Hazardous Substances) Act 1990, Planning (Consequential Provisions) Act 1990.

---

89. Effect on planning permission of modification or termination of scheme

(1) Modifications to an enterprise zone scheme do not affect planning permission under the scheme in any case where the development authorised by it has been begun before the modifications take effect.

(2) When an area ceases to be an enterprise zone, planning permission under the scheme shall cease to have effect except in a case where the development authorised by it has been begun.   **[96]**

NOTES
  Commencement: 24 August 1990.

Deemed planning permission

90. Development with government authorisation

(1) Where the authorisation of a government department is required by virtue of an enactment in respect of development to be carried out by a local authority [or National Park authority], or by statutory undertakers who are not a local authority [or National Park authority], that department may, on granting that authorisation, direct that planning permission for that development shall be deemed to be granted, subject to such conditions (if any) as may be specified in the direction.

(2) On granting a consent under section 36 or 37 of the Electricity Act 1989 in respect of any operation or change of use that constitutes development, the Secretary of State may direct that planning permission for that development and any ancillary development shall be deemed to be granted, subject to such conditions (if any) as may be specified in the direction.

[(2A) On making an order under section 1 or 3 of the Transport and Works Act 1992 which includes provision for development, the Secretary of State may direct that planning permission for that development shall be deemed to be granted, subject to be granted, subject to such conditions (if any) as may be specified in the direction.]

(3) The provisions of this Act (except [Part] XII) shall apply in relation to any planning permission deemed to be granted by virtue of a direction under this section as if it had been granted by the Secretary of State on an application referred to him under section 77.

(4) For the purposes of this section development is authorised by a government department if—

(a) any consent, authority or approval to or for the development is granted by the department in pursuance of an enactment;

(b) a compulsory purchase order is confirmed by the department authorising the purchase of land for the purpose of the development;

(c) consent is granted by the department to the appropriation of land for the purpose of the development or the acquisition of land by agreement for that purpose;

(d) authority is given by the department—

(i) for the borrowing of money for the purpose of the development, or

(ii) for the application for that purpose of any money not otherwise so applicable; or

(e) any undertaking is given by the department to pay a grant in respect of the development in accordance with an enactment authorising the payment of such grants;

and references in this section to the authorisation of a government department shall be construed accordingly.

(5) In subsection (2) "ancillary development", in relation to development consisting of the extension of a generating station, does not include any development which is not directly related to the generation of electricity by that station; and in this subsection "extension" and "generating station" have the same meanings as in Part I of the Electricity Act 1989.   **[97]**

NOTES
    Commencement: 24 August 1990 (sub-ss (1), (2), (3)–(5)); 1 January 1993 (sub-s (2A)).
    Words in square brackets in sub-s (1) inserted by the Environment Act 1995, s 78, Sch 10, para 32(4), as from a day to be appointed under s 125(3).
    Sub-s (2A) inserted by the Transport and Works Act 1992, s 16(1).
    Word in square brackets in sub-s (3) substituted by the Planning and Compensation Act 1991, s 31(4), Sch 6, paras 8, 12.

Duration of planning permission

91. General condition limiting duration of planning permission

(1) Subject to the provisions of this section, every planning permission granted or deemed to be granted shall be granted or, as the case may be, be deemed to be granted, subject to the condition that the development to which it relates must be begun not later than the expiration of—

>   (a) five years beginning with the date on which the permission is granted or, as the case may be, deemed to be granted; or
>   (b) such other period (whether longer or shorter) beginning with that date as the authority concerned with the terms of planning permission may direct.

(2) The period mentioned in subsection (1)(b) shall be a period which the authority consider appropriate having regard to the provisions of the development plan and to any other material considerations.

(3) If planning permission is granted without the condition required by subsection (1), it shall be deemed to have been granted subject to the condition that the development to which it relates must be begun not later than the expiration of five years beginning with the date of the grant.

(4) Nothing in this section applies—

>   (a) to any planning permission granted by a development order;
>   (b) to any planning permission [granted for development carried out before the grant of that permission];
>   (c) to any planning permission granted for a limited period;
>   [(d) to any planning permission for development consisting of the winning and working of minerals or involving the depositing of mineral waste which is granted (or deemed to be granted) subject to a condition that the development to which it relates must be begun before the expiration of a specified period after—
>   (i) the completion of other development consisting of the winning and working of minerals already being carried out by the applicant for the planning permission; or
>   (ii) the cessation of depositing of mineral waste already being carried out by the applicant for the planning permission;]
>   (e) to any planning permission granted by an enterprise zone scheme;
>   (f) to any planning permission granted by a simplified planning zone scheme; or
>   (g) to any outline planning permission, as defined by section 92.   **[98]**

NOTES
    Commencement: 24 August 1990.
    Words in square brackets in sub-s (4)(b), and the whole of sub-s (4)(d), substituted by the Planning and Compensation Act 1991, ss 21, 32, Sch 1, paras 1, 3, Sch 7, paras 8, 20.

92. Outline planning permission

(1) In this section and section 91 "outline planning permission" means planning permission granted, in accordance with the provisions of a development order, with

the reservation for subsequent approval by the local planning authority or the Secretary of State of matters not particularised in the application ("reserved matters").

(2) Subject to the following provisions of this section, where outline planning permission is granted for development consisting in or including the carrying out of building or other operations, it shall be granted subject to conditions to the effect—

    (a) that, in the case of any reserved matter, application for approval must be made not later than the expiration of three years beginning with the date of the grant of outline planning permission; and

    (b) that the development to which the permission relates must be begun not later than—

        (i) the expiration of five years from the date of the grant of outline planning permission; or

        (ii) if later, the expiration of two years from the final approval of the reserved matters or, in the case of approval on different dates, the final approval of the last such matter to be approved.

(3) If outline planning permission is granted without the conditions required by subsection (2), it shall be deemed to have been granted subject to those conditions.

(4) The authority concerned with the terms of an outline planning permission may, in applying subsection (2), substitute, or direct that there be substituted, for the periods of three years, five years or two years referred to in that subsection such other periods respectively (whether longer or shorter) as they consider appropriate.

(5) They may also specify, or direct that there be specified, separate periods under paragraph (a) of subsection (2) in relation to separate parts of the development to which the planning permission relates; and, if they do so, the condition required by paragraph (b) of that subsection shall then be framed correspondingly by reference to those parts, instead of by reference to the development as a whole.

(6) In considering whether to exercise their powers under subsections (4) and (5), the authority shall have regard to the provisions of the development plan and to any other material considerations. **[99]**

NOTES
    Commencement: 24 August 1990.

93. Provisions supplementary to ss 91 and 92

(1) The authority referred to in section 91(1)(b) or 92(4) is—

    (a) the local planning authority or the Secretary of State, in the case of planning permission granted by them,

    (b) in the case of planning permission deemed to be granted under section 90(1), the department on whose direction planning permission is deemed to be granted, and

    (c) in the case of planning permission deemed to be granted under section 90(2), the Secretary of State.

(2) For the purposes of section 92, a reserved matter shall be treated as finally approved—

    (a) when an application for approval is granted, or

    (b) in a case where the application is made to the local planning authority and on an appeal to the Secretary of State against the authority's decision on the application the Secretary of State grants the approval, when the appeal is determined.

(3) Where a local planning authority grant planning permission, the fact that any of the conditions of the permission are required by the provisions of section 91 or 92 to be imposed, or are deemed by those provisions to be imposed, shall not prevent the conditions being the subject of an appeal under section 78 against the decision of the authority.

(4) In the case of planning permission (whether outline or other) which has conditions attached to it by or under section 91 or 92—

(a) development carried out after the date by which the conditions require it to be carried out shall be treated as not authorised by the permission; and

(b) an application for approval of a reserved matter, if it is made after the date by which the conditions require it to be made, shall be treated as not made in accordance with the terms of the permission.   **[100]**

NOTES
  Commencement: 24 August 1990.
  Modification: section modified by the Town and Country Planning General Regulations 1992, SI 1992/1492, reg 5(1)(c), Sch 1 at **[829]**.

94. Termination of planning permission by reference to time limit: completion notices

(1) This section applies where—

(a) by virtue of section 91 or 92, a planning permission is subject to a condition that the development to which the permission relates must be begun before the expiration of a particular period, that development has been begun within that period, but that period has elapsed without the development having been completed; or

(b) development has been begun in accordance with planning permission under a simplified planning zone scheme but has not been completed by the time the area ceases to be a simplified planning zone; or

(c) development has been begun in accordance with planning permission under an enterprise zone scheme but has not been completed by the time the area ceases to be an enterprise zone.

(2) If the local planning authority are of the opinion that the development will not be completed within a reasonable period, they may serve a notice ("a completion notice") stating that the planning permission will cease to have effect at the expiration of a further period specified in the notice.

(3) The period so specified must not be less than 12 months after the notice takes effect.

(4) A completion notice shall be served—

(a) on the owner of the land,

(b) on the occupier of the land, and

(c) on any other person who in the opinion of the local planning authority will be affected by the notice.

(5) The local planning authority may withdraw a completion notice at any time before the expiration of the period specified in it as the period at the expiration of which the planning permission is to cease to have effect.

(6) If they do so they shall immediately give notice of the withdrawal to every person who was served with the completion notice.   **[101]**

NOTES
   Commencement: 24 August 1990.

95. Effect of completion notice

(1) A completion notice shall not take effect unless and until it is confirmed by the Secretary of State.

(2) In confirming a completion notice the Secretary of State may substitute some longer period for that specified in the notice as the period at the expiration of which the planning permission is to cease to have effect.

(3) If, within such period as may be specified in a completion notice (which must not be less than 28 days from its service) any person on whom the notice is served so requires, the Secretary of State, before confirming the notice, shall give him and the local planning authority an opportunity of appearing before and being heard by a person appointed by the Secretary of State for the purpose.

(4) If a completion notice takes effect, the planning permission referred to in it shall become invalid at the expiration of the period specified in the notice (whether the original period specified under section 94(2) or a longer period substituted by the Secretary of State under subsection (2)).

(5) Subsection (4) shall not affect any permission so far as development carried out under it before the end of the period mentioned in that subsection is concerned.

[102]

NOTES
   Commencement: 24 August 1990.
   Modification: section modified by the Town and Country Planning General Regulations 1992, SI 1992/1492, reg 5(1)(c), Sch 1 at **[829]**.

96. Power of Secretary of State to serve completion notices

(1) If it appears to the Secretary of State to be expedient that a completion notice should be served in respect of any land, he may himself serve such a notice.

(2) A completion notice served by the Secretary of State shall have the same effect as if it had been served by the local planning authority.

(3) The Secretary of State shall not serve such a notice without consulting the local planning authority.   **[103]**

NOTES
   Commencement: 24 August 1990.
   Modification: section modified by the Town and Country Planning General Regulations 1992, SI 1992/1492, reg 5(1)(c), Sch 1 at **[829]**.

Revocation and modification of planning permission

97. Power to revoke or modify planning permission

(1) If it appears to the local planning authority that it is expedient to revoke or modify any permission to develop land granted on an application made under this Part, the authority may by order revoke or modify the permission to such extent as they consider expedient.

(2) In exercising their functions under subsection (1) the authority shall have regard to the development plan and to any other material considerations.

(3) The power conferred by this section may be exercised—

(a) where the permission relates to the carrying out of building or other operations, at any time before those operations have been completed;

(b) where the permission relates to a change of the use of any land, at any time before the change has taken place.

(4) The revocation or modification of permission for the carrying out of building or other operations shall not affect so much of those operations as has been previously carried out.

(5) References in this section to the local planning authority are to be construed in relation to development consisting of the winning and working of minerals as references to the mineral planning authority, and . . .

[(6) Part II of Schedule 5 shall have effect for the purpose of making special provision with respect to the conditions that may be imposed by an order under this section which revokes or modifies permission for development—

(a) consisting of the winning and working of minerals; or

(b) involving the depositing of refuse or waste materials.]   **[104]**

NOTES
Commencement: 24 August 1990 (sub-ss (1)–(5)); 25 September 1991 (sub-s (6)).
Words omitted from sub-s (5) repealed, and sub-s (6) added, by the Planning and Compensation Act 1991, ss 21, 84(6), Sch 1, paras 1, 4, Sch 19, Pt I.

98. Procedure for s 97 orders: opposed cases

(1) Except as provided in section 99, an order under section 97 shall not take effect unless it is confirmed by the Secretary of State.

(2) Where a local planning authority submit such an order to the Secretary of State for confirmation, they shall serve notice on—

(a) the owner of the land affected,

(b) the occupier of the land affected, and

(c) any other person who in their opinion will be affected by the order.

(3) The notice shall specify the period within which any person on whom it is served may require the Secretary of State to give him an opportunity of appearing before, and being heard by, a person appointed by the Secretary of State for the purpose.

(4) If within that period such a person so requires, before the Secretary of State confirms the order he shall give such an opportunity both to him and to the local planning authority.

(5) The period referred to in subsection (3) must not be less than 28 days from the service of the notice.

(6) The Secretary of State may confirm an order submitted to him under this section either without modification or subject to such modifications as he considers expedient.   **[105]**

NOTES
Commencement: 24 August 1990.
Modification: section modified by the Town and Country Planning General Regulations 1992, SI 1992/1492, reg 5(1)(c), Sch 1 at **[829]**.

99. Procedure for s 97 orders: unopposed cases

(1) This section applies where—

(a) the local planning authority have made an order under section 97; and

(b) the owner and the occupier of the land and all persons who in the authority's opinion will be affected by the order have notified the authority in writing that they do not object to it.

(2) Where this section applies, instead of submitting the order to the Secretary of State for confirmation the authority shall advertise in the prescribed manner the fact that the order has been made, and the advertisement must specify—

(a) the period within which persons affected by the order may give notice to the Secretary of State that they wish for an opportunity of appearing before, and being heard by, a person appointed by the Secretary of State for the purpose; and

(b) the period at the expiration of which, if no such notice is given to the Secretary of State, the order may take effect by virtue of this section without being confirmed by the Secretary of State.

(3) The authority shall also serve notice to the same effect on the persons mentioned in subsection (1)(b).

(4) The period referred to in subsection (2)(a) must not be less than 28 days from the date the advertisement first appears.

(5) The period referred to in subsection (2)(b) must not be less than 14 days from the expiration of the period referred to in subsection (2)(a).

(6) The authority shall send a copy of any advertisement published under subsection (2) to the Secretary of State not more than three days after the publication.

(7) If—

(a) no person claiming to be affected by the order has given notice to the Secretary of State under subsection (2)(a) within the period referred to in that subsection, and

(b) the Secretary of State has not directed within that period that the order be submitted to him for confirmation,

the order shall take effect at the expiry of the period referred to in subsection (2)(b), without being confirmed by the Secretary of State as required by section 98(1).

(8) This section does not apply—

(a) to an order revoking or modifying a planning permission granted or deemed to have been granted by the Secretary of State under this Part or Part VII, or

(b) to an order modifying any conditions to which a planning permission is subject by virtue of section 91 or 92.   **[106]**

NOTES
Commencement: 24 August 1990.

---

100. Revocation and modification of planning permission by the Secretary of State

(1) If it appears to the Secretary of State that it is expedient that an order should be made under section 97, he may himself make such an order.

(2) Such an order which is made by the Secretary of State shall have the same effect as if it had been made by the local planning authority and confirmed by the Secretary of State.

(3) The Secretary of State shall not make such an order without consulting the local planning authority.

(4) Where the Secretary of State proposes to make such an order he shall serve notice on the local planning authority.

(5) The notice shall specify the period (which must not be less than 28 days from the date of its service) within which the authority may require an opportunity of appearing before and being heard by a person appointed by the Secretary of State for the purpose.

(6) If within that period the authority so require, before the Secretary of State makes the order he shall give the authority such an opportunity.

(7) The provisions of this Part and of any regulations made under this Act with respect to the procedure to be followed in connection with the submission by the local planning authority of any order under section 97 and its confirmation by the Secretary of State shall have effect, subject to any necessary modifications, in relation to any proposal by the Secretary of State to make such an order and its making by him.

[(8) Subsections (5) and (6) of section 97 apply for the purposes of this section as they apply for the purposes of that.] **[107]**

NOTES

Commencement: 24 August 1990 (sub-ss (1)–(7)); 25 September 1991 (sub-s (8)).
Sub-s (8) substituted by the Planning and Compensation Act 1991, s 21, Sch 1, paras 1, 5.
Modification: section modified by the Town and Country Planning General Regulations 1992, SI 1992/1492, reg 5(1)(c), Sch 1 at **[829]**.

References to Planning Inquiry Commission

101. Power to refer certain planning questions to Planning Inquiry Commission

(1) The Secretary of State may constitute a Planning Inquiry Commission to inquire into and report on any matter referred to them under subsection (2) in the circumstances mentioned in subsection (3).

(2) The matters that may be referred to a Planning Inquiry Commission are—

(a) an application for planning permission which the Secretary of State has under section 77 directed to be referred to him instead of being dealt with by a local planning authority;

(b) an appeal under section 78 (including that section as applied by or under any other provision of this Act);

(c) a proposal that a government department should give a direction under section 90(1) that planning permission shall be deemed to be granted for development by a local authority [or National Park authority] or by statutory undertakers which is required by any enactment to be authorised by that department;

(d) a proposal that development should be carried out by or on behalf of a government department.

(3) Any of those matters may be referred to any such commission under this section if it appears expedient to the responsible Minister or Ministers that the question whether the proposed development should be permitted to be carried out should be the subject of a special inquiry on either or both of the following grounds—

(a) that there are considerations of national or regional importance which are relevant to the determination of that question and require evaluation, but a proper evaluation of them cannot be made unless there is a special inquiry for the purpose;

(b) that the technical or scientific aspects of the proposed development are of so unfamiliar a character as to jeopardise a proper determination of that question unless there is a special inquiry for the purpose.

(4) Part I of Schedule 8 shall have effect as respects the constitution of any such commission and its functions and procedure on references to it under this section, and the references in subsection (3) and in that Schedule to ''the responsible Minister or Ministers'' shall be construed in accordance with Part II of that Schedule.

(5) In relation to any matter affecting both England and Wales, the functions of the Secretary of State under subsection (1) shall be exercised by the Secretaries of State for the time being having general responsibility in planning matters in relation to England and in relation to Wales acting jointly.   **[108]**

NOTES

Commencement: 24 August 1990.

Words in square brackets in sub-s (2)(c) inserted by the Environment Act 1995, s 78, Sch 10, para 32(4), as from a day to be appointed under s 125(3).

Other controls over development

102. Orders requiring discontinuance of use or alteration or removal of buildings or works

(1) If, having regard to the development plan and to any other material considerations, it appears to a local planning authority that it is expedient in the interests of the proper planning of their area (including the interests of amenity)—

(a) that any use of land should be discontinued or that any conditions should be imposed on the continuance of a use of land; or

(b) that any buildings or works should be altered or removed,

they may by order—

(i) require the discontinuance of that use, or

(ii) impose such conditions as may be specified in the order on the continuance of it, or

(iii) require such steps as may be so specified to be taken for the alteration or removal of the buildings or works,

as the case may be.

(2) An order under this section may grant planning permission for any development of the land to which the order relates, subject to such conditions as may be specified in the order.

(3) Section 97 shall apply in relation to any planning permission granted by an order under this section as it applies in relation to planning permission granted by the local planning authority on an application made under this Part.

[(4) The planning permission which may be granted by an order under this section includes planning permission, subject to such conditions as may be specified in the order, for development carried out before the date on which the order was submitted to the Secretary of State under section 103.

(5) Planning permission for such development may be granted so as to have effect from—

(a) the date on which the development was carried out; or
(b) if it was carried out in accordance with planning permission granted for a limited period, the end of that period.]

(6) Where the requirements of an order under this section will involve the displacement of persons residing in any premises, it shall be the duty of the local planning authority, in so far as there is no other residential accommodation suitable to the reasonable requirements of those persons available on reasonable terms, to secure the provision of such accommodation in advance of the displacement.

(7) Subject to section 103(8), in the case of planning permission granted by an order under this section, the authority referred to in sections 91(1)(b) and 92(4) is the local planning authority making the order.

(8) The previous provisions of this section do not apply to the use of any land for development [consisting of the winning and working of minerals or involving the depositing of refuse or waste materials] except as provided in Schedule 9, and that Schedule shall have effect for the purpose of making provision as respects land which is or has been so used.   **[109]**

NOTES
Commencement: 24 August 1990 (sub-ss (1)–(3), (6)–(8)); 2 January 1992 (sub-ss (4), (5)).
Sub-ss (4), (5), and words in square brackets in sub-s (8), substituted by the Planning and Compensation Act 1991, ss 21, 32, Sch 1, paras 1, 6, Sch 7, paras 8, 21.

103. Confirmation by Secretary of State of s 102 orders

(1) An order under section 102 shall not take effect unless it is confirmed by the Secretary of State, either without modification or subject to such modifications as he considers expedient.

(2) The power of the Secretary of State under this section to confirm an order subject to modifications includes power—
(a) to modify any provision of the order granting planning permission, as mentioned in subsections (2) to (5) of section 102;
(b) to include in the order any grant of planning permission which might have been included in the order as submitted to him.

(3) Where a local planning authority submit an order to the Secretary of State for his confirmation under this section, they shall serve notice—
(a) on the owner of the land affected,
(b) on the occupier of that land, and
(c) on any other person who in their opinion will be affected by the order.

(4) The notice shall specify the period within which any person on whom it is served may require the Secretary of State to give him an opportunity of appearing before, and being heard by, a person appointed by the Secretary of State for the purpose.

(5) If within that period such a person so requires, before the Secretary of State confirms the order, he shall give such an opportunity both to him and to the local planning authority.

(6) The period referred to in subsection (4) must not be less than 28 days from the service of the notice.

(7) Where an order under section 102 has been confirmed by the Secretary of State, the local planning authority shall serve a copy of the order on the owner and occupier of the land to which the order relates.

(8) Where the Secretary of State exercises his powers under subsection (2) in confirming an order granting planning permission, he is the authority referred to in sections 91(1)(b) and 92(4).   **[110]**

NOTES

Commencement: 24 August 1990.

Modification: section modified by the Town and Country Planning General Regulations 1992, SI 1992/1492, reg 5(1)(c), Sch 1 at **[829]**.

104. Power of the Secretary of State to make s 102 orders

(1) If it appears to the Secretary of State that it is expedient that an order should be made under section 102, he may himself make such an order.

(2) Such an order made by the Secretary of State shall have the same effect as if it had been made by the local planning authority and confirmed by the Secretary of State.

(3) The Secretary of State shall not make such an order without consulting the local planning authority.

(4) Where the Secretary of State proposes to make such an order he shall serve notice on the local planning authority.

(5) The notice shall specify the period within which the authority may require an opportunity of appearing before and being heard by a person appointed by the Secretary of State for the purpose.

(6) If within that period the authority so require, before the Secretary of State makes the order he shall give the authority such an opportunity.

(7) The period referred to in subsection (5) must not be less than 28 days from the date of the service of the notice.

(8) The provisions of this Part and of any regulations made under this Act with respect to the procedure to be followed in connection with the submission by the local planning authority of any order under section 102, its confirmation by the Secretary of State and the service of copies of it as confirmed shall have effect, subject to any necessary modifications, in relation to any proposal by the Secretary of State to make such an order, its making by him and the service of copies of it.

                                                                                        [111]

NOTES

Commencement: 24 August 1990.

Modification: section modified by the Town and Country Planning General Regulations 1992, SI 1992/1492, reg 5(1)(c), Sch 1 at **[829]**.

[105. Reviews by mineral planning authorities

(1) Every mineral planning authority shall undertake periodic reviews about the winning and working of minerals and the depositing of mineral waste in their area.

(2) Subject to regulations made by virtue of subsection (4), the duty under this section is, at such intervals as they think fit—

   (a) to review every mining site in their area; and
   (b) to consider whether they should make an order under section 97 or under paragraph 1, 3, 5 or 6 of Schedule 9, and if they do consider that they should make any such order, to make it.

(3) For the purposes of subsection (2) ''a mining site'' means a site which—

(a) is being used for the winning and working of minerals or the depositing of mineral waste;

(b) has been so used at any time during—

    (i) the period of five years preceding the date of the beginning of the review; or

    (ii) such other period preceding that date as may be prescribed; or

(c) is authorised to be so used.

(4) If regulations so require, the reviews shall be undertaken at prescribed intervals and shall cover such matters as may be prescribed.]   **[112]**

NOTES

  Commencement: 25 September 1991.

  Substituted by the Planning and Compensation Act 1991, s 21, Sch 1, paras 1, 7.

  Repealed by the Environment Act 1995, ss 96(4), 120(3), Sch 24, as from a day to be appointed under s 125(3).

[106. Planning obligations

(1) Any person interested in land in the area of a local planning authority may, by agreement or otherwise, enter into an obligation (referred to in this section and sections 106A and 106B as "a planning obligation"), enforceable to the extent mentioned in subsection (3)—

    (a) restricting the development or use of the land in any specified way;

    (b) requiring specified operations or activities to be carried out in, on, under or over the land;

    (c) requiring the land to be used in any specified way; or

    (d) requiring a sum or sums to be paid to the authority on a specified date or dates or periodically.

(2) A planning obligation may—

    (a) be unconditional or subject to conditions;

    (b) impose any restriction or requirement mentioned in subsection (1)(a) to (c) either indefinitely or for such period or periods as may be specified; and

    (c) if it requires a sum or sums to be paid, require the payment of a specified amount or an amount determined in accordance with the instrument by which the obligation is entered into and, if it requires the payment of periodical sums, require them to be paid indefinitely or for a specified period.

(3) Subject to subsection (4) a planning obligation is enforceable by the authority identified in accordance with subsection (9)(d)—

    (a) against the person entering into the obligation; and

    (b) against any person deriving title from that person.

(4) The instrument by which a planning obligation is entered into may provide that a person shall not be bound by the obligation in respect of any period during which he no longer has an interest in the land.

(5) A restriction or requirement imposed under a planning obligation is enforceable by injunction.

(6) Without prejudice to subsection (5), if there is a breach of a requirement in a planning obligation to carry out any operations in, on, under or over the land to which the obligation relates, the authority by whom the obligation is enforceable may—

> (a) enter the land and carry out the operations; and
> (b) recover from the person or persons against whom the obligation is enforceable any expenses reasonably incurred by them in doing so.

(7) Before an authority exercise their power under subsection (6)(a) they shall give not less than twenty-one days' notice of their intention to do so to any person against whom the planning obligation is enforceable.

(8) Any person who wilfully obstructs a person acting in the exercise of a power under subsection (6)(a) shall be guilty of an offence and liable on summary conviction to a fine not exceeding level 3 on the standard scale.

(9) A planning obligation may not be entered into except by an instrument executed as a deed which—

> (a) states that the obligation is a planning obligation for the purposes of this section;
> (b) identifies the land in which the person entering into the obligation is interested;
> (c) identifies the person entering into the obligation and states what his interest in the land is; and
> (d) identifies the local planning authority by whom the obligation is enforceable.

(10) A copy of any such instrument shall be given to the authority so identified.

(11) A planning obligation shall be a local land charge and for the purposes of the Local Land Charges Act 1975 the authority by whom the obligation is enforceable shall be treated as the originating authority as respects such a charge.

(12) Regulations may provide for the charging on the land of—

> (a) any sum or sums required to be paid under a planning obligation; and
> (b) any expenses recoverable by a local planning authority under subsection (6)(b),

and this section and sections 106A and 106B shall have effect subject to any such regulations.

(13) In this section "specified" means specified in the instrument by which the planning obligation is entered into and in this section and section 106A "land" has the same meaning as in the Local Land Charges Act 1975.]   **[113]**

NOTES

Commencement: 25 October 1991.

This section, and ss 106A, 106B, substituted for s 106 by the Planning and Compensation Act 1991, s 12(1).

[106A. Modification and discharge of planning obligations

(1) A planning obligation may not be modified or discharged except—

> (a) by agreement between the authority by whom the obligation is enforceable and the person or persons against whom the obligation is enforceable; or
> (b) in accordance with this section and section 106B.

(2) An agreement falling within subsection (1)(a) shall not be entered into except by an instrument executed as a deed.

(3) A person against whom a planning obligation is enforceable may, at any time after the expiry of the relevant period, apply to the local planning authority by whom the obligation is enforceable for the obligation—

    (a) to have effect subject to such modifications as may be specified in the
application; or

    (b) to be discharged.

(4) In subsection (3) "the relevant period" means—

    (a) such period as may be prescribed; or

    (b) if no period is prescribed, the period of five years beginning with the date
on which the obligation is entered into.

(5) An application under subsection (3) for the modification of a planning
obligation may not specify a modification imposing an obligation on any other
person against whom the obligation is enforceable.

(6) Where an application is made to an authority under subsection (3), the
authority may determine—

    (a) that the planning obligation shall continue to have effect without
modification;

    (b) if the obligation no longer serves a useful purpose, that it shall be
discharged; or

    (c) if the obligation continues to serve a useful purpose, but would serve that
purpose equally well if it had effect subject to the modifications specified
in the application, that it shall have effect subject to those modifications.

(7) The authority shall give notice of their determination to the applicant within
such period as may be prescribed.

(8) Where an authority determine that a planning obligation shall have effect
subject to modifications specified in the application, the obligation as modified shall
be enforceable as if it had been entered into on the date on which notice of the
determination was given to the applicant.

(9) Regulations may make provision with respect to—

    (a) the form and content of applications under subsection (3);

    (b) the publication of notices of such applications;

    (c) the procedures for considering any representations made with respect to
such applications; and

    (d) the notices to be given to applicants of determinations under subsection
(6).

(10) Section 84 of the Law of Property Act 1925 (power to discharge or modify
restrictive covenants affecting land) does not apply to a planning obligation.][**113A**]

NOTES
    Commencement: 25 November 1991 (certain purposes); 9 November 1992 (remaining purposes).
    Substituted as noted to s 106 at **[113]**.

[106B. Appeals

(1) Where a local planning authority—

    (a) fail to give notice as mentioned in section 106A(7); or

    (b) determine that a planning obligation shall continue to have effect without
modification,

the applicant may appeal to the Secretary of State.

(2) For the purposes of an appeal under subsection (1)(a), it shall be assumed
that the authority have determined that the planning obligation shall continue to have
effect without modification.

(3) An appeal under this section shall be made by notice served within such period and in such manner as may be prescribed.

(4) Subsections (6) to (9) of section 106A apply in relation to appeals to the Secretary of State under this section as they apply in relation to applications to authorities under that section.

(5) Before determining the appeal the Secretary of State shall, if either the applicant or the authority so wish, give each of them an opportunity of appearing before and being heard by a person appointed by the Secretary of State for the purpose.

(6) The determination of an appeal by the Secretary of State under this section shall be final.

(7) Schedule 6 applies to appeals under this section.]   **[113B]**

NOTES
  Commencement: 25 November 1991 (certain purposes); 9 November 1992 (remaining purposes).
  Substituted as noted to s 106 at **[113]**.

PART IV

COMPENSATION FOR EFFECTS OF CERTAIN ORDERS, NOTICES, ETC

Compensation for revocation of planning permission, etc

107. Compensation where planning permission revoked or modified

(1) Subject to section 116, where planning permission is revoked or modified by an order under section 97, then if, on a claim made to the local planning authority within the prescribed time and in the prescribed manner, it is shown that a person interested in the land or in minerals in, on or under it—

  (a) has incurred expenditure in carrying out work which is rendered abortive by the revocation or modification; or
  (b) has otherwise sustained loss or damage which is directly attributable to the revocation or modification,

the local planning authority shall pay that person compensation in respect of that expenditure, loss or damage.

(2) For the purposes of this section, any expenditure incurred in the preparation of plans for the purposes of any work, or upon other similar matters preparatory to it, shall be taken to be included in the expenditure incurred in carrying out that work.

(3) Subject to subsection (2), no compensation shall be paid under this section in respect—

  (a) of any work carried out before the grant of the permission which is revoked or modified, or
  (b) of any other loss or damage arising out of anything done or omitted to be done before the grant of that permission (other than loss or damage consisting of depreciation of the value of an interest in land).

(4) In calculating for the purposes of this section the amount of any loss or damage consisting of depreciation of the value of an interest in land, it shall be assumed that planning permission would be granted [—

  (a) subject to the condition set out in Schedule 10, for any development of the land of a class specified in paragraph 1 of Schedule 3;

(b) for any development of a class specified in paragraph 2 of Schedule 3.]

(5) In this Part any reference to an order under section 97 includes a reference to an order under the provisions of that section as applied by section 102(3) (or, subject to section 116, by paragraph [1(3)] of Schedule 9).   **[114]**

NOTES
Commencement: 24 August 1990.
Words in square brackets in sub-s (4) substituted in relation to claims made on or after 16 November 1990, and expression in square brackets in sub-s (5) substituted, by the Planning and Compensation Act 1991, ss 21, 31(4), Sch 1, paras 1, 8, Sch 6, paras 8, 13.

108. Compensation for refusal or conditional grant of planning permission formerly granted by development order

(1) Where—

(a) planning permission granted by a development order is withdrawn (whether by the revocation or amendment of the order or by the issue of directions under powers conferred by the order); and

(b) on an application made under Part III planning permission for development formerly permitted by that order is refused or is granted subject to conditions other than those imposed by that order,

section 107 shall apply as if the planning permission granted by the development order—

(i) had been granted by the local planning authority under Part III; and
(ii) had been revoked or modified by an order under section 97.

(2) Where planning permission granted by a development order is withdrawn by revocation or amendment of the order, this section applies only if the application referred to in subsection (1)(b) is made before the end of the period of 12 months beginning with the date on which the revocation or amendment came into operation.

(3) This section shall not apply in relation to planning permission for the development of operational land of statutory undertakers.

[(4) Regulations made by virtue of this subsection may provide that subsection (1) shall not apply where planning permission granted by a development order for demolition of buildings or any description of buildings is withdrawn by the issue of directions under powers conferred by the order.]   **[115]**

NOTES
Commencement: 24 August 1990 (sub-ss (1)–(3)); 27 July 1992 (sub-s (4)).
Sub-s (4) added by the Planning and Compensation Act 1991, s 13(3).

109. Apportionment of compensation for depreciation

(1) Where compensation becomes payable under section 107 which includes compensation for depreciation of an amount exceeding £20, the local planning authority—

(a) if it appears to them to be practicable to do so, shall apportion the amount of the compensation for depreciation between different parts of the land to which the claim for that compensation relates; and

(b) shall give particulars of any such apportionment to the claimant and to any other person entitled to an interest in land which appears to the authority to be substantially affected by the apportionment.

(2) In carrying out an apportionment under subsection (1)(a), the local planning authority shall divide the land into parts and shall distribute the compensation for

depreciation between those parts, according to the way in which different parts of the land appear to the authority to be differently affected by the order or, in a case falling within section 108, the relevant planning decision, in consequence of which the compensation is payable.

(3) Regulations under this section shall make provision, subject to subsection (4)—

    (a) for enabling the claimant and any other person to whom particulars of an apportionment have been given under subsection (1), or who establishes that he is entitled to an interest in land which is substantially affected by such an apportionment, if he wishes to dispute the apportionment, to require it to be referred to the Lands Tribunal;

    (b) for enabling the claimant and every other person to whom particulars of any such apportionment have been so given to be heard by the Tribunal on any reference under this section of that apportionment; and

    (c) for requiring the Tribunal, on any such reference, either to confirm or to vary the apportionment and to notify the parties of the decision of the Tribunal.

(4) Where on a reference to the Lands Tribunal under this section it is shown that an apportionment—

    (a) relates wholly or partly to the same matters as a previous apportionment, and

    (b) is consistent with that previous apportionment in so far as it relates to those matters,

the Tribunal shall not vary the apportionment in such a way as to be inconsistent with the previous apportionment in so far as it relates to those matters.

(5) On a reference to the Lands Tribunal by virtue of subsection (3), subsections (1) and (2), so far as they relate to the making of an apportionment, shall apply with the substitution, for references to the local planning authority, of references to the Lands Tribunal.

(6) In this section and [section 110]—

    "compensation for depreciation" means so much of any compensation payable under section 107 as is payable in respect of loss or damage consisting of depreciation of the value of an interest in land,

    "interest" (where the reference is to an interest in land) means the fee simple or a tenancy of the land and does not include any other interest in it, and

    "relevant planning decision" means the planning decision by which planning permission is refused, or is granted subject to conditions other than those previously imposed by the development order.   **[116]**

NOTES

    Commencement: 24 August 1990.

    Words in square brackets in sub-s (6) substituted by the Planning and Compensation Act 1991, s 31(4), Sch 6, paras 8, 14.

110. Registration of compensation for depreciation

(1) Where compensation becomes payable under section 107 which includes compensation for depreciation of an amount exceeding £20, the local planning authority shall give notice to the Secretary of State that such compensation has become payable, specifying the amount of the compensation for depreciation and any apportionment of it under section 109.

(2) Where the Secretary of State is given such notice he shall cause notice of that fact to be deposited—

(a) with the council of the district [, Welsh county, county borough] or London borough in which the land is situated, and

(b) if that council is not the local planning authority, with the local planning authority.

(3) Notices deposited under this section must specify—

(a) the order, or in a case falling within section 108 the relevant planning decision, and the land to which the claim for compensation relates; and

(b) the amount of compensation and any apportionment of it under section 109.

(4) Notices deposited under this section shall be local land charges, and for the purposes of the Local Land Charges Act 1975 the council with whom any such notice is deposited shall be treated as the originating authority as respects the charge constituted by it.

(5) In relation to compensation specified in a notice registered under this section, references in this Part to so much of the compensation as is attributable to a part of the land to which the notice relates shall be construed as follows—

(a) if the notice does not include an apportionment under section 109, the amount of the compensation shall be treated as distributed rateably according to area over the land to which the notice relates;

(b) if the notice includes such an apportionment—

(i) the compensation shall be treated as distributed in accordance with that apportionment as between the different parts of the land by reference to which the apportionment is made; and

(ii) so much of the compensation as, in accordance with the apportionment, is attributed to a part of the land shall be treated as distributed rateably according to area over that part.   **[117]**

NOTES
    Commencement: 24 August 1990.
    Words in square brackets in sub-s (2) inserted by the Local Government (Wales) Act 1994, s 20(4)(b), Sch 6, Pt II, para 24(2), as from a day to be appointed.

111. Recovery of compensation under s 107 on subsequent development

(1) No person shall carry out any . . . development to which this section applies on land in respect of which a notice ("a compensation notice") is registered under section 110 until any amount which is recoverable under this section in accordance with section 112 in respect of the compensation specified in the notice has been paid or secured to the satisfaction of the Secretary of State.

(2) Subject to subsections (3) [to (5)], this section applies to any . . . development—

(a) which is development of a residential, commercial or industrial character and consists wholly or mainly of the construction of houses, flats, shop or office premises, or industrial buildings (including warehouses), or any combination of them; or

(b) which consists in the winning and working of minerals; or

(c) to which, having regard to the probable value of the development, it is in the opinion of the Secretary of State reasonable that this section should apply.

(3) This section shall not apply to any development by virtue of subsection (2)(c) if, on an application made to him for the purpose, the Secretary of State has certified that, having regard to the probable value of the development, it is not in his opinion reasonable that this section should apply to it.

(4) Where the compensation under section 107 specified in the notice registered under section 110 became payable in respect of an order modifying planning permission or, in a case falling within section 108, of a relevant planning decision (within the meaning of section 109) granting conditional planning permission, this section shall not apply to development in accordance with that permission as modified by the order or, as the case may be, in accordance with those conditions.

[(5) This section does not apply to any development—

    (a) of a class specified in paragraph 1 of Schedule 3 which is carried out in accordance with the condition set out in Schedule 10; or

    (b) of a class specified in paragraph 2 of Schedule 3.]   **[118]**

NOTES
    Commencement: 24 August 1990.
    Words omitted from sub-ss (1), (2) repealed, words in square brackets in sub-s (2) substituted, and sub-s (5) substituted, by the Planning and Compensation Act 1991, ss 31(4), 84(6), Sch 6, paras 8, 15, Sch 19, Pt II.

112. Amount recoverable under s 111 and provisions for payment or remission of it

(1) Subject to the following provisions of this section, the amount recoverable under section 111 in respect of the compensation specified in a notice registered under section 110—

    (a) if the land on which the development is to be carried out ("the development area") is identical with, or includes (with other land) the whole of, the land comprised in the notice, shall be the amount of compensation specified in the notice;

    (b) if the development area forms part of the land comprised in the notice, or includes part of that land together with other land not comprised in the notice, shall be so much of the amount of the compensation specified in the notice as is attributable to land comprised in the notice and falling within the development area.

(2) Where, in the case of any land in respect of which such a notice has been so registered, the Secretary of State is satisfied, having regard to the probable value of any proper development of that land, that no such development is likely to be carried out unless he exercises his powers under this subsection, he may, in the case of any particular development, remit the whole or part of any amount otherwise recoverable under section 111.

(3) Where part only of any such amount has been remitted in respect of any land, the Secretary of State shall cause the notice registered under section 110 to be amended by substituting in it, for the statement of the amount of the compensation, in so far as it is attributable to that land, a statement of the amount which has been remitted under subsection (2).

(4) Where, in connection with the development of any land, an amount becomes recoverable under section 111 in respect of the compensation specified in such a notice, then, except where, and to the extent that, payment of that amount has been remitted under subsection (2), no amount shall be recoverable under that section in

respect of that compensation, in so far as it is attributable to that land, in connection with any subsequent development of it.

(5) No amount shall be recoverable under section 111 in respect of any compensation by reference to which a sum has become recoverable by the Secretary of State under section 308.

(6) An amount recoverable under section 111 in respect of any compensation shall be payable to the Secretary of State either—

    (a) as a single capital payment, or

    (b) as a series of instalments of capital and interest combined, or

    (c) as a series of other annual or periodical payments, of such amounts, and payable at such times, as the Secretary of State may direct.

(7) Before giving a direction under subsection (6)(c) the Secretary of State shall take into account any representations made by the person by whom the development is to be carried out.

(8) Except where the amount payable under subsection (6) is payable as a single capital payment, it shall be secured by the person by whom the development is to be carried out in such manner (whether by mortgage, covenant or otherwise) as the Secretary of State may direct.

(9) If any person initiates any . . . development to which section 111 applies in contravention of subsection (1) of that section, the Secretary of State may serve a notice on him—

    (a) specifying the amount appearing to the Secretary of State to be the amount recoverable under that section in respect of the compensation in question, and

    (b) requiring him to pay that amount to the Secretary of State within such period as may be specified in the notice.

(10) The period specified under subsection (9)(b) must not be less than three months after the service of the notice.

(11) Subject to subsection (12), any sum recovered by the Secretary of State under section 111 shall be paid to the local planning authority who paid the compensation to which that sum relates.

(12) Subject to subsection (13), in paying any such sum to the local planning authority, the Secretary of State shall deduct from it—

    (a) . . .

    (b) the amount of any grant paid by him under Part XIV in respect of that compensation.

(13) If the sum recovered by the Secretary of State under section 111—

    (a) is an instalment of the total sum recoverable, or

    (b) is recovered by reference to development of part of the land in respect of which the compensation was payable,

any deduction to be made under . . . subsection (12) shall be a deduction of such amount as the Secretary of State may determine to be the proper proportion of the amount referred to in that paragraph.   **[119–121]**

NOTES

    Commencement: 24 August 1990.

    Words omitted from sub-ss (9), (12), (13) repealed by the Planning and Compensation Act 1991, ss 31(4), 84(6), Sch 6, paras 8, 16, Sch 19, Pt II.

113. *(Repealed by the Planning and Compensation Act 1991, ss 31(4), 84(6), Sch 6, paras 8, 17, Sch 19, Pt II.)*

Compensation for other planning decisions

114. *(Repealed, in relation to an application for planning permission made on or after 16 November 1990, by the Planning and Compensation Act 1991, ss 31(2), (7), 84(6), Sch 19, Pt II.)*

115. Compensation in respect of orders under s 102, etc

(1) This section shall have effect where an order is made under section 102—

    (a) requiring a use of land to be discontinued,
    (b) imposing conditions on the continuance of it, or
    (c) requiring any buildings or works on land to be altered or removed.

(2) If, on a claim made to the local planning authority within the prescribed time and in the prescribed manner, it is shown that any person has suffered damage in consequence of the order—

    (a) by depreciation of the value of an interest to which he is entitled in the land or in minerals in, on or under it, or
    (b) by being disturbed in his enjoyment of the land or of such minerals,

that authority shall pay to that person compensation in respect of that damage.

(3) Without prejudice to subsection (2), any person who carries out any works in compliance with the order shall be entitled, on a claim made as mentioned in that subsection, to recover from the local planning authority compensation in respect of any expenses reasonably incurred by him in that behalf.

(4) Any compensation payable to a person under this section by virtue of such an order as is mentioned in subsection (1) shall be reduced by the value to him of any timber, apparatus or other materials removed for the purpose of complying with the order.

(5) Subject to section 116, this section applies where such an order as is mentioned in subsection (6) is made as it applies where an order is made under section 102.

(6) The orders referred to in subsection (5) are an order under paragraph 1 of Schedule 9—

    (a) requiring a use of land to be discontinued, or
    (b) imposing conditions on the continuance of it, or
    (c) requiring any buildings or works or plant or machinery on land to be altered or removed,

or an order under paragraph 3, 5 or 6 of that Schedule.   **[122]**

NOTES
   Commencement: 24 August 1990.

[116. Modification of compensation provisions in respect of mineral working etc

(1) Regulations made by virtue of this section with the consent of the Treasury may provide that where an order is made under—

(a) section 97 modifying planning permission for development consisting of the winning and working of minerals or involving the depositing of mineral waste; or

(b) paragraph 1, 3, 5 or 6 of Schedule 9 with respect to such winning and working or depositing,

sections 107, 115, 117, 279 and 280 shall have effect subject, in such cases as may be prescribed, to such modifications as may be prescribed.

(2) Any such regulations may make provision—

(a) as to circumstances in which compensation is not to be payable;

(b) for the modification of the basis on which any amount to be paid by way of compensation is to be assessed;

(c) for the assessment of any such amount on a basis different from that on which it would otherwise have been assessed,

and may also make different provision for different cases and incidental or supplementary provision.

(3) No such regulations shall be made unless a draft of the instrument is laid before and approved by a resolution of each House of Parliament.

(4) Before making any such regulations the Secretary of State shall consult such persons as appear to him to be representative—

(a) of persons carrying out mining operations;

(b) of owners of interests in land containing minerals; and

(c) of mineral planning authorities.   **[123]**

NOTES
Commencement: 25 September 1991.
Substituted by the Planning and Compensation Act 1991, s 21, Sch 1, paras 1, 9.
Savings: Regulations made or having effect as if made under Sch 11 to this Act, as repealed by the Planning and Compensation Act 1991, s 21, Sch 1, paras 1, 16(1), have effect as if made under this section, to the extent that they are in force on 25 September 1991 (ie the date of the coming into force of the repeal of Sch 11, by virtue of s 21 of, and Sch 1, paras 1, 16(2) to, the 1991 Act).

General and supplemental provisions

117. General provisions as to compensation for depreciation under Part IV

(1) For the purpose of assessing any compensation to which this section applies, the rules set out in section 5 of the Land Compensation Act 1961 shall, so far as applicable and subject to any necessary modifications, have effect as they have effect for the purpose of assessing compensation for the compulsory acquisition of an interest in land.

(2) Subject to regulations [by virtue of section 116], this section applies to any compensation which under the provisions of this Part is payable in respect of depreciation of the value of an interest in land.

(3) Where an interest in land is subject to a mortgage—

(a) any compensation to which this section applies, which is payable in respect of depreciation of the value of that interest, shall be assessed as if the interest were not subject to the mortgage;

(b) a claim for any such compensation may be made by any mortgagee of the interest, but without prejudice to the making of a claim by the person entitled to the interest;

(c) no compensation to which this section applies shall be payable in respect of the interest of the mortgagee (as distinct from the interest which is subject to the mortgage); and

(d) any compensation to which this section applies which is payable in respect of the interest which is subject to the mortgage shall be paid to the mortgagee, or, if there is more than one mortgagee, to the first mortgagee, and shall in either case be applied by him as if it were proceeds of sale.

[124]

NOTES

Commencement: 24 August 1990.

Words in square brackets in sub-s (2) substituted by the Planning and Compensation Act 1991, s 21, Sch 1, paras 1, 10.

118. Determination of claims for compensation

(1) Except in so far as may be otherwise provided by any regulations made under this Act, any question of disputed compensation under this Part shall be referred to and determined by the Lands Tribunal.

(2) In relation to the determination of any such question, the provisions of sections 2 and 4 of the Land Compensation Act 1961 shall apply subject to any necessary modifications and to the provisions of any regulations made under this Act.   **[125–143]**

NOTES

Commencement: 24 August 1990.

(Ss 119–136 and Sch 12 (Pt V) repealed by the Planning and Compensation Act 1991, ss 31(1), (5), 84(6), Sch 19, Pt II, with effect in relation to any compensation under Pt V unless the claim was made under s 127 prior to 25 September 1991 (ie the date on which this repeal came into force).)

PART VI

RIGHTS OF OWNERS ETC TO REQUIRE PURCHASE OF INTERESTS

CHAPTER I

INTERESTS AFFECTED BY PLANNING DECISIONS OR ORDERS

Service of purchase notices

137. Circumstances in which purchase notices may be served

(1) This section applies where—

(a) on an application for planning permission to develop any land, permission is refused or is granted subject to conditions; or

(b) by an order under section 97 planning permission in respect of any land is revoked, or is modified by the imposition of conditions; or

(c) an order is made under section 102 or paragraph 1 of Schedule 9 in respect of any land.

(2) If—

(a) in the case mentioned in subsection (1)(a) or (b), any owner of the land claims that the conditions mentioned in subsection (3) are satisfied with respect to it, or

(b) in the case mentioned in subsection (1)(c), any person entitled to an interest in land in respect of which the order is made claims that the conditions mentioned in subsection (4) are satisfied with respect to it,

he may, within the prescribed time and in the prescribed manner, serve on the council of the district [, Welsh county, county borough] or London borough in which the land is situated a notice (in this Act referred to as "a purchase notice") requiring that council to purchase his interest in the land in accordance with this Chapter.

(3) The conditions mentioned in subsection (2)(a) are—

(a) that the land has become incapable of reasonably beneficial use in its existing state; and

(b) in a case where planning permission was granted subject to conditions or was modified by the imposition of conditions, that the land cannot be rendered capable of reasonably beneficial use by the carrying out of the permitted development in accordance with those conditions; and

(c) in any case, that the land cannot be rendered capable of reasonably beneficial use by the carrying out of any other development for which planning permission has been granted or for which the local planning authority or the Secretary of State has undertaken to grant planning permission.

(4) The conditions mentioned in subsection (2)(b) are—

(a) that by reason of the order the land is incapable of reasonably beneficial use in its existing state; and

(b) that it cannot be rendered capable of reasonably beneficial use by the carrying out of any development for which planning permission has been granted, whether by that order or otherwise.

(5) For the purposes of subsection (1)(a) and any claim arising in the circumstances mentioned in that subsection, the conditions referred to in sections 91 and 92 shall be disregarded.

(6) A person on whom a repairs notice has been served under section 48 of the Planning (Listed Buildings and Conservation Areas) Act 1990 shall not be entitled to serve a notice under this section in the circumstances mentioned in subsection (1)(a) in respect of the building in question—

(a) until the expiration of three months beginning with the date of the service of the repairs notice; and

(b) if during that period the compulsory acquisition of the building is begun in the exercise of powers under section 47 of that Act, unless and until the compulsory acquisition is discontinued.

(7) For the purposes of subsection (6) a compulsory acquisition—

(a) is started when the notice required by section 12 of the Acquisition of Land Act 1981 or, as the case may be, paragraph 3 of Schedule 1 to that Act is served; and

(b) is discontinued—

(i) in the case of acquisition by the Secretary of State, when he decides not to make the compulsory purchase order; and

(ii) in any other case, when the order is withdrawn or the Secretary of State decides not to confirm it.

(8) No purchase notice shall be served in respect of an interest in land while the land is incapable of reasonably beneficial use by reason only of such an order as is

mentioned in subsection (1)(c), except by virtue of a claim under subsection (2)(b).
[144]

NOTES
Commencement: 24 August 1990.
Words in square brackets in sub-s (2) inserted by the Local Government (Wales) Act 1994, s 20(4)(b), Sch 6, Pt II, para 24(3), as from a day to be appointed.

138. Circumstances in which land incapable of reasonably beneficial use

(1) Where, for the purpose of determining whether the conditions specified in section 137(3) or (4) are satisfied in relation to any land, any question arises as to what is or would in any particular circumstances be a reasonably beneficial use of that land, then, in determining that question for that purpose, no account shall be taken of any unauthorised prospective use of that land.

(2) A prospective use of land shall be regarded as unauthorised for the purposes of subsection (1)—

(a) if it would involve the carrying out of [development other than any development specified in paragraph 1 or 2 of Schedule 3;] or

(b) in the case of a purchase notice served in consequence of a refusal or conditional grant of planning permission, if it would contravene the condition set out in Schedule 10.   **[145]**

NOTES
Commencement: 24 August 1990.
Words in square brackets in sub-s (2)(a) substituted by the Planning and Compensation Act 1991, s 31(4), Sch 6, paras 8, 18.

Duties of authorities on service of purchase notice

139. Action by council on whom purchase notice is served

(1) The council on whom a purchase notice is served shall serve on the owner by whom the purchase notice was served a notice (a ''response notice'') stating either—

(a) that the council are willing to comply with the purchase notice; or

(b) that another local authority or statutory undertakers specified in the response notice have agreed to comply with it in their place; or

(c) that for reasons so specified the council are not willing to comply with the purchase notice and have not found any other local authority or statutory undertakers who will agree to comply with it in their place, and that they have sent the Secretary of State a copy of the purchase notice and of the response notice.

(2) A response notice must be served before the end of the period of three months beginning with the date of service of the purchase notice.

(3) Where the council on whom a purchase notice is served by an owner have served a response notice on him in accordance with subsection (1)(a) or (b), the council or, as the case may be, the other local authority or statutory undertakers specified in the response notice shall be deemed—

(a) to be authorised to acquire the interest of the owner compulsorily in accordance with the relevant provisions, and

(b) to have served a notice to treat in respect of it on the date of service of the response notice.

(4) Where the council propose to serve such a response notice as is mentioned in subsection (1)(c), they must first send the Secretary of State a copy—

    (a) of the proposed response notice, and
    (b) of the purchase notice.

    (5) A notice to treat which is deemed to have been served by virtue of subsection (3)(b) may not be withdrawn under section 31 of the Land Compensation Act 1961.

[146]

NOTES
    Commencement: 24 August 1990.

140. Procedure on reference of purchase notice to Secretary of State

(1) Where a copy of a purchase notice is sent to the Secretary of State under section 139(4), he shall consider whether to confirm the notice or to take other action under section 141 in respect of it.

    (2) Before confirming a purchase notice or taking such other action, the Secretary of State must give notice of his proposed action—

    (a) to the person who served the purchase notice;
    (b) to the council on whom it was served;
    (c) [in England] outside Greater London—

        (i) to the country planning authority and also where that authority is a joint planning board, to the county council; and
       (ii) if the district council on whom the purchase notice in question was served is a constituent member of a joint planning board, to that board;

    [(cc) in Wales, to the local planning authority, where it is a joint planning board;] and
    (d) if the Secretary of State proposes to substitute any other local authority or statutory undertakers for the council on whom the notice was served, to them.

    (3) A notice under subsection (2) shall specify the period (which must not be less than 28 days from its service) within which any of the persons on whom it is served may require the Secretary of State to give those persons an opportunity of appearing before, and being heard by, a person appointed by the Secretary of State for the purpose.

    (4) If within that period any of those persons so require, before the Secretary of State confirms the purchase notice or takes any other action under section 141 in respect of it he must give those persons such an opportunity.

    (5) If, after any of those persons have appeared before and been heard by the appointed person, it appears to the Secretary of State to be expedient to take action under section 141 otherwise than in accordance with the notice given by him, the Secretary of State may take that action accordingly. **[147]**

NOTES
    Commencement: 24 August 1990.
    Words in square brackets in sub-s (2) inserted by the Local Government (Wales) Act 1994, s 20(4)(b), Sch 6, Pt II, para 24(4), as from a day to be appointed.

141. Action by Secretary of State in relation to purchase notice

(1) Subject to the following provisions of this section and to section 142(3), if the Secretary of State is satisfied that the conditions specified in subsection (3) or, as the case may be, subsection (4) of section 137 are satisfied in relation to a purchase notice, he shall confirm the notice.

(2) If it appears to the Secretary of State to be expedient to do so, he may, instead of confirming the purchase notice—

(a) in the case of a notice served on account of the refusal of planning permission, grant planning permission for the development in question;

(b) in the case of a notice served on account of planning permission for development being granted subject to conditions, revoke or amend those conditions so far as appears to him to be required in order to enable the land to be rendered capable of reasonably beneficial use by the carrying out of that development;

(c) in the case of a notice served on account of the revocation of planning permission by an order under section 97, cancel the order;

(d) in the case of a notice served on account of the modification of planning permission by such an order by the imposition of conditions, revoke or amend those conditions so far as appears to him to be required in order to enable the land to be rendered capable of reasonably beneficial use by the carrying out of the development in respect of which the permission was granted; or

(e) in the case of a notice served on account of the making of an order under section 102 or paragraph 1 of Schedule 9, revoke the order or, as the case may be, amend the order so far as appears to him to be required in order to prevent the land from being rendered incapable of reasonably beneficial use by the order.

(3) If it appears to the Secretary of State that the land, or any part of the land, could be rendered capable of reasonably beneficial use within a reasonable time by the carrying out of any other development for which planning permission ought to be granted, he may, instead of confirming the purchase notice, or, as the case may be, of confirming it so far as it relates to that part of the land, direct that, if an application for planning permission for that development is made, it must be granted.

(4) If it appears to the Secretary of State, having regard to the probable ultimate use of the land, that it is expedient to do so, he may, if he confirms the notice, modify it, either in relation to the whole or any part of the land, by substituting another local authority or statutory undertakers for the council on whom the notice was served.

(5) Any reference in section 140 to the taking of action by the Secretary of State under this section includes a reference to the taking by him of a decision not to confirm the purchase notice either on the grounds that any of the conditions referred to in subsection (1) are not satisfied or by virtue of section 142.　　　　**[148]**

NOTES
　　Commencement: 24 August 1990.

142. Power to refuse to confirm purchase notice where land has restricted use by virtue of previous planning permission

(1) This section applies where a purchase notice is served in respect of land which consists in whole or in part of land which has a restricted use by virtue of an existing planning permission.

(2) For the purposes of this section, land is to be treated as having a restricted use by virtue of an existing planning permission if it is part of a larger area in respect of which planning permission has previously been granted (and has not been revoked) and either—

(a) it remains a condition of the planning permission (however expressed) that that part shall remain undeveloped or be preserved or laid out in a particular way as amenity land in relation to the remainder; or

(b) the planning permission was granted on an application which contemplated (expressly or by necessary implication) that the part should not be comprised in the development for which planning permission was sought, or should be preserved or laid out as mentioned in paragraph (a).

(3) Where a copy of the purchase notice is sent to the Secretary of State under section 139(4), he need not confirm the notice under section 141(1) if it appears to him that the land having a restricted use by virtue of an existing planning permission ought, in accordance with that permission, to remain undeveloped or, as the case may be, remain or be preserved or laid out as amenity land in relation to the remainder of the large area for which that planning permission was granted.   **[149]**

NOTES
Commencement: 24 August 1990.

143. Effect of Secretary of State's action in relation to purchase notice

(1) Where the Secretary of State confirms a purchase notice—

(a) the council on whom the purchase notice was served, or

(b) if under section 141(4) the Secretary of State modified the purchase notice by substituting another local authority or statutory undertakers for that council, that other authority or those undertakers,

shall be deemed to be authorised to acquire the interest of the owner compulsorily in accordance with the relevant provisions, and to have served a notice to treat in respect of it on such date as the Secretary of State may direct.

(2) If, before the end of the relevant period, the Secretary of State has neither—

(a) confirmed the purchase notice, nor

(b) taken any such action in respect of it as is mentioned in section 141(2) or (3), nor

(c) notified the owner by whom the notice was served that he does not propose to confirm the notice,

the notice shall be deemed to be confirmed at the end of that period, and the council on whom the notice was served shall be deemed to be authorised as mentioned in subsection (1) and to have served a notice to treat in respect of the owner's interest at the end of that period.

(3) Subject to subsection (4), for the purposes of subsection (2) the relevant period is—

(a) the period of nine months beginning with the date of service of the purchase notice; or

(b) if it ends earlier, the period of six months beginning with the date on which a copy of the purchase notice was sent to the Secretary of State.

(4) The relevant period does not run if the Secretary of State has before him at the same time both—

(a) a copy of the purchase notice sent to him under section 139(4); and

(b) a notice of appeal under section 78, 174 or 195 of this Act or under section 20 or 39 of the Planning (Listed Buildings and Conservation Areas) Act 1990 (appeals against refusal of listed building consent, etc. and appeals against listed building enforcement notices) or under section 21 of the Planning (Hazardous Substances) Act 1990 (appeals against decisions and failure to take decisions relating to hazardous substances) relating to any of the land to which the purchase notice relates.

(5) Where—

(a) the Secretary of State has notified the owner by whom a purchase notice has been served of a decision on his part to confirm, or not to confirm, the notice; and

(b) that decision is quashed under Part XII,

the purchase notice shall be treated as cancelled, but the owner may serve a further purchase notice in its place.

(6) The reference in subsection (5) to a decision to confirm, or not to confirm, the purchase notice includes—

(a) any decision not to confirm the notice in respect of any part of the land to which it relates, and

(b) any decision to grant any permission, or give any direction instead of confirming the notice, either wholly or in part.

(7) For the purposes of determining whether a further purchase notice under subsection (5) was served within the period prescribed for the service of purchase notices, the planning decision in consequence of which the notice was served shall be treated as having been made on the date on which the decision of the Secretary of State was quashed.

(8) A notice to treat which is deemed to have been served by virtue of subsection (1) or (2) may not be withdrawn under section 31 of the Land Compensation Act 1961.   **[150]**

NOTES
Commencement: 24 August 1990.

Compensation

144. Special provisions as to compensation where purchase notice served

(1) Where compensation is payable by virtue of section 107 in respect of expenditure incurred in carrying out any works on land, any compensation payable in respect of the acquisition of an interest in the land in pursuance of a purchase notice shall be reduced by an amount equal to the value of those works.

(2) Where—

(a) the Secretary of State directs under section 141(3) that, if an application for it is made, planning permission must be granted for the development of any land, and

(b) on a claim made to the local planning authority within the prescribed time and in the prescribed manner, it is shown that the permitted development value of the interest in that land in respect of which the purchase notice was served is less than its [Schedule 3 value],

that authority shall pay the person entitled to that interest compensation of an amount equal to the difference.

(3) If the planning permission mentioned in subsection (2)(a) would be granted subject to conditions for regulating the design or external appearance, or the size or height of buildings, or for regulating the number of buildings to be erected on the land, the Secretary of State may direct that in assessing any compensation payable

under subsection (2) those conditions must be disregarded, either altogether or to such extent as may be specified in the direction.

(4) The Secretary of State may only give a direction under subsection (3) if it appears to him to be reasonable to do so having regard to the local circumstances.

(5) Sections 117 and 118 shall have effect in relation to compensation under subsection (2) as they have effect in relation to compensation to which those sections apply.

(6) In this section—

"permitted development value", in relation to an interest in land in respect of which a direction is given under section 141(3), means the value of that interest calculated with regard to that direction, but on the assumption that no planning permission would be granted otherwise than in accordance with that direction, and

["Schedule 3 value", in relation to such an interest, means the value of that interest calculated on the assumption that planning permission would be granted—

(a) subject to the condition in Schedule 10, for any development of a class specified in paragraph 1 of Schedule 3; and

(b) for any development of a class specified in paragraph 2 of Schedule 3].

(7) Where a purchase notice in respect of an interest in land is served in consequence of an order under section 102 or paragraph 1 of Schedule 9, then if—

(a) that interest is acquired in accordance with this Chapter; or

(b) compensation is payable in respect of that interest under subsection (2),

no compensation shall be payable in respect of that order under section 115.   **[151]**

NOTES

Commencement: 24 August 1990.

Words in square brackets in sub-ss (2)(b), (6) substituted by the Planning and Compensation Act 1991, s 31(4), Sch 6, paras 8, 19.

Special provisions for requiring purchase of whole or partially affected agricultural unit

145. Counter-notice requiring purchase of remainder of agricultural unit

(1) This section applies where—

(a) an acquiring authority is deemed under this Chapter to have served notice to treat in respect of any agricultural land on a person ("the claimant") who has a greater interest in the land than as tenant for a year or from year to year (whether or not he is in occupation of the land), and

(b) the claimant has such an interest in other agricultural land ("the unaffected area") comprised in the same agricultural unit as that to which the notice relates.

(2) Where this section applies the claimant may serve on the acquiring authority a counter-notice—

(a) claiming that the unaffected area is not reasonably capable of being farmed, either by itself or in conjunction with other relevant land, as a separate agricultural unit; and

(b) requiring the acquiring authority to purchase his interest in the whole of the unaffected area.

(3) Subject to subsection (4), "other relevant land" in subsection (2) means—

(a) land which is comprised in the same agricultural unit as the land to which the notice to treat relates and in which the claimant does not have such an interest as is mentioned in subsection (1); and

(b) land which is comprised in any other agricultural unit occupied by the claimant on the date on which the notice to treat is deemed to have been served and in respect of which he is then entitled to a greater interest than as tenant for a year or from year to year.

(4) Where a notice to treat has been served or is deemed under this Chapter or under Part III of the Compulsory Purchase (Vesting Declarations) Act 1981 to have been served in respect of any of the unaffected area or in respect of other relevant land as defined in subsection (3), then, unless and until the notice to treat is withdrawn, this section and section 146 shall have effect as if that land did not form part of the unaffected land or, as the case may be, did not constitute other relevant land.

(5) Where a counter-notice is served under subsection (2) the claimant shall also serve a copy of it on any other person who has an interest in the unaffected area (but failure to comply with this subsection shall not invalidate the counter-notice).

(6) A counter-notice under subsection (2) and any copy of that notice required to be served under subsection (5) must be served within the period of two months beginning with the date on which the notice to treat is deemed to have been served.

(7) This section is without prejudice to the rights conferred by sections 93 and 94 of the Lands Clauses (Consolidation) Act 1845 or section 8(2) and (3) of the Compulsory Purchase Act 1965 (provisions as to divided land).   **[152]**

NOTES

Commencement: 24 August 1990.

Special provisions for requiring purchase of whole of partially affected agricultural unit

146. Effect of counter-notice under s 145

(1) If the acquiring authority do not within the period of two months beginning with the date of service of a counter-notice under section 145 agree in writing to accept the counter-notice as valid, the claimant or the authority may, within two months after the end of that period, refer it to the Lands Tribunal.

(2) On such a reference the Tribunal shall determine whether the claim in the counter-notice is justified and declare the counter-notice valid or invalid accordingly.

(3) Where a counter-notice is accepted as valid under subsection (1) or declared to be valid under subsection (2), the acquiring authority shall be deemed—

(a) to be authorised to acquire compulsorily the interest of the claimant in the land to which the requirement in the counter-notice relates under the same provision of this Chapter as they are authorised to acquire the other land in the agricultural unit in question; and

(b) to have served a notice to treat in respect of it on the date on which notice to treat is deemed to have been served under that provision.

(4) A claimant may withdraw a counter-notice at any time before the compensation payable in respect of a compulsory acquisition in pursuance of the

counter-notice has been determined by the Lands Tribunal or at any time before the end of six weeks beginning with the date on which it is determined.

(5) Where a counter-notice is withdrawn by virtue of subsection (4) any notice to treat deemed to have been served in consequence of it shall be deemed to have been withdrawn.

(6) Without prejudice to subsection (5), a notice to treat deemed to have been served by virtue of this section may not be withdrawn under section 31 of the Land Compensation Act 1961.

(7) The compensation payable in respect of the acquisition of an interest in land in pursuance of a notice to treat deemed to have been served by virtue of this section shall be assessed on the assumptions mentioned in section 5(2), (3) and (4) of the Land Compensation Act 1973.

(8) Where by virtue of this section the acquiring authority become or will become entitled to a lease of any land but not to the interest of the lessor—

(a) the authority shall offer to surrender the lease to the lessor on such terms as the authority consider reasonable;

(b) the question of what is reasonable may be referred to the Lands Tribunal by the authority or the lessor and, if at the expiration of the period of three months after the date of the offer mentioned in paragraph (a) the authority and the lessor have not agreed on that question and that question has not been referred to the Tribunal by the lessor, it shall be so referred by the authority;

(c) if that question is referred to the Tribunal, the lessor shall be deemed—

(i) to have accepted the surrender of the lease at the expiry of one month after the date of the determination of the Tribunal or on such other date as the Tribunal may direct, and

(ii) to have agreed with the authority on the terms of surrender which the Tribunal has held to be reasonable.

(9) For the purposes of subsection (8) any terms as to surrender contained in the lease shall be disregarded.

(10) Where the lessor—

(a) refuses to accept any sum payable to him by virtue of subsection (8), or

(b) refuses or fails to make out his title to the satisfaction of the acquiring authority,

they may pay into court any such sum payable to the lessor and section 9(2) and (5) of the Compulsory Purchase Act 1965 (deposit of compensation in cases of refusal to convey etc.) shall apply to that sum with the necessary modifications.

(11) Where an acquiring authority who become entitled to the lease of any land as mentioned in subsection (8) are a body incorporated by or under any enactment, the corporate powers of the authority shall, if they would not otherwise do so, include the power to farm that land.   **[153]**

NOTES
    Commencement: 24 August 1990.

147. Provisions supplemental to ss 145 and 146

(1) Sections 145 and 146 apply in relation to the acquisition of interests in land by government departments which possess compulsory purchase powers as they apply

in relation to the acquisition of interests in land by authorities who are not government departments.

(2) In sections 145, 146 and this section—

"agricultural" and "agricultural land" have the meaning given in section 109 of the Agriculture Act 1947 and references to the farming of land include references to the carrying on in relation to the land of any agricultural activities;

"agricultural unit" has the meaning given in section 171(1);

"acquiring authority" has the same meaning as in the Land Compensation Act 1961; and

"government departments which possess compulsory purchase powers" means government departments being authorities possessing compulsory purchase powers within the meaning of that Act.   **[154]**

NOTES
Commencement: 24 August 1990.

Supplemental

[147A. Application of Chapter I to National Parks

This Chapter shall have effect as if—

(a) the bodies on whom a purchase notice may be served under section 137 included any National Park authority which is the local planning authority for the area in which the land is situated; and

(b) a National Park authority were a local authority for the purposes of this Act and the National Park for which it is the local planning authority were its area;

and the references in this Chapter and in section 288(10)(a) to a council and to a local authority shall be construed accordingly.]   **[154A]**

NOTES
Commencement: 19 September 1995.
Inserted by the Environment Act 1995, s 67(5).

148. Interpretation of Chapter I

(1) In this Chapter—

"the relevant provisions" means—

(a) the provisions of Part IX, or

(b) in the case of statutory undertakers, any statutory provision (however expressed) under which they have power, or may be authorised, to purchase land compulsorily for the purposes of their undertaking; and

"statutory undertakers" includes public telecommunications operators.

(2) In the case of a purchase notice served by such a person as is mentioned in subsection (2)(b) of section 137, references in this Chapter to the owner of the land include references to that person unless the context otherwise requires.   **[155]**

NOTES
Commencement: 24 August 1990.

CHAPTER II

INTERESTS AFFECTED BY PLANNING PROPOSALS: BLIGHT

Preliminary

149. Scope of Chapter II

(1) This Chapter shall have effect in relation to land falling within any paragraph of Schedule 13 (land affected by planning proposals of public authorities etc.); and in this Chapter such land is referred to as "blighted land".

(2) Subject to the provisions of sections 161 and 162, an interest qualifies for protection under this Chapter if—

  (a) it is an interest in a hereditament or part of a hereditament and on the relevant date it satisfies one of the conditions mentioned in subsection (3); or

  (b) it is an interest in an agricultural unit or part of an agricultural unit and on the relevant date it is the interest of an owner-occupier of the unit;

and in this Chapter such an interest is referred to as "a qualifying interest".

(3) The conditions mentioned in subsection (2)(a) are—

  (a) that the annual value of the hereditament does not exceed such amount as may be prescribed for the purposes of this paragraph by an order made by the Secretary of State, and the interest is the interest of an owner-occupier of the hereditament; or

  (b) that the interest is the interest of a resident owner-occupier of the hereditament.

(4) In this section "the relevant date", in relation to an interest, means the date of service of a notice under section 150 in respect of it.

(5) In this Chapter "blight notice" means a notice served under section 150, 161 or 162.   **[156]**

NOTES
  Commencement: 24 August 1990.

Blight notices

150. Notices requiring purchase of blighted land

(1) Where the whole or part of a hereditament or agricultural unit is comprised in blighted land and a person claims that—

  (a) he is entitled to a qualifying interest in that hereditament or unit;

  (b) he has made reasonable endeavours to sell that interest [or the land falls within paragraph 21 or paragraph 22 (disregarding the notes) of Schedule 13 and the powers of compulsory acquisition remain exercisable]; and

  (c) in consequence of the fact that the hereditament or unit or a part of it was, or was likely to be, comprised in blighted land, he has been unable to sell that interest except at a price substantially lower than that for which it might reasonably have been expected to sell if no part of the hereditament or unit were, or were likely to be, comprised in such land,

he may serve on the appropriate authority a notice in the prescribed form requiring that authority to purchase that interest to the extent specified in, and otherwise in accordance with, this Chapter.

(2) Subject to subsection (3), subsection (1) shall apply in relation to an interest in part of a hereditament or unit as it applies in relation to an interest in the whole of a hereditament or unit.

(3) Subsection (2) shall not enable any person—

    (a) if he is entitled to an interest in the whole of a hereditament or agricultural unit, to make any claim or serve any notice under this section in respect of his interest in part of a hereditament or unit; or

    (b) if he is entitled to an interest only in part of a hereditament or agricultural unit, to make or serve any such claim or notice in respect of his interest in less than the whole of that part.

(4) In this Chapter—

    (a) subject to section 161(1), "the claimant", in relation to a blight notice, means the person who served that notice, and

    (b) any reference to the interest of the claimant, in relation to a blight notice, is a reference to the interest which the notice requires the appropriate authority to purchase as mentioned in subsection (1).   **[157]**

NOTES

    Commencement: 24 August 1990.

    Words in square brackets in sub-s (1)(b) inserted by the Planning and Compensation Act 1991, s 70, Sch 15, Pt I, para 13.

151. Counter-notices objecting to blight notices

(1) Where a blight notice has been served in respect of a hereditament or an agricultural unit, the appropriate authority may serve on the claimant a counter-notice in the prescribed form objecting to the notice.

(2) A counter-notice under subsection (1) may be served at any time before the end of the period of two months beginning with the date of service of the blight notice.

(3) Such a counter-notice shall specify the grounds on which the appropriate authority object to the blight notice (being one or more of the grounds specified in subsection (4) or, as relevant, in section 159(1), 161(5) or 162(5)).

(4) Subject to the following provisions of this Act, the grounds on which objection may be made in a counter-notice to a notice served under section 150 are—

    (a) that no part of the hereditament or agricultural unit to which the notice relates is comprised in blighted land;

    (b) that the appropriate authority (unless compelled to do so by virtue of this Chapter) do not propose to acquire any part of the hereditament, or in the case of an agricultural unit any part of the affected area, in the exercise of any relevant powers;

    (c) that the appropriate authority propose in the exercise of relevant powers to acquire a part of the hereditament or, in the case of an agricultural unit, a part of the affected area specified in the counter-notice, but (unless compelled to do so by virtue of this Chapter) do not propose to acquire any other part of that hereditament or area in the exercise of any such powers;

    (d) in the case of land falling within paragraph 1, 3 or 13 but not 14, 15 or 16 of Schedule 13, that the appropriate authority (unless compelled to do so by virtue of this Chapter) do not propose to acquire in the exercise of any relevant powers any part of the hereditament or, in the case of an agricultural unit, any part of the affected area during the period of 15 years from the date of the counter-notice or such longer period from that date as may be specified in the counter-notice;

(e) that, on the date of service of the notice under section 150, the claimant was not entitled to an interest in any part of the hereditament or agricultural unit to which the notice relates;

(f) that (for reasons specified in the counter-notice) the interest of the claimant is not a qualifying interest;

(g) that the conditions specified in paragraphs (b) and (c) of section 150(1) are not fulfilled.

(5) Where the appropriate enactment confers power to acquire rights over land, subsection (4) shall have effect as if—

(a) in paragraph (b) after the word "acquire" there were inserted the words "or to acquire any rights over";

(b) in paragraph (c) for the words "do not propose to acquire" there were substituted the words "propose neither to acquire, nor to acquire any rights over";

(c) in paragraph (d) after the words "affected area" there were inserted "or to acquire any rights over any part of it".

(6) An objection may not be made on the grounds mentioned in paragraph (d) of subsection (4) if it may be made on the grounds mentioned in paragraph (b) of that subsection.

(7) The grounds on which objection may be made in a counter-notice to a blight notice served by virtue of paragraph 19 of Schedule 13 shall not include those mentioned in subsection (4)(b) or (c).

(8) In this section "relevant powers", in relation to blighted land falling within any paragraph of Schedule 13, means any powers under which the appropriate authority are or could be authorised—

(a) to acquire that land or to acquire any rights over it compulsorily as being land falling within that paragraph; or

(b) to acquire that land or any rights over it compulsorily for any of the relevant purposes;

and "the relevant purposes", in relation to any such land, means the purposes for which, in accordance with the circumstances by virtue of which that land falls within the paragraph in question, it is liable to be acquired or is indicated as being proposed to be acquired.   **[158]**

NOTES
Commencement: 24 August 1990.

152. Further counter-notices where certain proposals have come into force

(1) Where—

(a) an appropriate authority have served a counter-notice objecting to a blight notice in respect of any land falling within paragraph 1, 2, 3, 4 or 14 of Schedule 13 by virtue of Note(1) to that paragraph, and

(b) the relevant plan or alterations or, as the case may be, the relevant order or scheme comes into force (whether in its original form or with modifications),

the appropriate authority may serve on the claimant, in substitution for the counter-notice already served, a further counter-notice specifying different grounds of objection.

(2) Such a further counter-notice shall not be served—

    (a) at any time after the end of the period of two months beginning with the date on which the relevant plan or alterations come into force; or

    (b) if the objection in the counter-notice already served has been withdrawn or the Lands Tribunal has already determined whether or not to uphold that objection.   **[159]**

NOTES
Commencement: 24 August 1990.

153. Reference of objection to Lands Tribunal: general

(1) Where a counter-notice has been served under section 151 objecting to a blight notice, the claimant may require the objection to be referred to the Lands Tribunal.

(2) Such a reference may be required under subsection (1) at any time before the end of the period of two months beginning with the date of service of the counter-notice.

(3) On any such reference, if the objection is not withdrawn, the Lands Tribunal shall consider—

    (a) the matters set out in the notice served by the claimant, and

    (b) the grounds of the objection specified in the counter-notice;

and, subject to subsection (4), unless it is shown to the satisfaction of the Tribunal that the objection is not well-founded, the Tribunal shall uphold the objection.

(4) An objection on the grounds mentioned in section 151(4)(b), (c) or (d) shall not be upheld by the Tribunal unless it is shown to the satisfaction of the Tribunal that the objection is well-founded.

(5) If the Tribunal determines not to uphold the objection, the Tribunal shall declare that the notice to which the counter-notice relates is a valid notice.

(6) If the Tribunal upholds the objection, but only on the grounds mentioned in section 151(4)(c), the Tribunal shall declare that the notice is a valid notice in relation to the part of the hereditament, or in the case of an agricultural unit the part of the affected area, specified in the counter-notice as being the part which the appropriate authority propose to acquire as mentioned in that notice, but not in relation to any other part of the hereditament or affected area.

(7) In a case falling within subsection (5) or (6), the Tribunal shall give directions specifying the date on which notice to treat (as mentioned in section 154) is to be deemed to have been served.

(8) This section shall have effect in relation to a further counter-notice served by virtue of section 152(1) as it has effect in relation to the counter-notice for which it is substituted.   **[160]**

NOTES
Commencement: 24 August 1990.

154. Effect of valid blight notice

(1) Subsection (2) applies where a blight notice has been served and either—

    (a) no counter-notice objecting to that notice is served in accordance with this Chapter; or

    (b) where such a counter-notice has been served, the objection is withdrawn or, on a reference to the Lands Tribunal, is not upheld by the Tribunal.

(2) Where this subsection applies, the appropriate authority shall be deemed—

(a) to be authorised to acquire compulsorily under the appropriate enactment the interest of the claimant in the hereditament, or in the case of an agricultural unit the interest of the claimant in so far as it subsists in the affected area, and

(b) to have served a notice to treat in respect of it on the date mentioned in subsection (3).

(3) The date referred to in subsection (2)—

(a) in a case where, on a reference to the Lands Tribunal, the Tribunal determines not to uphold the objection, is the date specified in directions given by the Tribunal in accordance with section 153(7);

(b) in any other case, is the date on which the period of two months beginning with the date of service of the blight notice comes to an end.

(4) Subsection (5) applies where the appropriate authority have served a counter-notice objecting to a blight notice on the grounds mentioned in section 151(4)(c) and either—

(a) the claimant, without referring that objection to the Lands Tribunal, and before the time for so referring it has expired—

(i) gives notice to the appropriate authority that he accepts the proposal of the authority to acquire the part of the hereditament or affected area specified in the counter-notice, and

(ii) withdraws his claim as to the remainder of that hereditament or area; or

(b) on a reference to the Lands Tribunal, the Tribunal makes a declaration in accordance with section 153(6) in respect of that part of the hereditament or affected area.

(5) Where this subsection applies, the appropriate authority shall be deemed—

(a) to be authorised to acquire compulsorily under the appropriate enactment the interest of the claimant in so far as it subsists in the part of the hereditament or affected area specified in the counter-notice (but not in so far as it subsists in any other part of that hereditament or area), and

(b) to have served a notice to treat in respect of it on the date mentioned in subsection (6).

(6) The date referred to in subsection (5)—

(a) in a case falling within paragraph (a) of subsection (4), is the date on which notice is given in accordance with that paragraph; and

(b) in a case falling within paragraph (b) of that subsection, is the date specified in directions given by the Lands Tribunal in accordance with section 153(7).   **[161]**

NOTES

Commencement: 24 August 1990.

155. Effect on powers of compulsory acquisition of counter-notice disclaiming intention to acquire

(1) Subsection (2) shall have effect where the grounds of objection specified in a counter-notice served under section 151 consist of or include the grounds mentioned in paragraph (b) or (d) of subsection (4) of that section and either—

(a) the objection on the grounds mentioned in that paragraph is referred to and upheld by the Lands Tribunal; or

(b) the time for referring that objection to the Lands Tribunal expires without its having been so referred.

(2) If—

(a) a compulsory purchase order has been made under the appropriate enactment in respect of land which consists of or includes the whole or part of the hereditament or agricultural unit to which the counter-notice relates, or

(b) the land in question falls within paragraph 21 of Schedule 13,

any power conferred by that order or, as the case may be, by special enactment for the compulsory acquisition of the interest of the claimant in the hereditament or agricultural unit or any part of it shall cease to have effect.

(3) Subsection (4) shall have effect where the grounds of objection specified in a counter-notice under section 151 consist of or include the grounds mentioned in paragraph (c) of subsection (4) of that section and either—

(b) the objection on the grounds mentioned in that paragraph is referred to and upheld by the Lands Tribunal; or

(c) the time for referring that objection to the Lands Tribunal expires without its having been so referred;

and in subsection (4) any reference to "the part of the hereditament or affected area not required" is a reference to the whole of that hereditament or area except the part specified in the counter-notice as being the part which the appropriate authority proposes to acquire as mentioned in the counter-notice.

(4) If—

(a) a compulsory purchase order has been made under the appropriate enactment in respect of land which consists of or includes any of the part of the hereditament or affected area not required, or

(b) the land in question falls within paragraph 21 of Schedule 13,

any power conferred by that order or, as the case may be, by the special enactment for the compulsory acquisition of the interest of the claimant in any land comprised in the part of the hereditament or affected area not required shall cease to have effect.   **[162]**

NOTES
Commencement: 24 August 1990.

156. Withdrawal of blight notice

(1) Subject to subsection (3), the person by whom a blight notice has been served may withdraw the notice at any time before the compensation payable in respect of a compulsory acquisition in pursuance of the notice has been determined by the Lands Tribunal or, if there has been such a determination, at any time before the end of the period of six weeks beginning with the date of the determination.

(2) Where a blight notice is withdrawn by virtue of subsection (1) any notice to treat deemed to have been served in consequence of it shall be deemed to have been withdrawn.

(3) A person shall not be entitled by virtue of subsection (1) to withdraw a notice after the appropriate authority have exercised a right of entering and taking possession

of land in pursuance of a notice to treat deemed to have been served in consequence of that notice.

(4) No compensation shall be payable in respect of the withdrawal of a notice to treat which is deemed to have been withdrawn by virtue of subsection (2).   **[163]**

NOTES

Commencement: 24 August 1990.

Compensation

157. Special provisions as to compensation for acquisitions in pursuance of blight notices

(1) Where—

   (a) an interest in land is acquired in pursuance of a blight notice, and
   (b) the interest is one in respect of which a compulsory purchase order is in force under section 1 of the Acquisition of Land Act 1981, as applied by section 47 of the Planning (Listed Buildings and Conservation Areas) Act 1990, containing a direction for minimum compensation under section 50 of that Act of 1990,

the compensation payable for the acquisition shall be assessed in accordance with that direction and as if the notice to treat deemed to have been served in respect of the interest under section 154 had been served in pursuance of the compulsory purchase order.

(2) Where—

   (a) an interest in land is acquired in pursuance of a blight notice, and
   (b) the interest is one in respect of which a compulsory purchase order is in force under section 290 of the Housing Act 1985 (acquisition of land for clearance);

the compensation payable for the acquisition shall be assessed in accordance with that Act and as if the notice to treat deemed to have been served in respect of the interest under section 154 had been served in pursuance of the compulsory purchase order.

(3) The compensation payable in respect of the acquisition by virtue of section 160 of an interest in land comprised in—

   (a) the unaffected area of an agricultural unit; or
   (b) if the appropriate authority have served a counter-notice objecting to the blight notice on the grounds mentioned in section 151(4)(c), so much of the affected area of the unit as is not specified in the counter-notice,

shall be assessed on the assumptions mentioned in section 5(2), (3) and (4) of the Land Compensation Act 1973.

(4) In subsection (3) the reference to "the appropriate authority" shall be construed as if the unaffected area of an agricultural unit were part of the affected area.   **[164]**

NOTES

Commencement: 24 August 1990.

Special provisions for requiring purchase of whole of partially affected agricultural unit

158. Inclusion in blight notices of requirement to purchase parts of agricultural units unaffected by blight

(1) This section applies where—

    (a) a blight notice is served in respect of an interest in the whole or part of an agricultural unit, and

    (b) on the date of service that unit or part contains land ("the unaffected area") which is not blighted land as well as land ("the affected area") which is such land.

(2) Where this section applies the claimant may include in the blight notice—

    (a) a claim that the unaffected area is not reasonably capable of being farmed, either by itself or in conjunction with other relevant land, as a separate agricultural unit; and

    (b) a requirement that the appropriate authority shall purchase his interest in the whole of the unit or, as the case may be, in the whole of the part of it to which the notice relates.

(3) Subject to section 159(4), "other relevant land" in subsection (2) means—

    (a) if the blight notice is served only in respect of part of land comprised in the agricultural unit, the remainder of it; and

    (b) land which is comprised in any other agricultural unit occupied by the claimant on the date of service and in respect of which he is then entitled to an owner's interest as defined in section 168(4).   **[165]**

NOTES

Commencement: 24 August 1990.

159. Objections to s 158 notices

(1) The grounds on which objection may be made in a counter-notice to a blight notice served by virtue of section 158 shall include the grounds that the claim made in the notice is not justified.

(2) Objection shall not be made to a blight notice served by virtue of section 158 on the grounds mentioned in section 151(4)(c) unless it is also made on the grounds mentioned in subsection (1).

(3) The Lands Tribunal shall not uphold an objection to a notice served by virtue of section 158 on the grounds mentioned in section 151(4)(c) unless it also upholds the objection on the grounds mentioned in subsection (1).

(4) Where objection is made to a blight notice served by virtue of section 158 on the grounds mentioned in subsection (1) and also on those mentioned in section 151(4)(c), the Lands Tribunal, in determining whether or not to uphold the objection, shall treat that part of the affected area which is not specified in the counter-notice as included in "other relevant land" as defined in section 158(3).

(5) If the Lands Tribunal upholds an objection but only on the ground mentioned in subsection (1), the Tribunal shall declare that the blight notice is a valid notice in relation to the affected area but not in relation to the unaffected area.

(6) If the Tribunal upholds an objection both on the grounds mentioned in subsection (1) and on the grounds mentioned in section 151(4)(c) (but not on any other grounds) the Tribunal shall declare that the blight notice is a valid notice in

relation to the part of the affected area specified in the counter-notice as being the part which the appropriate authority propose to acquire as mentioned in that notice but not in relation to any other part of the affected area or in relation to the unaffected area.

(7) In a case falling within subsection (5) or (6), the Tribunal shall give directions specifying a date on which notice to treat (as mentioned in sections 154 and section 160) is to be deemd to have been served.

(8) Section 153(6) shall not apply to any blight notice served by virtue of section 158. **[166]**

NOTES

Commencement: 24 August 1990.

160. Effect of notices served by virtue of s 158

(1) In relation to a blight notice served by virtue of section 158—

    (a) subsection (2) of section 154 shall have effect as if for the words ''or in the case of an agricultural unit the interest of the claimant in so far as it subsists in the affected area'' there were substituted the words ''or agricultural unit''; and

    (b) subsections (4) and (5) of that section shall not apply to any such blight notice.

(2) Where the appropriate authority have served a counter-notice objecting to a blight notice on the grounds mentioned in section 159(1), then if either—

    (a) the claimant, without referring that objection to the Lands Tribunal and before the time for so referring it has expired, gives notice to the appropriate authority that he withdraws his claim as to the unaffected area; or

    (b) on a reference to the Tribunal, the Tribunal makes a declaration in accordance with section 159(5),

the appropriate authority shall be deemed—

    (i) to be authorised to acquire compulsorily under the appropriate enactment the interest of the claimant in so far as it subsists in the affected area (but not in so far as it subsists in the unaffected area), and

    (ii) to have served a notice to treat in respect of it on the date mentioned in subsection (3).

(3) The date referred to in subsection (2)—

    (a) in a case falling within paragraph (a) of subsection (2), is the date on which notice is given in accordance with that paragraph; and

    (b) in a case falling within paragraph (b) of that subsection, is the date specified in directions given by the Tribunal in accordance with section 159(7).

(4) Where the appropriate authority have served a counter-notice objecting to a blight notice on the grounds mentioned in section 159(1) and also on the grounds mentioned in section 151(4)(c), then if either—

    (a) the claimant, without referring that objection to the Lands Tribunal and before the time for so referring it has expired—

(i) gives notice to the appropriate authority that he accepts the proposal
of the authority to acquire the part of the affected area specified in
the counter-notice, and

(ii) withdraws his claim as to the remainder of that area and as to the
unaffected area; or

(b) on a reference to the Tribunal, the Tribunal makes a declaration in
accordance with section 159(6) in respect of that part of the affected area,

the appropriate authority shall be deemed to be authorised to acquire compulsorily
under the appropriate enactment the interest of the claimant in so far as it subsists in
the part of the affected area specified in the counter-notice (but not in so far as it
subsists in any other part of that area or in the unaffected area) and to have served a
notice to treat in respect of it on the date mentioned in subsection (5).

(5) The date referred to in subsection (4)—

(a) in a case falling within paragraph (a) of that subsection, is the date on
which notice is given in accordance with that paragraph; and

(b) in a case falling within paragraph (b) of that subsection, is the date
specified in directions given by the Tribunal in accordance with section
159(7).

(6) In relation to a blight notice served by virtue of section 158 references to
"the appropriate authority" and "the appropriate enactment" shall be construed as
if the unaffected area of an agricultural unit were part of the affected area.   **[167]**

NOTES
Commencement: 24 August 1990.

Personal representatives, mortgagees and partnerships

161. Powers of personal representatives in respect of blight notice

(1) In relation to any time after the death of a person who has served a blight notice,
sections 151(1), 152(1), 153(1), 154(4) and (5), 156(1) and 160(2) and (4) shall
apply as if any reference in them to the claimant were a reference to the claimant's
personal representatives.

(2) Where the whole or part of a hereditament or agricultural unit is comprised
in blighted land and a person claims that—

(a) he is the personal representative of a person ("the deceased") who at the
date of his death was entitled to an interest in that hereditament or unit;

(b) the interest was one which would have been a qualifying interest if a
notice under section 150 had been served in respect of it on that date;

(c) he has made reasonable endeavours to sell that interest [or the land falls
within paragraph 21 or paragraph 22 (disregarding the notes) of Schedule
13 and the powers of compulsory acquisition remain exercisable];

(d) in consequence of the fact that the hereditament or unit or a part of it was,
or was likely to be, comprised in blighted land, he has been unable to sell
that interest except at a price substantially lower than that for which it
might reasonably have been expected to sell if no part of the hereditament
or unit were, or were likely to be, comprised in such land; and

(e) one or more individuals are (to the exclusion of any body corporate)
beneficially entitled to that interest,

he may serve on the appropriate authority a notice in the prescribed form requiring
that authority to purchase that interest to the extent specified in, and otherwise in
accordance with, this Chapter.

(3) Subject to subsection (4), subsection (2) shall apply in relation to an interest in part of a hereditament or agricultural unit as it applies in relation to an interest in the whole of a hereditament or agricultural unit.

(4) Subsection (3) shall not enable any person—

(a) if the deceased was entitled to an interest in the whole of a hereditament or agricultural unit, to make any claim or serve any notice under this section in respect of the deceased's interest in part of the hereditament or unit; or

(b) if the deceased was entitled to an interest only in part of the hereditament or agricultural unit, to make or serve any such claim or notice in respect of the deceased's interest in less than the whole of that part.

(5) Subject to sections 151(7) and 159(2) and (3), the grounds on which objection may be made in a counter-notice under section 151 to a notice under this section are those specified in paragraphs (a) to (c) of subsection (4) of that section and, in a case to which it applies, the grounds specified in paragraph (d) of that subsection and also the following grounds—

(a) that the claimant is not the personal representative of the deceased or that, on the date of the deceased's death, the deceased was not entitled to an interest in any part of the hereditament or agricultural unit to which the notice relates;

(b) that (for reasons specified in the counter-notice) the interest of the deceased is not such as is specified in subsection (2)(b);

(c) that the conditions specified in subsection (2)(c), (d) or (e) are not satisfied. **[168]**

NOTES

Commencement: 24 August 1990.

Words in square brackets in sub-s (2)(c) inserted by the Planning and Compensation Act 1991, s 70, Sch 15, Pt I, para 13.

162. Power of mortgages to serve blight notice

(1) Where the whole or part of a hereditament or agricultural unit is comprised in blighted land and a person claims that—

(a) he is entitled as mortgagee (by virtue of a power which has become exercisable) to sell an interest in the hereditament or unit, giving immediate vacant possession of the land;

(b) he has made reasonable endeavours to sell that interest [or the land falls within paragraph 21 or paragraph 22 (disregarding the notes) of Schedule 13 and the powers of compulsory acquisition remain exercisable]; and

(c) in consequence of the fact that the hereditament or unit or a part of it was, or was likely to be, comprised in blighted land, he has been unable to sell that interest except at a price substantially lower than that for which it might reasonably have been expected to sell if no part of the hereditament or unit were, or were likely to be, comprised in such land,

then, subject to the provisions of this section, he may serve on the appropriate authority a notice in the prescribed form requiring that authority to purchase that interest to the extent specified in, and otherwise in accordance with, this Chapter.

(2) Subject to subsection (3), subsection (1) shall apply in relation to an interest in part of a hereditament or unit as it applies in relation to an interest in the whole of a hereditament or unit.

(3) Subsection (2) shall not enable a person—

(a) if his interest as mortgagee is in the whole of a hereditament or agricultural unit, to make any claim or serve any notice under this section in respect of any interest in part of the hereditament or unit; or

(b) if his interest as mortgagee is only in part of a hereditament or agricultural unit, to make or serve any such notice or claim in respect of any interest in less than the whole of that part.

(4) Notice under this section shall not be served unless the interest which the mortgagee claims he has the power to sell—

(a) could be the subject of a notice under section 150 served by the person entitled to it on the date of service of the notice under this section; or

(b) could have been the subject of such a notice served by that person on a date not more than six months before the date of service of the notice under this section.

(5) Subject to sections 151(7) and 159(2) and (3), the grounds on which objection may be made in a counter-notice under section 151 to a notice under this section are those specified in paragraphs (a) to (c) of subsection (4) of that section and, in a case to which it applies, the grounds specified in paragraph (d) of that subsection and also the following grounds—

(a) that, on the date of service of the notice under this section, the claimant had no interest as mortgagee in any part of the hereditament or agricultural unit to which the notice relates;

(b) that (for reasons specified in the counter-notice) the claimant had not on that date the power referred to in subsection (1)(a);

(c) that the conditions specified in subsection (1)(b) and (c) are not fulfilled;

(d) that (for reasons specified in the counter-notice) neither of the conditions specified in subsection (4) was, on the date of service of the notice under this section, satisfied with regard to the interest referred to in that subsection.　　　　**[169]**

NOTES

Commencement: 24 August 1990.

Words in square brackets in sub-s (1)(b) inserted by the Planning and Compensation Act 1991, s 70, Sch 15, Pt I, para 13.

163. Prohibition on service of simultaneous notices under ss 150, 161 and 162

(1) No notice shall be served under section 150 or 161 in respect of a hereditament or agricultural unit, or any part of it, at a time when a notice already served under section 162 is outstanding with respect to it, and no notice shall be served under section 162 at a time when a notice already served under section 150 or 161 is outstanding with respect to the relevant hereditament, unit or part.

(2) For the purposes of subsection (1), a notice shall be treated as outstanding with respect to a hereditament, unit or part—

(a) until it is withdrawn in relation to the hereditament, unit or part; or

(b) in a case where an objection to the notice has been made by a counter-notice under section 151, until either—

(i) the period of two months specified in section 153 elapses without the claimant having required the objection to be referred to the Lands Tribunal under that section; or

(ii) the objection, having been so referred, is upheld by the Tribunal with respect to the hereditament, unit or part.　　　　**[170]**

NOTES

Commencement: 24 August 1990.

164. Special provisions as to partnerships

(1) This section shall have effect for the purposes of the application of this Chapter to a hereditament or agricultural unit occupied for the purposes of a partnership firm.

(2) Occupation for the purposes of the firm shall be treated as occupation by the firm, and not as occupation by any one or more of the partners individually, and the definitions of "owner-occupier" in section 168(1) and (2) shall apply in relation to the firm accordingly.

(3) If, after the service by the firm of a blight notice, any change occurs (whether by death or otherwise) in the constitution of the firm, any proceedings, rights or obligations consequential upon that notice may be carried on or exercised by or against, or, as the case may be, shall be incumbent upon, the partners for the time being constituting the firm.

(4) Nothing in this Chapter shall be construed as indicating an intention to exclude the operation of the definition of "person" in Schedule 1 to the Interpretation Act 1978 (by which, unless the contrary intention appears, "person" includes any body of persons corporate or unincorporate) in relation to any provision of this Chapter.

(5) Subsection (2) shall not affect the definition of "resident owner-occupier" in section 168(3).   **[171]**

NOTES

Commencement: 24 August 1990.

Miscellaneous and supplementary provisions

165. Power of Secretary of State to acquire land affected by orders relating to new towns etc where blight notice served

(1) Where a blight notice has been served in respect of land falling within paragraph 7, 8 or 9 of Schedule 13, then until such time as a development corporation is established for the new town or, as the case may be, an urban development corporation is established for the urban development area the Secretary of State shall have power to acquire compulsorily any interest in the land in pursuance of the blight notice served by virtue of that paragraph.

(2) Where the Secretary of State acquires an interest under subsection (1), then—

    (a) if the land is or becomes land within paragraph 8 or, as the case may be, paragraph 9(b) of Schedule 13, the interest shall be transferred by him to the development corporation established for the new town or, as the case may be, the urban development corporation established for the urban development area; and

    (b) in any other case, the interest may be disposed of by him in such manner as he thinks fit.

(3) The Land Compensation Act 1961 shall have effect in relation to the compensation payable in respect of the acquisition of an interest by the Secretary of State under subsection (1) as if—

    (a) the acquisition were by a development corporation under the New Towns Act 1981 or, as the case may be, by an urban development corporation under Part XVI of the Local Government, Planning and Land Act 1980;

(b) in the case of land within paragraph 7 of Schedule 13, the land formed part of an area designated as the site of a new town by an order which has come into operation under section 1 of the New Towns Act 1981; and

(c) in the case of land within paragraph 9(a) of Schedule 13, the land formed part of an area designated as an urban development area by an order under section 134 of the Local Government, Planning and land Act 1980 which has come into operation.   **[172]**

NOTES
    Commencement: 24 August 1990.

166. Saving for claimant's right to sell whole hereditament, etc

(1) The provisions of sections 151(4)(c), 153(6), 154(4) and (5) and 155(3) and (4) relating to hereditaments shall not affect—

(a) the right of a claimant under section 92 of the Lands Clauses Consolidation Act 1845 to sell the whole of the hereditament or, in the case of an agricultural unit, the whole of the affected area, which he has required the authority to purchase; or

(b) the right of a claimant under section 8 of the Compulsory Purchase Act 1965 to sell (unless the Lands Tribunal otherwise determines) the whole of the hereditament or, as the case may be, affected area which he has required that authority to purchase.

(2) In accordance with subsection (1)(b), in determining whether or not to uphold an objection relating to a hereditament on the grounds mentioned in section 151(4)(c), the Lands Tribunal shall consider (in addition to the other matters which they are required to consider) whether—

(a) in the case of a house, building or factory, the part proposed to be acquired can be taken without material detriment to the house, building or factory; or

(b) in the case of a park or garden belonging to a house, the part proposed to be acquired can be taken without seriously affecting the amenity or convenience of the house.   **[173]**

NOTES
    Commencement: 24 August 1990.

167. No withdrawal of constructive notice to treat

Without prejudice to the provisions of section 156(1) and (2), a notice to treat which is deemed to have been served by virtue of this Chapter may not be withdrawn under section 31 of the Land Compensation Act 1961.   **[174]**

NOTES
    Commencement: 24 August 1990.

168. Meaning of "owner-occupier" and "resident owner-occupier"

(1) Subject to the following provisions of this section, in this Chapter "owner-occupier", in relation to a hereditament, means—

(a) a person who occupies the whole or a substantial part of the hereditament in right of an owner's interest in it, and has so occupied the hereditament or that part of it during the whole of the period of six months ending with the date of service; or

(b) if the whole or a substantial part of the hereditament was unoccupied for a period of not more than 12 months ending with that date, a person who so occupied the hereditament or as the case may be, that part of it during the whole of a period of six months ending immediately before the period when it was not occupied.

(2) Subject to the following provisions of this section, in this Chapter "owner-occupier", in relation to an agricultural unit, means a person who—

(a) occupies the whole of that unit and has occupied it during the whole of the period of six months ending with the date of service; or

(b) occupied the whole of that unit during the whole of a period of six months ending not more than 12 months before the date of service,

and, at all times material for the purposes of paragraph (a) or, as the case may be, paragraph (b) has been entitled to an owner's interest in the whole or part of that unit.

(3) In this Chapter "resident owner-occupier", in relation to a hereditament, means—

(a) an individual who occupies the whole or a substantial part of the hereditament as a private dwelling in right of an owner's interest in it, and has so occupied the hereditament or, as the case may be, that part during the whole of the period of six months ending with the date of service; or

(b) if the whole or a substantial part of the hereditament was unoccupied for a period of not more than 12 months ending with that date, an individual who so occupied the hereditament or, as the case may be, that part during the whole of a period of six months ending immediately before the period when it was not occupied.

(4) In this section—

"owner's interest", in relation to a hereditament or agricultural unit, means a freehold interest in it or a tenancy of it granted or extended for a term of years certain not less than three years of which remain unexpired on the date of service; and

"date of service", in relation to a hereditament or agricultural unit, means the date of service of a notice in respect of it under section 150.   **[175]**

NOTES
Commencement: 24 August 1990.

169. "Appropriate authority" for purposes of Chapter II

(1) Subject to the following provisions of this section, in this Chapter "the appropriate authority", in relation to any land, means the government department, local authority [National Park authority] or other body or person by whom, in accordance with the circumstances by virtue of which the land falls within any paragraph of Schedule 13, the land is liable to be acquired or is indicated as being proposed to be acquired or, as the case may be, any right over the land is proposed to be acquired.

(2) If any question arises—

(a) whether the appropriate authority in relation to any land for the purposes of this Chapter is the Secretary of State or a local highway authority; or

(b) which of two or more local highway authorities is the appropriate authority in relation to any land for those purposes; or

(c) which of two or more local authorities is the appropriate authority in relation to any land for those purposes,

that question shall be referred to the Secretary of State, whose decision shall be final.

(3) If any question arises which authority is the appropriate authority for the purposes of this Chapter—

(a) section 151(2) shall have effect as if the reference to the date of service of the blight notice were a reference to that date or, if it is later, the date on which that question is determined;

(b) section 162(4)(b) shall apply with the substitution for the period of six months of a reference to that period extended by so long as it takes to obtain a determination of the question; and

(c) section 168(1)(b), (2)(b) and (3)(b) shall apply with the substitution for the reference to 12 months before the date of service of a reference to that period extended by so long as it takes to obtain a determination of the question.

(4) In relation to land falling within paragraph 7, 8 or 9 of Schedule 13, until such time as a development corporaton is established for the new town or, as the case may be, an urban development corporation is established for the urban development area, this Chapter shall have effect as if "the appropriate authority" were the Secretary of State.

(5) In relation to land falling within paragraph 19 of Schedule 13, "the appropriate authority" shall be the highway authority for the highway in relation to which the order mentioned in that paragraph was made.   **[176]**

NOTES
    Commencement: 24 August 1990.
    Words in square brackets in sub-s (1) inserted by the Environment Act 1995, s 78, Sch 10, para 32(5), as from a day to be appointed under s 125(3).

170. "Appropriate enactment" for purposes of Chapter II

(1) Subject to the following provisions of this section, in this Chapter "the appropriate enactment", in relation to land falling within any paragraph of Schedule 13, means the enactment which provides for the compulsory acquisition of land as being land falling within that paragraph or, as respects paragraph 22(b), the enactment under which the compulsory purchase order referred to in that paragraph was made.

(2) In relation to land falling within paragraph 2, 3 or 4 of that Schedule, an enactment shall for the purposes of subsection (1) be taken to be an enactment which provides for the compulsory acquisition of land as being land falling within that paragraph if—

(a) the enactment provides for the compulsory acquisition of land for the purposes of the functions which are indicated in the development plan as being the functions for the purposes of which the land is allocated or is proposed to be developed; or

(b) where no particular functions are so indicated in the development plan, the enactment provides for the compulsory acquisition of land for the purposes of any of the functions of the government department, local authority [National Park authority] or other body for the purposes of whose functions the land is allocated or is defined as the site of proposed development.

(3) In relation to land falling within paragraph 2, 3 or 4 of that Schedule by virtue of Note (1) to that paragraph, "the appropriate enactment" shall be determined

in accordance with subsection (2) as if references in that subsection to the development plan were references to any such plan, proposal or modifications as are mentioned in paragraph (a), (b) or (c) of that Note.

(4) In relation to land falling within paragraph 5 or 6 of that Schedule, "the appropriate enactment" shall be determined in accordance with subsection (2) as if references in that subsection to the development plan were references to the resolution or direction in question.

(5) In relation to land falling within paragraph 7, 8 or 9 of that Schedule, until such time as a development corporation is established for the new town or, as the case may be, an urban development corporation is established for the urban development area, this Chapter shall have effect as if "the appropriate enactment" were section 165(1).

(6) In relation to land falling within paragraph 10 or 11 of that Schedule, "the appropriate enactment" shall be section 290 of the Housing Act 1985.

(7) In relation to land falling within paragraph 19 of that Schedule, "the appropriate enactment" shall be section 239(6) of the Highways Act 1980.

(8) In relation to land falling within paragraph 22 of that Schedule by vitue of Note (1) to that paragraph, "the appropriate enactment" shall be the enactment which would provide for the compulsory acquisition of the land or of the rights over the land if the relevant compulsory purchase order were confirmed or made.

(9) Where, in accordance with the circumstances by virtue of which any land falls within any paragraph of that Schedule, it is indicated that the land is proposed to be acquired for highway purposes, any enactment under which a highway authority are or (subject to the fulfilment of the relevant conditions) could be authorised to acquire that land compulsorily for highway purposes shall, for the purposes of subsection (1), be taken to be an enactment providing for the compulsory acquisition of that land as being land falling within that paragraph.

(10) In subsection (9) the reference to the fulfilment of the relevant conditions is a reference to such one or more of the following as are applicable to the circumstances in question—

    (a) the coming into operation of any requisite order or scheme made, or having effect as if made, under the provisions of Part II of the Highways Act 1980;

    (b) the coming into operation of any requisite scheme made, or having effect as if made, under section 106(3) of that Act;

    (c) the making or approval of any requisite plans.

(11) If, apart from this subsection, two or more enactments would be the appropriate enactment in relation to any land for the purposes of this Chapter, the appropriate enactment for those purposes shall be taken to be that one of those enactments under which, in the circumstances in question, it is most likely that (apart from this Chapter) the land would have been acquired by the appropriate authority.

(12) If any question arises as to which enactment is the appropriate enactment in relation to any land for the purposes of this Chapter, that question shall be referred—

    (a) where the appropriate authority are a government department, to the Minister in charge of that department;

    (b) where the appropriate authority are statutory undertakers, to the appropriate Minister; and

(c) in any other case, to the Secretary of State,

and the decision of the Minister or, as the case may be, the Secretary of State shall be final.   **[177]**

NOTES
Commencement: 24 August 1990.
Words in square brackets in sub-s (2)(b) inserted by the Environment Act 1995, s 78, Sch 10, para 32(5), as from a day to be appointed under s 125(3).

171. General interpretation of Chapter II

(1) Subject to the following provisions of this section, in this Chapter—

"the affected area", in relation to an agricultural unit, means so much of that unit as, on the date of service, consists of land falling within any paragraph of Schedule 13;

"agricultural" has the same meaning as in section 109 of the Agriculture Act 1947 and references to the farming of land include references to the carrying on in relation to the land of agricultural activities;

"agricultural unit" means land which is occupied as a unit for agricultural purposes, including any dwellinghouse or other building occupied by the same person for the purpose of farming the land;

"annual value" means—

(a) in the case of a hereditament which is shown in a local non-domestic rating list and none of which consists of domestic property or property exempt from local non-domestic rating, the value shown in that list as the rateable value of that hereditament on the date of service;

(b) in the case of a hereditament which is shown in a local non-domestic rating list and which includes domestic property or property exempt from local domestic rating, the sum of—

(i) the value shown in that list as the rateable value of that hereditament on the date of service; and

(ii) the value attributable to the non-rateable part of that hereditament in accordance with subsections (2) and (3);

(c) in the case of any other hereditament, the value attributable to that hereditament in accordance with subsections (2) and (3);

"blight notice" has the meaning given in section 149(5);

"the claimant" has the meaning given in section 150(4);

"hereditament" means a relevant hereditament within the meaning of section 64(4)(a) to (c) of the Local Government Finance Act 1988;

"special enactment" means a local enactment, or a provision contained in an Act other than a local or private Act, which is a local enactment or provision authorising the compulsory acquisition of land specifically identified in it; and in this definition "local enactment" means a local or private Act, or an order confirmed by Parliament or brought into operation in accordance with special parliamentary procedure.

(2) The value attributable to a hereditament, or the non-rateable part of it, in respect of domestic property shall be the value certified by the relevant valuation officer as being 5 per cent of the compensation which would be payable in respect of the value of that property if it were purchased compulsorily under statute with vacant

possession and the compensation payable were calculated in accordance with Part II of the Land Compensation Act 1961 by reference to the relevant date.

(3) The value attributable to a hereditament, or the non-rateable part of it, in respect of property exempt from local non-domestic rating shall be the value certified by the relevant valuation officer as being the value which would have been shown as the rateable value of that property on the date of service if it were a relevant non-domestic hereditament consisting entirely of non-domestic property, none of which was exempt from local non-domestic rating.

(4) Land which (apart from this subsection) would comprise separate hereditaments solely by reason of being divided by a boundary between rating areas shall be treated for the purposes of the definition of ''hereditament'' in subsection (1) as if it were not so divided.

(5) In this section—

''date of service'' has the same meaning as in section 168;

''relevant valuation officer'' means the valuation officer who would have determined the rateable value in respect of the hereditament for the purposes of Part III of the Local Government Finance Act 1988 if the hereditament had fulfilled the conditions set out in section 42(1)(b) to (d) of that Act;

''relevant date'' is the date by reference to which that determination would have been made;

and expressions used in the definition of ''annual value'' in subsection (1) or in subsection (2) or (3) which are also used in Part III of that Act have the same meaning as in that Part. **[178]**

NOTES
Commencement: 24 August 1990.

PART VII

ENFORCEMENT

[Introductory

171A. Expressions used in connection with enforcement

(1) For the purposes of this Act—

    (a) carrying out development without the required planning permission; or
    (b) failing to comply with any condition or limitation subject to which planning permission has been granted,

constitutes a breach of planning control.

(2) For the purposes of this Act—

    (a) the issue of an enforcement notice (defined in section 172); or
    (b) the service of a breach of condition notice (defined in section 187A),

constitutes taking enforcement action.

(3) In this Part ''planning permission'' includes permission under Part III of the 1947 Act, of the 1962 Act or of the 1971 Act.] **[178A]**

NOTES
Commencement: 2 January 1992 (except so far as relates to breach of condition notices); 27 July 1992 (so far as so relates).

This section, the cross-heading immediately preceding it, and s 171B, inserted by the Planning and Compensation Act 1991, s 4.

[171B. Time limits

(1) Where there has been a breach of planning control consisting in the carrying out without planning permission of building, engineering, mining or other operations in, on, over or under land, no enforcement action may be taken after the end of the period of four years beginning with the date on which the operations were substantially completed.

(2) Where there has been a breach of planning control consisting in the change of use of any building to use as a single dwellinghouse, no enforcement action may be taken after the end of the period of four years beginning with the date of the breach.

(3) In the case of any other breach of planning control, no enforcement action may be taken after the end of the period of ten years beginning with the date of the breach.

(4) The preceding subsections do not prevent—

   (a) the service of a breach of condition notice in respect of any breach of planning control if an enforcement notice in respect of the breach is in effect; or
   (b) taking further enforcement action in respect of any breach of planning control if, during the period of four years ending with that action being taken, the local planning authority have taken or purported to take enforcement action in respect of that breach.]   **[178B]**

NOTES
   Commencement: 2 January 1992 (except so far as relates to breach of condition notices); 27 July 1992 (so far as so relating).
   Inserted as noted to s 171A at **[178A]**.

[Planning contravention notices

171C Power to require information about activities on land

(1) Where it appears to the local planning authority that there may have been a breach of planning control in respect of any land, they may serve notice to that effect (referred to in this Act as a "planning contravention notice") on any person who—

   (a) is the owner or occupier of the land or has any other interest in it; or
   (b) is carrying out operations on the land or is using it for any purpose.

(2) A planning contravention notice may require the person on whom it is served to give such information as to—

   (a) any operations being carried out on the land, any use of the land and any other activities being carried out on the land; and
   (b) any matter relating to the conditions or limitations subject to which any planning permission in respect of the land has been granted,

as may be specified in the notice.

(3) Without prejudice to the generality of subsection (2), the notice may require the person on whom it is served, so far as he is able—

   (a) to state whether or not the land is being used for any purpose specified in the notice or any operations or activities specified in the notice are being or have been carried out on the land;

(b) to state when any use, operations or activities began;

(c) to give the name and address of any person known to him to use or have used the land for any purpose or to be carrying out, or have carried out, any operations or activities on the land;

(d) to give any information he holds as to any planning permission for any use or operations or any reason for planning permission not being required for any use or operations;

(e) to state the nature of his interest (if any) in the land and the name and address of any other person known to him to have an interest in the land.

(4) A planning contravention notice may give notice of a time and place at which—

(a) any offer which the person on whom the notice is served may wish to make to apply for planning permission, to refrain from carrying out any operations or activities or to undertake remedial works; and

(b) any representations which he may wish to make about the notice,

will be considered by the authority, and the authority shall give him an opportunity to make in person any such offer or representations at that time and place.

(5) A planning contravention notice must inform the person on whom it is served—

(a) of the likely consequences of his failing to respond to the notice and, in particular, that enforcement action may be taken; and

(b) of the effect of section 186(5)(b).

(6) Any requirement of a planning contravention notice shall be complied with by giving information in writing to the local planning authority.

(7) The service of a planning contravention notice does not affect any other power exercisable in respect of any breach of planning control.

(8) In this section references to operations or activities on land include operations or activities in, under or over the land.]   **[178C]**

NOTES

Commencement: 2 January 1992.

This section, the cross-heading immediately preceding it, and s 171D, inserted by the Planning and Compensation Act 1991, s 1.

[171D. Penalties for non-compliance with planning contravention notice

(1) If, at any time after the end of the period of twenty-one days beginning with the day on which a planning contravention notice has been served on any person, he has not complied with any requirement of the notice, he shall be guilty of an offence.

(2) An offence under subsection (1) may be charged by reference to any day or longer period of time and a person may be convicted of a second or subsequent offence under that subsection by reference to any period of time following the preceding conviction for such an offence.

(3) It shall be a defence for a person charged with an offence under subsection (1) to prove that he had a reasonable excuse for failing to comply with the requirement.

(4) A person guilty of an offence under subsection (1) shall be liable on summary conviction to a fine not exceeding level 3 on the standard scale.

(5) If any person—

    (a) makes any statement purporting to comply with a requirement of a planning contravention notice which he knows to be false or misleading in a material particular; or

    (b) recklessly makes such a statement which is false or misleading in a material particular,

he shall be guilty of an offence.

    (6) A person guilty of an offence under subsection (5) shall be liable on summary conviction to a fine not exceeding level 5 on the standard scale.]   **[178D]**

NOTES
    Commencement: 2 January 1992.
    Inserted as noted to s 171C at **[178C]**.

Enforcement notices

[172. Issue of enforcement notice

(1) The local planning authority may issue a notice (in this Act referred to as an "enforcement notice") where it appears to them—

    (a) that there has been a breach of planning control; and

    (b) that it is expedient to issue the notice, having regard to the provisions of the development plan and to any other material considerations.

(2) A copy of an enforcement notice shall be served—

    (a) on the owner and on the occupier of the land to which it relates; and

    (b) on any other person having an interest in the land, being an interest which, in the opinion of the authority, is materially affected by the notice.

(3) The service of the notice shall take place—

    (a) not more than twenty-eight days after its date of issue; and

    (b) not less than twenty-eight days before the date specified in it as the date on which it is to take effect.]   **[179]**

NOTES
    Commencement: 25 November 1991 (certain purposes); 2 January 1992 (remaining purposes).
    This section and ss 173, 173A substituted for ss 172, 173 by the Planning and Compensation Act 1991, s 5.

[173. Contents and effect of notice

(1) An enforcement notice shall state—

    (a) the matters which appear to the local planning authority to constitute the breach of planning control; and

    (b) the paragraph of section 171A(1) within which, in the opinion of the authority, the breach falls.

(2) A notice complies with subsection (1)(a) if it enables any person on whom a copy of it is served to know what those matters are.

(3) An enforcement notice shall specify the steps which the authority require to be taken, or the activities which the authority require to cease, in order to achieve, wholly or partly, any of the following purposes.

(4) Those purposes are—

    (a) remedying the breach by making any development comply with the terms (including conditions and limitations) of any planning permission which has been granted in respect of the land, by discontinuing any use of the land or by restoring the land to its condition before the breach took place; or

(b) remedying any injury to amenity which has been caused by the breach.

(5) An enforcement notice may, for example, require—

(a) the alteration or removal of any buildings or works;

(b) the carrying out of any building or other operations;

(c) any activity on the land not to be carried on except to the extent specified in the notice; or

(d) the contour of a deposit of refuse or waste materials on land to be modified by altering the gradient or gradients of its sides.

(6) Where an enforcement notice is issued in respect of a breach of planning control consisting of demolition of a building, the notice may require the construction of a building (in this section referred to as a "replacement building") which, subject to subsection (7), is as similar as possible to the demolished building.

(7) A replacement building—

(a) must comply with any requirement imposed by any enactment applicable to the construction of buildings;

(b) may differ from the demolished building in any respect which, if the demolished building had been altered in that respect, would not have constituted a breach of planning control;

(c) must comply with any regulations made for the purposes of this subsection (including regulations modifying paragraphs (a) and (b)).

(8) An enforcement notice shall specify the date on which it is to take effect and, subject to sections 175(4) and 289(4A), shall take effect on that date.

(9) An enforcement notice shall specify the period at the end of which any steps are required to have been taken or any activities are required to have ceased and may specify different periods for different steps or activities; and, where different periods apply to different steps or activities, references in this Part to the period for compliance with an enforcement notice, in relation to any step or activity, are to the period at the end of which the step is required to have been taken or the activity is required to have ceased.

(10) An enforcement notice shall specify such additional matters as may be prescribed, and regulations may require every copy of an enforcement notice served under section 172 to be accompanied by an explanatory note giving prescribed information as to the right of appeal under section 174.

(11) Where—

(a) an enforcement notice in respect of any breach of planning control could have required any buildings or works to be removed or any activity to cease, but does not do so; and

(b) all the requirements of the notice have been complied with,

then, so far as the notice did not so require, planning permission shall be treated as having been granted by virtue of section 73A in respect of development consisting of the construction of the buildings or works or, as the case may be, the carrying out of the activities.

(12) Where—

(a) an enforcement notice requires the construction of a replacement building; and

(b) all the requirements of the notice with respect to that construction have been complied with,

planning permission shall be treated as having been granted by virtue of section 73A in respect of development consisting of that construction.]   **[180]**

NOTES

Commencement: 25 November 1991 (certain purposes); 2 January 1992 (remaining purposes).
Substituted as noted to s 172 at **[179]**.
Modification: sub-s (10) modified by the Town and Country Planning (Special Enforcement Notices) Regulations 1992, SI 1992/1562, reg 2, Schedule at **[837]**.

[173A. Variation and withdrawal of enforcement notices

(1) The local planning authority may—

(a) withdraw an enforcement notice issued by them; or
(b) waive or relax any requirement of such a notice and, in particular, may extend any period specified in accordance with section 173(9).

(2) The powers conferred by subsection (1) may be exercised whether or not the notice has taken effect.

(3) The local planning authority shall, immediately after exercising the powers conferred by subsection (1), give notice of the exercise to every person who has been served with a copy of the enforcement notice or would, if the notice were reissued, be served with a copy of it.

(4) The withdrawal of an enforcement notice does not affect the power of the local planning authority to issue a further enforcement notice.]   **[180A]**

NOTES

Commencement: 25 November 1991 (certain purposes); 2 January 1992 (remaining purposes).
Substituted as noted to s 172 at **[179]**.
Modification: sub-s (1)(b) modified by the Town and Country Planning (Special Enforcement Notices) Regulations 1992, SI 1992/1562, reg 2, Schedule at **[837]**.

174. Appeal against enforcement notice

(1) A person having an interest in the land to which an enforcement notice relates or a relevant occupier may appeal to the Secretary of State against the notice, whether or not a copy of it has been served on him.

[(2) An appeal may be brought on any of the following grounds—

(a) that, in respect of any breach of planning control which may be constituted by the matters stated in the notice, planning permission ought to be granted or, as the case may be, the condition or limitation concerned ought to be discharged;
(b) that those matters have not occurred;
(c) that those matters (if they occurred) do not constitute a breach of planning control;
(d) that, at the date when the notice was issued, no enforcement action could be taken in respect of any breach of planning control which may be constituted by those matters;
(e) that copies of the enforcement notice were not served as required by section 172;
(f) that the steps required by the notice to be taken, or the activities required by the notice to cease, exceed what is necessary to remedy any breach of planning control which may be constituted by those matters or, as the case

may be, to remedy any injury to amenity which has been caused by any such breach;

(g) that any period specified in the notice in accordance with section 173(9) falls short of what should reasonably be allowed.

(3) An appeal under this section shall be made either—

(a) by giving written notice of the appeal to the Secretary of State before the date specified in the enforcement notice as the date on which it is to take effect; or

(b) by sending such notice to him in a properly addressed and pre-paid letter posted to him at such time that, in the ordinary course of post, it would be delivered to him before that date.]

(4) A person who gives notice under subsection (3) shall submit to the Secretary of State, either when giving the notice or within the prescribed time, a statement in writing—

(a) specifying the grounds on which he is appealing against the enforcement notice; and

(b) giving such further information as may be prescribed.

(5) If, where more than one ground is specified in that statement, the appellant does not give information required under subsection (4)(b) in relation to each of those grounds within the prescribed time, the Secretary of State may determine the appeal without considering any ground as to which the appellant has failed to give such information within that time.

(6) In this section "relevant occupier" means a person who—

(a) on the date on which the enforcement notice is issued occupies the land to which the notice relates by virtue of a licence . . .; and

(b) continues so to occupy the land when the appeal is brought. **[181]**

NOTES

Commencement: 24 August 1990 (sub-ss (1), (4)–(6)); 2 January 1992 (sub-ss (2), (3)).

Sub-ss (2), (3) substituted, and words omitted from sub-s (6)(a) repealed, by the Planning and Compensation Act 1991, ss 6(1), 32, Sch 7, paras 8, 22.

Modification: section modified by the Planning (Hazardous Substances) Regulations 1992, SI 1992/656, reg 18, Sch 4, Pt 1 at **[767]**.

175. Appeals: supplementary provisions

(1) The Secretary of State may by regulations prescribe the procedure which is to be followed on appeals under section 174 and, in particular, but without prejudice to the generality of this subsection, may—

(a) require the local planning authority to submit, within such time as may be prescribed, a statement indicating the submissions which they propose to put forward on the appeal;

(b) specify the matters to be included in such a statement;

(c) require the authority or the appellant to give such notice of such an appeal as may be prescribed;

(d) require the authority to send to the Secretary of State, within such period from the date of the bringing of the appeal as may be prescribed, a copy of the enforcement notice and a list of the persons served with copies of it.

(2) The notice to be prescribed under subsection (1)(c) shall be such notice as in the opinion of the Secretary of State is likely to bring the appeal to the attention of

persons in the locality in which the land to which the enforcement notice relates is situated.

(3) Subject to section 176(4), the Secretary of State shall, if either the appellant or the local planning authority so desire, give each of them an opportunity of appearing before and being heard by a person appointed by the Secretary of State for the purpose.

(4) Where an appeal is brought under section 174 the enforcement notice shall [subject to any order under section 289(4A)] be of no effect pending the final determination or the withdrawal of the appeal.

(5) Where any person has appealed to the Secretary of State against an enforcement notice, no person shall be entitled, in any other proceedings instituted after the making of the appeal, to claim that the notice was not duly served on the person who appealed.

(6) Schedule 6 applies to appeals under section 174, including appeals under that section as applied by regulations under any other provisions of this Act.

[(7) Subsection (5) of section 250 of the Local Government Act 1972 (which authorises a Minister holding an inquiry under that section to make orders with respect to the costs of the parties) shall apply in relation to any proceedings before the Secretary of State on an appeal under section 174 as if those proceedings were an inquiry held by the Secretary of State under section 250.]   **[182]**

NOTES

Commencement: 24 August 1990 (sub-ss (1)-(6)); for effect of sub-s (7) see annotations below.

Words in square brackets in sub-s (4) inserted by the Planning and Compensation Act 1991, s 6(2).

Sub-s (7): temporarily added by the Planning (Consequential Provisions) Act 1990, s 6, Sch 4, paras 1, 3, until such day as may be appointed by order made by the Secretary of State. The Planning (Consequential Provisions) Act 1990 (Appointed Day No 1 and Transitional Provisions) Order 1991, SI 1991/2698 appointed 2 January 1992 only for the purposes of awards of costs in relation to proceedings which give rise to a hearing.

Modification: section modified by the Planning (Hazardous Substances) Regulations 1992, SI 1992/656, reg 18, Sch 4, Pt 1 at **[767]**.

---

176. General provisions relating to determination of appeals

[(1) On an appeal under section 174 the Secretary of State may—

  (a) correct any defect, error or misdescription in the enforcement notice; or
  (b) vary the terms of the enforcement notice,

if he is satisfied that the correction or variation will not cause injustice to the appellant or the local planning authority.

(2) Where the Secretary of State determines to allow the appeal, he may quash the notice.

(2A) The Secretary of State shall give any directions necessary to give effect to his determination on the appeal.]

(3) The Secretary of State—

  (a) may dismiss an appeal if the appellant fails to comply with section 174(4) within the prescribed time; and
  (b) may allow an appeal and quash the enforcement notice if the local planning authority fail to comply with any requirement of regulations made by virtue of paragraph (a), (b), or (d) of section 175(1) within the prescribed period.

(4) If the Secretary of State proposes to dismiss an appeal under paragraph (a)

of subsection (3) or to allow an appeal and quash the enforcement notice under paragraph (b) of that subsection, he need not comply with section 175(3).

(5) Where it would otherwise be a ground for determining an appeal under section 174 in favour of the appellant that a person required to be served with a copy of the enforcement notice was not served, the Secretary of State may disregard that fact if neither the appellant nor that person has been substantially prejudiced by the failure to serve him.   **[183]**

NOTES
   Commencement: 24 August 1990 (sub-ss (3)–(5)); 2 January 1992 (sub-ss (1), (2), (2A)).
   Sub-ss (1), (2), (2A) substituted for sub-ss (1), (2), as originally enacted, by the Planning and Compensation Act 1991, s 32, Sch 7, paras 8, 23.
   Modification: section modified by the Planning (Hazardous Substances) Regulations 1992, SI 1992/656, reg 18, Sch 4, Pt 1 at **[767]**.

177. Grant or modification of planning permission on appeals against enforcement notices

(1) On the determination of an appeal under section 174, the Secretary of State may—

   [(a) grant planning permission in respect of the matters stated in the enforcement notice as constituting a breach of planning control, whether in relation to the whole or any part of those matters or in relation to the whole or any part of the land to which the notice relates;]

   (b) discharge any condition or limitation subject to which planning permission was granted;

   [(c) determine whether, on the date on which the appeal was made, any existing use of the land was lawful, any operations which had been carried out in, on, over or under the land were lawful or any matter constituting a failure to comply with any condition or limitation subject to which planning permission was granted was lawful and, if so, issue a certificate under section 191].

   [(1A) The provisions of sections 191 to 194 mentioned in subsection (1B) shall apply for the purposes of subsection (1)(c) as they apply for the purposes of section 191, but as if—

   (a) any reference to an application for a certificate were a reference to the appeal and any reference to the date of such an application were a reference to the date on which the appeal is made; and

   (b) references to the local planning authority were references to the Secretary of State.

   (1B) Those provisions are: sections 191(5) to (7), 193(4) (so far as it relates to the form of the certificate), (6) and (7) and 194.]

(2) In considering whether to grant planning permission under subsection (1), the Secretary of State shall have regard to the provisions of the development plan, so far as material to the subject matter of the enforcement notice, and to any other material considerations.

   [(3) The planning permission that may be granted under subsection (1) is any planning permission that might be granted on an application under Part III.]

(4) Where under subsection (1) the Secretary of State discharges a condition or limitation, he may substitute another condition or limitation for it, whether more or less onerous.

(5) Where an appeal against an enforcement notice is brought under section 174, the appellant shall be deemed to have made an application for planning permission [in respect of the matters stated in the enforcement notice as constituting a breach of planning control].

[(5A) Where—
- (a) the statement under subsection (4) of section 174 specifies the ground mentioned in subsection (2)(a) of that section;
- (b) any fee is payable under regulations made by virtue of section 303 in respect of the application deemed to be made by virtue of the appeal; and
- (c) the Secretary of State gives notice in writing to the appellant specifying the period within which the fee must be paid,

then, if that fee is not paid within that period, the appeal, so far as brought on that ground, and the application shall lapse at the end of that period.]

(6) Any planning permission granted under subsection (1) on an appeal shall be treated as granted on the application deemed to have been made by the appellant.

(7) In relation to a grant of planning permission or a determination under subsection (1) the Secretary of State's decision shall be final.

(8) For the purposes of section 69 the Secretary of State's decision shall be treated as having been given by him in dealing with an application for planning permission made to the local planning authority.   **[184]**

NOTES
Commencement: 24 August 1990 (sub-ss (1), (2), (4), (5), (6)–(8)); 2 January 1992 (sub-ss (3), (5A)); 27 July 1992 (sub-ss (1A), (1B)).
Sub-ss (1)(a), (c), (3) substituted, sub-s (5) amended, and sub-ss (1A), (1B), (5A) inserted, by the Planning and Compensation Act 1991, ss 6(3), 32, Sch 7, paras 8, 24.
Modification: section modified by the Planning (Hazardous Substances) Regulations 1992, SI 1992/ 656, reg 18, Sch 4, Pt 1 at [767].

178. Execution and cost of works required by enforcement notice

[(1) Where any steps required by an enforcement notice to be taken are not taken within the period for compliance with the notice, the local planning authority may—
- (a) enter the land and take the steps; and
- (b) recover from the person who is then the owner of the land any expenses reasonably incurred by them in doing so.]

(2) Where a copy of an enforcement notice has been served in respect of any breach of planning control . . . —
- (a) any expenses incurred by the owner or occupier of any land for the purpose of complying with the notice, and
- (b) any sums paid by the owner of any land under subsection (1) in respect of expenses incurred by the local planning authority in taking steps required by such a notice to be taken,

shall be deemed to be incurred or paid for the use and at the request of the person by whom the breach of planning control was committed.

(3) Regulations made under this Act may provide that—
- (a) section 276 of the Public Health Act 1936, (power of local authorities to sell materials removed in executing works under that Act subject to accounting for the proceeds of sale);
- (b) section 289 of that Act (power to require the occupier of any premises to permit works to be executed by the owner of the premises); and

(c) section 294 of that Act (limit on liability of persons holding premises as agents or trustees in respect of the expenses recoverable under that Act),

shall apply, subject to such adaptations and modifications as may be specified in the regulations, in relation to any steps required to be taken by an enforcement notice.

(4) Regulations under subsection (3) applying section 289 of the Public Health Act 1936 may include adaptations and modifications for the purpose of giving the owner of land to which an enforcement notice relates the right, as against all other persons interested in the land, to comply with the requirements of the enforcement notice.

(5) Regulations under subsection (3) may also provide for the charging on the land of any expenses recoverable by a local planning authority under subsection (1).

[(6) Any person who wilfully obstructs a person acting in the exercise of powers under subsection (1) shall be guilty of an offence and liable on summary conviction to a fine not exceeding level 3 on the standard scale.]   **[185]**

NOTES

Commencement: 24 August 1990 (sub-ss (2)–(5)); 2 January 1992 (sub-ss (1), (6)).

Sub-ss (1), (6) substituted for sub-ss (1), (6), (7), and the words omitted from sub-s (2) repealed, by the Planning and Compensation Act 1991, ss 7, 32, 84(6), Sch 7, paras 8, 25, Sch 19, Pt I.

Modification: section modified by the Planning (Hazardous Substances) Regulations 1992, SI 1992/ 656, reg 20, Sch 4, Pt 2 at **[768]**.

[179. Offence where enforcement notice not complied with

(1) Where, at any time after the end of the period for compliance with an enforcement notice, any step required by the notice to be taken has not been taken or any activity required by the notice to cease is being carried on, the person who is then the owner of the land is in breach of the notice.

(2) Where the owner of the land is in breach of an enforcement notice he shall be guilty of an offence.

(3) In proceedings against any person for an offence under subsection (2), it shall be a defence for him to show that he did everything he could be expected to do to secure compliance with the notice.

(4) A person who has control of or an interest in the land to which an enforcement notice relates (other than the owner) must not carry on any activity which is required by the notice to cease or cause or permit such an activity to be carried on.

(5) A person who, at any time after the end of the period for compliance with the notice, contravenes subsection (4) shall be guilty of an offence.

(6) An offence under subsection (2) or (5) may be charged by reference to any day or longer period of time and a person may be convicted of a second or subsequent offence under the subsection in question by reference to any period of time following the preceding conviction for such an offence.

(7) Where—

  (a) a person charged with an offence under this section has not been served with a copy of the enforcement notice; and
  (b) the notice is not contained in the appropriate register kept under section 188,

it shall be a defence for him to show that he was not aware of the existence of the notice.

(8) A person guilty of an offence under this section shall be liable—

(a) on summary conviction, to a fine not exceeding £20,000; and
(b) on conviction on indictment, to a fine.

(9) In determining the amount of any fine to be imposed on a person convicted of an offence under this section, the court shall in particular have regard to any financial benefit which has accrued or appears likely to accrue to him in consequence of the offence.]   **[186]**

NOTES
Commencement: 2 January 1992.
Substituted by the Planning and Compensation Act 1991, s 8.
Modification: section modified by the Town and Country Planning (Special Enforcement Notices) Regulations 1992, SI 1992/1562, reg 2, Schedule at **[837]**, and by the Planning (Hazardous Substances) Regulations 1992, SI 1992/656, reg 20, Sch 4, Pt 2 at **[768]**.

[180. Effect of planning permission, etc, on enforcement or breach of condition notice

(1) Where, after the service of—

(a) a copy of an enforcement notice; or
(b) a breach of condition notice,

planning permission is granted for any development carried out before the grant of that permission, the notice shall cease to have effect so far as inconsistent with that permission.

(2) Where after a breach of condition notice has been served any condition to which the notice relates is discharged, the notice shall cease to have effect so far as it requires any person to secure compliance with the condition in question.

(3) The fact that an enforcement notice or breach of condition notice has wholly or partly ceased to have effect by virtue of this section shall not affect the liability of any person for an offence in respect of a previous failure to comply, or secure compliance, with the notice.]   **[187]**

NOTES
Commencement: 2 January 1992 (except so far as relates to breach of condition notices); 27 July 1992 (otherwise).
Substituted by the Planning and Compensation Act 1991, s 32, Sch 7, para 26.
Modification: section modified by the Town and Country Planning (Special Enforcement Notices) Regulations 1992, SI 1992/1562, reg 2, Schedule at **[837]**, and by the Planning (Hazardous Substances) Regulations 1992, SI 1992/656, reg 20, Sch 4, Pt 2 at **[768]**.

181. Enforcement notice to have effect against subsequent development

(1) Compliance with an enforcement notice, whether in respect of—

(a) the completion, [removal] or alteration of any buildings or works;
(b) the discontinuance of any use of land; or
(c) any other requirements contained in the notice,

shall not discharge the notice.

(2) Without prejudice to subsection (1), any provision of an enforcement notice requiring a use of land to be discontinued shall operate as a requirement that it shall be discontinued permanently, to the extent that it is in contravention of Part III; and accordingly the resumption of that use at any time after it has been discontinued in compliance with the enforcement notice shall to that extent be in contravention of the enforcement notice.

(3) Without prejudice to subsection (1), if any development is carried out on land by way of reinstating or restoring buildings or works which have been [removed] or altered in compliance with an enforcement notice, the notice shall, notwithstanding that its terms are not apt for the purpose, be deemed to apply in relation to the buildings or works as reinstated or restored as it applied in relation to the buildings or works before they were [removed] or altered; and, subject to subsection (4), the provisions of section 178(1) and (2) shall apply accordingly.

(4) Where, at any time after an enforcement notice takes effect—

(a) any development is carried out on land by way of reinstating or restoring buildings or works which have been [removed] or altered in compliance with the notice; and

(b) the local planning authority propose, under section 178(1), to take any steps required by the enforcement notice for the [removal] or alteration of the buildings or works in consequence of the reinstatement or restoration,

the local planning authority shall, not less than 28 days before taking any such steps, serve on the owner and occupier of the land a notice of their intention to do so.

(5) Where without planning permission a person carries out any development on land by way of reinstating or restoring buildings or works which have been [removed] or altered in compliance with an enforcement notice—

(a) he shall be guilty of an offence and shall be liable on summary conviction to a fine not exceeding level 5 on the standard scale, and

(b) no person shall be liable under [section 179(2)] for failure to take any steps required to be taken by an enforcement notice by way of [removal] or alteration of what has been so reinstated or restored. **[188]**

NOTES

Commencement: 24 August 1990.

Words in square brackets in sub-ss (1), (3)–(5) substituted by the Planning and Compensation Act 1991, s 32, Sch 7, paras 8, 27.

Modification: section modified by the Town and Country Planning (Special Enforcement Notices) Regulations 1992, SI 1992/1562, reg 2, Schedule at **[837]**, and by the Planning (Hazardous Substances) Regulations 1992, SI 1992/656, reg 20, Sch 4, Pt 2 at **[768]**.

182. Enforcement by the Secretary of State

(1) If it appears to the Secretary of State to be expedient that an enforcement notice should be issued in respect of any land, he may issue such a notice.

(2) The Secretary of State shall not issue such a notice without consulting the local planning authority.

(3) An enforcement notice issued by the Secretary of State shall have the same effect as a notice issued by the local planning authority.

(4) In relation to an enforcement notice issued by the Secretary of State, sections 178 and 181 shall apply as if for any reference in those sections to the local planning authority there were substituted a reference to the Secretary of State. **[189]**

NOTES

Commencement: 24 August 1990.

183. Stop notices

[(1) Where the local planning authority consider it expedient that any relevant activity should cease before the expiry of the period for compliance with an enforcement notice, they may, when they serve the copy of the enforcement notice or afterwards, serve a notice (in this Act referred to as a "stop notice") prohibiting the carrying out of that activity on the land to which the enforcement notice relates, or any part of that land specified in the stop notice.

(2) In this section and sections 184 and 186 "relevant activity" means any activity specified in the enforcement notice as an activity which the local planning authority require to cease and any activity carried out as part of that activity or associated with that activity.

(3) A stop notice may not be served where the enforcement notice has taken effect.

(4) A stop notice shall not prohibit the use of any building as a dwellinghouse.

(5) A stop notice shall not prohibit the carrying out of any activity if the activity has been carried out (whether continuously or not) for a period of more than four years ending with the service of the notice; and for the purposes of this subsection no account is to be taken of any period during which the activity was authorised by planning permission.

(5A) Subsection (5) does not prevent a stop notice prohibiting any activity consisting of, or incidental to, building, engineering, mining or other operations or the deposit of refuse or waste materials.]

(6) A stop notice may be served by the local planning authority on any person who appears to them to have an interest in the land or to be engaged in any activity prohibited by the notice.

(7) The local planning authority may at any time withdraw a stop notice (without prejudice to their power to serve another) by serving notice to that effect on persons served with the stop notice.   **[190]**

NOTES
   Commencement: 24 August 1990 (sub-ss (6), (7)); 2 January 1992 (sub-ss (1)–(5), (5A)).
   Sub-ss (1)–(5), (5A) substituted for sub-ss (1)–(5) by the Planning and Compensation Act 1991, s 9(1).
   Modification: sub-s (6) modified by the Town and Country Planning (Special Enforcement Notices) Regulations 1992, SI 1992/1562, reg 2, Schedule at **[837]**.

184. Stop notices: supplementary provisions

(1) A stop notice must refer to the enforcement notice to which it relates and have a copy of that notice annexed to it.

(2) A stop notice must specify the date on which it will take effect (and it cannot be contravened until that date).

[3] That date—

   (a) must not be earlier than three days after the date when the notice is served, unless the local planning authority consider that there are special reasons for specifying an earlier date and a statement of those reasons is served with the stop notice; and

   (b) must not be later than twenty-eight days from the date when the notice is first served on any person.]

(4) A stop notice shall cease to have effect when—

   (a) the enforcement notice to which it relates is withdrawn or quashed; or

   (b) the [period for compliance with the enforcement notice] expires; or

(c) notice of the withdrawal of the stop notice is first served under section 183(7).

(5) A stop notice shall also cease to have effect if or to the extent that the activities prohibited by it cease, on a variation of the enforcement notice, to be [relevant activities].

(6) Where a stop notice has been served in respect of any land, the local planning authority may display there a notice (in this section and section 187 referred to as a "site notice")—

(a) stating that a stop notice has been served and that any person contravening it may be prosecuted for an offence under section 187,
(b) giving the date when the stop notice takes effect, and
(c) indicating its requirements.

(7) If under section 183(7) the local planning authority withdraw a stop notice in respect of which a site notice was displayed, they must display a notice of the withdrawal in place of the site notice.

(8) A stop notice shall not be invalid by reason that a copy of the enforcement notice to which it relates was not served as required by section [172] if it is shown that the local planning authority took all such steps as were reasonably practicable to effect proper service.   **[191]**

NOTES
Commencement: 24 August 1990 (sub-ss (1), (2), (4)–(8)); 2 January 1992 (sub-s (3)).
Sub-s (3), and words in square brackets in sub-ss (4)(b), (5), (8), substituted by the Planning and Compensation Act 1991, ss 9(2), 32, Sch 7, paras 8, 28.
Modification: sub-s (8) modified by the Town and Country Planning (Special Enforcement Notices) Regulations 1992, SI 1992/1562, reg 2, Schedule at **[837]**.

185. Service of stop notices by Secretary of State

(1) If it appears to the Secretary of State to be expedient that a stop notice should be served in respect of any land, he may himself serve such a notice.

(2) A notice served by the Secretary of State under subsection (1) shall have the same effect as if it had been served by the local planning authority.

(3) The Secretary of State shall not serve such a notice without consulting the local planning authority.   **[192]**

NOTES
Commencement: 24 August 1990.

186. Compensation for loss due to stop notice

(1) Where a stop notice is served under section 183 compensation may be payable under this section in respect of a prohibition contained in the notice only if—

(a) the enforcement notice is quashed on grounds other than those mentioned in paragraph (a) of section 174(2);
(b) the enforcement notice is varied (otherwise than on the grounds mentioned in that paragraph) so that [any activity the carrying out of which is prohibited by the stop notice ceases to be a relevant activity];
(c) the enforcement notice is withdrawn by the local planning authority otherwise than in consequence of the grant by them of planning permission for the development to which the notice relates . . .; or

(d) the stop notice is withdrawn.

(2) A person who, when the stop notice is first served, has an interest in or occupies the land to which the notice relates shall be entitled to be compensated by the local planning authority in respect of any loss or damage directly attributable to the prohibition contained in the notice or, in a case within subsection (1)(b), [the prohibition of such of the activities prohibited by the stop notice as cease to be relevant activities].

(3) A claim for compensation under this section shall be made to the local planning authority within the prescribed time and in the prescribed manner.

(4) The loss or damage in respect of which compensation is payable under this section in respect of a prohibition shall include any sum payable in respect of a breach of contract caused by the taking of action necessary to comply with the prohibition.

[(5) No compensation is payable under this section—

    (a) in respect of the prohibition in a stop notice of any activity which, at any time when the notice is in force, constitutes or contributes to a breach of planning control; or

    (b) in the case of a claimant who was required to provide information under section 171C or 330 or section 16 of the Local Government (Miscellaneous Provisions) Act 1976, in respect of any loss or damage suffered by him which could have been avoided if he had provided the information or had otherwise co-operated with the local planning authority when responding to the notice.]

(6) Except in so far as may be otherwise provided by any regulations made under this Act, any question of disputed compensation under this Part shall be referred to and determined by the Lands Tribunal.

(7) In relation to the determination of any such question, the provisions of sections 2 and 4 of the Land Compensation Act 1961 shall apply subject to any necessary modifications and to the provisions of any regulations made under this Act.   **[193]**

NOTES

    Commencement: 24 August 1990 (sub-ss (1)–(4), (6), (7)); 2 January 1992 (sub-s (5)).

    Words in square brackets in sub-ss (1)(b), (2), and the whole of sub-s (5), substituted, and words omitted from sub-s (1)(c) repealed, by the Planning and Compensation Act 1991, ss 9(3), 32, 84(6), Sch 7, paras 8, 29, Sch 19, Pt I.

    Modification: sub-s (1) modified by the Town and Country Planning (Special Enforcement Notices) Regulations 1992, SI 1992/1562, reg 2, Schedule at **[837]**.

187. Penalties for contravention of stop notice

[(1) If any person contravenes a stop notice after a site notice has been displayed or the stop notice has been served on him he shall be guilty of an offence.

(1A) An offence under this section may be charged by reference to any day or longer period of time and a person may be convicted of a second or subsequent offence under this section by reference to any period of time following the preceding conviction for such an offence.

(1B) References in this section to contravening a stop notice include causing or permitting its contravention.

(2) A person guilty of an offence under this section shall be liable—

(a) on summary conviction, to a fine not exceeding £20,000; and

(b) on conviction on indictment, to a fine.

(2A) In determining the amount of any fine to be imposed on a person convicted of an offence under this section, the court shall in particular have regard to any financial benefit which has accrued or appears likely to accrue to him in consequence of the offence.]

(3) In proceedings for an offence under this section it shall be a defence for the accused to prove—

(a) that the stop notice was not served on him, and

(b) that he did not know, and could not reasonably have been expected to know, of its existence.   **[194]**

NOTES

Commencement: 24 August 1990 (sub-s (3)); 2 January 1992 (sub-ss (1), (1A), (1B), (2), (2A)).

Sub-ss (1)–(2A) substituted for sub-ss (1), (2) by the Planning and Compensation Act 1991, s 9(4).

[Breach of condition

187A. Enforcement of conditions

(1) This section applies where planning permission for carrying out any development of land has been granted subject to conditions.

(2) The local planning authority may, if any of the conditions is not complied with, serve a notice (in this Act referred to as a "breach of condition notice") on—

(a) any person who is carrying out or has carried out the development; or

(b) any person having control of the land,

requiring him to secure compliance with such of the conditions as are specified in the notice.

(3) References in this section to the person responsible are to the person on whom the breach of condition notice has been served.

(4) The conditions which may be specified in a notice served by virtue of subsection (2)(b) are any of the conditions regulating the use of the land.

(5) A breach of condition notice shall specify the steps which the authority consider ought to be taken, or the activities which the authority consider ought to cease, to secure compliance with the conditions specified in the notice.

(6) The authority may by notice served on the person responsible withdraw the breach of condition notice, but its withdrawal shall not affect the power to serve on him a further breach of condition notice in respect of the conditions specified in the earlier notice or any other conditions.

(7) The period allowed for compliance with the notice is—

(a) such period of not less than twenty-eight days beginning with the date of service of the notice as may be specified in the notice; or

(b) that period as extended by a further notice served by the local planning authority on the person responsible.

(8) If, at any time after the end of the period allowed for compliance with the notice—

(a) any of the conditions specified in the notice is not complied with; and

(b) the steps specified in the notice have not been taken or, as the case may be, the activities specified in the notice have not ceased,

the person responsible is in breach of the notice.

(9) If the person responsible is in breach of the notice he shall be guilty of an offence.

(10) An offence under subsection (9) may be charged by reference to any day or longer period of time and a person may be convicted of a second or subsequent offence under that subsection by reference to any period of time following the preceding conviction for such an offence.

(11) It shall be a defence for a person charged with an offence under subsection (9) to prove—

    (a) that he took all reasonable measures to secure compliance with the conditions specified in the notice; or

    (b) where the notice was served on him by virtue of subsection (2)(b), that he no longer had control of the land.

(12) A person who is guilty of an offence under subsection (9) shall be liable on summary conviction to a fine not exceeding level 3 on the standard scale.

(13) In this section—

    (a) "conditions" includes limitations; and

    (b) references to carrying out any development include causing or permitting another to do so.]   **[194A]**

NOTES

    Commencement: 27 July 1992.

    This section, and the cross-heading immediately preceding it, inserted by the Planning and Compensation Act 1991, s 2.

[Injunctions

187B. Injunctions restraining breaches of planning control

(1) Where a local planning authority consider it necessary or expedient for any actual or apprehended breach of planning control to be restrained by injunction, they may apply to the court for an injunction, whether or not they have exercised or are proposing to exercise any of their other powers under this Part.

(2) On an application under subsection (1) the court may grant such an injunction as the court thinks appropriate for the purpose of restraining the breach.

(3) Rules of court may provide for such an injunction to be issued against a person whose identity is unknown.

(4) In this section "the court" means the High Court or the county court.]
     [194B]

NOTES

    Commencement: 25 November 1991 (certain purposes); 2 January 1992 (remaining purposes).

    This section, and the cross-heading immediately preceding it, inserted by the Planning and Compensation Act 1991, s 3.

Registers

188. Register of enforcement and stop notices

(1) Every district planning authority [, every local planning authority for an area in Wales] and the council of every metropolitan district or London borough shall keep,

in such manner as may be prescribed by a development order, a register containing such information as may be so prescribed with respect—

    (a) to enforcement notices; . . .
    (b) to stop notices,
    [(c) to breach of condition notices]

which relate to land in their area.

    (2) A development order may make provision—

    (a) for the entry relating to any enforcement notice [stop notice or breach of condition notice], and everything relating to any such notice, to be removed from the register in such circumstances as may be specified in the order; and

    (b) for requiring a county planning authority to supply to a district planning authority such information as may be so specified with regard to enforcement notices issued and stop notices [and breach of condition notices] served by the county planning authority.

    (3) Every register kept under this section shall be available for inspection by the public at all reasonable hours.   **[195]**

NOTES

Commencement: 24 August 1990.

Words omitted from sub-s (1)(a) repealed, sub-s (1)(c) and words in square brackets in sub-s (2)(b) inserted, and words in square brackets in sub-s (2)(a) substituted, by the Planning and Compensation Act 1991, s 32, Sch 7, paras 8, 30.

Words in square brackets in sub-s (1) inserted by the Local Government (Wales) Act 1994, s 20(4)(b), Sch 6, Pt II, para 24(5), as from a day to be appointed.

Modification: section modified by the Planning (Hazardous Substances) Regulations 1992, SI 1992/656, reg 21, Sch 4, Pt 3 at **[769]**.

Enforcement of orders for discontinuance of use, etc

189. Penalties for contravention of orders under s 102 and Schedule 9

(1) Any person who without planning permission—

    (a) uses land, or causes or permits land to be used—

        (i) for any purpose for which an order under section 102 or paragraph 1 of Schedule 9 has required that its use shall be discontinued; or

        (ii) in contravention of any condition imposed by such an order by virtue of subsection (1) of that section or, as the case may be, sub-paragraph (1) of that paragraph; or

    (b) resumes, or causes or permits to be resumed, development consisting of the winning and working of minerals [or involving the depositing of mineral waste] the resumption of which an order under paragraph 3 of that Schedule has prohibited; or

    (c) contravenes, or causes or permits to be contravened, any such requirement as is specified in sub-paragraph (3) or (4) of that paragraph,

shall be guilty of an offence.

    (2) Any person who contravenes any requirement of an order under paragraph 5 or 6 of that Schedule or who causes or permits any requirement of such an order to be contravened shall be guilty of an offence.

    (3) Any person guilty of an offence under this section shall be liable—

    (a) on summary conviction, to a fine not exceeding the statutory maximum; and

(b) on conviction on indictment, to a fine.

(4) It shall be a defence for a person charged with an offence under this section to prove that he took all reasonable measures and exercised all due diligence to avoid commission of the offence by himself or by any person under his control.

(5) If in any case the defence provided by subsection (4) involves an allegation that the commission of the offence was due to the act or default of another person or due to reliance on information supplied by another person, the person charged shall not, without the leave of the court, be entitled to rely on the defence unless, within a period ending seven clear days before the hearing, he has served on the prosecutor a notice in writing giving such information identifying or assisting in the identification of the other person as was then in his possession.   **[196]**

NOTES
  Commencement: 24 August 1990.
  Words in square brackets in sub-s (1)(b) inserted by the Planning and Compensation Act 1991, s 21, Sch 1, paras 1, 11.

190. Enforcement of orders under s 102 and Schedule 9

(1) This section applies where—

  (a) any step required by an order under section 102 or paragraph 1 of Schedule 9 to be taken for the alteration or removal of any buildings or works or any plant or machinery;

  (b) any step required by an order under paragraph 3 of that Schedule to be taken—

      (i) for the alteration or removal of plant or machinery; or
      (ii) for the removal or alleviation of any injury to amenity; or

  (c) any step for the protection of the environment required to be taken by an order under paragraph 5 or 6 of that Schedule,

has not been taken within the period specified in the order or within such extended period as the local planning authority or, as the case may be, the mineral planning authority may allow.

(2) Where this section applies the local planning authority or, as the case may be, the mineral planning authority may enter the land and take the required step.

(3) Where the local planning authority or, as the case may be, the mineral planning authority have exercised their power under subsection (2) they may recover from the person who is then the owner of the land any expenses reasonably incurred by them in doing so.

(4) ...

(5) Section 276 of the Public Health Act 1936 shall apply in relation to any works executed by an authority under subsection (2) as it applies in relation to works executed by a local authority under that Act.   **[197]**

NOTES
  Commencement: 24 August 1990.
  Sub-s (4) repealed by the Planning and Compensation Act 1991, ss 32, 84(6), Sch 7, paras 8, 31, Sch 19, Pt I.

[Certificate of lawful use or development

191. Certificate of lawfulness of existing use or development

(1) If any person wishes to ascertain whether—

    (a) any existing use of buildings or other land is lawful;

    (b) any operations which have been carried out in, on, over or under land are lawful; or

    (c) any other matter constituting a failure to comply with any condition or limitation subject to which planning permission has been granted is lawful,

he may make an application for the purpose to the local planning authority specifying the land and describing the use, operations or other matter.

(2) For the purposes of this Act uses and operations are lawful at any time if—

    (a) no enforcement action may then be taken in respect of them (whether because they did not involve development or require planning permission or because the time for enforcement action has expired or for any other reason); and

    (b) they do not constitute a contravention of any of the requirements of any enforcement notice then in force.

(3) For the purposes of this Act any matter constituting a failure to comply with any condition or limitation subject to which planning permission has been granted is lawful at any time if—

    (a) the time for taking enforcement action in respect of the failure has then expired; and

    (b) it does not constitute a contravention of any of the requirements of any enforcement notice or breach of condition notice then in force.

(4) If, on an application under this section, the local planning authority are provided with information satisfying them of the lawfulness at the time of the application of the use, operations or other matter described in the application, or that description as modified by the local planning authority or a description substituted by them, they shall issue a certificate to that effect; and in any other case they shall refuse the application.

(5) A certificate under this section shall—

    (a) specify the land to which it relates;

    (b) describe the use, operations or other matter in question (in the case of any use falling within one of the classes specified in an order under section 55(2)(f), identifying it by reference to that class);

    (c) give the reasons for determining the use, operations or other matter to be lawful; and

    (d) specify the date of the application for the certificate.

(6) The lawfulness of any use, operations or other matter for which a certificate is in force under this section shall be conclusively presumed.

(7) A certificate under this section in respect of any use shall also have effect, for the purposes of the following enactments, as if it were a grant of planning permission—

    (a) section 3(3) of the Caravan Sites and Control of Development Act 1960;

    (b) section 5(2) of the Control of Pollution Act 1974; and

   (c) section 36(2)(a) of the Environmental Protection Act 1990.]   **[198]**

NOTES

    Commencement: 27 July 1992.

    This section, and ss 192–194, substituted by the Planning and Compensation Act 1991, s 10.

[192. Certificate of lawfulness of proposed use or development

(1) If any person wishes to ascertain whether—

    (a) any proposed use of buildings or other land; or

    (b) any operations proposed to be carried out in, on, over or under land,

would be lawful, he may make an application for the purpose to the local planning authority specifying the land and describing the use or operations in question.

(2) If, on an application under this section, the local planning authority are provided with information satisfying them that the use or operations described in the application would be lawful if instituted or begun at the time of the application, they shall issue a certificate to that effect; and in any other case they shall refuse the application.

(3) A certificate under this section shall—

    (a) specify the land to which it relates;

    (b) describe the use or operations in question (in the case of any use falling within one of the classes specified in an order under section 55(2)(f), identifying it by reference to that class);

    (c) give the reasons for determining the use or operations to be lawful; and

    (d) specify the date of the application for the certificate.

(4) The lawfulness of any use or operations for which a certificate is in force under this section shall be conclusively presumed unless there is a material change, before the use is instituted or the operations are begun, in any of the matters relevant to determining such lawfulness.]   **[199]**

NOTES

    Commencement: 27 July 1992.

    Substituted as noted to s 191 at **[198]**.

[193. Certificates under sections 191 and 192: supplementary provisions

(1) An application for a certificate under section 191 or 192 shall be made in such manner as may be prescribed by a development order and shall include such particulars, and be verified by such evidence, as may be required by such an order or by any directions given under such an order or by the local planning authority.

(2) Provision may be made by a development order for regulating the manner in which applications for certificates under those sections are to be dealt with by local planning authorities.

(3) In particular, such an order may provide for requiring the authority—

    (a) to give to any applicant within such time as may be prescribed by the order such notice as may be so prescribed as to the manner in which his application has been dealt with; and

    (b) to give to the Secretary of State and to such other persons as may be prescribed by or under the order, such information as may be so prescribed with respect to such applications made to the authority, including information as to the manner in which any application has been dealt with.

(4) A certificate under either of those sections may be issued—

(a) for the whole or part of the land specified in the application; and

(b) where the application specifies two or more uses, operations or other matters, for all of them or some one or more of them;

and shall be in such form as may be prescribed by a development order.

(5) A certificate under section 191 or 192 shall not affect any matter constituting a failure to comply with any condition or limitation subject to which planning permission has been granted unless that matter is described in the certificate.

(6) In section 69 references to applications for planning permission shall include references to applications for certificates under section 191 or 192.

(7) A local planning authority may revoke a certificate under either of those sections if, on the application for the certificate—

(a) a statement was made or document used which was false in a material particular; or

(b) any material information was withheld.

(8) Provision may be made by a development order for regulating the manner in which certificates may be revoked and the notice to be given of such revocation.]

[200]

NOTES
Commencement: 27 July 1992.
Substituted as noted to s 191 at **[198]**.

[194. Offences

(1) If any person, for the purpose of procuring a particular decision on an application (whether by himself or another) for the issue of a certificate under section 191 or 192—

(a) knowingly or recklessly makes a statement which is false or misleading in a material particular;

(b) with intent to deceive, uses any document which is false or misleading in a material particular; or

(c) with intent to deceive, withholds any material information,

he shall be guilty of an offence.

(2) A person guilty of an offence under subsection (1) shall be liable—

(a) on summary conviction, to a fine not exceeding the statutory maximum; or

(b) on conviction on indictment, to imprisonment for a term not exceeding two years, or a fine, or both.

(3) Notwithstanding section 127 of the Magistrates' Courts Act 1980, a magistrates' court may try an information in respect of an offence under subsection (1) whenever laid.]   **[201]**

NOTES
Commencement: 27 July 1992.
Substituted as noted to s 191 at **[198]**.

195. Appeals against refusal or failure to give decision on application

(1) Where an application is made to a local planning authority for [a certificate under section 191 or 192] and—

(a) the application is refused or is refused in part, or

(b) the authority do not give notice to the applicant of their decision on the application within such period as may be prescribed by a development order or within such extended period as may at any time be agreed upon in writing between the applicant and the authority,

the applicant may by notice appeal to the Secretary of State.

(2) On any such appeal, if and so far as the Secretary of State is satisfied—

(a) in the case of an appeal under subsection (1)(a), that the authority's refusal is not well-founded, or

(b) in the case of an appeal under subsection (1)(b), that if the authority had refused the application their refusal would not have been well-founded,

he shall grant the appellant [a certificate under section 191 or, as the case may be, 192] accordingly or, in the case of a refusal in part, modify the certificate granted by the authority on the application.

(3) If and so far as the Secretary of State is satisfied that the authority's refusal is or, as the case may be, would have been well-founded, he shall dismiss the appeal.

[(4) References in this section to a refusal of an application in part include a modification or substitution of the description in the application of the use, operations or other matter in question.]

(5) For the purposes of the application of section 288(10)(b) in relation to an appeal in a case within subsection (1)(b) it shall be assumed that the authority decided to refuse the application in question.

(6) Schedule 6 applies to appeals under this section.   **[202]**

NOTES
    Commencement: 24 August 1990.
    Words in square brackets in sub-ss (1), (2), and the whole of sub-s (4), substituted by the Planning and Compensation Act 1991, s 32, Sch 7, paras 8, 32.

196. Further provisions as to references and appeals to the Secretary of State

(1) Before determining . . . an appeal to him under section 195(1), the Secretary of State shall, if either the [appellant] or the local planning authority so wish, give each of them an opportunity of appearing before, and being heard by, a person appointed by the Secretary of State for the purpose.

(2) Where the Secretary of State grants [a certificate under section 191 or 192 on] such an appeal, he shall give notice to the local planning authority of that fact.

(3) The decision of the Secretary of State on such an . . . appeal shall be final.

(4) The information which may be prescribed as being required to be contained in a register kept under section 69 shall include information with respect to [certificates under section 191 or 192] granted by the Secretary of State.

(5)–(7) . . .

[(8) Subsection (5) of section 250 of the Local Government Act 1972 (which authorises a Minister holding an inquiry under that section to make orders with respect to the costs of the parties) shall apply in relation to any proceedings before the Secretary of State on an appeal under section 195 as if those proceedings were an inquiry held by the Secretary of State under section 250.]   **[203]**

NOTES
    Commencement: 24 August 1990 (sub-ss (1)-(7)); for effect of sub-s (8) see annotations below.
    Words omitted from sub-ss (1), (3) and the whole of sub-ss (5)–(7) repealed, and words in square

brackets in sub-ss (1), (2), (4) substituted, by the Planning and Compensation Act 1991, ss 32, 84(6), Sch 7, paras 8, 33, Sch 19, Pt I.

Sub-s (8): temporarily inserted by the Planning (Consequential Provisions) Act 1990, s 6, Sch 4, paras 1, 4, until such day as may be appointed by order made by the Secretary of State. The Planning (Consequential Provisions) Act 1990 (Appointed Day No 1 and Transitional Provisions) Order 1991, SI 1991/2698, appointed 2 January 1992 only for the purposes of awards of costs in relation to proceedings which give rise to a hearing.

[Rights of entry for enforcement purposes

196A. Rights to enter without warrant

(1) Any person duly authorised in writing by a local planning authority may at any reasonable hour enter any land—

    (a) to ascertain whether there is or has been any breach of planning control on the land or any other land;

    (b) to determine whether any of the powers conferred on a local planning authority by this Part should be exercised in relation to the land or any other land;

    (c) to determine how any such power should be exercised in relation to the land or any other land;

    (d) to ascertain whether there has been compliance with any requirement imposed as a result of any such power having been exercised in relation to the land or any other land,

if there are reasonable grounds for entering for the purpose in question.

(2) Any person duly authorised in writing by the Secretary of State may at any reasonable hour enter any land to determine whether an enforcement notice should be issued in relation to the land or any other land, if there are reasonable grounds for entering for that purpose.

(3) The Secretary of State shall not so authorise any person without consulting the local planning authority.

(4) Admission to any building used as a dwellinghouse shall not be demanded as of right by virtue of subsection (1) or (2) unless twenty-four hours' notice of the intended entry has been given to the occupier of the building.] **[203A]**

NOTES

    Commencement: 2 January 1992.

    This section, ss 196B, 196C, and the cross-heading immediately before this section, inserted by the Planning and Compensation Act 1991, s 11(1).

[196B. Right to enter under warrant

(1) If it is shown to the satisfaction of a justice of the peace on sworn information in writing—

    (a) that there are reasonable grounds for entering any land for any of the purposes mentioned in section 196A(1) or (2); and

    (b) that—

        (i) admission to the land has been refused, or a refusal is reasonably apprehended; or

        (ii) the case is one of urgency,

the justice may issue a warrant authorising any person duly authorised in writing by a local planning authority or, as the case may be, the Secretary of State to enter the land.

(2) For the purposes of subsection (1)(b)(i) admission to land shall be regarded as having been refused if no reply is received to a request for admission within a reasonable period.

(3) A warrant authorises entry on one occasion only and that entry must be—

(a) within one month from the date of the issue of the warrant; and
(b) at a reasonable hour, unless the case is one of urgency.]   **[203B]**

NOTES
Commencement: 2 January 1992.
Inserted as noted to s 196A at **[203A]**.

[196C. Rights of entry: supplementary provisions

(1) A person authorised to enter any land in pursuance of a right of entry conferred under or by virtue of section 196A or 196B (referred to in this section as "a right of entry")—

(a) shall, if so required, produce evidence of his authority and state the purpose of his entry before so entering;
(b) may take with him such other persons as may be necessary; and
(c) on leaving the land shall, if the owner or occupier is not then present, leave it as effectively secured against trespassers as he found it.

(2) Any person who wilfully obstructs a person acting in the exercise of a right of entry shall be guilty of an offence and liable on summary conviction to a fine not exceeding level 3 on the standard scale.

(3) If any damage is caused to land or chattels in the exercise of a right of entry, compensation may be recovered by any person suffering the damage from the authority who gave the written authority for the entry or, as the case may be, the Secretary of State.

(4) The provisions of section 118 shall apply in relation to compensation under subsection (3) as they apply in relation to compensation under Part IV.

(5) If any person who enters any land, in exercise of a right of entry, discloses to any person any information obtained by him while on the land as to any manufacturing process or trade secret, he shall be guilty of an offence.

(6) Subsection (5) does not apply if the disclosure is made by a person in the course of performing his duty in connection with the purpose for which he was authorised to enter the land.

(7) A person who is guilty of an offence under subsection (5) shall be liable on summary conviction to a fine not exceeding the statutory maximum or on conviction on indictment to imprisonment for a term not exceeding two years or a fine or both.

(8) In sections 196A and 196B and this section references to a local planning authority include, in relation to a building situated in Greater London, a reference to the Historic Buildings and Monuments Commission for England.]   **[203C]**

NOTES
Commencement: 2 January 1992.
Inserted as noted to s 196A at **[203A]**.

PART VIII

SPECIAL CONTROLS

CHAPTER I

TREES

General duty of planning authorities as respects trees

197. Planning permission to include appropriate provision for preservation and planting of trees

It shall be the duty of the local planning authority—

(a) to ensure, whenever it is appropriate, that in granting planning permission for any development adequate provision is made, by the imposition of conditions, for the preservation or planting of trees; and

(b) to make such orders under section 198 as appear to the authority to be necessary in connection with the grant of such permission, whether for giving effect to such conditions or otherwise.   **[204]**

NOTES

Commencement: 24 August 1990.

Tree preservation orders

198. Power to make tree preservation orders

(1) If it appears to a local planning authority that it is expedient in the interests of amenity to make provision for the preservation of trees or woodlands in their area, they may for that purpose make an order with respect to such trees, groups of trees or woodlands as may be specified in the order.

(2) An order under subsection (1) is in this Act referred to as a "tree preservation order".

(3) A tree preservation order may, in particular, make provision—

(a) for prohibiting (subject to any exemptions for which provision may be made by the order) the cutting down, topping, lopping, uprooting, wilful damage or wilful destruction of trees except with the consent of the local planning authority, and for enabling that authority to give their consent subject to conditions;

(b) for securing the replanting, in such manner as may be prescribed by or under the order, of any part of a woodland area which is felled in the course of forestry operations permitted by or under the order;

(c) for applying, in relation to any consent under the order, and to applications for such consent, any of the provisions of this Act mentioned in subsection (4), subject to such adaptations and modifications as may be specified in the order.

(4) The provisions referred to in subsection (3)(c) are—

(a) the provisions of Part III relating to planning permission and to applications for planning permission, except sections 56, 62, 65 . . . , 69(3) and (4), 71, . . . , 91 to 96, 100 and 101 and Schedule 8; and

(b) sections 137 to 141, 143 and 144 (except so far as they relate to purchase notices served in consequence of such orders as are mentioned in section 137(1)(b) or (c));

(c) section 316.

(5) A tree preservation order may be made so as to apply, in relation to trees to be planted pursuant to any such conditions as are mentioned in section 197(a), as from the time when those trees are planted.

(6) Without prejudice to any other exemptions for which provision may be made by a tree preservation order, no such order shall apply—

(a) to the cutting down, uprooting, topping or lopping of trees which are dying or dead or have become dangerous, or

(b) to the cutting down, uprooting, topping or lopping of any trees in compliance with any obligations imposed by or under an Act of Parliament or so far as may be necessary for the prevention or abatement of a nuisance.

(7) This section shall have effect subject to—

(a) section 39(2) of the Housing and Planning Act 1986 (saving for effect of section 2(4) of the Opencast Coal Act 1958 on land affected by a tree preservation order despite its repeal); and

(b) section 15 of the Forestry Act 1967 (licences under that Act to fell trees comprised in a tree preservation order).   **[205]**

NOTES
Commencement: 24 August 1990.
Words omitted from sub-s (4)(a) repealed by the Planning and Compensation Act 1991, ss 31(4), 32, 84(6), Sch 6, paras 8, 20, Sch 7, paras 8, 34, Sch 19, Pts I, II.

199. Form of and procedure applicable to orders

(1) A tree preservation order shall not take effect until it is confirmed by the local planning authority and the local planning authority may confirm any such order either without modification or subject to such modifications as they consider expedient.

(2) Provision may be made by regulations under this Act with respect—

(a) to the form of tree preservation orders, and

(b) to the procedure to be followed in connection with the making and confirmation of such orders.

(3) Without prejudice to the generality of subsection (2), the regulations may make provision—

(a) that, before a tree preservation order is confirmed by the local planning authority, notice of the making of the order shall be given to the owners and occupiers of land affected by the order and to such other persons, if any, as may be specified in the regulations;

(b) that objections and representations with respect to the order, if duly made in accordance with the regulations, shall be considered before the order is confirmed by the local planning authority; and

(c) that copies of the order, when confirmed by the authority, shall be served on such persons as may be specified in the regulations.   **[206]**

NOTES
Commencement: 24 August 1990.

200. Orders affecting land where Forestry Commissioners interested

(1) In relation to land in which the Forestry Commissioners have an interest, a tree preservation order may be made only if—

(a) there is not in force in respect of the land a plan of operations or other working plan approved by the Commissioners under a forestry dedication covenant; and

(b) the Commissioners consent to the making of the order.

(2) For the purposes of subsection (1), the Forestry Commissioners are only to be regarded as having an interest in land if—

(a) they have made a grant or loan under section 1 of the Forestry Act 1979 in respect of it, or

(b) there is a forestry dedication covenant in force in respect of it.

(3) A tree preservation order in respect of such land shall not have effect so as to prohibit, or to require any consent for, the cutting down of a tree in accordance with a plan of operations or other working plan approved by the Forestry Commissioners, and for the time being in force, under a forestry dedication covenant or under the conditions of a grant or loan made under section 1 of the Forestry Act 1979.

(4) In this section—

(a) "a forestry dedication covenant" means a covenant entered into with the Commissioners under section 5 of the Forestry Act 1967; and

(b) references to provisions of the Forestry Act 1967 and the Forestry Act 1979 include references to any corresponding provisions replaced by those provisions or by earlier corresponding provisions.   **[207]**

NOTES
Commencement: 24 August 1990.

201. Provisional tree preservation orders

(1) If it appears to a local planning authority that a tree preservation order proposed to be made by that authority should take effect immediately without previous confirmation, they may include in the order as made by them a direction that this section shall apply to the order.

(2) Notwithstanding section 199(1), an order which contains such a direction—

(a) shall take effect provisionally on such date as may be specified in it, and

(b) shall continue in force by virtue of this section until—

(i) the expiration of a period of six months beginning with the date on which the order was made; or

(ii) the date on which the order is confirmed,

whichever first occurs.   **[208]**

NOTES
Commencement: 24 August 1990.

202. Power for Secretary of State to make tree preservation orders

(1) If it appears to the Secretary of State, after consultation with the local planning authority, to be expedient that a tree preservation order or an order amending or revoking such an order should be made, he may himself make such an order.

(2) Any order so made by the Secretary of State shall have the same effect as if

it had been made by the local planning authority and confirmed by them under this Chapter.

(3) The provisions of this Chapter and of any regulations made under it with respect to the procedure to be followed in connection with the making and confirmation of any order to which subsection (1) applies and the service of copies of it as confirmed shall have effect, subject to any necessary modifications—

(a) in relation to any proposal by the Secretary of State to make such an order,

(b) in relation to the making of it by the Secretary of State, and

(c) in relation to the service of copies of it as so made.   **[209]**

NOTES
  Commencement: 24 August 1990.

Compensation for loss or damage caused by orders, etc

203. Compensation in respect of tree preservation orders

A tree preservation order may make provision for the payment by the local planning authority, subject to such exceptions and conditions as may be specified in the order, of compensation in respect of loss or damage caused or incurred in consequence—

(a) of the refusal of any consent required under the order, or

(b) of the grant of any such consent subject to conditions.   **[210]**

NOTES
  Commencement: 24 August 1990.

204. Compensation in respect of requirement as to replanting of trees

(1) This section applies where—

(a) in pursuance of provision made by a tree preservation order, a direction is given by the local planning authority or the Secretary of State for securing the replanting of all or any part of a woodland area which is felled in the course of forestry operations permitted by or under the order; and

(b) the Forestry Commissioners decide not to make any grant or loan under section 1 of the Forestry Act 1979 in respect of the replanting by reason that the direction frustrates the use of the woodland area for the growing of timber or other forest products for commercial purposes and in accordance with the rules or practice of good forestry.

(2) Where this section applies, the local planning authority exercising functions under the tree preservation order shall be liable, on the making of a claim in accordance with this section, to pay compensation in respect of such loss or damage, if any, as is caused or incurred in consequence of compliance with the direction.

(3) The Forestry Commissioners shall, at the request of the person under a duty to comply with such a direction as is mentioned in subsection (1)(b), give a certificate stating—

(a) whether they have decided not to make such a grant or loan as is mentioned in subsection (1)(b), and

(b) if so, the grounds for their decision.

(4) A claim for compensation under this section must be served on the local planning authority—

(a) within 12 months from the date on which the direction was given, or

(b) where an appeal has been made to the Secretary of State against the decision of the local planning authority, within 12 months from the date of the decision of the Secretary of State on the appeal,

but subject in either case to such extension of that period as the local planning authority may allow. **[211]**

NOTES
Commencement: 24 August 1990.

205. Determination of compensation claims

(1) Except in so far as may be otherwise provided by any tree preservation order or any regulations made under this Act, any question of disputed compensation under section 203 or 204 shall be referred to and determined by the Lands Tribunal.

(2) In relation to the determination of any such question, the provisions of sections 2 and 4 of the Land Compensation Act 1961 shall apply subject to any necessary modifications and to the provisions of any regulations made under this Act. **[212]**

NOTES
Commencement: 24 August 1990.

Consequences of tree removal, etc

206. Replacement of trees

(1) If any tree in respect of which a tree preservation order is for the time being in force—

(a) is removed, uprooted or destroyed in contravention of the order, or
(b) except in the case of a tree to which the order applies as part of a woodland, is removed, uprooted or destroyed or dies at a time when its cutting down or uprooting is authorised only by virtue of section 198(6)(a),

it shall be the duty of the owner of the land to plant another tree of an appropriate size and species at the same place as soon as he reasonably can.

(2) The duty imposed by subsection (1) does not apply to an owner if on application by him the local planning authority dispense with it.

(3) In respect of trees in a woodland it shall be sufficient for the purposes of this section to replace the trees removed, uprooted or destroyed by planting the same number of trees—

(a) on or near the land on which the trees removed, uprooted or destroyed stood, or
(b) on such other land as may be agreed between the local planning authority and the owner of the land,

and in such places as may be designated by the local planning authority.

(4) In relation to any tree planted pursuant to this section, the relevant tree preservation order shall apply as it applied to the original tree.

(5) The duty imposed by subsection (1) on the owner of any land shall attach to the person who is from time to time the owner of the land. **[213]**

NOTES
Commencement: 24 August 1990.

207. Enforcement of duties as to replacement of trees

(1) If it appears to the local planning authority that—

    (a) the provisions of section 206, or

    (b) any conditions of a consent given under a tree preservation order which require the replacement of trees,

are not complied with in the case of any tree or trees, that authority may serve on the owner of the land a notice requiring him, within such period as may be specified in the notice, to plant a tree or trees of such size and species as may be so specified.

(2) A notice under subsection (1) may only be served within four years from the date of the alleged failure to comply with those provisions or conditions.

[(3) A notice under subsection (1) shall specify a period at the end of which it is to take effect.

(4) The specified period shall be a period of not less than twenty-eight days beginning with the date of service of the notice.]

(5) The duty imposed by section 206(1) may only be enforced as provided by this section and not otherwise.   **[214]**

NOTES

    Commencement: 24 August 1990 (sub-ss (1), (2), (5)); 2 January 1992 (sub-ss (3), (4)).

    Sub-ss (3), (4) substituted by the Planning and Compensation Act 1991, s 23(1).

208. Appeals against s 207 notices

(1) A person on whom a notice under section 207(1) is served may appeal to the Secretary of State against the notice on any of the following grounds—

    (a) that the provisions of section 206 or, as the case may be, the conditions mentioned in section 207(1)(b) are not applicable or have been complied with;

    [(aa) that in all the circumstances of the case the duty imposed by section 206(1) should be dispensed with in relation to any tree;]

    (b) that the requirements of the notice are unreasonable in respect of the period or the size or species of trees specified in it;

    (c) that the planting of a tree or trees in accordance with the notice is not required in the interests of amenity or would be contrary to the practice of good forestry;

    (d) that the place on which the tree is or trees are required to be planted is unsuitable for that purpose.

[(2) An appeal under subsection (1) shall be made either—

    (a) by giving written notice of the appeal to the Secretary of State before the end of the period specified in accordance with section 207(3); or

    (b) by sending such notice to him in a properly addressed and pre-paid letter posted to him at such time that, in the ordinary course of post, it would be delivered to him before the end of that period.]

(4) The notice shall indicate the grounds of the appeal and state the facts on which it is based.

(5) On any such appeal the Secretary of State shall, if either the appellant or the local planning authority so desire, give each of them an opportunity of appearing before and being heard by a person appointed by the Secretry of State for the purpose.

(6) Where such an appeal is brought, the notice under section 207(1) shall be of no effect pending the final determination or the withdrawal of the appeal.

[(7) On such an appeal the Secretary of State may—

(a) correct any defect, error or misdescription in the notice; or
(b) vary any of its requirements,

if he is satisfied that the correction or variation will not cause injustice to the appellant or the local planning authority.

(8) Where the Secretary of State determines to allow the appeal, he may quash the notice.

(8A) The Secretary of State shall give any directions necessary to give effect to his determination on the appeal.]

(9) Schedule 6 applies to appeals under this section.

(10) Where any person has appealed to the Secretary of State under this section against a notice, neither that person nor any other shall be entitled, in any other proceedings instituted after the making of the appeal, to claim that the notice was not duly served on the person who appealed.

[(11) Subsection (5) of section 250 of the Local Government Act 1972 (which authorises a Minister holding an inquiry under that section to make orders with respect to the costs of the parties) shall apply in relation to any proceedings before the Secretary of State on an appeal under this section as if those proceedings were an inquiry held by the Secretary of State under section 250.] **[215]**

NOTES
Commencement: 24 August 1990 (sub-ss (1), (4)-(6), (9), (10)); 2 January 1992 (sub-ss (2), (7), (8), (8A); for effect of sub-s (11) see annotations below.
Sub-s (1)(aa) inserted, sub-s (2) substituted for sub-ss (2), (3), sub-ss (7), (8), (8A) substituted for sub-ss (7), (8), by the Planning and Compensation Act 1991, s 23(2)–(4).
Sub-s (11): temporarily inserted by the Planning (Consequential Provisions) Act 1990, s 6, Sch 4, paras 1, 5, until such day as may be appointed by order made by the Secretary of State. The Planning (Consequential Provisions) Act 1990 (Appointed Day No 1 and Transitional Provisions) Order 1991, SI 1991/2698, appointed 2 January 1992 only for the purposes of awards of costs in relation to proceedings which give rise to a hearing.

209. Execution and cost of works required by s 207 notice

(1) If, within the period specified in a notice under section 207(1) for compliance with it, or within such extended period as the local planning authority may allow, any trees which are required to be planted by a notice under that section have not been planted, the local planning authority may—

(a) enter the land and plant those trees, and
(b) recover from the person who is then the owner of the land any expenses reasonably incurred by them in doing so.

(2) Where such a notice has been served—

(a) any expenses incurred by the owner of any land for the purpose of complying with the notice, and
(b) any sums paid by the owner of any land under subsection (1) in respect of expenses incurred by the local planning authority in planting trees required by such a notice to be planted,

shall be deemed to be incurred or paid for the use and at the request of any person, other than the owner, responsible for the cutting down, destruction or removal of the original tree or trees.

(3) Regulations made under this Act may provide that—

    (a) section 276 of the Public Health Act 1936 (power of local authorities to sell materials removed in executing works under that Act subject to accounting for the proceeds of sale);

    (b) section 289 of that Act (power to require the occupier of any premises to permit works to be executed by the owner of the premises); or

    (c) section 294 of that Act (limit on liability of persons holding premises as agents or trustees in respect of the expenses recoverable under that Act),

shall apply, subject to such adaptations and modifications as may be specified in the regulations, in relation to any steps required to be taken by a notice under section 207(1).

(4) Regulations under subsection (3) applying section 289 of the Public Health Act 1936 may include adaptations and modifications for the purpose of giving the owner of land to which such a notice relates the right, as against all other persons interested in the land, to comply with the requirements of the notice.

(5) Regulations under subsection (3) may also provide for the charging on the land of any expenses recoverable by a local authority [or National Park authority] under subsection (1).

[(6) Any person who wilfully obstructs a person acting in the exercise of the power under subsection (1)(a) shall be guilty of an offence and liable on summary conviction to a fine not exceeding level 3 on the standard scale.]   **[216]**

NOTES

    Commencement: 24 August 1990 (sub-ss (1)–(5)); 2 January 1992 (sub-s (6)).

    Words in square brackets in sub-s (5) inserted by the Environment Act 1995, s 78, Sch 10, para 32(6), as from a day to be appointed under s 125(3).

    Sub-s (6) substituted by the Planning and Compensation Act 1991, s 23(5).

210. Penalties for non-compliance with tree preservation orders

(1) If any person, in contravention of a tree preservation order—

    (a) cuts down, uproots or wilfully destroys a tree; or

    (b) wilfully damages, tops or lops a tree in such a manner as to be likely to destroy it,

he shall be guilty of an offence.

(2) A person guilty of an offence under subsection (1) shall be liable—

    [(a) on summary conviction to a fine not exceeding £20,000;] or

    (b) on conviction on indictment, to a fine.

(3) In determining the amount of any fine to be imposed on a person convicted ... of an offence under subsection (1), the court shall in particular have regard to any financial benefit which has accrued or appears likely to accrue to him in consequence of the offence.

(4) If any person contravenes the provisions of a tree preservation order otherwise than as mentioned in subsection (1), he shall be guilty of an offence and liable on summary conviction to a fine not exceeding level 4 on the standard scale.

(5) ...   **[217]**

NOTES

    Commencement: 24 August 1990.

    Sub-s (2)(a) substituted, and words omitted from sub-s (3) and the whole of sub-s (5) repealed, by the Planning and Compensation Act 1991, ss 23(6), 84(6), Sch 19, Pt I.

Trees in conservation areas

211. Preservation of trees in conservation areas

(1) Subject to the provisions of this section and section 212, any person who, in relation to a tree to which this section applies, does any act which might by virtue of section 198(3)(a) be prohibited by a tree preservation order shall be guilty of an offence.

(2) Subject to section 212, this section applies to any tree in a conservation area in respect of which no tree preservation order is for the time being in force.

(3) It shall be a defence for a person charged with an offence under subsection (1) to prove—

(a) that he served notice of his intention to do the act in question (with sufficient particulars to identify the tree) on the local planning authority in whose area the tree is or was situated; and

(b) that he did the act in question—

(i) with the consent of the local planning authority in whose area the tree is or was situated, or

(ii) after the expiry of the period of six weeks from the date of the notice but before the expiry of the period of two years from that date.

(4) Section 210 shall apply to an offence under this section as it applies to a contravention of a tree preservation order.   **[218]**

NOTES
    Commencement: 24 August 1990.

212. Power to disapply s 211

(1) The Secretary of State may by regulations direct that section 211 shall not apply in such cases as may be specified in the regulations.

(2) Without prejudice to the generality of subsection (1), the regulations may be framed so as to exempt from the application of that section cases defined by reference to all or any of the following matters—

(a) acts of such descriptions or done in such circumstances or subject to such conditions as may be specified in the regulations;

(b) trees in such conservation areas as may be so specified;

(c) trees of a size or species so specified; or

(d) trees belonging to persons or bodies of a description so specified.

(3) The regulations may, in relation to any matter by reference to which an exemption is conferred by them, make different provision for different circumstances.

(4) Regulations under subsection (1) may in particular, but without prejudice to the generality of that subsection, exempt from the application of section 211 cases exempted from section 198 by subsection (6) of that section.   **[219]**

NOTES
    Commencement: 24 August 1990.

213. Enforcement of controls as respects trees in conservation areas

(1) If any tree to which section 211 applies—

(a) is removed, uprooted or destroyed in contravention of that section; or

(b) is removed, uprooted or destroyed or dies at a time when its cutting down or uprooting is authorised only by virtue of the provisions of such regulations under subsection (1) of section 212 as are mentioned in subsection (4) of that section,

it shall be the duty of the owner of the land to plant another tree of an appropriate size and species at the same place as soon as he reasonably can.

(2) The duty imposed by subsection (1) does not apply to an owner if on application by him the local planning authority dispense with it.

(3) The duty imposed by subsection (1) on the owner of any land attaches to the person who is from time to time the owner of the land and may be enforced as provided by section 207 and not otherwise. **[220]**

NOTES
Commencement: 24 August 1990.

214. Registers of s 211 notices

It shall be the duty of a local planning authority to compile and keep available for public inspection free of charge at all reasonable hours and at a convenient place a register containing such particulars as the Secretary of State may determine of notices under section 211 affecting trees in their area. **[221]**

NOTES
Commencement: 24 August 1990.

[Injunctions

214A. Injunctions

(1) Where a local planning authority consider it necessary or expedient for an actual or apprehended offence under section 210 or 211 to be restrained by injunction, they may apply to the court for an injunction, whether or not they have exercised or are proposing to exercise any of their other powers under this Chapter.

(2) Subsections (2) to (4) of section 187B apply to an application under this section as they apply to an application under that section.] **[221A]**

NOTES
Commencement: 25 November 1991 (certain purposes); 2 January 1992 (remaining purposes).
This section, ss 214B–214D, and the cross-heading immediately preceeding this section, inserted by the Planning and Compensation Act 1991, s 23(7).

[Rights of entry

214B. Rights to enter without warrant

(1) Any person duly authorised in writing by a local planning authority may enter any land for the purpose of—

(a) surveying it in connection with making or confirming a tree preservation order with respect to the land;
(b) ascertaining whether an offence under section 210 or 211 has been committed on the land; or
(c) determining whether a notice under section 207 should be served on the owner of the land,

if there are reasonable grounds for entering for the purpose in question.

(2) Any person duly authorised in writing by the Secretary of State may enter any land for the purpose of surveying it in connection with making, amending or revoking a tree preservation order with respect to the land, if there are reasonable grounds for entering for that purpose.

(3) Any person who is duly authorised in writing by a local planning authority may enter any land in connection with the exercise of any functions conferred on the authority by or under this Chapter.

(4) Any person who is an officer of the Valuation Office may enter any land for the purpose of surveying it, or estimating its value, in connection with a claim for compensation in respect of any land which is payable by the local planning authority under this Chapter (other than section 204).

(5) Any person who is duly authorised in writing by the Secretary of State may enter any land in connection with the exercise of any functions conferred on the Secretary of State by or under this Chapter.

(6) The Secretary of State shall not authorise any person as mentioned in subsection (2) without consulting the local planning authority.

(7) Admission shall not be demanded as of right—

(a) by virtue of subsection (1) or (2) to any building used as a dwellinghouse; or

(b) by virtue of subsection (3), (4) or (5) to any land which is occupied,

unless twenty-four hours' notice of the intended entry has been given to the occupier.

(8) Any right to enter by virtue of this section shall be exercised at a reasonable hour.]   **[221B]**

NOTES
Commencement: 2 January 1992.
Inserted as noted to s 214A at **[221A]**.

214C. Right to enter under warrant

(1) If it is shown to the satisfaction of a justice of the peace on sworn information in writing—

(a) that there are reasonable grounds for entering any land for any of the purposes mentioned in section 214B(1) or (2); and

(b) that—

(i) admission to the land has been refused, or a refusal is reasonably apprehended; or

(ii) the case is one of urgency,

the justice may issue a warrant authorising any person duly authorised in writing by a local planning authority or, as the case may be, the Secretary of State to enter the land.

(2) For the purposes of subsection (1)(b)(i) admission to land shall be regarded as having been refused if no reply is received to a request for admission within a reasonable period.

(3) A warrant authorises entry on one occasion only and that entry must be—

(a) within one month from the date of the issue of the warrant; and

(b) at a reasonable hour, unless the case is one of urgency.]   **[221C]**

NOTES
Commencement: 2 January 1992.
Inserted as noted to s 214A at **[221A]**.

214D. Rights of entry: supplementary provisions

(1) Any power conferred under or by virtue of section 214B or 214C to enter land (referred to in this section as "a right of entry") shall be construed as including power to take samples from any tree and samples of the soil.

(2) A person authorised to enter land in the exercise of a right of entry—

    (a) shall, if so required, produce evidence of his authority and state the purpose of his entry before so entering;

    (b) may take with him such other persons as may be necessary; and

    (c) on leaving the land shall, if the owner or occupier is not then present, leave it as effectively secured against trespassers as he found it.

(3) Any person who wilfully obstructs a person acting in the exercise of a right of entry shall be guilty of an offence and liable on summary conviction to a fine not exceeding level 3 on the standard scale.

(4) If any damage is caused to land or chattels in the exercise of a right of entry, compensation may be recovered by any person suffering the damage from the authority who gave the written authority for the entry or, as the case may be, the Secretary of State.

(5) The provisions of section 118 shall apply in relation to compensation under subsection (4) as they apply in relation to compensation under Part IV.]   **[221D]**

NOTES
Commencement: 2 January 1992.
Inserted as noted to s 214A at **[221A]**.

CHAPTER II

LAND ADVERSELY AFFECTING AMENITY OF NEIGHBOURHOOD

215. Power to require proper maintenance of land

(1) If it appears to the local planning authority that the amenity of a part of their area, or of an adjoining area, is adversely affected by the condition of land in their area, they may serve on the owner and occupier of the land a notice under this section.

(2) The notice shall require such steps for remedying the condition of the land as may be specified in the notice to be taken within such period as may be so specified.

(3) Subject to the following provisions of this Chapter, the notice shall take effect at the end of such period as may be specified in the notice.

(4) That period shall not be less than 28 days after the service of the notice.

[222]

NOTES
Commencement: 24 August 1990.

216. Penalty for non-compliance with s 215 notice

(1) The provisions of this section shall have effect where a notice has been served under section 215.

(2) If any owner or occupier of the land on whom the notice was served fails to take steps required by the notice within the period specified in it for compliance with it, he shall be guilty of an offence and liable on summary conviction to a fine not exceeding level 3 on the standard scale.

(3) Where proceedings have been brought under subsection (2) against a person as the owner of the land and he has, at some time before the end of the compliance period, ceased to be the owner of the land, if he—

    (a) duly lays information to that effect, and
    (b) gives the prosecution not less than three clear days' notice of his intention,

he shall be entitled to have the person who then became the owner of the land brought before the court in the proceedings.

(4) Where proceedings have been brought under subsection (2) against a person as the occupier of the land and he has, at some time before the end of the compliance period, ceased to be the occupier of the land, if he—

    (a) duly lays information to that effect, and
    (b) gives the prosecution not less than three clear days' notice of his intention,

he shall be entitled to have brought before the court in the proceedings the person who then became the occupier of the land or, if nobody then became the occupier, the person who is the owner at the date of the notice.

(5) Where in such proceedings—

    (a) it has been proved that any steps required by the notice under section 215 have not been taken within the compliance period, and
    (b) the original defendant proves that the failure to take those steps was attributable, in whole or in part, to the default of a person specified in a notice under subsection (3) or (4)—

then—

    (i) that person may be convicted of the offence; and
    (ii) if the original defendant also proves that he took all reasonable steps to ensure compliance with the notice, he shall be acquitted of the offence.

(6) If, after a person has been convicted under the previous provisions of this section, he does not as soon as practicable do everything in his power to secure compliance with the notice, he shall be guilty of a further offence and liable on summary conviction to a fine not exceeding [one-tenth of level 3 on the standard scale] for each day following his first conviction on which any of the requirements of the notice remain unfulfilled.

(7) Any reference in this section to the compliance period, in relation to a notice, is a reference to the period specified in the notice for compliance with it or such extended period as the local planning authority who served the notice may allow for compliance. **[223]**

NOTES

    Commencement: 24 August 1990.
    Words in square brackets in sub-s (6) substituted by the Planning and Compensation Act 1991, s 32, Sch 7, paras 8, 35.

217. Appeal to magistrates' court against s 215 notice

(1) A person on whom a notice under section 215 is served, or any other person having an interest in the land to which the notice relates, may, at any time within the period specified in the notice as the period at the end of which it is to take effect, appeal against the notice on any of the following grounds—

(a) that the condition of the land to which the notice relates does not adversely affect the amenity of any part of the area of the local planning authority who served the notice, or of any adjoining area;

(b) that the condition of the land to which the notice relates is attributable to, and such as results in the ordinary course of events from, the carrying on of operations or a use of land which is not in contravention of Part III;

(c) that the requirements of the notice exceed what is necessary for preventing the condition of the land from adversely affecting the amenity of any part of the area of the local planning authority who served the notice, or of any adjoining area;

(d) that the period specified in the notice as the period within which any steps required by the notice are to be taken falls short of what should reasonably be allowed.

(2) Any appeal under this section shall be made to a magistrates' court acting for the petty sessions area in which the land in question is situated.

(3) Where such an appeal is brought, the notice to which it relates shall be of no effect pending the final determination or withdrawal of the appeal.

(4) On such an appeal the magistrates' court may correct any informality, defect or error in the notice if satisfied that the informality, defect or error is not material.

(5) On the determination of such an appeal the magistrates' court shall give directions for giving effect to their determination, including, where appropriate, directions for quashing the notice or for varying the terms of the notice in favour of the appellant.

(6) Where any person has appealed to a magistrates' court under this section against a notice, neither that person nor any other shall be entitled, in any other proceedings instituted after the making of the appeal, to claim that the notice was not duly served on the person who appealed.   **[224]**

NOTES
Commencement: 24 August 1990.

218. Further appeal to the Crown Court

Where an appeal has been brought under section 217, an appeal against the decision of the magistrates' court on that appeal may be brought to the Crown Court by the appellant or by the local planning authority who served the notice in question under section 215.   **[225]**

NOTES
Commencement: 24 August 1990.

219. Execution and cost of works required by s 215 notice

(1) If, within the period specified in a notice under section 215 in accordance with subsection (2) of that section, or within such extended period as the local planning authority who served the notice may allow, any steps required by the notice to be taken have not been taken, the local planning authority who served the notice may—

(a) enter the land and take those steps, and

(b) recover from the person who is then the owner of the land any expenses reasonably incurred by them in doing so.

(2) Where a notice has been served under section 215—

(a) any expenses incurred by the owner or occupier of any land for the purpose of complying with the notice, and

(b) any sums paid by the owner of any land under subsection (1) in respect of expenses incurred by the local planning authority in taking steps required by such a notice,

shall be deemed to be incurred or paid for the use and at the request of the person who caused or permitted the land to come to be in the condition in which it was when the notice was served.

(3) Regulations made under this Act may provide that—

(a) section 276 of the Public Health Act 1936 (power of local authorities to sell materials removed in executing works under that Act subject to accounting for the proceeds of sale);

(b) section 289 of that Act (power to require the occupier of any premises to permit works to be executed by the owner of the premises); or

(c) section 294 of that Act (limit on liability of persons holding premises as agents or trustees in respect of the expenses recoverable under that Act),

shall apply, subject to such adaptations and modifications as may be specified in the regulations, in relation to any steps required to be taken by a notice under section 215.

(4) Regulations under subsection (3) applying section 289 of the Public Health Act 1936 may include adaptations and modifications for the purpose of giving the owner of land to which a notice under section 215 relates the right, as against all other persons interested in the land, to comply with the requirements of the enforcement notice.

(5) Regulations under subsection (3) may also provide for the charging on the land of any expenses recoverable by a local authority under subsection (1).

(6) . . .   [226]

___

NOTES

Commencement: 24 August 1990.

Sub-s (6) repealed by the Planning and Compensation Act 1991, ss 32, 84(6), Sch 7, paras 8, 36, Sch 19, Pt I.

___

CHAPTER III

ADVERTISEMENTS

Advertisement regulations

220. Regulations controlling display of advertisements

(1) Regulations under this Act shall make provision for restricting or regulating the display of advertisements so far as appears to the Secretary of State to be expedient in the interests of amenity or public safety.

(2) Without prejudice to the generality of subsection (1), any such regulations may provide—

(a) for regulating the dimensions, appearance and position of advertisements which may be displayed, the sites on which advertisements may be displayed and the manner in which they are to be affixed to the land;

(b) for requiring the consent of the local planning authority to be obtained for the display of advertisements, or of advertisements of any class specified in the regulations;

(c) for applying, in relation to any such consent and to applications for such consent, any of the provisions mentioned in subsection (3), subject to such adaptations and modifications as may be specified in the regulations;

(d) for the constitution, for the purposes of the regulations, of such advisory committees as may be prescribed by the regulations, and for determining the manner in which the expenses of any such committee are to be defrayed.

(3) The provisions referred to in subsection (2)(c) are—

(a) the provisions of Part III relating to planning permission and to applications for planning permission, except sections 56, 62, 65 . . . , 69(3) and (4), 71, . . . , 91 to 96, 100 and 101 and Schedule 8;

(b) sections 137 to 141, 143 and 144 (except so far as they relate to purchase notices served in consequence of such orders as are mentioned in section 137(1)(b) or (c));

(c) section 316.

(4) Without prejudice to the generality of the powers conferred by this section, regulations made for the purposes of this section may provide that any appeal from the decision of the local planning authority, on an application for their consent under the regulations, shall be to an independent tribunal constituted in accordance with the regulations, instead of being an appeal to the Secretary of State.

(5) If any tribunal is so constituted, the Secretary of State may pay to the chairman and members of the tribunal such remuneration, whether by way of salaries or by way of fees, and such reasonable allowances in respect of expenses properly incurred in the performance of their duties, as he may with the consent of the Treasury determine.   **[227]**

NOTES

Commencement: 24 August 1990.

Words omitted from sub-s (3)(a) repealed by the Planning and Compensation Act 1991, ss 31(4), 32, 84(6), Sch 6, paras 8, 21, Sch 7, paras 8, 37, Sch 19, Pts I, II.

221. Power to make different advertisement regulations for different areas

(1) Regulations made for the purposes of section 220 may make different provision with respect to different areas, and in particular may make special provision—

(a) with respect to conservation areas;

(b) with respect to areas defined for the purposes of the regulations as experimental areas, and

(c) with respect to areas defined for the purposes of the regulations as areas of special control.

(2) An area may be defined as an experimental area for a prescribed period for the purpose of assessing the effect on amenity or public safety of advertisements of a prescribed description.

(3) An area may be defined as an area of special control if it is—

(a) a rural area, or

(b) an area which appears to the Secretary of State to require special protection on grounds of amenity.

(4) Without prejudice to the generality of subsection (1), the regulations may prohibit the display in an area of special control of all advertisements except advertisements of such classes (if any) as may be prescribed.

(5) Areas of special control for the purposes of regulations under this section may be defined by means of orders made or approved by the Secretary of State in accordance with the provisions of the regulations.

(6) Where the Secretary of State is authorised by the regulations to make or approve any such order as is mentioned in subsection (5), the regulations shall provide—

(a) for the publication of notice of the proposed order in such manner as may be prescribed,
(b) for the consideration of objections duly made to it, and
(c) for the holding of such inquiries or other hearings as may be prescribed,

before the order is made or approved.

(7) *Subject to subsection (8), regulations made under section 220 may be made so as to apply—*

(a) *to advertisements which are being displayed on the date on which the regulations come into force, or*
(b) *to the use for the display of the advertisements of any site which was being used for that purpose on that date.*

(8) *Any regulations made in accordance with subsection (7) shall provide for exempting from them—*

(a) *the continued display of any such advertisements as there mentioned; and*
(b) *the continued use for the display of advertisements of any such site as there mentioned,*

during such period as may be prescribed.

(9) *Different periods may be prescribed under subsection (8) for the purposes of different provisions of the regulations.* **[228]**

NOTES
Commencement: 24 August 1990.
Sub-ss (7)–(9) repealed by the Planning and Compensation Act 1991, s 84(6), Sch 19, Pt I, as from a day to be appointed.

222. Planning permission not needed for advertisements complying with regulations

Where the display of advertisements in accordance with regulations made under section 220 involves development of land—

(a) planning permission for that development shall be deemed to be granted by virtue of this section, and
(b) no application shall be necessary for that development under Part III.

[229]

NOTES
Commencement: 24 August 1990.

Repayment of expense of removing prohibited advertisements

223. Repayment of expense of removing prohibited advertisements

(1) Where, for the purpose of complying with any regulations made under section 220, works are carried out by any person—

(a) for removing an advertisement which was being displayed on 1st August 1948; or

(b) for discontinuing the use for the display of advertisements of a site used for that purpose on that date,

that person shall, on a claim made to the local planning authority within such time and in such manner as may be prescribed, be entitled to recover from that authority compensation in respect of any expenses reasonably incurred by him in carrying out those works.

(2) Except in so far as may be otherwise provided by any regulations made under this Act, any question of disputed compensation under this section shall be referred to and determined by the Lands Tribunal.

(3) In relation to the determination of any such question, the provisions of sections 2 and 4 of the Land Compensation Act 1961 shall apply subject to any necessary modifications and to the provisions of any regulations made under this Act.   **[230]**

NOTES
Commencement: 24 August 1990.

Enforcement of control over advertisements

224. Enforcement of control as to advertisements

(1) Regulations under section 220 may make provision for enabling the local planning authority to require—

(a) the removal of any advertisement which is displayed in contravention of the regulations, or

(b) the discontinuance of the use for the display of advertisements of any site which is being so used in contravention of the regulations.

(2) For that purpose the regulations may apply any of the provisions of Part VII with respect to enforcement notices or the provisions of section 186, subject to such adaptations and modifications as may be specified in the regulations.

(3) Without prejudice to any provisions included in such regulations by virtue of subsection (1) or (2), if any person displays an advertisement in contravention of the regulations he shall be guilty of an offence and liable on summary conviction to a fine of such amount as may be prescribed, not exceeding level 3 on the standard scale and, in the case of a continuing offence, [one-tenth of level 3 on the standard scale] for each day during which the offence continues after conviction.

(4) Without prejudice to the generality of subsection (3), a person shall be deemed to display an advertisement for the purposes of that subsection if—

(a) he is the owner or occupier of the land on which the advertisement is displayed; or

(b) the advertisement gives publicity to his goods, trade, business or other concerns.

(5) A person shall not be guilty of an offence under subsection (3) by reason only—

(a) of his being the owner or occupier of the land on which an advertisement is displayed, or

(b) of his goods, trade, business or other concerns being given publicity by the advertisement,

if he proves that it was displayed without his knowledge or consent. **[231]**

NOTES

Commencement: 24 August 1990.

Words in square brackets in sub-s (3) substituted by the Planning and Compensation Act 1991, s 32, Sch 7, paras 8, 38.

225. Power to remove or obliterate placards and posters

(1) Subject to subsections (2) and (3), the local planning authority may remove or obliterate any placard or poster—

(a) which is displayed in their area; and

(b) which in their opinion is so displayed in contravention of regulations made under section 220.

(2) Subsection (1) does not authorise the removal or obliteration of a placard or poster displayed within a building to which there is no public right of access.

(3) Subject to subsection (4), where a placard or poster identifies the person who displayed it or caused it to be displayed, the local planning authority shall not exercise any power conferred by subsection (1) unless they have first given him notice in writing—

(a) that in their opinion it is displayed in contravention of regulations made under section 220; and

(b) that they intend to remove or obliterate it on the expiry of a period specified in the notice.

(4) Subsection (3) does not apply if—

(a) the placard or poster does not give his address, and

(b) the authority do not know it and are unable to ascertain it after reasonable inquiry.

(5) The period specified in a notice under subsection (3) must be not less than two days from the date of service of the notice. **[232]**

NOTES

Commencement: 24 August 1990.

PART IX

ACQUISITION AND APPROPRIATION OF LAND FOR PLANNING PURPOSES, ETC

Acquisition for planning and public purposes

226. Compulsory acquisition of land for development and other planning purposes

(1) A local authority to whom this section applies shall, on being authorised to do so by the Secretary of State, have power to acquire compulsorily any land in their area which—

(a) is suitable for and required in order to secure the carrying out of development, redevelopment or improvement; or
(b) is required for a purpose which it is necessary to achieve in the interests of the proper planning of an area in which the land is situated.

(2) A local authority and the Secretary of State in considering for the purposes of subsection (1)(a) whether land is suitable for development, redevelopment or improvement shall have regard—

(a) to the provisions of the development plan, so far as material;
(b) to whether planning permission for any development on the land is in force; and
(c) to any other considerations which would be material for the purpose of determining an application for planning permission for development on the land.

(3) Where a local authority exercise their power under subsection (1) in relation to any land, they shall, on being authorised to do so by the Secretary of State, have power to acquire compulsorily—

(a) any land adjoining that land which is required for the purpose of executing works for facilitating its development or use; or
(b) where that land forms part of a common or open space or fuel or field garden allotment, any land which is required for the purpose of being given in exchange for the land which is being acquired.

(4) It is immaterial by whom the local authority propose that any activity or purpose mentioned in subsection (1) or (3)(a) should be undertaken or achieved (and in particular the local authority need not propose to undertake an activity or to achieve that purpose themselves).

(5) Where under subsection (1) the Secretary of State has power to authorise a local authority to whom this section applies to acquire any land compulsorily he may, after the requisite consultation, authorise the land to be so acquired by another authority, being a local authority within the meaning of this Act.

(6) Before giving an authorisation under subsection (5), the Secretary of State shall—

(a) if the land is in a non-metropolitan county [in England], consult with the councils of the county and the district;
(b) if the land is in a metropolitan district, consult with the council of the district;
[(bb) if the land is in Wales, consult with the council of the county or county borough;] and
(c) if the land is in a London borough, consult with the council of the borough.

(7) The Acquisition of Land Act 1981 shall apply to the compulsory acquisition of land under this section.

(8) The local authorities to whom this section applies are the councils of counties, [county boroughs,] districts and London boroughs.   **[233]**

NOTES
  Commencement: 24 August 1990.
  Words in square brackets in sub-ss (6), (8) inserted by the Local Government (Wales) Act 1994, s 20(4)(b), Sch 6, Pt II, para 24(6), as from a day to be appointed.

227. Acquisition of land by agreement

(1) The council of any county, [county borough,] district or London borough may acquire by agreement any land which they require for any purpose for which a local authority may be authorised to acquire land under section 226.

(2) The provisions of Part I of the Compulsory Purchase Act 1965 (so far as applicable), other than sections 4 to 8, section 10 and section 31, shall apply in relation to the acquisition of land under this section.   **[234]**

NOTES

Commencement: 24 August 1990.

Words in square brackets in sub-s (1) inserted by the Local Government (Wales) Act 1994, s 20(4)(b), Sch 6, Pt II, para 24(7), as from a day to be appointed.

228. Compulsory acquisition of land by the Secretary of State for the Environment

(1) The Secretary of State for the Environment may acquire compulsorily—

    (a) any land necessary for the public service; and

    (b) any land which it is proposed to use not only for the public service but also—

        (i) to meet the interests of proper planning of the area, or

        (ii) to secure the best or most economic development or use of the land, otherwise than for the public service.

(2) Where the Secretary of State has acquired or proposes to acquire any land under subsection (1) ("the primary land") and in his opinion other land ought to be acquired together with the primary land—

    (a) in the interests of the proper planning of the area concerned; or

    (b) for the purpose of ensuring that the primary land can be used, or developed and used, (together with that other land) in what appears to him to be the best or most economic way; or

    (c) where the primary land or any land acquired, or which he proposes to acquire, by virtue of paragraph (a) or (b) of this subsection or of section 122(1)(a) or (b) of the Local Government, Planning and Land Act 1980, forms part of a common, open space or fuel or field garden allotment, for the purpose of being given in exchange for that land,

he may compulsorily acquire that other land.

(3) Subject to subsection (4), the power of acquiring land compulsorily under this section shall include power to acquire an easement or other right over land by the grant of a new right.

(4) Subsection (3) shall not apply to an easement or other right over any land which would for the purposes of the Acquisition of Land Act 1981 form part of a common, open space or fuel or field garden allotment.

(5) References in this section to the public service include the service in the United Kingdom—

    (a) of any international organisation or institution whether or not the United Kingdom or Her Majesty's Government in the United Kingdom is or is to become a member;

    (b) of any office or agency established by such an organisation or institution or for its purposes, or established in pursuance of a treaty (whether or not the United Kingdom is or is to become a party to the treaty);

(c) of a foreign sovereign Power or the Government of such a Power.

(6) For the purposes of subsection (5)(b) "treaty" includes any international agreement and any protocol or annex to a treaty or international agreement.

(7) The Acquisition of Land Act 1981 shall apply to any compulsory acquisition by the Secretary of State for the Environment under this section. **[235]**

NOTES
Commencement: 24 August 1990.

229. Appropriation of land forming part of common, etc

(1) Any local authority may be authorised, by an order made by that authority and confirmed by the Secretary of State, to appropriate for any purpose for which that authority can be authorised to acquire land under any enactment any land to which this subsection applies which is for the time being held by them for other purposes.

(2) Subsection (1) applies to land which is or forms part of a common or fuel or field garden allotment (including any such land which is specially regulated by any enactment, whether public general or local or private), other than land which is Green Belt land within the meaning of the Green Belt (London and Home Counties) Act 1938.

(3) Section 19 of the Acquisition of Land Act 1981 (special provision with respect to compulsory purchase orders under that Act relating to land forming part of a common, open space or fuel or field garden allotment) shall apply to an order under this section authorising the appropriation of land as it applies to a compulsory purchase order under that Act.

(4) Where land appropriated under this section was acquired under an enactment incorporating the Lands Clauses Acts, any works executed on the land after the appropriation has been effected shall, for the purposes of section 68 of the Lands Clauses Consolidation Act 1845 and section 10 of the Compulsory Purchase Act 1965, be deemed to have been authorised by the enactment under which the land was acquired.

(5) On an appropriation of land by a local authority under this section, where—

 (a) the authority is not an authority to whom Part II of the 1959 Act applies;
 (b) the land was immediately before the appropriation held by the authority for the purposes of a grant-aided function (within the meaning of that Act); or
 (c) the land is appropriated by the authority for the purposes of such a function,

such adjustments shall be made in the accounts of the local authority as the Secretary of State may direct.

(6) On an appropriation under this section which does not fall within subsection (5), such adjustment of accounts shall be made as is required by section 24(1) of the 1959 Act. **[236]**

NOTES
Commencement: 24 August 1990.
1959 Act: Town and Country Planning Act 1959.

230. Acquisition of land for purposes of exchange

(1) Without prejudice to the generality of the powers conferred by sections 226 and 227, any power of a local authority to acquire land under those sections, whether compulsorily or by agreement, shall include power to acquire land required for giving in exchange—

    (a) for land appropriated under section 229; or

    (b) for Green Belt land appropriated in accordance with the Green Belt (London and Home Counties) Act 1938 for any purpose specified in a development plan.

(2) In subsection (1) "Green Belt land" has the same meaning as in that Act.

[237]

NOTES

Commencement: 24 August 1990.

231. Power of Secretary of State to require acquisition or development of land

(1) If the Secretary of State is satisfied after holding a local inquiry that the council of a county, [county borough,] district or London borough have failed to take steps for the acquisition of any land which in his opinion ought to be acquired by them under section 226 . . . , he may by order require the council to take such steps as may be specified in the order for acquiring the land.

(2) If the Secretary of State is satisfied after holding a local inquiry that a local authority have failed to carry out, on land acquired by them under section 226 (or section 68 of the 1962 Act or section 112 of the 1971 Act) or appropriated by them under section 229 (or section 121 of the 1971 Act), any development which in his opinion ought to be carried out, he may by order require the authority to take such steps as may be specified in the order for carrying out the development.

(3) An order under this section shall be enforceable on the application of the Secretary of State by mandamus. **[238]**

NOTES

Commencement: 24 August 1990.

Words omitted from sub-s (1) repealed by the Planning and Compensation Act 1991, ss 70, 84(6), Sch 15, Pt II, para 29, Sch 19, Pt III.

Words in square brackets in sub-s (1) inserted by the Local Government (Wales) Act 1994, s 20(4)(b), Sch 6, Pt II, para 24(8), as from a day to be appointed.

1962 Act: Town and Country Planning Act 1962.

1971 Act: Town and Country Planning Act 1971.

Appropriation, disposal and development of land held for planning purposes, etc

232. Appropriation of land held for planning purposes

(1) Where any land has been acquired or appropriated by a local authority for planning purposes and is for the time being held by them for the purposes for which it was so acquired or appropriated, the authority may appropriate the land for any purpose for which they are or may be authorised in any capacity to acquire land by virtue of or under any enactment not contained in this Part or in Chapter V of Part I of the Planning (Listed Buildings and Conservation Areas) Act 1990.

(2) Land which consists or forms part of a common, or formerly consisted or formed part of a common, and is held or managed by a local authority in accordance with a local Act shall not be appropriated under this section without the consent of the Secretary of State.

(3) Such consent may be given—

    (a) either in respect of a particular appropriation or in respect of appropriations of any class, and

    (b) either subject to or free from any conditions or limitations.

(4) Before appropriating under this section any land which consists of or forms part of an open space, a local authority—

    (a) shall publish a notice of their intention to do so for at least two consecutive weeks in a newspaper circulating in their area; and

    (b) shall consider any objections to the proposed appropriation which may be made to them.

(5) In relation to any appropriation under this section—

    (a) subsection (4) of section 122 of the Local Government Act 1972 (which relates to the operation of section 68 of the Lands Clauses Consolidation Act 1845 and section 10 of the Compulsory Purchase Act 1965) shall have effect as it has effect in relation to appropriations under section 122 of that Act of 1972; and

    (b) subsections (5) and (6) of section 229 of this Act shall have effect as they have effect in relation to appropriations under that section.

(6) In relation to any such land as is mentioned in subsection (1), this section shall have effect to the exclusion of the provisions of section 122(1) of the Local Government Act 1972.   **[239]**

NOTES

Commencement: 24 August 1990.

233. Disposal by local authorities of land held for planning purposes

(1) Where any land has been acquired or appropriated by a local authority for planning purposes and is for the time being held by them for the purposes for which it was so acquired or appropriated, the authority may dispose of the land to such person, in such manner and subject to such conditions as appear to them to be expedient in order—

    (a) to secure the best use of that or other land and any buildings or works which have been, or are to be, erected, constructed or carried out on it (whether by themselves or by any other person), or

    (b) to secure the erection, construction or carrying out on it of any buildings or works appearing to them to be needed for the proper planning of the area of the authority.

(2) Land which consists of or forms part of a common, or formerly consisted or formed part of a common, and is held or managed by a local authority in accordance with a local Act shall not be disposed of under this section without the consent of the Secretary of State.

(3) The consent of the Secretary of State is also required where the disposal is to be for a consideration less than the best that can reasonably be obtained and is not—

    (a) the grant of a term of seven years or less; or

    (b) the assignment of a term of years of which seven years or less are unexpired at the date of the assignment.

(4) Before disposing under this section of any land which consists of or forms part of an open space, a local authority—

(a) shall publish a notice of their intention to do so for at least two consecutive weeks in a newspaper circulating in their area; and

(b) shall consider any objections to the proposed disposal which may be made to them.

(5) In relation to land acquired or appropriated for planning purposes for a reason mentioned in section 226(1)(a) or (3) the powers conferred by this section on a local authority, and on the Secretary of State in respect of the giving of consent to disposals under this section, shall be so exercised as to secure to relevant occupiers, so far as may be practicable, a suitable opportunity for accommodation.

(6) A person is a relevant occupier for the purposes of subsection (5) if—

(a) he was living or carrying on business or other activities on any such land as is mentioned in that subsection which the authority have acquired as mentioned in subsection (1),

(b) he desires to obtain accommodation on such land, and

(c) he is willing to comply with any requirements of the authority as to the development and use of such land;

and in this subsection ''development'' includes redevelopment.

(7) In subsection (5) a suitable opportunity for accommodation means, in relation to any person, an opportunity to obtain accommodation on the land in question which is suitable to his reasonable requirements on terms settled with due regard to the price at which any such land has been acquired from him.

(8) In relation to any such land as is mentioned in subsection (1), this section shall have effect to the exclusion of section 123 of the Local Government Act 1972 (disposal of land by principal councils). **[240]**

NOTES
Commencement: 24 August 1990.

234. Disposal by Secretary of State of land acquired under s 228

(1) The Secretary of State may dispose of land held by him and acquired by him or any other Minister under section 228 to such person, in such manner and subject to such conditions as appear to him expedient.

(2) In particular, the Secretary of State may under subsection (1) dispose of land held by him for any purpose in order to secure its use for that purpose. **[241]**

NOTES
Commencement: 24 August 1990.

235. Development of land held for planning purposes

(1) A local authority may—

(a) erect, construct or carry out on any land to which this section applies any building or work other than a building or work for the erection, construction or carrying out of which, whether by that local authority or by any other person, statutory power exists by virtue of, or could be conferred under, an alternative enactment; and

(b) repair, maintain and insure any buildings or works on such land and generally deal with such land in a proper course of management.

(2) This section applies to any land which—

(a) has been acquired or appropriated by a local authority for planning purposes, and

(b) is for the time being held by the authority for the purposes for which it was so acquired or appropriated.

(3) A local authority may exercise the powers conferred by subsection (1) notwithstanding any limitation imposed by law on their capacity by virtue of their constitution.

(4) A local authority may enter into arrangements with an authorised association for the carrying out by the association of any operation which, apart from the arrangements, the local authority would have power under this section to carry out, on such terms (including terms as to the making of payments or loans by the authority to the association) as may be specified in the arrangements.

(5) Nothing in this section shall be construed—

(a) as authorising any act or omission on the part of a local authority which is actionable at the suit of any person on any grounds other than such a limitation as is mentioned in subsection (3); or

(b) as authorising an authorised association to carry out any operation which they would not have power to carry out apart from subsection (4).

(6) In this section—

"alternative enactment" means any enactment which is not contained in this Part, in section 2, 5 or 6 of the Local Authorities (Land) Act 1963, in section 14(1) or (4) or 17(3) of the Industrial Development Act 1982 or in Chapter V of Part I of the Planning (Listed Buildings and Conservation Areas) Act 1990; and

"authorised association" means any society, company or body of persons—

(a) whose objects include the promotion, formation or management of garden cities, garden suburbs or garden villages and the erection, improvement or management of buildings for the working classes and others, and

(b) which does not trade for profit or whose constitution forbids the issue of any share or loan capital with interest or dividend exceeding the rate for the time being fixed by the Treasury.   **[242]**

NOTES
   Commencement: 24 August 1990.

Extinguishment of certain rights affecting acquired or appropriated land

236. Extinguishment of rights over land compulsorily acquired

(1) Subject to the provisions of this section, upon the completion of a compulsory acquisition of land under section 226, 228 or 230—

(a) all private rights of way and rights of laying down, erecting, continuing or maintaining any apparatus on, under or over the land shall be extinguished, and

(b) any such apparatus shall vest in the acquiring authority.

(2) Subsection (1) shall not apply—

(a) to any right vested in, or apparatus belonging to, statutory undertakers for the purpose of the carrying on of their undertaking, or

(b) to any right conferred by or in accordance with the telecommunications code on the operator of a telecommunications code system, or

(c) to any telecommunications apparatus kept installed for the purposes of any such system.

(3) In respect of any right or apparatus not falling within subsection (2), subsection (1) shall have effect subject—

(a) to any direction given by the acquiring authority before the completion of the acquisition that subsection (1) shall not apply to any right or apparatus specified in the direction; and

(b) to any agreement which may be made (whether before or after the completion of the acquisition) between the acquiring authority and the person in or to whom the right or apparatus in question is vested or belongs.

(4) Any person who suffers loss by the extinguishment of a right or the vesting of any apparatus under this section shall be entitled to compensation from the acquiring authority.

(5) Any compensation payable under this section shall be determined in accordance with the Land Compensation Act 1961. **[243]**

NOTES
Commencement: 24 August 1990.

237. Power to override easements and other rights

(1) Subject to subsection (3), the erection, construction or carrying out or maintenance of any building or work on land which has been acquired or appropriated by a local authority for planning purposes (whether done by the local authority or by a person deriving title under them) is authorised by virtue of this section if it is done in accordance with planning permission, notwithstanding that it involves—

(a) interference with an interest or right to which this section applies, or

(b) a breach of a restriction as to the user of land arising by virtue of a contract.

(2) Subject to subsection (3), the interests and rights to which this section applies are any easement, liberty, privilege, right or advantage annexed to land and adversely affecting other land, including any natural right to support.

(3) Nothing in this section shall authorise interference with any right of way or right of laying down, erecting, continuing or maintaining apparatus on, under or over land which is—

(a) a right vested in or belonging to statutory undertakers for the purpose of the carrying on of their undertaking, or

(b) a right conferred by or in accordance with the telecommunications code on the operator of a telecommunications code system.

(4) In respect of any interference or breach in pursuance of subsection (1), compensation—

(a) shall be payable under section 63 or 68 of the Lands Clauses Consolidation Act 1845 or under section 7 or 10 of the Compulsory Purchase Act 1965, and

(b) shall be assessed in the same manner and subject to the same rules as in the case of other compensation under those sections in respect of injurious affection where—

(i) the compensation is to be estimated in connection with a purchase under those Acts, or

(ii) the injury arises from the execution of works on land acquired under those Acts.

(5) Where a person deriving title under the local authority by whom the land in question was acquired or appropriated—

    (a) is liable to pay compensation by virtue of subsection (4), and
    (b) fails to discharge that liability,

the liability shall be enforceable against the local authority.

(6) Nothing in subsection (5) shall be construed as affecting any agreement between the local authority and any other person for indemnifying the local authority against any liability under that subsection.

(7) Nothing in this section shall be construed as authorising any act or omission on the part of any person which is actionable at the suit of any person on any grounds other than such an interference or breach as is mentioned in subsection (1).   **[244]**

NOTES
Commencement: 24 August 1990.

238. Use and development of consecrated land

(1) Notwithstanding any obligation or restriction imposed under ecclesiastical law or otherwise in respect of consecrated land, any such land, which has been the subject of a relevant acquisition or appropriation, may subject to the following provisions of this section—

    (a) if it has been acquired by a Minister, be used in any manner by him or on his behalf for any purpose for which he acquired the land; and
    (b) in any other case, be used by any person in any manner in accordance with planning permission.

(2) Subsection (1) applies whether or not the land includes a building but it does not apply to land which consists of or forms part of a burial ground.

(3) Any use of consecrated land authorised by subsection (1) shall be subject—

    (a) to compliance with the prescribed requirements with respect—

        (i) to the removal and reinterment of any human remains, and
        (ii) to the disposal of monuments and fixtures and furnishings; and

    (b) to such provisions as may be prescribed for prohibiting or restricting the use of the land, either absolutely or until the prescribed consent has been obtained, so long as any church or other building used or formerly used for religious worship, or any part of it, remains on the land.

(4) Any use of land other than consecrated land which—

    (a) has been the subject of a relevant acquisition or appropriation, and
    (b) at the time of acquisition or appropriation included a church or other building used or formerly used for religious worship or the site of such a church or building,

shall be subject to compliance with such requirements as are mentioned in subsection (3)(a).

(5) Any regulations made for the purposes of subsection (3) or (4)—

    (a) shall contain such provisions as appear to the Secretary of State to be requisite for securing that any use of land which is subject to compliance with the regulations shall, as nearly as may be, be subject to the same control as is imposed by law in the case of a similar use authorised by an enactment not contained in this Act or by a Measure, or as it would be proper to impose on a disposal of the land in question otherwise than in pursuance of an enactment or Measure;

(b) shall contain such requirements relating to the disposal of any such land as is mentioned in subsection (3) or (4) as appear to the Secretary of State requisite for securing that the provisions of those subsections are complied with in relation to the use of the land; and

(c) may contain such incidental and consequential provisions (including provision as to the closing of registers) as appear to the Secretary of State to be expedient for the purposes of the regulations.

(6) Nothing in this section shall be construed as authorising any act or omission on the part of any person which is actionable at the suit of any person on any grounds other than contravention of any such obligation, restriction or enactment as is mentioned in subsection (1).   **[245]**

NOTES
Commencement: 24 August 1990.

239. Use and development of burial grounds

(1) Notwithstanding anything in any enactment relating to burial grounds or any obligation or restriction imposed under ecclesiastical law or otherwise in respect of them, any land consisting of a burial ground or part of a burial ground, which has been the subject of a relevant acquisition or appropriation, may—

(a) if it has been acquired by a Minister, be used in any manner by him or on his behalf for any purpose for which he acquired the land; and

(b) in any other case, be used by any person in any manner in accordance with planning permission.

(2) This section does not apply to land which has been used for the burial of the dead until the prescribed requirements with respect to the removal and reinterment of human remains, and the disposal of monuments, in or upon the land have been complied with.

(3) Nothing in this section shall be construed as authorising any act or omission on the part of any person which is actionable at the suit of any person on any grounds other than contravention of any such enactment, obligation or restriction as is mentioned in subsection (1).   **[246]**

NOTES
Commencement: 24 August 1990.

240. Provisions supplemental to ss 238 and 239

(1) Provision shall be made by any regulations made for the purposes of sections 238(3) and (4) and 239(2)—

(a) for requiring the persons in whom the land is vested to publish notice of their intention to carry out the removal and reinterment of any human remains or the disposal of any monuments;

(b) for enabling the personal representatives or relatives of any deceased person themselves to undertake—

(i) the removal and reinterment of the remains of the deceased, and

(ii) the disposal of any monument commemorating the deceased,

and for requiring the persons in whom the land is vested to defray the expenses of such removal, reinterment and disposal (not exceeding such amount as may be prescribed);

(c) for requiring compliance—

    (i) with such reasonable conditions (if any) as may be imposed in the case of consecrated land, by the bishop of the diocese, with respect to the manner of removal and the place and manner of reinterment of any human remains and the disposal of any monuments, and

    (ii) with any directions given in any case by the Secretary of State with respect to the removal and reinterment of any human remains.

(2) Subject to the provisions of any such regulations, no faculty is required—

(a) for the removal and reinterment in accordance with the regulations of any human remains, or

(b) for the removal or disposal of any monuments,

and section 25 of the Burial Act 1857 (prohibition of removal of human remains without the licence of the Secretary of State except in certain cases) does not apply to a removal carried out in accordance with the regulations.

(3) In sections 238 and 239 and this section—

"burial ground" includes any churchyard, cemetery or other ground, whether consecrated or not, which has at any time been set apart for the purposes of interment,

"monument" includes a tombstone or other memorial, and

"relevant acquisition or appropriation" means an acquisition made by a Minister, a local authority or statutory undertakers under this Part or Chapter V of Part I of the Planning (Listed Buildings and Conservation Areas) Act 1990 or compulsorily under any other enactment, or an appropriation by a local authority for planning purposes.   **[247]**

NOTES
Commencement: 24 August 1990.

241. Use and development of open spaces

(1) Notwithstanding anything in any enactment relating to land which is or forms part of a common, open space or fuel or field garden allotment or in any enactment by which the land is specially regulated, such land which has been acquired by a Minister, a local authority or statutory undertakers under this Part or under Chapter V of Part I of the Planning (Listed Buildings and Conservation Areas) Act 1990 or compulsorily under any other enactment, or which has been appropriated by a local authority for planning purposes—

(a) if it has been acquired by a Minister, may be used in any manner by him or on his behalf for any purpose for which he acquired the land; and

(b) in any other case, may be used by any person in any manner in accordance with planning permission.

(2) Nothing in this section shall be construed as authorising any act or omission on the part of any person which is actionable at the suit of any person on any grounds other than contravention of any such enactment as is mentioned in subsection (1).

    [248]

NOTES
Commencement: 24 August 1990.

242. Overriding of rights of possession

If the Secretary of State certifies that possession of a house which—

> (a) has been acquired or appropriated by a local authority for planning purposes, and
> (b) is for the time being held by the authority for the purposes for which it was acquired or appropriated,

is immediately required for those purposes, nothing in the Rent Act 1977 or Part I of the Housing Act 1988 shall prevent the acquiring or appropriating authority from obtaining possession of the house.   **[249]**

NOTES
Commencement: 24 August 1990.

Constitution of joint body to hold land for planning purposes

243. Constitution of joint body to hold land for planning purposes

(1) If it appears to the Secretary of State, after consultation with the local authorities concerned, to be expedient that any land acquired by a local authority for planning purposes should be held by a joint body, consisting of representatives of that authority and of any other local authority, he may by order provide for the establishment of such a joint body and for the transfer to that body of the land so acquired.

(2) Any order under this section providing for the establishment of a joint body may make such provision as the Secretary of State considers expedient with respect to the constitution and functions of that body.

(3) The provisions which may be included under subsection (2) include provisions—

> (a) for incorporating the joint body;
> (b) for conferring on them, in relation to land transferred to them as mentioned in subsection (1), any of the powers conferred on local authorities by this Part or Chapter V of Part I of the Planning (Listed Buildings and Conservation Areas) Act 1990 in relation to land acquired and held by such authorities for the purposes of this Part or that Chapter;
> (c) for determining the manner in which their expenses are to be defrayed.

(4) Regulations under this Act may make such provision consequential upon or supplementary to the provisions of this section as appears to the Secretary of State to be necessary or expedient.   **[250]**

NOTES
Commencement: 24 August 1990.

General and supplementary provisions

244. Powers of joint planning boards under this Part

(1) A joint planning board *or a board reconstituted under Schedule 17 to the Local Government Act 1972* shall, on being authorised to do so by the Secretary of State, have the same power to acquire land compulsorily as the local authorities to whom section 226 applies have under that section.

(2) Such a board shall have the same power to acquire land by agreement as the

local authorities mentioned in subsection (1) of section 227 have under that subsection.

(3) Sections 226(1) and (7), 227, 229, 230, 232, 233 and 235 to 242 apply with the necessary modifications as if any such board were a local authority to which those sections applied.

(4) On being authorised to do so by the Secretary of State such a board shall have, for any purpose for which by virtue of this section they may acquire land compulsorily, the power which section 13 of the Local Government (Miscellaneous Provisions) Act 1976 confers on the local authorities to whom subsection (1) of that section applies to purchase compulsorily rights over land not in existence when their compulsory purchase is authorised, and subsections (2) to (5) of that section shall accordingly apply to the purchase of rights under this subsection as they apply to the purchase of rights under subsection (1) of that section.   **[251]**

NOTES
    Commencement: 24 August 1990.
    Words in italics in sub-s (1) repealed by the Environment Act 1995, s 120(3), Sch 24, as from a day to be appointed under s 125(3).

[244A. Powers of National Park authorities under Part IX

(1) A National Park authority shall, on being authorised to do so by the Secretary of State, have the same power to acquire land compulsorily as the local authorities to whom section 226 applies have under that section.

(2) A National Park authority shall have the same power to acquire land by agreement as the local authorities mentioned in subsection (1) of section 227 have under that subsection.

(3) Sections 226(1) and (7), 227, 229, 230, 232, 233 and 235 to 242 shall apply with the necessary modifications as if a National Park authority were a local authority to which those sections applied and as if the Park in relation to which it carries out functions were the authority's area.]   **[251A]**

NOTES
    Commencement: 19 September 1995.
    Inserted by the Environment Act 1995, s 65(7), Sch 8, para 2 (1).

245. Modification of incorporated enactments for purposes of this Part

(1) Where—

   (a) it is proposed that land should be acquired compulsorily under section 226 or 228, and
   (b) a compulsory purchase order relating to that land is submitted to the confirming authority in accordance with Part II of the Acquisition of Land Act 1981 or, as the case may be, is made in draft by the Secretary of State for the Environment in accordance with Schedule 1 to that Act,

the confirming authority or, as the case may be, that Secretary of State may disregard for the purposes of that Part or, as the case may be, that Schedule any objection to the order or draft which, in the opinion of that authority or Secretary of State, amounts in substance to an objection to the provisions of the development plan defining the proposed use of that or any other land.

(2) Where a compulsory purchase order authorising the acquisition of any land under section 226 is submitted to the Secretary of State in accordance with Part II of the Acquisition of Land Act 1981, then if the Secretary of State—

(a) is satisfied that the order ought to be confirmed so far as it relates to part of the land comprised in it; but

(b) has not for the time being determined whether it ought to be confirmed so far as it relates to any other such land,

he may confirm the order so far as it relates to the land mentioned in paragraph (a) and give directions postponing consideration of the order, so far as it relates to any other land specified in the directions, until such time as may be so specified.

(3) Where the Secretary of State gives directions under subsection (2), the notices required by section 15 of the Acquisition of Land Act 1981 to be published and served shall include a statement of the effect of the directions.

(4) In construing the Compulsory Purchase Act 1965 in relation to any of the provisions of this Part—

(a) references to the execution of the works shall be construed as including references to any erection, construction or carrying out of buildings or works authorised by section 237;

(b) in relation to the erection, construction or carrying out of any buildings or works so authorised, references in section 10 of that Act to the acquiring authority shall be construed as references to the person by whom the buildings or works in question are erected, constructed or carried out; and

(c) references to the execution of the works shall be construed as including also references to any erection, construction or carrying out of buildings or works on behalf of a Minister or statutory undertakers on land acquired by that Minister or those undertakers, where the buildings or works are erected, constructed or carried out for the purposes for which the land was acquired. **[252]**

NOTES
Commencement: 24 August 1990.

246. Interpretation of this Part

(1) In this Part—

(a) any reference to the acquisition of land for planning purposes is a reference to the acquisition of it under section 226 or 227 of this Act or section 52 of the Planning (Listed Buildings and Conservation Areas) Act 1990 (or, as the case may be, under section 112 or 119 of the 1971 Act or section 68 or 71 of the 1962 Act); and

(b) any reference to the appropriation of land for planning purposes is a reference to the appropriation of it for purposes for which land can be (or, as the case may be, could have been) acquired under those sections.

(2) Nothing in sections 237 to 241 shall be construed as authorising any act or omission on the part of a local authority or body corporate in contravention of any limitation imposed by law on their capacity by virtue of their constitution.

(3) Any power conferred by section 238, 239 or 241 to use land in a manner mentioned in those sections shall be construed as a power so to use the land, whether or not it involves the erection, construction or carrying out of any building or work or the maintenance of any building or work. **[253]**

NOTES
Commencement: 24 August 1990.
1971 Act: Town and Country Planning Act 1971.
1962 Act: Town and Country Planning Act 1962.

PART X

HIGHWAYS

Orders made by Secretary of State

247. Highways affected by development: orders by Secretary of State

(1) The Secretary of State may by order authorise the stopping up or diversion of any highway if he is satisfied that it is necessary to do so in order to enable development to be carried out—

(a) in accordance with planning permission granted under Part III, or

(b) by a government department.

(2) Such an order may make such provision as appears to the Secretary of State to be necessary or expedient for the provision or improvement of any other highway.

(3) Such an order may direct—

(a) that any highway provided or improved by virtue of it shall for the purposes of the Highways Act 1980 be a highway maintainable at the public expense;

(b) that the Secretary of State, or any county council, [county borough council,] metropolitan district council or London borough specified in the order or, if it so specified, the Common Council of the City of London, shall be the highway authority for that highway;

(c) in the case of a highway for which the Secretary of State is to be the highway authority, that the highway shall, on such date as may be specified in the order, become a trunk road within the meaning of the Highways Act 1980.

(4) An order made under this section may contain such incidental and consequential provisions as appear to the Secretary of State to be necessary or expedient, including in particular—

(a) provision for authorising the Secretary of State, or requiring any other authority or person specified in the order—

(i) to pay, or to make contributions in respect of, the cost of doing any work provided for by the order or any increased expenditure to be incurred which is attributable to the doing of any such work; or

(ii) to repay, or to make contributions in respect of, any compensation paid by the highway authority in respect of restrictions imposed under section 1 or 2 of the Restriction of Ribbon Development Act 1935 in relation to any highway stopped up or diverted under the order;

(b) provision for the preservation of any rights of statutory undertakers in respect of any apparatus of theirs which immediately before the date of the order is under, in, on, over, along or across the highway to which the order relates.

(5) An order may be made under this section authorising the stopping up or diversion of any highway which is temporarily stopped up or diverted under any other enactment.

(6) The provisions of this section shall have effect without prejudice to—

(a) any power conferred on the Secretary of State by any other enactment to authorise the stopping up or diversion of a highway;

(b) the provisions of Part VI of the Acquisition of Land Act 1981; or

(c) the provisions of section 251(1). **[254]**

NOTES
Commencement: 24 August 1990.
Words in square brackets in sub-s (3)(b) inserted by the Local Government (Wales) Act 1994, s 20(4)(b), Sch 6, Pt II, para 24(9), as from a day to be appointed.

248. Highways crossing or entering route of proposed new highway, etc

(1) This section applies where—

    (a) planning permission is granted under Part III for constructing or improving, or the Secretary of State proposes to construct or improve, a highway (''the main highway''); and

    (b) another highway crosses or enters the route of the main highway or is, or will be, otherwise affected by the construction or improvement of the main highway.

(2) Where this section applies, if it appears to the Secretary of State expedient to do so—

    (a) in the interests of the safety of users of the main highway; or

    (b) to facilitate the movement of traffic on the main highway,

he may by order authorise the stopping up or diversion of the other highway.

(3) Subsections (2) to (6) of section 247 shall apply to an order under this section as they apply to an order under that section, taking the reference in subsection (2) of that section to any other highway as a reference to any highway other than that which is stopped up or diverted under this section and the references in subsection (3) to a highway provided or improved by virtue of an order under that section as including a reference to the main highway. **[255]**

NOTES
Commencement: 24 August 1990.

249. Order extinguishing right to use vehicles on highway

(1) This section applies where—

    (a) a local planning authority by resolution adopt a proposal for improving the amenity of part of their area, and

    (b) the proposal involves the public ceasing to have any right of way with vehicles over a highway in that area, being a highway which is neither a trunk road nor a road classified as a principal road.

(2) The Secretary of State may, on an application by a local planning authority who have so resolved, by order provide for the extinguishment of any right which persons may have to use vehicles on that highway.

(3) An order under subsection (2) may include such provision as the Secretary of State (after consultation with every authority who are a local planning authority for the area in question and the highway authority) thinks fit for permitting the use on the highway of vehicles (whether mechanically propelled or not) in such cases as may be specified in the order, notwithstanding the extinguishment of any such right as is mentioned in that subsection.

(4) Such provision as is mentioned in subsection (3) may be framed by reference to—

    (a) particular descriptions of vehicles, or

(b) particular persons by whom or on whose authority, vehicles may be used, or

(c) the circumstances in which, or the times at which, vehicles may be used for particular purposes.

(5) No provision contained in, or having effect under, any enactment, being a provision prohibiting or restricting the use of footpaths, footways or bridleways shall affect any use of a vehicle on a highway in relation to which an order under subsection (2) has effect, where the use is permitted in accordance with provisions of the order included by virtue of subsection (3).

(6) If any authority who are a local planning authority for the area in which a highway to which an order under subsection (2) relates is situated apply to the Secretary of State in that behalf, he may by order revoke that order, and, if he does so, any right to use vehicles on the highway in relation to which the order was made which was extinguished by virtue of the order under that subsection shall be reinstated.

(7) Such an order as is mentioned in subsection (6) may make provision requiring the removal of any obstruction of a highway resulting from the exercise of powers under Part VIIA of the Highways Act 1980.

(8) Before making an application under subsection (2) or (6) the local planning authority shall consult with the highway authority (if different) and any other authority who are a local planning authority for the area in question.

(9) Subsections (2), (3), (4) and (6) of section 247 shall apply to an order under this section as they apply to an order under that section.   **[256]**

NOTES
    Commencement: 24 August 1990.

250. Compensation for orders under s 249

(1) Any person who, at the time of an order under section 249(2) coming into force, has an interest in land having lawful access to a highway to which the order relates shall be entitled to be compensated by the local planning authority on whose application the order was made in respect of—

(a) any depreciation in the value of his interest which is directly attributable to the order; and

(b) any other loss or damage which is so attributable.

(2) . . .

(3) A claim for compensation under this section shall be made to the local planning authority on whose application the order was made within the prescribed time and in the prescribed manner.

(4) For the purpose of assessing any such compensation the rules set out in section 5 of the Land Compensation Act 1961 shall, so far as applicable and subject to any necessary modifications, have effect as they have effect for the purpose of assessing compensation for the compulsory acquisition of an interest in land.

(5) Where an interest in land is subject to a mortgage—

(a) any compensation to which this section applies which is payable in respect of depreciation of the value of that interest shall be assessed as if the interest were not subject to the mortgage;

(b) a claim for any such compensation may be made by any mortgagee of the interest, but without prejudice to the making of a claim by the person entitled to the interest;

(c) no compensation to which this section applies shall be payable in respect of the interest of the mortgagee (as distinct from the interest which is subject to the mortgage); and

(d) any compensation to which this section applies which is payable in respect of the interest which is subject to the mortgage shall be paid to the mortgagee (or, if there is more than one mortgagee, to the first mortgagee) and shall in either case be applied by him as if it were proceeds of sale.

(6) Except in so far as may be otherwise provided by any regulations made under this Act, any question of disputed compensation under this section shall be referred to and determined by the Lands Tribunal.

(7) In relation to the determination of any such question, the provisions of sections 2 and 4 of the Land Compensation Act 1961 shall apply subject to any necessary modifications and to the provisions of any regulations made under this Act.   **[257]**

NOTES
Commencement: 24 August 1990.
Sub-s (2) repealed by the Planning and Compensation Act 1991, ss 32, 84(6), Sch 7, paras 8, 29, Sch 19, Pt I.

251. Extinguishment of public rights of way over land held for planning purposes

(1) Where any land has been acquired or appropriated for planning purposes and is for the time being held by a local authority for the purposes for which it was acquired or appropriated, the Secretary of State may by order extinguish any public right of way over the land if he is satisfied—

(a) that an alternative right of way has been or will be provided; or

(b) that the provision of an alternative right of way is not required.

(2) In this section any reference to the acquisition or appropriation of land for planning purposes shall be construed in accordance with section 246(1) as if this section were in Part IX.

(3) Subsection (1) shall also apply (with the substitution of a reference to the Broads Authority for the reference to the local authority) in relation to any land within the Broads which is held by the Broads Authority and which was acquired by, or vested in, the Authority for any purpose connected with the discharge of any of its functions.   **[258]**

NOTES
Commencement: 24 August 1990.
Modification: sub-s (1) above, and ss 258(1), 260(1), 261, 271, 272, 274, 275, 276 and 324(6), have effect as if a National Park authority were a local authority for the purposes of this Act, by virtue of the Environment Act 1995, s 65(7), Sch 8, para 2(3).

252. Procedure for making of orders

(1) Before making an order under section 247, 248, 249 or 251 the Secretary of State shall publish in at least one local newspaper circulating in the relevant area, and in the London Gazette, a notice—

(a) stating the general effect of the order;

(b) specifying a place in the relevant area where a copy of the draft order and
of any relevant map or plan may be inspected by any person free of charge
at all reasonable hours during a period of 28 days from the date of the
publication of the notice ("the publication date"); and

(c) stating that any person may within that period by notice to the Secretary
of State object to the making of the order.

(2) Not later than the publication date, the Secretary of State shall serve a copy
of the notice, together with a copy of the draft order and of any relevant map or
plan—

(a) on every local authority in whose area any highway or, as the case may
be, any land to which the order relates is situated, and

[(aa) on any National Park authority which is the local planning authority for
the area in which any highway or, as the case may be, any land to which
the order relates is situated, and]

(b) on any water, sewerage, hydraulic power or electricity undertakers or
public gas supplier having any cables, mains, sewers, pipes or wires laid
along, across, under or over any highway to be stopped up or diverted, or,
as the case may be, any land over which a right of way is proposed to be
extinguished, under the order.

(3) Not later than the publication date, the Secretary of State shall also cause a
copy of the notice to be displayed in a prominent position at the ends of so much of
any highway as is proposed to be stopped up or diverted or, as the case may be, of
the right of way proposed to be extinguished under the order.

(4) If before the end of the period of 28 days mentioned in subsection (1)(b) an
objection is received by the Secretary of State from any local authority [National
Park authority] or undertakers or public gas supplier on whom a notice is required to
be served under subsection (2), or from any other person appearing to him to be
affected by the order, and the objection is not withdrawn, then unless subsection (5)
applies the Secretary of State shall cause a local inquiry to be held.

(5) If, in a case where the objection is made by a person other than such a local
authority or undertakers or supplier, the Secretary of State is satisfied that in the
special circumstances of the case the holding of such an inquiry is unnecessary he
may dispense with the inquiry.

(6) Subsections (2) to (5) of section 250 of the Local Government Act 1972
(local inquiries: evidence and costs) shall apply in relation to an inquiry caused to be
held by the Secretary of State under subsection (4).

(7) Where publication of the notice mentioned in subsection (1) takes place on
more than one day, the references in this section to the publication date are references
to the latest date on which it is published.

(8) After considering any objections to the order which are not withdrawn and,
where a local inquiry is held, the report of the person who held the inquiry, the
Secretary of State may, subject to subsection (9), make the order either without
modification or subject to such modifications as he thinks fit.

(9) Where—

(a) the order contains a provision requiring any such payment, repayment or
contribution as is mentioned in section 247(4)(a); and

(b) objection to that provision is duly made by an authority or person who
would be required by it to make such a payment, repayment or contribution;
and

(c) the objection is not withdrawn,

the order shall be subject to special parliamentary procedure.

(10) Immediately after the order has been made, the Secretary of State shall publish, in the manner specified in subsection (1), a notice stating that the order has been made and naming a place where a copy of the order may be seen at all reasonable hours.

(11) Subsections (2), (3) and (7) shall have effect in relation to a notice under subsection (10) as they have effect in relation to a notice under subsection (1).

(12) In this section—

"the relevant area", in relation to an order, means the area in which any highway or land to which the order relates is situated;

"local authority" means the council of a county, [county borough,] district, parish[, community] or London borough, [a police authority established under section 3 of the Police Act 1964,] a joint authority established by Part IV of the Local Government Act 1985, a housing action trust established under Part III of the Housing Act 1988 [, the Residuary Body for Wales (Corff Gweddilliol Cymru)] and the parish meeting of a rural parish not having a separate parish council;

and in subsection (2)—

(i) the reference to water undertakers shall be construed as including a reference to the National Rivers Authority, and

(ii) the reference to electricity undertakers shall be construed as a reference to holders of licences under section 6 of the Electricity Act 1989 who are entitled to exercise any power conferred by paragraph 1 of Schedule 4 to that Act. **[259]**

NOTES

Commencement: 24 August 1990.

Sub-s (2)(aa) and words in square brackets in sub-s (4) inserted by the Environment Act 1995, s 78, Sch 10, para 32(7), as from a day to be appointed under s 125(3).

In sub-s (12), in definition "local authority", words in first and second pairs of square brackets inserted by the Local Government (Wales) Act 1994, s 20(4)(b), Sch 6, Pt II, para 24(10), as from a day to be appointed; words in third pair of square brackets inserted by the Police and Magistrates' Courts Act 1994, s 43, Sch 4, Pt II, para 63; and words in fourth pair of square brackets inserted by the Local Government (Wales) Act 1994, s 39(2), Sch 13, para 32. For meaning of "local authority" in sub-s (12), see also the Local Government Act 1985, s 57(7), Sch 13, para 3(d) and the Local Government Residuary Body (England) Order 1995, SI 1995/401, art 18, Schedule, para 2(b).

253. Procedure in anticipation of planning permission

(1) Where—

(a) the Secretary of State would, if planning permission for any development had been granted under Part III, have power to make an order under section 247 or 248 authorising the stopping up or diversion of a highway in order to enable that development to be carried out, and

(b) subsection (2), (3) or (4) applies,

then, notwithstanding that such permission has not been granted, the Secretary of State may publish notice of the draft of such an order in accordance with section 252.

(2) This subsection applies where the relevant development is the subject of an application for planning permission and either—

(a) that application is made by a local authority [National Park authority] or statutory undertakers . . . ; or

    (b) that application stands referred to the Secretary of State in pursuance of a direction under section 77; or

    (c) the applicant has appealed to the Secretary of State under section 78 against a refusal of planning permission or of approval required under a development order or against a condition of any such permission or approval.

(3) This subsection applies where—

    (a) the relevant development is to be carried out by a local authority [National Park authority] or statutory undertakers and requires, by virtue of an enactment, the authorisation of a government department; and

    (b) the developers have made an application to the department for that authorisation and also requested a direction under section 90(1) that planning permission be deemed to be granted for that development.

(4) This subsection applies where the council of a county, [county borough,] metropolitan district or London borough [a National Park authority] or a joint planning board certify that they have begun to take such steps, in accordance with regulations made by virtue of section 316, as are required to enable them to obtain planning permission for the relevant development.

(5) Section 252(8) shall not be construed as authorising the Secretary of State to make an order under section 247 or 248 of which notice has been published by virtue of subsection (1) until planning permission is granted for the development which occasions the making of the order.   **[260]**

NOTES
> Commencement: 24 August 1990.
> Words in square brackets in sub-ss (2)(a), (3)(a) and second words in square brackets in sub-s (4) inserted by the Environment Act 1995, s 78, Sch 10, para 32(8), as from a day to be appointed under s 125(3).
> Words omitted from sub-s (2)(a) repealed by the Coal Industry Act 1994, s 67(1), (8), Sch 9, para 39(1), Sch 11, Pt II.
> First words in square brackets in sub-s (4) inserted by the Local Government (Wales) Act 1994, s 20(4)(b), Sch 6, Pt II, para 24(11), as from a day to be appointed.

254. Compulsory acquisition of land in connection with highways

(1) The Secretary of State, or a local highway authority on being authorised by the Secretary of State to do so, may acquire land compulsorily—

    (a) for the purpose of providing or improving any highway which is to be provided or improved in pursuance of an order under section 247, 248 or 249 or for any other purpose for which land is required in connection with the order; or

    (b) for the purpose of providing any public right of way which is to be provided as an alternative to a right of way extinguished under an order under section 251.

(2) The Acquisition of Land Act 1981 shall apply to the acquisition of land under this section.   **[261]**

NOTES
> Commencement: 24 August 1990.

255. Concurrent proceedings in connection with highways

(1) In relation to orders under sections 247, 248 and 249, regulations made under this Act may make provision for securing that any proceedings required to be taken

for the purposes of the acquisition of land under section 254 (as mentioned in subsection (1)(a) of that section) may be taken concurrently with any proceedings required to be taken for the purposes of the order.

(2) In relation to orders under section 251, regulations made under this Act may make provision for securing—

(a) that any proceedings required to be taken for the purposes of such an order may be taken concurrently with any proceedings required to be taken for the purposes of the acquisition of the land over which the right of way is to be extinguished; or

(b) that any proceedings required to be taken for the purposes of the acquisition of any other land under section 254 (as mentioned in subsection (1)(b) of that section) may be taken concurrently with either or both of the proceedings referred to in paragraph (a). **[262]**

NOTES
Commencement: 24 August 1990.

256. Telecommunication apparatus: orders by Secretary of State

(1) Where—

(a) in pursuance of an order under section 247, 248 or 249 a highway is stopped up or diverted or, as the case may be, any right to use vehicles on that highway is extinguished; and

(b) immediately before the date on which the order came into force there was under, in, on, over, along or across the highway any telecommunication apparatus kept installed for the purposes of a telecommunications code system,

the operator of that system shall have the same powers in respect of the apparatus as if the order had not come into force.

(2) Notwithstanding subsection (1), any person entitled to land over which the highway subsisted shall be entitled to require the alteration of the apparatus.

(3) Where—

(a) any such order provides for the improvement of a [highway for which the Secretary of State is not the highway authority], and

(b) immediately before the date on which the order came into force there was under, in, on, over, along or across the highway any telecommunication apparatus kept installed for the purposes of a telecommunications code system,

the local highway authority shall be entitled to require the alteration of the apparatus.

(4) Subsection (3) does not have effect so far as it relates to the alteration of any apparatus for the purpose of [major highway works, major bridge works or major transport works within the meaning of Part III of the New Roads and Street Works Act 1991].

(5) Paragraph 1(2) of the telecommunications code (alteration of apparatus to include moving, removal or replacement of apparatus) shall apply for the purposes of this section as it applies for the purposes of that code.

(6) Paragraph 21 of the telecommunications code (restriction on removal of telecommunication apparatus) shall apply in relation to any entitlement conferred by this section to require the alteration, moving or replacement of any telecommunication

apparatus as it applies in relation to an entitlement to require the removal of any such apparatus.   **[263]**

NOTES
    Commencement: 24 August 1990.
    Words in square brackets in sub-ss (3), (4) substituted by the New Roads and Street Works Act 1991, s 168(1), Sch 8, Pt III, para 126.

Orders by other authorities

257. Footpaths and bridleways affected by development: orders by other authorities

(1) Subject to section 259, a competent authority may by order authorise the stopping up or diversion of any footpath or bridleway if they are satisfied that it is necessary to do so in order to enable development to be carried out—

    (a) in accordance with planning permission granted under Part III, or

    (b) by a government department.

(2) An order under this section may, if the competent authority are satisfied that it should do so, provide—

    (a) for the creation of an alternative highway for use as a replacement for the one authorised by the order to be stopped up or diverted, or for the improvement of an existing highway for such use;

    (b) for authorising or requiring works to be carried out in relation to any footpath or bridleway for whose stopping up or diversion, creation or improvement provision is made by the order;

    (c) for the preservation of any rights of statutory undertakers in respect of any apparatus of theirs which immediately before the date of the order is under, in, on, over, along or across any such footpath or bridleway;

    (d) for requiring any person named in the order to pay, or make contributions in respect of, the cost of carrying out any such works.

(3) An order may be made under this section authorising the stopping up or diversion of a footpath or bridleway which is temporarily stopped up or diverted under any other enactment.

(4) In this section "competent authority" means—

    (a) in the case of development authorised by a planning permission, the local planning authority who granted the permission or, in the case of a permission granted by the Secretary of State, who would have had power to grant it; and

    (b) in the case of development carried out by a government department, the local planning authority who would have had power to grant planning permission on an application in respect of the development in question if such an application had fallen to be made.   **[264]**

NOTES
    Commencement: 24 August 1990.

258. Extinguishment of public rights of way over land held for planning purposes

(1) Where any land has been acquired or appropriated for planning purposes and is for the time being held by a local authority for the purposes for which it was acquired or appropriated, then, subject to section 259, the local authority may by order

extinguish any public right of way over the land, being a footpath or bridleway, if they are satisfied—

    (a) that an alternative right of way has been or will be provided; or

    (b) that the provision of an alternative right of way is not required.

(2) In this section any reference to the acquisition or appropriation of land for planning purposes shall be construed in accordance with section 246(1) as if this section were in Part IX.

(3) Subsection (1) shall also apply (with the substitution of a reference to the Broads Authority for the reference to the local authority) in relation to any land within the Broads which is held by the Broads Authority and which was acquired by, or vested in, the Authority for any purpose connected with the discharge of any of its functions.　　　　　　　　　　　　　　　　　　　　　　　　　**[265]**

NOTES
  Commencement: 24 August 1990.
  Modification: see the note to s 251 at **[258]**.

259. Confirmation of orders made by other authorities

(1) An order made under section 257 or 258 shall not take effect unless confirmed by the Secretary of State or unless confirmed, as an unopposed order, by the authority who made it.

(2) The Secretary of State shall not confirm any such order unless satisfied as to every matter as to which the authority making the order are required under section 257 or, as the case may be, section 258 to be satisfied.

(3) The time specified—

    (a) in an order under section 257 as the time from which a footpath or bridleway is to be stopped up or diverted; or

    (b) in an order under section 258 as the time from which a right of way is to be extinguished,

shall not be earlier than confirmation of the order.

(4) Schedule 14 shall have effect with respect to the confirmation of orders under section 257 or 258 and the publicity for such orders after they are confirmed.　**[266]**

NOTES
  Commencement: 24 August 1990.

260. Telecommunication apparatus: orders by or on application of other authorities

(1) This section applies where—

    (a) any order is made by a local authority under section 258(1), or on the application of a local authority under section 251(1), which extinguishes a public right of way; or

    (b) any order is made by a competent authority under section 257 which authorises the stopping up or diversion of a footpath or bridleway,

and at the time of the publication of the notice required by section 252(1) or, as the case may be, paragraph 1 of Schedule 14 any telecommunication apparatus was kept installed for the purposes of a telecommunications code system under, in, on, over, along or across the land over which the right of way subsided.

(2) In subsection (1) "competent authority" has the same meaning as in section

257 and in the following provisions of this section references to the authority are to the authority who made the order or, as the case may be, to the authority on whose application it was made.

(3) The power of the operator of the telecommunications code system to remove the apparatus—

(a) shall, notwithstanding the making of the order, be exercisable at any time not later than the end of the period of three months from the date on which the right of way is extinguished or authorised to be stopped up or diverted; and

(b) if before the end of that period the operator of the system has given notice to the authority of his intention to remove the apparatus or a part of it, shall be exercisable in respect of the whole or, as the case may be, that part of the apparatus after the end of that period.

(4) The operator of the system may by notice given in that behalf to the authority not later than the end of that period abandon the telecommunication apparatus or any part of it.

(5) Subject to subsection (4), the operator of the system shall be deemed at the end of that period to have abandoned any part of the apparatus which the operator has then neither removed nor given notice of his intention to remove.

(6) The operator of the system shall be entitled to recover from the authority the expense of providing, in substitution for the apparatus and any other telecommunication apparatus connected with it which is rendered useless in consequence of the removal or abandonment of the first-mentioned apparatus, any telecommunication apparatus in such other place as the operator may require.

(7) Where under the previous provisions of this section the operator of the system has abandoned the whole or any part of any telecommunication apparatus, that apparatus or that part of it shall vest in the authority and shall be deemed, with its abandonment, to cease to be kept installed for the purposes of a telecommunications code system.

(8) As soon as reasonably practicable after the making of any such order as is mentioned in paragraph (a) or (b) of subsection (1) in circumstances in which that subsection applies in relation to the operator of any telecommunications code system, the person by whom the order was made shall give notice to the operator of the making of the order.

(9) Subsections (5) and (6) of section 256 apply for the purposes of this section as they apply for the purposes of that section. **[267]**

NOTES
Commencement: 24 August 1990.
Modification: see the note to s 251 at **[258]**.

Temporary highway orders: mineral workings

261. Temporary stopping up of highways for mineral workings

(1) Where the Secretary of State is satisfied—

(a) that an order made by him under section 247 for the stopping up or diversion of a highway is required for the purpose of enabling minerals to be worked by surface working; and

(b) that the highway can be restored, after the minerals have been worked, to a condition not substantially less convenient to the public, the order may provide for the stopping up or diversion of the highway during such period as may be prescribed by or under the order and for its restoration at the expiration of that period.

(2) Where a competent authority within the meaning of section 257 are satisfied—

(a) that an order made by them under that section for the stopping up or diversion of a footpath or bridleway is required for the purpose of enabling minerals to be worked by surface working; and

(b) that the footpath or bridleway can be restored, after the minerals have been worked, to a condition not substantially less convenient to the public,

the order may provide for the stopping up or diversion of the footpath or bridleway during such period as may be prescribed by or under the order and for its restoration at the expiration of that period.

(3) Without prejudice to the provisions of section 247 or 257, any such order as is authorised by subsection (1) or (2) may contain such provisions as appear to the Secretary of State or, as the case may be, the competent authority to be expedient—

(a) for imposing upon persons who, apart from the order, would be subject to any liability with respect to the repair of the original highway during the period prescribed by or under the order a corresponding liability in respect of any highway provided in pursuance of the order;

(b) for the stopping up at the expiry of that period of any highway so provided and for the reconstruction and maintenance of the original highway;

and any provision included in the order in accordance with subsection (4) of section 247 or subsection (2) of section 257 requiring payment to be made in respect of any cost or expenditure under the order may provide for the payment of a capital sum in respect of the estimated amount of that cost or expenditure.

(4) In relation to any highway which is stopped up or diverted by virtue of an order under section 247 or 248, sections 271 and 272 shall have effect—

(a) as if for references to land which has been acquired as there mentioned and to the acquiring or appropriating authority there were substituted respectively references to land over which the highway subsisted and to the person entitled to possession of that land; and

(b) as if references in subsection (5) of each of those sections to a local authority or statutory undertakers included references to any person (other than a Minister) who is entitled to possession of that land,

and sections 275 to 278 shall have effect accordingly.

(5) Subsection (4) shall not apply to land constituting the site of a highway in respect of which opencast planning permission (within the meaning of section 51 of the Opencast Coal Act 1958) has been granted.   **[268]**

NOTES

Commencement: 24 August 1990.
Modification: see the note to s 251 at **[258]**.

PART XI

STATUTORY UNDERTAKERS

Preliminary

262. Meaning of "statutory undertakers"

(1) Subject to the following provisions of this section, in this Act "statutory undertakers" means persons authorised by any enactment to carry on any railway,

light railway, tramway, road transport, water transport, canal, inland navigation, dock, harbour, pier or lighthouse undertaking or any undertaking for the supply of hydraulic power and a relevant airport operator (within the meaning of Part V of the Airports Act 1986).

(2) Subject to the following provisions of this section, in this Act "statutory undertaking" shall be construed in accordance with subsection (1) and, in relation to a relevant airport operator (within the meaning of that Part), means an airport to which that Part of that Act applies.

(3) Subject to subsection (5), for the purposes of the provisions mentioned in subsection (4) any public gas supplier, water or sewerage undertaker, the National Rivers Authority, the Post Office and the Civil Aviation Authority shall be deemed to be statutory undertakers and their undertakings statutory undertakings.

(4) The provisions referred to in subsection (3) are sections 55, 90, 101, 108(3), ..., 139 to 141, 143, 148, 170(12)(b), 236(2)(a), 237 to 241, 245, 247(4)(b), 253, 257(2), 263(1) and (2), 264, 266 to 283, 288(10)(a), 306, 325(9), 336(2) and (3), paragraph 18 of Schedule 1 and Schedules 8, 13 and 14.

(5) Subsection (4) shall apply—

(a) as respects the Post Office, as if the reference to sections 55, 247(4)(b), 253 and 257(2) were omitted; and

(b) as respects the Post Office and the Civil Aviation Authority as if—

   (i) the references to sections 245, 263(1) and (2) and 336(2) and (3) were omitted; and

   (ii) after the words "266 to 283" there were inserted the words "(except section 271 as applied by section 13 of the Opencast Coal Act 1958)".

(6) Any holder of a licence under section 6 of the Electricity Act 1989 shall be deemed to be a statutory undertaker and his undertaking a statutory undertaking—

(a) for the purposes of the provisions mentioned in subsection (7)(a), if he holds a licence under subsection (1) of that section;

(b) for the purposes of the provisions mentioned in subsection (7)(b), if he is entitled to exercise any power conferred by Schedule 3 to that Act; and

(c) for the purposes of the provisions mentioned in subsection (7)(c), if he is entitled to exercise any power conferred by paragraph 1 of Schedule 4 to that Act.

(7) The provisions referred to in subsection (6) are—

(a) sections 55, 108(3), ..., 139 to 141, 143, 148, 236(2)(a), 237, 245, 253, 263(1) and (2), 264, 266 to 283, 288(10)(a), 306, 325(9) and 336(2) and (3), paragraph 18 of Schedule 1 and Schedule 13;

(b) sections 170(12)(b) and 238 to 241; and

(c) sections 247(4) and 257(2) and Schedule 14.   **[269]**

NOTES

Commencement: 24 August 1990.

Figure omitted from sub-ss (4), (7)(a) repealed by the Planning and Compensation Act 1991, ss 31(4), 84(6), Sch 6, paras 8, 22, Sch 19, Pt II.

263. Meaning of "operational land"

(1) Subject to the following provisions of this section and to section 264, in this Act "operational land" means, in relation to statutory undertakers—

(a) land which is used for the purpose of carrying on their undertaking; and

(b) land in which an interest is held for that purpose.

(2) Paragraphs (a) and (b) of subsection (1) do not include land which, in respect of its nature and situation, is comparable rather with land in general than with land which is used, or in which interests are held, for the purpose of the carrying on of statutory undertakings.

(3) In sections 108(3), . . . , 266 to 283 and Part II of Schedule 8 "operational land", in relation to the Post Office and the Civil Aviation Authority, means land of the Post Office's or, as the case may be, of the Authority's of any such class as may be prescribed by regulations.

(4) Such regulations—

(a) shall be made—

(i) in the case of the Post Office, by the appropriate Minister and the Secretary of State acting jointly; and

(ii) in the case of the Civil Aviation Authority, by the appropriate Minister;

(b) may define a class of land by reference to any circumstances whatsoever, and

(c) in the case of the Civil Aviation Authority, may make provision for different circumstances, including prescribing different classes of land for the purposes of different provisions.   **[270]**

NOTES
Commencement: 24 August 1990.
Words omitted from sub-s (3) repealed by the Planning and Compensation Act 1991, ss 31(4), 84(6), Sch 6, paras 8, 23, Sch 19, Pt II.

264. Cases in which land is to be treated as not being operational land

(1) This section applies where an interest in land is held by statutory undertakers for the purpose of carrying on their undertaking and—

(a) the interest was acquired by them on or after 6th December 1968; or

(b) it was held by them immediately before that date but the circumstances were then such that the land did not fall to be treated as operational land for the purposes of the 1962 Act.

(2) Where this section applies in respect of any land then, notwithstanding the provisions of section 263, the land shall not be treated as operational land for the purposes of this Act unless it falls within subsection (3) or (4).

(3) Land falls within this subsection if—

(a) there is, or at some time has been, in force with respect to it a specific planning permission for its development; and

(b) that development, if carried out, would involve or have involved its use for the purpose of the carrying on of the statutory undertakers' undertaking.

(4) Land falls within this subsection if—

(a) the undertakers' interest in the land was acquired by them as the result of a transfer under the provisions of the Transport Act 1968, the Transport (London) Act 1969, the Gas Act 1986, the Airports Act 1986 [the Water Act 1989 or the Water Industry Act 1991] from other statutory undertakers; and

(b) immediately before transfer the land was operational land of those other undertakers.

(5) A specific planning permission for the purpose of subsection (3)(a) is a planning permission—

(a) granted on an application in that behalf made under Part III; or
(b) granted by provisions of a development order granting planning permission generally for development which has received specific parliamentary approval; or
(c) granted by a special development order in respect of development specifically described in the order; or
(d) deemed to be granted by virtue of a direction of a government department under section 90(1).

(6) In subsection (5)—

(a) the reference in paragraph (a) to Part III includes a reference to Part III of the 1971 Act and the enactments in force before the commencement of that Act and replaced by Part III of it; and
(b) the reference in paragraph (b) to development which has received specific parliamentary approval is a reference to development authorised—

   (i) by a local or private Act of Parliament,
  (ii) by an order approved by both Houses of Parliament; or
 (iii) by an order which has been brought into operation in accordance with the provisions of the Statutory Orders (Special Procedure) Act 1945,

being an Act or order which designates specifically both the nature of the development authorised by it and the land upon which it may be carried out;

(c) the reference in paragraph (d) to section 90(1) includes a reference to section 40 of the 1971 Act, section 41 of the 1962 Act and section 35 of the 1947 Act.

(7) This section shall not apply to land in the case of which an interest of the Postmaster General's vested in the Post Office by virtue of section 16 of the Post Office Act 1969.

(8) Where an interest in land is held by the Civil Aviation Authority this section shall not apply for the purpose of determining whether the land is operational land in relation to the Authority for the purposes of this Act.   **[271]**

NOTES
   Commencement: 24 August 1990.
   Words in square brackets in sub-s (4)(a) substituted by the Water Consolidation (Consequential Provisions) Act 1991, s 2(1), Sch 1, para 54.
   1947 Act: Town and Country Planning Act 1947.
   1962 Act: Town and Country Planning Act 1962.
   1971 Act: Town and Country Planning Act 1971.

265. Meaning of "the appropriate Minister"

(1) Subject to the following provisions of this section, in this Act "the appropriate Minister" means—

(a) in relation to statutory undertakers carrying on any railway, light railway, tramway, road transport, dock, harbour, pier or lighthouse undertaking, the Civil Aviation Authority or a relevant airport operator (within the meaning of Part V of the Airports Act 1986), the Secretary of State for Transport;
(b) in relation to statutory undertakers carrying on an undertaking for the supply of hydraulic power, the Secretary of State for Energy;

(c) in relation to the Post Office, the Secretary of State for Trade and Industry; and

(d) in relation to any other statutory undertakers, the Secretary of State for the Environment.

(2) For the purposes of sections 170(12), 266 to 280, 325(9) and 336(2) and (3) and Part II of Schedule 8, "the appropriate Minister", in relation to a public gas supplier or a holder of a licence under section 6 of the Electricity Act 1989, means the Secretary of State for Energy.

(3) For the purposes of sections 170(12), 266 to 280, 325(9) and 336(2) and (3) and Part II of Schedule 8 and Schedule 14 "the appropriate Minister"—

(a) in relation to the National Rivers Authority, means the Secretary of State or the Minister of Agriculture, Fisheries and Food; and

(b) in relation to a water or sewerage undertaker, means the Secretary of State.

(4) References in this Act to the Secretary of State and the appropriate Minister—

(a) if the appropriate Minister is not the one concerned as the Secretary of State, shall be construed as references to the Secretary of State and the appropriate Minister; and

(b) if the one concerned as the Secretary of State is also the appropriate Minister, shall be construed as references to him alone,

and similarly with references to a Minister and the appropriate Minister and with any provision requiring the Secretary of State to act jointly with the appropriate Minister.   [272]

NOTES
Commencement: 24 August 1990.

Application of Part III to statutory undertakers

266. Applications for planning permission by statutory undertakers

(1) Where—

(a) an application for planning permission to develop land to which this subsection applies is made by statutory undertakers and is referred to the Secretary of State under Part III; or

(b) an appeal is made to the Secretary of State under that Part from the decision on such an application; or

(c) such an application is deemed to be made under subsection (5) of section 177 on an appeal under section 174 by statutory undertakers,

the application or appeal shall be dealt with by the Secretary of State and the appropriate Minister.

(2) Subsection (1) applies—

(a) to operational land; and

(b) to land in which the statutory undertakers hold or propose to acquire an interest with a view to its being used for the purpose of carrying on their undertaking, where the planning permission, if granted on the application or appeal, would be for development involving the use of the land for that purpose.

(3) ...

(4) Subject to the provisions of this Part as to compensation, the provisions of this Act shall apply to an application which is dealt with under this section by the

Secretary of State and the appropriate Minister as if it had been dealt with by the Secretary of State.

(5) Subsection (2)(b) shall have effect in relation to the Civil Aviation Authority as if for the reference to development involving the use of land for the purpose of carrying on the Civil Aviation Authority's undertaking there were substituted a reference to development involving the use of land for such of the purposes of carrying on that undertaking as may be prescribed by the appropriate Minister. **[273]**

NOTES
Commencement: 24 August 1990.
Sub-s (3) repealed by the Planning and Compensation Act 1991, ss 32, 84(6), Sch 7, paras 8, 40, Sch 19, Pt I.

267. Conditional grants of planning permission

Notwithstanding anything in Part III, planning permission to develop operational land of statutory undertakers shall not, except with their consent, be granted subject to conditions requiring—

    (a) that any buildings or works authorised by the permission shall be removed, or

    (b) that any use of the land so authorised shall be discontinued,

at the end of a specified period.   **[274]**

NOTES
Commencement: 24 August 1990.

268. Development requiring authorisation of government department

(1) The Secretary of State and the appropriate Minister shall not be required under section 266(1) to deal with an application for planning permission for the development of operational land if the authorisation of a government department is required in respect of that development.

(2) Subsection (1) does not apply where the relevant authorisation has been granted without any direction as to the grant of planning permission.

(3) For the purposes of this section development shall be taken to be authorised by a government department if—

    (a) any consent, authority or approval to or for the development is granted by the department in pursuance of an enactment;

    (b) a compulsory purchase order is confirmed by the department authorising the purchase of land for the purpose of the development;

    (c) consent is granted by the department to the appropriation of land for the purpose of the development or the acquisition of land by agreement for that purpose;

    (d) authority is given by the department for the borrowing of money for the purpose of the development, or for the application for that purpose of any money not otherwise so applicable; or

    (e) any undertaking is given by the department to pay a grant in respect of the development in accordance with an enactment authorising the payment of such grants,

and references in this section to the authorisation of a government department shall be construed accordingly.   **[275]**

NOTES
Commencement: 24 August 1990.

269. Revocation or modification of permission to develop operational land

In relation to any planning permission granted on the application of statutory undertakers for the development of operational land, the provisions of Part III with respect to the revocation and modification of planning permission shall have effect as if for any reference in them to the Secretary of State there were substituted a reference to the Secretary of State and the appropriate Minister.   **[276]**

NOTES
  Commencement: 24 August 1990.

270. Order requiring discontinuance of use etc of operational land

The provisions of Part III with respect to the making of orders—

  (a) requiring the discontinuance of any use of land;
  (b) imposing conditions on the continuance of it; or
  (c) requiring buildings or works on land to be altered or removed,

and the provisions of Schedule 9 with respect to the making of orders under that Schedule shall have effect in relation to operational land of statutory undertakers as if for any reference in them to the Secretary of State there were substituted a reference to the Secretary of State and the appropriate Minister.   **[277]**

NOTES
  Commencement: 24 August 1990.

Extinguishment of rights of statutory undertakers, etc

271. Extinguishment of rights of statutory undertakers: preliminary notices

(1) This section applies where any land has been acquired by a Minister, a local authority or statutory undertakers under Part IX of this Act or Chapter V of Part I of the Planning (Listed Buildings and Conservation Areas) Act 1990 or compulsorily under any other enactment or has been appropriated by a local authority for planning purposes, and—

  (a) there subsists over that land a right vested in or belonging to statutory undertakers for the purpose of the carrying on of their undertaking, being a right of way or a right of laying down, erecting, continuing or maintaining apparatus on, under or over the land; or
  (b) there is on, under or over the land apparatus vested in or belonging to statutory undertakers for the purpose of the carrying on of their undertaking.

(2) If the acquiring or appropriating authority is satisfied that the extinguishment of the right or, as the case may be, the removal of the apparatus, is necessary for the purpose of carrying out any development with a view to which the land was acquired or appropriated, they may serve on the statutory undertakers a notice—

  (a) stating that at the end of the relevant period the right will be extinguished; or
  (b) requiring that before the end of that period the apparatus shall be removed.

(3) The statutory undertakers on whom a notice is served under subsection (2) may, before the end of the period of 28 days from the date of service of the notice, serve a counter-notice on the acquiring or appropriating authority—

  (a) stating that they object to all or any of the provisions of the notice; and
  (b) specifying the grounds of their objection.

(4) If no counter-notice is served under subsection (3)—

(a) any right to which the notice relates shall be extinguished at the end of the relevant period; and

(b) if at the end of that period any requirement of the notice as to the removal of any apparatus has not been complied with, the acquiring or appropriating authority may remove the apparatus and dispose of it in any way the authority may think fit.

(5) If a counter-notice is served under subsection (3) on a local authority or on statutory undertakers, the authority or undertakers may either—

(a) withdraw the notice (without prejudice to the service of a further notice); or

(b) apply to the Secretary of State and the appropriate Minister for an order under this section embodying the provisions of the notice, with or without modification.

(6) If a counter-notice is served under subsection (3) on a Minister—

(a) he may withdraw the notice (without prejudice to the service of a further notice); or

(b) he and the appropriate Minister may make an order under this section embodying the provisions of the notice, with or without modification.

(7) In this section any reference to the appropriation of land for planning purposes shall be construed in accordance with section 246(1) as if this section were in Part IX.

(8) For the purposes of this section the relevant period, in relation to a notice served in respect of any right or apparatus, is the period of 28 days from the date of service of the notice or such longer period as may be specified in it in relation to that right or apparatus. **[278]**

NOTES
Commencement: 24 August 1990.
Modification: see the note to s 251 at **[258]**.

272. Extinguishment of rights of telecommunications code system operators: preliminary notices

(1) This section applies where any land has been acquired by a Minister, a local authority or statutory undertakers under Part IX of this Act or under Chapter V of Part I of the Planning (Listed Buildings and Conservation Areas) Act 1990 or compulsorily under any other enactment or has been appropriated by a local authority for planning purposes, and—

(a) there subsists over that land a right conferred by or in accordance with the telecommunications code on the operator of a telecommunications code system, being a right of way or a right of laying down, erecting, continuing or maintaining apparatus on, under or over the land; or

(b) there is on, under or over the land telecommunication apparatus kept installed for the purposes of any such system.

(2) If the acquiring or appropriating authority is satisfied that the extinguishment of the right or, as the case may be, the removal of the apparatus is necessary for the purpose of carrying out any development with a view to which the land was acquired or appropriated, they may serve on the operator of the telecommunications code system a notice—

(a) stating that at the end of the relevant period the right will be extinguished; or

(b) requiring that before the end of that period the apparatus shall be removed.

(3) The operator of the telecommunications code system on whom a notice is served under subsection (2) may, before the end of the period of 28 days from the date of service of the notice, serve a counter-notice on the acquiring or appropriating authority—

(a) stating that he objects to all or any of the provisions of the notice; and
(b) specifying the grounds of his objection.

(4) If no counter-notice is served under subsection (3)—

(a) any right to which the notice relates shall be extinguished at the end of the relevant period; and
(b) if at the end of that period any requirement of the notice as to the removal of any apparatus has not been complied with, the acquiring or appropriating authority may remove the apparatus and dispose of it in any way the authority may think fit.

(5) If a counter-notice is served under subsection (3) on a local authority or on statutory undertakers, the authority or undertakers may either—

(a) withdraw the notice (without prejudice to the service of a further notice); or
(b) apply to the Secretary of State and the Secretary of State for Trade and Industry for an order under this section embodying the provisions of the notice, with or without modification.

(6) If a counter-notice is served under subsection (3) on a Minister—

(a) he may withdraw the notice (without prejudice to the service of a further notice); or
(b) he and the Secretary of State for Trade and Industry may make an order under this section embodying the provisions of the notice, with or without modification.

(7) In this section any reference to the appropriation of land for planning purposes shall be construed in accordance with section 246(1) as if this section were in Part IX.

(8) For the purposes of this section the relevant period, in relation to a notice served in respect of any right or apparatus, is the period of 28 days from the date of service of the notice or such longer period as may be specified in it in relation to that right or apparatus.   [279]

NOTES
Commencement: 24 August 1990.
Modification: see the note to s 251 at [258].

273. Notice for same purposes as ss 271 and 272 but given by undertakers to developing authority

(1) Subject to the provisions of this section, where land has been acquired or appropriated as mentioned in section 271(1), and—

(a) there is on, under or over the land any apparatus vested in or belonging to statutory undertakers; and
(b) the undertakers claim that development to be carried out on the land is such as to require, on technical or other grounds connected with the carrying on of their undertaking, the removal or re-siting of the apparatus affected by the development,

the undertakers may serve on the acquiring or appropriating authority a notice claiming the right to enter on the land and carry out such works for the removal or re-siting of the apparatus or any part of it as may be specified in the notice.

(2) No notice under this section shall be served later than 21 days after the beginning of the development of land which has been acquired or appropriated as mentioned in section 271(1).

(3) Where a notice is served under this section, the authority on whom it is served may, before the end of the period of 28 days from the date of service, serve on the statutory undertakers a counter-notice—

(a) stating that they object to all or any of the provisions of the notice; and
(b) specifying the grounds of their objection.

(4) If no counter-notice is served under subsection (3), the statutory undertakers shall, after the end of that period, have the rights claimed in their notice.

(5) If a counter-notice is served under subsection (3), the statutory undertakers who served the notice under this section may either withdraw it or may apply to the Secretary of State and the appropriate Minister for an order under this section conferring on the undertakers the rights claimed in the notice or such modified rights as the Secretary of State and the appropriate Minister think it expedient to confer on them.

(6) Where, by virtue of this section or of an order of Ministers under it, statutory undertakers have the right to execute works for the removal or re-siting of apparatus, they may arrange with the acquiring or appropriating authority for the works to be carried out by that authority, under the superintendence of the undertakers, instead of by the undertakers themselves.

(7) In subsection (1)(a), the reference to apparatus vested in or belonging to statutory undertakers shall include a reference to telecommunication apparatus kept installed for the purposes of a telecommunications code system.

(8) For the purposes of subsection (7), in this section—

(a) references (except in subsection (1)(a)) to statutory undertakers shall have effect as references to the operator of any such system; and
(b) references to the appropriate Minister shall have effect as references to the Secretary of State for Trade and Industry.   **[280]**

NOTES
Commencement: 24 August 1990.

274. Orders under ss 271 and 272

(1) Where a Minister and the appropriate Minister propose to make an order under section 271(6) or 272(6), they shall prepare a draft of the order.

(2) Before making an order under subsection (5) or (6) of section 271, or under subsection (5) or (6) of section 272, the Ministers proposing to make the order shall give the statutory undertakers or, as the case may be, the operator of the telecommunications code system on whom notice was served under subsection (2) of section 271 or, as the case may be, under subsection (2) of section 272 an opportunity of objecting to the application for, or proposal to make, the order.

(3) If any such objection is made, before making the order the Ministers shall consider the objection and give those statutory undertakers or, as the case may be, that operator (and, in a case falling within subsection (5) of either of those sections,

the local authority or statutory undertakers on whom the counter-notice was served) an opportunity of appearing before, and being heard by, a person appointed for the purpose by the Secretary of State and the appropriate Minister.

(4) After complying with subsections (2) and (3) the Ministers may, if they think fit, make the order in accordance with the application or, as the case may be, in accordance with the draft order, either with or without modification.

(5) Where an order is made under section 271 or 272—

    (a) any right to which the order relates shall be extinguished at the end of the period specified in that behalf in the order; and

    (b) if, at the end of the period so specified in relation to any apparatus, any requirement of the order as to the removal of the apparatus has not been complied with, the acquiring or appropriating authority may remove the apparatus and dispose of it in any way the authority may think fit.

(6) In this section references to the appropriate Minister shall in the case of an order under section 272 be taken as references to the Secretary of State for Trade and Industry.   **[281]**

NOTES
    Commencement: 24 August 1990.
    Modification: see the note to s 251 at **[258]**.

Extension or modification of statutory undertakers' functions

275. Extension or modification of functions of statutory undertakers

(1) The powers conferred by this section shall be exercisable where, on a representation made by statutory undertakers, it appears to the Secretary of State and the appropriate Minister to be expedient that the powers and duties of those undertakers should be extended or modified, in order—

    (a) to secure the provision of services which would not otherwise be provided, or satisfactorily provided, for any purpose in connection with which a local authority or Minister may be authorised under Part IX of this Act or under Chapter V of Part I of the Planning (Listed Buildings and Conservation Areas) Act 1990 to acquire land or in connection with which any such person may compulsorily acquire land under any other enactment; or

    (b) to facilitate an adjustment of the carrying on of the undertaking necessitated by any of the acts and events mentioned in subsection (2).

(2) The said acts and events are—

    (a) the acquisition under Part IX of this Act or that Chapter or compulsorily under any other enactment of any land in which an interest was held, or which was used, for the purpose of the carrying on of the undertaking of the statutory undertakers in question;

    (b) the extinguishment of a right or the imposition of any requirement by virtue of section 271 or 272;

    (c) a decision on an application made by the statutory undertakers for planning permission to develop any such land as is mentioned in paragraph (a);

    (d) the revocation or modification of planning permission granted on any such application;

    (e) the making of an order under section 102 or paragraph 1 of Schedule 9 in relation to any such land.

(3) The powers conferred by this section shall also be exercisable where, on a

representation made by a local authority or Minister, it appears to the Secretary of State and the appropriate Minister to be expedient that the powers and duties of statutory undertakers should be extended or modified in order to secure the provision of new services, or the extension of existing services, for any purpose in connection with which the local authority or Minister making the representation may be authorised under Part IX of this Act or under Chapter V of Part I of the Planning (Listed Buildings and Conservation Areas) Act 1990 to acquire land or in connection with which the local authority or Minister may compulsorily acquire land under any other enactment.

(4) Where the powers conferred by this section are exercisable, the Secretary of State and the appropriate Minister may, if they think fit, by order provide for such extension or modification of the powers and duties of the statutory undertakers as appears to them to be requisite in order—

    (a) to secure the services in question, as mentioned in subsection (1)(a) or (3), or

    (b) to secure the adjustment in question, as mentioned in subsection (1)(b),

as the case may be.

(5) Without prejudice to the generality of subsection (4), an order under this section may make provision—

    (a) for empowering the statutory undertakers—

        (i) to acquire (whether compulsorily or by agreement) any land specified in the order, and

        (ii) to erect or construct any buildings or works so specified;

    (b) for applying in relation to the acquisition of any such land or the construction of any such works enactments relating to the acquisition of land and the construction of works;

    (c) where it has been represented that the making of the order is expedient for the purposes mentioned in subsection (1)(a) or (3), for giving effect to such financial arrangements between the local authority or Minister and the statutory undertakers as they may agree, or as, in default of agreement, may be determined to be equitable in such manner and by such tribunal as may be specified in the order;

    (d) for such incidental and supplemental matters as appear to the Secretary of State and the appropriate Minister to be expedient for the purposes of the order.   **[282]**

NOTES
  Commencement: 24 August 1990.
  Modification: see the note to s 251 at **[258]**.

276. Procedure in relation to orders under s 275

(1) As soon as possible after making such a representation as is mentioned in subsection (1) or subsection (3) of section 275 the statutory undertakers, the local authority or Minister making the representation shall—

    (a) publish notice of the representation; and

    (b) if the Secretary of State and the appropriate Minister so direct, serve a similar notice on such persons, or persons of such classes, as they may direct.

(2) A notice under subsection (1)—

    (a) shall be published in such form and manner as the Secretary of State and the appropriate Minister may direct;

(b) shall give such particulars as they may direct of the matters to which the representation relates; and

(c) shall specify the time within which, and the manner in which, objections to the making of an order on the representation may be made.

(3) Orders under section 275 shall be subject to special parliamentary procedure. **[283]**

NOTES
Commencement: 24 August 1990.
Modification: see the note to s 251 at **[258]**.

277. Relief of statutory undertakers from obligations rendered impracticable

(1) Where, on a representation made by statutory undertakers, the appropriate Minister is satisfied that the fulfilment of any obligation incurred by those undertakers in connection with the carrying on of their undertaking has been rendered impracticable by an act or event to which this subsection applies, the appropriate Minister may, if he thinks fit, by order direct that the statutory undertakers shall be relieved of the fulfilment of that obligation, either abosolutely or to such extent as may be specified in the order.

(2) Subsection (1) applies to the following acts and events—

(a) the compulsory acquisition under Part IX of this Act or under Chapter V of Part I of the Planning (Listed Buildings and Conservation Areas) Act 1990 or under any other enactment of any land in which an interest was held, or which was used, for the purpose of the carrying on of the undertaking of the statutory undertakers; and

(b) the acts and events specified in section 275(2)(b) to (e).

(3) The appropriate Minister may direct statutory undertakers who have made a representation to him under subsection (1) to publicise it in either or both of the following ways—

(a) by publishing in such form and manner as he may direct a notice, giving such particulars as he may direct of the matters to which the representation relates and specifying the time within which, and the manner in which, objections to the making of an order on the representation may be made; or

(b) by serving such a notice on such persons, or persons of such classes, as he may direct.

(4) The statutory undertakers shall comply with any direction given to them under subsection (3) as soon as possible after the making of the representation under subsection (1).

(5) If any objection to the making of an order under this section is duly made and is not withdrawn before the order is made, the order shall be subject to special parliamentary procedure.

(6) Immediately after an order is made under this section by the appropriate Minister, he shall—

(a) publish a notice stating that the order has been made and naming a place where a copy of it may be seen at all reasonable hours; and

(b) serve a similar notice—

(i) on any person who duly made an objection to the order and has sent to the appropriate Minister a request in writing to serve him with the notice required by this subsection, specifying an address for service; and

(ii) on such other persons (if any) as the appropriate Minister thinks fit.

(7) Subject to subsection (8), and to the provisions of Part XII, an order under this section shall become operative on the date on which the notice required by subsection (6) is first published.

(8) Where in accordance with subsection (5) the order is subject to special parliamentary procedure, subsection (7) shall not apply.   **[284]**

NOTES
Commencement: 24 August 1990.

278. Objections to orders under ss 275 and 277

(1) For the purposes of sections 275 to 277, an objection to the making of an order shall not be treated as duly made unless—

(a) the objection is made within the time and in the manner specified in the notice required by section 276 or, as the case may be, section 277; and
(b) a statement in writing of the grounds of the objection is comprised in or submitted with the objection.

(2) Where an objection to the making of such an order is duly made in accordance with subsection (1) and is not withdrawn, the following provisions of this section shall have effect in relation to it.

(3) Unless the appropriate Minister decides without regard to the objection not to make the order, or decides to make a modification which is agreed to by the objector as meeting the objection, before he makes a final decision he—

(a) shall consider the grounds of the objection as set out in the statement; and
(b) may, if he thinks fit, require the objector to submit within a specified period a further statement in writing as to any of the matters to which the objection relates.

(4) In so far as the appropriate Minister, after considering the grounds of the objection as set out in the original statement and in any such further statement, is satisfied that the objection relates to a matter which can be dealt with in the assessment of compensation, the appropriate Minister may treat the objection as irrelevant for the purpose of making a final decision.

(5) If—

(a) after considering the grounds of the objection as so set out, the appropriate Minister is satisfied that, for the purpose of making a final decision, he is sufficiently informed as to the matters to which the objection relates; or
(b) in a case where a further statement has been required, it is not submitted within the specified period,

the appropriate Minister may make a final decision without further investigation as to those matters.

(6) Subject to subsections (4) and (5), before making a final decision the appropriate Minister shall give the objector an opportunity of appearing before, and being heard by, a person appointed for the purpose by the appropriate Minister.

(7) If the objector takes that opportunity, the appropriate Minister shall give an opportunity of appearing and being heard on the same occasion to the statutory undertakers, local authority or Minister on whose representation the order is proposed

to be made, and to any other persons to whom it appears to him to be expedient to give such an opportunity.

(8) Notwithstanding anything in the previous provisions of this section, if it appears to the appropriate Minister that the matters to which the objection relates are such as to require investigation by public local inquiry before he makes a final decision, he shall cause such an inquiry to be held.

(9) Where the appropriate Minister determines to cause such an inquiry to be held, any of the requirements of subsections (3) to (7) to which effect has not been given at the time of that determination shall be dispensed with.

(10) In this section any reference to making a final decision in relation to an order is a reference to deciding whether to make the order or what modification (if any) ought to be made.

(11) In the application of this section to an order under section 275, any reference to the appropriate Minister shall be construed as a reference to the Secretary of State and the appropriate Minister.   **[285]**

NOTES
Commencement: 24 August 1990.

Compensation

279. Right to compensation in respect of certain decisions and orders

(1) Statutory undertakers shall, subject to the following provisions of this Part, be entitled to compensation from the local planning authority—

(a) in respect of any decision made in accordance with section 266 by which planning permission to develop operational land of those undertakers is refused or is granted subject to conditions where—

(i) planning permission for that development would have been granted by a development order but for a direction given under such an order that planning permission so granted should not apply to the development; and

(ii) it is not development which has received specific parliamentary approval (within the meaning of section 264(6));

(b) in respect of any order under section 97, as modified by section 269, by which planning permission which was granted on the application of those undertakers for the development of any such land is revoked or modified.

(2) Where by virtue of section 271—

(a) any right vested in or belonging to statutory undertakers is extinguished; or

(b) any requirement is imposed on statutory undertakers,

those undertakers shall be entitled to compensation from the acquiring or appropriating authority at whose instance the right was extinguished or the requirement imposed.

(3) Where by virtue of section 272—

(a) any right vested in or belonging to an operator of a telecommunications code system is extinguished; or

(b) any requirement is imposed on such an operator,

the operator shall be entitled to compensation from the acquiring or appropriating authority at whose instance the right was extinguished or the requirement imposed.

(4) Where—

    (a) works are carried out for the removal or re-siting of statutory undertakers' apparatus; and

    (b) the undertakers have the right to carry out those works by virtue of section 273 or an order of Ministers under that section,

the undertakers shall be entitled to compensation from the acquiring or appropriating authority.

(5) Subsection (1) shall not apply in respect of a decision or order if—

    (a) it relates to land acquired by the statutory undertakers after 7th January 1947; and

    (b) the Secretary of State and the appropriate Minister include in the decision or order a direction that subsection (1) shall not apply to it.

(6) The Secretary of State and the appropriate Minister may only give a direction under subsection (5) if they are satisfied, having regard to the nature, situation and existing development of the land and of any neighbouring land, and to any other material considerations, that it is unreasonable that compensation should be recovered in respect of the decision or order in question.

(7) For the purposes of this section the conditions referred to in sections 91 and 92 shall be disregarded.   **[286]**

NOTES

Commencement: 24 August 1990.

280. Measure of compensation to statutory undertakers, etc

(1) Where statutory undertakers are entitled to compensation—

    (a) as mentioned in subsection (1), (2) or (4) of section 279; or

    (b) under the provisions of section 115 in respect of an order made under section 102 or paragraph 1, 3, 5 or 6 of Schedule 9, as modified by section 270; or

    (c) in respect of a compulsory acquisition of land which has been acquired by those undertakers for the purposes of their undertaking, where the first-mentioned acquisition is effected under a compulsory purchase order confirmed or made without the appropriate Minister's certificate,

or the operator of a telecommunications code system is entitled to compensation as mentioned in section 279(3), the amount of the compensation shall (subject to section 281) be an amount calculated in accordance with this section.

(2) Subject to subsections (4) to (6), that amount shall be the aggregate of—

    (a) the amount of any expenditure reasonably incurred in acquiring land, providing apparatus, erecting buildings or doing work for the purpose of any adjustment of the carrying on of the undertaking or, as the case may be, the running of the telecommunications code system rendered necessary by the proceeding giving rise to compensation (a "business adjustment");

    (b) the appropriate amount for loss of profits; and

    (c) where the compensation is under section 279(2) or (3), and is in respect of the imposition of a requirement to remove apparatus, the amount of any expenditure reasonably incurred by the statutory undertakers or, as the case may be, the operator in complying with the requirement, reduced by the value after removal of the apparatus removed.

(3) In subsection (2) "the appropriate amount for loss of profits" means—

(a) where a business adjustment is made, the aggregate of—

    (i) the estimated amount of any decrease in net receipts from the carrying on of the undertaking or, as the case may be, the running of the telecommunications code system pending the adjustment, in so far as the decrease is directly attributable to the proceeding giving rise to compensation; and

    (ii) such amount as appears reasonable compensation for any estimated decrease in net receipts from the carrying on of the undertaking or, as the case may be, the running of the telecommunications code system in the period after the adjustment has been completed, in so far as the decrease is directly attributable to the adjustment;

(b) where no business adjustment is made, such amount as appears reasonable compensation for any estimated decrease in net receipts from the carrying on of the undertaking or, as the case may be, the running of the telecommunications code system which is directly attributable to the proceeding giving rise to compensation.

(4) Where a business adjustment is made, the aggregate amount mentioned in subsection (2) shall be reduced by such amount (if any) as appears to the Lands Tribunal to be appropriate to offset—

(a) the estimated value of any property (whether moveable or immoveable) belonging to the statutory undertakers or the operator and used for the carrying on of their undertaking or, as the case may be, the running of the telecommunications code system which in consequence of the adjustment ceases to be so used, in so far as the value of the property has not been taken into account under paragraph (c) of that subsection; and

(b) the estimated amount of any increase in net receipts from the carrying on of the undertaking or the running of the telecommunications code system in the period after the adjustment has been completed, in so far as that amount has not been taken into account in determining the amount mentioned in paragraph (b) of that subsection and is directly attributable to the adjustment.

(5) Where a business adjustment is made the aggregate amount mentioned in subsection (2) shall be further reduced by any amount which appears to the Lands Tribunal to be appropriate, having regard to any increase in the capital value of immoveable property belonging to the statutory undertakers or the operator which is directly attributable to the adjustment, allowance being made for any reduction made under subsection (4)(b).

(6) Where—

(a) the compensation is under section 279(4); and

(b) the acquiring or appropriating authority carry out the works,

then, in addition to any reduction falling to be made under subsection (4) or (5), the aggregate amount mentioned in subsection (2) shall be reduced by the actual cost to the authority of carrying out the works.

(7) References in this section to a decrease in net receipts shall be construed as references—

(a) to the amount by which a balance of receipts over expenditure is decreased; or

(b) to the amount by which a balance of expenditure over receipts is increased; or

(c) where a balance of receipts over expenditure is converted into a balance
of expenditure over receipts, to the aggregate of the two balances;

and references to an increase in net receipts shall be construed accordingly.

(8) In this section—

"proceeding giving rise to compensation" means—

(a) except in relation to compensation under section 279(4), the particular
action (that is to say, the decision, order, extinguishment of a right,
imposition of a requirement or acquisition) in respect of which
compensation falls to be assessed, as distinct from any development or
project in connection with which that action may have been taken;

(b) in relation to compensation under section 279(4), the circumstances
making it necessary for the apparatus in question to be removed or re-
sited;

"the appropriate Minister's certificate" means such a certificate as is mentioned
in section 16 of or paragraph 3 of Schedule 3 to the Acquisition of Land Act 1981.

[287]

NOTES
Commencement: 24 August 1990.

281. Exclusion of s 280 at option of statutory undertakers

(1) Where statutory undertakers are entitled to compensation in respect of such a
compulsory acquisition as is mentioned in section 280(1)(c), the statutory undertakers
may by notice in writing under this section elect that the compensation shall be
ascertained in accordance with the enactments (other than rule (5) of the rules set out
in section 5 of the Land Compensation Act 1961) which would be applicable apart
from section 280.

(2) If the statutory undertakers so elect the compensation shall be ascertained
accordingly.

(3) An election under this section may be made either in respect of the whole of
the land comprised in the compulsory acquisition in question or in respect of part of
that land.

(4) Any notice under this section shall be given to the acquiring authority before
the end of the period of two months from the date of service of notice to treat in
respect of the interest of the statutory undertakers.   **[288]**

NOTES
Commencement: 24 August 1990.

282. Procedure for assessing compensation

(1) Where the amount of any such compensation as is mentioned in subsection (1)
of section 280 falls to be ascertained in accordance with the provisions of that
section, the compensation shall, in default of agreement, be assessed by the Lands
Tribunal, if apart from this section it would not fall to be so assessed.

(2) For the purposes of any proceedings arising before the Lands Tribunal in
respect of compensation falling to be ascertained as mentioned in subsection (1), the
provisions of sections 2 and 4 of the Land Compensation Act 1961 shall apply as
they apply to proceedings on a question referred to the Tribunal under section 1 of
that Act, but with the substitution in section 4 of that Act, for references to the

acquiring authority, of references to the person from whom the compensation is claimed. **[289]**

NOTES
Commencement: 24 August 1990.

Advertisements

283. Display of advertisements on operational land

Sections 266 to 270 and 279(1), (5) and (6) do not apply in relation to the display of advertisements on operational land of statutory undertakers. **[290]**

NOTES
Commencement: 24 August 1990.

PART XII

VALIDITY

284. Validity of development plans and certain orders, decisions and directions

(1) Except in so far as may be provided by this Part, the validity of—

(a) a structure plan, local plan [minerals local plan, waste local plan] or unitary development plan or any alteration, . . . or replacement of any such plan, whether before or after the plan, alteration, . . . or replacement has been approved or adopted; or

(b) a simplified planning zone scheme or an alteration of such a scheme, whether before or after the adoption or approval of the scheme or alteration; or

(c) an order under any provision of Part X except section 251(1), whether before or after the order has been made; or

(d) an order under section 277, whether before or after the order has been made; or

(e) any such order as is mentioned in subsection (2), whether before or after it has been confirmed; or

(f) any such action on the part of the Secretary of State as is mentioned in subsection (3),

shall not be questioned in any legal proceedings whatsoever.

(2) The orders referred to in subsection (1)(e) are—

(a) any order under section 97 or under the provisions of that section as applied by or under any other provision of this Act;

(b) any order under section 102;

(c) any tree preservation order;

(d) any order made in pursuance of section 221(5);

(e) any order under paragraph 1, 3, 5 or 6 of Schedule 9.

(3) The action referred to in subsection (1)(f) is action on the part of the Secretary of State of any of the following descriptions—

(a) any decision on an application for planning permission referred to him under section 77;

(b) any decision on an appeal under section 78;

(c) . . .

(d) any decision to confirm a completion notice under section 95;

(e) any decision to grant planning permission under paragraph (a) of section 177(1) or to discharge a condition or limitation under paragraph (b) of that section;

(f) any decision to confirm or not to confirm a purchase notice including—

    (i) any decision not to confirm such a notice in respect of part of the land to which it relates, or

    (ii) any decision to grant any permission, or give any direction, instead of confirming such a notice, either wholly or in part;

(g) any decision . . . on an appeal under section 195(1);

(h) any decision relating—

    (i) to an application for consent under a tree preservation order,

    (ii) to an application for consent under any regulations made in accordance with section 220 or 221, or

    (iii) to any certificate or direction under any such order or regulations, whether it is a decision on appeal or a decision on an application referred to the Secretary of State for determination in the first instance.

(4) Nothing in this section shall affect the exercise of any jurisdiction of any court in respect of any refusal or failure on the part of the Secretary of State to take any such action as is mentioned in subsection (3).   **[291]**

NOTES

Commencement: 24 August 1990.

Words in square brackets in sub-s (1)(a) inserted, and words omitted from sub-ss (1)(a), (3)(g) and whole of sub-s (3)(c) repealed, by the Planning and Compensation Act 1991, ss 27, 31(4), 32, 84(6), Sch 4, Pt II, para 30, Sch 6, paras 8, 24, Sch 7, paras 8, 41, Sch 19, Pts I, II.

285. Validity of enforcement notices and similar notices

(1) . . . , the validity of an enforcement notice shall not, except by way of an appeal under Part VII, be questioned in any proceedings whatsoever on any of the grounds on which such an appeal may be brought.

(2) Subsection (1) shall not apply to proceedings brought under section 179 . . . against a person who—

(a) has held an interest in the land since before the enforcement notice was issued under that Part;

(b) did not have a copy of the enforcement notice served on him under that Part; and

(c) satisfies the court—

    (i) that he did not know and could not reasonably have been expected to know that the enforcement notice had been issued; and

    (ii) that his interests have been substantially prejudiced by the failure to serve him with a copy of it.

(3) Subject to subsection (4), the validity of a notice which has been served under section 215 on the owner and occupier of the land shall not, except by way of an appeal under Chapter II of Part VIII, be questioned in any proceedings whatsoever on either of the grounds specified in section 217(1)(a) or (b).

(4) Subsection (3) shall not prevent the validity of such a notice being questioned on either of those grounds in proceedings brought under section 216 against a person on whom the notice was not served, but who has held an interest in the land since

before the notice was served on the owner and occupier of the land, if he did not appeal against the notice under that Chapter.

(5), (6) . . . **[292]**

NOTES
Commencement: 24 August 1990.
Words omitted from sub-ss (1), (2), and the whole of sub-ss (5), (6), repealed by the Planning and Compensation Act 1991, ss 32, 84(6), Sch 7, paras 8, 42, Sch 19, Pt I.
Modification: section modified by the Town and Country Planning (Special Enforcement Notices) Regulations 1992, SI 1992/1562, reg 2, Schedule at **[837]**, and the Planning (Hazardous Substances) Regulations 1992, SI 1992/656, reg 22, Sch 4, Pt 4 at **[770]**.

286. Challenges to validity on ground of authority's powers

(1) The validity of any permission, determination or certificate granted, made or issued or purporting to have been granted, made or issued by a local planning authority in respect of—

   (a) an application for planning permission;
   (b) . . .
   (c) an application for [a certificate under section 191 or 192];
   (d) an application for consent to the display of advertisements under section 220; or
   (e) a determination under section 302 or Schedule 15,

shall not be called in question in any legal proceedings, or in any proceedings under this Act which are not legal proceedings, on the ground that the permission, determination or certificate should have been granted, made or given by some other local planning authority.

(2) The validity of any order under section 97 revoking or modifying planning permission, any order under section 102 or paragraph 1 of Schedule 9 requiring discontinuance of use, or imposing conditions on continuance of use, or requiring the alteration or removal of buildings or works, or any enforcement notice under section 172 or stop notice under section 183 [or a breach of condition notice under section 187A], being an order or notice purporting to have been made, issued or served by a local planning authority, shall not be called in question in any such proceedings on the ground—

   (a) in the case of an order or notice purporting to have been made, issued or served by a district planning authority, that they failed to comply with paragraph 11(2) of Schedule 1;
   (b) in the case of an order or notice purporting to have been made, issued or served by a county planning authority, that they had no power to make, issue or serve it because it did not relate to a county matter within the meaning of that Schedule. **[293]**

NOTES
Commencement: 24 August 1990.
Sub-s (1)(b) repealed, words in square brackets in sub-s (1)(c) substituted, and words in square brackets in sub-s (2) inserted, by the Planning and Compensation Act 1991, ss 32, 84(6), Sch 7, paras 8, 43, Sch 19, Pt I.

287. Proceedings for questioning validity of development plans and certain schemes and orders

(1) If any person aggrieved by a unitary development plan or a local plan [minerals local plan or waste local plan] or by any alteration, . . . or replacement of any such plan or structure plan, desires to question the validity of the plan or, as the case may be, the alteration, . . . or replacement on the ground—

(a) that it is not within the powers conferred by Part II, or

(b) that any requirement of that Part or of any regulations made under it has not been complied with in relation to the approval or adoption of the plan or, as the case may be, its alteration, repeal or replacement,

he may make an application to the High Court under this section.

(2) On any application under this section the High Court—

(a) may by interim order wholly or in part suspend the operation of the plan, or, as the case may be, the alteration, . . . or replacement, either generally or in so far as it affects any property of the applicant, until the final determination of the proceedings;

(b) if satisfied that the plan or, as the case may be, the alteration, . . . or replacement is wholly or to any extent outside the powers conferred by Part II, or that the interests of the applicant have been substantially prejudiced by the failure to comply with any requirement of that Part or of any regulations made under it, may wholly or in part quash the plan or, as the case may be, the alteration, . . . or replacement either generally or in so far as it affects any property of the applicant.

(3) Subsections (1) and (2) shall apply, subject to any necessary modifications, to a simplified planning zone scheme or an alteration of such a scheme or to an order under section 247, 248, 249, 251, 257, 258 or 277 as they apply to any plan or any alteration, . . . or replacement there mentioned.

(4) An application under this section must be made within six weeks from the relevant date.

(5) For the purposes of subsection (4) the relevant date is—

(a) in the case of an application in respect of such a plan as is mentioned in subsection (1), the date of the publication of the first notice of the approval or adoption of the plan, alteration, . . . or replacement required by regulations under section 26 or, as the case may be, section 53,

(b) in the case of an application by virtue of subsection (3) in respect of a simplified planning zone scheme or an alteration of such a scheme, the date of the publication of the first notice of the approval or adoption of the scheme or alteration required by regulations under paragraph 13 of Schedule 7,

(c) in the case of an application by virtue of subsection (3) in respect of an order under section 247, 248, 249, or 251, the date on which the notice required by section 252(10) is first published.

(d) in the case of an application by virtue of subsection (3) in respect of an order under section 257 or 258, the date on which the notice required by paragraph 7 of Schedule 14 is first published in accordance with that paragraph,

(e) in the case of an application by virtue of subsection (3) in respect of an order under section 277, the date on which the notice required by subsection (6) of that section is first published;

but subject, in the case of those orders mentioned in paragraphs (c) and (e) to which section 292 applies, to that section.

(6) In their application to simplified planning zone schemes and their alteration, subsections (1) and (2) shall have effect as if they referred to Part III instead of Part II.   **[294]**

NOTES

Commencement: 24 August 1990.

Words in square brackets in sub-s (1) inserted, and words omitted from sub-ss (1)–(3), (5), repealed, by the Planning and Compensation Act 1991, ss 27, 84(6), Sch 4, Pt II, para 31, Sch 19, Pt I. For transitional provisions, see Sch 4, Pt III, para 50 to the 1991 Act at **[547]**.

288. Proceedings for questioning the validity of other orders, decisions and directions

(1) If any person—

    (a) is aggrieved by any order to which this section applies and wishes to question the validity of that order on the grounds—

        (i) that the order is not within the powers of this Act, or

        (ii) that any of the relevant requirements have not been complied with in relation to that order; or

    (b) is aggrieved by any action on the part of the Secretary of State to which this section applies and wishes to question the validity of that action on the grounds—

        (i) that the action is not within the powers of this Act, or

        (ii) that any of the relevant requirements have not been complied with in relation to that action,

he may make an application to the High Court under this section.

(2) Without prejudice to subsection (1), if the authority directly concerned with any order to which this section applies, or with any action on the part of the Secretary of State to which this section applies, wish to question the validity of that order or action on any of the grounds mentioned in subsection (1), the authority may make an application to the High Court under this section.

(3) An application under this section must be made within six weeks from the date on which the order is confirmed (or, in the case of an order under section 97 which takes effect under section 99 without confirmation, the date on which it takes effect) or, as the case may be, the date on which the action is taken.

(4) This section applies to any such order as is mentioned in subsection (2) of section 284 and to any such action on the part of the Secretary of State as is mentioned in subsection (3) of that section.

(5) On any application under this section the High Court—

    (a) may, subject to subsection (6), by interim order suspend the operation of the order or action, the validity of which is questioned by the application, until the final determination of the proceedings;

    (b) if satisfied that the order or action in question is not within the powers of this Act, or that the interests of the applicant have been substantially prejudiced by a failure to comply with any of the relevant requirements in relation to it, may quash that order or action.

(6) Paragraph (a) of subsection (5) shall not apply to applications questioning the validity of tree preservation orders.

(7) In relation to a tree preservation order, or to an order made in pursuance of section 221(5), the powers conferred on the High Court by subsection (5) shall be exercisable by way of quashing or (where applicable) suspending the operation of the order either in whole or in part, as the court may determine.

(8) References in this section to the confirmation of an order include the

confirmation of an order subject to modifications as well as the confirmation of an order in the form in which it was made.

(9) In this section "the relevant requirements", in relation to any order or action to which this section applies, means any requirements of this Act or of the Tribunals and Inquiries Act [1992], or of any order, regulations or rules made under this Act or under that Act which are applicable to that order or action.

(10) Any reference in this section to the authority directly concerned with any order or action to which this section applies—

(a) in relation to any such decision as is mentioned in section 284(3)(f), is a reference to the council on whom the notice in question was served and, in a case where the Secretary of State has modified such a notice, wholly or in part, by substituting another local authority or statutory undertakers for that council, includes a reference to that local authority or those statutory undertakers;

(b) in any other case, is a reference to the authority who made the order in question or made the decision or served the notice to which the proceedings in question relate, or who referred the matter to the Secretary of State, or, where the order or notice in question was made or served by him, the authority named in the order or notice.   **[295]**

NOTES
Commencement: 24 August 1990.
Figure in square brackets in sub-s (9) substituted by the Tribunals and Inquiries Act 1992, s 18(1), Sch 3, para 25.

289. Appeals to High Court relating to enforcement notices and notices under s 207

(1) Where the Secretary of State gives a decision in proceedings on an appeal under Part VII against an enforcement notice the appellant or the local planning authority or any other person having an interest in the land to which the notice relates may, according as rules of court may provide, either appeal to the High Court against the decision on a point of law or require the Secretary of State to state and sign a case for the opinion of the High Court.

(2) Where the Secretary of State gives a decision in proceedings on an appeal under Part VIII against a notice under section 207, the appellant or the local planning authority or any person (other than the appellant) on whom the notice was served may, according as rules of court may provide, either appeal to the High Court against the decision on a point of law or require the Secretary of State to state and sign a case for the opinion of the High Court.

(3) At any stage of the proceedings on any such appeal as is mentioned in subsection (1), the Secretary of State may state any question of law arising in the course of the proceedings in the form of a special case for the decision of the High Court.

(4) A decision of the High Court on a case stated by virtue of subsection (3) shall be deemed to be a judgment of the court within the meaning of section 16 of the Supreme Court Act 1981 (jurisdiction of the Court of Appeal to hear and determine appeals from any judgment of the High Court).

[(4A) In proceedings brought by virtue of this section in respect of an enforcement notice, the High Court or, as the case may be, the Court of Appeal may, on such terms if any as the Court thinks fit (which may include terms requiring the local planning authority to give an undertaking as to damages or any other matter), order that the notice shall have effect, or have effect to such extent as may be specified in the order, pending the final determination of those proceedings and any re-hearing and determination by the Secretary of State.

(4B) Where proceedings are brought by virtue of this section in respect of any notice under section 207, the notice shall be of no effect pending the final determination of those proceedings and any re-hearing and determination by the Secretary of State.]

(5) In relation to any proceedings in the High Court or the Court of Appeal brought by virtue of this section the power to make rules of court shall include power to make rules—

> (a) prescribing the powers of the High Court or the Court of Appeal with respect to the remitting of the matter with the opinion or direction of the court for re-hearing and determination by the Secretary of State; and
>
> (b) providing for the Secretary of State, either generally or in such circumstances as may be prescribed by the rules, to be treated as a party to any such proceedings and to be entitled to appear and to be heard accordingly.

[(5A) Rules of court may also provide for the High Court or, as the case may be, the Court of Appeal to give directions as to the exercise, until such proceedings in respect of an enforcement notice are finally concluded and any re-hearing and determination by the Secretary of State has taken place, of any other powers in respect of the matters to which such a notice relates.

(6) No proceedings in the High Court shall be brought by virtue of this section except with the leave of that Court and no appeal to the Court of Appeal shall be so brought except with the leave of the Court of Appeal or of the High Court.]

(7) In this section ''decision'' includes a direction or order, and references to the giving of a decision shall be construed accordingly.   **[296–297]**

NOTES
    Commencement: 24 August 1990 (sub-ss (1)–(4), (5), (7)); 25 November 1991 (sub-ss (5A), (6) for certain purposes); 2 January 1992 (sub-ss (4A), (4B); sub-ss (5A), (6) for remaining purposes).
    Sub-ss (4A), (4B) inserted, and sub-ss (5A), (6) substituted for sub-s (6), by the Planning and Compensation Act 1991, s 6(4), (5).
    Modification: section modified by the Town and Country Planning (Special Enforcement Notices) Regulations 1992, SI 1992/1562, reg 2, Schedule at **[837]**, and the Planning (Hazardous Substances) Regulations 1992, SI 1992/656, reg 22, Sch 4, Pt 4 at **[770]**.

290. (*Repealed by the Planning and Compensation Act 1991, ss 32, 84(6), Sch 7, paras 8, 44, Sch 19, Pt I.*)

291. Special provisions as to decisions relating to statutory undertakers

In relation to any action which—

> (a) apart from the provisions of Part XI would fall to be taken by the Secretary of State and, if so taken, would be action falling within section 284(3); but
>
> (b) by virtue of that Part, is required to be taken by the Secretary of State and the appropriate Minister,

the provisions of sections 284 and 288 shall have effect (subject to section 292) as if any reference in those provisions to the Secretary of State were a reference to the Secretary of State and the appropriate Minister.   **[298]**

NOTES
    Commencement: 24 August 1990.

292. Special provisions as to orders subject to special parliamentary procedure

(1) Where an order under section 247, 248, 249 or 277 is subject to special parliamentary procedure, then—

    (a) if the order is confirmed by Act of Parliament under section 6 of the Statutory Orders (Special Procedure) Act 1945, sections 284 and 287 shall not apply to the order;

    (b) in any other case, section 287 shall have effect in relation to the order as if, in subsection (4) of that section, for the reference to the date there mentioned there were substituted a reference to the date on which the order becomes operative under section 6 of that Act ("the operative date").

(2) Where by virtue of Part XI any such action as is mentioned in section 291 is required to be embodied in an order, and that order is subject to special parliamentary procedure, then—

    (a) if the order in which the action is embodied is confirmed by Act of Parliament under section 6 of that Act, sections 284 and 288 shall not apply;

    (b) in any other case, section 288 shall apply with the substitution for any reference to the date on which the action is taken of a reference to the operative date.   **[299]**

NOTES
Commencement: 24 August 1990.

PART XIII

APPLICATION OF ACT TO CROWN LAND

Preliminary

293. Preliminary definitions

(1) In this Part—

"Crown land" means land in which there is a Crown interest or a Duchy interest;

"Crown interest" means an interest belonging to Her Majesty in right of the Crown or belonging to a government department or held in trust for Her Majesty for the purposes of a government department;

"Duchy interest" means an interest belonging to Her Majesty in right of the Duchy of Lancaster or belonging to the Duchy of Cornwall;

"private interest" means an interest which is neither a Crown interest nor a Duchy interest.

(2) For the purposes of this Part "the appropriate authority", in relation to any land—

    (a) in the case of land belonging to Her Majesty in right of the Crown and forming part of the Crown Estate, means the Crown Estate Commissioners;

    (b) in relation to any other land belonging to Her Majesty in right of the Crown, means the government department having the management of that land;

    (c) in relation to land belonging to Her Majesty in right of the Duchy of Lancaster, means the Chancellor of the Duchy;

(d) in relation to land belonging to the Duchy of Cornwall, means such person as the Duke of Cornwall, or the possessor for the time being of the Duchy of Cornwall, appoints;

(e) in the case of land belonging to a government department or held in trust for Her Majesty for the purposes of a government department, means that department.

(3) If any question arises as to what authority is the appropriate authority in relation to any land, that question shall be referred to the Treasury, whose decision shall be final.

(4) A person who is entitled to occupy Crown land by virtue of a licence in writing shall be treated for the purposes of section 296(1)(c), so far as applicable to Parts III, VII and VIII, and sections 294(2) to (7), 295, 299 and 300 as having an interest in land and references in section 299 to the disposal of an interest in Crown land, and in that section and sections 294(2) and 300 to a private interest in such land, shall be construed accordingly.   **[300]**

NOTES
Commencement: 24 August 1990.

Application of Act as respects Crown land

294. Control of development on Crown land: special enforcement notices

(1) No enforcement notice shall be issued under section 172 in respect of development carried out by or on behalf of the Crown after 1st July 1948 on land which was Crown land at the time when the development was carried out.

(2) The following provisions of this section apply to development of Crown land carried out otherwise than by or on behalf of the Crown at a time when no person is entitled to occupy it by virtue of a private interest.

(3) Where—

(a) it appears to a local planning authority that development to which this subsection applies has taken place in their area, and

(b) they consider it expedient to do so having regard to the provisions of the development plan and to any other material considerations,

they may issue a notice under this section (a "special enforcement notice").

(4) No special enforcement notice shall be issued except with the consent of the appropriate authority.

(5) A special enforcement notice shall specify—

(a) the matters alleged to constitute development to which this section applies; and

(b) the steps which the authority issuing the notice require to be taken for restoring the land to its condition before the development took place or for discontinuing any use of the land which has been instituted by the development.

(6) A special enforcement notice shall also specify—

(a) the date on which it is to take effect ("the specified date"), and

(b) the period within which any such steps as are mentioned in subsection (5)(b) are to be taken.

(7) A special enforcement notice may specify different periods for the taking of different steps.   **[301]**

NOTES
Commencement: 24 August 1990.

295. Supplementary provisions as to special enforcement notices

(1) Not later than 28 days after the date of the issue of a special enforcement notice and not later than 28 days before the specified date, the local planning authority who issued it shall serve a copy of it—

    (a) on the person who carried out the development alleged in the notice;
    (b) on any person who is occupying the land when the notice is issued; and
    (c) on the appropriate authority.

(2) The local planning authority need not serve a copy of the notice on the person mentioned in subsection (1)(a) if they are unable after reasonable enquiry to identify or trace him.

(3) Any such person as mentioned in subsection (1)(a) or (b) may appeal against the notice to the Secretary of State on the ground that the matters alleged in the notice—

    (a) have not taken place, or
    (b) do not constitute development to which section 294 applies.

(4) A person may appeal against a special enforcement notice under subsection (3) whether or not he was served with a copy of it.

(5) The provisions contained in or having effect under sections 174(3) to (5), 175(1) to (4) and 176(1) to (4) shall apply to special enforcement notices issued by local planning authorities and to appeals against them under subsection (3) as they apply to enforcement notices and to appeals under section 174.

(6) The Secretary of State may by regulations apply to special enforcement notices and to appeals under subsection (3) such other provisions of this Act (with such modifications as he thinks fit) as he thinks necessary or expedient.   **[302]**

NOTES
Commencement: 24 August 1990.

296. Exercise of powers in relation to Crown land

(1) Notwithstanding any interest of the Crown in Crown land, but subject to the following provisions of this section—

    (a) a plan approved, adopted or made under Part II of this Act or Part II of the 1971 Act may include proposals relating to the use of Crown land;
    (b) any power to acquire land compulsorily under Part IX may be exercised in relation to any interest in Crown land which is for the time being held otherwise than by or on behalf of the Crown;
    (c) any restrictions or powers imposed or conferred by Part III, VII [except sections 196A and 196B] or VIII, by the provisions of Part VI relating to purchase notices, or by any of the provisions of sections 266 to 270, shall apply and be exercisable in relation to Crown land, to the extent of any interest in it for the time being held otherwise than by or on behalf of the Crown.

(2) Except with the consent of the appropriate authority—

(a) no order or notice shall be made, issued or served under any of the provisions of section 102, 103, [171C, 172, 173A, 183, 187A, 187B], 198, 199 or 215 or Schedule 9 or under any of those provisions as applied by any order or regulations made under Part VIII, in relation to land which for the time being is Crown land;

[(aa) in relation to land which for the time being is Crown land—

    (i) a planning obligation shall not be enforced by injunction; and
    (ii) the power to enter land conferred by section 106(6) shall not be exercised;]

(b) no interest in land which for the time being is Crown land shall be acquired compulsorily under Part IX.

(3) No purchase notice shall be served in relation to any interest in Crown land unless—

(a) an offer has been previously made by the owner of that interest to dispose of it to the appropriate authority on equivalent terms, and
(b) that offer has been refused by the appropriate authority.

(4) In subsection (3) "equivalent terms" means that the price payable for the interest shall be equal to (and shall, in default of agreement, be determined in the same manner as) the compensation which would be payable in respect of it if it were acquired in pursuance of a purchase notice.

(5) The rights conferred by the provisions of Chapter II of Part VI shall be exercisable by a person who (within the meaning of those provisions) is an owner-occupier of a hereditament or agricultural unit which is Crown land, or is a resident owner-occupier of a hereditament which is Crown land, in the same way as they are exercisable in respect of a hereditament or agricultural unit which is not Crown land, and those provisions shall apply accordingly. **[303]**

NOTES
Commencement: 24 August 1990.
Words in square brackets in sub-s (1)(b) and the whole of sub-s (2)(aa) inserted, and the words in square brackets in sub-s (2)(a) substituted, by the Planning and Compensation Act 1991, ss 12(2), 32, Sch 7, paras 8, 45.
1971 Act: Town and Country Planning Act 1971.

297. Agreements relating to Crown land

(1) The appropriate authority and the local planning authority for the area in which any Crown land is situated may make agreements for securing the use of the land, so far as may be prescribed by any such agreement, in conformity with the provisions of the development plan applicable to it.

(2) Any such agreement may contain such consequential provisions, including provisions of a financial character, as may appear to be necessary or expedient having regard to the purposes of the agreement.

(3) An agreement made under this section by a government department shall not have effect unless it is approved by the Treasury.

(4) In considering whether to make or approve an agreement under this section relating—

(a) to land belonging to a government department, or
(b) to land held in trust for Her Majesty for the purposes of a government department,

the department and the Treasury shall have regard to the purposes for which the land is held by or for the department.   **[304]**

NOTES
  Commencement: 24 August 1990.

298. Supplementary provisions as to Crown and Duchy interests

[(1) Where there is a Crown interest in any land, sections 109 to 112 shall have effect in relation to any private interest or Duchy interest as if the Crown interest were a private interest.

(2) Where there is a Duchy interest in any land, those sections shall have effect in relation to that interest or any private interest as if the Duchy interest were a private interest.]

(3) Where, in accordance with an agreement under section 297, the approval of a local planning authority is required in respect of any development of land in which there is a Duchy interest, [sections 109 to 112] shall have effect in relation to the withholding of that approval, or the giving of it subject to conditions, as if it were a refusal of planning permission or, as the case may be, a grant of planning permission subject to conditions.   **[305]**

NOTES
  Commencement: 24 August 1990 (sub-s (3)); 2 January 1992 (sub-ss (1), (2)).
  Sub-ss (1), (2), and words in square brackets in sub-s (3), substituted by the Planning and Compensation Act 1991, s 31(4), Sch 6, paras 8, 25 (but not affecting the operation of the Planning (Consequential Provisions) Act 1990, Sch 3 at **[520]**, in relation to any private or Duchy interest (as defined by s 293 of this Act at **[300]**).

Provisions relating to anticipated disposal of Crown land

299. Application for planning permission etc in anticipation of disposal of Crown land

(1) This section has effect for the purpose of enabling Crown land, or an interest in Crown land, to be disposed of with the benefit of planning permission or a [certificate under section 192].

(2) Notwithstanding the interest of the Crown in the land in question, an application for any such permission [or certificate] may be made by—
  (a) the appropriate authority; or
  (b) any person authorised by that authority in writing;
and, subject to subsections (3) to (5), all the statutory provisions relating to the making and determination of any such application shall accordingly apply as if the land were not Crown land.

(3) Any planning permission granted by virtue of this section shall apply only—
  (a) to development carried out after the land in question has ceased to be Crown land; and
  (b) so long as that land continues to be Crown land, to development carried out by virtue of a private interest in the land.

[(4) Any application made by virtue of this section for a certificate under section 192 shall be determined as if the land were not Crown land.]

(5) The Secretary of State may by regulations—

(a) modify or exclude any of the statutory provisions referred to in subsection (2) in their application by virtue of that subsection and any other statutory provisions in their application to permissions or [certificates] granted or made by virtue of this section;

(b) make provision for requiring a local planning authority to be notified of any disposal of, or of an interest in, any Crown land in respect of which an application has been made by virtue of this section; and

(c) make such other provision in relation to the making and determination of applications by virtue of this section as he thinks necessary or expedient.

(6) This section shall not be construed as affecting any right to apply for any such permission or [certificate] as is mentioned in subsection (1) in respect of Crown land in a case in which such an application can be made by virtue of a private interest in the land.

(7) In this section "statutory provisions" means provisions contained in or having effect under any enactment.   **[306]**

NOTES
   Commencement: 24 August 1990.
   Words in square brackets in sub-ss (1), (2), (5)(a), (6), and the whole of sub-s (4), substituted by the Planning and Compensation Act 1991, s 32, Sch 7, paras 8, 46.

[299A. Crown planning obligations

(1) The appropriate authority in relation to any Crown interest or Duchy interest in land in the area of a local planning authority may enter into an obligation falling within any of paragraphs (a) to (d) of section 106(1) (in this section referred to as a "planning obligation") enforceable to the extent mentioned in subsection (3).

(2) A planning obligation may not be entered into except by an instrument executed as a deed which—

(a) states that the obligation is a planning obligation for the purposes of this section;

(b) identifies the land in relation to which the obligation is entered into;

(c) identifies the appropriate authority who are entering into the obligation and states what the Crown or Duchy interest in the land is; and

(d) identifies the local planning authority by whom the obligation is enforceable.

(3) A planning obligation entered into under this section is enforceable—

(a) against any person with a private interest deriving from the Crown or Duchy interest stated in accordance with subsection (2)(c);

(b) by the authority identified in accordance with subsection (2)(d).

(4) Subject to subsection (5), subsections (2), (4) to (8) and (10) to (13) of section 106 and sections 106A and 106B apply to a planning obligation entered into under this section as they apply to a planning obligation entered into under that section.

(5) The consent of the appropriate authority must be obtained to—

(a) the enforcement by injunction of a planning obligation against a person in respect of land which is Crown land; and

(b) the exercise, in relation to Crown land, of the power to enter land conferred by section 106(6) (as applied by subsection (4)).]   **[306A]**

NOTES
Commencement: 25 October 1991.
Inserted by the Planning and Compensation Act 1991, s 12(3).

300. Tree preservation orders in anticipation of disposal of Crown land

(1) A local planning authority may make a tree preservation order in respect of Crown land in which no interest is for the time being held otherwise than by or on behalf of the Crown, if they consider it expedient to do so for the purpose of preserving trees or woodlands on the land in the event of its ceasing to be Crown land or becoming subject to a private interest.

(2) No tree preservation order shall be made by virtue of this section except with the consent of the appropriate authority.

(3) A tree preservation order made by virtue of this section shall not take effect until the first occurrence of a relevant event.

(4) For the purposes of subsection (3), a relevant event occurs in relation to any land if it ceases to be Crown land or becomes subject to a private interest.

(5) A tree preservation order made by virtue of this section—

(a) shall not require confirmation under section 199 until after the occurrence of the event by virtue of which it takes effect; and

(b) shall by virtue of this subsection continue in force until—

(i) the expiration of the period of six months beginning with the occurrence of that event; or

(ii) the date on which the order is confirmed,

whichever first occurs.

(6) Where a tree preservation order takes effect in accordance with subsection (3), the appropriate authority shall as soon as practicable give to the authority who made the order a notice in writing of the name and address of the person who has become entitled to the land in question or to a private interest in it.

(7) The procedure prescribed under section 199 in connection with the confirmation of a tree preservation order shall apply in relation to an order made by virtue of this section as if the order were made on the date on which the notice under subsection (6) is received by the authority who made it. **[307]**

NOTES
Commencement: 24 August 1990.

301. Requirement of planning permission for continuance of use instituted by the Crown

(1) A local planning authority in whose area any Crown land is situated may agree with the appropriate authority that subsection (2) shall apply to such use of land by the Crown as is specified in the agreement, being a use resulting from a material change made or proposed to be made by the Crown in the use of the land.

(2) Where an agreement is made under subsection (1) in respect of any Crown land, then, if at any time the land ceases to be used by the Crown for the purposes specified in the agreement, this Act shall have effect in relation to any subsequent private use of the land as if—

(a) the specified use by the Crown had required planning permission, and

(b) that use had been authorised by planning permission granted subject to a condition requiring its discontinuance at that time.

(3) The condition referred to in subsection (2) shall not be enforceable against any person who had a private interest in the land at the time when the agreement was made unless the local planning authority by whom the agreement was made have notified him of the making of the agreement and of the effect of that subsection.

(4) An agreement made under subsection (1) by a local planning authority shall be a local land charge, and for the purposes of the Local Land Charges Act 1975 the local planning authority by whom such an agreement is made shall be treated as the originating authority as respects the charge constituted by the agreement.

(5) In this section "private use" means use otherwise than by or on behalf of the Crown, and references to the use of land by the Crown include references to its use on behalf of the Crown.   **[308]**

NOTES
Commencement: 24 August 1990.

Enforcement in respect of war-time breaches of planning control by Crown

302. Enforcement in respect of war-time breaches of planning control by Crown

(1) This section applies where during the war period—

(a) works not complying with planning control were carried out on land, or

(b) a use of land not complying with planning control was begun by or on behalf of the Crown.

(2) Subject to subsection (4), if at any time after the end of the war period there subsists in the land a permanent or long-term interest which is neither held by or on behalf of the Crown nor subject to any interest or right to possession so held, the planning control shall, so long as such an interest subsists in the land, be enforceable in respect of those works or that use notwithstanding—

(a) that the works were carried out or the land used by or on behalf of the Crown, or

(b) the subsistence in the land of any interest held by or on behalf of the Crown in reversion (whether immediate or not) expectant on the termination of that permanent or long-term interest.

(3) A person entitled to make an application under this subsection with respect to any land may apply at any time before the relevant date to an authority responsible for enforcing any planning control for a determination—

(a) whether works on the land carried out, or a use of the land begun, during the war period fail to comply with any planning control which the authority are responsible for enforcing, and

(b) if so, whether the works or use should be deemed to comply with that control.

(4) Where any works on land carried out, or use of land begun, during the war period remain or continues after the relevant date and no such determination has been given, the works or use shall by virtue of this subsection be treated for all purposes as complying with that control unless steps for enforcing the control have been begun before that date.

(5) Schedule 15 shall have effect for the purpose of making supplementary provision concerning the enforcement of breaches of planning control to which this section applies and the making and determination of applications under subsection (3).

(6) In this section and that Schedule—

"authority responsible for enforcing planning control" means, in relation to any works on land or use of land, the authority empowered by virtue of section 75 of the 1947 Act or of paragraph 34 of Schedule 24 to the 1971 Act (including that paragraph as it continues in effect by virtue of Schedule 3 to the Planning (Consequential Provisions) Act 1990) to serve an enforcement notice in respect of it or the authority who would be so empowered if the works had been carried out, or the use begun, otherwise than in compliance with planning control;

"the relevant date", in relation to any land, means the date with which the period of five years from the end of the war period ends, but for the purposes of this definition any time during which, notwithstanding subsection (2), planning control is unenforceable by reason of the subsistence in or over the land of any interest or right to possession held by or on behalf of the Crown shall be disregarded;

"owner" has the same meaning as in the Housing Act 1985 and "owned" shall be construed accordingly;

"permanent or long-term interest", in relation to any land, means the fee simple in the land, a tenancy of the land granted for a term of more than ten years and not subject to a subsisting right of the landlord to determine the tenancy at or before the expiration of ten years from the beginning of the term, or a tenancy granted for a term of ten years or less with a right of renewal which would enable the tenant to prolong the term of the tenancy beyond ten years;

"tenancy" includes a tenancy under an underlease and a tenancy under an agreement for a lease or underlease, but does not include an option to take a tenancy and does not include a mortgage;

"war period" means the period extending from 3rd September 1939 to 26th March 1946;

"works" includes any building, structure, excavation or other work on land.

(7) References in this section and that Schedule to non-compliance with planning control mean—

(a) in relation to works on land carried out, or a use of land begun, at a time when the land was subject to a resolution to prepare a scheme under the Town and Country Planning Act 1932, that the works were carried out or the use begun otherwise than in accordance with the terms of an interim development order or of permission granted under such an order;

(b) in relation to works on land carried out, or a use of land begun, at a time when the land was subject to such a scheme, that the works were carried out or the use begun otherwise than in conformity with the provisions of the scheme;

and references in this Act to compliance with planning control shall be construed accordingly.

(8) References in this section and that Schedule to the enforcement of planning control shall be construed as references to the exercise of the powers conferred by section 75 of the 1947 Act or by paragraph 34 of Schedule 24 to the 1971 Act (including that paragraph as it continues in effect by virtue of Schedule 3 to the Planning (Consequential Provisions) Act 1990).   **[309]**

NOTES

Commencement: 24 August 1990.
1947 Act: the Town and Country Planning Act 1947.
1971 Act: the Town and Country Planning Act 1971.

PART XIV

FINANCIAL PROVISIONS

303. Fees for planning applications, etc

(1) The Secretary of State may by regulations make such provision as he thinks fit for the payment of a fee of the prescribed amount to a local planning authority in respect of an application made to them under the planning Acts or any order or regulations made under them for any permission, consent, approval, determination or certificate.

(2) Regulations under subsection (1) may provide for the transfer of prescribed fees received in respect of any description of application by an authority to whom applications fall to be made to any other authority by whom applications of that description fall to be dealt with.

(3) The Secretary of State may by regulations make such provision as he thinks fit for the payment—

    [(a) of fees of prescribed amounts to him and to the local planning authority in respect of any application for planning permission deemed to be made under section 177(5); and

    (b) of a fee of the prescribed amount to him in respect of any other] application for planning permission which is deemed to be made to him under this Act or any order or regulations made under it.

(4) Regulations under subsection (1) or (3) may provide for the remission or refunding of a prescribed fee (in whole or in part) in prescribed circumstances.

(5) No such regulations shall be made unless a draft of the regulations has been laid before and approved by a resolution of each House of Parliament.

(6) The reference to the planning Acts in subsection (1) does not include a reference to section 302 of this Act [or the Planning (Hazardous Substances) Act 1990]. **[310]**

NOTES
    Commencement: 24 August 1990.
    Words in square brackets in sub-s (3) substituted by the Planning and Compensation Act 1991, s 6(6).
    Words in square brackets in sub-s (6) added by the Environmental Protection Act 1990, s 144, Sch 13, Pt I, para 10.
    Planning Acts: Town and Country Planning Act 1990, Planning (Listed Buildings and Conservation Areas) Act 1990, Planning (Hazardous Substances) Act 1990, Planning (Consequential Provisions) Act 1990.

304. Grants for research and education

The Secretary of State may, with the consent of the Treasury, make grants for assisting establishments engaged in promoting or assisting research relating to, and education with respect to, the planning and design of the physical environment.

[311]

NOTES
    Commencement: 24 August 1990.

305. Contributions by Ministers towards compensation paid by local authorities

(1) Where—

(a) compensation is payable by a local authority [or National Park authority] under this Act in consequence of any decision or order to which this section applies, and

(b) that decision or order was given or made wholly or partly in the interest of a service which is provided by a government department and the cost of which is defrayed out of money provided by Parliament,

the Minister responsible for the administration of that service may pay to that authority a contribution of such amount as he may with the consent of the Treasury determine.

(2) This section applies to any decision or order given or made under Part III, the provisions of Part VI relating to purchase notices, Part VII, Part VIII or Schedule 5, 6 or 9.   **[312]**

NOTES

Commencement: 24 August 1990.

Words in square brackets in sub-s (1)(a) inserted by the Environment Act 1995, s 78, Sch 10, para 32(9), as from a day to be appointed under s 125(3).

306. Contributions by local authorities and statutory undertakers

(1) Without prejudice to section 274 of the Highways Act 1980 (contributions by local authorities to expenses of highway authorities), any local authority may contribute towards any expenses incurred by a local highway authority—

(a) in the acquisition of land under Part IX of this Act or Chapter V of Part I of the Planning (Listed Buildings and Conservation Areas) Act 1990,

(b) in the construction or improvement of roads on land so acquired, or

(c) in connection with any development required in the interests of the proper planning of the area of the local authority.

(2) Any local authority and any statutory undertakers may contribute towards—

(a) any expenses incurred by a local planning authority in or in connection with the carrying out of a survey or the preparation of a unitary development plan or a local plan [minerals local plan or waste local plan] or the alteration, . . . or replacement of such a plan or a structure plan under Part II;

(b) any expenses incurred by a local planning authority or a mineral planning authority in or in connection with the performance of any of their functions under Part III, the provisions of Part VI relating to purchase notices, Part VII [except sections 196A and 196B], Part VIII (except section 207), Part IX or Schedule 5 or 9.

(3) Where any expenses are incurred by a local authority in the payment of compensation payable in consequence of anything done under Part III, the provisions of Part VI relating to purchase notices, Part VII [except sections 196A and 196B], Part VIII, or Schedule 5 or 9, the Secretary of State may, if it appears to him to be expedient to do so, require any other local authority to contribute towards those expenses such sum as appears to him to be reasonable, having regard to any benefit accruing to that authority by reason of the proceeding giving rise to the compensation.

(4) Subsection (3) shall apply in relation to payments made by a local authority to any statutory undertakers in accordance with financial arrangements to which effect is given under section 275(5)(c), as it applies in relation to compensation payable by such an authority in consequence of anything done under Part III, Part VIII or Schedule 5 or 9, and the reference in that subsection to the proceeding giving rise to the compensation shall be construed accordingly.

(5) For the purposes of this section, contributions made by a local planning authority towards the expenditure of a joint advisory committee shall be deemed to be expenses incurred by that authority for the purposes for which that expenditure is incurred by the committee.

[(6) This section shall have effect as if the references to a local authority included references to a National Park authority.]   **[313]**

NOTES

Commencement: 24 August 1990 (sub-ss (1)–(5)); to be appointed (sub-s (6)).

Words in square brackets in sub-ss (2), (3) inserted, and words omitted from sub-s (2)(a) repealed, by the Planning and Compensation Act 1991, ss 27, 32, 84(6), Sch 4, Pt II, para 32, Sch 7, paras 8, 47, Sch 19, Pt I.

Sub-s (6) inserted by the Environment Act 1995, s 78, Sch 10, para 32(10), as from a day to be appointed under s 125(3).

---

307. Assistance for acquisition of property where objection made to blight notice in certain cases

(1) The council of a county, [county borough,] district or London borough may advance money to any person for the purposes of enabling him to acquire a hereditament or agricultural unit in respect of which a counter-notice has been served under section 151 specifying the grounds mentioned in subsection (4)(d) of that section as, or as one of, the grounds of objection.

(2) No advance may be made under subsection (1) in the case of a hereditament if its annual value exceeds such amount as may be prescribed for the purposes of section 149(3)(a).

(3) An advance under subsection (1) may be made subject to such conditions as the council may think fit.   **[314]**

NOTES

Commencement: 24 August 1990.

Words in square brackets in sub-s (1) inserted by the Local Government (Wales) Act 1994, s 20(4)(b), Sch 6, Pt II, para 24(12), as from a day to be appointed.

---

308. Recovery from acquiring authorities of sums paid by way of compensation

(1) This section applies where—

    (a) an interest in land is compulsorily acquired or is sold to an authority possessing compulsory purchase powers, and

    (b) a notice is registered under section 110(2) . . . in respect of any of the land acquired or sold (whether before or after the completion of the acquisition or sale) in consequence of a planning decision or order made before the service of the notice to treat, or the making of the contract, in pursuance of which the acquisition or sale is effected.

(2) Where this section applies the Secretary of State shall, subject to the following provisions of this section, be entitled to recover from the acquiring authority a sum equal to so much of the amount of the compensation specified in the notice as (in accordance with section 110(5) . . .) is to be treated as attributable to that land.

(3) If, immediately after the completion of the acquisition or sale, there is outstanding some interest in the land acquired or sold to which a person other than the acquiring authority is entitled, the sum referred to in subsection (2) shall not

accrue due until that interest either ceases to exist or becomes vested in the acquiring authority.

(4) No sum shall be recoverable under this section in the case of a compulsory acquisition or sale where the Secretary of State is satisfied that the interest in question is being acquired for the purposes of the use of the land as a public open space.

(5) Where the Secretary of State recovers a sum under this section in respect of any land by reason that it is land in respect of which a notice is registered under the provisions of section 110, section 112(11) to (13) shall have effect in relation to that sum as if it were a sum recovered as mentioned in section 112(11).

(6) In this section . . . "interest" (where the reference is to an interest in land) means the fee simple or a tenancy of the land and does not include any other interest in it.   **[315–316]**

NOTES

Commencement: 24 August 1990.

Words omitted from sub-ss (1)(b), (2), (6) repealed (and any amount recoverable under this section by reason of a notice registered under s 132(1) (repealed) which has not been paid ceased to be recoverable) by the Planning and Compensation Act 1991, ss 31(4), 84(6), Sch 6, paras 8, 26, Sch 19, Pt II.

309. (*Repealed by the Planning and Compensation Act 1991, ss 31(4), 84(6), Sch 6, paras 8, 27, Sch 19, Pt II.*)

310. Sums recoverable from acquiring authorities reckonable for purposes of grant

Where—

(a) a sum is recoverable from any authority under section 308 . . . by reference to an acquisition or purchase of an interest in land, and

(b) a grant became or becomes payable to that or some other authority under an enactment in respect of that acquisition or purchase or of a subsequent appropriation of the land,

the power conferred by that enactment to pay the grant shall include, and shall be deemed always to have included, power to pay a grant in respect of that sum as if it had been expenditure incurred by the acquiring authority in connection with the acquisition or purchase.   **[317]**

NOTES

Commencement: 24 August 1990.

Words omitted repealed by the Planning and Compensation Act 1991, ss 31(4), 84(6), Sch 6, paras 8, 28, Sch 19, Pt II.

311. Expenses of government departments

(1) The following expenses of the Secretary of State shall be paid out of money provided by Parliament—

(a) any expenses incurred by the Secretary of State under subsection (5) of section 220 or in the payment of expenses of any committee established under that section;

(b) any sums necessary to enable the Secretary of State to make any payments becoming payable by him under Part IV . . . ;

(c) any expenses incurred by the Secretary of State under Part X;

(d) any expenses incurred by the Secretary of State in the making of grants under section 304;

(e) any administrative expenses incurred by the Secretary of State for the purposes of this Act.

(2) There shall be paid out of money provided by Parliament any expenses incurred by any government department (including the Secretary of State)—

    (a) in the acquisition of land under Part IX;
    (b) in the payment of compensation under section 236(4), 279(2) or 325;
    (c) under section 240(1)(b); or
    (d) under section 305.   **[318–319]**

NOTES
    Commencement: 24 August 1990.
    Words omitted from sub-s (1)(b) repealed by the Planning and Compensation Act 1991, ss 31(4), 84(6), Sch 6, paras 8, 29, Sch 19, Pt II.

312. *(Repealed by the Planning and Compensation Act 1991, ss 31(4), 84(6), Sch 6, paras 8, 30, Sch 19, Pt II.)*

313. General provision as to receipts of Secretary of State

. . . subject to the provisions of section 112, any sums received by the Secretary of State under any provision of this Act shall be paid into the Consolidated Fund. **[320]**

NOTES
    Commencement: 24 August 1990.
    Words omitted repealed by the Planning and Compensation Act 1991, ss 31(4), 84(6), Sch 6, paras 8, 31, Sch 19, Pt II.

314. Expenses of county councils

The council of a county may direct that any expenses incurred by them under the provisions specified in Parts I and II of Schedule 16 shall be treated as special expenses of a county council chargeable upon such part of the county as may be specified in the directions.   **[321]**

NOTES
    Commencement: 24 August 1990.

PART XV

MISCELLANEOUS AND GENERAL PROVISIONS

Application of Act in special cases

315. Power to modify Act in relation to minerals

(1) In relation to development consisting of the winning and working of minerals [or involving the depositing of mineral waste], the provisions specified in Parts I and II of Schedule 16 shall have effect subject to such adaptations and modifications as may be prescribed.

    (2) In relation to interests in land consisting of or comprising minerals (being either the fee simple or tenancies of such land), . . . the provisions specified in Part III of Schedule 16 shall have effect subject to such adaptations and modifications as may be prescribed.

    (3) Regulations made for the purposes of this section may only be made with the consent of the Treasury and shall be of no effect unless they are approved by resolution of each House of Parliament.

(4) Any regulations made by virtue of subsection (1) shall not apply—

(a) to the winning and working, on land held or occupied with land used for the purposes of agriculture of any minerals reasonably required for the purposes of that use, including the fertilisation of the land so used and the maintenance, improvement or alteration of buildings or works on it which are occupied or used for those purposes; . . .

(5) Nothing in subsection (1) or (4) shall be construed as affecting the prerogative right of Her Majesty (whether in right of the Crown or of the Duchy of Lancaster) or of the Duke of Cornwall to any gold or silver mine.   **[322]**

NOTES

Commencement: 24 August 1990.

Words in square brackets in sub-s (1) inserted, and words omitted from sub-s (2) repealed, by the Planning and Compensation Act 1991, ss 21, 31(4), 84(6), Sch 1, paras 1, 11, Sch 6, paras 8, 32, Sch 19, Pt II.

Words omitted from sub-s (4) repealed by the Coal Industry Act 1994, s 67(1), (8), Sch 9, para 39(2), Sch 11, Pt III.

[316. Land of interested planning authorities and development by them

(1) The provisions of Parts III, VII and VIII of this Act shall apply in relation to—

(a) land of interested planning authorities; and
(b) the development of any land by interested planning authorities or by such authorities jointly with any other persons,

subject to regulations made by virtue of this section.

(2) The regulations may, in relation to such land or such development—

(a) provide for any of those provisions to apply subject to prescribed exceptions or modifications or not to apply;
(b) make new provision as to any matter dealt with in any of those provisions;
(c) make different provision in relation to different classes of land or development.

(3) Without prejudice to subsection (2), the regulations may provide—

(a) subject to subsection (5), for applications for planning permission to develop such land, or for such development, to be determined by the authority concerned, by another interested planning authority or by the Secretary of State; and
(b) for the procedure to be followed on such applications,

and, in the case of applications falling to be determined by an interested planning authority, they may regulate the authority's arrangements for the discharge of their functions, notwithstanding anything in section 101 of the Local Government Act 1972.

(4) The regulations shall—

(a) provide for section 71(3), and any provision made by virtue of section 65 or 71 by a development order, to apply to applications for planning permission to develop such land, or for such development, subject to prescribed exceptions or modifications, or
(b) make corresponding provision.

(5) In the case of any application for planning permission to develop land of an interested planning authority where—

(a) the authority do not intend to develop the land themselves or jointly with any other person; and

(b) if it were not such land, the application would fall to be determined by another body,

the regulations shall provide for the application to be determined by that other body, unless the application is referred to the Secretary of State under section 77.

(6) In this section "interested planning authority", in relation to any land, means any body which exercises any of the functions of a local planning authority in relation to that land; and for the purposes of this section land is land of an authority if the authority have any interest in it.

(7) This section applies to any consent required in respect of any land as it applies to planning permission to develop land.

(8) Subsection (1) does not apply to sections 76, 90(2) and (5) and 223.]   **[323]**

NOTES
   Commencement: 17 July 1992.
   Substituted by the Planning and Compensation Act 1991, s 20.

[316A. Local planning authorities as statutory undertakers

In relation to statutory undertakers who are local planning authorities, section 283 and the provisions specified in that section shall have effect subject to such exceptions and modifications as may be prescribed.]   **[324]**

NOTES
   Commencement: 25 November 1991 (certain purposes); 17 July 1992 (remaining purposes).
   Inserted by the Planning and Compensation Act 1991, s 32, Sch 7, paras 8, 48.

317. *(Repealed by the Coal Industry Act 1994, s 67(1), (8), Sch 9, para 39(3), Sch 11, Pt III.)*

318. Ecclesiastical property

(1) Without prejudice to the provisions of the Acquisition of Land Act 1981 with respect to notices served under that Act, where under any of the provisions of this Act a notice or copy of a notice is required to be served on an owner of land, and the land is ecclesiastical property, a similar notice or copy of a notice shall be served on the Church Commissioners.

(2) Where the fee simple of any ecclesiastical property is in abeyance—

(a) if the property is situated elsewhere than in Wales, then for the purposes of the provisions specified in Part VI of Schedule 16 the fee simple shall be treated as being vested in the Church Commissioners;

(b) in any case, the fee simple shall, for the purposes of a compulsory acquisition of the property under Part IX, be treated as being vested in the Church Commissioners, and any notice to treat shall be served, or be deemed to have been served, accordingly.

(3) Any compensation payable under Part IV, section 186, Part VIII (except section 204) or section 250 in respect of land which is ecclesiastical property—

(a) shall [in the case of land which is not diocesan glebe land, be paid to the Church Commissioners, and

(b) shall, in the case of diocesan glebe land, be paid to the Diocesan Board of Finance in which the land is vested,

and shall (in either case)] be applied by them for the purposes for which the proceeds of a sale by agreement of the land would be applicable under any enactment or Measure authorising or disposing of the proceeds of such a sale.

(4) Any sum which under any of the provisions specified in Part III of Schedule 16 is payable in relation to land which is, or on 1st July 1948 was, ecclesiastical property, and apart from this subsection would be payable to an incumbent—

(a) shall be paid to the Church Commissioners, and
(b) shall be applied by them for the purposes mentioned in subsection [(3)]).

(5) Where any sum is recoverable under section 111, [or 112] in respect of any such land, the Church Commissioners may apply any money or securities held by them in the payment of that sum.

(6) In this section "ecclesiastical property" means land belonging to an ecclesiastical benefice, or being or forming part of a church subject to the jurisdiction of a bishop of any diocese or the site of such a church, or being or forming part of a burial ground subject to such jurisdiction [or being diocesan glebe land; and "Diocesan Board of Finance" and "diocesan glebe land" have the same meaning as in the Endowments and Glebe Measure 1976].   **[325]**

NOTES
Commencement: 24 August 1990.
Words in square brackets in sub-ss (3)–(5) substituted by the Planning and Compensation Act 1991, ss 31(4), 70, Sch 6, paras 8, 33, Sch 15, Pt II, para 30.

[319. The Isles of Scilly

(1) This Act applies to the Isles of Scilly subject to such exceptions, adaptations and modifications as the Secretary of State may by order direct.

(2) An order under this section may in particular provide for the exercise by the Council of the Isles of Scilly of any functions exercisable by a local planning authority or mineral planning authority.

(3) Before making an order under this section the Secretary of State shall consult with that Council.]   **[326]**

NOTES
Commencement: 25 November 1991 (certain purposes); 27 July 1992 (remaining purposes).
Substituted by the Planning and Compensation Act 1991, s 32, Sch 7, paras 8, 49.

Local inquiries and other hearings

320. Local inquiries

(1) The Secretary of State may cause a local inquiry to be held for the purposes of the exercise of any of his functions under any of the provisions of this Act.

(2) Subsections (2) to (5) of section 250 of the Local Government Act 1972 (local inquiries: evidence and costs) apply to an inquiry held by virtue of this section.   **[327]**

NOTES
Commencement: 24 August 1990.

321. Planning inquiries to be held in public subject to certain exceptions

(1) This section applies to any inquiry held under section 320(1), paragraph 6 of Schedule 6 or paragraph 5 of Schedule 8.

(2) Subject to subsection (3), at any such inquiry oral evidence shall be heard in public and documentary evidence shall be open to public inspection.

(3) If the Secretary of State is satisfied in the case of any such inquiry—

(a) that giving evidence of a particular description or, as the case may be, making it available for inspection would be likely to result in the disclosure of information as to any of the matters mentioned in subsection (4); and

(b) that the public disclosure of that information would be contrary to the national interest,

he may direct that evidence of the description indicated in the direction shall only be heard or, as the case may be, open to inspection at that inquiry by such persons or persons of such descriptions as he may specify in the direction.

(4) The matters referred to in subsection (3)(a) are—

(a) national security; and

(b) the measures taken or to be taken to ensure the security of any premises or property.   **[328]**

NOTES

Commencement: 24 August 1990.

322. Orders as to costs of parties where no local inquiry held

(1) *This section applies to proceedings under this Act where the Secretary of State is required, before reaching a decision, to give any person an opportunity of appearing before and being heard by a person appointed by him.*

(2) *The Secretary of State has the same power to make orders under section 250(5) of the Local Government Act 1972 (orders with respect to the costs of the parties) in relation to proceedings to which this section applies which do not give rise to a local inquiry as he has in relation to a local inquiry.*   **[329]**

NOTES

Commencement: 24 August 1990.

This section temporarily omitted by the Planning (Consequential Provisions) Act 1990, s 6, Sch 14, paras 1, 6, until such day as may be appointed by order made by the Secretary of State. The Planning (Consequential Provisions) Act 1990 (Appointed Day No 1 and Transitional Provisions) Order 1991, SI 1991/2698, appointed 2 January 1992 only for the purposes of awards of costs in relation to proceedings which give rise to a hearing.

[322A. Orders as to costs: supplementary

(1) This section applies where—

(a) for the purposes of any proceedings under this Act—

(i) the Secretary of State is required, before a decision is reached, to give any person an opportunity, or ask any person whether he wishes, to appear before and be heard by a person appointed by him; and

(ii) arrangements are made for a local inquiry or hearing to be held;

(b) the inquiry or hearing does not take place; and

(c) if it had taken place, the Secretary of State or a person appointed by him would have had power to make an order under section 250(5) of the Local Government Act 1972 requiring any party to pay any costs of any other party.

(2) Where this section applies the power to make such an order may be exercised, in relation to costs incurred for the purposes of the inquiry or hearing, as if it had taken place.]   **[329A]**

NOTES
    Commencement: 2 January 1992.
    Inserted by the Planning and Compensation Act 1991, s 30(1).

323. Procedure on certain appeals and applications

(1) The Secretary of State may by regulations prescribe the procedure to be followed in connection with proceedings under this Act where he is required, before reaching a decision, to give any person an opportunity of appearing before and being heard by a person appointed by him and which are to be disposed of without an inquiry or hearing to which rules under [section 9 of the Tribunals and Inquiries Act 1992] apply.

(2) The regulations may in particular make provision as to the procedure to be followed—

   (a) where steps have been taken with a view to the holding of such an inquiry or hearing which does not take place, or

   (b) where steps have been taken with a view to the determination of any matter by a person appointed by the Secretary of State and the proceedings are the subject of a direction that the matter shall instead be determined by the Secretary of State, or

   (c) where steps have been taken in pursuance of such a direction and a further direction is made revoking that direction,

and may provide that such steps shall be treated as compliance, in whole or in part, with the requirements of the regulations.

(3) The regulations may also—

   (a) provide for a time limit within which any party to the proceedings must submit representations in writing and any supporting documents;

   (b) prescribe the time limit (which may be different for different classes of proceedings) or enable the Secretary of State to give directions setting the time limit in a particular case or class of case;

   (c) empower the Secretary of State to proceed to a decision taking into account only such written representations and supporting documents as were submitted within the time limit; and

   (d) empower the Secretary of State, after giving the parties written notice of his intention to do so, to proceed to a decision notwithstanding that no written representations were made within the time limit, if it appears to him that he has sufficient material before him to enable him to reach a decision on the merits of the case.   **[330]**

NOTES
    Commencement: 24 August 1990.
    Words in square brackets in sub-s (1) substituted by the Tribunals and Inquiries Act 1992, s 18(1), Sch 3, para 26.

Rights of entry

324. Rights of entry

(1) Any person duly authorised in writing by the Secretary of State or by a local planning authority may at any reasonable time enter any land for the purpose of surveying it in connection with—

   (a) the preparation, approval, adoption or making of a unitary development plan or a local plan [minerals local plan or waste local plan] relating to the land under Part II or the alteration of such a plan or a structure plan relating to the land under that Part, including the carrying out of any survey under that Part;

(b) any application under Part III or sections . . . 220 or 221 or under any order or regulations made under any of those provisions, for any permission, consent or determination to be given or made in connection with that land or any other land under that Part or any of those sections or under any such order or regulations;

(c) any proposal by the local planning authority or by the Secretary of State to make, issue or serve any order or notice under Part III (other than sections 94 and 96), . . . [or Chapter 2 or 3 of Part VIII] or under any order or regulations made under any of those provisions.

(2) . . .

(3) Any person duly authorised in writing by the local planning authority may at any reasonable time enter any land for the purpose of exercising a power conferred on the authority by section 225 if—

(a) the land is unoccupied; and
(b) it would be impossible to exercise the power without entering the land.

(4) . . .

(5) Any person who is an officer of the Valuation Office or is duly authorised in writing by a local planning authority may at any reasonable time enter any land for the purpose of surveying it or estimating its value, in connection with a claim for compensation in respect of that land or any other land which is payable by the local planning authority under Part IV, section 186, [Chapter 2 or 3 of Part VIII], section 205(1) or Part XI (other than section 279(2) or (3) or 280(1)(c)).

(6) Any person who is an officer of the Valuation Office or is duly authorised in writing by a local authority or Minister authorised to acquire land under section 226 or 228 or by a local authority who have power to acquire land under Part IX may at any reasonable time enter any land for the purpose of surveying it, or estimating its value, in connection with any proposal to acquire that land or any other land or in connection with any claim for compensation in respect of any such acquisition.

(7) Any person duly authorised in writing by the Secretary of State or by a local planning authority may at any reasonable time enter any land in respect of which an order or notice has been made or served as mentioned in subsection (1)(c) for the purpose of ascertaining whether the order or notice has been complied with.

(8) Subject to section 325, any power conferred by this section to survey land shall be construed as including power to search and bore for the purpose of ascertaining the nature of the subsoil or the presence of minerals in it.

(9) In subsections (1)(c) and (7) references to a local planning authority include, in relation to a building situated in Greater London, a reference to the Historic Buildings and Monuments Commission for England. **[331]**

NOTES
Commencement: 24 August 1990.
Words in square brackets in sub-s (1)(a) inserted, words omitted from sub-s (1)(b), (c) and the whole of sub-ss (2), (4) repealed, and words in square brackets in sub-ss (1)(c), (5) substituted, by the Planning and Compensation Act 1991, ss 11(2), 23(8), 27, 31(4), 84(6), Sch 4, Pt II, para 33, Sch 6, paras 8, 34, Sch 19, Pts I, II.
Modification: see the note to s 251 at **[258]**.

325. Supplementary provisions as to rights of entry

(1) A person authorised under section 324 to enter any land—

    (a) shall, if so required, produce evidence of his authority [and state the purpose of his entry] before so entering, and

    (b) shall not demand admission as of right to any land which is occupied unless 24 hours' notice of the intended entry has been given to the occupier.

(2) Any person who wilfully obstructs a person acting in the exercise of his powers under section 324 shall be guilty of an offence and liable on summary conviction to a fine not exceeding [level 3] on the standard scale.

(3) If any person who, in compliance with the provisions of section 324, is admitted into a factory, workshop or workplace discloses to any person any information obtained by him in it as to any manufacturing process or trade secret, he shall be guilty of an offence.

(4) Subsection (3) does not apply if the disclosure is made by a person in the course of performing his duty in connection with the purpose for which he was authorised to enter the [land].

(5) A person who is guilty of an offence under subsection (3) shall be liable on summary conviction to a fine not exceeding the statutory maximum or on conviction on indictment to imprisonment for a term not exceeding two years or a fine or both.

(6) Where any [damage is caused to land or chattels]—

    (a) in the exercise of a right of entry conferred under section 324, or

    (b) in the making of any survey for the purpose of which any such right of entry has been so conferred,

compensation [may be recovered by any person suffering the damage] from the Secretary of State or authority on whose behalf the entry was effected.

(7) The provisions of section 118 shall apply in relation to compensation under subsection (6) as they apply in relation to compensation under Part IV.

(8) No person shall carry out under section 324 any works authorised by virtue of subsection (8) of that section unless notice of his intention to do so was included in the notice required by subsection (1).

(9) The authority of the appropriate Minister shall be required for the carrying out under that section of works so authorised if the land in question is held by statutory undertakers, and they object to the proposed works on the ground that the execution of the works would be seriously detrimental to the carrying on of their undertaking.   **[332–334]**

NOTES

    Commencement: 24 August 1990.

    Words in square brackets in sub-s (1)(a) inserted, and words in square brackets in sub-ss (2), (4), (6) substituted, by the Planning and Compensation Act 1991, ss 11(3), 32, Sch 7, paras 8, 50.

Miscellaneous and general provisions

326, 327. (*Repealed by the Planning and Compensation Act 1991, ss 31(4), 84(6), Sch 6, paras 8, 35, 36, Sch 19, Pt II.*)

328. Settled land and land of universities and colleges

(1) The purposes authorised for the application of capital money—

    (a) by section 73 of the Settled Land Act 1925 and by that section as applied by section 28 of the Law of Property Act 1925 in relation to trusts for sale; and

    (b) by section 26 of the Universities and College Estates Act 1925,

shall include the payment of any sum recoverable under section 111, [or 112].

(2) The purposes authorised as purposes for which money may be raised by mortgage—

    (a) by section 71 of the Settled Land Act 1925 and by that section as so applied; and

    (b) by section 30 of the Universities and College Estates Act 1925,

shall include the payment of any sum so recoverable.   [335]

NOTES
    Commencement: 24 August 1990.
    Words in square brackets in sub-s (1) substituted by the Planning and Compensation Act 1991, s 31(4), Sch 6, paras 8, 37.

329. Service of notices

(1) Any notice or other document required or authorised to be served or given under this Act may be served or given either—

    (a) by delivering it to the person on whom it is to be served or to whom it is to be given; or

    (b) by leaving it at the usual or last known place of abode of that person or, in a case where an address for service has been given by that person, at that address; or

    (c) by sending it in a prepaid registered letter, or by the recorded delivery service, addressed to that person at his usual or last known place of abode or, in a case where an address for service has been given by that person, at that address; or

    (d) in the case of an incorporated company or body, by delivering it to the secretary or clerk of the company or body at their registered or principal office or sending it in a prepaid registered letter, or by the recorded delivery service, addressed to the secretary or clerk of the company or body at that office.

(2) Where the notice or document is required or authorised to be served on any person as having an interest in premises, and the name of that person cannot be ascertained after reasonable inquiry, or where the notice or document is required or authorised to be served on any person as an occupier of premises, the notice or document shall be taken to be duly served if—

    (a) it is addressed to him either by name or by the description of ''the owner'' or, as the case may be, ''the occupier'' of the premises (describing them) and is delivered or sent in the manner specified in subsection (1)(a), (b) or (c); or

    (b) it is so addressed and is marked in such a manner as may be prescribed for securing that it is plainly identifiable as a communication of importance and—

        (i) it is sent to the premises in a prepaid registered letter or by the recorded delivery service and is not returned to the authority sending it, or

     (ii) it is delivered to some person on those premises, or is affixed conspicuously to some object on those premises.

(3) Where—

     (a) the notice or other document is required to be served on or given to all persons who have interests in or are occupiers of premises comprised in any land, and

     (b) it appears to the authority required or authorised to serve or give the notice or other document that any part of that land is unoccupied,

the notice or document shall be taken to be duly served on all persons having interests in, and on any occupiers of, premises comprised in that part of the land (other than a person who has given to that authority an address for the service of the notice or document on him) if it is addressed to ''the owners and any occupiers'' of that part of the land (describing it) and is affixed conspicuously to some object on the land.

[(4) This section is without prejudice to section 233 of the Local Government Act 1972 (general provisions as to service of notices by local authorities).] **[336]**

NOTES
    Commencement: 24 August 1990 (sub-ss (1)–(3)); 25 October 1991 (sub-s (4)).
    Sub-s (4) added by the Planning and Compensation Act 1991, s 32, Sch 7, paras 8, 51.

330. Power to require information as to interests in land

(1) For the purpose of enabling the Secretary of State or a local authority to make an order or issue or serve any notice or other document which, by any of the provisions of this Act, he or they are authorised or required to make, issue or serve, the Secretary of State or the local authority may by notice in writing require the occupier of any premises and any person who, either directly or indirectly, receives rent in respect of any premises to give in writing such information as to the matters mentioned in subsection (2) as may be so specified.

(2) Those matters are—

     (a) the nature of the interest in the premises of the person on whom the notice is served;

     (b) the name and address of any other person known to him as having an interest in the premises;

     (c) the purpose for which the premises are being used;

     (d) the time when that use began;

     (e) the name and address of any person known to the person on whom the notice is served as having used the premises for that purpose;

     (f) the time when any activities being carried out on the premises began.

(3) A notice under subsection (1) may require information to be given within 21 days after the date on which it is served, or such longer time as may be specified in it, or as the Secretary of State or, as the case may be, the local authority may allow.

(4) Any person who, without reasonable excuse, fails to comply with a notice served on him under subsection (1) shall be guilty of an offence and liable on summary conviction to a fine not exceeding level 3 on the standard scale.

(5) Any person who, having been required by a notice under subsection (1) to give any information, knowingly makes any misstatement in respect of it shall be guilty of an offence and liable on summary conviction to a fine not exceeding the statutory maximum or on conviction on indictment to imprisonment for a term not exceeding two years or to a fine, or both.

[(6) This section shall have effect as if the references to a local authority included references to a National Park authority.]   **[337]**

NOTES
    Commencement: 24 August 1990 (sub-ss (1)–(5)); to be appointed (sub-s (6)).
    Sub-s (6) inserted by the Environment Act 1995, s 78, Sch 10, para 32(11), as from a day to be appointed under s 125(3).

331. Offences by corporations

(1) Where an offence under this Act which has been committed by a body corporate is proved to have been committed with the consent or connivance of, or to be attributable to any neglect on the part of—

    (a) a director, manager, secretary or other similar officer of the body corporate, or

    (b) any person who was purporting to act in any such capacity,

he as well as the body corporate shall be guilty of that offence and be liable to be proceeded against accordingly.

(2) In subsection (1) ''director'', in relation to any body corporate—

    (a) which was established by or under an enactment for the purpose of carrying on under national ownership an industry or part of an industry or undertaking, and

    (b) whose affairs are managed by its members,

means a member of that body corporate.   **[338]**

NOTES
    Commencement: 24 August 1990.

332. Combined applications

(1) Regulations made under this Act may provide for the combination in a single document, made in such form and transmitted to such authority as may be prescribed of—

    (a) an application for planning permission in respect of any development; and

    (b) an application required, under any enactment specified in the regulations, to be made to a local authority in respect of that development.

(2) Before making any regulations under this section, the Secretary of State shall consult with such local authorities or associations of local authorities as appear to him to be concerned.

(3) Different provision may be made by any such regulations in relation to areas in which different enactments are in force.

(4) If an application required to be made to a local authority under an enactment specified in any such regulations is made in accordance with the provisions of the regulations, it shall be valid notwithstanding anything in that enactment prescribing, or enabling any authority to prescribe, the form in which, or the manner in which, such an application is to be made.

(5) Subsection (4) shall have effect without prejudice to—

    (a) the validity of any application made in accordance with the enactment in question; or

(b) any provisions of that enactment enabling a local authority to require further particulars of the matters to which the application relates.

(6) In this section "application" includes a submission.   **[339]**

NOTES
Commencement: 24 August 1990.

333. Regulations and orders

(1) The Secretary of State may make regulations under this Act—

   (a) for prescribing the form of any notice, order or other document authorised by or required by this Act to be served, made or issued by any local authority [or National Park authority];
   (b) for any purpose for which regulations are authorised or required to be made under this Act (other than a purpose for which regulations are authorised or required to be made by another Minister).

(2) Any power conferred by this Act to make regulations shall be exercisable by statutory instrument.

(3) Any statutory instrument containing regulations made under this Act (except regulations under section 88 and regulations which by virtue of this Act are of no effect unless approved by a resolution of each House of Parliament) shall be subject to annulment in pursuance of a resolution of either House of Parliament.

(4) The power to make development orders and orders under sections 2, 28, 55(2)(f), 87, 149(3)(a) and 319 shall be exercisable by statutory instrument.

(5) Any statutory instrument—

   (a) which contains an order under section 2 which has been made after a local inquiry has been held in accordance with subsection (2) of that section; or
   (b) which contains a development order or an order under section 28, 87 or 149(3)(a),

shall be subject to annulment in pursuance of a resolution of either House of Parliament.

(6) Without prejudice to subsection (5), where a development order makes provision for excluding or modifying any enactment contained in a public general Act (other than any of the enactments specified in Schedule 17) the order shall not have effect until that provision is approved by a resolution of each House of Parliament.

(7) Without prejudice to section 14 of the Interpretation Act 1978, any power conferred by any of the provisions of this Act to make an order, shall include power to vary or revoke any such order by a subsequent order.   **[340]**

NOTES
Commencement: 24 August 1990.
Words in square brackets in sub-s (1)(a) inserted by the Environment Act 1995, s 78, Sch 10, para 32(12), as from a day to be appointed under s 125(3).

334. Licensing planning areas

(1) Where the united district for which, by an order under section 2, a joint planning board is constituted comprises a licensing planning area, or the whole or part of such a united district is included in a licensing planning area, the Secretary of State may

by order revoke or vary any order in force under Part VII of the Licensing Act 1964 so far as may be necessary or expedient in consequence of the order under section 2.

(2) Subject to subsection (1), nothing in any order made under section 2 shall affect the validity of any order in force under Part VII of the Licensing Act 1964 if made before the date of the order under section 2.   **[341]**

NOTES
Commencement: 24 August 1990.

335. Act not excluded by special enactments

For the avoidance of doubt it is hereby declared that the provisions of this Act, and any restrictions or powers imposed or conferred by it in relation to land, apply and may be exercised in relation to any land notwithstanding that provision is made by any enactment in force at the passing of the 1947 Act, or by any local Act passed at any time during the Session of Parliament held during the regnal years 10 & 11 Geo. 6, for authorising or regulating any development of the land.   **[342]**

NOTES
Commencement: 24 August 1990.
1947 Act: Town and Country Planning Act 1947.

336. Interpretation

(1) In this Act, except in so far as the context otherwise requires and subject to the following provisions of this section and to any transitional provision made by the Planning (Consequential Provisions) Act 1990—

"the 1944 Act" means the Town and Country Planning Act 1944;

"the 1947 Act" means the Town and Country Planning Act 1947;

"the 1954 Act" means the Town and Country Planning Act 1954 ;

"the 1959 Act" means the Town and Country Planning Act 1959;

"the 1962 Act" means the Town and Country Planning Act 1962;

"the 1968 Act" means the Town and Country Planning Act 1968;

"the 1971 Act" means the Town and Country Planning Act 1971;

"acquiring authority", in relation to the acquisition of an interest in land (whether compulsorily or by agreement) or to a proposal so to acquire such an interest, means the government department, local authority or other body by whom the interest is, or is proposed to be, acquired;

"advertisement" means any word, letter, model, sign, placard, board, notice [awning, blind], device or representation, whether illuminated or not, in the nature of, and employed wholly or partly for the purposes of, advertisement, announcement or direction, and (without prejudice to the previous provisions of this definition) includes any hoarding or similar structure used [or designed], or adapted for use [and anything else principally used, or designed or adapted principally for use,] for the display of advertisements, and references to the display of advertisements shall be construed accordingly;

"aftercare condition" has the meaning given in paragraph 2(2) of Schedule 5;

"aftercare scheme" has the meaning given in paragraph 2(3) of Schedule 5;

"agriculture" includes horticulture, fruit growing, seed growing, dairy farming, the breeding and keeping of livestock (including any creature kept for the production of food, wool, skins or fur, or for the purpose of its use in the farming of land), the use of land as grazing land, meadow land, osier land, market gardens and nursery grounds, and the use of land for woodlands

where that use is ancillary to the farming of land for other agricultural
purposes, and "agricultural" shall be construed accordingly;
"the appropriate Minister" has the meaning given in section 265;
"authority possessing compulsory purchase powers", in relation to the
compulsory acquisition of an interest in land, means the person or body of
persons effecting the acquisition and, in relation to any other transaction
relating to an interest in land, means any person or body of persons who
could be or have been authorised to acquire that interest compulsorily for the
purposes for which the transaction is or was effected or a body (being a
parish council, community council or parish meeting) on whose behalf a
district council or county council [or county borough council] could be or
have been so authorised;
"authority to whom Part II of the 1959 Act applies" means a body of any of
the descriptions specified in Part I of Schedule 4 to the 1959 Act;
["breach of condition notice" has the meaning given in section 187A;
"breach of planning control" has the meaning given in section 171A]
"bridleway" has the same meaning as in the Highways Act 1980;
"the Broads" has the same meaning as in the Norfolk and Suffolk Broads Act
1988;
"building" includes any structure or erection, and any part of a building, as
so defined, but does not include plant or machinery comprised in a building;
"buildings or works" includes waste materials, refuse and other matters
deposited on land, and references to the erection or construction of buildings
or works shall be construed accordingly [and references to the removal of
buildings or works include demolition of buildings and filling in of trenches];
["building operations" has the meaning given by section 55]
"caravan site" has the meaning given in section 1(4) of the Caravan Sites and
Control of Development Act 1960;
"clearing", in relation to land, means the removal of buildings or materials
from the land, the levelling of the surface of the land, and the carrying out of
such other operations in relation to it as may be prescribed;
"common" includes any land subject to be enclosed under the Inclosure Acts
1845 to 1882, and any town or village green;
"compulsory acquisition" does not include the vesting in a person by an Act
of Parliament of property previously vested in some other person;
"conservation area" means an area designated under section 69 of the
Planning (Listed Buildings and Conservation Areas) Act 1990;
["depositing of mineral waste" means any process whereby a mineral-working
deposit is created or enlarged and "depositing of refuse or waste materials"
includes the depositing of mineral waste;]
"development" has the meaning given in section 55, and "develop" shall be
construed accordingly;

.   .   .   .   .

"development order" has the meaning given in section 59;
"development plan" shall be construed in accordance with sections 27 and 54
(but subject to the transitional provisions in Schedule 2 [and Part III of
Schedule 4 to the Planning and Compensation Act 1991]);
"disposal" means disposal by way of sale, exchange or lease, or by way of
the creation of any easement, right or privilege, or in any other manner,
except by way of appropriation, gift or mortgage, and "dispose of" shall be
construed accordingly;
"enactment" includes an enactment in any local or private Act of Parliament
and an order, rule, regulation, byelaw or scheme made under an Act of
Parliament;

"enforcement notice" means a notice under section 172;

"engineering operations" includes the formation or laying out of means of access to highways;

"enterprise zone scheme" means a scheme or modified scheme having effect to grant planning permission in accordance with section 88;

"erection", in relation to buildings as defined in this subsection, includes extension, alteration and re-erection;

.   .   .   .   .

"footpath" has the same meaning as in the Highways Act 1980;

"fuel or field garden allotment" means any allotment set out as a fuel allotment, or a field garden allotment, under an Inclosure Act;

"functions" includes powers and duties;

"government department" includes any Minister of the Crown;

"the Greater London Development Plan" means the development plan submitted to the Minister of Housing and Local Government under section 25 of the London Government Act 1963 and approved by the Secretary of State under section 5 of the 1962 Act or the corresponding provision of the 1971 Act;

"highway" has the same meaning as in the Highways Act 1980;

"improvement", in relation to a highway, has the same meaning as in the Highways Act 1980;

"joint planning board" has the meaning given in section 2;

"land" means any corporal hereditament, including a building, and, in relation to the acquisition of land under Part IX, includes any interest in or right over land;

"lease" includes an underlease and an agreement for a lease or underlease, but does not include an option to take a lease or a mortgage, and "leasehold interest" means the interest of the tenant under a lease as so defined;

"local authority" (except in section 252 and subject to subsection (10) [below and section 71(7) of the Environment Act 1995]) means—

> [(a) a billing authority or a precepting authority (except the Receiver for the Metropolitan Police District), as defined in section 69 of the Local Government Finance Act 1992;
>
> (aa) . . . a combined fire authority, as defined in section 144 of the Local Government Finance Act 1988;]
>
> (b) a levying body within the meaning of section 74 of that Act; and
>
> (c) a body as regards which section 75 of that Act applies;
>
> and includes any joint board or joint committee if all the constituent authorities are local authorities within paragraph (a), (b) or (c);

"local highway authority" means a highway authority other than the Secretary of State;

"local planning authority" shall be construed in accordance with Part I;

"London borough" includes the City of London, references to the council of a London borough or the clerk to such a council being construed, in relation to the City, as references to the Common Council of the City and the town clerk of the City respectively;

"means of access" includes any means of access, whether private or public, for vehicles or for foot passengers, and includes a street;

.   .   .   .   .

"mineral planning authority" has the meaning given in section 1(4);

"mineral-working deposit" means any deposit of material remaining after minerals have been extracted from land or otherwise deriving from the carrying out of operations for the winning and working of minerals in, on or under land;

"minerals" includes all [substances] of a kind ordinarily worked for removal by underground or surface working, except that it does not include peat cut for purposes other than sale;

"Minister" means any Minister of the Crown or other government department;

"mortgage" includes any charge or lien on any property for securing money or money's worth;

.   .   .   .   .

"open space" means any land laid out as a public garden, or used for the purposes of public recreation, or land which is a disused burial ground;

"operational land" has the meaning given in section 263;

"owner", in relation to any land, means . . . a person, other than a mortgagee not in possession, who, whether in his own right or as trustee for any other person, is entitled to receive the rack rent of the land or, where the land is not let at a rack rent, would be so entitled if it were so let;

"the planning Acts" means this Act, the Planning (Listed Buildings and Conservation Areas) Act 1990, the Planning (Hazardous Substances) Act 1990 and the Planning (Consequential Provisions) Act 1990;

["planning contravention notice" has the meaning given in section 171C]

"planning decision" means a decision made on an application under Part III;

"planning permission" means permission under Part III, . . .

"planning permission granted for a limited period" has the meaning given in section 72(2);

"prescribed" (except in relation to matters expressly required or authorised by this Act to be prescribed in some other way) means prescribed by regulations under this Act;

.   .   .   .   .

"public gas supplier" has the same meaning as in Part I of the Gas Act 1986;

"purchase notice" has the meaning given in section 137;

.   .   .   .   .

"replacement of open space", in relation to any area, means the rendering of land available for use as an open space, or otherwise in an undeveloped state, in substitution for land in that area which is so used;

"restoration condition" has the meaning given in paragraph 2(2) of Schedule 5;

.   .   .   .   .

"simplified planning zone" and "simplified planning zone scheme" shall be construed in accordance with sections 82 and 83;

.   .   .   .   .

"statutory undertakers" and "statutory undertaking" have the meanings given in section 262;

"steps for the protection of the environment" has the meaning given in paragraph 5(4) of Schedule 9;

"stop notice" has the meaning given in section 183;

"suspension order" has the meaning given in paragraph 5 of Schedule 9; and

"supplementary suspension order" has the meaning given in paragraph 6 of Schedule 9;

"tenancy" has the same meaning as in the Landlord and Tenant Act 1954;

"tree preservation order" has the meaning given in section 198;

"urban development area" and "urban development corporation" have the same meanings as in Part XVI of the Local Government, Planning and Land Act 1980;

"use", in relation to land, does not include the use of land for the carrying out of any building or other operations on it;

"Valuation Office" means the Valuation Office of the Inland Revenue Department;

"war damage" has the meaning given in the War Damage Act 1943

["the winning and working of minerals" includes the extraction of minerals from a mineral working deposit.]

[(1A) In this Act—

  (a) any reference to a county (other than one to a county planning authority) shall be construed, in relation to Wales, as including a reference to a county borough;

  (b) any reference to a county council shall be construed, in relation to Wales, as including a reference to a county borough council; and

  (c) section 17(4) and (5) of the Local Government (Wales) Act 1994 (references to counties and districts to be construed generally in relation to Wales as references to counties and county boroughs) shall not apply.]

(2) If, in relation to anything required or authorised to be done under this Act, any question arises as to which Minister is or was the appropriate Minister in relation to any statutory undertakers, that question shall be determined by the Treasury.

(3) If any question so arises whether land of statutory undertakers is operational land, that question shall be determined by the Minister who is the appropriate Minister in relation to those undertakers.

(4) Words in this Act importing a reference to service of a notice to treat shall be construed as including a reference to the constructive service of such a notice which, by virtue of any enactment, is to be deemed to be served.

(5) With respect to references in this Act to planning decisions—

  (a) in relation to a decision altered on appeal by the reversal or variation of the whole or part of it, such references shall be construed as references to the decision as so altered;

  (b) in relation to a decision upheld on appeal, such references shall be construed as references to the decision of the local planning authority and not to the decision of the Secretary of State on the appeal;

  (c) in relation to a decision given on an appeal in the circumstances mentioned in section 78(2), such references shall be construed as references to the decision so given;

  (d) the time of a planning decision, in a case where there is or was an appeal, shall be taken to be or have been the time of the decision as made by the local planning authority (whether or not that decision is or was altered on that appeal) or, in the case of a decision given on an appeal in the circumstances mentioned in section 78(2), the end of the period there mentioned.

(6) Section 56 shall apply for determining for the purposes of this Act when development of land shall be taken to be initiated.

(7) In relation to the sale or acquisition of an interest in land—

  (a) in a case where the interest is or was conveyed or assigned without a preliminary contract, references in this Act to a contract are references to the conveyance or assignment; and

  (b) references to the making of a contract are references to the execution of it.

(8) In this Act—

  (a) references to a person from whom title is derived by another person include references to any predecessor in title of that other person;

    (b) references to a person deriving title from another person include references to any successor in title of that other person;

    (c) references to deriving title are references to deriving title either directly or indirectly.

(9) References in the planning Acts to any of the provisions [of Parts III, VII and VIII] include, except where the context otherwise requires, references to those provisions as modified under section 316 . . .

(10) In section 90, Chapter I of Part VI, and [section] 330 "local authority", in relation to land in the Broads, includes the Broads Authority.   **[343]**

NOTES

Commencement: 24 August 1990.

Words and definitions in square brackets in sub-ss (1), (9), (10) (except those mentioned below) inserted, added or substituted, and words and definitions omitted from sub-ss (1), (9) (except those mentioned below) repealed by the Planning and Compensation Act 1991, ss 21, 24, 27, 31(4), 32, 84(6), Sch 1, paras 1, 12, Sch 4, Pt II, para 34, Sch 6, paras 8, 38, Sch 7, paras 8, 52, Sch 19, Pts I, II.

Words in square brackets in definition "authority possessing compulsory purchase powers" in sub-s (1) inserted, in definition "development plan" in sub-s (1), "27, 27A" substituted for "27", in definition "mineral planning authority" in sub-s (1), "1" substituted for "1(4)", and sub-s (1A) inserted by the Local Government (Wales) Act 1994, s 20(4)(b), Sch 6, Pt II, para 24(13), (14), as from a day to be appointed.

In definition "local authority" in sub-s (1), first words in square brackets inserted by the Environment Act 1995, s 78, Sch 10, para 32(13), as from a day to be appointed under s 125(3), paras (a), (aa) substituted for para (a) by the Local Government Finance Act 1992, s 117(1), Sch 13, para 91, and words omitted from para (aa) repealed by the Police and Magistrates' Courts Act 1994, s 93, Sch 9, Pt I.

337. Short title, commencement and extent

(1) This Act may be cited as the Town and Country Planning Act 1990.

(2) Except as provided in Part II and in Schedule 4 to the Planning (Consequential Provisions) Act 1990, this Act shall come into force at the end of the period of three months beginning with the day on which it is passed.

(3) This Act extends to England and Wales only.   **[344]**

NOTES

Commencement: 24 August 1990.

SCHEDULES

SCHEDULE 1

Section 1

LOCAL PLANNING AUTHORITIES: DISTRIBUTION OF FUNCTIONS

Preliminary

1.—(1) In this Schedule "county matter" means in relation to any application, order or notice—

    (a) the winning and working of minerals in, on or under land (whether by surface or underground working) or the erection of any building, plant or machinery—

        (i) which it is proposed to use in connection with the winning and working of minerals or with their treatment or disposal in or on land adjoining the site of the working; or

       (ii) which a person engaged in mining operations proposes to use in connection with the grading, washing, grinding or crushing of minerals;

    (b) the use of land, or the erection of any building, plant or machinery on land, for the carrying out of any process for the preparation or adaptation for sale of any mineral or the manufacture of any article from a mineral where—

(i) the land forms part of or adjoins a site used or proposed to be used for the winning and working of minerals; or

(ii) the mineral is, or is proposed to be, brought to the land from a site used, or proposed to be used, for the winning and working of minerals by means of a pipeline, conveyor belt, aerial ropeway, or similar plant or machinery, or by private road, private waterway or private railway;

(c) the carrying out of searches and tests of mineral deposits or the erection of any building, plant or machinery which it is proposed to use in connection with them;

(d) the [depositing] of mineral waste;

(e) the use of land for any purpose required in connection with the transport by rail or water of aggregates (that is to say, any of the following, namely—

(i) sand and gravel;

(ii) crushed rock;

(iii) artificial materials of appearance similar to sand, gravel or crushed rock and manufactured or otherwise derived from iron or steel slags, pulverised fuel ash, clay or mineral waste),

or the erection of any building, plant or machinery which it is proposed to use in connection with them;

(*f*) the erection of any building, plant or machinery which it is proposed to use for the coating of roadstone or the production of concrete or of concrete products or artificial aggregates, where the building, plant or machinery is to be erected in or on land which forms part of or adjoins a site used or proposed to be used—

(i) for the winning and working of minerals; or

(ii) for any of the purposes mentioned in paragraph (e) above;

(g) the erection of any building, plant or machinery which it is proposed to use for the manufacture of cement;

(h) the carrying out of operations in, on, over or under land, or a use of land, where the land is or forms part of a site used or formerly used for the winning and working of minerals and where the operations or use would conflict with or prejudice compliance with a restoration condition or an aftercare condition;

(i) the carrying out of operations in, on, over or under land, or any use of land, which is situated partly in and partly outside a National Park;

(j) the carrying out of any operation which is, as respects the area in question, a prescribed operation or an operation of a prescribed class or any use which is, as respects that area, a prescribed use or use of a prescribed class.

(2) . . .

Development plans

[2. The functions of a local planning authority—

(a) under sections 30 to 35B, 38(2) and 50(1), (4), (5) and (7) shall be exercisable by the county planning authority and not by the district planning authority;

(b) under section 36, 39, 40, 42 to 44 and 50(6), (7A) and (8) shall be exercisable by the district planning authority and not by the county planning authority;

and references to a local planning authority in those sections shall be construed accordingly.]

Planning and special control

3.—(1) The functions of a local planning authority of determining—

(a) applications for planning permission;

[(b) applications for a certificate under section 191 or 192];

shall, subject to sub-paragraph (2), be exercised by the district planning authority.

(2) The functions of a local planning authority of determining any such application as is mentioned in sub-paragraph (1) which [relates] to a county matter shall be exercised by the county planning authority.

(3)–(6) . . .

(7) The previous provisions of this paragraph shall not apply to applications relating to land in a National Park, but paragraph 4 shall apply to such applications instead.

4.—(1) ...

(2) Where any [application for planning permission, for a certificate under section 191 or 192 or for consent to the display of advertisements under section 220, relating in each case] to land in a National Park or an application so relating for approval of a matter reserved under an outline planning permission within the meaning of section 92 falls to be determined by a [National Park authority *or*] *county planning authority*, that authority shall before determining it consult with [any authority which (but for section 4A) would be *or, as the case may be, which is*] the district planning authority for the area in which the land to which the application relates is situated.

5.—(1) The Secretary of State may include in a development order such provisions as he thinks fit enabling a local highway authority to impose restrictions on the grant by the local planning authority of planning permission for the following descriptions of development relating to land in the area of the local highway authority—

    (a) the formation, laying out or alteration of any means of access to a road classified under section 12(3) of the Highways Act 1980 or section 27 of the Local Government Act 1966 or to a proposed road the route of which has been adopted by resolution of the local highway authority and notified as such to the local planning authority;

    (b) any other operations or use of land which appear to the local highway authority to be likely to result in a material increase in the volume of traffic entering or leaving such a classified or proposed road, to prejudice the improvement or construction of such a road or to result in a material change in the character of traffic entering, leaving or using such a road.

(2) The reference to a local planning authority in sub-paragraph (1) shall not be construed as including a reference to an urban development corporation who are the local planning authority by virtue of an order under section 149 of the Local Government, Planning and Land Act 1980, and no provision of a development order which is included in it by virtue of that paragraph is to be construed as applying to such a corporation.

(3) The Secretary of State may include in a development order provision enabling a local highway authority to impose restrictions on the grant by an urban development corporation who are the local planning authority of planning permission for such descriptions of development as may be specified in the order.

6.—(1) A development order may also include provision requiring a county planning authority who are determining any application mentioned in paragraph 3 and relating to a county matter, or an application for approval of a matter reserved under an outline planning permission within the meaning of section 92 and so relating, to give the district planning authority for the area in which the land to which the application relates is situated an opportunity to make recommendations to the county planning authority as to the manner in which the application is determined, and to take into account any such recommendations.

(2) It may also include provision requiring a county or district planning authority who have received any application so mentioned or any application for such approval *(including any such application relating to land in a National Park)* to notify the district or, as the case may be, county planning authority of the terms of their decision, or, where the application is referred to the Secretary of State, the date when it was so referred and, when notified to them, the terms of his decision.

7.—(1) It shall be the duty of a local planning authority in a non-metropolitan county when exercising their functions under [section 70] to seek the achievement of the general objectives of the structure plan for the time being in force in their area.

(2) Subject to sub-paragraph (4), the district planning authority shall consult the county planning authority for their area before determining any application to which this sub-paragraph applies.

(3) Sub-paragraph (2) applies to any application for planning permission for the carrying out—

(a) of any development of land which would materially conflict with or prejudice the
   implementation—

   [(i) of any policy contained in a structure plan which has been adopted or approved;
   (ii) of any policy contained in proposals made available for inspection under
       section 33(2);]
   (iv) of a fundamental provision of a development plan to which paragraph 2 of Part
       III of Schedule 2 applies, so far as the development plan is in force in the
       district planning authority's area;
   [(v) of any policy contained in a minerals local plan or a waste local plan which
       has been adopted or approved;
   (vi) of any policy contained in proposals for the making, alteration or replacement
       of a minerals local plan or a waste local plan which have been made available
       for inspection under section 40(2);
   (vii) of any proposal contained in a local plan which was prepared by the county
       planning authority and continued in operation by virtue of paragraph 44 of
       Schedule 4 to the Planning and Compensation Act 1991;
   (viii) of any proposal contained in proposals in respect of a local plan which have
       been prepared by the county planning authority and are adopted or approved
       by virtue of paragraph 43 of that Schedule or made available for inspection in
       pursuance of that paragraph;]

(b) of any development of land which would, by reason of its scale or nature or the
   location of the land, be of major importance for the implementation of a structure
   plan;
(c) of any development of land in an area which the county planning authority have
   notified to the district planning authority, in writing, as an area in which development
   is likely to affect or be affected by the winning and working of minerals, other than
   coal;
(d) of any development of land which the county planning authority have notified the
   district planning authority, in writing, that they themselves propose to develop;
(e) of any development of land which would prejudice the carrying out of development
   proposed by the county planning authority and notified to the district planning
   authority under paragraph (d);
(f) of any development of land in England in respect of which the county planning
   authority have notified the district planning authority, in writing, that it is proposed
   that it shall be used for waste disposal;
(g) of any development of land which would prejudice a proposed use of land for waste
   disposal notified to the district planning authority under paragraph (f).

(4) The district planning authority may determine any application to which sub-paragraph
(2) applies without the consultation required by that sub-paragraph if the county planning
authority have given them directions authorising them to do so.

(5) A direction under sub-paragraph (4) may relate to a class of applications or to a
particular application.

(6) Subject to sub-paragraph (7), where the district planning authority are required to
consult the county planning authority before determining an application for planning
permission—

   (a) they shall give the county planning authority notice that they propose to consider
       the application and send them a copy of it; and
   (b) they shall not determine it until the expiration of such period from the date of the
       notice as a development order may provide.

(7) A district planning authority may determine an application for planning permission
before the expiration of such a period as is mentioned in sub-paragraph (6)(b)—

   (a) if they have received representations concerning the application from the county
       planning authority before the expiration of that period; or
   (b) if the county planning authority have notified them that they do not wish to make
       representations.

(8) Where a district planning authority are required to consult the county planning
authority before determining an application for planning permission, they shall in determining

it take into account any representations relating to it which they have received from the county planning authority before the expiration of the period mentioned in sub-paragraph (6)(b).

[8.—(1) A local planning authority who have the function of determining applications for planning permission shall, if requested to do so by the council of any parish *or community* situated in their area, notify the council of—

    (a) any relevant planning application; and

    (b) any alteration to that application accepted by the authority.

(2) In sub-paragraph (1) "a relevant planning application" means an application which—

    (a) relates to land in the parish *or community*; and

    (b) is an application for—

        (i) planning permission; or

        (ii) approval of a matter reserved under an outline planning permission within the meaning of section 92.

(3) Any request made for the purposes of sub-paragraph (1) shall be in writing and state that the council wishes to be notified of all relevant applications or all applications of a description specified in the request.

(4) An authority shall comply with the duty to notify a council of an application by—

    (a) sending the council a copy of the application; or

    (b) indicating to the council the nature of the development which is the subject of the application and identifying the land to which it relates,

and any notification falling within paragraph (b) shall be in writing.

(5) An authority shall comply with their duty to notify a council of an alteration by—

    (a) sending a copy of the alteration to the council; or

    (b) informing the council in writing of its general effect,

but they need not notify a council of an alteration which in their opinion is trivial.

(6) A development order may require a local planning authority which is dealing with an application of which a council is entitled to be notified—

    (a) to give the council an opportunity to make representations to them as to the manner in which the application should be determined;

    (b) to take into account any such representations;

    (c) to notify the council of the terms of their decision or, where the application is referred to the Secretary of State, the date when it was so referred and, when notified to them, the terms of his decision.]

9.—(1) The functions of local planning authorities under the provisions of this Act relating to simplified planning zone schemes shall be exercised in non-metropolitan counties by the district planning authorities.

(2), (3) . . .

10. Elsewhere than in a National Park, the functions of a local planning authority under section 94 shall be exercisable by the district planning authority, except that where the relevant planning permission was granted by the county planning authority, those functions, so far as relating to that permission, shall be exercisable by the county planning authority and also by the district planning authority after consulting the county planning authority.

11.—(1) The functions of a local planning authority of—

    (a) making orders under section 97 revoking or modifying planning permission, or under section 102 requiring discontinuance of use, imposing conditions on continuance of use or requiring the alteration or removal of buildings or works, or

    (b) issuing enforcement notices under section 172 or serving [planning contravention notices under s 171C or] stop notices under section 183 [or breach of condition notices under section 187A],

shall, subject to sub-paragraphs (2) to (4), be exercisable by the district planning authority.

(2) In a case where it appears to the district planning authority of a district in a non-

metropolitan county that the functions mentioned in sub-paragraph (1) relate to county matters, they shall not exercise those functions without first consulting the county planning authority.

(3) Subject to sub-paragraph (4), in a non-metropolitan county those functions shall also be exercisable by a county planning authority in a case where it appears to that authority that they relate to a matter which should properly be considered a county matter.

(4) In relation to a matter which is a county matter by virtue of any of the provisions of paragraph 1(1)(a) to (h) the functions of a local planning authority specified in sub-paragraph (1)(b) shall only be exercisable by the county planning authority in their capacity as mineral planning authority.

12. In sections 178(1), 181(4)(b) and 190(2) to (5) any reference to the local planning authority shall be construed as a reference to the authority who issued the notice or made the order in question or, in the case of a notice issued or an order made by the Secretary of State, the authority named in the notice or order.

[12A. The functions of a local planning authority under section 187B are exercisable by any body having the function of taking enforcement action in respect of the breach in question.]

13.—(1) *A county planning authority* may only make a tree preservation order—

    (a) if they make it in pursuance of section 197(b);
    (b) if it relates to land which does not lie wholly within the area of a single district planning authority;
    (c) if it relates to land in which the county planning authority hold an interest; *or*
    (d) *if it relates to land in a National Park.*

(2) Where a local planning authority have made a tree preservation order under section 198 or the Secretary of State has made such an order by virtue of section 202, the powers of varying or revoking the order and the powers of dispensing with section 206 or serving, or appearing on an appeal relating to, a notice under section 207 shall be exercisable only by the authority who made the order or, in the case of an order made by the Secretary of State, the authority named in the order.

14. The functions of local planning authorities under sections 69, 211, 214, 220, 221, 224 and 225, and in non-metropolitan counties the functions under section 215, are exercisable by district planning authorities.

15.—(1) The copy of the notice required to be served by paragraph 4(5) of Schedule 8 on a local planning authority shall, in the case of a proposal that a government department should give a direction under section 90(1) or that development should be carried out by or on behalf of a government department, be served on the local planning authority who, in the opinion of the Secretary of State, would have been responsible for dealing with an application for planning permission for the development in question if such an application had fallen to be made.

(2) References in paragraphs 3(2) and 5(1) of that Schedule to the local planning authority shall be construed as references to the local planning authority on whom that copy is required to be served.

Compensation

16.—(1) Claims for payment of compensation under section 107 (including that section as applied by section 108) and sections . . . , 115(1) to (4), 186 and 223 shall, subject to sub-paragraph (3), be made to and paid by the local planning authority who took the action by virtue of which the claim arose or, where that action was taken by the Secretary of State, the local planning authority from whom the appeal was made to him or who referred the matter to him or, in the case of an order made or notice served by him by virtue of section 100, 104 or 185, the appropriate authority, and references in those sections to a local planning authority shall be construed accordingly.

(2) In this paragraph "appropriate authority" means—

    (a) in the case of a claim for compensation under section 107 or 108, the local planning authority who granted, or are to be treated for the purposes of section 107 as having

granted, the planning permission the revocation or modification of which gave rise
to the claim;

(b) in the case of a claim for compensation under section 115(1) to (4) or 186, the local
planning authority named in the relevant order or stop notice of the Secretary of
State;

(c) in the case of a claim for compensation under section 223, the district planning
authority.

(3) The Secretary of State may after consultation with all the authorities concerned direct
that where a local planning authority is liable to pay compensation under any of the provisions
mentioned in sub-paragraph (1) in any particular case or class of case they shall be entitled to
be reimbursed the whole of the compensation or such proportion of it as he may direct from
one or more authorities specified in the direction.

(4) The local planning authority by whom compensation is to be paid and to whom claims
for compensation are to be made under section 144(2) shall be the district planning authority.

17. Claims for payment of compensation under a tree preservation order by virtue of
section 203, and claims for payment of compensation under section 204 by virtue of directions
given in pursuance of such an order, shall be made to and paid by the local planning authority
who made the order or, in the case of an order made by the Secretary of State, the authority
named in the order; and the reference in section 204(2) to exercising functions under the tree
preservation order shall have effect subject to the provisions of this paragraph.

18. The local planning authority by whom compensation is to be paid under section
279(1)(a) to statutory undertakers shall be the authority who referred the application for
planning permission to the Secretary of State and the appropriate Minister, or from whose
decision the appeal was made to them or who served the enforcement notice appealed against,
as the case may be.

The Crown

19.—(1) Elsewhere than in a metropolitan county or a National Park the functions
conferred by section 302 and Schedule 15 on the authority responsible for enforcing planning
control shall, subject to sub-paragraph (3)—

(a) in the case of works on or a use of land which in the opinion of the district planning
authority relates to a county matter, be exercised by the county planning authority;

(b) in any other case be exercised by the district planning authority.

(2) *As respects an area in a National Park [to which section 4 applies] outside a
metropolitan county those functions shall be exercised by the county planning authority.*

[(2A) As respects the area of any National Park for which a National Park authority is the
local planning authority those functions shall be exercised by that authority.]

(3) Every application made under subsection (3) of that section to an authority responsible
for enforcing planning control shall be made to the district planning authority who, in the case
of an application falling to be determined by the county planning authority, shall send it on to
the latter.

(4) A county planning authority determining any such application shall give the district
planning authority for the area in which the land to which the application relates is situated an
opportunity to make recommendations to the county planning authority as to the manner in
which the application should be determined and shall take any such recommendations into
account.

(5) A county or district planning authority who have dealt with any such application shall
notify the district or, as the case may be, the county planning authority of the terms of their
determination or, in a case where the application has been referred to the Secretary of State,
the date when it was so referred.

Miscellaneous

20.—(1) The local planning authority whom the Secretary of State is required to consult
under section [100(3), 104(3) 196A(3), 202(1) or 214B(6)] or serve with a notice of his

proposals under section 100(4) or 104(4) shall be the county planning authority or the district planning authority, as he thinks appropriate, and references in sections 100(2), (3) and (4) and 104(2), (3) and (4) and 202 to the local planning authority shall be construed accordingly.

(2) In sections 96, 182 and 185 any reference to the local planning authority shall be construed as a reference to the county planning authority or the district planning authority, as the Secretary of State thinks appropriate.

[(3) In relation to land in the area of a joint planning board, a person entering into a planning obligation under section 106 or 299A may identify the council of the county in which the land is situated as the authority by whom the obligation is enforceable.]

(4) In paragraph 16 of Schedule 13 the reference to the local planning authority shall be construed—

    (a) *in relation to land in a National Park outside a metropolitan county, as a reference to the county planning authority*; and

    (b) in relation to land *elsewhere*, as a reference to the district planning authority.

21.—(1) Subject to sub-paragraph (2), the provisions of this Schedule do not apply in Greater London.

(2) Paragraph 5(3) of this Schedule applies in Greater London and paragraph 2(3) of Part I and of Part II of Schedule 2 shall apply as respects the temporary application of paragraph 7(1) of this Schedule in the metropolitan counties and in Greater London respectively. **[345]**

NOTES
Commencement: 24 August 1990.
Words in square brackets in paras 1(1)(d), 3(2), 20(1), first words in square brackets in para 4(2) and the whole of paras 2, 3(1)(b) (for original para 3(b), (c)), (3), 7(1), (3)(a)(i), (ii) (for original para 7(3)(a)(i)–(iii)), (v)–(viii) (for original para 7(3)(a)(v)–(vii)), 8, 20(3) substituted, paras 1(2), 3(3)–(6), 4(1), 9(2), (3) and figure omitted from para 16(1) repealed, and words in square brackets in para 11(1)(b) and whole of para 12A inserted, by the Planning and Compensation Act 1991, ss 19(2), 21, 27, 28, 31(4), 32, 84(6), Sch 1, paras 1, 13, Sch 4, Pt II, para 35, Sch 5, Pt II, para 3, Sch 6, paras 8, 39, Sch 7, paras 8, 53, Sch 19, Pts I, II.
Second and third words in square brackets in para 4(2) inserted and words in italics in that sub-para and in sub-para 6(2) repealed, words "In the case of any area for which there is both a district planning authority and a county planning authority" substituted for first words in italics in para 13(1) and sub-para 13(1)(d) and the word "or" preceding it repealed, words in square brackets in para 19(2), and para 19(2A), inserted, and para 19(2) repealed, words "which is land in an area the local planning authority for which comprises both a county planning authority and a district planning authority" substituted for words "outside a metropolitan county" in para 20(4)(a) and words "other land in an area the local planning authority for which comprises both a county planning authority and a district planning authority" substituted for word "elsewhere" in para 20(4)(b), and para 20(4)(a) and word "other" in para 20(4)(b) (as so substituted) repealed, by the Environment Act 1995, ss 78, 120(3), Sch 10, para 32(14), Sch 24, as from a day or days to be appointed under s 125(3).
Words in italics in para 8 repealed by the Local Government (Wales) Act 1994, ss 20(4)(b), 66(8), Sch 6, Pt II, para 24(15), Sch 18, as from a day to be appointed.

[SCHEDULE 1A

Section 18(7)

DISTRIBUTION OF LOCAL PLANNING AUTHORITY FUNCTIONS: WALES

1.—(1) Where a local planning authority are not the local highway authority, the Secretary of State may include in a development order such provisions as he thinks fit enabling the local highway authority to impose restrictions on the grant by the local planning authority of planning permission for the following descriptions of development relating to land in the area of the local highway authority—

    (a) the formation, laying out or alteration of any means of access to—

        (i) a road classified under section 12(3) of the Highways Act 1980 or section 27 of the Local Government Act 1966; or

        (ii) a proposed road the route of which has been adopted by resolution of the local highway authority and notified as such to the local planning authority;

(b) any other operations or use of land which appear to the local highway authority to be likely to—

    (i) result in a material increase in the volume of traffic entering or leaving such a classified or proposed road;

    (ii) prejudice the improvement or construction of such a road; or

    (iii) result in a material change in the character of traffic entering, leaving or using such a road.

(2) The reference to a local planning authority in sub-paragraph (1) shall not be construed as including a reference to an urban development corporation who are the local planning authority by virtue of an order under section 149 of the Local Government, Planning and Land Act 1980, and no provision of a development order which is included in it by virtue of that sub-paragraph is to be construed as applying to such a corporation.

(3) The Secretary of State may include in a development order provision enabling a local highway authority to impose restrictions on the grant by an urban development corporation who are the local planning authority of planning permission for such descriptions of development as may be specified in the order.

2.—(1) A local planning authority who have the function of determining applications for planning permission shall, if requested to do so by the council for any community or group of communities situated in their area, notify that council of—

(a) any relevant planning application; and

(b) any alteration to that application accepted by the authority.

(2) In sub-paragraph (1) ''relevant planning application'' means an application which—

(a) relates to land in the community or (as the case may be) one of the communities concerned; and

(b) is an application for—

    (i) planning permission; or

    (ii) approval of a matter reserved under an outline planning permission within the meaning of section 92.

(3) Any request made for the purposes of sub-paragraph (1) shall be in writing and shall state that the community council wishes to be notified of all relevant applications or all applications of a description specified in the request.

(4) An authority shall comply with the duty to notify a community council of an application by—

(a) sending the council a copy of the application; or

(b) indicating to the council the nature of the development which is the subject of the application and identifying the land to which it relates,

and any notification falling within paragraph (b) shall be in writing.

(5) An authority shall comply with their duty to notify a community council of an alteration by—

(a) sending a copy of the alteration to the council; or

(b) informing the council in writing of its general effect,

but they need not notify a community council of an alteration which in their opinion is trivial.

(6) A development order may require a local planning authority who are dealing with an application of which a community council is entitled to be notified—

(a) to give to the council an opportunity to make representations to them as to the manner in which the application should be determined;

(b) to take into account any such representations;

(c) to notify the council of the terms of their decision or, where the application is referred to the Secretary of State, the date when it was so referred and, when notified to them, the terms of his decision.

3. Paragraphs 4 to 10 apply only in relation to any area for which, by virtue of any provision of or made under section 6, 7 or 8, there is more than one local planning authority.

4. In sections 178(1), 181(4)(b) and 190(2), (3) and (5) any reference to the local planning authority shall be construed as a reference to the authority who issued the notice or made the order in question or, in the case of a notice issued or an order made by the Secretary of State, the authority named in the notice or order.

5. The functions of a local planning authority under section 187B are exercisable by any body having the function of taking enforcement action in respect of the breach in question.

6. Where a local planning authority have made a tree preservation order under section 198 or the Secretary of State has made such an order by virtue of section 202, the powers of varying or revoking the order and the powers of dispensing with section 206 or serving, or appearing on an appeal relating to, a notice under section 207 shall be exercisable only by the authority who made the order or, in the case of an order made by the Secretary of State, the authority named in the order.

7.—(1) The copy of the notice required to be served by paragraph 4(5) of Schedule 8 on a local planning authority shall, in the case of a proposal that a government department should give a direction under section 90(1) or that development should be carried out by or on behalf of a government department, be served on the local planning authority who, in the opinion of the Secretary of State, would have been responsible for dealing with an application for planning permission for the development in question if such an application had fallen to be made.

(2) References in paragraphs 3(2) and 5(1) of that Schedule to the local planning authority shall be construed as references to the local planning authority on whom that copy is required to be served.

Compensation

8.—(1) Claims for payment of compensation under section 107 (including that section as applied by section 108) and sections 115(1) to (4) and 186 shall, subject to sub-paragraph (3), be made to and paid by the local planning authority who took the action by virtue of which the claim arose or, where that action was taken by the Secretary of State, the local planning authority from whom the appeal was made to him or who referred the matter to him or, in the case of an order made or notice served by him by virtue of section 100, 104 or 185, the appropriate authority, and references in those sections to a local planning authority shall be construed accordingly.

(2) In this paragraph ''appropriate authority'' means—

(a) in the case of a claim for compensation under section 107 or 108, the local planning authority who granted, or are to be treated for the purposes of section 107 as having granted, the planning permission the revocation or modification of which gave rise to the claim; and

(b) in the case of a claim for compensation under section 115(1) to (4) or 186, the local planning authority named in the relevant order or stop notice of the Secretary of State.

(3) The Secretary of State may, after consultation with all the authorities concerned, direct that where a local planning authority is liable to pay compensation under any of the provisions mentioned in sub-paragraph (1) in any particular case or class of case they shall be entitled to be reimbursed the whole of the compensation or such proportion of it as he may direct from one or more authorities specified in the direction.

9. Claims for payment of compensation under a tree preservation order by virtue of section 203, and claims for payment of compensation under section 204 by virtue of directions given in pursuance of such an order, shall be made to and paid by the local planning authority who made the order or, in the case of an order made by the Secretary of State, the authority named in the order; and the reference in section 204(2) to the authority exercising functions under the tree preservation order shall have effect subject to the provisions of this paragraph.

10. The local planning authority by whom compensation is to be paid under section 279(1)(a) to statutory undertakers shall be the authority who referred the application for planning permission to the Secretary of State and the appropriate Minister, or from whose

decision the appeal was made to them or who served the enforcement notice appealed against, as the case maybe.

Miscellaneous

11. In relation to land in the area of a joint planning board, a person entering into a planning obligation under section 106 or 299A may identify the council of the county or county borough in which the land is situated as the authority by whom the obligation is enforceable.]   **[345A]**

NOTES

Inserted by the Local Government (Wales) Act 1994, s 18(7), Sch 4, as from a day to be appointed.

SCHEDULE 2

Sections 28, 54

DEVELOPMENT PLANS: TRANSITIONAL PROVISIONS

PART I

THE METROPOLITAN COUNTIES

Continuation of structure plans, local plans and old development plans

1.—(1) Subject to paragraphs 2 and 3—

(a) the structure plan,
(b) any local plan; and
(c) any old development plan,

which immediately before the commencement of this Act was in force in the area of a local planning authority in a metropolitan county (or in that and other areas) shall continue in force in respect of the area of that authority until a unitary development plan for that area becomes operative under Chapter I of Part II of this Act or, where parts of a unitary development plan become operative on different dates, until every part of it has become operative.

(2) A plan which continues in force by virtue of this paragraph shall, while it continues in force, be treated for the purposes of this Act, any other enactment relating to town and country planning, the Land Compensation Act 1961 and the Highways Act 1980 as being, or being comprised in, the development plan in respect of the area in question.

(3) In this paragraph "old development plan" means any plan which was in force in the area in question immediately before the commencement of this Act by virtue of Schedule 7 to the 1971 Act and paragraph 18 of Schedule 1 to the Local Government Act 1985.

Revocation of structure plan

2.—(1) Where under Chapter I of Part II of this Act the Secretary of State approves all or any of Part I of a unitary development plan he may by order—

(a) wholly or partly revoke a structure plan continued in force by paragraph 1, either in its application to the whole of the area of a local planning authority or in its application to part of that area; and
(b) make such consequential amendments to that plan as appear to him to be necessary or expedient.

(2) Before making an order under this paragraph the Secretary of State shall consult the local planning authority for the area to which the unitary development plan relates.

(3) Until the structure plan for an area in a metropolitan county ceases to be operative under paragraph 1 or this paragraph, paragraph 7(1) of Schedule 1 shall apply in that area with the omission of the words "in a non-metropolitan county".

3. . . .

Incorporation of current local plan in unitary development plan

4.—[(1) Sub-paragraph (2) applies where—

    (a) a local plan is in force in the area of a local planning authority;

    (b) a unitary development plan is being prepared;

    (c) the local planning authority who are preparing that plan have published in the prescribed manner a statement in the prescribed form identifying a policy included in the plan as an existing policy; and

    (d) a local inquiry or other hearing is held for the purpose of considering any objection to the plan.

(2) Where this sub-paragraph applies, the person holding the inquiry or other hearing need not allow an objector to appear if he is satisfied that—

    (a) the objection is to a policy identified in the statement published under sub-paragraph (1)(c);

    (b) the policy so identified is an existing policy; and

    (c) there has been no significant change in circumstances affecting the existing policy since it first formed part of the plan mentioned in sub-paragraph (1)(a).

(3) In this paragraph "existing policy" means a policy or proposal the substance of which (however expressed) was contained in a local plan in force as mentioned in sub-paragraph (1)(a).]

5, 6. . . .   **[346]**

NOTES

    Commencement: 24 August 1990 (paras 1, 2); 25 November 1991 (para 4 for certain purposes); 10 February 1992 (para 4 for remaining purposes).

    Paras 3, 5, 6 repealed, and para 4 substituted, by the Planning and Compensation Act 1991, ss 27, 84(6), Sch 4, Pt II, para 36(1)(a), (2), Sch 19, Pt I. For transitional provisions, see Sch 4, Pt III, para 41(2) to the 1991 Act at **[547]**.

    1971 Act: Town and Country Planning Act 1971.

[PART IA

WALES

Continuation of structure, local and old development plans

1.—(1) Every existing plan which relates to any part of Wales shall continue in force on and after 1st April 1996.

(2) When a unitary development plan has become fully operative for the area of a local planning authority in Wales—

    (a) any existing plan which is for the time being in force; and

    (b) any interim plan,

shall cease to have effect in respect of its plan area to the extent that it is comprised in the area of that local planning authority.

(3) Any existing plan or interim plan shall, while it continues in force in respect of the area, or part of the area, of any local planning authority in Wales, be treated for the purposes of—

    (a) this Act,

    (b) any other enactment relating to town and country planning,

    (c) the Land Compensation Act 1961, and

    (d) the Highways Act 1980,

as being, or as being comprised in, the development plan in respect of that area or, as the case may be, that part of that area.

(4) Sub-paragraphs (1) to (3) have effect subject to the provisions of this Part of this Schedule and the 1994 Act transitional provisions.

(5) In this paragraph—

"the 1994 Act transitional provisions" means the provisions of Part III of Schedule 5 to the Local Government (Wales) Act 1994;

"existing plan" means a—

 (a) structure plan;
 (b) local plan; or
 (c) old development plan,

to the extent that it was in force in respect of any area in Wales immediately before 1st April 1996 (and includes any alteration made to, or replacement of, the plan after that date under the 1994 Act transitional provisions);

"interim plan" means any modified plan (within the meaning of the 1994 Act transitional provisions) which comes into force in respect of any area in Wales on or after 1st April 1996 under those provisions;

"old development plan" means any plan which was in force immediately before 1st April 1996 by virtue of Schedule 7 to the Town and Country Planning Act 1971 and Part III of this Schedule; and

"plan area", in relation to an existing plan or interim plan, means the area in respect of which it was in force immediately before 1st April 1996 or, as the case may be, comes into force on or after that date.

Revocation of structure plan

2.—(1) Where under Chapter I of Part II of this Act the Secretary of State approves all or any of Part I of a unitary development plan for the whole or part of the area of a local planning authority in Wales ("the relevant whole or part area"), he may by order—

 (a) wholly or partly revoke an existing plan which is a structure plan in respect of the plan area, to the extent that it is comprised in the relevant whole or part area or any part of it; and
 (b) make such consequential amendments to that existing plan as appear to him to be necessary or expedient.

(2) Before making an order under this paragraph, the Secretary of State shall consult the local planning authority for the area to which the unitary development plan relates.

Incorporation of current policy in unitary development plan

3.—(1) This paragraph applies where—

 (a) a unitary development plan is being prepared for the area of a local planning authority in Wales;
 (b) the local planning authority preparing that plan have published in the prescribed manner a statement in the prescribed form identifying a policy included in the plan as an existing policy;
 (c) one or more local plans is or, as the case may be, are together in force throughout the policy area; and
 (d) a local inquiry or other hearing is held for the purpose of considering any objection to the plan.

(2) The person holding the inquiry or other hearing need not allow an objector to appear if he is satisfied that—

 (a) the objection is to a policy identified in the statement published under sub-paragraph (1)(b);
 (b) the policy so identified is an existing policy; and
 (c) there has been no significant change in circumstances affecting the existing policy since it first formed part of any plan mentioned in sub-paragraph (1)(c).

(3) In this paragraph—

"existing policy" means a policy the substance of which (however expressed) was contained in the local plan or local plans mentioned in sub-paragraph (1)(c);

"policy" includes a proposal; and

"policy area" means so much of the area of the local planning authority to which the policy concerned relates.

Meaning of "local plan"

4. In this Part of this Schedule, "local plan" includes—

   (a) a minerals local plan;
   (b) a waste local plan;
   (c) a local plan adopted or approved before the commencement of Part I of Schedule 4 to the Planning and Compensation Act 1991 or under Part III of that Schedule.]

[346A]

NOTES

Pt IA inserted by the Local Government (Wales) Act 1994, s 20(3)(b), Sch 5, Pt II, para 8, as from a day to be appointed.

PART II

GREATER LONDON

Continuation of Greater London Development Plan, local plans and old development plans

1.—(1) Subject to paragraphs 2 and 3—

   (a) the Greater London Development Plan,
   (b) any local plan; and
   (c) any old development plan,

which immediately before the commencement of this Act was in force in the area of a local planning authority in Greater London (or in that and other areas) shall continue in force in respect of the area of that authority until a unitary development plan for that area becomes operative under Chapter I of Part II of this Act or, where parts of a unitary development plan become operative on different dates, until every part of it has become operative.

(2) A plan which continues in force by virtue of this paragraph shall, while it continues in force, be treated for the purposes of this Act, any other enactment relating to town and country planning, the Land Compensation Act 1961 and the Highways Act 1980 as being, or being comprised in, the development plan in respect of the area in question.

(3) In this paragraph "old development plan" has the same meaning as in paragraph 1 of Part I of this Schedule.

Revocation of Greater London Development Plan

2.—(1) Where under Chapter I of Part II of this Act the Secretary of State approves all or any of Part I of a unitary development plan he may by order—

   (a) wholly or partly revoke the Greater London Development Plan, either in its application to the whole of the area of a local planning authority or in its application to part of that area; and
   (b) make such consequential amendments to that plan as appear to him to be necessary or expedient.

(2) Before making an order under this paragraph the Secretary of State shall consult the local planning authority for the area to which the unitary development plan relates.

(3) Until the Greater London Development Plan ceases to be operative in an area under paragraph 1 of this paragraph, paragraph 7(1) of Schedule 1 shall apply in that area—

   (a) with the omission of the words "in a non-metropolitan county"; and
   (b) with the substitution for the reference to the structure plan of a reference to that Plan.

3–16. . . .

Incorporation of current local plan in unitary development plan

17.—[(1) Sub-paragraph (2) applies where—

   (a) a local plan is in force in the area of a local planning authority;
   (b) a unitary development plan is being prepared;

(c) the local planning authority who are preparing that plan have published in the prescribed manner a statement in the prescribed form identifying a policy included in the plan as an existing policy; and

(d) a local inquiry or other hearing is held for the purpose of considering any objection to the plan.

(2) Where this sub-paragraph applies, the person holding the inquiry or other hearing need not allow an objector to appear if he is satisfied that—

(a) the objection is to a policy identified in the statement published under sub-paragraph (1)(c);

(b) the policy so identified is an existing policy; and

(c) there has been no significant change in circumstances affecting the existing policy since it first formed part of the plan mentioned in sub-paragraph (1)(a).

(3) In this paragraph ''existing policy'' means a policy or proposal the substance of which (however expressed) was contained in a local plan in force as mentioned in sub-paragraph (1)(a).]

18. . . .   **[347]**

NOTES
Commencement: 24 August 1990.
Paras 3–16, 18 repealed, and para 17 substituted, by the Planning and Compensation Act 1991, ss 27, 84(6), Sch 4, Pt II, para 36(1)(b), (2), Sch 19, Pt I. For transitional provisions, see Sch 4, Pt III, para 41(2) to the 1991 Act at **[547]**.

PART III

OLD DEVELOPMENT PLANS

Preliminary

1. In this Part of this Schedule ''old development plan'' means a development plan to which paragraph 2 of Schedule 7 to the 1971 Act (continuation in force of development plans prepared before structure plans became operative) applied immediately before the commencement of this Act.

Continuation in force of old development plans

2. Any old development plan which immediately before the commencement of this Act was in force as respects any district shall, subject to the provisions of this Part of this Schedule, continue in force as respects that district and be treated for the purposes of this Act, any other enactment relating to town and country planning, the Land Compensation Act 1961 and the Highways Act 1980 as being comprised in the development plan for that district.

Other plans to prevail over old development plans

3. Subject to the following provisions of this Part of this Schedule, where by virtue of paragraph 2 the old development plan for any district is treated as being comprised in a development plan for that district—

(a) if there is a conflict between any of its provisions and those of the structure plan for that district, or, in the case of Greater London, the Greater London Development Plan the provisions of the structure plan or, as the case may be, that Plan shall be taken to prevail for the purposes of Parts III, V, VI, VII, VIII and IX of this Act and of the Planning (Listed Buildings and Conservation Areas) Act 1990 and the Planning (Hazardous Substances) Act 1990; and

(b) if there is a conflict between any of its provisions and those of a local plan, the provisions of the local plan shall be taken to prevail for those purposes.

Street authorisation maps

4. Where immediately before the commencement of this Act a street authorisation map prepared in pursuance of the Town and Country Planning (Development Plans) Regulations

1965 or the Town and Country Planning (Development Plans for Greater London) Regulations 1966 was treated for the purposes of the 1971 Act as having been adopted as a local plan for a district by a local planning authority, it shall continue to be so treated.

Development plans for compensation purposes

5. Where there is no local plan in force in a district, then, for any of the purposes of the Land Compensation Act 1961—

(a) the development plan or current development plan shall as respects that district be taken as being whichever of the following plans gives rise to those assumptions as to the grant of planning permission which are more favourable to the owner of the land acquired, for that purpose, namely the structure plan or, as the case may be, the Greater London Development Plan, so far as applicable to the district, and any alterations to it, together with the Secretary of State's notice of approval of the plan and alterations, and the old development plan;

(b) land situated in an area defined in the current development plan as an area of comprehensive development shall be taken to be situated in whichever of the following areas leads to such assumptions as are mentioned in paragraph (a), namely any area wholly or partly within that district selected by the structure plan or, as the case may be, the Greater London Development Plan as an action area and the area so defined in the old development plan.

Discontinuance of old development plan on adoption of local plan

6. Subject to paragraph 8, on the adoption or approval of a local plan under section 43 or 45 or paragraph 10 of Part II of this Schedule so much of any old development plan as relates to the area to which the local plan relates shall cease to have effect.

7. The Secretary of State may by order direct that any of the provisions of the old development plan shall continue in force in relation to the area to which the local plan relates.

8. If the Secretary of State makes an order under paragraph 7, the provisions of the old development plan specified in the order shall continue in force to the extent so specified.

9. Subject to paragraph 10, the Secretary of State may by order wholly or partly revoke a development plan continued in force under this Schedule whether in its application to the whole of the area of a local planning authority or in its application to part of that area and make such consequential amendments to the plan as appear to him to be necessary or expedient.

10. Before making an order with respect to a development plan under paragraph 7 or 9, the Secretary of State shall consult with the local planning authority for the area to which the plan relates.   **[348]**

NOTES
Commencement: 24 August 1990.
1971 Act: Town and Country Planning Act 1971.

SCHEDULE 3
Sections 55, 107, 114

DEVELOPMENT NOT CONSTITUTING NEW DEVELOPMENT

PART I

DEVELOPMENT NOT RANKING FOR COMPENSATION UNDER S 114

1. The carrying out of—

(a) the rebuilding, as often as occasion may require, of any building which was in existence on 1st July 1948, or of any building which was in existence before that date but was destroyed or demolished after 7th January 1937, including the making good of war damage sustained by any such building;

(b) the rebuilding, as often as occasion may require, of any building erected after 1st July 1948 which was in existence at a material date;

    (c) the carrying out for the maintenance, improvement or other alteration of any building, of works which—

        (i) affect only the interior of the building, or do not materially affect the external appearance of the building, and
        (ii) are works for making good war damage,

so long as the cubic content of the original building is not substantially exceeded.

2. The use as two or more separate dwellinghouses of any building which at a material date was used as single dwellinghouse.   **[349–350]**

NOTES

  Commencement: 24 August 1990.

(Pt II (paras 3–8) repealed by the Planning and Compensation Act 1991, ss 31(4), 84(6), Sch 6, paras 8, 40(1), Sch 19, Pt II.)

PART III

SUPPLEMENTARY PROVISIONS

9. Where after 1st July 1948—

    (a) any buildings or works have been erected or constructed, or any use of land has been instituted, and
    (b) any condition imposed under Part III of this Act, limiting the period for which those buildings or works may be retained, or that use may be continued, has effect in relation to those buildings or works or that use,

this Schedule shall not operate except as respects the period specified in that condition.

10.—(1) Any reference in this Schedule to the cubic content of a building shall be construed as a reference to that content as ascertained by external measurement.

(2) For the purposes of [paragraph 1] the cubic content of a building is substantially increased or exceeded—

    (a) in the case of a dwellinghouse, :f it is increased or exceeded by more than one-tenth or 1,750 cubic feet, whichever is the greater; and
    (b) in any other case, if it is increased or exceeded by more than one-tenth.

11. . . .

12.—(1) In this Schedule "at a material date" means at either—

    (a) 1st July 1948; or
    (b) the date by reference to which this Schedule falls to be applied in the particular case in question.

(2) Sub-paragraph (1)(b) shall not apply in relation to any buildings, works or use of land in respect of which, whether before or after the date mentioned in that sub-paragraph, an enforcement notice served before that date has become or becomes effective.

13.—(1) In relation to a building erected after 1st July 1948 which results from the carrying out of any such works as are described in paragraph 1, any reference in this Schedule to the original building is a reference to the building in relation to which those works were carried out and not to the building resulting from the carrying out of those works.

[(2) This paragraph does not apply for the purposes of sections 111 and 138.]

14. . . .   **[351]**

NOTES

  Commencement: 24 August 1990.

  Words in square brackets in para 10(2) and the whole of para 13(2) substituted, and paras 11, 14 repealed, by the Planning and Compensation Act 1991, ss 31(4), 84(6), Sch 6, paras 8, 40, Sch 19, Pt II.

SCHEDULE 4

Section 57(7)

SPECIAL PROVISIONS AS TO LAND USE IN 1948

1. Where on 1st July 1948 land was being temporarily used for a purpose other than the purpose for which it was normally used, planning permission is not required for the resumption of the use of the land for the latter purpose before 6th December 1968.

2. Where on 1st July 1948 land was normally used for one purpose and was also used on occasions, whether at regular intervals or not, for another purpose, planning permission is not required in respect of the use of the land for that other purpose on similar occasions on or after 6th December 1968 if the land has been used for that other purpose on at least one similar occasion since 1st July 1948 and before the beginning of 1968.

3. Where land was unoccupied on 1st July 1948, but had before that date been occupied at some time on or after 7th January 1937, planning permission is not required in respect of any use of the land begun before 6th December 1968 for the purpose for which the land was last used before 1st July 1948.

4. Notwithstanding anything in paragraphs 1 to 3, the use of land as a caravan site shall not, by virtue of any of those paragraphs, be treated as a use for which planning permission is not required, unless the land was so used on one occasion at least during the period of two years ending with 9th March 1960.   **[352]**

NOTES
   Commencement: 24 August 1990.

SCHEDULE 5

Sections 72(5), 79(4), 97(5), Sch 9

CONDITIONS RELATING TO MINERAL WORKING

PART I

CONDITIONS IMPOSED ON GRANT OF PERMISSION

Duration of development

1.—(1) Every planning permission for development [—

   (a) consisting of the winning and working of minerals; or
   (b) involving the depositing of mineral waste,]

shall be subject to a condition as to the duration of the development.

(2) Except where a condition is specified under sub-paragraph (3), the condition in the case of planning permission granted or deemed to be granted after 22nd February 1982 is that the [winning and working of minerals or the depositing of mineral waste] must cease not later than the expiration of the period of 60 years beginning with the date of the permission.

(3) An authority granting planning permission after that date or directing after that date that planning permission shall be deemed to be granted may specify a longer or shorter period than 60 years, and if they do so, the condition is that the [winning and working of minerals or the depositing of mineral waste] must cease not later than the expiration of a period of the specified length beginning with the date of the permission.

(4) A longer or shorter period than 60 years may be prescribed for the purposes of sub-paragraphs (2) and (3).

(5) The condition in the case of planning permission granted or deemed to have been granted before 22nd February 1982 is that the [winning and working of minerals or the depositing of mineral waste] must cease not later than the expiration of the period of 60 years beginning with that date.

(6) A condition to which planning permission for development . . . is subject by virtue of this paragraph—

(a) is not to be regarded for the purposes of the planning Acts as a condition such as is mentioned in section 72(1)(b); but

(b) is to be regarded for the purposes of sections 78 and 79 as a condition imposed by a decision of the local planning authority, and may accordingly be the subject of an appeal under section 78.

Power to impose aftercare conditions

2.—(1) Where—

(a) planning permission for development consisting of the winning and working of minerals [or involving the depositing of refuse or waste materials] is granted, and

(b) the permission is subject to a condition requiring that after [the winning and working is completed or the depositing has ceased], the site shall be restored by the use of any or all of the following, namely subsoil, topsoil and soil-making material,

it may be granted subject also to any such condition as the mineral planning authority think fit requiring that such steps shall be taken as may be necessary to bring land to the required standard for whichever of the following uses is specified in the condition, namely—

    (i) use for agriculture;
    (ii) use for forestry; or
    (iii) use for amenity.

(2) In this Act—

(a) a condition such as is mentioned in paragraph (b) of sub-paragraph (1) is referred to as ''a restoration condition''; and

(b) a condition requiring such steps to be taken as are mentioned in that sub-paragraph is referred to as ''an aftercare condition''.

(3) An aftercare condition may either—

(a) specify the steps to be taken; or

(b) require that the steps be taken in accordance with a scheme (in this Act referred to as an ''aftercare scheme'') approved by the mineral planning authority.

(4) A mineral planning authority may approve an aftercare scheme in the form in which it is submitted to them or may modify it and approve it as modified.

(5) The steps that may be specified in an aftercare condition or an aftercare scheme may consist of planting, cultivating, fertilising, watering, draining or otherwise treating the land.

(6) Where a step is specified in a condition or a scheme, the period during which it is to be taken may also be specified, but no step may be required to be taken after the expiry of the aftercare period.

(7) In sub-paragraph (6) ''the aftercare period'' means a period of five years from compliance with the restoration condition or such other maximum period after compliance with that condition as may be prescribed; and in respect of any part of a site, the aftercare period shall commence on compliance with the restoration condition in respect of that part.

(8) The power to prescribe maximum periods conferred by sub-paragraph (7) includes power to prescribe maximum periods differing according to the use specified.

(9) In this paragraph ''forestry'' means the growing of a utilisable crop of timber.

Meaning of ''required standard''

3.—(1) In a case where—

(a) the use specified in an aftercare condition is a use for agriculture; and

(b) the land was in use for agriculture at the time of the grant of the planning permission or had previously been used for that purpose and had not at the time of the grant been used for any authorised purpose since its use for agriculture ceased; and

(c) the Minister has notified the mineral planning authority of the physical characteristics of the land when it was last used for agriculture,

the land is brought to the required standard when its physical characteristics are restored, so far as it is practicable to do so, to what they were when it was last used for agriculture.

(2) In any other case where the use specified in an aftercare condition is a use for agriculture, the land is brought to the required standard when it is reasonably fit for that use.

(3) Where the use specified in an aftercare condition is a use for forestry, the land is brought to the required standard when it is reasonably fit for that use.

(4) Where the use specified in an aftercare condition is a use for amenity, the land is brought to the required standard when it is suitable for sustaining trees, shrubs or other plants.

(5) In this paragraph—

"authorised" means authorised by planning permission;

"forestry" has the same meaning as in paragraph 2; and

"the Minister" means—

    (a) in relation to England, the Minister of Agriculture, Fisheries and Food; and
    (b) in relation to Wales, the Secretary of State.

Consultations

4.—(1) Before imposing an aftercare condition, the mineral planning authority shall consult—

    (a) the Minister, where they propose that the use specified in the condition shall be a use for agriculture; and
    (b) the Forestry Commission, where they propose that the use so specified shall be a use for forestry,

as to whether it is appropriate to specify that use.

(2) Where after consultations required by sub-paragraph (1) the mineral planning authority are satisfied that the use that they ought to specify is a use for agriculture or for forestry, they shall consult—

    (a) where it is for agriculture, the Minister; and
    (b) where it is for forestry, the Forestry Commission,

with regard to whether the steps to be taken should be specified in the aftercare condition or in an aftercare scheme.

(3) The mineral planning authority shall also consult the Minister or, as the case may be, the Forestry Commission—

    (a) as to the steps to be specified in an aftercare condition which specifies a use for agriculture or for forestry; and
    (b) before approving an aftercare scheme submitted in accordance with an aftercare condition which specifies such a use.

(4) The mineral planning authority shall also, from time to time as they consider expedient, consult the Minister or the Commission, as the case may be, as to whether the steps specified in an aftercare condition or an aftercare scheme are being taken.

[(4A) Without prejudice to the application of this paragraph in relation to consultation with the Forestry Commission, where the Minister is consulted pursuant to any provision of this paragraph—

    (a) he is not required to inspect any land or to express a view on any matter or question; and
    (b) he is not precluded from responding in general terms or otherwise in terms which are not specific to the land in question.]

(5) In this paragraph "forestry" and "the Minister" have the same meanings as in paragraph 3.

Certificate of compliance

5. If, on the application of any person with an interest in land in respect of which an aftercare condition has been imposed, the mineral planning authority are satisfied that the condition has been complied with they shall issue a certificate to that effect.

Recovery of expenses of compliance

6. A person who has complied with an aftercare condition but who has not himself [won and worked minerals or deposited refuse or waste materials] shall be entitled, subject to any condition to the contrary contained in a contract which is enforceable against him by the person who last carried out such operations, to recover from that person any expenses reasonably incurred in complying with the aftercare condition.   **[353]**

NOTES

Commencement: 24 August 1990.

Words in square brackets in paras 1(1)–(3), (5), (6), 2(1)(b), 6 substituted, words omitted from para 1(6) repealed, and words in square brackets in para 2(1)(a) inserted, by the Planning and Compensation Act 1991, ss 21, 84(6), Sch 1, paras 1, 14(1)–(5), Sch 19, Pt I.

Para 4(4A) inserted by the Environment Act 1995, s 120(1), Sch 22, para 43, as from a day to be appointed under s 125(3).

Modification: para 1 modified by the Town and Country Planning General Regulations 1992, SI 1992/1492, reg 5(1)(c), Sch 1 at **[829]**.

Planning Acts: Town and Country Planning Act 1990, Planning (Listed Buildings and Conservation Areas) Act 1990, Planning (Hazardous Substances) Act 1990, Planning (Consequential Provisions) Act 1990.

PART II

CONDITIONS IMPOSED ON REVOCATION OR MODIFICATION OF PERMISSION

7. An order under section 97 may in relation to planning permission for development consisting of the winning and working of minerals [or involving the depositing of refuse or waste materials], include such aftercare condition as the mineral planning authority think fit if—

    (a) it also includes a restoration condition; or
    (b) a restoration condition has previously been imposed in relation to the land by virtue of any provision of this Act.

8. Paragraphs 2(3) to (9) and 3 to 6 shall apply in relation to an aftercare condition so imposed as they apply in relation to such a condition imposed under paragraph 2.

[Interpretation

9. In this Schedule any reference to a mineral planning authority shall be construed, in relation to the exercise of functions with respect to the depositing of refuse or waste materials (other than mineral waste), as a reference to the authority entitled to discharge such functions.] **[354]**

NOTES

Commencement: 24 August 1990 (paras 7, 8); 25 September 1991 (para 9).

Words in square brackets in para 7 inserted, and para 9 and the cross-heading "Interpretation" added, by the Planning and Compensation Act 1991, s 21, Sch 1, paras 1, 14(6), (7).

SCHEDULE 6

Sections 79, 175, 195, 208

DETERMINATION OF CERTAIN APPEALS BY PERSON APPOINTED BY SECRETARY OF STATE

Determination of appeals by appointed person

1.—(1) The Secretary of State may by regulations prescribe classes of appeals under sections 78, [106B] 174, 195 and 208, [and paragraphs 6(11) and (12) and 11(1) of Schedule 13 and paragraph 9(1) of Schedule 14 to the Environment Act 1995,] which are to be determined by a person appointed by the Secretary of State for the purpose instead of by the Secretary of State.

(2) Those classes of appeals shall be so determined except in such classes of case—

    (a) as may for the time being be prescribed, or

(b) as may be specified in directions given by the Secretary of State.

(3) Regulations made for the purpose of this paragraph may provide for the giving of publicity to any directions given by the Secretary of State under this paragraph.

(4) This paragraph shall not affect any provision in this Act or any instrument made under it that an appeal shall lie to, or a notice of appeal shall be served on, the Secretary of State.

(5) A person appointed under this paragraph is referred to in this Schedule as "an appointed person".

Powers and duties of appointed person

2.—(1) An appointed person shall have the same powers and duties—

    (a) in relation to an appeal under section 78, as the Secretary of State has under [subsections (1), (4) and (6A)] of section 79;

[(aa) in relation to an appeal under section 106B, as he has under that section]

    (b) in relation to an appeal under section 174, as he has under sections 176(1), (2) [to (2A)] and (5) and 177(1) to (4);

    (c) in relation to an appeal under section 195, as he has under subsections (2) and (3) of that section . . .;

    (d) in relation to an appeal under section 208, as he has under subsections (7) [to (8A)] of that section.

(2) Sections 79(2), [106B(4)] 175(3), 196(1) and 208(5) shall not apply to an appeal which falls to be determined by an appointed person, but before it is determined the Secretary of State shall ask the appellant and the local planning authority whether they wish to appear before and be heard by the appointed person.

(3) If both the parties express a wish not to appear and be heard the appeal may be determined without their being heard.

(4) If either of the parties expresses a wish to appear and be heard, the appointed person shall give them both an opportunity of doing so.

(5) Sub-paragraph (2) does not apply in the case of an appeal under section 78 if the appeal is referred to a Planning Inquiry Commission under section 101.

(6) Where an appeal has been determined by an appointed person, his decision shall be treated as that of the Secretary of State.

(7) Except as provided by Part XII, the validity of that decision shall not be questioned in any proceedings whatsoever.

(8) It shall not be a ground of application to the High Court under section 288, or of appeal to the High Court under section 289 . . . that an appeal ought to have been determined by the Secretary of State and not by an appointed person, unless the appellant or the local planning authority challenge the appointed person's power to determine the appeal before his decision on the appeal is given.

(9) Where in any enactment (including this Act) there is a reference to the Secretary of State in a context relating or capable of relating to an appeal to which this Schedule applies or to anything done or authorised or required to be done by, to or before the Secretary of State on or in connection with any such appeal, then so far as the context permits it shall be construed, in relation to an appeal determined or falling to be determined by an appointed person, as a reference to him.

Determination of appeals by Secretary of State

3.—(1) The Secretary of State may, if he thinks fit, direct that an appeal which would otherwise fall to be determined by an appointed person shall instead be determined by the Secretary of State.

(2) Such a direction shall state the reasons for which it is given and shall be served on the person, if any, so appointed, the appellant, the local planning authority and any person who has made representations relating to the subject matter of the appeal which the authority are

required to take into account under [any provision of a development order made by virtue of] section 71(2)(a).

(3) Where in consequence of such a direction an appeal falls to be determined by the Secretary of State, the provisions of this Act which are relevant to the appeal shall, subject to the following provisions of this paragraph, apply to the appeal as if this Schedule had never applied to it.

(4) The Secretary of State shall give the appellant, the local planning authority and any person who has made any such representations as mentioned in sub-paragraph (2) an opportunity of appearing before and being heard by a person appointed by the Secretary of State for that purpose if—

(a) the reasons for the direction raise matters with respect to which any of those persons have not made representations; or

(b) in the case of the appellant or the local planning authority, either of them was not asked in pursuance of paragraph 2(2) whether they wished to appear before and be heard by the appointed person, or expressed no wish in answer to that question, or expressed a wish to appear and be heard, but was not given an opportunity of doing so.

(5) Sub-paragraph (4) does not apply in the case of an appeal under section 78 if the appeal is referred to a Planning Inquiry Commission under section 101.

(6) Except as provided by sub-paragraph (4), the Secretary of State need not give any person an opportunity of appearing before and being heard by a person appointed for the purpose, or of making fresh representations or making or withdrawing any representations already made.

(7) In determining the appeal the Secretary of State may take into account any report made to him by any person previously appointed to determine it.

4.—(1) The Secretary of State may by a further direction revoke a direction under paragraph 3 at any time before the determination of the appeal.

(2) Such a further direction shall state the reasons for which it is given and shall be served on the person, if any, previously appointed to determine the appeal, the appellant, the local planning authority and any person who has made representations relating to the subject matter of the appeal which the authority are required to take into account under [any provision of a development order made by virtue of] section 71(2)(a).

(3) Where such a further direction has been given, the provisions of this Schedule relevant to the appeal shall apply, subject to sub-paragraph (4), as if no direction under paragraph 3 had been given.

(4) Anything done by or on behalf of the Secretary of State in connection with the appeal which might have done by the appointed person (including any arrangements made for the holding of a hearing or local inquiry) shall, unless that person directs otherwise, be treated as having been done by him.

Appointment of another person to determine appeal

5.—(1) At any time before the appointed person has determined the appeal the Secretary of State may—

(a) revoke his appointment; and

(b) appoint another person under paragraph 1 to determine the appeal instead.

(2) Where such a new appointment is made the consideration of the appeal or any inquiry or other hearing in connection with it shall be begun afresh.

(3) Nothing in sub-paragraph (2) shall require—

(a) the question referred to in paragraph 2(2) to be asked again with reference to the new appointed person if before his appointment it was asked with reference to the previous appointed person (any answers being treated as given with reference to the new appointed person); or

(b) any person to be given an opportunity of making fresh representations or modifying or withdrawing any representations already made.

Local inquiries and hearings

6.—(1) Whether or not the parties to an appeal have asked for an opportunity to appear and be heard, an appointed person—

(a) may hold a local inquiry in connection with the appeal; and

(b) shall do so if the Secretary of State so directs.

(2) Where an appointed person—

(a) holds a hearing by virtue of paragraph 2(4); or

(b) holds an inquiry by virtue of this paragraph,

an assessor may be appointed by the Secretary of State to sit with the appointed person at the hearing or inquiry to advise him on any matters arising, notwithstanding that the appointed person is to determine the appeal.

(3) Subject to sub-paragraph (4), the costs of any such hearing or inquiry shall be defrayed by the Secretary of State.

(4) Subsections (2) to (5) of section 250 of the Local Government Act 1972 (local inquiries: evidence and costs) apply to an inquiry held under this paragraph with the following adaptations—

(a) with the substitution in subsection (4) (recovery of costs of holding the inquiry) for the references to the Minister causing the inquiry to be held of references to the Secretary of State; and

(b) with the substitution in subsection (5) (orders as to the costs of the parties) for the reference to the Minister causing the inquiry to be held of a reference to the appointed person or the Secretary of State.

(5) The appointed person or the Secretary of State has the same power to make orders under section 250(5) of that Act (orders with respect to costs of the parties) in relation to proceedings under this Schedule which do not give rise to an inquiry as he has in relation to such an inquiry.

Supplementary provisions

7. If before or during the determination of an appeal under section 78 which is to be or is being determined in accordance with paragraph 1, the Secretary of State forms the opinion mentioned in section 79(6), he may direct that the determination shall not be begun or proceeded with.

8.—(1) The Tribunals and Inquiries Act [1992] shall apply to a local inquiry or other hearing held in pursuance of this Schedule as it applies to a statutory inquiry held by the Secretary of State, but as if in [section 10(1)] of that Act (statement of reasons for decisions) the reference to any decision taken by the Secretary of State were a reference to a decision taken by an appointed person.

(2) Where an appointed person is an officer of the Department of the Environment or the Welsh Office the functions of determining an appeal and doing anything in connection with it conferred on him by this Schedule shall be treated for the purposes of the Parliamentary Commissioner Act 1967—

(a) if he was appointed by the Secretary of State for the time being having general responsibility in planning matters in relation to England, as functions of that Department; and

(b) if he was appointed by the Secretary of State for the time being having general responsibility in planning matters in relation to Wales, as functions of the Welsh Office. **[355]**

NOTES
Commencement: 24 August 1990.
Words in square brackets in para 2(1)(a), (c), (d) substituted, first words in square brackets in para 1(1) and words in square brackets in paras 2(1)(b), (2), 3(2), 4(2) and para 2(aa), inserted, and words omitted

from para 2(1)(c), (8) repealed, by the Planning and Compensation Act 1991, ss 32, 84(6), Sch 7, paras 8, 54, Sch 19, Pt I.

Second words in square brackets in para 1(1) inserted by the Environment Act 1995, s 120(1), Sch 22, para 44, as from a day to be appointed under s 125(3).

Words in square brackets in para 8(1) substituted by the Tribunals and Inquiries Act 1992, s 18(1), Sch 3, para 28.

Para 6: sub-para (5) temporarily omitted by the Planning (Consequential Provisions) Act 1990, s 6, Sch 4, paras 1, 7, until such day as may be appointed by order made by the Secretary of State. The Planning (Consequential Provisions) Act 1990 (Appointed Day No 1 and Transitional Provisions) Order 1991, SI 1991/2698, appointed 2 January 1992 only for the purposes of awards of costs in relation to proceedings which give rise to a hearing.

SCHEDULE 7
Section 83

SIMPLIFIED PLANNING ZONES

General

1.—(1) A simplified planning zone scheme shall consist of a map and a written statement, and such diagrams, illustrations and descriptive matter as the local planning authority think appropriate for explaining or illustrating the provisions of the scheme.

(2) A simplified planning zone scheme shall specify—

    (a) the development or classes of development permitted by the scheme,
    (b) the land in relation to which permission is granted, and
    (c) any conditions, limitations or exceptions subject to which it is granted;

and shall contain such other matters as may be prescribed.

Notification of proposals to make or alter scheme

2. An authority who decide under section 83(2) to make or alter a simplified planning zone scheme shall—

    (a) notify the Secretary of State of their decision as soon as practicable, and
    (b) determine the date on which they will begin to prepare the scheme or the alterations.

Power of Secretary of State to direct making or alteration of scheme

3.—(1) If a person requests a local planning authority to make or alter a simplified planning zone scheme but the authority—

    (a) refuse to do so, or
    (b) do not within the period of three months from the date of the request decide to so do,

he may, subject to sub-paragraph (2), require them to refer the matter to the Secretary of State.

(2) A person may not require the reference of the matter to the Secretary of State if—

    (a) in the case of a request to make a scheme, a simplified planning zone scheme relating to the whole or part of the land specified in the request has been adopted or approved within the 12 months preceding his request;
    (b) in the case of a request to alter the scheme, the scheme to which the request relates was adopted or approved, or any alteration to it has been adopted or approved, within that period.

(3) The Secretary of State shall, as soon as practicable after a matter is referred to him—

    (a) send the authority a copy of any representations made to him by the applicant which have not been made to the authority, and
    (b) notify the authority that if they wish to make any representations in the matter they should do so, in writing, within 28 days.

(4) After the Secretary of State has—

    (a) considered the matter and any written representations made by the applicant or the authority, and

(b) carried out such consultations with such persons as he thinks fit,

he may give the authority a simplified planning zone direction.

(5) The Secretary of State shall notify the applicant and the authority of his decision and of his reasons for it.

4.—(1) A simplified planning zone direction is—

(a) if the request was for the making of a scheme, a direction to make a scheme which the Secretary of State considers appropriate; and

(b) if the request was for the alteration of a scheme, a direction to alter it in such manner as he considers appropriate

[and, in either case, requires the local planning authority to take all the steps required by this Schedule for the adoption of proposals for the making or, as the case may be, alteration of a scheme].

(2) A direction under sub-paragraph (1)(a) or (b) may extend—

(a) to the land specified in the request to the authority,

(b) to any part of the land so specified, or

(c) to land which includes the whole or part of the land so specified;

and accordingly may direct that land shall be added to or excluded from an existing simplified planning zone.

[Steps to be taken before depositing proposals

5.—(1) A local planning authority proposing to make or alter a simplified planning zone scheme shall, before determining the content of their proposals, comply with this paragraph.

(2) They shall—

(a) consult the Secretary of State having responsibility for highways as to the effect any proposals they may make might have on existing or future highways,

(b) if they are the district planning authority, consult the county council—

(i) as county planning authority, and

(ii) as to the effect which any matters the district planning authority are considering including in the proposals might have on existing or future highways, and

(c) consult or notify such persons as regulations may require them to consult or, as the case may be, notify.

(3) They shall take such steps as may be prescribed or as the Secretary of State may, in a particular case, direct to publicise—

(a) the fact that they propose to make or alter a simplified planning zone scheme, and

(b) the matters which they are considering including in the proposals.

(4) They shall consider any representations that are made in accordance with regulations.

Procedure after deposit of proposals

6. Where a local planning authority have prepared a proposed simplified planning zone scheme, or proposed alterations to a simplified planning zone scheme, they shall—

(a) make copies of the proposed scheme or alterations available for inspection at such places as may be prescribed,

(b) take such steps as may be prescribed for the purpose of advertising the fact that the proposed scheme or alterations are so available and the places at which, and times during which, they may be inspected,

(c) take such steps as may be prescribed for inviting objections to be made within such period as may be prescribed, and

(d) send a copy of the proposed scheme or alterations to the Secretary of State and to the Secretary of State having responsibility for highways and, if they are the district planning authority, to the county council.]

[Procedure for dealing with objections

8.—(1) Where objections to the proposed scheme or alterations are made, the local planning authority may—

    (a) for the purpose of considering the objections, cause a local inquiry or other hearing to be held by a person appointed by the Secretary of State or, in such cases as may be prescribed, appointed by the authority, or

    (b) require the objections to be considered by a person appointed by the Secretary of State.

(2) A local planning authority shall exercise the power under sub-paragraph (1), or paragraph (a) or (b) of that sub-paragraph, if directed to do so by the Secretary of State.]

(4) Regulations may—

    (a) make provision with respect to the appointment, and qualifications for appointment, of persons [for the purposes of this paragraph];

    (b) include provision enabling the Secretary of State to direct a local planning authority to appoint a particular person, or one of a specified list or class of persons;

    (c) make provision with respect to the remuneration and allowances of the person appointed.

(5) Subsections (2) and (3) of section 250 of the Local Government Act 1972 (power to summon and examine witnesses) apply to an inquiry held under this paragraph.

(6) The Tribunals and Inquiries Act [1992] applies to a local inquiry or other hearing held under this paragraph as it applies to a statutory inquiry held by the Secretary of State, with the substitution in [section 10(1)] (statement of reasons for decision) for the references to a decision taken by the Secretary of State of references to a decision taken by a local authority.

Adoption of proposals by local planning authority

9.—[(1) After the expiry of the period for making objections or, if objections have been made in accordance with the regulations, after considering those objections and the views of any person holding an inquiry or hearing or considering the objections under paragraph 8, the local planning authority may by resolution adopt the proposals (subject to the following provisions of this paragraph and paragraph 10).]

(2) The authority may adopt the proposals as originally prepared or as modified so as to take account of—

    (a) any such objections as are mentioned in sub-paragraph (1) or any other objections to the proposals, or

    (b) any other considerations which appear to the authority to be material.

(3) If, before the proposals have been adopted by the local planning authority, it appears to the Secretary of State that they are unsatisfactory, he may direct the authority to [modify] the proposals in such respects as are indicated in the direction.

(4) An authority to whom such a direction is given shall not adopt the proposals unless—

    (a) they satisfy the Secretary of State that they have made the modifications necessary to conform with the direction, or

    (b) the direction is withdrawn.

Calling in of proposals for approval by Secretary of State

10.—(1) Before the proposals have been adopted by the local planning authority the Secretary of State may direct that they shall be sumitted to him for his approval.

(2) If the Secretary of State gives such a direction—

    (a) the authority shall not take any further steps for the adoption of the proposals, and in particular shall not hold or proceed with a local inquiry or other hearing [or any consideration of objections] in respect of the proposals under paragraph 8; and

    (b) the proposals shall not have effect unless approved by the Secretary of State and shall not require adoption by the authority.

Approval of proposals by Secretary of State

11.—(1) The Secretary of State may after considering proposals submitted to him under paragraph 10 either approve them, in whole or in part and with or without modifications, or reject them.

(2) In considering the proposals the Secretary of State may take into account any matters he thinks are relevant, whether or not they were taken into account in the proposals as submitted to him.

[(3) Where on taking the proposals into consideration the Secretary of State does not determine then to reject them he shall, before determining whether or not to approve them, consider any objections made in accordance with regulations (and not withdrawn) except objections which—

(a) have already been considered by the local planning authority or by a person appointed by the Secretary of State, or

(b) have already been considered at a local inquiry or other hearing.

(4) The Secretary of State may—

(a) for the purpose of considering any objections and the views of the local planning authority and of such other persons as he thinks fit, cause a local inquiry or other hearing to be held by a person appointed by him, or

(b) require such objections and views to be considered by a person appointed by him.

(5) In considering the proposals the Secretary of State may consult with, or consider the views of, any local planning authority or any other person; but he need not do so, or give an opportunity for the making or consideration of representations or objections, except so far as he is required to do so by sub-paragraph (3).]

Default powers

[12.—(1) Where—

(a) a local planning authority are directed under paragraph 3 to make a simplified planning zone scheme which the Secretary of State considers appropriate or to alter such a scheme in such manner as he considers appropriate, and

(b) the Secretary of State is satisfied, after holding a local inquiry or other hearing, that the authority are not taking within a reasonable period the steps required by this Schedule for the adoption of proposals for the making or, as the case may be, alteration of a scheme,

he may himself make a scheme or, as the case may be, the alterations.]

(2) Where under this paragraph anything which ought to have been done by a local planning authority is done by the Secretary of State, the previous provisions of this Schedule apply, so far as practicable, with any necessary modifications, in relation to the doing of that thing by the Secretary of State and the thing so done.

(3) Where the Secretary of State incurs expenses under this paragraph in connection with the doing of anything which should have been done by a local planning authority, so much of those expenses as may be certified by the Secretary of State to have been incurred in the performance of functions of that authority shall on demand be repaid by the authority to the Secretary of State.

Regulations and directions

13.—(1) Without prejudice to the previous provisions of this Schedule, the Secretary of State may make regulations with respect—

(a) to the form and content of simplified planning zone schemes, and

(b) to the procedure to be followed in connection with their preparation, withdrawal, adoption, submission, approval, making or alteration.

(2) Any such regulations may in particular—

(a) provide for the notice to be given of, or the publicity to be given to—

(i) matters included or proposed to be included in a simplified planning zone scheme, and

(ii) the adoption or approval of such a scheme, or of any alteration of it, or any other prescribed procedural step,

and for publicity to be given to the procedure to be followed in these respects;

(b) make provision with respect to the making and consideration of representations as to matters to be included in, or objections to, any such scheme or proposals for its alteration;

[(bb) make provision with respect to the circumstances in which representations with respect to the matters to be included in such a scheme or proposals for its alteration are to be treated, for the purposes of this Schedule, as being objections made in accordance with regulations;]

(c) without prejudice to paragraph (a), provide for notice to be given to particular persons of the adoption or approval of a simplified planning zone scheme, or an alteration to such a scheme, if they have objected to the proposals and have notified the local planning authority of their wish to receive notice, subject (if the regulations so provide) to the payment of a reasonable charge;

(d) require or authorise a local planning authority to consult with, or consider the views of, other persons before taking any prescribed procedural step;

(e) require a local planning authority, in such cases as may be prescribed or in such particular cases as the Secretary of State may direct, to provide persons making a request with copies of any document which has been made public . . ., subject (if the regulations so provide) to the payment of a reasonable charge;

(f) provide for the publication and inspection of a simplified planning zone scheme which has been adopted or approved, or any document adopted or approved altering such a scheme, and for copies of any such scheme or document to be made available on sale.

(3) Regulations under this paragraph may extend throughout England and Wales or to specified areas only and may make different provision for different cases.

(4) Subject to the previous provisions of this Schedule and to any regulations under this paragraph, the Secretary of State may give directions to any local planning authority or to local planning authorities generally—

(a) for formulating the procedure for the carrying out of their functions under this Schedule;

(b) for requiring them to give him such information as he may require for carrying out any of his functions under this Schedule.   **[356]**

NOTES

Commencement: 24 August 1990.

Words in square brackets in para 4(1) added, paras 5, 6 substituted for paras 5–7 as originally enacted, para 8(1), (2) substituted for para 8(1)–(3) as originally enacted, words in square brackets in para 8(4) substituted, para 9(1) and words in square brackets in para 9(3) substituted, words in square brackets in para 10(2)(a) inserted, para 11(3)–(5) substituted for para 11(3), (4) as originally enacted, para 12(1) substituted, para 13(2)(bb) inserted, and words omitted from para 13(2)(e) repealed, by the Planning and Compensation Act 1991, ss 28, 84(6), Sch 5, Pt I, paras 1, 2, Pt II, paras 4–10, Sch 19, Pt I.

Words in square brackets in para 8(6) substituted by the Tribunals and Inquiries Act 1992, s 18(1), Sch 3, para 29.

SCHEDULE 8

Section 101(4)

PLANNING INQUIRY COMMISSIONS

PART I

CONSTITUTION AND PROCEDURE ON REFERENCES

Constitution of Commissions

1.—(1) A Planning Inquiry Commission shall consist of a chairman and not less than two nor more than four other members appointed by the Secretary of State.

(2) The Secretary of State may—

(a) pay to the members of any such commission such remuneration and allowances as he may with the consent of the Treasury determine, and

(b) provide for each such commission such officers or servants, and such accommodation, as appears to him expedient to provide for the purpose of assisting the commission in the discharge of their functions.

(3) The validity of any proceedings of any such commission shall not be affected by any vacancy among the members of the commission or by any defect in the appointment of any member.

(4) In relation to any matter affecting both England and Wales—

(a) the functions of the Secretary of State under sub-paragraph (1) shall be exercised by the Secretaries of State for the time being having general responsibility in planning matters in relation to England and in relation to Wales acting jointly, and

(b) his functions under sub-paragraph (2) shall be exercised by one of those Secretaries of State authorised by the other to act on behalf of both of them for the purposes of that sub-paragraph.

Reference to a Planning Inquiry Commission

2.—(1) Two or more of the matters mentioned in section 101(2) may be referred to the same commission if it appears to the responsible Minister or Ministers that they relate to proposals to carry out development for similar purposes on different sites.

(2) Where a matter referred to a commission under section 101 relates to a proposal to carry out development for any purpose at a particular site, the responsible Minister or Ministers may also refer to the commission the question whether development for that purpose should instead be carried out at an alternative site.

(3) On referring a matter to a commission, the responsible Minister or Ministers—

(a) shall state in the reference the reasons for the reference, and

(b) may draw the attention of the commission to any points which seem to him or them to be relevant to their inquiry.

Functions of Planning Inquiry Commission on reference

3.—(1) A commission inquiring into a matter referred to them under section 101 shall—

(a) identify and investigate the considerations relevant to, or the technical or scientific aspects of, that matter which in their opinion are relevant to the question whether the proposed development should be permitted to be carried out, and

(b) assess the importance to be attached to those considerations or aspects.

(2) If—

(a) in the case of a matter mentioned in section 101(2)(a), (b) or (c), the applicant, or

(b) in any case, the local planning authority,

so wish, the commission shall give to each of them, and, in the case of an application or appeal mentioned in section 101(2)(a) or (b), also to any person who has made representations relating to the subject matter of the application or appeal which the authority are required to take into account [any provision of a development order made by virtue of section 71(2)(a)], an opportunity of appearing before and being heard by one or more members of the commission.

(3) The commission shall then report to the responsible Minister or Ministers on the matter referred to them.

(4) A commission may, with the approval of the Secretary of State and at his expense, arrange for the carrying out (whether by the commission themselves or by others) of research of any kind appearing to them to be relevant to a matter referred to them for inquiry and report.

(5) In sub-paragraph (4) "the Secretary of State," in relation to any matter affecting both England and Wales, means—

(a) the Secretary of State for the time being having general responsibility in planning matters in relation to England, or

(b) the Secretary of State for the time being having responsibility in relation to Wales,

acting, by arrangements between the two of them, on behalf of both.

Procedure on reference to a Planning Inquiry Commission

4.—(1) A reference to a Planning Inquiry Commission of a proposal that development should be carried out by or on behalf of a government department may be made at any time.

(2) A reference of any other matter mentioned in section 101 may be made at any time before, but not after, the determination of the relevant application referred under section 77 or the relevant appeal under section 78 or, as the case may be, the giving of the relevant direction under section 90(1).

(3) The fact that an inquiry or other hearing has been held into a proposal by a person appointed by any Minister for the purpose shall not prevent a reference of the proposal to a Planning Inquiry Commission.

(4) Notice of the making of a reference to any such commission shall be published in the prescribed manner.

(5) A copy of the notice must be served on the local planning authority for the area in which it is proposed that the relevant development will be carried out, and—

(a) in the case of an application for planning permission referred under section 77 or an appeal under section 78, on the applicant and any person who has made representations relating to the subject matter of the application or appeal which the authority are required to take into account under [any provision of a development order made by virtue of section 71(2)(a)];

(b) in the case of a proposal that a direction should be given under section 90(1) with respect to any development, on the local authority [National Park authority] or statutory undertakers applying for authorisation to carry out that development.

(6) Subject to the provisions of this paragraph and paragraph 5 and to any directions given to them by the responsible Minister or Ministers, a Planning Inquiry Commission shall have power to regulate their own procedure.

Local inquiries held by Planning Inquiry Commission

5.—(1) A Planning Inquiry Commission shall, for the purpose of complying with paragraph 3(2), hold a local inquiry; and they may hold such an inquiry, if they think it necessary for the proper discharge of their functions, notwithstanding that neither the applicant nor the local planning authority want an opportunity to appear and be heard.

(2) Where a Planning Inquiry Commission are to hold a local inquiry under sub-paragraph (1) in connection with a matter referred to them, and it appears to the responsible Minister or Ministers, in the case of some other matter falling to be determined by a Minister of the Crown and required or authorised by an enactment other than this paragraph to be the subject of a local inquiry, that the two matters are so far cognate that they should be considered together, he or, as the case may be, they may direct that the two inquiries be held concurrently or combined as one inquiry.

(3) An inquiry held by a commission under this paragraph shall be treated for the purposes of the Tribunals and Inquiries Act [1992] as one held by a Minister in pursuance of a duty imposed by a statutory provision.

(4) Subsections (2) to (5) of section 250 of the Local Government Act 1972 (local inquiries: evidence and costs) shall apply in relation to an inquiry held under sub-paragraph (1) as they apply in relation to an inquiry caused to be held by a Minister under subsection (1) of that section, with the substitution for references to the Minister causing the inquiry to be held (other than the first reference in subsection (4)) of references to the responsible Minister or Ministers. **[357]**

NOTES
Commencement: 24 August 1990.
Words in square brackets in paras 3(2), 4(5)(a) substituted by the Planning and Compensation Act 1991, s 32, Sch 7, paras 8, 55.
Words in square brackets in para 4(5)(b) inserted by the Environment Act 1995, s 78, Sch 10, para 32(15), as from a day to be appointed under s 125(3).
Figure in square brackets in para 5(3) substituted by the Tribunals and Inquiries Act 1992, s 18(1), Sch 3, para 30.

PART II

MEANING OF ''THE RESPONSIBLE MINISTER OR MINISTERS''

6. In relation to the matters specified in the first column of the Table below (which are matters mentioned in subsection (2)(a), (b), (c) or (d) of section 101 as matters which may be referred to a Planning Inquiry Commission under that section) ''the responsible Minister or Ministers'' for the purposes of that section and this Schedule—

(a) in the case of a matter affecting England only, are those specified opposite in the second column of the Table;

(b) in the case of a matter affecting Wales only, are those specified opposite in the third column of the Table; and

(c) in the case of a matter affecting both England and Wales, are those specified opposite in the fourth column of the Table.

7. Where an entry in the second, third or fourth columns of the Table specifies two or more Ministers, that entry shall be construed as referring to those Ministers acting jointly.

Table

Referred matter	Affecting England only	Affecting Wales only	Affecting both England and Wales
1. Application for planning permission or appeal under section 78 relating to land to which section 266(1) applies.	The Secretary of State for the time being having general responsibility in planning matters in relation to England and the appropriate Minister (if different).	The Secretary of State for the time being having general responsibility in planning matters in relation to Wales and the appropriate Minister (if different).	The Secretaries of State for the time being having general responsibility in planning matters in relation to England and in relation to Wales and the appropriate Minister (if different).
2. Application for planning permission or appeal under section 78 relating to land to which section 266(1) does not apply.	The Secretary of State for the time being having general responsibility in planning matters in relation to England.	The Secretary of State for the time being having general responsibility in planning matters in relation to Wales.	The Secretaries of State for the time being having general responsibility in planning matters in relation to England and in relation to Wales.
3. Proposal that a government department should give a direction under section 90(1) or that development should be carried out by or on behalf of a government department.	The Secretary of State for the time being having general responsibility in planning matters in relation to England and the Minister (if different) in charge of the government department concerned.	The Secretary of State for the time being having general responsibility in planning matters in relation to Wales and the Minister (if different) in charge of the government department concerned.	The Secretaries of State for the time being having general responsibility in planning matters in relation to England and in relation to Wales and the Minister (if different) in charge of the government department concerned.

NOTES
Commencement: 24 August 1990.

SCHEDULE 9

Section 102(8)

REQUIREMENTS RELATING TO DISCONTINUANCE OF MINERAL WORKING

Orders requiring discontinuance of mineral working

1.—(1) If, having regard to the development plan and to any other material considerations, it appears to a mineral planning authority that it is expedient in the interests of the proper planning of their area (including the interests of amenity)—

[(a) that any use of land for—

(i) development consisting of the winning and working of minerals; or
(ii) the depositing of refuse or waste materials,

should be discontinued or that any conditions should be imposed on the continuance of the winning and working or the depositing;] or

(b) that any buildings or works on land so used should be altered or removed; or
[(c) that any plant or machinery used for the winning and working or the depositing should be altered or removed,]

the mineral planning authority may by order require the discontinuance of that use, or impose such conditions as may be specified in the order on the continuance of it or, as the case may be, require such steps as may be so specified to be taken for the alteration or removal of the buildings or works or plant or machinery.

[(2) An order under this paragraph may grant planning permission for any development of the land to which the order relates, subject to such conditions as may be—

(a) required by paragraph 1 of Schedule 5; or
(b) specified in the order.

(3) Subsections (3) to (5) and (7) of section 102 and section 103 apply to orders under this paragraph as they apply to orders under section 102, but as if—

(a) references to the local planning authority were references to the mineral planning authority; and
(b) the reference in section 103(2)(a) to subsection (2) of section 102 were a reference to sub-paragraph (2).]

2.—[(1) An order under paragraph 1 may impose a restoration condition].

(2) If such an order—

(a) includes a restoration condition, or
(b) a restoration condition has previously been imposed in relation to the land by virtue of any provision of this Act,

the order may also include any such aftercare condition as the mineral planning authority think fit.

(3) Paragraphs 2(3) to (9) and 3 to 6 of Schedule 5 shall apply in relation to an aftercare condition imposed under this paragraph as they apply in relation to such a condition imposed under paragraph 2 of that Schedule, but with the substitution for sub-paragraphs (1) and (2) of paragraph 3 of that Schedule of sub-paragraphs (4) and (5) below.

(4) In a case where—

(a) the use specified in the aftercare condition is a use for agriculture;
(b) the land was in use for agriculture immediately [before the development began], or had previously been used for agriculture and had not been used for any authorised purpose since its use for agriculture ceased; and
(c) the Minister has notified the mineral planning authority of the physical characteristics of the land when it was last used for agriculture,

the land is brought to the required standard when its physical characteristics are restored, so far as it is practicable to do so, to what they were when it was last used for agriculture.

(5) In any other case where the use specified in the aftercare condition is a use for agriculture, the land is brought to the required standard when it is reasonably fit for that use.

Prohibition of resumption of mineral working

3.—[(1) Where it appears to the mineral planning authority—

    (a) that development of land—

        (i) consisting of the winning and working of minerals; or

        (ii) involving the depositing of mineral waste,

has occurred; but

    (b) the winning and working or depositing has permanently ceased, the mineral planning authority may by order—

        (i) prohibit the resumption of the winning and working or the depositing; and

        (ii) impose, in relation to the site, any such requirement as is specified in sub-paragraph (3).

(2) The mineral planning authority may assume that the winning and working or the depositing has permanently ceased only when—

    (a) no winning and working or depositing has occurred, to any substantial extent, at the site for a period of at least two years; and

    (b) it appears to the mineral planning authority, on the evidence available to them at the time when they make the order, that resumption of the winning and working or the depositing to any substantial extent at the site is unlikely.

(3) The requirements mentioned in sub-paragraph (1) are—

    (a) a requirement to alter or remove plant or machinery which was used for the purpose of the winning and working or the depositing or for any purpose ancillary to that purpose;

    (b) a requirement to take such steps as may be specified in the order, within such period as may be so specified, for the purpose of removing or alleviating any injury to amenity which has been caused by the winning and working or depositing, other than injury due to subsidence caused by underground mining operations;

    (c) a requirement that any condition subject to which planning permission for the development was granted or which has been imposed by virtue of any provision of this Act shall be complied with; and

    (d) a restoration condition.]

(4) If—

    (a) an order under this paragraph includes a restoration condition; or

    (b) a restoration condition has previously been imposed in relation to the site by virtue of any provision of this Act,

the order under this paragraph may include any such aftercare condition as the mineral planning authority think fit.

(5) Paragraphs 2(3) to (9) and 3 to 6 of Schedule 5 apply in relation to an aftercare condition imposed under this paragraph as they apply to such a condition imposed under paragraph 2 of this Schedule.

4.—(1) An order under paragraph 3 shall not take effect unless it is confirmed by the Secretary of State, either without modification or subject to such modifications as he considers expedient.

(2) Where a mineral planning authority submit such an order to the Secretary of State for his confirmation under this paragraph, the authority shall serve notice of the order—

    (a) on any person who is an owner or occupier of any of the land to which the order relates, and

    (b) on any other person who in their opinion will be affected by it.

(3) The notice shall specify the period within which any person on whom the notice is served may require the Secretary of State to give him an opportunity of appearing before, and being heard by, a person appointed by the Secretary of State for that purpose.

(4) If within that period such a person so requires, before the Secretary of State confirms the order he shall give such an opportunity both to him and to the mineral planning authority.

(5) The period referred to in sub-paragraph (3) must not be less than 28 days from the service of the notice.

(6) Where an order under paragraph 3 has been confirmed by the Secretary of State, the mineral planning authority shall serve a copy of the order on every person who was entitled to be served with notice under sub-paragraph (2).

(7) When an order under paragraph 3 takes effect any planning permission for the development to which the order relates shall cease to have effect.

(8) Sub-paragraph (7) is without prejudice to the power of the mineral planning authority, on revoking the order, to make a further grant of planning permission for development consisting of the winning and working of minerals [or involving the depositing of mineral waste].

Orders after suspension of winning and working of minerals

5.—[(1) Where it appears to the mineral planning authority—

(a) that development of land—

(i) consisting of the winning and working of minerals; or
(ii) involving the depositing of mineral waste,

has occurred; but

(b) the winning and working or depositing has been temporarily suspended,

the mineral planning authority may by order require that steps be taken for the protection of the environment.]

(2) An order under sub-paragraph (1) is in this Act referred to as a "suspension order".

[(3) The mineral planning authority may assume that the winning and working or the depositing has been temporarily suspended only when—

(a) no such winning and working or depositing has occurred, to any substantial extent, at the site for a period of at least twelve months; but
(b) it appears to the mineral planning authority, on the evidence available to them at the time when they make the order, that a resumption of such winning and working or depositing to a substantial extent is likely.

(4) In this Act "steps for the protection of the environment" means steps for the purpose—

(a) of preserving the amenities of the area in which the land in, on or under which the development was carried out is situated during the period while the winning and working or the depositing is suspended;
(b) of protecting that area from damage during that period; or
(c) of preventing any deterioration in the condition of the land during that period.]

(5) A suspension order shall specify a period, commencing with the date on which it is to take effect, within which any required step for the protection of the environment is to be taken and may specify different periods for the taking of different steps.

Supplementary suspension orders

6.—(1) At any time when a suspension order is in operation the mineral planning authority may by order direct—

(a) that steps for the protection of the environment shall be taken in addition to or in substitution for any of the steps which the suspension order or a previous order under this sub-paragraph specified as required to be taken; or
(b) that the suspension order or any order under this sub-paragraph shall cease to have effect.

(2) An order under sub-paragraph (1) is in this Act referred to as a "supplementary suspension order".

Confirmation and coming into operation of suspension orders

7.—(1) Subject to sub-paragraph (2), a suspension order or a supplementary suspension order shall not take effect unless it is confirmed by the Secretary of State, either without modification or subject to such modifications as he considers expedient.

(2) A supplementary suspension order revoking a suspension order or a previous supplementary suspension order and not requiring that any fresh step shall be taken for the protection of the environment shall take effect without confirmation.

(3) Sub-paragraphs (2) to (5) of paragraph 4 shall have effect in relation to a suspension order or supplementary suspension order submitted to the Secretary of State for his confirmation as they have effect in relation to an order submitted to him for his confirmation under that paragraph.

(4) Where a suspension order or supplementary suspension order has been confirmed by the Secretary of State, the mineral planning authority shall serve a copy of the order on every person who was entitled to be served with notice of the order by virtue of sub-paragraph (3).

Registration of suspension orders as local land charges

8. A suspension order or a supplementary suspension order shall be a local land charge.

Review of suspension orders

9.—(1) It shall be the duty of a mineral planning authority—

(a) to undertake in accordance with the following provisions of this paragraph reviews of suspension orders and supplementary suspension orders which are in operation in their area; and

(b) to determine whether they should make in relation to any land to which a suspension order or supplementary suspension order applies—

   (i) an order under paragraph 3; or
   (ii) a supplementary suspension order.

(2) The first review of a suspension order shall be undertaken not more than five years from the date on which the order takes effect.

(3) Each subsequent review shall be undertaken not more than five years after the previous review.

(4) If a supplementary suspension order is in operation for any part of the area for which a suspension order is in operation, they shall be reviewed together.

(5) If a mineral planning authority have made a supplementary suspension order which requires the taking of steps for the protection of the environment in substitution for all the steps required to be taken by a previous suspension order or supplementary suspension order, the authority shall undertake reviews of the supplementary suspension order in accordance with sub-paragraphs (6) and (7).

(6) The first review shall be undertaken not more than five years from the date on which the order takes effect.

(7) Each subsequent review shall be undertaken not more than five years after the previous review.

(8) The duties to undertake reviews imposed by this paragraph are in addition to and not in substitution for the duties imposed by section 105.

Resumption of mineral working after suspension order

10.—(1) Subject to sub-paragraph (2), nothing in a suspension order or a supplementary suspension order shall prevent the recommencement of development consisting of the winning and working of minerals [or involving the depositing of minerals waste at the site] in relation to which the order has effect.

(2) No person shall recommence such development without first giving the mineral planning authority notice of his intention to do so.

(3) A notice under sub-paragraph (2) shall specify the date on which the person giving the notice intends to recommence [the development].

[(4) The mineral planning authority shall revoke the order if the winning and working of minerals or the depositing of mineral waste has recommenced to a substantial extent at the site in relation to which the order has effect.]

(5) If the authority do not revoke the order before the end of the period of two months from the date specified in the notice under sub-paragraph (2), the person who gave that notice may apply to the Secretary of State for the revocation of the order.

(6) Notice of an application under sub-paragraph (5) shall be given by the applicant to the mineral planning authority.

(7) If he is required to do so by the person who gave the notice or by the mineral planning authority, the Secretary of State shall, before deciding whether to revoke the order, give him and the mineral planning authority an opportunity of appearing before, and being heard by, a person appointed by the Secretary of State for the purpose.

[(8) If the Secretary of State is satisfied that the winning and working of minerals or the depositing of mineral waste has recommenced to a substantial extent at the site in relation to which the order has effect, he shall revoke the order.]

(9) If the Secretary of State revokes an order by virtue of sub-paragraph (8), he shall give notice of its revocation—

    (a) to the person who applied to him for the revocation, and
    (b) to the mineral planning authority.

Default powers of Secretary of State

11.—(1) If it appears to the Secretary of State to be expedient that any order under paragraph 1, 3, 5 or 6 should be made, he may himself make such an order.

(2) Such an order which is made by the Secretary of State shall have the same effect as if it had been made by the mineral planning authority and confirmed by the Secretary of State.

(3) The Secretary of State shall not make such an order without consulting the mineral planning authority.

(4) Where the Secretary of State proposes to make an order under paragraph 1 he shall serve a notice of the proposal on the mineral planning authority.

(5) The notice shall specify the period (which must not be less than 28 days from the date of its service) within which the authority may require an opportunity of appearing before and being heard by a person appointed by the Secretary of State for the purpose.

(6) If within that period the authority so require, before the Secretary of State makes the order he shall give the authority such an opportunity.

(7) The provisions of this Schedule and of any regulations made under this Act with respect to the procedure to be followed in connection with the submission by the mineral planning authority of any order to which sub-paragraph (1) applies, its confirmation by the Secretary of State and the service of copies of it as confirmed shall have effect, subject to any necessary modifications, in relation to any proposal by the Secretary of State to make such an order, its making by him and the service of copies of it.

[Interpretation

12. In this Schedule any reference to a mineral planning authority shall be construed, in relation to the exercise of functions with respect to the depositing of refuse or waste materials (other than mineral waste), as a reference to the authority entitled to discharge such functions.]　　　　　　　　　　　　　　　　　　　　　　　　　　　　　　　　**[359]**

NOTES

    Commencement: 24 August 1990 (paras 1–11); 25 September 1991 (para 12).
    Paras 1(1)(a), (c), (2), (3), 2(1), 3(1)–(3), 5(1), (3), (4), 10(4), (8), and words in square brackets in paras 2(4)(b), 10(1), (3) substituted, words in square brackets in para 4(8) and the whole of para 12 (and

the cross-heading "Interpretation") added, by the Planning and Compensation Act 1991, s 21, Sch 1, paras 1, 15.

SCHEDULE 10

Sections 111, 114

CONDITION TREATED AS APPLICABLE TO REBUILDING AND ALTERATIONS

1. Where the building to be rebuilt or altered is the original building, the amount of gross floor space in the building as rebuilt or altered which may be used for any purpose shall not exceed by more than ten per cent. the amount of gross floor space which was last used for that purpose in the original building.

2. Where the building to be rebuilt or altered is not the original building, the amount of gross floor space in the building as rebuilt or altered which may be used for any purpose shall not exceed the amount of gross floor space which was last used for that purpose in the building before the rebuilding or alteration.

3. In determining under this Schedule the purpose for which floor space was last used in any building, no account shall be taken of any use in respect of which an effective enforcement notice has been or could be served or, in the case of a use which has been discontinued, could have been served immediately before the discontinuance.

4.—(1) For the purposes of this Schedule gross floor space shall be ascertained by external measurement.

(2) Where different parts of a building are used for different purposes, floor space common to those purposes shall be apportioned rateably.

5. In relation to a building erected after 1st July 1948 which is a building resulting from the carrying out of any such works as are described in paragraph 1 of Schedule 3, any reference in this Schedule to the original building is a reference to the building in relation to which those works were carried out and not to the building resulting from the carrying out of those works. **[360–362]**

NOTES
Commencement: 24 August 1990.

(Schs 11, 12 repealed by the Planning and Compensation Act 1991, ss 21, 31(1), 84(6), Sch 1, paras 1, 16(1), Sch 19, Pts I, II. For savings with respect to regulations made under Sch 11, see s 21 of, and Sch 1, para 16(2) to the 1991 Act; and for transitional provisions with respect to the repeal of Sch 12, see s 31(5), (6) of the 1991 Act at **[527]**.)

SCHEDULE 13

Section 149

BLIGHTED LAND

Land allocated for public authority functions in development plans etc.

1. Land indicated in a structure plan in force for the district in which it is situated either—

    (a) as land which may be required for the purposes—

        (i) of the functions of a government department, local authority [National Park authority] or statutory undertakers, . . . , or

        (ii) of the establishment or running by a public telecommunications operator of a telecommunication system, or

    (b) as land which may be included in an action area.

Notes

    (1) In this paragraph the reference to a structure plan in force includes a reference to—

    [(a) proposals for the alteration or replacement of a structure plan which have been made available for inspection under section 33(2);

(b) any proposed modifications to those proposals which have been published in accordance with regulations under section 53.]

(2) Note (1) shall cease to apply when the copies of the proposals made available for inspection have been withdrawn under section [34].

(3) Note (1) shall also cease to apply when—

(a) the relevant proposals become operative (whether in their original form or with modifications), or

(b) the Secretary of State decides to reject the proposals and notice of the decision has been given by advertisement.

(4) In Note (1) references to anything done under any provision include references to anything done under that provision as it applies by virtue of section 51.

(5) This paragraph does not apply to land situated in a district for which a local plan is [in operation], where that plan—

(a) allocates any land in the district for the purposes of such functions as are mentioned in this paragraph; or

(b) defines any land in the district as the site of proposed development for the purposes of any such functions.

[(5A) In Note (5) the reference to a local plan in operation includes a reference to a minerals local plan, a waste local plan, which in either case is in operation, and to a local plan continued in operation by virtue of paragraph 44 of Schedule 4 to the Planning and Compensation Act 1991.]

(6) This paragraph does not apply to land within paragraph 5 or 6.

(7) In the application of this paragraph to Greater London the reference to a structure plan shall be construed as a reference to the Greater London Development Plan [and Notes (1) to (4) shall be omitted].

2. Land which—

(a) is allocated for the purposes of any such functions as are mentioned in paragraph 1(a)(i) or (ii) by a local plan [in operation] for the district, or

(b) is land defined in such a plan as the site of proposed development for the purposes of any such functions.

Notes

[(1) In this paragraph the reference to a local plan in operation includes a reference to a minerals local plan, a waste local plan, which in either case is in operation, and to a local plan continued in operation by virtue of paragraph 44 of Schedule 4 to the Planning and Compensation Act 1991, and also includes—

(a) proposals for the making or alteration and replacement of any such plan where copies of the proposals have been made available for inspection under section 40(2) or by virtue of paragraph 43 of Schedule 4 to the Planning and Compensation Act 1991; and

(b) any proposed modifications to those proposals which have been published in accordance with regulations under section 53.]

(2) ...

(3) Note (1) shall ... cease to apply when—

(a) the relevant plan or proposals become operative (whether in their original form or with modifications), or

(b) the Secretary of State decides to reject, or the local planning authority decide to abandon, the plan or proposals and notice of the decision has been given by advertisement.

(4) In Note (1) references to anything done under any provision include references to anything done under that provision as it applies by virtue of section 51.

(5) ...

3. Land indicated in a unitary development plan in force *for the district in which it* is situated—

    (a) as land which may be required for the purpose of any such functions as are mentioned in paragraph 1(a)(i) or (ii), or

    (b) as land which may be included in an action area.

Notes

    (1) In this paragraph the reference to a unitary development plan includes references to—

    (a) a unitary development plan of which copies have been made available for inspection under section [13(2)];

    (b) proposals for the alteration or replacement of a unitary development plan of which copies have been made available for inspection under that provision as applied by section 21(2) . . .;

    (c) modifications proposed to be made by the local planning authority or the Secretary of State to any such plan or proposals as are mentioned in paragraph (a) or (b), being modifications of which notice has been given in accordance with regulations under Chapter I of Part II.

(2) Note (1) shall cease to apply when the copies of the plan or proposals made available for inspection have been withdrawn under section . . . 14(2) (but section 14(4) shall not invalidate any blight notice served by virtue of Note (1) before the withdrawal of copies of the plan or proposals).

    (3) Note (1) shall also cease to apply when—

    (a) the relevant plan or proposals become operative (whether in their original form or with modifications), or

    (b) the Secretary of State decides to reject, or the local planning authority decide to withdraw, the plan or proposals and notice of the decision has been given by advertisement.

(4) In Note (1) references to anything done under any provision include references to anything done under that provision as it applies by virtue of section 25(2).

4. Land which by a unitary development plan is allocated for the purposes, or defined as the site, of proposed development for any such functions as are mentioned in paragraph 1(a)(i) or (ii).

Notes

    (1) In this paragraph the reference to a unitary development plan includes references to—

    (a) a unitary development plan of which copies have been made available for inspection under section [13(2)]:

    (b) proposals for the alteration or replacement of a unitary development plan of which copies have been made available for inspection under that provision as applied by section 21(2) . . .;

    (c) modifications proposed to be be made by the local planning authority or the Secretary of State to any such plan or proposals as are mentioned in paragraph (a) or (b), being modifications of which notice has been given in accordance with regulations under Chapter I of Part II.

(2) Note (1) shall cease to apply when the copies of the plan or proposals made available for inspection have been withdrawn under section . . . 14(2) (but section 14(4) shall not invalidate any blight notice served by virtue of Note (1) before the withdrawal of copies of the plan or proposals).

    (3) Note (1) shall also cease to apply when—

    (a) the relevant plan or proposals become operative (whether in their original from or with modifications), or

    (b) the Secretary of State decides to reject, or the local planning authority decide to withdraw, the plan or proposals and notice of the decision has been given by advertisement.

(4) In Note (1) references to anything done under any provision include references to anything done under that provision as it applies by virtue of section 25(2).

5. Land indicated in a plan (other than a development plan) approved by a resolution passed by a local planning authority for the purpose of the exercise of their powers under Part III as land which may be required for the purposes of any [such functions as are mentioned in paragraph 1(a)(i) or (ii)].

6. Land in respect of which a local planning authority—

(a) have resolved to take action to safeguard it for development for the purposes of any such functions as are mentioned in paragraph 5, or

(b) have been directed by the Secretary of State to restrict the grant of planning permission in order to safeguard it for such development.

New towns and urban development areas

7. Land within an area described as the site of a proposed new town in the draft of an order in respect of which a notice has been published under paragraph 2 of Schedule 1 to the New Towns Act 1981.

Note

Land shall cease to be within this paragraph when—

(a) the order comes into operation (whether in the form of the draft or with modifications), or

(b) the Secretary of State decides not to make the order.

8. Land within an area designated as the site of a proposed new town by an order which has come into operation under section 1 of the New Towns Act 1981.

9. Land which is—

(a) within an area intended to be designated as an urban development area by an order which has been made under section 134 of the Local Government, Planning and Land Act 1980 but has not come into effect; or

(b) within an area which has been so designated by an order under that section which has come into effect.

Clearance and renewal areas

10. Land within an area declared to be a clearance area by a resolution under section 289 of the Housing Act 1985.

11. Land which—

(a) is surrounded by or adjoining an area declared to be a clearance area by a resolution under section 289 of the Housing Act 1985, and

(b) is land which a local authority have determined to purchase under section 290 of that Act.

12. Land indicated by information published in pursuance of section 92 of the Local Government and Housing Act 1989 as land which a local authority propose to acquire in exercise of their powers under Part VII of that Act (renewal areas).

Highways

13. Land indicated in a development plan (otherwise than by being dealt with in a manner mentioned in paragraphs 1, 2, 3 and 4) as—

(a) land on which a highway is proposed to be constructed, or

(b) land to be included in a highway as proposed to be improved or altered.

14. Land on or adjacent to the line of a highway proposed to be constructed, improved or altered, as indicated in an order or scheme which has come into operation under Part II of the Highways Act 1980 (or under the corresponding provisions of Part II of the Highways Act 1959 or section 1 of the Highways Act 1971), being land in relation to which a power of compulsory acquisition conferred by any of the provisions of Part XII of that Act of 1980 (including a power compulsorily to acquire any right by virtue of section 250) may become

exercisable, as being land required for purposes of construction, improvement or alteration as indicated in the order or scheme.

Notes

(1) In this paragraph the reference to an order or scheme which has come into operation includes a reference to an order or scheme which has been submitted for confirmation to, or been prepared in draft by, the Minister of Transport or the Secretary of State under Part II of that Act of 1980 and in respect of which a notice has been published under paragraph 1, 2 or 10 of Schedule 1 to that Act.

(2) Note (1) shall cease to apply when—

(a) the relevant order or scheme comes into operation (whether in its original form or with modifications), or

(b) the Secretary of State decides not to confirm or make the order or scheme.

(3) In this paragraph the reference to land required for purposes of construction, improvement or alteration as indicated in an order or scheme includes a reference to land required for the purposes of section 246(1) of the Highways Act 1980.

15. Land shown on plans approved by a resolution of a local highway authority as land comprised in the site of a highway as proposed to be constructed, improved or altered by that authority.

[16. Land comprised in the site of a highway as proposed to be constructed, improved or altered by the Secretary of State if he has given written notice of the proposal, together with maps or plans sufficient to identify the land in question, to the local planning authority.]

17. Land shown on plans approved by a resolution of a local highway authority as land proposed to be acquired by them for the purposes of section 246(1) of the Highways Act 1980.

18. Land shown in a written notice given by the Secretary of State to the local planning authority as land proposed to be acquired by him for the purposes of section 246(1) of the Highways Act 1980 in connection with a [highway] which he proposes to provide.

New streets

19. Land which—

(a) either—

(i) is within the outer lines prescribed by an order under section 188 of the Highways Act 1980 (orders prescribing minimum width of new streets) or section 159 of the Highways Act 1959 (which is the predecessor of that section); or

(ii) has a frontage to a highway declared to be a new street by an order under section 30 of the Public Health Act 1925 and lies within the minimum width of the street prescribed by any byelaws or local Act applicable by virtue of the order; and

(b) is, or is part of—

(i) a dwelling erected before, or under construction on, the date on which the order is made; or

(ii) the curtilage of any such dwelling.

Note

This paragraph does not include any land in which the appropriate authority have previously acquired an interest either in pursuance of a blight notice served by virtue of this paragraph or by agreement in circumstances such that they could have been required to acquire it in pursuance of such a notice.

General improvement areas

20. Land indicated by information published in pursuance of section 257 of the Housing Act 1985 as land which a local authority propose to acquire in the exercise of their powers under the provisions of Part VIII of that Act relating to general improvement areas.

Compulsory purchase

21. Land authorised by a special enactment to be compulsorily acquired, or land falling within the limits of deviation within which powers of compulsory acquisition conferred by a special enactment are exercisable.

22. Land in respect of which—

    (a) a compulsory purchase order is in force; or

    (b) there is in force a compulsory purchase order providing for the acquisition of a right or rights over that land;

and the appropriate authority have power to serve, but have not served, notice to treat in respect of the land or, as the case may be, the right or rights.

Notes

(1) This paragraph applies also to land in respect of which—

    (a) a compulsory purchase order has been submitted for confirmation to, or been prepared in draft by, a Minister, and

    (b) a notice has been published under paragraph 3(1)(a) of Schedule 1 to the Acquisition of Land Act 1981 or under any corresponding enactment applicable to it.

(2) Note (1) shall cease to apply when—

    (a) the relevant compulsory purchase order comes into force (whether in its original form or with modifications); or

    (b) the Minister concerned decides not to confirm or make the order.

[23. Land—

    (a) the compulsory acquisition of which is authorised by an order under section 1 or 3 of the Transport and Works Act 1992, or

    (b) which falls within the limits of deviation within which powers of compulsory acquisition conferred by such an order are exercisable, or

    (c) which is the subject of a proposal, contained in an application made in accordance with rules under section 6 of that Act or in a draft order prepared under section 7(3) of that Act, that it should be such land.]   **[363]**

NOTES

Commencement: 24 August 1990 (paras 1–22); 1 January 1993 (para 23).

Words in square brackets in para 1(a)(i) inserted by the Environment Act 1995, s 78, Sch 10, para 32(16), as from a day to be appointed under s 125(3).

Words omitted from para 1(a)(i) repealed, subject to transitional provisions, by the Coal Industry Act 1994, s 67(1), (7), (8), Sch 9, para 39(4), Sch 10, para 12, Sch 11, Pt II.

The whole of para 1 Note (1)(a), (b), para 2 Note (1) and para 16, and words in square brackets in para 1 Notes (2), (5), (7), para 2(a), para 3 Note (1)(a), para 4 Note (1)(a), para 5 and para 18, substituted; para 1 Note (5A) inserted; and the whole of para 2 Notes (2), (5), and words omitted from para 2 Note (3), para 3 Notes (1)(b), (2), para 4 Notes (1)(b), (2) repealed by the Planning and Compensation Act 1991, ss 27, 32, 70, 84(6), Sch 4, Pt II, para 37, Sch 7, paras 8, 56, Sch 15, Pt I, para 14, Sch 19, Pt I.

Words "where the land" substituted for words in italics in para 3 by the Local Government (Wales) Act 1994, s 20(4)(b), Sch 6, Pt II, para 24(16), as from a day to be appointed.

Para 23 added by the Transport and Works Act 1992, s 16(2).

Modification: paras 1, 2 modified by the Local Government (Wales) Act 1994, s 20(3)(c), Sch 5, Pt III, paras 9, 21, 22, as from a day to be appointed, as follows:

"Introductory

9.—(1) The provisions of this Part of this Schedule apply in relation to the area of any local planning authority in Wales during the period—

    (a) beginning on 1st April 1996, and

    (b) ending when a unitary development plan has become fully operative for that area.

(2) For the purposes of sub-paragraph (1), a unitary development plan for the area of a local planning authority in Wales has become fully operative—

    (a) when it has become operative under Chapter I of Part II of the planning Act; or

    (b) where different parts of it have become operative at different times, when all parts of it have become so operative.

(3) Sub-paragraphs (4) and (5) apply where the area of a local planning authority in Wales includes—

(a) the whole or any part of an area prescribed under section 23B(2) of the planning Act in relation to a National Park, and

(b) other land.

(4) The provisions of this Part of this Schedule apply separately in relation to—

(a) the Park area or, if there is more than one, each Park area, and

(b) the remaining area.

(5) Any reference in this Part of this Schedule to the area of the local planning authority (including any reference which falls to be so construed) shall be construed—

(a) in its application in relation to any Park area, as a reference to that Park area, and

(b) in its application in relation to the remaining area, as a reference to that area.

(6) In this paragraph—

"the Park area", in relation to a National Park, means the part of the local planning authority's area which is within the area prescribed under section 23B(2) of the planning Act in relation to that Park or, where there is more than one such part, those parts taken as a whole;

"the remaining area" means the part of the local planning authority's area which is not within an area so prescribed in relation to any National Park.

Planning blight: structure plans

21.—(1) Paragraph 1 of Schedule 13 to the planning Act (blighted land) shall apply with the omission of Notes (2), (5A) and (7) and as modified by sub-paragraphs (2) to (6).

(2) References to a structure plan in force for the district in which land is situated are to be read as if they were references to a structure plan in force where that land is situated by virtue of Part IA of Schedule 2 to the planning Act.

(3) Note (1) to that paragraph shall apply as if—

(a) in paragraph (a), after "inspection" there were inserted "before 1st April 1996" and at the end there were added "and not withdrawn before that date";

(b) after that paragraph there were inserted—

"(aa) modified structure plan proposals made available for inspection under that section as it is applied by virtue of Part III of Schedule 5 to the Local Government (Wales) Act 1994;";

(c) in paragraph (b), after "published" there were inserted "either before 1st April 1996" and at the end there were added "or after that date in accordance with regulations or a direction made by virtue of that Part of that Schedule".

(4) Note (3) to that paragraph shall apply as if, after paragraph (b), there were inserted—

"or

(c) copies of the unitary development plan for the area in which the land is situated have been made available under section 13(2).".

(5) Note (4) to that paragraph shall apply as if at the end there were added "or paragraph 13 of Schedule 5 to the Local Government (Wales) Act 1994".

(6) In Note (5) to that paragraph—

(a) the reference to a local plan is to be read as if it were a reference to—

(i) a local plan within the meaning of paragraph 4 of Part IA of Schedule 2 to the planning Act; or

(ii) a modified plan in force where that land is situated; and

(b) any reference to a district for which a local plan is in operation is to be read as if it were a reference to the area in which the plan mentioned in paragraph (a)(i) or (ii) is in force by virtue of Part IA of Schedule 2 to the planning Act.

Planning blight: local plans and modified plans

22.—(1) Paragraph 2 of Schedule 13 to the planning Act (blighted land) shall apply as modified by sub-paragraphs (2) to (5).

(2) Paragraph (a) shall apply as if for "for the district" there were substituted "where the land is situated".

(3) Note (1) to that paragraph shall apply as if—

(a) for the words from "includes a reference" to "also" there were substituted "is a reference to a local plan within the meaning of paragraph 4 of Part IA of Schedule 2 or a modified plan within the meaning of Part III of Schedule 5 to the Local Government (Wales) Act 1994, and, until copies of the unitary development plan for the area in which the land is situated have been made available under section 13(2),";

(b) in paragraph (a), after "proposals have" there were inserted "before 1st April 1996", and after "1991" there were inserted "and not withdrawn before that date"; and

(c) in paragraph (b)—

(i) after "published" there were inserted "either before 1st April 1996", and

(ii) at the end of that paragraph there were added "or after that date in accordance with regulations or a direction made by virtue of Part III of Schedule 5 to the Local Government (Wales) Act 1994''.

(4) Note (3) to that paragraph shall apply as if, in paragraph (b), the words ''the local planning authority decide to abandon'' were omitted.

(5) Note (4) to that paragraph shall apply as if, at the end, there were added ''or paragraph 13 of Schedule 5 to the Local Government (Wales) Act 1994''.''

SCHEDULE 14
Section 259

PROCEDURE FOR FOOTPATHS AND BRIDLEWAYS ORDERS

PART I
CONFIRMATION OF ORDERS

1.—(1) Before an order under section 257 or 258 is submitted to the Secretary of State for confirmation or confirmed as an unopposed order, the authority by whom the order was made shall give notice in the prescribed form—

(a) stating the general effect of the order and that it has been made and is about to be submitted for confirmation or to be confirmed as an unopposed order;

(b) naming a place in the area in which the land to which the order relates is situated where a copy of the order may be inspected free of charge and copies of it may be obtained at a reasonable charge at all reasonable hours; and

(c) specifying the time (which must not be less than 28 days from the date of the first publication of the notice) within which, and the manner in which, representations or objections with respect to the order may be made.

(2) Subject to sub-paragraphs (6) and (7), the notice to be given under sub-paragraph (1) shall be given—

(a) by publication in at least one local newspaper circulating in the area in which the land to which the order relates is situated; and

(b) by serving a similar notice on—

(i) every owner, occupier and lessee (except tenants for a month or a period less than a month and statutory tenants within the meaning of the Rent Act 1977) of any of that land;

(ii) every council, the council of every rural parish [or community] and the parish meeting of every rural parish not having a separate council, being a council or parish whose area includes any of that land; and

[(iia) any National Park authority for a National Park which includes any of that land; and]

(iii) any statutory undertakers to whom there belongs, or by whom there is used, for the purposes of their undertaking, any apparatus under, in, on, over, along or across that land; and

(iv) every person on whom notice is required to be served in pursuance of sub-paragraph (4); and

(v) such other persons as may be prescribed in relation to the area in which that land is situated or as the authority may consider appropriate; and

(c) by causing a copy of the notice to be displayed in a prominent position—

(i) at the ends of so much of any footpath or bridleway as is to be stopped up, diverted or extinguished by the order;

(ii) at council offices in the locality of the land to which the order relates; and

(iii) at such other places as the authority may consider appropriate.

(3) In sub-paragraph (2)—

''council'' means a county council, [a county borough council,] a district council, a London borough council or a joint authority established by Part IV of the Local Government Act 1985;

''council offices'' means offices or buildings acquired or provided by a council or by the council of a parish or community or the parish meeting of a parish not having a separate parish council.

(4) Any person may, on payment of such reasonable charge as the authority may consider appropriate, require an authority to give him notice of all such orders under section 257 or 258 as are made by the authority during a specified period, are of a specified description and relate to land comprised in a specified area.

(5) In sub-paragraph (4) "specified" means specified in the requirement.

(6) Except where an owner, occupier or lessee is a local authority [National Park authority] or statutory undertaker, the Secretary of State may in any particular case direct that it shall not be necessary to comply with sub-paragraph (2)(b)(i).

(7) If the Secretary of State gives a direction under sub-paragraph (6) in the case of any land, then—

(a) in addition to publication the notice shall be addressed to "the owners and any occupiers" of the land (describing it); and

(b) a copy or copies of the notice shall be affixed to some conspicuous object or objects on the land.

(8) Sub-paragraph (2)(b) and (c) and, where applicable, sub-paragraph (7) shall be complied with not less than 28 days before the expiry of the time specified in the notice.

(9) A notice required to be served by sub-paragraph (2)(b)(i), (ii), (iii) or (v) shall be accompanied by a copy of the order.

(10) A notice required to be displayed by sub-paragraph (2)(c)(i) at the ends of so much of any way as is affected by the order shall be accompanied by a plan showing the general effect of the order so far as it relates to that way.

2. If no representations or objections are duly made, or if any so made are withdrawn, the authority by whom the order was made may, instead of submitting the order to the Secretary of State, themselves confirm the order (but without any modification).

3.—(1) This paragraph applies where any representation or objection which has been duly made is not withdrawn.

(2) If the objection is made by a local authority [or a National Park authority] the Secretary of State shall, before confirming the order, cause a local inquiry to be held.

(3) If the representation or objection is made by a person other than a local authority the Secretary of State shall, before confirming the order, either—

(a) cause a local inquiry to be held; or

(b) give any person by whom any representation or objection has been duly made and not withdrawn an opportunity of being heard by a person appointed by the Secretary of State for the purpose.

(4) After considering the report of the person appointed under sub-paragraph (2) or (3) to hold the inquiry or hear representations or objections, the Secretary of State may confirm the order, with or without modifications.

(5) In the case of an order under section 257, if objection is made by statutory undertakers on the ground that the order provides for the creation of a public right of way over land covered by works used for the purpose of their undertaking, or over the curtilage of such land, and the objection is not withdrawn, the order shall be subject to special parliamentary procedure.

(6) Notwithstanding anything in the previous provisions of this paragraph, the Secretary of State shall not confirm an order so as to affect land not affected by the order as submitted to him, except after—

(a) giving such notice as appears to him requisite of his proposal so to modify the order, specifying the time (which must not be less than 28 days from the date of the first publication of the notice) within which, and the manner in which, representations or objections with respect to the proposal may be made;

(b) holding a local inquiry or giving any person by whom any representation or objection has been duly made and not withdrawn an opportunity of being heard by a person appointed by the Secretary of State for the purpose; and

(c) considering the report of the person appointed to hold the inquiry or, as the case may be, to hear representations or objections.

(7) In the case of an order under section 257, if objection is made by statutory undertakers on the ground that the order as modified would provide for the creation of a public right of way over land covered by works used for the purposes of their undertaking or over the curtilage of such land, and the objection is not withdrawn, the order shall be subject to special parliamentary procedure.

4.—(1) A decision of the Secretary of State under paragraph 3 shall, except in such classes of case as may for the time being be prescribed or as may be specified in directions given by the Secretary of State, be made by a person appointed by the Secretary of State for the purpose instead of by the Secretary of State.

(2) A decision made by a person so appointed shall be treated as a decision of the Secretary of State.

(3) The Secretary of State may, if he thinks fit, direct that a decision which, by virtue of sub-paragraph (1) and apart from this sub-paragraph, falls to be made by a person appointed by the Secretary of State shall instead be made by the Secretary of State.

(4) A direction under sub-paragraph (3) shall—

    (a) state the reasons for which it is given; and
    (b) be served on the person, if any, so appointed, the authority and any person by whom a representation or objection has been duly made and not withdrawn.

(5) Where the Secretary of State has appointed a person to make a decision under paragraph 3 the Secretary of State may, at any time before the making of the decision, appoint another person to make it instead of the person first appointed to make it.

(6) Where by virtue of sub-paragraph (3) or (5) a particular decision falls to be made by the Secretary of State or any other person instead of the person first appointed to make it, anything done by or in relation to the latter shall be treated as having been done by or in relation to the former.

(7) Regulations under this Act may provide for the giving of publicity to any directions given by the Secretary of State under this paragraph.

5.—(1) The Secretary of State shall not confirm an order under section 257 which extinguishes a right of way over land under, in, on, over, along or across which there is any apparatus belonging to or used by statutory undertakers for the purposes of their undertaking, unless the undertakers have consented to the confirmation of the order.

(2) Any such consent may be given subject to the condition that there are included in the order such provisions for the protection of the undertakers as they may reasonably require.

(3) The consent of statutory undertakers to any such order shall not be unreasonably withheld.

(4) Any question arising under this paragraph whether the withholding of consent is unreasonable, or whether any requirement is reasonable, shall be determined by whichever Minister is the appropriate Minister in relation to the statutory undertakers concerned.

6. Regulations under this Act may, subject to this Part of this Schedule, make such provision as the Secretary of State thinks expedient as to the procedure on the making, submission and confirmation of orders under sections 257 and 258. **[364]**

NOTES
Commencement: 24 August 1990.
Words in square brackets in para 1(2)(b)(ii), (3) inserted by the Local Government (Wales) Act 1994, s 20(4)(b), Sch 6, Pt II, para 24(17), as from a day to be appointed.
Sub-para 1(2)(b)(iia) and words in square brackets in paras 1(6) and 3(2) inserted by the Environment Act 1995, s 78, Sch 10, para 32(17), as from a day to be appointed under sub-s 125(3).
Para 1(3): as to meaning of "council", see also the Local Government Act 1985, s 57(7), Sch 3, para 19, and the Local Government Residuary Body Order 1995, SI 1995/401, art 18, Schedule, para 5.

PART II

PUBLICITY FOR ORDERS AFTER CONFIRMATION

7.—(1) As soon as possible after an order under section 257 or 258 has been confirmed by the Secretary of State or confirmed as an unopposed order, the authority to whom the order was made—

(a) shall publish, in the manner required by paragraph 1(2)(a), a notice in the prescribed form—

(i) describing the general effect of the order,

(ii) stating that it has been confirmed, and

(iii) naming a place in the area in which the land to which the order relates is situated where a copy of the order as confirmed may be inspected free of charge and copies of it may be obtained at a reasonable charge at all reasonable hours;

(b) shall serve a similar notice on any persons on whom notices were required to be served under paragraph 1(2)(b) or (7); and

(c) shall cause similar notices to be displayed in a similar manner as the notices required to be displayed under paragraph 1(2)(c).

(2) No such notice or copy need be served on a person unless he has sent to the authority a request in that behalf, specifying an address for service.

(3) A notice required to be served by sub-paragraph (1)(b) on—

(a) a person on whom notice was required to be served by paragraph 1(2)(b)(i), (ii) or (iii); or

(b) in the case of an order which has been confirmed with modifications, a person on whom notice was required to be served by paragraph 1(2)(b)(v),

shall be accompanied by a copy of the order as confirmed.

(4) As soon as possible after a decision not to confirm an order under section 257 or 258, the authority by whom the order was made shall give notice of the decision by serving a copy of it on any persons on whom notices were required to be served under paragraph 1(2)(b) or (7).

8. Where an order under section 257 or 258 has come into force otherwise than—

(a) on the date on which it was confirmed by the Secretary of State or confirmed as an unopposed order; or

(b) at the expiration of a specified period beginning with that date,

then as soon as possible after it has come into force the authority by whom it was made shall give notice of its coming into force by publication in at least one local newspaper circulating in the area in which the land to which the order relates is situated.   **[365]**

NOTES

Commencement: 24 August 1990.

SCHEDULE 15

Section 302(5)

ENFORCEMENT AS RESPECTS WAR-TIME BREACHES BY CROWN OF PLANNING CONTROL

Preliminary

1. In this Schedule an application under section 302(3) and a determination given on such an application are referred to respectively as "a compliance determination application" and "a compliance determination".

Making of compliance determination applications

2.—(1) A compliance determination application may be made with respect to any land—

(a) by the owner or occupier of the land, or

(b) by any person who proves that he has or intends to acquire an interest in the land which will be affected by a compliance determination or that he has borne any of the cost of carrying out works on the land during the war period.

(2) In the case of land owned or occupied by or on behalf of the Crown, or leased to, or to a person acting on behalf of, the Crown, or land with respect to which it is proved that there is held, or intended to be acquired, by or on behalf of the Crown an interest in the land which will be affected as mentioned in sub-paragraph (1) or that any of the cost there mentioned has been borne by the Crown, a compliance determination application may be made by any person acting on behalf of the Crown.

3. A compliance determination application shall be accompanied by such plans and other information as are necessary to enable the application to be determined.

4.—(1) The authority to whom a compliance determination application is made shall within 14 days from the receipt of the application publish notice of it in one or more local newspapers circulating in the area in which the land is situated and serve notice of it on any person appearing to the authority to be specially affected by the application.

(2) The authority shall taken into consideration any representations made to them in connection with the application within 14 days from the publication of the notice.

Determination of applications

5.—(1) Where a compliance determination application is made to an authority the authority shall determine whether the works or use in question fail to comply with any planning control which the authority are responsible for enforcing and, if so, shall specify the control in question.

(2) Where the authority determine that works or a use fail so to comply they shall further determine whether having regard to all relevant circumstances the works or use shall, notwithstanding the failure, be deemed so to comply, either unconditionally or subject to such conditions as to the time for which the works or use may be continued, the carrying out of alterations, or other matters, as the authority think expedient.

Appeals against compliance determinations or failure to make such determinations

6.—(1) Where the applicant is aggrieved by a compliance determination, or where a person by whom representations have been made as mentioned in paragraph 4 is aggrieved by such a determination, he may appeal to the Secretary of State.

(2) The applicant may also appeal if he is aggrieved by the failure of the authority to determine the application within two months from the last day on which representations under paragraph 4 may be made and has served notice on the authority that he appeals to the Secretary of State.

(3) An appeal under this paragraph must be made within the period of 28 days after the applicant has notice of the determination or, in the case of an appeal under sub-paragraph (2), after the applicant has served notice on the authority of the appeal, or within such extended period as the Secretary of State may allow.

7.—(1) On such an appeal the Secretary of State may give, in substitution for the determination, if any, given by the authority, such determination as appears to him to be proper having regard to all relevant circumstances, or, if he is satisfied that the applicant was not a person entitled to make the application, may decide that the application is not to be entertained.

(2) At any stage of the proceedings on such an appeal to him the Secretary of State may, and shall if so directed by the High Court, state in the form of a special case for the opinion of the High Court any question of law arising in connection with the appeal.

8. Subject to paragraph 9 and to any determination or decision of the Secretary of State on an appeal under paragraph 7, any compliance determination shall be final and any such failure to give a determination as mentioned in paragraph 6(2) shall be taken on the service of the notice there mentioned as a final refusal by the authority to entertain the application, and

any determination or decision of the Secretary of State on an appeal under paragraph 7 shall be final.

Fresh applications where alteration in circumstances

9. Where a compliance determination has been given that works on land or a use of land shall not be deemed to comply with planning control or shall be deemed to comply with it subject to conditions, then if a person entitled to make a compliance determination application with respect to the land satisfies the authority or on appeal the Secretary of State that there has been a material change of circumstances since the previous application was determined, he may make a subsequent application and on such an application the authority or on appeal the Secretary of State may substitute for the compliance determination such determination as appears proper having regard to all relevant circumstances.

References of application to Secretary of State

10.—(1) If it appears to the Secretary of State that it is expedient, having regard to considerations affecting the public interest (whether generally or in the locality concerned), that any compliance determination application to an authority or any class or description of such applications, should instead of being determined by the authority be referred to him for decision, he may give directions to the authority requiring that application, or applications of that class or description, to be so referred.

(2) This Schedule shall apply to any such reference as if it were an appeal under paragraph 6(2) following failure of the authority to entertain the application.

Information

11. The Secretary of State may give directions to any authority responsible for enforcing planning control requiring them to furnish him with such information with respect to compliance determination applications received by them as he considers necessary or expedient in connection with the exercise of his functions under this Schedule.

Opportunity for hearing

12. On any compliance determination application or any appeal under this Schedule the applicant or, in the case of an application referred to the Secretary of State for decision or an appeal to the Secretary of State, the applicant or the authority responsible for enforcing the planning control in question, may require the authority by whom the application is to be determined or, as the case may be, the Secretary of State to give him or them an opportunity before the application or appeal is determined of appearing before and being heard by a person appointed by the authority or, as the case may be, the Secretary of State for the purpose.

Notice of proposed enforcement

13.—(1) This paragraph applies where before the relevant date any person proposes to take steps for enforcing a planning control in the case of such works or such a use as mentioned in subsection (1) of section 302.

(2) Subject to sub-paragraph (4), unless a compliance determination application has been made in relation to the land which has not been finally determined, that person shall serve on every owner and occupier of the land not less than 28 days' notice of the proposal, and if within that period any person makes such an application in relation to the land and within seven days of making it serves on the person proposing to take steps as aforesaid notice that the application has been made, no steps for enforcing the control shall be taken until the final determination of the application.

(3) If such an application has been made which has not been finally determined, no such steps shall be taken until the final determination of it.

(4) No notice shall be required under sub-paragraph (2) if steps for enforcing a planning control in the case of any works on land are begun within 28 days of the final determination of a compliance determination application in relation to the land.

(5) For the purpose of this paragraph a compliance determination application shall be

treated as having been finally determined notwithstanding that a subsequent application may be made under paragraph 9.

Power of entry

14.—(1) At any time before the relevant date any officer of an authority responsible for enforcing planning control shall, on producing, if so required, some duly authenticated document showing his authority to act for the purposes of this paragraph, have a right, subject to the provisions of this paragraph, to enter any premises at all reasonable hours—

 (a) for the purpose of ascertaining whether there are on the premises any works carried out during the war period which do not comply with planning control, or whether a use of the premises continues which was begun during that period and does not comply with it;
 (b) where a compliance determination application has been made to the authority, for the purpose of obtaining any information required by the authority for the exercise of their functions under section 302 and this Schedule in relation to the application.

(2) Admission to any premises which are occupied shall not be demanded as of right unless 24 hours' notice of the intended entry has been served on the occupier.

(3) Any person who wilfully obstructs any officer of an authority acting in the exercise of his powers under this section shall be liable on summary conviction to a fine not exceeding level 1 on the standard scale.

(4) If any person who in compliance with this paragraph is admitted into a factory, workshop or workplace, discloses to any person any information obtained by him in it with regard to any manufacturing process or trade secret, he shall, unless such disclosure was made in the performance of his duty, be liable on summary conviction to a fine not exceeding level 3 on the standard scale or to imprisonment for a term not exceeding three months.

Service of notices

15.—(1) Any notice or other document required or authorised to be served under this Schedule may be served on any person either by delivering it to him, or by leaving it at his proper address or by post.

(2) Any such document required or authorised to be served upon an incorporated company or body shall be duly served if it is served upon the secretary or clerk of the company or body.

(3) For the purposes of this paragraph and of section 7 of the Interpretation Act 1978, the proper address of any person upon whom any such document is to be served is—

 (a) in the case of the secretary or clerk of any incorporated company or body, that of the registered or principal office of the company or body, and
 (b) in any other case, the last known address of the person to be served.

(4) If it is not practicable after reasonable enquiry to ascertain the name or address of an owner or occupier of land on whom any such document is to be served, the document may be served by addressing it to him by the description of "owner" or "occupier" of the premises (describing them) to which it relates, and by delivering it to some person on the premises or, if there is no person on the premises to whom it can be delivered, by affixing it, or a copy of it, to some conspicuous part of the premises.

Supplementary provisions

16. Parts XIV and XV do not apply to section 302 and this Schedule.   **[366]**

NOTES
  Commencement: 24 August 1990.

SCHEDULE 16

Sections 314-319

PROVISIONS OF THE PLANNING ACTS REFERRED TO IN SECTIONS 314 TO 319

PART I

Section 1(1), (2), (3) and (5).

Section 2.

Section 9.

Section 55.

Section 57.

Section 59.

Section 60 except subsection (4).

Sections 61 [and 62].

Section 69(1), (2) and (5).

Section 70.

[Section 7072A.]

Section 72(1) to (4).

[Section 73A.]

Section 74.

Section 75.

Section 77 with the omission in subsection (4) of the reference to sections 65 . . . .

Sections 78 and 79(1) to (5) . . .

Section 90(1), (3) and (4).

Sections 96 to 98 except subsection (5) of section 97.

Section 100.

Sections 102 to 104 except subsection (8) of section 102.

[Sections 106 to 106B.]

Section 107.

Section 108.

[Section 115].

Sections 117 and 118.

Section 137 except subsections (6) and (7).

Section 138.

Sections 139(1) to (4).

Sections 140 and 141.

Sections 143 and 144.

Section 148.

Section 175(5).

[Section 175(7).]

Sections 178 to 182.

Section 185.

Section 186(6) and (7).

Section 188.

Section 189.

Section 190 (in so far as it applies to orders under section 102).

[Section 192.

Sections 196A to 196C.]

[Section 196(8).]

Sections 198 to 200.

Sections 202 and 203.

Section 205.

Section 208(10).

[Section 208(11).]

Section 209(6).

Section 210.

Section 211(4).

[Sections 214A to 214D.]

Sections 215 to 224.

Section 227.

Sections 229 to 233.

Sections 235 to 247.

Sections 251 and 252.

Sections 254 to 256.

Section 260.

Section 263.

Section 265(1) and (4).

Sections 266 to 272.

Sections 274 to 278.

Section 279 except subsection (4).

Section 280 except subsections (6) and (8)(b).

Sections 281 to 283.

Section 284(1) except paragraphs (e) and (f).

Section 285 . . .

Section 287.

Section 289.

Section 292 with the omission in subsection (2) of the references to section 288.

Section 293(1) to (3).

Section 294(1).

Section 296(1) (the reference in paragraph (c) to Part III not being construed as referring to [section 65]), and (2) to (4).

Section 297.

Sections 305 and 306.

Section 314.

Section 315.

[Sections 316 and 316A.]

Section 318 except subsections (2)(a), (4) and (5).

Section 324(1), (3) and (5) to (9).

Section 325.

Section 330.

Section 334.

Paragraphs 13 and 20(3) of Schedule 1.

Schedule 3.

Paragraphs 1 to 3 of Schedule 4.

Schedule 17.

Any other provisions of the planning Acts in so far as they apply, or have effect for the purposes of, any of the provisions specified above.

PART II

Sections 30 to 49.

Section 50(5).

Section 51.

Sections 53 and 54.

Section 56(2) to (6) with the omission in subsection (3) of the references to sections 85, 86(6) and 87(4).

[Section 65.]

Section 69(3) and (4).

Section 79(6) [to] (7).

Sections 91 to 93.

Section 94(1)(a) and (2) to (6).

Section 95.

Section 99.

Section 101.

Section 137(6) and (7).

Section 142.

Section 157(1) and (2).

Sections 162 and 163.

Section 166.

[Sections 171A to 171D.]

Sections 172 to 174.

Section 175(1) to (4) and (6).

Sections 176 and 177.

Sections 183 and 184.

Section 186(1) to (5).

[Sections 187 to 187B.]

Sections 191 to 196.

Section 208(9).

Section 226.

Section 228(1), (3), (4) and (7).

Sections 248, 249 and 250.

Section 253.

Section 257.

Section 258(1).

Section 259.

Section 261.

Section 264(1) to (6).

Section 273.

Section 279(4).

Section 280(6) and (8)(b).

Section 304.

Section 307.

Section 331.

Paragraphs 3 to 12 of Part II of Schedule 2, Part III of Schedule 2, Schedules 6 and 14.

PART III

[Sections 109 to 112.]

Section 298.

Sections 308 to 310.

. . .

Section 318(4) and (5).

. . .

[Section 328.]

. . .

Any other provisions of the planning Acts in so far as they apply, or have effect for the purposes of, any of the provisions specified above.

* * * * *

PART VI

Section 60(4).

[Section 65.]

Section 71(1) [(2) and (2A)].

Sections 149 to 151.

Sections 153(1) to (7).

Sections 154 to 156.

Section 161(1) in so far as it relates to provisions mentioned in this Part of this Schedule.

Section 164.

Sections 168 to 171.

Section 284 except subsection (1)(a) to (d).

Section 285(5) and (6).

Section 288.

[Section 291.]

Section 292(2).

Section 296(1) (construed as if the reference to Part III were a reference only to [section 65] and (5).

Section 318(2) except paragraph (b).

. . .

Schedule 13, paragraphs 1 to 4, 12 to 16 and 20 to 22.

Any other provisions of this Act in so far as they apply, or have effect for the purpose of, any of the provisions specified above. **[367]**

NOTES

Commencement: 24 August 1990.

Words in square brackets in Pt I (except those referred to in the note "Temporary amendment" below) and words in square brackets in Pts II, III, VI inserted or substituted, and words omitted from Pts I, III, VI and the whole of Pts IV, V repealed, by the Planning and Compensation Act 1991, ss 31(4), 32, 84(6), Sch 6, paras 8, 41, Sch 7, paras 8, 57, Sch 19, Pts I, II.

Temporary amendment: in Pt I, the words "Section 175(7)", "Section 196(8)" and "Section 208(11)" in square brackets, and in Pt V, the words "Section 208(11)" in square brackets temporarily inserted by the Planning (Consequential Provisions) Act 1990, s 6, Sch 4, paras 1, 8, until such day as may be appointed by order made by the Secretary of State. The Planning (Consequential Provisions) Act 1990 (Appointed Day No 1 and Transitional Provisions) Order 1991, SI 1991/2698, appointed 2 January 1992 only for the purposes of awards of costs in relation to proceedings which give rise to a hearing.

Words in italics in Pt I substituted by words "Section 1(1) to (3), (5) and (6)" by the Local Government (Wales) Act 1994, s 20(4)(b), Sch 6, Pt II, para 24(18), as from a day to be appointed.

Planning Acts: Town and Country Planning Act 1990, Planning (Listed Buildings and Conservation Areas) Act 1990, Planning (Hazardous Substances) Act 1990, Planning (Consequential Provisions) Act 1990.

SCHEDULE 17

Section 333(6)

ENACTMENTS EXEMPTED FROM SECTION 333(6)

1. . . .

2. The following provisions of the Highways Act 1980—

section 73(1) to (3), (6) and (9) to (11)
section 74 (except subsection (6))
. . .
section 200(2) and (4)
section 241
section 261(5) and, so far as it relates to it, section 261(6)
section 307(5) and (7)
Schedule 9.

3. The following further provisions of the Highways Act 1980—

(a) . . .
(b) section 247(6) so far as applicable for the purposes of section 241 of that Act;
(c) in section 307—

(i) subsections (1) to (3) so far as applicable for the purposes of section 73 of that Act;
(ii) subsections (1), (3) and (6) so far as applicable for the purposes of section 74 of that Act;
(iii) . . .

(d) section 311 so far as applicable for the purposes of section 74 of that Act.

4. Section 279 of the Highways Act 1980 so far as the purposes in question are the purposes of the exercise by a county council [, county borough council] or metropolitan district council in relation to roads maintained by that council of their powers under section 73(1) to (3), (6) and (9) to (11) or section 241 of that Act.

5. Any enactment making such provision as might by virtue of any Act of Parliament have been made in relation to the area to which the order applies by means of a byelaw, order or regulation not requiring confirmation by Parliament.

6. Any enactment which has been previously excluded or modified by a development order, and any enactment having substantially the same effect as any such enactment. **[368]**

NOTES
Commencement: 24 August 1990.
Para 1 repealed by the Environmental Protection Act 1990, s 162(2), Sch 16, Pt III.
Words omitted from para 2, and the whole of para 3(a), (c)(iii), repealed by the Planning and Compensation Act 1991, s 84(6), Sch 19, Pt V, subject to savings set out in s 81(2) thereof.
Words in square brackets in para 4 inserted by the Local Government (Wales) Act 1994, s 20(4)(b), Sch 6, Pt II, para 24(19), as from a day to be appointed.

PLANNING (LISTED BUILDINGS AND CONSERVATION AREAS) ACT 1990

(c 9)

ARRANGEMENT OF SECTIONS

PART I

LISTED BUILDINGS

CHAPTER I

LISTING OF SPECIAL BUILDINGS

*An Act to consolidate certain enactments relating to special controls in respect of
buildings and areas of special architectural or historic interest with amendments
to give effect to recommendations of the Law Commission*   [24 May 1990]

PART I

LISTED BUILDINGS

CHAPTER I

LISTING OF SPECIAL BUILDINGS

1. Listing of buildings of special architectural or historic interest

(1) For the purposes of this Act and with a view to the guidance of local planning
authorities in the performance of their functions under this Act and the principal Act
in relation to buildings of special architectural or historic interest, the Secretary of
State shall compile lists of such buildings, or approve, with or without modifications,
such lists compiled by the Historic Buildings and Monuments Commission for
England (in this Act referred to as "the Commission") or by other persons or bodies
of persons, and may amend any list so compiled or approved.

(2) The Secretary of State shall not approve any list compiled by the Commission
if the list contains any building situated outside England.

(3) In considering whether to include a building in a list compiled or approved
under this section, the Secretary of State may take into account not only the building
itself but also—

(a) any respect in which its exterior contributes to the architectural or historic
interest of any group of buildings of which it forms part; and

(b) the desirability of preserving, on the ground of its architectural or historic
interest, any feature of the building consisting of a man-made object or
structure fixed to the building or forming part of the land and comprised
within the curtilage of the building.

(4) Before compiling, approving (with or without modifications) or amending
any list under this section the Secretary of State shall consult—

(a) in relation to buildings which are situated in England, with the Commission;
and

(b) with such other persons or bodies of persons as appear to him appropriate
as having special knowledge of, or interest in, buildings of architectural or
historic interest.

(5) In this Act "listed building" means a building which is for the time being included in a list compiled or approved by the Secretary of State under this section; and for the purposes of this Act—

(a) any object or structure fixed to the building;

(b) any object or structure within the curtilage of the building which, although not fixed to the building, forms part of the land and has done so since before 1st July 1948,

shall be treated as part of the building.

(6) Schedule 1 shall have effect for the purpose of making provision as to the treatment as listed buildings of certain buildings formerly subject to building preservation orders.   **[369]**

NOTES

Commencement: 24 August 1990.
The principal Act: Town and Country Planning Act 1990.

2. Publication of lists

(1) As soon as possible after any list has been compiled or approved under section 1 or any amendments of such a list have been made, a copy of so much of the list as relates to any district [, Welsh county, county borough,] or London borough or, as the case may be, of so much of the amendments as so relates, certified by or on behalf of the Secretary of State to be a true copy, shall be deposited—

(a) in the case of a London borough, with the borough and with the chief officer of the Commission; *and*

(b) in the case of a district—

(i) with the district council;

(ii) with the county planning authority whose area or any part of whose area includes the district, or any part of it; and

(iii) where the district council are not the district planning authority, with that authority.

[and

(c) in the case of a Welsh county or county borough—

(i) with the county council or (as the case may be) the county borough council; and

(ii) with the local planning authority, if different from that council.]

(2) Any copy deposited under subsection (1) shall be a local land charge, and the council with whom a copy is deposited shall be treated for the purposes of the Local Land Charges Act 1975 as the originating authority as respects the charge constituted by the deposit.

(3) As soon as possible after the inclusion of any building in a list under section 1 (whether it is included when the list is compiled, approved or amended) or as soon as possible after any such list has been amended by the exclusion of any building from it—

(a) the Secretary of State shall inform the council of the district [, Welsh county, county borough,] or London borough in whose area the building is situated of the inclusion or exclusion; and

(b) the council shall serve a notice in the prescribed form on every owner and occupier of the building, stating that the building has been included in or excluded from the list.

(4) The Secretary of State shall keep available for public inspection free of

charge at reasonable hours and at a convenient place, copies of all lists and amendments of lists, compiled, approved or made by him under section 1.

(5) Every authority with whom copies of any list or amendments are deposited under this section shall similarly keep available copies of so much of any such list or amendment as relates to buildings within their area.

(6) For the purposes of subsection (5) the Commission shall be taken to be an authority whose area is Greater London.   **[370]**

NOTES
 Commencement: 24 August 1990.
 Words in square brackets in sub-ss (1), (3) inserted and word in italics in sub-s (1) repealed by the Local Government (Wales) Act 1994, ss 20(4)(b), 66(8), Sch 6, Pt II, para 25(1), Sch 18, as from a day to be appointed.

3. Temporary listing: building preservation notices

(1) If it appears to a local planning authority, *other than* a county planning authority, that a building in their area which is not a listed building—

(a) is of special architectural or historic interest; and
(b) is in danger of demolition or of alteration in such a way as to affect its character as a building of such interest,

they may serve on the owner and occupier of the building a notice (in this Act referred to as a "building preservation notice").

(2) A building preservation notice served by a local planning authority shall—

(a) state that the building appears to them to be of special architectural or historic interest and that they have requested the Secretary of State to consider including it in a list compiled or approved under section 1; and
(b) explain the effect of subsections (3) to (5) and Schedule 2.

(3) A building preservation notice—

(a) shall come into force as soon as it has been served on both the owner and occupier of the building to which it relates; and
(b) subject to subsection (4), shall remain in force for six months from the date when it is served or, as the case may be, last served.

(4) A building preservation notice shall cease to be in force if the Secretary of State—

(a) includes the building in a list compiled or approved under section 1, or
(b) notifies the local planning authority in writing that he does not intend to do so.

(5) While a building preservation notice is in force with respect to a building, the provisions of this Act (other than section 59) and the principal Act shall have effect in relation to the building as if it were a listed building.

(6) If, following the service of a building preservation notice, the Secretary of State notifies the local planning authority that he does not propose to include the building in a list compiled or approved under section 1, the authority shall immediately give notice of that decision to the owner and occupier of the building.

(7) Following such a notification by the Secretary of State no further building preservation notice in respect of the building shall be served by the local planning authority within the period of 12 months beginning with the date of the notification.

(8) The Commission shall, as respects any London borough, have concurrently

with the council of that borough the functions of a local planning authority under this section; and references to the local planning authority shall be construed accordingly.   **[371]**

NOTES
Commencement: 24 August 1990.
Words in italics in sub-s (1) substituted by the words "in Wales, or to a local planning authority in England who are not" by the Local Government (Wales) Act 1994, s 20(4)(b), Sch 6, Pt II, para 25(2), as from a day to be appointed.
The principal Act: Town and Country Planning Act 1990.

4. Temporary listing in urgent cases

(1) If it appears to the local planning authority to be urgent that a building preservation notice should come into force, they may, instead of serving the notice on the owner and occupier of the building, affix the notice conspicuously to some object on the building.

(2) The affixing of a notice under subsection (1) shall be treated for all the purposes of section 3, this section, sections 5 and 10 to 26 and Schedule 2 as service of the notice.

(3) A notice which is so affixed must explain that by virtue of being so affixed it is treated as being served for those purposes.

(4) The Commission shall, as respects any London borough, have concurrently with the council of that borough the functions of a local planning authority under this section; and references to the local planning authority shall be construed accordingly.   **[372]**

NOTES
Commencement: 24 August 1990.

5. Provisions applicable on lapse of building preservation notice

Schedule 2 to this Act shall have effect as respects the lapse of building preservation notices.   **[373]**

NOTES
Commencement: 24 August 1990.

6. Issue of certificate that building not intended to be listed

(1) Where—

    (a) application has been made for planning permission for any development involving the alteration, extension or demolition of a building; or

    (b) any such planning permission has been granted;

the Secretary of State may, on the application of any person, issue a certificate stating that he does not intend to list the building.

(2) The issue of such a certificate in respect of a building shall—

    (a) preclude the Secretary of State for a period of 5 years from the date of issue from exercising in relation to that building any of the powers conferred on him by section 1; and

    (b) preclude the local planning authority for that period from serving a building preservation notice in relation to it.

(3) Notice of an application under subsection (1) shall be given to the local

planning authority within whose area the building is situated at the same time as the application is submitted to the Secretary of State.

(4) In this section "local planning authority", in relation to a building in Greater London, includes the Commission. **[374]**

NOTES
Commencement: 24 August 1990.

CHAPTER II

AUTHORISATION OF WORKS AFFECTING LISTED BUILDINGS

Control of works in respect of listed buildings

7. Restriction on works affecting listed buildings

Subject to the following provisions of this Act, no person shall execute or cause to be executed any works for the demolition of a listed building or for its alteration or extension in any manner which would affect its character as a building of special architectural or historic interest, unless the works are authorised. **[375]**

NOTES
Commencement: 24 August 1990.

8. Authorisation of works: listed building consent

(1) Works for the alteration or extension of a listed building are authorised if—

    (a) written consent for their execution has been granted by the local planning authority or the Secretary of State; and

    (b) they are executed in accordance with the terms of the consent and of any conditions attached to it.

(2) Works for the demolition of a listed building are authorised if—

    (a) such consent has been granted for their execution;

    (b) notice of the proposal to execute the works has been given to the Royal Commission;

    (c) after such notice has been given either—

        (i) for a period of at least one month following the grant of such consent, and before the commencement of the works, reasonable access to the building has been made available to members or officers of the Royal Commission for the purpose of recording it; or

        (ii) the Secretary of the Royal Commission, or another officer of theirs with authority to act on their behalf for the purposes of this section, has stated in writing that they have completed their recording of the building or that they do not wish to record it; and

    (d) the works are executed in accordance with the terms of the consent and of any conditions attached to it.

(3) Where—

    (a) works for the demolition of a listed building or for its alteration or extension are executed without such consent; and

    (b) written consent is granted by the local planning authority or the Secretary of State for the retention of the works,

the works are authorised from the grant of that consent.

(4) In this section "the Royal Commission" means—

(a) in relation to England, the Royal Commission on the Historical Monuments of England; and

(b) in relation to Wales, the Royal Commission on Ancient and Historical Monuments in Wales.

(5) The Secretary of State may by order provide that subsection (2) shall have effect with the substitution for the references to the Royal Commission of references to such other body as may be so specified.

(6) Such an order—

(a) shall apply in the case of works executed or to be executed on or after such date as may be specified in the order; and

(b) may apply in relation to either England or Wales, or both.

(7) Consent under subsection (1), (2) or (3) is referred to in this Act as "listed building consent".   **[376]**

NOTES
Commencement: 24 August 1990.

9. Offences

(1) If a person contravenes section 7 he shall be guilty of an offence.

(2) Without prejudice to subsection (1), if a person executing or causing to be executed any works in relation to a listed building under a listed building consent fails to comply with any condition attached to the consent, he shall be guilty of an offence.

(3) In proceedings for an offence under this section it shall be a defence to prove the following matters—

(a) that works to the building were urgently necessary in the interests of safety or health or for the preservation of the building;

(b) that it was not practicable to secure safety or health or, as the case may be, the preservation of the building by works of repair or works for affording temporary support or shelter;

(c) that the works carried out were limited to the minimum measures immediately necessary; and

(d) that notice in writing justifying in detail the carrying out of the works was given to the local planning authority as soon as reasonably practicable.

[(4) A person who is guilty of an offence under this section shall be liable—

(a) on summary conviction, to imprisonment for a term not exceeding six months or a fine not exceeding £20,000, or both; or

(b) on conviction on indictment, to imprisonment for a term not exceeding two years or a fine, or both.]

(5) In determining the amount of any fine to be imposed on a person convicted ... of an offence under this section, the court shall in particular have regard to any financial benefit which has accrued or appears likely to accrue to him in consequence of the offence.   **[377]**

NOTES
Commencement: 24 August 1990 (sub-ss (1)–(3), (5)); 25 September 1991 (sub-s (4)).
Sub-s (4) substituted, and words omitted from sub-s (5) repealed, by the Planning and Compensation Act 1991, ss 25, 84(6), Sch 3, Pt I, para 1, Sch 19, Pt I.

Applications for listed building consent

10. Making of applications for listed building consent

(1) Except as provided in sections 12 to 15, an application for listed building consent shall be made to and dealt with by the local planning authority.

(2) Such an application shall be made in such form as the authority may require and shall contain—

    (a) sufficient particulars to identify the building to which it relates, including a plan;

    (b) such other plans and drawings as are necessary to describe the works which are the subject of the application; and

    (c) such other particulars as may be required by the authority.

(3) Provision may be made by regulations under this Act with respect to—

    (a) the manner in which such applications are to be made;

    (b) the manner in which they are to be advertised; and

    (c) the time within which they are to be dealt with by local planning authorities or, as the case may be, by the Secretary of State. **[378]**

NOTES

    Commencement: 24 August 1990.

    Modification: section modified by the Transport and Works Application (Listed Buildings, Conservation Areas and Ancient Monuments Procedure) Regulations 1992, SI 1992/3138, reg 3(2), Sch 1, para 1, so as to assimilate the procedures for making applications in circumstances where proposals contained in an application under the Transport and Works Act 1992, s 6 give rise to a requirement for listed building consent or conservation area consent under this Act, and the application for consent made under this section is made not later than ten weeks after the application under the 1992 Act or where the Secretary of State considers it appropriate that the regulation should apply and has given a direction to that effect.

11. Certificates as to applicant's status etc

(1) Regulations under this Act may provide that an application for listed building consent shall not be entertained unless it is accompanied by one of the following certificates in the prescribed form and signed by or on behalf of the applicant—

    (a) a certificate stating that, at the beginning of the period of 21 days ending with the date of the application, no person (other than the applicant) was the owner of any of the building to which the application relates;

    (b) a certificate stating that the applicant has given the requisite notice of the application to all the persons (other than himself) who at the beginning of that period were owners of any of the building to which the application relates;

    (c) a certificate stating—

        (i) that the applicant is unable to issue a certificate in accordance with paragraph (a) or (b);

        (ii) that he has given the requisite notice of the application to such one or more of the persons mentioned in paragraph (b) as are specified in the certificate; and

        (iii) that he has taken such steps as are reasonably open to him (specifying them) to ascertain the names and addresses of the remainder of those persons but has been unable to do so;

    (d) a certificate stating that—

        (i) the applicant is unable to issue a certificate in accordance with paragraph (a); and

(ii) that he has taken such steps as are reasonably open to him (specifying them) to ascertain the names and addresses of the persons mentioned in paragraph (b) but has been unable to do so.

(2) Where such provision is made any such certificate as is mentioned in subsection (1)(b) or (c) must set out—

(a) the names of the persons to whom the applicant has given the requisite notice of the application;
(b) the addresses at which notice was given to them; and
(c) the date of service of each such notice.

(3) Such regulations may require that any such certificate as is mentioned in subsection (1)(c) or (d) shall also contain a statement that the requisite notice of the application, as set out in the certificate, has on a date specified in the certificate (which must not be earlier than the beginning of the period mentioned in subsection (1)(a)) been published in a local newspaper circulating in the locality in which the building is situated.

(4) Such regulations may also require that where an application is accompanied by such a certificate as is mentioned in subsection (1)(b), (c) or (d), the local planning authority—

(a) shall not determine the application before the end of the period of 21 days beginning with the date appearing from the certificate to be the latest of the dates of service of notices as mentioned in the certificate, or, if later, the date of publication of a notice as so mentioned;
(b) shall in determining the application take into account any representations relating to it which are made to them before the end of that period by any person who satisfies them that he is an owner of any of the building to which the application relates; and
(c) shall give notice of their decision to every person who has made representations which they were required to take into account in accordance with paragraph (b).

(5) Such regulations may also make provision as to who, in the case of any building, is to be treated as the owner for the purposes of any provision made by virtue of this section.

(6) If any person—

(a) issues a certificate which purports to comply with the requirements of regulations made by virtue of this section and contains a statement which he knows to be false or misleading in a material particular; or
(b) recklessly issues a certificate which purports to comply with those requirements and contains a statement which is false or misleading in a material particular,

he shall be guilty of an offence and liable on summary conviction to a fine not exceeding level 3 on the standard scale.

(7) Subject to subsection (5), in this section "owner" means a person who is for the time being the estate owner in respect of the fee simple or is entitled to a tenancy granted or extended for a term of years certain of which not less than seven years remain unexpired.   **[379]**

NOTES
Commencement: 24 August 1990.

12. Reference of certain applications to Secretary of State

(1) The Secretary of State may give directions requiring applications for listed building consent to be referred to him instead of being dealt with by the local planning authority.

(2) A direction under this section may relate either to a particular application, or to applications in respect of such buildings as may be specified in the direction.

(3) An application in respect of which a direction under this section has effect shall be referred to the Secretary of State accordingly.

[(3A) An application for listed building consent shall, without any direction by the Secretary of State, be referred to the Secretary of State instead of being dealt with by the local planning authority in any case where the consent is required in consequence of proposals included in an application for an order under section 1 or 3 of the Transport and Works Act 1992.]

(4) Before determining an application referred to him under this section, the Secretary of State shall, if either the applicant or the authority so wish, give each of them an opportunity of appearing before, and being heard by, a person appointed by the Secretary of State.

(5) The decision of the Secretary of State on any application referred to him under this section shall be final.   **[380]**

NOTES
  Commencement: 24 August 1990 (sub-ss (1)–(3), (4), (5)); 1 January 1993 (sub-s (3A)).
  Sub-s (3A) inserted by the Transport and Works Act 1992, s 17.

13. Duty to notify Secretary of State of applications

(1) A local planning authority, other than a London borough council, to whom application is made for listed building consent, and a London borough council to whom such an application is made by the Commission shall notify the Secretary of State of the application, giving particulars of the works for which the consent is required.

(2) The Secretary of State may within the period of 28 days beginning with the date of such a notification—

  (a) direct the reference of the application to him under section 12; or
  (b) give notice to the authority that he requires further time in which to consider whether to require such a reference.

(3) The local planning authority shall not grant listed building consent until—

  (a) the period mentioned in subsection (2) has expired without the Secretary of State directing the reference of the application to him or giving them notice under paragraph (b) of that subsection; or
  (b) the Secretary of State has notified them that he does not intend to require the reference of the application.   **[381]**

NOTES
  Commencement: 24 August 1990.

14. Duty of London borough councils to notify Commission

(1) Where an application for listed building consent is made to a local planning authority which is a London borough council—

(a) unless the authority have determined to refuse it, they shall notify the Commission of the application, giving particulars of the works for which the consent is required; and

(b) the authority shall not grant the consent unless they are authorised or directed to do so under subsection (2)(a).

(2) On receipt of such a notification the Commission may—

(a) subject to subsection (6), give the local planning authority directions as to the granting of the application or authorise them to determine the application as they think fit; or

(b) direct them to refuse the application.

(3) If the Commission intend to exercise either of their powers under subsection (2)(a), they shall notify the Secretary of State of the application giving particulars of the works for which the consent is required.

(4) Where the Commission direct the local planning authority under subsection (2)(b) to refuse listed building consent, the authority may, within 28 days from the date of the direction, notify the Secretary of State of the application giving particulars of the works for which the consent is required.

(5) The Secretary of State may within the period of 28 days beginning with the date of a notification under subsection (3) or (4)—

(a) direct the reference of the application to him; or

(b) give notice to the authority who notified him or, as the case may be, the Commission that he requires further time in which to consider whether to require such a reference.

(6) The Commission shall not direct the local planning authority under subsection (2)(a) to grant the application or authorise them to determine it as they think fit unless—

(a) the period mentioned in subsection (5) has expired without the Secretary of State directing the reference of the application to him or giving them notice under paragraph (b) of that subsection; or

(b) he has notified them that he does not intend to require the reference of the application.

(7) Where the local planning authority notify the Secretary of State as mentioned in subsection (4), they shall not refuse the application unless—

(a) a period of 28 days beginning with the date of the notification has expired without the Secretary of State directing the reference of the application to him or giving them notice under subsection (5)(b); or

(b) he has notified the authority that he does not intend to require the reference of the application.

(8) Where, after receiving notification under subsection (4), the Secretary of State directs the reference of the application to him, before determining the application he shall, if either the applicant or the authority or, as the case may be, the Commission so desire, give each of them an opportunity of appearing before, and being heard by, a person appointed by the Secretary of State.

(9) Subsection (1) shall not apply where the application for listed building consent is made by the Commission.   **[382]**

NOTES
Commencement: 24 August 1990.

15. Directions concerning notification of applications etc

(1) The Secretary of State may direct that, in the case of such descriptions of applications for listed building consent as he may specify, sections 13 and 14 shall not apply.

(2) Where a direction is in force under subsection (1) in respect of any description of application, local planning authorities may determine applications of that description in any manner they think fit, without notifying the Secretary of State or, as the case may be, the Commission.

(3) Before giving a direction under subsection (1) in respect of any description of application for consent to the demolition of a building in England, the Secretary of State shall consult the Commission.

(4) Where a direction is in force under subsection (1), the Secretary of State may direct a local planning authority that section 13 or, as the case may be, section 14 shall nevertheless apply—

(a) to a particular application for listed building consent; or
(b) to such descriptions of application for listed building consent as are specified in the direction;

and such a direction has effect in relation to any such application which has not been disposed of by the authority by their granting or refusing consent.

(5) Without prejudice to sections 10 to 14, the Secretary of State may give directions to local planning authorities requiring them, in such cases or classes of case as may be specified in the directions, to notify him and such other persons as may be so specified—

(a) of any applications made to the authorities for listed building consent; and
(b) of the decisions taken by the authorities on those applications.

(6) Directions under subsection (1) or (5) may be given to authorities generally or to particular authorities or descriptions of authority.   **[383]**

NOTES
 Commencement: 24 August 1990.

16. Decision on application

(1) Subject to the previous provisions of this Part, the local planning authority or, as the case may be, the Secretary of State may grant or refuse an application for listed building consent and, if they grant consent, may grant it subject to conditions.

(2) In considering whether to grant listed building consent for any works the local planning authority or the Secretary of State shall have special regard to the desirability of preserving the building or its setting or any features of special architectural or historic interest which it possesses.

(3) Any listed building consent shall (except in so far as it otherwise provides) enure for the benefit of the building and of all persons for the time being interested in it.   **[384]**

NOTES
 Commencement: 24 August 1990.

Grant of consent subject to conditions

17. Power to impose conditions on grant of listed building consent

(1) Without prejudice to the generality of section 16(1), the conditions subject to which listed building consent may be granted may include conditions with respect to—

    (a) the preservation of particular features of the building, either as part of it or after severance from it;

    (b) the making good, after the works are completed, of any damage caused to the building by the works;

    (c) the reconstruction of the building or any part of it following the execution of any works, with the use of original materials so far as practicable and with such alterations of the interior of the building as may be specified in the conditions.

(2) A condition may also be imposed requiring specified details of the works (whether or not set out in the application) to be approved subsequently by the local planning authority or, in the case of consent granted by the Secretary of State, specifying whether such details are to be approved by the local planning authority or by him.

(3) Listed building consent for the demolition of a listed building may be granted subject to a condition that the building shall not be demolished before—

    (a) a contract for the carrying out of works of redevelopment of the site has been made; and

    (b) planning permission has been granted for the development for which the contract provides. **[385]**

NOTES
    Commencement: 24 August 1990.

18. Limit of duration of listed building consent

(1) Subject to the provisions of this section, every listed building consent shall be granted subject to the condition that the works to which it relates must be begun not later than the expiration of—

    (a) five years beginning with the date on which the consent is granted; or

    (b) such other period (whether longer or shorter) beginning with that date as the authority granting the consent may direct, being a period which the authority considers appropriate having regard to any material considerations.

(2) If listed building consent is granted without the condition required by subsection (1), it shall be deemed to have been granted subject to the condition that the works to which it relates must be begun not later than the expiration of five years beginning with the date of the grant.

(3) Nothing in this section applies to any consent to the retention of works granted under section 8(3). **[386]**

NOTES
    Commencement: 24 August 1990.

19. Application for variation or discharge of conditions

(1) Any person interested in a listed building with respect to which listed building consent has been granted subject to conditions may apply to the local planning authority for the variation or discharge of the conditions.

(2) The application shall indicate what variation or discharge of conditions is applied for.

(3) Sections 10 to 15 apply to such an application as they apply to an application for listed building consent.

(4) On such an application the local planning authority or, as the case may be, the Secretary of State may vary or discharge the conditions attached to the consent, and may add new conditions consequential upon the variation or discharge, as they or he thinks fit.   **[387]**

NOTES
Commencement: 24 August 1990.

Appeals

20. Right to appeal against decision or failure to take decision

(1) Where a local planning authority—

  (a) refuse an application for listed building consent or grant it subject to conditions;

  (b) refuse an application for the variation or discharge of conditions subject to which such consent has been granted or grant it and add new conditions; or

  (c) refuse an application for approval required by a condition imposed on the granting of listed building consent with respect to details of works or grant it subject to conditions,

the applicant, if aggrieved by the decision, may appeal to the Secretary of State.

(2) A person who has made such an application may also appeal to the Secretary of State if the local planning authority have neither—

  (a) given notice to the applicant of their decision on the application; nor

  (b) in the case of such an application as is mentioned in paragraph (a) or (b) of subsection (1), given notice to the applicant that the application has been referred to the Secretary of State in accordance with directions given under section 12,

within the relevant period from the date of the receipt of the application, or within such extended period as may at any time be agreed upon in writing between the applicant and the authority.

(3) In this section "the relevant period" means—

  (a) in the case of such an application as is mentioned in paragraph (a) or (b) of subsection (1), such period as may be prescribed; and

  (b) in the case of such an application for approval as is mentioned in paragraph (c) of subsection (1), the period of eight weeks from the date of the receipt of the application.

(4) For the purposes of the application of sections 22(1) and 63(7)(b) in relation to an appeal under subsection (2) it shall be assumed that the authority decided to refuse the application in question.   **[388]**

NOTES
    Commencement: 24 August 1990.

21. Appeals: supplementary provisions

(1) An appeal under section 20 must be made by notice served in the prescribed manner within such period as may be prescribed.

(2) The period which may be prescribed under subsection (1) must not be less than—

    (a) in the case of an appeal under subsection (1) of section 20, 28 days from the receipt by the applicant of notification of the decision; or

    (b) in the case of an appeal under subsection (2) of that section, 28 days from the end of the relevant period (within the meaning of that section) or, as the case may be, the extended period there mentioned.

(3) The notice of appeal may include as the ground or one of the grounds of the appeal a claim that the building is not of special architectural or historic interest and ought to be removed from any list compiled or approved by the Secretary of State under section 1.

(4) In the case of a building with respect to which a listed building preservation notice is in force, the notice may include a claim that the building should not be included in such a list.

(5) Regulations under this Act may provide that an appeal in respect of an application for listed building consent or for the variation or discharge of conditions subject to which such consent has been granted shall not be entertained unless it is accompanied by a certificate in the prescribed form and corresponding to one of those described in subsection (1) of section 11.

(6) Any such regulations may also include provisions corresponding to those which may be included in the regulations which may be made by virtue of section 11.

(7) If any person—

    (a) issues a certificate which purports to comply with the requirements of regulations made by virtue of subsection (5) or (6) and contains a statement which he knows to be false or misleading in a material particular; or

    (b) recklessly issues a certificate which purports to comply with those requirements and contains a statement which is false or misleading in a material particular,

he shall be guilty of an offence and liable on summary conviction to a fine not exceeding level 3 on the standard scale.   **[389]**

NOTES
    Commencement: 24 August 1990.

22. Determination of appeals

(1) The Secretary of State may allow or dismiss an appeal under section 20 or may reverse or vary any part of the authority's decision (whether or not the appeal relates to that part), and—

    (a) may deal with the application as if it had been made to him in the first instance; and

(b) may exercise his power under section 1 to amend any list compiled or approved under that section by removing from it the building to which the appeal relates.

(2) Before determining the appeal, the Secretary of State shall, if either the applicant or the local planning authority so wish, give each of them an opportunity of appearing before, and being heard by, a person appointed by the Secretary of State for the purpose.

(3) The decision of the Secretary of State on the appeal shall be final.

(4) Schedule 3 applies to appeals under section 20. **[390]**

NOTES
Commencement: 24 August 1990.

Revocation and modification of consent

23. Revocation and modification of listed building consent by local planning authority

(1) If it appears to the local planning authority that it is expedient to revoke or modify any listed building consent granted on an application under this Act, the authority may by order revoke or modify the consent to such extent as they consider expedient.

(2) In performing their functions under subsection (1) the local planning authority shall have regard to the development plan and to any other material considerations.

(3) The power conferred by this section to revoke or modify listed building consent in respect of any works may be exercised at any time before those works have been completed, but the revocation or modification shall not affect so much of those works as has been previously carried out. **[391]**

NOTES
Commencement: 24 August 1990.

24. Procedure for s 23 orders: opposed cases

(1) Except as provided in section 25, an order made by a local planning authority under section 23 shall not take effect unless it is confirmed by the Secretary of State.

(2) Where a local planning authority submit such an order to the Secretary of State for confirmation they shall serve notice on—

(a) the owner of the building affected;
(b) the occupier of that building; and
(c) any other person who in their opinion will be affected by the order.

(3) The notice shall specify the period (which must not be less than 28 days after its service) within which any person on whom it is served may require an opportunity of appearing before and being heard by a person appointed by the Secretary of State for the purpose.

(4) If within that period a person on whom the notice is served so requires, the Secretary of State shall give such an opportunity both to that person and to the local planning authority before he confirms the order.

(5) The Secretary of State may confirm an order submitted to him under this

section either without modification or subject to such modifications as he considers expedient. **[392]**

NOTES
Commencement: 24 August 1990.

25. Procedure for s 23 orders: unopposed cases

(1) This section shall have effect where—

    (a) the local planning authority have made an order under section 23 revoking or modifying a listed building consent granted by them; and

    (b) the owner and occupier of the land and all persons who in the authority's opinion will be affected by the order have notified the authority in writing that they do not object to the order.

(2) Where this section applies, instead of submitting the order to the Secretary of State for confirmation the authority shall—

    (a) advertise in the prescribed manner the fact that the order has been made, specifying in the advertisement—

        (i) the period within which persons affected by the order may give notice to the Secretary of State that they wish for an opportunity of appearing before and being heard by a person appointed by him for the purpose; and

        (ii) the period at the end of which, if no such notice is given to the Secretary of State, the order may take effect by virtue of this section without being confirmed by him;

    (b) serve notice to the same effect on the persons mentioned in subsection (1)(b);

    (c) send a copy of any such advertisement to the Secretary of State not more than three days after its publication.

(3) If—

    (a) no person claiming to be affected by the order has given notice to the Secretary of State as mentioned in subsection (2)(a)(i) within the period referred to in that subsection; and

    (b) the Secretary of State has not directed within that period that the order be submitted to him for confirmation,

the order shall take effect at the end of the period referred to in subsection (2)(a)(ii) without being confirmed by the Secretary of State as required by section 24(1).

(4) The period referred to in subsection (2)(a)(i) must not be less than 28 days from the date on which the advertisement first appears.

(5) The period referred to in subsection (2)(a)(ii) must not be less than 14 days from the end of the period referred to in subsection (2)(a)(i). **[393]**

NOTES
Commencement: 24 August 1990.

26. Revocation and modification of listed building consent by the Secretary of State

(1) If it appears to the Secretary of State that it is expedient that an order should be made under section 23 revoking or modifying any listed building consent granted on an application under this Act, he may himself make such an order revoking or modifying the consent to such extent as he considers expedient.

(2) In performing his functions under subsection (1) the Secretary of State shall have regard to the development plan and to any other material considerations.

(3) The Secretary of State shall not make an order under that subsection without consulting the local planning authority.

(4) Where the Secretary of State proposes to make such an order he shall serve notice on—

    (a) the owner of the building affected;
    (b) the occupier of that building; and
    (c) any other person who in his opinion will be affected by the order.

(5) The notice shall specify the period (which must not be less than 28 days after its service) within which any person on whom it is served may require an opportunity of appearing before and being heard by a person appointed by the Secretary of State for the purpose.

(6) If within that period a person on whom it is served so requires, before the Secretary of State makes the order he shall give such an opportunity both to him and to the local planning authority.

(7) The power conferred by this section to revoke or modify listed building consent in respect of any works may be exercised at any time before those works have been completed, but the revocation or modification shall not affect so much of those works as has been previously carried out.

(8) An order under this section shall have the same effect as if it had been made by the local planning authority under section 23 and confirmed by the Secretary of State under section 24. **[394–395]**

NOTES
    Commencement: 24 August 1990.

CHAPTER III

RIGHTS OF OWNERS ETC

Compensation

27. (*Repealed by Planning and Compensation Act 1991, ss 31(3), (8), 84(6), Sch 19, Pt II, in relation to an application for listed building consent made on or after 16 November 1990.*)

28. Compensation where listed building consent revoked or modified

(1) This section shall have effect where listed building consent is revoked or modified by an order under section 23 (other than an order which takes effect by virtue of section 25).

(2) If on a claim made to the local planning authority within the prescribed time and in the prescribed manner, it is shown that a person interested in the building—

    (a) has incurred expenditure in carrying out works which are rendered abortive by the revocation or modification; or
    (b) has otherwise sustained loss or damage which is directly attributable to the revocation or modification,

the authority shall pay that person compensation in respect of that expenditure, loss or damage.

(3) Subject to subsection (4), no compensation shall be paid under this section in respect of—

    (a) any works carried out before the grant of the listed building consent which is revoked or modified; or

    (b) any other loss or damage (not being loss or damage consisting of depreciation of the value of an interest in land) arising out of anything done or omitted to be done before the grant of that consent.

(4) For the purposes of this section, expenditure incurred in the preparation of plans for the purposes of any works, or upon other similar matters preparatory to any works, shall be taken to be included in the expenditure incurred in carrying out those works.   **[396]**

NOTES

    Commencement: 24 August 1990.

29. Compensation for loss or damage caused by service of building preservation notice

(1) This section applies where a building preservation notice ceases to have effect without the building having been included in a list compiled or approved by the Secretary of State under section 1.

(2) Any person who at the time when the notice was served had an interest in the building shall, on making a claim to the authority within the prescribed time and in the prescribed manner, be entitled to be paid compensation by the local planning authority in respect of any loss or damage directly attributable to the effect of the notice.

(3) The loss or damage in respect of which compensation is payable under subsection (2) shall include a sum payable in respect of any breach of contract caused by the necessity of discontinuing or countermanding any works to the building on account of the building preservation notice being in force with respect to it.   **[397]**

NOTES

    Commencement: 24 August 1990.

30. Local planning authorities for compensation purposes

(1) Subject to subsection (2)—

    (a) . . .

    (b) claims under section 28 shall be made to and paid by the local planning authority who made the order in question or, where it was made by the Secretary of State under section 26, the local planning authority who are treated as having made it under that section;

    (c) claims under section 29 shall be made to and paid by the local planning authority who served the building preservation notice,

and references in those sections to a local planning authority shall be construed accordingly.

(2) The Secretary of State may after consultation with all the authorities concerned direct that where a local planning authority is liable to pay compensation under section . . . 28 or 29 in any particular case or class of case they shall be entitled to be reimbursed the whole of the compensation or such proportion of it as he may direct from one or more authorities specified in the direction.

(3) This section does not apply in Greater London.   **[398]**

NOTES
Commencement: 24 August 1990.
Sub-s (1)(a) and figure omitted from sub-s (2) repealed by the Planning and Compensation Act 1991,
ss 31(4), 84(6), Sch 6, para 42, Sch 19, Pt II.

31. General provisions as to compensation for depreciation under this Part

(1) For the purpose of assessing any compensation to which this section applies, the rules set out in section 5 of the Land Compensation Act 1961 shall, so far as applicable and subject to any necessary modifications, have effect as they have effect for the purpose of assessing compensation for the compulsory acquisition of an interest in land.

(2) This section applies to any compensation which is payable under sections [28 and] 29 in respect of depreciation of the value of an interest in land.

(3) Where an interest in land is subject to a mortgage—

    (a) any compensation to which this section applies, which is payable in respect of depreciation of the value of that interest, shall be assessed as if the interest were not subject to the mortgage;

    (b) a claim for any such compensation may be made by any mortgagee of the interest, but without prejudice to the making of a claim by the person entitled to the interest;

    (c) no compensation to which this section applies shall be payable in respect of the interest of the mortgagee (as distinct from the interest which is subject to the mortgage); and

    (d) any compensation to which this section applies which is payable in respect of the interest which is subject to the mortgage shall be paid to the mortgagee, or, if there is more than one mortgagee, to the first mortgagee, and shall in either case be applied by him as if it were proceeds of sale.

(4) Except in so far as may be otherwise provided by any regulations made under this Act, any question of disputed compensation under sections [28 and] 29 shall be referred to and determined by the Lands Tribunal.

(5) In relation to the determination of any such question, the provisions of sections 2 and 4 of the Land Compensation Act 1961 shall apply subject to any necessary modifications and to the provisions of any regulations made under this Act.   **[399]**

NOTES
Commencement: 24 August 1990.
Words in square brackets in sub-ss (2), (4) substituted by the Planning and Compensation Act 1991,
s 31(4), Sch 6, para 43.

Listed building purchase notices

32. Purchase notice on refusal or conditional grant of listed building consent

(1) Where—

    (a) listed building consent in respect of a building is refused, or granted subject to conditions, or is revoked or modified by an order under section 23 or 26; and

    (b) any owner of the building claims—

        (i) that the conditions mentioned in subsection (2) are satisfied with respect to it and any land comprising the building, or contiguous or adjacent to it, and owned with it; and

(ii) that the conditions mentioned in subsection (3) are satisfied with respect to that land,

he may, within the prescribed time and in the prescribed manner, serve on the council of the district [, Welsh county, county borough,] or London borough in which the building and land are situated a notice (in this Act referred to as a "listed building purchase notice") requiring that council to purchase his interest in the building and land in accordance with sections 33 to 37.

(2) The conditions mentioned in subsection (1)(b)(i) are—

(a) that the building and land in respect of which the notice is served have become incapable of reasonably beneficial use in their existing state;

(b) in a case where listed building consent has been granted subject to conditions with respect to the execution of the works or has been modified by the imposition of such conditions, that the land cannot be rendered capable of such use by the carrying out of the works in accordance with those conditions; and

(c) in any case, that the land cannot be rendered capable of such use by the carrying out of any other works for which listed building consent has been granted or for which the local planning authority or the Secretary of State has undertaken to grant such consent.

(3) The conditions mentioned in subsection (1)(b)(ii) are that the use of the land is substantially inseparable from that of the building and that it ought to be treated, together with the building, as a single holding.

(4) In determining for the purpose of subsection (2) what is or would in any particular circumstances be a reasonably beneficial use of land, no account shall be taken of any prospective use which would involve the carrying out of [development (other than any development specified in paragraph 1 or 2 of Schedule 3 to the principal Act)] or any works requiring listed building consent which might be executed to the building, other than works for which the local planning authority or the Secretary of State have undertaken to grant such consent.

[(4A) This section and sections 33 to 37 shall have effect as if—

(a) the bodies on whom a listed building purchase notice may be served under this section included any National Park authority which is the local planning authority for the area in which the building and land in question are situated; and

(b) a National Park authority were a local authority for the purposes of this Act and the Park for which it is the local planning authority were its area;

and the references in those sections and in section 63(7)(a) to a council and to a local authority shall be construed accordingly.]

(5) References in sections 33 to 37 to the land are to the building and the land in respect of which the notice under subsection (1) is served.   **[400]**

NOTES

Commencement: 24 August 1990 (sub-ss (1)–(4), (5)); to be appointed (sub-s (4A)).

Words in square brackets in sub-s (1) inserted by the Local Government (Wales) Act 1994, s 20(4)(b), Sch 6, Pt II, para 25(3), as from a day to be appointed.

Words in square brackets in sub-s (4) substituted by the Planning and Compensation Act 1991, s 31(4), Sch 6, para 44.

Sub-s (4A) inserted by the Environment Act 1995, s 78, Sch 10, para 33(2), as from a day to be appointed under s 125(3).

The principal Act: Town and Country Planning Act 1990.

33. Action by council on whom listed building purchase notice served

(1) The council on whom a listed building purchase notice is served by an owner shall serve on him a notice stating either—

   (a) that the council are willing to comply with the purchase notice; or
   (b) that another local authority or statutory undertakers specified in the notice under this subsection have agreed to comply with it in their place; or
   (c) that for reasons so specified the council are not willing to comply with the purchase notice and have not found any other local authority or statutory undertakers who will agree to comply with it in their place and that they have transmitted to the Secretary of State a copy of the purchase notice and of the notice under this subsection.

(2) A notice under subsection (1) must be served before the end of the period of three months beginning with the date of service of the listed building purchase notice.

(3) Where such a notice as is mentioned in paragraph (a) or (b) of subsection (1) has been duly served, the council or, as the case may be, the other local authority or statutory undertakers specified in the notice shall be deemed—

   (a) to be authorised to acquire the interest of the owner compulsorily in accordance with the provisions of section 47; and
   (b) to have served a notice to treat in respect of it on the date of service of the notice under that subsection.

(4) Where the council propose to serve such a notice as is mentioned in subsection (1)(c), they shall first send to the Secretary of State a copy of—

   (a) the proposed notice; and
   (b) the listed building purchase notice which was served on them.   **[401]**

NOTES
   Commencement: 24 August 1990.

34. Procedure on reference of listed building purchase notice to Secretary of State

(1) Where a copy of a listed building purchase notice is sent to the Secretary of State under section 33(4), he shall consider whether to confirm the notice or to take other action under section 35 in respect of it.

(2) Before confirming such a notice or taking such other action, the Secretary of State shall give notice of his proposed action—

   (a) to the person who served the notice;
   (b) to the council on whom it was served;
   (c) [in England] outside Greater London—

   (i) to the county planning authority and also, where that authority is a joint planning board, to the county council; and
   (ii) if the district council on whom the purchase notice in question was served is a constituent member of a joint planning board, to that board;

   [(cc) in Wales, to the local planning authority, where it is a joint planning board;] and
   (d) if the Secretary of State proposes to substitute any other local authority or statutory undertakers for the council on whom the notice was served, to them.

(3) A notice under subsection (2) shall specify the period (which must not be less than 28 days from its service) within which any of the persons on whom it is served may require the Secretary of State to give him an opportunity of appearing before and being heard by a person appointed by him for the purpose.

(4) If any of those persons so require, before the Secretary of State confirms the listed building purchase notice or takes any other action under section 35 in respect of it, he shall give such an opportunity to each of them.

(5) If after any of those persons have appeared before and been heard by the appointed person, it appears to the Secretary of State to be expedient to take action under section 35 otherwise than in accordance with the notice given by him, the Secretary of State may take that action accordingly.   **[402]**

NOTES
Commencement: 24 August 1990.
Words in square brackets in sub-s (2) inserted by the Local Government (Wales) Act 1994, s 20(4)(b), Sch 6, Pt II, para 25(4), as from a day to be appointed.

35. Action by Secretary of State in relation to listed building purchase notice

(1) Subject to the following provisions of this section, if the Secretary of State is satisfied that the conditions specified in section 32(2)(a) to (c) are satisfied in the case of any listed building purchase notice, he shall confirm the notice.

(2) If the Secretary of State is satisfied that those conditions are fulfilled only in respect of part of the land, he shall confirm the notice only in respect of that part and the notice shall have effect accordingly.

(3) The Secretary of State shall not confirm the notice unless he is satisfied that the land comprises such land contiguous or adjacent to the building as is in his opinion required—

(a) for preserving the building or its amenities, or
(b) for affording access to it, or
(c) for its proper control or management.

(4) If it appears to the Secretary of State to be expedient to do so he may, instead of confirming the notice—

(a) in the case of a notice served on account of the refusal of listed building consent for any works, grant such consent for those works;
(b) in the case of a notice served on account of such consent being granted subject to conditions, revoke or amend those conditions so far as it appears to him to be required in order to enable the land to be rendered capable of reasonably beneficial use by the carrying out of those works;
(c) in the case of a notice served on account of such consent being revoked by an order under section 23 or 26, cancel the order revoking the consent; or
(d) in the case of a notice served on account of such consent being modified by such an order by the imposition of conditions, revoke or amend those conditions so far as appears to him to be required in order to enable the land to be rendered capable of reasonably beneficial use by the carrying out of the works in respect of which the consent was granted.

(5) If it appears to the Secretary of State that the land (or any part of it) could be rendered capable of reasonably beneficial use within a reasonable time by the carrying out—

(a) of any other works for which listed building consent ought to be granted, or

(b) of any development for which planning permission ought to be granted,

he may, instead of confirming the listed building purchase notice (or confirming it so far as it relates to that part), direct that if an application is made for such consent for those works or, as the case may be, for planning permission for that development, it shall be granted.

(6) If it appears to the Secretary of State, having regard to the probable ultimate use of the building or its site, that it is expedient to do so, he may, if he confirms the notice, modify it either in relation to the whole or any part of the land, by substituting another local authority or statutory undertakers for the council on whom the notice was served.

(7) Any reference in section 34 to the taking of action by the Secretary of State under this section includes a reference to the taking by him of a decision not to confirm the notice on the grounds that any of the conditions referred to in subsection (1) are not satisfied.   **[403]**

NOTES
Commencement: 24 August 1990.

36. Effect of Secretary of State's action in relation to listed building purchase notice

(1) Where the Secretary of State confirms a listed building purchase notice, the council on whom the notice was served shall be deemed—

(a) to be authorised to acquire the owner's interest in the land compulsorily in accordance with the provisions of section 47; and

(b) to have served a notice to treat in respect of it on such date as the Secretary of State may direct.

(2) If before the end of the relevant period the Secretary of State has neither—

(a) confirmed the listed building purchase notice; nor
(b) notified the owner by whom it was served that he does not propose to confirm it; nor
(c) taken any such action in respect of it as is mentioned in subsection (4) or (5) of section 35,

the notice shall be deemed to be confirmed at the end of that period and the council on whom it was served shall be deemed to have been authorised as mentioned in subsection (1)(a) and to have served a notice to treat in respect of the owner's interest at the end of that period.

(3) Where a listed building purchase notice is confirmed in respect of only part of the land, references in this section to the owner's interest in the land are references to the owner's interest in that part.

(4) Where a listed building purchase notice is modified under section 35(6) by the substitution of another local authority or statutory undertakers for the council on whom the notice was served, the reference in subsection (1) to that council is to that other local authority or those statutory undertakers.

(5) In this section "the relevant period" means, subject to subsection (6) below—

(a) the period of nine months beginning with the date of the service of the listed building purchase notice; or

(b) if it ends earlier, the period of six months beginning with the date on which a copy of the notice was sent to the Secretary of State.

(6) The relevant period does not run if the Secretary of State has before him at the same time both—

(a) a copy of the listed building purchase notice sent to him under section 33(4); and

(b) a notice of appeal under section 20 or section 39 relating to any of the land to which the listed building purchase notice relates.

(7) Where any decision by the Secretary of State to confirm or not to confirm a listed building purchase notice (including any decision to confirm the notice only in respect of part of the land, or to give any direction as to the granting of listed building consent or planning permission) is quashed under section 63, the notice shall be treated as cancelled but the owner may serve a further notice in its place.

(8) For the purposes of determining whether such a further notice has been served within the period prescribed for the service of listed building purchase notices, the decision concerning listed building consent on account of which the notice has been served shall be treated as having been made on the date on which the Secretary of State's decision was quashed.   **[404]**

NOTES
Commencement: 24 August 1990.

37. Reduction of compensation on acquisition where s 28 compensation payable

Where compensation is payable under section 28 in respect of expenditure incurred in carrying out any works to a building, any compensation which then becomes payable in respect of the acquisition of an interest in the land in pursuance of a listed building purchase notice shall be reduced by an amount equal to the value of those works.   **[405]**

NOTES
Commencement: 24 August 1990.

CHAPTER IV
ENFORCEMENT

38. Power to issue listed building enforcement notice

(1) Where it appears to the local planning authority—

(a) that any works have been or are being executed to a listed building in their area; and

(b) that the works are such as to involve a contravention of section 9(1) or (2),

they may, if they consider it expedient to do so having regard to the effect of the works on the character of the building as one of special architectural or historic interest, issue a notice under this section (in this Act referred to as a "listed building enforcement notice").

(2) A listed building enforcement notice shall specify the alleged contravention and require such steps as may be specified in the notice to be taken . . .—

(a) for restoring the building to its former state; or

(b) if the authority consider that such restoration would not be reasonably practicable or would be undesirable, for executing such further works specified in the notice as they consider necessary to alleviate the effect of the works which were carried out without listed building consent; or

(c) for bringing the building to the state in which it would have been if the terms and conditions of any listed building consent which has been granted for the works had been complied with.

[(3) A listed building enforcement notice—

(a) shall specify the date on which it is to take effect and, subject to sections 39(3) and 65(3A), shall take effect on that date, and

(b) shall specify the period within which any steps are required to be taken and may specify different periods for different steps,

and, where different periods apply to different steps, references in this Part to the period for compliance with a listed building enforcement notice, in relation to any step, are to the period within which the step is required to be taken.]

(4) A copy of a listed building enforcement notice shall be served, not later than 28 days after the date of its issue and not later than 28 days before the [date specified in it as the date on which it is to take effect]—

(a) on the owner and on the occupier of the building to which it relates; and

(b) on any other person having an interest in that building which in the opinion of the authority is materially affected by the notice.

[(5) The local planning authority may—

(a) withdraw a listed building enforcement notice (without prejudice to their power to issue another); or

(b) waive or relax any requirement of such a notice and, in particular, may extend the period specified in accordance with section 38(3),

and the powers conferred by this subsection may be exercised whether or not the notice has taken effect.

(6) The local planning authority shall, immediately after exercising the powers conferred by subsection (5), give notice of the exercise to every person who has been served with a copy of the listed building enforcement notice or would, if the notice were re-issued, be served with a copy of it.]

(7) Where a listed building enforcement notice imposes any such requirement as is mentioned in subsection (2)(b), listed building consent shall be deemed to be granted for any works of demolition, alteration or extension of the 450building executed as a result of compliance with the notice.   **[406]**

NOTES

Commencement: 24 August 1990 (sub-ss (1), (2), (4), (7)); 2 January 1991 (sub-ss (3), (5), (6)).

Words omitted from sub-s (2) repealed, sub-ss (3), (5), (6) and words in square brackets in sub-s (4) substituted, by the Planning and Compensation Act 1991, ss 25, 84(6), Sch 3, Pt I, para 2, Pt II, para 19, Sch 19, Pt I.

39. Appeal against listed building enforcement notice

(1) A person having an interest in the building to which a listed building enforcement notice relates or a relevant occupier may appeal to the Secretary of State against the notice on any of the following grounds—

(a) that the building is not of special architectural or historic interest;

[(b) that the matters alleged to constitute a contravention of section 9(1) or (2) have not occurred;

(c) that those matters (if they occurred) do not constitute such a contravention];

(d) that works to the building were urgently necessary in the interests of safety or health or for the preservation of the building, that it was not practicable to secure safety or health or, as the case may be, the preservation of the building by works of repair or works for affording temporary support or shelter, and that the works carried out were limited to the minimum measures immediately necessary;

(e) that listed building consent ought to be granted for the works, or that any relevant condition of such consent which has been granted ought to be discharged, or different conditions substituted;

(f) that copies of the notice were not served as required by section 38(4);

(g) except in relation to such a requirement as is mentioned in section 38(2)(b) or (c), that the requirements of the notice exceed what is necessary for restoring the building to its condition before the works were carried out;

(h) that the period specified in the notice as the period within which any step required by the notice is to be taken falls short of what should reasonably be allowed;

(i) that the steps required by the notice for the purpose of restoring the character of the building to its former state would not serve that purpose;

(j) that steps required to be taken by virtue of section 38(2)(b) exceed what is necessary to alleviate the effect of the works executed to the building;

(k) that steps required to be taken by virtue of section 38(2)(c) exceed what is necessary to bring the building to the state in which it would have been if the terms and conditions of the listed building consent had been complied with.

[(2) An appeal under this section shall be made either—

(a) by giving written notice of the appeal to the Secretary of State before the date specified in the listed building enforcement notice as the date on which it is to take effect; or

(b) by sending such notice to him in a properly addressed and prepaid letter posted to him at such time that, in the ordinary course of post, it would be delivered to him before that date.]

(3) Where such an appeal is brought the listed building enforcement notice shall [subject to any order under section 65(3A)] be of no effect pending the final determination or the withdrawal of the appeal.

(4) A person who gives notice of appeal under this section shall submit to the Secretary of State, either when giving the notice or within such time as may be prescribed, a statement in writing—

(a) specifying the grounds on which he is appealing against the listed building enforcement notice; and

(b) giving such further information as may be prescribed.

(5) If, where more than one ground is specified in the statement, the appellant does not give information required under subsection (4)(b) in relation to each of those grounds within the prescribed time, the Secretary of State may determine the appeal without considering any ground as to which the appellant has failed to give such information within that time.

(6) Where any person has appealed to the Secretary of State under this section against a notice, no person shall be entitled, in any other proceedings instituted after the making of the appeal, to claim that the notice was not duly served on the person who appealed.

(7) In this section "relevant occupier" means a person who—

    (a) on the date on which the listed building enforcement notice is issued
       occupies the building to which the notice relates by virtue of a licence . . .;
       and

    (b) continues so to occupy the building when the appeal is brought.   **[407]**

NOTES
    Commencement: 24 August 1990 (sub-ss (1), (3)–(7)); 2 January 1992 (sub-s (2)).
    Sub-ss (1)(b), (c), (2) substituted, words in square brackets in sub-s (3) inserted, and words omitted
from sub-s (7) repealed, by the Planning and Compensation Act 1991, ss 25, 84(6), Sch 3, Pt I, para 3, Pt
II, para 20, Sch 19, Pt I.

40. Appeals: supplementary provisions

(1) The Secretary of State may by regulations prescribe the procedure which is to be
followed on appeals under section 39, and in particular, but without prejudice to the
generality of this subsection may—

    (a) require the local planning authority to submit, within such time as may be
       prescribed, a statement indicating the submissions which they propose to
       put forward on the appeal;

    (b) specify the matters to be included in such a statement;

    (c) require the authority or the appellant to give such notice of such an appeal
       as may be prescribed, being notice which in the opinion of the Secretary
       of State is likely to bring the appeal to the attention of persons in the
       locality in which the building in question is situated;

    (d) require the authority to send to the Secretary of State, within such period
       from the date of the bringing of the appeal as may be prescribed, a copy
       of the enforcement notice and a list of the persons served with copies of
       it.

(2) Subject to section 41(4), the Secretary of State shall, if either the appellant
or the local planning authority so wish, give each of them an opportunity of appearing
before and being heard by a person appointed by the Secretary of State for the
purpose.

(3) Schedule 3 applies to appeals under section 39.   **[408]**

NOTES
    Commencement: 24 August 1990.

41. Determination of appeals under s 39

[(1) On an appeal under section 39 the Secretary of State may—

    (a) correct any defect, error or misdescription in the listed building enforcement
       notice; or

    (b) vary the terms of the listed building enforcement notice,

if he is satisfied that the correction or variation will not cause injustice to the appellant
or the local planning authority.

(2) Where the Secretary of State determines to allow the appeal, he may quash
the notice.

(2A) The Secretary of State shall give any directions necessary to give effect to
his determination on the appeal.]

(3) The Secretary of State—

    (a) may dismiss such an appeal if the appellant fails to comply with section
       39(4) within the prescribed time; and

(b) may allow such an appeal and quash the listed building enforcement notice if the local planning authority fail to comply within the prescribed period with any requirement imposed by regulations made by virtue of section 40(1)(a), (b) or (d).

(4) If the Secretary of State proposes to dismiss an appeal under paragraph (a) of subsection (3) or to allow an appeal and quash the listed building enforcement notice under paragraph (b) of that subsection he need not comply with section 40(2).

(5) Where it would otherwise be a ground for determining an appeal in favour of the appellant that a person required to be served with a copy of the listed building enforcement notice was not served, the Secretary of State may disregard that fact if neither the appellant nor that person has been substantially prejudiced by the failure to serve him.

(6) On the determination of an appeal the Secretary of State may—

(a) grant listed building consent for the works to which the listed building enforcement notice relates or for part only of those works;
(b) discharge any condition or limitation subject to which listed building consent was granted and substitute any other condition, whether more or less onerous;
(c) if he thinks fit, exercise his power under section 1 to amend any list compiled or approved under that section by removing from it the building to which the appeal relates.

(7) Any listed building consent granted by the Secretary of State under subsection (6) shall be treated as granted on an application for the same consent under section 10 and the Secretary of State's decision in relation to the grant shall be final.

[(8) Subsection (5) of section 250 of the Local Government Act 1972 (which authorises a Minister holding an inquiry under that section to make orders with respect to the costs of the parties) shall apply in relation to any proceedings before the Secretary of State on an appeal under section 39 as if those proceedings were an inquiry held by the Secretary of State under section 250.]   **[409]**

NOTES
Commencement: 24 August 1990 (sub-ss (3)-(7), sub-s (8) (for effect see annotations)); 2 January 1992 (sub-ss (1), (2), (2A)).
Sub-ss (1), (2), (2A) substituted for sub-ss (1), (2) by the Planning and Compensation Act 1991, s 25, Sch 3, Pt I, para 4.
Sub-s (8): temporarily added by the Planning (Consequential Provisions) Act 1990, s 6, Sch 4, paras 1, 9 until such day as may be appointed by the Secretary of State. The Planning (Consequential Provisions) Act 1990 (Appointed Day No 1 and Transitional Provisions) Order 1991, SI 1991/2698, appointed 2 January 1992 only for the purposes of awards of costs in relation to proceedings which give rise to a hearing.

42. Execution of works required by listed building enforcement notice

(1) If any of the steps specified in the listed building enforcement notice have not been taken within the [period for compliance with the notice], the authority may—

(a) enter the land and take those steps, and
(b) recover from the person who is then the owner of the land any expenses reasonably incurred by them in doing so.

(2) Where a listed building enforcement notice has been served in respect of a building—

(a) any expenses incurred by the owner or occupier of the building for the purpose of complying with it, and

(b) any sums paid by the owner of the building under subsection (1) in respect of expenses incurred by the local planning authority in taking steps required by it,

shall be deemed to be incurred or paid for the use and at the request of the person who carried out the works to which the notice relates.

(3) Regulations under this Act may provide that all or any of the following sections of the Public Health Act 1936, namely—

(a) section 276 (power of local authorities to sell materials removed in executing works under that Act subject to accounting for the proceeds of sale);

(b) section 289 (power to require the occupier of any premises to permit works to be executed by the owner of the premises);

(c) section 294 (limit on liability of persons holding premises as agents or trustees in respect of the expenses recoverable under that Act),

shall apply, subject to such adaptations and modifications as may be specified in the regulations, in relation to any steps required to be taken by a listed building enforcement notice.

(4) Regulations under subsection (3) applying all or any of section 289 of that Act may include adaptations and modifications for the purpose of giving the owner of land to which such a notice relates the right, as against all other persons interested in the land, to comply with the requirements of the notice.

(5) Regulations under subsection (3) may also provide for the charging on the land on which the building stands of any expenses recoverable by a local planning authority under subsection (1).

[(6) Any person who wilfully obstructs a person acting in the exercise of powers under subsection (1) shall be guilty of an offence and liable on summary conviction to a fine not exceeding level 3 on the standard scale.]

(7) ...   **[410]**

NOTES
Commencement: 24 August 1990.
Words in square brackets in sub-s (1) and the whole of sub-s (6) substituted and sub-s (7) repealed, by the Planning and Compensation Act 1991, ss 25, 84(6), Sch 3, Pt I, para 5, Pt II, para 21, Sch 19, Pt I.

[43. Offence where listed building enforcement notice not complied with

(1) Where, at any time after the end of the period for compliance with the notice, any step required by a listed building enforcement notice to be taken has not been taken, the person who is then owner of the land is in breach of the notice.

(2) If at any time the owner of the land is in breach of a listed building enforcement notice he shall be guilty of an offence.

(3) An offence under this section may be charged by reference to any day or longer period of time and a person may be convicted of a second or subsequent offence under this section by reference to any period of time following the preceding conviction for such an offence.

(4) In proceedings against any person for an offence under this section, it shall be a defence for him to show—

(a) that he did everything he could be expected to do to secure that all the steps required by the notice were taken; or

(b) that he was not served with a copy of the listed building enforcement notice and was not aware of its existence.

(5) A person guilty of an offence under this section shall be liable—

(a) on summary conviction, to a fine not exceeding £20,000; and
(b) on conviction on indictment, to a fine.

(6) In determining the amount of any fine to be imposed on a person convicted of an offence under this section, the court shall in particular have regard to any financial benefit which has accrued or appears likely to accrue to him in consequence of the offence.]   **[411]**

NOTES

Commencement: 25 November 1991 (certain purposes); 2 January 1992 (remaining purposes).
Substituted by the Planning and Compensation Act 1991, s 25, Sch 3, Pt I, para 6.

44. Effect of listed building consent on listed building enforcement notice

(1) If, after the issue of a listed building enforcement notice, consent is granted under section 8(3)—

(a) for the retention of any work to which the notice relates; or
(b) permitting the retention of works without compliance with some condition subject to which a previous listed building consent was granted,

the notice shall cease to have effect in so far as it requires steps to be taken involving the works not being retained or, as the case may be, for complying with that condition.

(2) The fact that such a notice has wholly or partly ceased to have effect under subsection (1) shall not affect the liability of any person for an offence in respect of a previous failure to comply with that notice.   **[412]**

NOTES

Commencement: 24 August 1990.

[44A. Injunctions

(1) Where a local planning authority consider it necessary or expedient for any actual or apprehended contravention of section 9(1) or (2) to be restrained by injunction, they may apply to the court for an injunction, whether or not they have exercised or are proposing to exercise any of their other powers under this Part.

(2) On an application under subsection (1) the court may grant such an injunction as the court thinks appropriate for the purpose of restraining the contravention.

(3) Rules of court may, in particular, provide for such an injunction to be issued against a person whose identity is unknown.

(4) The references in subsection (1) to a local planning authority include, as respects England, the Commission.

(5) In this section "the court" means the High Court or the county court.]
                                                                           [412A]

NOTES

Commencement: 25 November 1991 (certain purposes); 2 January 1992 (remaining purposes).
Inserted by the Planning and Compensation Act 1991, s 25, Sch 3, Pt I, para 7.

45. Commission to have concurrent enforcement functions in London

The Commission shall, as respects any London borough, have concurrently with the council of that borough the functions of a local planning authority under sections 38 to 43; and references to the local planning authority in those provisions shall be construed accordingly.   **[413]**

NOTES
    Commencement: 24 August 1990.

46. Enforcement by the Secretary of State

(1) If it appears to the Secretary of State to be expedient that a listed building enforcement notice should be issued in respect of any land, he may issue such a notice.

(2) Before the Secretary of State serves a notice under subsection (1) he shall consult—
    (a) the local planning authority; and
    (b) if the land is situated in England, the Commission.

(3) A listed building enforcement notice issued by the Secretary of State shall have the same effect as a notice issued by the local planning authority.

(4) In relation to a listed building enforcement notice issued by the Secretary of State, [section 42] shall apply as if for any reference in [that section] to the local planning authority there were substituted a reference to the Secretary of State.

(5) References in this section to the local planning authority shall in the case of an authority for an area [in England] outside Greater London be construed as references to the district planning authority.   **[414]**

NOTES
    Commencement: 24 August 1990.
    Words in square brackets in sub-s (4) substituted by the Planning and Compensation Act 1991, s 25, Sch 3, Pt II, para 22.
    Words in square brackets in sub-s (5) inserted by the Local Government (Wales) Act 1994, s 20(4)(b), Sch 6, Pt II, para 25(5), as from a day to be appointed.

CHAPTER V
PREVENTION OF DETERIORATION AND DAMAGE
Compulsory acquisition of listed building in need of repair

47. Compulsory acquisition of listed building in need of repair

(1) If it appears to the Secretary of State that reasonable steps are not being taken for properly preserving a listed building he—
    (a) may authorise the appropriate authority to acquire compulsorily under this section the building and any relevant land; or
    (b) may himself compulsorily acquire them under this section.

(2) The Acquisition of Land Act 1981 shall apply to compulsory acquisition under this section.

(3) The Secretary of State shall not make or confirm a compulsory purchase order for the acquisition of any building by virtue of this section unless—
    (a) in the case of the acquisition of a building situated in England otherwise than by the Commission, he has consulted with the Commission; and

(b) in any case, he is satisfied that it is expedient to make provision for the preservation of the building and to authorise its compulsory acquisition for that purpose.

(4) Any person having an interest in a building which it is proposed to acquire compulsorily under this section may, within 28 days after the service of the notice required by section 12 of that Act of 1981 or, as the case may be, paragraph 3(1) of Schedule 1 to that Act, apply to a magistrates' court acting for the petty sessions area within which the building is situated for an order staying further proceedings on the compulsory purchase order.

(5) If on an application under subsection (4) the court is satisfied that reasonable steps have been taken for properly preserving the building, the court shall make an order accordingly.

(6) Any person aggrieved by the decision of a magistrates' court on an application under subsection (4) may appeal against the decision to the Crown Court.

(7) In this section—

"the appropriate authority" means—

(a) the council of the county [, county borough] or district in which the building is situated, or
(b) in the case of a building situated in Greater London, the Commission or the council of the London borough in which the building is situated, or
(c) in the case of a building situated outside Greater London, the joint planning board for the area in which the building is situated; or
(d) in the case of a building situated within the Broads, the Broads Authority;

"relevant land", in relation to any building, means the land comprising or contiguous or adjacent to it which appears to the Secretary of State to be required for preserving the building or its amenities, or for affording access to it, or for its proper control or management.   **[415]**

NOTES

Commencement: 24 August 1990.

Words in square brackets in sub-s (7) inserted by the Local Government (Wales) Act 1994, s 20(4)(b), Sch 6, Pt II, para 25(6), as from a day to be appointed.

Modification: in the case of a building situated in a National Park for which a National Park authority is the local planning authority, that authority and no other authority is the appropriate authority for the purposes of this section and ss 48–51; and the reference to a local authority in s 88(5) is to have effect accordingly, by virtue of the Environment Act 1995, s 70, Sch 9, para 13(1).

48. Repairs notice as preliminary to acquisition under s 47

(1) The compulsory purchase of a building under section 47 shall not be started by the appropriate authority or by the Secretary of State unless at least two months previously the authority or, as the case may be, the Secretary of State has served on the owner of the building a notice under this section (in this section referred to as a "repairs notice")—

(a) specifying the works which the appropriate authority or, as the case may be, the Secretary of State considers reasonably necessary for the proper preservation of the building; and
(b) explaining the effect of sections 47 to 50,

and the repairs notice has not been withdrawn.

(2) Where—

(a) a building is demolished after a repairs notice has been served in respect of it by an appropriate authority or the Secretary of State, but

(b) the Secretary of State is satisfied that he would have confirmed or, as the case may be, would have made a compulsory purchase order in respect of the building had it not been demolished,

the demolition of the building shall not prevent the authority or the Secretary of State from being authorised under section 47 to acquire compulsorily the site of the building.

(3) An appropriate authority or the Secretary of State may at any time withdraw a repairs notice served by them on any person; and if they do so, they shall immediately give him notice of the withdrawal.

(4) The Secretary of State shall consult with the Commission before he serves or withdraws a repairs notice in relation to a building situated in England.

(5) Where a repairs notice has been served on a person in respect of a building, he shall not be entitled to serve a listed building purchase notice in respect of it—

(a) until the expiration of three months beginning with the date of the service of the repairs notice; or

(b) if during that period the compulsory acquisition of the building is begun under section 47, unless and until the compulsory acquisition is discontinued.

(6) For the purposes of this section a compulsory acquisition—

(a) is started when the notice required by section 12 of the Acquisition of Land Act 1981 or, as the case may be, paragraph 3(1) of Schedule 1 to that Act is served; and

(b) is discontinued—

(i) in the case of acquisition by the Secretary of State, when he decides not to make the compulsory purchase order; and

(ii) in any other case, when the order is withdrawn or the Secretary of State decides not to confirm it.

(7) In this section ''appropriate authority'' has the same meaning as in section 47. **[416]**

NOTES
Commencement: 24 August 1990.
Modification: see the note to s 47 at **[415]**.

49. Compensation on compulsory acquisition of listed building

Subject to section 50, for the purpose of assessing compensation in respect of any compulsory acquisition of land including a building which immediately before the date of the compulsory purchase order was listed, it shall be assumed that listed building consent would be granted for any works—

(a) for the alteration or extension of the building; or

(b) for the demolition of the building for the purpose of development of any class specified in Schedule 3 to the principal Act (development not constituting new development),

. . . . . **[417]**

NOTES
Commencement: 24 August 1990.
Words omitted repealed by the Planning and Compensation Act 1991, ss 31(4), 84(6), Sch 6, para 45, Sch 19, Pt II.

The principal Act: Town and Country Planning Act 1990.
Modification: see the note to s 47 at **[415]**.

50. Minimum compensation in case of listed building deliberately left derelict

(1) Where the appropriate authority within the meaning of section 47—

    (a) propose to acquire a building compulsorily under section 47; and

    (b) are satisfied that the building has been deliberately allowed to fall into disrepair for the purpose of justifying its demolition and the development or redevelopment of the site or any adjoining site,

they may include in the compulsory purchase order as submitted to the Secretary of State for confirmation a direction for minimum compensation.

(2) Subject to the provisions of this section, where the Secretary of State acquires a building compulsorily under section 47, he may, if he is satisfied as mentioned in subsection (1)(b), include a direction for minimum compensation in the compulsory purchase order.

(3) Without prejudice to so much of section 12 of the Acquisition of Land Act 1981 or, as the case may be, paragraph 3(1) of Schedule 1 to that Act (notices stating effect of compulsory purchase order or, as the case may be, draft order) as requires the notice to state the effect of the order, the notice required to be served in accordance with that provision shall—

    (a) include a statement that a direction for minimum compensation has been included in the order or, as the case may be, in the draft order prepared by the Secretary of State in accordance with Schedule 1 to that Act; and

    (b) explain the meaning of the expression "direction for minimum compensation".

(4) A direction for minimum compensation, in relation to a building compulsorily acquired, is a direction that for the purpose of assessing compensation it is to be assumed, notwithstanding anything to the contrary in the Land Compensation Act 1961, the principal Act, or this Act—

    (a) that planning permission would not be granted for any development or re-development of the site of the building; and

    (b) that listed building consent would not be granted for any works for the demolition, alteration or extension of the building other than development or works necessary for restoring it to and maintaining it in a proper state of repair.

(5) If a compulsory purchase order is confirmed or made with the inclusion of a direction for minimum compensation, the compensation in respect of the compulsory acquisition shall be assessed in accordance with the direction.

(6) Where such a direction is included in a compulsory purchase order or, as the case may be, in a draft order prepared by the Secretary of State, any person having an interest in the building may, within 28 days after the service of the notice mentioned in subsection (3), apply to a magistrates' court acting for the petty sessions area in which the building is situated for an order that no such direction be included in the compulsory purchase order as confirmed or made by the Secretary of State.

(7) If the court to which an application is made under subsection (6) is satisfied that the building in respect of which the application is made has not been deliberately allowed to fall into disrepair for the purpose mentioned in subsection (1)(b) the court shall make the order applied for.

(8) A person aggrieved by the decision of a magistrates' court on an application under subsection (6) may appeal against the decision to the Crown Court.

(9) The rights conferred by subsections (6) and (8) shall not prejudice those conferred by section 47(4) and (6).   **[418]**

NOTES
   Commencement: 24 August 1990.
   The principal Act: Town and Country Planning Act 1990.
   Modification: see the note to s 47 at **[415]**.

51. Ending of rights over land compulsorily acquired

(1) Subject to the provisions of this section, upon the completion of a compulsory acquisition of land under section 47—

   (a) all private rights of way and rights of laying down, erecting, continuing or maintaining any apparatus on, under or over the land shall be extinguished, and

   (b) any such apparatus shall vest in the acquiring authority.

(2) Subsection (1) shall not apply—

   (a) to any rights vested in, or apparatus belonging to, statutory undertakers for the purpose of the carrying on of their undertaking, or

   (b) to any right conferred by or in accordance with the telecommunications code on the operator of a telecommunications code system, or

   (c) to any telecommunication apparatus kept installed for the purposes of any such system.

(3) In respect of any right or apparatus not falling within subsection (2), subsection (1) shall have effect subject—

   (a) to any direction given by the acquiring authority before the completion of the acquisition that subsection (1) shall not apply to any right or apparatus specified in the direction; and

   (b) to any agreement which may be made (whether before or after the completion of the acquisition) between the acquiring authority and the person in or to whom the right or apparatus in question is vested or belongs.

(4) Any person who suffers loss by the extinguishment of a right or the vesting of any apparatus under this section shall be entitled to compensation from the acquiring authority.

(5) Any compensation payable under this section shall be determined in accordance with the Land Compensation Act 1961.   **[419]**

NOTES
   Commencement: 24 August 1990.
   Modification: see the note to s 47 at **[415]**.

Acquisition by agreement

52. Acquisition of land by agreement

(1) The council of any county, [county borough,] district or London borough or a joint planning board for an area outside Greater London may acquire by agreement—

   (a) any building appearing to them to be of special architectural or historic interest; and

(b) any land comprising or contiguous or adjacent to such a building which appears to the Secretary of State to be required—

  (i) for preserving the building or its amenities, or
  (ii) for affording access to it, or
  (iii) for its proper control or management.

(2) The provisions of Part I of the Compulsory Purchase Act 1965 (so far as applicable), other than sections 4 to 8, 10 and 31, shall apply in relation to the acquisition of land under subsection (1), but references in that Part to the execution of the works shall be construed as including references to—

(a) any erection, construction or carrying out of buildings or works authorised by section 237 of the principal Act; and
(b) any erection, construction or carrying out of buildings or works on behalf of a Minister or statutory undertakers on land acquired by that Minister or those undertakers, where the buildings or works are erected, constructed or carried out for the purposes for which the land was acquired.   **[420]**

NOTES
Commencement: 24 August 1990.
Words in square brackets in sub-s (1) inserted by the Local Government (Wales) Act 1994, s 20(4)(b), Sch 6, Pt II, para 25(7), as from a day to be appointed.
The principal Act: Town and Country Planning Act 1990.
Modification: in relation to any building or land in any National Park for which a National Park authority is the local planning authority, the powers conferred on a county council or county borough council by this section are exercisable by the National Park authority, and not by any other authority, and sub-s (2) above is to have effect accordingly, by virtue of the Environment Act 1995, s 70, Sch 9, para 13(2).

Management of acquired buildings

53. Management of listed buildings acquired under this Act

(1) Where—

(a) a local authority or joint planning board acquire any building or other land under section 47(1) or 52(1)(a) or (b); or
(b) the Commission acquire any building or other land under section 47(1),

they may make such arrangements as to its management, use or disposal as they consider appropriate for the purpose of its preservation.

(2) Where the Secretary of State acquires any building or other land under section 47(1), he may—

(a) make such arrangements as he thinks fit as to the management, custody or use of the building or land; and
(b) dispose of or otherwise deal with any such building or land as he may from time to time determine.

(3) The Commission may be a party to such arrangements as are mentioned in subsection (2) if they relate to property situated in England.   **[421]**

NOTES
Commencement: 24 August 1990.
Modification: sub-s (1) above applies in relation to the powers conferred by virtue of the Environment Act 1995, Sch 9, para 13 (see the notes to ss 47, 52 at **[415]**, **[420]**) on a National Park authority as it applies in relation to the powers conferred by those sections on a local authority, by virtue of s 70 of, and Sch 9, para 13(3) to, the 1995 Act.

Urgent preservation

54. Urgent works to preserve unoccupied listed buildings

(1) A local authority may execute any works which appear to them to be urgently necessary for the preservation of a listed building in their area.

(2) If it appears to the Secretary of State that any works are urgently necessary for the preservation of a listed building—

> (a) if the building is in England, he shall authorise the Commission to execute any works specified in the authorisation which appear to him to be urgently necessary for its preservation; or
>
> (b) if the building is in Wales, he may himself execute any works which appear to him to be urgently necessary for its preservation.

(3) The works which may be executed under this section may consist of or include works for affording temporary support or shelter for the building.

(4) If the building is occupied works may be carried out only to those parts which are not in use.

(5) The owner of the building must be given not less than seven days notice in writing of the intention to carry out the works and, in the case of works authorised under subsection (2)(a), the Commission shall give that notice.

(6) A notice under subsection (5) shall describe the works proposed to be carried out.

(7) As respects buildings in Greater London, the functions of a local authority under this section are exercisable concurrently by the Commission and the relevant London borough council.   **[422]**

NOTES
Commencement: 24 August 1990.
Modification: this Act has effect as if a National Park authority were a local authority for the purposes of this section, and ss 55, 57, 58, and, in relation to those provisions, as if the relevant Park were the authority's area, by virtue of the Environment Act 1995, s 70, Sch 9, para 13(4).

55. Recovery of expenses of works under s 54

(1) This section has effect for enabling the expenses of works executed under section 54 to be recovered by the authority who carried out the works, that is to say the local authority, the Commission or the Secretary of State or, in the case of works carried out by the Commission on behalf of the Secretary of State, the Secretary of State.

(2) That authority may give notice to the owner of the building requiring him to pay the expenses of the works.

(3) Where the works consist of or include works for affording temporary support or shelter for the building—

> (a) the expenses which may be recovered include any continuing expenses involved in making available the apparatus or materials used; and
>
> (b) notices under subsection (2) in respect of any such continuing expenses may be given from time to time.

(4) The owner may within 28 days of the service of the notice represent to the Secretary of State—

> (a) that some or all of the works were unnecessary for the preservation of the building; or

(b) in the case of works for affording temporary support or shelter, that the temporary arrangements have continued for an unreasonable length of time; or

(c) that the amount specified in the notice is unreasonable; or

(d) that the recovery of that amount would cause him hardship,

and the Secretary of State shall determine to what extent the representations are justified.

(5) The Secretary of State shall give notice of his determination, the reasons for it and the amount recoverable—

(a) to the owner of the building; and

(b) if the authority who gave notice under subsection (2) is a local authority or the Commission, to them.

(6) ...   **[423]**

NOTES
Commencement: 24 August 1990.
Sub-s (6) repealed by the Planning and Compensation Act 1991, ss 25, 84(6), Sch 3, Pt II, para 23, Sch 19, Pt I.
Modification: see the note to s 54 at **[422]**.

56. Dangerous structure orders in respect of listed buildings

Before taking any steps with a view to—

(a) the making of an order in respect of a listed building under section 77(1)(a) of the Building Act 1984 or section 65 or 69(1) of the London Building Acts (Amendment) Act 1939; or

(b) the service of a notice under section 79(1) of that Act of 1984 or section 62(2) of that Act of 1939,

a local planning authority shall consider whether they should instead exercise their powers under sections 47 and 48 or section 54.   **[424]**

NOTES
Commencement: 24 August 1990.

Grants for repair and maintenance

57. Power of local authority to contribute to preservation of listed buildings etc

(1) A local authority may contribute towards the expenses incurred or to be incurred in the repair or maintenance—

(a) of a listed building which is situated in or in the vicinity of their area; or

(b) of a building in their area which is not listed but appears to them to be of architectural or historic interest.

(2) At the time of making such a contribution the local authority may also contribute towards the expenses incurred, or to be incurred, in the upkeep of any garden occupied with the building and contiguous or adjacent to it.

(3) A contribution under this section may be made by grant or loan.

(4) A contribution by way of loan may be made upon such terms and conditions as the local authority may determine including (but without prejudice to the foregoing) a term that the loan shall be free of interest.

(5) A local authority—

(a) may renounce their right to repayment of such a loan or any interest for the time being outstanding, and

(b) by agreement with the borrower may otherwise vary any of the terms and conditions on which such a loan is made.

(6) A local authority may require as a condition of the making by them of a contribution under this section by way of grant towards the expenses of the repair or maintenance or upkeep of any property that the person to whom the grant is made shall enter into an agreement with them for the purpose of enabling the public to have access to the property or part of it during such period and at such times as the agreement may provide.

(7) In this section and in section 58 "local authority" means—

(a) the council of a county, [county borough,] borough or district,

(b) a joint planning board constituted under section 2 of the principal Act, and

(c) in relation to a building or land in the Broads, the Broads Authority. **[425]**

NOTES
Commencement: 24 August 1990.
Words in square brackets in sub-s (7) inserted by the Local Government (Wales) Act 1994, s 20(4)(b), Sch 6, Pt II, para 25(8), as from a day to be appointed.
Modification: see the note to s 54 at **[422]**.
The principal Act: Town and Country Planning Act 1990.

58. Recovery of grants under s 57

(1) If, during the period of three years beginning with the day on which a grant is made under section 57 towards the repair or maintenance or upkeep of any property ("the grant property"), the grantee disposes of the interest held by him in the property on that day or any part of that interest, by way of sale or exchange or lease for a term of not less than 21 years, the local authority may recover the amount of the grant, or such part of it as they think fit, from the grantee in any court of competent jurisdiction.

(2) If the grantee gives the whole of that interest to any person (whether directly or indirectly, but otherwise than by will) subsection (1) shall have effect as if the donee were the grantee.

(3) If the grantee gives part of that interest to any person (whether directly or indirectly, but otherwise than by will) subsection (1) shall have effect as if any disposal or part disposal of that interest by the donee were a disposal by the grantee.

(4) If any condition imposed on the making of a grant to which this section applies is contravened or not complied with, the grantor may recover the amount of the grant, or such part of it as he thinks fit, from the grantee.

(5) Nothing in this section entitles a grantor to recover amounts in the aggregate exceeding the amount of the grant (for example by virtue of a breach of more than one condition or disposals of several parts of an interest in the grant property). **[426]**

NOTES
Commencement: 24 August 1990.
Modification: see the note to s 54 at **[422]**.
See further, in respect of sums recovered before the commencement of this Act: the Planning (Consequential Provisions) Act 1990, ss 3-5, Sch 3, para 17 at **[511]**–**[513]**, **[520]**.

Damage to listed buildings

59. Acts causing or likely to result in damage to listed buildings

(1) If, with the intention of causing damage to a listed building, any relevant person does or permits the doing of any act which causes or is likely to result in damage to the building, he shall be guilty of an offence and liable on summary conviction to a fine not exceeding level 3 on the standard scale.

(2) A person is a relevant person for the purpose of subsection (1) if apart from that subsection he would be entitled to do or permit the act in question.

(3) Subsection (1) does not apply to an act for the execution—

(a) of works authorised by planning permission granted or deemed to be granted in pursuance of an application under the principal Act; or

(b) of works for which listed building consent has been given under this Act.

(4) If a person convicted of an offence under this section fails to take such reasonable steps as may be necessary to prevent any damage or further damage resulting from the offence, he shall be guilty of a further offence and liable on summary conviction to a fine not exceeding [one-tenth of level 3 on the standard scale] for each day on which the failure continues.   **[427]**

NOTES
Commencement: 24 August 1990.
Words in square brackets in sub-s (4) substituted by the Planning and Compensation Act 1991, s 32, Sch 7, para 58.
The principal Act: Town and Country Planning Act 1990.

Exceptions for church buildings and ancient monuments

60. Exceptions for ecclesiastical buildings and redundant churches

(1) The provisions mentioned in subsection (2) shall not apply to any ecclesiastical building which is for the time being used for ecclesiastical purposes.

(2) Those provisions are sections 3, 4, 7 to 9, 47, 54 and 59.

(3) For the purposes of subsection (1), a building used or available for use by a minister of religion wholly or mainly as a residence from which to perform the duties of his office shall be treated as not being an ecclesiastical building.

(4) For the purposes of sections 7 to 9, a building shall be taken to be used for the time being for ecclesiastical purposes if it would be so used but for the works in question.

(5) The Secretary of State may by order provide for restricting or excluding the operation of subsections (1) to (3) in such cases as may be specified in the order.

(6) An order under this section may—

(a) make provision for buildings generally, for descriptions of buildings or for particular buildings;

(b) make different provision for buildings in different areas, for buildings of different religious faiths or denominations or according to the use made of the building;

(c) make such provision in relation to a part of a building (including, in particular, an object or structure falling to be treated as part of the building by virtue of section 1(5)) as may be made in relation to a building and make different provision for different parts of the same building;

(d) make different provision with respect to works of different descriptions or according to the extent of the works;

(e) make such consequential adaptations or modifications of the operation of any other provision of this Act or the principal Act, or of any instrument made under either of those Acts, as appear to the Secretary of State to be appropriate.

(7) Sections 7 to 9 shall not apply to the execution of works for the demolition, in pursuance of a pastoral or redundancy scheme (within the meaning of the Pastoral Measure 1983), of a redundant building (within the meaning of that Measure) or a part of such a building.   **[428]**

NOTES
   Commencement: 24 August 1990.
   The principal Act: Town and Country Planning Act 1990.

61. Exceptions for ancient monuments etc

(1) The provisions mentioned in subsection (2) shall not apply to any building for the time being included in the schedule of monuments compiled and maintained under section 1 of the Ancient Monuments and Archaeological Areas Act 1979.

(2) Those provisions are sections 3, 4, 7 to 9, 47, 54 and 59.   **[429]**

NOTES
   Commencement: 24 August 1990.

CHAPTER VI

MISCELLANEOUS AND SUPPLEMENTAL

Validity of instruments, decisions and proceedings

62. Validity of certain orders and decisions

(1) Except as provided by section 63, the validity of—

(a) any order under section 23 or 26 (whether before or after it has been confirmed); or

(b) any such decision by the Secretary of State as is mentioned in subsection (2),

shall not be questioned in any legal proceedings whatsoever.

(2) Those decisions are—

(a) any decision on an application referred to the Secretary of State under section 12 or on an appeal under section 20;

(b) any decision to confirm or not to confirm a listed building purchase notice including—

(i) any decision not to confirm such a notice in respect of part of the land to which it relates, and

(ii) any decision to grant any consent, or give any direction, in lieu of confirming such a notice, either wholly or in part;

(c) any decision to grant listed building consent under paragraph (a) of section 41(6) or to discharge a condition or limitation under paragraph (b) of that section.

(3) Nothing in this section shall affect the exercise of any jurisdiction of any

court in respect of any refusal or failure on the part of the Secretary of State to take any such decision as is mentioned in subsection (2).   **[430]**

NOTES

Commencement: 24 August 1990.

63. Proceedings for questioning validity of other orders, decisions and directions

(1) If any person is aggrieved by any such order or decision as is mentioned in section 62(1) and wishes to question its validity on the grounds—

(a) that it is not within the powers of this Act, or

(b) that any of the relevant requirements have not been complied with in relation to it,

he may make an application to the High Court under this section.

(2) Without prejudice to subsection (1), if the authority directly concerned with any such order or decision wish to question its validity on any of those grounds, the authority may make an application to the High Court under this section.

(3) An application under this section must be made within six weeks from the date on which the order is confirmed (or, in the case of an order under section 23 which takes effect under section 25 without confirmation, the date on which it takes effect) or, as the case may be, the date on which the action is taken.

(4) On any application under this section the High Court—

(a) may by interim order suspend the operation of the order or decision, the validity of which is questioned by the application, until the final determination of the proceedings; and

(b) if satisfied—

(i) that the order or decision is not within the powers of this Act, or

(ii) that the interests of the applicant have been substantially prejudiced by a failure to comply with any of the relevant requirements in relation to it,

may quash that order or decision.

(5) References in this section to the confirmation of an order include the confirmation of an order subject to modifications.

(6) In this section ''the relevant requirements'', in relation to any order or decision, means any requirements of this Act or of the Tribunals and Inquiries Act [1992] or of any order, regulations or rules made under either of those Acts which are applicable to that order or decision.

(7) For the purposes of subsection (2) the authority directly concerned with an order or decision is—

(a) in relation to any such decision as is mentioned in section 62(2)(b)—

(i) the council on whom the listed building purchase notice was served, and

(ii) in a case where the Secretary of State has modified the notice wholly or in part by substituting another local authority or statutory undertakers for that council, also that authority or those statutory undertakers; and

(b) otherwise, the authority who—

    (i) made the order or decision to which the proceedings in question relate, or

    (ii) referred the matter to the Secretary of State, or

    (iii) if the order was made by him, are the authority named in it.   **[431]**

NOTES
    Commencement: 24 August 1990.
    Figure in square brackets in sub-s (6) substituted by the Tribunals and Inquiries Act 1992, s 18(1), Sch 3, para 31.

64. Validity of listed building enforcement notices

The validity of a listed building enforcement notice shall not, except by way of an appeal under section 39, be questioned in any proceedings whatsoever on any of the grounds on which such an appeal may be brought.   **[432]**

NOTES
    Commencement: 24 August 1990.

65. Appeals to High Court relating to listed building enforcement notices

(1) Where the Secretary of State gives a decision in proceedings on an appeal under section 39 against a listed building enforcement notice, the appellant or the local planning authority or any other person having an interest in the land to which the notice relates may, according as rules of court may provide, either appeal to the High Court against the decision on a point of law or require the Secretary of State to state and sign a case for the opinion of the High Court.

(2) At any stage of the proceedings on any such appeal, the Secretary of State may state any question of law arising in the course of the proceedings in the form of a special case for the decision of the High Court.

(3) A decision of the High Court on a case stated by virtue of subsection (2) shall be deemed to be a judgment of the court within the meaning of section 16 of the Supreme Court Act 1981 (jurisdiction of the Court of Appeal to hear and determine appeals from any judgment of the High Court).

[(3A) In proceedings brought by virtue of this section, the High Court or, as the case may be, the Court of Appeal may, on such terms, if any, as the Court thinks fit (which may include terms requiring the local planning authority to give an undertaking as to damages or any other matter), order that the listed building enforcement notice shall have effect, or have effect to such extent as may be specified in the order, pending the final determination of those proceedings and any re-hearing and determination by the Secretary of State.]

(4) In relation to any proceedings in the High Court or the Court of Appeal brought by virtue of this section the power to make rules of court shall include power to make rules—

    (a) prescribing the powers of the High Court or the Court of Appeal with respect to the remitting of the matter with the opinion or direction of the court for re-hearing and determination by the Secretary of State; and

    (b) providing for the Secretary of State, either generally or in such circumstances as may be prescribed by the rules, to be treated as a party to any such proceedings and to be entitled to appear and to be heard accordingly.

[(5) No proceedings in the High Court shall be brought by virtue of this section except with the leave of that Court and no appeal to the Court of Appeal shall be so brought except with the leave of the Court of Appeal or of the High Court.]

(6) In this section "decision" includes a direction or order, and references to the giving of a decision shall be construed accordingly.

(7) In the case of a listed building enforcement notice issued by the Commission subsection (1) shall apply as if the reference to the local planning authority were a reference to the Commission.   **[433]**

NOTES
    Commencement: 24 August 1990 (sub-ss (1)–(3), (4), (6), (7)); 2 January 1992 (sub-ss (3A), (5)).
    Sub-s (3A) inserted, and sub-s (5) substituted, by the Planning and Compensation Act 1991, s 25, Sch 3, Pt I, para 8.

Special considerations affecting planning functions

66. General duty as respects listed buildings in exercise of planning functions

(1) In considering whether to grant planning permission for development which affects a listed building or its setting, the local planning authority or, as the case may be, the Secretary of State shall have special regard to the desirability of preserving the building or its setting or any features of special architectural or historic interest which it possesses.

(2) Without prejudice to section 72, in the exercise of the powers of appropriation, disposal and development (including redevelopment) conferred by the provisions of sections 232, 233 and 235(1) of the principal Act, a local authority shall have regard to the desirability of preserving features of special architectural or historic interest, and in particular, listed buildings.

(3) The reference in subsection (2) to a local authority includes a reference to a joint planning board *and a board reconstituted in pursuance of Schedule 17 to the Local Government Act 1972.*   **[434]**

NOTES
    Commencement: 24 August 1990.
    Words in italics in sub-s (3) repealed by the Environment Act 1995, s 120(3), Sch 24, as from a day to be appointed under s 125(3).
    Modification: the reference to a local authority in sub-s (2) is to include a reference to a National Park authority, by virtue of the Environment Act 1995, s 65(7), Sch 8, para 2(4).
    The principal Act: Town and Country Planning Act 1990.

67. Publicity for applications affecting setting of listed buildings

(1) This section applies where an application for planning permission for any development of land is made to a local planning authority and the development would, in the opinion of the authority, affect the setting of a listed building.

(2) The local planning authority shall—

(a) publish in a local newspaper circulating in the locality in which the land is situated; and

(b) for not less than seven days display on or near the land,

a notice indicating the nature of the development in question and naming a place within the locality where a copy of the application, and of all plans and other documents submitted with it, will be open to inspection by the public at all reasonable hours during the period of 21 days beginning with the date of publication of the notice under paragraph (a).

(3) In a case where the land is situated in England, the local planning authority shall send a copy of the notice to the Commission.

(4) Where the Secretary of State, after consulting with the Commission, notifies a local planning authority in writing that subsection (3) shall not affect the authority as regards any notice relating to any kind of application specified in the notification, then that subsection shall not affect the authority as regards any such notice.

(5) The Secretary of State shall send the Commission a copy of any notification made under subsection (4).

(6) The application shall not be determined by the local planning authority before—

   (a) the expiry of the period of 21 days referred to in subsection (2); or
   (b) if later, the expiry of the period of 21 days beginning with the date on which the notice required by that subsection to be displayed was first displayed.

(7) In determining any application for planning permission to which this section applies, the local planning authority shall take into account any representations relating to the application which are received by them before the periods mentioned in subsection (6) have elapsed.

[(8) In this section references to planning permission do not include references to planning permissions falling within section 73A of the principal Act.]   **[435]**

NOTES
   Commencement: 24 August 1990 (sub-ss (1)–(7)); 2 January 1992 (sub-s (8)).
   Sub-s (8) substituted by the Planning and Compensation Act 1991, s 32, Sch 7, para 59.
   The principal Act: Town and Country Planning Act 1990.

68. Reference to Commission of planning applications involving listed buildings in Greater London

(1) Without prejudice to his powers by virtue of section 74(1) of the principal Act, the Secretary of State may by regulations provide for any application for planning permission to which this section applies to be referred to the Commission before it is dealt with by the local planning authority.

(2) This section applies to an application for planning permission for any development in Greater London which would, in the opinion of the local planning authority to which the application is made, involve the demolition, in whole or in part, or a material alteration, of a listed building.

(3) Regulations under this section may—

   (a) provide for the Commission to give the referring authority directions as to the manner in which an application is to be dealt with; and
   (b) provide that an application which satisfies such conditions as may be specified in the regulations need not be referred to the Commission. **[436]**

NOTES
   Commencement: 24 August 1990.
   The principal Act: Town and Country Planning Act 1990.

PART II

CONSERVATION AREAS

Designation

69. Designation of conservation areas

(1) Every local planning authority—

    (a) shall from time to time determine which parts of their area are areas of special architectural or historic interest the character or appearance of which it is desirable to preserve or enhance, and

    (b) shall designate those areas as conservation areas.

(2) It shall be the duty of a local planning authority from time to time to review the past exercise of functions under this section and to determine whether any parts or any further parts of their area should be designated as conservation areas; and, if they so determine, they shall designate those parts accordingly.

(3) The Secretary of State may from time to time determine that any part of a local planning authority's area which is not for the time being designated as a conservation area is an area of special architectural or historic interest the character or appearance of which it is desirable to preserve or enhance; and, if he so determines, he may designate that part as a conservation area.

(4) The designation of any area as a conservation area shall be a local land charge.   **[437]**

NOTES
    Commencement: 24 August 1990.

70. Designation of conservation areas: supplementary provisions

(1) The functions of a local planning authority under section 69 and this section shall also be exercisable in Greater London by the Commission.

(2) Before making a determination under section 69 the Commission shall consult the council of each London borough of which any part is included in the area to which the proposed determination relates.

(3) Before making a determination under section 69(3) the Secretary of State shall consult the local planning authority.

(4) Before designating any area in Greater London as a conservation area the Commission shall obtain the consent of the Secretary of State.

(5) A local planning authority shall give notice of the designation of any part of their area as a conservation area under section 69(1) or (2) and of any variation or cancellation of any such designation—

    (a) to the Secretary of State; and

    (b) if it affects an area in England and the designation or, as the case may be, the variation or cancellation was not made by the Commission, to the Commission.

(6) The Secretary of State shall give notice of the designation of any part of the area of a local planning authority as a conservation area under section 69(3) and of any variation or cancellation of any such designation—

    (a) to the authority; and

(b) if it affects an area in England, to the Commission.

(7) A notice under subsection (5) or (6) shall contain sufficient particulars to identify the area affected.

(8) Notice of any such designation, variation or cancellation as is mentioned in subsection (5) or (6), with particulars of its effect, shall be published in the London Gazette and in at least one newspaper circulating in the area of the local planning authority, by that authority or, as the case may be, the Secretary of State.   **[438]**

NOTES
Commencement: 24 August 1990.

General duties of planning authorities

71. Formulation and publication of proposals for preservation and enhancement of conservation areas

(1) It shall be the duty of a local planning authority from time to time to formulate and publish proposals for the preservation and enhancement of any parts of their area which are conservation areas.

(2) Proposals under this section shall be submitted for consideration to a public meeting in the area to which they relate.

(3) The local planning authority shall have regard to any views concerning the proposals expressed by persons attending the meeting.   **[439]**

NOTES
Commencement: 24 August 1990.

72. General duty as respects conservation areas in exercise of planning functions

(1) In the exercise, with respect to any buildings or other land in a conservation area, of any [functions under or by virtue of] any of the provisions mentioned in subsection (2), special attention shall be paid to the desirability of preserving or enhancing the character or appearance of that area.

(2) The provisions referred to in subsection (1) are the planning Acts and Part I of the Historic Buildings and Ancient Monuments Act 1953 [and sections 70 and 73 of the Leasehold Reform, Housing and Urban Development Act 1993].   **[440]**

NOTES
Commencement: 24 August 1990.
Words in square brackets in sub-ss (1), (2) substituted and added respectively by the Leasehold Reform, Housing and Urban Development Act 1993, s 187(1), Sch 21, para 30.
The planning Acts: Town and Country Planning Act 1990, Planning (Hazardous Substances) Act 1990, Planning (Consequential Provisions) Act 1990 and this Act.

73. Publicity for applications affecting conservation areas

(1) Where an application for planning permission for any development of land is made to a local planning authority and the development would, in the opinion of the authority, affect the character or appearance of a conservation area, subsections (2) to (7) of section 67 shall apply as they apply in the circumstances mentioned in subsection (1) of that section.

[(2) In this section references to planning permission do not include references to planning permissions falling within section 73A of the principal Act.]   **[441]**

NOTES
Commencement: 24 August 1990 (sub-s (1)); 2 January 1992 (sub-s (2)).
Sub-s (2) substituted by the Planning and Compensation Act 1991, s 32, Sch 7, para 60.
The principal Act: Town and Country Planning Act 1990.

Control of demolition

74. Control of demolition in conservation areas

(1) A building in a conservation area shall not be demolished without the consent of the appropriate authority (in this Act referred to as "conservation area consent").

(2) The appropriate authority for the purposes of this section is—

(a) in relation to applications for consent made by local planning authorities, the Secretary of State; and

(b) in relation to other applications for consent, the local planning authority or the Secretary of State.

(3) Sections 7 to 26, 28, 32 to 46, 56, 62 to 65, 66(1), 82(2) to (4), 83(1)(b), (3) and (4) and 90(2) to (4) have effect in relation to buildings in conservation areas as they have effect in relation to listed buildings subject to such exceptions and modifications as may be prescribed by regulations.

(4) Any such regulations may make different provision—

(a) in relation to applications made by local planning authorities, and

(b) in relation to other applications.   **[442]**

NOTES
Commencement: 24 August 1990.

75. Cases in which s 74 does not apply

(1) Section 74 does not apply to—

(a) listed buildings;

(b) ecclesiastical buildings which are for the time being used for ecclesiastical purposes;

(c) buildings for the time being included in the schedule of monuments compiled and maintained under section 1 of the Ancient Monuments and Archaeological Areas Act 1979; or

(d) buildings in relation to which a direction under subsection (2) is for the time being in force.

(2) The Secretary of State may direct that section 74 shall not apply to any description of buildings specified in the direction.

(3) A direction under subsection (2) may be given either to an individual local planning authority exercising functions under that section or to local planning authorities generally.

(4) The Secretary of State may vary or revoke a direction under subsection (2) by a further direction under that subsection.

(5) For the purposes of subsection (1)(b), a building used or available for use by a minister of religion wholly or mainly as a residence from which to perform the duties of his office shall be treated as not being an ecclesiastical building.

(6) For the purposes of sections 7 to 9 as they apply by virtue of section 74(3) a building shall be taken to be used for the time being for ecclesiastical purposes if it would be so used but for the works in question.

(7) The Secretary of State may by order provide for restricting or excluding the operation of subsection (1)(b) in such cases as may be specified in the order.

(8) An order under subsection (7) may—

(a) make provision for buildings generally, for descriptions of buildings or for particular buildings;

(b) make different provision for buildings in different areas, for buildings of different religious faiths or denominations or according to the use made of the building;

(c) make such provision in relation to a part of a building (including, in particular, an object or structure falling to be treated as part of the building by virtue of section 1(5)) as may be made in relation to a building and make different provision for different parts of the same building;

(d) make different provision with respect to works of different descriptions or according to the extent of the works;

(e) make such consequential adaptations or modifications of the operation of any other provision of this Act or the principal Act, or of any instrument made under either of those Acts, as appear to the Secretary of State to be appropriate.

(9) Regulations under this Act may provide that subsections (5) to (8) shall have effect subject to such exceptions and modifications as may be prescribed, and any such regulations may make different provision—

(a) in relation to applications made by local planning authorities, and

(b) in relation to other applications.

(10) Any proceedings on or arising out of an application for conservation area consent made while section 74 applies to a building shall lapse if it ceases to apply to it, and any such consent granted with respect to the building shall also lapse.

(11) The fact that that section has ceased to apply to a building shall not affect the liability of any person to be prosecuted and punished for an offence under section 9 or 43 committed with respect to the building while that section did apply to it.

[443]

NOTES
Commencement: 24 August 1990.
The principal Act: Town and Country Planning Act 1990.

76. Urgent works to preserve unoccupied buildings in conservation areas

(1) If it appears to the Secretary of State that the preservation of a building in a conservation area is important for maintaining the character or appearance of that area, he may direct that section 54 shall apply to it as it applies to listed buildings.

(2) The Secretary of State shall consult the Commission before giving a direction under subsection (1) in respect of a building in England.   **[444]**

NOTES
Commencement: 24 August 1990.

Grants

77. Grants and loans for preservation or enhancement of conservation areas

(1) If in the opinion of the Commission any relevant expenditure has made or will make a significant contribution towards the preservation or enhancement of the character or appearance of any conservation area situated in England or any part of

such an area, they may make grants or loans for the purposes of defraying the whole or part of that expenditure.

(2) If in the opinion of the Secretary of State any relevant expenditure has made or will make a significant contribution towards the preservation or enhancement of the character or appearance of any conservation area situated in Wales or any part of such an area, he may make grants or loans for the purposes of defraying the whole or part of that expenditure.

(3) Expenditure is relevant for the purposes of subsection (1) or (2) if it has been or is to be incurred in or in connection with, or with a view to the promotion of, such preservation or enhancement as is mentioned in that subsection.

(4) A grant or loan under this section may be made subject to such conditions as the Commission or, as the case may be, the Secretary of State may think fit to impose.

(5) Any loan under subsection (1) shall be made on such terms as to repayment, payment of interest and otherwise as the Commission may determine.

(6) Any loan under subsection (2) shall be made on such terms as to repayment, payment of interest and otherwise as the Secretary of State may with the approval of the Treasury determine.

(7) Unless the making of a grant or loan under this section appears to the Secretary of State to be a matter of immediate urgency, before making the grant or loan, the Secretary of State shall consult the Historic Buildings Council for Wales as to its making and the conditions subject to which it should be made.

(8) The Secretary of State may pay such remuneration and allowances as he may with the approval of the Treasury determine to any member of the Historic Buildings Council for Wales by whom services are rendered in connection with any question as to the exercise of his powers under this section.

(9) If any such member is also a member of the House of Commons, those payments shall extend only to allowances in respect of travelling and subsistence expenses, and any other expenses necessarily incurred by him in connection with those services.   **[445]**

NOTES

Commencement: 24 August 1990.

78. Recovery of grants under s 77

(1) This section applies to any grant under section 77 made on terms that it shall be recoverable under this section.

(2) A grant shall only be regarded as made on those terms if before or on making the grant the grantor gives the grantee notice in writing—

    (a) summarising the effect of this section; and
    (b) if the grant is made for the purpose of defraying the whole or part of expenditure in relation to any particular property ("the grant property"), specifying the recovery period.

(3) In this section "the recovery period" means the period, beginning with the day on which the grant is made and ending not more than ten years after that day, during which the grant is to be recoverable in accordance with subsection (4).

(4) If during the recovery period the grantee disposes of the interest which was

held by him in the grant property on the day on which the grant was made or any part of that interest by way of sale or exchange or lease for a term of not less than 21 years, the grantor may recover the amount of the grant, or such part of it as the grantor thinks fit, from the grantee.

(5) If the grantee gives the whole of that interest to any person (whether directly or indirectly, but otherwise than by will) subsection (4) shall have effect as if the donee were the grantee.

(6) If the grantee gives part of that interest to any person (whether directly or indirectly, but otherwise than by will) subsection (4) shall have effect as if any disposal or part disposal of that interest by the donee were a disposal by the grantee.

(7) If any condition imposed on the making of a grant to which this section applies is contravened or not complied with, the grantor may recover the amount of the grant, or such part of it as he thinks fit, from the grantee.

(8) Nothing in this section entitles a grantor to recover amounts in the aggregate exceeding the amount of the grant (for example by virtue of a breach of more than one condition or disposals of several parts of an interest in the grant property). **[446]**

NOTES
    Commencement: 24 August 1990.
    See further, in respect of sums recovered before the commencement of this Act: the Planning (Consequential Provisions) Act 1990, ss 3-5, Sch 3, para 17 at **[511]**–**[513]**, **[520]**.

Town schemes

79. Town scheme agreements

(1) The Commission and one or more local authorities in England, or the Secretary of State and one or more local authorities in Wales, may enter an agreement (in this Act referred to as a "town scheme agreement") that a specified sum of money shall be set aside for a specified period of years for the purpose of making grants for the repair of buildings which are—

- (a) included in a list compiled for the purposes of such an agreement by the parties to the agreement, or by them and other such authorities, or
- (b) shown on a map prepared for those purposes by the parties, or by them and such other authorities.

(2) Before such a list is compiled or such a map is prepared by the Secretary of State and any local authorities as respects any buildings in Wales they shall consult the Historic Buildings Council for Wales.

(3) In this section "local authority" means—

- (a) a county council;
- [(aa) a county borough council;]
- (b) a district council;
- (c) in relation to any building situated within the Broads, the Broads Authority;
- [(ca) in relation to any building in a National Park for which a National Park authority is the local planning authority, that authority;]
- (d) a London borough council or the Common Council of the City of London;
- (e) the Council of the Isles of Scilly. **[447]**

NOTES
    Commencement: 24 August 1990.
    Sub-s (3)(aa) inserted by the Local Government (Wales) Act 1994, s 20(4)(b), Sch 6, Pt II, para 25(9), as from a day to be appointed.

Sub-s (3)(ca) inserted by the Environment Act 1995, s 78, Sch 10, para 33(3), as from a day to be appointed under s 120(3).

80. Grants for repairing of buildings in town schemes

(1) The Commission may make grants for the purpose of defraying the whole or part of any expenditure incurred or to be incurred in the repair of any building which—

    (a) is the subject of a town scheme agreement;
    (b) is situated in a conservation area in England; and
    (c) appears to the Commission to be of architectural or historic interest.

(2) The Secretary of State may make grants for the purpose of defraying the whole or part of any expenditure incurred or to be incurred in the repair of any building which—

    (a) is the subject of a town scheme agreement;
    (b) is situated in a conservation area in Wales; and
    (c) appears to him to be of architectural or historic interest.

(3) A grant under this section may be made subject to conditions imposed by the Commission or, as the case may be, the Secretary of State for such purposes as the Commission or, as the case may be, the Secretary of State thinks fit.

(4) Unless the making of a grant under this section appears to the Secretary of State to be a matter of immediate urgency, before he makes such a grant he may consult with the Historic Buildings Council for Wales as to the making of the grant and as to the conditions subject to which it should be made.

(5) The Commission or the Secretary of State may—

    (a) pay any grant under this section to any authority which is a party to a town scheme agreement; and
    (b) make arrangements with any such authority for the way in which the agreement is to be carried out.

(6) Those arrangements may include such arrangements for the offer and payment of grants under this section as the parties may agree.

(7) Section 78(4) to (8) shall apply to a grant under this section as it applies to a grant under that section, but taking the recovery period to be three years beginning with the day on which the grant is made.   **[448]**

NOTES
   Commencement: 24 August 1990.

PART III

GENERAL

Authorities exercising functions under Act

81. Authorities exercising functions under Act

In this Act "local planning authority" shall be construed in accordance with Part I of the principal Act and Schedule 4 to this Act (which makes further provision as to the exercise of functions under this Act).   **[449]**

NOTES
   Commencement: 24 August 1990.
   The principal Act: Town and Country Planning Act 1990.

Special cases

82. Application of Act to land and works of local planning authorities

(1) In relation to land of a local planning authority, section 1(1), (2) and (4) and sections 2, [and 39(6)] [41(8)] ... shall have effect subject to such exceptions and modifications as may be prescribed.

(2) The provisions mentioned in subsection (3) shall have effect for the purpose of applications by local planning authorities relating to the execution of works for the demolition, alteration or extension of listed buildings, subject to such exceptions and modifications as may be prescribed.

(3) Those provisions are sections 1(3), (5) and (6), 3 to 5, 7 to 29, 32 to 50 (except [section 39(6)], 60(1) to (4) (as it applies as respects the provisions mentioned in this subsection), 62 to 65, 67(2)(b), (6) and (7), 73(1), Schedules 1 and 2, paragraph 2 of Schedule 4 (as it applies to Schedule 1) and paragraph 4(1) of Schedule 4 (as it applies as respects the provisions mentioned in this subsection).

(4) Regulations under this section may in particular provide—

    (a) for the making of applications for listed building consent to the Secretary of State; and

    (b) for the issue or service by him of notices under section 2(3) and the provisions mentioned in subsection (3).   **[450]**

NOTES

Commencement: 24 August 1990.

Words in the first pair of square brackets and words omitted from sub-s (1), and words in square brackets in sub-s (3), substituted or repealed by the Planning and Compensation Act 1991, s 25, Sch 3, Pt II, para 24.

Sub-s (1): figure in second pair of square brackets temporarily added by the Planning (Consequential Provisions) Act 1990, s 6, Sch 4, paras 1, 10, until such day as may be appointed by order made by the Secretary of State. The Planning (Consequential Provisions) Act 1990 (Appointed Day No 1 and Transitional Provisions) Order 1991, SI 1991/2698, appointed 2 January 1992 only for the purposes of awards of costs in relation to proceedings which give rise to a hearing.

83. Exercise of powers in relation to Crown land

(1) Notwithstanding any interest of the Crown in Crown land, but subject to the following provisions of this section—

    (a) a building which for the time being is Crown land may be included in a list compiled or approved by the Secretary of State under section 1;

    (b) any restrictions imposed or powers conferred by sections 1 to 26, 32 to 46, 54 to 56, 59 to 61, 66(1), 67, 68, 73 or 76 or Schedule 1, 2 or 3 shall apply and be exercisable in relation to Crown land to the extent of any interest in it for the time being held otherwise than by or on behalf of the Crown;

    (c) any power to acquire land compulsorily under section 47 may be exercised in relation to any interest in the land which is for the time being held otherwise than by or on behalf of the Crown.

(2) Except with the consent of the appropriate authority—

    (a) no notice shall be issued or served under section 38 in relation to land which for the time being is Crown land;

    (b) no interest in land which for the time being is Crown land shall be acquired compulsorily under section 47.

(3) No listed building enforcement notice shall be issued in respect of works

executed by or on behalf of the Crown in respect of a building which was Crown land at the time when the works were executed.

(4) No listed building purchase notice shall be served in relation to any interest in Crown land unless—

    (a) an offer has been previously made by the owner of that interest to dispose of it to the appropriate authority on terms that the price payable for it—

        (i) shall be equal to the compensation which would be payable in respect of it if it were acquired in pursuance of such a notice, or

        (ii) in default of agreement, shall be determined in a similar manner to that in which that compensation would be determined; and

    (b) that offer has been refused by the appropriate authority.

(5) In this section—

"Crown land" means land in which there is a Crown interest or a Duchy interest;

"Crown interest" means an interest belonging to Her Majesty in right of the Crown, or belonging to a government department, or held in trust for Her Majesty for the purposes of a government department;

"Duchy interest" means an interest belonging to Her Majesty in right of the Duchy of Lancaster or belonging to the Duchy of Cornwall.

(6) A person who is entitled to occupy Crown land by virtue of a licence in writing shall be treated as having an interest in land for the purposes of subsection (1)(b) so far as applicable to sections 1 to 26, 38 to 46, 54 to 56, 59 to 61, 66(1), 67, 68, 73 and 76 and Schedule 1, 2 or 3.

(7) For the purposes of this section "the appropriate authority", in relation to any land—

    (a) in relation to land belonging to Her Majesty in right of the Crown and forming part of the Crown Estate, means the Crown Estate Commissioners;

    (b) in relation to any other land belonging to Her Majesty in right of the Crown, means the government department having the management of that land;

    (c) in relation to land belonging to Her Majesty in right of the Duchy of Lancaster, means the Chancellor of the Duchy;

    (d) in relation to land belonging to the Duchy of Cornwall, means such person as the Duke of Cornwall or the possessor for the time being of the Duchy of Cornwall appoints;

    (e) in the case of land belonging to a government department or held in trust for Her Majesty for the purposes of a government department, means that department.

(8) If any question arises as to what authority is the appropriate authority in relation to any land, that question shall be referred to the Treasury, whose decision shall be final. **[451]**

NOTES
    Commencement: 24 August 1990.

84. Application for listed building or conservation area consent in anticipation of disposal of Crown land

(1) This section has effect for the purpose of enabling Crown land, or an interest in Crown land, to be disposed of with the benefit of listed building consent or conservation area consent.

(2) Notwithstanding the interest of the Crown in the land in question, an application for any such consent may be made—

    (a) by the appropriate authority; or

    (b) by any person authorised by that authority in writing;

and, subject to subsections (3) and (4), all the statutory provisions relating to the making and determination of any such application shall accordingly apply as if the land were not Crown land.

(3) Any listed building consent or conservation area consent granted by virtue of this section shall apply only—

    (a) to works carried out after the land in question has ceased to be Crown land; and

    (b) so long as that land continues to be Crown land, to works carried out by virtue of a private interest in the land.

(4) The Secretary of State may by regulations—

    (a) modify or exclude any of the statutory provisions referred to in subsection (2) in their application by virtue of that subsection and any other statutory provisions in their application to consents granted or made by virtue of this section;

    (b) make provision for requiring a local planning authority to be notified of any disposal of, or of an interest in, any Crown land in respect of which an application has been made by virtue of this section; and

    (c) make such other provision in relation to the making and determination of applications by virtue of this section as he thinks necessary or expedient.

(5) This section shall not be construed as affecting any right to apply for any listed building consent or conservation area consent in respect of Crown land in a case in which such an application can be made by virtue of a private interest in the land.

(6) In this section—

    "statutory provisions" means provisions contained in or having effect under any enactment;

    "private interest" means an interest which is neither a Crown interest nor a Duchy interest;

and references to the disposal of an interest in Crown land include references to the grant of an interest in such land.

(7) Subsections (5), (7) and (8) of section 83 apply for the purposes of this section as they apply for the purposes of that section.

(8) A person who is entitled to occupy Crown land by virtue of a licence in writing shall be treated for the purposes of this section as having an interest in land and references to the disposal or grant of an interest in Crown land and to a private interest in such land shall be construed accordingly. **[452–453]**

NOTES
Commencement: 24 August 1990.

85. *(Repealed by the Coal Industry Act 1994, s 67(1), (8), Sch 9, para 40, Sch 11, Pt II.)*

86. Ecclesiastical property

(1) Without prejudice to the provisions of the Acquisition of Land Act 1981 with respect to notices served under that Act, where under any of the provisions of this Act a notice or copy of a notice is required to be served on an owner of land, and the land is ecclesiastical property, a similar notice or copy of a notice shall be served on the Church Commissioners.

(2) Where the fee simple of any ecclesiastical property is in abeyance—

- (a) if the property is situated in England, then for the purposes of section 11, this subsection (other than paragraph (b)) and sections 62, 63 and 83(1) and any other provisions of this Act so far as they apply or have effect for the purposes of any of those provisions, the fee simple shall be treated as being vested in the Church Commissioners;
- (b) in any case, the fee simple shall, for the purposes of a compulsory acquisition of the property under section 47, be treated as being vested in the Church Commissioners, and any notice to treat shall be served, or be deemed to have been served, accordingly.

(3) Any compensation payable under section 29 in respect of land which is ecclesiastical property—

- (a) shall [in the case of land which is not diocesan glebe land, be paid to the Church Commissioners; and
- (b) shall, in the case of diocesan glebe land, be paid to the Diocesan Board of Finance in which the land is vested,

and shall (in either case)] be applied by them for the purposes for which the proceeds of a sale by agreement of the land would be applicable under any enactment or Measure authorising or disposing of the proceeds of such a sale.

(4) In this section "ecclesiastical property" means land belonging to an ecclesiastical benefice, or being or forming part of a church subject to the jurisdiction of a bishop of any diocese or the site of such a church, or being or forming part of a burial ground subject to such jurisdiction [or being diocesan glebe land; and "Diocesan Board of Finance" and "diocesan glebe land" have the same meaning as in the Endowments and Glebe Measure 1976].   **[454]**

NOTES

Commencement: 24 August 1990.

Words in square brackets in sub-ss (3), (4) substituted by the Planning and Compensation Act 1991, s 70, Sch 15, Pt II, para 31.

87. Settled land

The classes of works specified in Part II of Schedule 3 to the Settled Land Act 1925 (which specifies improvements which may be paid for out of capital money, subject to provisions under which repayment out of income may be required to be made) shall include works specified by the Secretary of State as being required for properly maintaining a listed building which is settled land within the meaning of that Act.   **[455]**

NOTES

Commencement: 24 August 1990.

Miscellaneous provisions

88. Rights of entry

(1) Any person duly authorised in writing by the Secretary of State may at any reasonable time enter any land for the purpose of surveying any building on it [or

any other land] in connection with a proposal to include the building in, or exclude it from, a list compiled or approved under section 1.

(2) Any person duly authorised in writing by the Secretary of State, a local planning authority or, where the authorisation relates to a building situated in Greater London, the Commission may at any reasonable time enter any land for any of the following purposes—

(a) surveying it [or any other land] in connection with any proposal by the authority or the Secretary of State to make, issue or serve any order or notice under any of the provisions of sections 1 to 26, 38, 40, 46, 54, 55, 60, 68, 75 or 76 or under any order or regulations made under any of them, or any notice under section 48;

(b) ascertaining whether any such order or notice has been complied with [in relation to the land or any other land];

(c) ascertaining whether an offence has been, or is being, committed with respect to any building on the land [or any other land], under section 9, 11 or 43;

(d) ascertaining whether any [building on the land or any other land] is being maintained in a proper state of repair.

(3) Any person duly authorised in writing by the Secretary of State, a local authority or, where the authorisation relates to a building situated in Greater London, the Commission may at any reasonable time enter any land for any of the following purposes—

(a) ascertaining whether an offence has been or is being committed under section 59 [in relation to the land or any other land];

(b) ascertaining whether any of the functions conferred by section 54 should or may be exercised in connection with the land [or any other land]; or

(c) exercising any of those functions in connection with the land [or any other land].

(4) Any person who is an officer of the Valuation Office or is duly authorised in writing by a local planning authority may at any reasonable time enter any land for the purpose of surveying it, or estimating its value, in connection with a claim for compensation payable by the authority under section . . . 28 or 29 in respect of any land.

(5) Any person who is an officer of the Valuation Office or is duly authorised in writing by a local authority having power to acquire land under sections 47 to 52 may at any reasonable time enter any land for the purpose of surveying it, or estimating its value, in connection with any proposal to acquire that land or any other land or in connection with any claim for compensation in respect of any such acquisition.

(6) Subject to [section 88B(8)], any power conferred by this section to survey land shall be construed as including power to search and bore for the purpose of ascertaining the nature of the subsoil . . .

(7) . . .   **[456]**

NOTES
Commencement: 24 August 1990.
Words in square brackets in sub-ss (1)–(3), (6) inserted or substituted, words omitted from sub-ss (4), (6) repealed, and sub-s (7) substituted as noted to s 88A at **[456A]**, by the Planning and Compensation Act 1991, ss 25, 31(4), 84(6), Sch 3, Pt I, para 9, Pt II, para 25, Sch 6, para 46, Sch 19, Pts I, II.
Modification: see the note to s 47 at **[415]**. In relation to the powers conferred on a National Park authority by virtue of the Environment Act 1995, Sch 9, para 13 (see the notes to ss 47, 52, 53 and 54 at

[415], [420], [421] and [422]), this section has effect as if references to a local authority included references to a National Park authority, by virtue of s 70 of, and Sch 9, para 13(5) to, the 1995 Act.

[88A. Warrants to enter land

(1) If it is shown to the satisfaction of a justice of the peace on sworn information in writing—

    (a) that there are reasonable grounds for entering any land for any of the purposes mentioned in section 88; and

    (b) that—

        (i) admission to the land has been refused, or a refusal is reasonably apprehended; or

        (ii) the case is one of urgency,

the justice may issue a warrant authorising any person duly authorised in writing by the appropriate authority to enter the land.

(2) In subsection (1) ''the appropriate authority'' means the person who may authorise entry on the land under section 88 for the purpose in question.

(3) For the purposes of subsection (1)(b)(i) admission to land shall be regarded as having been refused if no reply is received to a request for admission within a reasonable period.

(4) A warrant authorises entry on one occasion only and that entry must be—

    (a) within one month from the date of the issue of the warrant; and

    (b) at a reasonable hour, unless the case is one of urgency.]   **[456A]**

NOTES
    Commencement: 2 January 1992.
    This section and s 88B at **[456B]** substituted for s 88(7) by the Planning and Compensation Act 1991, s 25, Sch 3, Pt I, para 9(2).

[88B. Rights of entry: supplementary provisions

(1) A person authorised under section 88 to enter any land shall not demand admission as of right to any land which is occupied unless twenty-four hours notice of the intended entry has been given to the occupier.

(2) A person authorised to enter land in pursuance of a right of entry conferred under or by virtue of section 88 or 88A (referred to in this section as ''a right of entry'')—

    (a) shall, if so required, produce evidence of his authority and state the purpose of his entry before so entering;

    (b) may take with him such other persons as may be necessary; and

    (c) on leaving the land shall, if the owner or occupier is not then present, leave it as effectively secured against trespassers as he found it.

(3) Any person who wilfully obstructs a person acting in the exercise of a right of entry shall be guilty of an offence and liable on summary conviction to a fine not exceeding level 3 on the standard scale.

(4) If any person who enters any land, in exercise of a right of entry, discloses to any person any information obtained by him while on the land as to any manufacturing process or trade secret, he shall be guilty of an offence.

(5) Subsection (4) does not apply if the disclosure is made by a person in the course of performing his duty in connection with the purpose for which he was authorised to enter the land.

(6) A person who is guilty of an offence under subsection (4) shall be liable—

(a) on summary conviction to a fine not exceeding the statutory maximum, or

(b) on conviction on indictment to imprisonment for a term not exceeding two years or a fine or both.

(7) If any damage is caused to land or chattels in the exercise of—

(a) a right of entry; or

(b) a power conferred by virtue of section 88(6) in connection with such a right,

compensation may be recovered by any person suffering the damage from the authority who gave the written authority for the entry or, as the case may be, the Secretary of State; and section 118 of the principal Act shall apply in relation to compensation under this subsection as it applies in relation to compensation under Part IV of that Act.

(8) No person shall carry out any works in exercise of a power conferred under section 88 unless notice of his intention to do so was included in the notice required by subsection (1).

(9) The authority of the appropriate Minister shall be required for the carrying out of works in exercise of a power conferred under section 88 if—

(a) the land in question is held by statutory undertakers; and

(b) they object to the proposed works on the ground that the execution of the works would be seriously detrimental to the carrying on of their undertaking.

(10) Section 265(1) and (3) of the principal Act (meaning of "appropriate Minister") applies for the purposes of subsection (9) as it applies for the purposes of section 325(9) of the principal Act.]   **[456B]**

NOTES
Commencement: 2 January 1992.
Substituted as noted to s 88A at **[456A]**.
The principal Act: Town and Country Planning Act 1990.

89. Application of certain general provisions of principal Act

(1) Subject to subsection (2), the following provisions of the principal Act shall apply for the purposes of this Act as they apply for the purposes of that Act, namely—

section 320 (local inquiries),
section 322 (orders as to costs of parties where no inquiry held),
[322A (orders as to costs: supplementary)]
section 323 (procedure on certain appeals and applications),
section 329 (service of notices),
section 330 (power to require information as to interests in land),
section 331 (offences by corporations).

(2) Section 331 of that Act shall not apply to offences under section 59 of this Act.

[(3) In the application of section 330 by virtue of this section, references to a local authority include the Commission.]   **[457]**

NOTES
Commencement: 24 August 1990 (sub-ss (1), (2)); 25 September 1991 (sub-s (3)).
Words in square brackets in sub-s (1) inserted, and sub-s (3) added, by the Planning and Compensation Act 1991, ss 29(2), 30(2).

Sub-s (1): words in italics temporarily omitted by the Planning (Consequential Provisions) Act 1990, s 6, Sch 4, paras 1, 11, until such day as may be appointed by order made by the Secretary of State. The Planning (Consequential Provisions) Act 1990 (Appointed Day No 1 and Transitional Provisions) Order 1991, SI 1991/2698, appointed 2 January 1992 only for the purposes of awards of costs in relation to proceedings which give rise to a hearing.
The principal Act: Town and Country Planning Act 1990.

90. Financial provisions

(1) Where—

- (a) compensation is payable by a local authority under this Act in consequence of any decision or order given or made under Chapters I, II or IV of Part I or sections 32 to 37, 60 or Schedule 3; and
- (b) the decision or order in consequence of which it is payable was given or made wholly or partly in the interest of a service which is provided by a government department and the cost of which is defrayed out of money provided by Parliament,

the Minister responsible for the administration of that service may pay that authority a contribution of such amount as he may with the consent of the Treasury determine.

(2) Any local authority and any statutory undertakers may contribute towards any expenses incurred by a local planning authority in or in connection with the performance of any of their functions under the provisions of Chapters I to V of Part I (other than sections [28] to 31, 53, 54, 55, 57, 58) and sections 66 and 68 and Schedule 1.

(3) Where any expenses are incurred by a local authority in the payment of compensation payable in consequence of anything done under Chapters I, II or IV of Part I or sections 32 to 37, 56, 59, 60, 66(1), 67, 68 or 73, the Secretary of State may, if it appears to him to be expedient to do so, require any other local authority to contribute towards those expenses such sum as appears to him to be reasonable, having regard to any benefit accruing to that authority by reason of the proceeding giving rise to the compensation.

(4) For the purposes of subsections (2) and (3), contributions made by a local planning authority towards the expenditure of a joint advisory committee shall be deemed to be expenses incurred by that authority for the purposes for which that expenditure is incurred by the committee.

(5) The council of a county may direct that any expenses incurred by them under the provisions specified in subsection (6) shall be treated as special expenses of a county council chargeable upon such part of the county as may be specified in the directions.

(6) Those provisions are—

- (a) sections 1(1) to (5), 2(1) to (3), [41(8)] 51, 52, 64, 65, 66(2), 82(1) and (4)(b), 83, 86 (except subsection (2)(a)), 87, 88 (except subsection (3)) and subsections (1) to (4) of this section and any other provisions of the planning Acts in so far as they apply, or have effect for the purposes of, any of those provisions; and
- (b) sections 1(6), 3, 4, 5, 7 to 29, 32 to 50 (except 39(6) . . .), 60(1) to (4), 61, 66(1), 67(2)(b), (6) and (7), 73(1) (so far as it applies to section 67(2)(b), (6) and (7)), 82(2), (3) and (4)(a) and Schedules 1, 2 and 3.

(7) There shall be paid out of money provided by Parliament—

- (a) any sums necessary to enable the Secretary of State to make any payments becoming payable by him under sections [28 or] 29;

(b) any expenses incurred by any government department (including the Secretary of State) in the acquisition of land under sections 47 to 52 or in the payment of compensation under section 51(4) or 88(7) or under subsection (1);

(c) any administrative expenses incurred by the Secretary of State for the purposes of this Act.

(8) Any sums received by the Secretary of State under this Act shall be paid into the Consolidated Fund. **[458]**

NOTES

Commencement: 24 August 1990.

Words in square brackets in sub-ss (2), (7)(a) substituted, and words omitted from sub-s (6)(b) repealed, by the Planning and Compensation Act 1991, ss 25, 31(4), 84(6), Sch 3, Pt II, para 26, Sch 6, para 47, Sch 19, Pt I.

Sub-s (6): figure in square brackets temporarily added by the Planning (Consequential Provisions) Act 1990, s 6, Sch 4, paras 1, 10, until such day as may be appointed by order made by the Secretary of State. The Planning (Consequential Provisions) Act 1990 (Appointed Day No 1 and Transitional Provisions) Order 1991, SI 1991/2698, appointed 2 January 1992 only for the purposes of the awards of costs in relation to proceedings which give rise to a hearing.

Modification: references to a local authority in sub-ss (1) to (4) above are deemed to include references to a National Park authority, by virtue of the Environment Act 1995, s 70, Sch 9, para 13(6).

The planning Acts: Town and Country Planning Act 1990, Planning (Hazardous Substances) Act 1990, Planning (Consequential Provisions) Act 1990 and this Act.

PART IV

SUPPLEMENTAL

91. Interpretation

(1) In this Act, except in so far as the context otherwise requires—

"building preservation notice" has the meaning given in section 3(1);

"the Commission" means the Historic Buildings and Monuments Commission for England;

"conservation area" means an area for the time being designated under section 69;

"conservation area consent" has the meaning given in section 74(1);

"listed building" has the meaning given in section 1(5);

"listed building consent" has the meaning given in section 8(7);

"listed building enforcement notice" has the meaning given in section 38(1);

"listed building purchase notice" has the meaning given in section 32(1);

"local planning authority" shall be construed in accordance with section 81;

"prescribed", except in relation to matters expressly required or authorised by this Act to be prescribed in some other way, means prescribed by regulations under this Act;

"the principal Act" means the Town and Country Planning Act 1990;

"town scheme agreement" has the meaning given in section 79.

(2) Subject to subsections (6) and (7) and except in so far as the context otherwise requires, the following expressions have the same meaning as in the principal Act—

"the 1962 Act"

"acquiring authority"

"the Broads"

"building"

"compulsory acquisition"

"development"

"development order"

"development plan"
"disposal"
"enactment"
"functions"
"government department"
"joint planning board"
"land"
"lease"
"local authority"
"London borough"
"minerals"
"Minister"
...
"owner"
"the planning Acts"
"planning permission"
"public gas supplier"
"use"
"Valuation Office",

but this subsection does not affect the meaning of "owner" in section 11.

(3) In this Act "statutory undertakers" has the same meaning as in the principal Act except that—

    (a) in sections 33 to 36 it shall be deemed to include references to a public telecommunications operator;

    (b) in sections 33 to 36, 51(2)(a) and 90(2) it shall be deemed to include the Post Office, the Civil Aviation Authority, a public gas supplier, a holder of a licence under section 6 of the Electricity Act 1989, the National Rivers Authority and every water or sewerage undertaker.

(4) References in the planning Acts to any of the provisions mentioned in section 82 include, except where the context otherwise requires, references to those provisions as modified under that section.

(5) Words in this Act importing a reference to service of a notice to treat shall be construed as including a reference to the constructive service of such a notice which, by virtue of any enactment, is to be deemed to be served.

(6) In sections 33 to 36, 53(1), 54, 55 and 88(3) "local authority", in relation to a building or land in the Broads, includes the Broads Authority.

(7) For the purposes of subsection (1)(b) of section 57 and subsection (2) of that section as it applies for the purposes of that subsection the definition of "building" in the principal Act shall apply with the omission of the words "but does not include any plant or machinery comprised in a building".   **[459]**

NOTES
    Commencement: 24 August 1990.
    Words omitted from sub-s (2) repealed by Planning and Compensation Act 1991, ss 31(4), 84(6), Sch 6, para 48, Sch 19, Pt II.

92. Application of Act to Isles of Scilly

(1) The Secretary of State shall, after consultation with the Council of the Isles of Scilly, by order provide for the application to those Isles of the provisions of this Act specified in subsection (2) as if those Isles were a separate county.

(2) The provisions referred to in subsection (1) are—

  (a) sections 1(1) to (5), 2(1) to (3), [41(8)], 51, 52, 64, 65, 66(2), 82(1) and (4)(b), 83, 84, 86 (except subsection (2)(a)), 87, 88 (except subsection (3)), 90(1) to (4) and any other provisions of the planning Acts in so far as they apply, or have effect for the purposes of, any of those provisions; and

  (b) sections 1(6), 3, 4, 5, 7 to 29, 32 to 50 (except 39(6) . . .), 60(1) to (4), 61, 66(1), 67(2)(b), (6) and (7), 73(1) (so far as it applies to section 67(2)(b), (6) and (7)), 75(1), (5) and (6), 82(2), (3) and (4)(a) and Schedules 1, 2 and 3.

(3) The Secretary of State, may, after consultation with the Council of the Isles of Scilly, by order provide for the application to those Isles of sections 2(4) and (5), 53 to 55, 59, 67(1) to (6), 69 to 72, 73(1), 74 to 76 and 88(3) and paragraph 4 of Schedule 4 as if those Isles were a separate county or district.

(4) Any order under this section may provide for the application of provisions to the Isles subject to such modifications as may be specified in the order.   **[460]**

NOTES
Commencement: 24 August 1990.
Sub-s (2): in para (a) figure in square brackets temporarily added by the Planning (Consequential Provisions) Act 1990, s 6, Sch 4, paras 1, 10, until such day as may be appointed by the Secretary of State. The Planning (Consequential Provisions) Act 1990 (Appointed Day No 1 and Transitional Provisions) Order 1991, SI 1991/2698, appointed 2 January 1992 only for the purposes of awards of costs in relation to proceedings which give rise to a hearing.
Words omitted from sub-s (2)(b) repealed by the Planning and Compensation Act 1991, ss 25, 84(6), Sch 3, Pt II, para 27, Sch 19, Pt I.
The planning Acts: Town and Country Planning Act 1990, Planning (Hazardous Substances) Act 1990, Planning (Consequential Provisions) Act 1990 and this Act.

93. Regulations and orders

(1) The Secretary of State may make regulations under this Act—

  (a) for prescribing the form of any notice, order or other document authorised or required by any of the provisions of this Act to be served, made or issued by any local authority [or National Park authority];

  (b) for any purpose for which regulations are authorised or required to be made under this Act.

(2) Any power conferred by this Act to make regulations shall be exercisable by statutory instrument.

(3) Any statutory instrument containing regulations made under this Act shall be subject to annulment in pursuance of a resolution of either House of Parliament.

(4) The power to make orders under sections 8(5), 60, 75(7) and 92 shall be exercisable by statutory instrument.

(5) Any statutory instrument which contains an order under section 60 or 75(7) shall be subject to annulment in pursuance of a resolution of either House of Parliament.

(6) Any order under section 60 or 75(7) may contain such supplementary and incidental provisions as may appear to the Secretary of State appropriate.

(7) Without prejudice to section 14 of the Interpretation Act 1978, any power conferred by this Act to make an order shall include power to vary or revoke any such order by a subsequent order.   **[461]**

NOTES
Commencement: 24 August 1990.
Words in square brackets in sub-s (1)(a) inserted by the Environment Act 1995, s 78, Sch 10, para 33(4), as from a day to be appointed under s 125(3).

94. Short title, commencement and extent

(1) This Act may be cited as the Planning (Listed Buildings and Conservation Areas) Act 1990.

(2) Except as provided in Schedule 4 to the Planning (Consequential Provisions) Act 1990, this Act shall come into force at the end of the period of three months beginning with the day on which it is passed.

(3) This Act extends to England and Wales only.

(4) Nothing in this Act shall impose any charge on the people or on public funds, or vary the amount or incidence of or otherwise alter any such charge in any manner, or affect the assessment, levying, administration or application of any money raised by any such charge. **[462]**

NOTES
Commencement: 24 August 1990.

SCHEDULES

SCHEDULE 1

Section 1(6)

BUILDINGS FORMERLY SUBJECT TO BUILDING PRESERVATION ORDERS

1. Subject to paragraph 2, every building which immediately before 1st January 1969 was subject to a building preservation order under Part III of the 1962 Act, but was not then included in a list compiled or approved under section 32 of that Act, shall be deemed to be a listed building.

2.—(1) The Secretary of State may at any time direct, in the case of any building, that paragraph 1 shall no longer apply to it.

(2) The local planning authority in whose area a building in respect of which such a direction is given is situated shall, on being notified of the direction, give notice of it to the owner and occupier of the building.

(3) Before giving such a direction in relation to a building situated in England, the Secretary of State shall consult with the Commission who shall in turn consult with the local planning authority and the owner and the occupier of the building.

(4) Before giving such a direction in relation to a building not situated in England, the Secretary of State shall consult with the local planning authority and the owner and occupier of the building.

3. In the case of a building to which paragraph 1 applies—

   (a) a notice of appeal under section 20 may include a claim that the Secretary of State should give a direction under paragraph 2 with respect to the building and on such an appeal the Secretary of State may give such a direction; and
   (b) such a direction may also be given on an appeal under section 39. **[463]**

NOTES
Commencement: 24 August 1990.
The 1962 Act: Town and Country Planning Act 1962.

SCHEDULE 2

Section 5

Lapse of Building Preservation Notices

1. This Schedule applies where a building preservation notice ceases to be in force by virtue of—

    (a) the expiry of the six month period mentioned in subsection (3)(b) of section 3; or

    (b) the service of a notification by the Secretary of State under subsection (4)(b) of that section.

2. The fact that the notice has ceased to be in force shall not affect the liability of any person to be prosecuted and punished for an offence under section 9 or 43 committed with respect to the building while it was in force.

3. Any proceedings on or arising out of an application for listed building consent with respect to the building made while the notice was in force and any such consent granted while it was in force shall lapse.

4.—(1) Any listed building enforcement notice served by the local planning authority while the building preservation notice was in force shall cease to have effect.

(2) Any proceedings on it under sections 38 to 40 shall lapse.

(3) Notwithstanding sub-paragraph (1), section 42(1) and (2) shall continue to have effect as respects any expenses incurred by the local authority, owner or occupier as mentioned in that section and with respect to any sums paid on account of such expenses.

[(4) The reference to a local authority in sub-paragraph (3) above includes a reference to any National Park authority which is the local planning authority for any area.]   **[464]**

NOTES

    Commencement: 24 August 1990.

    Para 4(4) inserted by the Environment Act 1995, s 78, Sch 10, para 33(5), as from a day to be appointed under s 125(3).

SCHEDULE 3

Sections 22, 40

Determination of Certain Appeals by Person Appointed by Secretary of State

Determination of appeals by appointed person

1.—(1) The Secretary of State may by regulations prescribe the classes of appeals under sections 20 and 39 which are to be determined by a person appointed by the Secretary of State for the purpose instead of by the Secretary of State.

(2) Appeals of a prescribed class shall be so determined except in such classes of case as may for the time being be prescribed or as may be specified in directions given by the Secretary of State.

(3) Regulations made for the purpose of this paragraph may provide for the giving of publicity to any directions given by the Secretary of State under this paragraph.

(4) This paragraph shall not affect any provision in this Act or any instrument made under it that an appeal shall lie to, or a notice of appeal shall be served on, the Secretary of State.

(5) A person appointed under this paragraph is referred to in this Schedule as ''an appointed person''.

Powers and duties of appointed person

2.—(1) An appointed person shall have the same powers and duties—

    (a) in relation to an appeal under section 20, as the Secretary of State has under subsection (1) of section 22 and paragraph 2 of Schedule 1; and

    (b) in relation to an appeal under section 39, as he has under section 41(1), (2) [2A], (5) or (6) and paragraph 2 of Schedule 1.

(2) Sections 22(2) and 40(2) shall not apply to an appeal which falls to be determined by an appointed person, but before it is determined the Secretary of State shall ask the appellant and the local planning authority whether they wish to appear before and be heard by the appointed person.

(3) If both the parties express a wish not to appear and be heard the appeal may be determined without their being heard.

(4) If either of the parties expresses a wish to appear and be heard, the appointed person shall give them both an opportunity of doing so.

(5) Where an appeal has been determined by an appointed person, his decision shall be treated as that of the Secretary of State.

(6) Except as provided by sections 62 to 65, the validity of that decision shall not be questioned in any proceedings whatsoever.

(7) It shall not be a ground of application to the High Court under section 63, or of appeal to the High Court under section 65, that an appeal ought to have been determined by the Secretary of State and not by an appointed person, unless the appellant or the local planning authority challenge the appointed person's power to determine the appeal before his decision on the appeal is given.

(8) Where in any enactment (including this Act) there is a reference to the Secretary of State in a context relating or capable of relating—

    (a) to an appeal under section 20 or 39, or
    (b) to anything done or authorised or required to be done by, to or before the Secretary of State on or in connection with any such appeal,

then so far as the context permits it shall be construed, in relation to an appeal determined or falling to be determined by an appointed person, as a reference to him.

Determination of appeals by Secretary of State

3.—(1) The Secretary of State may, if he thinks fit, direct that an appeal which would otherwise fall to be determined by an appointed person shall instead be determined by the Secretary of State.

(2) Such a direction shall state the reasons for which it is given and shall be served on the appellant, the local planning authority, any person who made representations relating to the subject matter of the appeal which the authority were required to take into account by regulations made under section 11(4) and, if any person has been appointed under paragraph 1, on him.

(3) Where in consequence of such a direction an appeal under section 20 or 39 falls to be determined by the Secretary of State himself, the provisions of this Act which are relevant to the appeal shall, subject to the following provisions of this paragraph, apply to the appeal as if this Schedule had never applied to it.

(4) The Secretary of State shall give the appellant, the local planning authority and any person who has made such representations as are referred to in sub-paragraph (2) an opportunity of appearing before and being heard by a person appointed by the Secretary of State for that purpose if—

    (a) the reasons for the direction raise matters with respect to which any of those persons have not made representations; or
    (b) in the case of the appellant and the local planning authority, either of them was not asked in pursuance of paragraph 2(2) whether they wished to appear before and be heard by the appointed person, or expressed no wish in answer to that question, or expressed a wish to appear and be heard but was not given an opportunity of doing so.

(5) Except as provided by sub-paragraph (4), the Secretary of State need not give any person an opportunity of appearing before and being heard by a person appointed for the purpose, or of making fresh representations or making or withdrawing any representations already made.

(6) In determining the appeal the Secretary of State may take into account any report made to him by any person previously appointed to determine it.

4.—(1) The Secretary of State may by a further direction revoke a direction under paragraph 3 at any time before the determination of the appeal.

(2) Such a further direction shall state the reasons for which it is given and shall be served on the person, if any, previously appointed to determine the appeal, the appellant, the local planning authority and any person who made representations relating to the subject matter of the appeal which the authority were required to take into account by regulations made under section 11(4).

(3) Where such a further direction has been given the provisions of this Schedule relevant to the appeal shall apply, subject to sub-paragraph (4), as if no direction under paragraph 3 had been given.

(4) Anything done by or on behalf of the Secretary of State in connection with the appeal which might have been done by the appointed person (including any arrangements made for the holding of a hearing or local inquiry) shall unless that person directs otherwise, be treated as having been done by him.

Appointment of another person to determine appeal

5.—(1) At any time before the appointed person has determined the appeal the Secretary of State may—

(a) revoke his appointment; and
(b) appoint another person under paragraph 1 to determine the appeal instead.

(2) Where such a new appointment is made the consideration of the appeal or any inquiry or other hearing in connection with it shall be begun afresh.

(3) Nothing in sub-paragraph (2) shall require—

(a) the question referred to in paragraph 2(2) to be asked again with reference to the new appointed person if before his appointment it was asked with reference to the previous appointed person (any answers being treated as given with reference to the new appointed person); or
(b) any person to be given an opportunity of making fresh representations or modifying or withdrawing any representations already made.

Local inquiries and hearings

6.—(1) Whether or not the parties to an appeal have asked for an opportunity to appear and be heard, an appointed person—

(a) may hold a local inquiry in connection with the appeal; and
(b) shall do so if the Secretary of State so directs.

(2) Where an appointed person—

(a) holds a hearing by virtue of paragraph 2(4); or
(b) holds an inquiry by virtue of this paragraph,

an assessor may be appointed by the Secretary of State to sit with the appointed person at the hearing or inquiry to advise him on any matters arising, notwithstanding that the appointed person is to determine the appeal.

(3) Subject to sub-paragraph (4), the costs of any such hearing or inquiry shall be paid by the Secretary of State.

(4) Section 250(2) to (5) of the Local Government Act 1972 (local inquiries: evidence and costs) applies to an inquiry held by virtue of this paragraph with the following adaptations—

(a) for the references in subsection (4) (recovery of costs of holding the inquiry) to the Minister causing the inquiry to be held, there shall be substituted references to the Secretary of State; and

(b) for the reference in subsection (5) (orders as to the costs of the parties) to the Minister causing the inquiry to be held, there shall be substituted a reference to the appointed person or the Secretary of State.

(5) Subject to sub-paragraph (6), at any such inquiry oral evidence shall be heard in public and documentary evidence shall be open to public inspection.

(6) If the Secretary of State is satisfied in the case of any such inquiry—

(a) that giving evidence of a particular description or, as the case may be, making it available for inspection would be likely to result in the disclosure of information as to any of the matters mentioned in sub-paragraph (7); and

(b) that the public disclosure of that information would be contrary to the national interest,

he may direct that evidence of the description indicated in the direction shall only be heard or, as the case may be, open to inspection at that inquiry by such persons or persons of such descriptions as he may specify in that direction.

(7) The matters referred to in sub-paragraph (6)(a) are—

(a) national security; and

(b) the measures taken or to be taken to ensure the security of any premises or property.

(8) *The appointed person or the Secretary of State has the same power to make orders under section 250(5) of the Local Government Act 1972 (orders with respect to costs of the parties) in relation to proceedings under this Schedule which do not give rise to an inquiry as he has in relation to such an inquiry.*

Supplementary provisions

7.—(1) The Tribunals and Inquiries Act [1992] shall apply to a local inquiry or other hearing held in pursuance of this Schedule as it applies to a statutory inquiry held by the Secretary of State, but as if in [section 10(1)] of that Act (statement of reasons for decisions) the reference to any decision taken by the Secretary of State were a reference to a decision taken by an appointed person.

(2) Where an appointed person is an officer of the Department of the Environment or the Welsh Office the functions of determining an appeal and doing anything in connection with it conferred on him by this Schedule shall be treated for the purposes of the Parliamentary Commissioner Act 1967—

(a) if he was appointed by the Secretary of State for the time being having general responsibility in planning matters in relation to England, as functions of that Department; and

(b) if he was appointed by the Secretary of State for the time being having general responsibility in planning matters in relation to Wales, as functions of the Welsh Office.   **[465]**

NOTES
Commencement: 24 August 1990.
Figure in square brackets in para 2(1)(b) inserted by the Planning and Compensation Act 1991, s 25, Sch 3, Pt II, para 28.
Para 6: sub-para (8) temporarily omitted by the Planning (Consequential Provisions) Act 1990, s 6, Sch 4, paras 1, 12, until such day as may be appointed by order made by the Secretary of State. The Planning (Consequential Provisions) Act 1990 (Appointed Day No 1 and, Transitional Provisions) Order 1991, SI 1991/2698, appointed 2 January 1991 only for the purposes of awards of costs in relation to proceedings which give rise to a hearing.
Words in square brackets in para 7(1) substituted by the Tribunals and Inquiries Act 1992, s 18(1), Sch 3, para 32.

SCHEDULE 4
Section 81

FURTHER PROVISIONS AS TO EXERCISE OF FUNCTIONS BY DIFFERENT AUTHORITIES

1.[—(1)] Subsection (3) of section 1 of the principal Act (which provides that outside London, the metropolitan counties and the Isles of Scilly planning functions are exercisable by both county and district planning authorities) shall have effect subject to paragraphs 2, 4, and 5, and that section and section 2 of the principal Act (joint planning boards) shall have effect subject to paragraph 3.

[(2) This Schedule shall apply in relation to Wales as if—

(a) paragraphs 2 to 5 were omitted;

(b) in paragraph 7, each reference to a district planning authority (or which is to be construed as such a reference) were a reference to the local planning authority.]

2. Subject to sections *4* [4A], 6, 7 [8 and 8A] of the principal Act (which make provision as to the exercise of planning functions in National Parks, enterprise zones, urban development areas and housing action areas) and to the following provisions, outside Greater London the functions of a local planning authority under sections 7 to 26, 38, 42, paragraph 2(2) of Schedule 1 and Schedule 2 shall be exercised by the district planning authority.

[3. Where an application for listed building consent under section 10 relating to land in a National Park falls to be determined by a [National Park authority *or*] *county planning authority*, that authority—

(a) shall send a copy of the application, as soon as practicable and in any event not later than seven days after they have received it, to [any authority which (but for section 4A) would be *or, as the case may be, which is*] the district planning authority for the area in which the land to which the application relates is situated; and

(b) shall before determining the application consult *the district planning* authority.]

4.—(1) Subject to sections *4(3) and (4)*, 6, 7 [8 and 8A] of the principal Act, the functions of a local planning authority under sections 67(2) and (3), 69, 70 and 74 and paragraph 2(3) and (4) of Schedule 1 shall be exercisable—

(a) in Greater London or a metropolitan county [or in any National Park for which a National Park authority is the local planning authority], by the local planning authority;

(b) in any part of a National Park *outside a metropolitan county*, by the county planning authority; and

(c) elsewhere, by the district planning authority;

but outside a National Park a county planning authority shall also have power to make determinations and designations under section 69.

(2) Before making a determination under section 69 a county planning authority [or National Park authority] shall consult the council of each district of which any part is included in the area to which the proposed determination relates.

(3) Where it is the duty of the district planning authority to take the steps required by section 67(2) in relation to an application which falls to be determined by the county planning authority, the district planning authority shall as soon as possible after taking those steps notify the county planning authority of the steps which they have taken and the date on which they took them.

5. For the purposes of sections 3 and 4, 7 to 26, 38, 42, 56, 66(1), 67, 69 to 75, 82, 84 and 88(2)(c) and (d) and the provisions of this Schedule so far as they relate to those provisions, the Broads Authority shall be the sole district planning authority in respect of the Broads, and in relation to a building or land within the Broads—

(a) the references to the district planning authority in section 2(1)(b)(iii) and in paragraph 4(1)(c) of this Schedule, so far as that paragraph relates to paragraph 2(3) and (4) of Schedule 1, include that Authority; and

(b) for the purposes of sections 6 [44A, 88(2)(a) and (b) and 88A] "local planning authority" includes that Authority.

6. The validity of any consent or determination granted or made or purported to be granted or made by a local planning authority in respect of an application for listed building consent or conservation area consent shall not be called in question in any legal proceedings, or in any proceedings under this Act which are not legal proceedings, on the ground that the consent or determination should have been granted or made by some other local planning authority.

7.—(1) The Secretary of State may from time to time direct a district planning authority to submit to him for his approval within a period specified in the direction the arrangements which the authority propose to make to obtain specialist advice in connection with their functions under sections 3, 4, 8, 10 to 26, 38, 42, 66(1), 69 to 72, 74 and 75.

(2) If the Secretary of State is not satisfied about any such arrangements he may direct the district planning authority and another local planning authority specified in the direction—

    (a) to enter into an agreement under section 113 of the Local Government Act 1972 for the placing at the disposal of the district planning authority, for the purpose of giving them any such specialist advice, of the services of officers employed by that other authority who are qualified to give such advice; or

    (b) to enter into arrangements, containing terms specified in the direction or terms on lines laid down by him, for the discharge by that other authority of any of those functions.

(3) Before giving a direction under sub-paragraph (2) the Secretary of State shall consult with the district planning authority and the other authority concerned.   **[466]**

NOTES

Commencement: 24 August 1990 (paras 1, 2, 4–7); 2 January 1992 (para 3).

Provisions of para 1 numbered para 1(1) and para 1(2) added by the Local Government (Wales) Act 1994, s 20(4)(b), Sch 6, Pt II, para 25(10), as from a day to be appointed.

Figure in italics in para 2 repealed and first figure in square brackets therein inserted, words in square brackets in para 3 inserted, first and second words in italics therein repealed and words "any such" substituted for third words in italics therein, and words in italics in para 4(1) repealed, words in square brackets in para 4(1)(a) and 4(2) inserted, and words "to which paragraph (a) above does not apply" substituted for words in italics in para 4(1)(b), by the Environment Act 1995, ss 78, 120(3), Sch 10, para 33(6), (7), (8), Sch 24, as from a day or days to be appointed under s 125(3).

Second words in square brackets in para 2 and words in square brackets at beginning of para 4(1) substituted by the Leasehold Reform, Housing and Urban Development Act 1993, s 187(1), Sch 21, para 31.

Para 3, and words in square brackets in para 5(b), substituted by the Planning and Compensation Act 1991, ss 25, 32, Sch 3, Pt II, para 29, Sch 7, para 61.

The principal Act: Town and Country Planning Act 1990.

PLANNING (HAZARDOUS SUBSTANCES) ACT 1990
(c 10)

ARRANGEMENT OF SECTIONS

An Act to consolidate certain enactments relating to special controls in respect of hazardous substances with amendments to give effect to recommendations of the Law Commission   [24 May 1990]

Hazardous substances authorities

1. Hazardous substances authorities: general

The council of the district [, Welsh county, county borough] or London borough in which land is situated shall be the hazardous substances authority in relation to the land except in cases where section . . . 3 applies.   **[467–468]**

NOTES
Commencement: Whole Act brought into force as follows—

11 March 1992 (so far as provisions of this Act confer on the Secretary of State a power or impose
on him a duty to make regulations, or make provision with respect to the exercise of any such
power or duty, for the purpose only of enabling or requiring the Secretary of State to make
regulations;
1 June 1992 (for all remaining purposes).
Words in square brackets inserted by the Local Government (Wales) Act 1994, s 20(4)(b), Sch 6,
Pt II, para 26(1), as from a day to be appointed.
Words omitted repealed by the Environmental Protection Act 1990, s 162(2), Sch 16, Pt VIII.
Hazardous substances authority: for the purposes of this Act, where a National Park authority is the
local planning authority for any National Park, that authority, and no other authority, is the hazardous
substances authority for land in the relevant Park; see the Environment Act 1995, s 70, Sch 9, para 14(1).

2. *(Repealed by the Environmental Protection Act 1990, ss 144, 162(2), Sch 13,
Pt I, paras 1, 2(1), Sch 16, Pt VII.)*

3. Hazardous substances authorities: other special cases

(1) The county council shall be the hazardous substances authority for land which is
in a non-metropolitan county [in England] and—

   (a) *is situated in a National Park;*
   (b) is used for the winning and working of minerals (including their extraction
   from a mineral-working deposit); or
   (c) is situated in England and used for the disposal of refuse or waste
   materials,

unless subsection (2) applies.

   (2) *If the land is in a National Park for which a joint planning board or special
planning board has been constituted, the board shall be the hazardous substances
authority for the land.*

   (3) The Broads Authority is the hazardous substances authority for the Broads
unless subsection (1) *or (2)* applies.

   (4) If the land is in an area for which an urban development corporation is the
local planning authority in relation to all kinds of development, the corporation shall
be the hazardous substances authority for the land unless subsection (1) *or (2)*
applies.

   (5) If the land is in an area for which a housing action trust established under
Part III of the Housing Act 1988 is the local planning authority in relation to all
kinds of development, the trust shall be the hazardous substances authority for the
land unless subsection (1) *or (2)* applies.

   [(5A) If the land is in an area for which the Urban Regeneration Agency is the
local planning authority in relation to all kinds of development, the Agency shall be
the hazardous substances authority for the land unless subsection (1) *or (2)* applies.]

(6) ...   **[469]**

NOTES
Commencement: 11 March 1992, 1 June 1992 (sub-ss (1)–(5)); see the note to s 1 at **[467–468]**;
10 November 1993 (sub-s (5A)).
Words in square brackets in sub-s (1) inserted by the Local Government (Wales) Act 1994, s 20(4)(b),
Sch 6, Pt II, para 26(2), as from a day to be appointed.
Sub-s (5A) inserted by the Leasehold Reform, Housing and Urban Development Act 1993, s 187(1),
Sch 21, para 32.
Sub-s (6) repealed by the Environmental Protection Act 1990, s 162(2), Sch 16, Pt VII.
Words in italics in this section repealed by the Environment Act 1995, s 120(3), Sch 24, as from a day
to be appointed under s 125(3).

Control over presence of hazardous substances

4. Requirement of hazardous substances consent

(1) Subject to the provisions of this Act, the presence of a hazardous substance on, over or under land requires the consent of the hazardous substances authority (in this Act referred to as "hazardous substances consent").

(2) Subsection (1) does not apply if the aggregate quantity of the substance—

(a) on, over or under the land;

(b) on, over or under other land which is within 500 metres of it and controlled by the same person; or

(c) in or on a structure controlled by the same person any part of which is within 500 metres of it,

is less than the quantity prescribed as the controlled quantity for that substance.

(3) The temporary presence of a hazardous substance while it is being transported from one place to another is not to be taken into account unless it is unloaded.

(4) The Secretary of State may by regulations provide that hazardous substances consent is not required or is only required—

(a) in relation to land of prescribed descriptions;

(b) by reason of the presence of hazardous substances in prescribed circumstances.

(5) Regulations under this section may make different provision for different cases or descriptions of cases.   **[470]**

NOTES
   Commencement: 11 March 1992, 1 June 1992; see the note to s 1 at **[467–468]**.

5. Power to prescribe hazardous substances

(1) For the purposes of this Act the Secretary of State—

(a) shall by regulations specify—

(i) the substances that are hazardous substances; and

(ii) the quantity which is to be the controlled quantity of any such substance; and

(b) may by regulations provide that, except in such circumstances as may be prescribed, all hazardous substances falling within a group specified in the regulations are to be treated as a single substance.

(2) Regulations which—

(a) are made by virtue of subsection (1)(a)(i); or

(b) are made by virtue of subsection (1)(a)(ii) and reduce the controlled quantity of a substance,

may make such transitional provision as appears to the Secretary of State to be appropriate.

(3) The power to make such transitional provision includes, without prejudice to its generality, power to apply sections 11 and 26 subject to such modifications as appear to the Secretary of State to be appropriate.

(4) Regulations under this section may make different provision for different cases or descriptions of cases.   **[471]**

NOTES
Commencement: 11 March 1992, 1 June 1992; see the note to s 1 at **[467–468]**.

Obtaining hazardous substances consent

6. Hazardous substances consent: general

(1) Hazardous substances consent—

(a) may be granted on an application under this Act, or

(b) may be deemed to have been granted by virtue of section 11 or 12.

(2) Without prejudice to the provisions of this Act, any hazardous substances consent shall (except in so far as it otherwise provides) enure for the benefit of the land to which it relates and of all persons for the time being interested in the land.

[472]

NOTES
Commencement: 11 March 1992, 1 June 1992; see the note to s 1 at **[467–468]**.

7. Applications for hazardous substances consent

(1) Provision may be made by regulations with respect to—

(a) the form and manner in which applications [under this Act] for hazardous substances consent are to be made;

(b) the particulars which they are to contain and the evidence by which they are to be verified;

(c) the manner in which they are to be advertised; and

(d) the time within which they are to be dealt with.

(2) Regulations—

(a) may require an applicant for hazardous substances consent or the hazardous substances authority or both to give publicity to an application for hazardous substances consent in such manner as may be prescribed;

(b) may require hazardous substances authorities to conduct appropriate consultations before determining applications for hazardous substances consent;

(c) may provide for the manner in which such a consultation is to be carried out and the time within which—

(i) such a consultation; or

(ii) any stage in such a consultation,

is to be completed;

(d) may require hazardous substances authorities to determine applications for hazardous substances consent within such time as may be prescribed;

(e) may require hazardous substances authorities to give prescribed persons or bodies prescribed information about applications for hazardous substances consent, including information as to the manner in which such applications have been dealt with.

(3) In subsection (2) above ''appropriate consultations'' [means consultations with the Health and Safety Executive and with] such persons or bodies as may be prescribed.

(4) Regulations under this section may make different provision for different cases or descriptions of cases.   **[473]**

NOTES
  Commencement: 11 March 1992, 1 June 1992; see the note to s 1 at **[467–468]**.
  Words in square brackets in sub-s (1)(a) inserted, and words in square brackets in sub-s (3) substituted, by the Environmental Protection Act 1990, s 144, Sch 13, Pt I, paras 1, 2(2), 3.

8. Certificates as to applicant's status etc

(1) Regulations under this Act may provide that an application for hazardous substances consent or an appeal against the refusal of such an application or against the imposition of a condition on such a consent shall not be entertained unless it is accompanied by one of the following certificates in the prescribed form and signed by or on behalf of the applicant—

   (a) a certificate stating that, at the beginning of the period of 21 days ending with the date of the application, no person (other than the applicant) was the owner of any of the land to which the application relates;

   (b) a certificate stating that the applicant has given the requisite notice of the application to all the persons (other than himself) who, at the beginning of that period, were owners of any of the land to which the application relates;

   (c) a certificate stating that—

       (i) the applicant is unable to issue a certificate in accordance with paragraph (a) or (b);

       (ii) he has given the requisite notice of the application to such one or more of the persons mentioned in paragraph (b) as are specified in the certificate;

       (iii) he has taken such steps as are reasonably open to him (specifying them) to ascertain the names and addresses of the remainder of those persons but has been unable to do so;

   (d) a certificate stating that—

       (i) the applicant is unable to issue a certificate in accordance with paragraph (a);

       (ii) he has taken such steps as are reasonably open to him (specifying them) to ascertain the names and addresses of the persons mentioned in paragraph (b) but has been unable to do so.

(2) Where such provision is made any such certificate as is mentioned in subsection (1)(b) or (c) must set out—

   (a) the names of those persons to whom the applicant has given the requisite notice of the application;

   (b) the addresses at which notice was given to them;

   (c) the date of service of each such notice.

(3) Such regulations may require that any such certificate as is mentioned in subsection (1)(c) or (d) shall also contain a statement that the requisite notice of the application, as set out in the certificate, has on a date specified in the certificate (which must not be earlier than the beginning of the period mentioned in subsection (1)(a)) been published in a local newspaper circulating in the locality in which the land in question is situated.

(4) Such regulations may also require that where an application is accompanied by such a certificate as is mentioned in subsection (1)(b), (c) or (d) the hazardous substances authority—

   (a) shall not determine the application before the end of the period of 21 days beginning with the date appearing from the certificate to be the latest of the dates of service of notices as mentioned in the certificate or, if later, the date of publication of a notice as so mentioned;

(b) in determining the application, shall take into account any representations relating to it which are made to them before the end of that period by any person who satisfies them that he is an owner of any land to which the application relates; and

(c) shall give notice of their decision to every person who has made representations which they were required to take into account in accordance with paragraph (b).

(5) Such regulations may also make provision as to who is to be treated as the owner of land for the purposes of any provisions of the regulations.

(6) If any person—

(a) issues a certificate which purports to comply with the requirements of regulations made by virtue of this section and contains a statement which he knows to be false or misleading in a material particular; or

(b) recklessly issues a certificate which purports to comply with those requirements and contains such a statement,

he shall be guilty of an offence and liable on summary conviction to a fine not exceeding level 3 on the standard scale.

(7) Regulations under this section may make different provision for different cases or descriptions of cases.

(8) Subject to subsection (5), in this section "owner", in relation to any land, means a person who is for the time being the estate owner in respect of the fee simple in the land or is entitled to a tenancy of the land granted or extended for a term of years certain, of which not less than seven years remain unexpired.   **[474]**

NOTES
Commencement: 11 March 1992, 1 June 1992; see the note to s 1 at **[467–468]**.

9. Determination of applications for hazardous substances consent

(1) Subject to the following provisions of this Act, where an application is made to a hazardous substances authority for hazardous substances consent, that authority—

(a) may grant hazardous substances consent, either unconditionally or subject to such conditions as they think fit; or

(b) may refuse hazardous substances consent.

(2) In dealing with such an application the hazardous substances authority shall have regard to any material considerations and, in particular, but without prejudice to the generality of the foregoing—

(a) to any current or contemplated use of the land to which the application relates;

(b) to the way in which land in the vicinity is being used or is likely to be used;

(c) to any planning permission that has been granted for development of land in the vicinity;

(d) to the provisions of the development plan; and

(e) to any advice which the Health and Safety Executive ... have given following consultations in pursuance of regulations under section 7(2).

(3) If an application relates to more than one hazardous substance, the authority may make different determinations in relation to each.

(4) It shall be the duty of a hazardous substances authority, when granting hazardous substances consent, to include in that consent—

(a) a description of the land to which the consent relates;

(b) a description of the hazardous substance or substances to which it relates; and

(c) in respect of each hazardous substance to which it relates, a statement of the maximum quantity allowed by the consent to be present at any one time.   **[475]**

NOTES

Commencement: 11 March 1992, 1 June 1992; see the note to s 1 at **[467–468]**.

Words omitted from sub-s (2)(e) repealed by the Environmental Protection Act 1990, s 162(2), Sch 16, Pt VII.

10. Power to impose conditions on grant of hazardous substances consent

(1) Without prejudice to the generality of section 9(1), a hazardous substances authority may make the grant of hazardous substances consent conditional on the commencement or partial or complete execution of development on the land which is authorised by a specified planning permission or may grant hazardous substances consent subject to conditions with respect to any of the following—

(a) how and where any hazardous substance to which the consent relates is to be kept or used;

(b) the times between which any such substance may be present;

(c) the permanent removal of any such substance—

(i) on or before a date specified in the consent; or

(ii) before the end of a period specified in it and commencing on the date on which it is granted.

(2) [A hazardous substances authority] may only grant consent subject to conditions as to how a hazardous substance is to be kept or used if the conditions are conditions to which the Health and Safety Executive have advised the authority that any consent they might grant should be subject.

(3) It shall be the duty of a hazardous substances authority when granting hazardous substances consent to include in that consent in respect of each hazardous substance to which it relates a statement of all conditions relating to that substance subject to which the consent is granted.   **[476]**

NOTES

Commencement: 11 March 1992, 1 June 1992; see the note to s 1 at **[467–468]**.

Words in square brackets in sub-s (2) substituted by the Environmental Protection Act 1990, s 144, Sch 13, Pt I, paras 1, 2(3).

11. Deemed hazardous substances consent: established presence

(1) Where a hazardous substance was present on, over or under any land at any time within the establishment period hazardous substances consent may be claimed in respect of its presence.

(2) A claim shall be made in the prescribed form before the end of the transitional period and shall contain the prescribed information as to the presence of the substance during the establishment period and as to how and where it was kept and used [while it was so present].

(3) Subject to subsections (4) to (6), the hazardous substances authority shall be deemed to have granted any hazardous substances consent which is claimed under subsection (1).

(4) If at the relevant date notification in respect of the substance was required by regulation 3 or 5 of the Notification Regulations, hazardous substances consent is only to be deemed to be granted under this section if notification in respect of the substance was given before that date in accordance with those regulations.

(5) If at the relevant date such notification was not so required, hazardous substances consent is only to be deemed to be granted under this section if an aggregate quantity of the substance not less than the controlled quantity was present at any one time within the establishment period.

(6) If it appears to the hazardous substances authority that a claim for hazardous substances consent does not comply with subsection (2), it shall be their duty, before the end of the period of two weeks from their receipt of the claim—

(a) to notify the claimant that in their opinion the claim is invalid; and
(b) to give their reasons for that opinion.

(7) Hazardous substances consent which is deemed to be granted under this section is subject . . .—

(a) [to the condition that] the maximum aggregate quantity of the substance that may be present—

(i) on, over or under the land to which the claim for the consent relates;
(ii) on, over or under other land which is within 500 metres of it and controlled by the same person; or
(iii) in or on a structure controlled by the same person any part of which is within 500 metres of it,
at any one time shall not exceed the established quantity [, and

(b) to any other such conditions (if any) as are prescribed for the purposes of this section and are applicable in the case of that consent].

(8) In this section—

"establishment period" means the period of 12 months immediately preceding the relevant date;

"established quantity" means, in relation to any land—

(a) where before the relevant date there was a notification in respect of a substance in accordance with any of the Notification Regulations—

(i) the quantity notified or last notified before that date; or
(ii) a quantity equal to twice the quantity which was so notified or last notified before the start of the establishment period,
whichever is the greater;

(b) where a notification was not required before that date by any of those regulations, a quantity exceeding by 50 per cent the maximum which was present on, over or under the land at any one time within that period;

"Notification Regulations" means the Notification of Installations Handling Hazardous Substances Regulations 1982;

"the relevant date" means the date on which Part IV of the Housing and Planning Act 1986 came into force or, if that Part of that Act is not in force immediately before the date on which this Act comes into force, that date.

"the transitional period" means the period of 6 months beginning with the relevant date. **[477]**

NOTES
Commencement: 11 March 1992, 1 June 1992; see the note to s 1 at **[467–468]**.
Words in square brackets in sub-ss (2), (7) substituted, and words omitted from sub-s (7) repealed, by the Environmental Protection Act 1990, ss 144, 162(2), Sch 13, Pt I, paras 1, 4, Sch 16, Pt VII.

12. Deemed hazardous substances consent: government authorisation

(1) Where—

    (a) the authorisation of a government department is required by virtue of an enactment in respect of development to be carried out by a local authority, or by statutory undertakers who are not a local authority; and

    (b) the development would involve the presence of a hazardous substance in circumstances requiring hazardous substances consent,

the department may, on granting that authorisation, also direct that hazardous substances consent shall be deemed to be granted subject to such conditions (if any) as may be specified in the direction.

(2) On granting a consent under section 36 of the Electricity Act 1989 in respect of any operation or change of use that would involve the presence of a hazardous substance in circumstances requiring hazardous substances consent, the Secretary of State may direct that hazardous substances consent shall be deemed to be granted, subject to such conditions (if any) as may be specified in the direction.

[(2A) On making an order under section 1 or 3 of the Transport and Works Act 1992 which includes any provision that would involve the presence of a hazardous substance in circumstances requiring hazardous substances consent, the Secretary of State may direct that hazardous substances consent shall be deemed to be granted, subject to such conditions (if any) as may be specified in the direction.]

(3) The department or, as the case may be, the Secretary of State shall consult the Health and Safety Commission before giving any such direction.

(4) For the purposes of this section development shall be taken to be authorised by a government department if—

    (a) any consent, authority or approval to or for the development is granted by the department in pursuance of an enactment;

    (b) a compulsory purchase order is confirmed by the department authorising the purchase of land for the purpose of the development;

    (c) consent is granted by the department to the appropriation of land for the purpose of the development or the acquisition of land by agreement for that purpose;

    (d) authority is given by the department for the borrowing of money for the purpose of the development, or for the application for that purpose of any money not otherwise so applicable; or

    (e) any undertaking is given by the department to pay a grant in respect of the development in accordance with an enactment authorising the payment of such grants,

and references in this section to the authorisation of a government department shall be construed accordingly.

(5) The provisions of this Act (except section 22) shall apply in relation to any hazardous substances consent deemed to be granted by virtue of directions under this section as if it had been granted by the Secretary of State on an application referred to him under section 20.

[(6) A government department or the Secretary of State shall, as respects any hazardous substances consent deemed to be granted by virtue of directions under this section, send to the hazardous substances authority concerned any such information as appears to be required by them for the purposes of a register under section 28.]

[478]

NOTES

 Commencement: 11 March 1992, 1 June 1992 (sub-ss (1), (2), (3)–(5)); see the note to s 1 at **[467–468]**; 1 January 1993 (sub-s (2A)); 1 January 1992 (sub-s (6)) (but note that the rest of this Act came into force on later dates; see the note to s 1 at **[467–468]**).

 Sub-s (2A) inserted by the Transport and Works Act 1992, s 18.

 Sub-s (6) added by the Environmental Protection Act 1990, s 144, Sch 13, Pt I, paras 1, 5.

 Modification: references to a local authority in this section and s 38(1)–(4) deemed to include references to a National Park authority, by virtue of the Environment Act 1995, s 70, Sch 9, para 14(2).

Variation and revocation of consents

13. Application for hazardous substances consent without condition attached to previous consent

(1) This section applies to an application for hazardous substances consent without a condition subject to which a previous hazardous substances consent was granted.

(2) On such an application the hazardous substances authority shall consider only the question of the conditions subject to which hazardous substances consent should be granted.

(3) If on such an application the hazardous substances authority determine—

 (a) that hazardous substances consent should be granted subject to conditions differing from those subject to which the previous consent was granted; or
 (b) that it should be granted unconditionally,

they shall grant hazardous substances consent accordingly.

(4) If on such an application the hazardous substances authority determine that hazardous substances consent should be granted subject to the same conditions as those subject to which the previous consent was granted, they shall refuse the application.

(5) Where—

 (a) hazardous substances consent has been granted or is deemed to have been granted for the presence on, over or under land of more than one hazardous substance; and
 (b) an application under this section does not relate to all the substances,

the hazardous substances authority shall only have regard to any condition relating to a substance to which the application does not relate to the extent that it has implications for a substance to which the application does relate.

(6) Where—

 (a) more than one hazardous substances consent has been granted or is deemed to have been granted in respect of the same land; and
 (b) an application under this section does not relate to all the consents,

the hazardous substances authority shall only have regard to any consent to which the application does not relate to the extent that it has implications for consent to which the application does relate.

(7) . . .   **[479]**

NOTES
Commencement: 11 March 1992, 1 June 1992; see the note to s 1 at **[467–468]**.
Sub-s (7) repealed by the Environmental Protection Act 1990, ss 144, 162(2), Sch 13, Pt I, paras 1, 6, Sch 16, Pt VII.

14. General power by order to revoke or modify hazardous substances consent

(1) The hazardous substances authority may by order revoke a hazardous substances consent or modify it to such extent as they consider expedient if it appears to them, having regard to any material consideration, that it is expedient to revoke or modify it.

(2) The hazardous substances authority may also by order revoke a hazardous substances consent if it appears to them—

(a) that there has been a material change of use of land to which a hazardous substances consent relates; or

(b) that planning permission has been granted for development the carrying out of which would involve a material change of use of such land and the development to which the permission relates has been commenced; or

(c) in the case of a hazardous substances consent which relates only to one substance, that that substance has not for at least five years been present on, over or under the land to which the consent relates in a quantity equal to or exceeding the controlled quantity; or

(d) in the case of a hazardous substances consent which relates to a number of substances, that none of those substances has for at least five years been so present.

(3) An order made by virtue of subsection (2)(a) or (b) in the case of a consent relating to more than one substance may revoke it entirely or only so far as it relates to a specified substance.

(4) An order under this section shall specify the grounds on which it is made.

[480]

NOTES
Commencement: 11 March 1992, 1 June 1992; see the note to s 1 at **[467–468]**.

15. Confirmation by Secretary of State of s 14 orders

(1) An order under section 14 . . . shall not take effect unless it is confirmed by the Secretary of State.

(2) The Secretary of State may confirm any such order submitted to him either without modification or subject to such modification as he considers expedient.

(3) Where a hazardous substances authority submit an order under section 14 to the Secretary of State for his confirmation under this section, the authority shall serve notice of the order—

(a) on any person who is an owner of the whole or any part of the land to which the order relates;

(b) on any person other than an owner who appears to them to be in control of the whole or any part of that land;

(c) on any other person who in their opinion will be affected by the order.

(4) A notice under subsection (3) shall specify the period (which must not be less than 28 days from the service of it) within which any person on whom the notice is served may require an opportunity of appearing before and being heard by a person appointed by the Secretary of State for that purpose.

(5) If such a person so requires, the Secretary of State, before confirming the order, shall give that person and the hazardous substances authority such an opportunity.

(6) Where an order under section 14 has been confirmed by the Secretary of State, the hazardous substances authority shall serve a copy of the order on every person who was entitled to be served with notice under subsection (3).   **[481]**

NOTES
Commencement: 11 March 1992, 1 June 1992; see the note to s 1 at **[467–468]**.
Words omitted from sub-s (1) repealed by the Environmental Protection Act 1990, s 162(2), Sch 16, Pt VII.

16. Compensation in respect of s 14 orders

(1) This section applies where an order is made under section 14(1) revoking or modifying a hazardous substances consent.

(2) If, on a claim made to the hazardous substances authority within the prescribed time and in the prescribed manner, it is shown that any person has suffered damage in consequence of the order—

  (a) by depreciation of the value of an interest to which he is entitled in the land or in minerals in, on or under it; or
  (b) by being disturbed in his enjoyment of the land or of minerals in, on or under it,

the authority shall pay him compensation in respect of that damage.

(3) Without prejudice to subsection (2), any person who carries out any works in compliance with the order shall be entitled, on a claim made as mentioned in that subsection, to recover from the hazardous substances authority compensation in respect of any expenses reasonably incurred by him in that behalf.

(4) Any compensation payable to a person under this section by virtue of an order shall be reduced by the value to him of any timber, apparatus or other materials removed for the purpose of complying with the order.

(5) Sections 117 and 118 of the principal Act (which contain general provisions as to the assessment of and the determination of claims for compensation) shall apply as if compensation under this section were compensation under section 115 of that Act.   **[482]**

NOTES
Commencement: 11 March 1992, 1 June 1992; see the note to s 1 at **[467–468]**.
The principal Act: Town and Country Planning Act 1990.

17. Revocation of hazardous substances consent on change of control of land

(1) A hazardous substances consent is revoked if there is a change in the person in control of part of the land to which it relates, unless an application for the continuation of the consent has previously been made to the hazardous substances authority.

(2) Regulations may make provision in relation to applications under subsection (1) corresponding to any provision that may be made by regulations under section 7 or 8 in relation to applications for hazardous substances consent.   **[483]**

NOTES
Commencement: 11 March 1992, 1 June 1992; see the note to s 1 at **[467–468]**.

18. Determination of applications for continuation of hazardous substances consent

(1) When an application is made under section 17 for the continuation of a hazardous substances consent the hazardous substances authority—

    (a) may modify the consent in any way they consider appropriate; or

    (b) may revoke it.

(2) In dealing with such an application the authority shall have regard to any material consideration and, in particular, but without prejudice to the generality of the foregoing—

    (a) to the matters to which a hazardous substances authority are required to have regard by section 9(2)(a) to (d); and

    (b) to any advice which the Health and Safety Executive ... have given following consultations in pursuance of regulations under section 17(2).

(3) If an application relates to more than one consent, the authority may make different determinations in relation to each.

(4) If a consent relates to more than one hazardous substance, the authority may make different determinations in relation to each.

(5) It shall be the duty of a hazardous substances authority, when continuing hazardous substances consent, to attach to the consent either—

    (a) a statement that it is unchanged in relation to the matters included in it by virtue of sections 9(4) and 10(3); or

    (b) a statement of any change in respect of those matters.

(6) The modifications which a hazardous substances authority may make by virtue of subsection (1)(a) include, without prejudice to the generality of that subsection, the making of the consent subject to conditions with respect to any of the matters mentioned in subsection (1) of section 10; and subsection (2) of that section shall apply as respects those conditions as it applies to the grant of consent subject to conditions.

(7) Where any application under section 17(1) is made to a hazardous substances authority then, unless within such period as may be prescribed, or within such extended period as may at any time be agreed upon in writing between the applicant and the hazardous substances authority, the hazardous substances authority either—

    (a) give notice to the applicant of their decision on the application; or

    (b) give notice to him that the application has been referred to the Secretary of State in accordance with directions given under section 20,

the application shall be deemed to have been granted. **[484]**

NOTES

    Commencement: 11 March 1992, 1 June 1992; see the note to s 1 at **[467–468]**.

    Words omitted from sub-s (2)(b) repealed by the Environmental Protection Act 1990, s 162(2), Sch 16, Pt VII.

19. Compensation on revocation or modification of consent under s 18

Where on an application under section 17(1) the hazardous substances authority modify or revoke the hazardous substances consent, they shall pay to the person in control of the whole of the land before the change in control by virtue of which the application was made compensation in respect of any loss or damage sustained by him and directly attributable to the modification or revocation. **[485]**

NOTES
    Commencement: 11 March 1992, 1 June 1992; see the note to s 1 at **[467–468]**.

Secretary of State's powers

20. Reference of applications to Secretary of State

(1) The Secretary of State may give directions requiring applications for hazardous substances consent or applications under section 17(1) to be referred to him instead of being dealt with by hazardous substances authorities.

(2) A direction under this section—

    (a) may be given either to a particular hazardous substances authority or to hazardous substances authorities generally; and

    (b) may relate either to a particular application or to applications of a class specified in the direction.

(3) Any application in respect of which a direction under this section has effect shall be referred to the Secretary of State accordingly.

(4) Before determining an application referred to him under this section, the Secretary of State shall, if either the applicant or the hazardous substances authority so wish, give to each of them an opportunity of appearing before, and being heard by, a person appointed by the Secretary of State for the purpose.

(5) The decision of the Secretary of State on any application referred to him under this section shall be final.

(6) ...   **[486]**

NOTES
    Commencement: 11 March 1992, 1 June 1992; see the note to s 1 at **[467–468]**.
    Sub-s (6) repealed by the Environmental Protection Act 1990, s 162(2), Sch 16, Pt VII.

21. Appeals against decisions or failure to take decisions relating to hazardous substances

(1) Where a hazardous substances authority refuse an application for hazardous substances consent or an application under section 17(1) or an application for any consent, agreement or approval of the authority required by a condition imposed on the grant of such consent, or grant it subject to conditions, the applicant may, if he is aggrieved by their decision, appeal to the Secretary of State.

(2) A person who has made an application for hazardous substances consent may also appeal to the Secretary of State if the hazardous substances authority have neither—

    (a) given notice to the applicant of their decision on the application; nor

    (b) given notice to him that the application has been referred to the Secretary of State in accordance with directions given under section 20,

within such period as may be prescribed, or within such extended period as may at any time be agreed upon in writing between the applicant and the hazardous substances authority; and for the purposes of this Act in such a case the authority shall be deemed to have decided to refuse the application.

(3) An appeal under this section must be made by notice served in the prescribed manner within such period as may be prescribed.

(4) The Secretary of State may allow or dismiss an appeal under this section or

may reverse or vary any part of the decision of the hazardous substances authority (whether or not the appeal relates to that part of it) and may deal with the application as if it had been made to him in the first instance.

(5) Before determining an appeal under this section, the Secretary of State shall, if either the applicant or the hazardous substances authority so wish, give each of them an opportunity of appearing before and being heard by a person appointed by the Secretary of State for the purpose.

(6) The decision of the Secretary of State on any appeal under this section shall be final.

(7) . . .

(8) The Schedule to this Act applies to appeals under this section.   [487]

NOTES
    Commencement: 11 March 1992, 1 June 1992; see the note to s 1 at [467–468].
    Sub-s (7) repealed by the Environmental Protection Act 1990, s 162(2), Sch 16, Pt VII.

22. Validity of decisions as to applications

(1) If any person is aggrieved by any decision of the Secretary of State under section 20 or 21 and wishes to question the validity of that decision on the grounds—

    (a) that it is not within the powers of this Act; or

    (b) that any of the relevant requirements have not been complied with in relation to that decision,

he may within six weeks from the date on which the decision is taken make an application to the High Court under this section.

(2) Without prejudice to subsection (1), if the hazardous substances authority who made the decision on the application to which the proceedings relate or, as the case may be, referred the application wish to question the validity of any such decision as is mentioned in that subsection on any of the grounds there mentioned, the authority may within six weeks from the date on which the decision is taken make an application to the High Court under this section.

(3) On any application under this section the High Court—

    (a) may by interim order suspend the operation of the decision the validity of which is questioned by the application until the final determination of the proceedings;

    (b) if satisfied that the decision in question is not within the powers of this Act, or that the interests of the applicant have been substantially prejudiced by a failure to comply with any of the relevant requirements in relation to it, may quash that decision.

(4) In this section "the relevant requirements", in relation to any decision, means any requirements of this Act or the [principal Act] or of [the Tribunals and Inquiries Act 1992], or of any order, regulations or rules made under this Act or under either of those Acts which are applicable to that decision.

(5) Except as provided by this section, the validity of any such decision as is mentioned in subsection (1) shall not be questioned in any legal proceedings whatsoever.

(6) Nothing in subsection (5) shall affect the exercise of any jurisdiction of any court in respect of any refusal or failure on the part of the Secretary of State to take any such decision as is there mentioned.   [488]

NOTES
Commencement: 11 March 1992, 1 June 1992; see the note to s 1 at **[467–468]**.
First words in square brackets in sub-s (4) substituted by the Environmental Protection Act 1990,
s 144, Sch 13, Pt I, paras 1, 7; second words in square brackets in sub-s (4) substituted by the Tribunals
and Inquiries Act 1992, s 18(1), Sch 3, para 33.
The principal Act: Town and Country Planning Act 1990.

Contraventions of hazardous substances control

23. Offences

(1) Subject to the following provisions of this section, if there is a contravention of hazardous substances control, the appropriate person shall be guilty of an offence.

(2) There is a contravention of hazardous substances control—

(a) if a quantity of a hazardous substance equal to or exceeding the controlled quantity is or has been present on, over or under land and either—

(i) there is no hazardous substances consent for the presence of the substance; or

(ii) there is hazardous substances consent for its presence but the quantity present exceeds the maximum quantity permitted by the consent;

(b) if there is or has been a failure to comply with a condition subject to which a hazardous substances consent was granted.

(3) In subsection (1) "the appropriate person" means—

(a) in relation to a contravention falling within paragraph (a) of subsection (2)—

(i) any person knowingly causing the substance to be present on, over or under the land;

(ii) any person allowing it to be so present; and

(b) in relation to a contravention falling within paragraph (a) or (b) of that subsection, the person in control of the land.

(4) A person guilty of an offence under this section shall be liable—

(a) on summary conviction, to a fine not exceeding [£20,000]; or

(b) on conviction on indictment, to a fine,

[(4A) In determining the amount of any fine to be imposed on a person convicted of an offence under this section, the court shall in particular have regard to any financial benefit which has accrued or appears likely to accrue to him in consequence of the offence].

(5) In any proceedings for an offence under this section it shall be a defence for the accused to prove—

(a) that he took all reasonable precautions and exercised all due diligence to avoid commission of the offence, or

(b) that commission of the offence could be avoided only by the taking of action amounting to a breach of a statutory duty.

(6) In any proceedings for an offence consisting of a contravention falling within subsection (2)(a), it shall be a defence for the accused to prove that at the time of the alleged commission of the offence he did not know, and had no reason to believe—

(a) if the case falls within paragraph (a)(i)—

(i) that the substance was present; or

(ii) that it was present in a quantity equal to or exceeding the controlled quantity;

(b) if the case falls within paragraph (a)(ii), that the substance was present in a quantity exceeding the maximum quantity permitted by the consent.

(7) In any proceedings for an offence consisting of a contravention falling within subsection (2)(b), it shall be a defence for the accused to prove that he did not know, and had no reason to believe, that there was a failure to comply with a condition subject to which hazardous substances consent had been granted.   **[489]**

NOTES
Commencement: 11 March 1992, 1 June 1992; see the note to s 1 at **[467–468]**
Words in square brackets in sub-s (4)(a), and the whole of sub-s (4A), substituted by the Planning and Compensation Act 1991, s 25, Sch 3, Pt I, para 10.

24. Power to issue hazardous substances contravention notice

(1) Where it appears to the hazardous substances authority that there is or has been a contravention of hazardous substances control, they may issue a notice—

(a) specifying an alleged contravention of hazardous substances control; and
(b) requiring such steps as may be specified in the notice to be taken to remedy [wholly or partly] the contravention,

if they consider it expedient to do so having regard to any material consideration.

(2) Such a notice is referred to in this Act as a "hazardous substances contravention notice".

(3) A hazardous substances authority shall not issue a hazardous substances contravention notice where it appears to them that a contravention of hazardous substances control can be avoided only by the taking of action amounting to a breach of a statutory duty.

(4) A copy of a hazardous substances contravention notice shall be served—

(a) on the owner of the land to which it relates;
(b) on any person other than the owner who appears to the hazardous substances authority to be in control of the land; and
(c) on such other persons as may be prescribed.

(5) A hazardous substances contravention notice shall also specify—

(a) a date not less than 28 days from the date of service of copies of the notice as the date on which it is to take effect;
(b) in respect of each of the steps required to be taken to remedy the contravention of hazardous substances control, the period from the notice taking effect within which the step is to be taken.

(6) Where a hazardous substances authority issue a hazardous substances contravention notice the steps required by the notice may, without prejudice to the generality of subsection (1)(b), if the authority think it expedient, include a requirement that the hazardous substance be removed from the land.

(7) Where a notice includes such a requirement, it may also contain a direction that at the end of such period as may be specified in the notice any hazardous substances consent for the presence of the substance shall cease to have effect or, if it relates to more than one substance, shall cease to have effect so far as it relates to the substances which are required to be removed.

(8) The hazardous substances authority may withdraw a hazardous substances

contravention notice (without prejudice to their power to issue another) at any time before [or after] it takes effect.

(9) If they do so, they shall immediately give notice of the withdrawal to every person who was served with a copy of the notice [or would, if the notice were reissued, be served with a copy of it]. **[490]**

NOTES
    Commencement: 11 March 1992, 2 June 1992; see the note to s 1 at **[467–468]**.
    Words in square brackets in sub-ss (1)(b), (8), (9) inserted or added by the Planning and Compensation Act 1991, s 25, Sch 3, Pt I, para 11.

[24A. Variation of hazardous substances contravention notices

(1) A hazardous substances authority may waive or relax any requirement of a hazardous substances contravention notice issued by them and, in particular, may extend any period specified in accordance with section 24(5)(b) in the notice.

(2) The powers conferred by subsection (1) may be exercised before or after the notice takes effect.

(3) The hazardous substances authority shall, immediately after exercising those powers, give notice of the exercise to every person who has been served with a copy of the hazardous substances contravention notice or would, if the notice were reissued, be served with a copy of it.] **[490A]**

NOTES
    Commencement: 2 January 1992 (but note that the rest of this Act came into force on later dates; see the note to s 1 at **[467–468]**).
    Inserted by the Planning and Compensation Act 1991, s 25, Sch 3, Pt I, para 12.

25. Hazardous substances contravention notices: supplementary provisions

(1) The Secretary of State may by regulations—

    (a) specify matters which are to be included in hazardous substances contravention notices, in addition to those which are required to be included in them by section 24;
    (b) provide—
        (i) for appeals to him against hazardous substances contravention notices;
       (ii) for the persons by whom, grounds upon which and time within which such an appeal may be brought;
      (iii) for the procedure to be followed on such appeals;
      (iv) for the directions that may be given on such an appeal;
       (v) for the application to such appeals, subject to such modifications as the regulations may specify, of any of the provisions of sections 174, [175(1) to (3)] and (6), 176, 177, 285 and 289 of the principal Act;
    (c) direct that any of the provisions of sections 178 . . . , 179 to 181, 183, 184, [186,] 187 and 188 of that Act shall have effect in relation to hazardous substances contravention notices subject to such modifications as he may specify in the regulations;
    (d) make such other provision as he considers necessary or expedient in relation to hazardous substances contravention notices.

(2) If any person appeals against a hazardous substances contravention notice, the notice shall [subject to regulations under this section] be of no effect pending the final determination or the withdrawal of the appeal.

(3) Regulations under section 24 or this section may make different provision for different cases or descriptions of cases.

(4) Where any person has appealed to the Secretary of State under this section against a hazardous substances contravention notice, no person shall be entitled, in any other proceedings instituted after the making of the appeal, to claim that the notice was not duly served on the person who appealed.

[(5) Subsection (5) of section 250 of the Local Government Act 1972 (which authorises a Minister holding an inquiry under that section to make orders with respect to the costs of the parties) shall apply in relation to any proceedings before the Secretary of State on an appeal under this section as if those proceedings were an inquiry held by the Secretary of State under section 250.]   **[491]**

NOTES
Commencement: 11 March 1992, 1 June 1992; see the note to s 1 at **[467–468]**.
Words in square brackets in sub-s (1)(b)(v) substituted, words omitted from sub-s (1)(c) repealed, and words in square brackets in sub-s (2) inserted, by the Planning and Compensation Act 1991, ss 25, 84(6), Sch 3, Pt I, para 13, Pt II, para 30, Sch 19, Pt I.
Figure in square brackets in sub-s (1)(c) inserted by the Environmental Protection Act 1990, s 144, Sch 13, Pt I, paras 1, 8.
Sub-s (5): temporarily added by the Planning (Consequential Provisions) Act 1990, s 6, Sch 4, paras 1, 13, until such day as may be appointed by order made by the Secretary of State. The Planning (Consequential Provisions) Act 1990 (Appointed Day No 1 and Transitional Provisions) Order 1991, SI 1991/2698, appointed 2 January 1992 only for the purposes of awards of costs in relation to proceedings which give rise to a hearing.
The principal Act: Town and Country Planning Act 1990.

26. Transitional exemptions

(1) No offence is committed under section 23 and no hazardous substances contravention notice may be issued in relation to a hazardous substance which is on, over or under any land, if—

    (a) the substance was present on, over or under the land at any time within the establishment period; and

    (b) in a case in which at the relevant date notification in respect of that substance was required by any of the Notification Regulations, both the conditions specified in subsection (2) were satisfied; and

    (c) in a case in which at that date such notification was not so required, the condition specified in paragraph (b) of that subsection is satisfied.

(2) The conditions mentioned in subsection (1) are—

    (a) that notification required by the Notification Regulations was given before the relevant date; and

    (b) that the substance has not been present during the transitional period in a quantity greater in aggregate than the established quantity.

[(2A) This section shall have effect until the end of the transitional period.]

(3) Expressions used in this section and in section 11 have the same meanings as in that section.   **[492]**

NOTES
Commencement: 11 March 1992, 1 June 1992 (sub-ss (1), (2), (3)); see the note to s 1 at **[467–468]**; 2 January 1992 (sub-s (2A)) (but note that the rest of this Act came into force on later dates; see the note to s 1 at **[467–468]**).
Sub-s (2A) inserted by the Planning and Compensation Act 1991, s 25, Sch 3, Pt I, para 14.

[26AA. Injunctions

(1) Where a hazardous substances authority consider it necessary or expedient for any actual or apprehended contravention of hazardous substances control to be restrained by injunction, they may apply to the court for an injunction, whether or not they have exercised or are proposing to exercise any of their other powers under this Act.

(2) On an application under subsection (1) the court may grant such an injunction as the court thinks appropriate for the purpose of restraining the contravention.

(3) Rules of court may, in particular, provide for such an injunction to be issued against a person whose identity is unknown.

(4) In this section ''the court'' means the High Court or the county court.]

[492A]

NOTES
Commencement: 25 November 1991 (certain purposes); 2 January 1992 (remaining purposes) (but note that the rest of this Act came into force on later dates; see the note to s 1 at **[467–468]**).
Inserted by the Planning and Compensation Act 1991, s 25, Sch 3, Pt I, para 15.

Miscellaneous provisions

[26A. Fees for consent applications

(1) Provision may be made by regulations for the payment of a fee of the prescribed amount to a hazardous substances authority in respect of an application for, or for the continuation of, hazardous substances consent.

(2) Regulations under this section may provide for the payment to the Secretary of State of a fee of the prescribed amount in respect of any application which is, by virtue of regulations under section 25, deemed to have been made for hazardous subtances consent.

(3) Regulations under this section may provide—
  (a) for the transfer of prescribed fees received by a hazardous substances authority in respect of any application which is referred to the Secretary of State under section 20;
  (b) for the remission of refunding of a prescribed fee (in whole or in part) in prescribed circumstances or in pursuance of a direction given by the Secretary of State;

and the regulations may make different provision for different areas or for different cases or descriptions of cases.]

[492B]

NOTES
Commencement: 1 January 1992 (but note that the rest of this Act was brought into force on later dates; see the note to s 1 at **[467–468]**).
Inserted by the Environmental Protection Act 1990, s 144, Sch 13, Pt I, paras 1, 9.

27. Temporary exemption directions

(1) If it appears to the Secretary of State—
  (a) either—
    (i) that the community or part of it is being or is likely to be deprived of an essential service or commodity; or
    (ii) that there is or is likely to be a shortage of such a service or commodity affecting the community or part of it; and

(b) that the presence of a hazardous substance on, over or under land specified in the direction in circumstances such that hazardous substances consent would be required, is necessary for the effective provision of that service or commodity,

he may direct that, subject to such conditions or exceptions as he thinks fit, the presence of the substance on, over or under the land is not to constitute a contravention of hazardous substances control so long as the direction remains in force.

(2) A direction under this section—

(a) may be withdrawn at any time;
(b) shall in any case cease to have effect at the end of the period of three months beginning with the day on which it was given, but without prejudice to the Secretary of State's power to give a further direction.

(3) The Secretary of State shall send a copy of any such direction to the authority who are the hazardous substances authority for the land.

(4) ...   **[493]**

NOTES
Commencement: 11 March 1992, 1 June 1992; see the note to s 1 at **[467–468]**.
Sub-s (4) repealed by the Environmental Protection Act 1990, s 162(2), Sch 16, Pt VII.

28. Registers etc

(1) Every ... hazardous substances authority ... shall keep, in such manner as may be prescribed, a register containing such information as may be prescribed with respect—

(a) to applications for hazardous substances consent [made to that authority;
(aa) to applications under s 17(1) made to that authority;]
(b) to hazardous substances consent having effect by virtue of section 11 or 12 with respect to land for which that authority is, ... the hazardous substances authority;
(c) to revocations or modifications of hazardous substances consent granted with respect to such land; and
(d) to directions under section 27 sent to the authority by the Secretary of State;

and every such register shall also contain such information as may be prescribed as to the manner in which applications for hazardous substances consent have been dealt with].

(2) ...

(3) Every register kept under this section shall be available for inspection by the public at all reasonable hours.   **[494]**

NOTES
Commencement: 11 March 1992, 1 June 1992; see the note to s 1 at **[467–468]**.
Words omitted from sub-s (1) and the whole of sub-s (2) repealed, and words in square brackets in sub-s (1) substituted or added, by the Environmental Protection Act 1990, ss 144, 162(2), Sch 13, Pt I, paras 1, 2(4), Sch 16, Pt VII.

29. Health and safety requirements

(1) Nothing in—

(a) any hazardous substances consent granted or deemed to be granted or having effect by virtue of this Act; or

(b) any hazardous substances contravention notice issued under section 24,

shall require or allow anything to be done in contravention of any of the relevant statutory provisions or any prohibition notice or improvement notice served under or by virtue of any of those provisions.

(2) To the extent that such a consent or notice purports to require or allow any such thing to be done, it shall be void.

(3) Where it appears to a hazardous substances authority who have granted, or are deemed to have granted, a hazardous substances consent or who have issued a hazardous substances contravention notice that the consent or notice or part of it is rendered void by subsection (2), the authority shall, as soon as is reasonably practicable, consult the [Health and Safety Executive] with regard to the matter.

(4) If the [Health and Safety Executive] advise the authority that the consent or notice is rendered wholly void, the authority shall revoke it.

(5) If they advise that part of the consent or notice is rendered void, the authority shall so modify it as to render it wholly operative.

(6) In this section—

.   .   .   .   .   .

"relevant statutory provisions", "improvement notice" and "prohibition notice" have the same meanings as in Part I of the Health and Safety at Work etc. Act 1974.   **[495]**

NOTES

Commencement: 11 March 1992, 1 June 1992; see the note to s 1 at **[467–468]**.

Words in square brackets in sub-ss (3), (4) substituted, and words omitted from sub-s (6) repealed, by the Environmental Protection Act 1990, ss 144, 162(2), Sch 13, Pt I, paras 1, 2(5), Sch 16, Pt VII.

General

30. Application of this Act to certain authorities and persons

(1) The provisions of this Act shall have effect, subject to such exceptions and modifications as may be prescribed, in relation to granting hazardous substances consent for authorities who are hazardous substances authorities . . .

(2) Subject to the provisions of section 12, any such regulations may in particular provide for securing—

(a) that any application by such an authority for hazardous substances consent in respect of the presence of a hazardous substance on, over or under land shall be made to the Secretary of State and not to the hazardous substances authority;

(b) that any order or notice authorised to be made, issued or served under those provisions shall be made, issued or served by the Secretary of State and not by the hazardous substances authority.   **[496]**

NOTES

Commencement: 11 March 1992, 1 June 1992; see the note to s 1 at **[467–468]**.

Words omitted from sub-s (1) repealed by the Environmental Protection Act 1990, s 162(2), Sch 16, Pt VII.

31. Exercise of powers in relation to Crown land

(1) Notwithstanding any interest of the Crown in Crown land, but subject to subsection (2), any restrictions imposed or powers conferred by sections 4 to 29 (except section 22) shall apply and be exercisable in relation to Crown land to the extent of any interest in it for the time being held otherwise than by or on behalf of the Crown.

(2) Except with the consent of the appropriate authority, no order or notice shall be made, issued or served under any of the provisions of section 14, 15 [24 or 26AA] in relation to land which for the time being is Crown land.

(3) In this section—

"Crown land" means land in which there is a Crown interest or a Duchy interest;

"Crown interest" means an interest belonging to Her Majesty in right of the Crown, or belonging to a government department or held in trust for Her Majesty for the purposes of a government department;

"Duchy interest" means an interest belonging to Her Majesty in right of the Duchy of Lancaster, or belonging to the Duchy of Cornwall.

(4) A person who is entitled to occupy Crown land by virtue of a licence in writing shall be treated for the purposes of subsection (1) as having an interest in land.

(5) For the purposes of this section "the appropriate authority", in relation to any land—

    (a) in the case of land belonging to Her Majesty in right of the Crown and forming part of the Crown Estate, means the Crown Estate Commissioners, and, in relation to any other land belonging to Her Majesty in right of the Crown, means the government department having the management of that land;

    (b) in relation to land belonging to Her Majesty in right of the Duchy of Lancaster, means the Chancellor of the Duchy;

    (c) in relation to land belonging to the Duchy of Cornwall, means such person as the Duke of Cornwall, or the possessor for the time being of the Duchy of Cornwall, appoints;

    (d) in the case of land belonging to a government department or held in trust for Her Majesty for the purposes of a government department, means that department.

(6) If any question arises as to what authority is the appropriate authority in relation to any land, that question shall be referred to the Treasury, whose decision shall be final.   [497]

NOTES
    Commencement: 11 March 1992, 1 June 1992; see the note to s 1 at [467–468].
    Words in square brackets in sub-s (2) substituted by the Planning and Compensation Act 1991, s 25, Sch 3, Pt II, para 31.

32. Application for hazardous substances consent in anticipation of disposal of Crown land

(1) Subsections (2) to (4) have effect for the purposes of enabling Crown land, or an interest in Crown land, to be disposed of with the benefit of hazardous substances consent.

(2) Notwithstanding the interest of the Crown in the land in question, an application for such consent may be made—

  (a) by the appropriate authority; or
  (b) by any person authorised by that authority in writing;

and, subject to subsections (3) and (4), all the statutory provisions relating to the making and determination of such an application shall accordingly apply as if the land were not Crown land.

(3) Any hazardous substances consent granted by virtue of this section shall apply only—

  (a) to the presence of the substance to which the consent relates after the land in question has ceased to be Crown land; and
  (b) so long as that land continues to be Crown land, to the presence of the substance by virtue of a private interest in the land.

(4) The Secretary of State may by regulations—

  (a) modify or exclude any of the statutory provisions referred to in subsection (2) in their application by virtue of that subsection and any other statutory provisions in their application to consents granted by virtue of this section;
  (b) make provision for requiring a hazardous substances authority to be notified of any disposal of, or of an interest in, any Crown land in respect of which an application has been made by virtue of this section; and
  (c) make such other provision in relation to the making and determination of applications by virtue of this section as he thinks necessary or expedient.

(5) This section shall not be construed as affecting any right to apply for hazardous substances consent in respect of Crown land in a case in which such an application can be made by virtue of a private interest in the land.

(6) In this section—

"private interest" means an interest which is neither a Crown interest nor a Duchy interest;

"statutory provisions" means provisions contained in or having effect under any enactment;

and references to the disposal of an interest in Crown land include references to the grant of an interest in such land.

(7) Subsections (3), (5) and (6) of section 31 apply for the purposes of this section as they apply for the purposes of that section.

(8) A person who is entitled to occupy Crown land by virtue of a licence in writing shall be treated for the purposes of this section as having an interest in land and references to the disposal or grant of an interest in Crown land and to a private interest in such land shall be construed accordingly.   **[498–499]**

NOTES
Commencement: 11 March 1992, 1 June 1992; see the note to s 1 at **[467–468]**.

33. (*Repealed by the Environmental Protection Act 1990, s 162(2), Sch 16, Pt VII.*)

34. Ecclesiastical property

(1) Where under any of the provisions of this Act a notice or copy of a notice is required to be served on an owner of land and the land is ecclesiastical property, a similar notice or copy of a notice shall be served on the Church Commissioners.

(2) Where the fee simple of any ecclesiastical property is in abeyance and the property is situated elsewhere than in Wales, then for the purposes of this section, sections 8 and 22 and section 31(1), so far as it applies to section 8, and any other provisions of the planning Acts so far as they apply, or have effect for the purpose of, any of those provisions, the fee simple shall be treated as being vested in the Church Commissioners.

(3) Any compensation payable under section 16 in respect of land which is ecclesiastical property—

(a) shall [in the case of land which is not diocesan glebe land, be paid to the Church Commissioners, and

(b) shall, in the case of diocesan glebe land, be paid to the Diocesan Board of Finance in which the land is vested,

and shall (in either case)] be applied by them for the purposes for which the proceeds of a sale by agreement of the land would be applicable under any enactment or Measure authorising or disposing of the proceeds of such a sale.

(4) In this section "ecclesiastical property" means land belonging to an ecclesiastical benefice, or being or forming part of a church subject to the jurisdiction of a bishop of any diocese or the site of such a church, or being or forming part of a burial ground subject to such jurisdiction [or being diocesan glebe land; and "Diocesan Board of Finance" and "diocesan glebe land" have the same meaning as in the Endowments and Glebe Measure 1976]. **[500]**

NOTES

Commencement: 11 March 1992, 1 June 1992; see the note to s 1 at **[467–468]**.

Words in square brackets in sub-ss (3), (4) substituted or inserted by the Planning and Compensation Act 1991, s 70, Sch 15, Pt II, para 32.

The planning Acts: Town and Country Planning Act 1990, Planning (Listed Buildings and Conservation Areas) Act 1990, Planning (Hazardous Substances) Act 1990, Planning (Consequential Provisions) Act 1990.

35. Applicaton of Act to Isles of Scilly

In relation to land in the Isles of Scilly the provisions of this Act, and any other provisions of the planning Acts in so far as they apply or have effect for the purposes of those provisions, shall have effect as if those Isles were a district and the Council of the Isles were the council of that district. **[501]**

NOTES

Commencement: 11 March 1992, 1 June 1992; see the note to s 1 at **[467–468]**.

The planning Acts: Town and Country Planning Act 1990, Planning (Listed Buildings and Conservation Areas) Act 1990, Planning (Hazardous Substances) Act 1990, Planning (Consequential Provisions) Act 1990.

36. Rights of entry

(1) Any person duly authorised in writing by the Secretary of State or by a hazardous substances authority may at any reasonable time enter any land for the purpose of surveying it in connection with—

(a) any application for hazardous substances consent;

(b) any proposal to issue a hazardous substances contravention notice.

(2) Any person duly authorised in writing by the Secretary of State or by a hazardous substances authority may at any reasonable time enter any land for the purpose of ascertaining whether an offence appears to have been committed under section 23.

(3) Any person who is an officer of the Valuation Office or a person duly authorised in writing by a hazardous substances authority may at any reasonable time enter any land for the purpose of surveying it, or estimating its value, in connection with a claim for compensation in respect of that land or any other land made by virtue of section 16 or 19.

(4) Any person duly authorised in writing by the Secretary of State or by a hazardous substances authority may at any reasonable time enter any land in respect of which a hazardous substances contravention notice [or notice under section 183 of the principal Act (as applied by regulations made by virtue of section 25)] has been issued for the purpose of ascertaining whether the notice has been complied with.

(5) ... any power conferred by this section to survey land shall be construed as including power to search and bore for the purpose of ascertaining the nature of the subsoil or the presence of minerals in it.

(6) ... **[502]**

NOTES
Commencement: 11 March 1992, 2 June 1992; see the note to s 1 at **[467–468]**.
Words in square brackets in sub-s (4) inserted, words omitted from sub-s (5) repealed, and sub-s (6) substituted as noted to s 36A at **[502A]**, by the Planning and Compensation Act 1991, ss 25, 84(6), Sch 3, Pt I, para 16, Pt II, para 32, Sch 19, Pt I.
The principal Act: Town and Country Planning Act 1990.

[36A. Warrants to enter land

(1) If it is shown to the satisfaction of a justice of the peace on sworn information in writing—

    (a) that there are reasonable grounds for entering any land for any of the purposes mentioned in section 36; and
    (b) that—

        (i) admission to the land has been refused, or a refusal is reasonably apprehended; or
        (ii) the case is one of urgency,

the justice may issue a warrant authorising any person duly authorised in writing by a hazardous substances authority to enter the land.

(2) For the purposes of subsection (1)(b)(i) admission to land shall be regarded as having been refused if no reply is received to a request for admission within a reasonable period.

(3) A warrant authorises entry on one occasion only and that entry must be—

    (a) within one month from the date of the issue of the warrant; and
    (b) at a reasonable hour, unless the case is one of urgency.] **[502A]**

NOTES
Commencement: 2 January 1992 (but note that the rest of this Act was brought into force on later dates; see the note to s 1 at **[467–468]**).
This section and s 36B substituted for s 36(6) by the Planning and Compensation Act 1991, s 25, Sch 3, Pt I, para 16(1), (3).

[36B. Rights of entry: supplementary provisions

(1) A person authorised to enter land in pursuance of a right of entry conferred under or by virtue of section 36 or 36A (referred to in this section as "a right of entry")—

    (a) shall, if so required, produce evidence of his authority and state the purpose of his entry before so entering;

    (b) may take with him such other persons as may be necessary; and

    (c) on leaving the land shall, if the owner or occupier is not then present, leave it as effectively secured against trespassers as he found it.

(2) Any person who wilfully obstructs a person acting in the exercise of a right of entry shall be guilty of an offence and liable on summary conviction to a fine not exceeding level 3 on the standard scale.

(3) If any person who enters any land, in exercise of a right of entry, discloses to any person any information obtained by him while on the land as to any manufacturing process or trade secret, he shall be guilty of an offence.

(4) Subsection (3) does not apply if the disclosure is made by a person in the course of performing his duty in connection with the purpose for which he was authorised to enter the land.

(5) A person who is guilty of an offence under subsection (3) shall be liable—

    (a) on summary conviction to a fine not exceeding the statutory maximum, or

    (b) on conviction on indictment to imprisonment for a term not exceeding two years or a fine or both.

(6) If any damage is caused to land or chattels in the exercise of—

    (a) a right of entry; or

    (b) a power conferred by virtue of section 36(5) in connection with such a right,

compensation may be recovered by any person suffering the damage from the authority who gave the written authority for the entry or, as the case may be, the Secretary of State; and section 118 of the principal Act shall apply in relation to compensation under this section as it applies in relation to compensation under Part IV of that Act.

(7) The authority of the appropriate Minister shall be required for the carrying out of works in the exercise of a power under section 36 if—

    (a) the land in question is held by statutory undertakers, and

    (b) they object to the proposed works on the ground that the execution of the works would be seriously detrimental to the carrying on of their undertaking.

(8) Section 265(1) and (3) of the principal Act (meaning of "appropriate Minister") applies for the purposes of subsection (7) as it applies for the purposes of section 325(9) of the principal Act.]   **[502B]**

NOTES
    Commencement: 2 January 1992 (but note that the rest of this Act was brought into force on later dates; see the note to s 1 at **[467–468]**).
    Substituted as noted to s 36A at **[502A]**.

37. Application of certain general provisions of principal Act

(1) The provisions of the principal Act specified in subsection (2) shall apply for the purposes of this Act as they apply for the purposes of that Act.

(2) Those provisions are—

    section 320 (local inquiries)
    section 322 (orders as to costs of parties where no inquiry held)
    [322A (orders as to costs: supplementary)]

section 323 (procedure on certain appeals and applications)
section 329 (service of notices)
section 330 (power to require information as to interests in land)
section 331 (offences by corporations).   **[503]**

NOTES

Commencement: 11 March 1992, 1 June 1992; see the note to s 1 at **[467–468]**.

Sub-s (2): words in italics temporarily omitted by the Planning (Consequential Provisions) Act 1990, s 6, Sch 4, paras 1, 14 until such day as may be appointed by order made by the Secretary of State. The Planning (Consequential Provisions) Act 1990 (Appointed Day No 1 and Transitional Provisions) Order 1991, SI 1991/2698, appointed 2 January 1992 only for the purposes of awards of costs in relation to proceedings which give rise to a hearing.

Words in square brackets in sub-s (2) inserted by the Planning and Compensation Act 1991, s 30(2).

The principal Act: Town and Country Planning Act 1990.

38. Financial provisions

(1) Where—

     (a) compensation is payable by a local authority under this Act in consequence of any decision or order given or made under sections 4 to 21 or the Schedule,

     (b) that decision or order was given or made wholly or partly in the interest of a service which is provided by a government department and the cost of which is defrayed out of money provided by Parliament,

the Minister responsible for the administration of that service may pay to that authority a contribution of such amount as he may with the consent of the Treasury determine.

(2) Any local authority and any statutory undertakers may contribute towards any expenses incurred by a hazardous substances authority . . . in or in connection with the performance of any of their functions under sections 4 to 29.

(3) Where any expenses are incurred by a local authority in the payment of compensation payable in consequence of anything done under sections 4 to 21, the Secretary of State may, if it appears to him to be expedient to do so, require any other local authority to contribute towards those expenses such sum as appears to him to be reasonable, having regard to any benefit accruing to that authority by reason of the proceeding giving rise to the compensation.

(4) For the purposes of subsections (2) and (3), contributions made by an authority towards the expenditure of a joint advisory committee shall be deemed to be expenses incurred by that authority for the purposes for which that expenditure is incurred by the committee.

(5) The council of a county may direct that any expenses incurred by them under sections [1, 3], 16, 20, 21, [25(5)], 31, 34 and 36, the previous provisions of this section or the Schedule shall be treated as special expenses of a county council chargeable upon such part of the county as may be specified in the directions.

(6) There shall be paid out of money provided by Parliament any expenses of the Secretary of State or any government department under this Act.

(7) Any sums received by the Secretary of State under this Act shall be paid into the Consolidated Fund.   **[504]**

NOTES

Commencement: 11 March 1992, 1 June 1992; see the note to s 1 at **[467–468]**.

Words omitted from sub-s (2) repealed, and first figures in square brackets in sub-s (5) substituted, by the Environmental Protection Act 1990, ss 144, 162(2), Sch 13, Pt I, paras 1, 2(6), Sch 16, Pt VII.

Sub-s (5): second figure in square brackets temporarily added by the Planning (Consequential

Provisions) Act 1990, s 6, Sch 4, paras 1, 15 until such day as may be appointed by order made by the Secretary of State. The Planning (Consequential Provisions) Act 1990 (Appointed Day No 1 and Transitional Provisions) Order 1991, SI 1991/2698, appointed 2 January 1992 only for the purposes of awards of costs in relation to proceedings which give rise to a hearing.

Modification: see the note to s 12 at **[478]**.

Supplemental

39. Interpretation

(1) In this Act—

"contravention of hazardous substances control" has the meaning given in section 23(2);

"hazardous substances authority" is to be construed in accordance with sections 1 [and] 3;

"hazardous substances consent" means consent required by section 4;

"hazardous substances contravention notice" means such a notice as is mentioned in section 24(1);

"the principal Act" means the Town and Country Planning Act 1990.

(2) In this Act, except in so far as the context otherwise requires and subject to the following provisions of this section, the following expressions have the same meaning as in the principal Act—

...
"the Broads";
"development";
"development plan";
"enactment";
"functions";
"government department";
"joint planning board";
"land";
"local authority";
"local planning authority";
"London borough";
"mineral working deposit";
"minerals";
"Minister";
...
"owner";
"the planning Acts";
"prescribed";
"public gas supplier";
"statutory undertakers";
"tenancy";
"urban development area" and "urban development corporation";
"use";
"Valuation Office";

but this subsection does not affect the meaning of "owner" in section 8.

(3) For the purposes of sections 4 to 21 and 23 to 26 any two bodies corporate are to be treated as being one person if—

    (a) one of them is a body corporate of which the other is a subsidiary (within the meaning of section 736 of the Companies Act 1985); or

    (b) both of them are subsidiaries (within the meaning of that Act) of one and the same body corporate.

(4) For the purposes of sections . . . 12 and 38(2) a public gas supplier shall be deemed to be a statutory undertaker . . .

(5) For the purposes of sections . . . 12 and 38(2) the National Rivers Authority and every water or sewerage undertaker shall be deemed to be a statutory undertaker . . .

(6) For the purposes of section 38(2) the Post Office, the Civil Aviation Authority and any holder of a licence under section 6(1) of the Electricity Act 1989 shall be deemed to be statutory undertakers . . .

(7), (8) . . .   **[505]**

NOTES

Commencement: 11 March 1992, 1 June 1992; see the note to s 1 at **[467–468]**.

Word in square brackets in sub-s (1) substituted, and words omitted from sub-ss (2), (4)–(6) and the whole of sub-ss (7), (8) repealed, by the Environmental Protection Act 1990, ss 144, 162(2), Sch 13, Pt I, paras 1, 2(7), Sch 16, Pt VII.

40. Regulations

(1) The Secretary of State may make regulations under this Act for any purpose for which regulations are authorised or required to be made under this Act, not being a purpose for which regulations are authorised or required to be made by another Minister.

(2) Any power conferred by this Act to make regulations shall be exercisable by statutory instrument.

(3) Any statutory instrument containing regulations made under this Act shall be subject to annulment in pursuance of a resolution of either House of Parliament.

    [506]

NOTES

Commencement: 11 March 1992, 1 June 1992; see the note to s 1 at **[467–468]**.

41. Short title, commencement and extent

(1) This Act may be cited as the Planning (Hazardous Substances) Act 1990.

(2) If an order has been made under section 57(2) of the Housing and Planning Act 1986 appointing a date during or at the end of the period of three months beginning with the day on which this Act is passed as the date on which all or any of the provisions of that Act relating to control over hazardous substances come into force, then the corresponding provisions of this Act (and, subject to Schedule 4 to the Planning (Consequential Provisions) Act 1990, the remaining provisions of it so far as they relate to them) shall come into force at the end of that period.

(3) Except so far as subsection (2) applies, the provisions of this Act (other than this section) shall come into force on such day as may be appointed by the Secretary of State by order made by statutory instrument and—

    (a) different days may be appointed for different provisions or for different purposes; and

(b) an order may make such transitional provision as the Secretary of State thinks appropriate.

(4) This Act extends to England and Wales only.   **[507]**

NOTES
  Commencement: 24 May 1990.

SCHEDULE
Section 21

DETERMINATION OF APPEALS BY PERSON APPOINTED BY SECRETARY OF STATE

Determination of appeals by appointed person

1.—(1) The Secretary of State may by regulations prescribe the classes of appeals under section 21 which are to be determined by a person appointed by the Secretary of State for the purpose instead of by the Secretary of State.

(2) Appeals of a prescribed class shall be so determined except in such classes of case as may for the time being be prescribed or as may be specified in directions given by the Secretary of State.

(3) Regulations made for the purpose of this paragraph may provide for the giving of publicity to any directions given by the Secretary of State under this paragraph.

(4) This paragraph shall not affect any provision in this Act or any instrument made under it that an appeal shall lie to, or a notice of appeal shall be served on, the Secretary of State.

(5) A person appointed under this paragraph is referred to in this Schedule as "an appointed person".

Powers and duties of appointed person

2.—(1) An appointed person shall have the same powers and duties as the Secretary of State has under subsection (4) of section 21.

(2) Subsection (5) of that section shall not apply to an appeal which falls to be determined by an appointed person, but before it is determined the Secretary of State shall ask the appellant and the hazardous substances authority whether they wish to appear before and be heard by the appointed person.

(3) If both the parties express a wish not to appear and be heard the appeal may be determined without their being heard.

(4) If either of the parties expresses a wish to appear and be heard, the appointed person shall give them both an opportunity of doing so.

(5) Where an appeal has been determined by an appointed person, his decision shall be treated as that of the Secretary of State.

(6) Except as provided by section 22, the validity of that decision shall not be questioned in any proceedings whatsoever.

(7) It shall not be a ground of application to the High Court under that section, that an appeal ought to have been determined by the Secretary of State and not by an appointed person, unless the appellant or the hazardous substances authority challenge the appointed person's power to determine the appeal before his decision on the appeal is given.

(8) Where in any enactment (including this Act) there is a reference to the Secretary of State in a context relating or capable of relating—

(a) to an appeal under section 21, or
(b) to any thing done or authorised or required to be done by, to or before the Secretary of State on or in connection with any such appeal,

then so far as the context permits it shall be construed, in relation to an appeal determined or falling to be determined by an appointed person, as a reference to him.

Determination of appeals by Secretary of State

3.—(1) The Secretary of State may, if he thinks fit, direct that an appeal which would otherwise fall to be determined by an appointed person shall instead be determined by the Secretary of State.

(2) Such a direction shall state the reasons for which it is given and shall be served on the appellant, the hazardous substances authority, any person who made representations relating to the subject matter of the appeal which the authority were required to take into account by regulations made under section 8(4) or, as the case may be, regulations made under section 17(2) making provision corresponding to section 8(4) and, if any person has been appointed under paragraph 1, on him.

(3) Where in consequence of such a direction an appeal under section 21 falls to be determined by the Secretary of State, the provisions of this Act which are relevant to the appeal shall, subject to the following provisions of this paragraph, apply to the appeal as if this Schedule had never applied to it.

(4) The Secretary of State shall give the appellant, the hazardous substances authority and any person who has made such representations as are referred to in sub-paragraph (2) an opportunity of appearing before and being heard by a person appointed by the Secretary of State for that purpose if—

(a) the reasons for the direction raise matters with respect to which any of those persons have not made representations; or

(b) in the case of the appellant or the hazardous substances authority, either of them was not asked in pursuance of paragraph 2(2) whether they wished to appear before and be heard by the appointed person, or expressed no wish in answer to that question, or expressed a wish to appear and be heard but was not given an opportunity of doing so.

(5) Except as provided by sub-paragraph (4), the Secretary of State need not give any person an opportunity of appearing before and being heard by a person appointed for the purpose, or of making fresh representations or making or withdrawing any representations already made.

(6) In determining the appeal the Secretary of State may take into account any report made to him by any person previously appointed to determine it.

4.—(1) The Secretary of State may by a further direction revoke a direction under paragraph 3 at any time before the determination of the appeal.

(2) Such a further direction shall state the reasons for which it is given and shall be served on the person, if any, previously appointed to determine the appeal, the appellant, the hazardous substances authority and any person who made representations relating to the subject matter of the appeal which the authority were required to take into account by regulations made under section 8(4) or, as the case may be, regulations made under section 17(2) making provision corresponding to section 8(4).

(3) Where such a further direction has been given the provisions of this Schedule relevant to the appeal shall apply, subject to sub-paragraph (4), as if no direction under paragraph 3 had been given.

(4) Anything done by or on behalf of the Secretary of State in connection with the appeal which might have been done by the appointed person (including any arrangements made for the holding of a hearing or local inquiry) shall, unless that person directs otherwise, be treated as having been done by him.

Appointment of another person to determine appeal

5.—(1) At any time before the appointed person has determined the appeal the Secretary of State may—

(a) revoke his appointment; and

(b) appoint another person under paragraph 1 to determine the appeal instead.

(2) Where such a new appointment is made the consideration of the appeal or any inquiry or other hearing in connection with it shall be begun afresh.

(3) Nothing in sub-paragraph (2) shall require—

(a) the question referred to in paragraph 2(2) to be asked again with reference to the new appointed person if before his appointment it was asked with reference to the previous appointed person (any answers being treated as given with reference to the new appointed person); or

(b) any person to be given an opportunity of making fresh representations or modifying or withdrawing any representations already made.

Local inquiries and hearings

6.—(1) Whether or not the parties to an appeal have asked for an opportunity to appear and be heard, an appointed person—

(a) may hold a local inquiry in connection with the appeal; and

(b) shall do so if the Secretary of State so directs.

(2) Where an appointed person—

(a) holds a hearing by virtue of paragraph 2(4); or

(b) holds an inquiry by virtue of this paragraph,

an assessor may be appointed by the Secretary of State to sit with the appointed person at the hearing or inquiry to advise him on any matters arising, notwithstanding that the appointed person is to determine the appeal.

(3) Subject to sub-paragraph (4), the costs—

(a) of any hearing held by virtue of paragraph 2(4); and

(b) of any inquiry held under this paragraph,

shall be defrayed by the Secretary of State.

(4) Section 250(2) to (5) of the Local Government Act 1972 (local inquiries: evidence and costs) applies to an inquiry held by virtue of this paragraph with the following adaptations—

(a) for the references in subsection (4) (recovery of costs of holding the inquiry) to the Minister causing the inquiry to be held there shall be substituted references to the Secretary of State; and

(b) for the reference in subsection (5) (orders as to the costs of the parties) to the Minister causing the inquiry to be held there shall be substituted a reference to the appointed person or the Secretary of State.

(5) Subject to sub-paragraph (6), at any such inquiry oral evidence shall be heard in public and documentary evidence shall be open to public inspection.

(6) If the Secretary of State is satisfied in the case of any such inquiry—

(a) that giving evidence of a particular description or, as the case may be, making it available for inspection would be likely to result in the disclosure of information as to any of the matters mentioned in sub-paragraph (7); and

(b) that the public disclosure of that information would be contrary to the national interest,

he may direct that evidence of the description indicated in the direction shall only be heard or, as the case may be, open to inspection at that inquiry by such persons or persons of such descriptions as he may specify in that direction.

(7) The matters referred to in sub-paragraph (6)(a) are—

(a) national security; and

(b) the measures taken or to be taken to ensure the security of any premises or property.

(8) *The appointed person or the Secretary of State has the same power to make orders under section 250(5) of the Local Government Act 1972 (orders with respect to costs of the*

parties) in relation to proceedings under this Schedule which do not give rise to an inquiry as he has in relation to such an inquiry.

Supplementary provisions

7.—(1) The Tribunals and Inquiries Act [1992] shall apply to a local inquiry or other hearing held in pursuance of this Schedule as it applies to a statutory inquiry held by the Secretary of State, but as if in [section 10(1)] of that Act (statement of reasons for decisions) the reference to any decision taken by the Secretary of State were a reference to a decision taken by an appointed person.

(2) Where an appointed person is an officer of the Department of the Environment or the Welsh Office the functions of determining an appeal and doing anything in connection with it conferred on him by this Schedule shall be treated for the purposes of the Parliamentary Commissioner Act 1967—

(a) if he was appointed by the Secretary of State for the time being having general responsibility in planning matters in relation to England, as functions of that Department; and

(b) if he was appointed by the Secretary of State for the time being having general responsibility in planning matters in relation to Wales, as functions of the Welsh Office.   **[508]**

NOTES

Commencement: 11 March 1992, 1 June 1992; see the note to s 1 at **[467–468]**.

Para 6: sub-para (8) temporarily omitted by the Planning (Consequential Provisions) Act 1990, s 6, Sch 4, paras 1, 16, until such day as may be appointed by order made by the Secretary of State. The Planning (Consequential Provisions) Act 1990 (Appointed Day No 1 and Transitional Provisions) Order 1991, SI 1991/2698, appointed 2 January 1992 only for the purposes of awards of costs in relation to proceedings which give rise to a hearing.

Words in square brackets in para 7 substituted by the Tribunals and Inquiries Act 1992, s 18(1), Sch 3, para 34.

PLANNING (CONSEQUENTIAL PROVISIONS) ACT 1990
(c 11)

ARRANGEMENT OF SECTIONS

An Act to make provision for repeals, consequential amendments, transitional and transitory matters and savings in connection with the consolidation of enactments in the Town and Country Planning Act 1990, the Planning (Listed Buildings and Conservation Areas) Act 1990 and the Planning (Hazardous Substances) Act 1990 (including provisions to give effect to recommendations of the Law Commission)   [24 May 1990]

1. Meaning of "the consolidating Acts", "the repealed enactments", etc

(1) In this Act—

"the consolidating Acts" means the principal Act, the Planning (Listed Buildings and Conservation Areas) Act 1990, the Planning (Hazardous Substances) Act 1990 and, so far as it reproduces the effect of the repealed enactments, this Act,

"the principal Act" means the Town and Country Planning Act 1990, and

"the repealed enactments" means the enactments repealed by this Act.

(2) Expressions used in this Act and in any of the other consolidating Acts have the same meaning as in those Acts.   **[509]**

NOTES
Commencement: 24 August 1990.

2. Continuity, and construction of references to old and new law

(1) The substitution of the consolidating Acts for the repealed enactments does not affect the continuity of the law.

(2) Anything done or having effect as if done under or for the purposes of a provision of the repealed enactments has effect, if it could have been done under or for the purposes of the corresponding provision of the consolidating Acts, as if done under or for the purposes of that corresponding provision.

(3) Any reference, whether express or implied, in the consolidating Acts or any other enactment, instrument or document to a provision of the consolidating Acts shall, so far as the context permits, be construed as including, in relation to the times, circumstances and purposes in relation to which the corresponding provision of the repealed enactments has effect, a reference to that corresponding provision.

(4) Any reference, whether express or implied, in any enactment, instrument or document to a provision of the repealed enactments shall be construed, so far as is required for continuing its effect, as including a reference to the corresponding provision of the consolidating Acts.   **[510]**

NOTES
Commencement: 24 August 1990.
The consolidating Acts: Town and Country Planning Act 1990, Planning (Listed Buildings and Conservation Areas) Act 1990, Planning (Hazardous Substances) Act 1990 and this Act (to the extent that it reproduces the effect of the repealed enactments—see s 1 at **[509]**).

3. Repeals

(1) The enactments specified in Schedule 1 are repealed to the extent specified in the third column of that Schedule.

(2) Those repeals include the repeal, in accordance with Recommendations of the Law Commission, of section 105(4) and (5) of the 1968 Act and section 21(7A) and (8) of the 1971 Act as no longer of practical utility.

(3) The repeals have effect subject to any relevant savings in Schedule 3.   **[511]**

NOTES
Commencement: 24 August 1990.
The 1968 Act: Town and Country Planning Act 1968.
The 1971 Act: Town and Country Planning Act 1971.

4. Consequential amendments

Schedule 2 (which makes consequential amendments) shall have effect, subect to any relevant transitional provisions in Schedule 3. **[512]**

NOTES
Commencement: 24 August 1990.

5. Transitional provisions and savings

(1) Schedule 3 (which makes transitional provision and contains savings in connection with the repeals made by this Act) shall have effect.

(2) Nothing in that Schedule affects the general operation of section 16 of the Interpretation Act 1978 (general savings implied on repeal) or of the previous provisions of this Act. **[513]**

NOTES
Commencement: 24 August 1990.

6. Transitory modifications

Schedule 4 (which makes transitory modifications of the consolidating enactments) which shall have effect. **[514]**

NOTES
Commencement: 24 August 1990.
The consolidating Acts: Town and Country Planning Act 1990, Planning (Listed Buildings and Conservation Areas) Act 1990, Planning (Hazardous Substances) Act 1990 and this Act (to the extent that it reproduces the effect of the repealed enactments—see s 1 at **[509]**).

7. Short title, commencement and extent

(1) This Act may be cited as the Planning (Consequential Provisions) Act 1990.

(2) This Act shall come into force at the end of the period of three months beginning with the day on which it is passed.

(3) This Act does not extend to Scotland or Northern Ireland except (subject to subsection (4)) so far as it affects other enactments so extending.

(4) The repeals in Part II of Schedule 1 extend to England and Wales only and those in Part III of that Schedule to Scotland only. **[515]**

NOTES
Commencement: 24 August 1990.

SCHEDULES

SCHEDULE 1

Section 3

REPEALS

PART I

GENERAL

Chapter	Short title	Extent of repeal
10 & 11 Geo 6 c 51	The Town and Country Planning Act 1947	The whole Act.

Chapter	Short title	Extent of repeal
10 & 11 Eliz 2 c 36	The Local Authorities (Historic Buildings) Act 1962	The whole Act.
10 & 11 Eliz 2 c 38	The Town and Country Planning Act 1962	The whole Act.
1963 c 33	The London Government Act 1963	In section 85, in subsection (3) the words from "or by" to "1971" and from "(or as" to "paragraph 6)" and in subsection (4) the words from "or of" to "1971".
1967 c 69	The Civic Amenities Act 1967	In section 5, paragraph (a) and in section 30(1), the definition of "the Planning Act".
1968 c 72	The Town and Country Planning Act 1968	The whole Act.
1969 c 22	The Redundant Churches and Other Religious Buildings Act 1969	Section 2.
1969 c 48	The Post Office Act 1969	In Schedule 4, paragraph 89 and in paragraph 93, sub-paragraphs (1)(xxxiii) and (4)(j).
1971 c 78	The Town and Country Planning Act 1971	The whole Act.
1972 c 5	The Local Employment Act 1972	In Schedule 3, the entry relating to the Town and Country Planning Act 1971.
1972 c 70	The Local Government Act 1972	In section 182, subsections (1) and (2), in subsection (3) paragraphs (a) and (c) and subsections (4) to (6). Section 183. In Schedule 16, paragraphs 4 to 54, 58 and 59.
1973 c 26	The Land Compensation Act 1973	In section 53(5) the words from "sections 180" to "or". Sections 68 to 82.
1973 c 37	The Water Act 1973	In Schedule 8, paragraph 94.
1974 c 7	The Local Government Act 1974	In Schedule 6, paragraph 25.
1974 c 32	The Town and Country Amenities Act 1974	Section 1(1). Section 4(1). In section 6, the words from "section 116" to "and in" and the words from "Schedule 8" to "or". Section 7(1). Section 8. Section 10. Section 13(1)(a).
1975 c 76	The Local Land Charges Act 1975	In Schedule 1, the entry relating to the Town and Country Planning Act 1971.
1977 c 29	The Town and Country Planning (Amendment) Act 1977	The whole Act.
1979 c 46	The Ancient Monuments Act and Archaeological Areas 1979	In Schedule 4, paragraph 11.
1980 c 65	The Local Government, Planning and Land Act 1980	Section 86(1) to (6). Sections 89 and 90.

Chapter	Short title	Extent of repeal
1980 c 65—*cont*	The Local Government, Planning and Land Act 1980—*cont*	Section 91(1). Section 119. In section 122, in subsection (1) the words "section 113 of the Town and Country Planning Act 1971" and "and 113", and in subsections (2), (3), (6) and (8) the word "113". In section 147, in subsection (1) the words from the beginning to "and", in subsection (3) the words from "sections 192" to "Act and" and in subsection (5) the words from the beginning to "Scotland". In section 149, in subsection (1) the words from "in place" to "planning authority", in subsection (3)(a) the words from "and in place" to "them" and subsection (5). Section 150. Schedule 14. In Schedule 15, paragraphs 2 to 15, 17 to 20, 22, 23 and 25 to 28. In Schedule 23, paragraphs 8 to 11. In Schedule 32, paragraph 5(7), in paragraph 15(2)(b), sub-paragraph (i), in paragraph 17(7) the words "the 1971 Act or", in the first place where they occur, and "Part III of the 1971 Act or", paragraphs 18, 20(1), 22(2)(a), 23 and 26(1A)(a). In Schedule 33, paragraph 12.
1980 c 66	The Highways Act 1980	In Schedule 24, paragraphs 20 and 22, and in paragraph 23, sub-paragraphs (d) to (h).
1981 c 36	The Town and Country Planning (Minerals) Act 1981	Sections 1 to 18. In section 34, the words from the beginning to "Act, and" and the words "in each case". Schedule 1.
1981 c 38	The British Telecommunications Act 1981	In Schedule 3, paragraph 10(2)(c).
1981 c 41	The Local Government and Planning (Amendment) Act 1981	The whole Act.
1981 c 43	The Disabled Persons Act 1981	Section 3.
1981 c 54	The Supreme Court Act 1981	In Schedule 5, the entry relating to the Town and Country Planning Act 1971.
1981 c 64	The New Towns Act 1981	In Schedule 12, paragraph 11.
1981 c 67	The Acquisition of Land Act 1981	In Schedule 4, in the Table in paragraph 1, the entry relating to the Town and Country Planning Act 1971 and paragraph 21.

Chapter	Short title	Extent of repeal
1981 c 69	The Wildlife and Countryside Act 1981	In Schedule 16, paragraphs 1 to 4.
1982 c 16	The Civil Aviation Act 1982	In Schedule 2, in paragraphs 4 and 5 the entries relating to the Town and Country Planning Act 1971 and paragraph 6. In Schedule 10, in paragraphs 4(c) and 8(c), the words from "either" to "or".
1982 c 21	The Planning Inquiries (Attendance of Public) Act 1982	The whole Act.
1982 c 30	The Local Government (Miscellaneous Provisions) Act 1982	Sections 35 and 36. In Schedule 5, paragraphs 2 and 3. In Schedule 6, paragraph 7.
1982 c 52	The Industrial Development Act 1982	In Part II of Schedule 2, paragraph 7(2).
1983 c 47	The National Heritage Act 1983	In Schedule 4, paragraphs 15 to 17 and 19 to 21, 22(1) to (5) and (7), 23 and 24.
1984 c 12	The Telecommunications Act 1984	In Schedule 4, paragraph 53.
1984 c 32	The London Regional Transport Act 1984	In Schedule 6, paragraph 9
1985 c 19	The Town and Country Planning (Compensation) Act 1985	Section 1.
1985 c 51	The Local Government Act 1985	In section 3, subsections (1), (3) and (4). Sections 4 and 5. Schedule 1. In Schedule 2, paragraph 1. In Schedule 3, paragraphs 2 and 3(1) and in paragraph 4 the words "54(2) and ". In Schedule 4, paragraph 50. In Schedule 14, paragraph 48.
1985 c 52	The Town and Country Planning (Amendment) Act 1985	Section 1.
1985 c 68	The Housing Act 1985	In section 256(4), paragraph (b).
1985 c 71	The Housing (Consequential Provisions) Act 1985	In Schedule 2, paragraphs 22 and 24(8).
1986 c 31	The Airports Act 1986	In Schedule 2, in paragraph 1(1) and (2), the words "the Town and Country Planning Act 1971". In Schedule 4, paragraph 1.
1986 c 44	The Gas Act 1986	In Schedule 7, in paragraph 2, sub-paragraph (1)(xxiv) and (xxvi) and in (xxvii) the words "and 71" and sub-paragraphs (2)(c) and (9)(e) and paragraph 12.
1986 c 63	The Housing and Planning Act 1986	Section 25. Sections 30 to 34. Section 41. Sections 45 and 46.

Chapter	Short title	Extent of repeal
1986 c 63—*cont*	The Housing and Planning Act 1986—*cont*	In section 58(1), the words from "in Part II" to "Schedule 6" and the words from "in Part IV" to "Schedule 7". In Schedule 6, Parts I and II. In Schedule 7, Part I. In Schedule 9, paragraphs 1 to 5, 6(1) and 7 to 12. Schedule 10. In Schedule 11, paragraphs 1 to 24, 26 and 27.
1987 c 3	The Coal Industry Act 1987	In Schedule 1, paragraph 19.
1988 c 4	The Norfolk and Suffolk Broads Act 1988	In Schedule 3, paragraphs 4, 7 to 28, 32 and 48.
1988 c 40	The Education Reform Act 1988	In Schedule 12, paragraphs 40 and 70.
1988 c 50	The Housing Act 1988	In section 67, in subsection (1) the words from "in place" onwards and in subsection (3) the words from "and in place" to "them", and sub-sections (5) and (6). In Schedule 17, paragraph 18.
1989 c 15	The Water Act 1989	In Schedule 25, in paragraph 1, in sub-paragraph (2), para-graphs (xvi) and (xvii) and in paragraph (xviii) the words "and 71", and sub-paragraphs (10)(iv) and (11)(ii), and paragraph 42.
1989 c 29	The Electricity Act 1989	In Schedule 16, in paragraph 1, in sub-paragraph (1), para-graphs (xxii) and (xxiv) and in paragraph (xxv) the words "and 71", paragraphs 2(2)(c), (4)(c) and (5)(b) and 3(1)(d).
1989 c 42	The Local Government and Housing Act 1989	In Schedule 11, paragraphs 19 and 20.

[516]

NOTES
 Commencement: 24 August 1990.

PART II
ENGLAND AND WALES ONLY

Chapter	Short title	Extent of repeal
9 & 10 Geo 6 c 35	The Building Restrictions (War-Time Contraventions) Act 1946	The whole Act.
14 & 15 Geo 6 c 60	The Mineral Workings Act 1951	Section 32 Section 40(6).
1969 c 48	The Post Office Act 1969	In Schedule 9, paragraph 27(8).
1972 c 42	The Town and Country Planning (Amendment) Act 1972	The whole Act.

Chapter	Short title	Extent of repeal
1980 c 65	The Local Government, Planning and Land Act 1980	Section 87.
1984 c 10	The Town and Country Planning Act 1984	The whole Act.
1989 c 29	The Electricity Act 1989	In Schedule 8, paragraph 7.

[517]

NOTES
  Commencement: 24 August 1990.

PART III

SCOTLAND ONLY

Chapter	Short title	Extent of repeal
14 & 15 Geo 6 c 60	The Mineral Workings Act 1951	In section 40(6), the words "section forty-nine of the principal Act or" and "as the case may be".
1972 c 42	The Town and Country Planning (Amendment) Act 1972	In section 10, in subsection (1), the words from "Subject" to "this section" and "section 277" to "1971 or", subsection (1AA), in subsection (2) the words from "or" to "Commission", subsections (3A) and (3B), in subsection (4) the words from "the appropriate" to "Monmouthshire)" and the words from "or the" to "Wales".
		In section 10A, in subsection (1) the words from "or" to "Commission", in subsections (3) and (5) the words "or (as the case may be) the Commission" and "or (as the case may be) they think", in subsection (8) the words "or (as the case may be) the Commission" and subsection (9).
1980 c 65	The Local Government Planning and Land Act 1980	In section 87, in subsection (1) the words "a local planning authority in England or Wales or", in subsection (2) paragraph (a) and in subsection (8) paragraph (a).
1984 c 10	The Town and Country Planning Act 1984	In section 1, in subsection (1)(b) the words from "section 53" to "or", in subsection (5)(b) the words from "a local" to "Scotland" and in subsection (6) the words from "section 277A" to "1971 or".

Chapter	Short title	Extent of repeal
1984 c 10—*cont*	The Town and Country Planning Act 1984—*cont*	In section 2, in subsection (1) the words from the beginning to "Scotland" and in subsection (4) the words from "section 60" to "1971 or". In section 3, in subsection (2), the words "a local planning authority or, in Scotland" and subsection (8). In section 4, in subsection (1) the words "a licence in writing or, in Scotland" and the words from "section 266(1)(b)" to "be" and subsections (2) and (3). In section 5, in subsection (1) the words from the beginning to "Scotland", in subsection (2) the words "the Act of 1971 or, as the case may be", in subsection (3) the words "local planning authority or" and subsection (4). In section 6, in subsection (1), the definition of "the Act of 1971" and in the definition of "the appropriate authority" the words from "section 266(7)" to "Scotland" and subsections (2) and (3). Section 7(2)(b).
1989 c 29	The Electricity Act 1989	In Schedule 8, in paragraph 7(4), in the definition of "the Planning Act" the words from "the Town and Country Planning Act 1971" to "Wales and" and in the definition of "the relevant section" the words from "section 35" to "1971 and".

[518]

NOTES
   Commencement: 24 August 1990.

SCHEDULE 2

Section 4

CONSEQUENTIAL AMENDMENTS

...   **[519]**

NOTES
   Commencement: 24 August 1990.
   This Schedule contains amendments only.
   Repealed in part by the Planning and Compensation Act 1991, s 84(6), Sch 19, Pts I–III, the Water Consolidation (Consequential Provisions) Act 1991, s 3(1), Sch 3, Pt I, the Education Act 1993, s 307(1), (3), Sch 19, para 159, Sch 21, Pt I, the Leasehold Reform, Housing and Urban Development Act 1993,

s 187(2), Sch 22, the Radioactive Substances Act 1993, s 50, Sch 6, Pt I, the Coal Industry Act 1994, s 67(8), Sch 11, Pt II and the Value Added Tax Act 1994, s 100(2), Sch 15.

Repealed in part by the Environmental Protection Act 1990, s 162(2), Sch 16, Pt VII, as from a day to be appointed under s 164(3) thereof and by the Environment Act 1995, s 120(3), Sch 24, as from a day to be appointed under s 125(3) thereof.

SCHEDULE 3

Sections 3, 4, 5

TRANSITIONAL PROVISIONS AND SAVINGS

1. The repeal by this Act of a provision relating to the coming into force of a provision reproduced in the consolidation Acts does not affect the operation of that provision, in so far as it is not specifically reproduced in the consolidating Acts but remains capable of having effect, in relation to the corresponding provision of the consolidating Acts.

2.—(1) The repeal by this Act of an enactment previously repealed subject to savings does not affect the continued operation of those savings.

(2) The repeal by this Act of a saving to which a previous repeal of an enactment is subject does not affect the operation of the saving in so far as it is not specifically reproduced in the consolidating Acts but remains capable of having effect.

3. Without prejudice to the generality of paragraphs 1 and 2, notwithstanding the repeal by this Act of Schedule 24 to the 1971 Act, the provisions of that Schedule shall continue to have effect, in so far as they are not specifically reproduced in this Schedule and remain capable of having effect, with any reference in those provisions to any provision of the repealed enactments which is reproduced in the consolidating Acts being taken, so far as the context permits, as including a reference to the corresponding provision of those Acts.

4. The repeal by this Act of an enactment which has effect as respects any provision of the repealed enactments (being a provision which is not reproduced in the consolidating Acts but continues in effect by virtue of this Schedule or the Interpretation Act 1978) does not affect its operation as respects that provision.

5. Any document made served or issued after this Act comes into force which contains a reference to any of the repealed enactments shall be construed, except so far as a contrary intention appears, as referring or, as the context may require, including a reference to the corresponding provision of the consolidating Acts.

6. Where any provision of the repealed enactments amends an enactment (not being an enactment reproduced in the consolidating Acts) which is repealed or partly repealed by another enactment which is not in force when this Act comes into force, that provision shall continue to have effect, notwithstanding its repeal by this Act, but subject to section 2(4) of this Act.

7.—(1) In any regulations in force under section 91 of the 1971 Act (execution and cost of works required by enforcement notice) references to an enforcement notice, and an enforcement notice a copy of which has been served in respect of any breach of planning control, include a reference to a notice served under section 103 of that Act or 207 of the principal Act (enforcement of duties as to replacement of trees).

(2) Section 319(3) of the principal Act shall apply to this paragraph as it applies to the provisions there mentioned.

8.—(1) Where the planning permission referred to in section 257 of the principal Act relates to a transferred matter, as defined in section 86(11) of the Local Government, Planning and Land Act 1980, but was granted by a county planning authority before the transfer date, as so defined, the district planning authority [or, in Wales, the local planning authority] shall be the competent authority for the purposes of that section.

(2) Section 319(1) of the principal Act shall apply to this paragraph as it applies to the provisions there mentioned.

9. The expression "statutory undertakers" in any provision of the consolidating Acts shall, as respects any time when the corresponding provision in the repealed enactments (or

any enactment replaced by them) was in force, have the same meaning as that expression had at that time in that provision.

10.—(1) In the case of an enforcement notice served before 27th July 1981, section 285(2) of the principal Act has effect with the following modifications.

(2) In paragraph (a) for the words "issued under that Part" there shall be substituted the words "served under Part V of the 1971 Act".

(3) For paragraph (b) there shall be substituted—

"(b) did not have the enforcement notice or a copy of it served on him under that Part of that Act".

(4) In paragraph (c)—

(a) in sub-paragraph (i) for the word "issued" there shall be substituted the word "served"; and

(b) in sub-paragraph (ii) the words "with a copy of it" shall be omitted.

(5) References in the principal Act to section 285(2) shall, so far as the context permits, be construed as including references to this paragraph.

11.—(1) The repeal by Part II of Schedule 1 to this Act of section 1(8) of the Town and Country Planning Act 1984 (which validates certain permissions granted in respect of Crown land before 12th August 1984) shall not affect any permission to which that section applies immediately before the date on which the principal Act comes into force (and accordingly any such permission has effect and is deemed always to have had effect as provided in section 299(3) of the principal Act).

(2) The repeal by that Part of that Schedule of section 2(7) of that Act of 1984 (which makes similar provision as to orders for the preservation of trees) shall not affect any order to which that section applies immediately before the date on which the principal Act comes into force (and accordingly any such order has effect and is deemed always to have had effect as provided in section 300(3) of the principal Act).

(3) The repeal by that Part of that Schedule of section 1(8) of that Act of 1984 (which makes similar provision as to listed building consents and conservation area consents) shall not affect any order to which that section applies immediately before the date on which the Planning (Listed Buildings and Conservation Areas) Act 1990 comes into force (and accordingly any such consent has effect and is deemed always to have had effect as provided in section 84(3) of the Planning (Listed Buildings) and Conservation Areas) Act 1990).

(4) Section 319(1) of the principal Act applies to sub-paragraphs (1) and (2) as it applies to the provisions there mentioned, and section 92(1) of the Planning (Listed Buildings and Conservation Areas) Act 1990 applies to sub-paragraph (3) as it applies to the provisions mentioned in subsection (2)(a) of that section.

12. The repeal by this Act of section 266(1)(a) of the 1971 Act shall not affect the validity of anything contained in the Greater London Development Plan.

13. The expression "local authority" in any provision of the consolidating Acts shall, as respects any time when the corresponding provision in the repealed enactments (or any enactment replaced by them) was in force, have the same meaning as that expression had at that time in that provision.

14. References in the consolidating Acts to the British Coal Corporation have effect as respects any time before 5th March 1987 as references to the National Coal Board.

15.—(1) Where the functions of a Minister under any enactment re-enacted or referred to in this Act have at any time been exercisable by another Minister or other Ministers, references in the relevant provision of this Act shall as respects any such time, be construed as references to the other Minister or Ministers.

(2) In this paragraph "Minister" includes the Board of Trade and the Treasury.

16. The repeal by this Act of section 56A of the 1971 Act (duration of listed building consents granted before 13th November 1980) shall not affect any consent to which that section applies immediately before this Act comes into force.

17. No sum may be recovered under section 58(4) of the Planning (Listed Buildings and Conservation Areas) Act 1990 or under subsection (7) of section 78 of that Act, as applied by section 80(7) of that Act, in respect of any grant made before that Act comes into force. **[520]**

NOTES
Commencement: 24 August 1990.
Para 3: saving made by this para is to cease to have effect in relation to any right to or claim for any liability in respect of any payment under a scheme made under the Town and Country Planning Act 1947, s 59 (repealed) or under any provision of the Town and Country Planning Act 1954, Pt I or V, by virtue of the Planning and Compensation Act 1991, s 31(4), Sch 6, para 49 at **[548]**.
Words in square brackets in para 8(1) inserted by the Local Government (Wales) Act 1994, s 20(4)(b), Sch 6, Pt II, para 27, as from a day to be appointed.
The principal Act: Town and Country Planning Act 1990.
The consolidating Acts: Town and Country Planning Act 1990, Planning (Listed Buildings and Conservation Areas) Act 1990, Planning (Hazardous Substances) Act 1990 and this Act (to the extent that it reproduces the effect of the repealed enactments—see s 1 at **[509]**).
The 1971 Act: Town and Country Planning Act 1971.

SCHEDULE 4

Section 6

TRANSITORY MODIFICATIONS

1.—(1) If—

(a) no date has been appointed as the date on which a provision mentioned in column 1 of the following Table is to come into force before the relevant commencement date for a paragraph of this Schedule mentioned in column 2 of the Table opposite that provision, or

(b) a date has been appointed which is later than the relevant commencement date for that paragraph,

then that paragraph shall have effect until the appointed day.

TABLE

Provision	*Paragraph of this Schedule*
. . .	. . .
Paragraph 9(1) of Schedule 11 to the Housing and Planning Act 1986 (c 63)	Paragraphs 6, 11 and 14.
Paragraph 9(2) of Schedule 11 to the Housing and Planning Act 1986 (c 63)	Paragraphs 7, 12 and 16.
The repeal of section 110(1) of the 1971 Act in Part III of Schedule 12 to the Housing and Planning Act 1986 (c 63)	Paragraphs 3, 4, 5, 8, 9, 10, 13 and 15.

(2) If—

(a) a date has been appointed as the date on which a provision mentioned in column 1 of the Table in sub-paragraph (1) is to come into force for some purposes of that provision but not for others, and

(b) that date is on or before the relevant commencement date for a paragraph of this Schedule mentioned in column 2 of the Table opposite that provision,

then that paragraph shall have effect for those other purposes of that provision (in so far as it is capable of doing so) until the relevant appointed day.

(3) In this paragraph—

"the relevant commencement date", in relation to a paragraph of this Schedule, means the date on which the provision of the consolidating Acts referred to in that paragraph comes into force;
"the appointed day" means—

(a) in the case mentioned in paragraph (a) of sub-paragraph (1), such day as may be appointed by the Secretary of State by order made by statutory instrument; and

(b) in the case mentioned in paragraph (b) of that sub-paragraph, the day appointed as the day on which the provision mentioned in column 1 of the Table is to come into force.

(4) An order under sub-paragraph (3) (other than an order appointing a day until which paragraph 2 has effect) may—

(a) appoint different days for different provisions and for different purposes, and

(b) make such transitional provision as the Secretary of State thinks appropriate;

and in sub-paragraph (2) "the relevant appointed day", in relation to any purpose of a provision, means the day appointed as the day on which the provision is to come into force for that purpose.

The principal Act

2. . . .

3. At the end of section 175 of that Act there shall be inserted—

"(7) Subsection (5) of section 250 of the Local Government Act 1972 (which authorises a Minister holding an inquiry under that section to make orders with respect to the costs of the parties) shall apply in relation to any proceedings before the Secretary of State on an appeal under section 174 as if those proceedings were an inquiry held by the Secretary of State under section 250.".

4. At the end of section 196 of that Act there shall be inserted—

"(8) Subsection (5) of section 250 of the Local Government Act 1972 (which authorises a Minister holding an inquiry under that section to make orders with respect to the costs of the parties) shall apply in relation to any proceedings before the Secretary of State on an appeal under section 195 as if those proceedings were an inquiry held by the Secretary of State under section 250.".

5. At the end of section 208 of that Act there shall be inserted—

"(1) Subsection (5) of section 250 of the Local Government Act 1972 (which authorises a Minister holding an inquiry under that section to make orders with respect to the costs of the parties) shall apply in relation to any proceedings before the Secretary of State on an appeal under this section as if those proceedings were an inquiry held by the Secretary of State under section 250.".

6. Section 322 of that Act shall be omitted.

7. In paragraph 6 of Schedule 6 to that Act sub-paragraph (5) shall be omitted.

8. In Schedule 16 to that Act—

(a) in Part I the words "Section 175(7)", "Section 196(8)" and "Section 208(11)"; and

(b) in Part V the words "Section 208(11)",

shall be inserted at the appropriate places.

The Planning (Listed Buildings and Conservation Areas) Act 1990

9. At the end of section 41 of the Planning (Listed Buildings and Conservation Areas) Act 1990 there shall be inserted—

"(8) Subsection (5) of section 250 of the Local Government Act 1972 (which authorises a Minister holding an inquiry under that section to make orders with respect to the costs of the parties) shall apply in relation to any proceedings before the Secretary of State on an appeal under section 39 as if those proceedings were an inquiry held by the Secretary of State under section 250.".

10. In sections 85(1), 90(6)(a) and 92(2)(a) of that Act after "2(1) to (3)", and in section 82(1) after "39(6)", there shall be inserted "41(8)".

11. In section 89(1) of that Act the words from section 322" to "held)" shall be omitted.

12. In paragraph 6 of Schedule 3 to that Act sub-paragraph (8) shall be omitted.

The Planning (Hazardous Substances) Act 1990

13. In section 25 of the Planning (Hazardous Substances) Act 1990, at the end there shall be inserted—

''(5) Subsection (5) of section 250 of the Local Government Act 1972 (which authorises a Minister holding an inquiry under that section to make orders with respect to the costs of the parties) shall apply in relation to any proceedings before the Secretary of State on an appeal under this section as if those proceedings were an inquiry held by the Secretary of State under section 250.''.

14. In section 37 of that Act the words from ''section 322'' to ''held)'' shall be omitted.

15. In section 38(5) of that Act, after ''21'' there shall be inserted ''25(5)''.

16. In paragraph 6 of the Schedule to that Act sub-paragraph (8) shall be omitted.

17. ...   **[521]**

NOTES
   Commencement: 24 August 1990.
   Words omitted from the Table in para 1 (part), and the whole of para 2, repealed by the Planning and Compensation Act 1991, ss 27, 84(6), Sch 4, Pt II, para 38, Sch 19, Pt I.
   Words omitted from the Table in para 1 (remainder), and the whole of para 17, repealed by the Radioactive Substances Act 1993, s 50, Sch 6, Pt I.
   The principal Act: Town and Country Planning Act 1990.
   The consolidating Acts: Town and Country Planning Act 1990, Planning (Listed Buildings and Conservation Areas) Act 1990, Planning (Hazardous Substances) Act 1990 and this Act (to the extent that it reproduces the effect of the repealed enactments - see s 1 at **[509]**).
   The 1971 Act: Town and Country Planning Act 1971.

PLANNING AND COMPENSATION ACT 1991
(1991 c 34)

ARRANGEMENT OF SECTIONS

PART I

TOWN AND COUNTRY PLANNING

ENGLAND AND WALES

*An Act to amend the law relating to town and country planning; to extend the powers
to acquire by agreement land which may be affected by carrying out public
works; to amend the law relating to compulsory acquisition of land and to
compensation where persons are displaced from land or the value of land or its
enjoyment may be affected by public works; to provide, in the case of
compensation payable in respect of things done in the exercise of statutory
powers, for advance payments and payments in interest; and to repeal Part X
of the Highways Act 1980*   [25th July 1991]

PART I

TOWN AND COUNTRY PLANNING

ENGLAND AND WALES

1–3. (*Amend the Town and Country Planning Act 1990 as follows: s 1 adds ss 171C, 171D; s 2 adds s 187A; s 3 adds s 187B.*)

Other changes relating to enforcement

4. Time limits on enforcement action

(1) ...

(2) If, in the case of any breach of planning control, the time for issuing an enforcement notice has expired, before the coming into force of this section, by virtue of section 172(4)(b) of the principal Act (as originally enacted), nothing in this section enables any enforcement action to be taken in respect of the breach.

[522]

NOTES

Commencement: See the table at **[559]**.
Sub-s (1) adds the Town and Country Planning Act 1990, ss 171A, 171B.

5–9. (*Amend the Town and Country Planning Act 1990 as follows: s 5 substitutes ss 172, 173, 173A for ss 172, 173 as originally enacted; s 6 substitutes s 174(2), (3), adds ss 177(5A), 289(4A), (4B), substitutes s 289(5A), (6) for s 289(6) as originally enacted and amends ss 175(4), 303(3); s 7 substitutes s 178(1) and substitutes s 178(6) for s 178(6), (7) as originally enacted; s 8 substitutes s 179; s 9 substitutes s 183(1)–(5A) for s 183(1)–(5) as originally enacted, substitutes ss 184(3), 186(5) and substitutes s 187(1), (1A), (1B), (2), (2A) for s 187(1), (2) as originally enacted.*)

10. Certificate of lawful use or development

(1) ...

(2) An order under section 84(2) of this Act may provide for established use certificates to have effect, in such circumstances and to such extent as may be specified in the order, for the purposes of section 191 of the principal Act as substituted by this section. **[523]**

NOTES

Commencement: See the table at **[559]**.
Sub-s (1) substitutes the Town and Country Planning Act 1990, ss 191–194.

11. (*Adds the Town and Country Planning Act 1990, ss 196A–196C and amends ss 324(1)(c), 325(6).*)

Control over development

12, 13. (*S 12 substitutes the Town and Country Planning Act 1990, ss 106–106B for s 106 as originally enacted and adds ss 296(2)(aa), 299A; s 13 adds the Town and Country Planning Act 1990, ss 55(1A), (2)(g), 108(4).*)

14. Fish farming

(1) ...

(2) This section does not apply to the placing or assembly of any structure before this section comes into force. **[524]**

NOTES
Commencement: See the table at **[559]**.
Sub-s (1) adds the Town and Country Planning Act 1990, s 55(4A).

15–19. (*Amend the Town and Country Planning Act 1990 as follows: s 15 inserts s 71A; s 16 substitutes s 65 for ss 65–68, as originally enacted and substitutes s 71(1)–(2A) for s 71(1), (2), as originally enacted; s 17 adds s 70A and amends s 78(2); s 18 adds s 79(6A); s 19 adds s 74(1A), amends Sch 1, para 3(2), and repeals Sch 1, paras 3(3)–(6), 4(1).*)

Controls over particular matters

20, 21. (*S 20 substitutes the Town and Country Planning Act 1990, s 316; s 21 introduces Sch 1 to this Act.*)

22. Old mining permissions

(1) In this section and Schedule 2 to this Act, "old mining permission" means any planning permission for development—

(a) consisting of the winning and working of minerals; or

(b) involving the depositing of mineral waste,

which was deemed to be granted under Part III of the Town and Country Planning Act 1947 by virtue of section 77 of that Act (development authorised under interim development orders after 21st July 1943).

(2) An old mining permission shall, if an application under that Schedule to determine the conditions to which the permission is to be subject is finally determined, have effect as from the final determination as if granted on the terms required to be registered.

(3) If no such development has, at any time in the period of two years ending with 1st May 1991, been carried out to any substantial extent anywhere in, on or under the land to which an old mining permission relates, that permission shall not authorise any such development to be carried out at any time after the coming into force of this section unless—

(a) the permission has effect in accordance with subsection (2) above; and

(b) the development is carried out after such an application is finally determined.

(4) An old mining permission shall—

(a) if no application for the registration of the permission is made under that Schedule, cease to have effect on the day following the last date on which such an application may be made; and

(b) if such an application is refused, cease to have effect on the day following the date on which the application is finally determined.

(5) An old mining permission shall, if—

(a) such an application is granted; but

(b) an application under that Schedule to determine the conditions to which the permission is to be subject is required to be served before the end of any period and is not so served,

cease to have effect on the day following the last date on which the application to determine those conditions may be served.

(6) Subject to subsection (3) above, this section—

(a) shall not affect any development carried out under an old mining permission before an application under that Schedule to determine the conditions to which the permission is to be subject is finally determined or, as the case may be, the date on which the permission ceases to have effect; and

(b) shall not affect any order made or having effect as if made under section 102 of or Schedule 9 to the principal Act (discontinuance, etc. orders).

(7) This section and that Schedule, and the principal Act, shall have effect as if the section and Schedule were included in Part III of that Act.   **[525]**

NOTES
Commencement: See the table at **[559]**.
Principal Act: Town and Country Planning Act 1990.

23–28. (*S 23 substitutes the Town and Country Planning Act 1990, ss 207(3), (4), 209(6), amends ss 208, 210, 324 of that Act, and adds ss 214A–214D of that Act; s 24 amends the Town and Country Planning Act 1990, s 336(1); s 25 introduces Sch 3 to this Act; s 26 adds the Town and Country Planning Act 1990, Pt II, Chapter III, s 54A; s 27 introduces Sch 4 to this Act; s 28 introduces Sch 5 to this Act.*)

Miscellaneous
29. Functions of Historic Buildings and Monuments Commission

(1) In section 33 of the National Heritage Act 1983 (general functions of Commission) after subsection (2) there is inserted—

"(2A) In relation to England, the Commission may—

(a) prosecute any offence under Part I of the Ancient Monuments and Archaeological Areas Act 1979 or under the Planning (Listed Buildings and Conservation Areas) Act 1990, or

(b) institute in their own name proceedings for an injunction to restrain any contravention of any provision of that Part or of that Act of 1990."

(2) . . .   **[526]**

NOTES
Commencement: See the table at **[559]**.
Sub-s (2) adds the Planning (Listed Buildings and Conservation Areas) Act 1990, s 89(3).

30. (*Adds the Town and Country Planning Act 1990, s 322A, and amends the Planning (Listed Buildings and Conservation Areas) Act 1990, s 89(1) and the Planning (Hazardous Substances) Act 1990, s 37(2).*)

31. Planning compensation repeals

(1)–(3) . . .

(4) Schedule 6 to this Act (compensation repeals: minor and consequential amendments) shall have effect.

(5) Subsection (1) above shall have effect in relation to any compensation under Part V of the principal Act unless a claim for the compensation has been made in accordance with section 127 of that Act before the repeal of that section comes into force.

(6) Any amount recoverable under section 133 of that Act which has not been paid, including any interest on any such amount, shall cease to be recoverable and

any mortgage, covenant or other obligation by which the payment of any such amount, or interest on it, is secured is discharged.

(7) The repeal of section 114 of that Act shall have effect, or be treated as having had effect, where the application for planning permission was made on or after 16th November 1990.

(8) The repeal of section 27 of the Planning (Listed Buildings and Conservation Areas) Act 1990 shall have effect, or be treated as having had effect, where the application for listed building consent was made on or after 16th November 1990.

[527]

NOTES

Commencement: See the table at **[559]**.

Sub-ss (1)–(3) repeal the Town and Country Planning Act 1990, ss 114, 119–136, Sch 12 and the Planning (Listed Buildings and Conservation Areas) Act 1990, s 27.

32. Planning: minor and consequential amendments

Schedule 7 to this Act (which makes minor and consequential amendments of the enactments relating to planning) shall have effect. **[528]**

NOTES

Commencement: See the table at **[559]**.

33–61. (*(Pt II) applies to Scotland only.*)

PART III

LAND COMPENSATION, ETC

ENGLAND AND WALES

Acquisition of land

62. Powers to acquire land which will be affected by public works

(1) After section 26(2) of the Land Compensation Act 1973 (responsible authority may acquire land by agreement where enjoyment of land affected by public works) there is inserted—

"(2A) Where the responsible authority—

(a) propose to carry out works on blighted land for the construction or alteration of any public works, and

(b) are, in relation to the land, the appropriate authority,

they may, subject to the provisions of this section, acquire by agreement land the enjoyment of which will in their opinion be seriously affected by the carrying out of the works or the use of the public works if the interest of the vendor is a qualifying interest.

(2B) In this section—

"qualifying interest" has the meaning given in section 149(2) of the Town and Country Planning Act 1990, taking references to the relevant date as references to the date on which the purchase agreement is made, and

"appropriate authority" and "blighted land" have the meanings given respectively in sections 169(1) and 149(1) of that Act."

(2) After section 246(2) of the Highways Act 1980 (acquisition of land by agreement where enjoyment of land affected by works) there is inserted—

"(2A) Where the highway authority propose to carry out works on blighted land for the construction or improvement of a highway, they may acquire by agreement land the enjoyment of which will in their opinion be seriously affected by the carrying out of the works or the use of the highway if the interest of the vendor is a qualifying interest.

(2B) In this section—

"qualifying interest" has the meaning given in section 149(2) of the Town and Country Planning Act 1990, taking references to the relevant date as references to the date on which the purchase agreement is made, and

"blighted land" has the meaning given in section 149(1) of that Act."

[529]

NOTES

Commencement: See the table at **[559]**.

63. Advance payments of compensation and interest

(1) In section 52 of the Land Compensation Act 1973 (right to advance payment of compensation) for subsection (5) there is substituted—

"(4A) Where, at any time after an advance payment has been made on the basis of the acquiring authority's estimate of the compensation, it appears to the acquiring authority that their estimate was too low, they shall, if a request in that behalf is made in accordance with subsection (2) above, pay to the claimant the balance of the amount of the advance payment calculated as at that time.

(5) Where the amount, or aggregate amount, of any payment under this section made on the basis of the acquiring authority's estimate of the compensation exceeds the compensation as finally determined or agreed, the excess shall be repaid; and if after any payment under this section has been made to any person it is discovered that he was not entitled to it, the amount of the payment shall be recoverable by the acquiring authority."

(2) After that section there is inserted—

"52A. Right to interest where advance payment made

(1) This section applies where the compensation to be paid by the acquiring authority for the compulsory acquisition of any interest in land would (apart from this section) carry interest under section 11(1) of the Compulsory Purchase Act 1965 or any bond under Schedule 3 to that Act or section 85 of the Lands Clauses Consolidation Act 1845.

(2) If the authority make a payment under section 52(1) above to any person on account of the compensation—

(a) they shall at the same time make a payment to that person of accrued interest, for the period beginning with the date of entry, on the amount by reference to which the payment under section 52(1) above was calculated; and

(b) the difference between the amount of the payment under section 52(1) above and the amount by reference to which it was calculated is an unpaid balance for the purposes of this section.

(3) If the authority make a payment under section 52(4A) above to any person

on account of the compensation, they shall at the same time make a payment to him of accrued interest, for the period beginning with the date of entry, on—

(a) the amount by reference to which the payment under section 52(4A) above was calculated; less

(b) the amount by reference to which the preceding payment under section 52(1) or (4A) above was calculated.

(4) Where the authority make a payment under section 52(4A) above on account of the compensation, the difference between—

(a) the amount of the payment; and

(b) the amount by reference to which it was calculated less the amount by reference to which the preceding payment under section 52(1) or (4A) above was calculated,

is an unpaid balance for the purposes of this section.

(5) If, on an anniversary of the date on which the authority made a payment to any person under section 52(1) above on account of the compensation—

(a) the amount of accrued interest on the unpaid balance under subsection (2) above or, as the case may be,

(b) the aggregate amount of the accrued interest on any unpaid balances,

exceeds £1,000, the authority shall make a payment to the claimant of the amount or aggregate amount.

(6) The acquiring authority shall, on paying the outstanding compensation, pay the amount of the accrued interest on the unpaid balance under subsection (2) above or, as the case may be, the aggregate amount of the accrued interest on any unpaid balances.

(7) For the purposes of subsections (5) and (6) above, interest accrues on any unpaid balance for the period beginning with—

(a) the making of the payment under section 52(1) or, as the case may be, 52(4A) above; or

(b) if any payment has already been made in respect of that balance under subsection (5) above, the date of the preceding payment under that subsection.

(8) For the purposes of this section—

(a) interest accrues at the rate prescribed under section 32 of the Land Compensation Act 1961 or, in the case of a bond under section 85 of the Lands Clauses Consolidation Act 1845, at the rate specified in section 85; and

(b) the amount by reference to which a payment under section 52(1) or (4A) was calculated is the amount referred to in section 52(3)(a) or (b) for the purposes of that calculation.

(9) Where any payment has been made under section 52(1) above on account of any compensation, the acquiring authority is not required to pay interest under section 11(1) of the Compulsory Purchase Act 1965 or any bond under Schedule 3 to that Act or under section 85 of the Lands Clauses Consolidation Act 1845.

(10) Where the amount, or aggregate amount, of any payment under section 52 above made on the basis of the acquiring authority's estimate of the compensation is greater than the compensation as finally determined or agreed and, accordingly, the interest paid under this section is excessive, the excess shall be repaid.

(11) If after any interest has been paid to any person under this section on any amount it is discovered that he was not entitled to the amount, the interest shall be recoverable by the acquiring authority.

(12) The Secretary of State may from time to time by order substitute another sum for the sum specified in subsection (5) above; and the power to make orders under this subsection shall be exercisable by statutory instrument which shall be subject to annulment in pursuance of a resolution of either House of Parliament.''

[530]

NOTES
 Commencement: See the table at **[559]**.

64. Planning assumptions in connection with highway schemes

At the end of section 14 of the Land Compensation Act 1961 (assumptions as to planning permission) there is added—

''(5) If, in a case where—
  (a) the relevant land is to be acquired for use for or in connection with the construction of a highway, or
  (b) the use of the relevant land for or in connection with the construction of a highway is being considered by a highway authority,

a determination mentioned in subsection (7) of this section falls to be made, that determination shall be made on the following assumption.

(6) The assumption is that, if the relevant land were not so used, no highway would be constructed to meet the same or substantially the same need as the highway referred to in paragraph (a) or (b) of subsection (5) of this section would have been constructed to meet.

(7) The determinations referred to in subsection (5) of this section are—
  (a) a determination, for the purpose of assessing compensation in respect of any compulsory acquisition, whether planning permission might reasonably have been expected to be granted for any development if no part of the relevant land were proposed to be acquired by any authority possessing compulsory purchase powers, and
  (b) a determination under section 17 of this Act as to the development for which, in the opinion of the local planning authority, planning permission would or would not have been granted if no part of the relevant land were proposed to be acquired by any authority possessing compulsory purchase powers.

(8) The references in subsections (5) and (6) of this section to the construction of a highway include its alteration or improvement.''   **[531]**

NOTES
 Commencement: See the table at **[559]**.

65. Certification of appropriate alternative development

(1) For section 17(1) of the Land Compensation Act 1961 (certificate of appropriate alternative development may be issued only if land is not in an area defined in development plan as an area of comprehensive development or shown in the plan as allocated for residential, commercial or industrial use) there is substituted—

''(1) Where an interest in land is proposed to be acquired by an authority possessing compulsory purchase powers, either of the parties directly concerned may, subject to subsection (2) of this section, apply to the local planning authority for a certificate under this section.''

(2) In subsection (4) of that section (certificate stating that permission for development would or would not be granted) for paragraphs (a) and (b) there is substituted—

"(a) that planning permission would have been granted for development of one or more classes specified in the certificate (whether specified in the application or not) and for any development for which the land is to be acquired, but would not have been granted for any other development; or

(b) that planning permission would have been granted for any development for which the land is to be acquired, but would not have been granted for any other development,

and for the purposes of this subsection development is development for which the land is to be acquired if the land is to be acquired for purposes which involve the carrying out of proposals of the acquiring authority for that development.''

(3) After subsection (9) of that section there is inserted—

"(9A) In assessing the compensation payable to any person in respect of any compulsory acquisition, there shall be taken into account any expenses reasonably incurred by him in connection with the issue of a certificate under this section (including expenses incurred in connection with an appeal under section 18 of this Act where any of the issues on the appeal are determined in his favour).''   **[532]**

NOTES
Commencement: See the table at **[559]**.

66. Compensation where permission for additional development granted after acquisition

(1) Schedule 14 to this Act (which revives Part IV of the Land Compensation Act 1961) shall have effect.

(2) This section applies to an acquisition or sale of an interest in land if the date of completion (within the meaning of that Part) falls on or after the day on which this section comes into force.   **[533]**

NOTES
Commencement: See the table at **[559]**.

67. Time limit on validity of notice to treat

In section 5 of the Compulsory Purchase Act 1965 (notice to treat) after subsection (2) there is inserted—

"(2A) A notice to treat shall cease to have effect at the end of the period of three years beginning with the date on which it is served unless—

(a) the compensation has been agreed or awarded or has been paid or paid into court,

(b) a general vesting declaration has been executed under section 4 of the Compulsory Purchase (Vesting Declarations) Act 1981,

(c) the acquiring authority have entered on and taken possession of the land specified in the notice, or

(d) the question of compensation has been referred to the Lands Tribunal.

(2B) If the person interested in the land, or having power to sell and convey or release it, and the acquiring authority agree to extend the period referred to in subsection (2A) of this section, the notice to treat shall cease to have effect at the end of the period as extended unless—

(a) any of the events referred to in that subsection have then taken place, or
(b) the parties have agreed to a further extension of the period (in which case this subsection shall apply again at the end of the period as further extended, and so on).

(2C) Where a notice to treat ceases to have effect by virtue of subsection (2A) or (2B) of this section, the acquiring authority—

(a) shall immediately give notice of that fact to the person on whom the notice was served and any other person who, since it was served, could have made an agreement under subsection (2B) of this section, and
(b) shall be liable to pay compensation to any person entitled to such a notice for any loss or expenses occasioned to him by the giving of the notice and its ceasing to have effect.

(2D) The amount of any compensation payable under subsection (2C) shall, in default of agreement, be determined by the Lands Tribunal.

(2E) Compensation payable to any person under subsection (2C) shall carry interest at the rate prescribed under section 32 of the Land Compensation Act 1961 from the date on which he was entitled to be given notice under that subsection until payment.''   [534]

NOTES
  Commencement: See the table at [559].

Home loss payments

68. Home loss payments

(1) For section 29(2) of the Land Compensation Act 1973 (home loss payment where person displaced from dwelling: period and nature of occupation) there is substituted—

   ''(2) A person shall not be entitled to a home loss payment unless the following conditions have been satisfied throughout the period of one year ending with the date of displacement—

   (a) he has been in occupation of the dwelling, or a substantial part of it, as his only or main residence; and
   (b) he has been in such occupation by virtue of an interest or right to which this section applies,

but, if those conditions are satisfied on the date of displacement, a payment (referred to in this section and sections 32 and 33 below as a ''discretionary payment'') may be made to him of an amount not exceeding the amount to which he would have been entitled if he had satisfied those conditions throughout that period.''

(2) Subsection (5) of that section (no payments where acquisition is in pursuance of blight notice) is omitted.

(3) For section 30 of that Act (amount of home loss payment in England and Wales) there is substituted—

"30. Amount of home loss payment in England and Wales

(1) In the case of a person who on the date of displacement is occupying, or is treated for the purposes of section 29 above as occupying, the dwelling by virtue of an interest in it which is an owner's interest, the amount of the home loss payment shall be 10 per cent of the market value of his interest in the dwelling or, as the case may be, the interest in the dwelling vested in trustees, subject to a maximum of £15,000 and a minimum of £1,500.

(2) In any other case, the amount of the home loss payment shall be £1,500.

(3) For the purposes of this section and section 32 below the market value of an interest in a dwelling—

(a) in a case where the interest is compulsorily acquired, is the amount assessed for the purposes of the acquisition as the value of the interest; and

(b) in any other case, is the amount which, if the interest were being compulsorily acquired in pursuance of a notice to treat served on the date of displacement, would be assessed for the purposes of the acquisition as the value of the interest,

and any dispute as to the amount referred to in paragraph (b) above shall be determined by the Lands Tribunal.

(4) In determining for the purposes of this section and section 32 below the market value of an interest in a dwelling, the dwelling shall be taken to include any garden, yard, outhouses and appurtenances belonging to or usually enjoyed with that dwelling.

(5) The Secretary of State may from time to time by regulations prescribe a different maximum or minimum for the purposes of subsection (1) above and a different amount for the purposes of subsection (2) above.

(6) The power to make regulations under subsection (5) above shall be exercisable by statutory instrument which shall be subject to annulment in pursuance of a resolution of either House of Parliament.

(7) In this section "owner's interest" means the interest of a person who is an owner as defined in section 7 of the Acquisition of Land Act 1981."

(4) For section 32(1) to (3) of that Act (supplementary provisions about home loss payments) there is substituted—

"(1) No home loss payment or discretionary payment shall be made except on a claim in writing made by the claimant giving such particulars as the authority responsible for making the payment may reasonably require for the purpose of determining whether the payment should be made and, if so, its amount.

(2) Where a person is entitled to a home loss payment, the payment shall be made on or before the latest of the following dates—

(a) the date of displacement;

(b) the last day of the period of three months beginning with the making of the claim; and

(c) where the amount of the payment is to be determined in accordance with section 30(1) above, the day on which the market value of the interest in question is agreed or finally determined.

(2A) Where the amount of the payment is to be determined in accordance with section 30(1) above—

(a) the acquiring authority may at any time make a payment in advance; and

(b) if, on the later of the dates referred to in subsection (2)(a) and (b) above, the market value of the interest in question has not been agreed or finally determined, the acquiring authority shall make a payment in advance (where they have not already done so).

(2B) The amount of the payment in advance shall be the lesser of—

(a) the maximum amount for the purposes of section 30(1) above,

(b) 10 per cent of the amount agreed to be the market value of the interest in question or, if there is no such agreement, 10 per cent of the acquiring authority's estimate of that amount.

(2C) Where the amount of a payment in advance differs from the amount of the home loss payment, the shortfall or excess shall be paid by or, as the case may be, repaid to the acquiring authority when the market value of the interest in question is agreed or finally determined.

(3) Where the claimant has satisfied, throughout any period, the conditions mentioned in section 29(2) above, that period shall be treated for the purposes of that subsection as including any immediately preceding period throughout which—

(a) he has resided in the dwelling as his only or main residence but without satisfying those conditions, and

(b) another person or other persons have satisfied those conditions,

and references in this subsection and subsection (3A) below to a dwelling include a reference to a substantial part of it.

(3A) Where the claimant has satisfied, throughout any period, the conditions mentioned in section 29(2) above, that period (or that period as extended under subsection (3) above) shall be treated for the purposes of section 29(2) above as including any immediately preceding period, or successive periods, throughout which he satisfied the conditions mentioned in section 29(2) above in relation to another dwelling or, as the case may be, other dwellings (applying subsection (3) above to determine the length of any period or periods)."

(5) In section 32(4) of that Act for "five years" there is substituted "one year".

(6) In section 32(5) of that Act, for "(3) and (4)" there is substituted "(3) to (4)".

(7) In section 32(7) and (7B) of that Act, after "home loss payment" (in both places) there is inserted "or discretionary payment" and after "required" (in both places) there is inserted "or authorised".

(8) In section 33 of that Act (caravan dwellers)—

(a) in subsection (2) after "home loss payment" there is inserted "or discretionary payment",

(b) in subsection (3), for the words following "substituted" (in the second place) there is substituted—

"(a) he has been in occupation of the caravan site by using a caravan stationed on it as his only or main residence; and

(b) he has been in such occupation of the site by virtue of an interest or right to which this section applies."";

(c) for subsection (4) there is substituted—

"(4) Section 30 above shall have effect as if the references to a person occupying a dwelling by virtue of an interest in it and to his interest in the dwelling were to a person occupying a caravan site by virtue of an interest in it and to that interest.'',

    (d) in subsection (5), for paragraph (a) there is substituted—

    ''(a) as if in subsections (3) and (3A) the references to a dwelling were to a caravan site;'',

and in paragraph (c) for ''(3) and (4)'' there is substituted ''(3) to (4)''.

(9) This section shall have effect in relation to displacements occurring on or after 16th November 1990 but, in the case of claims made before the date on which this section comes into force, no amount is required or authorised to be paid by virtue only of this section before the expiry of the period of one month beginning with the date on which this section comes into force.   **[535]**

NOTES

    Commencement: See the table at **[559]**.

69. Home loss payments: spouses having statutory rights of occupation

After section 29 of the Land Compensation Act 1973 there is inserted—

''29A. Spouses having statutory rights of occupation

(1) This section applies where, by reason of the entitlement of one spouse (''A'') to occupy a dwelling by virtue of an interest or right to which section 29 above applies, the other spouse (''B'') acquires rights of occupation (within the meaning of the Matrimonial Homes Act 1983).

    (2) So long as—

    (a) those rights of occupation continue,

    (b) B is in occupation of the dwelling and A is not, and

    (c) B is not, apart from this section, treated as occupying the dwelling by virtue of an interest or right to which that section applies,

B shall be treated for the purposes of that section as occupying the dwelling by virtue of such an interest (but not an owner's interest within the meaning of section 30 below).

(3) References in this section to a dwelling include a reference to a substantial part of it.''   **[536]**

NOTES

    Commencement: See the table at **[559]**.

70–79. (*S 70 introduces Sch 15 to this Act; ss 71–79 (Pt IV) apply to Scotland only.*)

PART V

MISCELLANEOUS AND GENERAL

80. Interest on compensation and payments on account

(1) Compensation payable under any provision mentioned in column 1 of an entry in Part I of Schedule 18 to this Act shall carry interest at the rate for the time being prescribed under section 32 of the Land Compensation Act 1961 or, in relation to Scotland, section 40 of the Land Compensation (Scotland) Act 1963 from the date shown against that provision in column 2 of the entry until payment.

(2) If it appears to any person that he may become liable to pay to another—

(a) compensation under any provision mentioned in Schedule 18 to this Act, or

(b) interest under subsection (1) above, under any provision mentioned in Part II of Schedule 18 to this Act or under any bond under section 85 of the Lands Clauses Consolidation Act 1845 or Schedule 3 to the Compulsory Purchase Act 1965,

he may, if the other person requests him in writing to do so, make one or more payments on account of such compensation or interest.

(3) If after a payment has been made by any person under subsection (2) above—

(a) it is agreed or determined that he is not liable to pay the compensation or interest, or

(b) by reason of any agreement or determination, any payment under that subsection is shown to have been excessive,

the payment or, as the case may be, excess shall be recoverable by that person.

(4) The Secretary of State may by order amend that Schedule by adding further entries or provisions to Part I or Part II.

(5) An order under this section shall be made by statutory instrument which shall be subject to annulment in pursuance of a resolution of either House of Parliament.   **[537]**

NOTES
Commencement: See the table at **[559]**.

81. Abolition of new street byelaws

(1) Part X of the Highways Act 1980 (new street byelaws) is repealed.

(2) Nothing in this section affects—

(a) any order made before the day on which this section comes into force under section 188 of that Act (new street orders) or under any enactment from which that section is derived; or

(b) any powers of a local authority exercisable under Part X of that Act in respect of such an order.

(3) The Secretary of State may by order made by statutory instrument repeal any local enactment so far as it makes provision having similar effect to any provision of Part X of that Act.   **[538]**

NOTES
Commencement: See the table at **[559]**.

82. Home loss payments: Northern Ireland

An Order in Council under paragraph 1(1)(b) of Schedule 1 to the Northern Ireland Act 1974 (exercise of legislative functions for Northern Ireland) which states that it is made only for purposes corresponding to the purposes of sections 68 and 69 of this Act—

(a) shall not be subject to paragraph 1(4) and (5) of that Schedule (affirmative resolution procedure and procedure in cases of urgency), but

(b) shall be subject to annulment in pursuance of a resolution of either House of Parliament.   **[539]**

NOTES
Commencement: See the table at **[559]**.

83. Consequential amendment of section 91A of the Income and Corporation Taxes Act 1988

In section 91A of the Income and Corporation Taxes Act 1988 (Waste disposal: restoration payments)—

    (a) in subsection (4)(b) for "any term of a relevant agreement" there is substituted "any relevant obligation"; and

    (b) for subsection (7) there is substituted—

"(7) For the purposes of this section a relevant obligation is—

    (a) an obligation arising under an agreement made under—

        (i) section 106 of the Town and Country Planning Act 1990, as originally enacted;

        (ii) section 50 of the Town and Country Planning (Scotland) Act 1972;

    (b) a planning obligation entered into under section 106 of the Act of 1990, as substituted by section 12 of the Planning and Compensation Act 1991, or under section 299A of the Act of 1990;

    (c) an obligation arising under or under an agreement under any provision—

        (i) corresponding to section 106 of the Town and Country Planning Act 1990, as originally enacted or as substituted by the Act of 1991 or to section 299A of the Act of 1990; and

        (ii) for the time being in force in Northern Ireland."   **[540]**

NOTES

Commencement: See the table at **[559]**.

84. Short title, commencement, etc

(1) This Act may be cited as the Planning and Compensation Act 1991.

(2) Subject to subsection (4) below, this Act shall come into force on such day as the Secretary of State may by order made by statutory instrument appoint, and different days may be appointed for different provisions and for different purposes.

(3) An order under subsection (2) above may contain such supplementary, incidental, consequential and transitional provisions as the Secretary of State thinks fit.

(4) Sections 31(2), (3), (7) and (8) and 60(2), (3) and (5), paragraphs 1, 5 and 13 of Schedule 6 and the related repeals shall come into force on the day on which this Act is passed.

(5) Nothing in any provision of this Act affects the punishment for an offence committed before the provision comes into force.

(6) The enactments mentioned in Schedule 19 to this Act are repealed to the extent specified in the third column.

(7) Parts I and III of this Act and section 81 extend to England and Wales only.

(8) Parts II and IV of this Act extend to Scotland only.

(9) This Act, apart from sections 82 and 83, does not extend to Northern Ireland.   **[541]**

NOTES

Commencement: See the table at **[559]**.

SCHEDULES

(Sch 1 amends the Town and Country Planning Act 1990 as follows: para 1 introduces the amendments to that Act; para 2 amends s 72(5); para 3 substitutes s 91(4)(d); para 4 amends s 97(5) and adds s 97(6); para 5 substitutes s 100(8); para 6 amends s 102(8); para 7 substitutes s 105; para 8 amends s 107(5); para 9 substitutes s 116; para 10 amends s 117(2); para 11 amends ss 189(1)(b), 315(1); para 12 amends s 336(1); para 13 amends Sch 1, para 1(1)(d) and repeals Sch 1, para 1(2); para 14 amends Sch 5, paras 1(1)–(3), (5), (6), 2(1), 6, 7, and adds Sch 5, para 9; para 15 substitutes Sch 9, paras 1(1)(a), (c), (2), (3), 2(1), 3(1)–(3), amends Sch 9, paras 2(4)(b), 4(8), 10(1), (3), substitutes Sch 9, para 5(1), (3), (4), 10(4), (8), and adds Sch 9, para 12; para 16 repeals Sch 11, subject to savings with respect to regulations made thereunder.)

SCHEDULE 2

Section 22

REGISTRATION OF OLD MINING PERMISSIONS

Application for registration

1.—(1) Any person who is an owner of any land to which an old mining permission relates, or is entitled to an interest in a mineral to which such a permission relates, may apply to the mineral planning authority for the permission to be registered.

(2) The application must specify the development which the applicant claims is authorised by the permission, including the land to which the permission relates, and the conditions (if any) to which the permission is subject.

(3) The application must be served on the mineral planning authority before the end of the period of six months beginning with the day on which this Schedule comes into force.

(4) On an application under this paragraph, the mineral planning authority must—

    (a) if they are satisfied that (apart from section 22(3) of this Act) the permission authorises development consisting of the winning and working of minerals or involving the depositing of mineral waste, ascertain—

        (i) the area of land to which the permission relates, and
        (ii) the conditions (if any) to which the permission is subject, and grant the application, and

    (b) in any other case, refuse the application.

(5) Where—

    (a) application has been made under this paragraph, but
    (b) the mineral planning authority have not given the applicant notice of their determination within the period of three months beginning with the service of notice of the application (or within such extended period as may at any time be agreed upon in writing between the applicant and the authority),

the application is to be treated for the purposes of section 22 of this Act and this Schedule as having been refused by the authority.

Determination of conditions

2.—(1) The conditions to which an old mining permission is to be subject—

    (a) may include any conditions which may be imposed on a grant of planning permission for development consisting of the winning and working of minerals or involving the depositing of mineral waste,
    (b) may be imposed in addition to, or in substitution for, any conditions ascertained under paragraph 1(4)(a) above, and
    (c) must include a condition that the winning and working of minerals or depositing of mineral waste must cease not later than 21st February 2042.

(2) Where an application for the registration of an old mining permission has been granted, any person who is an owner of any land to which the permission relates, or is entitled to an

interest in a mineral to which the permission relates, may apply to the mineral planning authority to determine the conditions to which the permission is to be subject.

(3) The application must set out proposed conditions.

(4) The application must be served on the mineral planning authority—

(a) after the date mentioned in sub-paragraph (5) below, and

(b) except where section 22(3) of this Act applies, before the end of the period of twelve months beginning with that date or such extended period as may at any time be agreed upon in writing between the applicant and the authority.

(5) The date referred to in sub-paragraph (4) above is—

(a) the date on which the application for registration is granted by the mineral planning authority, if no appeal is made to the Secretary of State under paragraph 5 below, and

(b) in any other case, the date on which the application for registration is finally determined.

(6) On an application under this paragraph—

(a) the mineral planning authority must determine the conditions to which the permission is to be subject, and

(b) if, within the period of three months beginning with the service of notice of the application (or within such extended period as may at any time be agreed upon in writing between the applicant and the authority) the authority have not given the applicant notice of their determination, the authority shall be treated for the purposes of section 22 of this Act and this Schedule as having determined that the permission is to be subject to the conditions set out in the application.

(7) The condition to which an old mining permission is to be subject by reason of sub-paragraph (1)(c) above is not to be regarded for the purposes of the planning Acts as a condition such as is mentioned in section 72(1)(b) of the principal Act (planning permission granted for a limited period).

(8) This paragraph does not apply to an old mining permission which has ceased to have effect since the application under paragraph 1 above was granted.

Registration

3.—(1) Where an application for the registration of an old mining permission is granted, the permission must be entered in the appropriate part of the register kept under section 69 of the principal Act and the entry must specify the area of land ascertained under paragraph 1(4)(a) above.

(2) Where an application to determine the conditions to which an old mining permission is to be subject is finally determined, the conditions must be entered in the appropriate part of that register.

(3) The matters required to be entered in the register under this paragraph must be entered as soon as reasonably practicable.

General provisions about applications

4.—(1) An application under paragraph 1 or 2 above is an application which is—

(a) made on an official form, and

(b) accompanied by an appropriate certificate.

(2) The applicant must, so far as reasonably practicable, give the information required by the form.

(3) Where the mineral planning authority receive an application under paragraph 1 or 2 above, they must as soon as reasonably practicable give to the applicant a written acknowledgement of the application.

(4) Where the mineral planning authority determine an application under either of those

paragraphs, they must as soon as reasonably practicable give written notice of their determination to the applicant.

(5) An appropriate certificate is such a certificate—

(a) as would be required under the provisions mentioned in sub-paragraph (6) or, as the case may be, (7) below to accompany the application if it were an application for planning permission for development consisting of the winning and working of minerals or, as the case may be, involving the depositing of mineral waste, but

(b) with such modifications as are required for the purposes of this Schedule.

(6) For the purposes of paragraph 1 above, the provisions referred to in sub-paragraph (5) above are—

(a) sections 66 to 68 of the principal Act (notification of owners and agricultural tenants) and any provisions of a development order made by virtue of those sections, or

(b) where section 16(1) of this Act is in force, any provision, corresponding to the provisions referred to in paragraph (a) above, of section 65 of that Act (notice etc. of applications) and of a development order made by virtue of that section.

(7) For the purposes of paragraph 2 above, the provisions referred to in sub-paragraph (5) above are—

(a) sections 65 to 68 of the principal Act (publicity for applications) and any provision of a development order made by virtue of those sections, or

(b) where section 16(1) of this Act is in force, section 65 of that Act and any provision of a development order made by virtue of that section.

(8) Section 68(1) or, as the case may be, 65(5) of that Act (offences) shall also have effect in relation to any certificate purporting to be an appropriate certificate.

Right of appeal

5.—(1) Where the mineral planning authority—

(a) refuse an application under paragraph 1 above, or

(b) in granting such an application, ascertain an area of land, or conditions, which differ from those specified in the application,

the applicant may appeal to the Secretary of State.

(2) Where on an application under paragraph 2 above, the mineral planning authority determine conditions that differ in any respect from the conditions set out in the application, the applicant may appeal to the Secretary of State.

(3) An appeal under this paragraph must be made by giving notice of appeal to the Secretary of State.

(4) In the case of an appeal under sub-paragraph (1) above, the notice must be given to the Secretary of State before the end of the period of three months beginning with the determination or, in the case of an application treated as refused by virtue of paragraph 1(5) above, beginning at the end of the period or extended period referred to in paragraph 1(5)(b).

(5) In the case of an appeal under sub-paragraph (2) above, the notice must be given to the Secretary of State before the end of the period of six months beginning with the determination.

(6) A notice of appeal under this paragraph is a notice which—

(a) is made on an official form, and

(b) is accompanied by an appropriate certificate.

(7) The appellant must, so far as reasonably practicable, give the information required by the form.

(8) Paragraph 4(5) to (8) above shall apply for the purposes of sub-paragraph (7) above as it applies for the purposes of paragraph 4(1) above.

Determination of appeal

6.—(1) On an appeal under paragraph 5 above the Secretary of State may—

    (a) allow or dismiss the appeal, or

    (b) reverse or vary any part of the decision of the mineral planning authority (whether the appeal relates to that part of it or not),

and may deal with the application as if it had been made to him in the first instance.

(2) Before determining such an appeal the Secretary of State must, if either the appellant or the mineral planning authority so wish, give each of them an opportunity of appearing before and being heard by a person appointed by the Secretary of State for the purpose.

(3) If at any time before or during the determination of such an appeal it appears to the Secretary of State that the appellant is responsible for undue delay in the progress of the appeal, he may—

    (a) give the appellant notice that the appeal will be dismissed unless the appellant takes, within the period specified in the notice, such steps as are specified in the notice for the expedition of the appeal, and

    (b) if the appellant fails to take those steps within that period, dismiss the appeal accordingly.

(4) The decision of the Secretary of State on such an appeal shall be final.

Reference of applications to Secretary of State

7.—(1) The Secretary of State may give directions requiring applications under this Schedule to any mineral planning authority to be referred to him for determination instead of being dealt with by the authority.

(2) The direction may relate either to a particular application or to applications of a class specified in the direction.

(3) Where an application is referred to him under this paragraph—

    (a) subject to paragraph (b) and sub-paragraph (4) below, the following provisions of this Schedule—

        (i) paragraph 1(1) to (4),
        (ii) paragraph 2(1) to (6)(a), (7) and (8),
        (iii) paragraphs 3 and 4, and
        (iv) paragraphs 8 to 10,

    shall apply, with any necessary modifications, as they apply to applications which fall to be determined by the mineral planning authority,

    (b) before determining the application the Secretary of State must, if either the applicant or the mineral planning authority so wish, give each of them an opportunity of appearing before and being heard by a person appointed by the Secretary of State for the purpose, and

    (c) the decision of the Secretary of State on the application shall be final.

(4) Where an application under paragraph 1 above is so referred to him, paragraph 2(5) above shall apply as if for paragraphs (a) and (b) there were substituted "the date on which the application for registration is finally determined".

Two or more applicants

8.—(1) Where a person has served an application under paragraph 1 or 2 above in respect of an old mining permission—

    (a) he may not serve any further application under the paragraph in question in respect of the same permission, and

    (b) if the application has been determined, whether or not it has been finally determined, no other person may serve an application under the paragraph in question in respect of the same permission.

(2) Where—

(a) a person has served an application under paragraph 1 or 2 above in respect of an old mining permission, and

(b) another person duly serves an application under the paragraph in question in respect of the same permission,

then for the purpose of the determination of the applications and any appeal against such a determination, this Schedule shall have effect as if the applications were a single application served on the date on which the later application was served and references to the applicant shall be read as references to either or any of the applicants.

Application of provisions of principal Act

9.—(1) Subject to paragraph 3 above, section 69 of the principal Act (registers of applications, etc.), and any provision of a development order made by virtue of that section, shall have effect with any necessary modifications as if references to applications for planning permission included applications under paragraph 1 or 2 above.

(2) Where the mineral planning authority is not the authority required to keep the register under that section, the mineral planning authority must provide the authority required to keep the register with such information and documents as that authority requires to comply with paragraph 3 above and with that section as applied by this paragraph.

(3) Sections 284 and 288 of the principal Act (validity of certain decisions and proceedings for questioning their validity) shall have effect as if the action mentioned in section 284(3) included any decision of the Secretary of State on an appeal under paragraph 5 above or on an application referred to him under paragraph 7 above.

Interpretation

10.—(1) In this Schedule—

"official form" means, in relation to an application or appeal, a document supplied by or on behalf of the Secretary of State for use for the purpose in question, and

"owner" in relation to any land means any person who—

(a) is the estate owner in respect of the fee simple, or

(b) is entitled to a tenancy granted or extended for a term of years certain of which not less than seven years remain unexpired.

(2) For the purposes of section 22 of this Act and this Schedule, an application under paragraph 1 or 2 above is finally determined when the following conditions are met—

(a) the proceedings on the application, including any proceedings on or in consequence of an application under section 288 of the principal Act, have been determined, and

(b) any time for appealing under paragraph 5 above, or applying or further applying under that section, (where there is a right to do so) has expired.   **[542]**

NOTES

Commencement: See the table at **[559]**.

SCHEDULE 3

Section 25

LISTED BUILDINGS, CONSERVATION AREAS AND HAZARDOUS SUBSTANCES

PART I

CHANGES RELATING TO ENFORCEMENT

1–16. ...   **[543]**

NOTES

Commencement: See the table at **[559]**.

Paras 1–9 amend the Planning (Listed Buildings and Conservation Areas) Act 1990 as follows: para 1 substitutes s 9(4) and amends s 9(5); para 2 substitutes s 38(5), (6); para 3 substitutes s 39(1)(b), (c), (2) and amends s 39(3); para 4 substitutes s 41 (1), (2) (2A) for s 41(1), (2) as originally enacted; para 5 substitutes s 42(6); para 6 substitutes s 43; para 7 adds s 44A; para 8 adds s 65(3A) and substitutes s 65(5); para 9 amends s 88 (1)–(3) and substitutes ss 88A, 88B for s 88(7) as originally enacted.

Paras 10–16 amend the Planning (Hazardous Substances) Act 1990 as follows: para 10 amends s 23(4) and adds s 23(4A); para 11 amends s 24(1)(b), (8), (9); para 12 adds s 24A; para 13 amends s 25(2); para 14 adds s 26(2A); para 15 adds s 26AA; para 16 amends s 36(4) and substitutes ss 36A, 36B for s 36(6) as originally enacted.

PART II

MINOR AND CONSEQUENTIAL AMENDMENTS

Local Government, Planning and Land Act 1980 (c. 65)

17. In Part I of Schedule 29 to the Local Government, Planning and Land Act 1980, the following are inserted at the appropriate places among the provisions of the Planning (Listed Buildings and Conservation Areas) Act 1990 there listed: 44A, 88 and 88A.

Housing Act 1988 (c. 50)

18. In section 67(3A) of the Housing Act 1988 for "25 and 36" there is substituted "26AA, 36 and 36A".

19–32. ....   **[544]**

NOTES
Commencement: See the table at **[559]**.
Paras 19–29 amend the Planning (Listed Buildings and Conservation Areas) Act 1990 as follows: para 19 amends s 38(2) and substitutes s 38(3); para 20 amends s 39(7); para 21 amends s 42(1) and repeals s 42(7); para 22 amends s 46(4); para 23 repeals s 55(6); para 24 amends s 82(1), (3); para 25 amends s 88(6); para 26 amends s 90(6)(b); para 27 amends s 92(2)(b); para 28 amends Sch 3, para 2(1)(b); para 29 amends Sch 4, para 5(b).
Paras 30–32 amend the Planning (Hazardous Substances) Act 1990, ss 25(1)(b)(v), (c), 31(2), 36(5).

Section 27

SCHEDULE 4

DEVELOPMENT PLANS

PART I

STREAMLINING OF DEVELOPMENT PLAN SYSTEM

1–29. ....   **[545]**

NOTES
Commencement: See the table at **[559]**.
Paras 1–29 amend the Town and Country Planning Act 1990 as follows: para 1 introduces the amendments to that Act; para 2 amends s 12(3), (4)(a), adds s 12(3A), (3B), (7A), (10), and substitutes s 12(6); para 3 inserts s 12A; para 4 substitutes s 13; para 5 amends s 14(2), (4) and repeals s 14(3); para 6 substitutes s 15(1); para 7 substitutes s 16(1), (1A), (1B) for s 16(1) as originally enacted; para 8 amends s 17(1); para 9 amends ss 17(1), 18(1); para 10 amends s 19(2); para 11 amends s 20(1); para 12 substitutes s 21(1), (1A), (1B) for s 21(1) as originally enacted, and amends s 21(2); para 13 repeals s 22; para 14 repeals s 23(2)–(4), (9), (10) and amends s 23(5), (6), (8); para 15 adds s 26(2)(cc), (ff) and amends s 26(2)(f); para 16 substitutes s 31(2)–(10) for s 31(2)–(5) as originally enacted; para 17 substitutes ss 32–35, 35A–35C, 36–40 for ss 32–41 as originally enacted; para 18 substitutes s 42(1), (2), (2A) for s 42(1), (2) as originally enacted; para 19 substitutes s 43(1) for s 43(1), (2) as originally enacted and amends s 43(4); para 20 amends s 44(1) and substitutes s 44(2); para 21 amends s 45(3)(a) and adds s 45(5); para 22 substitutes s 46 for ss 46–48 as originally enacted; para 23 amends s 49; para 24 amends s 50(1), (4)–(6), (8), repeals s 50(2), (3) and substitutes s 50(7), (7A), (9) for the original s 50(7), (9); para 25 amends s 51(1); para 26 adds s 51A; para 27 amends s 52(1) and repeals s 52(2), (3); para 28 amends s 53(1), (2)(b), (f), (g), inserts s 53(2)(cc), (ff) and repeals s 53(5); para 29 substitutes s 54(1)(a)–(d) and amends s 54(4).

PART II
MINOR AND CONSEQUENTIAL AMENDMENTS

30–38. ....

39. In Schedule 17 to the Local Government Act 1972 (discharge of planning functions in national parks) in paragraph 6(a) for "Part II" there is substituted "sections 30 to 35C, 46(2) and 50(1), (4), (5) and (7)".   **[546]**

NOTES

Commencement: See the table at **[559]**.

Paras 30–37 amend the Town and Country Planning Act 1990 as follows: para 30 amends s 284(1)(a); para 31 amends s 287(1)–(3), (5); para 32 amends s 306(2); para 33 amends s 324(1)(a); para 34 amends s 336(1); para 35 substitutes Sch 1, para 2 and Sch 1, para 7(3)(a)(i), (ii), (v)–(viii) for Sch 1, para 7(3)(a)(i)–(iii), (v)–(vii); para 36 repeals Sch 2, Pt I, paras 3, 5, 6, Pt II, paras 3–16, 18 and substitutes Sch 2, Pt I, para 4, Pt II para 17; para 37 amends Sch 13, in para 1, Notes (1), (2), (5), (7), para 2(a), in para 2, Note (3), in para 3, Notes (1)(a), (b), (2), in para 4, Notes (1)(a), (b), (2), inserts Sch 13, in para 1, Note (5A), substitutes Sch 13, in para 2, Note (1), and repeals Sch 13, in para 2, Notes (2), (5).

Para 38 amends the Planning (Consequential Provisions) Act 1990, Sch 4, para 1, and repeals Sch 4, para 2 thereto.

Para 39: repealed by the Environment Act 1995, s 120(3), Sch 24, as from a day to be appointed under s 125(3) of that Act.

PART III
TRANSITIONAL PROVISIONS

Interpretation

40. In this Part of this Schedule—

"commencement" means the commencement of Part I of this Schedule;

"the old law" means the principal Act in the form in which it was in force immediately before commencement;

"the new law" means the principal Act as amended by this Act;

"prescribed" means prescribed by regulations made by the Secretary of State;

"winning and working of minerals", "depositing of mineral waste", "policies" in relation to such winning and working or depositing, and "waste policies" have the same meaning as they have under the new law.

Unitary development plans

41.—(1) Where a local planning authority have, under section 13(3) of the old law, made available copies of proposals for the making, alteration or replacement of a unitary development plan but the proposals are not adopted or approved before commencement—

(a) the proposals shall be treated on and after commencement as if made available under section 13(2) of the the new law; and

(b) any other step taken before commencement for the purpose of complying with any requirement of the old law with respect to such making, alteration or replacement may be treated on and after commencement as having been taken for the purpose of complying with any similar requirement imposed by or under the new law.

(2) Sub-paragraph (3) below applies where, at any time within the period of two years beginning with the date of commencement—

(a) a unitary development plan is in operation which by virtue of paragraph 4 of Part I or paragraph 17 of Part II of Schedule 2 to the old law includes a local plan (whether subject to alteration or otherwise);

(b) proposals are made for the alteration or replacement of the unitary development plan;

(c) the local planning authority who are making those proposals have published in the prescribed manner a statement in the prescribed form identifying a policy included in the plan as an existing policy; and

(d) a local inquiry or other hearing is held for the purpose of considering an objection to the proposals.

(3) Where this sub-paragraph applies, the person holding the inquiry or other hearing need not allow an objector to appear if he is satisfied that—

(a) the objection is to a policy identified in the statement published under sub-paragraph (2)(c) above;

(b) the policy so identified is an existing policy; and

(c) there has been no significant change in circumstances affecting the existing policy since it was included in the unitary development plan.

(4) In this paragraph "existing policy" means a policy or proposal the substance of which (however expressed) was contained in a plan included as mentioned in sub-paragraph (2)(a) above.

Structure plans

42.—(1) Where a local planning authority have, under section 32(3) of the old law, submitted to the Secretary of State copies of proposals for the alteration or repeal and replacement of a structure plan but the proposals are not approved before commencement—

(a) the submission of the proposals shall on and after commencement be treated for the purposes of the new law as the sending of the copy under section 33(2)(b) of that law; and

(b) any other step taken before commencement for the purpose of complying with any requirement of the old law with respect to such alteration or repeal and replacement may on and after commencement be treated as having been taken for the purpose of complying with any similar requirement imposed by or under Part II of the new law.

(2) Where sub-paragraph (1) above applies the proposals may be adopted or approved under the new law as if they had been prepared after commencement.

Local plans

43. Where a local planning authority have made available under section 39(5) or 40(2) of the old law copies of proposals for the making, alteration, repeal or replacement of a local plan but the proposals are not adopted or approved before commencement, the proposals may after commencement be adopted or as the case may be, approved as if the old law were still in force.

44.—(1) A local plan which—

(a) immediately before commencement is in operation in the area of a local planning authority, or

(b) is brought into operation after commencement by virtue of paragraph 43 above,

(in this Schedule referred to as "a saved local plan") shall, subject to the following provisions of this paragraph, continue in operation.

(2) Where a saved local plan—

(a) complies with section 36 of the new law and was prepared by the authority who are entitled to prepare the plan required by that section, or

(b) contains only those policies required or permitted to be included in a minerals local plan or a waste local plan in accordance with sections 36 to 38 of the new law and was made by the authority who are entitled to prepare a minerals local plan or, as the case may be, a waste local plan,

it shall be treated as if it were a local plan, a minerals local plan or, as the case may be, a waste local plan which had been adopted or, as the case may be, approved under the new law (and accordingly may be altered or replaced under the new law).

(3) In sub-paragraphs (4) to (8) below the references to saved local plans do not include a reference to saved local plans treated, by virtue of sub-paragraph (2) above, as if adopted or approved under the new law.

(4) Any saved local plan shall have effect subject to a local plan, minerals local plan or waste local plan which is adopted or approved under the new law and shall not be treated as mentioned in sub-paragraph (2) above (and accordingly may not be altered or replaced under the new law).

(5) Where the last of the plans, or the plan, required to be prepared for an area under sections 36 to 38 of the new law is prepared for that area—

(a) any saved local plan, and

(b) any old development plan,

shall cease to have effect in relation to that area.

(6) If the Secretary of State so directs, any specified provisions of a saved local plan shall continue in operation—

(a) for such period as may be specified or determined in accordance with the direction;

(b) in relation to the area or any specified part of the area to which the saved local plan relates.

(7) The Secretary of State may revoke any direction given under sub-paragraph (6) above.

(8) Before giving or revoking any such direction the Secretary of State shall consult any local planning authority for the area in which the plan is in operation.

(9) A saved local plan shall, while it continues in operation, be treated for the purposes of the new law, any other enactment relating to town and country planning, the Land Compensation Act 1961 and the Highways Act 1980 as being comprised in the development plan in respect of the area in question.

(10) In this paragraph—

"old development plan" has the same meaning as in Part III of Schedule 2 to the principal Act; and

"specified" means specified in the direction.

45.—(1) Sub-paragraph (2) below applies where after commencement—

(a) there is in operation in the area of a local planning authority a saved local plan which does not fall within paragraph 44(2)(a) above;

(b) proposals are made in pursuance of the new law for the making, alteration or replacement of a local plan for that area;

(c) the local planning authority who are making those proposals have published in the prescribed manner a statement in the prescribed form identifying a policy included in the plan as an existing policy; and

(d) a local inquiry or other hearing is held for the purpose of considering any objection to the proposals.

(2) Where this sub-paragraph applies, the person holding the inquiry or other hearing need not allow an objector to appear if he is satisfied that—

(a) the objection is to a policy identified in the statement published under sub-paragraph (1)(c) above;

(b) the policy so identified is an existing policy; and

(c) there has been no significant change in circumstances affecting the existing policy since it first formed part of the saved local plan.

(3) In this paragraph "existing policy" means a policy or proposal the substance of which (however expressed) was contained in the saved local plan falling within sub-paragraph (1)(a) above.

Minerals and waste local plans

46.—(1) Sub-paragraph (2) below applies where after commencement—

(a) there is in operation in the area of a local planning authority a saved local plan which does not fall within paragraph 44(2)(b) above and which contains—

(i) any detailed policies for development consisting of the winning and working of minerals or involving the depositing of mineral waste; or

(ii) any waste policies;

(b) proposals are made in pursuance of the new law for the making, alteration or replacement of a minerals local plan or a waste local plan for that area;

    (c) the local planning authority who are making those proposals have published in the prescribed manner a statement in the prescribed form identifying a policy included in the plan as an existing policy; and

    (d) a local inquiry or other hearing is held for the purpose of considering any objection to the proposals.

(2) Where this sub-paragraph applies, the person holding the inquiry or other hearing need not allow an objector to appear if he is satisfied that—

    (a) the objection is to a policy identified in the statement published under sub-paragraph (1)(c) above;

    (b) the policy so identified is an existing policy; and

    (c) there has been no significant change in circumstances affecting the existing policy since it first formed part of the saved local plan.

(3) In this paragraph "existing policy" means any policy falling within sub-paragraph (1)(a) above the substance of which (however expressed) was contained in the saved local plan falling within that sub-paragraph.

Duty of structure plan authority to notify authorities responsible for saved local plans etc.

47.—(1) In this paragraph the references to saved local plans do not include a reference to saved local plans treated, by virtue of paragraph 44(2) above, as if adopted or approved under the new law.

(2) Where at any time after commencement any proposals for the alteration or replacement of a structure plan are adopted or approved, the authority concerned shall—

    (a) notify any local planning authority in their area that the proposals have been adopted or approved;

    (b) supply that authority with a statement that any saved local plan in operation in that authority's area is or, as the case may be, is not in general conformity with the altered or new structure plan.

(3) A statement that a saved local plan is not in general conformity with a structure plan shall specify the respects in which it is not in such conformity.

(4) Where at any time after commencement any proposals for the alteration or replacement of a structure plan are withdrawn, the authority concerned shall notify any authority who prepared any saved local plan which is in operation in their area that the proposals have been withdrawn.

(5) Nothing in this paragraph requires an authority to notify or supply a statement to themselves.

(6) The provisions of a saved local plan shall prevail for all purposes over any conflicting provisions in the relevant structure plan unless the saved local plan is one stated under sub-paragraph (2) above not to be in general conformity with the structure plan.

(7) Sub-paragraph (6) above is subject to any regulations made by the Secretary of State with respect to conflict between plans.

Consultation

48. Any consultation undertaken before commencement for the purposes of any provision contained in or made under Part II of the old law shall be as effective for the purposes of any similar provision contained in or made under Part II of the new law as if undertaken after commencement.

Joint plans

49.—(1) The Secretary of State may give directions applying with modifications the provisions of this part of this Schedule to cases where—

    (a) any plan has been or is being jointly prepared; or

(b) any proposals for the alteration, repeal or replacement of such a plan have been or are being jointly prepared.

(2) Any such directions may be of a general or particular character.

Proceedings for questioning validity of development plans

50. An application may be made after commencement under and in accordance with section 287 of the old law with respect to any plan adopted, altered, repealed or replaced under the old law.

The Isles of Scilly

51. An order under section 319 of the new law may make transitional provision in connection with any development plan in force in the Isles of Scilly.   **[547]**

NOTES
Commencement: See the table at **[559]**.

(Sch 5 amends the Town and Country Planning Act 1990 as follows: para 1 substitutes Sch 7, paras 5, 6 (for paras 5–7 as originally enacted); para 2 substitutes paras 8(1), (2) (for para 8(1)–(3) as originally enacted), 11(3)–(5) (for para 11 (3), (4) as originally enacted); para 3 repeals Sch 1, para 9(2), (3); para 4 introduces further amendments to Sch 7 to that Act; para 5 amends Sch 7, para 4(1); para 6 amends Sch 7, para 8(4); para 7 substitutes Sch 7, para 9(1), and amends Sch 7, para 9(3); para 8 amends para 10(2)(a); para 9 substitutes para 12(1); para 10 adds Sch 7, para 13(2)(bb), and amends Sch 7, para 13(2)(e).)

SCHEDULE 6
Section 31

PLANNING COMPENSATION REPEALS: MINOR AND CONSEQUENTIAL AMENDMENTS

Land Compensation Act 1961 (c. 33)

1.—(1) In section 15 of the Land Compensation Act 1961 (assumptions not directly derived from development plans—

(a) for subsection (3) there is substituted—

"(3) Subject to subsection (4) of this section, it shall be assumed that, in respect of the relevant land or any part of it, planning permission would be granted—

(a) subject to the condition set out in Schedule 10 to the Town and Country Planning Act 1990, for any development of a class specified in paragraph 1 of Schedule 3 to that Act; and
(b) for any development of a class specified in paragraph 2 of Schedule 3 to that Act."; " and

(b) in subsection (4), paragraphs (a) and (b) are omitted.

(2) This paragraph shall have effect, or be treated as having had effect, in relation to compensation which fell or falls to be assessed by reference to prices current on 16th November 1990 or on any subsequent date.

Gas Act 1965 (c. 36)

2. In Schedule 3 to the Gas Act 1965, paragraph 3 is omitted.

Public Expenditure and Receipts Act 1968 (c.14)

3. In Schedule 3 to the Public Expenditure and Receipts Act 1968 (variation of fees) in paragraph 7, sub-paragraph (b) is omitted.

Post Office Act 1969 (c. 48)

4. In Schedule 9 to the Post Office Act 1969 (transitional provisions) in paragraph 27(7) for "Parts V and XII of the Town and Country Planning Act 1990" there is substituted "Part XII of the Town and Country Planning Act 1990".

Land Compensation Act 1973 (c. 26)

5.—(1) In section 5 of the Land Compensation Act 1973 (assessment of compensation: assumptions as to planning permissions)—

(a) for subsection (2) there is substituted—

"(2) Subject to subsection (3) below, it shall be assumed that, in respect of the land in which the interest subsists ("the relevant land") or any part of it, planning permission would be granted—

(a) subject to the condition set out in Schedule 10 to the Town and Country Planning Act 1990, for any development of a class specified in paragraph 1 of Schedule 3 to that Act; and

(b) for any development of a class specified in paragraph 2 of Schedule 3 to that Act."; and

(b) in subsection (3), paragraphs (a) and (b) are omitted.

(2) This paragraph shall have effect, or be treated as having had effect, where the relevant date for the purposes of Part I of the Land Compensation Act 1973 fell or falls on or after 16th November 1990.

Civil Aviation Act 1982 (c. 16)

6. In section 53(1)(a) of the Civil Aviation Act 1982 "114," is omitted.

Airports Act 1986 (c. 31)

7. In section 61(1)(a) of the Airports Act 1986 "114," is omitted.

8–48. ....

Planning (Consequential Provisions) Act 1990 (c. 11)

49. The saving made by paragraph 3 of Schedule 3 to the Planning (Consequential Provisions) Act 1990 (transitional provisions and savings) shall cease to have effect in relation to any right to or claim for or any liability in respect of any payment—

(a) under a scheme made under section 59 of the Town and Country Planning Act 1947;

(b) under any provision of Part I or V of the Town and Country Planning Act 1954.

[548]

NOTES

Commencement: See the table at **[559]**.

Paras 8–41 amend the Town and Country Planning Act 1990 as follows: para 8 introduces the amendments to that Act; para 9 repeals s 55(6); para 10 substitutes s 56(5)(b); para 11 repeals ss 80, 81; para 12 amends s 90(3); para 13 amends s 107(4) with effect, or treated as having effect, in relation to claims made on or after 16 November 1990; para 14 amends s 109(6); para 15 amends s 111(1), (2) and substitutes s 111(5); para 16 amends s 112(9), (12), (13); para 17 repeals s 113; para 18 amends s 138(2); para 19 amends s 144(2)(b), (6); para 20 amends s 198(4)(a); para 21 amends s 220(3)(a); para 22 amends s 262(4), (7)(a); para 23 amends s 263(3); para 24 repeals s 284(3)(c); para 25 substitutes s 298(1), (2) and amends s 298(3), but does not affect the operation of the Planning (Consequential Provisions) Act 1990, Sch 3 in relation to any private interest or Duchy interest; para 26 amends s 308(1)(b), (2), (6) (and any amount recoverable under that section, by reason of a notice registered under s 132(1), which has not been paid ceases to be recoverable); para 27 repeals s 309; para 28 amends s 310; para 29 amends s 311(1)(b); para 30 repeals s 312; para 31 amends s 313; para 32 amends s 315(2); para 33 amends s 318(5); para 34 repeals s 324(4); para 35 repeals s 326; para 36 repeals s 327; para 37 amends s 328(1); para 38 amends s 336(1); para 39 amends Sch 1, para 16(1); para 40 repeals Sch 3, paras 3–8, 11, 14, amends Sch 3, para 10(2) and substitutes Sch 3, para 13(2); para 41 amends Sch 16, Pts I, III, VI.

Paras 42–48 amend the Planning (Listed Buildings and Conservation Areas) Act 1990 as follows: para 42 repeals s 30(1)(a) and amends s 30(2); para 43 amends s 31(2), (4); para 44 amends s 32(4); para 45 amends s 49; para 46 amends s 88(4); para 47 amends s 90(2), (7)(a); para 48 amends s 91(2).

SCHEDULE 7

Section 32

PLANNING IN ENGLAND AND WALES: MINOR AND CONSEQUENTIAL AMENDMENTS

Agricultural Land (Removal of Surface Soil) Act 1953 (c. 10)

1. In section 2(3) of the Agricultural Land (Removal of Surface Soil) Act 1953 for the words from "it was determined" to the end there is substituted "a certificate was issued under section 192 of the Town and Country Planning Act 1990 that the operations would be lawful."

Local Government Act 1972 (c. 70)

2. In Part III of Schedule 12A to the Local Government Act 1972, in the definition of "protected informant", for "172(3)" there is substituted "171A".

Local Government (Miscellaneous Provisions) Act 1976 (c. 57)

3. In section 7(5) of the Local Government (Miscellaneous Provisions) Act 1976 paragraph (a)(iii) is omitted.

Rent (Agriculture) Act 1976 (c. 80)

4. In section 33(4) of the Rent (Agriculture) Act 1976 for the words from "section 63(2)(b)" to the end there is substituted "section 73A of the Town and Country Planning Act 1990".

Local Government, Planning and Land Act 1980 (c. 65)

5. In Part I of Schedule 29 to the Local Government, Planning and Land Act 1980, the following are inserted at the appropriate places among the provisions of the principal Act there listed: 171C, 173A, 187A, 187B, 196A to 196C and 324(1)(b) and (c) and (7).

Local Government (Miscellaneous Provisions) Act 1982 (c. 30)

6. In section 33 of the Local Government (Miscellaneous Provisions) Act 1982, in subsection (1) for paragraphs (a) to (c) there is substituted—

"(a) is executed for the purpose of securing the carrying out of works on land in the council's area in which the other person has an interest, or

(b) is executed for the purpose of regulating the use of or is otherwise connected with land in or outside the council's area in which the other person has an interest,

and which is neither executed for the purpose of facilitating nor connected with the development of the land in question."

Housing Act 1988 (c. 50)

7. In section 67(3A) of the Housing Act 1988 after "104" there is inserted "171C, 171D".

8.–61. ....   [549]

NOTES
Commencement: See the table at [559].
Paras 8–57 amend the Town and Country Planning Act 1990 as follows: para 8 introduces the amendments to that Act; para 9 amends s 5(1), (3); para 10 amends s 56(3), and adds s 56(4)(aa); para 11 repeals s 63; para 12 repeals s 64; para 13 amends s 69(1), (3); para 14 amends s 70(3); para 15 amends s 71(4); para 16 adds s 73A; para 17 amends s 74(2); para 18 amends s 77(4); para 19 amends s 79(4); para 20 amends s 91(4)(b); para 21 substitutes s 102(4), (5); para 22 amends s 174(6); para 23 substitutes s 176(1), (2), (2A) for s 176(1), (2) as originally enacted; para 24 substitutes s 177(1)(a), (3), substitutes s 177(1)(c), (1A), (1B) for s 177(1)(c) as originally enacted, and amends s 177(5); para 25 amends s 178(2); para 26 substitutes s 180; s 27 amends s 181(1), (3)–(5); para 28 amends s 184(4)(b), (5), (8); para 29 amends s 186(1)(b), (c), (2); para 30 amends s 188(1), (2); para 31 repeals s 190(4); para 32 amends s 195(1), (2), and substitutes s 195(4); para 33 amends s 196(1)–(4), and repeals s 196(5)–(7); para 34 amends s 198(4)(a); para 35 amends s 216(6); para 36 repeals s 219(6); para 37 amends s 220(3)(a); para 38 amends s 224(3); para 39 repeals s 250(2); para 40 repeals s 266(3); para 41 amends s 284(3)(g); para 42 amends s 285(1), (2), and repeals s 285(5), (6); para 43 repeals s 286(1)(b), and amends s 286(1)(c), (2); para 44 repeals s 290; para 45 amends s 296(1)(c), (2)(a); para 46 amends

s 299(1), (2), (5)(a), (6), and substitutes s 299(4); para 47 amends s 306(2)(b), (3); para 48 adds s 316A; para 49 substitutes s 319; para 50 amends s 325(1)(a), (2), (4); para 51 adds s 329(4); para 52 amends s 336(1), (9), (10); para 53 substitutes Sch 1, paras 3(1)(b) (for para 3(1)(b), (c) as originally enacted), 8, 20(3), amends Sch 1, paras 4(2), 7(1), 11(1)(b), 20(1), and adds Sch 1, para 12A; para 54 amends Sch 6, paras 1(1), 2(1)(a)–(d), (2), (8), 3(2), 4(2) and adds Sch 6, para 2(aa); paras 55, 56 amend Sch 8, paras 3(2), 4(5)(a), Sch 13, para 5; para 57 amends Sch 16, Pts I–III, VI, and repeals Sch 16, Pts IV, V.

    Paras 58–61 amend the Planning (Listed Buildings and Conservation Areas) Act 1990, s 59(4), and substitute ss 67(8), 73(2) of, and Sch 4, para 3 to, that Act.

(Schs 8–13 apply to Scotland only.)

SCHEDULE 14

Section 66

COMPENSATION WHERE PERMISSION FOR ADDITIONAL DEVELOPMENT GRANTED AFTER ACQUISITION

1. After section 22 of the Land Compensation Act 1961 there is inserted—

"PART IV

COMPENSATION WHERE PERMISSION FOR ADDITIONAL DEVELOPMENT GRANTED AFTER ACQUISITION

23. Compensation where planning decision made after acquisition

(1) Where—

    (a) any interest in land is compulsorily acquired or is sold to an authority possessing compulsory purchase powers and, before the end of the period of ten years beginning with the date of completion, a planning decision is made granting permission for the carrying out of additional development of any of the land; and

    (b) the principal amount of the compensation which was payable in respect of the compulsory acquisition or, in the case of a sale by agreement, the amount of the purchase price, was less than the amount specified in subsection (2) of this section,

then, subject to the following provisions of this section, the person to whom the compensation or purchase price was payable shall be entitled, on a claim duly made by him, to compensation from the acquiring authority of an amount equal to the difference.

(2) The amount referred to in subsection (1)(b) of this section is the principal amount of the compensation which would have been payable in respect of a compulsory acquisition of the interest by the acquiring authority, in pursuance of a notice to treat served on the relevant date if—

    (a) the planning decision mentioned in subsection (1)(a) of this section had been made before that date; and

    (b) the permission granted by it had been in force on that date.

(3) No compensation shall be payable by virtue of this section in respect of a planning decision in so far as it relates to land acquired by the acquiring authority, whether compulsorily or by agreement—

    (a) under section 142 or 143 of the Local Government, Planning and Land Act 1980 (acquisitions by urban development corporations and by highway authorities in connection with urban development areas);

    (b) under the New Towns Act 1981 (acquisitions by development corporations and by highway authorities in connection with new town areas); or

    (c) where the compulsory purchase order included a direction under section 50 of the Planning (Listed Buildings and Conservation Areas) Act 1990 (minimum compensation where building deliberately allowed to fall into disrepair).

(4) If—

    (a) in accordance with the preceding provisions of this section the person referred to in subsection (1) of this section would be entitled to compensation under this section; but

(b) before the planning decision in question that person has died, or any other act or event has occurred whereby the right to compensation under this section, if vested in him immediately before that act or event, would thereupon have vested in some other person,

the right to compensation under this section shall be treated as having devolved as if that right had been vested in him immediately before his death or immediately before that act or event, as the case may be, and the compensation shall be payable to the persons claiming under him accordingly.

(5) Compensation under this section shall carry interest at the rate prescribed under section 32 of this Act from the date of the planning decision in question until payment.

(6) The provisions of Part I of this Act (so far as applicable) shall apply (subject to the following provisions) in relation to the assessment of compensation under this section as they apply in relation to the assessment of compensation in respect of the compulsory acquisition of an interest in land.

24. Provisions as to claims under section 23

(1) For the purpose of facilitating the making of claims for compensation under section 23 of this Act—

(a) the person entitled to receive the compensation or purchase price in respect of such an acquisition or sale as is mentioned in section 23(1)(a) of this Act; or

(b) any person claiming under him as being a person who, if compensation under that section became payable, would be entitled to it by virtue of subsection (4) of that section,

may give to the acquiring authority an address for service under this section.

(2) Where, at any time—

(a) after a person has given an acquiring authority an address for service under this section; and

(b) before the end of the period mentioned in paragraph (a) of section 23(1) of this Act,

such a planning decision is made as is mentioned in that paragraph, the acquiring authority shall, subject to subsection (3) of this section, give notice of the decision in the prescribed form to that person at that address.

(3) If—

(a) an address for service has been given by such a person as is mentioned in subsection (1)(b) of this section; and

(b) the acquiring authority have reasonable grounds for believing that the person mentioned in subsection (1)(a) of this section is dead or that any other act or event has occurred as mentioned in section 23(4)(b) of this Act,

the acquiring authority need not give a notice to the person mentioned in subsection (1)(a).

(4) A claim for compensation under section 23 of this Act in respect of a planning decision shall not have effect if made more than six months after the following date, that is to say—

(a) if the claim is made by a person who has not given the acquiring authority an address for service under this section, the date of the decision;

(b) if the claim is made by a person who has given the acquiring

authority such an address, the date on which notice of the decision is given to him in accordance with subsection (2) of this section;

but, where there is an appeal against the planning decision, the reference in paragraph (a) of this subsection to the date of the planning decision shall be read as a reference to the date of the decision on the appeal.

(5) The references in subsection (4) of this section to an appeal against a planning decision include an appeal made by virtue of section 78(2) of the Town and Country Planning Act 1990.

(6) Where—

(a) a person has given to an acquiring authority an address for service under this section; and

(b) that authority, before the end of the period mentioned in section 23(1)(a) of this Act, cease to be entitled to an interest in the whole or part of the land comprised in the acquisition or sale, without remaining or becoming entitled to a freehold interest in, or tenancy of that land or that part of it, as the case may be,

they shall notify the local planning authority; and after that it shall be the duty of the local planning authority to give notice to the acquiring authority of any planning decision of which the acquiring authority are required to give notice under subsection (2) of this section.

(7) Notice under subsection (6) of this section of a planning decision—

(a) in the case of a decision made by the local planning authority, shall be given within seven days after the making of the decision; and

(b) in any other case, shall be given within seven days after the making of the decision has been notified to the local planning authority.

25. Extension to planning permission where no planning decision made

(1) The provisions of sections 23 and 24(1) of this Act shall have effect in relation to any planning permission falling within column 1 of the following table for any development as if a planning decision granting that permission had been made on the date shown in column 2.

Planning permission	Date of decision
Permission granted by a development order	When development is initiated
Permission granted by the adoption or approval of a simplified planning zone scheme	When the scheme is approved or adopted
Permission granted by an order designating an enterprise zone	When the designation takes effect
Permission deemed to be granted by a direction under section 90 of the Town and Country Planning Act 1990	When the direction is given
Permission deemed to be granted by a local planning authority	The occurrence of the event in consequence of which the permission is deemed to be granted

(2) Where the provisions of section 23 of this Act have effect as applied by subsection (1) of this section in relation to any planning permission falling within column 1 of that table for any development, then if—

(a) before the date shown in column 2, a person who (under section 24(1) of this Act as so applied) is entitled to give an address for service under that section has given such an address to the acquiring authority; and

(b) the development is proposed to be carried out by the acquiring authority or, if it is proposed to be carried out by a person other than the acquiring authority, notice of that proposal is given to the acquiring authority by the person proposing to carry out the development,

it shall, subject to subsection (3) of this section, be the duty of the acquiring authority to give notice of that proposal in the prescribed form to the person mentioned in paragraph (a) of this subsection at the address given by him to the authority.

(3) An acquiring authority shall not be required by virtue of subsection (2) of this section to give notice of proposed development to the person mentioned in section 24(1)(a) of this Act if—

(a) an address for service has been given to them by such a person as is mentioned in section 24(1)(b) of this Act; and

(b) they have reasonable grounds for believing that the former person is dead or that any other act or event has occurred as mentioned in section 23(4)(b) of this Act.

(4) A claim for compensation under section 23 of this Act in respect of a planning permission falling within column 1 of that table shall not have effect if made more than six months after the following date, that is to say—

(a) if the claim is made by a person to whom notice has been given under subsection (2) of this section, the date on which the notice was given;

(b) in any other case, the date shown in column 2.

26. Extension to Crown development

(1) Where—

(a) any interest in land is compulsorily acquired or is sold to an authority possessing compulsory purchase powers, and before the end of the period of ten years beginning with the date of completion there is initiated any additional development of any of the land which was comprised in the acquisition or sale; and

(b) by reason of any such circumstances as are mentioned in subsection (2) of this section the development in question is development for which planning permission is not required,

the provisions of sections 23 and 24(1) of this Act shall apply as if a planning decision granting permission for that development had been made at the time when the additional development is so initiated.

(2) The circumstances referred to in subsection (1) of this section are either or both of the following—

(a) that the development is initiated by or on behalf of the Crown;

(b) that there is a Crown or Duchy interest in the land and the development is initiated in right of that interest.

(3) Where—

(a) the provisions of section 23 of this Act have effect as applied by subsection (1) of this section in relation to the initiation of any development; and

(b) before the development is initiated a person who (under section 24(1) of this Act as so applied) is entitled to give an address for service under that section has given such an address to the acquiring authority,

it shall, subject to subsections (4) and (5) of this section, be the duty of the acquiring authority to give notice in the prescribed form of the initiation of the development to the person mentioned in paragraph (b) of this subsection at the address given by him to the authority.

(4) Where—

(a) by virtue of subsection (3) of this section, it is the duty of a government department to give notice of development initiated by or on behalf of that department; and

(b) the Minister in charge of the department certifies that for reasons of national security it is necessary that the nature of the development should not be disclosed, except to the extent specified in the certificate,

the department shall give notice of development, but shall not be required to give any particulars of the nature of the development except to the extent specified in the certificate.

(5) An acquiring authority shall not be required by virtue of subsection (3) of this section to give notice of proposed development to the person mentioned in section 24(1)(a) of this Act if—

(a) an address for service has been given to them by such a person as is mentioned in section 24(1)(b) of this Act; and

(b) they have reasonable grounds for believing that the former person is dead or that any other act or event has occurred as mentioned in section 23(4)(b) of this Act.

(6) A claim for compensation under section 23 of this Act in respect of the initiation of any development shall not have effect if made more than six months after the following date, that is to say—

(a) if the claim is made by a person to whom notice has been given under subsection (3) of this section, the date on which the notice was given;

(b) in any other case, the time the development is initiated.

(7) In this section "Crown or Duchy interest" means an interest belonging to Her Majesty in right of the Crown or of the Duchy of Lancaster, or belonging to the Duchy of Cornwall, or belonging to a government department or held in trust for Her Majesty for the purposes of a government department.

27. Application of Part IV to certain cases

The preceding provisions of this Part of this Act shall have effect subject to the provisions of the Third Schedule to this Act.

28. Regulations for purposes of Part IV

(1) The Secretary of State may by statutory instrument make regulations for prescribing the form of any notice required by this Part of this Act to be given in the prescribed form.

(2) Any statutory instrument containing such regulations shall be subject to annulment in pursuance of a resolution of either House of Parliament.

29. Interpretation of Part IV

(1) In this Part of this Act—

"additional development", in relation to an acquisition or sale of an interest in land, means any development of the land other than the following, that is to say—

(a) where the acquiring authority are a local authority, and acquired the interest for the purposes of any of their functions, development for the purposes of the functions for which they acquired it;

(b) where the acquiring authority are not a local authority, development for the purposes of the project, in connection with which they acquired the interest;

(c) development for which planning permission was in force on the relevant date;

(d) in the case of compulsory acquisition, development for which it was assumed (in accordance with the provisions of sections 14 to 16 of this Act) for the purpose of assessing compensation that planning permission would be granted; and

(e) in the case of a sale by agreement, development for which, if the interest (instead of being sold by agreement) had been compulsorily acquired by the acquiring authority in pursuance of a notice to treat served on the relevant date, it would have been so assumed;

"date of completion", in relation to an acquisition or sale of an interest in land, means the date on which the acquisition or sale is completed by the vesting of that interest in the acquiring authority;

"local authority" means—

(a) a charging authority, a precepting authority, a combined police authority or a combined fire authority, as defined in section 144 of the Local Government Finance Act 1988;

(b) a levying board within the meaning of section 74 of that Act;

(c) a body as regards which section 75 of that Act applies;

(d) any joint board or joint committee if all the constituent authorities are such authorities as are described in paragraphs (a) to (c); and

(e) the Honourable Society of the Inner Temple or the Honourable Society of the Middle Temple;

and includes any internal drainage board under section 6 of the Land Drainage Act 1976;

"prescribed" means prescribed by regulations under this Part of this Act;

"the relevant date", in relation to a compulsory acquisition of an interest in land, means the date of service of the notice to treat and, in relation to a sale of such an interest by agreement, means the date of the making of the contract in pursuance of which the sale was effected.

(2) In this Part of this Act any reference to the granting of permission for the carrying out of development of any land is a reference to the granting of permission (including where applicable outline permission) for that development—

(a) either unconditionally or subject to conditions; and

(b) either in respect of that land taken by itself or in respect of an area including that land.''

2. After Schedule 2 to that Act there is inserted—

''THIRD SCHEDULE

Section 66

APPLICATION OF PART IV TO CERTAIN CASES

Disturbance, severance and injurious affection

1. Subject to paragraph 2 of this Schedule, any reference in section 23 of this Act to the principal amount of any compensation shall be construed as including any sum attributable to disturbance, severance or injurious affection.

2. If the person entitled to the compensation under section 23 of this Act—

(a) was, at the time of the compulsory acquisition or sale mentioned in subsection (1) of that section, entitled to an interest in other land contiguous or adjacent to the land acquired or purchased; but

(b) is, at the time of the planning decision in question, no longer entitled to that interest, either in respect of the whole or in respect of part of that land;

any reference in section 23 of this Act to the principal amount of any compensation or the amount of the purchase price shall be construed as excluding so much of the compensation or purchase price as was or would have been attributable to severance or injurious affection of that land or, as the case may be, of that part.

Increase in value of contiguous or adjacent land

3. In determining for the purposes of section 23 of this Act the difference between the principal amount of the compensation specified in subsection (2) of that section and the principal amount of the compensation or the amount of the purchase price mentioned in subsection (1) of that section, in a case where—

(a) the compensation or the purchase price was or would have been reduced (whether by virtue of section 7 of this Act or otherwise) by reason of an increase in the value of an interest in contiguous or adjacent land; but

(b) at the time of the planning decision the person entitled to the compensation under section 23 of this Act is not entitled to the interest or is entitled to it only as respects part of the contiguous or adjacent land,

the amount specified in section 23(2) and the principal amount or purchase price mentioned in section 23(1) shall be calculated as if the circumstances by reason of which it was or would have been so reduced had not existed or, as the case may be, as if the interest in the contiguous or adjacent land had subsisted only in that part of the land.

Mortgaged land

4. Subject to the provisions of this Schedule relating to settled land, where, in a case falling within section 23(1) of this Act, the interest in land which was acquired or sold was subject to a mortgage, any reference (however expressed) in section 23 or section 24 of this Act to the person entitled to the compensation or purchase price shall be construed as a reference to the person who, subject to the mortgage, was entitled to that interest, and not as a reference to the mortgagee.

5. For the purposes of the application of section 23 of this Act, and of the provisions of this Schedule other than this paragraph, to a case falling within the preceding paragraph, any reference to the principal amount of the compensation which was or would have been

payable in respect of any compulsory acquisition shall be construed as a reference to the principal amount of the compensation which would have been payable if the interest in question had not been subject to a mortgage.

6. No compensation shall be payable by virtue of section 23 of this Act in respect of a compulsory acquisition or sale by agreement where the interest acquired or sold was the interest of a mortgagee (as distinct from an interest subject to a mortgage).

Settled land

7.—(1) Where, in a case falling within section 23(1) of this Act, the interest in land which was acquired or sold was subject to a settlement, and accordingly the compensation or purchase price was payable to the trustees of that settlement, any reference (however expressed) in section 23 or section 24 of this Act to the person entitled to the compensation or purchase price shall be construed as a reference to the trustees for the time being of the settlement.

(2) Where sub-paragraph (1) of this paragraph applies, section 23(4) of this Act shall not apply.

(3) Any compensation paid to the trustees of the settlement by virtue of section 23 of this Act in respect of a compulsory acquisition or sale by agreement shall be applicable by the trustees as if it were proceeds of the sale of the interest acquired or sold.

(4) In this paragraph "settlement" means a settlement within the meaning of the Settled Land Act 1925, or a trust for sale within the meaning of the Law of Property Act 1925.

Interpretation

8. References in this Schedule to sections 23 and 24 of this Act include references to those sections as applied by section 25 or 26 of this Act, and references to the time of any planning decision shall be construed accordingly.''

[550]

NOTES

Commencement: See the table at **[559]**.

SCHEDULE 15

Section 70

AMENDMENTS RELATING TO LAND COMPENSATION

PART I

MISCELLANEOUS AMENDMENTS

Rules for assessment of compensation

1. In section 5 of the Land Compensation Act 1961 (rules for assessing compensation), in rule (3) (disregard of special suitability of land for any purpose where, in particular, there is no market for that purpose apart from the special needs of a particular purchaser or the requirements of an authority possessing compulsory purchase powers) "the special needs of a particular purchaser or" is omitted.

Expenses in acquiring replacement land

2. After section 10 of the Land Compensation Act 1961 there is inserted—

"10A Expenses of owners not in occupation.

Where, in consequence of any compulsory acquisition of land—

(a) the acquiring authority acquire an interest of a person who is not then in occupation of the land; and

(b) that person incurs incidental charges or expenses in acquiring, within the period of one year beginning with the date of entry, an interest in other land in the United Kingdom,

the charges or expenses shall be taken into account in assessing his compensation as they would be taken into account if he were in occupation of the land.''

Compensation otherwise than in the form of money

3. In section 3 of the Compulsory Purchase Act 1965 (acquisition by agreement for a consideration in money) after ''money'' there is inserted ''or money's worth''.

Tenants at will, etc. part acquisitions

4. In section 20(2) of the Compulsory Purchase Act 1965 (tenant at will, etc., entitled to compensation for damage done to him in his tenancy), for ''in his tenancy by severing the'' there is substituted ''by severing''.

Caravans etc. affected by noise of public works

5.—(1) After section 20 of the Land Compensation Act 1973 there is inserted—

''20A Power to make payments in respect of caravans and other structures affected by noise of public works.

(1) The Secretary of State may make regulations empowering responsible authorities to make a payment, not exceeding an amount specified in the regulations, in respect of any dwelling which—

(a) is not a building;
(b) is occupied by a person as his only or main residence; and
(c) is affected or likely to be affected by noise caused by the construction or use of public works.

(2) Regulations under this section may—

(a) make provision as to the level of noise giving rise to a power under the regulations and the area in which a dwelling must be situated if a power is to arise in respect of it;
(b) specify the classes of public works and of dwellings in respect of which a power is to arise, and the classes of persons entitled to make claims, under the regulations; and
(c) make provision as to the funds out of which expenses incurred by responsible authorities under the regulations are to be defrayed.

(3) The power to make regulations under this section shall be exercisable by statutory instrument which shall be subject to annulment in pursuance of a resolution of either House of Parliament.

(4) Subsections (3), (7) and (12) of section 20 above apply for the purposes of this section as they apply for the purposes of that.''.

(2) This paragraph does not apply in relation to any public works if the relevant date for the purposes of Part I of the Land Compensation Act 1973 fell more than twelve months before the date on which this paragraph comes into force.

Farm loss payments

6.—(1) Section 34 of the Land Compensation Act 1973 (right to farm loss payment where person displaced from agricultural unit) is amended as follows.

(2) For subsection (1)(a) (section applies only if whole of land is acquired) there is substituted—

''(a) in consequence of the compulsory acquisition of his interest in the whole, or a sufficient part, of that land, he is displaced from the land acquired''.

(3) In subsection (2) (interests qualifying for compensation) for the words following ''tenancy'' there is substituted ''where his interest is as tenant for a year or from year to year

or a greater interest, and "sufficient part" means not less than 0.5 hectares or such other area as the Secretary of State may by order specify".

(4) After that subsection there is inserted—

"(2A) The power to make an order under subsection (2) above shall be exercisable by statutory instrument which shall be subject to annulment in pursuance of a resolution of either House of Parliament."

(5) At the end of subsection (3)(a) (meaning of displacement) there is added "or on any date after the making or confirmation of the compulsory purchase order but before being required to do so by the acquiring authority".

(6) Subsection (6) is omitted.

Notice to quit agricultural holding: right to opt for notice of entry compensation

7. At the end of section 59(7) of the Land Compensation Act 1973 (which does not apply where land was Crown land at time of agreement to acquire it) there is inserted "and the reference in that subsection to an authority possessing compulsory purchase powers includes a person or body of persons who would be an authority possessing compulsory purchase powers if the landlord's interest were not an interest in Crown land (as defined by section 293 of the Town and Country Planning Act 1990)."

Service of documents

8. In section 6(4) of the Acquisition of Land Act 1981 (service of documents where not practicable to ascertain name or address of owner, etc.), for the words from "premises or" to the end there is substituted "land or, if there is no person on the land to whom it may be delivered, by leaving it or a copy of it on or near the land".

Meaning of "owner"

9. In section 7 of the Acquisition of Land Act 1981 (interpretation) at the end of the definition of "owner" there is inserted "and a person who would have power to sell and convey or release the land to the acquiring authority if a compulsory purchase order were operative".

Local authority and statutory undertakers' land

10.—(1) At the end of section 16(1) of, and paragraph 3(1) of Schedule 3 to, the Acquisition of Land Act 1981 (statutory undertakers' land excluded from compulsory purchase if objection made and no certificate given) there is added "and the representation is not withdrawn."

(2) For section 31(2) and (3) of that Act (acquisition under certain enactments without a certificate) there is substituted—

"(2) Section 16(2) of, and paragraph 3(2) of Schedule 3 to, this Act shall not apply to an order confirmed or made by the appropriate Minister jointly with the Minister or Ministers who would (apart from this subsection) have power to make or confirm it."

11. In section 17(3) of, and paragraph 4(3) of Schedule 3 to, that Act (certain compulsory acquisitions to be subject to special parliamentary procedure, unless acquirer is local authority, etc.), before "the Land Authority for Wales" there is inserted "an urban development corporation".

Commons, open spaces, etc.

12.—(1) In section 19 of the Acquisition of Land Act 1981 (compulsory acquisition of commons, etc., to be subject to special parliamentary procedure, with exceptions)—

(a) at the end of subsection (1)(a) there is inserted—

"(aa) that the land is being purchased in order to secure its preservation or improve its management", and

(b) in subsection (2) after "shall" there is inserted "direct the acquiring authority to",

(c) after that subsection there is inserted—

"(2A) Notice under subsection (2) above shall be given in such form and manner as the Secretary of State may direct.", and

(d) at the end of subsection (3) there is added "except where the Secretary of State has given a certificate under subsection (1)(aa) above."

(2) In paragraph 6 of Schedule 3 to that Act—

(a) after sub-paragraph (1)(a) there is inserted—

"(aa) that the right is being acquired in order to secure the preservation or improve the management of the land", and

(b) in sub-paragraph (3) after "shall" there is inserted "direct the acquiring authority to",

(c) after that sub-paragraph there is inserted—

"(3A) Notice under sub-paragraph (3) above shall be given in such form and manner as the Secretary of State may direct.", and

(d) in sub-paragraph (4), after "mentioned, and" there is inserted "except where the Secretary of State has given his certificate under sub-paragraph (1)(aa) above."

Blighted land

13, 14. . . .   **[551]**

NOTES

Commencement: See the table at **[559]**.
Para 13 amends the Town and Country Planning Act 1990, ss 150(1)(b), 161(2)(c), 162(1)(b) and para 14 substitutes Sch 13, para 16 and amends Sch 13, para 18 to that Act.

PART II

MINOR AND CONSEQUENTIAL AMENDMENTS

Land Compensation Act 1961 (c. 33)

15.—(1) In section 14(1) of the Land Compensation Act 1961 after "shall" there is inserted "(subject to subsection (3A) of this section)".

(2) In section 14(3) of that Act, for the words from "but" to the end there is substituted—

"(3A) In determining—

(a) for the purpose referred to in subsection (1) of this section whether planning permission for any development could in any particular circumstances reasonably have been expected to be granted in respect of any land; or

(b) whether any of the assumptions mentioned in section 16 of this Act (but not section 15) are applicable to the relevant land or any part thereof,

regard shall be had to any contrary opinion expressed in relation to that land in any certificate issued under Part III of this Act."

16. In section 17 of that Act—

(a) for the words from the beginning of subsection (2) to "acquire it" there is substituted "If the authority proposing to acquire the interest", and

(b) subsection (8) is omitted.

17. In section 19(1) of that Act for "in the circumstances mentioned in subsection (1) of section 17 of this Act" there is substituted "by an authority possessing compulsory purchase powers".

18. Section 22(3) of that Act is omitted.

Compulsory Purchase Act 1965 (c. 56)

19. In section 31 of the Compulsory Purchase Act 1965—

(a) after "but" there is inserted "in the case of land which is not diocesan glebe land",

(b) for "to be applied" there is substituted "and, in the case of diocesan glebe land, shall be paid to the Diocesan Board of Finance in which the land is vested and, in either case, shall be applied", and

(c) at the end of that section there is added—

"In this section "Diocesan Board of Finance" and "diocesan glebe land" have the same meaning as in the Endowments and Glebe Measure 1976."

Land Compensation Act 1973 (c. 26)

20. In section 13 of the Land Compensation Act 1973—

    (a) in subsection (1) for "to the Church Commissioners to" there is substituted—

        "(a) in the case of land which is not diocesan glebe land, to the Church Commissioners; and

        (b) in the case of diocesan glebe land, to the Diocesan Board of Finance in which the land is vested,

        and (in either case) shall", and

    (b) at the end of subsection (2) there is added "or being diocesan glebe land; and "Diocesan Board of Finance" and "diocesan glebe land" have the same meaning as in the Endowments and Glebe Measure 1976".

21. In section 26 of that Act—

    (a) in subsection (2) for "of the kind mentioned in section 22(2) above" there is substituted "a qualifying interest", and

    (b) in subsection (5) for "and (2)" there is substituted "(2) and (2A)".

22.—(1) Section 29 of that Act is amended as follows.

(2) In subsection (1)—

    (a) in paragraph (ii) "passed the resolution" is omitted;
    (b) "and" following paragraph (iii) is omitted;
    (c) after paragraph (iv) there is inserted "and"; and
    (d) in paragraph (v) after "(e)" there is inserted "above".

(3) In subsection (3A) the words from "of the service" to "(1)(b) above" are omitted.

(4) In subsection (4)—

    (a) for paragraph (b) there is substituted—

        "(b) a right to occupy the dwelling—
        (i) as a statutory tenant within the meaning of the Rent (Agriculture) Act 1976 or the Rent Act 1977, or
        (ii) under a contract to which section 19 of the Rent Act 1977 (restricted contracts) applies or would apply if the contract or dwelling were not excluded by section 19(3) to (5) or 144 of that Act", and

    (b) for paragraph (e) there is substituted—

        "(e) a right to occupy the dwelling under a licence where—
        (i) it is a right to occupy as a protected occupier within the meaning of the Rent (Agriculture) Act 1976,
        (ii) Part IV of the Housing Act 1985 (secure tenancies) applies to the licence, or
        (iii) the licence is an assured agricultural occupancy within the meaning of Part I of the Housing Act 1988."

23. In section 32(7B) of that Act for "the person giving up possession" there is substituted "any person giving up possession or occupation".

24. In section 52 of that Act—

    (a) in subsection (9) after "the amount of the advance payment" there is inserted "together with any amount paid under section 52A", and

(b) in subsection (10) the words following "unpaid" are omitted.

Local Government, Planning and Land Act 1980 (c. 65)

25. After section 141(5) of the Local Government, Planning and Land Act 1980 there is inserted—

"(5A) No compensation is payable, by virtue of an order under this section, under Part IV of the Land Compensation Act 1961."

Highways Act 1980 (c. 66)

26. In section 246(2) of the Highways Act 1980, for the words following paragraph (b) there is substituted "if the interest of the vendor is a qualifying interest".

Acquisition of Land Act 1981 (c. 67)

27. At the end of section 12(3) of, and paragraph 3(3) of Schedule 1 to, the Acquisition of Land Act 1981 there is added "or being diocesan glebe land within the meaning of the Endowments and Glebe Measure 1976".

28. Section 20 of, and paragraph 7 of Schedule 3 to, that Act are repealed.

29–32. . . .   **[552]**

NOTES
Commencement: See the table at **[559]**.
Paras 29, 30 amend the Town and Country Planning Act 1990, ss 231, 318(3), (4), (6).
Para 31 amends the Planning (Listed Buildings and Conservation Areas) Act 1990, s 86(3), (4).
Para 32 amends the Planning (Hazardous Substances) Act 1990, s 34(3), (4).)

(Schs 16, 17 apply to Scotland only.)

SCHEDULE 18

Section 80

COMPENSATION PROVISIONS REFERRED TO IN SECTION 80

PART I

PROVISIONS THAT DO NOT PROVIDE FOR INTEREST

(1) Enactment	(2) Date from which interest payable
Enactments extending to Great Britain	
Section 10(4)(a) of the Forestry Act 1967	Date of claim for compensation
Section 18(1)(a) of the Reservoirs Act 1975	Date of entry on the land
Section 18(1)(b) of that Act	Date of claim for disturbance
Section 7 of the Ancient Monuments and Archaeological Areas Act 1979	Date of the refusal, or grant subject to conditions, of scheduled monument consent
Section 9 of that Act	Date works ceased to be authorised
Section 46 of that Act	Date of entry on the land
Enactments extending to England and Wales	
Section 31(3) of the Land Compensation Act 1961	Date of withdrawal of notice to treat
Section 11(3) of the Compulsory Purchase Act 1965	Date of entry on the land
. . . Section 44(3) of that Act	Date of claim

(1) Enactment	(2) Date from which interest payable
Section 93(7) of that Act	Date of claim
Section 23 of the Highways Act 1980	Date which would be the date from which interest is payable if the works were executed under Part V by a highway authority
Section 28(1) of that Act	Date of claim
Section 73(9) of that Act	Date of claim
Section 74(8) of that Act	Date of claim
Section 77(2) of that Act	In the case of damage sustained by reason of expenditure, the date on which the damage is sustained; otherwise the date of claim
Section 79(11) of that Act	In the case of loss, the date of the notice; and in the case of injurious affection, the date of claim
Section 79(12) of that Act	Date of service of the notice
Section 126(2) of that Act	Date of claim
Section 231 of that Act	In the case of damage sustained by reason of expenditure, the date on which the damage is sustained, otherwise the date of claim
Section 292(1) of that Act	In the case of damage, the date of entry; in the case of disturbance, the date of claim
Section 57 of the Public Health (Control of Disease) Act 1984	In the case damage sustained by reason of expenditure, the date on which the damage is sustained, otherwise the date of claim
Section 106 of the Building Act 1984	In the case damage sustained by reason of expenditure, the date on which the damage is sustained, otherwise the date of claim
. . . Section 107(1) of the principal Act	Date of order under section 97
Section 107(1) of that Act as applied by section 108(1)	Date planning permission is refused or granted subject to conditions
Section 115 of that Act	Date damage suffered or expenses incurred
Section 144(2) of that Act	Date of direction under section 141(3)
Section 186 of that Act	Date of service of stop notice
Section 203 of that Act	Date consent required by tree preservation order is refused or granted subject to conditions
Section 204 of that Act	Date direction is given by local planning authority or Secretary of State
Section 223 of that Act	Date expenses incurred
Section 250 of that Act	Date of order under section 249(2)
Section 279(1) of that Act	Date of decision made in accordance with section 266 or of order under section 97
Section 279(2) of that Act	Date right extinguished or requirement imposed
Section 28 of Planning (Listed Buildings and Conservation Areas) Act 1990	Date of order under section 23
Section 29 of that Act	Date building preservation notice served
Section 16 of the Planning (Hazardous Substances) Act 1990	Date of order under section 14(1)
Section 19 of that Act	Date of modification or revocation of hazardous substances consent
[Paragraph 1 of Schedule 9 to the Water Resources Act 1991	Date of entry upon or occupation or use of land
Paragraph 2(2) or (3) of that Schedule	Date of the ordinary drought order

(1) Enactment	(2) Date from which interest payable
Paragraph 2(4) of that Schedule	Date of decision to prohibit or limit the taking of water
Paragraph 2(5) of that Schedule	Date of suspension or variation of consent to make discharges or of the attachment of conditions to such consent
Paragraph 2(1) of Schedule 21 to that Act	Date of claim
Paragraph 2(2) or (3) of that Schedule	In the case of damage sustained by reason of expenditure, the date on which the damage is sustained; otherwise the date of claim
Paragraph 4(1)(b) of that Schedule	Date loss is caused or damage done
Paragraph 5(1) of that Schedule (including that provision as applied by paragraph 5(3)(b) of that Schedule)	Date of claim
Paragraph 2(1) of Schedule 12 to the Water Industry Act 1991	Date of claim
Paragraph 2(2) or (3) of that Schedule	In the case of damage sustained by reason of expenditure, the date on which the damage is sustained; otherwise the date of claim
Paragraph 6(1)(b) of that Schedule	Date loss is caused or damage done
Section 14 of the Land Drainage Act 1991 (including that provision as applied by section 25(4)(b))	Date of claim
Section 22 of that Act	Date of claim
Section 29(5) of that Act (including that provision as applied by sections 30(3) and 31(5))	Date of claim]

Enactments extending to Scotland

Section 2 of the Land Drainage (Scotland) Act 1930	Date loss is caused or damage done
Section 1 of the Land Drainage (Scotland) Act 1941	Date of injury or damage
Section 4 of the Land Drainage (Scotland) Act 1958	Date damage is suffered
Section 39(3) of the Land Compensation (Scotland) Act 1963	Date of withdrawal of notice to treat
Section 56J(8) of the 1972 Act	Date of order revoking or modifying consent
Section 56K(12) of the 1972 Act	Date of modification or revocation of consent
Section 153 of the 1972 Act	Date of order under section 42
Section 154 of the 1972 Act	Date permission is refused or granted subject to conditions
Section 159 of the 1972 Act	Date damage suffered or expenses incurred
Section 161 of the 1972 Act	Date of order under paragraph 9 of Schedule 10
Section 162 of the 1972 Act	Date building preservation notice served
Section 163 of the 1972 Act	Date consent required by tree preservation order is refused or granted subject to conditions
Section 164 of the 1972 Act	Date requirement is imposed by planning authority or Secretary of State
Section 165 of the 1972 Act	Date expenses incurred
Section 166 of the 1972 Act	Date of service of stop notice
Section 167A of the 1972 Act	Date order made

(1) Enactment	(2) Date from which interest payable
Section 176 of the 1972 Act	Date of direction under section 172(3)
Section 201(5) of the 1972 Act	Date on which order takes effect
Section 226 of the 1972 Act	Date planning permission refused or granted subject to conditions
Section 10 of the Water (Scotland) Act 1980	Date damage sustained
Schedule 6 to that Act	Date source or land is affected or injury is sustained
Section 71 of the Roads (Scotland) Act 1984	Date access stopped up or limited
Section 72 of that Act	Date access stopped up
Section 83(8) of that Act	As regards expenses, date expenses incurred; as regards injurious effect, date injury sustained
Section 88(2) of that Act	Date on which damage sustained
Section 106 of that Act	As regards compulsory acquisition, date on which compulsory purchase notice first published; as regards acquisition by agreement, date agreement made.
Section 116 of that Act	Date on which damage sustained
Section 121 of that Act	Date on which damage done or materials removed
Section 140 of that Act	Date of damage or disturbance

[553]

NOTES

Commencement: See the table at **[559]**.

Entries in square brackets inserted by the Water Consolidation (Consequential Provisions) Act 1991, s 2, Sch 1, para 58, and those omitted repealed by s 3(1) of, and Sch 3, Pt I to, that Act.

PART II

PROVISIONS THAT PROVIDE FOR INTEREST

Enactments extending to England and Wales

Section 23 of the Land Compensation Act 1961 (permission for additional development granted after acquisition).

The following provisions of the Compulsory Purchase Act 1965—

section 5 (notice to treat ceasing to have effect), and
section 11(1) (entry on land under compulsory purchase powers).

The following provisions of the Land Compensation Act 1973—

section 18 (claims under Part I of that Act),
section 36(6) (farm loss payment),
section 37(6) (disturbance payments), and
section 63(1) (injurious affection payments under section 10 of the Compulsory Purchase Act 1965).

Rule 38 of the Lands Tribunal Rules 1975 (awards with interest by Lands Tribunal).

Enactments extending to Scotland

Sections 84 to 86 of the Lands Clauses Consolidation (Scotland) Act 1845.

Paragraph 3 of Schedule 2 to the Acquisition of Land (Authorisation Procedure) (Scotland) Act 1947.

Section 31 (compensation where planning decision made after acquisition) of the Land Compensation (Scotland) Act 1963.

The following provisions of the Land Compensation (Scotland) Act 1973—

section 16 (interest on compensation),
section 33(6) (supplementary provisions about farm loss payments),
section 34(5) (disturbance payments for people without compensatable interests),
section 59 (interest on compensation for injurious affection where no land taken).

Section 78 of this Act.   **[554]**

NOTES
    Commencement: See the table at **[559]**.

SCHEDULE 19

Section 84

REPEALS

PART I

PLANNING: ENGLAND AND WALES

Chapter	Short title	Extent of Repeal
1976 c. 57.	Local Government (Miscellaneous Provisions) Act 1976.	In section 7(5) paragraph (a)(iii).
1990 c. 8.	Town and Country Planning Act 1990.	In section 12(4)(a), ''other'' (in the second place where it occurs) and ''or for any description of development or other use of such land''. Section 14(3). In section 21(2) ''Subject to section 22''. Section 22. Section 23(2) to (4), (9) and (10). In section 49 ''repeal''. In section 50, in subsection (1) ''for the repeal and'', subsections (2) and (3), in subsections (4) and (5) ''repeal and'', in subsection (6) ''repeal'', in paragraph (a) the words from the beginning to ''except that'', ''or 40(2)(a)'' and ''or 40(3)'' and in paragraph (b) ''and they may do so as respects any part of their area to which the proposals relate'' and in subsection (8) ''repeal'' and ''in accordance with the provisions of the relevant local plan scheme''. In section 51(1) ''repeal'' (in both places). Section 52(2) and (3).

Chapter	Short title	Extent of Repeal
1990 c. 8—*contd*	Town and Country Planning Act 1990—*contd*	In section 53, in subsections (1) and (2)(b) ''repeal'', in subsection (2)(g) ''repealing'' and subsection (5).
		Section 55(6).
		Section 63.
		Section 64.
		In section 69, in subsection (1) ''made to that authority'' and in subsection (3) ''made to the authority''.
		In section 74(2) ''section 71 of this Act and''.
		In section 97(5) the words from ''and Part II of Schedule 5'' to the end.
		In section 176(4) ''in writing''.
		In section 178(2) ''(as defined in section 172(3))''.
		In section 186(1)(c) the words from ''or for its retention'' to ''granted''.
		In section 188(1) the ''and'' immediately preceding paragraph (b).
		Section 190(4).
		In section 196 ''an application referred to him under section 192(5) or'' (in subsection (1)), and ''an application or'' (in subsection (3)), and subsections (5) to (7).
		In section 198(4)(a) ''to 68''.
		In section 210, in subsection (3) ''on indictment'' and subsection (5).
		Section 219(6).
		In section 220(3)(a) ''to 68''.
		Section 221(7) to (9).
		Section 250(2).
		Section 266(3).
		In section 284, in subsection (1)(a) ''repeal'' (in both places) and in subsection (3)(g) the words from ''on an application'' to ''or''.
		In section 285, in subsection (1) ''Subject to the provisions of this section'', in subsection (2) ''(6) to (8)'' and subsections (5) and (6).
		Section 286(1)(b).
		In section 287(1), (2), (3) and (5) ''repeal'' in each place where it occurs.
		Section 290.
		In section 306(2) ''repeal''.
		In section 324, in subsection (1)(b) ''198 to 200'', in subsection (1)(c) ''Part VII'' and subsection (2).

Chapter	Short title	Extent of Repeal
1990 c. 8—*contd*	Town and Country Planning Act 1990—*contd*	In section 336(1), the definitions of "development consisting of the winning and working of minerals", "established use certificate" and "mineral compensation modifications", in the definition of "owner" the words "(except in sections 66, 67 and 71)", in the definition of "planning permission" the words from "and in construing" to the end, the definitions of "relevant order", "restriction on the winning and working of minerals" and "special consultations" and in section 336(9) "(1) to (3)". In Schedule 1, paragraphs 1(2), 3(3) to (6), 4(1) and 9(2) and (3). In Schedule 2, in Part I paragraphs 3, 5 and 6, and in Part II paragraphs 3 to 16 and 18. In Schedule 5, in paragraph 1(6) "consisting of the winning and working of minerals". In Schedule 6, in paragraph 2, in sub-paragraph (1)(c) "and subsection (5) of section 196" and in sub-paragraph (8) "or 290". In Schedule 7, in paragraph 13(2)(e) the words from "for the purpose" to "6(2)". Schedule 11. In Schedule 13, Notes (2) and (5) to paragraph 2, in Note (3) to paragraph 2 "also", in Note (1)(b) to paragraph 3 "or under section 22", in Note (2) to paragraph 3 "13(7) or", in Note (1)(b) to paragraph 4 "or under section 22" and in Note (2) to paragraph 4 "13(7) or". In Schedule 16, in Part I, in the entry relating to section 77 "(2) and (9), 66 and 67", in the entry relating to sections 78 and 79 the words from "with" to the end and in the entry relating to section 285 "except subsections (5) and (6)"; and in Part III, the entries relating to sections 312(2) and 324(4); and Parts IV and V.

Chapter	Short title	Extent of Repeal
1990 c. 9.	Planning (Listed Building and Conservation Areas) Act 1990.	In section 9(5) "on indictment". In section 38(2) "within such period as may be so specified". In section 39(7) "in writing". Section 55(6). In section 88(6) "or the presence of minerals in it". In section 90(6)(b) "and 42(6)". In section 92(2)(b) "and 42(6)".
1990 c. 10.	Planning (Hazardous Substances) Act 1990.	In section 25(1)(c) "(1) to (5) and (7)" In section 36(5) "Subject to subsection (6)".
1990 c. 11.	Planning (Consequential Provisions) Act 1990.	In Schedule 2, paragraphs 3(2), 35(1)(b) and 38. In Schedule 4, in paragraph 1, in the Table the entry relating to section 9(4) of the 1971 Act and paragraph 2 of the Schedule, and paragraph 2 of the Schedule.

[555]

NOTES

Commencement: See the table at **[559]**.

PART II

PLANNING COMPENSATION REPEALS

Chapter	Short title	Extent of Repeal
1961 c. 33.	Land Compensation Act 1961.	In section 15(4) paragraphs (a) and (b).
1965 c. 36.	Gas Act 1965.	In Schedule 3, paragraph 3.
1968 c. 14.	Public Expenditure and Receipts Act 1968.	In Schedule 3, paragraph 7(b).
1973 c. 26.	Land Compensation Act 1973.	In section 5(3), paragraphs (a) and (b).
1982 c. 16.	Civil Aviation Act 1982.	In section 53(1)(a) "114".
1986 c. 31.	Airports Act 1986.	In section 61(1)(a) "114".
1990 c. 8.	Town and Country Planning Act 1990.	Section 55(6). Sections 80 and 81. In section 111(1) and (2) "new" (in both places). In section 112, in subsection (9) "new", subsection (12)(a) and in subsection (13) "paragraph (a) or paragraph (b) of". Sections 113 and 114. Part V. In section 198(4)(a) "80, 81". In section 220(3)(a) "80, 81".

Chapter	Short title	Extent of Repeal
1990 c. 8—*contd*	Town and Country Planning Act 1990—*contd*	In section 262(4) and (7)(a) "123". In section 263(3) "123(3) and (4)". Section 284(3)(c). In section 308, in subsection (1)(b) "or 132(1)", in subsection (2) "or, as the case may be, section 132(4)" and in subsection (6) "and in section 309". Section 309. In section 310 "or 309". In section 311(1)(b) "or V". Section 312. In section 313 "Without prejudice to section 312, and". In section 315(2), the words from "and in relation" to "in respect of such land". Section 324(4). Sections 326 and 327. In section 336(1) the definitions of "new development" and "previous apportionment". In Schedule 1, in paragraph 16(1) "114". In Schedule 3, paragraphs 3 to 8, 11 and 14. Schedule 12. In Schedule 16, in Parts III and VI, the entries relating to Schedule 12.
1990 c. 9.	Planning (Listed Buildings and Conservation Areas) Act 1990.	Section 27. In section 30, subsection (1)(a) and in subsection (2) "27". In section 49 the words from "other than" to the end. In section 88(4) "27". In section 91(2) "new development".
1990 c. 11.	Planning (Consequential Provisions) Act 1990.	In Schedule 2, paragraphs 12(3)(a), 18, 24(3)(a)(i) and, in paragraph 29(2) paragraph (a) and, in paragraph (b), sub-paragraphs (i) and (ii).

The repeals in Part II have effect subject to section 31(7) and (8) of this Act and paragraphs 1(2), 5(2) and 13(2) of Schedule 6.   **[556]**

NOTES
   Commencement: See the table at **[559]**.

PART III

LAND COMPENSATION: ENGLAND AND WALES

Chapter	Short title	Extent of Repeal
1961 c. 33.	Land Compensation Act 1961.	In section 5, in rule (3), "the special needs of a particular purchaser or". Section 17(8). Section 22(3).
1973 c. 26.	Land Compensation Act 1973.	In section 29, in subsection (1) "passed the resolution" in paragraph (ii) and the "and" following paragraph (iii), in subsection (3A) the words from "of the service" to "(1)(b) above" and subsection (5). Section 34(6). In section 52(10), the words following "unpaid".
1973 c. 56.	Land Compensation (Scotland) Act 1973.	In Part II of Schedule 2, the entry for section 33(4) of the Land Compensation Act 1973.
1980 c. 65.	Local Government, Planning and Land Act 1980	Section 114(2).
1981 c. 67.	Acquisition of Land Act 1981.	Section 20. Paragraph 7 of Schedule 3.
1985 c. 71.	Housing (Consequential Provisions) Act 1985.	In Schedule 2, paragraph 24(2)(c).
1986 c. 63.	Housing and Planning Act 1986.	Section 9(3)(c).
1990 c. 8.	Town and Country Planning Act 1990.	In section 231, the words from "for a purpose" to "is situated".
1990 c. 11.	Planning (Consequential Provisions) Act 1990.	In Schedule 2, paragraph 29(4).

[557]

NOTES

Commencement: See the table at **[559]**.

(Pt IV applies to Scotland only.)

PART V

NEW STREET BYLAWS

Chapter	Short title	Extent of Repeal
1980 c. 66.	Highways Act 1980.	Part X. Section 203(2)(b)(ii). In section 232(9), in the definition of "byelaw width", the word "byelaws". In section 307(1) the words "193, 200(2)". Section 325(1)(c).

Chapter	Short title	Extent of Repeal
1980 c. 66—*contd*	Highways Act 1980—*contd*	In section 326(1) the words ''or 186''. In Schedule 22 paragraph 4. In Schedule 23 paragraphs 10 and 11.
1985 c. 51.	Local Government Act 1985.	In Schedule 4, paragraphs 29 to 32.
1985 c. 68.	Housing Act 1985.	In section 622, in the definition of ''building regulations'', paragraph (b).
1990 c. 8.	Town and Country Planning Act 1990.	In paragraph 2 of Schedule 17 the words— ''Sections 188, 193 and 196 Section 200(2) and (4)''. In Schedule 17, in paragraph 3, sub-paragraphs (a) and (c)(iii).

The repeals in Part V are subject to the savings in section 81(2) of this Act. **[558]**

NOTES
    Commencement: See the table at **[559]**.

TABLE

COMMENCEMENT OF PLANNING AND COMPENSATION ACT 1991

Royal Assent: 25 Jul 1991

Commencement provisions: s 84(2)–(4); Planning and Compensation Act 1991 (Commencement No 1 and Transitional Provisions) Order 1991, SI 1991/2067; Planning and Compensation Act 1991 (Commencement No 2 and Transitional Provisions) (Scotland) Order 1991, SI 1991/2092; Planning and Compensation Act 1991 (Commencement No 3) Order 1991, SI 1991/2272; Planning and Compensation Act 1991 (Commencement No 4 and Transitional Provisions) Order 1991, SI 1991/2728; Planning and Compensation Act 1991 (Commencement No 5 and Transitional Provisions) Order 1991, SI 1991/2905; Planning and Compensation Act 1991 (Commencement No 6) (Scotland) Order 1992, SI 1992/71; Planning and Compensation Act 1991 (Commencement No 7 and Transitional Provisions) Order 1992, SI 1992/334; Planning and Compensation Act 1991 (Commencement No 8) Order 1992, SI 1992/665; Planning and Compensation Act 1991 (Commencement No 9 and Transitional Provision) Order 1992, SI 1992/1279; Planning and Compensation Act 1991 (Commencement No 10 and Transitional Provision) Order 1992, SI 1992/1491; Planning and Compensation Act 1991 (Commencement No 11 and Transitional Provisions) Order 1992, SI 1992/1630; Planning and Compensation Act 1991 (Commencement No 12 and Transitional Provisions) (Scotland) Order 1992, SI 1992/1937; Planning and Compensation Act 1991 (Commencement No 13 and Transitional Provision) Order 1992, SI 1992/2413; Planning and Compensation Act 1991 (Commencement No 14 and Transitional Provision) Order 1992, SI 1992/2831; Planning and Compensation Act 1991 (Commencement No 15) (Scotland) Order 1993, SI 1993/275; Planning and Compensation Act 1991 (Commencement No 16) (Scotland) Order 1994, SI 1994/398; Planning and Compensation Act 1991 (Commencement No 17 and Transitional Provision) (Scotland) Order 1994, SI 1994/3292

Abbreviation: ''rules, etc'' means ''so much of the provision as enables provision to be made by rules of court, confers on the Secretary of State a power or imposes on him a duty to make or to make provision by development order or other order or regulations or to give or revoke directions, or makes provision with respect to the exercise of any such power or performance of any such duty, is brought into force on the specified date''

s 1   2 Jan 1992 (SI 1991/2905)
 2   27 Jul 1992 (SI 1992/1630)

3	25 Nov 1991 (rules, etc) (SI 1991/2728)
	2 Jan 1992 (otherwise) (SI 1991/2905)
4	2 Jan 1992 (except so far as relates to breach of condition notices) (SI 1991/2905)
	27 Jul 1992 (exception noted above) (SI 1992/1630)
5	25 Nov 1991 (rules, etc) (SI 1991/2728)
6	2 Jan 1992 (otherwise) (SI 1991/2905)
6(1)–(4)	2 Jan 1992 (SI 1991/2905)
(5)	25 Nov 1991 (rules, etc) (SI 1991/2728)
	2 Jan 1992 (otherwise) (SI 1991/2905)
(6)	13 Oct 1991 (SI 1991/2272)
7–9	2 Jan 1992 (SI 1991/2905)
10	25 Nov 1991 (rules, etc) (SI 1991/2728)
	27 Jul 1992 (otherwise) (SI 1992/1630)
11	2 Jan 1992 (SI 1991/2905)
12(1)	25 Oct 1991 (so far as substitutes Town and Country Planning Act 1990, s 106) (SI 1991/2272)
	25 Nov 1991 (so far as substitutes Town and Country Planning Act 1990, ss 106A, 106B) (rules, etc) (SI 1991/2728)
	9 Nov 1992(otherwise) (SI 1992/2831)
(2), (3)	25 Oct 1991 (SI 1991/2272)
13(1)	27 Jul 1992 (SI 1992/1279)
(2)	25 Nov 1991 (rules, etc) (SI 1991/2728)
	27 Jul 1992 (otherwise) (SI 1992/1279)
(3)	27 Jul 1992 (SI 1992/1279)
14	2 Jan 1992 (SI 1991/2905)
15	25 Sep 1991 (SI 1991/2067)
16	25 Nov 1991 (rules, etc) (SI 1991/2728)
	17 Jul 1992 (otherwise) (SI 1992/1491)
17, 18	25 Sep 1991 (SI 1991/2067)
19	25 Nov 1991 (rules, etc) (SI 1991/2728)
	2 Jan 1992(otherwise, except so far as relates to Town and Country Planning Act 1990, Sch 1, para 4(1), as it concerns applications for consent to the display of advertisements) (SI 1991/2905)
	6 Apr 1992 (exception noted above) (SI 1992/665)
20	25 Nov 1991 (rules, etc) (SI 1991/2728)
	17 Jul 1992 (otherwise) (SI 1992/1491)
21	See Sch 1 below
22	25 Sep 1991 (SI 1991/2067)
23(1)–(6)	2 Jan 1992 (SI 1991/2905)
(7)	25 Nov 1991 (so far as relates to Town and Country Planning Act 1990, s 214A(2)) (rules, etc) (SI 1991/2728)
	2 Jan 1992 (otherwise) (SI 1991/2905)
(8)	2 Jan 1992 (SI 1991/2905)
24	6 Apr 1992 (SI 1992/665)
25	See Sch 3 below
26	25 Sep 1991 (SI 1991/2067)
27	See Sch 4 below
28	See Sch 5 below
29	25 Sep 1991 (SI 1991/2067)
30	2 Jan 1992 (subject to certain exceptions and savings; see SI 1991/2728, arts 3, 4) (SI 1991/2728)
	Not in force (exceptions referred to above)
31(1)	25 Sep 1991 (SI 1991/2067)

(2), (3)	25 Jul 1991 (s 84(4))
(4)	See Sch 6 below
(5), (6)	25 Sep 1991 (SI 1991/2067)
(7), (8)	25 Jul 1991 (s 84(4))
32	See Sch 7 below
33	26 Mar 1992 (SI 1992/334)
34	10 Aug 1992 (so far as inserts definition of breach of condition notice into Town and Country Planning (Scotland) Act 1972) (SI 1992/1937)
	25 Sep 1992 (otherwise) (SI 1992/1937)
35	26 Mar 1992 (SI 1992/334)
36	26 Mar 1992 (except so far as relates to breach of condition notices) (SI 1992/334)
	25 Sep 1992 (exception noted above) (SI 1992/1937)
37	24 Feb 1992 (for purpose of enabling Secretary of State to make regulations under Town and Country Planning (Scotland) Act 1972, s 84AA(10)) (SI 1992/334)
	26 Mar 1992 (otherwise) (SI 1992/334)
38–41	26 Mar 1992 (SI 1992/334)
42	10 Aug 1992 (for purpose of enabling Secretary of State to make regulations or development order under Town and Country Planning (Scotland) Act 1972, s 90B) (SI 1992/1937)
	25 Sep 1992 (otherwise) (SI 1992/1937)
43	26 Mar 1992 (SI 1992/334)
44	3 Feb 1995 (subject to a transitional provision) (SI 1994/3292)
45	10 Aug 1992 (SI 1992/1937)
46	3 Feb 1995 (SI 1994/3292)
47, 48	25 Sep 1991 (SI 1991/2092)
49	24 Jan 1992 (SI 1992/71)
50	25 Sep 1991 (SI 1991/2092)
51	See Sch 8 below
52, 53	24 Jan 1992 (SI 1992/71)
54	26 Mar 1992 (SI 1992/334)
55	10 Aug 1992 (SI 1992/1937)
56	26 Mar 1992 (SI 1992/334)
57	See Sch 10 below
58	7 Mar 1994 (SI 1994/398)
59	See Sch 11 below
60(1)	25 Sep 1991 (SI 1991/2092)
(2), (3)	25 Jul 1991 (s 84(4))
(4)	25 Sep 1991 (SI 1991/2092)
(5)	25 Jul 1991 (s 84(4))
(6)	See Sch 12 below
(7), (8)	25 Sep 1991 (SI 1991/2092)
61	See Sch 13 below
62–69	25 Sep 1991 (SI 1991/2067)
70	See Sch 15 below
71–78	25 Sep 1991 (SI 1991/2092)
79	See Sch 17 below
80	25 Sep 1991 (except in relation to entries noted to Sch 18 below) (EW) (SI 1991/2067)
	25 Sep 1991 (except in relation to entries noted to Sch 18 below) (S) (SI 1991/2092)
	2 Jan 1992 (otherwise) (EW) (SI 1991/2728)
	Not in force (otherwise) (S)
81	25 Sep 1991 (SI 1991/2067)
82	26 Mar 1992 (SI 1992/334)

83	25 Oct 1991 (SI 1991/2272)
84(1)–(5)	25 Jul 1991 (RA)
(6)	See Sch 19 below
(7)–(9)	25 Jul 1991 (RA)
Sch 1, 2	25 Sep 1991 (SI 1991/2067)
3, para 1	25 Sep 1991 (SI 1991/2067)
2–6	2 Jan 1992 (SI 1991/2905)
7	25 Nov 1991 (rules, etc) (SI 1991/2728)
	2 Jan 1992 (otherwise) (SI 1991/2905)
8–14	2 Jan 1992 (SI 1991/2905)
15	25 Nov 1991 (rules, etc) (SI 1991/2728)
	2 Jan 1992 (otherwise) (SI 1991/2905)
16–32	2 Jan 1992 (SI 1991/2905)
4, para 1, 2	25 Nov 1991 (rules, etc) (SI 1991/2728)
	10 Feb 1992 (otherwise) (SI 1991/2905)
3	10 Feb 1992 (SI 1991/2905)
4–25	25 Nov 1991 (rules, etc) (SI 1991/2728)
	10 Feb 1992 (otherwise) (SI 1991/2905)
26	10 Feb 1992 (SI 1991/2905)
27–51	25 Nov 1991 (rules, etc) (SI 1991/2728)
	10 Feb 1992 (otherwise) (SI 1991/2905)
5	25 Nov 1991 (rules, etc) (SI 1991/2728)
	9 Nov 1992 (otherwise; but note that amendments do not apply with respect to proposals which are or have been made available for inspection in accordance with Town and Country Planning Act 1990, Sch 7, para 5 or 6 before 12 Oct 1992 but simplified planning zone scheme had not yet come into operation on that date) (SI 1992/2413)
6, para 1	25 Jul 1991 (s 84(4))
2–4	25 Sep 1991 (SI 1991/2067)
5	25 Jul 1991 (s 84(4))
6–12	25 Sep 1991 (SI 1991/2067)
13	25 Jul 1991 (s 84(4))
14–49	25 Sep 1991 (SI 1991/2067)
7, para 1	27 Jul 1992 (SI 1992/1630)
2	2 Jan 1992 (SI 1991/2905)
3	27 Jul 1992 (SI 1992/1630)
4	2 Jan 1992 (SI 1991/2905)
5	2 Jan 1992 (except so far as relates to reference to s 187A) (SI 1991/2905)
	27 Jul 1992 (exception noted above) (SI 1992/1630)
6	25 Oct 1991 (SI 1991/2272)
7	2 Jan 1992 (SI 1991/2905)
8	25 Sep 1991 (SI 1991/2067)
9(1)	2 Jan 1992 (SI 1991/2905)
(2)(a)	10 Feb 1992 (SI 1991/2905)
(b)	27 Jul 1992 (SI 1992/1630)
(c)	25 Sep 1991 (SI 1991/2067)
(d)	2 Jan 1992 (so far as relates to reference to s 171C) (SI 1991/2905)
	9 Nov 1992 (otherwise) (SI 1992/2831)
(e)	2 Jan 1992 (SI 1991/2905)
(f)	2 Jan 1992 (so far as relates to reference to s 187B) (SI 1991/2905)
	27 Jul 1992 (otherwise) (SI 1992/1630)
(g)	2 Jan 1992 (SI 1991/2905)
(h)	25 Oct 1991 (SI 1991/2272)

(i)	2 Jan 1992 (except so far as relates to substitution of reference to ''section 316(1) to (3)'' by reference to ''section 316'') (SI 1991/2905)
	17 Jul 1992 (exception noted above) (SI 1992/ 1491)
10(1)	25 Sep 1991 (SI 1991/2067)
(2)	27 Jul 1992 (SI 1992/1279)
11	2 Jan 1992 (SI 1991/2905)
12	27 Jul 1992 (SI 1992/1630)
13	2 Jan 1992 (SI 1991/2905)
14, 15	17 Jul 1992 (SI 1992/1491)
16	2 Jan 1992 (SI 1991/2905)
17	17 Jul 1992 (SI 1992/1491)
18, 19	2 Jan 1992 (so far as relate to inclusion in Town and Country Planning Act 1990, ss 77(4), 79(4), of reference to s 73A) (SI 1991/ 2905)
	17 Jul 1992 (otherwise) (SI 1992/1491)
20–23	2 Jan 1992 (SI 1991/2905)
24(1)(a)	2 Jan 1992 (SI 1991/2905)
(b)	27 Jul 1992 (SI 1992/1630)
(2), (3)	2 Jan 1992 (SI 1991/2905)
25	2 Jan 1992 (SI 1991/2905)
26	2 Jan 1992 (except so far as relates to breach of condition notices) (SI 1991/2905)
	27 Jul 1992 (exception noted above) (SI 1992/ 1630)
27–29	2 Jan 1992 (SI 1991/2905)
30	27 Jul 1992 (SI 1992/1630)
31	2 Jan 1992 (SI 1991/2905)
32, 33	27 Jul 1992 (SI 1992/1630)
34	17 Jul 1992 (SI 1992/1491)
35	2 Jan 1992 (SI 1991/2905)
36	25 Sep 1991 (SI 1991/2067)
37	17 Jul 1992 (SI 1992/1491)
38	6 Apr 1992 (SI 1992/665)
39–41	27 Jul 1992 (SI 1992/1630)
42	2 Jan 1992 (SI 1991/2905)
43, 44	27 Jul 1992 (SI 1992/1630)
45(1)	2 Jan 1992 (SI 1991/2905)
(2)	2 Jan 1992 (except so far as relates to reference to s 187A) (SI 1991/2905)
	27 Jul 1992 (exception noted above) (SI 1992/ 1630)
46	27 Jul 1992 (SI 1992/1630)
47	2 Jan 1992 (SI 1991/2905)
48	25 Nov 1991 (rules, etc) (SI 1991/2728)
	17 Jul 1992 (otherwise) (SI 1992/1491)
49	25 Nov 1991 (rules, etc) (SI 1991/2728)
	27 Jul 1992 (otherwise) (SI 1992/1630)
50	2 Jan 1992 (SI 1991/2905)
51	25 Sep 1991 (SI 1991/2067)
52(1)	2 Jan 1992 (SI 1991/2905)
(2)(a)	2 Jan 1992 (except so far as relates to definition ''breach of condition notice'') (SI 1991/ 2905)
	27 Jul 1992 (exception noted above) (SI 1992/ 1630)
(b)	2 Jan 1992 (SI 1991/2905)
(c)	27 Jul 1992 (but not relating to demolition of building on land where, before 27 Jul 1992,

	planning permission has been granted under Town and Country Planning Act 1990, Pt III, or has been deemed to have been granted under that Part of that Act, for the redevelopment of the land) (SI 1992/1279)
(d)	27 Jul 1992 (SI 1992/1630)
(e)	17 Jul 1992 (SI 1992/1491)
(f), (g)	2 Jan 1992 (SI 1991/2905)
(3)	17 Jul 1992 (SI 1992/1491)
(4)	2 Jan 1992 (SI 1991/2905)
53(1)	See sub-paras (2)–(9) below
(2)	27 Jul 1992 (SI 1992/1630)
(3)	2 Jan 1992 (except so far as relates to applications for consent to the display of advertisements) (SI 1991/2905)
	6 Apr 1992 (exception noted above) (SI 1992/665)
(4)	17 Jul 1992 (SI 1992/1491)
(5)	2 Jan 1992 (so far as confers on the Secretary of State a power to make provision by development order) (SI 1991/2905)
	9 Nov 1992 (otherwise; but note that does not apply to application for planning permission or application for approval of matter reserved under outline planning permission (within meaning of Town and Country Planning Act 1990, s 92, made before 6 Nov 1992 nor to any alteration to that application accepted by the authority) (SI 1992/2831)
(6)	2 Jan 1992 (so far as relates to insertion of the words ''planning contravention notices under s 171C or'') (SI 1991/2905)
	27 Jul 1992 (otherwise) (SI 1992/1630)
(7), (8)	2 Jan 1992 (SI 1991/2905)
(9)	25 Oct 1991 (SI 1991/2272)
54(1)	25 Sep 1991 (SI 1991/2067)
(2)	9 Nov 1992 (SI 1992/2831)
(3)(a)	25 Sep 1991 (SI 1991/2067)
(b)	9 Nov 1992 (SI 1992/2831)
(c)	2 Jan 1992 (SI 1991/2905)
(d)	27 Jul 1992 (SI 1992/1630)
(e)	2 Jan 1992 (SI 1991/2905)
(f)	9 Nov 1992 (SI 1992/2831)
(g)	27 Jul 1992 (SI 1992/1630)
(4)	17 Jul 1992 (SI 1992/1491)
55	17 Jul 1992 (SI 1992/1491)
56	25 Sep 1991 (SI 1991/2067)
57(1)	25 Sep 1991 (SI 1991/2067)
(2)(a)	2 Jan 1992 (so far as relates to omission of reference to s 63) (SI 1991/2905)
	27 Jul 1992 (otherwise) (SI 1992/1630)
(b)	25 Sep 1991 (SI 1991/2067)
(c)	2 Jan 1992 (SI 1991/2905)
(d), (e)	17 Jul 1992 (SI 1992/1491)
(f)	9 Nov 1992 (SI 1992/2831)
(g)	2 Jan 1992 (so far as relates to references to ss 196A–196C) (SI 1991/2905)
	27 Jul 1992 (otherwise) (SI 1992/1630)
(h), (i)	2 Jan 1992 (SI 1991/2905)
(j), (k)	17 Jul 1992 (SI 1992/1491)
(3)(a)	17 Jul 1992 (SI 1992/1491)
(b)	25 Sep 1991 (SI 1991/2067)

(c)	2 Jan 1992 (SI 1991/2905)
(d)	2 Jan 1992 (except so far as relates to s 187A) (SI 1991/2905)
	27 Jul 1992 (exception noted above) (SI 1992/1630)
(4)	25 Sep 1991 (SI 1991/2067)
(5)	17 Jul 1992 (except so far as relates to omission of reference to Part IV) (SI 1992/1491)
	27 Jul 1992 (exception noted above) (SI 1992/1630)
(6)(a), (b)	17 Jul 1992 (SI 1992/1491)
(c)	27 Jul 1992 (SI 1992/1630)
(d)	17 Jul 1992 (SI 1992/1491)
58–61	2 Jan 1992 (SI 1991/2905)
8, 9	24 Jan 1992 (SI 1992/71)
10, para 1, 2	25 Sep 1991 (SI 1991/2092)
3	18 Feb 1993 (SI 1993/275)
4–8	26 Mar 1992 (SI 1992/334)
9	18 Feb 1993 (SI 1993/275)
10	26 Mar 1992 (SI 1992/334)
11	1 May 1993 (SI 1993/275)
12, 13	26 Mar 1992 (SI 1992/334)
11	*Not in force*
12	25 Sep 1991 (SI 1991/2092)
13, para 1	25 Sep 1992 (SI 1992/1937)
2	25 Sep 1991 (SI 1991/2092)
3, 4	7 Mar 1994 (SI 1994/398)
5, 6	25 Sep 1991 (SI 1991/2092)
7(a)(i)	3 Feb 1995 (SI 1994/3292)
(ii), (iii)	25 Sep 1991 (SI 1991/2092)
(b)	25 Sep 1991 (SI 1991/2092)
8	26 Mar 1992 (SI 1992/334)
9	25 Sep 1991 (SI 1991/2092)
10(a)	26 Mar 1992 (so far as relates to substitution of reference to "27(1), 27A, 28A and 29") (SI 1992/334)
	3 Feb 1995 (otherwise) (SI 1994/3292)
(b)	3 Feb 1995 (SI 1994/3292)
11(a)	25 Sep 1991 (SI 1991/2092)
(b)(i), (ii)	3 Feb 1995 (SI 1994/3292)
(iii)	26 Mar 1992 (SI 1992/334)
(iv)	3 Feb 1995 (SI 1994/3292)
(c)	25 Sep 1991 (SI 1991/2092)
12	25 Sep 1991 (SI 1991/2092)
13	26 Mar 1992 (SI 1992/334)
14	25 Sep 1991 (SI 1991/2092)
15	3 Feb 1995 (SI 1994/3292)
16	26 Mar 1992 (SI 1992/334)
17, 18	25 Sep 1992 (SI 1992/1937)
19	26 Mar 1992 (SI 1992/334)
20(a), (b)	26 Mar 1992 (SI 1992/334)
(c)	26 Mar 1992 (except so far as para 20(c)(ii) relates to substitution of Town and Country Planning (Scotland) Act 1972, s 85(5)(d)) (SI 1992/334)
	25 Sep 1992 (exception noted above) (SI 1992/1937)
(d)	25 Sep 1992 (SI 1992/1937)
(e)–(g)	26 Mar 1992 (SI 1992/334)
21	26 Mar 1992 (SI 1992/334)
22	10 Aug 1992 (SI 1992/1937)
23, 24	26 Mar 1992 (SI 1992/334)

25	26 Mar 1992 (except so far as substituted s 89A relates to breach of condition notice) (SI 1992/334)
	25 Sep 1992 (exception noted above) (SI 1992/1937)
26	25 Sep 1992 (SI 1992/1937)
27	26 Mar 1992 (SI 1992/334)
28	25 Sep 1991 (SI 1991/2092)
29, 30	26 Mar 1992 (SI 1992/334)
31–34	25 Sep 1992 (SI 1992/1937)
35	26 Mar 1992 (SI 1992/334)
36	25 Sep 1991 (SI 1991/2092)
37	26 Mar 1992 (except insertion of reference to s 87AA) (SI 1992/334)
	25 Sep 1992 (exception noted above) (SI 1992/1937)
38(a)–(d)	26 Mar 1992 (SI 1992/334)
(e)	25 Sep 1991 (SI 1991/2092)
(f)	26 Mar 1992 (SI 1992/334)
39	26 Mar 1992 (SI 1992/334)
40(1)(a)	26 Mar 1992 (so far as inserts definition "breach of planning control") (SI 1992/334)
	10 Aug 1992 (otherwise) (SI 1992/1937)
(b), (c)	3 Feb 1995 (SI 1994/3292)
(d)	25 Sep 1992 (SI 1992/1937)
(e), (f)	26 Mar 1992 (SI 1992/334)
(2)	*Not in force*
41(1)	25 Sep 1991 (SI 1991/2092)
(2)	26 Mar 1992 (SI 1992/334)
(3), (4)	3 Feb 1995 (SI 1994/3292)
42	3 Feb 1995 (SI 1994/3292)
43(a)(i)	25 Sep 1991 (SI 1991/2092)
(ii)	25 Sep 1992 (SI 1992/1937)
(iii)	26 Mar 1992 (except insertion of reference to "section 90A") (SI 1992/334)
	25 Sep 1992 (exception noted above) (SI 1992/1937)
(iv)	26 Mar 1992 (SI 1992/334)
(b)(i)	25 Sep 1991 (SI 1991/2092)
(ii)	26 Mar 1992 (SI 1992/334)
(iii)	25 Sep 1992 (SI 1992/1937)
(c)	26 Mar 1992 (SI 1992/334)
44	*Not in force*; prospectively repealed by Local Government etc (Scotland) Act 1994, s 180(2), Sch 14
45	13 Oct 1991 (SI 1991/2272; but note that SI 1992/334 also purports to bring this provision into force on 26 Mar 1992)
46	26 Mar 1992 (except insertion of reference to "section 87AA") (SI 1992/334)
	25 Sep 1992 (exception noted above) (SI 1992/1937)
47	25 Sep 1992 (SI 1992/1937)
14	25 Sep 1991 (SI 1991/2067)
15, para 1–31	25 Sep 1991 (SI 1991/2067)
32	2 Jan 1992 (SI 1991/2728)
16, 17	25 Sep 1991 (SI 1991/2092)
18, Pt I	25 Sep 1991 (except entries relating to Planning (Hazardous Substances) Act 1990) (EW) (SI 1991/2067)
	25 Sep 1991 (except entries relating to Town and Country Planning (Scotland) Act 1972) (S) (SI 1991/2092)

II
19, Pt I

2 Jan 1992 (exception noted above) (EW) (SI 1991/2728

Not in force (exception noted above) (S)

25 Sep 1991 (SI 1991/2067; SI 1991/2092))

25 Sep 1991 (repeals of or in Town and Country Planning Act 1990, ss 55(6), 97(5), 219(6), 336(1) (definitions of "development consisting of the winning and working of minerals", "mineral compensation modifications", "relevant order", "restriction on the winning and working of minerals" and "special consultations"), Sch 1, para 1(2), Sch 5, para 1(6), Sch 11, Sch 16, Pt III (entries relating to ss 312(2), 324(4)); Planning (Listed Buildings and Conservation Areas) Act 1990, s 9(5)) (SI 1991/2067)

2 Jan 1992 (repeals of or in Town and Country Planning Act 1990, ss 63, 69(1), (3), 178(2), 186(1)(c), 190(4), 210(3), (5), 285(1), (2), (5), (6), 324(1)(b), (c), (2), 336(1) (definition of "planning permission"), Sch 1, para 4(1) (except so far as concerns applications for consent to the display of advertisements), Sch 16 (entry relating to s 285); Planning (Listed Buildings and Conservation Areas) Act 1990, ss 38(2), 39(7), 42(7), 55(6), 88(6), 90(6)(b), 92(2)(b); Planning (Hazardous Substances) Act 1990, ss 25(1)(c), 36(5); Planning (Consequential Provisions) Act 1990, Sch 2, para 38) (SI 1991/2905)

10 Feb 1992 (repeals of or in Town and Country Planning Act 1990, ss 12(4)(a), 14(3), 21(2), 22, 23(2)–(4), (9), (10), 49, 50, 51(1), 52(2), (3), 53(1), (2)(b), (g), (5), 284(1)(a), 287(1)–(3), (5), 306(2), Sch 2, Pt I, paras 3, 5, 6, Pt II, paras 3–16, 18, Sch 13; Planning (Consequential Provisions) Act 1990, Sch 4) (SI 1991/2905)

6 Apr 1992 (repeal of Town and Country Planning Act 1990, Sch 1, para 4(1) (so far as not already in force)) (SI 1992/665)

17 Jul 1992 (repeals of or in Town and Country Planning Act 1990, ss 74(2), 198(4)(a), 220(3)(a), 336(1), (9), Sch 16, Pt I, entries relating to ss 77, 78, 79, Pt V) (SI 1992/1491)

27 Jul 1992 (repeals of or in Local Government (Miscellaneous Provisions) Act 1976, s 7(5)(a)(iii); Town and Country Planning Act 1990, ss 64, 188(1), 196, 250(2), 266(3), 284(3)(g), 286(1)(b), 290, 336(1), Sch 6, para 2(1)(c), (8), Sch 16, Pt IV; Planning (Consequential Provisions) Act 1990, Sch 2, paras 3(2), 35(1)(b)) (SI 1992/1630)

9 Nov 1992 (repeals of or in Town and Country Planning Act 1990, Sch 1, para 9(2), (3), Sch 7, para 13(2)(e)) (SI 1992/2831)

25 Jul 1991 (repeals of Land Compensation Act 1961, s 15(4)(a), (b); Land Compensation Act 1973, s 5(3)(a), (b); Town and Country Planning Act 1990, s 114; Planning (Listed Buildings and Conservation Areas) Act 1990, s 27) (s 84(4))

	25 Sep 1991 (otherwise) (SI 1991/2067)
III	25 Sep 1991 (SI 1991/2067)
IV	25 Jul 1991 (repeals of Town and Country Planning (Scotland) Act 1972, ss 158, 160) (s 84(4))
	25 Sep 1991 (repeal in Land Compensation (Scotland) Act 1973, Sch 2, Pt II) (SI 1991/2067)
	25 Sep 1991 (repeals of or in Land Compensation (Scotland) Act 1963, ss 12, 23(4)(a), (b), 25(8), 30(3); Gas Act 1965, Sch 3, para 3; Public Expenditure and Receipts Act 1968, Sch 3, para 7(a); Town and Country Planning (Scotland) Act 1972, ss 19(5), 35, 36, 58(2)(a), 106, Pt VII (except s 145), 155(5), (6), 156, 157(1), (3), (4), 158, 160, 169(3), 231(3)(c), 244(2), 245, 246, 248, 249, 263, 264, 265, 275(1) (definitions of "new development" and "previous apportionment"), Sch 6, paras 3–9, 12, Sch 19, Pt I; Land Compensation (Scotland) Act 1973, ss 5(3)(a), (b), 27(1), (5), 31(6), 48(9)(b); Local Government, Planning and Land Act 1980, s 114(2); Civil Aviation Act 1982, s 53(1)(a); Airports Act 1986, s 61(1)(a)) (SI 1991/2092)
	26 Mar 1992 (repeals of or in Town and Country Planning (Scotland) Act 1972, ss 85(5), (11), 88(1), (2), 93(1)(k), (5), 98(1), (3), 166(2)(c), 265(1)(b), (2A)(a), (4), 275(1) (in definition "planning permission", words from "and in construing" to the end)) (SI 1992/334)
	25 Sep 1992 (repeals of or in Town and Country Planning (Scotland) Act 1972, ss 51, 91(3), (5), 201(5), 214(3), 234, 275(1)) (subject to transitional provisions) (SI 1992/1937)
	3 Feb 1995 (repeal in Town and Country Planning (Scotland) Act 1972, s 28(1)) (SI 1994/3292)
	Not in force (otherwise)
V	25 Sep 1991 (SI 1991/2067)

Note: the orders bringing this Act into force, as noted above, contain numerous transitional and saving provisions which are too complex to set out in this work   **[559]**

TRANSPORT AND WORKS ACT 1992
(1992 c 42)

ARRANGEMENT OF SECTIONS

PART I

ORDERS AUTHORISING WORKS ETC

Power to make orders

PART II

SAFETY OF RAILWAYS ETC

CHAPTER II

OTHER SAFETY PROVISIONS

General

An Act to provide for the making of orders relating to, or to matters ancillary to, the construction or operation of railways, tramways, trolley vehicle systems, other guided transport systems and inland waterways, and orders relating to, or to matters ancillary to, works interfering with rights of navigation; to make further provision in relation to railways, tramways, trolley vehicle systems and other guided transport systems; to amend certain enactments relating to harbours; and for connected purposes   [16th March 1992]

PART I

ORDERS AUTHORISING WORKS ETC

Power to make orders

1. Orders as to railways, tramways etc

(1) The Secretary of State may make an order relating to, or to matters ancillary to, the construction or operation of a transport system of any of the following kinds, so far as it is in England and Wales—

    (a) a railway;
    (b) a tramway;
    (c) a trolley vehicle system;
    (d) a system using a mode of guided transport prescribed by order made under section 2 below.

(2) The power to make orders under this section shall be exercisable by statutory instrument. **[559A]**

NOTES
    Commencement: 1 January 1993.
    See further: the Conservation (Natural Habitats, &c) Regulations 1994, SI 1994/2716, regs 10, 48 et seq, 79–82 at **[930]** et seq.

2. Extension of section 1 to other guided transport systems

(1) The Secretary of State may by order prescribe modes of guided transport for the purposes of section 1(1)(d) above.

(2) The power to make orders under this section shall be exercisable by statutory instrument; but no order shall be made unless a draft of it has been laid before, and approved by a resolution of, each House of Parliament. **[559B]**

NOTES
    Commencement: 1 January 1993.

3. Orders as to inland waterways etc

(1) The Secretary of State may make an order relating to, or to matters ancillary to—

    (a) the construction or operation of an inland waterway in England and Wales;
    (b) the carrying out of works which—

        (i) interfere with rights of navigation in waters within or adjacent to England and Wales, up to the seaward limits of the territorial sea, and
        (ii) are of a description prescribed by order made under section 4 below.

(2) The Secretary of State shall not make an order under this section if in his opinion the primary object of the order could be achieved by means of an order under the Harbours Act 1964.

(3) The power to make orders under this section shall be exercisable by statutory instrument. **[559C]**

NOTES
    Commencement: 1 January 1993.
    See further: the Conservation (Natural Habitats, &c) Regulations 1994, SI 1994/2716, regs 10, 48 et seq, 79–82 at **[930]** et seq.

4. Description of works for purposes of section 3

(1) The Secretary of State may by order prescribe descriptions of works for the purposes of section 3(1)(b) above.

(2) The power to make orders under this section shall be exercisable by statutory instrument; but no order shall be made unless a draft of it has been laid before, and approved by a resolution of, each House of Parliament.   **[559D]**

NOTES
Commencement: 1 January 1993.

5. Subject matter of orders under sections 1 and 3

(1) Without prejudice to the generality of sections 1 and 3 above, the matters as to which provision may be made by an order under either of those sections include those set out in Schedule 1 to this Act.

(2) An order under section 1 or 3 above may make provision in relation to more than one scheme, system or mode of transport.

(3) An order under section 1 or 3 above may—

(a) apply, modify or exclude any statutory provision which relates to any matter as to which an order could be made under section 1 or, as the case may be, 3, and

(b) make such amendments, repeals and revocations of statutory provisions of local application as appear to the Secretary of State to be necessary or expedient in consequence of any provision of the order or otherwise in connection with the order;

and for the purposes of this subsection ''statutory provision'' means provision of an Act of Parliament or of an instrument made under an Act of Parliament.

(4) The provisions that may be made by an order under section 1 or 3 above include—

(a) any provision that appears to the Secretary of State to be necessary or expedient for giving full effect to—

(i) any other provision of the order,

(ii) any provision of an earlier order under the section concerned, or

(iii) any provision which is contained in an Act of Parliament passed before the time when this Part of this Act is first wholly in force, or in an instrument made under an Act of Parliament before that time, and which is of a kind which could be included in an order under section 1 or 3 above;

(b) such supplemental and transitional provisions as appear to him to be necessary or expedient in connection with the order.

(5) A provision of an order under section 1 or 3 above relating to offences shall not authorise the imposition on persons convicted of an offence of a term of imprisonment or of a fine exceeding level 3 on the standard scale.

(6) An order under section 1 or 3 above shall not extinguish any public right of way over land unless the Secretary of State is satisfied—

(a) that an alternative right of way has been or will be provided, or

(b) that the provision of an alternative right of way is not required.

(7) Where an order under sections 104(3), 105(3) or 112 of the Transport Act 1968 (classification and maintenance of the British Waterways Board's waterways,

and maintenance and use of other waterways) is required so as to give effect to any proposal, no provision shall be included in an order under section 1 or 3 above which would—

(a) remove that requirement, or

(b) alter the requirements of sections 104, 105 or 112 of, or Schedule 13 to, that Act relating to orders under those sections.   **[559E]**

NOTES

Commencement: 1 January 1993.

Procedure for making orders

6. Applications for orders under sections 1 and 3

(1) Subject to section 7 below, the Secretary of State shall not make an order under section 1 or 3 above except on an application made to him in accordance with rules made under this section.

(2) The Secretary of State may make rules as to—

(a) the form of an application under this section;

(b) the documents and information that must be submitted with it;

(c) the giving and publication of notices of an application;

(d) any other steps that must be taken before an application is made or in connection with the making of an application.

(3) Any provision made by rules as to the consultation that must be carried out before an application is made may include provision requiring compliance with general or special directions given by the Secretary of State.

(4) Rules under this section may make different provision for different cases, and may include provision authorising the Secretary of State—

(a) to dispense with compliance with rules that would otherwise apply, or

(b) to require compliance with rules that would not otherwise apply, in any case where he considers it appropriate to do so.

(5) Rules may provide for fees of such amounts as may be determined by or in accordance with the rules to be payable to the Secretary of State on the making of applications under this section.

(6) The power to make rules under this section shall be exercisable by statutory instrument which shall be subject to annulment in pursuance of a resolution of either House of Parliament.   **[559F]**

NOTES

Commencement: 1 January 1993.

7. Orders under sections 1 and 3 made otherwise than on application

(1) The Secretary of State may without any application being made to him make—

(a) an order under section 1 above which relates to, or to matters ancillary to, the construction for naval, military, air force or other defence purposes of a railway, tramway or other system within section 1(1), or the operation of a railway, tramway or other system constructed for those purposes;

(b) an order under section 1 or 3 above making any provision which appears to the Secretary of State to be necessary or expedient, in the interests of safety,—

(i) for the purpose of suspending or discontinuing any operations, or

(ii) in consequence of the abandonment or neglect of any works;

(c) an order under section 1 or 3 above repealing or revoking provisions which appear to the Secretary of State to be spent.

(2) An order made by virtue of subsection (1)(b) above may include provision for the recovery by the Secretary of State of the costs of making the order and of carrying its provisions into effect.

(3) Where the Secretary of State proposes to make an order by virtue of this section, he shall—

(a) prepare a draft of the order,
(b) publish a notice of the proposal, containing such particulars as may be prescribed, in the London Gazette and in a local newspaper circulating in the area (or each of the areas) in which any proposed works are to be carried out, and
(c) give such further notices of the proposal as may be prescribed.

(4) The power to make provision by rules under section 6 above in relation to applications shall include power to make such corresponding provision as the Secretary of State considers appropriate in relation to proposals to make orders by virtue of this section; and in subsection (3) above "prescribed" means prescribed by rules under section 6. **[559G]**

NOTES
Commencement: 1 January 1993.

8. Model clauses

(1) The Secretary of State may by order prescribe model provisions for incorporation in any draft orders which, in accordance with rules made under section 6 above, may be required to be submitted with applications under that section.

(2) Different provisions may be prescribed under this section for different cases.

(3) The prescribing under this section of a model provision shall not of itself make it mandatory for a provision in the terms of the model to be incorporated in a draft order or in any order eventually made by the Secretary of State under section 1 or 3 above.

(4) The power to make orders under this section shall be exercisable by statutory instrument. **[559H]**

NOTES
Commencement: 1 January 1993.

9. Schemes of national significance

(1) This section applies where an application made under section 6 above relates (wholly or in part) to proposals which in the opinion of the Secretary of State are of national significance.

(2) Before the end of the period of 56 days beginning with the day on which he receives the application, the Secretary of State shall publish in the London Gazette a notice identifying the application and the proposals which in his opinion are of national significance.

(3) On, or as soon as practicable after, the day on which the notice required by subsection (2) above is published, the Secretary of State shall—

    (a) publish a like notice in a local newspaper circulating in the area (or each of the areas) in which any proposed works are to be carried out, and

    (b) send a copy of the notice to the applicant and to every person within section 11(4) below who objected to the application in accordance with rules made under section 10 below.

(4) The Secretary of State shall not make an order on the application unless each House of Parliament, on a motion moved by a Minister of the Crown which identifies the proposals referred to above, passes a resolution approving them at some time later than 56 days after the day of publication of the notice required by subsection (2) above.

(5) An order made on the application shall not include any provision that is inconsistent with a proposal approved by a resolution in accordance with this section unless that provision gives effect to modifications of the proposal which have themselves been approved by a resolution of each House of Parliament passed on a motion moved by a Minister of the Crown.

(6) This section shall apply in relation to an order which the Secretary of State makes or proposes to make by virtue of section 7 above as it applies in relation to an order for which an application is made to him, except that in such a case—

    (a) subsections (2) and (3) above shall not apply, and

    (b) subsection (4) above shall apply as if the reference to the notice required by subsection (2) above were a reference to the notice required by section 7(3) above to be published in the London Gazette;

and any proposals which in the opinion of the Secretary of State are of national significance shall be identified as such in any notice required by or under section 7(3) above. **[559I]**

NOTES

    Commencement: 1 January 1993.

10. Objections

(1) The Secretary of State may make rules as to—

    (a) the making of objections to an application under section 6 above or to a proposal to make an order by virtue of section 7 above;

    (b) the information to be comprised within or submitted with an objection;

    (c) the submission by the person making the application of written representations or information in relation to objections;

    (d) the submission of further written representations or information;

    (e) such other matters relating to the consideration of objections as appear to the Secretary of State to be appropriate.

(2) Subject to the following provisions of this section, the Secretary of State shall not make a determination under section 13(1) below to make an order without first taking into consideration the grounds of any objection in respect of which rules under this section have been complied with.

(3) If an objection is withdrawn or appears to the Secretary of State—

    (a) to be frivolous or trivial, or

    (b) to relate to matters which fall to be determined by a tribunal concerned with the assessment of compensation,

he may make a determination under section 13(1) below without further consideration of the objection.

(4) Subsection (2) above shall not apply where the Secretary of State causes an inquiry to be held under section 11(1) below or causes an objection to be dealt with in accordance with section 11(2) below, but the Secretary of State shall not make a determination under section 13(1) below without first taking into consideration the report of the person holding the inquiry, or as the case may be of the person appointed under section 11(2).

(5) Rules under this section may make different provision for different cases, and may include provision authorising the Secretary of State—

    (a) to dispense with compliance with rules that would otherwise apply, or
    (b) to require compliance with rules that would not otherwise apply,

in any case where he considers it appropriate to do so.

(6) The power to make rules under this section shall be exercisable by statutory instrument which shall be subject to annulment in pursuance of a resolution of either House of Parliament.   **[559J]**

NOTES
Commencement: 1 January 1993.

11. Inquiries and hearings

(1) The Secretary of State may cause a public local inquiry to be held for the purposes of an application under section 6 above or a proposal by the Secretary of State to make an order by virtue of section 7 above.

(2) The Secretary of State may give to a person who makes an objection in accordance with rules under section 10 above an opportunity of appearing before and being heard by a person appointed by the Secretary of State for the purpose.

(3) Where an objection is made by a person within subsection (4) below who informs the Secretary of State in writing that he wishes the objection to be referred to an inquiry or dealt with in accordance with subsection (2) above, then, unless section 10(3) above applies, the Secretary of State shall either cause an inquiry to be held or, if he so determines, cause the objection to be dealt with in accordance with subsection (2).

(4) The persons within this subsection are—

    (a) any local authority for an area in which any works authorised by the proposed order are to be carried out, and
    (b) where the proposals include the compulsory acquisition of land, any person who, if Part II of the Acquisition of Land Act 1981 (notice to owners, lessees and occupiers) applied to the acquisition, would be entitled to a notice under section 12 of that Act;

and for the purposes of paragraph (a) above "local authority" means a county council, a district council, a London borough council, the Common Council of the City of London, the Council of the Isles of Scilly[, a county borough council,] and a Passenger Transport Executive.

(5) Subsections (2) to (5) of section 250 of the Local Government Act 1972 (attendance and evidence at, and costs of, inquiries) shall apply to an inquiry held under subsection (1) above; but—

    (a) in its application by virtue of this subsection, section 250(4) shall have effect with the omission of the words "and any amount" onwards, and

(b) the power to make an order as to costs under section 250(5) as applied by this subsection shall be exercisable not only where the inquiry takes place but also where arrangements are made for it but it does not take place.

(6) Subsections (4) and (5) of section 250 of the Local Government Act 1972 (costs) shall apply in relation to proceedings under subsection (2) above as they apply in relation to an inquiry under subsection (1) above. **[559K]**

NOTES

Commencement: 1 January 1993.

Words in square brackets in sub-s (4) inserted by the Local Government (Wales) Act 1994, s 22(1), Sch 7, Pt I, para 34(1), as from a day to be appointed.

Modification: sub-s (4) modified by the Transport and Works Applications (Inland Waterways Procedure) Regulations 1993, SI 1993/1119, regs 3, 4, 5, Sch 2.

See further, in relation to the procedure for any inquiry which is caused by the Secretary of State to be held pursuant to this section, the Transport and Works (Inquiries Procedure) Rules 1992, SI 1992/2817.

12. Special parliamentary procedure

(1) An order under section 1 or 3 above authorising a compulsory purchase shall be subject to special parliamentary procedure to the same extent as it would be, by virtue of section 18 or 19 of the Acquisition of Land Act 1981 (or by virtue of paragraph 5 or 6 of Schedule 3 to that Act) (National Trust land, commons etc), if the purchase were authorised by an order under section 2(1) of that Act.

(2) In section 3 of the Statutory Orders (Special Procedure) Act 1945 (petitions against orders subject to special parliamentary procedure) after subsection (4) there shall be inserted—

"(4A) The Chairmen shall not certify that a petition is proper to be received if the order to which it relates is made under section 1 of the Transport and Works Act 1992 and either—

(a) the petition is a petition of general objection and the order relates to proposals which have been approved by each House of Parliament in accordance with section 9 of that Act, or

(b) the petition is a petition for amendment and any of the amendments asked for would in the opinion of the Chairmen be inconsistent with such proposals."

(3) In relation to an order under section 1 or 3 above which is subject to special parliamentary procedure—

(a) section 13(5) below shall not apply,

(b) section 22 below shall not apply if the order is confirmed by Act of Parliament under section 6 of the Statutory Orders (Special Procedure) Act 1945, and

(c) in any other case, section 22(1) below shall have effect as if for the reference to the day on which the notice required by section 14(1)(b) is published there were substituted a reference to the day on which the order comes into operation under the Statutory Orders (Special Procedure) Act 1945. **[559L]**

NOTES

Commencement: 1 January 1993.

13. Making or refusal of orders under section 1 or 3

(1) Where an application has been made to the Secretary of State under section 6 above, or he proposes to make an order by virtue of section 7 above, and (in either

case) the requirements of the preceding provisions of this Act in relation to any objections have been satisfied, he shall determine—

(a) to make an order under section 1 or 3 above which gives effect to the proposals concerned without modifications, or

(b) to make an order which gives effect to those proposals with modifications, or

(c) not to make an order.

(2) Where an application has been made to the Secretary of State under section 6 above and he considers that any of the objects of the order applied for could be achieved by other means, he may on that ground determine not to make the order (but this subsection is without prejudice to subsection (3) below).

(3) The power of the Secretary of State to make a determination under subsection (1) above includes power to make a determination in respect of some only of the proposals concerned, while making a separate determination in respect of, or deferring consideration of, others (and accordingly the power to make an order under section 1 or 3 above includes power to make two or more orders on the same application).

(4) Where the Secretary of State proposes to make an order which gives effect to the proposals concerned with modifications which will in his opinion make a substantial change in the proposals—

(a) he shall notify any person who appears to him to be likely to be affected by the modifications,

(b) he shall give that person an opportunity of making representations to him about the modifications within such period as he may specify in the notice, and

(c) he shall before making the order consider any representations duly made to him.

(5) An order under section 1 or 3 above shall come into operation on the date on which the notice required by subsection (1)(b) of section 14 below is first published, or on such later date, if any, as may be specified in the order.   **[559M]**

NOTES
Commencement: 1 January 1993.

14. Publicity for making or refusal of orders

(1) As soon as practicable after making a determination under section 13(1) above, the Secretary of State shall—

(a) give notice of the determination to the person (if any) who applied for the order and to every person who made an objection which was referred to an inquiry or hearing in accordance with section 11(3) above, and

(b) publish a notice of the determination in the London Gazette.

(2) A notice under subsection (1)(a) above shall state the reasons for the determination.

(3) A notice under subsection (1) above of a determination to make an order shall give such particulars of the terms of the order as the Secretary of State considers appropriate, and in particular shall (except where the order is made by virtue of section 7 above) state the name and address of the person who applied for the order.

[(3A) Where a determination under section 13(1) above relates to an application or proposal to which this subsection applies, the notices under subsection (1) above shall state that, before the Secretary of State made the determination—

    (a) he considered the environmental statement, and

    (b) he complied with any obligations under section 10 above in respect of any objection made in accordance with rules under that section which relates to the environmental statement, and

    (c) he considered, or referred to an inquiry under section 11(1) above or a person appointed under section 11(2), any representation duly made to him (other than an objection) which relates to the environmental statement.

(3B) Subsection (3A) above applies to any application under section 6 above for an order, and any proposal to make an order by virtue of section 7 above, where the order would authorise—

    (a) works or other projects in a class listed in Annex I to Council Directive 85/337/EEC on the assessment of the effects of certain public and private projects on the environment, or

    (b) works or other projects in a class listed in Annex II to that Directive which are, by virtue of their nature, size or location, likely to have significant effects on the environment.

(3C) The Secretary of State shall send a copy of any notice to which subsection (3A) above applies to any person who made—

    (a) an objection to which paragraph (b) of that subsection refers, which was not referred to an inquiry or hearing in accordance with section 11(3) above, or

    (b) a representation to which subsection (3A)(c) above refers.

(3D) For the purposes of subsection (3A) above, "environmental statement" means a statement—

    (a) which is required by virtue of rules made under section 6 above—

        (i) to accompany an application under that section for an order; or

       (ii) to be prepared in connection with the publication of a notice of a proposal to make an order by virtue of section 7 above, and

    (b) which sets out particulars of the likely impact on the environment of the implementation of the order applied for or proposed.]

(4) Where the Secretary of State determines to make an order, the person who applied for the order (or, where the order is made by virtue of section 7 above, the Secretary of State) shall publish a copy of the notice given to him under subsection (1) above in a local newspaper circulating in the area (or each of the areas) in which any works authorised by the order are to be carried out.

(5) As soon as practicable after the making of an order under section 1 or 3 above, the person who applied for the order (or, where the order is made by virtue of section 7 above, the Secretary of State) shall—

    (a) deposit in the office of the Clerk of the Parliaments a copy of the order, and of any plan or book of reference prepared in connection with the application (or proposed order), and

    (b) deposit with each of the councils mentioned in subsection (7) below in whose area works authorised by the order are to be carried out a copy of each of those documents, or of so much of them as is relevant to those works.

(6) Where a plan or book of reference is revised before the order is made, the reference in subsection (5)(a) above is to the latest version.

(7) The councils referred to in subsection (5) above are district councils, London borough councils and the Common Council of the City of London [but are, in relation to Wales, county councils and county borough councils].

(8) A council with which documents are deposited in accordance with subsection (5) above shall make them available for inspection free of charge at all reasonable hours.   **[559N]**

NOTES
Commencement: 1 January 1993 (sub-ss (1)–(3), (4)–(8)); 1 August 1995 (sub-ss (3A)–(3D)).
Sub-ss (3A)–(3D) inserted by SI 1995/1541, reg 2, as from 1 August 1995.
Words in square brackets in sub-s (7) added by the Local Government (Wales) Act 1994, s 22(1), Sch 7, Pt I, para 34(2), as from a day to be appointed.

Consents etc under other enactments

15. Assimilation of procedures

(1) This section applies to applications made under section 6 above relating to proposals for the purposes of which the giving of a consent, permission or licence under any enactment, or the making or confirmation of an order under any enactment, is required.

(2) The Secretary of State may make regulations for securing that, where the requirement referred to in subsection (1) above would not be removed by the order to which the application relates—

  (a) the procedure for obtaining, or otherwise relating to, the consent, permission, licence, order or confirmation, and
  (b) the procedure relating to the application made under section 6 above,

are wholly or partly assimilated (and in particular that proceedings relating to the one may be held concurrently with proceedings relating to the other).

(3) Regulations under this section may include provision—

  (a) excluding or modifying the application of any enactment;
  (b) authorising the Secretary of State to give directions or take such other steps as may be appropriate for the purpose of securing the object mentioned in subsection (2) above.

(4) The power to make regulations under this section shall be exercisable by statutory instrument, which shall be subject to annulment in pursuance of a resolution of either House of Parliament.

(5) This section shall apply to proposals by the Secretary of State to make orders by virtue of section 7 above as it applies to applications under section 6 above.
     [559O]

NOTES
Commencement: 1 January 1993.

16. (*Inserts the Town and Country Planning Act 1990, s 90(2A) and adds Sch 13, para 23 thereto.*)

17. (*Inserts the Planning (Listed Buildings and Conservation Areas) Act 1990, s 12(3A).*)

18. (*Inserts the Planning (Hazardous Substances) Act 1990, s 12(2A).*)

19. Coast Protection Act 1949

In section 35 of the Coast Protection Act 1949 (which excepts certain operations from the requirement to obtain the Secretary of State's consent under section 34) in subsection (1) there shall be added after paragraph (g)—

> "(h) any operations authorised by an order under section 1 or 3 of the Transport and Works Act 1992." **[559P]**

NOTES
Commencement: 1 January 1993.

20. Power to apply for, or object to, orders

(1) A body which has power to promote or power to oppose Bills in Parliament shall also have power to apply for, or as the case may be power to object to, orders under sections 1 and 3 above.

(2) Where the power of a body to promote or to oppose Bills is subject to any condition, then, except as provided by subsection (3) below, the corresponding power conferred on the body by subsection (1) above shall be subject to the like condition.

(3) The powers conferred by subsection (1) above on—

    (a) the British Railways Board,
    (b) the British Waterways Board, and
    (c) London Regional Transport,

shall be exercisable without the consent of the Secretary of State. **[559Q]**

NOTES
Commencement: 1 January 1993.

21. Transport Consultative Committees

(1) In section 56 of the Transport Act 1962 (which establishes a Central Transport Consultative Committee and Area Transport Users Consultative Committees) after subsection (6) there shall be inserted—

> "(6A) An Area Committee may consider, and if they think fit object to, any proposal for the discontinuance of railway services made in an application for an order under section 1 of the Transport and Works Act 1992 or made by the Secretary of State by virtue of section 7 of that Act."

(2) In section 41 of the London Regional Transport Act 1984 (which provides for the London Regional Passenger Committee to be treated as an Area Transport Users Consultative Committee for certain purposes) in subsection (2)(c) for "(7)" there shall be substituted "(6A)". **[559R]**

NOTES
Commencement: 1 January 1993.

Miscellaneous

22. Validity of orders under section 1 or 3

(1) If a person aggrieved by an order under section 1 or 3 above desires to question the validity of it, or of any provision contained in it, on the ground—

(a) that it is not within the powers of this Act, or

(b) that any requirement imposed by or under this Act or the Tribunals and Inquiries Act 1971 has not been complied with,

he may, within the period of 42 days beginning with the day on which the notice required by section 14(1)(b) above is published, make an application for the purpose to the High Court.

(2) On any such application, the court—

(a) may by interim order suspend the operation of the order, or of any provision contained in it, either generally or in so far as it affects any property of the applicant, until the final determination of the proceedings, and

(b) if satisfied that the order or any provision contained in it is not within the powers of this Act, or that the interests of the applicant have been substantially prejudiced by a failure to comply with any requirement imposed by or under this Act or the Tribunals and. Inquiries Act 1971, may quash the order or any provision contained in it, either generally or in so far as it affects any property of the applicant.

(3) Subject to subsections (1) and (2) above, an order under section 1 or 3 above shall not, either before or after it has been made, be questioned in any legal proceedings whatever.   **[559S]**

NOTES
Commencement: 1 January 1993.

23. Exercise of Secretary of State's functions by appointed person

(1) The Secretary of State may by regulations prescribe classes of application which are to be dealt with by a person appointed by the Secretary of State for the purpose instead of by the Secretary of State.

(2) The Secretary of State may if he thinks fit direct that an application which would otherwise fall to be determined by an appointed person shall be determined by the Secretary of State.

(3) Subject to subsection (4) below, a person appointed under this section shall have in relation to the application—

(a) the same powers and duties as the Secretary of State has under sections 1 and 3 above, and

(b) such other powers and duties conferred on the Secretary of State under or by virtue of this Part of this Act as may be specified in the regulations;

and for that purpose any reference in any Act or instrument (including this Act and any instrument made under it) to the Secretary of State, or to anything done or authorised or required to be done by or to the Secretary of State, shall be construed, so far as the context permits and subject to regulations under this section, as a reference to that person.

(4) An order made on an application dealt with by a person appointed under this section shall not authorise the compulsory acquisition of land, or the compulsory creation or extinguishment of rights over land (including rights of navigation over water).

(5) Where an application has been dealt with by a person appointed under this section, any order made by him under section 1 or 3 shall be treated as made by the Secretary of State.

(6) At any time before the appointed person has determined the application the Secretary of State may—

(a) revoke his appointment, and

(b) appoint another person under subsection (1) above to deal with the application instead;

and where such a new appointment is made the consideration of the application shall begin afresh, except to the extent that regulations under this section provide otherwise.

(7) If the Secretary of State exercises the power conferred on him by subsection (6)(a) above, he shall give reasons to the appointed person for revoking his appointment.

(8) Regulations under this section may provide for the giving of publicity to any directions given by the Secretary of State under subsection (2) above and to any appointment made by virtue of subsection (6) above.

(9) The Tribunals and Inquiries Act 1971 shall apply to a local inquiry or other hearing by a person appointed under this section as it applies to a statutory inquiry held by the Secretary of State, but as if in section 12(1) of that Act (statement of reasons for decisions) the reference to any decision taken by the Secretary of State were a reference to a decision taken by an appointed person.

(10) Where a person appointed under this section is an officer of the Department of Transport, the Department of the Environment, the [Department of Trade and Industry] or the Welsh Office, his functions shall be treated for the purposes of the Parliamentary Commissioner Act 1967—

(a) if he was appointed by the Secretary of State for the time being having general responsibility in transport matters, as functions of the Department of Transport;

(b) if he was appointed by the Secretary of State for the time being having general responsibility in planning matters in relation to England, as functions of the Department of the Environment;

(c) if he was appointed by the Secretary of State for the time being having general responsibility in energy matters, as functions of the [Department of Trade and Industry];

(d) if he was appointed by the Secretary of State for the time being having general responsibility in planning matters in relation to Wales, as functions of the Welsh Office.

(11) The power to make regulations under this section shall be exercisable by statutory instrument, which shall be subject to annulment in pursuance of a resolution of either House of Parliament. **[559T]**

NOTES

Commencement: 1 January 1993.

Words in square brackets in sub-s (10) substituted by the Transfer of Functions (Energy) Order 1992, SI 1992/1314, art 3(3), Schedule, para 2(b).

24. (*Applies to Scotland only.*)

25. Crown land

(1) If the appropriate authority agrees—

    (a) an interest which—

        (i) subsists in land in which there is a Crown or Duchy interest, but

        (ii) is not itself a Crown or Duchy interest,

    may be acquired compulsorily by virtue of an order under section 1 or 3 above, and

    (b) any provision of this Act or of such an order (other than a provision by virtue of which an interest in land is compulsorily acquired) may apply in relation to land in which there is a Crown or Duchy interest.

(2) In this section "Crown or Duchy interest" means an interest belonging to Her Majesty in right of the Crown or of the Duchy of Lancaster, or belonging to the Duchy of Cornwall, or belonging to a government department, or held in trust for Her Majesty for the purposes of a government department.

(3) In this section "the appropriate authority" means—

    (a) in the case of land belonging to Her Majesty in right of the Crown and forming part of the Crown Estate, the Crown Estate Commissioners;

    (b) in the case of other land belonging to Her Majesty in right of the Crown, the government department having the management of the land;

    (c) in the case of land belonging to Her Majesty in right of the Duchy of Lancaster, the Chancellor of the Duchy;

    (d) in the case of land belonging to the Duchy of Cornwall, such person as the Duke of Cornwall, or the possessor for the time being of the Duchy of Cornwall, appoints;

    (e) in the case of land belonging to a government department or held in trust for Her Majesty for the purposes of a government department, that department.

(4) If any question arises as to what authority is the appropriate authority in relation to any land, that question shall be referred to the Treasury, whose decision shall be final.   **[559U]**

NOTES

    Commencement: 1 January 1993.

PART II

SAFETY OF RAILWAYS ETC

26—40. ((*Chapter I*): *these sections are outside the scope of this work.*)

CHAPTER II

OTHER SAFETY PROVISIONS

General

41. Approval of works, plant and equipment

(1) For the purpose of securing the safe operation of railways, tramways, trolley vehicle systems and prescribed systems of guided transport, the Secretary of State may make regulations requiring that his approval be obtained before—

(a) new works, plant or equipment are first brought into use, or
(b) works, plant or equipment are first brought into use after alterations have been made to them.

(2) Regulations under this section—

(a) shall prescribe the cases in which approval is required and the procedure for obtaining it;
(b) may include provision as to the time when works, plant or equipment are to be treated as first brought into use, including provision for disregarding periods of testing and other periods of use before sufficient information is available for a decision to be made on an application for approval;
(c) may include provision prohibiting the giving of false information to the Secretary of State.

(3) Regulations under this section may make different provision for different cases, and may include provision authorising the Secretary of State—

(a) to dispense (conditionally or unconditionally) with compliance with regulations that would otherwise apply, or
(b) to require compliance with regulations that would not otherwise apply,

either in the case of any particular works, plant, equipment or alterations, or in the case of works, plant, equipment or alterations of such descriptions as he may determine.

(4) Regulations under this section may provide that any person who without reasonable cause contravenes any specified provision of the regulations, or does so in specified circumstances, shall be guilty of an offence under this section.

(5) Where the commission by any person of an offence under this section is due to the act or default of some other person, that other person shall be guilty of the offence, and a person may be charged with and convicted of the offence by virtue of this subsection whether or not proceedings are taken against the first-mentioned person.

(6) A person guilty of an offence under this section shall be liable on summary conviction to a fine not exceeding level 5 on the standard scale.

(7) In this section—

"equipment" includes vehicles;
"prescribed systems of guided transport" means systems using a mode of guided transport prescribed by regulations under this section.

(8) The power to make regulations under this section shall be exercisable by statutory instrument, which shall be subject to annulment in pursuance of a resolution of either House of Parliament.   **[559V]**

NOTES
Commencement: 31 January 1993.

42. Inspectors

(1) The functions of inspectors appointed under section 3 of the Regulation of Railways Act 1871 shall extend not only to railways (as defined by section 2 of that Act) but also to other railways and tramways, to trolley vehicle systems and to any system using a mode of guided transport prescribed by regulations under section 41 above; and in any enactment relating to those functions—

(a) references to railways or matters relating to railways shall be construed accordingly, and

(b) references to a company working a railway shall have effect as references to an operator of a railway, tramway, trolley vehicle system or system using a mode of guided transport prescribed by such regulations.

(2) In section 3 of the Regulation of Railways Act 1871, the proviso (which prohibits an inspector from interfering in the affairs of a company) shall cease to have effect.   **[559W]**

NOTES
Commencement: 31 January 1993.

43. Accidents, etc

(1) The Secretary of State may make regulations requiring the reporting to him of—

(a) accidents involving death or personal injury, and

(b) circumstances involving a danger of death or personal injury,

which occur in the operation of railways, tramways, trolley vehicle systems and systems using a mode of guided transport prescribed by the regulations.

(2) Regulations under this section shall prescribe the cases in which reports are required, the persons required to make them, the time and manner in which they are to be made, and the particulars to be included in them.

(3) Regulations under this section may make different provision for different cases, and may include provision authorising the Secretary of State—

(a) to dispense with compliance with any provision of the regulations that would otherwise apply, or

(b) to require compliance with any provision that would not otherwise apply,

in any case where he considers it appropriate to do so.

(4) A person who, without reasonable excuse, fails to make a report as required by regulations under this section shall be guilty of an offence.

(5) A person guilty of an offence under this section shall be liable on summary conviction to a fine not exceeding level 2 on the standard scale.

(6) The power to make regulations under this section shall be exercisable by statutory instrument, which shall be subject to annulment in pursuance of a resolution of either House of Parliament.   **[559X]**

NOTES
Commencement: to be appointed.

44. Accidents, etc: consequential amendments

(1) Section 6 of the Regulation of Railways Act 1871 (which is superseded by section 43 above) shall cease to have effect.

(2) In section 7 of that Act (inquiries into accidents etc)—

(a) for the words "this Act" (in the words preceding the paragraphs) there shall be substituted the words "regulations under section 43 of the Transport and Works Act 1992";

(b) after paragraph (4) there shall be added—

"In this section any reference to an accident includes a reference to circumstances involving a danger of death or personal injury."

(3) In section 8 of that Act (appointment of assessor to coroner) for the words "of this Act" there shall be substituted the words "of regulations under section 43 of the Transport and Works Act 1992".   **[559Y]**

NOTES
Commencement: to be appointed.

45. Directions limiting speeds and loads

(1) The Secretary of State may give a direction under this section to any person carrying on an undertaking which includes the provision of transport services on a railway, tramway or system using any other mode of guided transport.

(2) A direction under this section may impose—

(a) maximum speeds at which vehicles in use on the system may travel, and
(b) maximum weights that may be transmitted to the rails (or other structures which support vehicles in use on the system) by any one pair of wheels, or by such other parts of the vehicles as may be specified in the direction.

(3) Directions under this section may make different provision for different vehicles, different parts of the system, or otherwise for different circumstances.

(4) Before giving a direction under this section, the Secretary of State shall consult the person to whom he proposes to give it.

(5) If a direction under this section is contravened in the course of the provision of transport services by the person to whom the direction was given, that person shall be guilty of an offence.

(6) A person guilty of an offence under this section shall be liable on summary conviction to a fine not exceeding level 5 on the standard scale. **[559Z]**

NOTES
Commencement: 15 July 1992.

46. Directions requiring insurance

(1) The Secretary of State may give a direction under this section to an operator of a railway, tramway, trolley vehicle system or system using any other mode of guided transport.

(2) A direction under this section may require the person to whom it is given to ensure that there are at all times in force such policies of insurance against liability in respect of death or personal injury as comply with the requirements of the direction.

(3) Before giving a direction under this section, the Secretary of State shall consult the person to whom he proposes to give it.

(4) If a direction under this section is contravened, the person to whom the direction was given shall be guilty of an offence.

(5) A person guilty of an offence under this section shall be liable on summary conviction to a fine not exceeding level 5 on the standard scale. **[559AA]**

NOTES
Commencement: 15 July 1992.

Rail crossings

47. Stopping up and diversion of crossings

(1) Schedule 2 to this Act (which amends the Highways Act 1980 so as to provide for the stopping up or diversion of footpaths and bridleways crossing railways and tramways) shall have effect.

(2) Where a public right of way over a footpath or bridleway where it crosses a railway or tramway is extinguished by an order under sections 18 to 119A of the Highways Act 1980, any obligation (however imposed) to maintain the crossing for the benefit of the public shall cease to have effect. **[559BB]**

NOTES

Commencement: 22 December 1992 (sub-s (1), certain purposes); 31 January 1993 (sub-s (1) remaining purposes, sub-s (2)).

48. Footpaths and bridleways over railways

(1) This section applies where—
  (a) a public right of way over a footpath or bridleway crosses a railway or tramway otherwise than by a tunnel or bridge,
  (b) the operator of the railway or tramway has made a closure or diversion application in respect of the crossing, and
  (c) in the opinion of the Secretary of State the crossing constitutes a danger to members of the public using it or likely to use it.

(2) The Secretary of State may by order require the operator to provide a tunnel or a bridge, or to improve an existing tunnel or bridge, to carry the path or way over or under the railway or tramway at or reasonably near to the crossing to which the closure or diversion application relates.

(3) An order under this section may include particulars as to the tunnel or bridge which is to be provided or as to the improvements which are to be made.

(4) The Secretary of State shall not make an order under this section after the end of the period of two years beginning with the day on which the closure or diversion application is made, and not less than two months before making an order he shall give written notice of his proposal to make the order to the operator and to each local authority in whose area the crossing (or any proposed new crossing) is situated.

(5) A notice given under subsection (4) above must be accompanied by a draft of the proposed order under this section; and any order eventually made may include modifications of the draft.

(6) An operator shall not be regarded as in breach of a duty imposed by an order under this section if he has used his best endeavours to comply with the order.

(7) Where an operator is required by an order under this section to provide or improve a bridge or tunnel, but is unable to do so because he does not have the powers or rights (including rights over land) needed for the purpose, he shall not be taken to have used his best endeavours to comply with the order unless he has used his best endeavours to obtain those powers or rights (whether by means of an order under section 1 above or otherwise).

(8) In this section—
  "bridleway" has the same meaning as in the Highways Act 1980;
  "closure or diversion application" means—
      (a) an application made under section 6 above, or

(b) a request made in accordance with section 120(3A)(b) of the Highways Act 1980,

for an order by virtue of which a public right of way would be extinguished or diverted;

''footpath'' has the same meaning as in the Highways Act 1980;

''local authority'' means a county council, a district council, a London borough council, the Common Council of the City of London[, a county borough council,] a parish or community council and a parish meeting of a parish not having a separate parish council;

''operator'', in relation to a railway or tramway, means any person carrying on an undertaking which includes maintaining the permanent way. **[559CC]**

NOTES

Commencement: 31 January 1993.

In definition ''local authority'' in sub-s (8) words in square brackets inserted by the Local Government (Wales) Act 1994, s 22(1), Sch 7, Pt I, para 34(3), as from a day to be appointed.

49. Securing of gates and barriers

(1) Section 75 of the Railways Clauses Consolidation Act 1845 and section 68 of the Railways Clauses Consolidation (Scotland) Act 1845 (which make it an offence for any person to fail to fasten gates) shall be amended as follows.

(2) After the word ''gate'' there shall be inserted the words ''or to lower any barrier''.

(3) For the words ''not exceeding'' onwards there shall be substituted the words ''not exceeding level 3 on the standard scale''. **[559DD]**

NOTES

Commencement: 15 July 1992.

50. Orders under Transport Act 1968

Section 124 of the Transport Act 1968 (which gives the Secretary of State power to impose obligations in respect of level crossings), in its application in England and Wales, shall cease to have effect. **[559EE]**

NOTES

Commencement: to be appointed.

51. Amendment of Level Crossings Act 1983

In section 1 of the Level Crossings Act 1983 (safety arrangements at level crossings) in subsection (11), for the definition of ''operator'' there shall be substituted—

''''operator'', in relation to a crossing, means any person carrying on an undertaking which includes maintaining the permanent way;''. **[559FF]**

NOTES

Commencement: 31 January 1993.

Signs and barriers at private crossings

52. Placing of signs and barriers

(1) Subject to any directions under subsection (2) below, the operator of a railway or tramway which is crossed in any place by a private road or path may cause or permit crossing signs or barriers of a character—

(a) prescribed in regulations made by the Secretary of State, or
(b) otherwise authorised by him,

to be placed on or near the road or path near the crossing.

(2) The Secretary of State may give directions to the operator of a railway or tramway which is crossed in any place by a private road or path for the placing of crossing signs or barriers of a character specified in the directions on or near the road or path near the crossing.

(3) For the purposes of this section—

(a) the size and colour of a crossing sign and whether or not it is illuminated (by lighting or the use of reflectors or reflecting material), and
(b) the nature of the warnings, information, requirements, restrictions or prohibitions conveyed by it,

shall be regarded as part of the sign's character.

(4) The power to make regulations under this section shall be exercisable by statutory instrument, which shall be subject to annulment in pursuance of a resolution of either House of Parliament.

(5) Regulations under this section may make different provision for different cases.   **[559GG]**

NOTES
Commencement: to be appointed.

53. Rights to enter land

(1) The operator of a railway or tramway shall not enter or do anything on any land for the purpose of exercising his powers under section 52(1) above except—

(a) with the consent of every owner of the land, or
(b) in accordance with an authorisation given by the Secretary of State under subsection (4) below.

(2) Where the operator of a railway or tramway proposes to enter or do anything on any land for the purpose of exercising his powers under section 52(1) above but has not obtained the consent of every owner of the land to his proposals (after making reasonable efforts to do so), he shall serve on every owner whose consent he has not obtained a notice giving details of the proposals and stating that—

(a) he is referring the proposals to the Secretary of State for a decision as to whether or not they should be carried out, and
(b) in making that decision, the Secretary of State will consider any written representations made to him by the owner within the period of forty-two days beginning with the date of the notice.

(3) Where subsection (2) above applies, the operator shall—

(a) submit a copy of every notice served by him under that subsection to the Secretary of State, and
(b) provide the Secretary of State with such further information about the proposals as he may require.

(4) Where proposals are referred to the Secretary of State under this section, he shall after the expiry of the period of forty-two days beginning with the date of the latest notice served under subsection (2) above and after considering any representations made to him in accordance with that subsection—

(a) authorise the operator to carry out the proposals (either without modifications or with such modifications as the Secretary of State may specify), or

(b) direct him not to carry out the proposals,

and shall serve notice of his decision on every owner served with a notice under subsection (2) above.

(5) Any authorisation under subsection (4) above may be given subject to such conditions as the Secretary of State may specify, including conditions that compensation shall be payable by the operator.

(6) Any dispute as to the amount of any compensation payable by virtue of subsection (5) above shall be referred to and determined by the Lands Tribunal or, in relation to land in Scotland, the Lands Tribunal for Scotland.

(7) The operator of a railway or tramway may enter any land and do anything necessary on it (without the consent of the owners of the land) for the purpose of—

(a) complying with any directions given under section 52(2) above,

or

(b) maintaining a crossing sign or barrier lawfully placed on or near a private road or path near a place where it crosses the railway or tramway.

(8) The Secretary of State may enter any land and do anything necessary on it (without the consent of the owners of the land) for the purpose of exercising his powers under section 54(1) below.

(9) In this section ''owner''—

(a) in relation to any land in England and Wales, means a person, other than a mortgagee not in possession, who is for the time being entitled to dispose of the fee simple (whether in possession or reversion) and includes also a person holding, or entitled to the rents and profits of, the land under a tenancy, other than a tenancy for a month or any period less than a month;

(b) in relation to any land in Scotland, means a person who, under the Land Clauses Acts, would be entitled to sell and convey land to the promoters of an undertaking and includes also a person who is or would be entitled to receive the rent of the land under a tenancy, other than a tenancy for a month or any period less than a month.   **[559HH]**

NOTES
Commencement: to be appointed.

54. Default powers of Secretary of State

(1) If the operator of a railway or tramway fails—

(a) to comply with a direction given under section 52(2) above, or

(b) to maintain a crossing sign or barrier lawfully placed on or near a private road or path near a place where it crosses the railway or tramway,

the Secretary of State may himself carry out the work required by the direction or necessary to maintain the crossing sign or barrier.

(2) Any expenses incurred by the Secretary of State in doing so shall be recoverable by him from the operator.

(3) A direction given under section 52(2) above—

(a) if relating to a private road or path in England and Wales, shall be enforceable on the application of the Secretary of State by an order of mandamus;

(b) if relating to a private road or path in Scotland, shall be enforceable by order of the Court of Session on an application by the Lord Advocate under section 45 of the Court of Session Act 1988. **[559II]**

NOTES

Commencement: to be appointed.

55. Offence of failing to comply with sign

(1) A person who fails to comply with any requirement, restriction or prohibition conveyed by a crossing sign lawfully placed on or near a private road or path near a place where it crosses a railway or tramway shall be guilty of an offence.

(2) In any proceedings for an offence under this section, a crossing sign on or near a private road or path near a place where it crosses a railway or tramway shall be taken to have been lawfully placed there unless the contrary is proved.

(3) A person guilty of an offence under this section shall be liable on summary conviction to a fine not exceeding level 3 on the standard scale. **[559JJ]**

NOTES

Commencement: to be appointed.

56. Interpretation of sections 52 to 55

(1) In sections 52 to 55 above (and this section)—

"barrier" includes gate;

"cross" means cross otherwise than by tunnel or bridge;

"crossing sign", in relation to a private road or path and any place where it crosses a railway or tramway, means—

(a) any object or device (whether fixed or portable), or

(b) any line or mark on the road or path,

for conveying to users of the road or path warnings, information, requirements, restrictions or prohibitions relating to the crossing;

"fail" includes refuse;

"lawfully placed" means placed in accordance with sections 52 to 54 above;

"maintain" includes repair and replace;

"place" includes erect and (in relation to a sign) display;

"private road or path" means any length of road or path to which the public does not have access.

(2) In the case of a railway or tramway which has more than one operator, the powers conferred by sections 52 to 54 above shall only be exercisable by or in relation to the operator carrying on the undertaking which includes maintaining the permanent way. **[559KK]**

NOTES

Commencement: to be appointed.

CHAPTER III

SUPPLEMENTARY

57. Duty to consult

It shall be the duty of the Secretary of State, before he makes regulations under section 32, [or 38(2)] above, to consult such organisations as he considers to be representative of persons who will be affected by the regulations.   **[559LL]**

NOTES
  Commencement: 15 July 1992.
  Words in square brackets substituted by the Railways Act 1993, s 117(5)(a).

58. Prosecutions

No proceedings shall be instituted in England and Wales in respect of an offence under this Part[, other than an offence under section 41 or 43 above,] except by or with the consent of the Secretary of State or the Director of Public Prosecutions.
                                                                                    [559MM]

NOTES
  Commencement: 15 July 1992.
  Words in square brackets inserted by the Railways Act 1993, s 117(5)(b).

59. Offences by bodies corporate etc

(1) Where an offence under this Part committed by a body corporate is committed with the consent or connivance of, or is attributable to any neglect on the part of, a director, manager, secretary or other similar officer of the body, or a person purporting to act in such a capacity, he as well as the body corporate shall be guilty of the offence.

(2) In subsection (1) above "director", in relation to a body corporate whose affairs are managed by its members, means a member of the body corporate.

(3) Where, in Scotland, an offence under this Part committed by a partnership or by an unincorporated association other than a partnership is committed with the consent or connivance of, or is attributable to any neglect on the part of, a partner in the partnership or (as the case may be) a person concerned in the management or control of the association, he, as well as the partnership or association, shall be guilty of the offence.   **[559NN]**

NOTES
  Commencement: 15 July 1992.

PART III

MISCELLANEOUS AND GENERAL

Tramways

60. Powers of leasing

(1) A person authorised by or under an enactment to operate a tramway ("the lessor") may with the consent of the Secretary of State grant to another person ("the lessee"), for a period agreed between the lessor and the lessee, the right to operate the tramway (or any part of it) and such related statutory rights as may be so agreed.

(2) The terms of any agreement made by virtue of subsection (1) above shall be subject to the approval of the Secretary of State.

(3) Where an agreement is made by virtue of subsection (1) above, references in any enactment to the lessor shall, if and to the extent that the agreement so provides, have effect as references to the lessee.

(4) This section shall apply only to tramways in operation at the passing of this Act.   **[559OO]**

NOTES
Commencement: 15 July 1992.

61. Amendment of Public Passenger Vehicles Act 1981

(1) The Public Passenger Vehicles Act 1981 shall be amended as follows.

(2) In section 24 (regulation of conduct of drivers, inspectors and conductors)—

    (a) at the end of subsection (1) there shall be added the words "and

        (c) drivers, inspectors and conductors of tramcars";

    (b) in subsection (2), after the word "driver" there shall be inserted the words "of a public service vehicle".

(3) In section 25(1) (regulation of conduct of passengers), after the words "public service vehicles" there shall be inserted the words "or tramcars" and after the words "public service vehicle" wherever they occur there shall be inserted the words "or tramcar".

(4) In section 27(1) (returns to be provided by persons operating public service vehicles) after the words "public service vehicles" there shall be inserted the words "or tramcars".

(5) In section 60(1) (general power to make regulations)—

    (a) at the end of paragraph (j) (carriage of luggage and goods on public service vehicles) there shall be added the words "or tramcars";

    (b) in paragraph (k)(custody of property left on a public service vehicle) after the word "vehicle" there shall be inserted the words "or tramcar".

(6) After subsection (1A) of section 60 there shall be inserted—

"(1B) Regulations made under any provision of this Act and applying to tramcars may amend or exclude any provision of an Act or instrument of local application whose subject-matter is the same as that of the regulations." **[559PP]**

NOTES
Commencement: 31 January 1993.

62. Exclusion of hackney carriage legislation

(1) In section 4 of the Metropolitan Public Carriage Act 1869 (interpretation) in the definition of "hackney carriage", for the words "not a stage carriage" there shall be substituted the words "neither a stage carriage nor a tramcar".

(2) In section 4 of the London Cab Act 1968 (display of signs etc) in subsection (5) in the definition of "private hire-car", after the words "public service vehicle" there shall be inserted the words "or tramcar".

(3) In section 80 of the Local Government (Miscellaneous Provisions) Act 1976

(interpretation) in subsection (1) in the definition of "private hire vehicle", after the words "London cab" there shall be inserted the words "or tramcar".   **[559QQ]**

NOTES
  Commencement: to be appointed.

Harbours

63. Harbours

(1) The Harbours Act 1964 shall have effect with the amendments set out in Schedule 3 to this Act.

(2) In section 37 of the Docks and Harbours Act 1966 (which gives to harbour authorities powers to acquire harbour businesses, and to subscribe for or acquire securities of bodies engaged, or to be engaged, in harbour businesses)—

   (a) in subsection (1), for the words "harbour operations" and the words "such operations" there shall be substituted the words "activities relating to harbours";
   (b) in subsection (2), for the words "harbour operations" there shall be substituted the words "activities relating to harbours";
   (c) after subsection (2) there shall be inserted—

   "(2A) Nothing in subsection (2) above shall be construed as authorising a harbour authority to delegate to another body any function that it could not delegate apart from that subsection.";

   (d) subsection (3) shall be omitted.

(3) In section 35 of the Coast Protection Act 1949 (which excepts certain operations from the requirement to obtain the Secretary of State's consent under section 34) in subsection (1) there shall be added after paragraph (h)—

   "(i) any operations authorised by an order under section 14 or 16 of the Harbours Act 1964."   **[559RR]**

NOTES
  Commencement: 15 July 1992 (subject to transitional provisions in SI 1992/1347).

Miscellaneous

64. Maintenance of footpaths and bridleways

(1) Section 36 of the Highways Act 1980 (highways maintainable at public expense) shall be amended as follows.

(2) In subsection (2), at the end of paragraph (c), the word "and" shall be omitted.

(3) After paragraph (d) of subsection (2), there shall be added—

   "(e) a highway, being a footpath or bridleway, created in consequence of a rail crossing diversion order, or of an order made under section 14 or 16 of the Harbours Act 1964, or of an order made under section 1 or 3 of the Transport and Works Act 1992."

(4) After subsection (3) there shall be inserted—

   "(3A) Paragraph (e) of subsection (2) above shall not apply to a footpath or bridleway, or to any part of a footpath or bridleway, which by virtue of an order of a kind referred to in that subsection is maintainable otherwise than at the public expense."   **[559SS]**

NOTES
Commencement: 31 January 1993.

65. Certain enactments to cease to have effect

(1) The following enactments shall cease to have effect—

    (a) the General Pier and Harbour Act 1861;

    (b) in the Tramways Act 1870—

> section 3 (except as incorporated in, or otherwise applied by, any Act of Parliament or Provisional Order),
> sections 4 to 21,
> sections 22 to 24 (except as incorporated in, or otherwise applied by, any Act of Parliament or Provisional Order),
> in section 25, the words from the beginning to "surface of the road" (except as incorporated in, or otherwise applied by, any Act of Parliament or Provisional Order),
> in section 25, the words "and shall not be opened" onwards,
> sections 26 to 40 (except as incorporated in, or otherwise applied by, any Act of Parliament or Provisional Order),
> sections 41 and 42,
> sections 43 to 47 (except as incorporated in, or otherwise applied by, any Act of Parliament or Provisional Order),
> section 48,
> sections 49 to 64 (except as incorporated in, or otherwise applied by, any Act of Parliament or Provisional Order),
> Parts I and II of Schedule A (except as incorporated in, or otherwise applied by, any Act of Parliament or Provisional Order),
> Part III of Schedule A,
> Schedule B, and
> Schedule C (except as incorporated in, or otherwise applied by, any Act of Parliament or Provisional Order);

    (c) the Military Tramways Act 1887;

    (d) the Railways (Electrical Power) Act 1903;

    (e) the Fishery Harbours Act 1915;

    (f) section 220(1)(a) of the Insolvency Act 1986.

(2) In the Coast Protection Act 1949, in sections 2(8)(a) and 17(8)(b), for the words "to which the Fishery Harbours Act 1915 applies" there shall be substituted the words "which is a fishery harbour for the purposes of section 21 of the Sea Fish Industry Act 1951".   **[559TT]**

NOTES
Commencement: 15 July 1992 (sub-ss (1)(a), (e), (2)); 1 January 1993 (sub-s (1)(b) (in part), sub-s (1)(c), (d), (f)); 5 April 1994 (sub-s (1)(b) (in part)); to be appointed (sub-s (1)(b) (remainder)).

General

66. Service of notices

(1) A notice or other document required or authorised to be served for the purposes of this Act may be served by post.

(2) Where the person on whom a notice or other document to be served for the purposes of this Act is a body corporate, the notice or document is duly served if it is served on the secretary or clerk of that body.

(3) For the purposes of section 7 of the Interpretation Act 1978 as it applies for

the purposes of this section, the proper address of any person in relation to the service on him of a notice or document under subsection (1) above is, if he has given an address for service, that address, and otherwise—

    (a) in the case of the secretary or clerk of a body corporate, the registered or principal office of that body;

    (b) in any other case, his last known address at the time of service.

(4) Where for the purposes of this Act a notice or other document is required or authorised to be served on a person as having any interest in, or as the occupier of, land and his name or address cannot be ascertained after reasonable inquiry, the notice may be served by—

    (a) addressing it to him by name or by the description of "owner", or as the case may be "occupier", of the land (describing it), and

    (b) either leaving it in the hands of a person who is or appears to be resident or employed on the land or leaving it conspicuously affixed to some building or object on the land.

(5) This section shall not be taken to exclude the employment of any method of service not expressly provided for by it.

(6) This section shall not apply to anything required or authorised to be served under section 35 above. **[559UU]**

NOTES
    Commencement: 15 July 1992.

67. Interpretation

(1) In this Act, except where the context otherwise requires—

    "carriageway" has the same meaning as in the Highways Act 1980, or in Scotland the Roads (Scotland) Act 1984;

    "guided transport" means transport by vehicles guided by means external to the vehicles (whether or not the vehicles are also capable of being operated in some other way);

    "inland waterway" includes both natural and artificial waterways, and waterways within parts of the sea that are in Great Britain, but not any waterway managed or maintained by a person who is a harbour authority (within the meaning of the Harbours Act 1964) in relation to the waterway;

    "operator", in relation to a transport system, means any person carrying on an undertaking which includes the system or any part of it or the provision of transport services on the system;

    "railway" means a system of transport employing parallel rails which—

    (a) provide support and guidance for vehicles carried on flanged wheels, and

    (b) form a track which either is of a gauge of at least 350 millimetres or crosses a carriageway (whether or not on the same level),

    but does not include a tramway;

    "street" means—

    (a) in England and Wales, a street within the meaning of section 48 of the New Roads and Street Works Act 1991, together with land on the verge of a street or between two carriageways;

    (b) in Scotland, a road within the meaning of section 107 of the New Roads and Street Works Act 1991, together with land on the verge of a road or between two carriageways;

"tramway" means a system of transport used wholly or mainly for the carriage of passengers and employing parallel rails which—

(a) provide support and guidance for vehicles carried on flanged wheels, and

(b) are laid wholly or mainly along a street or in any other place to which the public has access (including a place to which the public has access only on making a payment);

"trolley vehicle system" means a system of transport by vehicles constructed or adapted for use on roads without rails under electric power transmitted to them by overhead wires (whether or not there is in addition a source of power on board the vehicles);

"vehicle" includes mobile traction unit.

(2) References in this Act to rights over land include references to rights to do, or to place and maintain, anything in, on or under land or in the air-space above its surface.   **[559VV]**

NOTES
Commencement: 15 July 1992.

68. Repeals

(1) The enactments mentioned in Schedule 4 to this Act (which include spent enactments) are hereby repealed to the extent specified in the third column of that Schedule.

(2) The repeal by this Act of the Notice of Accidents Act 1894 shall not affect section 75 of the Civil Aviation Act 1982 (by virtue of which regulations may include provisions applying section 3 of the 1894 Act).   **[559WW]**

NOTES
Commencement: 15 July 1992 (sub-s (1), certain purposes); 7 December 1992 (sub-s (1), certain purposes); 1 January 1993 (sub-s (1), certain purposes); 31 January 1993 (sub-s (1), certain purposes); 5 April 1994 (sub-s (1), certain purposes); to be appointed (sub-s (1) remaining purposes, sub-s (2)).

69. Expenses

There shall be paid out of money provided by Parliament—

(a) any expenses incurred by the Secretary of State under this Act, and

(b) any increase attributable to this Act in the sums payable out of money so provided under any other enactment.   **[559XX]**

NOTES
Commencement: 15 July 1992.

70. Commencement

(1) The preceding sections of, and the Schedules to, this Act shall come into force on such day as the Secretary of State may appoint by order made by statutory instrument; and different days may be appointed for different purposes.

(2) An order under subsection (1) above may include such transitional provisions and savings as appear to the Secretary of State to be necessary or expedient.

[559YY]

NOTES
Commencement: 16 March 1992.

71. Extent

This Act shall not extend to Northern Ireland. **[559ZZ]**

NOTES
Commencement: 16 March 1992.

72. Short title

This Act may be cited as the Transport and Works Act 1992. **[559ZA]**

NOTES
Commencement: 16 March 1992.

SCHEDULE 1

Section 5

MATTERS WITHIN SECTIONS 1 AND 3

1. The construction, alteration, repair, maintenance, demolition and removal of railways, tramways, trolley vehicle systems and other transport systems within section 1(1) of this Act, waterways, roads, watercourses, buildings and other structures.

2. The carrying out of any other civil engineering or other works.

3. The acquisition of land, whether compulsorily or by agreement.

4. The creation and extinguishment of rights over land (including rights of navigation over water), whether compulsorily or by agreement.

5. The abrogation and modification of agreements relating to land.

6. The conferring on persons providing transport services of rights to use systems belonging to others.

7. The protection of the property or interests of any person.

8. The imposition and exclusion of obligations or of liability in respect of any acts or omissions.

9. The making of agreements to secure the provision of police services.

10. The carrying out of surveys and the taking of soil samples.

11. The payment of compensation.

12. The charging of tolls, fares (including penalty fares) and other charges, and the creation of summary offences in connection with non-payment (or in connection with a person's failure to give his name or address in accordance with provisions relating to penalty fares).

13. The making of byelaws by any person and their enforcement, including the creation of summary offences.

14. The payment of rates.

15. The transfer, leasing, discontinuance and revival of undertakings.

16. The submission of disputes to arbitration.

17. The imposition of requirements to obtain the consent of the Secretary of State.
[559ZB]

NOTES
Commencement: 1 January 1993.

SCHEDULE 2

Section 47

STOPPING UP AND DIVERSION OF RAIL CROSSINGS

1. The Highways Act 1980 shall be amended as follows.

2.—(1) Section 118 (stopping up of footpaths and bridleways) shall be amended as follows.

(2) In subsection (5), for—

(a) the words "or public path diversion order made under section 119 below", and
(b) the words "or the public path diversion order",

there shall be substituted the words ", public path diversion order or rail crossing diversion order".

(3) In subsection (7), for "119" there shall be substituted "118A".

3. After section 118 there shall be inserted—

"118A. Stopping up of footpaths and bridleways crossing railways

(1) This section applies where it appears to a council expedient in the interests of the safety of members of the public using it or likely to use it that a footpath or bridleway in their area which crosses a railway, otherwise than by tunnel or bridge, should be stopped up.

(2) Where this section applies, the council may by order made by them and submitted to and confirmed by the Secretary of State, or confirmed as an unopposed order, extinguish the public right of way over the path or way—

(a) on the crossing itself, and
(b) for so much of its length as they deem expedient from the crossing to its intersection with another highway over which there subsists a like right of way (whether or not other rights of way also subsist over it).

(3) An order under this section is referred to in this Act as a "rail crossing extinguishment order".

(4) The Secretary of State shall not confirm a rail crossing extinguishment order, and a council shall not confirm such an order as an unopposed order, unless he or, as the case may be, they are satisfied that it is expedient to do so having regard to all the circumstances, and in particular to—

(a) whether it is reasonably practicable to make the crossing safe for use by the public, and
(b) what arrangements have been made for ensuring that, if the order is confirmed, any appropriate barriers and signs are erected and maintained.

(5) Before determining to make a rail crossing extinguishment order on the representations of the operator of the railway crossed by the path or way, the council may require him to enter into an agreement with them to defray, or to make such contribution as may be specified in the agreement towards, any expenses which the council may incur in connection with the erection or maintenance of barriers and signs.

(6) A rail crossing extinguishment order shall be in such form as may be prescribed by regulations made by the Secretary of State and shall contain a map, on such scale as may be so prescribed, defining the land over which the public right of way is thereby extinguished.

(7) Schedule 6 to this Act has effect as to the making, confirmation, validity and date of operation of rail crossing extinguishment orders.

(8) In this section—

"operator", in relation to a railway, means any person carrying on an undertaking which includes maintaining the permanent way;

"railway" includes tramway but does not include any part of a system where rails are laid along a carriageway."

4. After section 119 (diversion of footpaths and bridleways) there shall be inserted—

"119A. Diversion of footpaths and bridleways crossing railways

(1) This section applies where it appears to a council expedient in the interests of the safety of members of the public using it or likely to use it that a footpath or bridleway in their area which crosses a railway, otherwise than by tunnel or bridge, should be diverted (whether on to land of the same or of another owner, lessee or occupier).

(2) Where this section applies, the council may by order made by them and submitted to and confirmed by the Secretary of State, or confirmed as an unopposed order—

(a) create, as from such date as may be specified in the order, any such new path or way as appears to the council requisite for effecting the diversion, and

(b) extinguish, as from such date as may be so specified, the public right of way over the crossing and over so much of the path or way of which the crossing forms part as appears to the council requisite as aforesaid.

(3) An order under this section is referred to in this Act as a "rail crossing diversion order".

(4) The Secretary of State shall not confirm a rail crossing diversion order, and a council shall not confirm such an order as an unopposed order, unless he or, as the case may be, they are satisfied that it is expedient to do so having regard to all the circumstances, and in particular to—

(a) whether it is reasonably practicable to make the crossing safe for use by the public, and

(b) what arrangements have been made for ensuring that, if the order is confirmed, any appropriate barriers and signs are erected and maintained.

(5) A rail crossing diversion order shall not alter a point of termination of a path or way diverted under the order—

(a) if that point is not on a highway over which there subsists a like right of way (whether or not other rights of way also subsist over it), or

(b) (where it is on such a highway) otherwise than to another point which is on the same highway, or another such highway connected with it.

(6) A rail crossing diversion order may make provision requiring the operator of the railway to maintain all or part of the footpath or bridleway created by the order.

(7) Where it appears to the council that work requires to be done to provide necessary facilities for the convenient exercise of any such new right of way as is mentioned in subsection (2)(a) above, the date specified under subsection (2)(b) shall be later than the date specified under subsection (2)(a) by such time as appears to the council requisite for enabling the work to be carried out.

(8) Before determining to make a rail crossing diversion order on the representations of the operator of the railway crossed by the path or way, the council may require him to enter into an agreement with them to defray, or to make such contribution as may be specified in the agreement towards,—

(a) any compensation which may become payable under section 28 above as applied by section 121(2) below;

(b) any expenses which the council may incur in connection with the erection or maintenance of barriers and signs;

(c) where the council are the highway authority for the path or way in question, any expenses which they may incur in bringing the new site of the path or way into fit condition for use by the public;

(d) where the council are not the highway authority, any expenses which may become recoverable from them by the highway authority under the provisions of section 27(2) above as applied by subsection (11) below.

(9) A rail crossing diversion order shall be in such form as may be prescribed by

regulations made by the Secretary of State and shall contain a map, on such scale as may be so prescribed—

(a) showing the existing site of so much of the line of the path or way as is to be diverted by the order and the new site to which it is to be diverted,

(b) indicating whether a new right of way is created by the order over the whole of the new site or whether some part of it is already comprised in a footpath or bridleway, and

(c) where some part of the new site is already so comprised, defining that part.

(10) Schedule 6 to this Act has effect as to the making, confirmation, validity and date of operation of rail crossing diversion orders.

(11) Section 27 above (making up of new footpaths and bridleways) applies to a footpath or bridleway created by a rail crossing diversion order with the substitution, for references to a public path creation order, of references to a rail crossing diversion order and, for references to section 26(2) above, of references to section 120(3) below.

(12) In this section and in section 120 below—

"operator", in relation to a railway, means any person carrying on an undertaking which includes maintaining the permanent way;

"railway" includes tramway but does not include any part of a system where rails are laid along a carriageway."

5.—(1) Section 120 (exercise of powers of making public path extinguishment and diversion orders) shall be amended as follows.

(2) In subsection (1), for the words "and 119" there shall be substituted the words "to 119A".

(3) In subsection (2), for the words from "public path extinguishment" to "and 119" there shall be substituted the words "orders under sections 118 to 119A".

(4) In subsection (3)—

(a) after "118(1)" there shall be inserted "or 118A(1) or 119A(1)";

(b) after the words "stopped up" there shall be inserted the words "or diverted";

(c) after the words "extinguishment order" there shall be added the words ", a rail crossing extinguishment order, a rail crossing diversion order";

(d) for the words "and 119" there shall be substituted the words "to 119A";

(e) after the word "consultation" there shall be inserted the words "(subject to subsection (3A) below)".

(5) After subsection (3) there shall be inserted—

"(3A) Where—

(a) the operator of a railway makes a request to a council to make an order under section 118A or 119A above in respect of a crossing over the railway,

(b) the request is in such form and gives such particulars as are prescribed by regulations made by the Secretary of State, and

(c) the council have neither confirmed the order nor submitted it to the Secretary of State within 6 months of receiving the request,

the power conferred on the Secretary of State by subsection (3) above may be exercised without consultation with the council."

(6) In subsection (4), after the words "public path diversion order" there shall be inserted the words "or a rail crossing diversion order".

(7) In subsection (5)—

(a) for the words "he may require the owner, lessee or occupier" there shall be substituted the words "or, on the representations of the operator of the railway concerned, a rail crossing diversion order, he may require the person";

(b) for the words "for the owner, lessee or occupier" there shall be substituted the words "for that person";

(c) after "119(5)" there shall be inserted the words ", or as the case may be 119A(8),".

6.—(1) Section 121 (supplementary provisions) shall be amended as follows.

(2) In subsection (1)—

   (a) for the words "or a public path diversion order" there shall be substituted the words ", a rail crossing extinguishment order, a public path diversion order or a rail crossing diversion order";

   (b) after the words "and a public path diversion order" there shall be added the words "or a rail crossing diversion order".

(3) In subsection (2), for the words "and to public path diversion orders" there shall be substituted the words ", rail crossing extinguishment orders, public path diversion orders and rail crossing diversion orders".

(4) In subsection (3), for the words "and public path diversion orders" there shall be substituted the words ", rail crossing extinguishment orders, public path diversion orders and rail crossing diversion orders".

(5) In subsection (4), for the words "or a public path diversion order" there shall be substituted the words ", a rail crossing extinguishment order, a public path diversion order or a rail crossing diversion order".

7. In section 293 (powers of entry for purposes connected with certain orders relating to footpaths and bridleways) in subsection (1) for the words "or a public path diversion order" there shall be substituted the words ", a rail crossing extinguishment order, a public path diversion order or a rail crossing diversion order".

8. In section 325 (provisions as to regulations, schemes and orders) in subsection (2)(a), after the word "section", there shall be inserted the words "120(3A) or".

9. In section 329(1) (interpretation) after the definition of "rack rent" there shall be inserted—

   "rail crossing diversion order" means an order under section 119A above;
   "rail crossing extinguishment order" means an order under section 118A above;".

10.—(1) Schedule 6 shall be amended as follows.

(2) In paragraph 1—

   (a) in sub-paragraphs (1) and (2) for the words "or a public path diversion order" there shall be substituted the words ", a rail crossing extinguishment order, a public path diversion order or a rail crossing diversion order";

   (b) in sub-paragraph (3A) for the words "and public path diversion orders" there shall be substituted the words ", rail crossing extinguishment orders, public path diversion orders and rail crossing diversion orders";

   (c) in sub-paragraph (3B) for the words "and draft public path diversion orders" there shall be substituted the words ", draft rail crossing extinguishment orders, draft public path diversion orders and draft rail crossing diversion orders".

(3) In paragraph 2A(1), after the words "shall, except in" there shall be inserted the words "the case of a rail crossing extinguishment order, the case of a rail crossing diversion order and".

(4) In paragraph 3(2)—

   (a) after the words "public path extinguishment order" there shall be inserted the words "or a rail crossing extinguishment order";

   (b) for the words "or a public path diversion order" there shall be substituted the words ", a public path diversion order or a rail crossing diversion order".   **[559ZC]**

NOTES

Commencement: 22 December 1992 (certain purposes); 31 January 1993 (remaining purposes).

SCHEDULE 3

Section 63

AMENDMENT OF HARBOURS ACT 1964

1.—(1) Section 14 (harbour revision orders) shall be amended as follows.

(2) In subsection (2)(b) at the end there shall be added the words "or in the interests of the recreational use of sea-going ships".

(3) After subsection (2A) there shall be inserted—

"(2B) Nothing in subsection (2)(b) of this section shall prevent the making of an order for facilitating—

(a) the closing of part of the harbour,
(b) a reduction in the facilities available in the harbour, or
(c) the disposal of property not required for the purposes of the harbour,

if the appropriate Minister is satisfied that the making of the order is desirable on grounds other than those specified in that subsection."

(4) In subsection (3)—

(a) for the words from "a provision" to "said objects" there shall be substituted the words "any other provision of the order";
(b) after the words "for the purposes of" there shall be inserted the words ", or in connection with,";
(c) for the words "repealing and amending" there shall be substituted the words "excluding or modifying any provision of any Act or of any instrument made under any Act (including this Act) and for repealing".

(5) After subsection (4) there shall be inserted—

"(4A) Where two or more harbours are being improved, maintained or managed by the same harbour authority or by harbour authorities which are members of the same group, a harbour revision order may relate to more than one of the harbours; and for this purpose two authorities are members of the same group if one is a subsidiary (within the meaning of the Companies Act 1985) of the other or both are subsidiaries of another company (within the meaning of that Act)."

(6) In subsection (5), for the words "large-scale map" there shall be substituted the words "map of a scale not less than 1:2500".

(7) After subsection (5) there shall be inserted—

"(5A) Where a harbour revision order includes provision for extinguishing or diverting a public right of way over a footpath or bridleway, there must be annexed to the order a map of a scale not less than 1:2500 on which the path or way concerned, and in the case of a diversion the new path or way, are plainly delineated."

2.—(1) Section 16 (harbour empowerment orders) shall be amended as follows.

(2) At the end of subsection (5) there shall be added the words "or in the interests of the recreational use of sea-going ships".

(3) In subsection (6), after the words "any other enactment" there shall be inserted the words "and provisions for excluding or modifying any provision of any Act or of any instrument made under any Act (including this Act)".

(4) In subsection (7), for the words "large-scale map" there shall be substituted the words "map of a scale not less than 1:2500".

(5) After subsection (7) there shall be inserted—

"(7A) Where a harbour empowerment order includes provision for extinguishing or diverting a public right of way over a footpath or bridleway, there must be annexed to the order a map of a scale not less than 1:2500 on which the path or way concerned, and in the case of a diversion the new path or way, are plainly delineated."

3. In section 17 (procedure for making harbour revision and empowerment orders) after subsection (2) there shall be inserted—

"(2A) Neither the Secretary of State nor the Minister of Agriculture, Fisheries and Food shall make a harbour revision or empowerment order which provides for extinguishing a public right of way over a footpath or bridleway unless he is satisfied—

(a) that an alternative right of way has been or will be provided, or
(b) that the provision of an alternative right of way is not required.

(2B) Neither the Secretary of State nor the Minister of Agriculture, Fisheries and Food shall make a harbour revision or empowerment order which provides for diverting a public right of way over a footpath or bridleway unless he is satisfied that the path or way will not be substantially less convenient to the public in consequence of the diversion."

4. In section 18 (harbour reorganisation schemes) in subsection (3), for the words "large-scale map" there shall be substituted the words "map of a scale not less than 1:2500".

5.—(1) Section 47 (provisions as to inquiries and hearings) shall be amended as follows.

(2) After subsection (1) there shall be inserted—

"(1A) The power to make an order as to costs under section 250(5) of the Local Government Act 1972 as applied by subsection (1) above shall be exercisable not only where the inquiry or hearing takes place but also where arrangements are made for it but it does not take place."

(3) (*Applies to Scotland only.*)

(4) In subsection (3), for the words from "required by paragraph 4(3)" to "Schedule 4" there shall be substituted the words "into an order subject to the provisions of paragraph 4B of Schedule 3".

6. After section 48 (service of documents) there shall be inserted—

"48A. Environmental duties of harbour authorities

It shall be the duty of a harbour authority in formulating or considering any proposals relating to its functions under any enactment to have regard to—

(a) the conservation of the natural beauty of the countryside and of flora, fauna and geological or physiographical features of special interest;
(b) the desirability of preserving for the public any freedom of access to places of natural beauty; and
(c) the desirability of maintaining the availability to the public of any facility for visiting or inspecting any building, site or object of archaeological, architectural or historic interest;

and to take into account any effect which the proposals may have on the natural beauty of the countryside, flora, fauna or any such feature or facility."

7.—(1) Section 57 (interpretation) shall be amended as follows.

(2) After the definition of "the Boards" there shall be inserted—

""bridleway", in relation to England and Wales, has the same meaning as in the Highways Act 1980 and, in relation to Scotland, has the same meaning as in Part III of the Countryside (Scotland) Act 1967;".

(3) After the definition of "fishery harbour" there shall be inserted—

""footpath", in relation to England and Wales, has the same meaning as in the Highways Act 1980 and, in relation to Scotland, has the same meaning as in the Roads (Scotland) Act 1984;".

8. Section 62 (saving for private Bills etc) shall be omitted.

9.—(1) Schedule 2 (objects for whose achievement harbour revision orders may be made) shall be amended as follows.

(2) In paragraph 3(c) for the words from "out" to "others of" there shall be substituted the words "on by others of activities relating to the harbour or of".

(3) After paragraph 7 there shall be inserted—

"**7A.** Extinguishing or diverting public rights of way over footpaths or bridleways for the purposes of works described in the order or works ancillary to such works.

7B. Extinguishing public rights of navigation for the purposes of works described in the order or works ancillary to such works, or permitting interference with the enjoyment of such rights for the purposes of such works or for the purposes of works carried out by a person authorised by the authority to carry them out."

(4) After paragraph 8 there shall be inserted—

"**8A.** Enabling the authority to close part of the harbour or to reduce the facilities available in the harbour."

(5) After paragraph 9 there shall be inserted—

"**9A.** Empowering the authority (alone or with others) to develop land not required for the purposes of the harbour with a view to disposing of the land or of interests in it, and to acquire land by agreement for the purpose of developing it together with such land.

9B. Empowering the authority to delegate the performance of any of the functions of the authority except—

    (a) a duty imposed on the authority by or under any enactment;
    (b) the making of byelaws;
    (c) the levying of ship, passenger and goods dues;
    (d) the appointment of harbour, dock and pier masters;
    (e) the nomination of persons to act as constables;
    (f) functions relating to the laying down of buoys, the erection of lighthouses and the exhibition of lights, beacons and sea-marks, so far as those functions are exercisable for the purposes of the safety of navigation."

(6) After paragraph 16 there shall be inserted—

"**16A.** Imposing or conferring on the authority duties or powers (including powers to make byelaws) for the conservation of the natural beauty of all or any part of the harbour or of any of the fauna, flora or geological or physiographical features in the harbour and all other natural features."

10.—(1) Schedule 3 (procedure for making harbour orders) shall be amended as follows.

(2) After paragraph 1A there shall be inserted—

"**1B.** Such fees as may be determined by the Secretary of State shall be payable on the making of an application for a harbour revision order."

(3) In paragraph 3, after sub-paragraph (b) there shall be inserted—

"(ba) if provision is proposed to be included in the order extinguishing or diverting a public right of way over a footpath or bridleway, the applicant shall—

    (i) serve on every local authority for the area in which the path or way is situated a notice stating the effect of the provision, naming a place where a copy of the draft of the proposed order (and of any relevant map accompanying the application for the order) may be seen at all reasonable hours and stating that, if the local authority desire to make to the Secretary of State objection to the inclusion of the provision in the order, they should do so in writing (stating the grounds of their objection) before the expiration of the period of forty-two days from the date on which the notice is served on them;

    (ii) cause a copy of the notice to be displayed in a prominent position at the ends of so much of any path or way as would by virtue of the order cease to be subject to a public right of way;

and for the purposes of this sub-paragraph, "local authority" means, in England and Wales, a county council, a district council, a London borough council, the Common Council of the City of London, the Council of the Isles of Scilly, a parish or community council and a parish meeting of a parish not having a separate parish council and, in Scotland, a regional, islands or district council;".

(4) In paragraph 4A, in sub-paragraph (1) for the words "is opposed" there shall be substituted the words "authorises the compulsory purchase of land", and for sub-paragraphs (2) to (4) there shall be substituted—

"(2) Where this paragraph has effect in relation to an order, it shall be subject to special parliamentary procedure to the same extent as it would be, by virtue of section 18 or 19 of the Acquisition of Land Act 1981 (or by virtue of paragraph 5 or 6 of Schedule 3 to that Act) (National Trust land, commons etc), if the purchase were authorised by an order under section 2(1) of that Act."

(5) (*Applies to Scotland only.*)

(6) In paragraph 5(a), for the words from "to which" to "so affected" there shall be substituted the words "which is not subject to special parliamentary procedure,".

(7) Paragraphs 8A and 8B shall be omitted.

(8) In paragraph 14(3), for the words "(b) and (c)" there shall be substituted the words "(b) to (c)".   **[559ZD]**

NOTES

Commencement: 15 July 1992 (subject to transitional provisions in SI 1992/1347).

SCHEDULE 4

Section 68

REPEALS

PART I

RAILWAYS AND TRAMWAYS

Chapter	Short title	Extent of repeal
5 & 6 Vict. c. 55.	The Railway Regulation Act 1842	In section 17, the words "who shall be found drunk while so employed upon the said railway".
33 & 34 Vict. c. 78	The Tramways Act 1870	Section 3 (except as incorporated in, or otherwise applied by, any Act of Parliament or Provisional Order).
		Sections 4 to 21.
		Sections 22 to 24 (except as incorporated in, or otherwise applied by, any Act of Parliament or Provisional Order).
		In section 25, the words from the beginning to "surface of the road" (except as incorporated in, or otherwise applied by, any Act of Parliament or Provisional Order).
		In section 25, the words "and shall not be opened" onwards.

Chapter	Short title	Extent of repeal
33 & 34 Vict. c. 78— *contd*	The Tramways Act 1870— *contd*	Sections 26 to 40 (except as incorporated in, or otherwise applied by, any Act of Parliament or Provisional Order). Sections 41 and 42. Sections 43 to 47 (except as incorporated in, or otherwise applied by, any Act of Parliament or Provisional Order). Section 48. Sections 49 to 64 (except as incorporated in, or otherwise applied by, any Act of Parliament or Provisional Order). Parts I and II of Schedule A (except as incorporated in, or otherwise applied by, any Act of Parliament or Provisional Order). Part III of Schedule A. Schedule B. Schedule C (except as incorporated in, or otherwise applied by, any Act of Parliament or Provisional Order).
34 & 35 Vict. c. 78	The Regulation of Railways Act 1871	In section 3, the words "Provided that" onwards. Section 6.
45 & 46 Vict. c. 50	The Municipal Corporations Act 1882	In Part I of Schedule 9, the entry relating to the Tramways Act 1870 (except as incorporated in, or otherwise applied by, any Act of Parliament or Provisional Order).
50 & 51 Vict. c. 65	The Military Tramways Act 1887	The whole Act.
52 & 53 Vict. c. 14	The Town Police Clauses Act 1889	In section 3, the words from "duly licensed" to "Act of Parliament."
57 & 58 Vict. c. 28	The Notice of Accidents Act 1894	The whole Act, so far as unrepealed.
59 & 60 Vict. c. 48	The Light Railways Act 1896	The whole Act, so far as unrepealed (except as it applies in Scotland).
63 & 64 Vict. c. 27	The Railway Employment (Prevention of Accidents) Act 1900	Section 13(2).
3 Edw. 7 c. 30.	The Railways (Electrical Power) Act 1903	The whole Act.
6 Edw. 7 c. 53.	The Notice of Accidents Act 1906	The whole Act, so far as unrepealed.
2 & 3 Geo. 5 c. 19	The Light Railways Act 1912	The whole Act, so far as unrepealed (except as it applies in Scotland).

Chapter	Short title	Extent of repeal
11 & 12 Geo. 5 c. 55	The Railways Act 1921	Sections 68 and 69 (except as they apply in Scotland). Section 71 (except as it applies in Scotland). Sections 73 and 74 (except as they apply in Scotland).
24 & 25 Geo. 5 c. 53	The Road and Rail Traffic Act 1933	Section 41. Section 43.
2 & 3 Eliz. 2 c. 64.	The Transport Charges &c (Miscellaneous Provisions) Act 1954	Section 9. In section 13(1)— the definition of ''railway of the nature of a tramway''; the definition of ''tramcar''; the words ''and references to'' to ''Road Traffic Act 1960''. Section 14(5).
8 & 9 Eliz. 2 c. 16.	The Road Traffic Act 1960	In Schedule 17, the entry relating to the Transport Charges &c (Miscellaneous Provisions) Act 1954.
10 & 11 Eliz. 2 c.46.	The Transport Act 1962	In section 83— subsections (1) to (5) (except as they apply in Scotland); subsection (6).
1965 c. 2.	The Administration of Justice Act 1965	In Schedule 1— the entry relating to the Tramways Act 1870; the entry relating to the Light Railways Act 1896.
1965 c. xxi.	The British Railways Act 1965	Section 35(3) and (8).
1965 c. xli.	The London Transport Act 1965	Section 34(3).
1967 c. 80.	The Criminal Justice Act 1967	In Part I of Schedule 3— the entry relating to section 75 of the Railways Clauses Consolidation Act 1845; the entry relating to section 68 of the Railways Clauses Consolidation (Scotland) Act 1845.
1968 c. 73.	The Transport Act 1968	Section 121(4) (except as it applies in Scotland). In section 121(5), the words ''or by virtue of subsection (4) thereof''(except as they apply in Scotland). In section 121(6), the words ''or by virtue of subsection (4)'' (except as they apply in Scotland). Section 124 (except as it applies in Scotland). Section 125(4).
1972 c. 70.	The Local Government Act 1972	Section 131(2)(c).
1975 c. 9.	The Supply Powers Act 1975	In Schedule 1, the entry relating to the Military Tramways Act 1887.

Chapter	Short title	Extent of repeal
1975 c. 53.	The Public Service Vehicles (Arrest of Offenders) Act 1975	The whole Act, so far as unrepealed.
1977 c. xii.	The London Transport Act 1977	In the Schedule, the entry relating to section 75 of the Railways Clauses Consolidation Act 1845.
1977 c. xvii.	The British Railways Act 1977	In Schedule 1— the entry relating to section 75 of the Railways Clauses Consolidation Act 1845; the entry relating to section 68 of the Railways Clauses Consolidation (Scotland) Act 1845.
1980 c. 66.	The Highways Act 1980	In section 36(2), at the end of paragraph (c), the word "and".
1982 c. 53.	The Administration of Justice Act 1982	Section 46(2)(b)(i). Section 46(2)(d).
1984 c. 12.	The Telecommunications Act 1984	In Schedule 4, paragraph 7.
1984 c. 54.	The Roads (Scotland) Act 1984	In Schedule 9— paragraph 6 (except as incorporated in, or otherwise applied by, any Act of Parliament or Provisional Order); paragraph 12.
1986 c. 45.	The Insolvency Act 1986	Section 220(1)(a).
1987 c. 53.	The Channel Tunnel Act 1987	In paragraph 3 of Schedule 6— in the entry relating to the Regulation of Railways Act 1871, the words "and 6" and the words "returns of and"; the entry relating to the Road and Rail Traffic Act 1933.

[559ZE]

NOTES
    Commencement: 15 July 1992 (in part); 7 December 1992 (in part); 1 January 1993 (in part); 31 January 1993 (in part); 5 April 1994 (in part); to be appointed (remainder).

PART II

HARBOURS

Chapter	Short title	Extent of repeal
24 & 25 Vict. c. 45	The General Pier and Harbour Act 1861	The whole Act, so far as unrepealed.
25 & 26 Vict. c. 19	The General Pier and Harbour Act 1861, Amendment Act	The whole Act, so far as unrepealed.
25 & 26 Vict. c. 69	The Harbours Transfer Act 1862	Sections 13 and 14.
5 & 6 Geo. 5 c. 48	The Fishery Harbours Act 1915	The whole Act, so far as unrepealed.

Chapter	Short title	Extent of repeal
1 Edw. 8 & 1 Geo. 6 c. 28.	The Harbours, Piers and Ferries (Scotland) Act 1937	Sections 4 and 5.
14 & 15 Geo. 6 c. 30	The Sea Fish Industry Act 1951	Section 21(4). In section 21(5), the words "in section two of the said Act of 1915 or". In section 21(8), the word "either" and the words from "or of the Fishery Harbours Act 1915" to "the Minister of Transport)".
1964 c. 40.	The Harbours Act 1964	Section 17(3) and (4). In section 57(1), the definition of "large–scale". Section 62. In Schedule 3— paragraph 5A; paragraph 8A; paragraph 8B; in paragraph 9, the words from "and further stating" to "or will come into operation"; paragraph 9A.
1966 c. 28.	The Docks and Harbours Act 1966	Section 37(3).
1973 c. 65.	The Local Government (Scotland) Act 1973	In Schedule 19— paragraph 5; paragraph 8.
1981 c. 56.	The Transport Act 1981	In Schedule 6, paragraph 4(4) to (7).

[559ZF]

NOTES

Commencement: 15 July 1992 (subject to transitional provisions in SI 1992/1347).

LEASEHOLD REFORM, HOUSING AND URBAN DEVELOPMENT ACT 1993

(1993 c 28)

ARRANGEMENT OF SECTIONS

PART III

DEVELOPMENT OF URBAN AND OTHER AREAS

The Urban Regeneration Agency

SCHEDULES:

An Act to confer rights to collective enfranchisement and lease renewal on tenants of flats; to make further provision with respect to enfranchisement by tenants of houses; to make provision for auditing the management, by landlords or other persons, of residential property and for the approval of codes of practice relating thereto; to amend Parts III and IV of the Landlord and Tenant Act 1987; to confer jurisdiction on leasehold valuation tribunals as respects Crown land; to make provision for rendering void agreements preventing the occupation of leasehold property by persons with mental disorders; to amend Parts II, IV and V of the Housing Act 1985, Schedule 2 to the Housing Associations Act 1985, Parts I and III and sections 248 and 299 of the Housing (Scotland) Act 1987, Part III of the Housing Act 1988, and Part VI of the Local Government and Housing Act 1989; to make provision with respect to certain disposals requiring consent under Part II of the Housing Act 1985, including provision for the payment of a levy; to alter the basis of certain contributions by the Secretary of State under section 569 of that Act; to establish and confer functions on a body to replace the English Industrial Estates Corporation and to be known as the Urban Regeneration Agency; to provide for the designation of certain urban and other areas and to make provision as to the effect of such designation; to amend section 23 of the Land Compensation Act 1961, section 98 of the Local Government, Planning and Land Act 1980 and section 27 of the Housing and Planning Act 1986; to make further provision with respect to urban development corporations and urban development areas; and for connected purposes   [20 July 1993]

PART III

DEVELOPMENT OF URBAN AND OTHER AREAS

The Urban Regeneration Agency

158. The Agency

(1) There shall be a body corporate to be known as the Urban Regeneration Agency ("the Agency") for the purpose of exercising the functions conferred on it by the following provisions of this Part.

(2) Schedule 17 to this Act shall have effect with respect to the constitution of the Agency and Schedule 18 to this Act shall have effect with respect to the finances of the Agency.

(3) It is hereby declared that, except as provided by section 175, the Agency is not to be regarded as the servant or agent of the Crown or as enjoying any status, immunity or privilege of the Crown and that its property is not to be regarded as the property of, or property held on behalf of, the Crown.   **[560]**

NOTES
Commencement: 10 November 1993.

159. Objects of Agency

(1) The main object of the Agency shall be to secure the regeneration of land in England—

   (a) which is land of one or more of the descriptions mentioned in subsection (2); and

   (b) which the Agency (having regard to guidance, and acting in accordance with directions, given by the Secretary of State under section 167) determines to be suitable for regeneration under this Part.

(2) The descriptions of land referred to in subsection (1)(a) are—

   (a) land which is vacant or unused;

   (b) land which is situated in an urban area and which is under-used or ineffectively used;

   (c) land which is contaminated, derelict, neglected or unsightly; and

   (d) land which is likely to become derelict, neglected or unsightly by reason of actual or apprehended collapse of the surface as the result of the carrying out of relevant operations which have ceased to be carried out;

and in this subsection "relevant operations" has the same meaning as in section 1 of the Derelict Land Act 1982.

(3) The Agency shall also have the object of securing the development of land in England which the Agency—

   (a) having regard to guidance given by the Secretary of State under section 167;

   (b) acting in accordance with directions given by the Secretary of State under that section; and

   (c) with the consent of the Secretary of State,

determines to be suitable for development under this Part.

(4) The objects of the Agency are to be achieved in particular by the following means (or by such of them as seem to the Agency to be appropriate in any particular case), namely—

   (a) by securing that land and buildings are brought into effective use;

   (b) by developing, or encouraging the development of, existing and new industry and commerce;

   (c) by creating an attractive and safe environment;

   (d) by facilitating the provision of housing and providing, or facilitating the provision of, social and recreational facilities.   **[561]**

NOTES

Commencement: 10 November 1993.

160. General powers of Agency

(1) Subject to the following provisions of this Part, for the purpose of achieving its objects the Agency may—

   (a) acquire, hold, manage, reclaim, improve and dispose of land, plant, machinery, equipment and other property;

   (b) carry out the development or redevelopment of land, including the conversion or demolition of existing buildings;

   (c) carry out building and other operations;

   (d) provide means of access, services or other facilities for land;

   (e) seek to ensure the provision of water, electricity, gas, sewerage and other services;

(f) carry on any business or undertaking for the purposes of its objects;

(g) with the consent of the Secretary of State, form, or acquire interests in, bodies corporate;

(h) act with other persons, whether in partnership or otherwise;

(i) give financial assistance to other persons;

(j) act as agent for other persons;

(k) provide advisory or other services and facilities; and

(l) generally do anything necessary or expedient for the purposes of its objects or for purposes incidental to those purposes.

(2) Nothing in section 159 or this section shall empower the Agency—

(a) to provide housing otherwise than by acquiring existing housing accommodation and making it available on a temporary basis for purposes incidental to the purposes of its objects;

(b) to acquire an interest in a body corporate which at the time of the acquisition is carrying on a trade or business, if the effect of the acquisition would be to make the body corporate a subsidiary of the Agency; or

(c) except with the consent of the Secretary of State, to dispose of any land otherwise than for the best consideration which can reasonably be obtained.

(3) For the avoidance of doubt it is hereby declared that subsection (1) relates only to the capacity of the Agency as a statutory corporation and nothing in section 159 or this section authorises it to disregard any enactment or rule of law.

(4) In this section—

"improve", in relation to land, includes refurbish, equip and fit out;

"subsidiary" has the meaning given by section 736 of the Companies Act 1985;

and in this section and the following provisions of this Part references to land include land not falling within subsection (1) or (3) of section 159. **[562]**

NOTES

Commencement: 10 November 1993.

161. Vesting of land by order

(1) Subject to subsections (2) and (3), the Secretary of State may by order provide that land specified in the order which is vested in a local authority, statutory undertakers or other public body, or in a wholly-owned subsidiary of a public body, shall vest in the Agency.

(2) An order under subsection (1) may not specify land vested in statutory undertakers which is used for the purpose of carrying on their statutory undertakings or which is held for that purpose.

(3) In the case of land vested in statutory undertakers, the power to make an order under subsection (1) shall be exercisable by the Secretary of State and the appropriate Minister.

(4) An order under subsection (1) shall have the same effect as a declaration under the Compulsory Purchase (Vesting Declarations) Act 1981 except that, in relation to such an order, the enactments mentioned in Schedule 19 to this Act shall have effect with the modifications specified in that Schedule.

(5) Compensation under the Land Compensation Act 1961, as applied by subsection (4) and Schedule 19 to this Act, shall be assessed by reference to values current on the date the order under subsection (1) comes into force.

(6) No compensation is payable, by virtue of an order under subsection (1), under Part IV of the Land Compensation Act 1961.

(7) In this section—

"the appropriate Minister"—

    (a) in relation to statutory undertakers who are or are deemed to be statutory undertakers for the purposes of any provision of Part XI of the Town and Country Planning Act 1990, shall be construed as if contained in that Part;

    (b) in relation to any other statutory undertakers, shall be construed in accordance with an order made by the Secretary of State;

and the reference to the Secretary of State and the appropriate Minister shall be similarly construed;

"local authority" means a county council, [a county borough council,] a district council, a London borough council or the Common Council of the City of London;

"statutory undertakers", except where the context otherwise requires, means—

    (a) persons authorised by any enactment to carry on any railway, light railway, tramway, road transport, water transport, canal, inland navigation, dock, harbour, pier or lighthouse undertaking, or any undertaking for the supply of hydraulic power;

    (b) British Shipbuilders, the Civil Aviation Authority, *the British Coal Corporation* and the Post Office;

    (c) any other authority, body or undertakers specified in an order made by the Secretary of State;

    (d) any wholly-owned subsidiary of any person, authority or body mentioned in paragraphs (a) and (b) or of any authority, body or undertakers specified in an order made under paragraph (c);

and "statutory undertaking" shall be construed accordingly;

"wholly-owned subsidiary" has the meaning given by section 736 of the Companies Act 1985.

(8) If any question arises as to which Minister is the appropriate Minister in relation to any statutory undertakers, that question shall be determined by the Treasury.

(9) An order under subsection (1) shall be made by statutory instrument but no such order shall be made unless a draft of the order has been laid before and approved by resolution of each House of Parliament.

(10) An order under subsection (7) shall be made by statutory instrument which shall be subject to annulment in pursuance of a resolution of either House of Parliament.   **[563]**

NOTES

Commencement: 10 November 1993.

Sub-s (7): words in square brackets in definition "local authority" inserted by the Local Government (Wales) Act 1994, s 66(6), Sch 16, para 104, as from a day to be appointed; words in italics in definition "statutory undertakers" repealed by the Coal Industry Act 1994, s 67(1), (8), Sch 9, para 45, Sch 11, Pt IV, as from a day to be appointed as the "dissolution date" as defined in ss 23(2), 65(1) of that Act.

162. Acquisition of land

(1) The Agency may, for the purpose of achieving its objects or for purposes incidental to that purpose, acquire land by agreement or, on being authorised to do so by the Secretary of State, compulsorily.

(2) The Agency may, for those purposes, be authorised by the Secretary of State, by means of a compulsory purchase order, to acquire compulsorily such new rights over land as are specified in the order.

(3) Where the land referred to in subsection (1) or (2) forms part of a common, open space or fuel or field garden allotment, the Agency may acquire (by agreement or, on being authorised to do so by the Secretary of State, compulsorily) land for giving in exchange for the land or, as the case may be, rights acquired.

(4) Subject to section 169, the Acquisition of Land Act 1981 shall apply to the compulsory acquisition of land by virtue of subsection (1) or (3).

(5) Schedule 3 to that Act shall apply to the compulsory acquisition of a right by virtue of subsection (2) but with the modification that the reference in paragraph 4(3) to statutory undertakers includes a reference to the Agency.

(6) The provisions of Part I of the Compulsory Purchase Act 1965 (so far as applicable), other than section 31, shall apply to the acquisition by the Agency of land by agreement; and in that Part as so applied ''land'' has the meaning given by the Interpretation Act 1978.

(7) In subsection (2)—

    ''new rights over land'' means rights over land which are not in existence when the order specifying them is made;

    ''compulsory purchase order'' has the same meaning as in the Acquisition of Land Act 1981.   **[564]**

NOTES

    Commencement: 10 November 1993.

163. Power to enter and survey land

(1) Any person who is duly authorised in writing by the Agency may at any reasonable time enter any land for the purpose of surveying it, or estimating its value, in connection with—

    (a) any proposal to acquire that land or any other land; or

    (b) any claim for compensation in respect of any such acquisition.

(2) The power to survey land shall be construed as including power to search and bore for the purpose of ascertaining the nature of the subsoil or the presence of minerals in it.

(3) A person authorised under this section to enter any land—

    (a) shall, if so required, produce evidence of his authority before entry, and

    (b) shall not demand admission as of right to any land which is occupied unless 28 days' notice of the intended entry has been given to the occupier by the Agency.

(4) Any person who wilfully obstructs a person acting in exercise of his powers under this section shall be guilty of an offence and liable on summary conviction to a fine not exceeding level 2 on the standard scale.

(5) If any person who, in compliance with the provisions of this section, is admitted into a factory, workshop or workplace discloses to any person any information obtained by him in it as to any manufacturing process or trade secret, he shall be guilty of an offence.

(6) Subsection (5) does not apply if the disclosure is made by a person in the

course of performing his duty in connection with the purpose for which he was authorised to enter the premises.

(7) A person who is guilty of an offence under subsection (5) shall be liable on summary conviction to a fine not exceeding the statutory maximum or on conviction on indictment to imprisonment for a term not exceeding two years or a fine or both.

(8) Where any land is damaged—

(a) in the exercise of a right of entry under this section, or
(b) in the making of any survey under this section,

compensation in respect of that damage may be recovered by any person interested in the land from the Agency.

(9) The provisions of section 118 of the Town and Country Planning Act 1990 (determination of claims for compensation) shall apply in relation to compensation under subsection (8) as they apply in relation to compensation under Part IV of that Act.

(10) No person shall carry out under this section any works authorised by virtue of subsection (2) unless notice of his intention to do so was included in the notice required by subsection (3).

(11) The authority of the appropriate Minister shall be required for the carrying out of any such works if—

(a) the land in question is held by statutory undertakers; and
(b) they object to the proposed works on the ground that the execution of the works would be seriously detrimental to the carrying on of their undertaking;

and expressions used in this subsection have the same meanings as they have in section 325(9) of the Town and Country Planning Act 1990 (supplementary provisions as to rights of entry).   **[565]**

NOTES

Commencement: 10 November 1993.

164. Financial assistance

(1) The consent of the Secretary of State is required for the exercise of the Agency's power to give financial assistance; and such assistance—

(a) may be given by the Agency only in respect of qualifying expenditure; and
(b) may be so given on such terms and conditions as the Agency, with the consent of the Secretary of State, considers appropriate.

(2) Expenditure incurred in connection with any of the following matters is qualifying expenditure—

(a) the acquisition of land;
(b) the reclamation, improvement or refurbishment of land;
(c) the development or redevelopment of land, including the conversion or demolition of existing buildings;
(d) the equipment or fitting out of land;
(e) the provision of means of access, services or other facilities for land;
(f) environmental improvements.

(3) Financial assistance may be given in any form and may, in particular, be given by way of—

    (a) grants;
    (b) loans;
    (c) guarantees; or
    (d) incurring expenditure for the benefit of the person assisted;

but the Agency shall not in giving financial assistance purchase loan or share capital in a company.

    (4) A consent under subsection (1) may be given only with the approval of the Treasury.

    (5) The terms and conditions on which financial assistance is given may, in particular, include provision as to—

      (a) the circumstances in which the assistance must be repaid, or otherwise made good, to the Agency, and the manner in which that is to be done;
      (b) the circumstances in which the Agency is entitled to recover the proceeds or part of the proceeds of any disposal of land in respect of which the assistance was provided.

    (6) Any person receiving financial assistance shall comply with the terms and conditions on which it is given and compliance may be enforced by the Agency.

[566]

NOTES

Commencement: 10 November 1993.

---

165. Connection of private streets to highway

(1) For the purpose of achieving its objects or for purposes incidental to that purpose, the Agency may serve a notice (a ''connection notice'') on the local highway authority requiring the authority to connect a private street to an existing highway (whether or not it is a highway which for the purposes of the Highways Act 1980 is a highway maintainable at the public expense).

    (2) A connection notice must specify—

      (a) the private street and the existing highway;
      (b) the works which appear to the Agency to be necessary to make the connection; and
      (c) the period within which those works should be carried out.

    (3) Before serving a connection notice the Agency shall consult the local highway authority about the proposed contents of the notice.

    (4) Within the period of two months beginning with the date on which the connection notice was served, the local highway authority may appeal against the notice to the Secretary of State.

    (5) After considering any representations made to him by the Agency and the local highway authority, the Secretary of State shall determine an appeal under subsection (4) by setting aside or confirming the connection notice (with or without modifications).

    (6) A connection notice becomes effective—

      (a) where no appeal is made within the period of two months referred to in subsection (4), upon the expiry of that period;
      (b) where an appeal is made within that period but is withdrawn before it has been determined by the Secretary of State, on the date following the expiry

of the period of 21 days beginning with the date on which the Secretary of
State is notified of the withdrawal;

(c) where an appeal is made and the connection notice is confirmed by a
determination under subsection (5), on such date as the Secretary of State
may specify in the determination.

(7) Where a connection notice becomes effective, the local highway authority
shall carry out the works specified in the notice within such period as may be so
specified and may recover from the Agency the expenses reasonably incurred by
them in doing so.

(8) If the local highway authority do not carry out the works specified in the
notice within such period as may be so specified, the Agency may itself carry out or
complete those works or arrange for another person to do so.

(9) In this section "local highway authority" has the same meaning as in the
Highways Act 1980.   **[567]**

NOTES
Commencement: 10 November 1993.

The Agency: supplemental

166. Consents of Secretary of State

A consent of the Secretary of State under the foregoing provisions of this Part—

(a) may be given unconditionally or subject to conditions;

(b) may be given in relation to a particular case or in relation to such
descriptions of case as may be specified in the consent; and

(c) except in relation to anything already done or agreed to be done on the
authority of the consent, may be varied or revoked by a notice given by
the Secretary of State to the Agency.   **[568]**

NOTES
Commencement: 10 November 1993.

167. Guidance and directions by Secretary of State

(1) The Agency shall have regard to guidance from time to time given by the
Secretary of State in deciding—

(a) which land is suitable for regeneration or development under this Part;
and

(b) which of its functions under this Part it is to exercise for securing the
regeneration or development of any particular land and how it is to
exercise those functions.

(2) Without prejudice to any of the foregoing provisions of this Part requiring
the consent of the Secretary of State to be obtained for anything to be done by the
Agency, he may give directions to the Agency—

(a) for restricting the exercise by it of any of its functions under this Part; or

(b) for requiring it to exercise those functions in any manner specified in the
directions.

(3) Directions under subsection (2) may be of a general or particular nature and
may be varied or revoked by subsequent directions.   **[569]**

NOTES
Commencement: 10 November 1993.

168. Validity of transactions

(1) A transaction between a person and the Agency shall not be invalidated by reason only of any failure by the Agency to observe its objects or the requirement in subsection (1) of section 160 that the Agency shall exercise the powers conferred by that subsection for the purpose of achieving its objects, and such a person shall not be concerned to see or enquire whether there has been any such failure.

(2) A transaction between a person and the Agency acting in purported exercise of its functions under this Part shall not be invalidated by reason only that it was carried out in contravention of any direction given under subsection (2) of section 167, and such a person shall not be concerned to see or enquire whether any directions under that subsection have been given or complied with. **[570]**

NOTES
Commencement: 10 November 1993.

169. Supplementary provisions as to vesting and acquisition of land

(1) Schedule 20 to this Act shall have effect.

(2) Part I of that Schedule modifies the Acquisition of Land Act 1981 as applied by section 162.

(3) Part II of that Schedule contains supplementary provisions about land vested in or acquired by the Agency under this Part.

(4) Part III of that Schedule contains supplementary provisions about the acquisition by the Agency of rights over land by virtue of section 162(2). **[571]**

NOTES
Commencement: 10 November 1993.

Designation orders and their effect

170. Power to make designation orders

(1) Where, as respects any area in England which is an urban area or which, in the opinion of the Secretary of State, is suitable for urban development, it appears to the Secretary of State—

- (a) that all or any of the provisions authorised by section 171 should be made in relation to the whole or any part of it; or
- (b) that either or both of sections 172 and 173 should apply in relation to it,

the Secretary of State may by order designate that area and either so make the provision or provisions, or direct that the section or sections shall so apply, or (as the case may require) do both of those things.

(2) In this Part "designation order" means an order under this section and "designated area" means, subject to subsection (5), an area designated by a designation order.

(3) Before making a designation order the Secretary of State shall consult every local authority any part of whose area is intended to be included in the proposed designated area.

(4) A designation order—

- (a) shall be made by statutory instrument which shall be subject to annulment in pursuance of a resolution of either House of Parliament; and

(b) may contain such savings and transitional and supplementary provisions as may be specified in the order.

(5) The power to amend a designation order conferred by section 14 of the Interpretation Act 1978 includes power to amend the boundaries of the designated area; and where any such amendment is made, any reference in this Part to a designated area is a reference to the designated area as so amended.

(6) In this section "local authority" means a county council, a district council, a London borough council or the Common Council of the City of London.   **[572]**

NOTES
Commencement: 10 November 1993.

171. Agency as local planning authority

(1) If a designation order so provides, the Agency shall be the local planning authority for the whole or any part of the designated area—

(a) for such purposes of Part III of the Town and Country Planning Act 1990 and sections 67 and 73 of the Planning (Listed Buildings and Conservation Areas) Act 1990 as may be specified in the order; and

(b) in relation to such kinds of development as may be so specified.

(2) A designation order making such provision as is mentioned in subsection (1) may also provide—

(a) that any enactment relating to local planning authorities shall not apply to the Agency; and

(b) that any such enactment which applies to the Agency shall apply to it subject to such modifications as may be specified in the order.

(3) If a designation order so provides—

(a) subject to any modifications specified in the order, the Agency shall have, in the whole or any part of the designated area, such of the functions conferred by the provisions mentioned in subsection (4) as may be so specified; and

(b) such of the provisions of Part VI and sections 249 to 251 and 258 of the Town and Country Planning Act 1990 and sections 32 to 37 of the Planning (Listed Buildings and Conservation Areas) Act 1990 as are mentioned in the order shall have effect, in relation to the Agency and to land in the designated area, subject to the modifications there specified.

(4) The provisions referred to in subsection (3)(a) are—

(a) sections 171C, 171D, 172 to 185, 187 to 202, 206 to 222, 224, 225, 231 and 320 to 336 of, and paragraph 11 of Schedule 9 to, the Town and Country Planning Act 1990;

(b) Chapters I, II and IV of Part I and sections 54 to 56, 59 to 61, 66, 68 to 72, 74 to 76 and 88 of the Planning (Listed Buildings and Conservation Areas) Act 1990; and

(c) sections 4 to 15, 17 to 21, 23 to 26AA, 36 and 36A of the Planning (Hazardous Substances) Act 1990.

(5) A designation order making such provision as is mentioned in subsection (3) may also provide that, for the purposes of any of the provisions specified in the order, any enactment relating to local planning authorities shall apply to the Agency subject to such modifications as may be so specified.   **[573]**

NOTES
Commencement: 10 November 1993.

172. Adoption of private streets

(1) Where—

    (a) this section applies in relation to a designated area; and

    (b) any street works have been executed on any land in the designated area which was then or has since become a private street (or part of a private street),

the Agency may serve a notice (an ''adoption notice'') on the street works authority requiring the authority to declare the street (or part) to be a highway which for the purposes of the Highways Act 1980 is a highway maintainable at the public expense.

(2) Within the period of two months beginning with the date on which the adoption notice was served, the street works authority may appeal against the notice to the Secretary of State.

(3) After considering any representations made to him by the Agency and the street works authority, the Secretary of State shall determine an appeal under subsection (2) by setting aside or confirming the adoption notice (with or without modifications).

(4) Where, under subsection (3), the Secretary of State confirms the adoption notice—

    (a) he may at the same time impose conditions (including financial conditions) upon the Agency with which it must comply in order for the notice to take effect; and

    (b) with effect from such date as the Secretary of State may specify, the street (or part) shall become a highway which for the purposes of the Highways Act 1980 is a highway maintainable at the public expense.

(5) Where a street works authority neither complies with the adoption notice, nor appeals under subsection (2), the street (or part) shall become, upon the expiry of the period of two months referred to in subsection (2), a highway which for the purposes of the Highways Act 1980 is a highway maintainable at the public expense.

(6) In this section ''street works'' and ''street works authority'' have the same meanings as in Part XI of the Highways Act 1980. **[574]**

NOTES
Commencement: 10 November 1993.

173. Traffic regulation orders for private streets

(1) Where—

    (a) this section applies in relation to a designated area;

    (b) the Agency submits to the Secretary of State that an order under this section should be made in relation to any road in the designated area which is a private street; and

    (c) it appears to the Secretary of State that the traffic authority do not intend to make an order under section 1 or, as the case may be, section 6 of the Road Traffic Regulation Act 1984 (orders concerning traffic regulation) in relation to the road,

the Secretary of State may by order under this section make in relation to the road any such provision as he might have made by order under that section if he had been the traffic authority.

(2) The Road Traffic Regulation Act 1984 applies to an order under this section as it applies to an order made by the Secretary of State under section 1 or, as the case may be, section 6 of that Act in relation to a road for which he is the traffic authority.

(3) In this section "road" and "traffic authority" have the same meanings as in the Road Traffic Regulation Act 1984.   **[575]**

NOTES
Commencement: 10 November 1993.

Other functions of Secretary of State

174. Financial assistance for urban regeneration

For section 27 of the Housing and Planning Act 1986 (power to give financial assistance) there shall be substituted the following section—

"27 Power to give assistance

(1) The Secretary of State may, with the consent of the Treasury, give financial assistance to any person in respect of expenditure incurred in connection with activities contributing to the regeneration of an urban area.

(2) Activities contributing to the regeneration of an urban area include in particular—

    (a) securing that land and buildings are brought into effective use;
    (b) developing, or encouraging the development of, existing and new industry and commerce;
    (c) creating an attractive and safe environment;
    (d) providing housing or social and recreational facilities so as to encourage people to live or work in the area;
    (e) providing employment for people who live in the area;
    (f) providing training, educational facilities or health services for people who live in the area."   **[576]**

NOTES
Commencement: 11 October 1993.
This section also extends to Scotland.

175. Power to appoint Agency as agent

(1) The Secretary of State may, on such terms as he may with the approval of the Treasury specify, appoint the Agency to act as his agent in connection with such of the functions mentioned in subsection (2) as he may specify; and where such an appointment is made, the Agency shall act as such an agent in accordance with the terms of its appointment.

(2) The functions referred to in subsection (1) are—

    (a) functions under section 1 of the Derelict Land Act 1982 or any enactment superseded by that section (grants for reclaiming or improving land or bringing land into use), other than the powers to make orders under subsections (5) and (7) of that section; and
    (b) so far as exercisable in relation to England, functions under sections 27 to 29 of the Housing and Planning Act 1986 (financial assistance for urban regeneration).

(3) In so far as an appointment under subsection (1) relates to functions mentioned in subsection (2)(b), the terms of the appointment shall preclude the Agency from giving financial assistance in respect of expenditure which is not qualifying expenditure within the meaning of section 164. **[577]**

NOTES
Commencement: 10 November 1993.

176. Power to direct disposal of unused etc land held by public bodies

(1) In subsection (1) of section 98 (disposal of land by public bodies at direction of Secretary of State) of the Local Government, Planning and Land Act 1980 ("the 1980 Act")—

  (a) in paragraph (a), for the words "is for the time being entered on a register maintained by him under section 95 above" there shall be substituted the words "for the time being satisfies the conditions specified in section 95(2) above"; and
  (b) in paragraph (b), for the words "is for the time being entered on such a register" there shall be substituted the words "for the time being satisfies those conditions".

(2) In section 99A of that Act (powers of entry), subsection (2) (which precludes entry on land which is not for the time being entered on a register maintained under section 95) shall cease to have effect. **[578]**

NOTES
Commencement: 11 October 1993.

Urban development corporations

177. Power to act as agents of Agency

(1) The Agency may, with the consent of the Secretary of State, appoint an urban development corporation, on such terms as may be agreed, to act as its agent in connection with such of its functions (other than its power to give financial assistance) as may be specified in the appointment; and where such an appointment is made, the urban development corporation shall act as such an agent in accordance with the terms of its appointment.

(2) For the purpose of assisting the Agency to carry out any of its functions, an urban development corporation, on being so requested by the Agency, may arrange for any of its property or staff to be made available to the Agency for such period and on such other terms as it thinks fit.

(3) In this section "urban development corporation" means a corporation established by an order under section 135 of the 1980 Act. **[579]**

NOTES
Commencement: 10 November 1993.
1980 Act: the Local Government, Planning and Land Act 1980.

178. Powers with respect to private streets

For section 157 of the 1980 Act (highways) there shall be substituted the following sections—

"Private streets

157 Adoption of private streets

(1) Where any street works have been executed on any land in an urban development area which was then or has since become a private street (or part of a private street), the urban development corporation may serve a notice (an "adoption notice") on the street works authority requiring the authority to declare the street (or part) to be a highway which for the purposes of the Highways Act 1980 is a highway maintainable at the public expense.

(2) Within the period of two months beginning with the date on which the adoption notice was served, the street works authority may appeal against the notice to the Secretary of State.

(3) After considering any representations made to him by the corporation and the street works authority, the Secretary of State shall determine an appeal under subsection (2) above by setting aside or confirming the adoption notice (with or without modifications).

(4) Where, under subsection (3) above, the Secretary of State confirms the adoption notice—

  (a) he may at the same time impose conditions (including financial conditions) upon the corporation with which it must comply in order for the notice to take effect; and

  (b) with effect from such date as the Secretary of State may specify, the street (or part) shall become a highway which for the purposes of the Highways Act 1980 is a highway maintainable at the public expense.

(5) Where a street works authority neither complies with the adoption notice, nor appeals under subsection (2) above, the street (or part) shall become, upon the expiry of the period of two months referred to in subsection (2) above, a highway which for the purposes of the Highways Act 1980 is a highway maintainable at the public expense.

(6) In this section—

  "highway" has the same meaning as in the Highways Act 1980;
  "private street", "street works" and "street works authority" have the same meanings as in Part XI of that Act.

(7) This section does not extend to Scotland.

157A Connection of private streets to highway

(1) An urban development corporation may serve a notice (a "connection notice") on the local highway authority requiring the authority to connect a private street in the urban development area to an existing highway (whether or not it is a highway which for the purposes of the Highways Act 1980 is a highway maintainable at the public expense).

(2) A connection notice must specify—

  (a) the private street and the existing highway;

  (b) the works which appear to the corporation to be necessary to make the connection; and

(c) the period within which those works should be carried out.

(3) Before serving a connection notice an urban development corporation shall consult the local highway authority about the proposed contents of the notice.

(4) Within the period of two months beginning with the date on which the connection notice was served, the local highway authority may appeal against the notice to the Secretary of State.

(5) After considering any representations made to him by the corporation and the local highway authority, the Secretary of State shall determine an appeal under subsection (4) above by setting aside or confirming the connection notice (with or without modifications).

(6) A connection notice becomes effective—

(a) where no appeal is made within the period of two months referred to in subsection (4) above, upon the expiry of that period;

(b) where an appeal is made within that period but is withdrawn before it has been determined by the Secretary of State, on the date following the expiry of the period of 21 days beginning with the date on which the Secretary of State is notified of the withdrawal;

(c) where an appeal is made and the connection notice is confirmed by a determination under subsection (5) above, on such date as the Secretary of State may specify in the determination.

(7) Where a connection notice becomes effective, the local highway authority shall carry out the works specified in the notice within such period as may be so specified and may recover from the corporation the expenses reasonably incurred by them in doing so.

(8) If the local highway authority do not carry out the works specified in the notice within such period as may be so specified, the corporation may themselves carry out or complete those works or arrange for another person to do so.

(9) In this section—

"highway" and "local highway authority" have the same meanings as in the Highways Act 1980;

"private street" has the same meaning as in Part XI of that Act.

(10) This section does not extend to Scotland.

157B Traffic regulation orders for private streets

(1) Where—

(a) an urban development corporation submits to the Secretary of State that an order under this section should be made in relation to any road in the urban development area which is a private street; and

(b) it appears to the Secretary of State that the traffic authority do not intend to make an order under section 1 or, as the case may be, section 6 of the Road Traffic Regulation Act 1984 (orders concerning traffic regulation) in relation to the road,

the Secretary of State may by order under this section make in relation to the road any such provision as he might have made by order under that section if he had been the traffic authority.

(2) The Road Traffic Regulation Act 1984 applies to an order under this section as it applies to an order made by the Secretary of State under section 1 or,

as the case may be, section 6 of that Act in relation to a road for which he is the traffic authority.

(3) In this section—

"private street" has the same meaning as in Part XI of the Highways Act 1980;

"road" and "traffic authority" have the same meanings as in the Road Traffic Regulation Act 1984.

(4) This section does not extend to Scotland.''   **[580]**

NOTES
Commencement: 11 October 1993 (subject to savings).
1980 Act: the Local Government, Planning and Land Act 1980.

179. Adjustment of areas

(1)-(4) . . .

(5) In section 171 of that Act (interpretation of Part XVI: general), for the definition of "urban development area" there shall be substituted the following definition—

"urban development area" means so much of an area designated by an order under subsection (1) of section 134 above as is not excluded from it by an order under subsection (3A) of that section;''.   **[581]**

NOTES
Commencement: 11 October 1993.
Sub-ss (1)-(4) amend the Local Government, Planning and Land Act 1980, ss 134, 135.
That Act: the Local Government, Planning and Land Act 1980.
This section also extends to Scotland.

180. Transfers of property, rights and liabilities

(1) In subsection (1) of section 165 of the 1980 Act (power to transfer undertaking of urban development corporation), after the words "local authority", in both places where they occur, there shall be inserted the words "or other body".

(2) Subsection (3) of that section (transfer of liabilities by order) shall cease to have effect; and after that section there shall be inserted the following section—

"165A Transfers of property, rights and liabilities by order

(1) Subject to this section, the Secretary of State may at any time by order transfer to himself, upon by such terms as he thinks fit, any property, rights or liabilities which—

(a) are for the time being vested in an urban development corporation, and
(b) are not proposed to be transferred under an agreement made under section 165 above and approved by the Secretary of State with the Treasury's concurrence.

(2) An order under this section may terminate—

(a) any appointment of the corporation under subsection (1) of section 177 of the Leasehold Reform, Housing and Urban Development Act 1993 (power of corporations to act as agents of the Urban Regeneration Agency); and
(b) any arrangements made by the corporation under subsection (2) of that section.

(3) Before making an order under this section, the Secretary of State shall consult each local authority in whose area all or part of the urban development area is situated.

(4) An order under this section shall be made by statutory instrument which shall be subject to annulment in pursuance of a resolution of either House of Parliament.'

(3) In subsection (9) of that section—

(a) after the words "this section" there shall be inserted the words "and sections 165A and 166 below";
(b) for the words "the section", in both places where they occur, there shall be substituted the words "the sections".

(4) For subsection (1) of section 166 of that Act (dissolution of urban development corporations) there shall be substituted the following subsection—

"(1) Where all property, rights and liabilities of an urban development corporation have been transferred under or by one or more relevant instruments, the Secretary of State may make an order by statutory instrument under this section."

(5) For subsection (5) of that section there shall be substituted the following subsection—

"(5) In this section "relevant instrument" means an agreement made under section 165 above or an order made under section 165A above."   **[582]**

NOTES
    Commencement: 10 November 1993 (certain purposes); 11 October 1993 (remaining purposes).
    1980 Act: the Local Government, Planning and Land Act 1980.
    This section also extends to Scotland.

Miscellaneous

181. No compensation where planning decision made after certain acquisitions

(1) Section 23(3) of the Land Compensation Act 1961 (no compensation where planning decision made after certain acquisitions) shall be amended as follows.

(2) After paragraph (a) there shall be inserted the following paragraph—

"(aa) under section 104 of that Act (acquisition by the Land Authority for Wales);".

(3) After paragraph (c) there shall be inserted the words

"or
(d) under Part III of the Leasehold Reform, Housing and Urban Development Act 1993 (acquisition by the Urban Regeneration Agency)."

(4) Subsection (2) above shall apply to an acquisition or sale of an interest in land if the date of completion (within the meaning of Part IV of that Act) falls on or after the day on which this Act is passed.   **[583]**

NOTES
    Commencement: 20 July 1993 (sub-ss (1), (2), (4)); 10 November 1993 (sub-s (3)).
    That Act: the Local Government, Planning and Land Act 1980.

182. Powers of housing action trusts with respect to private streets

(1) In subsection (1) of section 69 of the Housing Act 1988 (powers of housing action trusts with respect to private streets), for the words "in a private street (or part of a private street) in a designated area" there shall be substituted the words "on any land in a designated area which was then or has since become a private street (or part of a private street)".

(2) In subsection (2) of that section, the words from "on grounds" onwards shall be omitted.   **[584]**

NOTES
Commencement: 11 October 1993.

Supplemental

183. Notices

(1) This section has effect in relation to any notice required or authorised by this Part to be given to or served on any person.

(2) Any such notice may be given to or served on the person in question either by delivering it to him, or by leaving it at his proper address, or by sending it by post to him at that address.

(3) Any such notice may—

- (a) in the case of a body corporate, be given to or served on the secretary or clerk of that body; and
- (b) in the case of a partnership, be given to or served on a partner or a person having the control or management of the partnership business.

(4) For the purposes of this section and of section 7 of the Interpretation Act 1978 (service of documents by post) in its application to this section, the proper address of any person to or on whom a notice is to be given or served shall be his last known address, except that—

- (a) in the case of a body corporate or its secretary or clerk, it shall be the address of the registered or principal office of that body; and
- (b) in the case of a partnership, a partner or a person having the control or management of the partnership business, it shall be that of the principal office of the partnership;

and for the purposes of this subsection the principal office of a company registered outside the United Kingdom or of a partnership carrying on business outside the United Kingdom shall be its principal office within the United Kingdom.

(5) If the person to be given or served with any notice mentioned in subsection (1) has specified an address within the United Kingdom other than his proper address within the meaning of subsection (4) as the one at which he or someone on his behalf will accept documents of the same description as that notice, that address shall also be treated for the purposes of this section and section 7 of the Interpretation Act 1978 as his proper address.

(6) If the name or address of any owner, lessee or occupier of land to or on whom any notice mentioned in subsection (1) is to be served cannot after reasonable inquiry be ascertained, the document may be served either by leaving it in the hands of a person who is or appears to be resident or employed on the land or by leaving it conspicuously affixed to some building or object on the land.   **[585]**

NOTES
Commencement: 10 November 1993.

184. Dissolution of English Industrial Estates Corporation

(1) The English Industrial Estates Corporation shall cease to exist on the commencement of this section.

(2) All the property, rights and liabilities to which that Corporation was entitled or subject immediately before that commencement shall become by virtue of this section property, rights and liabilities of the Agency. **[586]**

NOTES
Commencement: 1 April 1994 (subject to transitional provisions).

185. Interpretation of Part III

In this Part—

"the 1980 Act" means the Local Government, Planning and Land Act 1980;
"the Agency" means the Urban Regeneration Agency;
"designation order" and "designated area" have the meanings given by section 170;
"highway" has the same meaning as in the Highways Act 1980;
"private street" has the same meaning as in Part XI of that Act. **[587]**

NOTES
Commencement: 10 November 1993.

PART IV

SUPPLEMENTAL

186. Financial provisions

(1) There shall be paid out of money provided by Parliament—

(a) any expenses of the Secretary of State incurred in consequence of this Act; and

(b) any increase attributable to this Act in the sums payable out of money so provided under any other enactment.

(2) There shall be paid into the Consolidated Fund any increase attributable to this Act in the sums payable into that Fund under any other enactment. **[588]**

NOTES
Commencement: 20 July 1993.

187. (*Introduces Schs 21 and 22 to this Act.*)

188. Short title, commencement and extent

(1) This Act may be cited as the Leasehold Reform, Housing and Urban Development Act 1993.

(2) This Act, except—

(a) this section;

(b) sections 126 and 127, 135 to 140, 149 to 151, 181(1), (2) and (4) and 186; and

(c) the repeal in section 80(1) of the Local Government and Housing Act 1989, shall come into force on such day as the Secretary of State may by order made by statutory instrument appoint; and different days may be so appointed for different provisions or for different purposes.

(3) An order under subsection (2) may contain such transitional provisions and savings (whether or not involving the modification of any statutory provision) as appear to the Secretary of State necessary or expedient in connection with the provisions thereby brought into force by the order.

(4) The following, namely—

    (a) Part I of this Act;

    (b) Chapter I of Part II of this Act; and

    (c) subject to subsection (6), Part III of this Act,

extend to England and Wales only.

(5) Chapter II of Part II of this Act extends to Scotland only.

(6) In Part III of this Act—

    (a) sections 174, 179 and 180 also extend to Scotland;

    (b) paragraph 8 of Schedule 17 also extends to Scotland and Northern Ireland.

(7) This Part, except this section, paragraph 3 of Schedule 21 and the repeals in the House of Commons Disqualification Act 1975 and the Northern Ireland Assembly Disqualification Act 1975, does not extend to Northern Ireland.   **[589]**

NOTES

Commencement: 20 July 1993.

SCHEDULES

SCHEDULE 17

Section 158(2)

CONSTITUTION OF THE AGENCY

Membership

1.—(1) The Agency shall consist of such number of members (being not less than six) as the Secretary of State may from time to time appoint.

(2) The Secretary of State shall appoint one of the members to be chairman and may, if he thinks fit, appoint another of them to be deputy chairman.

(3) Subject to the provisions of this paragraph, a member of the Agency shall hold and vacate office in accordance with the terms of his appointment.

(4) A person who ceases to be a member of the Agency shall be eligible for reappointment.

(5) A member of the Agency may resign his office by notice in writing to the Secretary of State.

(6) The Secretary of State may remove a member of the Agency from office if he is satisfied that he—

    (a) is unable or unfit to carry out the functions of a member;

    (b) has not complied with the terms of his appointment; or

    (c) has become bankrupt or made an arrangement with his creditors.

(7) A person shall cease to be chairman or deputy chairman of the Agency—

    (a) if he resigns as such by notice in writing to the Secretary of State; or

(b) if he ceases to be a member of the Agency.

Remuneration, pensions etc

2.—(1) The Agency shall pay to its members such remuneration, and such allowances, as the Secretary of State may determine.

(2) The Agency may—

(a) pay such pensions, allowances or gratuities to or in respect of any persons who have been or are its members as the Secretary of State may determine;

(b) make such payments as the Secretary of State may determine towards provision for the payment of pensions, allowances or gratuities to or in respect of any such persons.

(3) If, when a person ceases to be a member of the Agency, the Secretary of State determines that there are special circumstances which make it right that he should receive compensation, the Agency shall pay to him a sum by way of compensation of such amount as the Secretary of State may determine.

(4) The approval of the Treasury shall be required for any determination of the Secretary of State under this paragraph.

Staff

3.—(1) There shall be a chief executive of the Agency who shall be responsible to the Agency for the general exercise of the Agency's functions.

(2) The chief executive shall be appointed by the Agency but no person shall be appointed as chief executive unless the Secretary of State has consented to the appointment.

(3) The Agency may appoint such other number of staff as the Secretary of State may approve.

(4) The terms and conditions of appointment of any person appointed by the Agency under this paragraph shall be determined by the Agency with the consent of the Secretary of State.

(5) The Agency shall pay to members of its staff such remuneration, and such allowances, as it may, with the consent of the Secretary of State, determine.

(6) The Agency may—

(a) pay such pensions, allowances or gratuities to or in respect of any persons who have been or are members of its staff;

(b) make such payments towards provision for the payment of pensions, allowances or gratuities to or in respect of any such persons,

as it may, with the consent of the Secretary of State, determine.

(7) Any reference in sub-paragraph (6) to pensions, allowances or gratuities to or in respect of any such persons as are mentioned in that sub-paragraph includes a reference to payments by way of compensation to or in respect of any members of the Agency's staff who suffer loss of office or employment or loss or diminution of emoluments.

(8) The approval of the Treasury shall be required for the giving of any consent under sub-paragraph (4), (5) or (6).

Delegation of powers

4. Anything authorised or required to be done by the Agency under this Part—

(a) may be done by any member of the Agency, or of its staff, who has been authorised for the purpose, whether generally or specially, by the Agency; or

(b) may be done by any committee or sub-committee of the Agency which has been so authorised.

Proceedings

5.—(1) Subject to the following provisions of this Schedule, the Agency may regulate both its own procedure (including quorum) and that of any committee or sub-committee.

(2) The Secretary of State may give directions as to the exercise by the Agency of its power under sub-paragraph (1) to regulate procedure; and directions under this sub-paragraph may be of a general or particular nature and may be varied or revoked by subsequent directions.

(3) The validity of any proceedings of the Agency or of any committee or sub-committee of the Agency shall not be affected—

(a) by a vacancy amongst the members of the Agency, committee or sub-committee;
(b) by a defect in the appointment of a member of the Agency, committee or sub-committee; or
(c) by a contravention of directions under sub-paragraph (2) or of paragraph 6.

(4) With the consent of the Secretary of State, persons who are not members of the Agency may be appointed as members of a committee or sub-committee of the Agency, but any such committee or sub-committee may not consist entirely of persons who are neither members of the Agency nor members of its staff

(5) The Agency may pay to any person who is a member of a committee or sub-committee but who is not a member of the Agency such remuneration, and such allowances, as the Secretary of State may, with the approval of the Treasury, determine.

Members' interests

6.—(1) A member of the Agency or of any committee or sub-committee who is directly or indirectly interested in any matter brought up for consideration at a meeting of the Agency or of the committee or sub-committee shall disclose the nature of his interest to the meeting.

(2) Where the matter in respect of which such a disclosure is made is a contract or agreement of any description, the member shall not take part in any deliberation or decision of the Agency, committee or sub-committee with respect to the matter.

(3) Where the matter in respect of which such a disclosure is made is one other than a contract or agreement, the member may take part in any deliberation or decision of the Agency, committee or sub-committee with respect to the matter unless the rest of the members decide that the interest disclosed might prejudicially affect the member's consideration of the matter.

Application of seal and proof of instruments

7.—(1) The application of the seal of the Agency shall be authenticated by the signature of any member of the Agency, or of its staff, who has been authorised by the Agency, whether generally or specially, for the purpose.

(2) Every document purporting to be an instrument issued by the Agency and to be duly sealed with the seal of the Agency or to be signed on behalf of the Agency shall be received in evidence and, unless the contrary is shown, shall be deemed to be an instrument so issued.

House of Commons disqualification

8. In Schedule 1 to the House of Commons Disqualification Act 1975 (bodies of which all members are disqualified for membership of the House of Commons), in Part II there shall be inserted, at the appropriate place, the following entry—

"The Urban Regeneration Agency.";

and the like insertion shall be made in Part II of Schedule 1 to the Northern Ireland Assembly Disqualification Act 1975. **[590]**

NOTES

Commencement: 10 November 1993.
Para 8 of this Schedule also extends to Scotland.

SCHEDULE 18

Section 158(2)

FINANCES OF THE AGENCY

Financial year

1. The financial years of the Agency shall be as follows—

    (a) the period beginning with the commencement of this Schedule and ending with the next following 31st March; and

    (b) each successive period of twelve months;

and references in this Schedule to a financial year shall be construed accordingly.

Financial duties

2.—(1) After consultation with the Agency, the Secretary of State may, with the approval of the Treasury, determine the financial duties of the Agency; and different determinations may be made in relation to different functions of the Agency.

(2) The Secretary of State shall give the Agency notice of every determination, and a determination may—

    (a) relate to a period beginning before the date on which it is made;

    (b) contain incidental or supplementary provisions; and

    (c) be varied or revoked by a subsequent determination.

Government grants

3.—(1) The Secretary of State may, out of moneys provided by Parliament and with the approval of the Treasury, pay to the Agency, in respect of the exercise of its functions and in respect of its administrative expenses, such sums as he may, with the approval of the Treasury, determine.

(2) The payment may be made on such terms as the Secretary of State may, with the approval of the Treasury, determine.

Borrowing

4.—(1) The Agency may borrow temporarily, by way of overdraft or otherwise, such sums as it may require for meeting its obligations and exercising its functions—

    (a) in sterling from the Secretary of State; or

    (b) with the consent of the Secretary of State, or in accordance with any general authority given by the Secretary of State, either in sterling or in a currency other than sterling from a person other than the Secretary of State.

(2) The Agency may borrow otherwise than by way of temporary loan such sums as it may require—

    (a) in sterling from the Secretary of State; or

    (b) with the consent of the Secretary of State, in a currency other than sterling from a person other than the Secretary of State.

(3) The Secretary of State may lend to the Agency any sums it has power to borrow from him under sub-paragraph (1) or (2).

(4) The Treasury may issue to the Secretary of State out of the National Loans Fund any sums necessary to enable him to make loans under sub-paragraph (3).

(5) Loans made under sub-paragraph (3) shall be repaid to the Secretary of State at such times and by such methods, and interest on the loans shall be paid to him at such times and at such rates, as he may determine.

(6) All sums received by the Secretary of State under sub-paragraph (5) shall be paid into the National Loans Fund.

(7) The approval of the Treasury shall be required for the giving of any consent or

authority under sub-paragraph (1) or (2), the making of any loan under sub-paragraph (3) or the making of any determination under sub-paragraph (5).

Guarantees

5.—(1) The Treasury may guarantee, in such manner and on such conditions as they think fit, the repayment of the principal of, and the payment of interest on, any sums which the Agency borrows from a person other than the Secretary of State.

(2) Immediately after a guarantee is given under this paragraph, the Treasury shall lay a statement of the guarantee before each House of Parliament; and, where any sum is issued for fulfilling a guarantee so given, the Treasury shall lay before each House of Parliament a statement relating to that sum, as soon as possible after the end of each financial year—

(a) beginning with that in which the sum is issued; and
(b) ending with that in which all liability in respect of the principal of the sum and in respect of interest on it is finally discharged.

(3) Any sums required by the Treasury for fulfilling a guarantee under this paragraph shall be charged on and issued out of the Consolidated Fund.

(4) If any sums are issued in fulfilment of a guarantee given under this paragraph, the Agency shall make to the Treasury, at such times and in such manner as the Treasury may from time to time direct, payments of such amounts as the Treasury so direct in or towards repayment of the sums so issued and payments of interest, at such rates as the Treasury so direct, on what is outstanding for the time being in respect of sums so issued.

(5) Any sums received by the Treasury in pursuance of sub-paragraph (4) shall be paid into the Consolidated Fund.

Surplus funds

6.—(1) This paragraph applies where it appears to the Secretary of State, after consultation with the Treasury and the Agency, that the Agency has a surplus, whether on capital or on revenue account, after making allowance by way of transfer to reserve or otherwise for its future requirements.

(2) The Agency shall, if the Secretary of State with the approval of the Treasury and after consultation with the Agency so directs, pay to the Secretary of State such sum not exceeding the amount of the surplus as may be specified in the direction.

(3) Any sum received by the Secretary of State under this paragraph shall, subject to sub-paragraph (5), be paid into the Consolidated Fund.

(4) The whole or part of any payment made to the Secretary of State by the Agency under sub-paragraph (2) shall, if the Secretary of State with the approval of the Treasury so determines, be treated as made—

(a) by way of repayment of such part of the principal of loans under paragraph 4(3); and
(b) in respect of the repayments due at such times,

as may be so determined.

(5) Any sum treated under sub-paragraph (4) as a repayment of a loan shall be paid by the Secretary of State into the National Loans Fund.

Financial limits

7.—(1) The aggregate amount at any time of borrowed sums shall not exceed £200 million or such greater sum not exceeding £300 million as the Secretary of State may by order made by statutory instrument specify.

(2) In sub-paragraph (1) "borrowed sums" means sums borrowed by the Agency under paragraph 4 minus repayments made or treated as made in respect of those sums.

(3) No order shall be made under sub-paragraph (1) unless a draft of the order has been laid before and approved by resolution of the House of Commons.

Grants and loans: accounts

8.—(1) The Secretary of State shall prepare in respect of each financial year an account—

    (a) of the sums issued to him under paragraph 4(4) and the sums received by him under paragraph 4(5) and of the disposal by him of those sums; and

    (b) of the sums paid into the Consolidated Fund or National Loans Fund under paragraph 6.

(2) The Secretary of State shall send the account to the Comptroller and Auditor General before the end of the month of November next following the end of that year.

(3) The Comptroller and Auditor General shall examine, certify and report on the account and lay copies of it and of his report before each House of Parliament.

(4) The form of the account and the manner of preparing it shall be such as the Treasury may direct.

Accounts

9.—(1) The Agency shall keep proper accounts and other records in relation to them.

(2) The accounts and records shall show, in respect of the financial year to which they relate, a true and fair view of the Agency's activities.

(3) The Agency shall prepare in respect of each financial year a statement of accounts complying with any requirement which the Secretary of State has, with the approval of the Treasury, notified in writing to the Agency relating to—

    (a) the information to be contained in the statement;

    (b) the manner in which the information is to be presented; and

    (c) the methods and principles according to which the statement is to be prepared.

(4) Subject to any requirement notified to the Agency under sub-paragraph (3), in preparing any statement of accounts in accordance with that sub-paragraph the Agency shall follow, with respect to each of the matters specified in paragraphs (a) to (c) of that sub-paragraph, such course as may for the time being be approved by the Secretary of State with the consent of the Treasury.

Audit

10. The Agency's accounts and statements of accounts shall be audited by an auditor to be appointed annually by the Secretary of State.

(2) A person shall not be qualified for appointment under sub-paragraph (1) unless—

    (a) he is eligible for appointment as a company auditor under Part II of the Companies Act 1989 (eligibility for appointment as company auditor); and

    (b) if the Agency were a body to which section 384 of the Companies Act 1985 (duty to appoint auditors) applies, he would not be ineligible for appointment as company auditor of the Agency by virtue of section 27 of the Companies Act 1989 (ineligibility on ground of lack of independence).

Transmission to Secretary of State

11. As soon as the accounts and statement of accounts of the Agency for any financial year have been audited, it shall send to the Secretary of State a copy of the statement, together with a copy of any report made by the auditor on the statement or on the accounts.

Reports

12.—(1) As soon as possible after the end of each financial year, the Agency—

    (a) shall make to the Secretary of State a report dealing generally with its operations during the year; and

    (b) shall include in the report a copy of its audited statement of accounts for that year and such information as the Secretary of State may specify.

(2) The Secretary of State shall lay a copy of the report before each House of Parliament.

Information

13. Without prejudice to paragraph 12, the Agency shall provide the Secretary of State with such information relating to its activities as he may require, and for that purpose—

(a) shall permit any person authorised by the Secretary of State to inspect and make copies of the accounts, books, documents or papers of the Agency; and

(b) shall afford such explanation of them as that person or the Secretary of State may reasonably require.   **[591]**

NOTES

Commencement: 10 November 1993.

SCHEDULE 19

Section 161(4)

VESTING OF LAND IN THE AGENCY: MODIFICATIONS OF ENACTMENTS

Land Compensation Act 1961 (c. 33)

1. The Land Compensation Act 1961 shall have effect in relation to orders under section 161(1) of this Act with the modifications specified in paragraphs 2 to 5.

2. References to the date of service of a notice to treat shall be treated as references to the date on which an order under section 161(1) of this Act comes into force.

3. Section 17(2) (certification of appropriate alternative development) shall be treated as if for the words "the authority proposing to acquire the interest have served a notice to treat in respect thereof, or an agreement has been made for the sale thereof to that authority" there were substituted the words "an order under section 161 of the Leasehold Reform, Housing and Urban Development Act 1993 vesting the land in which the interest subsists in the Urban Regeneration Agency has come into force, or an agreement has been made for the sale of the interest to the Agency".

4. Section 22(2) (interpretation of Part III) shall be treated as if at the end of paragraph (c) there were added the words

"or

(ca) where an order has been made under section 161(1) of the Leasehold Reform, Housing and Urban Development Act 1993 vesting the land in which the interest subsists in the Urban Regeneration Agency".

5. Any reference to a notice to treat in section 39(2) (interpretation) shall be treated as a reference to an order under section 161(1) of this Act.

Compulsory Purchase (Vesting Declarations) Act 1981 (c. 66)

6. In section 15 of the Compulsory Purchase (Vesting Declarations) Act 1981 (application to orders under section 141 of Local Government, Planning and Land Act 1980) after the words "vesting declaration)" there shall be inserted the words "or under subsection (1) of section 161 of the Leasehold Reform, Housing and Urban Development Act 1993 (subsection (4) of which makes similar provision)".

7.—(1) In Schedule 2 to that Act (vesting of land in urban development corporation), in paragraph 1 after the words "similar provision)" there shall be inserted the words "or under subsection (1) of section 161 of the Leasehold Reform, Housing and Urban Development Act 1993 (subsection (4) of which contains similar provision)".

(2) In paragraph 3(a) of that Schedule for the words "or, as the case may be, the housing action trust" there shall be substituted the words "the housing action trust or the Urban Regeneration Agency (as the case may be)".   **[592]**

NOTES

Commencement: 10 November 1993.

SCHEDULE 20

Section 169

THE AGENCY: LAND

PART I

MODIFICATIONS OF ACQUISITION OF LAND ACT 1981

1. The Acquisition of Land Act 1981 (in this Part of this Schedule referred to as "the 1981 Act") shall have effect in relation to the compulsory acquisition of land under this Part of this Act with the modifications specified in paragraphs 2 and 3.

2.—(1) Where a compulsory purchase order authorising the acquisition of any land is submitted to the Secretary of State in accordance with section 2(2) of the 1981 Act (procedure for authorisation), then if the Secretary of State—

    (a) is satisfied that the order ought to be confirmed so far as it relates to part of the land comprised in it, but

    (b) has not for the time being determined whether it ought to be confirmed so far as it relates to any other such land,

he may confirm the order so far as it relates to the land mentioned in paragraph (a), and give directions postponing the consideration of the order, so far as it relates to any other land specified in the directions, until such time as may be so specified.

(2) Where the Secretary of State gives directions under sub-paragraph (1), the notices required by section 15 of the 1981 Act (notices after confirmation of order) to be published and served shall include a statement of the effect of the directions.

3. The reference in section 17(3) of the 1981 Act (local authority and statutory undertakers' land) to statutory undertakers includes a reference to the Agency. **[593]**

NOTES

    Commencement: 10 November 1993.

PART II

LAND: SUPPLEMENTARY

Extinguishment of rights over land

4.—(1) Subject to this paragraph, on an order under section 161(1) of this Act coming into force or the completion by the Agency of a compulsory acquisition of land under this Part of this Act—

    (a) all private rights of way and rights of laying down, erecting, continuing or maintaining any apparatus on, under or over the land shall be extinguished; and

    (b) any such apparatus shall vest in the Agency.

(2) Sub-paragraph (1) does not apply—

    (a) to any right vested in, or apparatus belonging to, statutory undertakers for the purpose of carrying on their undertaking; or

    (b) to any right conferred by or in accordance with the telecommunications code on the operator of a telecommunications code system or to any telecommunications apparatus kept installed for the purposes of any such system.

(3) In respect of any right or apparatus not falling within sub-paragraph (2), sub-paragraph (1) shall have effect subject to—

    (a) any direction given by the Secretary of State before the coming into force of the order or by the Agency before the completion of the acquisition (as the case may be) that sub-paragraph (1) shall not apply to any right or apparatus specified in the direction, and

    (b) any agreement which may be made (whether before or after the coming into force of the order or completion of the acquisition) between the Secretary of State or the

Agency and the person in or to whom the right or apparatus in question is vested or belongs.

(4) Any person who suffers loss by the extinguishment of a right or the vesting of any apparatus under this paragraph shall be entitled to compensation from the Agency.

(5) Any compensation payable under this paragraph shall be determined in accordance with the Land Compensation Act 1961.

Power to override easements

5.—(1) The erection, construction, carrying out, or maintenance of any building or work on land which has been vested in or acquired by the Agency under this Part of this Act, whether done by the Agency or by any other person, is authorised by virtue of this paragraph if it is done in accordance with planning permission, notwithstanding that it involves—

(a) interference with an interest or right to which this paragraph applies; or
(b) a breach of a restriction as to the user of land arising by virtue of a contract.

(2) Nothing in sub-paragraph (1) shall authorise interference with any right of way or right of laying down, erecting, continuing or maintaining apparatus on, under or over land, being—

(a) a right vested in or belonging to statutory undertakers for the purpose of the carrying on of their undertaking; or
(b) a right conferred by or in accordance with the telecommunications code on the operator of a telecommunications code system.

(3) This paragraph applies to the following interests and rights, that is to say, any easement, liberty, privilege, right or advantage annexed to land and adversely affecting other land, including any natural right to support.

(4) In respect of any interference or breach in pursuance of sub-paragraph (1), compensation shall be payable under section 7 or 10 of the Compulsory Purchase Act 1965, to be assessed in the same manner and subject to the same rules as in the case of other compensation under those sections in respect of injurious affection where the compensation is to be estimated in connection with a purchase by the Agency or the injury arises from the execution of works on land acquired by the Agency.

(5) Where a person other than the Agency—

(a) is liable to pay compensation by virtue of sub-paragraph (4); and
(b) fails to discharge that liability,

the liability shall (subject to sub-paragraph (6)) be enforceable against the Agency.

(6) Nothing in sub-paragraph (5) shall be construed as affecting any agreement between the Agency and any other person for indemnifying the Agency against any liability under that sub-paragraph.

(7) Nothing in this paragraph shall be construed as authorising any act or omission on the part of any person which is actionable at the suit of any person on any grounds other than such an interference or breach as is mentioned in sub-paragraph (1).

(8) Nothing in this paragraph shall be construed as authorising any act or omission on the part of the Agency or any body corporate in contravention of any limitation imposed by law on its capacity by virtue of its constitution.

Consecrated land and burial grounds

6.—(1) Any consecrated land, whether including a building or not, which has been vested in or acquired by the Agency under this Part of this Act may (subject to the following provisions of this paragraph) be used by the Agency, or by any other person, in any manner in accordance with planning permission, notwithstanding any obligation or restriction imposed under ecclesiastical law or otherwise in respect of consecrated land.

(2) Sub-paragraph (1) does not apply to land which consists or forms part of a burial ground.

(3) Any use of consecrated land authorised by sub-paragraph (1), and the use of any land, not being consecrated land, vested or acquired as mentioned in that sub-paragraph which at the time of vesting or acquisition included a church or other building used or formerly used for religious worship or the site thereof, shall be subject to compliance with the prescribed requirements with respect to—

(a) the removal and reinterment of any human remains; and
(b) the disposal of monuments,

and, in the case of consecrated land, shall be subject to such provisions as may be prescribed for prohibiting or restricting the use of the land, either absolutely or until the prescribed consent has been obtained, so long as any church or other building used or formerly used for religious worship, or any part thereof, remains on the land.

(4) Any regulations made for the purposes of sub-paragraph (3)—

(a) shall contain such provisions as appear to the Secretary of State to be requisite for securing that any use of land which is subject to compliance with the regulations shall, as nearly as may be, be subject to the like control as is imposed by law in the case of a similar use authorised by an enactment not contained in this Act or by a Measure, or as it would be proper to impose on a disposal of the land in question otherwise than in pursuance of an enactment or Measure;

(b) shall contain requirements relating to the disposal of any such land as is mentioned in sub-paragraph (3) such as appear to the Secretary of State requisite for securing that the provisions of that sub-paragraph shall be complied with in relation to the use of the land; and

(c) may contain such incidental and consequential provisions (including provision as to the closing of registers) as appear to the Secretary of State to be expedient for the purposes of the regulations.

(5) Any land consisting of a burial ground or part of a burial ground which has been vested in or acquired by the Agency under this Part of this Act may be used by the Agency in any manner in accordance with planning permission, notwithstanding anything in any enactment relating to burial grounds or any obligation or restriction imposed under ecclesiastical law or otherwise in respect of burial grounds.

(6) Sub-paragraph (5) shall not have effect in respect of any land which has been used for the burial of the dead until the prescribed requirements with respect to the removal and reinterment of human remains and the disposal of monuments in or upon the land have been complied with.

(7) Provision shall be made by any regulations made for the purposes of sub-paragraphs (3) and (6)—

(a) for requiring the persons in whom the land is vested to publish notice of their intention to carry out the removal and reinterment of any human remains or the disposal of any monuments;

(b) for enabling the personal representatives or relatives of any deceased person themselves to undertake the removal and reinterment of the remains of the deceased and the disposal of any monument commemorating the deceased, and for requiring the persons in whom the land is vested to defray the expenses of such removal, reinterment and disposal, not exceeding such amount as may be prescribed;

(c) for requiring compliance with such reasonable conditions (if any) as may be imposed, in the case of consecrated land, by the bishop of the diocese, with respect to the manner of removal and the place and manner of reinterment of any human remains and the disposal of any monuments; and

(d) for requiring compliance with any directions given in any case by the Secretary of State with respect to the removal and reinterment of any human remains.

(8) Subject to the provisions of any such regulations as are referred to in sub-paragraph (7), no faculty shall be required—

(a) for the removal and reinterment in accordance with the regulations of any human remains; or

(b) for the removal or disposal of any monuments;

and the provisions of section 25 of the Burial Act 1857 (which prohibits the removal of human remains without the licence of the Secretary of State except in certain cases) shall not apply to a removal carried out in accordance with the regulations.

(9) Any power conferred by this paragraph to use land in a manner therein mentioned shall be construed as a power so to use the land, whether or not it involves—

    (a) the erection, construction or carrying out of any building or work; or

    (b) the maintenance of any building or work.

(10) Nothing in this paragraph shall be construed as authorising any act or omission on the part of any person which is actionable at the suit of any person on any grounds other than contravention of any such obligation, restriction or enactment as is mentioned in sub-paragraph (1) or (5).

(11) Sub-paragraph (8) of paragraph 5 shall apply in relation to this paragraph as it applies in relation to that.

(12) In this paragraph—

    "burial ground" includes any churchyard, cemetery or other ground, whether consecrated or not, which has at any time been set apart for the purposes of interment; and

    "monument" includes a tombstone or other memorial.

(13) In this paragraph "prescribed" means prescribed by regulations made by the Secretary of State.

(14) The power to make regulations under this paragraph shall be exercisable by statutory instrument which shall be subject to annulment in pursuance of a resolution of either House of Parliament.

Open spaces

7.—(1) Any land being, or forming part of, a common, open space or fuel or field garden allotment, which has been vested in or acquired by the Agency under this Part of this Act may be used by the Agency, or by any other person, in any manner in accordance with planning permission, notwithstanding anything in any enactment—

    (a) relating to land of that kind; or

    (b) by which the land is specially regulated.

(2) Nothing in this paragraph shall be construed as authorising any act or omission on the part of any person which is actionable at the suit of any person on any grounds other than contravention of any such enactment as is mentioned in sub-paragraph (1).

(3) Sub-paragraph (8) of paragraph 5 shall apply in relation to this paragraph as it applies in relation to that.

Displacement of persons

8. If the Secretary of State certifies that possession of a house which—

    (a) has been vested in or acquired by the Agency under this Part of this Act; and

    (b) is for the time being held by the Agency for the purposes of its objects,

is immediately required for those purposes, nothing in the Rent (Agriculture) Act 1976, the Rent Act 1977 or the Housing Act 1988 shall prevent the Agency from obtaining possession of the house.

Extinguishment of public rights of way

9.—(1) Where any land—

    (a) has been vested in or acquired by the Agency under this Part of this Act; and

    (b) is for the time being held by the Agency for the purposes of its objects,

the Secretary of State may by order extinguish any public right of way over the land.

(2) Where the Secretary of State proposes to make an order under this paragraph, he shall—

    (a) publish in such manner as appears to him to be requisite a notice—

(i) stating the effect of the order, and

(ii) specifying the time (not being less than 28 days from the publication of the notice) within which, and the manner in which, objections to the proposal may be made; and

(b) serve a like notice—

(i) on the local planning authority in whose area the land is situated; and

(ii) on the relevant highway authority.

(3) In sub-paragraph (2) "the relevant highway authority" means any authority which is a highway authority in relation to the right of way proposed to be extinguished by the order under this paragraph.

(4) Where an objection to a proposal to make an order under this paragraph is duly made and is not withdrawn, the provisions of paragraph 10 shall have effect in relation to the proposal.

(5) For the purposes of this paragraph an objection to such a proposal shall not be treated as duly made unless—

(a) it is made within the time and in the manner specified in the notice required by this paragraph; and

(b) a statement in writing of the grounds of the objection is comprised in or submitted with the objection.

10.—(1) In this paragraph any reference to making a final decision, in relation to an order, is a reference to deciding whether to make the order or what modification, if any, ought to be made.

(2) Unless the Secretary of State decides apart from the objection not to make the order, or decides to make a modification which is agreed to by the objector as meeting the objection, the Secretary of State—

(a) shall, before making a final decision, consider the grounds of the objection as set out in the statement comprised in or submitted with the objection; and

(b) may, if he thinks fit, require the objector to submit within a specified period a further statement in writing as to any of the matters to which the objection relates.

(3) In so far as the Secretary of State, after considering the grounds of the objection as set out in the original statement and in any such further statement, is satisfied that the objection relates to a matter which can be dealt with in the assessment of compensation, he may treat the objection as irrelevant for the purpose of making a final decision.

(4) In any case where—

(a) after considering the grounds of the objection as set out in the original statement and in any such further statement, the Secretary of State is satisfied that, for the purpose of making a final decision, he is sufficiently informed as to the matters to which the objection relates; or

(b) a further statement has been required but is not submitted within the specified period,

the Secretary of State may make a final decision without further investigation as to the matters to which the objection relates.

(5) Subject to sub-paragraphs (3) and (4), the Secretary of State, before making a final decision, shall afford to the objector an opportunity of appearing before, and being heard by, a person appointed for the purpose by the Secretary of State; and if the objector avails himself of that opportunity, the Secretary of State shall afford an opportunity of appearing and being heard on the same occasion—

(a) to the Agency; and

(b) to any other persons to whom it appears to the Secretary of State to be expedient to afford such an opportunity.

(6) Notwithstanding anything in the preceding provisions of this paragraph, if it appears to the Secretary of State that the matters to which the objection relates are such as to require investigation by public local inquiry before he makes a final decision, he shall cause such an inquiry to be held; and where he determines to cause such an inquiry to be held, any of the

requirements of those provisions to which effect has not been given at the time of that determination shall be dispensed with.

Telegraphic lines

11.—(1) Where an order under paragraph 9 extinguishing a public right of way is made and at the time of the publication of the notice required by sub-paragraph (2) of that paragraph any telecommunication apparatus was kept installed for the purposes of a telecommunications code system under, in, on, over, along or across the land over which the right of way subsisted—

(a) the power of the operator of the system to remove the apparatus shall, notwithstanding the making of the order, be exercisable at any time not later than the end of the period of three months from the date on which the right of way is extinguished and shall be exercisable in respect of the whole or any part of the apparatus after the end of that period if before the end of that period the operator of the system has given notice to the Agency of his intention to remove the apparatus or that part of it, as the case may be;

(b) the operator of the system may by notice given in that behalf to the Agency not later than the end of the said period of three months abandon the telecommunication apparatus or any part of it;

(c) subject to paragraph (b), the operator of the system shall be deemed at the end of that period to have abandoned any part of the apparatus which he has then neither removed nor given notice of his intention to remove;

(d) the operator of the system shall be entitled to recover from the Agency the expense of providing, in substitution for the apparatus and any other telecommunication apparatus connected with it which is rendered useless in consequence of the removal or abandonment of the first-mentioned apparatus, any telecommunication apparatus in such other place as the operator may require; and

(e) where under the preceding provisions of this sub-paragraph the operator of the system has abandoned the whole or any part of any telecommunication apparatus, that apparatus or that part of it shall vest in the Agency and shall be deemed, with its abandonment, to cease to be kept installed for the purposes of a telecommunications code system.

(2) As soon as practicable after the making of an order under paragraph 9 extinguishing a public right of way in circumstances in which sub-paragraph (1) applies in relation to the operator of any telecommunications code system, the Secretary of State shall give notice to the operator of the making of the order.

Statutory undertakers

12.—(1) Where any land has been vested in or acquired by the Agency under this Part of this Act and—

(a) there subsists over that land a right vested in or belonging to statutory undertakers for the purpose of the carrying on of their undertaking, being a right of way or a right of laying down, erecting, continuing or maintaining apparatus on, under or over that land, or

(b) there is on, under or over the land apparatus vested in or belonging to statutory undertakers for the purpose of the carrying on of their undertaking,

the Agency may serve on the statutory undertakers a notice stating that, at the end of the period of 28 days from the date of service of the notice or such longer period as may be specified therein, the right will be extinguished or requiring that, before the end of that period, the apparatus shall be removed.

(2) The statutory undertakers on whom a notice is served under sub-paragraph (1) may, before the end of the period of 28 days from the service of the notice, serve a counter-notice on the Agency stating that they object to all or any provisions of the notice and specifying the grounds of their objection.

(3) If no counter-notice is served under sub-paragraph (2)—

(a) any right to which the notice relates shall be extinguished at the end of the period specified in that behalf in the notice; and

(b) if, at the end of the period so specified in relation to any apparatus, any requirement of the notice as to the removal of the apparatus has not been complied with, the Agency may remove the apparatus and dispose of it in any way it may think fit.

(4) If a counter-notice is served under sub-paragraph (2) on the Agency, it may either withdraw the notice (without prejudice to the service of a further notice) or apply to the Secretary of State and the appropriate Minister for an order under this paragraph embodying the provisions of the notice with or without modification.

(5) Where by virtue of this paragraph any right vested in or belonging to statutory undertakers is extinguished, or any requirement is imposed on statutory undertakers, those undertakers shall be entitled to compensation from the Agency.

(6) Sections 280 and 282 of the Town and Country Planning Act 1990 (measure of compensation to statutory undertakers) shall apply to compensation under sub-paragraph (5) as they apply to compensation under section 279(4) of that Act.

(7) Except in a case where paragraph 11 applies—

(a) the reference in paragraph (a) of sub-paragraph (1) to a right vested in or belonging to statutory undertakers for the purpose of the carrying on of their undertaking shall include a reference to a right conferred by or in accordance with the telecommunications code on the operator of a telecommunications code system; and

(b) the reference in paragraph (b) of that sub-paragraph to apparatus vested in or belonging to statutory undertakers for the purpose of the carrying on of their undertaking shall include a reference to telecommunication apparatus kept installed for the purposes of any such system.

(8) Where paragraph (a) or (b) of sub-paragraph (1) has effect as mentioned in sub-paragraph (7), in the rest of this paragraph and in paragraph 13—

(a) any reference to statutory undertakers shall have effect as a reference to the operator of any such system as is referred to in sub-paragraph (7); and

(b) any reference to the appropriate Minister shall have effect as a reference to the Secretary of State for Trade and Industry.

13.—(1) Before making an order under paragraph 12 the Secretary of State and the appropriate Minister—

(a) shall afford to the statutory undertakers on whom notice was served under paragraph 12(1) an opportunity of objecting to the application for the order; and

(b) if any objection is made, shall consider the objection and afford to those statutory undertakers and to the Agency an opportunity of appearing before and being heard by a person appointed by the Secretary of State and the appropriate Minister for the purpose;

and the Secretary of State and the appropriate Minister may then, if they think fit, make the order in accordance with the application either with or without modification.

(2) Where an order is made under paragraph 12—

(a) any right to which the order relates shall be extinguished at the end of the period specified in that behalf in the order; and

(b) if, at the end of the period so specified in relation to any apparatus, any requirement of the order as to the removal of the apparatus has not been complied with, the Agency may remove the apparatus and dispose of it in any way it may think fit.

14.—(1) Subject to this paragraph, where any land has been vested in or acquired by the Agency under this Part of this Act and—

(a) there is on, under or over the land apparatus vested in or belonging to statutory undertakers, and

(b) the undertakers claim that development to be carried out on the land is such as to require, on technical or other grounds connected with the carrying on of their undertaking, the removal or re-siting of the apparatus affected by the development,

the undertakers may serve on the Agency a notice claiming the right to enter on the land and carry out such works for the removal or re-siting of the apparatus or any part of it as may be specified in the notice.

(2) Where, after the land has been vested or acquired as mentioned in sub-paragraph (1), development of the land is begun to be carried out, no notice under this paragraph shall be served later than 21 days after the beginning of the development.

(3) Where a notice is served under this paragraph the Agency may, before the end of the period of 28 days from the date of service, serve on the statutory undertakers a counter-notice stating that it objects to all or any of the provisions of the notice and specifying the grounds of its objection.

(4) If no counter-notice is served under sub-paragraph (3), the statutory undertakers shall, after the end of the said period of 28 days, have the rights claimed in their notice.

(5) If a counter-notice is served under sub-paragraph (3), the statutory undertakers who served the notice under this paragraph may either withdraw it or apply to the Secretary of State and the appropriate Minister for an order under this paragraph conferring on the undertakers—

(a) the rights claimed in the notice; or
(b) such modified rights as the Secretary of State and the appropriate Minister think it expedient to confer on them.

(6) Where by virtue of this paragraph or an order made by the Secretary of State and the appropriate Minister under it, statutory undertakers have the right to execute works for the removal or re-siting of apparatus, they may arrange with the Agency for the works to be carried out by the Agency, under the superintendence of the undertakers, instead of by the undertakers themselves.

(7) Where works are carried out for the removal or re-siting of statutory undertakers' apparatus, being works which the undertakers have the right to carry out by virtue of this paragraph or an order made by the Secretary of State and the appropriate Minister under it, the undertakers shall be entitled to compensation from the Agency.

(8) Sections 280 and 282 of the Town and Country Planning Act 1990 (measure of compensation to statutory undertakers) shall apply to compensation under sub-paragraph (7) as they apply to compensation under section 279(4) of that Act.

(9) In sub-paragraph (1)(a), the reference to apparatus vested in or belonging to statutory undertakers shall include a reference to telecommunication apparatus kept installed for the purposes of a telecommunications code system.

(10) Where sub-paragraph (1)(a) has effect as mentioned in sub-paragraph (9), in the rest of this paragraph—

(a) any reference to statutory undertakers shall have effect as a reference to the operator of any such system as is referred to in sub-paragraph (9); and
(b) any reference to the appropriate Minister shall have effect as a reference to the Secretary of State for Trade and Industry.

15.—(1) The powers conferred by this paragraph shall be exercisable where, on a representation made by statutory undertakers, it appears to the Secretary of State and the appropriate Minister to be expedient that the powers and duties of those undertakers should be extended or modified, in order—

(a) to secure the provision of services which would not otherwise be provided, or which would not otherwise be satisfactorily provided, in relation to relevant land; or
(b) to facilitate an adjustment of the carrying on of the undertaking necessitated by any of the acts and events mentioned in sub-paragraph (2).

(2) The said acts and events are—

(a) the vesting in or acquisition by the Agency under this Part of this Act of any land in which an interest was held, or which was used, for the purpose of the carrying on of the undertaking of the statutory undertakers in question; and
(b) the extinguishment of a right or the imposition of any requirement by virtue of paragraph 12.

(3) The powers conferred by this paragraph shall also be exercisable where, on a representation made by the Agency, it appears to the Secretary of State and the appropriate

Minister to be expedient that the powers and duties of statutory undertakers should be extended or modified, in order to secure the provision of new services, or the extension of existing services, in relation to relevant land.

(4) Where the powers conferred by this paragraph are exercisable, the Secretary of State and the appropriate Minister may, if they think fit, by order provide for such extension or modification of the powers and duties of the statutory undertakers as appears to them to be requisite in order to secure—

    (a) the provision of the services in question, as mentioned in sub-paragraph (1)(a) or sub-paragraph (3); or

    (b) the adjustment in question, as mentioned in sub-paragraph (1)(b),

as the case may be.

(5) Without prejudice to the generality of sub-paragraph (4), an order under this paragraph may make provision—

    (a) for empowering the statutory undertakers to acquire (whether compulsorily or by agreement) any land specified in the order, and to erect or construct any buildings or works so specified;

    (b) for applying, in relation to the acquisition of any such land or the construction of any such works, enactments relating to the acquisition of land and the construction of works;

    (c) where it has been represented that the making of the order is expedient for the purposes mentioned in sub-paragraph (1)(a) or (3), for giving effect to such financial arrangements between the Agency and the statutory undertakers as they may agree, or as, in default of agreement, may be determined to be equitable in such manner and by such tribunal as may be specified in the order; and

    (d) for such incidental and supplemental matters as appear to the Secretary of State and the appropriate Minister to be expedient for the purposes of the order.

(6) In this paragraph "relevant land" means land in respect of which any of the functions of the Agency under this Part of this Act are being or have been exercised.

16.—(1) As soon as may be after making such a representation as is mentioned in sub-paragraph (1) or (3) of paragraph 15—

    (a) the statutory undertakers, in a case falling within sub-paragraph (1), or

    (b) the Agency, in a case falling within sub-paragraph (3),

shall publish, in such form and manner as may be directed by the Secretary of State and the appropriate Minister, a notice giving such particulars as may be so directed of the matters to which the representation relates, and specifying the time within which, and the manner in which, objections to the making of an order on the representation may be made, and shall also, if it is so directed by the Secretary of State and the appropriate Minister, serve a like notice on such persons, or persons of such classes, as may be so directed.

(2) Orders under paragraph 15 shall be subject to special parliamentary procedure.

17.—(1) Where, on a representation made by statutory undertakers, the appropriate Minister is satisfied that the fulfilment of any obligations incurred by those undertakers in connection with the carrying on of their undertaking has been rendered impracticable by an act or event to which this sub-paragraph applies, the appropriate Minister may, if he thinks fit, by order direct that the statutory undertakers shall be relieved of the fulfilment of that obligation, either absolutely or to such extent as may be specified in the order.

(2) Sub-paragraph (1) applies to the following acts and events—

    (a) the vesting in or acquisition by the Agency under this Part of this Act of any land in which an interest was held, or which was used, for the purpose of the carrying on of the undertaking of the statutory undertakers; and

    (b) the extinguishment of a right or the imposition of any requirement by virtue of paragraph 12.

(3) As soon as may be after making a representation to the appropriate Minister under sub-paragraph (1), the statutory undertakers shall, as may be directed by the appropriate Minister, do either or both of the following, that is to say—

(a) publish (in such form and manner as may be so directed) a notice—

    (i) giving such particulars as may be so directed of the matters to which the representation relates; and

    (ii) specifying the time within which, and the manner in which, objections to the making of an order on the representation may be made; and

(b) serve a like notice on such persons, or persons of such classes, as may be so directed.

(4) If any objection to the making of an order under this paragraph is duly made and is not withdrawn before the order is made, the order shall be subject to special parliamentary procedure.

(5) Immediately after an order is made under this paragraph by the appropriate Minister, he shall publish a notice stating that the order has been made and naming a place where a copy of it may be seen at all reasonable hours, and shall serve a like notice—

(a) on any person who duly made an objection to the order and has sent to the appropriate Minister a request in writing to serve him with the notice required by this sub-paragraph, specifying an address for service; and

(b) on such other persons (if any) as the appropriate Minister thinks fit.

(6) Subject to the following provisions of this paragraph, an order under this paragraph shall become operative on the date on which the notice required by sub-paragraph (5) is first published.

(7) Where in accordance with sub-paragraph (4) the order is subject to special parliamentary procedure, sub-paragraph (6) shall not apply.

(8) If any person aggrieved by an order under this paragraph wishes to question the validity of the order on the ground—

(a) that it is not within the powers conferred by this paragraph, or

(b) that any requirement of this paragraph has not been complied with in relation to the order,

he may, within six weeks from the date on which the notice required by sub-paragraph (5) is first published, make an application to the High Court under this paragraph.

(9) On any application under sub-paragraph (8) the High Court—

(a) may by interim order wholly or in part suspend the operation of the order, either generally or in so far as it affects any property of the applicant, until the final determination of the proceedings; and

(b) if satisfied—

    (i) that the order is wholly or to any extent outside the powers conferred by this paragraph; or

    (ii) that the interests of the applicant have been substantially prejudiced by the failure to comply with any requirement of this paragraph,

may wholly or in part quash the order, either generally or in so far as it affects any property of the applicant.

(10) Subject to sub-paragraph (8), the validity of an order under this paragraph shall not be questioned in any legal proceedings whatsoever, either before or after the order has been made.

18.—(1) For the purposes of paragraphs 15 and 17, an objection to the making of an order thereunder shall not be treated as duly made unless—

(a) the objection is made within the time and in the manner specified in the notice required by paragraph 16 or 17 (as the case may be); and

(b) a statement in writing of the grounds of the objection is comprised in or submitted with the objection.

(2) Where an objection to the making of such an order is duly made in accordance with sub-paragraph (1) and is not withdrawn, the following provisions of this paragraph shall have effect in relation thereto; but, in the application of those provisions to an order under paragraph

15, any reference to the appropriate Minister shall be construed as a reference to the Secretary of State and the appropriate Minister.

(3) Unless the appropriate Minister decides apart from the objection not to make the order, or decides to make a modification which is agreed to by the objector as meeting the objection, the appropriate Minister, before making a final decision—

    (a) shall consider the grounds of the objection as set out in the statement; and

    (b) may, if he thinks fit, require the objector to submit within a specified period a further statement in writing as to any of the matters to which the objection relates.

(4) In so far as the appropriate Minister after considering the grounds of the objection as set out in the original statement and in any such further statement, is satisfied that the objection relates to a matter which can be dealt with in the assessment of compensation, the appropriate Minister may treat the objection as irrelevant for the purpose of making a final decision.

(5) In any case where—

    (a) after considering the grounds of the objection as set out in the original statement and in any such further statement, the appropriate Minister is satisfied that, for the purpose of making a final decision, he is sufficiently informed as to the matters to which the objection relates; or

    (b) a further statement has been required but is not submitted within the specified period,

the appropriate Minister may make a final decision without further investigation as to the matters to which the objection relates.

(6) Subject to sub-paragraphs (4) and (5), the appropriate Minister, before making a final decision, shall afford to the objector an opportunity of appearing before, and being heard by, a person appointed for the purpose by the appropriate Minister; and if the objector avails himself of that opportunity, the appropriate Minister shall afford an opportunity of appearing and being heard on the same occasion—

    (a) to the person (being the Agency or the statutory undertakers) on whose representation the order is proposed to be made; and

    (b) to any other persons to whom it appears to the appropriate Minister to be expedient to afford such an opportunity.

(7) Notwithstanding anything in the preceding provisions of this paragraph, if it appears to the appropriate Minister that the matters to which the objection relates are such as to require investigation by public local inquiry before he makes a final decision, he shall cause such an inquiry to be held; and where he determines to cause such an inquiry to be held, any of the requirements of those provisions to which effect has not been given at the time of that determination shall be dispensed with.

(8) In this paragraph any reference to making a final decision, in relation to an order, is a reference to deciding whether to make the order or what modification (if any) ought to be made.

Interpretation

19.—(1) Any expression used in this Part of this Schedule to which a meaning is assigned by paragraph 1 of Schedule 4 to the Telecommunications Act 1984 has that meaning in this Part.

(2) In this Part of this Schedule "statutory undertakers" means persons who are or are deemed to be statutory undertakers for the purposes of any provision of Part XI of the Town and Country Planning Act 1990; and "statutory undertaking" shall be construed in accordance with section 262 of that Act (meaning of "statutory undertaker").

(3) In this Part of this Schedule "the appropriate Minister" shall be construed as if contained in Part XI the Town and Country Planning Act 1990; and any reference to the Secretary of State and the appropriate Minister shall be similarly construed. **[594]**

NOTES

Commencement: 10 November 1993.

PART III

ACQUISITION OF RIGHTS

20.—(1) The Compulsory Purchase Act 1965 (in this Part of this Schedule referred to as "the 1965 Act") shall have effect with the modifications necessary to make it apply to the compulsory acquisition of rights by virtue of section 162(2) of this Act as it applies to the compulsory purchase of land so that, in appropriate contexts, references in the 1965 Act to land are read as referring, or as including references, to the rights or to land over which the rights are or are to be exercisable, according to the requirements of the particular context.

(2) Without prejudice to the generality of sub-paragraph (1), in relation to the acquisition of rights by virtue of section 162(2) of this Act—

(a) Part I of the 1965 Act (which relates to compulsory purchases under the Acquisition of Land Act 1981) shall have effect with the modifications specified in paragraphs 21 to 23; and

(b) the enactments relating to compensation for the compulsory purchase of land shall apply with the necessary modifications as they apply to such compensation.

21. For section 7 of the 1965 Act (which relates to compensation) there shall be substituted the following section—

"**7.**—(1) In assessing the compensation to be paid by the acquiring authority under this Act regard shall be had not only to the extent, if any, to which the value of the land over which the right is purchased is depreciated by the purchase but also to the damage, if any, to be sustained by the owner of the land by reason of injurious affection of other land of the owner by the exercise of the right.

(2) The modifications subject to which subsection (1) of section 44 of the Land Compensation Act 1973 (compensation for injurious affectation) is to have effect, as applied by subsection (2) of that section to compensation for injurious affection under this section, are that for the words "land is acquired or taken" there shall be substituted the words "a right over land is acquired' and for the words "acquired or taken from him" there shall be substituted the words "over which the right is exercisable"."

22. For section 8 of the 1965 Act (which relates to cases in which a vendor cannot be required to sell part only of a building or garden) there shall be substituted the following section—

"**8.**—(1) Where in consequence of the service on a person in pursuance of section 5 of this Act of a notice to treat in respect of a right over land consisting of a house, building or manufactory or of a park or garden belonging to a house ("the relevant land")—

(a) a question of disputed compensation in respect of the purchase of the right would apart from this section fall to be determined by the Lands Tribunal ("the Tribunal"); and

(b) before the Tribunal has determined that question the person satisfies the Tribunal that he has an interest which he is able and willing to sell in the whole of the relevant land and—

(i) where that land consists of a house, building or manufactory, that the right cannot be purchased without material detriment to that land, or

(ii) where that land consists of such a park or garden, that the right cannot be purchased without seriously affecting the amenity or convenience of the house to which that land belongs,

the compulsory purchase order to which the notice to treat relates shall, in relation to that person, cease to authorise the purchase of the right and be deemed to authorise the purchase of that person's interest in the whole of the relevant land including, where the land consists of such a park or garden, the house to which it belongs, and the notice shall be deemed to have been served in respect of that interest on such date as the Tribunal directs.

(2) Any question as to the extent of the land in which a compulsory purchase order is deemed to authorise the purchase of an interest by virtue of the preceding subsection shall be determined by the Tribunal.

(3) Where in consequence of a determination of the Tribunal that it is satisfied as mentioned in subsection (1) of this section a compulsory purchase order is deemed by

virtue of that subsection to authorise the purchase of an interest in land, the acquiring authority may, at any time within the period of six weeks beginning with the date of the determination, withdraw the notice to treat in consequence of which the determination was made; but nothing in this subsection prejudices any other power of the authority to withdraw the notice.

(4) The modifications subject to which subsection (1) of section 58 of the Land Compensation Act 1973 (determination of material detriment) is to have effect, as applied by subsection (2) of that section to the duty of the Tribunal in determining whether it is satisfied as mentioned in subsection (1) of this section, are that—

(a) at the beginning of paragraphs (a) and (b) there shall be inserted the words "a right over";

(b) for the word "severance" there shall be substituted the words "right on the whole of the house, building or manufactory or of the house and the park or garden"; and

(c) for the words "part proposed" and "part is" there shall be substituted respectively the words "right proposed" and "right is"."

23.—(1) The following provisions of the 1965 Act (which state the effect of a deed poll executed in various circumstances where there is no conveyance by persons with interests in the land), namely—

(a) section 9(4) (failure of owners to convey);
(b) paragraph 10(3) of Schedule 1 (owners under incapacity);
(c) paragraph 2(3) of Schedule 2 (absent and untraced owners); and
(d) paragraphs 2(3) and 7(2) of Schedule 4 (common land),

shall be so modified as to secure that, as against persons with interests in the land which are expressed to be overridden by the deed, the right which is to be acquired compulsorily is vested absolutely in the acquiring authority.

(2) Section 11 of the 1965 Act (powers of entry) shall be so modified as to secure that, as from the date on which the acquiring authority has served notice to treat in respect of any right, it has power, exercisable in the like circumstances and subject to the like conditions, to enter for the purpose of exercising that right (which shall be deemed for this purpose to have been created on the date of service of the notice); and sections 12 (penalty for unauthorised entry) and 13 (entry on sheriff's warrant in the event of obstruction) of the 1965 Act shall be modified correspondingly.

(3) Section 20 of the 1965 Act (compensation for short-term tenants) shall apply with the modifications necessary to secure that persons with such interests as are mentioned in that section are compensated in a manner corresponding to that in which they would be compensated on a compulsory purchase of the interests but taking into account only the extent (if any) of such interference with such interests as is actually caused, or likely to be caused, by the exercise of the right in question.

(4) Section 22 of the 1965 Act (protection of acquiring authority's possession of land where by inadvertence an interest in the land has not been purchased) shall be so modified as to enable the acquiring authority, in circumstances corresponding to those referred to in that section, to continue to be entitled to exercise the right in question, subject to compliance with that section as respects compensation.   **[595]**

NOTES
Commencement: 10 November 1993.

ENVIRONMENT ACT 1995
(1995 c 25)

ARRANGEMENT OF SECTIONS

SCHEDULES:

*An Act to provide for the establishment of a body corporate to be known as the
Environment Agency and a body corporate to be known as the Scottish
Environment Protection Agency; to provide for the transfer of functions,
property, rights and liabilities to those bodies and for the conferring of other
functions on them; to make provision with respect to contaminated land and
abandoned mines; to make further provision in relation to National Parks; to
make further provision for the control of pollution, the conservation of natural
resources and the conservation or enhancement of the environment; to make
provision for imposing obligations on certain persons in respect of certain
products or materials; to make provision in relation to fisheries; to make
provision for certain enactments to bind the Crown; to make provision with
respect to the application of certain enactments in relation to the Isles of Scilly;
and for connected purposes.*   [19th July 1995]

1—60. *((Parts I and II): these sections are outside the scope of this work.)*

PART III

NATIONAL PARKS

Purposes of National Parks

61. Purposes of National Parks

(1) In section 5 of the National Parks and Access to the Countryside Act 1949
(National Parks) for subsection (1) (which provides that Part II of that Act has effect
for the purpose of preserving and enhancing the natural beauty of the areas specified
in subsection (2) of that section and for the purpose of promoting their enjoyment by
the public) there shall be substituted—

"(1) The provisions of this Part of this Act shall have effect for the purpose—

(a) of conserving and enhancing the natural beauty, wildlife and cultural
heritage of the areas specified in the next following subsection; and

(b) of promoting opportunities for the understanding and enjoyment of the
special qualities of those areas by the public."

(2) The amendment made by subsection (1) above is without prejudice to the
continuing validity of any designation of an area as a National Park under subsection
(3) of that section.

(3) The following enactments (which refer to the purposes specified in section
5(1) of the National Parks and Access to the Countryside Act 1949), that is to say—

(a) sections 6(3) and (4)(g), 11 and 101(3) of that Act, and
(b) sections 2(5)(b) and 13(4) of the Countryside Act 1968,

shall have effect in accordance with subsection (4) below.

(4) In the application of any provision specified in subsection (3) above, any
reference to the purposes specified in subsection (1) of section 5 of the National
Parks and Access to the Countryside Act 1949—

(a) in relation to any particular National Park, shall be construed as a reference to the substituted purposes as from the time when a National Park authority becomes the local planning authority for that Park; and

(b) in relation to National Parks generally, shall be construed as a reference—

(i) to the original purposes, so far as relating to National Parks in the case of which the National Park authority has not become the local planning authority since the coming into force of this section, and

(ii) to the substituted purposes, so far as relating to National Parks in the case of which the National Park authority has become the local planning authority since the coming into force of this section.

(5) In subsection (4) above—

"original purposes" means the purposes specified in subsection (1) of section 5 of that Act, as originally enacted;

"substituted purposes" means the purposes specified in that subsection as substituted by subsection (1) above.   **[595A]**

NOTES

Commencement: 19 September 1995.

62. Duty of certain bodies and persons to have regard to the purposes for which National Parks are designated

(1) After section 11 of the National Parks and Access to the Countryside Act 1949 (general powers of local planning authorities in relation to National Parks) there shall be inserted—

"11A Duty of certain bodies and persons to have regard to the purposes for which National Parks are designated

(1) A National Park authority, in pursuing in relation to the National Park the purposes specified in subsection (1) of section five of this Act, shall seek to foster the economic and social well-being of local communities within the National Park, but without incurring significant expenditure in doing so, and shall for that purpose co-operate with local authorities and public bodies whose functions include the promotion of economic or social development within the area of the National Park.

(2) In exercising or performing any functions in relation to, or so as to affect, land in any National Park, a relevant authority shall have regard to the purposes specified in subsection (1) of section five of this Act and if it appears that there is a conflict between those purposes, shall attach greater weight to the purpose of conserving and enhancing the natural beauty, wildlife and cultural heritage of the area comprised in the National Park.

(3) For the purposes of this section "relevant authority" means—

(a) any Minister of the Crown,

(b) any public body,

(c) any statutory undertaker, or

(d) any person holding public office.

(4) In subsection (3) of this section—

"public body" includes—

(a) any local authority, joint board or joint committee;

(b) any National Park authority;

"public office" means—

    (a) an office under Her Majesty;

    (b) an office created or continued in existence by a public general Act of Parliament; or

    (c) an office the remuneration in respect of which is paid out of money provided by Parliament.

(5) In subsection (4) of this section, "joint board" and "joint committee" mean—

    (a) a joint or special planning board for a National Park reconstituted by order under paragraph 1 or 3 of Schedule 17 to the Local Government Act 1972, or a joint planning board within the meaning of section 2 of the Town and Country Planning Act 1990;

    (b) a joint committee appointed under section 102(1)(b) of the Local Government Act 1972.

(6) In this section, "local authority"—

    (a) in relation to England, means a county council, district council or parish council;

    (b) in relation to Wales, means a county council, county borough council, district council or community council."

(2) The duty imposed by subsection (1) of the section 11A inserted by subsection (1) above shall take effect, in the case of any particular National Park, as from the time when a National Park authority becomes the local planning authority for that Park. **[595B]**

NOTES
Commencement: 19 September 1995.

Establishment of National Park authorities

63. Establishment of National Park authorities

(1) The Secretary of State may—

    (a) in the case of any National Park for which there is an existing authority, or

    (b) in connection with the designation of any area as a new such Park,

by order establish an authority (to be known as "a National Park authority") to carry out in relation to that Park the functions conferred on such an authority by or under this Part.

(2) An order under this section may provide, in relation to any National Park for which there is an existing authority—

    (a) for the existing authority to cease to have any functions in relation to that Park as from the time when a National Park authority becomes the local planning authority for that Park;

    (b) for such (if any) of the functions of the existing authority as, by virtue of this Part, are not as from that time to be functions of the National Park authority for that Park to become functions of the person on whom they would be conferred if the area in question were not in a National Park; and

    (c) for the winding up of the existing authority and for that authority to cease to exist, or to be dissolved, as from such time as may be specified in the order.

(3) Subject to any order under subsection (4) below, where there is a variation of the area of a National Park for which there is or is to be a National Park authority, the Park for which that authority is or is to be the authority shall be deemed, as from the time when the variation takes effect, to be that area as varied.

(4) Where provision is made for the variation of the area of a National Park for which there is or is to be a National Park authority, the Secretary of State may by order make such transitional provision as he thinks fit with respect to—

(a) any functions which, in relation to any area that becomes part of the National Park, are by virtue of the variation to become functions of that authority; and

(b) any functions which, in relation to any area that ceases to be part of the National Park, are by virtue of the variation to become functions of a person other than that authority.

(5) Schedule 7 to this Act shall have effect with respect to National Park authorities. **[595C]**

NOTES
Commencement: 19 September 1995.

64. National Park authorities in Wales

(1) Where a National Park planning board has been constituted for the area of any particular existing National Park in Wales, the Secretary of State may exercise his power under section 63 above to establish a National Park authority in relation to that National Park by making an order under that section designating for the body corporate constituted as that board a date earlier than 31st March 1997 on which that body—

(a) shall cease to be a National Park planning board, and

(b) shall be constituted the National Park authority in relation to that National Park,

without affecting its corporate status (and an order made under or by virtue of that section may make provision re-naming that body accordingly).

(2) Any order under—

(a) paragraph 3A of Schedule 17 to the 1972 Act (special planning boards), or

(b) section 2(1B) of the Town and Country Planning Act 1990 (joint planning boards),

relating to the body corporate constituted as the National Park planning board in question shall have effect on and after the designated date for that body as an order under section 63 above relating to that body in its capacity as the National Park authority in relation to the National Park in question.

(3) For the purposes of any order establishing a National Park authority under section 63 above by virtue of subsection (1) above, or any order which, by virtue of subsection (2) above, has effect as an order under that section—

(a) the requirements of paragraph 2(3) of Schedule 7 to this Act with respect to consultation with councils for principal areas shall, by virtue of the establishment of the National Park planning board, be deemed to have been complied with as respects any provision of the order;

(b) in the case of any member of the National Park planning board immediately before the designated date who was holding that office by virtue of his

appointment as such by the Secretary of State under and in accordance
with paragraph 11 of Schedule 17 to the 1972 Act (which requires prior
consultation), the appointment shall, on and after the designated date, have
effect for the remainder of the period for which it was made as an
appointment as a member of the National Park authority made by the
Secretary of State in accordance with paragraph 4(1) of Schedule 7 to this
Act;

(c) in the case of any other member of the National Park planning board
immediately before the designated date who is on that date a member of a
principal council for an area which includes the whole or any part of the
National Park in question, his appointment as a member of that board
shall, on and after the designated date, have effect for the remainder of the
period for which it was made as an appointment as a local authority
member of the National Park authority made in accordance with paragraph
2 of that Schedule; and

(d) any other requirement, whether statutory or otherwise, which must be
complied with in connection with the establishment of a National Park
authority shall be deemed to have been complied with by virtue of the
establishment of the National Park planning board;

and, except as provided by paragraphs (b) and (c) above, no person who is a member
of the National Park planning board immediately before the designated date shall, by
virtue of the order, become a member of the National Park authority.

(4) The functions of a National Park planning board shall include the duty to
take such steps as it considers necessary to enable it (that is to say, the body corporate
constituted as that board) on being constituted the National Park authority in relation
to the National Park in question by an order made by virtue of subsection (1) above,
to perform its functions as a National Park authority on and after the designated date;
and the functions conferred on such a board by this subsection—

(a) shall be exercisable before (as well as on or after) 1st April 1996; and
(b) are in addition to any other functions which are exercisable by such a
board before that date by virtue of paragraph 13 of Schedule 17 to the
Local Government (Wales) Act 1994.

(5) The functions of a principal council for an area which includes the whole or
any part of the area of a National Park planning board shall include the duty to take
such steps as it considers necessary to enable the body corporate constituted as that
board, on being constituted the National Park authority in relation to the National
Park in question by an order made by virtue of subsection (1) above, to perform
those functions which would, apart from the order, be exercisable by a principal
council but which will become functions of that body, as the National Park authority,
on the designated date.

(6) Where the Secretary of State—

(a) has taken any steps with a view to, or otherwise in connection with, the
establishment of a National Park planning board for the area of an existing
National Park in Wales (''the proposed board''), but
(b) decides not to proceed with the establishment of the proposed board and
to establish instead a National Park authority in relation to that National
Park (''the proposed authority''), and
(c) the proposed authority is, or is to be, established before 31st March 1997,

the doing of anything by or in relation to the Secretary of State (other than the
making by the Secretary of State of an instrument of a legislative character) with a
view to, or otherwise in connection with, establishing the proposed board shall be
treated, as respects the proposed authority, as the doing of any corresponding or

reasonably similar thing falling to be done for the purposes of, or otherwise in connection with, the establishment of that authority.

(7) Without prejudice to the generality of subsection (6) above, in any case falling within paragraphs (a) to (c) of that subsection—

(a) any consultation with a principal council after 15th December 1994 by the Secretary of State as respects the proposed board (whether or not required by or under any enactment) shall be deemed, as respects the proposed authority, to have been carried out for the purposes of the consultation with councils for principal areas required by paragraph 2(3) of Schedule 7 to this Act;

(b) anything done by or in relation to the Secretary of State for the purposes of the consultation required by paragraph 11 of Schedule 17 to the 1972 Act (appointment of members by Secretary of State) preparatory to the appointment of a person as a member of the proposed board shall be deemed, as respects the proposed authority, to have been done for the purposes of the consultation required by paragraph 4(1) of Schedule 7 to this Act preparatory to the appointment of that person as a member of that authority;

(c) anything done by or in relation to the Secretary of State (other than the making by the Secretary of State of an instrument of a legislative character) for the purposes of, or otherwise in connection with, any other requirement, whether statutory or otherwise, of a consultative or procedural nature—

(i) which relates to a National Park planning board, and
(ii) for which there is a corresponding or reasonably similar requirement which relates to a National Park authority,

shall be treated, as respects the proposed authority, as done for the purposes of, or otherwise in connection with, that other corresponding or reasonably similar requirement.

(8) Section 54 of the Local Government (Wales) Act 1994 (powers to make incidental, consequential, transitional or supplemental provision) shall have effect as if this Part were contained in that Act, except that subsection (2)(e) of that section shall have effect as if this Part were contained in an Act passed in the same Session as that Act.

(9) In this section—

"the designated date", in the case of any body corporate constituted as a National Park planning board which becomes, or is to become, a National Park authority by virtue of this section, means the date designated by virtue of subsection (1) above in the order relating to that body;

"existing National Park" means a National Park in respect of which there was in force on 15th December 1994 an order under section 5 of the National Parks and Access to the Countryside Act 1949 (designation of areas as National Parks);

"National Park planning board" means—

(a) a special planning board constituted by order under paragraph 3A of Schedule 17 to the 1972 Act to discharge, as respects the area of a National Park in Wales, the functions to which Part I of that Schedule applies, or

(b) a joint planning board constituted by order under subsection (1B) of section 2 of the Town and Country Planning Act 1990 for a united district comprising the area of a National Park in Wales.   **[595D]**

NOTES
Commencement: 19 September 1995.

Functions of National Park authorities

65. General purposes and powers

(1) This Part so far as it relates to the establishment and functions of National Park authorities shall have effect for the purposes specified in section 5(1) of the National Parks and Access to the Countryside Act 1949 (purposes of conserving and enhancing the natural beauty, wildlife and cultural heritage of National Parks and of promoting opportunities for the understanding and enjoyment of the special qualities of those Parks by the public).

(2) Sections 37 and 38 of the Countryside Act 1968 (general duties as to the protection of interests of the countryside and the avoidance of pollution) shall apply to National Park authorities as they apply to local authorities.

(3) The functions of a National Park authority in the period (if any) between the time when it is established and the time when it becomes the local planning authority for the relevant Park shall be confined to the taking of such steps as the authority, after consultation with the Secretary of State and any existing authority for that Park, considers appropriate for securing that it is able properly to carry out its functions after that time.

(4) In the application of subsection (3) above in the case of a National Park authority established in relation to a National Park in Wales, the reference to any existing authority for that Park shall have effect as respects consultation carried out during so much of that period as falls before 1st April 1996 as including a reference to any principal council whose area is wholly or partly comprised in that Park.

(5) The powers of a National Park authority shall include power to do anything which, in the opinion of that authority, is calculated to facilitate, or is conducive or incidental to—

(a) the accomplishment of the purposes mentioned in subsection (1) above; or

(b) the carrying out of any functions conferred on it by virtue of any other enactment.

(6) The powers conferred on a National Park authority by subsection (5) above shall not include either—

(a) power to do anything in contravention of any restriction imposed by virtue of this Part in relation to any express power of the authority; or

(b) a power to raise money (whether by borrowing or otherwise) in a manner which is not authorised apart from that subsection;

but the things that may be done in exercise of those powers shall not be treated as excluding anything by reason only that it involves the expenditure, borrowing or lending of money or the acquisition or disposal of any property or rights.

(7) Schedule 8 to this Act shall have effect with respect to the supplemental and incidental powers of a National Park authority. **[595E]**

NOTES
Commencement: 19 September 1995.

66. National Park Management Plans

(1) Subject to subsection (2) below, every National Park authority shall, within three years after its operational date, prepare and publish a plan, to be known as a National Park Management Plan, which formulates its policy for the management of the relevant Park and for the carrying out of its functions in relation to that Park.

(2) A National Park authority for a Park wholly or mainly comprising any area which, immediately before the authority's operational date, was or was included in an area for which there was a National Park Plan prepared and published under paragraph 18 of Schedule 17 to the 1972 Act (National Park plans) shall not be required to prepare a Management Plan under subsection (1) above if, within six months of that date, it adopts the existing National Park Plan as its Management Plan and publishes notice that it has done so.

(3) Where a National Park authority is proposing to adopt a plan under subsection (2) above, it may review the plan before adopting it and shall do so if the plan would have fallen to be reviewed under paragraph 18 of Schedule 17 to the 1972 Act in the period of twelve months beginning with the authority's operational date.

(4) A National Park authority shall review its National Park Management Plan within the period of five years of its operational date and, after the first review, at intervals of not more than five years.

(5) Where a National Park authority has adopted a plan under subsection (2) above as its National Park Management Plan and has not reviewed that Plan before adopting it, the first review of that Plan under subsection (4) above shall take place no later than the time when the adopted plan would otherwise have fallen to be reviewed under paragraph 18 of Schedule 17 to the 1972 Act.

(6) Where a National Park authority reviews any plan under this section, it shall—

    (a) determine on that review whether it would be expedient to amend the plan and what (if any) amendments would be appropriate;

    (b) make any amendments that it considers appropriate; and

    (c) publish a report on the review specifying any amendments made.

(7) A National Park authority which is proposing to publish, adopt or review any plan under this section shall—

    (a) give notice of the proposal to every principal council whose area is wholly or partly comprised in the relevant Park and, according to whether that Park is in England or in Wales, to the Countryside Commission and the Nature Conservancy Council for England or to the Countryside Council for Wales;

    (b) send a copy of the plan, together (where appropriate) with any proposed amendments of the plan, to every body to which notice of the proposal is required to be given by paragraph (a) above, and

    (c) take into consideration any observations made by any such body.

(8) A National Park authority shall send to the Secretary of State a copy of every plan, notice or report which it is required to publish under this section.

(9) In this section "operational date", in relation to a National Park authority, means the date on which the authority becomes the local planning authority for the relevant Park.   **[595F]**

NOTES
  Commencement: 19 September 1995.

67. National Park authority to be local planning authority

(1) ...

(2) The Secretary of State may by order make provision—

    (a) for applying Chapter I of Part II of that Act of 1990 (unitary development plans), instead of provisions of Chapter II of that Part (structure and local plans), in relation to the area of any National Park; or

    (b) for applying Chapter II of that Part in relation to the area of such a Park—

        (i) as if functions under that Chapter of a planning authority of any description were functions of such public authority as may be specified in the order (and not of the National Park authority); and

        (ii) as if that Part had effect with such other modifications as may be so specified in relation to the carrying out of those functions by an authority so specified.

(3) Without prejudice to any power conferred by virtue of section 75 below, the Secretary of State shall have power by order, for the purposes of any provision made by virtue of this section, to modify the provisions of Part II of that Act of 1990 (development plans) in relation to any such area of a local planning authority as, but for any exclusion by virtue of section 4A of that Act, would include the whole or any part of a National Park.

(4) References in this section to provisions of Part II of that Act of 1990 include references to any provisions for modifying those provisions which are contained in any enactment passed after this Act.

    (5) ...   [595G]

NOTES
  Commencement: 19 September 1995.
  Sub-ss (1), (5) insert the Town and Country Planning Act 1990, ss 4A, 147A respectively.
  That Act of 1990: ie the Town and Country Planning Act 1990.

68. Planning authority functions under National Parks legislation etc

(1) Where a National Park authority is the local planning authority for any National Park, section 184 of the 1972 Act and paragraph 37 of Schedule 17 to that Act (functions under certain legislation relating to the National Parks and the countryside) shall not apply as respects that Park in relation to any of the functions conferred by or under—

    (a) the National Parks and Access to the Countryside Act 1949 ("the 1949 Act"), or

    (b) the Countryside Act 1968 ("the 1968 Act"),

on a planning authority of any description.

(2) In consequence of subsection (1) above, but subject to subsections (3) to (7) below—

    (a) functions which are conferred on a local planning authority by or under the 1949 Act or the 1968 Act, and the functions conferred on a county planning authority (or, in relation to Wales, a local planning authority) by section 69 of the 1949 Act (suspension of access to avoid risk of fire), shall, as respects the whole or any part of a National Park for which a

National Park authority is the local planning authority, be functions of that authority and not of any other authority;

(b) references in those Acts to a local planning authority whose area consists of or includes the whole or any part of a National Park shall be construed, in relation to any National Park for which a National Park authority is the local planning authority, as references to the National Park authority; and

(c) other references in those Acts to a local planning authority and the references to a local authority in section 103 of the 1949 Act and sections 10 and 43 to 45 of the 1968 Act (which contain provision applying in relation to local authorities in their capacity as local planning authorities) shall have effect accordingly.

(3) Section 11 of the 1949 Act (which makes provision in relation to a local planning authority that corresponds to provision made by section 65 above in relation to a National Park authority) shall not apply in relation to any National Park authority.

(4) The functions conferred by or under section 12 of the 1949 Act or section 12 of the 1968 Act (facilities for National Parks) which are exercisable by virtue of this section by a National Park authority in a National Park—

(a) shall be exercisable by that authority outside the relevant Park on any land in the neighbourhood of that Park; but

(b) shall be so exercisable only under arrangements made with the local planning authority for the area where they are exercised.

(5) Sections 61 to 63 of the 1949 Act (survey of access requirements and action in response to the survey) shall have effect in accordance with subsection (2) above as respects the area of any National Park for which a National Park authority has become the local planning authority—

(a) in the case of a Park designated after the commencement of this section, as if section 61(1) applied with the substitution for the reference to the commencement of that Act of a reference to the time when that authority became the local planning authority for that Park;

(b) as if no area were required by virtue of subsection (3) of section 61 of that Act, or of any previous review under that section, to be excluded from any area to be reviewed by virtue of paragraph (a) above; and

(c) in the case of a Park designated before the commencement of this section, as if—

(i) the power (if any) to make a resolution for the purposes of the proviso to that subsection (3) as respects any part of the area of the Park which has not previously been reviewed under that section, and

(ii) the functions which, where such a resolution has been so made, are conferred on the authority which made it or on any authority which has conducted a review in pursuance of the resolution,

were a power or, as the case may be, functions of the National Park authority, and not of any other authority.

(6) The following functions, so far as exercisable by a National Park authority in relation to land or countryside in a National Park in England for which that authority is the local planning authority, that is to say—

(a) those conferred by or under section 89 of the 1949 Act (planting of trees and treatment of derelict land), and

(b) those conferred by section 10 of the 1968 Act (camping and picnic sites),

shall be exercisable in relation to so much of that Park as is comprised in a district for which there is a district council, concurrently with the National Park authority, by that district council.

(7) For the purposes of any enactment relating to the functions of a district planning authority, the functions of a district council by virtue of subsection (6) above shall be deemed to be conferred on them as a district planning authority and as if the district were the area for which they are such an authority.

(8) The following powers, that is to say—

   (a) those conferred on a local authority by or under section 92 of the 1949 Act (wardens), and
   (b) those conferred on a local authority by or under section 41 of the 1968 Act (byelaws),

so far as they are conferred in relation to any of the functions which by virtue of this section are functions of a National Park authority as respects the relevant Park, shall be exercisable by that authority and also, in the case of those conferred by or under section 41 of the 1968 Act, by a district council in relation to that council's functions by virtue of subsection (6)(b) above, but not by any other authority.

(9) Section 104 of the 1949 Act (general provisions as to appropriation and disposal of land), except subsection (11), shall have effect as if references in that section to a local authority included references to a National Park authority.

(10) For the purposes of any functions conferred on a National Park authority by virtue of this section references in any enactment to the area of the authority shall be construed as references to the relevant Park.   **[595H]**

NOTES
Commencement: 19 September 1995.

69. Planning authority functions under the Wildlife and Countryside Act 1981

(1) A National Park authority which is the local planning authority for any National Park, and not any other authority, shall have all the functions under the Wildlife and Countryside Act 1981 which are conferred as respects that Park on a planning authority of any description.

(2) Accordingly—

   (a) a National Park authority shall be the relevant authority for the purposes of sections 39, 41 and 50 of that Act (management agreements and duties of agriculture Ministers in relation to the countryside) as respects any land in any National Park for which that authority is the local planning authority; and
   (b) section 52(2) of that Act (construction of references to a local planning authority) shall not apply as respects any National Park for which a National Park authority is the local planning authority.

(3) Section 43 of that Act (maps of National Parks) shall have effect in accordance with the preceding provisions of this section—

   (a) in the case of a National Park designated after the commencement of this section, as if the relevant date for the purposes of that section were the date on which a National Park authority becomes the local planning authority for the Park; and
   (b) in any other case, as if the function of reviewing and revising any map of a part of the Park in question included a power, in pursuance of the review

and revisions, to consolidate that map with other maps prepared under that section as respects other parts of that Park.

(4) In section 44 of that Act (grants and loans for purposes of National Parks), after subsection (1) there shall be inserted the following subsection—

"(1A) Subsection (1) above shall not apply in relation to any National Park for which a National Park authority is the local planning authority; but the National Park authority for such a Park may give financial assistance by way of grant or loan, or partly in one way and partly in the other, to any person in respect of expenditure incurred by him in doing anything which, in the opinion of the authority, is conducive to the attainment in the Park in question of any of the purposes mentioned in section 5(1) of the 1949 Act (purposes of conserving and enhancing the natural beauty, wildlife and cultural heritage of National Parks and of promoting opportunities for the understanding and enjoyment of the special qualities of those Parks by the public)."   **[595I]**

NOTES
Commencement: 19 September 1995.

70. Other statutory functions

In addition to its functions under the enactments mentioned in sections 67 to 69 above and to such of its functions under any other enactment as are conferred by virtue of its being a local planning authority within the meaning of the Town and Country Planning Act 1990, a National Park authority shall have the further miscellaneous functions conferred on it by virtue of Schedule 9 to this Act.   **[595J]**

NOTES
Commencement: 19 September 1995.

Finances of National Park authorities

71. National Park authorities to be levying bodies

(1) A National Park authority shall have power in respect of every financial year beginning after the establishment of that authority to issue levies to the councils by whom the local authority members of that authority fall to be appointed.

(2) Subject to the following provisions of this section, a levy issued by virtue of this section shall be issued in accordance with regulations under section 74 of the Local Government Finance Act 1988 (power to make regulations authorising a levying body to issue a levy); and, accordingly, a National Park authority shall be deemed to be a levying body within the meaning of that section.

(3) Subject to any maximum specified in or determined in accordance with any regulations under that section 74, the amount of the levies issued by a National Park authority in respect of any financial year shall be equal to the sum by which the aggregate of the amounts specified in subsection (4) below is exceeded by the aggregate of the sums which it estimates it will require in respect of that year for the following purposes, that is to say—

(a) meeting the expenditure of the authority which will fall to be charged for that year to any revenue account;

(b) making such provision as may be appropriate for meeting contingencies the expenditure on which would fall to be so charged;

(c) securing the availability to the authority of adequate working balances on its revenue accounts; and

(d) providing the authority with the funds required for covering any deficit carried forward from a previous financial year in any revenue account.

(4) The amounts mentioned in subsection (3) above in relation to any financial year are—

(a) any amounts to be received by the authority in respect of that year by way of grant under section 72 below;

(b) the authority's estimate of the amounts which are likely for that year to be credited to any revenue account in respect of sums payable to the authority for things done in the course of, or in connection with, the carrying out of its functions; and

(c) the authority's estimate of the amounts not falling within paragraph (a) or (b) above which apart from this section are, or are likely to be, available to it for that year for the purposes mentioned in subsection (3) above.

(5) Where agreement as to the apportionment of the amount to be raised by a National Park authority in respect of any financial year by way of levies is entered into, before 1st December in the immediately preceding financial year, by all the authorities to whom the levies in respect of that year may be issued by that authority, that amount shall be apportioned between those authorities in accordance with the agreement, instead of in accordance with any provision made by virtue of that section 74.

(6) Regulations under that section 74 may include provision for requiring an authority to anticipate a levy by virtue of this section when making any calculations which fall, for the financial year following that in which any National Park authority is established, to be made (whether originally or by way of substitute) under section 32 or 43 of the Local Government Finance Act 1992 (calculation of budget requirement).

(7) A National Park authority shall not by virtue of this section be a local authority within the meaning of the Town and Country Planning Act 1990. **[595K]**

NOTES
Commencement: 19 September 1995.

72. National Park grant

(1) The Secretary of State may make grants to a National Park authority for such purposes, of such amounts and on such terms and such conditions as he thinks fit.

(2) Before determining the amount of any grant which he proposes to make to a National Park authority under this section, or the purpose for which it is to be made, the Secretary of State shall consult, according to whether the relevant Park is in England or in Wales, either the Countryside Commission or the Countryside Council for Wales.

(3) The consent of the Treasury shall be required for the making of a grant under this section. **[595L]**

NOTES
Commencement: 19 September 1995.

73. Capital finances and borrowing

In section 39(1) of the Local Government and Housing Act 1989 (which specifies the authorities to which the provisions of Part IV of that Act relating to capital accounts and borrowing powers apply), after paragraph (i) there shall be inserted—

"(ia) a National Park authority;". **[595M]**

NOTES
Commencement: 19 September 1995.

74. Validation of certain grants paid to local authorities in respect of expenditure relating to National Parks

(1) No payment made for any year beginning on or after 1st April 1990 and ending on or before 31st March 1996 by the Secretary of State by way of grant to the council of a county or a metropolitan district in respect of the council's expenditure or estimated expenditure in connection with National Parks shall be regarded as made otherwise than under and in accordance with the relevant enactments by reason only of—

(a) the aggregate amount of such grants for the year to such councils not having been duly prescribed;

(b) the method of determining the proportion of such aggregate amount payable to that council not having been duly prescribed; or

(c) payment of the grant being, or having been, made—

(i) otherwise than in accordance with an approved Rate Support Grant Report or such a Report as varied by an approved supplementary report for the year; or

(ii) without there being an approved Rate Support Grant Report for the year.

(2) Any reference in this section to a payment by way of grant made under and in accordance with the relevant enactments is a reference to a payment of grant made under section 7 of the Local Government Act 1974 (supplementary grants towards expenditure with respect to National Parks) in accordance with the provisions of that section and those of section 60 or 61 of the Local Government, Planning and Land Act 1980 (rate support grant reports and supplementary reports) as they apply in relation to grants under the said section 7.

(3) In this section—

"approved Rate Support Grant Report" means a Rate Support Grant Report which has been laid before and approved by a resolution of the House of Commons;

"approved supplementary report" means a supplementary report which has been laid before and approved by a resolution of the House of Commons;

"duly prescribed" means prescribed by a Rate Support Grant Report or a supplementary report;

"Rate Support Grant Report" means a Rate Support Grant Report made under section 60 of the Local Government, Planning and Land Act 1980;

"supplementary report" means a supplementary report made under section 61 of that Act; and

"year" means a period of 12 months beginning with 1st April. **[595N]**

NOTES
Commencement: 19 July 1995.

Supplemental provisions

75. Powers to make orders

(1) This section applies to every power of the Secretary of State under the preceding provisions of this Part to make an order.

(2) The powers to which this section applies shall, in each case, be exercisable by statutory instrument; and, except in the case of a statutory instrument made by virtue of section 64 above which only—

    (a) designates a date,

    (b) specifies a time for the purposes of section 4A of the Town and Country Planning Act 1990,

    (c) renames a body,

    (d) makes provision under paragraph 2 of Schedule 7 to this Act—

        (i) for excluding a council from the councils by whom the local authority members of a National Park authority are to be appointed, or

        (ii) for so increasing the number of local authority members of a National Park authority to be appointed by any council as to secure that the number of local authority members of that authority remains unchanged notwithstanding any such exclusion of a council, or

    (e) makes provision under section 63(2) above,

any such statutory instrument shall be subject to annulment in pursuance of a resolution of either House of Parliament.

(3) The powers to which this section applies shall, in each case, include power to make such incidental, supplemental, consequential and transitional provision as the Secretary of State thinks necessary or expedient.

(4) A power of the Secretary of State by an order under this Part to make incidental, supplemental, consequential or transitional provision shall include power for any incidental, supplemental, consequential or, as the case may be, transitional purpose—

    (a) to apply with or without modifications,

    (b) to extend, exclude or modify, or

    (c) to repeal or revoke with or without savings,

any enactment or any instrument made under any enactment.

(5) The provision that may be made for incidental, supplemental, consequential or transitional purposes in the case of any order under this Part which—

    (a) establishes a National Park authority or winds up the existing authority for any National Park, or

    (b) otherwise has the effect of transferring functions from one person to another or of providing for functions to become exercisable concurrently by two or more persons or to cease to be so exercisable,

shall include provision for the transfer of property, rights and liabilities from one person to another.

(6) A power of the Secretary of State under this Part to provide by order for the transfer of any property, rights or liabilities, or to make transitional provision in connection with any such transfer or with any order by which functions become or cease to be exercisable by any authority, shall include power to provide, in particular—

    (a) for the management and custody of any transferred property (whether real or personal);

(b) for any liabilities transferred to include liabilities under any enactment;

(c) for legal proceedings commenced by or against any person to be continued by or against a person to whom property, rights or liabilities are transferred or, as the case may be, any authority by whom any functions are to become exercisable;

(d) for the transfer of staff, compensation for loss of office, pensions and other staffing matters; and

(e) for treating any person to whom a transfer of property, rights or liabilities is made or, as the case may be, by whom any functions are to become exercisable as, for some or all purposes, the same person in law as the person from whom the transfer is made or the authority by whom the functions have previously been exercisable.

(7) The powers to which this section applies shall, in each case, include power to make different provision for different cases, including different provision for different areas or localities and for different authorities.

(8) The powers to which this section applies shall be without prejudice to any powers conferred by Part II of the Local Government Act 1992 or any other enactment.

(9) In this section "enactment" includes an enactment contained in an Act passed after this Act. **[595O]**

NOTES

Commencement: 19 September 1995.

76. Agreements as to incidental matters

(1) Any public authorities affected by an order under this Part may from time to time make agreements with respect to—

(a) any property, income, rights, liabilities or expenses (so far as affected by the order) of the parties to the agreement; or

(b) any financial relations between those parties.

(2) Such an agreement may provide—

(a) for the transfer or retention of any property, rights and liabilities, with or without conditions, and for the joint use of any property;

(b) for the making of payments by any party to the agreement in respect of—

(i) property, rights and liabilities transferred or retained,

(ii) the joint use of any property, or

(iii) remuneration or compensation payable to any person;

and

(c) for the making of any such payment either by way of a capital sum or of a terminable annuity.

(3) In default of agreement as to any disputed matter, the matter shall be referred to the arbitration of a single arbitrator agreed on by the parties or, in default of agreement, appointed by the Secretary of State; and the award of the arbitrator may make any provision that might be contained in an agreement under this section.

(4) In subsection (3) above "disputed matter" means any matter which—

(a) might be the subject of provision contained in an agreement under this section; and

(b) is the subject of such a dispute between two or more public authorities as is not resolved by or under provision contained in any order under this Part. **[595P]**

NOTES
Commencement: 19 September 1995.

77. Isles of Scilly

(1) This Part shall have effect in relation to the Isles of Scilly subject to any such modifications as may be provided for by the Secretary of State by order made by statutory instrument.

(2) Before making an order under this section the Secretary of State shall consult with the Council of the Isles of Scilly.

(3) The power to make an order under this section shall include power to make such incidental, supplemental, consequential or transitional provision as the Secretary of State thinks necessary or expedient. **[595Q]**

NOTES
Commencement: 19 September 1995.

78. Minor and consequential amendments relating to National Parks

The enactments mentioned in Schedule 10 to this Act shall have effect subject to the amendments contained in that Schedule (being minor amendments and consequential amendments in connection with the provisions of this Part). **[595R]**

NOTES
Commencement: to be appointed.

79. Interpretation of Part III

(1) In this Part, except in so far as the context otherwise requires—

"the 1972 Act" means the Local Government Act 1972;
"existing authority", in relation to a National Park, means—

(a) any such joint or special planning board for that Park or for any area wholly or partly comprised in that Park as was reconstituted by an order under paragraph 1 or 3 of Schedule 17 to the 1972 Act or constituted by an order under paragraph 3A of that Schedule or section 2(1B) of the Town and Country Planning Act 1990; or
(b) any National Park Committee for that Park or for any such area;

"liability", in relation to the transfer of liabilities from one person to another, does not include any criminal liability;
"principal council" and "principal area" have the same meanings as in the 1972 Act;
"public authority" means any local authority within the meaning of the 1972 Act (including any such authority in their capacity as a local planning authority), any National Park authority, any existing authority for a National Park, any joint authority or residuary body established under Part II of the Local Government Act 1992, any joint authority established under section 34 of the Local Government (Wales) Act 1994 or the Residuary Body for Wales established by section 39 of that Act;

"the relevant Park", in relation to a National Park authority, means the area for which that authority is or is to be the National Park authority.

(2) Where—

(a) any enactment that is applied by virtue of this Part in relation to National Park authorities refers, or falls to be construed as referring, to any other enactment, and

(b) that other enactment is also one which is so applied,

the reference shall be construed (so far as it would not be so construed apart from this subsection) as including a reference to the other enactment as it is applied in relation to National Park authorities.   **[595S]**

NOTES
Commencement: 19 September 1995.

80—91. ((*Part IV): these sections are outside the scope of this work.*)

PART V

MISCELLANEOUS, GENERAL AND SUPPLEMENTAL PROVISIONS

92—95. (*These sections are outside the scope of this work.*)

Mineral planning permissions

96. Mineral planning permissions

(1) Schedules 13 and 14 to this Act shall have effect.

(2) This section, those Schedules as they apply to England and Wales, and the 1990 Act shall have effect as if this section and those Schedules (as so applying) were included in Part III of that Act.

(3) This section, those Schedules as they apply to Scotland, and the 1972 Act shall have effect as if this section and those Schedules (as so applying) were included in Part III of that Act.

(4) Section 105 of the 1990 Act and section 251A of the 1972 Act shall cease to have effect.

(5) Without prejudice to the generality of sections 59 to 61 of the 1990 Act or, as the case may be, section 21 of the 1972 Act, a development order may make, in relation to any planning permission which is granted by a development order for minerals development, provision similar to any provision made by Schedule 13 or 14 to this Act.

(6) In this section and those Schedules—

"the 1972 Act" means the Town and Country Planning (Scotland) Act 1972;

"the 1990 Act" means the Town and Country Planning Act 1990;

"the 1991 Act" means the Planning and Compensation Act 1991; and

"minerals development" means development consisting of the winning and working of minerals, or involving the depositing of mineral waste. **[595T]**

NOTES
Commencement: to be appointed.

97—118. (*These sections are outside the scope of this work.*)

Miscellaneous and supplemental

119—124. (*These sections are outside the scope of this work.*)

125. Short title, commencement, extent, etc

(1) This Act may be cited as the Environment Act 1995.

(2) Part III of this Act, except for section 78, paragraph 7(2) of Schedule 7 and Schedule 10, shall come into force at the end of the period of two months beginning with the day on which this Act is passed.

(3) Except as provided in subsection (2) above and except for this section, section 74 above and paragraphs 76(8)(a) and 135 of Schedule 22 to this Act (which come into force on the passing of this Act) and the repeal of sub-paragraph (1) of paragraph 22 of Schedule 10 to this Act (which comes into force in accordance with sub-paragraph (7) of that paragraph) this Act shall come into force on such day as the Secretary of State may specify by order made by statutory instrument; and different days may be so specified for different provisions or for different purposes of the same provision.

(4) Without prejudice to the provisions of Schedule 23 to this Act, an order under subsection (3) above may make such transitional provisions and savings as appear to the Secretary of State necessary or expedient in connection with any provision brought into force by the order.

(5) The power conferred by subsection (4) above includes power to modify any enactment contained in this or any other Act.

(6) An Order in Council under paragraph 1(1)(b) of Schedule 1 to the Northern Ireland Act 1974 (legislation for Northern Ireland in the interim period) which states that it is made only for purposes corresponding to those of section 98 of this Act—

(a) shall not be subject to paragraph 1(4) and (5) of that Schedule (affirmative resolution of both Houses of Parliament); but

(b) shall be subject to annulment in pursuance of a resolution of either House of Parliament.

(7) Except for this section and any amendment or repeal by this Act of any provision contained in—

(a) the Parliamentary Commissioner Act 1967,

(b) the Sea Fish (Conservation) Act 1967,

(c) the House of Commons Disqualification Act 1975, or

(d) the Northern Ireland Assembly Disqualification Act 1975,

this Act shall not extend to Northern Ireland.

(8) Part III of this Act, and Schedule 24 to this Act so far as relating to that Part, extends to England and Wales only.

(9) Section 106 of, and Schedule 16 to, this Act extend to Scotland only.

(10) Subject to the foregoing provisions of this section and to any express provision made by this Act to the contrary, any amendment, repeal or revocation made by this Act shall have the same extent as the enactment or instrument to which it relates.   **[595U]**

NOTES
Commencement: 19 July 1995.

SCHEDULES
(Schs 1-6 are outside the scope of this work.)

SCHEDULE 7

Section 63

NATIONAL PARK AUTHORITIES

Status and constitution of authorities

1.—(1) A National Park authority shall be a body corporate.

(2) A National Park authority shall consist of—

(a) such number of local authority members as may be specified in the relevant order; and

(b) such number of members to be appointed by the Secretary of State as may be so specified.

(3) In the case of a National Park authority for a National Park in England, such number as may be specified in the relevant order of the number of members of the authority to be appointed by the Secretary of State shall be parish members.

(4) The number specified in the relevant order for any National Park authority as the number of members of that authority who are to be appointed by the Secretary of State shall—

(a) as respects any National Park authority for a National Park in England, be two less than the number of local authority members specified in the order; and

(b) as respects any National Park authority for a National Park in Wales, be equal to half the number of local authority members specified in the order.

(5) As respects any National Park authority for a National Park in England, the number specified in the relevant order as the number of parish members to be appointed by the Secretary of State shall be one less than one half of the total number of the members of the authority to be appointed by the Secretary of State.

(6) Accordingly—

(a) in the case of a National Park authority for a National Park in England, the effect of the relevant order shall be such that the total number of members of the authority will be an even number which is not a whole number multiple of four; and

(b) in the case of a National Park authority for a National Park in Wales, the number of local authority members specified in the relevant order shall be an even number.

[595V]

NOTES
Commencement: 19 September 1995.

Local authority members

2.—(1) The local authority members of a National Park authority shall be appointed by such of the councils for the principal areas wholly or partly comprised in the relevant Park as may be specified in or determined under the relevant order.

(2) Each of the councils who are to appoint the local authority members of a National Park authority shall be entitled to appoint such number of those members as may be so specified or determined and to make any appointment required by reason of a vacancy arising in respect of a member appointed by that council.

(3) Before making any provision by the relevant order as to—

(a) the number of members of a National Park authority who are to be local authority members,

(b) the councils by whom the local authority members of a National Park authority are to be appointed, or

(c) the number of members to be appointed by each such council,

the Secretary of State shall consult the council for every principal area the whole or any part of which is comprised in the relevant Park; and the Secretary of State may make provision for excluding the council for any such area from the councils by whom the local authority members of a National Park authority are to be appointed only at the request of that council.

(4) A person shall not be appointed as a local authority member of a National Park authority unless he is a member of a principal council the area of which is wholly or partly comprised in the relevant Park; and, in appointing local authority members of a National Park authority, a principal council shall have regard to the desirability of appointing members of the council who represent wards, or (in Wales) electoral divisions, situated wholly or partly within the relevant Park.

(5) Subject to the following provisions of this Schedule, where a person who qualifies for his appointment by virtue of his membership of any council is appointed as a local authority member of a National Park authority—

(a) he shall hold office from the time of his appointment until he ceases to be a member of that council; but

(b) his appointment may, before any such cessation, be terminated for the purposes of, and in accordance with, sections 15 to 17 of the Local Government and Housing Act 1989 (political balance).

(6) Sub-paragraph (5)(a) above shall have effect so as to terminate the term of office of a person who, on retiring from any council, immediately becomes such a member again as a newly elected councillor; but a person who so becomes a member again shall be eligible for re-appointment to the National Park authority.

(7) The appointment of any person as a local authority member of a National Park authority may provide that he is not to be treated for the purposes of sub-paragraph (5) above as qualifying for his appointment by virtue of his membership of any council other than that specified in the appointment.

(8) In paragraph 2(1) of Schedule 1 to the Local Government and Housing Act 1989 (bodies to which appointments have to be made taking account of political balance), after paragraph (b) there shall be inserted the following paragraph—

"(ba) a National Park authority;". **[595W]**

NOTES
Commencement: 19 September 1995.

Parish members of English National Park authorities

3.—(1) The parish members of an English National Park authority shall be appointed by the Secretary of State.

(2) A person shall not be appointed as a parish member of an English National Park authority unless he is—

(a) a member of the parish council for a parish the whole or any part of which is comprised in the relevant Park; or

(b) the chairman of the parish meeting of a parish—

(i) which does not have a separate parish council; and

(ii) the whole or any part of which is comprised in the relevant Park.

(3) Subject to the following provisions of this Schedule, where a person who qualifies for his appointment by virtue of his membership of a parish council is appointed as a parish member of an English National Park authority, he shall hold office from the time of his appointment until he ceases to be a member of that parish council.

(4) Sub-paragraph (3) above shall have effect so as to terminate the term of office of a person who on retiring from any parish council immediately becomes such a member again as

a newly elected councillor; but a person who so becomes a member again shall be eligible for re-appointment to the National Park authority.

(5) Subject to the following provisions of this Schedule, where a person who qualifies for his appointment by virtue of his being the chairman of a parish meeting is appointed as a parish member of an English National Park authority, he shall hold office from the time of his appointment until he ceases to be the chairman of that parish meeting.

(6) Sub-paragraph (5) above shall have effect so as to terminate the term of office of a person who is elected to succeed himself as chairman of any parish meeting; but a person who so becomes the chairman again shall be eligible for re-appointment to the National Park authority.

(7) Subject to the provisions of this Schedule, a parish member of an English National Park authority shall hold office in accordance with the terms of his appointment.

(8) In this paragraph, "English National Park authority" means a National Park authority for a National Park in England. **[595X]**

NOTES
Commencement: 19 September 1995.

Members (other than parish members) appointed by the Secretary of State

4.—(1) Before appointing any person as a member of a National Park authority the Secretary of State shall consult, according to whether the relevant Park is in England or in Wales, either the Countryside Commission or the Countryside Council for Wales.

(2) Subject to the following provisions of this Schedule, a person appointed as a member of a National Park authority by the Secretary of State—

    (a) shall hold office for such period of not less than one year nor more than three years as may be specified in the terms of his appointment; but

    (b) on ceasing to hold office shall be eligible for re-appointment.

(3) The term of office of a person appointed by the Secretary of State to fill such a vacancy in the membership of a National Park authority as occurs where a person appointed by the Secretary of State ceases to be a member of the authority before the end of his term of office may be for a period of less than one year if it is made to expire with the time when the term of office of the person in respect of whom the vacancy has arisen would have expired.

(4) Subject to the provisions of this Schedule, a member of a National Park authority appointed by the Secretary of State shall hold office in accordance with the terms of his appointment.

(5) This paragraph shall not apply to persons appointed as parish members of a National Park authority for a National Park in England or to their appointment as such members.

[595Y]

NOTES
Commencement: 19 September 1995.

Chairman and deputy chairman

5.—(1) The members of a National Park authority shall elect, from amongst their members, both a chairman and a deputy chairman of the authority.

(2) Subject to sub-paragraphs (3) and (4) below, the chairman and deputy chairman of a National Park authority shall be elected for a period not exceeding one year; but a person so elected shall, on ceasing to hold office at the end of his term of office as chairman or deputy chairman, be eligible for re-election.

(3) A person shall cease to hold office as chairman or deputy chairman of a National Park authority if he ceases to be a member of the authority.

(4) Where a vacancy occurs in the office of chairman or deputy chairman of a National Park authority, it shall be the duty of the members of that authority to secure that that vacancy is filled as soon as possible. **[595Z]**

NOTES
Commencement: 19 September 1995.

Removal of members

6.—(1) The Secretary of State may, by giving a local authority member of a National Park authority such written notice of the termination of his appointment as the Secretary of State considers appropriate, remove that member from office; but he shall do so only where he considers it appropriate to remove that member from office in consequence of the provisions of any order for varying either the area of the relevant Park or the number of local authority members of that authority.

(2) The Secretary of State may remove from office any member of a National Park authority appointed by him, other than any parish member of a National Park authority for a National Park in England, either—

(a) by giving that member three months' written notice of the termination of the appointment; or

(b) in such other manner as may be provided for in the terms of that member's appointment.

(3) The Secretary of State may remove from office any parish member of a National Park authority for a National Park in England either—

(a) by giving that member such written notice of the termination of his appointment as the Secretary of State considers appropriate; or

(b) in such other manner as may be provided for in the terms of that member's appointment;

but a parish member shall only be removed from office in the manner mentioned in paragraph (a) above where the Secretary of State considers it appropriate to do so in consequence of the provisions of any order for varying either the area of the relevant Park or the number of parish members of the National Park authority in question. **[596]**

NOTES
Commencement: 19 September 1995.

Disqualification of members

7.—(1) A person is disqualified for becoming or remaining a member of a National Park authority if he holds any paid office or employment appointments to which are or may be made or confirmed by—

(a) the authority itself or any council by whom a local authority member of the authority is appointed;

(b) any committee or sub-committee of the authority or of any such council;

(c) any joint committee on which the authority or any such council is represented;

(d) as respects a National Park authority for a National Park in England—

(i) any parish council for, or parish meeting of, a parish the whole or any part of which is comprised in the relevant Park;

(ii) any committee or sub-committee of any such parish council or any committee of any such parish meeting; or

(iii) any joint committee on which any such parish council or parish meeting is represented; or

(e) any person himself holding an office or employment which disqualifies him for becoming a member of the authority.

(2) A person is also disqualified for becoming or remaining a member of a National Park authority if he holds any employment in a company which, in accordance with Part V of the

Local Government and Housing Act 1989 other than section 73, is under the control of that authority.

(3) Section 92 of the 1972 Act (proceedings for disqualification) shall have effect in relation to a person who acts or claims to be entitled to act as a member of a National Park authority as it applies in relation to a person who acts or claims to be entitled to act as a member of a local authority, but as if—

(a) references in that section to a local government elector for the area concerned were references to a local government elector for any principal area the whole or any part of which is comprised in the relevant Park; and

(b) in subsection (6)(b) of that section (failure to deliver declaration of acceptance of office), the words from "of failure" to "or by reason" were omitted.

(4) Sections 1 to 3 of the Local Government and Housing Act 1989 (disqualification of persons holding politically restricted posts) shall have effect as if a National Park authority were a local authority for the purposes of Part I of that Act.

(5) In Part III of Schedule 1 to the House of Commons Disqualification Act 1975 (other disqualifying offices), in the entry inserted by section 1(2) of that Act of 1989 (politically restricted post), after "that Part" there shall be inserted "or a National Park authority".

[596A]

NOTES
Commencement: 19 September 1995 (sub-paras (1), (3)-(5)); to be appointed (sub-para (2)).

Vacation of office for failure to attend meetings

8. Section 85 of the 1972 Act (failure to attend meetings) shall have effect in relation to a National Park authority as it has effect in relation to a local authority. **[596B]**

NOTES
Commencement: 19 September 1995.

Code of conduct for members

9. Section 31 of the Local Government and Housing Act 1989 (code of conduct for members of local authorities) shall have effect as if a National Park authority were a local authority for the purposes of that section. **[596C]**

NOTES
Commencement: 19 September 1995.

Restrictions on voting on account of interests etc

10.—(1) Sections 94 to 98 of the 1972 Act (restrictions on voting) shall have effect in relation to meetings of a National Park authority as they have effect in relation to meetings of a local authority.

(2) Section 19 of the Local Government and Housing Act 1989 (members' interests) shall have effect as if a National Park authority were a local authority for the purposes of Part I of that Act. **[596D]**

NOTES
Commencement: 19 September 1995.

Allowances and time off for members

11.—(1) National Park authority shall be a body to which sections 174 to 176 of the 1972 Act (allowances for travelling, conferences and visits) shall apply and shall also be deemed to be a relevant authority for the purposes of section 18 of the Local Government and Housing Act 1989 (basic attendance and special responsibility allowances).

(2) For the purposes of sub-paragraph (1) above references in section 18 of that Act of 1989 to a member of an authority who is a councillor shall be deemed, in relation to a National Park authority, to include references to a member of that authority who is appointed as such a member by the Secretary of State.

(3) In section 29(1) of the Employment Protection (Consolidation) Act 1978 (time off for public duties), after paragraph (b) there shall be inserted the following paragraph—

"(ba) a National Park authority;"

but section 10 of that Act of 1989 (limit on paid leave for local authority duties) shall have effect as if a National Park authority were a relevant council for the purposes of that section.

[596E]

NOTES
Commencement: 19 September 1995.

Meetings and proceedings of the authority

12.—(1) The following provisions, that is to say—

    (a) the provisions of Part VI of Schedule 12 to the 1972 Act (proceedings and meetings of local authorities) and of section 99 of that Act so far as it relates to that Part of that Schedule; and

    (b) the provisions of section 100 of that Act (admission of the public and press),

shall have effect as if a National Park authority were a local authority for the purposes of those provisions.

(2) In section 100J of the 1972 Act (bodies in addition to principal councils to which provisions as to access to meetings etc apply)—

    (a) in subsection (1), after paragraph (cc) there shall be inserted the following paragraph—

      "(cd) a National Park authority;"

    (b) in subsection (3), after "(cc)" there shall be inserted "(cd)"; and

    (c) in subsection (4)(aa)—

      (i) after "Navigation Committee" there shall be inserted "or any National Park authority"; and

      (ii) for "body which" there shall be substituted "person who".

(3) Section 20 of the Local Government and Housing Act 1989 (power to require adoption of certain procedural standing orders) shall have effect as if a National Park authority were a relevant authority for the purposes of that section.

(4) The validity of any proceedings of a National Park authority shall not be affected by a vacancy amongst its members, by any defect in the appointment of a member of the authority or by the want of qualification, or the disqualification, of any such member. **[596F]**

NOTES
Commencement: 19 September 1995.

Committees and sub-committees and officers

13.—(1) Sections 101 to 106 of the 1972 Act (arrangements for committees and sub-committees) shall have effect as if a National Park authority were a local authority for the purposes of those sections.

(2) Accordingly, section 13 of the Local Government and Housing Act 1989 (voting rights of members of certain committees) shall have effect as if a National Park authority were a relevant authority for the purposes of that section.

(3) It shall be the duty of a National Park authority, in relation to any committee or sub-committee to which this sub-paragraph applies, to secure—

    (a) that the membership of the committee or sub-committee consists of or includes both local authority members of the authority and at least one member appointed to the authority by the Secretary of State;

    (b) that the division of members of the authority who are members of the committee or sub-committee between—

        (i) local authority members, and

        (ii) members appointed to the authority by the Secretary of State,

    is (as nearly as possible using whole numbers) in the same proportions as required, by virtue of paragraph 1(2) above, in the case of the authority itself; and

    (c) that the quorum of the committee or sub-committee includes at least one local authority member of the authority and at least one member appointed to the authority by the Secretary of State.

(4) Sub-paragraph (3) above applies in the case of any National Park authority to the following committees and sub-committees, except those appointed under section 102(4) or (4A) of the 1972 Act (advisory committees), that is to say—

    (a) any committee or sub-committee of the authority;

    (b) any joint committee on which the authority is represented; and

    (c) any sub-committee of such a joint committee.

(5) The proceedings of a committee or sub-committee to which sub-paragraph (3) above applies shall not be invalidated by any failure of a National Park authority to perform its duty under that sub-paragraph.

(6) The provisions of sections 112 to 119 and 151 of the 1972 Act (staff of local authorities) and of section 30 of the Local Government (Miscellaneous Provisions) Act 1976 (power to forgo repayment of remuneration) shall have effect as if a National Park authority were a local authority for the purposes of those provisions.

(7) The following provisions of the Local Government and Housing Act 1989 shall apply in relation to a National Park authority as they apply in relation to the authorities which are relevant authorities for the purposes of those provisions, that is to say—

    (a) section 4 (designation and reports of head of paid service);

    (b) section 5 (designation and reports of monitoring officer); and

    (c) with the omission of subsection (4)(d) (assistants for political groups), section 8 (standing orders with respect to staff);

and section 7 of that Act (staff to be appointed on merit) shall apply to any appointment to paid office or employment under a National Park authority as it applies to an appointment to paid office or employment under a body which is a local authority for the purposes of Part I of that Act.

(8) Section 12 of that Act of 1989 (conflict of interest in staff negotiations) shall have effect as if references in that section to a local authority included references to a National Park authority. **[596G]**

NOTES

    Commencement: 19 September 1995.

National Park Officer

14.—(1) Every National Park authority for a National Park shall secure that there is at all times an officer appointed by that authority to be responsible to the authority for the manner in which the carrying out of its different functions is co-ordinated.

(2) For the purposes of this paragraph a National Park authority may adopt—

    (a) any appointment which an existing authority has made under paragraph 15 of Schedule 17 to the 1972 Act in relation to any area wholly or partly comprised in the relevant Park; or

(b) if the relevant Park is in Wales, any appointment—

    (i) which was made under that paragraph in relation to any such area, and

    (ii) which was adopted by a National Park planning board, as defined in section 64 of this Act, by virtue of an order under paragraph 3A of Schedule 17 to the 1972 Act or section 2(1B) of the Town and Country Planning Act 1990.

(3) Before making or adopting an appointment under this paragraph or assigning additional responsibilities to a person holding such an appointment, a National Park authority shall consult, according to whether the Park in question is in England or in Wales, either the Countryside Commission or the Countryside Council for Wales.

(4) Sub-paragraph (3) above shall not apply in relation to the adoption of an appointment under this paragraph in relation to a National Park in Wales in any case where—

(a) the National Park authority in question is the National Park authority in relation to that National Park by virtue of an order under section 63 of this Act made by virtue of section 64(1) of this Act;

(b) the appointment in question was made or adopted by the body corporate which has so become that National Park authority, but in its capacity as the National Park planning board, as defined in section 64 of this Act, for the area of the National Park in question; and

(c) no additional responsibilities are, on the occasion of the adoption of the appointment, to be assigned to the person holding the appointment.

(5) A person who holds office with a National Park authority by virtue of an appointment made or adopted under this paragraph—

(a) may at the same time hold the office of head of that authority's paid service, the office of monitoring officer in relation to that authority or both those offices; but

(b) shall not at the same time be that authority's chief finance officer (within the meaning of section 5 of the Local Government and Housing Act 1989) or hold any office under any principal council.

(6) An officer holding office with a National Park authority by virtue of an appointment made or adopted under this paragraph shall be known as a National Park officer. **[596H]**

NOTES

Commencement: 19 September 1995.

Personal liability of members and officers

15. Section 265 of the Public Health Act 1875 (personal liability of members and officers of certain authorities) shall have effect as if—

(a) a National Park authority were an authority such as is mentioned in that section;

(b) the references in that section to a member of the authority included, in relation to a National Park authority, references to any person who is not such a member but for the time being serves as a member of a committee or sub-committee of such an authority;

(c) the references in that section to the purpose of executing that Act and to the purposes of that Act were each, in relation to a National Park authority, references to the purpose of carrying out the functions of that authority by virtue of Part III of this Act; and

(d) the words "or rate" were omitted. **[596I]**

NOTES

Commencement: 19 September 1995.

Liaison with parish and community councils

16. A National Park authority shall make arrangements—

(a) in the case of a National Park in England, with each parish council the area of which is comprised wholly or partly within the Park, or

(b) in the case of a National Park in Wales, with each community council the area of which is so comprised,

for the purpose of informing and consulting that council about the authority's discharge of its functions.   **[596J]**

Documents, notices, records, byelaws etc

17.—(1) The Local Government (Records) Act 1962 shall have effect in relation to a National Park authority as if that authority were a local authority for the purposes of that Act.

(2) Subject to sub-paragraph (3) below, the following provisions of the 1972 Act, that is to say—

(a) sections 224 and 225(1) (custody and deposit of documents with a proper officer of the local authority),
(b) sections 228 and 229 (inspection of documents and photocopies),
(c) section 230 (reports and returns),
(d) sections 231 to 234 (service and authentication of documents), and
(e) without prejudice to their application by virtue of any other provision of Part III of this Act, sections 236 to 238 (byelaws),

shall have effect as if for the purposes of those provisions a National Park authority were a local authority or, in the case of section 224, a principal council.

(3) References in section 228 of the 1972 Act to a local government elector shall have effect for the purposes of that section as applied by sub-paragraph (2) above as if, in relation to a National Park authority, they were references to a local government elector for any principal area the whole or any part of which is comprised in the relevant Park.

(4) Section 41 of the Local Government (Miscellaneous Provisions) Act 1976 (evidence of resolutions and minutes of proceedings) shall have effect as if a National Park authority were a local authority for the purposes of that Act.

(5) Where a National Park authority has made any byelaws and those byelaws have been confirmed, that authority shall send a copy of the byelaws as confirmed to every council for a principal area the whole or any part of which is comprised in the relevant Park.   **[596K]**

Investigation in connection with maladministration etc

18.—(1) In section 25(1) of the Local Government Act 1974 (bodies subject to investigation under Part III of that Act), after paragraph (aa) there shall be inserted the following paragraph—

"(ab) a National Park authority;".

(2) In section 26(7) of that Act (no investigation where complaint relates to all or most of the inhabitants of an area), before paragraph (a) there shall be inserted the following paragraph—

"(aa) where the complaint relates to a National Park authority, the area of the Park for which it is such an authority;".

(3) In section 34(1) of that Act (interpretation), in the definition of "member", after "the joint board" there shall be inserted "and in relation to a National Park authority, includes a member of any of the councils by whom a local authority member of the authority is appointed".   **[596L]**

NOTES
Commencement: 19 September 1995.

Audit by Audit Commission auditor etc

19.—(1) In section 12(2) of the Local Government Finance Act 1982 (bodies whose accounts are subject to audit), after paragraph (ff) there shall be inserted the following paragraph—

"(fg) a National Park authority;"

and sections 1 to 7 of the Local Government Act 1992 (performance standards and further provisions relating to audit) shall have effect accordingly.

(2) Sections 19 and 20 of that Act of 1982 (unlawful payments etc) shall have effect as if references in those sections to a local authority included references to a National Park authority.

(3) In section 36 of that Act of 1982 (interpretation), after subsection (3) there shall be inserted the following subsection—

"(3A) In the application of Part III of this Act in relation to a National Park authority, any reference to a local government elector for the area of the authority shall be construed as a reference to a local government elector for any area the whole or any part of which is comprised in the Park for which that authority is the local planning authority." **[596M]**

NOTES
Commencement: 19 September 1995.

Meaning of "relevant order"

20. In this Schedule "the relevant order", in relation to a National Park authority, means—

   (a) the order under section 63 of this Act establishing that authority;
   (b) any order under that section relating to that authority; or
   (c) any order made in relation to that authority in exercise of the power to amend an order under that section. **[596N]**

NOTES
Commencement: 19 September 1995.

SCHEDULE 8
Section 65

SUPPLEMENTAL AND INCIDENTAL POWERS OF NATIONAL PARK AUTHORITIES

Powers in relation to land etc

1.—(1) Subject to sub-paragraph (2) below, the following provisions, that is to say—

   (a) sections 120, 122 and 123 of the 1972 Act (powers of local authorities to acquire and dispose of land), and
   (b) sections 128 to 131 of that Act (general provisions in relation to land transactions),

shall have effect as if, for the purposes of those provisions, a National Park authority were a principal council and the relevant Park were the authority's area.

(2) The following provisions of the Local Government (Miscellaneous Provisions) Act 1976, that is to say—

   (a) section 13 (compulsory acquisition of rights over land),
   (b) section 15 (survey of land for the purposes of compulsory purchase),
   (c) section 16 (obtaining information about land), and

(d) section 29 (repayment of unclaimed compensation),

shall apply in relation to a National Park authority as if the authority were a local authority for the purposes of that Act.

(3) Section 33 of the Local Government (Miscellaneous Provisions) Act 1982 (enforceability by local authorities of certain covenants relating to land) shall have effect as if references to a principal council included references to a National Park authority and as if the relevant Park were that authority's area; and for the purposes of this paragraph the reference in subsection (1) of that section to section 111 of the 1972 Act shall have effect as a reference to section 65 of this Act.

(4) This paragraph shall be without prejudice to any power conferred on a National Park authority by virtue of paragraph 2 below.   **[596O]**

NOTES
Commencement: 19 September 1995.

2.—(1) . . .

(2) Every such reference in that Act to the acquisition or appropriation of land for planning purposes as falls to be construed in accordance with section 246 of that Act shall be taken (so far as it would not otherwise do so) to include a reference to an acquisition or appropriation of land under any power conferred by virtue of sub-paragraph (1) above.

(3) The following provisions of that Act, that is to say—

    (a) sections 251(1), 258(1), 260(1), 261, 271, 272 and 274 (extinguishing rights of way and other rights),
    (b) sections 275 and 276 (extension and modification of functions of statutory undertakers), and
    (c) section 324(6) (rights of entry),

shall have effect as if a National Park authority were a local authority for the purposes of that Act.

(4) The reference to a local authority in section 66(2) of the Planning (Listed Buildings and Conservation Areas) Act 1990 (which refers to the powers of a local authority under sections 232, 233 and 235(1) of the Town and Country Planning Act 1990) shall include a reference to a National Park authority.   **[596P]**

NOTES
Commencement: 19 September 1995.
Sub-para (1) inserts the Town and Country Planning Act 1990, s 244A.

Miscellaneous transactions and powers

3.—(1) The following provisions of the 1972 Act shall also have effect as if a National Park authority were a principal council for the purposes of that Act and as if the relevant Park were the authority's area, that is to say—

    (a) section 132 (use of premises);
    (b) section 135 (contracts of local authorities);
    (c) section 136 (contributions towards expenditure on concurrent functions);
    (d) section 139 (acceptance of gifts of property);
    (e) sections 140, 140A and 140C (insurance);
    (f) section 143 (subscriptions to local government associations); and
    (g) sections 222 and 223 (conduct of prosecutions and participation in other legal proceedings).

(2) Section 38 of the Local Government (Miscellaneous Provisions) Act 1976 (use of spare capacity of local authority computers) shall have effect as if a National Park authority were a local authority for the purposes of that Act.

(3) Section 41 of the Local Government (Miscellaneous Provisions) Act 1982 (lost

property) shall have effect as if a National Park authority were a local authority for the purposes of that Act.

(4) Section 45 of that Act of 1982 (arrangements under the Employment and Training Act 1973) shall have effect as if a National Park authority were a local authority to which that section applies.   **[596Q]**

NOTES
Commencement: 19 September 1995.

Transfer of securities on alteration of area

4. Section 146 of the 1972 Act (transfer of securities on alteration of area) shall have effect as if a National Park authority were a local authority for the purposes of that Act and as if the reference in subsection (1)(b) of that section to an enactment similar to a provision of the 1972 Act included a reference to any provision of Part III of this Act.   **[596R]**

NOTES
Commencement: 19 September 1995.

The Local Authorities (Goods and Services) Act 1970

5. The Local Authorities (Goods and Services) Act 1970 (supply of goods and services by local authorities) shall have effect as if a National Park authority were both a local authority and a public body for the purposes of that Act.   **[596S]**

NOTES
Commencement: 19 September 1995.

Power to execute works outside Park

6. Any power to execute works which is conferred on a National Park authority by virtue of Part III of this Act or any other enactment shall be taken, except in so far as the contrary intention appears, to include power, for the purposes of the carrying out of the authority's functions in relation to the relevant Park, to execute works of the relevant description outside, as well as inside, that Park.   **[596T]**

NOTES
Commencement: 19 September 1995.

Power to promote Bills

7.—(1) Section 239 of the 1972 Act (power of local authority to promote local or personal Bills) shall have effect in relation to a National Park authority as if it were a local authority for the purposes of that Act and as if the relevant Park were the authority's area.

(2) A National Park authority shall have no power by virtue of Part III of this Act to promote a Bill for—

    (a) modifying the area of any National Park or any local government area;

    (b) modifying the authority's own constitution or that of any other National Park authority; or

    (c) modifying the status or the electoral arrangements of any such local government area.

(3) In sub-paragraph (2) above—

    "electoral arrangements" means any electoral arrangements within the meaning of section 14(4) of the Local Government Act 1992 or any corresponding arrangements in relation to any area in Wales; and "local government area" means any local government area within the meaning of that Act or any area in Wales for which any council carries out functions of local government. **[596U]**

NOTES
Commencement: 19 September 1995.

Competitive tendering etc

8.—(1) Part III of the Local Government, Planning and Land Act 1980 (direct labour organisations) shall have effect in relation to a National Park authority as if such an authority were a local authority for the purposes of that Part.

(2) In section 1(1) of the Local Government Act 1988 (defined authorities for the purposes of the provisions of that Act relating to competition), after paragraph (a) there shall be inserted the following paragraph—

"(aa) a National Park authority;".

(3) In Schedule 2 to that Act of 1988 (bodies to which Part II of that Act applies), after the entry relating to the Broads Authority there shall be inserted—

"Any National Park authority".

(4) In section 18 of that Act of 1988 (race relations matters), after subsection (7) there shall be inserted the following subsection—

"(7A) Any reference in this section to a local authority shall be deemed to include a reference to a National Park authority."

(5) In section 33(3)(c) of that Act of 1988 (definition of "relevant public body" for the purposes of provisions relating to contracts with associated companies), after "within" there shall be inserted "paragraph (aa) or".

(6) References in sections 8 to 10 of the Local Government Act 1992 (competition) to any provisions of that Act of 1980 or of that Act of 1988 shall include references to those provisions as they have effect by virtue of this paragraph. **[596V]**

NOTES
Commencement: 19 September 1995.

Restrictions on publicity

9. Part II of the Local Government Act 1986 (restrictions on publicity) shall have effect as if a National Park authority were a local authority for the purposes of that Part. **[596W]**

NOTES
Commencement: 19 September 1995.

Provisions applying in relation to companies in which authorities have interests

10. In section 67(3) of the Local Government and Housing Act 1989 (local authorities for the purposes of Part V of that Act), after paragraph (m) there shall be inserted the following paragraph—

"(ma) a National Park authority;". **[596X]**

NOTES
Commencement: 19 September 1995.

Provisions as to charges

11. In section 152(2) of that Act of 1989 (provisions as to charges), after paragraph (j) there shall be inserted the following paragraph—

"(ja) a National Park authority;"

and section 151 of that Act (power to amend existing provisions as to charges) shall have effect as if references to an existing provision included references to any such provision as applied by Part III of this Act. **[596Y]**

NOTES

Commencement: 19 September 1995.

Service agency agreements

12. Section 25 of the Local Government (Wales) Act 1994 (service agency agreements) shall have effect as if a National Park authority for any National Park in Wales were a new principal council for the purposes of that section. **[596Z]**

NOTES

Commencement: 19 September 1995.

Contracting out

13. Part II of the Deregulation and Contracting Out Act 1994 (contracting out) shall have effect as if a National Park authority were a local authority for the purposes of that Part. **[597]**

NOTES

Commencement: 19 September 1995.

SCHEDULE 9

Section 70

MISCELLANEOUS STATUTORY FUNCTIONS OF NATIONAL PARK AUTHORITIES

Common land etc

1.—(1) The enactments specified in sub-paragraph (2) below shall have effect in relation to any registered common which—

    (a) is within any National Park for which a National Park authority is the local planning authority, and

    (b) is not owned by, or vested in, any other body which is a local authority,

as if the National Park authority were a local authority for the purposes of those enactments and as if the relevant Park were that authority's area.

(2) The enactments mentioned in sub-paragraph (1) above are—

    (a) section 1 of the Commons Act 1899 (scheme for regulation);
    (b) section 194(2) of the Law of Property Act 1925 (application for removal of works);
    (c) section 23 of and Schedule 2 to the Caravan Sites and Control of Development Act 1960 (power of district council to prohibit caravans on commons); and
    (d) section 9 of the Commons Registration Act 1965 (protection of unclaimed common land).

(3) In the Commons Act 1899 references to the council by which a scheme is made under section 1 of that Act shall be construed accordingly; and the powers conferred by sections 7 and 12 of that Act (acquisition of land and contributions to expenses) shall be exercisable by a National Park authority in relation to the relevant Park as they are exercisable by a district council in relation to their district.

(4) A National Park authority shall have the same power to make an application under

section 18 of the Commons Act 1899 (modification of provisions for recreation grounds) as a local authority.

(5) References in this paragraph, in relation to an enactment specified in sub-paragraph (2) above or to any enactment contained in section 18 of the Commons Act 1899, to a local authority are references to any such local authority, within the meaning of the 1972 Act, as has functions conferred on it by or by virtue of that enactment.

(6) In this paragraph "registered common" means any land registered as common land or as a town or village green under the Commons Registration Act 1965.　　　　**[597A]**

NOTES

Commencement: 19 September 1995.

Open spaces

2. The Open Spaces Act 1906 shall have effect as if references in that Act to a local authority included references to a National Park authority.　　　　**[597B]**

NOTES

Commencement: 19 September 1995.

Nature reserves

3. Sections 21 and 22 of the National Parks and Access to the Countryside Act 1949 (establishment of nature reserves and application of enactments to local authority reserves) shall have effect as if the bodies on whom powers are conferred by section 21 of that Act included every National Park authority and as if the relevant Park were the authority's area; and references in those sections to a local authority and to their area shall be construed accordingly.　　　　**[597C]**

NOTES

Commencement: 19 September 1995.

Caravan sites

4. In the Caravan Sites and Control of Development Act 1960—

    (a) section 24 (power to provide sites for caravans), and
    (b) paragraph 11 of Schedule 1 to that Act (no licence required for land occupied by a local authority),

shall have effect as if a National Park authority were a local authority for the purposes of that Act and as if the relevant Park were that authority's area.　　　　**[597D]**

NOTES

Commencement: 19 September 1995.

Country Parks

5. The Countryside Act 1968 shall have effect as if a National Park authority were a local authority for the purposes of—

    (a) sections 6 to 8 of that Act (country parks);
    (b) section 9 of that Act (powers exercisable over or near common land); and
    (c) section 41 of that Act (byelaws) in so far as it has the effect in relation to—

        (i) any country park provided under section 7 of that Act, or
        (ii) any land as respects which any powers under section 9 of that Act have been exercised,

of conferring powers on a local authority or of applying provisions of section 92 of the National Parks and Access to the Countryside Act 1949 (wardens);

and the references to a local authority in sections 43 to 45 of that Act of 1968 (general provisions as to the powers of local authorities) shall have effect accordingly.   **[597E]**

NOTES

Commencement: 19 September 1995.

Provision of information and encouragement of visitors

6. Sections 142 and 144 of the 1972 Act (provision of information about local services and encouragement of visitors) shall have effect (subject to paragraph 9 of Schedule 8 to this Act) as if a National Park authority were a local authority for the purposes of that Act and as if the relevant Park were the authority's area.   **[597F]**

NOTES

Commencement: 19 September 1995.

Derelict land etc

7. The provisions of section 16 of the Welsh Development Agency Act 1975 and of section 1 of the Derelict Land Act 1982 (powers for the improvement of land) shall have effect in relation to land in a National Park for which a National Park authority is the local planning authority as if references in those provisions to a local authority included references to the National Park authority and as if the relevant Park were the authority's area.   **[597G]**

NOTES

Commencement: 19 September 1995.

Recreational facilities

8. Section 19 of the Local Government (Miscellaneous Provisions) Act 1976 (recreational facilities) shall have effect as if the powers conferred by that section on local authorities were also conferred, so as to be exercisable within a National Park for which a National Park authority is the local planning authority, on that authority.   **[597H]**

NOTES

Commencement: 19 September 1995.

Refuse Disposal

9.—(1) Subject to sub-paragraph (2) below, references to a local authority in the Refuse Disposal (Amenity) Act 1978 shall have effect in relation to land in a National Park for which a National Park authority is the local planning authority as if they included references to that authority and as if the relevant Park were the authority's area.

(2) Sub-paragraph (1) above shall not apply, in relation to any time before the coming into force of the repeal of section 1 of that Act, to any reference in that section.   **[597I]**

NOTES

Commencement: 19 September 1995.

Ancient Monuments and Archaeological Areas

10.—(1) Subject to sub-paragraph (2) below, Parts I and II of the Ancient Monuments and Archaeological Areas Act 1979 shall have effect as if in relation—

   (a) to any monument in a National Park for which a National Park authority is the local planning authority, or

(b) to any area the whole or any part of which is comprised in such a Park,

the references in those Parts to a local authority included references to that National Park authority.

(2) Section 35 of that Act (notice of operations affecting area of archaeological importance) shall have effect in relation to land in such a National Park as is mentioned in sub-paragraph (1) above as if—

(a) any notice required to be served on a local authority under that section were required, instead, to be served on the National Park authority; and

(b) the functions conferred on a local authority by virtue of that section had been conferred instead on the National Park authority.

(3) Section 45(2) and (3) of that Act (assistance for archaeological investigations) shall have effect as if a National Park authority were a local authority for the purposes of that Act and as if the relevant Park were the authority's area.   **[597J]**

NOTES
Commencement: 19 September 1995.

Footpaths and bridleways

11. The following provisions of the Highways Act 1980, that is to say—

(a) sections 25 to 29 (footpaths and bridleways),
(b) section 72(2) (widening of public paths),
(c) sections 118 to 121 (stopping up and diversion of public paths), and
(d) Schedule 6 (procedure for orders),

shall have effect as if references in those sections to a local authority or council included references to a National Park authority and as if the relevant Park were the authority's area.   **[597K]**

NOTES
Commencement: 19 September 1995.

Litter

12. The following provisions, that is to say—

(a) section 4 of the Litter Act 1983 (consultations and proposals for the abatement of litter), and
(b) section 88 of the Environmental Protection Act 1990 (fixed penalty notices for leaving litter),

shall have effect as if a National Park authority were a litter authority for the purposes of those provisions, as if the relevant Park were the authority's area and as if the reference in that section 4 to the authority's area were a reference to any part of the relevant Park.   **[597L]**

NOTES
Commencement: 19 September 1995.

Listed and historic buildings

13.—(1) In the case of a building situated in a National Park for which a National Park authority is the local planning authority, that authority and no other authority shall be the appropriate authority for the purposes of sections 47 to 51 of the Planning (Listed Buildings and Conservation Areas) Act 1990 (purchase of listed buildings etc in need of repair); and the reference to a local authority in section 88(5) of that Act (rights of entry) and in section 6 of the Historic Buildings and Ancient Monuments Act 1953 (under which grants for the acquisition of buildings in Wales may be made) shall have effect accordingly.

(2) In relation to any building or land in any such National Park, the powers conferred on

a county council or county borough council by section 52 of that Act of 1990 (power to acquire building and land by agreement) shall be exercisable by the National Park authority, and not (without prejudice to their powers apart from that section) by any other authority; and subsection (2) of that section shall have effect accordingly.

(3) Section 53(1) of that Act (management of listed buildings etc acquired under the Act) shall apply in relation to the powers conferred by virtue of this paragraph on a National Park authority as it applies in relation to the powers conferred by sections 47 and 52 of that Act on a local authority.

(4) That Act shall have effect as if a National Park authority were a local authority for the purposes of—

    (a) sections 54 and 55 of that Act (urgent works to preserve listed buildings etc), and
    (b) sections 57 and 58 of that Act (power of local authorities to contribute towards preservation of listed buildings etc),

and, in relation to those provisions, as if the relevant Park were the authority's area.

(5) In relation to the powers conferred on a National Park authority by virtue of this paragraph, section 88 of that Act (powers of entry) shall have effect as if references in that section to a local authority included references to a National Park authority.

(6) References to a local authority in section 90(1) to (4) of that Act (financial provisions) shall be deemed to include references to a National Park authority. **[597M]**

NOTES
Commencement: 19 September 1995.

Hazardous substances

14.—(1) For the purposes of the Planning (Hazardous Substances) Act 1990, where a National Park authority is the local planning authority for any National Park, that authority, and no other authority, shall be the hazardous substances authority for land in the relevant Park.

(2) References to a local authority in sections 12 and 38(1) to (4) of that Act (government consent to local authority activities and financial provisions) shall be deemed to include references to a National Park authority. **[597N]**

NOTES
Commencement: 19 September 1995.

Local Charities

15. Sections 76 to 78 of the Charities Act 1993 (local charities) shall have effect as if the references to a council for any area included references to a National Park authority and as if the relevant Park were the authority's area. **[597O]**

NOTES
Commencement: 19 September 1995.

Overseas Assistance

16. The Local Government (Overseas Assistance) Act 1993 shall have effect as if a National Park authority were a local authority for the purposes of that Act. **[597P]**

NOTES
Commencement: 19 September 1995.

(Sch 10 contains minor and consequential amendments relating to National Parks, with effect as from a day to be appointed; Schs 11, 12 are outside the scope of this work.)

SCHEDULE 13

Section 96

REVIEW OF OLD MINERAL PLANNING PERMISSIONS

Interpretation

1.—(1) In this Schedule—

"dormant site" means a Phase I or Phase II site in, on or under which no minerals development has been carried out to any substantial extent at any time in the period beginning on 22nd February 1982 and ending with 6th June 1995 otherwise than by virtue of a planning permission which is not a relevant planning permission relating to the site;

"first list", in relation to a mineral planning authority, means the list prepared by them pursuant to paragraph 3 below;

"mineral planning authority"—

(a) as respects England and Wales, means a mineral planning authority within the meaning of the 1990 Act, and

(b) as respects Scotland, means a planning authority for the purposes of the 1972 Act;

"mineral site" has the meaning given by sub-paragraph (2) below;

"National Park" means an area designated as such under section 5(3) of the National Parks and Access to the Countryside Act 1949;

"old mining permission" has the meaning given—

(a) as respects England and Wales, by section 22(1) of the 1991 Act, and

(b) as respects Scotland, by section 49H(1) of the 1972 Act;

"owner", in relation to any land—

(a) as respects England and Wales, means any person who—

(i) is the estate owner in respect of the fee simple, or

(ii) is entitled to a tenancy granted or extended for a term of years certain of which not less than seven years remains unexpired; and

(b) as respects Scotland, has the meaning given by paragraph 10(1) of Schedule 10A to the 1972 Act;

"Phase I site" and "Phase II site" have the meaning given by paragraph 2 below;

"relevant planning permission" means any planning permission, other than an old mining permission or a planning permission granted by a development order, granted after 30th June 1948 for minerals development; and

"second list", in relation to a mineral planning authority, means the list prepared by them pursuant to paragraph 4 below.

(2) For the purposes of this Schedule, but subject to sub-paragraph (3) below, "mineral site" means—

(a) in a case where it appears to the mineral planning authority to be expedient to treat as a single site the aggregate of the land to which any two or more relevant planning permissions relate, the aggregate of the land to which those permissions relate; and

(b) in any other case, the land to which a relevant planning permission relates.

(3) In determining whether it appears to them to be expedient to treat as a single site the aggregate of the land to which two or more relevant planning permissions relate a mineral planning authority shall have regard to any guidance issued for the purpose by the Secretary of State.

(4) Any reference (however expressed) in this Schedule to an old mining permission or a relevant planning permission relating to a mineral site is a reference to the mineral site, or some part of it, being the land to which the permission relates; and where any such permission authorises the carrying out of development consisting of the winning and working of minerals but only in respect of any particular mineral or minerals, that permission shall not be taken, for the purposes of this Schedule, as relating to any other mineral in, on or under the land to which the permission relates.

(5) For the purposes of this Schedule, a mineral site which is a Phase I site or a Phase II site is active if it is not a dormant site.

(6) For the purposes of this Schedule, working rights are restricted in respect of a mineral site if any of—

(a) the size of the area which may be used for the winning and working of minerals or the depositing of mineral waste;

(b) the depth to which operations for the winning and working of minerals may extend;

(c) the height of any deposit of mineral waste;

(d) the rate at which any particular mineral may be extracted;

(e) the rate at which any particular mineral waste may be deposited;

(f) the period at the expiry of which any winning or working of minerals or depositing of mineral waste is to cease; or

(g) the total quantity of minerals which may be extracted from, or of mineral waste which may be deposited on, the site,

is restricted or reduced in respect of the mineral site in question.

(7) For the purposes of this Schedule, where an application is made under paragraph 9 below for the determination of the conditions to which the relevant planning permissions relating to the mineral site to which the application relates are to be subject, those conditions are finally determined when—

(a) the proceedings on the application, including any proceedings on or in consequence of an application under section 288 of the 1990 Act or, as the case may be, section 233 of the 1972 Act, have been determined, and

(b) any time for appealing under paragraph 11(1) below, or applying or further applying under paragraph 9 below, (where there is a right to do so) has expired.   **[597Q]**

NOTES

Commencement: to be appointed.
The 1990 Act: ie the Town and Country Planning Act 1990.
The 1972 Act: ie the Town and Country Planning (Scotland) Act 1972.
The 1991 Act: ie the Planning and Compensation Act 1991.

Phase I and II sites

2.—(1) This paragraph has effect for the purposes of determining which mineral sites are Phase I sites, which are Phase II sites, and which are neither Phase I nor Phase II sites.

(2) A mineral site is neither a Phase I site nor a Phase II site where—

(a) all the relevant planning permissions which relate to the site have been granted after 21st February 1982; or

(b) some only of the relevant planning permissions which relate to the site have been granted after 21st February 1982, and the parts of the site to which those permissions relate constitute the greater part of that site.

(3) With the exception of those mineral sites which, by virtue of sub-paragraph (2) above, are neither Phase I nor Phase II sites, every mineral site is either a Phase I site or a Phase II site.

(4) Subject to sub-paragraph (2) above, where any part of a mineral site is situated within—

(a) a National Park;

(b) a site in respect of which a notification under section 28 of the Wildlife and Countryside Act 1981 (sites of special scientific interest) is in force;

(c) an area designated under section 87 of the National Parks and Access to the Countryside Act 1949 as an area of outstanding natural beauty;

(d) an area designated as a National Scenic Area under section 262C of the 1972 Act; or

(e) an area designated as a Natural Heritage Area under section 6 of the Natural Heritage (Scotland) Act 1991,

that site is a Phase I site.

(5) Subject to sub-paragraphs (2) and (4) above, where—

  (a) all the relevant planning permissions which relate to a mineral site, and which were not granted after 21st February 1982, were granted after the relevant day in 1969; or

  (b) the parts of a mineral site to which relate such of the relevant planning permissions relating to the site as were granted after the relevant day in 1969 but before 22nd February 1982 constitute a greater part of the site than is constituted by those parts of the site to which no such relevant planning permission relates but to which a relevant planning permission granted on or before the relevant day in 1969 does relate,

the mineral site is a Phase II site.

(6) In sub-paragraph (5) above, "the relevant day in 1969" means—

  (a) as respects England and Wales, 31st March 1969; and

  (b) as respects Scotland, 7th December 1969.

(7) Every other mineral site, that is to say any mineral site other than one—

  (a) which is, by virtue of sub-paragraph (2) above, neither a Phase I nor a Phase II site; or

  (b) which is a Phase I site by virtue of sub-paragraph (4) above; or

  (c) which is a Phase II site by virtue of sub-paragraph (5) above,

is a Phase I site.

(8) In ascertaining, for the purposes of sub-paragraph (2) or (5) above, whether any parts of a mineral site constitute the greater part of that site, or whether a part of a mineral site is greater than any other part, that mineral site shall be treated as not including any part of the site—

  (a) to which an old mining permission relates; or

  (b) which is a part where minerals development has been (but is no longer being) carried out and which has, in the opinion of the mineral planning authority, been satisfactorily restored;

but no part of a site shall be treated, by virtue of paragraph (b) above, as being not included in the site unless the mineral planning authority are satisfied that any aftercare conditions which relate to that part have, so far as relating to that part, been complied with.   **[597R]**

NOTES

Commencement: to be appointed.

The 1972 Act: ie the Town and Country Planning (Scotland) Act 1972.

The "first list"

3.—(1) A mineral planning authority shall, in accordance with the following provisions of this paragraph, prepare a list of mineral sites in their area ("the first list").

(2) A site shall, but shall only, be included in the first list if it is a mineral site in the area of the mineral planning authority and is either—

  (a) an active Phase I site;

  (b) an active Phase II site; or

  (c) a dormant site.

(3) In respect of each site included in the first list, the list shall indicate whether the site is an active Phase I site, an active Phase II site or a dormant site.

(4) In respect of each active Phase I site included in the first list, that list shall specify the date by which an application is to be made to the mineral planning authority under paragraph 9 below.

(5) Any date specified pursuant to sub-paragraph (4) above shall be a date—

  (a) not earlier than the date upon which expires the period of 12 months from the date on which the first list is first advertised in accordance with paragraph 5 below, and

(b) not later than the date upon which expires the period of three years from the date upon which the provisions of this Schedule come into force.

(6) The preparation of the first list shall be completed before the day upon which it is first advertised in accordance with paragraph 5 below. **[597S]**

NOTES
Commencement: to be appointed.

The "second list"

4.—(1) A mineral planning authority shall, in accordance with the following provisions of this paragraph, prepare a list of the active Phase II sites in their area ("the second list").

(2) The second list shall include each mineral site in the mineral planning authority's area which is an active Phase II site.

(3) In respect of each site included in the second list, that list shall indicate the date by which an application is to be made to the mineral planning authority under paragraph 9 below.

(4) Subject to paragraph (5) below, any date specified pursuant to sub-paragraph (3) above shall be a date—

(a) not earlier than the date upon which expires the period of 12 months from the date on which the second list is first advertised in accordance with paragraph 5 below, and

(b) not later than the date upon which expires the period of six years from the date upon which the provisions of this Schedule come into force.

(5) The Secretary of State may by order provide that sub-paragraph (4)(b) above shall have effect as if for the period of six years referred to in that paragraph there were substituted such longer period specified in the order.

(6) The power of the Secretary of State to make an order under sub-paragraph (5) above shall be exercisable by statutory instrument; and any statutory instrument containing such an order shall be subject to annulment in pursuance of a resolution of either House of Parliament.

(7) The preparation of the second list shall be completed before the day upon which it is first advertised in accordance with paragraph 5 below. **[597T]**

NOTES
Commencement: to be appointed.

Advertisement of the first and second lists

5.—(1) This paragraph makes provision for the advertisement of the first and second lists prepared by a mineral planning authority.

(2) The mineral planning authority shall advertise each of the first and second lists by causing to be published, in each of two successive weeks, in one or more newspapers circulating in its area, notice of the list having been prepared.

(3) In respect of each of those lists, such notice shall—

(a) state that the list has been prepared by the authority; and
(b) specify one or more places within the area of the authority at which the list may be inspected, and in respect of each such place specify the times (which shall be reasonable times) during which facilities for inspection of the list will be afforded.

(4) In respect of the first list, such notice shall—

(a) be first published no later than the day upon which expires the period of three months from the date upon which the provisions of this Schedule come into force;
(b) explain the general effect of a mineral site being classified as a dormant site or, as the case may be, as an active Phase I site or an active Phase II site;

    (c) explain the consequences which will occur if no application is made under paragraph 9 below in respect of an active Phase I site included in the list by the date specified in the list for that site;

    (d) explain the effects for any dormant or active Phase I or II site not included in the list of its not being included in the list and—

        (i) set out the right to make an application to the authority for that site to be included in the list;

        (ii) set out the date by which such an application must be made; and

        (iii) state that the owner of such a site has a right of appeal against any decision of the authority upon such an application; and

    (e) explain that the owner of an active Phase I site has a right to apply for postponement of the date specified in the list for the making of an application under paragraph 9 below, and set out the date by which an application for such postponement must be made.

(5) In respect of the second list, such notice shall—

    (a) be first published no later than the day upon which expires the period of three years, or such longer period as the Secretary of State may by order specify, from the date upon which the provisions of this Schedule come into force; and

    (b) explain the consequences which will occur if no application is made under paragraph 9 below in respect of an active Phase II site included in the list by the date specified in the list for that site.

(6) The power of the Secretary of State to make an order under sub-paragraph (5) above shall be exercisable by statutory instrument; and any statutory instrument containing such an order shall be subject to annulment in pursuance of a resolution of either House of Parliament.   **[597U]**

NOTES

Commencement: to be appointed.

Applications for inclusion in the first list of sites not included in that list as originally prepared and appeals from decisions upon such applications

6.—(1) Any person who is the owner of any land, or is entitled to an interest in a mineral, may, if that land or interest is not a mineral site included in the first list and does not form part of any mineral site included in that list, apply to the mineral planning authority for that land or interest to be included in that list.

(2) An application under sub-paragraph (1) above shall be made no later than the day upon which expires the period of three months from the day when the first list was first advertised in accordance with paragraph 5 above.

(3) Where the mineral planning authority consider that—

    (a) the land or interest is, or forms part of, any dormant or active Phase I or II site, they shall accede to the application; or

    (b) part only of the land or interest is, or forms part of, any dormant or active Phase I or II site, they shall accede to the application so far as it relates to that part of the land or interest,

but shall otherwise refuse the application.

(4) On acceding, whether in whole or in part, to an application made under sub-paragraph (1) above, the mineral planning authority shall amend the first list as follows—

    (a) where they consider that the land or interest, or any part of the land or interest, is a dormant site or an active Phase I or II site, they shall add the mineral site consisting of the land or interest or, as the case may be, that part, to the first list and shall cause the list to indicate whether the site is an active Phase I site, an active Phase II site or a dormant site;

(b) where they consider that the land or interest, or any part of the land or interest, forms part of any mineral site included in the first list, they shall amend the entry in the first list for that site accordingly.

(5) Where the mineral planning authority amend the first list in accordance with sub-paragraph (4) above, they shall also—

(a) in a case where an active Phase I site is added to the first list pursuant to paragraph (a) of that sub-paragraph, cause that list to specify, in respect of that site, the date by which an application is to be made to the mineral planning authority under paragraph 9 below;

(b) in a case where—

(i) the entry for an active Phase I site included in the first list is amended pursuant to paragraph (b) of that sub-paragraph; and

(ii) the date specified in that list in respect of that site as the date by which an application is to be made to the mineral planning authority under paragraph 9 below is a date falling less than 12 months after the date upon which the authority make their decision upon the application in question,

cause that date to be amended so as to specify instead the date upon which expires the period of 12 months from the date on which the applicant is notified under sub-paragraph (10) below of the authority's decision upon his application.

(6) Any date specified pursuant to sub-paragraph (5)(a) above shall be a date—

(a) not earlier than the date upon which expires the period of 12 months from the date on which the applicant is notified under sub-paragraph (10) below of the mineral planning authority's decision upon his application, and

(b) not later than the later of—

(i) the date upon which expires the period of three years from the date upon which the provisions of this Schedule come into force; and

(ii) the date mentioned in paragraph (a) above.

(7) On acceding, whether in whole or in part, to an application made under sub-paragraph (1) above, the mineral planning authority shall, if the second list has been first advertised in accordance with paragraph 5 above prior to the time at which they make their decision on the application, amend the second list as follows—

(a) where they consider that the land or interest, or any part of the land or interest, is an active Phase II site, they shall add the mineral site consisting of the land or interest or, as the case may be, that part, to the second list;

(b) where they consider that the land or interest, or any part of the land or interest, forms part of any active Phase II site included in the second list, they shall amend the entry in that list for that site accordingly.

(8) Where the mineral planning authority amend the second list in accordance with sub-paragraph (7) above, they shall also—

(a) in a case where an active Phase II site is added to the second list pursuant to paragraph (a) of that sub-paragraph, cause that list to specify, in respect of that site, the date by which an application is to be made to the authority under paragraph 9 below;

(b) in a case where—

(i) the entry for an active Phase II site included in the second list is amended pursuant to paragraph (b) of that sub-paragraph; and

(ii) the date specified in that list in respect of that site as the date by which an application is to be made to the authority under paragraph 9 below is a date falling less than 12 months after the date upon which the authority make their decision upon the application in question,

cause that date to be amended so as to specify instead the date upon which expires the period of 12 months from the date on which the applicant is notified under sub-paragraph (10) below of the authority's decision upon his application.

(9) Any date specified pursuant to sub-paragraph (8)(a) above shall be a date—

    (a) not earlier than the date upon which expires the period of 12 months from the date on which the applicant is notified under sub-paragraph (10) below of the mineral planning authority's decision upon his application, and

    (b) not later than the later of—

        (i) the date upon which expires the period of six years from the date upon which the provisions of this Schedule come into force; and

        (ii) the date mentioned in paragraph (a) above.

(10) When a mineral planning authority determine an application made under sub-paragraph (1) above, they shall notify the applicant in writing of their decision and, in a case where they have acceded to the application, whether in whole or in part, shall supply the applicant with details of any amendment to be made to the first or second list in accordance with sub-paragraph (4) or (8) above.

(11) Where a mineral planning authority—

    (a) refuse an application made under sub-paragraph (1) above; or

    (b) accede to such an application only so far as it relates to part of the land or interest in respect of which it was made,

the applicant may by notice appeal to the Secretary of State.

(12) A person who has made such an application may also appeal to the Secretary of State if the mineral planning authority have not given notice to the applicant of their decision on the application within eight weeks of their having received the application or within such extended period as may at any time be agreed upon in writing between the applicant and the authority.

(13) An appeal under sub-paragraph (11) or (12) above must be made by giving notice of appeal to the Secretary of State before the end of the period of six months beginning with—

    (a) in the case of an appeal under sub-paragraph (11) above, the determination; or

    (b) in the case of an appeal under sub-paragraph (12) above, the end of the period of eight weeks mentioned in that sub-paragraph or, as the case may be, the end of the extended period mentioned in that sub-paragraph.   **[597V]**

NOTES

Commencement: to be appointed.

Postponement of the date specified in the first or second list for review of the permissions relating to a Phase I or II site in cases where the existing conditions are satisfactory

7.—(1) Any person who is the owner of any land, or of any interest in any mineral, comprised in—

    (a) an active Phase I site included in the first list; or

    (b) an active Phase II site included in the second list,

may apply to the mineral planning authority for the postponement of the date specified in that list in respect of that site as the date by which an application is to be made to the authority under paragraph 9 below (in this paragraph referred to as "the specified date").

(2) Subject to sub-paragraph (3) below, an application under sub-paragraph (1) above shall be made no later than the day upon which expires the period of three months from the day when—

    (a) in the case of an active Phase I site, the first list; or

    (b) in the case of an active Phase II site, the second list,

was first advertised in accordance with paragraph 5 above.

(3) In the case of—

    (a) an active Phase I site—

        (i) added to the first list in accordance with paragraph 6(4)(a) above; or

        (ii) in respect of which the entry in the first list was amended in accordance with paragraph 6(4)(b) above;

    or

(b) an active Phase II site—

    (i) added to the second list in accordance with paragraph 6(7)(a) above; or

    (ii) in respect of which the entry in the second list was amended in accordance with paragraph 6(7)(b) above,

an application under sub-paragraph (1) above shall be made no later than the day upon which expires the period of three months from the day on which notice was given under paragraph 6(10) above of the mineral planning authority's decision to add the site to or, as the case may be, so to amend the list in question.

(4) An application under sub-paragraph (1) above shall be in writing and shall—

    (a) set out the conditions to which each relevant planning permission relating to the site is subject;

    (b) set out the applicant's reasons for considering those conditions to be satisfactory;

    (c) set out the date which the applicant wishes to be substituted for the specified date; and

    (d) be accompanied by the appropriate certificate (within the meaning of sub-paragraph (5) or (6) below).

(5) For the purposes of sub-paragraph (4) above, as respects England and Wales the appropriate certificate is such a certificate—

    (a) as would be required, under section 65 of the 1990 Act (notice etc of applications for planning permission) and any provision of a development order made by virtue of that section, to accompany the application if it were an application for planning permission for minerals development, but

    (b) with such modifications as are required for the purposes of this paragraph,

and section 65(6) of that Act (offences) shall also have effect in relation to any certificate purporting to be the appropriate certificate.

(6) For the purposes of sub-paragraph (4) above, the appropriate certificate is, as respects Scotland, each of the certificates which would be required, under or by virtue of sections 23 and 24 of the 1972 Act (notice etc of applications for planning permission), to accompany the application if it were an application for planning permission for minerals development, but with such modifications as are required for the purposes of this paragraph; and sections 23(3) and 24(5) of that Act (offences) shall have effect in relation to any certificate purporting to be the appropriate certificate.

(7) Where the mineral planning authority receive an application made under sub-paragraph (1) above—

    (a) if they consider the conditions referred to in sub-paragraph (4)(a) above to be satisfactory they shall agree to the specified date being postponed in which event they shall determine the date to be substituted for that date;

    (b) in any other case they shall refuse the application.

(8) Where the mineral planning authority agree to the specified date being postponed they shall cause the first or, as the case may be, the second list to be amended accordingly.

(9) When a mineral planning authority determine an application made under sub-paragraph (1) above, they shall notify the applicant in writing of their decision and, in a case where they have agreed to the postponement of the specified date, shall notify the applicant of the date which they have determined should be substituted for the specified date.

(10) Where, within three months of the mineral planning authority having received an application under sub-paragraph (1) above, or within such extended period as may at any time be agreed upon in writing between the applicant and the authority, the authority have not given notice, under sub-paragraph (9) above, to the applicant of their decision upon the application, the authority shall be treated as—

    (a) having agreed to the specified date being postponed; and

    (b) having determined that the date referred to in sub-paragraph (4)(c) above be substituted for the specified date,

and sub-paragraph (8) above shall apply accordingly. **[597W]**

NOTES
Commencement: to be appointed.
The 1990 Act: ie the Town and Country Planning Act 1990.
The 1972 Act: ie the Town and Country Planning (Scotland) Act 1972.

Service on owners etc of notice of preparation of the first and second lists

8.—(1) The mineral planning authority shall, no later than the date upon which the first list is first advertised in accordance with paragraph 5 above, serve notice in writing of the first list having been prepared on each person appearing to them to be the owner of any land, or entitled to an interest in any mineral, included within a mineral site included in the first list, but this sub-paragraph is subject to sub-paragraph (7) below.

(2) A notice required to be served by sub-paragraph (1) above shall—

(a) indicate whether the mineral site in question is a dormant site or an active Phase I or II site; and

(b) where that site is an active Phase I site—

(i) indicate the date specified in the first list in relation to that site as the date by which an application is to be made to the mineral planning authority under paragraph 9 below;

(ii) explain the consequences which will occur if such an application is not made by the date so specified; and

(iii) explain the right to apply to have that date postponed, and indicate the date by which such an application must be made.

(3) Where, in relation to any land or mineral included in an active Phase I site, the mineral planning authority—

(a) has served notice on any person under sub-paragraph (1) above; and

(b) has received no application under paragraph 9 below from that person by the date falling eight weeks before the date specified in the first list as the date by which such applications should be made in respect of the site in question,

the authority shall serve a written reminder on that person, and such a reminder shall—

(i) indicate that the land or mineral in question is included in an active Phase I site;

(ii) comply with the requirements of sub-paragraph (2)(b)(i) and (ii) above; and

(iii) be served on that person on or before the date falling four weeks before the date specified in the first list in respect of that site as the date by which an application is to be made to the authority under paragraph 9 below.

(4) The mineral planning authority shall, no later than the date upon which the second list is first advertised in accordance with paragraph 5 above, serve notice in writing of the second list having been prepared on each person appearing to them to be the owner of any land, or entitled to an interest in any mineral, included within an active Phase II site included in the second list, but this sub-paragraph is subject to sub-paragraph (7) below.

(5) A notice required to be served by sub-paragraph (4) above shall—

(a) indicate that the mineral site in question is an active Phase II site; and

(b) indicate the date specified in the second list in relation to that site as the date by which an application is to be made to the mineral planning authority under paragraph 9 below;

(c) explain the consequences which will occur if such an application is not made by the date so specified; and

(d) explain the right to apply to have that date postponed, and indicate the date by which such an application must be made.

(6) Where, in relation to any land or mineral included in an active Phase II site, the mineral planning authority—

(a) has served notice on any person under sub-paragraph (4) above; and

(b) has received no application under paragraph 9 below from that person by the date falling eight weeks before the date specified in the second list as the date by which such applications should be made in respect of the site in question, the authority shall serve a written reminder on that person, and such a reminder shall—

    (i) comply with the requirements of sub-paragraph (5)(a) to (c) above; and

    (ii) be served on that person on or before the date falling four weeks before the date specified in the second list in respect of that site as the date by which an application is to be made to the authority under paragraph 9 below.

(7) Sub-paragraph (1) or (4) above shall not require the mineral planning authority to serve notice under that sub-paragraph upon any person whose identity or address for service is not known to and cannot practicably, after reasonable inquiry, be ascertained by them, but in any such case the authority shall cause to be firmly affixed, to each of one or more conspicuous objects on the land or, as the case may be, on the surface of the land above the interest in question, a copy of the notice which they would (apart from the provisions of this sub-paragraph) have had to serve under that sub-paragraph on the owner of that land or interest.

(8) If, in a case where sub-paragraph (7) above applies, no person makes an application to the authority under paragraph 9 below in respect of the active Phase I or II site which includes the land or interest in question by the date falling eight weeks before the date specified in the first or, as the case may be, the second list as the date by which such applications should be made in respect of that site, the authority shall cause to be firmly affixed, to each of one or more conspicuous objects on the land or, as the case may be, on the surface of the land above the interest in question, a copy of the written reminder that would, in a case not falling within sub-paragraph (7) above, have been served under sub-paragraph (3) or (6) above.

(9) Where by sub-paragraph (7) or (8) above a copy of any notice is required to be affixed to an object on any land that copy shall—

    (a) be displayed in such a way as to be easily visible and legible;

    (b) be first displayed—

        (i) in a case where the requirement arises under sub-paragraph (7) above, no later than the date upon which the first or, as the case may be, the second list is first advertised in accordance with paragraph 5 above; or

        (ii) in a case where the requirement arises under sub-paragraph (8) above, no later than the date falling four weeks before the date specified in the first or, as the case may be, the second list in respect of the site in question as the date by which an application is to be made to the authority under paragraph 9 below; and

    (c) be left in position for at least the period of 21 days from the date when it is first displayed, but where the notice is, without fault or intention of the authority, removed, obscured or defaced before that period has elapsed, that requirement shall be treated as having been complied with if the authority has taken reasonable steps for protection of the notice and, if need be, its replacement.

(10) In sub-paragraphs (7) and (8) above, any reference to a conspicuous object on any land includes, in a case where the person serving a notice considers that there are no or insufficient such objects on the land, a reference to a post driven into or erected upon the land by the person serving the notice for the purpose of having affixed to it the notice in question.

(11) Where the mineral planning authority, being required—

    (a) by sub-paragraph (3) or (6) above to serve a written reminder on any person; or

    (b) by sub-paragraph (8) above to cause a copy of such a reminder to be displayed in the manner set out in that sub-paragraph,

fail to comply with that requirement by the date specified for the purpose, they may at any later time serve or, as the case may be, cause to be displayed, such a written reminder and, in any such case, the date by which an application in relation to the mineral site in question is to be made under paragraph 9 below is the date upon which expires the period of three months from the date when the reminder was served or posted in accordance with the provisions of this sub-paragraph.   **[597X]**

NOTES

Commencement: to be appointed.

*Applications for approval of conditions and appeals in cases where the conditions approved
are not those proposed*

9.—(1) Any person who is the owner of any land, or who is entitled to an interest in a mineral, may, if that land or mineral is or forms part of a dormant site or an active Phase I or II site, apply to the mineral planning authority to determine the conditions to which the relevant planning permissions relating to that site are to be subject.

(2) An application under this paragraph shall be in writing and shall—

(a) identify the mineral site to which the application relates;

(b) specify the land or minerals comprised in the site of which the applicant is the owner or, as the case may be, in which the applicant is entitled to an interest;

(c) identify any relevant planning permissions relating to the site;

(d) identify, and give an address for, each other person that the applicant knows or, after reasonable inquiry, has cause to believe to be an owner of any land, or entitled to any interest in any mineral, comprised in the site;

(e) set out the conditions to which the applicant proposes the permissions referred to in paragraph (c) above should be subject; and

(f) be accompanied by the appropriate certificate (within the meaning of sub-paragraph (3) or (4) below).

(3) For the purposes of sub-paragraph (2) above, as respects England and Wales the appropriate certificate is such a certificate—

(a) as would be required, under section 65 of the 1990 Act (notice etc of applications for planning permission) and any provision of a development order made by virtue of that section, to accompany the application if it were an application for planning permission for minerals development, but

(b) with such modifications as are required for the purposes of this paragraph,

and section 65(6) of that Act (offences) shall also have effect in relation to any certificate purporting to be the appropriate certificate.

(4) For the purposes of sub-paragraph (2) above, the appropriate certificate is, as respects Scotland, each of the certificates which would be required, under or by virtue of sections 23 and 24 of the 1972 Act (notice etc of applications for planning permission), to accompany the application if it were an application for planning permission for minerals development, but with such modifications as are required for the purposes of this paragraph; and sections 23(3) and 24(5) of that Act (offences) shall have effect in relation to any certificate purporting to be the appropriate certificate.

(5) Section 65 of the 1990 Act or, as respects Scotland, section 24 of the 1972 Act (by virtue of which a development order may provide for publicising applications for planning permission) shall have effect, with any necessary modifications, as if subsection (1) of that section also authorised a development order to provide for publicising applications under this paragraph.

(6) Where the mineral planning authority receive an application under this paragraph in relation to a dormant site or an active Phase I or II site they shall determine the conditions to which each relevant planning permission relating to the site is to be subject; and any such permission shall, from the date when the conditions to which it is to be subject are finally determined, have effect subject to the conditions which are determined under this Schedule as being the conditions to which it is to be subject.

(7) The conditions imposed by virtue of a determination under sub-paragraph (6) above—

(a) may include any conditions which may be imposed on a grant of planning permission for minerals development;

(b) may be in addition to, or in substitution for, any existing conditions to which the permission in question is subject.

(8) In determining that a relevant planning permission is to be subject to any condition relating to development for which planning permission is granted by a development order, the mineral planning authority shall have regard to any guidance issued for the purpose by the Secretary of State.

(9) Subject to sub-paragraph (10) below, where, within the period of three months from the mineral planning authority having received an application under this paragraph, or within such extended period as may at any time be agreed upon in writing between the applicant and the authority, the authority have not given notice to the applicant of their decision upon the application, the authority shall be treated as having at the end of that period or, as the case may be, that extended period, determined that the conditions to which any relevant planning permission to which the application relates is to be subject are those specified in the application as being proposed in relation to that permission; and any such permission shall, from that time, have effect subject to those conditions.

(10) Where a mineral planning authority, having received an application under this paragraph, are of the opinion that they are unable to determine the application unless further details are supplied to them, they shall within the period of one month from having received the application give notice to the applicant—

    (a) stating that they are of such opinion; and
    (b) specifying the further details which they require,

and where the authority so serve such a notice the period of three months referred to in sub-paragraph (9) above shall run not from the authority having received the application but from the time when the authority have received all the further details specified in the notice.

(11) Without prejudice to the generality of sub-paragraph (10) above, the further details which may be specified in a notice under that sub-paragraph include any—

    (a) information, plans or drawings; or
    (b) evidence verifying any particulars of details supplied to the authority in respect of the application in question,

which it is reasonable for the authority to request for the purpose of enabling them to determine the application. **[597Y]**

NOTES
    Commencement: to be appointed.
    The 1990 Act: ie the Town and Country Planning Act 1990.
    The 1972 Act: ie the Town and Country Planning (Scotland) Act 1972.

Notice of determination of conditions to be accompanied by additional information in certain cases

10.—(1) This paragraph applies in a case where—

    (a) on an application made to the mineral planning authority under paragraph 9 above in respect of an active Phase I or II site the authority determine under that paragraph the conditions to which the relevant planning permissions relating to the site are to be subject;
    (b) those conditions differ in any respect from the proposed conditions set out in the application; and
    (c) the effect of the conditions, other than any restoration or aftercare conditions, so determined by the authority, as compared with the effect of the conditions, other than any restoration or aftercare conditions, to which the relevant planning permissions in question were subject immediately prior to the authority making the determination, is to restrict working rights in respect of the site.

(2) In a case where this paragraph applies, the mineral planning authority shall, upon giving to the applicant notice of the conditions determined by the authority under paragraph 9 above, also give to the applicant notice—

    (a) stating that the conditions determined by the authority differ in some respect from the proposed conditions set out in the application;
    (b) stating that the effect of the conditions, other than any restoration or aftercare conditions, determined by the authority, as compared with the effect of the conditions, other than any restoration or aftercare conditions, to which the relevant planning permissions relating to the site in question were subject immediately prior to the making of the authority's determination, is to restrict working rights in respect of the site;

(c) identifying the working rights so restricted; and

(d) stating whether, in the opinion of the authority, the effect of that restriction of working rights would be such as to prejudice adversely to an unreasonable degree—

      (i) the economic viability of operating the site; or

      (ii) the asset value of the site.

(3) In determining whether, in their opinion, the effect of that restriction of working rights would be such as is mentioned in sub-paragraph (2)(d) above, a mineral planning authority shall have regard to any guidance issued for the purpose by the Secretary of State.

(4) In this paragraph, "the applicant" means the person who made the application in question under paragraph 9 above.   **[597Z]**

NOTES

Commencement: to be appointed.

Right to appeal against mineral planning authority's determination of conditions etc

11.—(1) Where the mineral planning authority—

(a) on an application under paragraph 9 above determine under that paragraph conditions that differ in any respect from the proposed conditions set out in the application; or

(b) give notice, under paragraph (d) of paragraph 10(2) above, stating that, in their opinion, the restriction of working rights in question would not be such as to prejudice adversely to an unreasonable degree either of the matters referred to in sub-paragraphs (i) and (ii) of the said paragraph (d),

the person who made the application may appeal to the Secretary of State.

(2) An appeal under sub-paragraph (1) above must be made by giving notice of appeal to the Secretary of State before the end of the period of six months beginning with the date on which the authority give notice to the applicant of their determination or, as the case may be, stating their opinion.   **[598]**

NOTES

Commencement: to be appointed.

Permissions ceasing to have effect

12.—(1) Subject to paragraph 8(11) above, where no application under paragraph 9 above in respect of an active Phase I or II site has been served on the mineral planning authority by the date specified in the first or, as the case may be, the second list as the date by which applications under that paragraph in respect of that site are to be made, or by such later date as may at any time be agreed upon in writing between the applicant and the authority, each relevant planning permission relating to the site shall cease to have effect, except insofar as it imposes any restoration or aftercare condition, on the day following the last date on which such an application may be made.

(2) The reference in sub-paragraph (1) above to the date specified in the first or, as the case may be, the second list as the date by which applications under paragraph 9 above are to be made in respect of any Phase I or II site is a reference to the date specified for that purpose in respect of that site in that list as prepared by the mineral planning authority or, where that date has been varied by virtue of any provision of this Schedule, to that date as so varied.

(3) Subject to sub-paragraph (4) below, no relevant planning permission which relates to a dormant site shall have effect to authorise the carrying out of minerals development unless—

(a) an application has been made under paragraph 9 above in respect of that site; and

(b) that permission has effect in accordance with sub-paragraph (6) of that paragraph.

(4) A relevant planning permission which relates to a Phase I or II site not included in the first list shall cease to have effect, except insofar as it imposes any restoration or aftercare condition, on the day following the last date on which an application under sub-paragraph (1)

of paragraph 6 above may be made in respect of that site unless an application has been made under that sub-paragraph by that date in which event, unless the site is added to that list, such a permission shall cease to have effect when the following conditions are met—

    (a) the proceedings on that application, including any proceedings on or in consequence of the application under section 288 of the 1990 Act or, as the case may be, section 233 of the 1972 Act, have been determined, and

    (b) any time for appealing under paragraph 6(11) or (12) above, or applying or further applying under paragraph 6(1) above, (where there is a right to do so) has expired.

                                                     [598A]

NOTES
    Commencement: to be appointed.
    The 1990 Act: ie the Town and Country Planning Act 1990.
    The 1972 Act: ie the Town and Country Planning (Scotland) Act 1972.

Reference of applications to the Secretary of State

13.—(1) The Secretary of State may give directions requiring applications under paragraph 9 above to any mineral planning authority to be referred to him for determination instead of being dealt with by the authority.

(2) Any such direction may relate either to a particular application or to applications of a class specified in the direction.

(3) Where an application is referred to the Secretary of State in accordance with such a direction—

    (a) subject to paragraph (b) below, the following provisions of this Schedule—

        (i) paragraph 9(6) and (7),
        (ii) paragraph 10, and
        (iii) paragraph 14 so far as relating to applications under paragraph 9 above,

    shall apply, with any necessary modifications, as they apply to applications which fall to be determined by the mineral planning authority;

    (b) before determining the application the Secretary of State must, if either the applicant or the mineral planning authority so wish, give each of them an opportunity of appearing before and being heard by a person appointed by the Secretary of State for the purpose; and

    (c) the decision of the Secretary of State on the application shall be final.   **[598B]**

NOTES
    Commencement: to be appointed.

Two or more applicants

14.—(1) Where a mineral planning authority has received from any person a duly made application under paragraph 7(1) or 9 above—

    (a) that person may not make any further application under the paragraph in question in respect of the same site; and

    (b) if the application has been determined, whether or not in the case of an application under paragraph 9 above it has been finally determined, no other person may make an application under the paragraph in question in respect of the same site.

(2) Where—

    (a) a mineral planning authority has received from any person in respect of a mineral site a duly made application under paragraph 7(1) or 9 above; and

    (b) the authority receives from another person a duly made application under the paragraph in question in respect of the same site,

then for the purpose of the determination of the applications and any appeal against such a determination, this Schedule shall have effect as if the applications were a single application received by the authority on the date on which the later application was received by the authority and references to the applicant shall be read as references to either or any of the applicants.   **[598C]**

NOTES

Commencement: to be appointed.

Compensation

15.—(1) This paragraph applies in a case where—

    (a) an application made under paragraph 9 above in respect of an active Phase I or II site is finally determined; and

    (b) the requirements of either sub-paragraph (2) or (3) below are satisfied.

(2) The requirements, referred to in sub-paragraph (1)(b) above, of this sub-paragraph are—

    (a) that the conditions to which the relevant planning permissions relating to the site are to be subject were determined by the mineral planning authority;

    (b) no appeal was made under paragraph 11(1)(a) above in respect of that determination or any such appeal was withdrawn or dismissed; and

    (c) the authority gave notice under paragraph (d) of paragraph 10(2) above and either—

        (i) that notice stated that, in the authority's opinion, the restriction of working rights in question would be such as to prejudice adversely to an unreasonable degree either of the matters referred to in sub-paragraphs (i) and (ii) of the said paragraph (d); or

        (ii) that notice stated that, in the authority's opinion, the restriction in question would not be such as would so prejudice either of those matters but an appeal under paragraph 11(1) above in respect of the giving of the notice has been allowed.

(3) The requirements, referred to in sub-paragraph (1)(b) above, of this sub-paragraph are that the conditions to which the relevant planning permissions are to be subject were determined by the Secretary of State (whether upon an appeal under paragraph 11(1)(a) above or upon a reference under paragraph 13 above) and—

    (a) in a case where those conditions were determined upon an appeal under paragraph 11(1)(a) above either—

        (i) the mineral planning authority gave notice under paragraph (d) of paragraph 10(2) above stating that, in their opinion, the restriction of working rights in question would be such as to prejudice adversely to an unreasonable degree either of the matters referred to in sub-paragraphs (i) and (ii) of the said paragraph (d), or

        (ii) the authority gave a notice under the said paragraph (d) stating that, in their opinion, the restriction in question would not be such as would so prejudice either of those matters but an appeal under paragraph 11(1)(b) above in respect of the giving of that notice has been allowed;

    or

    (b) in a case where those conditions were determined upon a reference under paragraph 13 above, the Secretary of State gave notice under paragraph (d) of paragraph 10(2) above stating that, in his opinion, the restriction of working rights in question would be such as to prejudice adversely to an unreasonable degree either of the matters referred to in sub-paragraphs (i) and (ii) of the said paragraph (d).

(4) In a case to which this paragraph applies—

    (a) as respects England and Wales, Parts IV and XI of the 1990 Act, or

    (b) as respects Scotland, Parts VIII and XI of the 1972 Act,

shall have effect as if an order made under section 97 of the 1990 Act or, as the case may be, section 42 of the 1972 Act, had been confirmed by the Secretary of State under section 98 of the 1990 Act or, as the case may be, section 42 of the 1972 Act at the time when the application in question was finally determined and, as so confirmed, had effect to modify those permissions to the extent specified in sub-paragraph (5) below.

(5) For the purposes of sub-paragraph (4) above, the order which is treated by virtue of that sub-paragraph as having been made under section 97 of the 1990 Act or section 42 of the 1972 Act is one whose only effect adverse to the interests of any person having an interest in the land or minerals comprised in the mineral site is to restrict working rights in respect of the site to the same extent as the relevant restriction.

(6) For the purposes of section 116 of the 1990 Act and section 167A of the 1972 Act and of any regulations made under those sections, the permissions treated as being modified by the order mentioned in sub-paragraph (4) above shall be treated as if they were planning permissions for development which neither consists of nor includes any minerals development. **[598D]**

NOTES

Commencement: to be appointed.
The 1990 Act: ie the Town and Country Planning Act 1990.
The 1972 Act: ie the Town and Country Planning (Scotland) Act 1972.

Appeals: general procedural provisions

16.—(1) This paragraph applies to appeals under any of the following provisions of this Schedule—

(a) paragraph 6(11) or (12) above; or
(b) paragraph 11(1) above.

(2) Notice of appeal in respect of an appeal to which this paragraph applies shall be given on a form supplied by or on behalf of the Secretary of State for use for that purpose, and giving, so far as reasonably practicable, the information required by that form.

(3) Paragraph 6 of Schedule 2 to the 1991 Act (determination of appeals) shall, as respects England and Wales, apply to an appeal to which this paragraph applies as it applies to an appeal under paragraph 5 of that Schedule.

(4) As respects England and Wales, sections 284 to 288 of the 1990 Act (validity of certain decisions and proceedings for questioning their validity) shall have effect as if the action mentioned in section 284(3) of that Act included any decision of the Secretary of State

(a) on an appeal to which this paragraph applies; or
(b) on an application under paragraph 9 above referred to him under paragraph 13 above.

(5) Paragraph 6 of Schedule 10A to the 1972 Act (determination of appeals) shall, as respects Scotland, apply to an appeal to which this paragraph applies as it applies to appeals under paragraph 5 of that Schedule.

(6) As respects Scotland, sections 231 to 233 of the 1972 Act (validity of certain decisions and proceedings for questioning their validity) shall have effect as if the action mentioned in section 231(3) included any decision of the Secretary of State—

(a) on an appeal to which this paragraph applies; or
(b) on an application under paragraph 9 above referred to him under paragraph 13 above.

(7) As respects Scotland, Schedule 7 to the 1972 Act shall apply to appeals to which this paragraph applies. **[598E]**

NOTES

Commencement: to be appointed.
The 1991 Act: ie the Planning and Compensation Act 1991.
The 1990 Act: ie the Town and Country Planning Act 1990.
The 1972 Act: ie the Town and Country Planning (Scotland) Act 1972.

SCHEDULE 14

Section 96

PERIODIC REVIEW OF MINERAL PLANNING PERMISSIONS

Duty to carry out periodic reviews

1. The mineral planning authority shall, in accordance with the provisions of this Schedule, cause periodic reviews to be carried out of the mineral permissions relating to a mining site.

[598F]

NOTES

Commencement: to be appointed.

Interpretation

2.—(1) For the purposes of this Schedule—

"first review date", in relation to a mining site, shall, subject to paragraph 5 below, be ascertained in accordance with paragraph 3 below;

"mineral permission" means any planning permission, other than a planning permission granted by a development order, for minerals development;

"mineral planning authority"—

    (a) as respects England and Wales, means a mineral planning authority within the meaning of the 1990 Act, and

    (b) as respects Scotland, means a planning authority for the purposes of the 1972 Act;

"mining site" means—

    (a) in a case where it appears to the mineral planning authority to be expedient to treat as a single site the aggregate of the land to which any two or more mineral permissions relate, the aggregate of the land to which those permissions relate; and

    (b) in any other case, the land to which a mineral permission relates;

"old mining permission" has the meaning given—

    (a) as respects England and Wales, by section 22(1) of the 1991 Act, and

    (b) as respects Scotland, by section 49H(1) of the 1972 Act; and

"owner", in relation to any land—

    (a) as respects England and Wales, means any person who—

        (i) is the estate owner in respect of the fee simple, or

        (ii) is entitled to a tenancy granted or extended for a term of years certain of which not less than seven years remains unexpired; and

    (b) as respects Scotland, has the meaning given by paragraph 10(1) of Schedule 10A to the 1972 Act.

(2) In determining whether it appears to them to be expedient to treat as a single site the aggregate of the land to which two or more mineral permissions relate a mineral planning authority shall have regard to any guidance issued for the purpose by the Secretary of State.

(3) Any reference (however expressed) in this Schedule to a mining site being a site to which relates—

    (a) an old mining permission; or

    (b) a mineral permission,

is a reference to the mining site, or some part of it, being the land to which the permission relates.

(4) For the purposes of this Schedule, an application made under paragraph 6 below is finally determined when—

(a) the proceedings on the application, including any proceedings on or in consequence of an application under section 288 of the 1990 Act or section 233 of the 1972 Act, have been determined, and

(b) any time for appealing under paragraph 9(1) below, or applying or further applying under paragraph 6 below, (where there is a right to do so) has expired.   **[598G]**

NOTES

Commencement: to be appointed.
The 1990 Act: ie the Town and Country Planning Act 1990.
The 1972 Act: ie the Town and Country Planning (Scotland) Act 1972.
The 1991 Act: ie the Planning and Compensation Act 1991.

The first review date

3.—(1) Subject to sub-paragraph (7) below, in a case where the mineral permissions relating to a mining site include an old mining permission, the first review date means—

(a) the date falling fifteen years after the date upon which, pursuant to an application made under paragraph 2 of Schedule 2 to the 1991 Act or, as the case may be, paragraph 2 of Schedule 10A to the 1972 Act, the conditions to which that old mining permission is to be subject are finally determined under that Schedule; or

(b) where there are two or more old mining permissions relating to that site, and the date upon which those conditions are finally determined is not the same date for each of those permissions, the date falling fifteen years after the date upon which was made the last such final determination to be so made in respect of any of those permissions,

and paragraph 10(2) of Schedule 2 to the 1991 Act or, as the case may be, paragraph 10(2) of Schedule 10A to the 1972 Act (meaning of "finally determined") shall apply for the purposes of this sub-paragraph as it applies for the purposes of section 22 of and Schedule 2 to the 1991 Act or, as the case may be, section 49H of and Schedule 10A to the 1972 Act.

(2) Subject to sub-paragraph (7) below, in the case of a mining site which is a Phase I or II site within the meaning of Schedule 13 to this Act, the first review date means the date falling fifteen years after the date upon which, pursuant to an application made under paragraph 9 of that Schedule, there is determined under that paragraph the conditions to which the relevant planning permissions (within the meaning of that Schedule) relating to the site are to be subject.

(3) Subject to sub-paragraphs (4) and (7) below, in the case of a mining site—

(a) which is not a Phase I or II site within the meaning of Schedule 13 to this Act; and

(b) to which no old mining permission relates,

the first review date is the date falling fifteen years after the date upon which was granted the most recent mineral permission which relates to the site.

(4) Where, in the case of a mining site falling within sub-paragraph (3) above, the most recent mineral permission relating to that site relates, or the most recent such permissions (whether or not granted on the same date) between them relate, to part only of the site, and in the opinion of the mineral planning authority it is expedient, for the purpose of ascertaining, under that sub-paragraph, the first review date in respect of that site, to treat that permission or those permissions as having been granted at the same time as the last of the other mineral permissions relating to the site, the first review date for that site shall be ascertained under that sub-paragraph accordingly.

(5) A mineral planning authority shall, in deciding whether they are of such an opinion as is mentioned in sub-paragraph (4) above, have regard to any guidance issued by the Secretary of State for the purpose.

(6) Subject to sub-paragraph (7) below, in the case of a mining site—

(a) to which relates a mineral permission in respect of which an order has been made under section 97 of the 1990 Act or section 42 of the 1972 Act, or

(b) in respect of which, or any part of which, an order has been made under paragraph 1 of Schedule 9 to the 1990 Act or section 49 of the 1972 Act, the first review date shall be the date falling fifteen years after the date upon which the order took effect or, in a case where there is more than one such order, upon which the last of those orders to take effect took effect.

(7) In the case of a mining site for which the preceding provisions of this paragraph have effect to specify two or more different dates as the first review date, the first review date shall be the latest of those dates. **[598H]**

NOTES

Commencement: to be appointed.
The 1991 Act: ie the Planning and Compensation Act 1991.
The 1972 Act: ie the Town and Country Planning (Scotland) Act 1972.
The 1990 Act: ie the Town and Country Planning Act 1990.

Service of notice of first periodic review

4.—(1) The mineral planning authority shall, in connection with the first periodic review of the mineral permissions relating to a mining site, no later than 12 months before the first review date, serve notice upon each person appearing to them to be the owner of any land, or entitled to an interest in any mineral, included in that site.

(2) A notice required to be served under sub-paragraph (1) above shall—

   (a) specify the mining site to which it relates;
   (b) identify the mineral permissions relating to that site;
   (c) state the first review date;
   (d) state that the first review date is the date by which an application must be made for approval of the conditions to which the mineral permissions relating to the site are to be subject and explain the consequences which will occur if no such application is made by that date; and
   (e) explain the right to apply for postponement of the first review date and give the date by which such an application has to be made.

(3) Where, in relation to any land or mineral included in a mining site, the mineral planning authority—

   (a) has served notice on any person under sub-paragraph (1) above; and
   (b) has received no application under paragraph 6 below from that person by the date falling eight weeks before the first review date,

the authority shall serve a written reminder on that person.

(4) A reminder required to be served under sub-paragraph (3) above shall—

   (a) indicate that the land or mineral in question is included in a mining site;
   (b) comply with the requirements of sub-paragraph (2)(a) to (d) above; and
   (c) be served on the person in question on or before the date falling four weeks before the first review date.

(5) Sub-paragraph (1) above shall not require the mineral planning authority to serve notice under that sub-paragraph upon any person whose identity or address for service is not known to and cannot practicably, after reasonable inquiry, be ascertained by them, but in any such case the authority shall cause to be firmly affixed, to each of one or more conspicuous objects on the land or, as the case may be, on the surface of the land above the interest in question, a copy of the notice which they would (apart from the provisions of this sub-paragraph) have had to serve under that sub-paragraph on the owner of that land or interest.

(6) If, in a case where sub-paragraph (5) above applies, no person makes an application to the authority under paragraph 6 below in respect of the mining site which includes the land or interest in question by the date falling eight weeks before the first review date, the authority shall cause to be firmly affixed, to each of one or more conspicuous objects on the land or, as the case may be, on the surface of the land above the interest in question, a copy of the written reminder that would, in a case not falling within sub-paragraph (5) above, have been served under sub-paragraph (3) above.

(7) Where by sub-paragraph (5) or (6) above a copy of any notice is required to be affixed to an object on any land that copy shall—

(a) be displayed in such a way as to be easily visible and legible;

(b) be first displayed—

(i) in a case where the requirement arises under sub-paragraph (5) above, no later than 12 months before the first review date; or

(ii) in a case where the requirement arises under sub-paragraph (6) above, no later than the date falling four weeks before the first review date;

and

(c) be left in position for at least the period of 21 days from the date when it is first displayed, but where the notice is, without fault or intention of the authority, removed, obscured or defaced before that period has elapsed, that requirement shall be treated as having been complied with if the authority has taken reasonable steps for protection of the notice and, if need be, its replacement.

(8) In sub-paragraphs (5) and (6) above, any reference to a conspicuous object on any land includes, in a case where the person serving a notice considers that there are no or insufficient such objects on the land, a reference to a post driven into or erected upon the land by the person serving the notice for the purpose of having affixed to it a copy of the notice in question.   **[598I]**

NOTES

Commencement: to be appointed.

Application for postponement of the first review date

5.—(1) Any person who is the owner of any land, or of any interest in any mineral, comprised in a mining site may, no later than the day upon which expires the period of three months from the day upon which notice was served upon him under paragraph 4 above, apply under this paragraph to the mineral planning authority for the postponement of the first review date.

(2) An application under this paragraph shall be in writing and shall set out—

(a) the conditions to which each mineral permission relating to the site is subject;

(b) the applicant's reasons for considering those conditions to be satisfactory; and

(c) the date which the applicant wishes to have substituted for the first review date.

(3) Where the mineral planning authority receive an application made under this paragraph—

(a) if they consider the conditions referred to in sub-paragraph (2)(a) above to be satisfactory they shall agree to the first review date being postponed in which event they shall determine the date to be substituted for that date;

(b) in any other case they shall refuse the application.

(4) When a mineral planning authority determine an application made under this paragraph, they shall notify the applicant in writing of their decision and, in a case where they have agreed to the postponement of the first review date, shall notify the applicant of the date which they have determined should be substituted for the first review date.

(5) Where, within the period of three months of the mineral planning authority having received an application under this paragraph, or within such extended period as may at any time be agreed upon in writing between the applicant and the authority, the authority have not given notice, under sub-paragraph (4) above, to the applicant of their decision upon the application, the authority shall be treated as having, at the end of that period or, as the case may be, that extended period—

(a) agreed to the first review date being postponed; and

(b) determined that the date referred to in sub-paragraph (2)(c) above be substituted for the first review date.   **[598J]**

NOTES
Commencement: to be appointed.

Application to determine the conditions to which the mineral permissions relating to a mining site are to be subject

6.—(1) Any person who is the owner of any land, or who is entitled to an interest in a mineral, may, if that land or mineral is or forms part of a mining site, apply to the mineral planning authority to determine the conditions to which the mineral permissions relating to that site are to be subject.

(2) An application under this paragraph shall be in writing and shall—

(a) identify the mining site in respect of which the application is made and state that the application is made in connection with the first periodic review of the mineral permissions relating to that site;

(b) specify the land or minerals comprised in the site of which the applicant is the owner or, as the case may be, in which the applicant is entitled to an interest;

(c) identify the mineral permissions relating to the site;

(d) identify, and give an address for, each other person that the applicant knows or, after reasonable inquiry, has cause to believe to be an owner of any land, or entitled to any interest in any mineral, comprised in the site;

(e) set out the conditions to which the applicant proposes the permissions referred to in paragraph (c) above should be subject; and

(f) be accompanied by the appropriate certificate (within the meaning of sub-paragraph (3) or (4) below).

(3) For the purposes of sub-paragraph (2) above, as respects England and Wales the appropriate certificate is such a certificate—

(a) as would be required, under section 65 of the 1990 Act and any provision of a development order made by virtue of that section, to accompany the application if it were an application for planning permission for minerals development, but

(b) with such modifications as are required for the purposes of this paragraph,

and section 65(6) of the 1990 Act shall also have effect in relation to any certificate purporting to be the appropriate certificate.

(4) For the purposes of sub-paragraph (2) above, the appropriate certificate is, as respects Scotland, each of the certificates which would be required, under or by virtue of sections 23 and 24 of the 1972 Act (notice etc of applications for planning permission), to accompany the application if it were an application for planning permission for minerals development, but with such modifications as are required for the purposes of this paragraph; and sections 23(3) and 24(5) of that Act (offences) shall have effect in relation to any certificate purporting to be the appropriate certificate.

(5) Where the mineral planning authority receive an application under this paragraph in relation to a mining site they shall determine the conditions to which each mineral permission relating to the site is to be subject.

(6) The conditions imposed by virtue of a determination under sub-paragraph (5) above—

(a) may include any conditions which may be imposed on a grant of planning permission for minerals development;

(b) may be in addition to, or in substitution for, any existing conditions to which the permission in question is subject.

(7) In determining that a mineral permission is to be subject to any condition relating to development for which planning permission is granted by a development order, the mineral planning authority shall have regard to any guidance issued for the purpose by the Secretary of State.

(8) Subject to sub-paragraph (9) below, where, within the period of three months of the mineral planning authority having received an application under this paragraph, or within such extended period as may at any time be agreed upon in writing between the applicant and the authority, the authority have not given notice to the applicant of their decision upon the application, the authority shall be treated as having at the end of that period or, as the case

may be, that extended period, determined that the conditions to which any mineral permission to which the application relates is to be subject are those specified in the application as being proposed in relation to that permission; and any such permission shall, from that time, have effect subject to those conditions.

(9) Where a mineral planning authority, having received an application under this paragraph, are of the opinion that they are unable to determine the application unless further details are supplied to them, they shall within the period of one month from having received the application give notice to the applicant—

(a) stating that they are of such opinion; and
(b) specifying the further details which they require,

and where the authority so serve such a notice the period of three months referred to in sub-paragraph (8) above shall run not from the authority having received the application but from the time when the authority have received all the further details specified in the notice.

(10) Without prejudice to the generality of sub-paragraph (9) above, the further details which may be specified in a notice under that sub-paragraph include any—

(a) information, plans or drawings; or
(b) evidence verifying any particulars of details supplied to the authority in respect of the application in question,

which it is reasonable for the authority to request for the purpose of enabling them to determine the application.   **[598K]**

NOTES
    Commencement: to be appointed.
    The 1990 Act: ie the Town and Country Planning Act 1990.
    The 1972 Act: ie the Town and Country Planning (Scotland) Act 1972.

Permissions ceasing to have effect

7. Where no application under paragraph 6 above in respect of a mining site has been served on the mineral planning authority by the first review date, or by such later date as may at any time be agreed upon in writing between the applicant and the authority, each mineral permission—

(a) relating to the site; and
(b) identified in the notice served in relation to the site under paragraph 4 above,

shall cease to have effect, except insofar as it imposes any restoration or aftercare condition, on the day following the first review date or, as the case may be, such later agreed date.

[598L]

NOTES
    Commencement: to be appointed.

Reference of applications to the Secretary of State

8.—(1) The Secretary of State may give directions requiring applications made under paragraph 6 above to any mineral planning authority to be referred to him for determination instead of being dealt with by the authority.

(2) A direction under sub-paragraph (1) above may relate either to a particular application or to applications of a class specified in the direction.

(3) Where an application is referred to the Secretary of State in accordance with a direction under sub-paragraph (1) above—

(a) subject to paragraph (b) below, paragraph 6(5) and (6) above, and paragraph 11 below so far as relating to applications under paragraph 6 above, shall apply, with any necessary modifications, to his determination of the application as they apply to the determination of applications by the mineral planning authority;

(b) before determining the application the Secretary of State must, if either the applicant or the mineral planning authority so wish, give each of them an opportunity of appearing before and being heard by a person appointed by the Secretary of State for the purpose; and

(c) the decision of the Secretary of State on the application shall be final.   **[598M]**

NOTES

Commencement: to be appointed.

Appeals

9.—(1) Where on an application under paragraph 6 above the mineral planning authority determine conditions that differ in any respect from the proposed conditions set out in the application, the applicant may appeal to the Secretary of State.

(2) An appeal under sub-paragraph (1) above must be made by giving notice of appeal to the Secretary of State, before the end of the period of six months beginning with the determination, on a form supplied by or on behalf of the Secretary of State for use for that purpose, and giving, so far as reasonably practicable, the information required by that form.

(3) Paragraph 6 of Schedule 2 to the 1991 Act (determination of appeals) shall, as respects England and Wales, apply to appeals under sub-paragraph (1) above as it applies to appeals under paragraph 5 of that Schedule.

(4) As respects England and Wales, sections 284 to 288 of the 1990 Act shall have effect as if the action mentioned in section 284(3) of that Act included any decision of the Secretary of State—

(a) on an appeal under sub-paragraph (1) above; or

(b) on an application under paragraph 6 above referred to him under paragraph 8 above.

(5) Paragraph 6 of Schedule 10A to the 1972 Act (determination of appeals) shall, as respects Scotland, apply to appeals under sub-paragraph (1) above as it applies to appeals under paragraph 5 of that Schedule.

(6) As respects Scotland, sections 231 to 233 of the 1972 Act shall have effect as if the action mentioned in section 231(3) included any decision of the Secretary of State—

(a) on an appeal under sub-paragraph (1) above; or

(b) on an application under paragraph 6 above referred to him under paragraph 8 above.

(7) As respects Scotland, Schedule 7 to the 1972 Act shall apply to appeals under sub-paragraph (1) above.   **[598N]**

NOTES

Commencement: to be appointed.
The 1991 Act: ie the Planning and Compensation Act 1991.
The 1990 Act: ie the Town and Country Planning Act 1990.
The 1972 Act: ie the Town and Country Planning (Scotland) Act 1972.

Time from which conditions determined under this Schedule are to take effect

10.—(1) Where an application has been made under paragraph 6 above in respect of a mining site, each of the mineral permissions relating to the site shall, from the time when the application is finally determined, have effect subject to the conditions to which it is determined under this Schedule that permission is to be subject.

(2) Sub-paragraph (1) above is without prejudice to paragraph 6(8) above.   **[598O]**

NOTES

Commencement: to be appointed.

Two or more applicants

11.—(1) Where a mineral planning authority have received from any person a duly made application under paragraph 5 or 6 above—

(a) that person may not make any further application under the paragraph in question in respect of the same site; and

(b) if the application has been determined, whether or not in the case of an application under paragraph 6 above it has been finally determined, no other person may make an application under the paragraph in question in respect of the same site.

(2) Where—

(a) a mineral planning authority have received from any person in respect of a mineral site a duly made application under paragraph 5 or 6 above; and

(b) the authority receives from another person a duly made application under the paragraph in question in respect of the same site,

then for the purpose of the determination of the applications and any appeal against such a determination, this Schedule shall have effect as if the applications were a single application received by the authority on the date on which the later application was received by the authority and references to the applicant shall be read as references to either or any of the applicants. **[598P]**

NOTES
Commencement: to be appointed.

Second and subsequent periodic reviews

12.—(1) In this paragraph, in relation to a mining site, but subject to paragraph 5 above as applied by sub-paragraph (2) below, ''review date'' means—

(a) in the case of the second periodic review, the date falling fifteen years after the date upon which was finally determined an application made under paragraph 6 above in respect of the site; and

(b) in the case of subsequent periodic reviews, the date falling fifteen years after the date upon which there was last finally determined under this Schedule an application made in respect of that site under paragraph 6 above as applied by sub-paragraph (2) below.

(2) Paragraphs 4 to 11 above shall apply in respect of the second or any subsequent periodic review of the mineral permissions relating to a mining site as they apply to the first such periodic review, but as if—

(a) any reference in those paragraphs to the ''first review date'' were a reference to the review date; and

(b) the references in paragraphs 4(1) and 6(2)(a) above to the first periodic review were references to the periodic review in question. **[598Q]**

NOTES
Commencement: to be appointed.

Compensation

13.—(1) This paragraph applies where—

(a) an application made under paragraph 6 above in respect of a mining site is finally determined; and

(b) the conditions to which the mineral permissions relating to the site are to be subject, as determined under this Schedule, differ in any respect from the proposed conditions set out in the application; and

(c) the effect of the new conditions, except insofar as they are restoration or aftercare conditions, as compared with the effect of the existing conditions, except insofar as they were restoration or aftercare conditions, is to restrict working rights in respect of the site.

(2) For the purposes of this paragraph—

"the new conditions", in relation to a mining site, means the conditions, determined under this Schedule, to which the mineral permissions relating to the site are to be subject; and

"the existing conditions", in relation to a mining site, means the conditions to which the mineral permissions relating to the site were subject immediately prior to the final determination of the application made under paragraph 6 above in respect of that site.

(3) For the purposes of this paragraph, working rights are restricted in respect of a mining site if any of—

(a) the size of the area which may be used for the winning and working of minerals or the depositing of mineral waste;

(b) the depth to which operations for the winning and working of minerals may extend;

(c) the height of any deposit of mineral waste;

(d) the rate at which any particular mineral may be extracted;

(e) the rate at which any particular mineral waste may be deposited;

(f) the period at the expiry of which any winning or working of minerals or depositing of mineral waste is to cease; or

(g) the total quantity of minerals which may be extracted from, or of mineral waste which may be deposited on, the site,

is restricted or reduced in respect of the mining site in question.

(4) In a case to which this paragraph applies, but subject to sub-paragraph (6) below, as respects England and Wales, Parts IV and XI of the 1990 Act and, as respects Scotland, Parts VIII and XI of the 1972 Act, shall have effect as if an order made under section 97 of the 1990 Act or, as the case may be, section 42 of the 1972 Act—

(a) had been confirmed by the Secretary of State under section 98 of the 1990 Act or, as the case may be, section 42 of the 1972 Act at the time when the application in question was finally determined; and

(b) as so confirmed, had effect to modify those permissions to the extent specified in sub-paragraph (6) below.

(5) For the purposes of this paragraph, the order referred to in sub-paragraph (4) above is one whose only effect adverse to the interests of any person having an interest in the land or minerals comprised in the mineral site is to restrict working rights in respect of the site to the same extent as the relevant restriction.

(6) For the purposes of section 116 of the 1990 Act and section 167A of the 1972 Act and of any regulations made under those sections, the permissions treated as being modified by the order mentioned in sub-paragraph (4) above shall be treated as if they were planning permissions for development which neither consists of nor includes any minerals development. **[598R–600]**

NOTES

Commencement: to be appointed.
The 1990 Act: ie the Town and Country Planning Act 1990.
The 1972 Act: ie the Town and Country Planning (Scotland) Act 1972.

(Schs 15-24 are outside the scope of this work.)

PART II
SECONDARY LEGISLATION

TOWN AND COUNTRY PLANNING (TREE PRESERVATION ORDER) REGULATIONS 1969
(SI 1969/17)

NOTES

Made: 7 January 1969

Commencement: 10 February 1969

Authority: Town and Country Planning Act 1962, ss 29, 217, Civic Amenities Act 1967, s 16, Town and Country Planning Act 1968, s 81; subsequently had effect under Town and Country Planning Act 1971, ss 60, 61, 287; now have effect under Town and Country Planning Act 1990, s 199

ARRANGEMENT OF REGULATIONS

1. Citation and commencement

These regulations may be cited as the Town and Country Planning (Tree Preservation Order) Regulations 1969 and shall come into operation on 10th February 1969.

[601]

2. Interpretation

(1) In these regulations, unless the context otherwise requires—

"the Act" means the Town and Country Planning Act 1962;

"the Act of 1967" means the Civic Amenities Act 1967;

"authority" includes a local planning authority making an order as hereinafter defined, and a local authority making such an order under powers delegated by a local planning authority;

"The Conservator of Forests" means in relation to an order the Forestry Commissioners' Conservator of Forests for the conservancy in which the trees included in the order are situated;

"District Valuer" means in relation to an order the officer of the Commissioners of Inland Revenue for the time being appointed to be District Valuer and Valuation Officer for the area in which the trees included in the order are situated;

"the Minister" means, except as respects Wales, the Minister of Housing and Local Government and as respects Wales the Secretary of State;

"order" means a tree preservation order made under section 29 of the Act and includes an order amending or revoking such an order;

"Wales" includes Monmouthshire.

(2) The Interpretation Act 1889 shall apply to the interpretation of these regulations as it applies to the interpretation of an Act of Parliament.   **[602]**

4. Form and contents of order

(1) An order shall be in the form (or substantially in the form) set out in the Schedule hereto.

(2) The order shall define the position of the trees, groups of trees, or woodlands to which it relates, and for that purpose shall include a map. **[603]**

5. Procedure

An authority shall, on making an order—

(a) place on deposit for inspection at a place or places convenient to the locality in which the trees, or groups of trees, or woodlands are situated a certified copy or copies of the order and of the map;

(b) send a copy of the order and the map to the Conservator of Forests and the District Valuer together with a list of all the persons served under (c) of this regulation;

(c) serve on the owners and occupiers of the land affected by the order, and on any other person then known to them to be entitled to work by surface working any minerals in that land or to fell any of the trees affected by the order, a copy of the order and the map together with a notice stating—

   (i) the grounds for making the order;

   (ii) the address or addresses of the place or places where a certified copy or copies of the order and map have been deposited for inspection, and the hours during which they may be inspected;

   (iii) that objections and representations with respect to the order may be made to [the authority] in accordance with regulation 7 hereof, a copy of which regulation shall be included in or appended to the notice;

   (iv) ...

   (v) where the order contains a direction under section 16 of the Act of 1967, the effect of the direction. **[604]**

NOTES
Amended by SI 1981/14, reg 2(a).

6. *(Revoked by SI 1981/14, reg 2(b).)*

7. Objections and representations

(1) Every objection or representation with respect to an order shall be made in writing to [the authority, and shall state the grounds thereof], and specify the particular trees, groups of trees, or woodlands in respect of which it is made.

(2) An objection or representation shall be duly made if it complies with paragraph (1) of this regulation and is received by [the authority] within 28 days from the date of the service of the notice of the making of the order. **[605]**

NOTES
Amended by SI 1981/14, reg 2(c).

8. Consideration by the Minister

(1) ...

(2) [The authority] shall, before deciding whether to confirm the order, take into consideration any objections and representations duly made in accordance with regulation 7 hereof, and, if a local inquiry is held, the report of that inquiry. **[606]**

NOTES
Amended by SI 1981/14, reg 2(d).

9. Action on receipt of Minister's decision

[The authority shall, as soon as practicable after reaching a decision on the order, inform the owners and occupiers of the land to which the order relates, the Conservator of Forests, the District Valuer and any other person on whom notice has been served in accordance with the provisions of regulation 5 hereof, of their decision; and, in addition, where the order has been confirmed subject to modifications, the authority shall serve on every such person a copy of the order and the map as confirmed.]   **[607]**

NOTES

Substituted by SI 1981/14, reg 2(e).

SCHEDULE

Form of Tree Preservation Order

Town and Country Planning Acts 1962 and 1968

[Civic Amenities Act 1967]
(Include only where order contains a direction under section 16 of the Civic Amenities Act 1967)

(Insert title of order)

[The   Council (Insert name of local planning authority)] [The
Council (Insert name), on behalf of   Council (Insert name of local planning authority)] in
this order called "the authority", in pursuance of the powers conferred in that behalf by section 29 of the Town and Country Planning Act 1962 [and section 16 of the Civic Amenities Act 1967] (Include only where order contains a direction under section 16 of the Civic Amenities Act 1967), and subject to the provisions of the Forestry Act 1967, hereby makes the following order:

1. In this Order—

"the Act" means the Town and Country Planning Act 1962;

"owner" means the owner in fee simple, either in possession or who has granted a lease or tenancy of which the unexpired portion is less than three years; lessee (including a sub-lessee) or tenant in possession, the unexpired portion of whose lease or tenancy is three years or more; and a mortgagee in possession; and "the Minister" means the [Minister of Housing and Local Government] [Secretary of State for Wales].

2. Subject to the provisions of this Order and to the exemptions specified in the Second Schedule hereto, no person shall, except with the consent of the authority and in accordance with the conditions, if any, imposed on such consent, cut down, top, lop [uproot, wilfully damage] or wilfully destroy or cause or permit the cutting down, topping, lopping [uprooting, wilfully damaging] or wilful destruction of any tree specified in the First Schedule hereto or comprised in a group of trees or in a woodland therein specified, the position of which trees, groups of trees and woodlands is defined in the manner indicated in the said First Schedule on the map annexed hereto (Map to be to a scale of not less than 25 inches to one mile, except in the case of large woodlands when the scale shall be 6 inches to one mile.) which map shall, for the purpose of such definition as aforesaid, prevail where any ambiguity arises between it and the specification in the said First Schedule.

3. An application for consent made to the authority (When Tree Preservation Order is made by a District Council on behalf of a County Council an application for consent should be made to the District Council. See also note at foot of this page) under Article 2 of this Order shall be in writing stating the reasons for making the application, and shall by reference if necessary to a plan specify the trees to which the application relates, and the operations for the carrying out of which consent is required.

4.—(1) Where an application for consent is made to the authority (When Tree Preservation Order is made by a District Council on behalf of a County Council an application for consent should be made to the District Council. See also note at foot of this page) under this Order, the authority may grant such consent either unconditionally, or subject to such conditions (including conditions requiring the replacement of any tree by one or more trees on the site or in the immediate vicinity thereof), as the authority may think fit, or may refuse consent:

Provided that where the application relates to any woodland specified in the First Schedule to this Order the authority shall grant consent so far as accords with the principles of good forestry, except where, in the opinion of the authority, it is necessary in the interests of amenity to maintain the special character of the woodland or the woodland character of the area, and shall not impose conditions on such consent requiring replacement or replanting.

(2) The authority shall keep a register of all applications for consent under this Order containing information as to the nature of the application, the decision of the authority thereon, any compensation awarded in consequence of such decision and any directions as to replanting of woodlands; and every such register shall be available for inspection by the public at all reasonable hours.

5. Where the authority refuse consent under this Order or grant such consent subject to conditions they may when refusing or granting consent certify in respect of any trees for which they are so refusing or granting consent that they are satisfied—

   (a) that the refusal or condition is in the interests of good forestry; or
   [(b) in the case of trees, other than trees comprised in a group of trees or in a woodland, that the trees have an outstanding or special amenity value; or
   (c) in the case of trees which are comprised in a group of trees or in a woodland, that the group of trees or the woodland, as the case may be, has an outstanding or special amenity value,

but a certificate shall not be given in the case of trees falling within (c) above if the application in respect of them has been referred by the Forestry Commissioners under section 15(1)(b) or 15(2)(a) of the Forestry Act 1967].

6.—(1) Where consent is granted under this Order to fell any part of a woodland other than consent for silvicultural thinning then unless—

   (a) such consent is granted for the purpose of enabling development to be carried out in accordance with a permission to develop land under Part III of the Act, or
   (b) the authority with the approval of the Minister dispense with replanting.

the authority shall give to the owner of the land on which that part of the woodland is situated a direction in writing specifying the manner in which and the time within which he shall replant such land and where such a direction is given and the part is felled the owner shall, subject to the provision of this Order and section 25 of the Countryside Act 1968, replant the said land in accordance with the direction.

(2) Any direction given under paragraph (1) of this Article may include requirements as to—

   (a) species;
   (b) number of trees per acre;
   (c) the erection and maintenance of fencing necessary for protection of the replanting;
   (d) the preparation of ground, draining, removal of brushwood, lop and top; and
   (e) protective measures against fire.

7. On imposing any condition requiring the replacement of any tree under Article 4 of the Order, or on giving a direction under Article 6 of this Order with respect to the replanting of woodlands, the authority shall if such condition or direction relates to land in respect of which byelaws made by a river authority, a drainage board, the Conservators of the River Thames or the Lee Conservancy Catchment Board restrict or regulate the planting of trees, notify the applicant or the owner of the land, as the case may be, of the existence of such byelaws and that any such condition or direction has effect subject to the requirements of the river authority,

---

NOTE: If it is desired to fell any of the trees included in this Order, whether included as trees, groups of trees or woodlands, and the trees are trees for the felling of which a licence is required under the Forestry Act 1967, application should be made *not* to the authority for consent under this Order but to the Conservator of Forests for a licence under that Act (section 15(5)).

drainage board, the Conservators of the River Thames or the Lee Conservancy Catchment Board under those byelaws and the condition or direction shall have effect accordingly.

8. The provisions set out in the Third Schedule to this Order, being provisions of Part III of the Act and of section 80 of the Town and Country Planning Act 1968 adapted and modified for the purposes of this Order, shall apply in relation thereto.

9. Subject to the provisions of this Order, any person who has suffered loss or damage in consequence of any refusal (including revocation or modification) of consent under this Order or of any grant of any such consent subject to conditions, shall, if he makes a claim on the authority within the time and in the manner prescribed by this Order, be entitled to recover from the authority compensation in respect of such loss or damage:

Provided that no compensation shall be payable in respect of loss or damage suffered by reason of such refusal or grant of consent in the case of any trees the subject of a certificate in accordance with Article 5 of this Order.

10. In assessing compensation payable under the last preceding Article account shall be taken of:

   (a) any compensation or contribution which has been paid whether to the claimant or any other person, in respect of the same trees under the terms of this or any other Tree Preservation Order under section 29 of the Act or under the terms of any Interim Preservation Order made under section 8 of the Town and Country Planning (Interim Development) Act 1943, or any compensation which has been paid or which could have been claimed under any provision relating to the preservation of trees or protection of woodlands contained in an operative scheme under the Town and Country Planning Act 1932, and

   (b) any injurious affection to any land of the owner which would result from the felling of the trees the subject of the claim.

11.—(1) A claim for compensation under this Order shall be in writing and shall be made by serving it on the authority, such service to be effected by delivering the claim at the offices of the authority addressed to the Clerk thereof or by sending it by prepaid post so addressed.

(2) The time within which any such claim shall be made as aforesaid shall be a period of twelve months from the date of the decision of the authority, or of the Minister, as the case may be, or where an appeal has been made to the Minister against the decision of the authority, from the date of the decision of the Minister on the appeal.

12. Any question of disputed compensation shall be determined in accordance with the provisions of section 128 of the Act.

13.—[(1) The provisions of section 16 of the Civic Amenities Act 1967 shall apply to this Order and the Order shall take effect on   ]
(This provision is not to be included unless it appears to the authority that the Order should take effect immediately.)

[(2) This order shall apply to any tree specified in the First Schedule hereto, which is to be planted as mentioned therein, as from the time when that tree is planted]. (This provision may be included in relation to trees to be planted pursuant to a condition imposed under Section 12(1) of the Civic Amenities Act 1967.)

[NOTE: Any person contravening the provisions of this Order by cutting down, uprooting or wilfully destroying a tree, or by wilfully damaging, topping or lopping a tree in such a manner as to be likely to destroy it is guilty of an offence and liable on summary conviction to a fine not exceeding £400 or twice the sum which appears to the court to be the value of the tree, whichever is the greater, or on indictment to a fine. The penalty for any other contravention of this Order is a fine not exceeding £200 on summary conviction and, in the case of a continuing offence when the contravention is continued after conviction, a person is liable on summary conviction to an additional fine not exceeding £5 for every day on which the contravention is so continued.

If a tree other than one to which an Order applies as part of a woodland is removed, uprooted or destroyed in contravention of an Order or is removed, uprooted or destroyed or dies at a time when its cutting down or uprooting is authorised only by section 60(6) of the

Town and Country Planning Act 1971 relating to trees which are dying or dead or have become dangerous, it is the duty of the owner of the land, unless on his application the local planning authority dispense with the requirement, to plant another tree of appropriate size and species at the same place as soon as he reasonably can. Except in emergency, not less than 5 days previous notice of the removal, etc., should be given to the authority to enable the latter to decide whether or not to dispense with the requirement.]

FIRST SCHEDULE*

Trees Specified Individually
(encircled in black on the map)

No. on Map	Description	Situation
[T1]	[Oak]	
[T2]	[Ash]	

Trees Specified by References to an Area
(within a dotted black line on the map)

No. on Map	Description	Situation
[A1]	[The several trees of whatever species standing in the area numbered A1 on the map	]
[A2]	[The several oak, beech, and larch trees standing in the area numbered A2 on the map	]

Groups of Trees
(within a broken black line on the map)

No. on Map	Description	Situation
[G1]	[Group consisting of 3 oak, 2 ash and 3 elm]	
[G2]	[Group consisting of 10 beech]	

Woodlands
(within a continuous black line on the map)

No. on Map	Description	Situation
[W1]	[Mixed hardwoods consisting mainly of	]
[W2]	[Mixed conifers and deciduous trees consisting mainly of	]

SECOND SCHEDULE

This Order shall not apply so as to require the consent of the authority to

(1) the cutting down of any tree on land which is subject to a forestry dedication covenant where

(a) any positive covenants on the part of the owner of the land contained in the same deed as the forestry dedication covenant and at the time of the cutting down binding on the then owner of the land are fulfilled;

(b) the cutting down is in accordance with a plan of operations approved by the Forestry Commission under such deed.

[(2) the cutting down of any tree which is in accordance with a plan of operations approved by the Forestry Commission under the approved woodlands scheme or other grant scheme under section 4 of the Forestry Act 1967 except a scheme which applies to a forestry dedication covenant;

---

* Every heading should be included in the Schedule, and the word "NONE" written in where necessary. The entries above are shown as examples in each category.

*(3) the cutting down, uprooting, topping or lopping of a tree]

(a) in pursuance of the power conferred on the Postmaster General by virtue of section 5 of the Telegraph (Construction) Act 1908;

(b) by or at the request of

   (i) a statutory undertaker [or holder of a licence under section 6(1) of the Electricity Act 1989] where the land on which the tree is situated is operational land as defined by the Act and either works on such land cannot otherwise be carried out or the cutting down, topping or lopping is for the purpose of securing safety in the operation of the undertaking;

   (ii) [a licence holder within the meaning of the Electricity Act 1989], where any tree obstructs the construction by the [licence holder] of any . . . electric line within the meaning [of Part I of the said Act of 1989] or interferes or would interfere with the maintenance or working of any such line;

   (iii) a river authority established under the Water Resources Act 1963, a drainage board constituted or treated as having been constituted under the Land Drainage Act 1930, the Conservators of the River Thames, or the Lee Conservancy Catchment Board, where the tree interferes or would interfere with the exercise of any of the functions of such river authority, drainage board, Conservators of the River Thames or Lee Conservancy Catchment Board in relation to the maintenance, improvement or construction of water courses or of drainage works; or

   (iv) the Minister of Defence for the Royal Air Force, the Minister of Technology or the Board of Trade where in the opinion of such Minister or Board the tree obstructs the approach of aircraft to, or their departure from, any aerodrome or hinders the safe and efficient use of aviation or defence technical installations;

(c) where immediately required for the purpose of carrying out development authorised by the planning permission granted on an application made under Part III of the Act, or deemed to have been so granted for any of the purposes of that Part;

(d) which is a fruit tree cultivated for fruit production growing or standing on land comprised in an orchard or garden;

[Where the trees are within the area administered by the Conservators of the River Thames]

[(e) in pursuance of the powers conferred on the Conservators of the River Thames by virtue of section 105 of the Thames Conservancy Act 1932].

THIRD SCHEDULE

Provisions of the following parts of (a) Part III of the Town and Country Planning Act 1962 and (b) section 80 of the Town and Country Planning Act 1968 as adapted and modified to apply to this Order.

(a) Part III of the Town and Country Planning Act 1962

21.—(1) Without prejudice to the following provisions as to the revocation or modification of consents, any consent under the Order, including any direction as to replanting given by the authority on the granting of such consent, shall (except in so far as the consent otherwise provides), enure for the benefit of the land and of all persons for the time being interested therein.

Reference of applications to the Minister

22.—(1) The Minister may give directions to the authority requiring applications for consent under the Order to be referred to him instead of being dealt with by the authority.

(2) A direction under this section may relate either to a particular application or to applications of a class specified in the direction.

---

* NOTE: Section 13(1) of the Civic Amenities Act 1967 requires, unless on the application of the owner the local authority dispense with the requirement, that any tree removed or destroyed under section 29(7) of the Town and Country Planning Act 1962, shall be replaced by another tree of appropriate size and species. In order to enable the local planning authority to come to a decision, on whether or not to dispense with the requirement, notice of the proposed action should be given to the local planning authority which except in a case of emergency shall be of not less than five days.

(3) Any application in respect of which a direction under this section has effect shall be referred to the Minister accordingly.

(4) Where an application for consent under the Order is referred to the Minister under this section, the provisions of Articles 4 and 5 of the Order shall apply as they apply to an application which falls to be determined by the authority.

(5) Before determining an application referred to him under this section the Minister shall, if either the applicant or the authority so desire, afford to each of them an opportunity of appearing before, and being heard by, a person appointed by the Minister for the purpose.

(6) The decision of the Minister on any application referred to him under this section shall be final.

Appeals against decisions

23.—(1) Where an application is made to the authority (when Tree Preservation Order is made by a District Council on behalf of a County Council an application for consent should be made to the District Council) for consent under the Order and that consent is refused by that authority or is granted by them subject to conditions, or where any certificate or direction is given by the authority, the applicant, if he is aggrieved by their decision on the application, or by any such certificate, or the person directed if he is aggrieved by the direction, may by notice under this section appeal to the Minister.

(2) A notice under this section shall be served in writing within twenty-eight days from the receipt of notification of the decision, certificate or direction, as the case may be, or such longer period as the Minister may allow.

(4) Where an appeal is brought under this section from a decision, certificate or direction of the authority, the Minister, subject to the following provisions of this section, may allow or dismiss the appeal, or may reverse or vary any part of the decision of the authority, whether the appeal relates to that part thereof or not, or may cancel any certificate or cancel or vary any direction, and may deal with the application as if it had been made to him in the first instance.

(5) Before determining an appeal under this section, the Minister shall, if either the appellant or the authority so desire, afford to each of them an opportunity of appearing before, and being heard by, a person appointed by the Minister for the purpose.

(7) The decision of the Minister on any appeal under this section shall be final.

Appeal in default of decision

24. Where an application for consent under the Order is made to the authority, then unless within two months from the date of receipt of the application, or within such extended period as may at any time be agreed upon in writing between the applicant and the authority, the authority either—

(a) give notice to the applicant of their decision on the application; or
(b) give notice to him that the application has been referred to the Minister in accordance with directions given under section 22 above;

the provisions of the last preceding section shall apply in relation to the application as if the consent to which it relates had been refused by the authority, and as if notification of their decision had been received by the applicant at the end of the said period of two months, or at the end of the said extended period, as the case may be.

Power to revoke or modify the consent under the Order

27.—(1) If it appears to the authority that it is expedient to revoke or modify any consent under the Order granted on an application made under Article 3 of the Order, the authority may by Order revoke or modify the consent to such an extent as they consider expedient.

(2) (Subject to the provisions of section 16 of the Civic Amenities Act 1967 and section 80 of the Town and Country Planning Act 1968) an Order under this section shall not take effect unless it is confirmed by the Minister; and the Minister may confirm any such Order

submitted to him either without modification or subject to such modifications as he considers expedient.

(3) Where an authority submit an Order to the Minister for his confirmation under this section, the authority shall furnish the Minister with a statement of their reason for making the Order and shall serve notice together with a copy of the aforesaid statement on the owner and on the occupier of the land affected, and on any other person who in their opinion will be affected by the Order, and if within the period of twenty-eight days from the service thereof any person on whom the notice is served so requires, the Minister, before confirming the Order, shall afford to that person, and to the authority, an opportunity of appearing before, and being heard by, a person appointed by the Minister for the purpose.

(4) The power conferred by this section to revoke or modify a consent may be exercised at any time before the operations for which consent has been given have been completed:

Provided that the revocation or modification of consent shall not affect so much of these operations as has been previously carried out.

(5) Where a notice has been served in accordance with the provisions of subsection (3) of this section, no operations or further operations as the case may be, in pursuance of the consent granted, shall be carried out pending the decision of the Minister under subsection (2) of this section.

(b) Town and Country Planning Act 1968

Unopposed revocation or modification of consent

80.—(1) The following provisions shall have effect where the local planning authority have made an Order (hereinafter called "such Order") under section 27 above revoking or modifying any consent granted on an appplication made under a tree preservation order but have not submitted such Order to the Minister for confirmation by him and the owner and the occupier of the land and all persons who in the authority's opinion will be affected by such Order have notified the authority in writing that they do not object to such Order.

(2) The authority shall advertise the fact that such Order has been made and the advertisement shall specify (a) the period (not less than twenty-eight days from the date on which the advertisement first appears) within which persons affected by such Order may give notice to the Minister that they wish for an opportunity of appearing before, and being heard by, a person appointed by the Minister for the purpose and (b) the period (not less than 14 days from the expiration of the period referred to in paragraph (a) above) at the expiration of which, if no such notice is given to the Minister, such Order may take effect by virtue of this section and without being confirmed by the Minister.

(3) The authority shall also serve notices to the same effect on the persons mentioned in subsection (1) above.

(4) The authority shall send a copy of any advertisement published under subsection (2) above to the Minister, not more than three days after the publication.

(5) If within the period referred to in subsection (2)(a) above no person claiming to be affected by such Order has given notice to the Minister as aforesaid and the Minister has not directed that such Order be submitted to him for confirmation, such Order shall at the expiration of the period referred to in subsection (2)(b) of this section take effect by virtue of this section and without being confirmed by the Minister as required by section 27(2) of the Town and Country Planning Act 1962.

(6) This section does not apply to such Order revoking or modifying a consent granted or deemed to have been granted by the Minister under Part III or Part IV of the Town and Country Planning Act 1962 or under Part II or Part V of the Town and Country Planning Act 1968. **[608]**

NOTES
Amended by SI 1975/148, SI 1988/963, reg 2 and SI 1990/526, art 2, Schedule.

TOWN AND COUNTRY PLANNING (TREE PRESERVATION ORDER) (AMENDMENT) AND (TREES IN CONSERVATION AREAS) (EXEMPTED CASES) REGULATIONS 1975
(SI 1975/148)

NOTES
    Made: 11 February 1975
    Commencement: 12 March 1975
    Authority: Town and Country Planning Act 1971, ss 60, 61A, 287; now have effect under Town and Country Planning Act 1990, ss 199, 212

1. Citation, commencement and interpretation

(1) These regulations may be cited as the Town and Country Planning (Tree Preservation Order) (Amendment) and (Trees in Conservation Areas) (Exempted Cases) Regulations 1975 and shall come into operation on 12th March 1975.

(2) The Interpretation Act 1889 shall apply for the interpretation of these regulations as it applies for the interpretation of an Act of Parliament.   **[609]**

2. (*Amends SI 1969/17, Schedule.*)

3. Trees in conservation areas—exempted cases

Section 61A of the Town and Country Planning Act 1971 shall not apply where the act is—

    (i) the cutting down, uprooting, topping or lopping of a tree in the circumstances mentioned in sub-section (6) of section 60 of that Act;

    (ii) the cutting down of a tree in the circumstances mentioned in paragraph (1) or (2), or the cutting down, uprooting, topping or lopping of a tree in the circumstances mentioned in paragraph (3), of the Second Schedule to the Form of Tree Preservation Order contained in the Schedule to the Town and Country Planning (Tree Preservation Order) Regulations 1969 (as amended by these regulations);

    (iii) the cutting down of a tree in accordance with a felling licence granted by the Forestry Commissioners;

    (iv) the cutting down, uprooting, topping or lopping of a tree on land in the occupation of a local planning authority and the act is done by or with the consent of that authority;

    (v) the cutting down, uprooting, topping or lopping of a tree having a diameter not exceeding 75 millimetres, or the cutting down or uprooting of a tree having a diameter not exceeding 100 millimetres where the act is carried out to improve the growth of the other trees, the reference to "diameter" herein being construed as a reference to the diameter, measured over the bark, at a point 1.5 metres above the ground level.   **[610]**

NOTES
    Section 61A: see now the Town and Country Planning Act 1990, ss 211–214.

TOWN AND COUNTRY PLANNING (PRESCRIPTION OF COUNTY MATTERS) REGULATIONS 1980
(SI 1980/2010)

NOTES
Made: 19 December 1980
Commencement: 13 January 1991
Authority: Local Government Act 1972, ss 266(1), 270(1), Sch 16, para 32(f); now have effect under Town and Country Planning Act 1990, s 1, Sch 1, para 1

1. These regulations may be cited as the Town and Country Planning (Prescription of County Matters) Regulations 1980 and shall come into operation on 13th January 1981. **[611]**

2. The following classes of operations and uses of land are prescribed for the purposes of paragraph 32 of Schedule 16 to the Local Government Act 1972 as respects England:—

    (a) the use of land or the carrying out of operations in or on land for the deposit of refuse or waste materials;

    (b) the erection of any building, plant or machinery designed to be used wholly or mainly for purposes of treating, storing, processing or disposing of refuse or waste materials. **[612]**

NOTES
Local Government Act 1972, Sch 16, para 32: see now the Town and Country Planning Act 1990, Sch 1, para 1.

TOWN AND COUNTRY PLANNING (DETERMINATION OF APPEALS BY APPOINTED PERSONS) (PRESCRIBED CLASSES) REGULATIONS 1981
(SI 1981/804)

NOTES
Made: 3 June 1981
Commencement: 1 July 1981
Authority: Town and Country Planning Act 1971, s 287, Sch 9, para 1; see now the Town and Country Planning Act 1990, Sch 6, para 1, the Planning (Listed Buildings and Conservation Areas) Act 1990, Sch 3, para 1

1. Application, citation and commencement

(1) These regulations may be cited as the Town and Country Planning (Determination of appeals by appointed persons) (Prescribed Classes) Regulations 1981 and shall come into operation on 1st July 1981.

(2) These regulations apply to appeals within the classes prescribed in regulation 3 of which notice is given on or after the date when they come into operation. **[613]**

2. Interpretation

In these regulations, unless the context otherwise requires—

    "the Act" means the Town and Country Planning Act 1971;

    "local planning authority" means—

(a) a district [council] or a London borough council;
(b) an urban development corporation which is the local planning
    authority for its area, for the purposes of determining applications for
    planning permission under Part III of the Act, by virtue of the
    provisions of an order made under section 149 of the Local
    Government, Planning and Land Act 1980; or
(c) an enterprise zone authority which is the local planning authority for
    an enterprise zone, for the purposes of determining applications for
    planning permission under Part III of the Act, by virtue of the
    provisions of an order made under paragraph 5 of Schedule 32 to the
    Local Government, Planning and Land Act 1980;

"statutory undertakers" means persons authorised by any enactment to carry
on any railway, light railway, tramway, road transport, water transport, canal,
inland navigation, dock, harbour, pier or lighthouse undertaking or any
undertaking for the supply of . . . , . . . hydraulic power or water and includes
the British Airports Authority, the Civil Aviation Authority, the Post Office
[, public gas suppliers within the meaning of Part I of the Gas Act 1986 and
holders of a licence under section 6(1) of the Electricity Act 1989] and
companies which are deemed to be statutory undertakers by virtue of section
141(2) of the Transport Act 1968   **[614]**

NOTES
  Definition "local planning authority" amended by SI 1986/443, reg 2, Sch 1, para 7; definition
"statutory undertakers" amended by SI 1986/1356, art 2, Schedule, SI 1990/526, art 2, Schedule.

3. Classes of appeal for determination by appointed persons

Subject to the provisions of regulation 4 of these regulations, the following classes
of appeal are prescribed for the purposes of paragraph 1(1) of Schedule 9 to the Act
as appeals to be determined by a person appointed by the Secretary of State instead
of by the Secretary of State—

(a) appeals under section 36 of the Act (appeals against planning decisions),
    including appeals under that section as applied by section 37 (appeals in
    default of planning decision) of the Act; . . .
(b) appeals under section 88 of the Act (appeals against enforcement notices)
[(c) appeals under section 97 of the Act (listed building enforcement notices),
    including appeals under that section as having effect by virtue of section
    277A of the Act (conservation areas); and
(d) appeals under paragraph 8 of Schedule 11 to the Act (listed building
    consent) including appeals under that paragraph as having effect by virtue
    of section 277A).]   **[615]**

NOTES
  Word omitted from para (a) revoked, and paras (c), (d) added by SI 1986/623, reg 2(1), (2).

4. Classes of appeal received for determination by the Secretary of State

The following classes of case are prescribed for the purposes of paragraph 1(1) of
Schedule 9 to the Act as appeals which are not to be determined in the manner set
out in that paragraph—

(a) appeals under section 36 of the Act, or under that section as applied by
    section 37 of the Act, by statutory undertakers where the relevant
    application related to land to which section 225(1) of the Act applies; . . .
(b) appeals by statutory undertakers under section 88 of the Act where the
    breach of planning control alleged in the enforcement notice consists in

the carrying out of development of land to which section 225(1) of the Act applies, or failure to comply with a condition or limitation on a grant of planning permission for development of any such land.

[(c) appeals under section 97 of the Act (listed building enforcement notices) concerned with Grade I and II* listed buildings;

(d) appeals under paragraph 8 of Schedule 11 to the Act (listed building consent) concerned with Grade I and II* listed buildings,]

[(e) appeals relating to buildings for which grants have been made under sections 3A or 4 of the Historic Buildings and Ancient Monuments Act 1953; and

(f) appeals referred to in regulation 3(c) or (d) above relating to buildings in Wales.] **[616]**

NOTES

Para (a): word omitted revoked by SI 1986/623, reg 2(1), (3).

Paras (c), (d): originally added by SI 1986/623, reg 2(1), (3), subsequently substituted by SI 1989/1087, reg 2.

Paras (e), (f): added (together with substituted paras (c), (d)) by SI 1986/623, reg 2(1), (3).

5. Publicity for directions under paragraph 1(1) of Schedule 9 to the Act

On the making by the Secretary of State of a direction under paragraph 1(1) of Schedule 9 to the Act he may by notice in writing enclosing a copy of the direction require the local planning authority for every area in respect of which the direction has effect to publish as soon as may be a notice in at least one newspaper circulating in the area; and such notice shall contain a concise statement of the effect of the direction and shall specify the place or places where a copy of the direction may be seen at all reasonable hours. **[617]**

6. (*Revoked by SI 1986/623, reg 2(1), (4).*)

TOWN AND COUNTRY PLANNING (APPEALS) (WRITTEN REPRESENTATIONS PROCEDURE) REGULATIONS 1987
(SI 1987/701)

NOTES

Made: 9 April 1987

Commencement: 5 May 1987

Authority: Town and Country Planning Act 1971, s 282B; now have effect under Town and Country Planning Act 1990, s 323

ARRANGEMENT OF REGULATIONS

1. Citation and commencement

These Regulations may be cited as the Town and Country Planning (Appeals) (Written Representations Procedure) Regulations 1987 and shall come into force on 5th May 1987. **[618]**

2. Interpretation

In these Regulations, unless the context otherwise requires—

"the Act" means the Town and Country Planning Act 1971;

"appeals questionnaire" means a document in the form supplied by the Secretary of State to local planning authorities for the purpose of proceedings under these Regulations; and

"local planning authority" means the body who were responsible for dealing with the application occasioning the appeal.   **[619]**

3. Application

(1) These Regulations apply where, after they come into force, a person giving notice of appeal to the Secretary of State under section 36 of the Act ("the appellant") informs the Secretary of State in the notice that he wishes the appeal to be disposed of on the basis of written representations and other documents.

(2) Where an appeal under section 36 of the Act is being disposed of otherwise than on the basis of written representations and other documents and the appellant and the local planning authority inform the Secretary of State that they wish it to be disposed of on that basis, these Regulations thereafter apply to the proceedings to such extent as the Secretary of State may specify having regard to any steps already taken in relation to those proceedings.

(3) These Regulations cease to apply as respects proceedings if the Secretary of State informs the appellant and the local planning authority that he will afford to them an opportunity of appearing before and being heard by a person appointed by him for the purpose.

(4) In this regulation references to section 36 of the Act include a reference to that section as applied by section 37.   **[620]**

4. Notification of receipt of appeal

The Secretary of State shall forthwith upon receipt of the notice of appeal advise the appellant and the local planning authority of—

(a) the date of receipt ("the starting date");

(b) the reference number allocated to the appeal; and

(c) the address to which written communications to the Secretary of State about the appeal are to be sent.   **[621]**

5. Notice to interested persons

(1) The local planning authority shall not later than 5 working days after receiving notification of the appeal give written notice of it to—

(a) any authority or any person notified or consulted in accordance with the Act or a development order about the application which has given rise to the appeal; and

(b) any other person who made representations to the local planning authority about that application.

(2) A notice under paragraph (1) shall—

(a) state the name of the appellant and the address of the site to which the appeal relates;

(b) describe the application;

(c) set out the matters notified to the authority under regulation 4;

    (d) state that copies of any representations made by any authority or person mentioned in paragraph (1), other than representations which the maker has asked to be treated as confidential, will be sent to the Secretary of State and the appellant; and will be considered by the Secretary of State when determining the appeal unless, within 28 days of the starting date, the authority or person who made the representations asks the Secretary of State to disregard them;

    (e) state that further written representations may be submitted to the Secretary of State within 28 days of the starting date.   **[622]**

6. Appeals questionnaire

(1) The local planning authority shall not later than 14 days after the starting date submit to the Secretary of State—

    (a) an appropriately completed appeals questionnaire;

    (b) a copy of all documents relating to the case which are referred to in the completed questionnaire other than any written representations which the maker has asked to be treated as confidential.

(2) The appeals questionnaire shall state the date on which it is submitted and the local planning authority shall simultaneously send to the appellant a copy of the questionnaire and of all documents submitted to the Secretary of State under paragraph (1).   **[623]**

7. Representations

(1) The notice of appeal and the documents accompanying it shall comprise the appellant's representations in relation to the appeal.

(2) The local planning authority may elect to treat the appeals questionnaire and the documents submitted with it as their representations in relation to the appeal; and, where they do so, they shall notify the Secretary of State and the appellant accordingly when submitting the questionnaire or sending the copy in accordance with regulation 6.

(3) Where the local planning authority do not elect as described in paragraph (2), they may submit representations to the Secretary of State not later than 28 days after the starting date.

(4) The appellant may make further representations by way of reply to the local planning authority not later than 17 days after—

    (a) in a case where the authority have elected as described in paragraph (2), the date stated on the appeals questionnaire as the date on which it was submitted to the Secretary of State; or

    (b) in a case where the authority have not so elected, the date of submission of the authority's representations in accordance with paragraph (3).

(5) Any representations made by the local planning authority or the appellant shall be dated and submitted to the Secretary of State on the date they bear; and the local planning authority shall on that date send to the appellant a copy of any representations they make and the appellant shall similarly send to the local planning authority a copy of any further representations he makes.

(6) Any interested party may submit representations to the Secretary of State not later than 28 days after the starting date; and where the Secretary of State sends to

the appellant and the local planning authority a copy of any such representations, he shall allow them a period of not less than 7 days in which to reply to them.

(7) In this regulation references to representations include a reference to supporting documents. **[624]**

8. Power to set later time limits

The Secretary of State may in a particular case give directions setting later time limits than those prescribed by these Regulations. **[625]**

9. Decision on appeal

(1) The Secretary of State may proceed to a decision on an appeal taking into account only such written representations and supporting documents as have been submitted within the relevant time limits.

(2) The Secretary of State may, after giving the appellant and the local planning authority written notice of his intention to do so, proceed to a decision on an appeal notwithstanding that no written representations have been made within the relevant time limits if it appears to him that he has sufficient material before him to enable him to reach a decision on the merits of the case.

(3) In this regulation, "relevant time limits" means the time limits prescribed by these Regulations or, where the Secretary of State has given directions under regulation 8, the time limits set by those directions. **[626]**

TOWN AND COUNTRY PLANNING (USE CLASSES) ORDER 1987
(SI 1987/764)

NOTES
Made: 28 April 1987
Commencement: 1 June 1987
Authority: Town and Country Planning Act 1971, ss 22(2)(f), 287(3); now has effect under Town and Country Planning Act 1990, ss 55(2)(f), 333(7).

ARRANGEMENT OF ARTICLES

1. Citation and commencement

This Order may be cited as the Town and Country Planning (Use Classes) Order 1987 and shall come into force on 1 June 1987. **[627]**

2. Interpretation

In this Order, unless the context otherwise requires:—

"care" means personal care for people in need of such care by reason of old age, disablement, past or present dependence on alcohol or drugs or past or present mental disorder, and in class C2 also includes the personal care of children and medical care and treatment;

"day centre" means premises which are visited during the day for social or recreational purposes or for the purposes of rehabilitation or occupational training, at which care is also provided;

. . .

"industrial process" means a process for or incidental to any of the following purposes:—

(a) the making of any article or part of any article (including a ship or vessel, or a film, video or sound recording);

(b) the altering, repairing, maintaining, ornamenting, finishing, cleaning, washing, packing, canning, adapting for sale, breaking up or demolition of any article; or

(c) the getting, dressing or treatment of minerals;

in the course of any trade or business other than agriculture, and other than a use carried out in or adjacent to a mine or quarry;

"Schedule" means the Schedule to this Order;

"site" means the whole area of land within a single unit of occupation. **[628]**

NOTES

Amended by SI 1992/657, art 2(1).

3. Use Classes

(1) Subject to the provisions of this Order, where a building or other land is used for a purpose of any class specified in the Schedule, the use of that building or that other land for any other purpose of the same class shall not be taken to involve development of the land.

(2) References in paragraph (1) to a building include references to land occupied with the building and used for the same purposes.

(3) A use which is included in and ordinarily incidental to any use in a class specified in the Schedule is not excluded from the use to which it is incidental merely because it is specified in the Schedule as a separate use.

(4) Where land on a single site or on adjacent sites used as parts of a single undertaking is used for purposes consisting of or including purposes falling [within classes B1 and B2] in the Schedule, those classes may be treated as a single class in considering the use of that land for the purposes of this Order, so long as the area used for a purpose falling [within class B2] is not substantially increased as a result.

(5) . . .

(6) No class specified in the Schedule includes use—

(a) as a theatre,

(b) as an amusement arcade or centre, or a funfair,

[(c) as a launderette,]

(d) for the sale of fuel for motor vehicles,

(e) for the sale or display for sale of motor vehicles,

(f) for a taxi business or business for the hire of motor vehicles,

(g) as a scrapyard, or a yard for the storage or distribution of minerals or the breaking of motor vehicles.

[(h) for any work registrable under the Alkali, etc Works Regulation Act 1906] [(i) as a hostel.]   **[629]**

NOTES
   Amended by SI 1991/1567, art 2(1), SI 1992/610, art 2(1), SI 1992/657, art 2(2), SI 1994/724, art 2(1),
SI 1995/297, art 2(1).

4. Change of use of part of building or land

In the case of a building used for a purpose within class C3 (dwelling-houses) in the
Schedule, the use as a separate dwelling-house of any part of the building or of any
land occupied with and used for the same purposes as the building is not, by virtue
of this Order, to be taken as not amounting to development.   **[630]**

5. Revocation

The Town and Country Planning (Use Classes) Order 1972 and the Town and
Country Planning (Use Classes) (Amendment) Order 1983 are hereby revoked.

[631]

SCHEDULE
PART A

Class A1. Shops

Use for all or any of the following purposes—

   (a) for the retail sale of goods other than hot food,
   (b) as a post office,
   (c) for the sale of tickets or as a travel agency,
   (d) for the sale of sandwiches or other cold food for consumption off the premises,
   (e) for hairdressing,
   (f) for the direction of funerals,
   (g) for the display of goods for sale,
   (h) for the hiring out of domestic or personal goods or articles,
   [(i) for the washing or cleaning of clothes or fabrics on the premises,
   (j) for the reception of goods to be washed, cleaned or repaired,]

where the sale, display or service is to visiting members of the public.

Class A2. Financial and professional services

   Use for the provision of—

   (a) financial services, or
   (b) professional services (other than health or medical services), or
   (c) any other services (including use as a betting office) which it is appropriate to
       provide in a shopping area,

where the services are provided principally to visiting members of the public.

Class A3. Food and drink

   Use for the sale of food or drink for consumption on the premises or of hot food for
consumption off the premises.

PART B

Class B1. Business

   Use for all or any of the following purposes—

   (a) as an office other than a use within class A2 (financial and professional services),
   (b) for research and development of products or processes, or

(c) for any industrial process,

being a use which can be carried out in any residential area without detriment to the amenity of that area by reason of noise, vibration, smell, fumes, smoke, soot, ash, dust or grit.

Class B2. *General industrial*

Use for the carrying on of an industrial process other than one falling within class B1 above . . .

*   *   *   *   *

Class B8. *Storage or distribution*

Use for storage or as a distribution centre.

PART C

[Class C1. *Hotels*

Use as a hotel or as a boarding or guest house where, in each case, no significant element of care is provided.]

Class C2. *Residential institutions*

Use for the provision of residential accommodation and care to people in need of care (other than a use within class C3 (dwelling houses)).
Use as a hospital or nursing home.
Use as a residential school, college or training centre.

Class C3. *Dwellinghouses*

Use as a dwellinghouse (whether or not as a sole or main residence)—

    (a) by a single person or by people living together as a family, or
    (b) by not more than 6 residents living together as a single household (including a household where care is provided for residents).

PART D

Class D1. *Non-residential institutions*

Any use not including a residential use—

    (a) For the provision of any medical or health services except the use of premises attached to the residence of the consultant or practitioner,
    (b) as a crèche, day nursery or a day centre,
    (c) for the provision of education,
    (d) for the display of works of art (otherwise than for sale or hire),
    (e) as a museum,
    (f) as a public library or public reading room,
    (g) as a public hall or exhibition hall,
    (h) for, or in connection with, public worship or religious instruction.

Class D2. *Assembly and leisure*

Use as—

    (a) a cinema,
    (b) a concert hall,
    (c) a bingo hall or casino,
    (d) a dance hall,
    (e) a swimming bath, skating rink, gymnasium or area for other indoor or outdoor sports or recreations, not involving motorised vehicles or firearms.   **[632]**

NOTES
    Amended by SI 1991/1567, art 2(2), SI 1992/610, art 2(2), SI 1994/724, art 2(2), SI 1995/297, art 2(2).

TOWN AND COUNTRY PLANNING (ASSESSMENT OF ENVIRONMENTAL EFFECTS) REGULATIONS 1988
(SI 1988/1199)

NOTES
   Made: 12 July 1988
   Commencement: 15 July 1988
   Authority: European Communities Act 1972, s 2(2)

ARRANGEMENT OF REGULATIONS

1. Citation, commencement and application

(1) These Regulations may be cited as the Town and Country Planning (Assessment of Environmental Effects) Regulations 1988.

(2) These Regulations shall come into force on the third day after the day on which they are made.

[(3) Subject to paragraph (4), these Regulations apply throughout England and Wales.

(4) Paragraphs (2) and (5)(a) of regulation 13 shall not apply to the Isles of Scilly and, in relation to the Isles of Scilly, the reference in paragraph (6) of that regulation to paragraph (5) of that regulation shall be construed as a reference to paragraph (5)(b).

(5) These regulations apply to local authority applications mentioned in paragraph (1) of regulation 25A in accordance with the modifications set out in that paragraph.]   **[633]**

NOTES

Amended by SI 1992/1494, reg 3, Schedule, para 1.

2. Interpretation

(1) In these Regulations, unless the contrary intention appears—

"the Act" means the Town and Country Planning Act 1971, references to sections are references to sections of that Act and expressions used in that Act and these Regulations have the meaning they have in the Act save that, in relation to an appeal, references to the Secretary of State shall not be construed as references to an inspector;

"aerodrome" means a defined area on land or water (including any buildings and other installations) intended to be used either wholly or in part for the arrival, departure and surface movement of aircraft;

"controlled waste" has the meaning assigned to it by section 30(1) of the Control of Pollution Act 1974;

"documents" include photographs, drawings, maps and plans;

"environmental information" means the environmental statement prepared by the applicant or appellant . . ., any representations made by any body required by these Regulations to be invited to make representations or to be consulted and any representations duly made by any other person about the likely environmental effects of the proposed development;

"environmental statement" means such a statement as is described in Schedule 3;

"exempt development" means particular proposed development which is the subject of a direction by the Secretary of State that these Regulations do not apply in relation to it;

"the General Development Order" means the Town and Country Planning General Development Order 1977;

*   *   *   *   *

"inspector" means a person appointed by the Secretary of State pursuant to Schedule 9 to the Act to determine an appeal;

"the land" means the land on which proposed development would be carried out;

"local planning authority" means the body to whom it falls or would but for a direction under section 35 fall, to determine an application for planning permission, or to whom it would fall (but for any such direction) to determine a proposed application;

"principal council" has the meaning assigned to that term by section 270(1) of the Local Government Act 1972;

"register" means a register kept pursuant to section 34 and "appropriate register" means the register on which particulars of an application for planning permission for the relevant development would fall to be placed when such an application is made;

"Schedule" means a Schedule to these Regulations;

"Schedule 1 application" means an application for planning permission (other than an application made pursuant to section 31A or section 32) for the carrying out of development of any description mentioned in Schedule 1, which is not exempt development;

"Schedule 2 application" means, subject to paragraph (2), an application for planning permission (other than an application made pursuant to section 31A or section 32) for the carrying out of development of any description mentioned in Schedule 2, which is not exempt development and which would be likely to have significant effects on the environment by virtue of factors such as its nature, size or location;

"special road" means [any road which for the purposes of Part I of the New Roads and Street Works Act 1991 is a road subject to a concession and any other road] authorised by a scheme made by a local highway authority under section 16 of the Highways Act 1980 for the use of traffic within Classes I and II of Schedule 4 to that Act; and

"special waste" means waste to which that term is applied by regulation 2 of the Control of Pollution (Special Waste) Regulations 1980.

(2) Where the Secretary of State gives a direction which includes a statement that in his opinion proposed development would be likely, or would not be likely, to have significant effects on the environment by virtue of factors such as its nature, size or location, or includes such a statement in a notification under regulation 10(1), that statement shall determine whether an application for planning permission for that development is, or is not, a Schedule 2 application by reason of the effects the development would be likely to have; and references in these Regulations to a Schedule 2 application shall be interpreted accordingly.   **[634]**

NOTES
Words omitted revoked by SI 1992/1494, reg 3, Schedule 6, para 2.
Words in square brackets in definition "special road" substituted by SI 1994/677, reg 2, Schedule, para 1, subject to transitional provisions in reg 3.

3. Extension of the power to provide in a development order for the giving of directions as respects the manner in which planning applications are dealt with

The provisions enabling the Secretary of State to give directions which may be included in a development order by virtue of section 31 shall include provisions enabling him to direct—

(a) that particular proposed development of a description set out in Schedule 1 or 2 is exempt development to which these Regulations do not apply [in accordance with Article 2(3) of Council Directive 85/337/EEC];

(b) that particular proposed development is not development in respect of which the consideration of environmental information is required before planning permission can be granted;

(c) that particular proposed development or development of any class is development in respect of which such consideration is required.   **[635]**

NOTES
Amended by SI 1994/677, reg 2, Schedule, para 2.

4. Prohibition on the grant of planning permission without consideration of environmental information

(1) This regulation applies to any Schedule 1 or Schedule 2 application received by the authority with whom it is lodged on or after 15th July 1988 . . .

For the purposes of this paragraph, the date of receipt of an application by an authority shall be determined in accordance with article 7(6A) of the General Development Order.

(2) The local planning authority or the Secretary of State or an inspector shall not grant planning permission pursuant to an application to which this regulation applies unless they have first taken the environmental information into consideration [and state in their decision that they have done so].

(3) Subject to any direction of the Secretary of State, the occurrence of an event mentioned in paragraph (4) shall determine in the case of an application for planning permission for development, other than exempt development, that, for the purposes of this regulation, the application is a Schedule 1 or 2 application.

(4) The events referred to in paragraph (3) are—

- (i) the submission by the applicant of an environmental statement expressed to be for the purposes of these Regulations;
- (ii) a failure by the applicant to apply to the Secretary of State for a direction where the local planning authority have given such an opinion as is mentioned in regulation 5(6)(a); and
- (iii) the making to that authority by the applicant of a written statement agreeing or conceding that the submission of an environmental statement is required. **[636]**

NOTES
Words omitted revoked by SI 1992/1494, reg 3, Schedule, para 3.
Para (2): amended by SI 1994/677, reg 2, Schedule, para 3.

5. Opinion as to whether an application will be a Schedule 1 or 2 application

(1) A person who is minded to apply for planning permission may ask the local planning authority to state in writing whether in their opinion the proposed development would be within a description mentioned in Schedule 1 or 2 and, if so,—

- (a) within which such description; and
- (b) if it falls within a description in Schedule 2, whether its likely effects would be such that regulation 4 would apply.

(2) A request made pursuant to paragraph (1) shall be accompanied by—

- (a) a plan sufficient to identify the land;
- (b) a brief description of the nature and purpose of the proposed development and of its possible effects on the environment;
- (c) such other information or representations as the person making the request may wish to provide or make.

(3) An authority receiving a request under paragraph (1) shall, if they consider that they have not been provided with sufficient information to give an opinion on the questions raised, notify the person making the request of particular points on which they require further information.

(4) An authority shall respond to a request under paragraph (1) within 3 weeks

beginning with the date [of receipt of the request] or such longer period as may be agreed in writing with the person making the request; and if they express an opinion to the effect that the consideration of environmental information would be required before planning permission could be granted for the proposed development, they shall provide with the opinion a written statement giving clearly and precisely their full reasons for their conclusion.

(5) An authority shall make a copy of any opinion given pursuant to a request under paragraph (1), and any accompanying statement of reasons and a copy of the relevant request and the accompanying documents available for public inspection at any reasonable hour at the place where the appropriate register (or relevant section of that register) is kept until such time, if any, as a copy of that opinion is required by regulation 7 to be placed on Part I of that register.

(6) Where an authority—

    (a) give an opinion to the effect mentioned in paragraph (4); or
    (b) fail to give an opinion within the relevant period mentioned in paragraph (4),

the person who requested the opinion may apply in accordance with regulation 6 to the Secretary of State for a direction on the matter.

(7) Paragraph (6)(b) applies notwithstanding that the authority may not have received further information which they have sought under paragraph (3).   **[637]**

NOTES
    Amended by SI 1994/677, reg 2, Schedule, para 4.

6. Pre-application directions

(1) A person applying to the Secretary of State for a direction pursuant to regulation 5(6) shall submit with his application—

    (a) a copy of his request under regulation 5(1) to the local planning authority and the documents which accompanied it;
    (b) a copy of any notification under regulation 5(3) which he has received and of any response;
    (c) a copy of any opinion given by the authority and of the accompanying statement of reasons; and
    (d) any representations he wishes to make.

(2) A person applying as aforesaid shall, when he makes the application, send the local planning authority a copy of the application and of any representations he makes to the Secretary of State.

(3) The Secretary of State shall notify an applicant in writing of any points on which he considers the information provided pursuant to paragraph (1) is insufficient to enable him to give a direction; and may request the local planning authority to provide such information as they can on any of those points.

(4) The Secretary of State shall issue a direction within 3 weeks beginning with the date of [receipt of the application] or such longer period as he may reasonably require.

(5) The Secretary of State shall upon giving a direction send a copy to the applicant and the local planning authority; and where he gives a direction that the proposed application would be a Schedule 1 or Schedule 2 application, he shall at the same time send them a written statement giving his full reasons for his conclusion clearly and precisely.   **[638]**

NOTES
    Amended by SI 1994/677, reg 2, Schedule, para 5.

7. Availability of directions etc for inspection

(1) Where particulars of a planning application are placed on Part I of the register, the local planning authority shall take steps to secure that there is also placed on that Part a copy of any direction which the Secretary of State has given as to whether the application is, or is not, a Schedule 1 or 2 application; and of any relevant opinion given pursuant to regulation 5.

(2) Where the Secretary of State gives any such direction as is mentioned in paragraph (1) after particulars of the relevant application have been placed on Part I of the register or sends the applicant a notification under regulation 10, the local planning authority shall take steps to secure that a copy of that direction or notification is also placed on that Part of the register.

(3) Where the local planning authority notify an applicant under regulation 9 that they consider his application cannot be granted unless he submits an environmental statement, they shall take steps to secure that a copy of that notification is placed on Part I of the register.

(4) Where the Secretary of State gives, otherwise than pursuant to regulation 6, a direction as to whether the consideration of environmental information is required before planning permission can be granted for a particular proposed development he shall forthwith send a copy of the direction to the local planning authority and to such other persons as he considers it desirable to send a copy together, where necessary, with documents sufficient to identify the land and the development.

(5) Where a copy of a direction is received by the local planning authority before application is made for planning permission for the development in question, the authority shall take steps to secure that a copy of the direction and any documents sent with it are available for public inspection at all reasonable hours at the place where the appropriate register (or section of that register) is kept.   **[639]**

8. Procedure to facilitate preparation for environmental statements

(1) A prospective applicant may give the local planning authority notice in writing that he intends to make a Schedule 1 or Schedule 2 application and to submit an environmental statement with his application.

(2) A notice under paragraph (1) shall include the information necessary to identify, or be accompanied by documents identifying, the land and the nature and purpose of the proposed development, and shall indicate the main environmental consequences to which the prospective applicant proposes to refer in his environmental statement.

(3) Paragraph (4) applies where—

    (a) the local planning authority receive in relation to a proposed planning application—

        (i) such a notice as is mentioned in paragraph (1); or

        (ii) such a statement as is mentioned in regulation 4(4)(iii); or

        (iii) a copy of a direction by the Secretary of State under regulation 6 that a proposed application would be a Schedule 1 or Schedule 2 application; . . .

(4) Where this paragraph applies, the authority in question shall—

   (a) notify the bodies mentioned in paragraph (5) in writing of the name and address of the prospective applicant and of the duty imposed upon them by regulation 22 to make information available to the prospective applicant;

   (b) inform the prospective applicant in writing of the names and addresses of the bodies so notified.

(5) The bodies referred to in paragraph (4) are—

   (a) any body which the local planning authority would be required by article 15 of the General Development Order or any direction under that article to consult if the application were before them;

   (b) the following bodies if not referred to in sub-paragraph (a),—

      (i) any principal council for the area where the land is situated, if not the local planning authority;
      (ii) the Countryside Commission;
      (iii) the Nature Conservancy Council;

   (c) where the proposed development is a development of a description referred to in paragraph (6), [the chief inspector for England and Wales appointed under Part I of the Environmental Protection Act 1990].

(6) The development referred to in paragraph (5)(c) is any development which in the opinion of the local planning authority will—

   (a) involve mining operations, or manufacturing industry or the disposal of waste; and

   (b) is likely either—

      (i) to give rise to waste, the disposal of which requires an authorisation under the Radioactive Substances Act 1960, or to discharges (other than of domestic sewage) which are controlled waste or special waste or are likely to require the licence or consent of [the National Rivers Authority]; or
      (ii) to involve works specified in Schedule 1 to the Health and Safety (Emissions to the Atmosphere) Regulations 1983.

(7) Paragraph (4) shall apply (but subject to the modifications mentioned in paragraph (8)) where a Schedule 1 or Schedule 2 application has been made without an environmental statement and—

      (i) the Secretary of State has given a direction to the effect that the consideration of environmental information is required before planning permission can be granted; or
      (ii) the applicant has informed the local planning authority or, where the application has been referred to the Secretary of State or is the subject of an appeal, the Secretary of State, that he proposes to submit an environmental statement.

(8) In its application by virtue of paragraph (7), paragraph (4) shall have effect—

   (a) as if references to the prospective applicant were references to the applicant or appellant, as appropriate; and

   (b) where the application has been referred to the Secretary of State or is the subject of an appeal, as if references to the local planning authority in paragraphs (4) and (6) were references to the Secretary of State and regulation (5)(a) referred to such bodies as the Secretary of State considers would be required to be consulted by or under article 15 of the General Development Order if the case were before the local planning authority.

[640]

NOTES

Amended by SI 1989/1968, reg 3, Sch 2, SI 1992/1494, reg 3, Schedule, para 4, SI 1994/677, reg 2, Schedule, para 6.

9. Application made to a planning authority without an environmental statement

(1) Where it appears to the local planning authority that an application for planning permission is a Schedule 1 or a Schedule 2 application, and it is not accompanied by an environmental statement, they shall (unless the application is the subject of a direction under section 35) within 3 weeks beginning with the date of receipt of the application, or such longer period as they may agree with the applicant in writing, notify the applicant in writing that they consider the submission of such a statement is required, giving their full reasons for their view clearly and precisely.

(2) An applicant receiving a notification pursuant to paragraph (1) may within 3 weeks beginning with the date of the notification write to the authority to inform them that he—

    (i) accepts their view and is providing an environmental statement; or

    (ii) is applying in writing to the Secretary of State for his direction on the matter.

(3) If the applicant does not write in accordance with paragraph (2), the permission sought shall be deemed to be refused at the end of the 3 week period; but no appeal shall lie to the Secretary of State by virtue of section 36 or 37.

The deemed refusal shall be treated as a decision of the authority for the purposes of article 21(2)(c) of the General Development Order.

(4) Except where the Secretary of State gives a direction to the effect that regulation 4 does not apply, an authority which has given a notification in accordance with paragraph (1) shall determine the relevant application only by refusing planning permission if the applicant does not submit an environmental statement and comply with regulation 13(5).

(5) A person applying to the Secretary of State for a direction pursuant to paragraph (2) shall send with his application copies of—

    (a) his application for planning permission;

    (b) all documents sent to the authority as part of the application; and

    (c) all correspondence with the authority relating to the development proposed,

and paragraphs [(2)] to (5) of regulation 6 shall apply in relation to the application.

[641]

NOTES

Amended by SI 1994/677, reg 2, Schedule, para 7.

10. Application referred to the Secretary of State without an environmental statement

(1) Where it appears to the Secretary of State that an application for planning permission which has been referred to him for determination is a Schedule 1 or a Schedule 2 application, and it is not accompanied by an environmental statement, he shall within 3 weeks beginning with the date he received the application, or such longer period as he may reasonably require, notify the applicant in writing that the

submission of an environmental statement is required, giving his full reasons for his view clearly and precisely.

(2) An applicant receiving a notification pursuant to paragraph (1) may within 3 weeks beginning with the date of the notification write to the Secretary of State to inform him that he proposes to provide an environmental statement.

(3) If the applicant does not write in accordance with paragraph (2), the Secretary of State shall be under no duty to deal with the application: and at the end of the 3 week period he shall inform the applicant in writing that no further action is being taken on the application.

(4) Where the Secretary of State has given a notification in accordance with paragraph (1), he shall determine the relevant application only by refusing planning permission if the applicant does not submit an environmental statement and comply with regulation 13(5).

(5) The Secretary of State shall send a copy of any notification under paragraph (1) to the local planning authority. **[642]**

11. Appeal to the Secretary of State without an environmental statement

(1) Where the Secretary of State on consideration of an appeal under section 36 forms the view that the relevant application is a Schedule 1 or a Schedule 2 application, and the documents sent to him for the purposes of the appeal do not include a copy of an environmental statement, regulation 10 shall apply subject to any necessary modifications.

(2) Where an inspector is dealing with an appeal and any question arises as to whether the relevant application is a Schedule 1 or a Schedule 2 application and it appears to the inspector that it may be such an application and no environmental statement has been submitted, the inspector shall refer the matter to the Secretary of State.

(3) Where a question is referred pursuant to paragraph (2), the Secretary of State shall direct whether or not the application is a Schedule 1 or Schedule 2 application; and the inspector shall not determine the appeal, except by refusing planning permission, before he receives a direction.

(4) Where the Secretary of State directs as aforesaid, he shall forthwith send copies of the direction to the appellant, the local planning authority and the inspector, and to any other person he considers desirable, and where he directs that the application is a Schedule 1 or Schedule 2 application he shall at the same time send those persons a written statement giving his full reasons for his conclusions clearly and precisely.

(5) Where the Secretary of State directs that the application is a Schedule 1 or Schedule 2 application, the appellant may within 3 weeks beginning with the date of the direction write to the Secretary of State to inform him that he proposes to provide an environmental statement.

(6) If the appellant does not write in accordance with paragraph (5), the inspector shall be under no duty to deal with the appeal; and at the end of the 3 week period he shall inform the appellant that no further action is being taken on the appeal.

(7) Where the Secretary of State has directed that the relevant application is a Schedule 1 or Schedule 2 application, the inspector shall determine the appeal only

by refusing planning permission if the appellant does not submit an environmental statement and comply with regulation 13(5). **[643]**

12. (*Revoked by SI 1992/1494, reg 3, Schedule, para 5.*)

13. Publicity where an environmental statement is submitted in course of planning procedures

(1) Where a Schedule 1 or a Schedule 2 application has been made without an environmental statement and the applicant proposes to submit one, he shall before submitting it, comply with paragraphs (2) to (5).

(2) The applicant shall publish in a local newspaper circulating in the locality in which the land is situated (hereinafter referred to as ''the locality'') a notice stating—

(a) his name and that he is the applicant for planning permission and the name and address of the local planning authority;

(b) the date on which the application was made and, if it be the case, that it has been referred to the Secretary of State for determination or is the subject of an appeal to him;

(c) the address or location and the nature of the proposed development;

(d) that a copy of the application and of the plans and other documents submitted with it together with a copy of the environmental statement may be inspected by members of the public at all reasonable hours;

(e) an address in the locality at which those documents may be inspected, and the latest date on which they will be available for inspection (being a date not less than 20 days later than the date on which the notice is published);

(f) an address in the locality (whether or not the same as that given pursuant to sub-paragraph (e)) at which copies of the environmental statement may be obtained;

(g) that copies may be obtained there so long as stocks last;

(h) if a charge is to be made for a copy, the amount of the charge; and

(i) that any person wishing to make representations about the application should make them in writing, before the date named in accordance with sub-paragraph (e), to the local planning authority or (in the case of an application referred to the Secretary of State or an appeal) to the Secretary of State.

(3) The applicant shall, unless he has not, and was not reasonably able to acquire, such rights as would enable him to do so, post on the land a notice containing the information specified in paragraph (2), except that the date named as the latest date on which the documents will be available for inspection shall be not less than 20 days later than the date on which the notice is first posted.

(4) The notice mentioned in paragraph (3) must—

(a) be left in position for not less than 7 days in the month immediately preceding the date of the submission of the environmental statement; and

(b) be affixed firmly to some object on the land and sited and displayed in such a way as to be easily visible to, and readable by, members of the public without going on to the land.

(5) The environmental statement, when submitted, shall be accompanied by—

(a) a copy of the notice mentioned in paragraph (2) certified by or on behalf of the applicant as having been published in a named newspaper on a date specified in the certificate; and

(b) a certificate by or on behalf of the applicant which states either—

(i) that he has posted a notice on the land in compliance with this regulation and when he did so, and that the notice was left in position for not less than 7 days in the month immediately preceding the date of the submission of the statement, or that, without any fault or intention on his part, it was removed, obscured or defaced before 7 days had elapsed and he took reasonable steps for its protection or replacement, specifying the steps taken; or

(ii) that the applicant was unable to comply with paragraph (3) and (4) above because he did not have the necessary rights to do so; that he has taken such reasonable steps as are open to him to acquire those rights; and has been unable to do so, specifying the steps taken.

(6) Where an applicant proposes to provide an environmental statement in the circumstances mentioned in paragraph (1), the local planning authority, the Secretary of State or the inspector, as the case may be, shall (unless disposed to refuse the permission sought) suspend consideration of the application or appeal until receipt of the statement and the other documents mentioned in paragraph (5); and shall not determine it during the period of 21 days beginning with the date of receipt of the statement and the other documents so mentioned.

(7) If any person issues a certificate which purports to comply with the requirements of paragraph (5)(b) and which contains a statement which he knows to be false or misleading in a material particular, or recklessly issues a certificate which purports to comply with those requirements and which contains a statement which is false or misleading in a material particular, he shall be guilty of an offence and liable on summary conviction to a fine not exceeding level 3 on the standard scale.

(8) The reference in paragraph (7) to a fine not exceeding level 3 on the standard scale shall be construed in accordance with section 37 (standard scale of fines for summary offences) of the Criminal Justice Act 1982.

(9) Where it is proposed to submit an environmental statement in connection with an appeal, this regulation applies with the substitution, except in paragraph 2(a), of references to the appellant for references to the applicant. **[644]**

14. Procedure where the planning authority receive an environmental statement

(1) When an applicant making a Schedule 1 or Schedule 2 application submits an environmental statement to the local planning authority he shall provide the authority with [three additional copies] of the statement for transmission to the Secretary of State and, if at the same time he serves a copy of the statement or of a part of it on any other body, he shall—

(a) serve with it a copy of the application and any plan submitted with it (unless he has already served these documents on the body in question);

(b) inform the body that representations may be made to the local planning authority;

(c) inform the authority of the name of every body whom he has so served, of the date of service and, where he has not served a copy of the whole of the statement, of the part of which a copy was served.

(2) When a local planning authority receive an environmental statement in connection with a Schedule 1 or Schedule 2 application the authority shall—

(a) take steps to secure that a copy of the statement is placed on Part I of the register with the application;

(b) send to the Secretary of State [three copies of the statement, and a copy] of the relevant application and of any documents submitted with the application;

(c) advise any body mentioned in regulation 8(5) on whom the applicant has not served a copy of the statement or a part of it, that a statement will be taken into consideration in determining the application, elicit whether they wish to receive a copy of the statement or any part of it and inform them that they may make representations;

(d) inform the applicant of the copies required by those bodies and of the names and addresses of the bodies concerned and enquire of him whether he proposes to serve the required copy on each of those bodies or send the required copies to the authority for service;

(e) serve on the relevant body any copy sent to them by the applicant for service.

(3) The applicant shall inform the authority which of the courses mentioned in paragraph 2(d) he proposes to follow and shall serve copies of the environmental statement or a part of it on each body on whom he has said he will serve a copy or send the necessary copies to the authority, as the case may be. Where the applicant elects to send copies to the bodies directly he shall inform the authority as mentioned in paragraph (1)(c).

(4) The local planning authority shall not determine the application until the expiry of 14 days from the last date on which a copy of the environmental statement or a part of it was served in accordance with this regulation.   **[645]**

NOTES
    Amended by SI 1994/677, reg 2, Schedule, paras 8, 9, subject to transitional provisions in reg 3.

15. Procedure where the Secretary of State receives an environmental statement

(1) This regulation applies where an applicant submits to the Secretary of State an environmental statement relating to a Schedule 1 or Schedule 2 application which is before the Secretary of State for determination or is the subject of an appeal to him.

(2) The applicant shall submit [four] copies of the statement to the Secretary of State who shall transmit one copy to the local planning authority.

(3) The local planning authority shall take steps to secure that the copy so transmitted is placed on the register.

(4) If at the same time as he submits a statement to the Secretary of State the applicant serves a copy of it or a part of it on any other body, the applicant shall comply with regulation 14(1)(a) and (b) and inform the Secretary of State of the matters mentioned in regulation 14(1)(c).

(5) The Secretary of State shall comply with regulation 14(2)(c) to (e) and the applicant with regulation 14(3) as if—

(a) references in any of those provisions and regulation 8(6) to the local planning authority were references to the Secretary of State; and

(b) regulation 8(5)(a) referred to such bodies as the Secretary of State considers would be required to be consulted by or under article 15 of the General Development Order if the matter were before the local planning authority;

and the Secretary of State or the inspector shall comply with regulation 14(4) as if it referred to him instead of to the local planning authority.

(6) ...

(7) In this regulation, references to the applicant include references to an appellant. **[646]**

NOTES
   Para (2): amended by SI 1994/677, reg 2, Schedule, para 10, subject to transitional provisions in reg 3.
   Para (6) revoked by SI 1992/1494, reg 3, Schedule, para 6.
   General Development Order: see now SI 1995/418, 419.

16. Extension of the period for an authority's decision on a planning application

(1) In determining for the purposes of section 37 (appeal in default of planning decision) the time which has elapsed without the local planning authority giving notice to the applicant of their decision in a case where—

   (a) the authority have notified an applicant in accordance with regulation 9(1) that the submission of an environmental statement is required; and

   (b) the Secretary of State has given a direction in the matter,

no account shall be taken of any period before the issue of the direction.

[(2) Where it falls to an authority determining an application for planning permission to take environmental information into consideration, article 23 of the Town and Country Planning General Development Order 1988 shall have effect as if—

   (a) for the reference in paragraph (2)(a) of that article to a period of 8 weeks there was substituted a reference to a period of 16 weeks;

   (b) after paragraph (3)(b) of that article there was inserted—

   "(ba) the environmental statement required to be submitted in respect of the application has been submitted, together with the documents required to accompany that statement; and"]. **[647]**

NOTES
   Amended by SI 1992/1494, reg 3, Schedule, para 7.

17. (*Revoked by SI 1992/1494, reg 3, Schedule, para 8.*)

18. Availability of copies of an environmental statement

An applicant for planning permission or an appellant who submits an environmental statement in connection with his application or appeal shall ensure that a reasonable number of copies of the statement are available at the address named in the notices published or posted pursuant to [article 12B of the Town and Country Planning General Development Order 1988 or regulation 13] as the address at which such copies may be obtained. **[648]**

NOTES
   Amended by SI 1992/1494, reg 3, Schedule, para 9.

19. Provision of a copy of an environmental statement for the Secretary of State

Where an applicant for planning permission has submitted an environmental statement in connection with his application and the application—

   (a) is directed to be referred to the Secretary of State under section 35; or

(b) occasions an appeal under section 36,

the applicant shall supply the Secretary of State with [three copies] of the statement unless, in the case of a referred application, the local planning authority have done so when referring the application to him.   **[649]**

NOTES

Amended by SI 1994/677, reg 2, Schedule, para 11, subject to transitional provisions in reg 3.

20. Charges

(1) A reasonable charge reflecting printing and distribution costs may be made to a member of the public for a copy of an environmental statement made available in accordance with regulation . . . 18 and for any copy, in excess of one, of the whole or part of a statement supplied to a body pursuant to regulation 14, [or 15].

(2) A reasonable charge reflecting the cost of making the relevant information available may be made by a body supplying in accordance with regulation 22(1) information sought by an applicant or appellant.   **[650]**

NOTES

Amended by SI 1992/1494, reg 3, Schedule, para 10.

21. Further information and evidence respecting environmental statements

(1) The local planning authority or the Secretary of State or an inspector, when dealing with an application or appeal in relation to which an environmental statement has been provided, may in writing require the applicant or appellant to provide such further information as may be specified concerning any matter which is required to be, or may be, dealt with in the statement; and where in the opinion of the authorty or the Secretary of State or the inspector—

(a) the applicant or appellant could (having regard in particular to current knowledge and methods of assessment) provide further information about any matter mentioned in paragraph 3 of Schedule 3; and

(b) that further information is reasonably required to give proper consideration to the likely environmental effects of the proposed development,

they or he shall notify the applicant or appellant in writing accordingly, and the applicant or appellant shall provide that further information.

[(2) Paragraphs (3) to (9) shall apply in relation to further information required of an applicant or appellant after those paragraphs come into force except in so far as such further information is required to be provided for the purposes of a local inquiry held under the Act and the request for such further information states that it is to be provided for such purposes.

(3) The recipient of the further information shall publish in a local newspaper circulating in the locality in which the land is situated (hereinafter referred to as "the locality") a notice stating—

(a) the name of the applicant for planning permission or the appellant (as the case may be) and the name and address of the local planning authority;

(b) the date on which the application was made and, if it be the case, that it has been referred to the Secretary of State for determination or is the subject of an appeal to him;

(c) the address or location and the nature of the proposed development;

(d) that further information is available in relation to an environmental statement which has already been provided;

(e) that a copy of the further information may be inspected by members of the public at all reasonable hours;

(f) an address in the locality at which the further information may be inspected and the latest date on which it will be available for inspection (being a date not less than 20 days later than the date on which the notice is published);

(g) an address in the locality (whether or not the same as that given pursuant to sub-paragraph (f)) at which copies of the further information may be obtained;

(h) that copies may be obtained there so long as stocks last;

(i) if a charge is to be made for a copy, the amount of the charge; and

(j) that any person wishing to make representations about the further information should make them in writing, before the date specified in accordance with sub-paragraph (f), to the local planning authority, the Secretary of State or the inspector (as the case may be).

(4) The recipient of the further information shall send a copy of it to each person to whom the environmental statement to which it relates was sent.

(5) Where the recipient of the further information is a local planning authority they shall—

(a) take steps to secure that a copy of the further information is placed on Part I of the register with the application and the environmental statement; and

(b) send to the Secretary of State three copies of the further information.

(6) The recipient of the further information may by notice in writing require the applicant or appellant to provide such number of copies of the further information as is specified in the notice (being the number required for the purposes of paragraph (4) or (5)).

(7) Where further information is required to be provided, the local planning authority, the Secretary of State or the inspector, as the case may be, shall suspend determination of the application or appeal; and shall not determine it before the expiry of 14 days after the date on which the further information was sent to all persons to whom the environmental statement was sent or the expiry of 21 days after the date that notice of it was published in a local newspaper, whichever is the later.

(8) The applicant or appellant who provides further information in accordance with paragraph (1) shall ensure that a reasonable number of copies of the information is available at the address named in the notice published pursuant to paragraph (3) as the address at which such copies may be obtained.

(9) A reasonable charge reflecting printing and distribution costs may be made to a member of the public for a copy of the further information made available in accordance with paragraph (8) and for any copy, in excess of one, of the whole or part of the further information supplied to a person pursuant to paragraph (4).]

[(10)] The local planning authority or the Secretary of State or an inspector may in writing require an applicant or appellant to produce such evidence as they may reasonably call for to verify any information in his environmental statement. **[651]**

NOTES
Amended by SI 1994/677, reg 2, Schedule, para 12.

22. Provision of information

(1) Subject to paragraph (2), the local planning authority and any body notified in accordance with these Regulations that a person has made or is proposing to make a

Schedule 1 or Schedule 2 application, shall, if requested by the applicant (or prospective applicant) or may without such a request, enter into consultation with him to determine whether the body has in its possession any information which he or they consider relevant to the preparation of an environmental statement and, if they have, the body shall make any such information available to him.

(2) Paragraph (1) shall not require the disclosure by a body of confidential information.   **[652]**

23. Duty to inform the Secretary of State

[Where, after environmental information has been taken into consideration, a local planning authority determine an application for planning permission, they shall inform the Secretary of State of the decision taken and provide details of any conditions subject to which any planning permission was granted.]   **[653]**

NOTES
  Substituted by SI 1992/1494, reg 3, Schedule, para 11.

24. Service of notices etc

Any notice or other document to be sent, served or given under these Regulations may be served or given in a manner specified in section 283(1).   **[654]**

25. Application to the High Court

For the purposes of Part XII of the Act (validity of certain decisions), the reference in section 245 to action of the Secretary of State which is not within the powers of the Act shall be taken to extend to a grant of planning permission in contravention of regulation 4 of these Regulations.   **[655]**

[25A. Local authority applications

(1) In the application of these Regulations to a Schedule 1 or Schedule 2 application (or proposed application) where the local planning authority is also (or would also be) the applicant (whether alone or jointly with any other person), the following modifications shall apply—

  (a) regulations 5 and 6 shall not apply;
  (b) regulation 8(1) to (3) shall not apply but regulation 8(4)(a) shall apply
      where an authority proposes to make a Schedule 1 or Schedule 2
      application and to submit an environmental statement with that application;
  (c) regulation 9 shall not apply;
  (d) regulation 10(5) shall not apply;
  (e) save for the purposes of regulation 15(4) and (5), regulation 14 shall apply
      as if—

      (i) in paragraph (1), for "When an applicant" to "other body, he shall"
          was substituted "When an applicant making a Schedule 1 or Schedule
          2 application submits an environmental statement and at the same
          time serves a copy of the statement or of a part of it on any other
          body, he shall" and subparagraph (c) was omitted;
      (ii) in paragraph (2), for subparagraphs (d) and (e) was substituted—

          "(d) serve on any such body that has expressed a wish to receive
              a copy of the statement or any part of it such a copy.";

      (iii) paragraph (3) was omitted;

  (f) regulation 15 shall apply as if—

       (i) paragraph (2) was omitted;

      (ii) for paragraph (3) was substituted—

         ''(3) The local planning authority shall take steps to secure that a copy of the environmental statement is placed on the register.''.

(2) An authority which is minded to make a planning application in relation to which it would be the local planning authority may request the Secretary of State in writing for a direction as to whether the proposed application would be a Schedule 1 or a Schedule 2 application.

(3) A request made pursuant to paragraph (2) shall be accompanied by—

    (a) a plan sufficient to identify the land;

    (b) a brief description of the nature and purpose of the proposed development and of its possible effects on the environment;

    (c) such other information or representations as the authority may wish to provide or make.

(4) An authority making a request under paragraph (2) shall send to the Secretary of State any further information he may request in writing to enable him to give a direction.]   **[656]**

NOTES

   Inserted by SI 1992/1494, reg 2.

26. *(Revoked by SI 1992/1494, reg 3, Schedule, para 12.)*

SCHEDULES
SCHEDULE 1

Regulation 2(1)

DESCRIPTIONS OF DEVELOPMENT

(1) The carrying out of building or other operations, or the change of use of buildings or other land (where a material change) to provide any of the following—

1. A crude-oil refinery (excluding an undertaking manufacturing only lubricants from crude oil) or an installation for the gasification and liquefaction of 500 tonnes or more of coal or bituminous shale per day.

[2.(a) A thermal power station or other combustion installation with a heat output of 300 megawatts or more (not being an installation falling within paragraph (b)); and

    (b) A nuclear power station or other nuclear reactor (excluding a research installation for the production and conversion of fissionable and fertile materials, the maximum power of which does not exceed 1 kilowatt continuous thermal load).]

3. An installation designed solely for the permanent storage or final disposal of radioactive waste.

4. An integrated works for the initial melting of cast-iron and steel.

5. An installation for the extraction of asbestos or for the processing and transformation of asbestos or products containing asbestos:—

    (a) where the installation produces asbestos-cement products, with an annual production of more than 20,000 tonnes of finished products; or

    (b) where the installation produces friction material, with an annual production of more than 50 tonnes of finished products; or

    (c) in other cases, where the installation will utilise more than 200 tonnes of asbestos per year.

6. An integrated chemical installation, that is to say, an industrial installation or group of

installations where two or more linked chemical or physical processes are employed for the manufacture of olefins from petroleum products, or of sulphuric acid, nitric acid, hydrofluoric acid, chlorine or fluorine.

7. A special road; a line for long-distance railway traffic; or an aerodrome with a basic runway length of 2,100m or more.

8. A trading port, an inland waterway which permits the passage of vessels of over 1,350 tonnes or a port for inland waterway traffic capable of handling such vessels.

9. A waste-disposal installation for the incineration or chemical treatment of special waste.

(2) The carrying out of operations whereby land is filled with special waste, or the change of use of land (where a material change) to use for the   **[657]**

NOTES

Para (1): sub-para 2 substituted by SI 1990/367, reg 2.

SCHEDULE 2
Regulation 2(1)

DESCRIPTIONS OF DEVELOPMENT

Development for any of the following purposes—

1. *Agriculture*
   - (a) water-management for agriculture
   - (b) poultry-rearing
   - (c) pig-rearing
   - (d) a salmon hatchery
   - (e) an installation for the rearing of salmon
   - (f) the reclamation of land from the sea

2. *Extractive industry*
   - (a) extracting peat
   - (b) deep drilling, including in particular—
       - (i) geothermal drilling
       - (ii) drilling for the storage of nuclear waste material
       - (iii) drilling for water supplies
       but excluding drilling to investigate the stability of the soil
   - (c) extracting minerals (other than metalliferous and energy-producing minerals) such as marble, sand, gravel, shale, salt, phosphates and potash
   - (d) extracting coal or lignite by underground or open-cast mining
   - (e) extracting petroleum
   - (f) extracting natural gas
   - (g) extracting ores
   - (h) extracting bituminous shale
   - (i) extracting minerals (other than metalliferous and energy-producing minerals) by open-cast mining
   - (j) a surface industrial installation for the extraction of coal, petroleum, natural gas or ores or bituminous shale
   - (k) a coke oven (dry distillation of coal)
   - (l) an installation for the manufacture of cement

3. *Energy industry*
   - (a) a non-nuclear thermal power station, not being an installation falling within Schedule 1, or an installation for the production of electricity, steam and hot water
   - (b) an industrial installation for carrying gas, steam or hot water; or the transmission of electrical energy by overhead cables
   - (c) the surface storage of natural gas
   - (d) the underground storage of combustible gases
   - (e) the surface storage of fossil fuels

(f) the industrial briquetting of coal or lignite
(g) an installation for the production or enrichment of nuclear fuels
(h) an installation for the reprocessing of irradiated nuclear fuels
(i) an installation for the collection or processing of radioactive waste, not being an installation falling within Schedule 1
(j) an installation for hydroelectric energy production
[(k) a wind generator]

4. *Processing of metals*

(a) an ironworks or steelworks including a foundry, forge, drawing plant or rolling mill (not being a works falling within Schedule 1)
(b) an installation for the production (including smelting, refining, drawing and rolling) of non-ferrous metals, other than precious metals
(c) the pressing, drawing or stamping of large castings
(d) the surface treatment and coating of metals
(e) boilermaking or manufacturing reservoirs, tanks and other sheet-metal containers
(f) manufacturing or assembling motor vehicles or manufacturing motor-vehicle engines
(g) a shipyard
(h) an installation for the construction or repair of aircraft
(i) the manufacture of railway equipment
(j) swaging by explosives
(k) an installation for the roasting or sintering of metallic ores

5. *Glass making*

the manufacture of glass

6. *Chemical industry*

(a) the treatment of intermediate products and production of chemicals, other than development falling within Schedule 1
(b) the production of pesticides or pharmaceutical products, paints or varnishes, elastomers or peroxides
(c) the storage of petroleum or petrochemical or chemical products

7. *Food industry*

(a) the manufacture of vegetable or animal oils or fats
(b) the packing or canning of animal or vegetable products
(c) the manufacture of dairy products
(d) brewing or malting
(e) confectionery or syrup manufacture
(f) an installation for the slaughter of animals
(g) an industrial starch manufacturing installation
(h) a fish-meal or fish-oil factory
(i) a sugar factory

8. *Textile, leather, wood and paper industries*

(a) a wool scouring, degreasing and bleaching factory
(b) the manufacture of fibre board, particle board or plywood
(c) the manufacture of pulp, paper or board
(d) a fibre-dyeing factory
(e) a cellulose-processing and production installation
(f) a tannery or a leather dressing factor

9. *Rubber industry*

the manufacture and treatment of elastomer-based products

10. *Infrastructure projects*

(a) an industrial estate development project
(b) an urban development project
(c) a ski-lift or cable-car

    (d) the construction of a road, or a harbour, including a fishing harbour, or an aerodrome, not being development falling within Schedule 1

    (e) canalisation or flood-relief works

    (f) a dam or other installation designed to hold water or store it on a long-term basis

    (g) a tramway, elevated or underground railway, suspended line or similar line, exclusively or mainly for passenger transport

    (h) an oil or gas pipeline installation

    (i) a long-distance aqueduct

    (j) a yacht marina

    [(k) a motorway service area

    (l) coast protection works]

11. *Other projects*

    (a) a holiday village or hotel complex

    (b) a permanent racing or test track for cars or motor cycles

    (c) an installation for the disposal of controlled waste or waste from mines and quarries, not being an installation falling within Schedule 1

    (d) a waste water treatment plant

    (e) a site for depositing sludge

    (f) the storage of scrap iron

    (g) a test bench for engines, turbines or reactors

    (h) the manufacture of artificial mineral fibres

    (i) the manufacture, packing, loading or placing in cartridges of gunpowder or other explosives

    (j) a knackers' yard

12. The modification of a development which has been carried out, where that development is within a description mentioned in Schedule 1.

13. Development within a description mentioned in Schedule 1, where it is exclusively or mainly for the development and testing of new methods or products and will not be permitted for longer than one year.   **[658]**

NOTES

Amended by SI 1994/677, reg 2, Schedule, paras 13, 14, subject to transitional provisions in reg 3.

SCHEDULE 3

Regulation 2(1)

1. An environmental statement comprises a document or series of documents providing for the purpose of assessing the likely impact upon the environment of the development proposed to be carried out, the information specified in paragraph 2 (referred to in this Schedule as "the specified information").

2. The specified information is—

    (a) a description of the development proposed, comprising information about the site and the design and size or scale of the development;

    (b) the data necessary to identify and assess the main effects which that development is likely to have on the environment;

    (c) a description of the likely significant effects, direct and indirect, on the environment of the development, explained by reference to its possible impact on—

        human beings;

        flora;

        fauna;

        soil;

        water;

        air;

        climate;

        the landscape;

        the inter-action between any of the foregoing;

material assets;
the cultural heritage;

(d) where significant adverse effects are identified with respect to any of the foregoing, a description of the measures envisaged in order to avoid, reduce or remedy those effects; and

(e) a summary in non-technical language of the information specified above.

3. An environmental statement may include, by way of explanation or amplification of any specified information, further information on any of the following matters—

(a) the physical characteristics of the proposed development, and the land-use requirements during the construction and operational phases;

(b) the main characteristics of the production processes proposed, including the nature and quality of the materials to be used;

(c) the estimated type and quantity of expected residues and emissions (including pollutants of water, air or soil, noise, vibration, light, heat and radiation) resulting from the proposed development when in operation;

(d) (in outline) the main alternatives (if any) studied by the applicant, appellant or authority and an indication of the main reasons for choosing the development proposed, taking into account the environmental effects;

(e) the likely significant direct and indirect effects on the environment of the development proposed which may result from—

(i) the use of natural resources;

(ii) the emission of pollutants, the creation of nuisances, and the elimination of waste;

(f) the forecasting methods used to assess any effects on the environment about which information is given under subparagraph (e); and

(g) any difficulties, such as technical deficiencies or lack of know-how, encountered in compiling any specified information.

In paragraph (e), "effects" includes secondary, cumulative, short, medium and long term, permanent, temporary, positive and negative effects.

4. Where further information is included in an environmental statement pursuant to paragraph 3, a non-technical summary of that information shall also be provided. **[659]**

TOWN AND COUNTRY PLANNING (APPLICATIONS) REGULATIONS 1988
(SI 1988/1812)

NOTES
Made: 21 October 1988
Commencement: 5 December 1988
Authority: Town and Country Planning Act 1971, ss 25, 287(1); now have effect under Town and Country Planning Act 1990, ss 62, 333(1)–(3).

ARRANGEMENT OF REGULATIONS

1. Citation and commencement

These Regulations may be cited as the Town and Country Planning (Applications) Regulations 1988 and shall come into force on 5th December 1988. **[660]**

2. Interpretation

In these regulations, unless the context otherwise requires—

"the Act" means the Town and Country Planning Act 1971;

"building" does not include any plant or machinery or a structure or erection of the nature of plant or machinery;

"outline planning permission" means planning permission for the erection of a building, subject to a condition requiring the subsequent approval of the local planning authority with respect to one or more reserved matters, that is to say—

    (a) siting,
    (b) design,
    (c) external appearance,
    (d) means of access,
    (e) the landscaping of the site. **[661]**

3. Applications for planning permission

(1) Subject to the following provisions of this regulation, an application for planning permission shall—

    (a) be made on a form provided by the local planning authority;
    (b) include the particulars specified in the form and be accompanied by a plan which identifies the land to which it relates and any other plans and drawings and information necessary to describe the development which is the subject of the application; and
    (c) except where the authority indicate that a lesser number is required, be accompanied by 3 copies of the form and the plans and drawings submitted with it.

(2) In the case of an application for outline planning permission, details need not be given of any proposed reserved matters.

(3) An application—

    (a) for renewal of planning permission where—

        (i) a planning permission has previously been granted for development which has not yet begun, and
        (ii) a time limit was imposed under section 41 (limit of duration of planning permission) or section 42 (outline planning permission) of the Act which has not yet expired, or

    (b) under section 31A (an application for the variation of a condition subject to which the planning permission was granted) or 32(1)(b) (an application for permission to retain buildings or works or continue the use of land without compliance with a condition),

shall be made in writing and give sufficient information to enable the authority to identify the previous grant of planning permission and any condition in question.

[662]

4. Directions by the local planning authority

The local planning authority who are to determine an application may direct an applicant in writing to—

    (a) supply any further information and, except in the case of outline applications, plans and drawings necessary to enable them to determine the application; or

(b) provide one of their officers with any evidence in respect of the application as is reasonable for them to call for to verify any particulars of information given to them. **[663]**

PLANNING (LISTED BUILDINGS AND CONSERVATION AREAS) REGULATIONS 1990
(SI 1990/1519)

NOTES
Made: 29 July 1990
Commencement: 24 August 1990
Authority: Planning (Listed Buildings and Conservation Areas) Act 1990, ss 2, 10, 11, 19–21, 25, 27–29, 32, 42, 74, 82, 84, 91, 93

ARRANGEMENT OF REGULATIONS

1. Citation and Commencement

These Regulations may be cited as the Planning (Listed Buildings and Conservation Areas) Regulations 1990 and shall come into force on 24th August 1990. **[664]**

2. Interpretation

In these Regulations "the Act" means the Planning (Listed Buildings and Conservation Areas) Act 1990. **[665]**

3. Applications for listed building consent or for conservation area consent

(1) An application to a local planning authority for listed building consent or for conservation area consent shall be made on a form issued by the local planning authority and obtainable from that authority and shall, subject to regulation 7, be lodged with the local planning authority together with two further copies of the form, plans and drawings.

(2) On receipt of any such application with a certificate under regulation 6 the local planning authority shall send to the applicant an acknowledgement thereof in the terms (or substantially in the terms) set out in Part I of Schedule 1 hereto.

(3) Where, after the sending of an acknowledgement as required by paragraph (2), the local planning authority form the opinion that the application is invalid by reason of failure to comply with requirements of paragraph (1) or with any other statutory requirement, they shall as soon as may be notify the applicant that his application is invalid.

(4) Where a valid application under paragraph (1) has been received by a local planning authority, the time within which the authority shall give notice to an applicant of their decision or of the reference of an application to the Secretary of State shall be a period of 8 weeks from the date when the form of application and the certificate under regulation 6 were lodged with the local planning authority or (except where the applicant has already given notice of appeal to the Secretary of State) such other period as may at any time be agreed upon in writing between the applicant and the local planning authority.

(5) Every such notice of decision or reference to the Secretary of State shall be in writing and where the local planning authority decide to grant listed building consent or conservation area consent subject to conditions or to refuse it, the notice shall state the reasons for the decision and shall be accompanied by a notification in the terms (or substantially in the terms) set out in Part II of Schedule 1 hereto. **[666]**

NOTES

Modification: where listed building consent or conservation area consent is required for the purposes of proposals included in an application made under the Transport and Works Act 1992, s 6, and either the application for the relevant consent has been made not later than 10 weeks after the application under the said s 6, or the Secretary of State considers it appropriate that the Transport and Works Applications (Listed Buildings, Conservation Areas and Ancient Monuments Procedure) Regulations 1992, SI 1992/3138, reg 3, should apply (and he has give a direction to that effect), this regulation and regs 5, 6, Sch 2, Pt I, have effect with the modifications indicated in the notes thereto. This regulation is accordingly modified as if, in para (1), for the words "plans and drawings" there were substituted the words "and of such plans, drawings, sections, models, photographs and other materials as are submitted with it".

4. Applications to vary or discharge conditions attached to listed building consent or conservation area consent

(1) An application to a local planning authority by a person interested in a building for the variation or discharge of conditions attached to a listed building consent or conservation area consent granted in respect of that building shall be made on a form issued by the local planning authority and obtainable from that authority, and shall, subject to regulation 7, be lodged with the local planning authority and obtainable from that authority, and shall, subject to regulation 7, be lodged with the local planning authority together with two further copies of the form, plans and drawings.

(2) Regulations 3(2) to 3(5) shall have effect in relation to an application under this regulation as they have effect in relation to an application under regulation 3(1), except that for the reference in regulation 3(5) to a notification in the terms set out in Part II of Schedule 1, there shall be substituted a reference to a notification in the terms set out in Part III of that Schedule. **[667]**

5. Advertisement of applications

(1) Subject to paragraph (3), where an application under regulation 3 or 4 is made to a local planning authority in respect of any building the authority shall—

    (a) publish in a local newspaper circulating in the locality in which the building is situated a notice indicating the nature of the works which are the subject of the application and naming a place within the locality where a copy of the application, and of all plans and other documents submitted with it, will be open to inspection by the public at all reasonable hours during the period of 21 days beginning with the date of publication of the notice; and

(b) for not less than 7 days display on or near the said building a notice containing the same particulars as are required to be contained in the notice to be published in accordance with sub-paragraph (a).

(2) Subject to paragraph (3), an application under regulation 3 or 4 shall not be determined by the local planning authority before both of the following periods have elapsed, namely—

(a) the period of 21 days referred to in sub-paragraph (a) of paragraph (1) above; and

(b) the period of 21 days beginning with the date on which the notice required by sub-paragraph (b) of the said paragraph (1) was first displayed;

and in determining the application the authority shall take into account any representations relating to the application which are received by them before both of those periods have elapsed.

(3) Paragraphs (1) and (2) shall not apply to any application for—

(a) listed building consent to carry out works affecting only the interior of a building which when last notified to the authority by the Secretary of State as a building of special architectural or historic interest was classified as a Grade II (unstarred) listed building; or

(b) the variation or discharge of conditions attached to a listed building consent in respect of the interior of such a Grade II (unstarred) listed building. **[668]**

NOTES

Modification: in the circumstances noted to reg 3 this regulation is modified by SI 1992/3138 so that for para (1) there is substituted:

"(1) Subject to paragraph (3), where an application is made under regulation 3 or 4—

(a) the applicant shall, not more than 14 days before nor later than the date of the application, publish in a local newspaper circulating in the area in which the building is situated a notice—

(i) indicating the nature of works which are, or are to be, the subject of the application, and

(ii) naming all the places in the area (or as close as reasonably possible to that area) where a copy of the application, and of all plans, drawings, sections and other materials submitted with it, may be inspected free of charge at all reasonable hours during a period specified in the notice, being a period of not less than 42 days from the date of the application.

and such notice may be combined with such notice of the concurrent application as the applicant is required, by rules made under section 6 of the Transport and Works Act 1992, to publish in a local newspaper; and

(b) the local planning authority shall for not less than 7 days, during the period of 42 days prescribed by sub-paragraph (a) above, display on or near the said building a notice containing the same particulars as are required to be published in accordance with sub-paragraph (a).";

and as if the following paragraph was inserted:

"(3A) In this regulation and in regulation 6 below, "concurrent application" means an application made under section 6 of the Transport and Works Act 1992 relating to proposals for the purposes of which the granting of listed building consent or conservation area consent is required in respect of the building to which the application relates.".

6. Certificate to accompany applications and appeals

(1) A local planning authority shall not entertain any application under regulation 3 or 4 unless it is accompanied by one of the following certificates signed by or on behalf of the applicant—

    (a) a certificate stating that, at the beginning of the period of 21 days ending with the date of the application, no person (other than the applicant) was the owner of any of the building to which the application relates:

    (b) a certificate stating that the applicant has given the requisite notice of the application to all persons (other than himself) who at the beginning of that period were owners of any of the building to which the application relates, and setting out the names of those persons, the addresses at which notice of the application was given to them respectively, and the date of service of each such notice;

    (c) a certificate stating that the applicant is unable to issue a certificate in accordance with either sub-paragraphs (a) or (b), that he has given the requisite notice of the application to such one or more of the persons mentioned in sub-paragraph (b) as are specified in the certificate (setting out their names, the addresses at which notice of the application was given to them respectively, and the date of service of each such notice), that he has taken such steps as are reasonably open to him (specifying them) to ascertain the names and addresses of the remainder of those persons and that he has been unable to do so;

    (d) a certificate stating that the applicant is unable to issue a certificate in accordance with sub-paragraph (a), that he has taken such steps as are reasonably open to him (specifying them) to ascertain the names and addresses of the persons mentioned in sub-paragraph (b) but has been unable to do so.

(2) Any such certificate as is mentioned in sub-paragraph (c) or sub-paragraph (d) of paragraph (1) shall also contain a statement that the requisite notice of the application, as set out in the certificate, has on a date specified in the certificate (which must not be earlier than the beginning of the period mentioned in sub-paragraph (a) of paragraph (1)) been published in a local newspaper circulating in the locality in which the building is situated.

(3) Where an application under regulation 3 or 4 is accompanied by such a certificate as is mentioned in sub-paragraph (b), sub-paragraph (c), or sub-paragraph (d) of paragraph (1), the local planning authority—

    (a) shall not determine the application before the end of the period of 21 days beginning with the date appearing from the certificate to be the latest of the dates of service of notices as mentioned in the certificate, or, if later, the date of publication of a notice as so mentioned;

    (b) shall in determining the application take into account any representations relating to it which are made to them before the end of that period by any person who satisfies them that he is an owner of any of the building to which the application relates; and

    (c) shall give notice of their decision to every person who has made representations which they were required to take into account in accordance with sub-paragraph (b).

(4) For the purposes of this regulation, "owner" means a person who is for the time being the estate owner in respect of the fee simple or is entitled to a tenancy granted or extended for a term of years certain of which not less than seven years remain unexpired.

(5) The provisions of this regulation shall apply, with any necessary modifications, where an application under regulation 3 or 4 is referred (or is deemed to have been referred) to the Secretary of State under section 12 of the Act or, in relation to an appeal to the Secretary of State under sections 20 or 21 of the Act, as they apply in relation to an application which falls to be determined by the local planning authority.

(6) Certificates issued for the purposes of this regulation shall be in the forms set out in Part 1 of Schedule 2 hereto.

(7) The requisite notices for the purposes of the provisions of this regulation in relation to applications shall be in the forms set out in Part II of Schedule 2 hereto.

(8) The requisite notices for the purposes of the provisions of this regulation in relation to appeals shall be in the forms set out in Part III of Schedule 2 hereto. **[669]**

NOTES
    Modification: in the circumstances noted to reg 3 this regulation is modified by SI 1992/3138 so that, after sub-para (1)(a), there is inserted:

    "(aa) a certificate stating—

        (i) notice of the concurrent application has been given in accordance with rules made under section 6 of the Transport and Works Act 1992 to all of the persons (other than the applicant) who were, at the beginning of a period of 28 days ending with the date of the concurrent application, the owners of the building; and

        (ii) every such notice contains a statement that an application for listed building consent or conservation area consent has been, or is to be, made inrespect of the building.";

and as if for para (4) there was substituted the following:

    "(4) For the purposes of this regulation, "owner" means a person, other than a mortgagee not in possession, who is for the time being entitled to dispose of the fee simple of the building (whether in possession or reversion) and includes also a person holding, or entitled to the rents and profits of the land under, a lease or agreement the unexpired term whereof exceeds three years.".

7. Applications in National Parks

(1) An application under regulation 3 or 4 as respects a building situated in an area of a National Park outside a metropolitan county shall be made to the council of the district who shall send it on, together with all accompanying documents required by these Regulations, to the body authorised to exercise the functions relating to such application (being the council of the county, the joint planning board or the special planning board, as the case may be).

(2) An application under regulation 3 or 4 as respects a building situated in an area of a National Park within a metropolitan county shall be made to the joint planning board. **[670]**

8. Appeals

(1) An applicant who desires to appeal—

    (a) against a decision of a local planning authority—

        (i) refusing listed building consent or conservation area consent or granting either such consent subject to conditions; or

        (ii) refusing to vary or discharge the conditions attached to a listed building consent or a conservation area consent, or in respect of the addition of new conditions consequential upon any such variation or discharge; or

    (b) on the failure of a local planning authority to give notice of their decision or of the reference of the application to the Secretary of State;

shall give notice of appeal to the Secretary of State (on a form obtained from the

Secretary of State) within six months of notice of the decision or of the expiry of the appropriate period allowed under regulation 3(4), as the case may be, or such longer period as the Secretary of State may at any time allow.

(2) Such a person shall also furnish to the Secretary of State a copy of each of the following documents—

(i) the application;
(ii) all relevant plans, drawings, particulars and documents submitted with the application, including a copy of the certificate given in accordance with regulation 6;
(iii) the notice of the decision, if any;
(iv) all other relevant correspondence with the local planning authority.
[671]

9. Claims for compensation and listed building purchase notices

(1) A claim for compensation made to a local planning authority under sections 27, 28, 29 of the Act, or a listed building purchase notice served on the council of a district, or on the Common Council or on the council of a London borough under section 32 of the Act, shall be in writing and shall be served on that authority or council by delivering it at the offices of the authority or council addressed to the clerk thereof, or by sending it so addressed by prepaid post.

(2) The time within which any such claim or notice as is mentioned in paragraph (1) shall be served, shall be—

(a) in the case of a claim for compensation, 6 months; and
(b) in the case of a listed building purchase notice, 12 months from the date of the decision in respect of which the claim or notice is made or given, or such longer period as the Secretary of State may allow in any particular case.   **[672]**

10. Advertisement of unopposed revocation or modification order

Where by virtue of the provisions of section 25(2) of the Act the making of an order under section 23 of the Act in respect of works to a building is required to be advertised, the local planning authority shall publish the advertisement in a local newspaper circulating in the area in which the building is situated.   **[673]**

11. Application of the Public Health Act 1936 to listed building enforcement notices

[(1)] The provisions of sections 276, 289 and 294 of the Public Health Act 1936 shall apply in relation to steps required to be taken by a listed building enforcement notice, as if—

(a) references to a local authority were references to the local planning authority who issued the enforcement notice or where the enforcement notice was issued by the Commission, to the Commission;
(b) references (in whatever form) to the execution of works under the said Act of 1936 were references to the taking of steps required to be taken under the notice;
(c) references in the said section 289 to the occupier were references to a person having an interest in the premises other than the owner; and
(d) the reference in the said section 294 to "expenses under this Act" were a reference to expenses incurred in the taking of such steps as aforementioned.

[(2) The expenses recoverable by a local planning authority under section 42(1) of the Planning (Listed Buildings and Conservation Areas) Act 1990 are, until recovered, a charge that is binding on successive owners of the land to which the listed building enforcement notice related and the charge shall take effect as from the date of the completion by the local planning authority of the steps required to be taken by the listed building enforcement notice.] **[674]**

NOTES
  Para (1): renumbered as such by SI 1991/2804, art 10(2)(a).
  Para (2): added by SI 1991/2804, art 10(2)(b).

12. Demolition of unlisted buildings in conservation areas

In their application to buildings in conservation areas, the provisions of the Act referred to in section 74(3) and which are set out in column (1) of Schedule 3 hereto shall have effect as they have effect in relation to listed buildings subject to—

  (a) the substitution of "conservation area enforcement notice" for any reference to "listed building enforcement notice", and the substitution of "conservation area purchase notice" for any reference to "listed building purchase notice", and
  (b) the exceptions and additional modifications (if any) set out opposite such provisions in column 2 of that Schedule. **[675]**

13. Applications by local planning authorities

(1) In relation to applications by local planning authorities relating to the execution of works for the demolition, alteration or extension of listed buildings or for the demolition of unlisted buildings in conservation areas, the provisions of the Act specified in section 82(3) of the Act shall have effect subject to the exceptions and modifications prescribed in this regulation.

(2) Where a local planning authority require listed building consent for the demolition, alteration or extension of a listed building in their area or conservation area consent for the demolition of a building within a conservation area in their area, the authority shall, subject to paragraph (7), make application to the Secretary of State for that consent.

(3) Any such application shall be in the form of an application to the local planning authority, and shall be deemed to have been referred to the Secretary of State under section 12 of the Act and the provisions of that section shall apply to the determination of the application by the Secretary of State.

(4) Where a local planning authority have made an application for consent under paragraph (2) they shall, before sending it to the Secretary of State—

  (a) publish in a local newspaper circulating in the locality in which the building is situated a notice indicating the nature of the works which are the subject of the application and naming a place within the locality where a copy of the application, and of all the plans and other documents which it is intended to submit to the Secretary of State with it, will be open to inspection by the public at all reasonable hours during the period of 21 days beginning with the date of publication of the notice; and
  (b) for not less than 7 days display on or near the said building a notice containing the same particulars as are required to be contained in the notice to be published in accordance with sub-paragraph (a) above.

(5) Paragraph (4) does not apply to any application by a local planning authority relating to works affecting only the interior of a building which when last notified to

the authority by the Secretary of State as a building of special architectural or historic interest was classified as a Grade II (unstarred) listed building.

(6) An application by a local planning authority to the Secretary of State under paragraph (2) above shall be accompanied by a copy of all representations duly made in relation thereto.

(7) An application by the council of a county to the Secretary of State under paragraph (2) above, together with any accompanying documents required by this regulation, shall be made to the council of the district who shall forthwith send it on to the Secretary of State.

(8) In relation to a listed building, or a building in a conservation area, belonging to a local planning authority, the Secretary of State may serve any notice authorised to be served by a local planning authority in relation to a listed building or a building in a conservation area.   **[676]**

14. Form of notice that a building has become, or ceased to be, listed

The forms set out in Schedule 4 hereto (or forms substantially to the like effect) are the prescribed forms of notice for the purposes of section 2(3) of the Act.   **[677]**

15. Application for listed building or conservation area consent in anticipation of disposal of Crown land

(1) The following provisions of these Regulations shall, in their application to the making and determination of applications for listed building consent and conservation area consent made by virtue of section 84(2) of the Act, have effect subject to the following modifications—

    (a) in regulation 3(2), for the words "a certificate under regulation 6" substitute the words "the certificate or other document required by regulation 6 below";

    (b) in regulation 6(1), after the words "accompanied by" insert the words "the documents described in paragraph (1A) below or"; and

    (c) after paragraph (1), add the following paragraph; "(1A) Where an application for listed building consent or conservation area consent is made in respect of Crown land by the appropriate authority or by a person authorised by that authority in writing, and where there is no interest in the land which is for the time being held otherwise than by or on behalf of the Crown, the application shall be accompanied by—

        (a) a statement that there is for the time being no private interest in the land; and

        (b) where the application is made by a person authorised by the appropriate authority, a copy of the relevant authorisation.".

(2) The appropriate authority shall, as soon as may be, after disposing of, or disposing of an interest in, any Crown land in respect of which an application has been made by virtue of section 84(2) of the Act, give notice in writing to the local planning authority of such disposal.   **[678]**

16. Revocations

The Town and Country Planning (Listed Buildings and Buildings in Conservation Areas) Regulations 1987 are hereby revoked.   **[679]**

SCHEDULES

SCHEDULE 1

Regulations 3 and 4

PART 1

NOTIFICATION TO BE SENT TO APPLICANT ON RECEIPT OF APPLICATION

Your application dated   was received on   (a).

*[Examination of the form of application and accompanying plans and documents to ascertain whether your application complies with the statutory requirement has not been completed.

If on further examination it is found that the application is invalid for failure to comply with such requirements (or for any other reason) a further communication will be sent to you as soon as possible.]

If by   (b) *[you have not received notification that your application is invalid and] this authority have not given you notice of their decision (and you have not agreed with them in writing that the period within which their decision shall be given may be extended) you may appeal to the Secretary of State in accordance with sections 20 and 21 of the Planning (Listed Buildings and Conservation Areas) Act 1990 by notice sent within six months from that date (unless the application has already been referred by this authority to the [Secretary of State for the Environment] [Secretary of State for Wales]). Appeals must be made on a form which is obtainable from the [Department of the Environment] [Welsh Office].

   (a) Insert date when relevant document(s) referred to in regulation [3(1)], [4(1)]* were received.
   (b) Insert date 8 weeks from date of receipt of application (as given at (a)).
* Delete as appropriate.

PART II

NOTIFICATION TO BE SENT TO APPLICANT ON REFUSAL OF LISTED BUILDING CONSENT OR CONSERVATION AREA CONSENT, OR GRANT OF CONSENT SUBJECT TO CONDITIONS (TO BE ENDORSED ON NOTICES OF DECISION)

(1) If the applicant is aggrieved by the decision of the local planning authority to refuse listed building consent or conservation area consent for the proposed works, or to grant consent subject to conditions, he may appeal to the [Secretary of State for the Environment] [Secretary of State for Wales] in accordance with sections 20 and 21 of the Planning (Listed Buildings and Conservation Areas) Act 1990 within six months of receipt of this notice. (Appeals must be made on a form which is obtainable from the [Department of the Environment] [Welsh Office]). The Secretary of State has power to allow a longer period for the giving of a notice of appeal but he will not normally be prepared to exercise this power unless there are special circumstances which excuse the delay in giving notice of appeal.

(2) If listed building consent or conservation area consent is refused, or granted subject to conditions, whether by the local planning authority or by the [Secretary of State for the Environment] [Secretary of State for Wales], and the owner of the land claims that the land has become incapable of reasonably beneficial use in its existing state and cannot be rendered capable of reasonably beneficial use by the carrying out of any works which have been or would be permitted, he may serve on the council of the district, or London borough in which the land is situated (or, where appropriate, on the Common Council of the City of London) a purchase notice requiring that council to purchase his interest in the land in accordance with the provisions of section 32 of the Planning (Listed Buildings and Conservation Areas) Act 1990.

(3) In certain circumstances a claim may be made against the local planning authority for compensation where permission is refused or granted subject to conditions by the Secretary of State on appeal or on a reference of the application to him. The circumstances in which such compensation is payable are set out in section 27 of the Planning (Listed Buildings and Conservation Areas) Act 1990.

PART III

NOTIFICATION TO BE SENT TO APPLICANT ON REFUSAL TO VARY OR DISCHARGE CONDITIONS ATTACHED TO LISTED BUILDING CONSENT OR CONSERVATION AREA CONSENT, OR ON THE ADDITION OF NEW CONDITIONS CONSEQUENTIAL UPON VARIATION OR DISCHARGE

If the applicant is aggrieved by the decision of the local planning authority—

(a) to refuse to vary or discharge the conditions attached to a listed building consent or a conservation area consent; or

(b) to add new conditions consequential upon any such variation or discharge.

he may appeal to the [Secretary of State for the Environment] [Secretary of State for Wales] in accordance with sections 20 and 21 of the Planning (Listed Buildings and Conservation Areas) Act 1990 within six months of receipt of this notice. (Appeals must be made on a form which is obtainable from the [Department of the Environment] [Welsh Office]). The Secretary of State has power to allow a longer period for the giving of a notice of appeal but he will not normally be prepared to exercise this power unless there are special circumstances which excuse the delay in giving notice of appeal.   **[680]**

SCHEDULE 2

Regulation 6

PART I

PLANNING (LISTING BUILDINGS AND CONSERVATION AREAS) ACT 1990

I hereby certify that:

No person other than [myself] [the applicant] [the appellant]* was the owner (a) of any of the building to which the [application] [appeal]* relates at the beginning of the period of 21 days ending with the date of the accompanying [application] [appeal]*.

or

Certificate B*

I hereby certify that:

[I have] [The applicant has] [the appellant has]* given the requisite notice to all the persons other than [myself] [the applicant] [the appellant]* who, at the beginning of the period of 21 days ending with the date of the accompanying [application] [appeal]*, were owners (a) of the building to which the [application] [appeal]* relates—

Name of owner   Address   Date of
                                                                      service of
                                                                      notice

or

Certificate C*

I hereby certify that:

1. [I am] [The applicant is] [The appellant is]* unable to issue a certificate in accordance with either sub-paragraph (a) or sub-paragraph (b) of regulation 6(1) of the Planning (Listed Buildings and Conservation Areas) Regulations 1990 in respect of the accompanying [application] [appeal]* dated

2. [I have] [The applicant has]* [The appellant has]* given the requisite notice to the following persons other than [myself] [the applicant] [the appellant]* who, at the beginning of the period of 21 days ending with the date of the [application] [appeal]*, were owners (a) of the building to which the [application] [appeal]* relates—

Name of owner	Address	Date of service of notice

3. [I have] [The applicant has] [The appellant has]* taken the steps listed below, being steps reasonably open to [me] [him]* to ascertain the names and addresses of the other owners (a) of the building and [have] [has]* been unable to so so:

> (b).

4. Notice of the [application] [appeal]* as set out below has been published in the
> (c) on   (d).

Copy of notice as published

or

Certificate D*

I hereby certify that:

1. [I am] [The applicant is] [The appellant is]* unable to issue a certificate in accordance with sub-paragraph (a) of regulation 6(1) of the Planning (Listed Buildings and Conservation Areas) Regulations 1990 in respect of the accompanying [application] [appeal]* dated
and [have] [has]* taken the steps listed below, being steps reasonably open to [me] [him]*, to ascertain the names and addresses of all the persons other than [myself] [himself]* who, at the beginning of the period of 21 days ending with the date of the [application] [appeal]*, were owners (a) of the building to which the [application] [appeal]* relates and [have] [had]* been unable to do so: (b).

2. Notice of the [application] [appeal]* as set out below has been published in the
> (c) on   (d).

Copy of notice as published

Signed   .   .   .   .
[on behalf of   .   .   .   ]*
Date   .   .   .   .   .

*Delete where inappropriate.

Notes

> (a) "Owner" means a person having a freehold interest or a leasehold interest of which not less than 7 years remain unexpired.
> (b) Insert description of steps taken.
> (c) Insert name of local newspaper circulating in the locality in which the land is situated.
> (d) Insert date of publication (which must not be earlier than 20 days before the application or appeal).

PART II

PLANNING (LISTED BUILDINGS AND CONSERVATION AREAS) ACT 1990

NOTICE FOR SERVICE ON INDIVIDUALS

Proposal for [demolishing] [altering] [extending] [varying or discharging conditions]*

TAKE NOTICE that application is being made to the   (b) Council by
> (c) for [listed building consent] [conservation area consent]
[variation or discharge of conditions]*   (d).

If you wish to make representations about the application, you should make them in writing, not later than   (e) to the Council at   (f).

Signed　　.　　　.　　　.　　　.　　　.
[on behalf of　　.　　　.　　　.　　　]*
Date　　.　　　.　　　.　　　.　　　.

PLANNING (LISTED BUILDINGS AND CONSERVATION AREAS) ACT 1990

NOTICE FOR PUBLICATION IN LOCAL NEWSPAPERS WHERE NOT ALL THE OWNERS ARE KNOWN, PURSUANT TO REGULATION 6(2) OF THE PLANNING (LISTED BUILDINGS AND CONSERVATION AREAS) REGULATIONS 1990

Proposal for [demolishing] [altering] [extending] [varying or discharging conditions]*

(a).

Notice is hereby given that application is being made to the　　　　　(b) Council by　　　　　　　　(c) for [listed building consent] [conservation area consent] [variation or discharge of conditions]*

(d).

Any owner of the building (namely a freeholder, or a leaseholder entitled to an unexpired term of at least seven years) who wishes to make representations to the above-mentioned Council about the application should make them in writing not later than

(e) to the Council at　　　　　　　　(f).

Signed　　.　　　.　　　.　　　.　　　.
[on behalf of　　.　　　.　　　.　　　]*
Date　　.　　　.　　　.　　　.　　　.

*Delete where inappropriate.

Notes

(a) Insert name, address or location of building with sufficient precision to ensure identification of it.
(b) Insert name of council.
(c) Insert name of applicant.
(d) Insert description of proposed works and name, address or location of building, or in the case of an application to vary or discharge conditions, insert description of the proposed variation or discharge.
(e) Insert date not less than 20 days later than the date on which the notice is served or published.
(f) Insert address of council.

PART III

PLANNING (LISTED BUILDINGS AND CONSERVATION AREAS) ACT 1990

NOTICE FOR SERVICE ON INDIVIDUALS

Proposal for [demolishing] [altering] [extending] [varying or discharging conditions]*

(a)

TAKE NOTICE that an appeal is being made to the [Secretary of State for the Environment] [Secretary of State for Wales]* by　　　　(b) [against the decision of the (c) Council] [on the failure of the　　　　(c) Council to give notice of a decision]* on an application to　　　　(d).

If you should wish to make representations to the Secretary of State about the appeal you should make them not later than　　　　(e), to the [Secretary of State for the Environment] [Secretary of State for Wales]* at

Signed   .   .   .   .
[on behalf of   .   .   .   ]*
Date   .   .   .   .

PLANNING (LISTED BUILDINGS AND CONSERVATION AREAS) ACT 1990

NOTICE FOR PUBLICATION IN LOCAL NEWSPAPERS

Proposal for [demolishing] [altering] [extending] [varying or discharging conditions]*

(a).

Notice is hereby given that an appeal is being made to the [Secretary of State for the Environment] [Secretary of State for Wales]* by   (b)
[against the decision of the   (c) Council] [on the failure of the
(c) Council to give notice of a decision]* on an application to   (d).

Any owner of the building (namely, a freeholder, or a leaseholder entitled to an unexpired term of at least seven years) who wishes to make representations to the Secretary of State about the appeal should make them in writing, not later than   (e), to the [Secretary of State for the Environment] [Secretary of State for Wales]* at

Signed   .   .   .   .
[on behalf of   .   .   .   ]*
Date   .   .   .   .

*Delete where inappropriate.

Notes

(a) Insert name, address or location of building with sufficient precision to ensure identification of it.
(b) Insert name of appellant.
(c) Insert name of council.
(d) Insert description of proposed works and name, address or location of building, or in the case of an application to vary or discharge conditions, insert description of the proposed variation or discharge.
(e) Insert date not less than 20 days later than the date on which the notice is served or published.   **[681]**

SCHEDULE 3

Regulation 12

(1) *Provisions of the Act relating to listed building control*	(2) *Exceptions and additional modifications (if any)*
Section 7	Omit the words "or for its alteration or extension in any manner which would affect its character as a building of special architectural or historical interest".
Section 8	1. Omit subsection (1). 2. In subsection (2), omit paragraphs (b) and (c). 3. In subsection (3)(a), omit the words "or for its alteration or extension". 4. Omit subsections (4) to (7).
Sections 9 to 12	None.
Section 13	Omit.

(1) *Provisions of the Act relating to listed building control*	(2) *Exceptions and additional modifications (if any)*
Section 14	Substitute the following— "14. Where application for conservation area consent is made as respects a building situated in Greater London, the local planning authority shall notify the Historic Buildings and Monuments Commission for England of that application, shall not determine such application until the expiry of a period of 28 days from such notification, shall take into account any representations made by the Commission within such period in respect of that application, and shall notify the Commission of their decision on that application.".
Section 15	1. Omit subsections (1) to (4). 2. In subsection (6) omit "(1) or".
Section 16	Omit subsection (2).
Sections 17 to 20	None.
Section 21	Omit subsections (3) and (4).
Section 22	Omit subsection (1) (b).
Sections 23 to 26	None.
Section 28.	None.
Sections 32 to 37	None.
Section 38	In subsection (1), for the words "the character of the building as one of special architectural or historic interest", substitute the words "the character or appearance of the conservation area in which the building is situated".

Section 39	In subsection (1)8
	  (i) substitute the following paragraph for paragraph (a)—
	    "(a) that retention of the building is not necessary in the interests of preserving or enhancing the character or appearance of the conservation area in which it is situated;".
	  (ii) omit paragraph (i).

Section 40	None.
Section 41	Omit subsection (6)(c).
Sections 42 to 46	None.
Section 56	For the words "sections 47 and 48 or section 54", substitute the words "section 54 where a direction has been made in respect of that building under section 76(1)".
Sections 62 to 65	None.
Section 66(1)	Omit.
Section 82(2) to (40	1. In subsection (2) omit the words "alteration or extension". 2. In subsections (2)–(4) the exceptions and modifications mentioned in regulation 13 and also as mentioned in this column, shall have effect in relation to the appropriate provision mentioned in section 82(3).
Section 83(1)(b), (3) and (4)	None.
Section 90(2) to (4)	None.

SCHEDULE 4

Regulation 14

Notice that a building has become listed

IMPORTANT—THIS COMMUNICATION AFFECTS YOUR PROPERTY

PLANNING (LISTED BUILDINGS AND CONSERVATION AREAS) ACT 1990

BUILDINGS OF SPECIAL ARCHITECTURAL OR HISTORIC INTEREST

To:

NOTICE IS HEREBY GIVEN that the building known as   situated in
          has on   19   been included in a list of buildings of special architectural
or historic interest compiled by the [Secretary of State for Environment] [Secretary of State
for Wales] under section 1 of the Planning (Listed Buildings and Conservation Areas) Act
1990.

Date   19   [Town Clerk]
                                                               [Clerk of the Council]
                                                               [Chief Executive]

Note

Listing of Buildings of Special Architectural or Historic Interest

The above notice is addressed to you as owner or occupier of the building named, which has
been included in one of the lists of buildings of special architectural or historic interest under
section 1 of the Planning (Listed Buildings and Conservation Areas) Act 1990 by the
[Secretary of State for the Environment] [Secretary of State for Wales]. The lists are compiled
by the Secretary of State as a statutory duty after consultation with [the Historic Buildings and
Monuments Commission for England and with such other]* persons or bodies as appear to
him appropriate as having special knowledge of, or interest in, buildings of architectural or
historic interest.

This notice does not call for any action on your part unless you propose at any time to
demolish the building or to do any works (either to the exterior or the interior) which would
affect its character. In that event you will need to seek "listed building consent", that is to
say, the consent of the local planning authority (the   Council) to the work
you wish to do.

You should however note that it is an offence to carry out any of these works without obtaining
listed building consent. A conviction for this offence could result in a fine or even
imprisonment. Nevertheless where works which were urgently necessary in the interests of
safety or of health or for the preservation of the building were carried out without consent it is
a defence to prove that—

(a) it was not practicable to secure safety or health or the preservation of the building
by works of repair or works for affording temporary support or shelter:
(b) the works carried out were limited to the minimum measures immediately necessary;
and
(c) notice in writing justifying in detail the carrying out of the works was given to the
local planning authority as soon as reasonably practicable.

Certain buildings are exempt from the requirement to obtain listed building consent, notably
ecclesiastical buildings which are for the time being used for ecclesiastical purposes (but it
should also be noted that this exemption does not apply to a building used or available for use
as a residence by a minister of religion and that the exemption may be restricted or excluded
by an order of the Secretary of State under section 60 of the 1990 Act).

Although there is no statutory right of appeal as such against the listing of a building, you are
not precluded at any time from writing to the Secretary of State claiming that the building
should cease to be listed on the ground that it is not in fact of special architectural or historic
interest; and any such claim, with the evidence supporting it, will be carefully considered by

the Secretary of State in consultation with his statutory advisers. A guidance note on the procedure is available from the Secretary of State. In addition, where listed building consent is refused by a local planning authority or is granted subject to conditions, there is a right of appeal to the [Secretary of State for the Environment] [Secretary of State for Wales]; and one of the grounds for an appeal may be that the building is not of special architectural or historic interest.

If at any time you propose to take action which may affect the character of your building, you would be well advised to refer to the provisions of the Planning (Listed Buildings and Conservation Areas) Act 1990, and of the Planning (Listed Buildings and Conservation Areas) Regulations 1990 (S.I. 1990/1519). Further details can be obtained from your local planning authority.

NOTICE THAT A BUILDING HAS CEASED TO BE LISTED

IMPORTANT—THIS COMMUNICATION AFFECTS YOUR PROPERTY

PLANNING (LISTED BUILDINGS AND CONSERVATION AREAS) ACT 1990

BUILDINGS OF SPECIAL ARCHITECTURAL OR HISTORIC INTEREST

To:

NOTICE IS HEREBY GIVEN that the building known as   situated in   has, by an amendment made by the [Secretary of State for the Environment] [Secretary of State for Wales] under section 1(1) of the Planning (Listed Buildings and Conservation Areas) Act 1990 on   19 , been excluded from the list of buildings of special architectural or historic interest compiled by the Secretary of State.

Date: 19   [Town Clerk]
                 [Clerk of the Council]
                 [Chief Executive]

[683]

TOWN AND COUNTRY PLANNING (DEVELOPMENT PLAN) REGULATIONS 1991

(SI 1991/2794)

NOTES

  Made: 10 December 1991

  Authority: Town and Country Planning Act 1990, ss 12, 13, 26, 31, 33, 36, 37(4), 38(5), 40, 46, 53, 336(1) Sch 2, Pt I, para 4, Sch 2, Pt II, para 17; Planning and Compensation Act 1991, Sch 4, paras 40, 41(2), 45(1), 46(1), 47(7)

ARRANGEMENT OF REGULATIONS

PART I

GENERAL

PART 3

ACTION AREAS

PART 4

PROCEDURE

PART 5

INTERVENTION BY THE SECRETARY OF STATE

PART 6

AVAILABILITY OF DOCUMENTS AND INDEX

PART 7

CONFORMITY AND CONFLICT

PART 8

TRANSITIONAL PROVISIONS

PART 9

REVOCATION AND SAVINGS

PART 1

GENERAL

1. Citation and commencement

These Regulations may be cited as the Town and Country Planning (Development Plan) Regulations 1991 and shall come into force on 10th February 1992. **[684]**

NOTES
Commencement: 10 February 1992.

2. Interpretation

(1) In these Regulations—

"the 1990 Act" means the Town and Country Planning Act 1990;

"the 1991 Act" means the Planning and Compensation Act 1991;

"by advertisement" means by publication in the London Gazette and by local advertisement;

"by local advertisement" means by publication on at least one occasion in two successive weeks in a local newspaper circulating in the area of the local planning authority;

"statutory plan" means a unitary development plan, structure plan, local plan, minerals local plan or waste local plan.

(2) In these Regulations—

(a) a reference to the section of an Act is a reference to that section of the 1990 Act;

(b) a reference to a numbered form is a reference to the correspondingly numbered form in the Schedule to these Regulations;

(c) in relation to the making, alteration or replacement of a statutory plan by two or more local planning authorities jointly, a reference to a local planning authority shall be read as a reference to all of the local planning authorities making, altering or replacing the plan.

(3) Part 8 of these Regulations shall be interpreted in accordance with regulation 38. **[685]**

NOTES
Commencement: 10 February 1992.

3. Application

These Regulations apply with respect to—

(a) the form and content of unitary development plans and the procedure to be followed in connection with the making, alteration and replacement of such plans under Chapter I of Part II of the 1990 Act;

(b) the form and content of structure plans and the procedure to be followed in connection with the alteration and replacement of such plans under Chapter II of Part II of the 1990 Act;

(c) the form and content of local plans, minerals local plans and waste local plans and the procedure to be followed in connection with the making, alteration and replacement of such plans under Chapter II of Part II of the 1990 Act. **[686]**

NOTES
Commencement: 10 February 1992.

PART 2

FORM AND CONTENT OF STATUTORY PLANS

4. Title

(1) The title of a statutory plan shall consist of the name of the area of the local planning authority followed by "unitary development plan", "structure plan", "local plan", "minerals local plan" or "waste local plan", as the case may be.

(2) Where policies in respect of development consisting of the winning and working of minerals or involving the depositing of mineral waste ("mineral policies") are included in a local plan or waste policies are included in a local plan or a minerals local plan, the local plan or minerals local plan including such policies shall have a sub-title consisting of the words "including mineral policies", "including waste" or "including mineral and waste policies", as the case may be.

[687]

NOTES
Commencement: 10 February 1992.

5. Structure plan diagrams

(1) A structure plan shall contain a diagram, called the key diagram, illustrating the general policies formulated in the plan's written statement.

(2) A structure plan may also contain a diagram, called an inset diagram, drawn to a larger scale than the key diagram, and illustrating the application of the general policies to part of the area covered by the structure plan.

(3) Where an inset diagram is included in a structure plan, the area covered by the inset diagram shall be identified on the key diagram and the application of the general policies to that area shall be illustrated on that inset diagram only.

(4) No key diagram or inset diagram contained in a structure plan shall be on a map base.

(5) The title of a structure plan shall be set out on the key diagram and on any inset diagram contained in the plan and the key diagram and any inset diagram shall include an explanation of any symbol or notation used in the diagram.   **[688]**

NOTES
Commencement: 10 February 1992.

6. Maps

(1) The map required by section 12(4)(b) to be included in a unitary development plan, and by section 36(6)(a) to be included in a local plan, a minerals local plan and a waste local plan, shall be called the proposals map and shall be a map of the authority's area reproduced from, or based upon, an Ordnance Survey map and shall show National Grid lines and reference numbers.

(2) Policies for any part of the authority's area may be illustrated on a separate map on a larger scale than the proposals map, called an inset map.

(3) Where an inset map is included in a plan, the area covered by the inset map shall be identified on the proposals map and the policies for that area shall be illustrated on that inset map only.

(4) The title (and any sub-title) of a statutory plan mentioned in paragraph (1)

shall be set out on the proposals map and any inset map contained in the plan and the proposals map and any inset map shall show the scale to which it has been prepared and include an explanation of any symbol or notation used in the map.

[689]

NOTES

Commencement: 10 February 1992.

7. Reasoned justification

(1) A local plan, minerals local plan and waste local plan shall contain a reasoned justification of the policies formulated in the plan.

(2) The reasoned justification shall be set out so as to be readily distinguishable from the other contents of the plan. **[690]**

NOTES

Commencement: 10 February 1992.

PART 3

ACTION AREAS

8. Action areas: prescribed period

The period prescribed for the purpose of section 12(8) and 36(7) (period for the commencement of comprehensive treatment of an action area) is a period of 10 years beginning with the date on which the relevant plan is first made available for inspection in accordance with section 13(2)(a) or 40(2)(a), as the case may be. **[691]**

NOTES

Commencement: 10 February 1992.

PART 4

PROCEDURE

9. Regard to be had to certain matters and statement of regard

(1) In formulating their general policies in Part I of a unitary development plan or in a structure plan, the local planning authority shall, in addition to the matters specified in section 12(6), in the case of a unitary development plan, and in section 31(6), in the case of a structure plan, have regard to—

    (a) social and economic considerations;

    (b) environmental considerations; and

    (c) any policies and proposals of an urban development corporation which affect, or may be expected to affect, their area.

(2) In formulating their waste policies in Part II of a unitary development plan, or in a waste local plan, or in a local plan or minerals local plan containing waste policies, a local planning authority shall have regard to any waste disposal plan for their area under section 50 of the Environmental Protection Act 1990.

(3) The reasoned justification of the general policies in Part I and of the policies in Part II of a unitary development plan shall contain a statement of—

    (a) the regard which the local planning authority have had in formulating their general policies in Part I to the matters specified in section 12(6) and paragraph (1);

    (b) the regard which the authority have had in formulating their waste policies in Part II to any waste disposal plan for their area and the reason for any inconsistency between their waste policies and the waste disposal plan; and

(e) the account which the authority have taken of any enterprise zone scheme in their area.

(4) The explanatory memorandum accompanying proposals for the alteration or replacement of a structure plan shall contain a statement of the regard which the local planning authority have had in formulating their general policies to the matters specified in section 31(6) and paragraph (1).

(5) The reasoned justification of the policies formulated in a local plan, minerals local plan or waste local plan shall contain a statement of—

(a) in the case of a local plan, the regard which the local planning authority have had in formulating their policies to any enterprise zone scheme in their area;

(b) in the case of a waste local plan, or a local plan or a minerals local plan containing waste policies, the regard which the local planning authority have had in formulating their waste policies to any waste disposal plan and the reason for any inconsistency between their waste policies and the waste disposal plan. **[692]**

NOTES
Commencement: 10 February 1992.

10. Pre-deposit consultation

(1) When preparing proposals for a statutory plan or for the alteration or replacement of such a plan under section 13(1), 33(1) or 40(1), and before finally determining the contents of the proposals, the local planning authority shall consult—

(a) the Secretary of State for the Environment and the Secretary of State for Transport, in England, or the Secretary of State for Wales, in Wales;

(b) any other local planning authority for the area covered by the proposals;

(c) any local planning authority for an area adjacent to the area covered by the proposals;

(d) except in the case of structure plan proposals, the council of any parish or community for the area covered by the proposals;

(e) the National Rivers Authority;

(f) the Countryside Commission and the Nature Conservancy Council for England, in England, or the Countryside Council for Wales, in Wales;

(g) the Historic Buildings and Monuments Commission for England, in England.

(2) The local planning authority shall consider any representations made by the consultees before finally determining the contents of the proposals.

(3) The local planning authority shall prepare a statement of any other persons they have consulted when preparing their proposals, in addition to those listed in paragraph (1), and of any steps they have taken to publicise their proposals and to provide persons with an opportunity of making representations in respect of those proposals. **[693]**

NOTES
Commencement: 10 February 1992.

11. Deposit of proposals

(1) A local planning authority making proposals for a statutory plan or for the alteration or replacement of a statutory plan available for inspection in accordance with section 13(2)(a), 33(2)(a) or 40(2)(a), shall—

  (a) make the proposals available at their principal office and at such other places within their area as they consider appropriate;
  (b) give notice by advertisement in Form 1; and
  (c) give notice in similar form to any consultee under regulation 10(1) and to any other person whom they consider should be given notice.

  (2) Proposals made available for inspection shall be accompanied by—

  (a) the statement prepared pursuant to regulation 10(3);
  (b) in the case of local plan, minerals local plan or waste local plan proposals made available in accordance with section 40(2)(a), any statement supplied under section 46(2);
  (c) in the case of structure plan proposals made available in accordance with section 33(2)(a), the explanatory memorandum.

  (3) The local planning authority shall send 4 copies of the documents made available for inspection to the Secretary of State.   **[694]**

NOTES
Commencement: 10 February 1992.

12. Objections and representations

(1) The period within which objections and representations may be made to the local planning authority with respect to proposals for a statutory plan, or for the alteration or replacement of such a plan, made available for inspection under section 13(2)(a), 33(2)(a) or 40(2)(a), shall be six weeks beginning with the date on which a notice given pursuant to regulation 11(1)(b) is first published in a local newspaper.

  (2) Objections and representations shall be made in writing and addressed to the local planning authority in accordance with the details given in the published notice.

  (3) In addition to the requirement to consider objections imposed by sections 13(6), 33(6) or 40(7), as the case may be, the local planning authority shall also consider any representations made in accordance with this regulation.

  (4) In the case of deposited proposals for a statutory plan or for the replacement of a statutory plan, a representation that matters relating to the development and use of land not included in the deposited proposals ought to have been so included shall be treated as an objection made to the proposals in accordance with the regulations for the purpose of—

  (a) regulation 17;
  (b) in the case of statutory plan proposals other than structure plan proposals, regulation 14 and sections 16 and 42,

if the representation is made within the time and in the manner required by this regulation.   **[695]**

NOTES
Commencement: 10 February 1992.

13. Withdrawal of proposals

(1) On the withdrawal of proposals for a local plan, minerals local plan or waste local plan, or for the alteration or replacement of such a plan, the local planning authority shall—

(a) withdraw the copies of the proposals made available for inspection under section 40(2)(a); and

(b) give notice that the proposals have been withdrawn to every person who has made an objection or representation with respect to the proposals.

(2) On the withdrawal of proposals for a unitary development plan, or for the alteration or replacement of a unitary development plan or a structure plan, the local planning authority shall, in addition to the persons specified in section 14(2)(b), in the case of unitary development plan proposals, or in section 34(2)(b), in the case of structure plan proposals, give notice of the withdrawal to every person who has made a representation with respect to the proposals.

(3) A local planning authority withdrawing proposals for a statutory plan, or for the alteration or replacement of such a plan, shall also give notice by advertisement.

(4) The notice of withdrawal required by sections 14(2)(b), 34(2)(b) and by this regulation shall be in Form 2. **[696]**

NOTES
Commencement: 10 February 1992.

14. Local inquiry or other hearing

(1) A local planning authority shall, at least six weeks before the opening of any local inquiry or other hearing which they cause to be held to consider objections to proposals for a statutory plan or for the alteration or replacement of a statutory plan made available for inspection under section 13(2) or 40(2)—

(a) give any person who has objected to, or made a representation in respect of, the proposals in accordance with these regulations and not withdrawn the objection or representation, notice of the time and place at which the inquiry or other hearing is to be held, the name of the person appointed to hold it, and its purpose; and

(b) in the case of a local inquiry, give notice of that information by local advertisement.

(2) A local inquiry referred to in paragraph (1) shall be held in public. **[697]**

NOTES
Commencement: 10 February 1992.

15. Examination in public

(1) A local planning authority shall, at least six weeks before the opening of an examination in public which they cause to be held of matters affecting the consideration of proposals for the alteration or replacement of a structure plan—

(a) make available for inspection at any place at which the plan proposals have been made available for inspection a list of the matters with which the examination in public will be concerned and the persons who have been invited to take part in it;

(b) give any person who has objected to, or made a representation in respect of, the proposals in accordance with these regulations and not withdrawn the objection or representation, notice of the time and place at which the examination in public is to be held, the name of the person or persons appointed to hold it and its purpose, and the availability for inspection of the list mentioned in sub-paragraph (a); and

(c) give notice of that information by local advertisement.

(2) Any notice given under paragraph (1) shall invite representations to be made to the local planning authority on the list referred to in paragraph (1)(a) within 28 days of the date on which the notice is first published in a local newspaper. **[698]**

NOTES
Commencement: 10 February 1992.

16. Consideration of proposals following a local inquiry or other hearing or examination in public

(1) Where a local planning authority cause a local inquiry or other hearing to be held for a purpose mentioned in regulation 14(1), or an examination in public to be held for a purpose mentioned in regulation 15, the authority shall, after considering the report of the person holding the inquiry, other hearing, or examination in public, as the case may be, prepare a statement of—

(a) the decisions they have reached in the light of the report and any recommendations contained in the report; and

(b) the reasons for those decisions.

(2) Where a list of proposed modifications to the statutory plan proposals is made available for inspection under regulation 18(1) after the statement of decisions and reasons is prepared, the report mentioned in paragraph (1) and that statement shall be made available for inspection from the date on which, and at the places at which, the list is made available for inspection.

(3) Where such a list is not made available for inspection under regulation 18(1) after the statement of decisions and reasons is prepared, the local planning authority shall—

(a) give notice by local advertisement in Form 3;

(b) serve a notice in similar form on any person who has objected to, or made a representation in respect of, the plan proposals in accordance with these regulations and not withdrawn the objection or representation; and

(c) make copies of the report mentioned in paragraph (1) and the statement of decisions and reasons available for inspection at any place at which the plan proposals have been made available for inspection.

(4) Where the report of the person holding the inquiry, other hearing, or examination in public, as the case may be, contains recommendations that the statutory plan proposals should be modified in a manner specified in the report and the local planning authority intend not to accept one or more of those recommendations—

(a) the authority shall make a list of the recommendations that they do not intend to accept available for inspection from the date on which, and at the places at which, the report is made available for inspection;

(b) the notice given in Form 3, or in Form 4, as the case may be, shall record the authority's intention not to accept those recommendations and invite objections and representations to be made in respect of that intention within six weeks of the date on which the notice is first published in a local newspaper;

(c) paragraphs (3) and (4) of regulation 18 shall apply to any objection and representation made in respect of that intention as they apply to objections and representations made in respect of proposed modifications;

(d) where a local inquiry or other hearing is held to consider objections made to that intention, regulation 14 shall apply, and where an examination in public is held to consider matters in connection with that intention, regulation 15 shall apply, as those regulations apply in the case of statutory plan proposals, and this regulation shall apply following such a local inquiry or other hearing or examination in public as it applies to a local inquiry or other hearing or examination in public mentioned in paragraph (1); and

(e) where objections have been made to that intention in accordance with these regulations and not withdrawn and the local planning authority do not cause a local inquiry or other hearing or examination in public to be held, regulation 17 shall apply to the consideration of the objections as it applies to the consideration of objections to statutory plan proposals.

(5) Where notice is given in Form 3 and paragraph (4) does not apply, the notice shall give 28 days notice of the local planning authority's intention to adopt the statutory plan proposals. **[699]**

NOTES
Commencement: 10 February 1992.

17. Consideration of objections without a local inquiry or other hearing or examination in public

(1) Where objections have been made to statutory plan proposals in accordance with these regulations and not withdrawn and the local planning authority do not cause a local inquiry or other hearing or examination in public to be held, the authority shall prepare a statement of their decisions as respects all the objections and their reasons for each decision.

(2) Paragraphs (2), (3) and (5) of regulation 16 shall apply where a statement is prepared pursuant to paragraph (1) as they apply where a statement is prepared pursuant to regulation 16(1). **[700]**

NOTES
Commencement: 10 February 1992.

18. Modification of proposals

(1) Subject to paragraph (7), a local planning authority proposing to modify proposals for a statutory plan or for the alteration or replacement of a statutory plan (whether to comply with a direction given by the Secretary of State or on their own initiative) shall, unless they are satisfied that the modifications they intend to make will not materially affect the content of the proposals—

(a) prepare a list of the modifications with their reasons for proposing them;

(b) make copies of that list available for inspection at any place at which the plan proposals have been made available for inspection;

(c) give notice by local advertisement in Form 4; and

(d) serve a notice in similar form on any person who has objected to, or made a representation in respect of, the plan proposals in accordance with these regulations and not withdrawn the objection or representation.

(2) The period within which objections and representations may be made to the local planning authority in respect of proposed modifications is six weeks beginning

with the date on which a notice given pursuant to paragraph (1) is first published in a local newspaper.

(3) Objections and representations shall be made in writing and addressed in accordance with the details given in the notice.

(4) An objection to, or representation in respect of, proposed modifications, made in accordance with this regulation, shall be treated as an objection made in accordance with the regulations for the purpose of section 13(6), in the case of unitary development plan proposals, section 33(6), in the case of structure plan proposals, and section 40(7), in the case of local plan, minerals local plan or waste local plan proposals.

(5) Where a local inquiry or other hearing is held to consider objections made to proposed modifications, regulation 14 shall apply, and where an examination in public is held to consider matters in connection with proposed modifications, regulation 15 shall apply, as those regulations apply in the case of statutory plan proposals, and regulation 16 shall apply following such a local inquiry or other hearing or examination in public as it applies to a local inquiry or other hearing or examination in public mentioned in paragraph (1) of that regulation.

(6) Where objections have been made to proposed modifications in accordance with this regulation and not withdrawn and the local planning authority do not cause a local inquiry or other hearing or examination in public to be held, regulation 17 shall apply to the consideration of the objections as it applies to the consideration of objections to statutory plan proposals.

(7) Unless a list of proposed modifications contains only modifications proposed by the local planning authority in order to comply with a direction given by the Secretary of State under section 17(1), 35(2) or 43(4), it shall not be made available for inspection, and the notice referred to in paragraph (1) shall not be given or served, until after—

(a) the period for objecting to the statutory plan proposals after they have been made available for inspection has expired, or, in the case of a second or subsequent list of proposed modifications, the period for objecting to the previous list of proposed modifications has expired; and

(b) any statement (or further statement) required by regulation 16(1) or 17(1), as the case may be, has been prepared. **[701]**

NOTES
Commencement: 10 February 1992.

19. Notice of intention to adopt

Without prejudice to sections 13(6), 32(7) and 40(7), proposals for a statutory plan or for the alteration or replacement of such a plan shall not be adopted by a local planning authority until the period given by the authority in their notice of intention to adopt in Form 1, or where the authority has also given notice of their intention to adopt in Form 3 or Form 4, the period in the last such notice to be given by the authority, has expired. **[702]**

NOTES
Commencement: 10 February 1992.

20. Adoption

(1) When a local planning authority adopt proposals for a statutory plan or for the alteration or replacement of a statutory plan they shall—

(a) give notice by advertisement in Form 5; and
(b) serve notice in similar form on any person who has asked to be notified of the adoption.

(2) A copy of the notice given pursuant to paragraph (1) and of the adopted proposals shall be made available for inspection at any place at which the proposals were made available for inspection under regulation 11(1)(a).

(3) The local planning authority shall, not later than the date on which notice is first given by advertisement pursuant to paragraph (1), send 4 copies of the adopted proposals to the Secretary of State. **[703]**

NOTES
Commencement: 10 February 1992.

PART 5

INTERVENTION BY THE SECRETARY OF STATE

21. Documents to be supplied to the Secretary of State

A local planning authority shall supply the Secretary of State with a copy of every notice published by the authority in accordance with these Regulations when the notice is first published, together with a copy of every document made available for inspection in accordance with these regulations. **[704]**

NOTES
Commencement: 10 February 1992.

22. Direction to modify proposals

(1) Where the Secretary of State directs a local planning authority to modify their proposals under section 17(1), 35(2) or 43(4) the authority shall make a copy of the direction available for inspection with any subsequent list of modifications made so available pursuant to regulation 18(1), and that list shall indicate—

(a) which modifications have been proposed to comply with the direction; or
(b) where modifications have not been proposed to comply, or to comply fully, with the direction, the authority's reasons for not doing so.

(2) Any notice of adoption of the proposals given pursuant to regulation 20(1) shall state that the local planning authority have satisfied the Secretary of State that they have made the modifications necessary to conform with the direction to modify or that the direction has been withdrawn, as the case may be.

(3) A copy of any notification by the Secretary of State that he is satisfied with the modifications made or that the direction is withdrawn shall be made available for inspection from the date on which, and at the places at which, the adopted proposals are made available for inspection. **[705]**

NOTES
Commencement: 10 February 1992.

23. Direction not to adopt proposals

If, before the local planning authority have adopted proposals for a statutory plan or for the alteration or replacement of such a plan, the Secretary of State directs them not to adopt the proposals until he has decided whether to give them a direction under section 18(1), 35A(1) or 44(1), as the case may be, they shall not adopt the proposals until he has notified them of his decision. **[706]**

NOTES
Commencement: 10 February 1992.

24. Called-in proposals

(1) Where the Secretary of State is minded to approve with modifications proposals for a statutory plan or for the alteration or replacement of a statutory plan submitted to him for his approval, he shall, unless, in his opinion, the proposed modifications will not materially affect the content of the plan proposals, send a list of the proposed modifications to the local planning authority, and the authority shall, upon receipt of the list—

  (a) make copies of the list available for inspection at any place at which the plan proposals have been made available for inspection;
  (b) give notice by local advertisement in Form 6; and
  (c) serve notice in similar form on any person who has objected to, or made a representation in respect of, the plan in accordance with these regulations and not withdrawn the objection or representation and on any other person on whom the Secretary of State directs them to serve such a notice.

(2) The period within which objections or representations may be made to the Secretary of State in respect of the proposed modifications is six weeks beginning with the date on which a notice given pursuant to paragraph (1) is first published in a local newspaper.

(3) Objections and representations shall be made in writing and addressed in accordance with the details given in the notice.

(4) Where the Secretary of State causes a local inquiry or other hearing to be held for the purpose of considering objections to statutory plan proposals submitted to him for his approval, or to modifications which he proposes to make to such proposals, he shall give such notice as the local planning authority would be required to give by regulation 14(1) if they were proposing to hold an inquiry or other hearing.

(5) Where the Secretary of State causes an examination in public to be held under section 20(4) or 35B(2) of matters affecting his consideration of proposals submitted to him for his approval, or modifications which he proposes to make to such proposals, he shall—

  (a) send a list of the matters with which the examination in public will be concerned and the persons who have been invited to take part in it to the local planning authority; and
  (b) give such notice as the local planning authority would be required to give by regulation 15 if they were proposing to hold an examination in public.

(6) The local planning authority shall, on receipt of a list sent to then, pursuant to paragraph (5), make that list available for inspection at any place at which the plan proposals have been made available for inspection.

(7) The local planning authority shall, on being notified by the Secretary of State of his decision on statutory plan proposals submitted to him for his approval—

  (a) give notice by advertisement in Form 7;
  (b) serve a notice in similar form on any person who has asked to be notified of the decision reached on the proposals and on any other person on whom the Secretary of State directs them to serve such a notice; and

(c) make a copy of the Secretary of State's notification and of the approved or rejected proposals available for inspection at any place at which the proposals were made available for inspection under regulation 11(1)(a).

[707]

NOTES
Commencement: 10 February 1992.

25. Making, alteration and replacement of statutory plans by the Secretary of State

(1) These Regulations apply, so far as practicable and with any necessary modifications, to the making, alteration and replacement of a statutory plan by the Secretary of State as they apply to the making, alteration or replacement of a statutory plan by a local planning authority.

(2) When a statutory plan or alteration made by the Secretary of State becomes operative, the local planning authority entitled to prepare proposals for the alteration or replacement of the plan made or altered by the Secretary of State shall comply with regulation 27 in respect of that plan.   **[708]**

NOTES
Commencement: 10 February 1992.

PART 6

AVAILABILITY OF DOCUMENTS AND INDEX

26. Availability of documents for inspection

(1) Subject to paragraph (3), documents made available for inspection pursuant to Part II of the 1990 Act or these Regulations by a local planning authority making, altering or replacing a statutory plan shall be made so available at the place and time specified by the authority when giving notice of their availability for inspection, and shall, unless the statutory plan proposals are withdrawn, remain so available until the expiration of six weeks from the date of publication of the notice of adoption, approval or rejection of the proposals.

(2) The local planning authority shall, on request and on payment of a reasonable charge, provide, as soon as practicable, a copy of any document made available for inspection mentioned in paragraph (1).

(3) Adopted proposals made available for inspection under regulation 20(2) and approved proposals made available for inspection under regulation 24(7)(c) shall remain so available until printed copies of the proposals are made available for inspection under regulation 27(1).   **[709]**

NOTES
Commencement: 10 February 1992.

27. Availability of plans after adoption or approval

(1) As soon as practicable after proposals for a statutory plan or for the alteration or replacement of a statutory plan have been adopted or approved, the local planning authority which prepared the proposals shall secure that printed copies of the statutory plan, the statutory plan as altered, or the replacement plan, as the case may be, are available for inspection during normal office hours at their principal office and at such other places within their area as they consider appropriate and, on payment of a reasonable charge, for purchase.

(2) A local planning authority shall continue to make printed copies of a statutory plan, altered statutory plan, or replacement plan made available for inspection and purchase under paragraph (1) so available until the relevant plan is altered, further altered, or replaced, as the case may be. **[710]**

NOTES

Commencement: 10 February 1992.

28. Index

(1) A local planning authority shall keep an index containing the following information in respect of the development plan for their area—

  (a) the title of any plan forming part of or constituting the development plan for their area;

  (b) the date on which that plan was adopted or approved;

  (c) the title and date of adoption or approval of any alteration to that plan;

  (d) the date of the first publication of any notice given under these Regulations in respect of proposals for the making of a plan which will form part of or constitute the development plan for their area or for the alteration or replacement of such a plan; and

  (e) the places at which any plan, alteration or notice listed in the index may be inspected.

(2) In a non-metropolitan area, the index kept by the local planning authority shall also contain the date of any statement supplied under section 35C or paragraph 47 of Schedule 4 to the 1991 Act, or prepared under regulations 30 or 36, in relation to a plan listed in the index and shall identify the places at which the statement may be inspected.

(3) A local planning authority shall also keep a map showing the boundary of any plan listed in their index.

(4) The index and map kept in accordance with this regulation shall be made available for inspection during normal office hours at the local planning authority's principal office and at such other places within their area as they consider appropriate. **[711]**

NOTES

Commencement: 10 February 1992.

PART 7

CONFORMITY AND CONFLICT

29. Statement of conformity of proposals with structure plan: prescribed period

The prescribed period for the purpose of section 46(1)(b) is 28 days. **[712]**

NOTES

Commencement: 10 February 1992.

30. Statement of conformity on adoption or approval of structure plan

(1) An authority responsible for a structure plan shall, where any proposals of theirs for the alteration or replacement of a structure plan are adopted or approved, prepare a statement in respect of any local plan for which the authority is responsible, and any minerals local plan and waste local plan for their area, stating whether the plan is, or as the case may be, is not, in general conformity with the altered or new structure plan.

(2) A statement prepared under paragraph (1) stating that a local plan, minerals local plan or waste local plan is not in general conformity with a structure plan shall specify the respects in which it is not in such conformity.

(3) A local planning authority which makes available for inspection a plan to which a statement under section 35C or paragraph (1) relates, shall make a copy of the statement available for inspection at any place at which the plan is made available for inspection.

(4) In this regulation, references to an authority responsible for a structure plan or a local plan shall be construed in accordance with section 35C(5).   **[713]**

NOTES
Commencement: 10 February 1992.

31. Conflict between structure plans and local plans, minerals local plans and waste local plans

The provisions of a local plan prevail for all purposes over any conflicting provisions in a structure plan made by the same authority, and the provisions of a minerals local plan and of a waste local plan prevail for all purposes over any conflicting provisions in a structure plan, unless the local plan, minerals local plan or waste local plan is one—

    (a) stated under regulation 30(1) not to be in general conformity with the structure plan; and

    (b) neither altered nor replaced after the statement was prepared.   **[714]**

NOTES
Commencement: 10 February 1992.

32. Conflict between local plans and mineral local plans or waste local plans

Where there is a conflict between provisions in a local plan and provisions in a minerals local plan or waste local plan, the more recently adopted or approved provisions prevail.   **[715]**

NOTES
Commencement: 10 February 1992.

33. Conflict within statutory plans

Where there is a conflict between the written statement of a statutory plan and any other document forming part of the plan, the provisions of the written statement prevail.   **[716]**

NOTES
Commencement: 10 February 1992.

PART 8

TRANSITIONAL PROVISIONS

34. Unitary development plan proposals deposited under the old law

(1) This regulation applies to proposals for a unitary development plan treated as if made available for inspection under section 13(2) by virtue of paragraph 41(1) of Schedule 4 to the 1991 Act.

(2) Where this regulation applies and the six week period afforded under the old

law for making objections to the unitary development plan proposals made available for inspection under section 13(3) of the old law has not expired at commencement—

    (a) the local planning authority which made the proposals available for inspection under the old law shall, as soon as practicable, give notice by advertisement that objections may be made under the new law to any policy contained in the proposals, including local plan policies incorporated into the proposals under the old law, and that the period given for making objections to the proposals is to be treated as expiring six weeks after the date on which the notice is first published in a local newspaper; and

    (b) the period for making objections to the proposals shall be so treated for all purposes.   **[717]**

NOTES
    Commencement: 10 February 1992.

35. Existing policy statement

(1) An existing policy statement shall be made in Form 8.

(2) A local planning authority intending to publish an existing policy statement shall—

    (a) make copies of their existing policy statement available for inspection at any place at which the statutory plan proposals are made available for inspection for the purpose of regulation 11(1)(a);

    (b) where the statutory plan proposals are first made available for inspection on or after commencement, publish the statement with the notice of deposit of those proposals on each occasion on which that notice is published pursuant to regulation 11(1)(b) and include a copy of the statement with any notice given pursuant to regulation 11(1)(c);

    (c) where the statutory plan proposals were made available for inspection under the old law and the authority is required to give notice by regulation 34(2)(a), publish the statement with that notice on each occasion on which that notice is published pursuant to that regulation.

(5) In this regulation "existing policy statement" means a statement made for the purpose of paragraph 4 of Part I or paragraph 17 of Part II of Schedule 2 to the 1990 Act or paragraphs 41(2), 45(1), or 46(1) of Schedule 4 to the 1991 Act.   **[718]**

NOTES
    Commencement: 10 February 1992.
    Para (5): it is thought that the numbering of this para is erroneous and that it should be numbered as para (3).

36. Conflict between structure plans and saved local plans

(1) Where proposals for the alteration or replacement of a structure plan are adopted or approved and the local planning authority concerned are the only local planning authority in their area, that authority shall prepare a statement that any saved local plan in operation in the area is, or, as the case may be, is not, in general conformity with the altered or new structure plan.

(2) A statement prepared under paragraph (1) stating that a saved local plan is not in general conformity with a structure plan shall specify the respects in which it is not in such conformity.

(3) A local planning authority which make available for inspection a saved local plan to which a statement under paragraph 47(2) of Schedule 4 to the 1991 Act or

paragraph (1) relates, shall make a copy of the statement available for inspection at any place at which the plan is made available for inspection.

(4) The provisions of a saved local plan mentioned in paragraph (1) prevail for all purposes over any conflicting provisions in the structure plan unless the saved local plan is one stated under that paragraph not to be in general conformity with the structure plan.

(5) In this regulation, the references to a saved local plan do not include a reference to a saved local plan to which paragraph 44(2) of Schedule 4 to the 1991 Act applies. **[719]**

NOTES
    Commencement: 10 February 1992.

37. Availability of plans adopted or approved before commencement

Where, immediately before commencement, a local planning authority are making a plan forming part of or constituting the development plan for their area available for inspection, that authority shall continue to make that plan available for inspection until the plan ceases to have effect in relation to the authority's area. **[720]**

NOTES
    Commencement: 10 February 1992.

38. Interpretation of Part 8

In this Part, "commencement", "the old law" and "the new law" have the meaning given to those expressions by paragraph 40 of Schedule 4 to the 1991 Act. **[721]**

NOTES
    Commencement: 10 February 1992.

PART 9

REVOCATION AND SAVINGS

39. Revocation and savings

(1) Subject to paragraph (2), the Town and Country Planning (Structure and Local Plans) Regulations 1982, the Town and Country Planning (Local Plans for Greater London) Regulations 1983, the Town and Country Planning (Structure and Local Plans) (Amendment) Regulations 1984, paragraphs 8 to 14 of Schedule 1 to the Town and Country Planning (Local Government Reorganisation) (Miscellaneous Amendments) Regulations 1986, the Town and Country Planning (Structure and Local Plans) (Amendment) Regulations 1987 and the Town and Country Planning (Unitary Development Plans) Regulations 1988 are hereby revoked.

(2) The Town and Country Planning (Structure and Local Plans) Regulations 1982 shall continue to apply for the purpose of the preparation and adoption or approval of a local plan under the old law in accordance with paragraph 43 of Schedule 4 to the 1991 Act.

(3) In paragraph (2), "old law" has the meaning given to that expression in paragraph 40 of that Schedule. **[722]**

NOTES
    Commencement: 10 February 1992.

SCHEDULE

Regulation 11

PRESCRIBED FORMS

FORM 1:

NOTICE OF DEPOSIT OF PROPOSALS FOR A STATUTORY PLAN OR FOR THE ALTERATION OR REPLACEMENT OF A STATUTORY PLAN.

Town and Country Planning Act 1990
*Notice of Deposit of Proposals for [the [Alteration] [Replacement] of] a [Unitary
Development Plan] [Structure Plan] [Local Plan] [Minerals Local Plan]
[Waste Local Plan]*
(Title of plan)

(1) have prepared proposals for [the [alteration] [replacement] of] the above plan.

Copies of the proposals are available for public inspection at (2) free of charge on (3).

Objections to, and representations in respect of, the proposals should be sent in writing to (4) before (5). Objections and representations should specify the matters to which they relate and the grounds on which they are made, and may be accompanied by a request to be notified at a specified address of the withdrawal, adoption, approval or rejection of the proposals.

Only objectors whose objections are made in writing and sent to the address specified above within the six week period ending on (5) will have a right to have their objections considered at a local inquiry.

Notice of Intention to Adopt Proposals

If no objections are received during the period given for making objections (1) intend to adopt the proposals on the expiry of that period.

Notes

1 Omit any expression within square brackets which is inappropriate.

2 Insert:

    (1) the name of the local planning authority;
    (2) the address of the local planning authority's principal office and of any other places at which the documents are available for inspection;
    (3) the days on which, and hours between which, the documents are available for inspection;
    (4) the name or title of the officer to whom objections and representations should be sent and the address to which they are to be sent;
    (5) the date which provides a period of six weeks beginning with the date on which the notice is first published in a local newspaper for the making of objections and representations.

FORM 2:

NOTICE OR WITHDRAWAL OF PROPOSALS FOR A STATUTORY PLAN OR FOR THE ALTERATION OR REPLACEMENT OF A STATUTORY PLAN.

Regulation 13

Town and Country Planning Act 1990
*Notice of Withdrawal of Proposals for [the [Alteration] [Replacement] of] a [Unitary
Development Plan] [Structure Plan] [Local Plan] [Minerals Local plan] [Waste Local
Plan]*
(Title of plan)

Copies of these proposals made available for inspection by (1) have been withdrawn because (2)

Notes

1 Omit any expression within square brackets which is inappropriate.

2 Insert:

(1) the name of the local planning authority;
(2) the reasons why the proposals have been withdrawn.

FORM 3:

NOTICE OR INTENTION TO ADOPT PROPOSALS FOR A STATUTORY PLAN OR FOR THE ALTERATION OR REPLACEMENT OF A STATUTORY PLAN WITHOUT PROPOSING MODIFICATIONS OR FURTHER MODIFICATIONS.

Regulations 16 and 17

Town and Country Planning Act 1990
Notice of Withdrawal of Proposals for [the [Alteration] [Replacement] of] a [Unitary Development Plan] [Structure Plan] [Local Plan] [Minerals Local plan] [Waste Local Plan]
(Title of plan)

(1) propose to adopt these plan proposals without proposing any [further] modifications. Copies of the plan proposals [, the report of the person who held the [local inquiry] [hearing] [examination in public] and the authority's statement of reasons and decisions in the light of the report] [and the authority's statement of reasons and decisions as respects objections to the plan proposals] are available for inspection at (2) on (3).

[The authority do not intend to accept the recommendations in the report that the proposals should be modified. A list of the recommendations which the authority do not intend to accept is available for inspection with the above documents. Objections to, and representations in respect of, the intention not to modify the plan proposals in accordance with the recommendations in the report should be sent in writing to (4) before (5). Objections and representations should specify the matters to which they relate and the grounds on which they are made, and may be accompanied by a request to be notified at a specified address of the withdrawal, adoption, approval or rejection of the plan proposals. (1) will adopt the proposals after that date if no objections are received.][(1) will adopt the proposals after (6)]

Notes

1 Omit any expression within square brackets which is inappropriate.

2. Insert—

(1) the name of the local planning authority;
(2) the address of the local planning authority's principal office and of any other places at which the documents are available for inspection;
(3) the days on which, and hours between which, the documents are available for inspection;
(4) the name or title of the officer to whom objections and representations should be sent and the address to which they are to be sent;
(5) the date which provides a period of six weeks beginning with the date on which the notice is first published in a local newspaper for the making of objections and representations;
(6) the date which is 28 days after the date on which the notice is first published in a local newspaper.

FORM 4:

NOTICE OF PROPOSED MODIFICATIONS TO PROPOSALS FOR A STATUTORY PLAN OR FOR THE ALTERATION OR REPLACEMENT OF A STATUTORY PLAN.

Regulation 18

Town and Country Planning Act 1990
Notice of Proposed Modifications to Proposals for [the [Alteration] [Replacement] of] a

[Unitary Development Plan] [Structure Plan] [Local Plan] [Minerals Local Plan] [Waste Local Plan]
(Title of plan)

(1) propose to modify these plan proposals.

A list of the proposed modifications (other than modifications which the authority are satisfied will not materially affect the content of the plan proposals) with the authority's reasons for proposing them are available for inspection at (2) on (3). Copies of the plan proposals [, a direction from the Secretary of State directing the authority to modify the plan proposals,] [, the report of the person who held the [local inquiry] [hearing] [examination in public] and the authority's statement of reasons and decisions in the light of the report] [and the authority's statement of reasons and decisions as respects objections to the plan proposals] are similarly available for inspection.

[The authority do not intend to accept all of the recommendations in the report. A list of the recommendations which the authority do not intend to accept is available for inspection with the above documents.]

Objections to, and representations in respect of, the proposed modifications [and to the intention not to modify the plan proposals in accordance with certain of the recommendations in the report] should be sent in writing to (4) before (5). Objections and representations should specify the matters to which they relate and the grounds on which they are made, and may be accompanied by a request to be notified at a specified address of the withdrawal, adoption, approval or rejection of the plan proposals.

Notice of Intention to Adopt Proposals

If no objections are received during the period given for making objections [and the Secretary of State is satisfied that the modifications proposed conform with his direction or the direction is withdrawn] (1) intend to adopt the proposals on the expiry of that period.

Notes

1 Omit any expression within square brackets which is inappropriate.

2 Insert—

  (1) the name of the local planning authority;
  (2) the address of the local planning authority's principal office and of any other places at which the documents are available for inspection;
  (3) the days on which, and hours between which, the documents are available for inspection;
  (4) the name or title of the officer to whom objections and representations should be sent and the address to which they are to be sent;
  (5) the date which provides a period of six weeks beginning with the date on which the notice is first published in a local newspaper for the making of objections and representations.

FORM 5:

NOTICE OF PROPOSED ADOPTION OR PROPOSALS FOR A STATUTORY PLAN OR FOR THE ALTERATION OR REPLACEMENT OF A STATUTORY PLAN.

Regulation 20

Town and Country Planning Act 1990
Notice of Proposed Modifications to Proposals for [the [Alteration] [Replacement] of] a
[Unitary Development Plan] [Structure Plan] [Local Plan] [Minerals Local Plan] [Waste Local Plan]

On (1) (2) adopted these plan proposals [with modifications]. [The Secretary of State [was satisfied that the necessary modifications had been made to comply with] [withdrew] his direction to the authority to modify [the proposals].

Copies of the adopted proposals [and of the Secretary of State's notification [that he was satisfied with the modifications made to comply with] [withdrawing] his direction] are available for inspection at (3) on (4).

The proposals become operative on their adoption, but any person aggrieved by the proposals who desires to question their validity on the ground that they are not within the powers conferred by Part II of the Town and Country Planning Act 1990 or that any requirement of that Act or of any regulation made under it has not been complied with in relation to the adoption of the proposals, may, within six weeks from (5), make an application to the High Court under section 287 of the 1990 Act.

Notes

1 Omit any expression within square brackets which is inappropriate.

2 Insert—

(1) the date on which the proposals were adopted;
(2) the name of the local planning authority;
(3) the address of the local planning authority's principal office and of any other place at which the documents are available for inspection;
(4) the days on which and hours between which, the documents are available for inspection;
(5) the date on which this notice is first published.

FORM 6:

NOTICE OF PROPOSED MODIFICATIONS BY THE SECRETARY OF STATE TO PROPOSALS FOR A STATUTORY PLAN OR THE ALTERATION OR REPLACEMENT OF A STATUTORY PLAN SUBMITTED TO HIM FOR HIS APPROVAL.

Regulation 24

Town and Country Planning Act 1990
Notice of Proposed Modifications to Proposals for [the [Alteration] [Replacement] of] a
[Unitary Development Plan] [Structure Plan] [Local Plan] [Minerals Local Plan] [Waste
Local Plan]
(Title of plan)

The Secretary of State for [the Environment] [Wales] proposes to modify these plan proposals prepared by (1) and submitted to the Secretary of State for his approval.

A copy of the plan in proposals and a list of the proposed modifications (other than modifications which the Secretary of State is satisfied will not materially affect the content of the plan proposals) are available for inspection at (2) on (3).

Objections to, and representations in respect of, the proposed modifications should be sent in writing to (4) before (5) and may be accompanied by a request to be notified at a specified address of the approval or rejection of the plan proposals.

Notes

1. Omit any expression within square brackets which is inappropriate.
2. Insert—

(1) the name of the local planning authority;
(2) the address of the local authority's principal office and of any other places at which the documents are available for inspection;
(3) the days on which, and hours between which, the documents are available for inspection;
(4) the name and address of the appropriate Regional Director of the Department of the Environment or the Welsh Office to whom such objections and representations should be sent;
(5) the date which provides a period of six weeks beginning with the date on which the notice is first published in a local newspaper for the making of objections and representations.

FORM 7:

NOTICE OF APPROVAL OR REJECTION BY THE SECRETARY OF STATE OF PROPOSALS FOR A STATUTORY PLAN OR THE ALTERATION OR REPLACEMENT OF A STATUTORY PLAN SUBMITTED TO HIM FOR HIS APPROVAL

Regulation 24

Town and Country Planning Act 1990
Notice of [Approval] [Rejection] by the Secretary of State of Proposals for [the [Alteration]
[Replacement] of] a [Unitary Development Plan] [Structure Plan] [Local Plan] [Minerals
Local Plan] [Waste Local Plan]
(Title of plan)

The Secretary of State for [the Environment] [Wales] [approved] [rejected] these plan proposals prepared by (1) [in part] [and] [with modifications] [and] [with reservations].

Copies of the proposals and of the Secretary of State's letter notifying his decision are available for inspection at (2) on (3).

[The proposals [became] [become] Operative on (4), but any person aggrieved by the proposals who desires to question their validity on the ground that they are not within the powers conferred by Part II of the Town and Country Planning Act 1990 or that any requirement of that Act or of any regulation made under it has not been complied with in relation to the approval of the proposals, may, within six weeks from (5), make an application to the High Court under section 287 of the 1990 Act.]

Notes

1 Omit any expression within square brackets which is inappropriate.

2 Insert—

    (1) the name of the local planning authority;
    (2) the address of the local planning authority's principal office and of any other place at which the documents are available for inspection;
    (3) the days on which, and hours between which, the documents are available for inspection;
    (4) the appropriate date;
    (5) the date on which this notice is first published.

FORM 8:

EXISTING POLICY STATEMENT

Regulation 35

Town and Country Planning Act 1990
Notice of [Approval] [Rejection] by the Secretary of State of Proposals for [the [Alteration]
[Replacement] of] a [Unitary Development Plan] [Structure Plan] [Local Plan] [Minerals
Local Plan] [Waste Local Plan]
(Title of plan)

The proposals for [the [alteration] [replacement] of] the above plan, made available for inspection by (1) at (2), include policies which were, in the opinion of the authority, previously contained in a local plan for the area("existing policies"). A list of the policies contained in the proposals which have been identified by the authority as existing policies is set out below.

[Objections may be made to these policies at the same time and in the same manner as objections may be made to the other policies in the proposals.] [The period for objecting to the above proposals set out in the notice of deposit first published locally on (3) is extended and such objections, including objections to policies identified as existing policies, should be sent in writing to (4) before (5).] However, the person holding any local inquiry or other hearing need not allow a person who objects to a policy which has been identified as an existing policy to appear at the local inquiry or other hearing if he is satisfied that the policy so identified is an existing policy and that there has been no significant change in circumstances affecting the existing policy since it first formed part of the local plan.

(List of policies identified by the local authority as existing policies)

Notes

1 Omit any expression within square brackets which is inappropriate.

2 Insert—

    (1) the name of the local planning authority;

    (2) the address of the local planning authority's principal office and of any other place at which the documents are available for inspection;

    (3) the date on which the notice of deposit was first published in a local newspaper;

    (4) the name or title of the officer to whom objections should be sent and the address to which they are to be sent;

    (5) the date which provides a period of six weeks beginning with the date on which the notice is first published in a local newspaper for the making of objections.   **[723]**

NOTES
  Commencement: 10 February 1992.

TOWN AND COUNTRY PLANNING (ENFORCEMENT NOTICES AND APPEALS) REGULATIONS 1991
(SI 1991/2804)

NOTES
  Made: 11 December 1991
  Authority: Town and Country Planning Act 1990, ss 173(10), 174(4), 175(1), 178(3), (5), 336(1); Planning (Listed Buildings and Conservation Areas) Act 1990, ss 39(4), 40(1), 42(3), (5), 91(1)

ARRANGEMENT OF REGULATIONS

PART I

CITATION, COMMENCEMENT AND INTERPRETATION

PART II

ENFORCEMENT NOTICES UNDER SECTION 172

PART III

APPEALS

PART IV

NOTICES ISSUED BY THE SECRETARY OF STATE

PART I

CITATION, COMMENCEMENT AND INTERPRETATION

1. Citation and commencement

These Regulations may be cited as the Town and Country Planning (Enforcement Notices and Appeals) Regulations 1991 and shall come into force on 2nd January 1992.   **[724]**

NOTES
 Commencement: 2 January 1992.

2. Interpretation

In these Regulations, unless the context otherwise requires—

"the principal Act" means the Town and Country Planning Act 1990;
"the Listed Buildings Act" means the Planning (Listed Buildings and Conservation Areas) Act 1990;
"enforcement notice" means a notice issued under section 172(1) of the principal Act or section 38(1) of the Listed Buildings Act;
"local planning authority" means the local authority or other body who issue the relevant enforcement notice.   **[725]**

NOTES
 Commencement: 2 January 1992.

PART II

ENFORCEMENT NOTICES UNDER SECTION 172

3. Additional matters to be specified in enforcement notice

An enforcement notice issued under section 172 of the principal Act shall specify—

(a) the reasons why the local planning authority consider it expedient to issue the notice; and
(b) the precise boundaries of the land to which the notice relates, whether by reference to a plan or otherwise.   **[726]**

NOTES
 Commencement: 2 January 1992.

4. Explanatory note to accompany copy enforcement notices

Every copy of an enforcement notice served by a local planning authority under section 172(2) of the principal Act shall be accompanied by an explanatory note which shall include the following—

(a) a copy of sections 171A[, 171B and 172] to 177 of the principal Act, or a summary of those sections including the following information

(i) that there is a right of appeal to the Secretary of State against the enforcement notice;

(ii) that an appeal must be made by giving written notice of the appeal to the Secretary of State before the date specified in the enforcement notice as the date on which it is to take effect or by sending such notice to him in a properly addressed, pre-paid letter posted to him at such time that, in the ordinary course of post, it would bed delivered to him before that date;

(iii) the grounds on which an appeal may be brought under section 174 of the principal Act;

(b) notification that an appellant must submit to the Secretary of State, either when giving notice of appeal or within 14 days from the date on which the Secretary of State sends him a notice so requiring him, a statement in writing specifying the grounds on which he is appealing against the enforcement notice and stating briefly the facts on which he proposes to rely in support of each of those grounds. **[727]**

NOTES
Commencement: 2 January 1992.
Amended by SI 1992/1904, reg 2(1).

PART III

APPEALS

5. Statement by appellant

A person who makes an appeal to the Secretary of State under section 174(3) of the principal Act or section 39(2) of the Listed Buildings Act against an enforcement notice and who does not include with it a statement in writing specifying the grounds on which he is appealing against the notice and stating briefly the facts on which he proposes to rely in support of each of those grounds, shall deliver such a statement to the Secretary of State not later than 14 days from the date on which the Secretary of State sends him a notice so requiring him. **[728]**

NOTES
Commencement: 2 January 1992.

6. Local planning authority to send copy of notice to Secretary of State

Where an appeal has been made to the Secretary of State against an enforcement notice the local planning authority who issued the notice shall if so required by the Secretary of State send to him, not later than 14 days from the date on which the Secretary of State gives them notice that the appeal has been made, a copy of the enforcement notice and a list of the names and addresses of the persons on whom a copy of the notice was served under section 172(2) of the principal Act or section 38(4) of the Listed Buildings Act, as the case may be. **[729]**

NOTES
Commencement: 2 January 1992.

7. Statement by local planning authority

(1) Where an appeal has been made to the Secretary of State against an enforcement notice issued by a local planning authority, the authority shall [serve on the Secretary of State and] on the appellant a statement indicating the submissions which they propose to put forward on the appeal, including the following matters—

    (a) a summary of the authority's response to each ground of appeal pleaded by the appellant;

    (b) a statement whether the authority would be prepared to grant planning permission for the matters alleged in the enforcement notice to constitute the breach of planning control, or to grant listed building consent or conservation area consent for the works to which the listed building enforcement notice or conservation area enforcement notice relates, as the case may be, and, if so, particulars of the conditions, if any, which they would wish to impose on such permission or consent.

[(2) Any statement which is required to be served by paragraph (1) of this regulation shall be served—

    (a) where a local inquiry is to be held, and the date fixed for the holding of the inquiry is less than 18 weeks after the relevant date, at least 6 weeks before the date fixed for the holding of the inquiry;

    (b) where a local inquiry is to be held and paragraph (a) does not apply, not later than 12 weeks after the relevant date;

    (c) where no local inquiry is to be held, not later than 28 days from the date on which the Secretary of State sends to the authority a notice requesting the statement.

(3) In paragraph (2), "relevant date" means the date of the Secretary of State's written notice to the appellant and the local planning authority of his intention to cause an inquiry to be held.]   **[730]**

NOTES

    Commencement: 2 January 1992.

    Words in square brackets in para (1), and paras (2), (3) substituted for para (2) as originally enacted, by SI 1992/1904, reg 2(2).

    Transitional provision: substitution of paras (2), (3) does not apply to an appeal made before 1 September 1992 (SI 1992/1904, reg 3).

8. Public notice of appeal

(1) Where an appeal has been made to the Secretary of State against an enforcement notice issued by a local planning authority and he proposes not to hold a local inquiry, the authority shall give notice of the appeal to occupiers of properties in the locality of the site to which the enforcement notice relates and to any other persons who in the opinion of the authority are affected by the breach of planning control or contravention of listed building or conservation area control which is alleged in the enforcement notice.

(2) Any notice given under paragraph (1) of this regulation shall include—

    (a) a description of the alleged breach of control;

    (b) in the case of an appeal against an enforcement notice issued under section 172 of the principal Act, a statement of the reasons specified in the notice under regulation 3(a) of these Regulations;

    (c) the grounds on which the appellant appealed against the enforcement notice; and

    (d) a statement inviting interested persons to submit comments in writing to the local planning authority within such time as may be specified in the notice.   **[731]**

NOTES

    Commencement: 2 January 1992.

PART IV

NOTICES ISSUED BY THE SECRETARY OF STATE

9. Application of Regulations

These Regulations, except regulation 6, shall apply with respect to enforcement notices issued by the Secretary of State under section 182 of the principal Act, to appeals made to the Secretary of State against such notices, and to appeals against notices issued by him under section 46 of the Listed Buildings Act as they apply with respect to such notices issued by local planning authorities and to appeals made against them as if—

(a) for references to a local planning authority there were substituted references to the Secretary of State;

(b) in regulation 3, for "section 172" there were substituted "section 182";

(c) in regulation 4—

(i) for "section 172(2)" there were substituted "section 182(1)"; and

(ii) in paragraph (a), after "sections 171A[, 171B and 172] to 177" there were inserted "and section 182"; and

(d) for regulation 7 the following were substituted—

"**7.**—(1) Where an appeal has been made to the Secretary of State against an enforcement notice which he has issued, the Secretary of State shall serve on the appellant a statement indicating the submissions which he proposes to put forward on the appeal including a summary of his response to each ground of appeal pleaded by the appellant.

(2) Any statement which is required to be served by paragraph (1) of this regulation shall, where a local inquiry is to be held, be served not later than 28 days before the date of the inquiry.".   [732]

NOTES
Commencement: 2 January 1992.
Amended by SI 1992/1904, reg 2(1).

PART V

RECOVERY OF LOCAL AUTHORITY EXPENSES

10. Charge on land

. . .   [733]

NOTES
Commencement: 2 January 1992.
Para (1): revoked by SI 1992/1492.
Para (2): amends SI 1990/1519, reg 11.

PART VI

REVOCATION

11. The Town and Country Planning (Enforcement Notices and Appeals) Regulations 1981 are hereby revoked.   [734]

NOTES
Commencement: 2 January 1992.

PLANNING (HAZARDOUS SUBSTANCES) REGULATIONS 1992
(SI 1992/656)

NOTES
    Made: 11 March 1992
    Authority: Planning (Hazardous Substances) Act 1990, ss 4, 5(1), 7, 8, 11(2),(7), 17(2), 21(2),(3), 24(4), 25, 26A, 28(1), 30, 39(2), 40(1)

ARRANGEMENT OF REGULATIONS

PART 1

General

PART 2

Hazardous Substances, Controlled Quantities and Exemptions

PART 3

Express Consent

PART 4

Deemed Consent

PART 5

Enforcement

PART 6

PART I

GENERAL

1. Citation and commencement

These Regulations may be cited as the Planning (Hazardous Substances) Regulations 1992 and shall come into force on 1st June 1992.   **[735]**

_____

NOTES
    Commencement: 1 June 1992.

_____

2. Interpretation

(1) In these Regulations, unless the context otherwise requires—

"the Act" means the Planning (Hazardous Substances) Act 1990;
"buried or mounded vessel" includes a vessel which is only partially buried or mounded;
"moveable container" means any container designed or adapted to contain hazardous substances other than a vessel;
"vessel" means any container designed or adapted to contain hazardous substances which is affixed to the land, and includes a container which forms part of plant or machinery which is affixed to the land but does not include a pipeline.

(2) In these Regulations—

(a) a reference to a section is a reference to that section of the Act, unless there is a contrary indication;

(b) a reference to a numbered form is a reference to the correspondingly numbered form in Schedule 2.

(3) Part 4, Form 8 and Schedule 3 (deemed consents) shall be construed in accordance with regulation 16.

(4) Schedule 1 (hazardous substances and controlled quantities) shall be construed in accordance with Part D of that Schedule.

(5) References to sections of the principal Act mentioned in regulations 18, 20, 21 and 22 (enforcement) shall, in those sections and these Regulations, be construed as references to those sections as modified by these Regulations in relation to hazardous substances control.   **[736]**

NOTES
Commencement: 1 June 1992.

PART 2

HAZARDOUS SUBSTANCES, CONTROLLED QUANTITIES AND EXEMPTIONS

3. Hazardous substances and controlled quantities

(1) Subject to paragraph (2), the substances specified in column 1 of Schedule 1 are hazardous substances for the purposes of the Act.

(2) A substance which is controlled waste, as defined by section 75(4) of the Environmental Protection Act 1990, or radioactive waste, as defined in section 18(4) of the Radioactive Substances Act 1960, is not a hazardous substance for the purposes of the Act.

(3) The quantity specified in column 2 of Schedule 1 is the controlled quantity of the corresponding hazardous substance in column 1 of that Schedule for the purposes of the Act.   **[737]**

NOTES
Commencement: 1 June 1992.

4. Exemptions

(1) Hazardous substances consent is not required for the temporary presence of a hazardous substance during the period between it being unloaded from one means of transport and loaded onto another while it is being transported from one place to another.

(2) Hazardous substances consent is not required for the presence of a hazardous substance contained in an aerosol dispenser if—

(a) the capacity of the dispenser does not exceed 1000 millilitres; or
(b) the dispenser—
    (i) does not contain a substance or mixture of substances which is flammable within the meaning of paragraph 2 of Part III of Schedule 1 to the Classification, Packaging and Labelling of Dangerous Substances Regulations 1984; and
    (ii) does not contain a substance numbered 7, 8, 18, 21, 22, 24, 25, 27, 29, 30, 33, 34 or 65 in column 1 of Schedule 1 or, if it does, the aggregate quantity of that substance contained in aerosol dispensers with a capacity in excess of 1000 millilitres on the relevant site is less than the controlled quantity for that substance.

(3) Hazardous substances consent is not required for the presence of a hazardous substance contained in an exempt pipe-line or a service pipe.

(4) Hazardous substances consent is not required for the presence of a hazardous substance which has been unloaded from a ship or other sea going craft in an emergency until the expiry of the period of 14 days beginning with the day on which it was so unloaded; and for the purpose of this paragraph a substance shall be treated as having been unloaded from a craft in an emergency if—

(a) it was unloaded from a craft to which a direction under section 3(1) of the Dangerous Vessels Act 1985 (directions by Secretary of State to harbour master) applied; or

(b) it was unloaded from a craft after having been brought into a harbour or harbour area, within the meaning of regulation 2 of the Dangerous Substances in Harbour Areas Regulations 1987, without requiring notification under paragraph (1) of regulation 6 of those regulations by virtue of an exemption under paragraph (5) of that regulation.

(5) Where hazardous substances consent is deemed to have been granted under section 11 for the presence of substance number 40 in column 1 of Schedule 1, consent is not required for the presence of an additional quantity of that substance not exceeding one third of the established quantity provided that all the conditions set out in Schedule 3 and applying to that substance under the deemed consent are also complied with in relation to the additional quantity present.

(6) The presence of a substance to which paragraphs (1), (2), (3) and (4) apply shall not be taken into account when calculating the quantity of a hazardous substance present on, over or under land for any purpose of the Act or these Regulations.

(7) In this regulation—

(a) "exempt pipe-line" means a pipe-line used to convey a hazardous substance to or from a site, but does not include—

(i) that part of the pipe-line on, over, or under a site to which it has an outlet or inlet;

(ii) a service pipe;

(b) "service pipe" means a pipe-line used by a public gas supplier (within the meaning of section 7(1) of the Gas Act 1986) to supply gas to an individual consumer from a main of that supplier. **[738]**

NOTES
Commencement: 1 June 1992.

PART 3
EXPRESS CONSENT

5. Applications for hazardous substances consent

(1) Subject to paragraph (2) and regulation 26, an application for hazardous substances consent shall—

(a) be made to the hazardous substances authority on Form 1;

(b) include the information specified in the form, a site map, and a substance location plan;

(c) be accompanied by 3 copies of the form, the map and plan submitted with it and the notices and certificates required by regulations 6 and 7.

(2) Subject to regulation 26, an application to which section 13 applies (application for hazardous substances consent without a condition subject to which a previous consent was granted) shall—

(a) be made to the hazardous substances authority on Form 2;

(b) include the particulars specified in the form, a change of location plan, if required by paragraph (6), and particulars of the relevant consent;

(c) be accompanied by 3 copies of the form, the relevant consent, any plan submitted with it and the notices and certificates required by regulations 6 and 7.

(3) An application under section 17 (application for the continuation of consent following a change of control) shall—

(a) be made to the hazardous substances authority on Form 2;

(b) include the particulars specified in the form, a change of control plan, and particulars of the relevant consent;

(c) be accompanied by 3 copies of the form, the relevant consent, the change of control plan and the notices and certificates required by regulations 6 and 7.

(4) The site map required by paragraph (1)(b) shall be a map, reproduced from, or based upon, an Ordnance Survey map with a scale of not less than 1 to 10,000, which identifies the land to which the application relates and shows National Grid lines and reference numbers.

(5) The substance location plan required by paragraph (1)(b) shall be a plan of the land to which the application relates, drawn to a scale of not less than 1 to 2,500, which identifies—

(a) any area of the site intended to be used for the storage of the substance;

(b) where the substance is to be used in a manufacturing, treatment or other industrial process, the location of the major items of plant involved in that process in which the substance will be present;

(c) access points to and from the land.

(6) A change of location plan shall be required in the case of an application to which section 13 applies which relates to a condition restricting the location of a hazardous substance, and shall be a plan of the land to which the application relates, drawn to a scale of not less than 1 to 2,500, which identifies the location of the hazardous substance at the date of the application and the proposed location requiring the application.

(7) The change of control plan required by paragraph (3) shall be a plan of the land to which the application relates, drawn to a scale of not less than 1 to 2,500, which identifies each area of the site under separate control after the proposed change of control.

(8) The relevant consent referred to in paragraphs (2)(b) and (3)(b) is the existing hazardous substances consent which applies to the hazardous substance to which the application applies; and the particulars of the relevant consent to be supplied shall be a copy of the consent, in the case of a consent granted on an application under the Act, a copy of the relevant claim, in the case of a consent deemed to be granted under section 11 or a copy of the relevant direction, in the case of a consent deemed to be granted under section 12.

(9) Where an application referred to in paragraphs (2) or (3) relates to more than one relevant consent, particulars of each such consent shall be included in the application.

(10) Regulations 6 to 13 shall apply to applications made under section 17 as they apply to applications for hazardous substances consent.   **[739]**

NOTES
Commencement: 1 June 1992.

6. Publication of notices of applications

(1) Before making an application for hazardous substances consent to the hazardous substances authority, the applicant shall, during the 21 day period immediately preceding the application—

(a) publish in a local newspaper circulating in the locality in which the land to which the application relates is situated a notice of the application on Form 3; and

(b) subject to paragraphs (3) and (4), post that notice on the land for not less than 7 days during that 21 day period, sited and displayed in such a way as to be easily legible without entering onto the land.

(2) The notice required by paragraph (1) shall invite representations on the application to be made to the hazardous substances authority within 21 days of the publication or posting of the notice, as the case may be.

(3) An applicant shall not be required to comply with paragraph (1)(b) if—

(a) he has no right of access or other rights in respect of the land which would enable him to post the notice as required; and

(b) he has taken all reasonable steps to acquire such rights but has failed.

(4) The applicant shall not be treated as having failed to comply with paragraph (1)(b) if the notice is, without any fault or intention of his, removed, obscured or defaced before the 7 days referred to in that paragraph have elapsed, so long as he has taken reasonable steps for its protection and, if need be, replacement.

(5) An application for hazardous substances consent shall not be entertained by the hazardous substances authority unless it is accompanied by—

(a) a copy of the notice referred to in paragraph (1), certified by, or on behalf of, the applicant as having been published in a local newspaper in accordance with paragraph (1)(a) and specifying the name of the newspaper and the date of its publication; and

(b) the appropriate certificate on Form 4, signed by or on behalf of the applicant.   **[740]**

NOTES
Commencement: 1 June 1992.

7. Notification of applications to owners

(1) An application for hazardous substances consent shall not be entertained by the hazardous substances authority unless it is accompanied by which ever of certificates A to D set out in Form 5 is appropriate, signed by or on behalf of the applicant.

(2) The required notice referred to in certificates B and C
of Form 5 shall, in the case of an application for hazardous substances consent, be a notice given on Form 6 and shall invite any owner on whom the notice is served to make representations on the application to the hazardous substances authority within 21 days of service of the notice.   **[741]**

NOTES
Commencement: 1 June 1992.

8. Inspection of applications

The applicant shall make a copy of the application available for inspection at a place within the locality of the application site during the period or periods allowed for making representations pursuant to regulation 6(2) and 7(2).   **[742]**

NOTES
Commencement: 1 June 1992.

9. Receipt of applications by hazardous substances authority

(1) When the hazardous substances authority receive an application for hazardous substances consent or an application for any consent, agreement or approval required by a condition imposed on a grant of hazardous substance consent, they shall, as soon as practicable, acknowledge receipt in writing.

(2) Where, in the opinion of the hazardous substances authority, the application is invalid, the authority shall, as soon as practicable, notify the applicant of their opinion, giving their reasons.

(3) For the purposes of this regulation and regulations 10 and 11, an application for hazardous substances consent shall be taken to have been received when each of the following events has occurred—

   (a) the application form has been served on the hazardous substances authority;
   (b) any certificate or documents required by regulations 6 and 7 have been served on that authority; and
   (c) any fee required to be paid in respect of the application has been paid to that authority and, for this purpose, lodging a cheque for the amount of a fee is to be taken as payment.   **[743]**

NOTES
Commencement: 1 June 1992.

10. Consultation before the grant of hazardous substances consent

(1) Except where the body or person concerned has notified the hazardous substances authority that they do not wish to be consulted, the authority shall, before determining an application for hazardous substances consent, consult—

   (a) the Health and Safety Executive;
   (b) the district or London borough council or county council concerned, where that council is not also the hazardous substances authority;
   (c) the parish or community council concerned;
   (d) the fire and civil defence authority concerned, where that authority is not also the hazardous substances authority;
   (e) the National Rivers Authority;
   (f) the public gas supplier concerned;
   (g) the electricity board concerned;
   (h) where the land to which the application relates is within 2 kilometres of a royal palace, park or residence, the Secretary of State;
   (i) where the land to which the application relates is in an area designated as a new town, the development corporation for the new town;
   (j) where the land to which the application relates is situated within 2000 metres of—
      (i) an adjacent county, district or London borough, the council for that county, district or London borough;
      (ii) the area of an adjacent fire authority and civil defence authority, that authority;

(iii) an adjacent new town, the development corporation for the new town;

(k) where it appears to the hazardous substances authority dealing with the application that land in the area of any other hazardous substances authority may be affected, that authority;

(l) where the application relates to land in an area to which section 28(1) of the Wildlife and Countryside Act 1981 applies (sites of special scientific interest), in England, the Nature Conservancy Council or, in Wales, the Countryside Council for Wales;

(m) where the application relates to land in an area of coal working notified to the hazardous substances authority by the British Coal Corporation [or the Coal Authority, the Coal Authority;]

(n) where the application relates to land which is used for disposal or storage of controlled waste, the waste disposal authority concerned, where that authority is not also the hazardous substances authority.

(2) Where, under this regulation, a hazardous substances authority is required to consult in respect of an application, they shall, unless a copy of the application has been served on the consultee by the applicant, serve the consultee with a copy of the application within 7 days of its receipt by the authority.

(3) In paragraph (1)(n), "controlled waste" has the meaning given to that expression by section 75(4) of the Environmental Protection Act 1990 and "waste disposal authority" shall be construed in accordance with section 30(2) of that Act.

[744]

NOTES

Commencement: 1 June 1992.

Amended by SI 1994/2567, art 2, Schedule, subject to transitional provisions in art 6.

11. Determination of applications for hazardous substances consent

(1) A hazardous substances authority shall not determine an application for hazardous substances consent before the expiry of—

(a) the period or periods allowed for making representations pursuant to regulation 6(2) and 7(2); and

(b) where the authority is required to consult under regulation 10, a period of 28 days beginning with the date on which the consultee is served with a copy of the application, or, where the authority is required to consult more than one consultee, beginning with the date by which all consultees have been so served.

(2) Subject to paragraph (1), a hazardous substances authority shall, within the period specified in paragraph (3), give the applicant written notice of their decision or notice that the application has been referred to the Secretary of State for determination by him.

(3) The period specified for the purposes of paragraph (2) is—

(a) a period of 8 weeks from the date when the application is received by the hazardous substances authority;

(b) except where the applicant has already given notice of appeal to the Secretary of State, such extended period as may be agreed in writing by the applicant and the hazardous substances authority; or

(c) where a fee due in respect of an application has been paid by a cheque which is subsequently dishonoured, the appropriate period specified in (a) or (b) above calculated without regard to any time between the date when the authority sent the applicant written notice of the dishonouring of the cheque and the date when the authority are satisfied that they have received the full amount of the fee.

(4) When a hazardous substances authority give notice of a decision on an application the notice shall, where hazardous substances consent is refused or is granted subject to conditions—

(a) state, clearly and precisely, their full reasons for the refusal or for any condition imposed;
(b) include a statement to the effect that if the applicant is aggrieved by the decision he may appeal to the Secretary of State under section 21 within 6 months of the date of the notice of the decision, or such longer period as the Secretary of State may at any time allow.

(5) The hazardous substances authority shall, as soon as is practicable, inform the following persons of the terms of their decision—

(a) the Health and Safety Executive;
(b) the district or London borough council or county council, where that council is not the hazardous substances authority concerned;
(c) any other consultees who have made representations to them on the application; and
(d) any owners who have made representations to them on the application.

[745]

NOTES
Commencement: 1 June 1992.

12. Notice of reference of applications to the Secretary of State

On referring any application to the Secretary of State pursuant to a direction under section 20, a hazardous substance authority shall serve on the applicant a notice—

(a) informing the applicant that the application has been referred to the Secretary of State;
(b) setting out the reasons given by the Secretary of State for issuing the direction; and —
(c) containing a statement that the Secretary of State will, if the applicant so desires, give the applicant an opportunity of appearing before and being heard by a person appointed by the Secretary of State for that purpose.

[746]

NOTES
Commencement: 1 June 1992.

13. Appeals

(1) An appeal to the Secretary of State under section 21 shall be made within 6 months of—

(a) the date of the notice of the decision giving rise to the appeal; or
(b) in the case of an appeal under section 21(2), the expiry of the period specified in regulation 11(3),

or within such longer period as the Secretary of State may, at any time, allow.

(2) An appeal under section 21 shall—

(a) be made to the Secretary of State on a form obtained from him;
(b) include the information specified in the form; and
(c) be accompanied by the documents specified in paragraph (3) and the certificate required by paragraph (4).

(3) The documents mentioned in paragraph (2)(c) are—

(a) the application made to the hazardous substances authority which has occasioned the appeal;

(b) any notices and certificates required by regulations 6 and 7 which accompanied the application;

(c) any correspondence with the authority relating to the application; and

(d) the notice of decision, if any.

(4) An appeal under section 21 shall not be entertained by the Secretary of State unless it is accompanied by which ever of certificates A to D is appropriate set out in Form 5, signed by or on behalf of the appellant.

(5) The required notice referred to in certificates B and C shall, in the case of an appeal under section 21, be a notice given on Form 7.

(6) The appellant shall send a copy of the completed notice of appeal form and accompanying certificate to the hazardous substances authority at the same time as the appeal is made to the Secretary of State.   **[747]**

NOTES

Commencement: 1 June 1992.

PART 4

DEEMED CONSENT

14. Claim for deemed consent

(1) A claim for deemed consent under section 11 shall—

(a) be made to the hazardous substances authority on Form 8;

(b) include the information specified by the form, a site map, and, where applicable, a moveable container storage area plan and a vessel location plan for each hazardous substance included in the claim;

(c) be accompanied by 3 copies of the form and the map and any plan submitted with it.

(2) The site map required by paragraph (1)(b) shall be a map, reproduced from, or based upon, an Ordnance Survey map with a scale of not less than 1 to 10,000, which identifies the land to which the claim relates and shows National Grid lines and reference numbers.

(3) The moveable container storage area plan required by paragraph (1)(b) shall be a plan of the land to which the claim relates, drawn to a scale of not less than 1 to 2,500, which identifies any area of the site where the hazardous substance has been stored in moveable containers at any time during the establishment period.

(4) The vessel location plan required by paragraph (1)(b) shall be a plan of the land to which the claim relates, drawn to a scale of not less than 1 to 2,500, which identifies any area of the site where the hazardous substance has been present in a vessel at any time during the establishment period; provided that—

(a) no point on the boundary of the area so identified shall be more than 75 metres away from—

(i) a building which is or was within the area and which at any time during the establishment period contained a vessel in which the substance was present;

(ii) plant and machinery (other than pipe work) which is or was affixed to land within the area and which, at any time during the establishment period whilst it was so affixed, was used for an industrial process involving the substance; or

(iii) a vessel which is or was located outside a building and within the area and in which, at any time during the establishment period whilst it was so located, the substance was present;

(b) no area identified in accordance with this paragraph shall overlap with any other area so identified in respect of the same substance. **[748]**

NOTES
Commencement: 1 June 1992.

15. Conditions on deemed consent

The conditions set out in Schedule 3 are the prescribed conditions for the purposes of section 11(7)(b). **[749]**

NOTES
Commencement: 1 June 1992.

16. Interpretation of deemed consent provisions

(1) For the purpose of paragraph (3) of regulation 14 and the condition set out in paragraph 7(1) of Schedule 3, no account shall be taken of the storage of a hazardous substance in moveable containers in an area, if the quantity of the substance so stored in that area does not exceed 10% of the substance's controlled quantity.

(2) For the purpose of the 75 metre limit in paragraph (4)(a) of regulation 14, where a petroleum – spirit licence under the Petroleum (Consolidation) Act 1928 applying to the site was in force at any time during the establishment period, the reference to a vessel in which the hazardous substance was present shall, in relation to hazardous substance number 71 in column 1 of Schedule 1, include any vessel identified in the licence.

(3) For the purpose of paragraph (4) of regulation 14 and the conditions set out in paragraphs 1 to 6 of Schedule 3, and for the purpose of completing Table C in Form 8, no account shall be taken of the presence in a vessel of a hazardous substance if the quantity present in the vessel does not exceed 10% of the substance's controlled quantity.

(4) For the purpose of the conditions set out in paragraphs 1 to 5 of Schedule 3, and for the purpose of completing Table C in Form 8, a hazardous substance shall not be treated as being present in a vessel at other than ambient temperature by virtue only of—

(a) the heating of the substance to maintain its fluidity during seasonal variations in temperature; or

(b) any cooling effect resulting from the vaporisation of the substance during the withdrawal of vapour from the vessel; or

(c) the presence of the substance at above or below ambient temperature on entry into the vessel, if the temperature of the substance is allowed to move to ambient temperature upon entry.

(5) For the purpose of the conditions set out in paragraphs 1 to 5 of Schedule 3, and for the purpose of completing Table C in Form 8, a hazardous substance shall not be treated as being present at above atmospheric pressure unless the pressure at which it is present exceeds 1.5 bar absolute.

(6) For the purpose of the conditions set out in paragraphs 1 to 5 of Schedule 3,

no account shall be taken of an increase in pressure during the operation of a pressure relief system.

(7) In Schedule 3 and Table C in Form 8 "vessel area" means an area identified in a vessel location plan in accordance with paragraph (4) of regulation 14.

(8) In Schedule 3, references to a column of Table C refer to the relevant column of Table C of the form on which the claim for deemed consent is made which applies to the relevant hazardous substance and vessel area.   **[750]**

NOTES
Commencement: 1 June 1992.

PART 5

ENFORCEMENT

17. Hazardous substances contravention notices

(1) A hazardous substances contravention notice shall identify the land to which the notice relates, whether by reference to a plan or otherwise.

(2) The persons prescribed pursuant to section 24(4)(c) (other persons to be given notice) are all persons having an interest in the land which in the opinion of the authority issuing the notice is materially affected by the notice.

(3) Every copy of a hazardous substances contravention notice served pursuant to section 24(4) shall be accompanied by a statement setting out—

    (a) the hazardous substances authority's reasons for issuing the notice;
    (b) the right of appeal to the Secretary of State against the notice, and the persons by whom, grounds upon which and time within which such an appeal may be brought under section 174 of the principal Act.   **[751]**

NOTES
Commencement: 1 June 1992.

18. Appeals against hazardous substances contravention notices

(1) Sections 174, 175(3), (6), 176 and 177 of the principal Act shall apply to appeals against hazardous substances contravention notices, subject to the modifications set out in Part 1 of Schedule 4.

(2) The provisions of those sections, as modified under paragraph (1), are set out in Part 5 of Schedule 4.   **[752]**

NOTES
Commencement: 1 June 1992.

19. Appeals: supplementary

(1) A person who appeals against a hazardous substances contravention notice shall, at the same time as notice of the appeal is given or sent to the Secretary of State under section 174(3) of the principal Act, serve on the hazardous substances authority a copy of the notice of appeal and accompanying material required by section 174(4) of that Act.

(2) The hazardous substances authority shall, within 28 days of being served with the notice of appeal, serve on the Secretary of State and on the appellant a statement—

    (a) setting out their submissions in relation to each ground of appeal; and

(b) indicating whether they would be prepared to grant hazardous substances consent for the presence on, over or under the land of any quantity of the hazardous substance to which the hazardous substances contravention notice relates and, if so, particulars of the conditions, if any, which they would wish to impose on such consent.

(3) The hazardous substances authority shall, within that 28 day period, give notice of the appeal to occupiers of properties in the locality of the site to which the hazardous substances contravention notice relates.   **[753]**

NOTES
Commencement: 1 June 1992.

20. Effect of hazardous substances contravention notices, etc

(1) Sections 178 to 181 of the principal Act shall have effect in relation to hazardous substances contravention notices, subject to the modifications set out in Part 2 of Schedule 4.

(2) The provisions of those sections, as modified under paragraph (1) are set out in Part 5 of Schedule 4.   **[754]**

NOTES
Commencement: 1 June 1992.

21. Enforcement register

(1) Section 188 of the principal Act (register of enforcement and stop notices) shall have effect in relation to hazardous substances contravention notices, subject to the modifications set out in Part 3 of Schedule 4.

(2) The provisions of that section, as modified under paragraph (1), are set out in Part 5 of Schedule 4.   **[755]**

NOTES
Commencement: 1 June 1992.

22. Validity

(1) Sections 285 and 289 of the principal Act shall apply to appeals against hazardous substances contravention notices, subject to the modifications set out in Part 4 of Schedule 4.

(2) Section 25(2) is subject to any order under section 289(4A) of the principal Act, as applied by paragraph (1).

(3) The provisions of sections 285 and 289 of the principal Act, as modified under paragraph (1), are set out in Part 5 of Schedule 4.   **[756]**

NOTES
Commencement: 1 June 1992.

PART 6
CONSENTS REGISTER

23. Consents register

(1) The register required by section 28(1) shall be kept in 6 parts—

(a) Part 1 shall contain a copy of every application for hazardous substances consent made to the hazardous substances authority and not finally determined;

(b) Part 2 shall contain, in respect of every application for hazardous substance consent made to the hazardous substances authority—

   (i) a copy of the application;

   (ii) particulars of any direction given under section 20;

   (iii) the decision (if any) of the authority, including details of any conditions subject to which consent was granted and the date of the decision;

   (iv) the reference number, date and effect of any decision of the Secretary of State, whether on a reference under section 20 or on an appeal under section 21;

(c) Part 3 shall contain a copy of every order revoking or modifying hazardous substances consent made by the hazardous substance authority and the date and effect of any confirmation by the Secretary of State in accordance with section 15.

(d) Part 4 shall contain, in respect of every hazardous substances consent deemed to be granted under section 11(3), a copy of the relevant claim form;

(e) Part 5 shall contain a copy of every hazardous substance consent deemed to be granted by virtue of a direction given by a Government Department under section 12;

(f) Part 6 shall contain a copy of any direction under section 27 sent to the authority by the Secretary of State.

(2) Where the Secretary of State grants hazardous substances consent under section 177 of the principal Act on the determination of an appeal against a hazardous substances contravention notice, the hazardous substances authority for the land covered by the consent shall enter the date and effect of that decision in Part 2 of the register.

(3) The register shall include an index to enable any person to trace an entry in the register.

(4) Every entry in the register shall be made within 14 days of the relevant information being available to the hazardous substances authority.

(5) The register shall be kept at the principal office of the hazardous substances authority.

(6) For the purpose of paragraph (1)(a), an application shall not be treated as finally determined unless—

(a) it has been decided by the hazardous substances authority (or the period specified in regulation 11(3) has expired without their giving a decision) and the period specified in regulation 13(1) has expired without any appeal having been made to the Secretary of State;

(b) it has been referred to the Secretary of State under section 20 or an appeal has been made to the Secretary of State under section 21, the Secretary of State has issued his decision and the period of 6 weeks specified in section 22(1) has expired without any application having been made to the High Court under that section;

(c) an application has been made to the High Court under section 22 and the matter has been determined, either by final dismissal of the application by a Court or by the quashing of the Secretary of State's decision and the issue of a fresh decision (without a further application under the said section 22 being duly made); or

(d) it has been withdrawn by the applicant before being determined or an appeal has been withdrawn by the applicant before the Secretary of State has issued his decision.   **[757]**

NOTES
Commencement: 1 June 1992.

PART 7
MISCELLANEOUS

24. Fees for applications

(1) Subject to paragraph (3), a fee shall be payable to a hazardous substances authority on an application for hazardous substances consent as follows—

(a) if section 13(1) applies (new consent without previous conditions), £200;
(b) if section 13(1) does not apply and the quantity specified in the application as the maximum quantity proposed to be present exceeds twice the controlled quantity, £400;
(c) in all other cases, £250.

(2) Subject to paragraph (3), a fee shall be payable to a hazardous substances authority on an application for the continuation of hazardous substances consent under section 17(1) of £200.

(3) Where applications relating to the same site are made to two or more hazardous substances authorities, a fee shall be payable only to the authority in whose area the largest part of the site is situated and the amount payable shall be the amount that would have been payable if application had fallen to be made to one authority in relation to the whole site.

(4) Any fee due in respect of an application shall accompany the application when it is made to the hazardous substances authority.

(5) Any fee paid pursuant to this regulation shall be refunded if the application is rejected as invalidly made.   **[758]**

NOTES
Commencement: 1 June 1992.

25. Fees for deemed applications

(1) Subject to paragraph (4), a fee shall be paid to the Secretary of State in every case where an application for hazardous substances consent is deemed to have been made by virtue of section 177(5) of the principal Act (in consequence of an appeal under section 174 of that Act against a hazardous substances contravention notice) by every person who has made a valid appeal against the relevant hazardous substances contravention notice and whose appeal has not been withdrawn before the date on which the Secretary of State issues a notice under paragraph (3).

(2) Subject to paragraph (6), the fee payable shall be the amount which would be payable under regulation 24 if the application were an application to which that regulation applied.

(3) The fee due shall be paid at such time as the Secretary of State may in the particular case specify by notice in writing to the appellant.

(4) This regulation shall not apply where the appellant had—

  (a) before the date when the hazardous substances contravention notice was
      issued, applied to the hazardous substances authority for hazardous
      substances consent for the presence of the quantity of the substance to
      which the notice relates, and had paid to the authority the fee payable in
      respect of that application; or
  (b) before the date specified in the notice as the date on which it is to take
      effect, made an appeal to the Secretary of State against the refusal of the
      hazardous substances authority to grant such consent,

and at the date when the relevant notice was issued that application or, in the case of
an appeal made before that date, that appeal, had not been determined.

(5) Any fee paid in respect of the deemed application shall be refunded to the
appellant by the Secretary of State if—

  (a) the Secretary of State declines jurisdiction on the relevant appeal on the
      grounds that it does not comply with one or more of the requirements of
      subsections (1) to (3) of section 174 of the principal Act;
  (b) the Secretary of State dismisses the relevant appeal in exercise of his
      powers under section 176(3)(a) of the principal Act (on the grounds that
      the appellant has failed to comply with section 174(4) of that Act);
  (c) the Secretary of State allows the relevant appeal and quashes the relevant
      hazardous substances contravention notice in exercise of his powers under
      section 176(3)(b) of the principal Act (on the grounds that the hazardous
      substances authority have failed to comply with regulation 19(2) of these
      Regulations);
  (d) the relevant appeal is withdrawn with the result that there are at least 21
      days between the date on which notice in writing of the withdrawal is
      received by the Secretary of State and—

      (i) the date (or in the event of postponement, the latest date) appointed
          for the holding of an inquiry or hearing into that appeal; or
      (ii) in the case of an appeal which is being dealt with by written
           representations, the date (or in the event of postponement, the latest
           date) appointed for the inspection of the site to which the notice
           relates;

  (e) the hazardous substances authority withdraws the relevant hazardous
      substances contravention notice before it takes effect, or the Secretary of
      State decides that the notice is a nullity;
  (f) the Secretary of State allows the relevant appeal on any of the grounds set
      out in section 174(2)(b) to (e) of the principal Act; or
  (g) the Secretary of State allows the relevant appeal on the ground that the
      notice is invalid, or that it contains a defect, error or misdescription which
      cannot be corrected under section 176(1)(a) of the principal Act.

(6) Where a hazardous substances contravention notice is varied under section
176(1) of the principal Act otherwise than to take account of a grant of hazardous
substances consent under section 177(1), and the fee calculated in accordance with
paragraph (2) would have been a lesser amount if the original notice had been in the
terms of the varied notice, the fee payable shall be that lesser amount and any excess
amount already paid shall be refunded.

(7) In determining a fee under paragraph (6) no account shall be taken of any
change in fees which takes effect after the making of the deemed application. **[759]**

NOTES
  Commencement: 1 June 1992.

26. Application of the Act to hazardous substances authorities

(1) Any application by a hazardous substances authority for hazardous substances consent shall be made to the Secretary of State.

(2) Regulations 5 to 8 shall apply to the making of such applications as they apply to applications made to a hazardous substances authority.

(3) For the purpose of regulation 23, an application made to the Secretary of State by a hazardous substances authority shall be treated as an application made to the hazardous substances authority and referred to the Secretary of State under section 20.

(4) Section 9 (other than subsection (2)(e)) shall apply in relation to an application made to the Secretary of State by a hazardous substances authority as it applies in relation to an application made to a hazardous substances authority.

(5) For the purpose of section 22, a decision of the Secretary of State on an application made to him by a hazardous substances authority shall be treated as a decision under section 20.   **[760]**

NOTES
Commencement: 1 June 1992.

SCHEDULE 1

Regulation 3

HAZARDOUS SUBSTANCES AND CONTROLLED QUANTITIES

PART A

TOXIC SUBSTANCES

Column 1 *Hazardous substances*		*Column 2* *Controlled quantities*
		(in *tonnes*, unless otherwise stated)
1	Acetone Cyanohydrin (2-Cyanopropan-2-ol)	200
2	Acrolein (2-Propenal)	200
3	Acrylonitrile	20
4	Allyl alcohol (2-Propen-1-ol)	200
5	Allylamine	200
6	Ammonia (anhydrous or as solution containing more than 50% by weight of ammonia)	100
7	Arsenic trioxide, Arsenious (III) acid and salts	1
8	Arsine (Arsenic hydride)	1
9	Bromine	40
10	Carbon disulphide	20
11	Chlorine	10
12	Ethylene dibromide (1, 2-Dibromoethane)	50
13	Ethyleneimine	50
14	Formaldehyde (>90%)	50
15	Hydrogen chloride (liquefied gas)	250
16	Hydrogen cyanide	20
17	Hydrogen fluoride	10
18	Hydrogen selenide	1
19	Hydrogen sulphide	50
20	Methyl bromide (Bromoethane)	200
21	Methyl isocyanate	150 kilograms
22	Nickel tetracarbonyl	1

Column 1 Hazardous substances	Column 2 Controlled quantities
23 Nitrogen oxides	50
24 Oxygen difluoride	1
25 Pentaborane	1
26 Phosgene	750 kilograms
27 Phosphine (Hydrogen phosphide)	1
28 Propyleneimine	50
29 Selenium hexafluoride	1
30 Stibine (Antimony hydride)	1
31 Sulphur dioxide	20
32 Sulphur trioxide (including the sulphur trioxide content in oleum)	15
33 Tellurium hexafluoride	1
34 2, 3, 7, 8-Tetrachlorodibenzo-p-dioxin (TCDD)	1 kilogram
35 Tetraethyl lead	50
36 Tetramethyl lead	50

[761]

NOTES
    Commencement: 1 June 1992.

PART B

HIGHLY REACTIVE SUBSTANCES AND EXPLOSIVE SUBSTANCES

Column 1 Hazardous substances	Column 2 Controlled quantities
	(in *tonnes*, unless otherwise stated)
37 Acetylene (Ethyne) when a gas subject to a pressure not exceeding 620 millibars above that of the atmosphere, and not otherwise deemed to be an explosive by virtue of Order in Council No 30 as amended by the Compressed Acetylene Order 1947, or when contained in a homogeneous porous substance in cylinders in accordance with Order of Secretary of State No 9, made under the Explosives Act 1875	50
38 Ammonium nitrate and mixtures containing ammonium nitrate where the nitrogen content derived from the ammonium nitrate exceeds 28% of the mixture by weight other than—	500
(i) mixtures to which the Explosives Act 1875 applies;	
(ii) ammonium nitrate based products manufactured chemically for use as fertiliser which comply with Council Directive 80/876/EEC; or	
(iii) compound fertilisers.	
39 Aqueous solutions containing more than 90 parts by weight of ammonium nitrate per 100 parts by weight of solution	500
40 Ammonium nitrate based products manufactured chemically for use as fertilisers which comply with Council Directive 80/876/EEC and compound fertilisers where the nitrogen content derived from the ammonium nitrate exceeds 28% of the mixture by weight	1000
41 2,2-Bis(tert-butylperoxy)butane (>70%)	5
42 1,1 -Bis(tert-butylperoxy)cyclohexane (>80%)	5

Column 1 Hazardous substances	Column 2 Controlled quantities
43 tert-Butyl peroxyacetate (>70%)	5
44 tert-Butyl peroxyisobutyrate (>80%)	5
45 tert-Butyl peroxyisopropylcarbonate (>80%)	5
46 tert-Butyl peroxymaleate (>80%)	5
47 tert-Butyl peroxypivalate (>77%)	5
48 Cellulose nitrate other than—	50
(i) cellulose nitrate to which the Explosives Act 1875 applies; or	

(ii) solutions of cellulose nitrate where the nitrogen
        content of the cellulose nitrate does not exceed
        12.3% by weight and the solution contains not
        more than 55 parts of cellulose nitrate per 100
        parts by weight of solution	

49 Dibenzyl peroxydicarbonate (>90%)	5
50 Diethyl peroxydicarbonate (>30%)	5
51 2,2-Dihydroperoxypropane (>30%)	5
52 Di-isobutyryl peroxide (>50%)	5
53 Di-n-propyl peroxydicarbonate (>80%)	5
54 Di-sec-butyl peroxydicarbonate (>80%)	5
55 Ethylene oxide	5
56 Ethyl nitrate	50
57 3,3,6,6,9,9, Hexamethyl-1,2,4,5-tetroxacyclononane (>75%)	5 (in *tonnes*, unless otherwise stated)
58 Hydrogen	2
59 Liquid Oxygen	500
60 Methyl ethyl ketone peroxide (>60%)	5
61 Methyl isobutyl ketone peroxide (>60%)	5
62 Peracetic acid (>60%)	5
63 Propylene oxide	5
64 Sodium chlorate	25
65 Sulphur dichloride	1

[762]

NOTES
     Commencement: 1 June 1992.

PART C

FLAMMABLE SUBSTANCES (UNLESS SPECIFICALLY NAMED IN PARTS A AND B)

Column 1 Hazardous substances	Column 2 Controlled quantities
	(in *tonnes*, unless otherwise stated)

66   Liquefied petroleum gas, such as commercial propane and
     commercial butane, and any mixtures thereof, when held
     at a pressure greater than 1.4 bar absolute
	25

67   Liquefied petroleum gas, such as commercial propane and
     commercial butane, and any mixture thereof, when held
     under refrigeration at a pressure of 1.4 bar absolute or less
	50

68 Gas or any mixture of gases which is flammable in air, when held as a gas	15

Column 1 *Hazardous substances*	Column 2 *Controlled quantities*
69 A substance or any mixture of substances, which is flammable in air, when held above its boiling point (measured at l bar absolute) as a liquid or as a mixture of liquid and gas at a pressure of more than 1.4 bar absolute	25
70 A liquefied gas or any mixture of liquefied gases, which is flammable in air and has a boiling point of less than 0°C (measured at 1 bar absolute), when held under refrigeration or cooling at a pressure of 1.4 bar absolute or less	50
71 A liquid or any mixture of liquids not included in entries 68 to 70 above, which has a flash point of less than 21°C	10,000

[763]

NOTES
Commencement: 1 June 1992.

PART D

INTERPRETATION

In this Schedule—

(a) references to percentages are references to parts by weight of the substance per 100 parts by weight of the solution;

(b) ''compound fertiliser'' means a fertiliser containing ammonium nitrate and phosphate or potash;

(c) Part C does not include a substance which is within Part A or Part B;

(d) a substance, or any mixture of substances, shall only be treated as a hazardous substance by virtue of satisfying a description in entry number 37, 66, 67, 68, 69 or 70 when it is in a state in which it satisfies the description;

(e) the controlled quantity of 25 tonnes in entry 69 refers, in the case of a mixture of substances, to the quantity of substances within that mixture held above heir boiling point (measured at 1 bar absolute);

(f) the controlled quantity of 50 tonnes in entry 70 refers, in the case of a mixture of substances, to the quantity of substances within that mixture having boiling points below 0°C. **[764]**

NOTES
Commencement: 1 June 1992.

SCHEDULE 2

Form 1

PRESCRIBED FORMS, NOTICES AND CERTIFICATES

The Planning (Hazardous Substances) Act 1990 – Section 7(1)
The Planning (Hazardous Substances) Regulations 1992 (Regulation 5)

General application for Hazardous Substances Consent

1. **Applicant** *(IN BLOCK CAPITALS)*
   Address

   Tel No

   Agent *(if any)* to whom correspondence should be sent *(IN BLOCK CAPITALS)*
   Address

   Tel No
   Contact

2. **Address or location of application site**

3. **Substance(s) covered by application**

Name	Entry number in Schedule 1 to the 1992 Regulations	Maximum quantity proposed to be present (in tonnes)†

   † or kilograms in the case of substances with entry numbers 21, 26 or 34

4. **Manner in which substance(s) to be kept and used**
   Provide the following information for each substance covered by the application *(referring to the substance location plan where appropriate)*

   (a) Tick one box below to show whether the substance will be present for storage only **or** will be stored and involved in a manufacturing, treatment or other industrial process:

Substance Entry number	Storage only	Stored **and** involved in industrial process

(b) For each vessel to be used for **storing** the substance(s), give the following information:

Vessel No*	Entry No of substance(s) to be stored in vessel	Installed above ground (yes†/no)	Buried (yes/no)	Mounded (yes/no)	Max capacity (cubic metres)	Highest vessel design temperature (°C)	Highest vessel design pressure (bar absolute)

* identify by reference to substance location plan
† if "yes", specify whether or not it will be provided with full secondary containment

(c) State for each substance the largest size *(capacity in cubic metres)* of any **moveable** container to be used for that substance:

(d) Where the substance is to be used in a **manufacturing, treatment or other industrial process***(es)*, give a general description of the process*(es)*, describe the major items of plant which will contain the substance; and state the maximum quantity *(in tonnes)* which is liable to be present in the major items of the plant, and the maximum temperature (°C) and pressure *(bar absolute)* at which the substance is liable to be present:

Substance entry No	Description of process(es)	Major items of plant*	Max quantity (tonnes)	Max temp (°C)	Max pressure (bar absolute)

* identify by reference to substance location plan

5. Additional Information

(a) Has any application for hazardous substance consent or planning permission relating to the application site been made which has not yet been determined?   **YES/NO**

(b) Will any such application be submitted at the same time as this application?   **YES/NO**

If you have answered **"YES"** to either of the preceding questions, give sufficient details to enable the application(s) to be identified.

(c) **Plans.** Please list the maps or plans or any explanatory scale drawings of plant/buildings submitted with this application.

(d) Give any further information which you consider to be relevant to the determination of this application.

I/we hereby apply for hazardous substances consent in accordance with the proposals described in the application

                 Signed ....

                 on behalf of ....

                 (insert applicant's name if signed by agent)

                 Date ....

The Planning (Hazardous Substances) Act 1990 – Sections 13 and 17
The Planning (Hazardous Substances) Regulations 1992 (Regulation 5)

Application for either: *(tick appropriate box)*

☐ **Hazardous Substances Consent**
without a condition(s) imposed on a
previous consent (section 13)

OR

☐ **Continuation of Hazardous Substances Consent**
following a change in control of part of the land (section 17)

1. **Applicant** *(IN BLOCK CAPITALS)*
Address

Tel No

Agent *(if any)* to whom correspondence should be sent *(IN BLOCK CAPITALS)*
Address

Tel No
Contact

2. **Address or location of Application Site**

3. **Substances covered by application**

Name	Entry number in Schedule 1 to the 1992 Regulations	Maximum quantity proposed to be present (in tonnes)†

† or kilograms in the case of substances with entry numbers 21, 26 or 34

4. In the case of an application for hazardous substances consent without a condition imposed on a previous consent (section 13)

(a) identify the condition(s) previously imposed which it is intended should not be imposed on the consent, or should only be imposed in a modified form *(in the latter case, indicate the proposed modification)*–

(b) give the reasons why the condition(s) referred to in (a) should not be imposed or should only be imposed in a modified form–

(c) describe any relevant changes in circumstances since the previous consent was granted–

5. In the case of an application for the continuation of hazardous substances consent(s) following a change in the person in control of part of the land (section 17)

(a) describe the use of each area of the site identified in the accompanying change of control plan.

(b) describe any relevant changes in circumstances since the existing consent was granted.

6. Additional information

Give any further information which you consider to be relevant to the determination of the application–

I/we* hereby apply for hazardous substances consent/the continuation of hazardous substances consent* in accordance with this application.

* delete where inappropriate

Signed ....

on behalf of ....

(insert applicant's name if signed by agent)

Date ....

Form 3

The Planning (Hazardous Substances) Act 1990
The Planning (Hazardous Substances) Regulations 1992 (Regulation 6)

Notice of Application for Hazardous Substances Consent/
Continuation of Hazardous Substances Consent*

I give notice that *(a)* ....

is applying to the *(b)* ....

for hazardous substances consent/the continuation of hazardous substance consent* *(c)* ....

....

....

at *(d)* ....

....

....

Members of the public may inspect a copy of the application at *(e)* ....

....

....

during all reasonable hours until *(f)* ....

Anyone who wishes to make representations about this application should write to the *(b)* ....

....

at *(g)* ....

....

....

by *(f)* ....

Signed: ....

*on behalf of ....

Date ....

* *delete where inappropriate*

Insert:

(a) applicant's name
(b) name of Council or other body to whom the application is to be made
(c) brief details of the consent being sought
(d) address or location of the application site
(e) address at which the application may be inspected (the applicant is required to make the application available for inspection at a place within the locality of the application site)
(f) date giving a period of not less than 21 days, beginning with the date when the notice is published or first displayed on site (as the case may be)
(g) address of Council or other body to whom the application is to be made

Form 4

The Planning (Hazardous Substances) Act 1990
The Planning (Hazardous Substances) Regulations 1992 (Regulation 6)

Posting of Notice of Application Certificate

Certificate A

I certify that:

- I/The applicant* posted the notice required by regulation 6(1)(b) of the above Regulations on the land which is the subject of the accompanying application.

- The notice was left in position for not less than 7 days during the 21 day period preceding the application.

or

Certificate B

I certify that:

I have/The applicant has* been unable to post the notice required by regulation 6(1)(b) of the above Regulations on the land which is the subject of the accompanying application because I have/the applicant has* no right of access or other rights in respect of the land that would enable me/the applicant* to do so.

I have/The applicant has* taken the following steps to acquire those rights, but have/has* been unsuccessful.

(Give description of steps taken) ....

....

....

or

Certificate C

I certify that:

- I/The applicant* posted the notice required by regulation 6(1)(b) of the above Regulations on the land which is the subject of the accompanying application.

- It was, however, left in position for less than 7 days during the 21 day period preceding the application.

- This happened because it was removed/obscured/defaced* before 7 days had elapsed.

- This was not my/the applicant's* fault or intention.

- I/The applicant* took the following steps to protect and replace the notice:

(Give description of steps taken)

....

....

Signed ....

*On behalf of ....

Date ....

* *delete where inappropriate*

Form 5

The Planning (Hazardous Substances) Act 1990
The Planning (Hazardous Substances) Regulations 1992

Certificates under Regulation 7(1)* or 13(4)**(a)**

Certificate A

I certify that:

at the beginning of the period of 21 days ending with the date of the accompanying application/appeal* nobody, except the applicant/appellant*, was the owner *(b)* of any part of the land to which the application/appeal* relates.

Signed ....

*on behalf of ....

Date ....

Certificate B

I certify that:

I have/The applicant has/The appellant has* given the required notice *(c)* to everyone else who, at the beginning of the period of 21 days ending with the date of the accompanying application/appeal, was the owner *(b)* of any part of the land to which the application/appeal*relates, as listed below.

Owner's name	Address at which notice was served	Date at which notice was served

Signed ....

*on behalf of ....

Date ....

Certificate C

I certify that:

I/The applicant/The appellant* cannot issue a Certificate A or B in respect of the accompanying application/appeal*.

I have/The applicant has/The appellant has* given the required notice *(c)* to the persons specified below, being persons who at the beginning of the period of 21 days ending with the date of the application/appeal*, were owners *(b)* of any part of the land to which the application/appeal *relates.

Owner's name	Address at which notice was served	Date at which notice was served

I have/The applicant has/The appellant has* taken all reasonable steps open to me/him/her* to find out the names and addresses of the remaining owners *(b)* of the land, or of a part of it, but have/has* been unable to do so. These steps were as follows:–

(d) ....

....

....

....

Signed ....

*On behalf of ....

Date ....

Certificate D

I certify that:

I/The applicant/The appellant* cannot issue a Certificate A in respect of the accompanying application/appeal*

I/The applicant/The appellant* have/has* taken all reasonable steps open to me/him/her* to find out the names and addresses of everyone else who, at the beginning of the period of 21 days ending with the date of the application/appeal*, was the owner *(b)* of any part of the land to which the application/appeal* relates, but have/has* been unable to do so. These steps were as follows:–

(d) ....

....

....

....

Signed ....

*On behalf of ....

Date ....

* delete where inappropriate

(a) These Certificates are for use both with applications and appeals for hazardous substances consent. References to either regulation 7(1) or 13(4) should therefore be deleted as appropriate. One of certificates A, B, C or D must be completed.

(b) "Owner" means a person having a freehold interest or a tenancy the unexpired term of which is not less than 7 years.

(c) Form 6 (for applications) or Form 7 (for appeals).

(d) Insert description of steps taken.

Form 6

The Planning (Hazardous Substances) Act 1990
The Planning (Hazardous Substances) Regulations 1992

Notice of Application for Hazardous Substances Consent/
Continuation of Hazardous Substances Consent*

To be served on an owner
("owner" means a person having a freehold interest or a tenancy the unexpired term of which is not less than 7 years.)

I give notice that *(a)* ....

is applying to the *(b)* ....

for hazardous substances consent/the continuation of hazardous substances consent* *(c)* ....

....

....

at *(d)* ....

....

....

You may inspect a copy of the application at *(e)* ....

....

....

within 21 days of the service of this notice.

If you wish to make representations about this application you should write to the *(b)* ....

....

at *(f)* ....

....

....

within 21 days of the service of this notice.

Signed: ....

*on behalf of ....

Date ....

*   delete where inappropriate

Insert:
(a) applicant's name
(b) name of Council or other body to whom the applicaton is to be made
(c) brief details of the consent being sought
(d) address or location of the application site
(e) address at which the application may be inspected (the applicant is required to make the application available for inspection at a place within the locality of the application site)
(f) address of Council or other body to whom the application is to be made

Form 7

The Planning (Hazardous Substances) Act 1990
The Planning (Hazardous Substances) Regulations 1992 (Regulation 13)

Notice of Appeal

To be served on an owner
("owner" means a person having a freehold interest or a tenancy the unexpired term of which is not less than 7 years.)

I give notice that *(a)* ....

having applied to the *(b)* ....

for hazardous substances consent/the continuation of hazardous substances consent* *(c)* ....

....

....

at *(d)* ....

....

....

is appealing to the Secretary of State for the Environment/Secretary of State for Wales*

– against the decision of the (b) ....

– on the failure of the (b) .... to give notice of a decision*

If you wish to make representations about this appeal you should write to the Planning Inspectorate, Tollgate House, Houlton Street, Bristol BS2 9DJ/the Planning Inspectorate, Cathays Park, Cardiff CF1 3NQ* within 21 days of the date of service of this notice.

Signed: ....

*on behalf of ....

Date ....

* delete where inappropriate

Insert:

(a) appellant's name
(b) name of Council or other body to whom the application was made
(c) brief details of the consent being sought
(d) address or location of the application site

Form 8

The Planning (Hazardous Substances) Act 1990 – Section 11
The Planning (Hazardous Substances) Regulations 1992 (Regulation 14)

Part 1 Claimant and Site

1. **Claimant** *(IN BLOCK CAPITALS)*
    Address

    Tel No

    Agent *(if any)* to whom correspondence should be sent *(IN BLOCK CAPITALS)*
    Address

    Tel No
    Contact

2. **Full postal address or location of land to which the claim relates**

3. **General description of activities carried on at the site during the establishment period**

Part 2 – Substances for which consent is being claimed and established quantity

Table A

To be completed for substances notified to HSE*(a)* under NIHHS*(b)* before the relevant date*(c)*

1 Name of Substance(s) present during establishment period*(d)*	2 Entry number in Schedule 1 to the 1992 Regulations*(e)*	3 Quantity last notified to HSE(a) before the relevant date*(c)*	4 Quantity notified before start of the establishment period*(d)* (if applicable)	5 Established quantity*(f)*

Table B

To be completed for substances **not** required to be notified under NIHHS before the relevant date*(c)* and where a quantity not less than the controlled quantity *(h)* was present at any one time during the establishment period*(d)*.

1 Name of Substance(s) present during establishment period*(d)*	2 Entry number in Schedule 1 to the 1992 Regulations*(e)*	3 Maximum quantity present during establishment period*(d)*	4 Established quantity*(g)*

Notes to part 2

(a) "HSE" stands for the Health and Safety Executive.

(b) 'NIHHS" stands for the Notification of Installations Handling Hazardous Substances Regulations 1982.

(c) The relevant date is 1st June 1992.

(d) The establishment period is the 12 months period immediately preceding the relevant date.

(e) The "1992 Regulations" means the Planning (Hazardous Substances) Regulations 1992.

(f) The established quantity in Table A for a substance is the quantity in column (3) of that table for the substance, or twice the quantity specified in column (4) for that substance, if greater.

(g) The established quantity in Table B for a substance is the quantity specified in column (3) of that table for that substance multiplied by 1.5.

(h) The "controlled quantity" means the quantity specified for that substance in column 2 of the table in Part 1 of Schedule 1 to the 1992 Regulations.

Part 3 – Moveable Container Storage Areas

For each area identified in any moveable container storage area plan which accompanies this
claim specify–

(a) the maximum quantity of the hazardous substance stored in the area in moveable
containers at any time during the establishment period–

(b) whether the substance was stored in a moveable container with a capacity in excess of
10% of the substance's controlled quantity in that area during that period and, if so, the
capacity (in tonnes) of the largest moveable container in which the substance was so
stored–

Part 4 – Vessel Capacity, Temperature, and Pressure

(see next page)

Part 4 Vessel Capacity, Temperature and Pressure – Table C

Vessel area (a)	Entry number of substance in Schedule 1 to the 1992 Regulations	Below ambient temperature (b)		At ambient temperature (c)				Above ambient temperature (d)				
		1(e)	2(f)	3(g)	4(h)	5(i)	6(j)	7(k)	8(l)	9(m)	10(n)	11(o)
		Largest capacity vessel	Highest vessel design pressure	Buried or mounded vessels largest capacity vessel	Buried or mounded vessels highest vessel design pressure	Non buried or non mounded vessels largest capacity vessel	Non buried or non mounded vessels highest vessel design pressure	Present at or below boiling point at 1 bar largest capacity vessel	Present at or below boiling point at 1 bar highest vessel design pressure	Highest design temperature	Present at or above boiling point at 1 bar largest capacity vessel	Present at above boiling point at 1 bar highest vessel design pressure

Notes to Part 4 – Table C

(a) This table should be completed for each vessel area identified in any vessel location plan which accompanies this claim, with a separate row being completed for each hazardous substance in that vessel area.

(b) Only complete columns 1 and 2 in respect of a vessel area in which the substance was present in a vessel at below ambient temperature at any time during the establishment period.

(c) Only complete columns 3 to 6 in respect of a vessel area in which the substance was present in a vessel at ambient temperature at any time during the establishment period.

(d) Only complete columns 7 to 11 in respect of a vessel area in which the substance was present in a vessel at above ambient temperature at any time during the establishment period.

(e) **Column 1** Enter the capacity *(in cubic metres)* of the largest capacity vessel in which the substance was present in the relevant vessel area at below ambient temperature at any time during the establishment period.

(f) **Column 2** Only complete if the substance was present in a vessel at above atmospheric pressure at below ambient temperature in the relevant vessel area at any time during the establishment period.

To complete, enter the highest vessel design pressure of any vessel in which the substance was present in the relevant vessel area at above atmospheric pressure at below ambient temperature at any time during the establishment period.

(g) **Column 3** Only complete if the substance was present at ambient temperature in a vessel which was buried or mounded in the relevant vessel area at any time during the establishment period.

To complete, enter the capacity *(in cubic metres)* of the largest capacity buried or mounded vessel in which the substance was present at ambient temperature in the relevant vessel area at any time during the establishment period.

(h) **Column 4** Only complete if the substance was present at above atmospheric pressure at ambient temperature in a vessel which was buried or mounded in the relevant vessel area at any time during the establishment period.

To complete, enter the highest vessel design operating pressure of any buried or mounded vessel in which the substance was present in the relevant vessel area at above atmospheric pressure at ambient temperature at any time during the establishment period.

(i) **Column 5** Only complete if the substance was present at ambient temperature in a non-buried or non-mounded vessel in the relevant vessel area at any time during the establishment period.

To complete, enter the capacity *(in cubic metres)* of the largest capacity non-buried or non-mounded vessel in which the substance was present at ambient temperature in the relevant vessel area at any time during the establishment period.

(j) **Column 6** Only complete if the substance was present at above atmospheric pressure at ambient temperature in a non-buried or non-mounded vessel in the relevant vessel area at any time during the establishment period.

To complete, enter the highest vessel design operating pressure of any non-buried or non-mounded vessel in which the substance was present in the relevant vessel area at above atmospheric pressure at ambient temperature at any time during the establishment period.

(k) **Column 7** Only complete if the substance was present in a vessel at above ambient temperature at or below its boiling point at 1 bar absolute in the relevant vessel area at any time during the establishment period.

To complete, enter the capacity *(in cubic metres)* of the largest capacity vessel in which the substance was present at above ambient temperature at or below its boiling point at 1 bar absolute in the relevant vessel area at any time during the establishment period.

(*l*) **Column 8** Only complete if the substance was present at above atmospheric pressure at above ambient temperature at or below its boiling point at 1 bar absolute in a vessel in the relevant vessel area at any time during the establishment period.

To complete, enter the highest vessel design operating pressure of any vessel in which the substance was present at above atmospheric pressure at above ambient temperature at or below its boiling point at 1 bar absolute in a vessel in the relevant vessel area at any time during the establishment period.

(*m*) **Column 9** Enter the highest design operating temperature *(in centigrade)* of any vessel in which the substance was present at above ambient temperature in the relevant vessel area at any time during the establishment period.

(*n*) **Column 10** Only complete if the substance was present in a vessel at above its boiling point at 1 bar absolute in the relevant vessel area at any time during the establishment period.

To complete, enter the capacity *(in cubic metres)* of the largest capacity vessel in which the substance was present at above its boiling point at 1 bar absolute in the relevant vessel area at any time during the establishment period.

(*o*) **Column 11** Only complete if the substance was present at above atmospheric pressure above its boiling point at 1 bar absolute in a vessel in the relevant vessel area at any time during the establishment period.

To complete, enter the highest vessel design operating pressure of any vessel in which the substance was present at above atmospheric pressure at above its boiling point at 1 bar absolute in a vessel in the relevant vessel area at any time during the establishment period.

Part 5

I/We hereby claim hazardous substances consent in accordance with the information provided(a).

Signed ....

on behalf of ....

Date ....

Notes to Part 5

(*a*) The hazardous substances authority is required to notify you within 2 weeks from receipt of the claim if, in their opinion, the claim is invalid and to give their reasons for that opinion. If the claim is valid that authority shall be deemed to have granted the hazardous substances consent claimed, subject to the conditions set out in section 11(7) of the Planning (Hazardous Substances) Act 1990 and Schedule 3 to the Planning (Hazardous Substances) Regulations 1992.

SCHEDULE 3

Regulation 15

DEEMED CONSENT CONDITIONS

Below ambient temperature vessel conditions

1. A hazardous substance shall only be present at below ambient temperature in a vessel in a vessel area if—

   (a) it was present at below ambient temperature in a vessel in that vessel area at any time during the establishment period;

   (b) the vessel in which it is present does not have a greater capacity than that specified in column 1 of Table C; and

   (c) the pressure at which it is present does not exceed—

      (i) atmospheric pressure, if the substance was not present at above atmospheric pressure at below ambient temperature in a vessel in that vessel area at any time during the establishment period; or

      (ii) the pressure specified in column 2 of Table C, in any other case.

Ambient temperature vessel conditions

2. A hazardous substance shall only be present at ambient temperature in a buried or mounded vessel in a vessel area if—

   (a) it was present at ambient temperature in a buried or mounded vessel in that vessel area at any time during the establishment period;

   (b) the buried or mounded vessel in which it is present does not have a greater capacity than that specified in column 3 of Table C; and

   (c) the pressure at which it is present in the buried or mounded vessel does not exceed—

      (i) atmospheric pressure, if the substance was not present at above atmospheric pressure at ambient temperature in a buried or mounded vessel in that vessel area at any time during the establishment period; or

      (ii) the pressure specified in column 4 of Table C, in any other case.

3. A hazardous substance shall only be present at ambient temperature in a non-buried or non-mounded vessel in a vessel area if—

   (a) it was present at ambient temperature in a non-buried or non-mounded vessel in that vessel area at any time during the establishment period;

   (b) the non-buried or non-mounded vessel in which it is present does not have a greater capacity than that specified in column 5 of Table C; and

   (c) the pressure at which it is present in the non-buried or non-mounded vessel does not exceed—

      (i) atmospheric pressure, if the substance was not present at above atmospheric pressure at ambient temperature in a non-buried or non-mounded vessel in that vessel area at any time during the establishment period; or

      (ii) the pressure specified in column 6 of Table C, in any other case.

Above ambient temperature vessel conditions

4. A hazardous substance shall only be present at above ambient temperature and at or below its boiling point at 1 bar absolute in a vessel in a vessel area if—

   (a) it was present at above ambient temperature and at or below its boiling point at 1 bar absolute in a vessel in that vessel area at any time during the establishment period;

   (b) the vessel in which it is present does not have a greater capacity than that specified in column 7 of Table C; and

   (c) the pressure at which it is present does not exceed—

      (i) atmospheric pressure, if the substance was not present at above atmospheric pressure at above ambient temperature and at or below its boiling point at 1 bar absolute in a vessel in that vessel area at any time during the establishment period; or

      (ii) the pressure specified in column 8 of Table C, in any other case.

5. A hazardous substance shall only be present at above its boiling point at 1 bar absolute in a vessel area if—

(a) it was present at above its boiling point at 1 bar absolute in a vessel in that vessel area at any time during the establishment period;

(b) the temperature at which it is present does not exceed the temperature specified in column 9 of Table C;

(c) the vessel in which it is present does not have a greater capacity than that specified in column 10 of Table C; and

(d) the pressure at which it is present does not exceed—

(i) atmospheric pressure, if the substance was not present at above atmospheric pressure at above its boiling point at 1 bar absolute in a vessel in that vessel area at any time during the establishment period; or

(ii) the pressure specified in column 11 of Table C, in any other case.

Vessel location condition

6. A hazardous substance shall not be present in a vessel outside of a vessel area.

Moveable container storage area conditions

7. (1) A hazardous substance shall only be stored in moveable containers in an area identified in a moveable container storage area plan for that substance in accordance with regulation 14(3).

(2) The quantity of a hazardous substance stored in such an area shall not exceed twice the maximum quantity of the substance stored in moveable containers in that area at any time during the establishment period.

(3) A hazardous substance shall not be stored in such an area in a moveable container with a capacity in excess of—

(a) 10% of the substance's controlled quantity, if it was not stored in a moveable container with a capacity in excess of 10% of that quantity in that area at any time during the establishment period; or

(b) the capacity of the largest moveable container in which it was stored during that period in that area, in any other case. **[766]**

NOTES
Commencement: 1 June 1992.

SCHEDULE 4

Regulations 18, 20 21 and 22

ENFORCEMENT—MODIFICATION OF THE PRINCIPAL ACT

PART I

APPEALS AGAINST HAZARDOUS SUBSTANCES CONTRAVENTION NOTICES

1. In section 174 of the principal Act (appeals against enforcement notice)—

(a) in subsection (1), for "an enforcement notice" substitute "a hazardous substances contravention notice";

(b) for subsection (2) substitute—

"(2) An appeal may be brought on any of the following grounds—

(a) that, in respect of any contravention of hazardous substances control specified in the notice, hazardous substances consent ought to be granted for the quantity of the hazardous substance present on, over or under the land or, as the case may be, the condition concerned ought to be discharged;

(b) that the matters alleged to constitute a contravention of hazardous substances control have not occurred;

(c) that those matters (if they occurred) do not constitute a contravention of hazardous substances control;

(d) that copies of the hazardous substances contravention notice were not served as required by or under section 24(4) of the Planning (Hazardous Substances) Act 1990;

(e) that the steps required by the notice to be taken exceed what is necessary to remedy any contravention of hazardous substances control;

(f) that any period specified in the notice in accordance with section 24(5)(b) of that Act falls short of what should reasonably be allowed.'';

(c) in subsection (3)(a), for ''enforcement notice'' substitute ''hazardous substances contravention notice'';

(d) for subsection (4) substitute—

''(4) A notice under subsection (3) shall be accompanied by a copy of the hazardous substances contravention notice, together with a statement—

(a) specifying the grounds on which the appeal is being made against the hazardous substances contravention notice; and

(b) setting out the appellant's submissions in relation to each ground of appeal.'';

(e) in subsection (5), after ''does not'' and ''failed'' insert ''in that statement'' and omit ''within the prescribed time'' and ''within that time'';

(f) in subsection (6), for ''enforcement notice'' substitute ''hazardous substances contravention notice''.

2. In section 175 of the principal Act (appeals—supplementary provisions)—

(a) in subsection (3), for ''local planning authority'' substitute ''hazardous substances authority'';

(b) in subsection (6), for ''any other provisions of this Act'' substitute ''section 25(1) of the Planning (Hazardous Substances) Act 1990''.

3. In section 176 of the principal Act (general provisions relating to determination of appeals)—

(a) in subsection (1)—

(i) for ''enforcement notice'' in both places where it occurs, substitute ''hazardous substances contravention notice'';

(ii) for ''local planning authority'' substitute ''hazardous substances authority'';

(b) in subsection (3)—

(i) in paragraph (a) omit ''within the prescribed time'';

(ii) for paragraph (b) substitute—

''(b) may allow an appeal and quash the hazardous substances contravention notice if the hazardous substances authority fail to comply with regulation 19(2) of the Planning (Hazardous Substances) Regulations 1992.'';

(c) in subsections (4) and (5), for ''enforcement notice'' substitute ''hazardous substances contravention notice''.

4. In section 177 of the principal Act (grant or modification of planning permission on appeal against enforcement notice)—

(a) for subsection (1) substitute—

''(1) On the determination of an appeal under section 174, the Secretary of State may—

(a) grant hazardous substances consent for the presence of the hazardous substance on, over or under the land to which the hazardous substances contravention notice relates or on, over or under part of that land;

(b) discharge any condition subject to which hazardous substances consent was granted.'';

(b) omit subsections (1A) and (1B);

(c) for subsection (2) substitute—

''(2) In considering whether to grant hazardous substances consent under subsection (1), the Secretary of State shall have regard to the considerations specified in section 9(2) of the Planning (Hazardous Substances) Act 1990.'';

(d) in subsection (3), for ''planning permission'' in both places where it occurs substitute ''hazardous substances consent'' and for ''Part III'' substitute ''the Planning (Hazardous Substances) Act 1990'';

(e) in subsection (4) omit ''or limitation'' in both places where it occurs;

(f) for subsection (5) substitute—

"(5) Where an appeal against a hazardous substances contravention notice is brought under section 174, the appellant shall be deemed to have made an application for hazardous substances consent in respect of the matters specified in the hazardous substances contravention notice as constituting a contravention of hazardous substances control.";

(g) in subsection (5A), for "section 303" substitute "section 26A of the Planning (Hazardous Substances) Act 1990";

(h) in subsections (6) and (7), for "planning permission" substitute "hazardous substances consent";

(i) for subsection (8) substitute—

"(8) For the purposes of section 28 of the Planning (Hazardous Substances) Act 1990 the Secretary of State's decision shall be treated as having been given by him in dealing with an application for hazardous substances consent made to the hazardous substances authority.".

[767]

NOTES
   Commencement: 1 June 1992.

PART 2
EFFECT OF HAZARDOUS SUBSTANCES CONTRAVENTION NOTICES, ETC.

5. In section 178 of the principal Act (execution and cost of works required by enforcement notices)—

(a) for "an enforcement notice" in each place where it occurs substitute "a hazardous substances contravention notice";

(b) for "local planning authority" in each place where it occurs substitute "hazardous substances authority";

(c) in subsection (2) for "breach of planning control" in both places where it occurs substitute "contravention of hazardous substances control";

(d) in subsection (4) for "the enforcement notice" substitute "the hazardous substances contravention notice";

(e) after subsection (6) insert—

"(7) Where different periods are specified for different steps under section 24(5)(b) of the Planning (Hazardous Substances) Act 1990 in relation to a hazardous substances contravention notice, references in this section and in section 179 to the period for compliance with a hazardous substances contravention notice, in relation to any step, are to the period at the end of which the step is required to have been taken.".

6. In section 179 (offence where enforcement notice not complied with)—

(a) for subsection (1) substitute—

"(1) Where, at any time after the end of the period for compliance with a hazardous substances contravention notice, any steps required by the notice to be taken have not been taken, the person who is then the owner of the land and any person other than the owner who is in control of the land is in breach of the notice.";

(b) in subsection (2) for "the owner of the land" substitute "a person" and for "an enforcement notice" substitute "a hazardous substances contravention notice";

(c) omit subsections (4) and (5);

(d) in subsection (6) omit "or (5)";

(e) in subsection (7)(a) for "enforcement notice" substitute "hazardous substance contravention notice".

7. In Section 180 (effect of planning permission etc. on enforcement or breach of condition notice)—

(a) for subsection (1) substitute—

"(1) Where, after the service of a copy of a hazardous substances contravention notice, hazardous substances consent is granted for the presence of a hazardous substance on, over or under the land to which the notice relates, the notice shall cease to have effect so far as inconsistent with that consent.''

(b) omit subsection (2);
(c) in subsection (3), for ''enforcement notice or breach of conditions notice'' substitute ''a hazardous substances contravention notice''.

8. For Section 181 (enforcement notice to have effect against subsequent development) substitute—

''(1) Compliance with a hazardous substances contravention notice shall not discharge that notice.

(2) Without prejudice to subsection (1), where a provision of a hazardous substances contravention notice requires a hazardous substance to be removed from the land to which the notice relates, the presence on, over or under that land of a quantity of that substance equal to or exceeding its controlled quantity at any time after the substance has been removed in compliance with the hazardous substances contravention notice shall be in contravention of that notice.

(3) Without prejudice to subsection (1), where a provision of a hazardous substances contravention notice requires the quantity of a hazardous substance on, over or under the land to which the notice relates to be reduced below a specified quantity (being greater than the controlled quantity), the presence on, over or under that land of a quantity of that substance equal to or in excess of the specified quantity at any time after the quantity of that substance has been reduced below the specified quantity in compliance with the hazardous substances contravention notice, shall be in contravention of that notice.

(4) Without prejudice to subsection (1), where a provision of a hazardous substances contravention notice requires Steps to be taken to remedy a failure to comply with a condition subject to which a hazardous substances consent was granted, after those steps have been taken no further steps shall be taken which would constitute a breach of that condition, and the taking of such further steps shall be in contravention of that notice.

(5) Sections 178 and 179 shall apply to the contravention of a hazardous substances contravention notice to which this section applies as if the period for compliance with the notice had expired on the date the contravention took place, but the hazardous substances authority shall not enter the land under section 178(1) without, at least 28 days before their entry, Serving on the owner or occupier of the land a notice of their intention to do so.''.

[768]

NOTES
Commencement: 1 June 1992.

PART 3

REGISTERS

9. In section 188 of the principal Act (register of enforcement and stop notices)—

(a) for subsections (1) and (2) substitute—

''(1) Every hazardous substances authority shall keep an enforcement register containing the following information in respect of each hazardous substances contravention notice issued by them—

(a) the address of the land to which the notice relates;
(b) the date of service of copies of the notice;
(c) a statement of the alleged contravention of hazardous substances control, the steps required by the notice to remedy the contravention, and the period within which such steps are to be taken;
(d) the date specified in the notice as the date on which it is to take effect;
(e) the date and effect of any variation of the notice;
(f) the date of any appeal to the Secretary of State against the notice and the date of the final determination of the appeal.

(1A) The entry relating to the hazardous substances contravention notice and everything relating to any such notice shall be removed from the register if the notice is quashed by the Secretary of State or withdrawn.

(1B) The register shall include an index to enable any person to trace an entry in the register.

(1C) Every entry in the register shall be made within 14 days of the relevant information being available to the hazardous substances authority.

(2) The register shall be kept at the principal office of the hazardous substances authority.''.

[769]

NOTES
Commencement: 1 June 1992.

PART 4
VALIDITY

10. In section 285 of the principal Act (validity of enforcement notices and similar notices)—

    (a) in subsection (1), for "an enforcement notice" substitute "a hazardous substances contravention notice";

    (b) in subsection (2), for "enforcement notice" in each place where it occurs substitute "hazardous substances contravention notice";

    (c) omit subsections (3) and (4).

11. In section 289 of the principal Act (appeals to the High Court relating to enforcement notices etc.)—

    (a) in subsections (1), (4A) and (5A) for "an enforcement notice" in each place where it occurs substitute "a hazardous substances contravention notice" and in subsections (1) and (4A) for "local planning authority" in each place where it occurs substitute "hazardous substances authority";

    (b) omit subsections (2) and (4B).   **[770]**

NOTES
Commencement: 1 June 1992.

PART 5
SECTIONS OF THE PRINCIPAL ACT AS MODIFIED

174.—(1) A person having an interest in the land to which a hazardous substances contravention notice relates or a relevant occupier may appeal to the Secretary of State against the notice, whether or not a copy of it has been served on him.

(2) An appeal may be brought on any of the following grounds—

    (a) that, in respect of any contravention of hazardous substances control specified in the notice, hazardous substances consent ought to be granted for the quantity of the hazardous substance present on, over or under the land or, as the case may be, the condition concerned ought to be discharged;

    (b) that the matters alleged to constitute a contravention of hazardous substances control have not occurred;

    (c) that these matters (if they occurred) do not constitute a contravention of hazardous substances control;

    (d) that copies of the hazardous substances contravention notice were not served as required by or under section 24(4) of the Planning (Hazardous Substances) Act 1990;

    (e) that the steps required by the notice to be taken exceed what is necessary to remedy any contravention of hazardous substances control;

    (f) that any period specified in the notice in accordance with section 24(5)(b) of that Act falls short of what should reasonably be allowed.

(3) An appeal under this section shall be made either—

   (a) by giving written notice of the appeal to the Secretary of State before the date specified in the hazardous substances contravention notice as the date on which it is to take effect; or
   (b) by sending such notice to him in a properly addressed and pre-paid letter posted to him at such time that, in the ordinary course of post, it would be delivered to him before that date.

(4) A notice under subsection (3) shall be accompanied by a copy of the hazardous substances contravention notice, together with a statement—

   (a) specifying the grounds on which the appeal is being made against the hazardous substances contravention notice; and
   (b) setting out the appellant's submissions in relation to each ground of appeal.

(5) If where more than one ground is specified in that Statement, the appellant does not in that statement give information required under subsection (4)(b) in relation to each of those grounds the Secretary of State may determine the appeal without considering any ground as to which the appellant has failed in that statement to give such information.

(6) In this section "relevant occupier" means a person who—

   (a) on the date on which the hazardous substances contravention notice is issued occupies the land to which the notice relates by virtue of a licence; and
   (b) continues so to occupy the land when the appeal is brought.

175.—(3) Subject to Section 176(4), the Secretary of State shall, if either the appellant or the hazardous substances authority so desire, give each of them an opportunity of appearing before and being heard by a person appointed by the Secretary of State for the purpose.

*   *   *   *   *

(6) Schedule 6 applies to appeals under section 174, including appeals under that section as applied by regulations under section 25(1) of the Planning (Hazardous Substances) Act 1990.

176.—(1) On an appeal under section 174 the Secretary of State may—

   (a) correct any defect, error or misdescription in the hazardous substances contravention notice; or
   (b) vary the terms of the hazardous substances contravention notice,

if he is satisfied that the correction or variation will not cause injustice to the appellant or the hazardous substances authority.

(2) Where the Secretary of State determines to allow the appeal, he may quash the notice.

(2A) The Secretary of State shall give any directions necessary to give effect to his determination on the appeal.

(3) The Secretary of State—

   (a) may dismiss an appeal if the appellant fails to comply with section 174(4); and
   (b) may allow an appeal and quash the hazardous substances contravention notice if the hazardous substances authority fail to comply with regulation 19(2) of the Planning (Hazardous Substances) Regulations 1992.

(4) If the Secretary of State proposes to dismiss an appeal under paragraph (a) of subsection (3) or to allow an appeal and quash the hazardous substances contravention notice under paragraph (b) of that subsection, he need not comply with Section 175(3).

(5) Where it would otherwise be a ground for determining an appeal under section 174 in favour of the appellant that a person required to be served with a copy of the hazardous substances contravention notice was not served, the Secretary of State may disregard that fact if neither the appellant nor that person has been substantially prejudiced by the failure to serve him.

177.—(1) On the determination of an appeal under section 174, the Secretary of State may—

   (a) grant hazardous substances consent for the presence of the hazardous substance on, over or under the land to which the hazardous substances contravention notice relates or on, over or under part of that land;

(b) discharge any condition subject to which hazardous substances consent was granted.

(2) In considering whether to grant hazardous substances consent under subsection (1), the Secretary of State shall have regard to the considerations specified in section 9(2) of the Planning (Hazardous Substances) Act 1990.

(3) The hazardous substances consent that may be granted under subsection (1) is any hazardous substances consent that might be granted on an application under the Planning (Hazardous Substances) Act 1990.

(4) Where under subsection (1) the Secretary of State discharges a condition he may substitute another condition for it, whether more or less onerous.

(5) Where an appeal against a hazardous substances contravention notice is brought under section 174, the appellant shall be deemed to have made an application for hazardous substances consent in respect of the matters specified in the hazardous substances contravention notice as constituting a contravention of hazardous substances control.

(5A) Where—

   (a) the statement under subsection (4) of section 174 specifies the ground mentioned in subsection (2)(a) of that section;

   (b) any fee is payable under regulations made by virtue of section 26A of the Planning (Hazardous Substances) Act 1990 in respect of the application deemed to be made by virtue of the appeal; and

   (c) the Secretary of State gives notice in writing to the appellant specifying the period within which the fee must be paid,

then, if that fee is not paid within that period, the appeal, so far as brought on that ground, and the application shall lapse at the end of that period.

(6) Any hazardous substances consent granted under subsection (1) on an appeal shall be treated as granted on the application deemed to have been made by the appellant.

(7) In relation to a grant of hazardous substances consent or a determination under subsection (1) the Secretary of State's decision shall be final.

(8) For the purposes of section 28 of the Planning (Hazardous Substances) Act 1990 the Secretary of State's decision shall be treated as having been given by him in dealing with an application for hazardous substances consent made to the hazardous substances authority.

178.—(1) Where any steps required by a hazardous substances contravention notice to be taken are not taken within the period for compliance with the notice, the hazardous substances authority may—

   (a) enter the land and take the steps; and

   (b) recover from the person who is then the owner of the land any expenses reasonably incurred by them in doing so.

(2) Where a copy of a hazardous substances contravention notice has been served in respect of any contravention of hazardous substances control—

   (a) any expenses incurred by the owner or occupier of any land for the purpose of complying with the notice, and

   (b) any sums paid by the owner of any land under subsection (1) in respect of expenses incurred by the hazardous substances authority in taking steps required by such a notice to be taken,

shall be deemed to be incurred or paid for the use and at the request of the person by whom the contravention of hazardous substances control was committed.

(3) Regulations made under this Act may provide that—

   (a) section 276 of the Public Health Act 1936, (power of local authorities to sell materials removed in executing works under that Act subject to accounting for the proceeds of sale);

   (b) section 289 of that Act (power to require the occupier of any premises to permit works to be executed by the owner of the premises); and

   (c) section 294 of that Act (limit on liability of persons holding premises as agents or trustees in respect of the expenses recoverable under that Act), shall apply, subject to such adaptations and modifications as may be specified in the regulations, in relation to any steps required to be taken by a hazardous substances contravention notice.

(4) Regulations under subsection (3) applying section 289 of the Public Health Act 1936 may include adaptations and modifications for the purpose of giving the owner of land to which a hazardous substances contravention notice relates the right, as against all other persons interested in the land, to comply with the requirements of the hazardous substances contravention notice.

(5) Regulations under subsection (3) may also provide for the charging on the land of any expenses recoverable by a hazardous substances authority under subsection (1).

(6) Any person who wilfully obstructs a person acting in the exercise of powers under subsection (1) shall be guilty of an offence and liable on summary conviction to a fine not exceeding level 3 on the standard scale.

(7) Where different periods are specified for different steps under section 24(5)(b) of the Planning (Hazardous Substances) Act 1990 in relation to a hazardous substances contravention notice, references in this section and in section 179 to the period for compliance with a hazardous substances contravention notice, in relation to any step, are to the period at the end of which the step is required to have been taken.

179.—(1) Where, at any time after the end of the period for compliance with a hazardous substances contravention notice, any steps required by the notice to be taken have not been taken, the person who is then the owner of the land and any person other than the owner who is in control of the land is in breach of the notice.

(2) Where a person is in breach of a hazardous substances contravention notice he shall be guilty of an offence.

(3) In proceedings against any person for an offence under subsection (2), it shall be a defence for him to show that he did everything he could be expected to do to secure compliance with the notice.

*   *   *   *   *

(6) An offence under subsection (2) may be charged by reference to any day or longer period of time and a person may be convicted of a second or subsequent offence under the subsection in question by reference to any period of time following the preceding conviction for such an offence.

(7) Where—
    (a) a person charged with an offence under this section has not been served with a copy of the hazardous substances contravention notice; and
    (b) the notice is not contained in the appropriate register kept under section 188,

it shall be a defence for him to show that he was not aware of the existence of the notice.

(8) A person guilty of an offence under this section shall be liable—
    (a) on summary conviction, to a fine not exceeding £20,000; and
    (b) on conviction on indictment, to a fine.

(9) In determining the amount of any fine to be imposed on a person convicted of an offence under this section, the court shall in particular have regard to any financial benefit which has accrued or appears likely to accrue to him in consequence of the offence.

180.—(1) Where, after the service of a copy of a hazardous substances contravention notice, hazardous substances consent is granted for the presence of a hazardous substance on, over or under the land to which the notice relates, the notice shall cease to have effect so far as inconsistent with that consent.

*   *   *   *   *

(3) The fact that a hazardous substances contravention notice has wholly or partly ceased to have effect by virtue of this section shall not affect the liability of any person for an offence in respect of a previous failure to comply, or secure compliance, with the notice.

181.—(1) Compliance with a hazardous substances contravention notice shall not discharge that notice.

(2) Without prejudice to subsection (1), where a provision of a hazardous substances contravention notice requires a hazardous substance to be removed from the land to which the notice relates, the presence on, over or under that land of a quantity of that substance equal to or exceeding its controlled quantity at any time after the substance has been removed in compliance with the hazardous substances contravention notice shall be in contravention of that notice.

(3) Without prejudice to subsection (1), where a provision of a hazardous substances contravention notice requires the quantity of a hazardous substance on, over or under the land to which the notice relates to be reduced below a specified quantity (being greater than the controlled quantity), the presence on, over or under that land of a quantity of that substance equal to or in excess of the specified quantity at any time after the quantity of that substance has been reduced below the specified quantity in compliance with the hazardous substances contravention notice, shall be in contravention of that notice.

(4) Without prejudice to subsection (1), where a provision of a hazardous substances contravention notice requires steps to be taken to remedy a failure to comply with a condition subject to which a hazardous substances consent was granted, after those steps have been taken no further steps shall be taken which would constitute a breach of that condition, and the taking of such further steps shall be in contravention of that notice.

(5) Sections 178 and 179 shall apply to the contravention of a hazardous substances contravention notice to which this section applies as if the period for compliance with the notice had expired on the date the contravention took place, but the hazardous substances authority shall not enter the land under section 178(1) without, at least 28 days before their entry, serving on the owner or occupier of the land a notice of their intention to do so.

*   *   *   *   *

188.—(1) Every hazardous substances authority shall keep an enforcement register containing the following information in respect of each hazardous substances contravention notice issued by them—

    (a) the address of the land to which the notice relates;
    (b) the date of service of copies of the notice;
    (c) a statement of the alleged contravention of hazardous substances control, the steps required by the notice to remedy the contravention, and the period within which such steps are to be taken;
    (d) the date specified in the notice as the date on which it is to take effect;
    (e) the date and effect of any variation of the notice;
    (f) the date of any appeal to the Secretary of State against the notice and the date of the final determination of the appeal.

(1A) The entry relating to the hazardous substances contravention notice and everything relating to any such notice shall be removed from the register if the notice is quashed by the Secretary of State or withdrawn.

(1B) The register shall include an index to enable any person to trace an entry in the register.

(1C) Every entry in the register shall be made within 14 days of the relevant information being available to the hazardous substances authority.

(2) The register shall be kept at the principal office of the hazardous substances authority.

(3) Every register kept under this section shall be available for inspection by the public at all reasonable hours.

*   *   *   *   *

285.—(1) The validity of a hazardous substances contravention notice shall not, except by way of an appeal under Part VII, be questioned in any proceedings whatsoever on any of the grounds on which such an appeal may be brought.

(2) Subsection (1) shall not apply to proceedings brought under section 179 against a person who—

(a) has held an interest in the land since before the hazardous substances contravention notice was issued under that Part;

(b) did not have a copy of the hazardous substances contravention served on him under that Part; and

(c) satisfies the court—

(i) that he did not know and could not reasonably have been expected to know that the hazardous substances contravention notice had been issued; and

(ii) that his interests have been substantially prejudiced by the failure to serve him with a copy of it.

*   *   *   *   *

289.—(1) Where the Secretary of State gives a decision in proceedings on an appeal under Part VII against a hazardous substances contravention notice the appellant or the hazardous substances authority or any other person having an interest in the land to which the notice relates may, according as rules of court may provide, either appeal to the High Court against the decision on a point of law or require the Secretary of State to state and sign a case for the opinion of the High Court.

*   *   *   *   *

(3) At any stage of the proceedings on any such appeal as is mentioned in subsection (1), the Secretary of State may state any question of law arising in the course of the proceedings in the form of a special case for the decision of the High Court.

(4) A decision of the High Court on a case stated by virtue of subsection (3) shall be deemed to be a judgment of the court within the meaning of section 16 of the Supreme Court Act 1981 (jurisdiction of the Court of Appeal to hear and determine appeals from any judgment of the High Court).

(4A) In proceedings brought by virtue of this section in respect of a hazardous substances contravention notice, the High Court or, as the case may be, the Court of Appeal may, on such terms if any as the Court thinks fit (which may include terms requiring the hazardous substances authority to give an undertaking as to damages or any other matter), order that the notice shall have effect, or have effect to such extent as may be specified in the order, pending the final determination of those proceedings and any rehearing and determination by the Secretary of State.

(5) In relation to any proceedings in the High Court or the Court of Appeal brought by virtue of this section the power to make rules of court shall include power to make rules—

(a) prescribing the powers of the High Court or the Court of Appeal with respect to the remitting of the matter with the opinion or direction of the court for rehearing and determination by the Secretary of State; and

(b) providing for the Secretary of State, either generally or in such circumstances as may be prescribed by the rules, to be treated as a party to any such proceedings and to be entitled to appear and to be heard accordingly.

(5A) Rules of court may also provide for the High Court or, as the case may be, the Court of Appeal to give directions as to the exercise, until such proceedings in respect of a hazardous substances contravention notice are finally concluded and any re-hearing and determination by the Secretary of State has taken place, of any other powers in respect of the matters to which such a notice relates.

(6) No proceedings in the High Court shall be brought by virtue of this section except with the leave of that Court and no appeal to the Court of Appeal shall be so brought except with the leave of the Court of Appeal or of the High Court.

(7) In this section "decision" includes a direction or order, and references to the giving of a decision shall be construed accordingly.   **[771]**

NOTES
Commencement: 1 June 1992.

TOWN AND COUNTRY PLANNING (CONTROL OF ADVERTISEMENTS) REGULATIONS 1992
(SI 1992/666)

NOTES
Made: 11 March 1992
Authority: Town and Country Planning Act 1990, ss 220, 221, 223(1), 224(3), 333(1)

ARRANGEMENT OF REGULATIONS

PART I

General

PART I

GENERAL

1. Citation and commencement

These Regulations may be cited as the Town and Country Planning (Control of Advertisements) Regulations 1992 and shall come into force on 6th April 1992.

[772]

NOTES
    Commencement: 6 April 1992.

2. Interpretation

(1) In these Regulations—

    "the Act" means the Town and Country Planning Act 1990;

    "advertisement" does not include anything employed wholly as a memorial or as a railway signal;

    "area of outstanding natural beauty" means an area designated as such by an order made under section 87 of the National Parks and Access to the Countryside Act 1949;

    "area of special control" means an area designated by an order under regulation 18;

    "balloon" means a tethered balloon or similar object;

    "deemed consent" has the meaning given by regulation 5;

    "discontinuance notice" means a notice served under regulation 8;

    "express consent" has the meaning given by regulation 5;

    "illuminated advertisement" means an advertisement which is designed or adapted to be illuminated by artificial lighting, directly or by reflection, and which is so illuminated;

    "National Park" has the meaning given by section 5 of the National Parks and Access to the Countryside Act 1949;

"site" means any land or building, other than an advertisement, on which an advertisement is displayed;

"standard conditions" means the conditions specified in Schedule 1;

"statutory undertaker" includes, in addition to any person mentioned in section 262(1) of the Act, the Civil Aviation Authority, the British Airports Authority, [the Coal Authority or any licensed operator within the meaning of section 65(1) of the Coal Industry Act 1994], any public gas supplier within the meaning of Part I of the Gas Act 1986, any public electricity supplier within the meaning of Part I of the Electricity Act 1989, [any person who is a licence holder, or who has the benefit of a licence exemption, within the meaning of Part I of the Railways Act 1993,] the Post Office, the National Rivers Authority, any water or sewerage undertaker and any telecommunications code system operator; and statutory undertaking shall be interpreted accordingly;

"telecommunications code system operator" means a person who has been granted under section 7 of the Telecommunications Act 1984 a licence which applies the telecommunications code to him in pursuance of section 10 of that Act;

"vehicle" includes a vessel on any inland waterway; and

"waterway" includes coastal waters.

(2) In these Regulations, "local planning authority" means—

(a) for land in the area of an urban development corporation, except in regulation 18, that corporation where it is the local planning authority for the purposes of sections 220 and 224 of the Act;

(b) for land in a National Park which is land that is not in a metropolitan county, the county planning authority for the area where the land is situated; and

(c) in any other case, the relevant district planning authority or metropolitan district or London borough council.

(3) Any reference in these Regulations to a person displaying an advertisement includes—

(a) the owner and occupier of the land on which the advertisement is displayed;

(b) any person to whose goods, trade, business or other concerns publicity is given by the advertisement; and

(c) the person who undertakes or maintains the display of the advertisement.

(4) Except in Class A in Schedule 2, any reference in these Regulations to the land, the building, the site or the premises on which an advertisement is displayed includes, in the case of an advertisement which is displayed on, or which consists of, a balloon, a reference to the land, the building, the site or other premises to which the balloon is attached and to all land, buildings or other premises normally occupied therewith.   [773]

NOTES

Commencement: 6 April 1992.

Para (1): amended by SI 1994/2351, reg 3.

3. Application

(1) These Regulations apply to the display on any site in England and Wales of any advertisement.

(2) Parts II and III of these Regulations do not apply to any advertisement falling

within a description set out in Schedule 2 provided it complies with any conditions and limitations specified in that Schedule; and—

    (a) in the case of an advertisement falling within Class G, it complies with the standard conditions set out in paragraphs 1, 2, 3, and 5 of Schedule 1; or

    (b) in any other case, it complies with all the standard conditions.   **[774]**

NOTES
    Commencement: 6 April 1992.

4. Powers to be exercised in the interests of amenity and public safety

(1) A local planning authority shall exercise their powers under these Regulations only in the interests of amenity and public safety, taking account of any material factors, and in particular—

    (a) in the case of amenity, the general characteristics of the locality, including the presence of any feature of historic, architectural, cultural or similar interest, disregarding, if they think fit, any advertisement being displayed there;

    (b) in the case of public safety—

        (i) the safety of any person who may use any road, railway, waterway, dock, harbour or aerodrome;

       (ii) whether any display of advertisements is likely to obscure, or hinder the ready interpretation of, any road traffic sign, railway signal or aid to navigation by water or air.

(2) In determining an application for consent for the display of advertisements, or considering whether to make an order revoking or modifying a consent, the local planning authority may have regard to any material change in circumstances likely to occur within the period for which the consent is required or granted.

(3) Unless it appears to the local planning authority to be required in the interests of amenity or public safety, an express consent for the display of advertisements shall not contain any limitation or restriction relating to the subject matter, content or design of what is to be displayed.

(4) A consent for the display of advertisements shall take effect as consent for the use of the site for the purposes of the display, whether by the erection of structures or otherwise, and for the benefit of any person interested in the site.   **[775]**

NOTES
    Commencement: 6 April 1992.

5. Requirement for consent

(1) No advertisement may be displayed without consent granted by the local planning authority or by the Secretary of State on an application in that behalf (referred to in these Regulations as "express consent"), or granted by regulation 6 (referred to in these Regulations as "deemed consent"), except an advertisement displayed in accordance with paragraph (2) below.

    (2) The display—

    (a) outside any area of special control, of such an advertisement as is mentioned in regulation 3(2); or

    (b) within an area of special control, of such an advertisement as is so mentioned, other than one falling within Class A in Schedule 2,

is in accordance with this paragraph.   **[776]**

NOTES
Commencement: 6 April 1992.

PART II
DEEMED CONSENT

6. Deemed consent for the display of advertisements

(1) Subject to regulations 7 and 8, and in the case of an area of special control also to regulation 19, deemed consent is hereby granted for the display of an advertisement falling within any class specified in Part I of Schedule 3, subject—

(a) to any conditions and limitations specified in that Part in relation to that class;

and

(b) to the standard conditions.

(2) Part II of Schedule 3 applies for the interpretation of that Schedule.   **[777]**

NOTES
Commencement: 6 April 1992.

7. Directions restricting deemed consent

(1) If the Secretary of State is satisfied, upon a proposal made to him by the local planning authority, that the display of advertisements of any class or description specified in Schedule 3, other than Class 12 or 13, should not be undertaken in any particular area or in any particular case without express consent, he may direct that the consent granted by regulation 6 for that class or description shall not apply in that area or in that case, for a specified period or indefinitely.

(2) Before making any such direction, the Secretary of State shall—

(a) where the proposal relates to a particular area, publish, or cause to be published, in at least one newspaper circulating in the locality, and on the same or a subsequent date in the London Gazette, a notice that such a proposal has been made, naming a place or places in the locality where a map or maps defining the area concerned may be inspected at all reasonable hours; and

(b) where the proposal relates to a particular case, serve, or cause to be served, on the owner and occupier of the land affected and on any other person who, to his knowledge, proposes to display on such land an advertisement of the class or description concerned, a notice that a proposal has been made, specifying the land and the class or description of advertisement in question.

(3) Any notice under paragraph (2) above shall state that any objection to the making of a direction may be made to the Secretary of State in writing within such period (not being less than 21 days from the date when the notice was given) as is specified in the notice.

(4) The Secretary of State shall not make a direction under this regulation until after the expiry of the specified period.

(5) In determining whether to make a direction, the Secretary of State—

(a) shall take into account any objections made in accordance with paragraph (3) above;

(b) may modify the proposal of the local planning authority if—

   (i) he has notified, in writing, that authority and any person who has made an objection or representation to him of his intention and his reasons for it and has given them a reasonable opportunity to respond; and

   (ii) the intended modification does not extend the area of land specified in the proposal.

(6) Where the Secretary of State makes a direction, he shall send it to the local planning authority, with a statement of his reasons for making it, and shall send a copy of that statement to any person who has made an objection in accordance with paragraph (3) above.

(7) Notice of the making of any direction for a particular area shall be published by the local planning authority in at least one newspaper circulating in the locality and, unless the Secretary of State otherwise directs, on the same or a subsequent date in the London Gazette, and such notice shall—

(a) contain a full statement of the effect of the direction;

(b) name a place or places in the locality where a copy of the direction and of a map defining the area concerned may be seen at all reasonable hours; and

(c) specify a date when the direction shall come into force, being at least 14 and not more than 28 days after the first publication of the notice.

(8) Notice of the making of any direction for a particular case shall be served by the local planning authority on the owner and on any occupier of the land to which the direction relates, and on any other person who, to the knowledge of the authority, proposes to display on such land an advertisement of the class or description affected.

(9) A direction for an area shall come into force on the date specified in the notice given under paragraph (7) above, and a direction for a particular case shall come into force on the date on which notice is served on the occupier or, if there is no occupier, on the owner of the land affected.   **[778]**

NOTES

Commencement: 6 April 1992.

8. Discontinuance of deemed consent

(1) The local planning authority may serve a notice requiring the discontinuance of the display of an advertisement, or of the use of a site for the display of an advertisement, for which deemed consent is granted under regulation 6 if they are satisfied that it is necessary to do so to remedy a substantial injury to the amenity of the locality or a danger to members of the public: but in the case of an advertisement within Class 12 in Schedule 3, they may not do so if the advertisement is also within Class F or Class G in Schedule 2.

(2) A discontinuance notice—

(a) shall be served on the advertiser and on the owner and occupier of the site on which the advertisement is displayed;

(b) may, if the local planning authority think fit, also be served on any other person displaying the advertisement;

(c) shall specify the advertisement or the site to which it relates;

(d) shall specify a period within which the display or the use of the site (as the case may be) is to be discontinued; and

(e) shall contain a full statement of the reasons why action has been taken under this regulation.

(3) Subject to paragraphs (4) and (5) below, a discontinuance notice shall take effect at the end of the period (being at least 8 weeks after the date on which it is served) specified in the notice.

(4) If an appeal is made to the Secretary of State under regulation 15, the notice shall be of no effect pending the final determination or withdrawal of the appeal.

(5) The local planning authority, by a notice served on the advertiser, may withdraw a discontinuance notice at any time before it takes effect or may, where no appeal to the Secretary of State is pending, from time to time vary a discontinuance notice by extending the period specified for the taking effect of the notice.

(6) The local planning authority shall, on serving on the advertiser a notice of withdrawal or variation under paragraph (5) above, send a copy to every other person served with the discontinuance notice. **[779]**

NOTES
Commencement: 6 April 1992.

PART III
EXPRESS CONSENT

9. Applications for express consent

(1) An application for express consent shall be made to the local planning authority.

(2) Such an application shall be made on a form provided by the local planning authority and give the particulars required by that form. There shall be annexed to the form such plans as the authority require.

(3) An applicant shall provide the local planning authority with 2 additional copies of the completed form and the annexed plans.

(4) The local planning authority may, if they think fit, accept an application notwithstanding that the requirements of paragraph (2) or (3) above are not complied with, provided the application is in writing.

(5) A local planning authority shall not employ a form or require the submission of plans or information inconsistently with any direction which the Secretary of State may have given as to the matter.

(6) An application for the renewal of an express consent may not be made at a date earlier than 6 months before the expiry of that consent. **[780]**

NOTES
Commencement: 6 April 1992.

10. Secretary of State's directions

The Secretary of State may give directions to a local planning authority, either generally or in relation to a particular case or class of case, specifying the kinds of particulars, plans or information to be contained in an application for express consent. **[781]**

NOTES
Commencement: 6 April 1992.

11. Receipt of applications

On receipt of an application for express consent, the local planning authority—

    (a) shall send an acknowledgement in writing to the applicant and, in the case of a county planning authority, shall also send a copy of the application and the accompanying plans to the district planning authority within whose area any part of the application site is situated;

    (b) may direct the applicant in writing to provide one of their officers with such evidence as may reasonably be called for to verify any particulars or information given to them.   **[782]**

NOTES

Commencement: 6 April 1992.

12. Duty to consult

(1) Before granting an express consent, a local planning authority shall consult—

    (a) any neighbouring local planning authority, any part of whose area appears likely to be affected;

    (b) where the application relates to land in a National Park which is land that is not in a metropolitan county, the district planning authority for the area in which the land is situated;

    (c) where they consider that a grant of consent may affect the safety of persons using any trunk road (as defined in section 329 of the Highways Act 1980) in England, the Secretary of State for Transport;

    (d) where they consider that a grant of consent may affect the safety of persons using any railway, waterway, dock, harbour or aerodrome (civil or military), the person responsible for the operation thereof, and, in the case of coastal waters, the Corporation of Trinity House.

(2) The local planning authority shall give anyone whom they are required to consult at least 14 days' notice that the relevant application is to be considered and shall take into account any representations made by any such person.   **[783]**

NOTES

Commencement: 6 April 1992.

13. Power to deal with applications

(1) Subject to regulation 19, where an application for express consent is made to the local planning authority, they may—

    (a) grant consent, in whole or in part, subject to the standard conditions and, subject to paragraphs (3) to (6) below, to such additional conditions as they think fit; or

    (b) refuse consent; or

    (c) decline to determine the application in accordance with section 70A of the Act, which shall apply in relation to the application subject to the modifications specified in Part I of Schedule 4, the provisions of that section as modified being set out in Part II of that Schedule.

(2) An express consent may be—

    (a) for the display of a particular advertisement or advertisements with or without illumination, as the applicant specifies;

    (b) for the use of a particular site for the display of advertisements in a specified manner, whether by reference to the number, siting, size or illumination of the advertisements, or the structures intended for such display, or the design or appearance of any such structure, or otherwise; or

(c) for the retention of any display of advertisements or the continuation of the use of a site begun before the date of the application.

(3) The conditions imposed under paragraph (1)(a) above may in particular include conditions—

(a) regulating the display of advertisements to which the consent relates;
(b) regulating the use for the display of advertisements of the site to which the application relates or any adjacent land under the control of the applicant, or requiring the carrying out of works on any such land;
(c) requiring the removal of any advertisement or the discontinuance of any use of land authorised by the consent, at the end of a specified period, and the carrying out of any works required for the reinstatement of the land.

(4) The local planning authority shall not, under paragraph (1)(a) above, impose any condition in relation to the display of an advertisement within any class specified in Schedule 3 more restrictive than those imposed by that Schedule in relation to that class.

(5) Subject to paragraph (4) above, an express consent shall be subject to the condition that it expires at the end of—

(a) such period as the local planning authority may specify in granting the consent; or
(b) where no period is so specified, a period of 5 years.

(6) A local planning authority may specify a period under paragraph (5)(a) above as a period running from the earlier of the following, namely the date of the commencement of the display or a specified date not later than 6 months after the date on which the consent is granted.   **[784]**

NOTES
Commencement: 6 April 1992.

14. Notification of decision

(1) The grant or refusal of an express consent by a local planning authority shall be notified in writing to the applicant within a period of 8 weeks from the date of the receipt of the application or such longer period as the applicant may, before the expiry of that period, agree in writing.

(2) The authority shall state in writing their reasons for—

(a) any refusal of consent in whole or in part;
(b) any decision to impose any condition under regulation 13(1)(a) on a consent, except a condition specified in Schedule 3 in relation to a class within which the advertisement falls; and
(c) any condition whereby the the consent expires before the expiry of 5 years from the date on which it is granted, except when the consent is granted for the period for which it was applied for.   **[785]**

NOTES
Commencement: 6 April 1992.

15. Appeals to the Secretary of State

(1) Sections 78 and 79 of the Act shall apply, in relation to applications for express consent under these Regulations, subject to the modifications specified in Part III of Schedule 4.

(2) The provisions of those sections, as modified under paragraph (1) above, are set out in Part IV of that Schedule.

(3) Where a discontinuance notice is served under regulation 8, sections 78 and 79 of the Act shall apply subject to the modifications specified in Part V of Schedule 4. [786]

NOTES
Commencement: 6 April 1992.

16. Revocation or modification of express consent

(1) If a local planning authority are satisfied that it is expedient, they may by order revoke or modify an express consent, subject to paragraphs (2) to (7) below.

(2) An order under paragraph (1) above shall not take effect without the approval of the Secretary of State.

(3) When an authority submit an order under paragraph (1) above to the Secretary of State for approval, they shall serve notice on the person who applied for the express consent, the owner and the occupier of the land affected and any other person who, in their opinion, will be affected by the order, specifying a period of at least 28 days from the service of the notice within which objection may be made.

(4) If, within the period specified in the notice, an objection to the order is received by the Secretary of State from any person on whom notice was served, the Secretary of State shall, before approving the order, give to that person and to the local planning authority an opportunity of appearing before and being heard by a person appointed by him.

(5) The power to make an order under this regulation may be exercised—

(a) in a case which involves the carrying out of building or other operations, at any time before those operations have been completed;

(b) in any other case, at any time before the display of advertisements is begun.

(6) In a case to which paragraph (5)(a) above applies, the revocation or modification of consent shall not affect such operations as have already been carried out.

(7) The Secretary of State may approve an order submitted to him under this regulation either without modification or subject to such modifications as he considers expedient. [787]

NOTES
Commencement: 6 April 1992.

17. Compensation for revocation or modification

(1) Where—

(a) an order under regulation 16 takes effect; and

(b) within 6 months of its approval a claim in writing is served on the local planning authority, either by delivery at or by post to their offices,

the authority shall pay compensation to the claimant for any loss or damage suffered in the circumstances and to the extent specified in paragraph (2) below.

(2) Compensation is payable if, and to the extent that, the claimant has—

(a) incurred expenditure in carrying out abortive work, including the preparation of plans or similar material;

(b) otherwise sustained loss or damage directly attributable to the order, other
than loss or damage consisting of any depreciation in value of any interest
in land,

but excluding any work done, or loss or damage arising out of anything done or not
done, before the grant of consent.   **[788]**

NOTES

Commencement: 6 April 1992.

PART IV

AREAS OF SPECIAL CONTROL

18. Area of Special Control Orders

(1) Every local planning authority shall from time to time consider whether any part
or additional part of their area should be designated as an area of special control.

(2) An area of special control shall be designated by an area of special control
order made by the local planning authority and approved by the Secretary of State,
in accordance with the provisions of Schedule 5.

(3) An area of special control order may be revoked or modified by a subsequent
order made by the authority and approved by the Secretary of State, in accordance
with the provisions of Schedule 5.

(4) Where an area of special control order is in force, the local planning authority
shall consider at least once in every 5 years whether it should be revoked or modified.

(5) Before making an order under this regulation, a local planning authority shall
consult—

(a) where it appears to them that the order will be likely to affect any part of
the area of a neighbouring local planning authority, that authority;
(b) where the order will relate to any land in a National Park which is land
that is not in a metropolitan county, any district planning authority within
whose area any of that land is situated.

(6) A local planning authority shall not exercise their power under this regulation
in the interests of public safety within the meaning of regulation 4(1).   **[789]**

NOTES

Commencement: 6 April 1992.

19. Control in areas of special control

(1) Subject to the provisions of this regulation, no advertisements may be displayed
in an area of special control unless they fall within—

(a) Classes B to J in Schedule 2;
(b) Classes 1 to 3, 5 to 7 and 9 to 14 in Schedule 3;
(c) paragraph (2) below.

(2) Advertisements of the following descriptions displayed with express consent
come within this paragraph—

(a) hoardings or similar structures to be used only for the display of notices
relating to local events, activities or entertainments;
(b) any advertisement for the purpose of announcement or direction in relation
to buildings or other land in the locality, where reasonably required having
regard to the nature and situation of such buildings or other land;

(c) any advertisement required in the interests of public safety;

(d) any advertisement which could be displayed by virtue of paragraph (1)(b) above but for some non-compliance with a condition or limitation imposed by Schedule 3 as respects size, height from the ground, number or illumination or but for a direction under regulation 7;

(e) any advertisement within Class 4A, 4B or 8 in Schedule 3.

(3) Express consent may not be given for the display in an area of special control of an illuminated advertisement falling within sub-paragraph (2)(a) or (b) above.

(4) Without prejudice to paragraph (2) above, where an area is designated as an area of special control, advertisements within paragraph (5) below which are being displayed immediately before the relevant order comes into force may continue to be displayed, but only for the period specified in relation thereto in that paragraph.

(5) The advertisements and specified periods mentioned in paragraph (4) above are—

(a) any advertisement within Class 4A or 4B in Schedule 3 for which express consent has not been granted, 5 years from the date on which the order comes into force;

(b) any advertisement within Class 8 for which express consent has not been granted, 1 year from the date on which the order comes into force or 2 years from the date on which the advertisement was first displayed, whichever period expires later;

(c) any advertisement for which express consent has been granted, 6 months from the date on which the order comes into force or for the remainder of the period of the express consent, whichever period expires later.

(6) Nothing in paragraphs (1) to (5) above shall—

(a) affect a notice served at any time under regulation 8;

(b) override any condition imposed on a consent, whereby an advertisement is required to be removed;

(c) restrict the powers of a local planning authority, or of the Secretary of State, in regard to any contravention of these Regulations;

(d) render unlawful the display, pursuant to express consent or to Class 14 in Schedule 3, of an advertisement mentioned in paragraph 2(d) or (e) above.   **[790]**

NOTES

Commencement: 6 April 1992.

PART V

MISCELLANEOUS

20. Repayment of expense of removing prohibited advertisements

The time limit prescribed for the purpose of making a claim for compensation under section 223 of the Act for the recovery of expenses reasonably incurred is a period of 6 months from the completion of the works.   **[791]**

NOTES

Commencement: 6 April 1992.

21. Register of applications

(1) Every local planning authority shall keep a register containing particulars of—

(a) any application made to them for express consent for the display of an advertisement, including the name and address of the applicant, the date of the application and the type of advertisement concerned;

(b) any direction given under these Regulations relating to the application;

(c) the date and effect of any decision of the local planning authority on the application;

(d) the date and effect of any decision of the Secretary of State on an appeal.

(2) The register shall include an index to enable a person to trace any entry therein.

(3) Any part of the register which relates to land within a particular part of the area of a local planning authority may be kept at a place within or convenient to that part of their area.

(4) Subject to paragraph (3) above, the register shall be kept at the office of the local planning authority.

(5) Every entry in the register consisting of particulars of an application shall be made within 14 days of the receipt of that application.

(6) The register shall be open to public inspection at all reasonable hours. **[792]**

NOTES
Commencement: 6 April 1992.

22. Directions requiring information

The Secretary of State may give a direction to a local planning authority, or to such authorities generally, requiring them to provide him with information required for the purpose of any of his functions under these Regulations. **[793]**

NOTES
Commencement: 6 April 1992.

23. Exercise of powers by the Secretary of State

(1) If it appears to the Secretary of State, after consultation with the local planning authority, that—

(a) a discontinuance notice should be served under regulation 8; or

(b) an area of special control order, or an order revoking such an order, should be made under regulation 18,

he may himself serve such a notice or make such an order.

(2) Where the Secretary of State proposes to exercise his powers under paragraph (1) above, the provisions of regulations 8 and 15 (in relation to sub-paragraph (a)), and of regulation 18 and Schedule 5 (in relation to sub-paragraph (b)), shall apply as they apply to the action of a local planning authority, with such modifications as may be necessary. **[794]**

NOTES
Commencement: 6 April 1992.

24. Discontinuance notice in respect of authority's advertisement

(1) If the Secretary of State is satisfied that it is necessary to remedy a substantial injury to the amenity of the locality or a danger to members of the public, he may serve a discontinuance notice under regulation 8 in relation to an advertisement within Class 1B in Schedule 3.

(2) Paragraphs (2), (5) and (6) of regulation 8 shall apply to a discontinuance notice to which paragraph (1) above applies as if references to the local planning authority were references to the Secretary of State.

(3) Paragraph (3) of regulation 15 shall apply to a discontinuance notice to which paragraph (1) above applies, with such modifications as may be necessary.

[795]

NOTES
Commencement: 6 April 1992.

25. Extension of time limits

The Secretary of State may, in any particular case, extend the time within which anything is required to be done under these Regulations or within which any objection, representation or claim for compensation may be made. **[796]**

NOTES
Commencement: 6 April 1992.

26. Cancellation or variation of directions

Any power conferred by these Regulations to give a direction includes power to cancel or vary the direction by a subsequent direction. **[797]**

NOTES
Commencement: 6 April 1992.

27. Contravention of Regulations

A person displaying an advertisement in contravention of these Regulations shall be liable on summary conviction of an offence under section 224(3) of the Act to a fine of an amount not exceeding level 3 on the standard scale and, in the case of a continuing offence, one-tenth of level 3 on the standard scale for each day during which the offence continues after conviction. **[798]**

NOTES
Commencement: 6 April 1992.

28. Statutory Instruments revoked

The Town and Country Planning (Control of Advertisements) Regulations 1989, the Town and Country Planning (Control of Advertisements) (Amendment) Regulations 1990 and the Town and Country Planning (Control of Advertisements) (Amendment) (No. 2) Regulations 1990 are hereby revoked. **[799]**

NOTES
Commencement: 6 April 1992.

SCHEDULE 1

Regulation 2(1)

STANDARD CONDITIONS

1. Any advertisements displayed, and any site used for the display of advertisements, shall be maintained in a clean and tidy condition to the reasonable satisfaction of the local planning authority.

2. Any structure or hoarding erected or used principally for the purpose of displaying advertisements shall be maintained in a safe condition.

3. Where an advertisement is required under these Regulations to be removed, the removal shall be carried out to the reasonable satisfaction of the local planning authority.

4. No advertisement is to be displayed without the permission of the owner of the site or any other person with an interest in the site entitled to grant permission.

5. No advertisement shall be sited or displayed so as to obscure, or hinder the ready interpretation of, any road traffic sign, railway signal or aid to navigation by water or air, or so as otherwise to render hazardous the use of any highway, railway, waterway or aerodrome (civil or military). **[800]**

NOTES
Commencement: 6 April 1992.

SCHEDULE 2

Regulation 3(2)

CLASSES OF ADVERTISEMENTS TO WHICH PARTS II AND III OF THESE REGULATIONS DO NOT APPLY

Description of advertisement	*Conditions, limitations and interpretation*
CLASS A The display of an advertisement on or consisting of a balloon not more than 60 metres above ground level.	1 The site of the advertisement is not within an area of outstanding natural beauty, a conservation area, a National Park, the Broads or an area of special control. 2 Not more than one such advertisement may be displayed on the site at any one time. 3 The site may not be used for the display of advertisements on more than 10 days in total in any calendar year. 4 For the purposes of Class A, "the site" means— (a) in a case where the advertisement is being displayed by a person (other than the occupier of the land) who is using, or proposing to use, the land to which the balloon is attached for a particular activity (other than the display of advertisements) for a temporary period, the whole of the land used, or to be used, for that activity; or (b) in any other case, the land to which the balloon is attached and all land normally occupied together therewith.
CLASS B An advertisement displayed on enclosed land.	1 The advertisement is not readily visible from outside the enclosed land or from any place to which the public have a right of access. 2 For the purposes of Class B, "enclosed land" includes any railway station (and its yards) or bus station, together with its forecourt, whether enclosed or not; but does not include any public park, public garden or other land held for the use or enjoyment of the public, or (save as herein specified) any enclosed railway land normally used for the carriage of passengers or goods by rail.

Description of advertisement	Conditions, limitations and interpretation
CLASS C An advertisement displayed on or in a vehicle.	1 The vehicle is not— (a) normally employed except as a moving vehicle; or (b) used principally for the display of advertisements.
CLASS D An advertisement incorporated in the fabric of a building.	1 The building or any external face of it is not used principally for the display of advertisements. 2 For the purposes of Class D— (a) an advertisement fixed to, or painted on, a building is not to be regarded as incorporated in its fabric; (b) a hoarding or similar structure is to be regarded as a building used principally for the display of advertisements.
CLASS E An advertisement displayed on an article for sale or on the container in, or from which, an article is sold.	1 The advertisement refers only to the article for sale. 2 The advertisement may not be illuminated. 3 It may not exceed 0.1 square metre in area. 4 For the purposes of Class E, ''article'' includes a gas or liquid.
CLASS F An advertisement relating specifically to a pending Parliamentary, [European Parliamentary] or local government election.	1 The advertisement shall be removed within 14 days after the close of the poll in the election to which it relates.
CLASS G An advertisement required to be displayed by Standing Orders of either House of Parliament or by any enactment or any condition imposed by any enactment on the exercise of any power or function.	1 If the advertisement would, if it were not within this Class, fall within any Class in Schedule 3, any conditions imposed on that Class as to size, height or number of advertisements displayed shall apply to it. 2 In a case to which paragraph 1 does not apply, the size, height, and number of advertisements displayed shall not exceed what is necessary to achieve the purpose for which the advertisement is required. 3 The advertisement may not be displayed after the expiry of the period during which it is required or authorised to be displayed, or if there is no such period, the expiry of a reasonable time after its purpose has been satisfied.
CLASS H A traffic sign.	1 For the purposes of Class H, a traffic sign means a traffic sign as defined in section 64(1) of the Road Traffic Regulation Act 1984.
CLASS I The national flag of any country.	1 Each flag is to be displayed on a single vertical flagstaff. 2 Neither the flag nor the flagstaff may display any advertisement or subject matter additional to the design of the flag.

Description of advertisement	*Conditions, limitations and interpretation*
CLASS J An advertisement displayed inside a building.	1 The advertisement may not be illuminated. 2 The building in which the advertisement is displayed is not used principally for the display of advertisements. 3 No part of the advertisement may be within 1 metre of any external door, window or other opening, through which it is visible from outside the building.

[801]

NOTES
    Commencement: 6 April 1992.
    Class F: amended by SI 1994/2351, reg 4.

SCHEDULE 3

Regulation 6

CLASSES OF ADVERTISEMENTS WHICH MAY BE DISPLAYED WITH DEEMED CONSENT

PART I

SPECIFIED CLASSES AND CONDITIONS

Class 1—Functional advertisements of local authorities, statutory undertakers and public transport undertakers

1A Description

An advertisement displayed wholly for the purpose of announcement or direction in relation to any of the functions of a local authority or to the operation of a statutory undertaking or a public transport undertaking, which—

(a) is reasonably required to be displayed for the safe or efficient performance of those functions, or operation of that undertaking, and
(b) cannot be displayed by virtue of any other specified class.

1A Conditions and Limitations

(1) Illumination is not permitted unless reasonably required for the purpose of the advertisement.

1B Description

An advertisement displayed by a local planning authority on land in their area.

1B Conditions and Limitations

(1) In an area of special control, such an advertisement may be displayed only if the authority could have granted express consent for its display.

Class 2—Miscellaneous advertisements relating to the premises on which they are displayed

2A Description

An advertisement displayed for the purpose of identification, direction or warning, with respect to the land or building on which it is displayed.

2A Conditions and Limitations

(1) No such advertisement may exceed 0.3 square metre in area.

(2) Illumination is not permitted.

(3) No character or symbol on the advertisement may be more than 0.75 metre in height, or 0.3 metre in an area of special control.

(4) No part of the advertisement may be more than 4.6 metres above ground level, or 3.6 metres in an area of special control.

2B Description

An advertisement relating to any person, partnership or company separately carrying on a profession, business or trade at the premises where it is displayed.

2B Conditions and Limitations

(1) No advertisement may exceed 0.3 square metre in area.

(2) No character or symbol on the advertisement may be more than 0.75 metre in height, or 0.3 metre in an area of special control.

(3) No part of the advertisement may be more than 4.6 metres above ground level, or 3.6 metres in an area of special control.

(4) Not more than one such advertisement is permitted for each person, partnership or company or, in the case of premises with entrances on different road frontages, one such advertisement at each of two such entrances.

(5) Illumination is not permitted unless the advertisement states that medical or similar services or supplies are available on the premises and the illumination is in a manner reasonably required to fulfil the purpose of the advertisement.

2C Description

An advertisement relating to any institution of a religious, educational, cultural, recreational or medical or similar character, or to any hotel, inn or public house, block of flats, club, boarding house or hostel, at the premises where it is displayed.

2C Conditions and Limitations

(1) Not more than one such advertisement is permitted in respect of each premises or, in the case of premises with entrances on different road frontages, one such advertisement at each of two such entrances.

(2) No such advertisement may exceed 1.2 square metres in area.

(3) No character or symbol on the advertisement may be more than 0.75 metre in height, or 0.3 metre in an area of special control.

(4) No part of the advertisement may be more than 4.6 metres above ground level, or 3.6 metres in an area of special control.

(5) Illumination is not permitted unless the advertisement states that medical or similar services or supplies are available at the premises and the illumination is in a manner reasonably required to fulfil the purpose of the advertisement.

Class 3—Miscellaneous temporary advertisements

3A Description

An advertisement relating to the sale or letting, for residential, agricultural, industrial or commercial use or for development for such use, of the land or premises on which it is displayed.

3A Conditions and Limitations

(1) (a) Not more than one such advertisement, consisting of a single board or two joined boards, is permitted.

(b) Where more than one such advertisement is displayed, the first to be displayed shall be taken to be the one permitted.

(2) No advertisement may be displayed indicating that land or premises have been sold or let, other than by the addition to an existing advertisement of a statement that a sale or letting has been agreed, or that the land or premises have been sold or let, subject to contract.

(3) Any such advertisement shall be removed within 14 days after the sale is completed or a tenancy is granted.

(4) No such advertisement may exceed in area—

(a) where the advertisement relates to residential use or development, 0.5 square metre or, in the case of two joined boards together, 0.6 square metre in aggregate;

(b) where the advertisement relates to any other use or development, 2 square metres or, in the case of two joined boards together, 2.3 square metres in aggregate.

(5) Where the advertisement is displayed on a building, the maximum projection permitted from the face of the building is 1 metre.

(6) Illumination is not permitted.

(7) No character or symbol on the advertisement may be more than 0.75 metre in height, or 0.3 metre in an area of special control.

(8) No part of the advertisement may be higher above ground level than 4.6 metres, or 3.6 metres in an area of special control or, in the case of a sale or letting of part only of a building, the lowest level of that part of the building on which display is reasonably practicable.

3B Description

An advertisement announcing the sale of goods or livestock, and displayed on the land where the goods or livestock are situated or where the sale is held, not being land which is normally used, whether at regular intervals or otherwise, for the purpose of holding such sales.

3B Conditions and Limitations

(1) (a) Not more than one such advertisement may be displayed at any one time on the land concerned.

(b) Where more than one such advertisement is displayed, the first to be displayed shall be taken to be the one permitted.

(2) No such advertisement may be displayed earlier than 28 days before the day (or first day) on which the sale is due to take place.

(3) Any such advertisement shall be removed within 14 days after the sale is completed.

(4) No such advertisement may exceed 1.2 square metres in area.

(5) Illumination is not permitted.

(6) No character or symbol on the advertisement may be more than 0.75 metre in height, or 0.3 metre in an area of special control.

(7) No part of the advertisement may be more than 4.6 metres above ground level, or 3.6 metres in an area of special control.

3C Description

An advertisement relating to the carrying out of building or similar work on the land on which it is displayed, not being land which is normally used, whether at regular intervals or otherwise, for the purposes of carrying out such work.

3C Conditions and Limitations

(1) (a) Not more than one such advertisement shall be displayed at any one time, on each road frontage of the land, in respect of each separate development project, except in the case mentioned in paragraph (4) below.

(b) Where more than one such advertisement is displayed, the first to be displayed on any frontage shall be taken to be the one permitted.

(2) No such advertisement may be displayed except while the relevant works are being carried out.

(3) No such advertisement may exceed in aggregate—

(a) in the case of an advertisement referring to one person—
  (i) if the display is more than 10 metres from a highway, 3 square metres in area; or
  (ii) in any other case, 2 square metres;

(b) in the case of an advertisement referring to more than one person—
  (i) if the display is more than 10 metres from a highway, 3 square metres plus 0.6 square metre for each additional person, or
  (ii) in any other case, 2 square metres plus 0.4 square metre for each additional person,

together with 0.2 of the area permitted under sub-paragraph (a) or (b) above for the name, if any, of the development project.

(4) Where any such advertisement does not refer to any person carrying out such work, that person may display a separate advertisement with a maximum area of 0.5 square metre, which does so refer, on each frontage of the land for a maximum period of 3 months.

(5) Illumination is not permitted.

(6) No character or symbol on the advertisement may be more than 0.75 metre in height, or 0.3 metre in an area of special control.

(7) No part of the advertisement may be more than 4.6 metres above ground level, or 3.6 metres in an area of special control.

3D Description

An advertisement—

(i) announcing any local event of a religious, educational, cultural, political, social or recreational character,
(ii) relating to any temporary matter in connection with an event or local activity of such a character,

not being an event or activity promoted or carried on for commercial purposes.

3D Conditions and Limitations

(1) No such advertisement may exceed 0.6 square metre in area.

(2) No such advertisement may be displayed earlier than 28 days before the day (or first day) on which the event or activity is due to take place.

(3) Any such advertisement shall be removed within 14 days after the end of the event or activity.

(4) Illumination is not permitted.

(5) No character or symbol on the advertisement may be more than 0.75 metre in height, or 0.3 metre in an area of special control.

(6) No part of the advertisement may be more than 4.6 metres above ground level, or 3.6 metres in an area of special control.

3E Description

An advertisement relating to any demonstration of agricultural methods or processes, on the land on which it is displayed.

3E Conditions and Limitations

(1) Advertisements of this Class may not be displayed on any land for more than 6 months in any period of 12 months.

(2) The maximum area of display permitted in respect of each demonstration is 1.2 square metres.

(3) No single advertisement within such a display may exceed 0.4 square metre in area.

(4) No such advertisement may be displayed earlier than 28 days before the day (or first day) on which the demonstration is due to take place and shall be removed within 14 days after the end of the demonstration.

(5) Illumination is not permitted.

(6) No character or symbol on the advertisement may be more than 0.75 metre in height, or 0.3 metre in an area of special control.

(7) No part of the advertisement may be more than 4.6 metres above ground level, or 3.6 metres in an area of special control.

3F Description

An advertisement relating to the visit of a travelling circus, fair or similar travelling entertainment to any specified place in the district.

3F Conditions and Limitations

(1) No such advertisement may exceed 0.6 square metre in area.

(2) No such advertisement may be displayed earlier than 14 days before the first performance or opening of the entertainment at the place specified.

(3) Any such advertisement shall be removed within 7 days after the last performance or closing of the specified entertainment.

(4) At least 14 days before the advertisement is first displayed, the local planning authority are to be notified in writing of the first date on which, and of the site at which, it is to be displayed.

(5) Illumination is not permitted.

(6) No part of the advertisement may be more than 3.6 metres above ground level.

Class 4—Illuminated advertisements on business premises

4A Description

An illuminated advertisement displayed on the frontage of premises within a retail park, which overlook or face on to a communal car park wholly bounded by the retail park, where the advertisement refers wholly to any or all of the following matters, namely the business carried on [, the goods sold or services provided, or the name or qualifications of the persons carrying on the business, or supplying the goods or services, on those premises].

4A Conditions and Limitations

(1) Subject to paragraph (11) below, no such advertisement is permitted within a conservation area, an area of outstanding natural beauty, a National Park or the Broads.

(2) In the case of a shop, no such advertisement may be displayed except on a wall containing a shop window.

(3) Not more than one such advertisement parallel to a wall and one projecting at right angles from such a wall is permitted, and in the case of any projecting advertisement—

(a) no surface may be greater than 1 square metre in area;
(b) the advertisement may not project more than 1 metre from the wall; and
(c) it may not be more than 1.5 metres high.

(4) Each character of the advertisement but no part of the background is to be illuminated from within.

(5) No such advertisement may include any intermittent light source, moving feature, exposed cold cathode tubing, animation or reflective material.

(6) The luminance of any such advertisement may not exceed the limits specified in paragraph 2 of Part II of this Schedule.

(7) In the case of any advertisement consisting of a built-up box containing the light source, the distance between—

(a) the face of the advertisement and any wall parallel to which it is displayed, at the point where it is affixed, or
(b) the two faces of an advertisement projecting from a wall,

may not exceed 0.25 metre.

(8) The lowest part of any such advertisement must be at least 2.5 metres above ground level.

(9) No character or symbol on the advertisement may be more than 0.75 metre in height.

(10) No part of the advertisement may be higher above ground level than 4.6 metres or the bottom level of any first floor window in the wall on which the advertisement is displayed, whichever is the lower.

(11) Paragraph (1) above does not preclude the continued display of an advertisement being displayed at the date of designation of the relevant area until the expiry of 5 years from that date.

4B Description

An illuminated advertisement, other than one falling within Class 4A, displayed on business premises wholly with reference to any or all of the following matters, namely the business carried on or the name or qualifications of the person carrying on a business from those premises.

4B Conditions and Limitations

(1) Subject to paragraph (12) below, no such advertisement is permitted within a conservation area, an area of outstanding natural beauty, a National Park or the Broads.

(2) In the case of a shop, no such advertisement may be displayed except on a wall containing a shop window.

(3) Not more than one such advertisement parallel to a wall and one projecting at right angles from such a wall is permitted, and in the case of any projecting advertisement—

(a) no surface may be greater than 0.75 square metre in area;
(b) the advertisement may not project more than 1 metre from the wall or two-thirds of the width of any footway or pavement below, whichever is the less;
(c) it may not be more than 1 metre high; and
(d) it may not project over any carriageway.

[(4) Illumination may be—

(a) by halo illumination, or
(b) so long as no part of the background of the advertisement is illuminated, by illumination of each character or symbol of the advertisement from within.]

(5) No such advertisement may include any intermittent light source, moving feature, exposed cold cathode tubing, [or animation].

(6) [Where the method of illumination is that described in paragraph (4)(b), the luminance]

of any such advertisement may not exceed the limits specified in paragraph 2 of Part II of this Schedule.

(7) In the case of any such advertisement consisting of a built-up box containing the light source, the distance between—

    (a) the face of the advertisement and any wall parallel to which it is displayed, at the point where it is affixed, or

    (b) the 2 faces of an advertisement projecting from a wall,

may not exceed 0.25 metre.

(8) The lowest part of any such advertisement shall be at least 2.5 metres above ground level.

(9) No surface of any advertisement may exceed one-sixth of the frontage on which it is displayed, measured up to a height of 4.6 metres from ground level or 0.2 of the frontage measured to the top of the advertisement, whichever is the less.

(10) No character or symbol on the advertisement may be more than 0.75 metre in height.

(11) No part of the advertisement may be higher above ground level than 4.6 metres or the bottom level of any first floor window in the wall on which the advertisement is displayed, whichever is the lower.

(12) Paragraph (1) above does not preclude the continued display of an advertisement being displayed at the date of designation of the relevant area until the expiry of 5 years from that date.

Class 5—Advertisements on business premises

5 Description

Any advertisement which does not fall within Class 4A or 4B displayed on business premises wholly with reference to any or all of the following matters, namely the business carried on, the goods sold or services provided, or the name or qualifications of the person carrying on the business, or supplying the goods or services, on those premises.

5 Conditions and Limitations

(1) In the case of a shop, no such advertisement may be displayed, except on a wall containing a shop window.

(2) In an area of special control, the space occupied by any such advertisement may not exceed 0.1 of the overall area of the face of the building on which it is displayed, up to a height of 3.6 metres from ground level; and the area occupied by any such advertisement shall, notwithstanding that it is displayed in some other manner, be calculated as if the whole advertisement were displayed flat against the face of the building.

(3) Illumination is not permitted unless the advertisement states that medical or similar services or supplies are available at the premises on which the advertisement is displayed and the illumination is in a manner reasonably required to fulfil the purpose of the advertisement.

(4) No character or symbol on the advertisement may be more than 0.75 metre in height, or 0.3 metre in an area of special control.

(5) No part of the advertisement may be higher above ground level than whichever is the lower of—

    (a) 4.6 metres, or 3.6 metres in an area of special control; or

    (b) the bottom level of any first floor window in the wall on which the advertisement is displayed.

Class 6—An advertisement on a forecourt of business premises

6 Description

An advertisement displayed on any forecourt of business premises, wholly with reference to all or any of the matters specified in Class 5.

6 Conditions and Limitations

(1) Advertisements displayed on any such forecourt or, in the case of a building with a forecourt on two or more frontages on each of those frontages, shall not exceed in aggregate 4.5 square metres in area.

(2) Illumination is not permitted.

(3) No character or symbol on the advertisement may be more than 0.75 metre in height, or 0.3 metre in an area of special control.

(4) No part of the advertisement may be more than 4.6 metres above ground level, or 3.6 metres in an area of special control.

[Class 7—Flag advertisements

7A Description

An advertisement in the form of a flag attached to a single flagstaff projecting vertically from the roof of a building.

7A Conditions and Limitations

(1) No such advertisement is permitted other than one—

  (a) bearing the name or device of any person occupying the building; or
  (b) referring to a specific event (other than the offering of named goods for sale) of limited duration, which is taking place in the building, for the duration of that event.

(2) No character or symbol on the flag may be more than 0.75 metre in height, or 0.3 metre in an area of special control.

7B Description

An advertisement in the form of a flag attached to a single vertical flagstaff erected on a site which forms part of an area of land in respect of which planning permission has been granted for development of which the only or principal component is residential development and on which—

  (a) operations for the construction of houses are in progress pursuant to that permission, or
  (b) such operations having been completed, at least one of the houses remains unsold.

7B Conditions and Limitations

(1) No such advertisement is permitted within a conservation area, an area of outstanding natural beauty, a National Park, the Broads or an area of special control.

(2) The number of such advertisements on the land concerned shall not exceed—

  (a) where the aggregate number of houses on that land does not exceed 10, one;
  (b) where the aggregate number of houses on that land exceeds 10 but does not exceed 100, two;
  (c) where the aggregate number of houses on that land exceeds 100, three.

(3) No part of the flagstaff may be more than 4.6 metres above ground level.

(4) No flag shall exceed 2 square metres in area.

(5) No such advertisement shall be displayed after the expiration of the period of 1 year commencing on the day on which building operations on the land concerned have been substantially completed.]

Class 8—Advertisements on hoardings

8 Description

An advertisement on a hoarding which encloses, either wholly or in part, land on which building operations are taking place or are about to take place, if those operations are in accordance with a grant of planning permission (other than outline permission) for development primarily for use for commercial, industrial or business purposes.

8 Conditions and Limitations

(1) Subject to paragraph (7) below, no such advertisement shall be displayed in a conservation area, a National Park, an area of outstanding natural beauty or the Broads.

(2) No such advertisement may be displayed earlier than [three months] before the commencement of the building operations.

(3) Any such advertisement shall be at least 1.5 metres high and 1 metre long and not more than 3.1 metres high and [12.1 metres long].

(4) At least 14 days before the advertisement is first displayed, the local planning authority shall be notified in writing by the person displaying it of the date on which it will first be displayed and shall be sent a copy of the relevant planning permission.

(5) No such advertisement shall be displayed for more than [3 years].

(6) Illumination is permitted in a manner and to the extent reasonably required to achieve the purpose of the advertisement.

(7) Paragraph (1) above does not preclude the continued display of an advertisement being displayed at the date of designation of the relevant area until the expiry of 1 year from that date or 2 years from the date of commencement of the display, whichever is the later.

Class 9—Advertisements on highway structures

9 Description

An advertisement displayed on a part of an object or structure designed to accommodate four-sheet panel displays, the use of which for the display of such advertisements is authorised under section 115E(1)(a) of the Highways Act 1980.

9 Conditions and Limitations

(1) No such advertisement may exceed [2.16 square metres] in area.

(2) Illumination is not permitted.

(3) No character or symbol on the advertisement may be more than 0.75 metre in height, or 0.3 metre in an area of special control.

(4) No part of the advertisement may be more than 4.6 metres above ground level, or 3.6 metres in an area of special control.

Class 10—Advertisements for neighbourhood watch and similar schemes

10 Description

An advertisement displayed on or near highway land (but not in the window of a building), to give notice that a neighbourhood watch scheme or a similar scheme established jointly by the police authority and a local committee or other body of persons is in operation in the area.

10 Conditions and Limitations

(1) No such advertisement may exceed 0.2 square metre in area.

(2) No such advertisement may be displayed on highway land without the consent of the highway authority.

(3) The local planning authority shall, at least 14 days before the advertisement is first displayed, be given particulars in writing of the place at which it is to be displayed and a certificate—

    (a) that the scheme has been properly established;
    (b) that the police authority have agreed to the display of the advertisement; and

(c) where relevant, that the consent of the highway authority has been given.

(4) Any such advertisement shall be removed within 14 days after—

(a) the relevant scheme ceases to operate;
(b) the relevant scheme ceases to be approved by the police authority; or
(c) the highway authority withdraw their consent to its display.

(5) Illumination is not permitted.

(6) No character or symbol on the advertisement may be more than 0.75 metre in height, or 0.3 metre in an area of special control.

(7) No part of the advertisement may be more than 3.6 metres above ground level.

Class 11—Directional advertisements

11 Description

An advertisement on a single flat surface directing potential buyers and others to a site where residential development is taking place.

11 Conditions and Limitations

(1) No such advertisement may exceed 0.15 square metre in area.

(2) No part of the advertisement may be of a reflective material.

(3) The design of the advertisement may not be similar to that of a traffic sign.

(4) The advertisement is to be displayed on land adjacent to highway land, in a manner which makes it reasonably visible to an approaching driver, but not within 50 metres of a traffic sign intended to be observed by persons approaching from the same direction.

(5) No advertisement may be more than two miles from the main entrance of the site.

(6) The local planning authority shall, at least 14 days before the advertisement is first displayed, be notified in writing of the place at which, and the first date on which, it will be displayed.

(7) No such advertisement may be displayed after the development of the site is completed or, in any event, for more than 2 years.

(8) Illumination is not permitted.

(9) Any character or symbol on the advertisement shall be at least 0.04 metre high.

(10) No character or symbol on the advertisement may be more than 0.25 metre high.

(11) No part of the advertisement may be more than 4.6 metres above ground level, or 3.6 metres in an area of special control.

Class 12—Advertisements inside buildings

12 Description

An advertisement displayed inside a building which does not fall within Class J in Schedule 2.

Class 13—Sites used for the display of advertisements on 1st April 1974

13 Description

An advertisement displayed on a site which was used for the display of advertisements without express consent on 1st April 1974 and has been so used continually since that date.

13 Conditions and Limitations

(1) No substantial increase in the extent, or substantial alteration in the manner, of the use of the site for the display of advertisements on 1st April 1974 is permitted.

(2) If any building or structure on which such an advertisement is displayed is required

by or under any enactment to be removed, no erection of any building or structure to continue the display is permitted.

Class 14—Advertisements displayed after expiry of express consent

14 Description

An advertisement displayed with express consent, after the expiry of that consent, unless—

(a) a condition to the contrary was imposed on the consent,
(b) a renewal of consent was applied for and refused.

14 Conditions and Limitations

(1) Any condition imposed on the relevant express consent is to continue to apply to any such advertisement.

(2) No advertisement may be displayed under this class except on a site which has been continually used for the purpose since the expiry of the express consent.   **[802]**

NOTES
Commencement: 6 April 1992.
Amended by SI 1994/2351, regs 5–8.

PART II
INTERPRETATION

1.—(1) In this Schedule—

"business premises" means any building or part of a building normally used for the purpose of any professional, commercial or industrial undertaking, or for providing services to members of the public or of any association, and includes a public restaurant, licensed premises and a place of public entertainment, but not—

(a) a building used as an institution of a religious, educational, cultural, recreational, or medical or similar character;
(b) a building designed for use as one or more separate dwellings, unless it was normally used, immediately before 1st September 1949, for any such purpose or has been adapted for use for any such purpose by the construction of a shop front or the making of a material alteration of a similar kind to its external appearance;
(c) any forecourt or other land forming part of the curtilage of a building;
(d) any fence, wall or similar screen or structure, unless it forms part of the fabric of a building;

"forecourt" includes any fence, wall or similar screen or structure enclosing a forecourt and not forming part of the fabric of a building constituting business premises;
"ground level", in relation to the display of advertisements on any building, means the ground-floor level of that building;
"highway land" means any land within the boundaries of a highway;
"joined boards" means boards joined at an angle, so that only one surface of each is usable for advertising;
"public transport undertaking" means an undertaking engaged in the carriage of passengers in a manner similar to that of a statutory undertaking;
"retail park" means a group of 3 or more retail stores, at least one of which has a minimum internal floor area of 1,000 square metres and which—

(a) are set apart from existing shopping centres but within an existing or proposed urban area;
(b) sell primarily goods other than food;
(c) share one or more communal car parks.

"traffic sign" means a sign falling within Class H of Schedule 2 to these Regulations.

(2) Where a maximum area is specified, in relation to any class in this Schedule, in the case of a double-sided board, the area of one side only shall be taken into account.

2.—(1) Subject to sub-paragraph (2), the permitted limits of luminance for advertisements falling within Class 4A or 4B are, for an illuminated area measuring not more than—

(a) 0.5 square metre, 1,000 candela per square metre,
(b) 2 square metres, 800 candela per square metre,
(c) 10 square metres, 600 candela per square metre,

and for any greater area, 400 candela per square metre.

(2) For the purposes of calculating the relevant area for the permitted limits—

(a) each advertisement, or in the case of a double-sided projecting advertisement, each side of the advertisement is to be taken separately;
(b) no unilluminated part of the advertisement is to be taken into account.

[3. In relation to advertisements within Class 4A or Class 4B ''halo illumination'' means illumination from within built-up boxes comprising characters or symbols where the only source of light is directed through the back of the box onto an otherwise unilluminated backing panel.

4.—(1) For the purposes of Class 7B—

''aggregate number'' means the aggregate of the number of houses constructed, in the course of construction or proposed to be constructed on the land concerned;

''flat'' mans a separate and self-contained set of premises constructed for the purpose of a dwelling and forming part of a building from some other part of which it is divided horizontally;

''house'' includes a flat;

''planning permission'' does not include any outline planning permission in relation to which some or all of the matters reserved for subsequent approval remain to be approved; and

''the land concerned'', in relation to any development, means—

(a) except in a case to which sub-paragraph (2) or (3) applies, the land to which the planning permission for the development relates;
(b) in a case to which sub-paragraph (2) applies, the land on which a particular phase of that development was or, as the case may be, is being or is about to be carried out;
(c) in a case to which sub-paragraph (3) applies, the part of the land to which the permission relates on which a person has carried out part of that development, or, as the case may be, is carrying it out or is about to carry it out.

(2) Subject to sub-paragraph (3), this sub-paragraph applies where the development is carried out in phases.

(3) This sub-paragraph applies where the development is carried out by two or more persons who each carry out part of it on a discrete part of the land to which the planning permission relates (whether the whole of the development or any part of it is carried out in phases or otherwise).]   **[803]**

NOTES
Commencement: 6 April 1992.
Paras 3, 4: added by SI 1994/2351, reg 9.

SCHEDULE 4
Regulations 13 and 15

MODIFICATIONS OF THE ACT

PART I

MODIFICATIONS OF SECTION 70A OF THE ACT (POWER OF LOCAL PLANNING AUTHORITY TO DECLINE TO DETERMINE APPLICATIONS)

1. In section 70A of the Act—

(a) in subsection (1)—

(i) for "planning permission for the development of any land" substitute "express consent";

(ii) in paragraph (a), omit the words "has refused a similar application referred to him under section 77 or"; and

(iii) for paragraph (b) substitute—

"(b) in the opinion of the authority there has been no significant change since the dismissal mentioned in paragraph (a) in any material consideration.";

(b) in subsection (2)—

(i) for "planning permission for the development of any land" substitute "express consent";

(ii) for "development" substitute "subject matter of the applications"; and

(iii) for "the applications" substitute "they".   **[804]**

NOTES
Commencement: 6 April 1992.

PART II

SECTION 70A OF THE ACT AS MODIFIED

70A.—(1) A local planning authority may decline to determine an application for express consent if—

(a) within the period of two years ending with the date on which the application is received, the Secretary of State has dismissed an appeal against the refusal of a similar application;

and

(b) in the opinion of the authority there has been no significant change since the dismissal mentioned in paragraph (a) in any material consideration.

(2) For the purposes of this section an application for express consent shall be taken to be similar to a later application if the subject matter of the applications and the land to which they relate are in the opinion of the local planning authority the same or substantially the same.   **[805]**

NOTES
Commencement: 6 April 1992.

PART III

MODIFICATIONS OF SECTIONS 78 AND 79 OF THE ACT (APPLICATIONS FOR EXPRESS CONSENT)

1. In section 78 of the Act—

(a) in subsection (1), for paragraphs (a), (b) and (c) substitute "refuse an application for express consent or grant it subject to conditions,";

(b) for subsection (2) substitute—

"(2) A person who has made an application for express consent may also appeal to the Secretary of State if within the period of 8 weeks from the date when the application was received by the local planning authority, that authority have neither given him notice of their decision on it nor given him notice that they have exercised their power under section 70A to decline to determine the application.";

(c) for subsection (3) substitute the following subsections—

"(3) Any appeal under subsection (1) or (2) shall be made by notice served within 8 weeks from the date of receipt of the local planning authority's decision, or, as the case may be, within 8 weeks from the expiry of the period mentioned in subsection (2), or within such longer period as the Secretary of State may in either case at any time allow.

(3A) The notice mentioned in subsection (3) shall be accompanied by a copy of each of the following documents—

(a) the application made to the local planning authority;
(b) all relevant plans and particulars submitted to them;
(c) any notice of decision; and
(d) any other relevant correspondence with the authority.'';

(d) for subsection (4) substitute—

"(4) Where an appeal is made to the Secretary of State as mentioned in subsection (3), he may require the appellant or the local planning authority to submit to him, within such period as he may specify, a statement in writing in respect of such matters relating to the application as he may specify, and if, after considering the grounds of appeal and any such statement, the Secretary of State is satisfied that he has sufficient information to enable him to determine the appeal he may, with the agreement in writing of both the appellant and the local planning authority, determine the appeal without complying with section 79(2).'';

(e) in subsection (5), omit references to sections 253(2)(c) and 266(1)(b).

2. In section 79 of the Act—

(a) after subsection (1) insert—

"(1A) The Secretary of State may, in granting an express consent, specify that the term thereof shall run for such longer or shorter period than 5 years as he considers expedient, having regard to regulation 4 of the Town and Country Planning (Control of Advertisements) Regulations 1992 and to any period specified in the application for consent.'';

(b) omit subsection (4);
(c) in subsection (5), for "such an appeal shall be final", substitute "an appeal under section 78 shall be final, and shall otherwise have effect as if it were a decision of the local planning authority.'';
(d) in subsection (6), for the words from "in respect of an application for planning permission" to "planning permission for that development", substitute "in respect of an application for express consent, the Secretary of State forms the opinion that, having regard to the Regulations mentioned in subsection (1A) and to any direction given under them, consent";
(e) in subsection (6A), after the word "appeal" the first time it appears, insert "as is mentioned in subsection (6)''.   **[806]**

NOTES

Commencement: 6 April 1992.

PART IV

SECTIONS 78 AND 79 OF THE ACT AS MODIFIED (APPLICATIONS FOR EXPRESS CONSENT)

78.—(1) Where a local planning authority refuse an application for express consent or grant it subject to conditions, the applicant may by notice appeal to the Secretary of State.

(2) A person who has made an application for express consent may also appeal to the Secretary of State if within the period of 8 weeks from the date when the application was received by the local planning authority, that authority have neither given him notice of their decision on it nor given him notice that they have exercised their power under section 70A to decline to determine the application.

(3) Any appeal under subsection (1) or (2) shall be made by notice served within 8 weeks from the date of receipt of the local planning authority's decision, or, as the case may be, within 8 weeks from the expiry of the period mentioned in subsection (2), or within such longer period as the Secretary of State may in either case at any time allow.

(3A) The notice mentioned in subsection (3) shall be accompanied by a copy of each of the following documents—

(a) the application made to the local planning authority;
(b) all relevant plans and particulars submitted to them;
(c) any notice of decision; and

(d) any other relevant correspondence with the authority.

(4) Where an appeal is made to the Secretary of State as mentioned in subsection (3), he may require the appellant or the local planning authority to submit to him, within such period as he may specify, a statement in writing in respect of such matters relating to the application as he may specify, and if, after considering the grounds of appeal and any such statement, the Secretary of State is satisfied that he has sufficient information to enable him to determine the appeal he may, with the agreement in writing of both the appellant and the local planning authority, determine the appeal without complying with section 79(2).

(5) For the purposes of the application of sections 79(1) and 288(10)(b) in relation to an appeal under subsection (2), it shall be assumed that the authority decided to refuse the application in question.

79.—(1) On an appeal under section 78 the Secretary of State may—

(a) allow or dismiss the appeal, or
(b) reverse or vary any part of the decision of the local planning authority (whether the appeal relates to that part of it or not),

and may deal with the application as if it had been made to him in the first instance.

(1A) The Secretary of State may, in granting an express consent, specify that the term thereof shall run for much longer or shorter period than 5 years as he considers expedient, having regard to regulation 4 of the Town and Country Planning (Control of Advertisements) Regulations 1992 and to any period specified in the application for consent.

(2) Before determining an appeal under section 78 the Secretary of State shall, if either the appellant or the local planning authority so wish, give each of them an opportunity of appearing before and being heard by a person appointed by the Secretary of State for the purpose.

(3) Subsection (2) does not apply to an appeal referred to a Planning Inquiry Commission under section 101.

(5) The decision of the Secretary of State on an appeal under section 78 shall be final, and shall otherwise have effect as if it were a decision of the local planning authority.

(6) If, before or during the determination of such an appeal in respect of an application for express consent, the Secretary of State forms the opinion that, having regard to the Regulations mentioned in subsection (1A) and to any direction given under them, consent—

(a) could not have been granted by the local planning authority; or
(b) could not have been granted otherwise than subject to the conditions imposed, he may decline to determine the appeal or to proceed with the determination.

(6A) If at any time before or during the determination of such an appeal as is mentioned in subsection (6) it appears to the Secretary of State that the appellant is responsible for undue delay in the progress of the appeal, he may—

(a) give the appellant notice that the appeal will be dismissed unless the appellant takes, within the period specified in the notice, such steps as are specified in the notice for the expedition of the appeal; and
(b) if the appellant fails to take those steps within that period, dismiss the appeal accordingly.

(7) Schedule 6 applies to appeals under section 78, including appeals under that section as applied by or under any other provision of this Act.   **[807]**

NOTES
Commencement: 6 April 1992.

PART V

MODIFICATIONS OF THE ACT (DISCONTINUANCE NOTICES)

1. In section 78 for subsections (1) to (5) substitute—

    "(1) Where a discontinuance notice has been served on any person by a local planning authority under regulation 8 of the Town and Country Planning (Control of Advertisements) Regulations 1992 that person may, if he is aggrieved by the notice, appeal by notice under this section to the Secretary of State.

(2) Notice of appeal shall be given in writing to the Secretary of State at any time before the date on which the discontinuance notice is due to take effect under regulation 8(3), taking account where appropriate of any extension of time under regulation 8(5), of those Regulations, or such longer period as the Secretary of State may allow, and the notice shall be accompanied by a copy of each of the following documents—

(a) the discontinuance notice;
(b) any notice of variation thereof, and
(c) any relevant correspondence with the authority.

(3) Where an appeal is brought under this section, the Secretary of State may require the appellant or the local planning authority to submit to him, within such period as he may specify, a statement in writing in respect of such matters relating to the discontinuance notice as he may specify and if, after considering the grounds of appeal and any such statement, the Secretary of State is satisfied that he has sufficient information to enable him to determine the appeal, he may, with the agreement in writing of both the appellant and the local planning authority, determine the appeal without complying with section 79(2).''.

2. In section 79—

(a) for subsection (1) substitute—

"(1) Where an appeal is brought in respect of a discontinuance notice the Secretary of State may—

(a) allow or dismiss the appeal, or
(b) reverse or vary any part of the discontinuance notice (whether the appeal relates to that part of it or not),

and may deal with the matter as if an application for express consent had been made and refused for the reasons stated for the taking of discontinuance action.'';

(b) for subsection (4) substitute—

"(4) On the determination of an appeal under section 78 the Secretary of State shall give such directions as may be necessary for giving effect to his determination, including, where appropriate, directions for quashing the discontinuance notice or for varying its terms in favour of the appellant.'';

(c) omit subsection (6);
(d) in subsection (6A), after the word "appeal" the first time it appears, insert "in respect of a discontinuance notice".　　　　　　　　　　　　　　　**[808]**

NOTES
Commencement: 6 April 1992.

SCHEDULE 5

Regulation 18

AREA OF SPECIAL CONTROL ORDERS

PART I

PROCEDURE FOR AREA OF SPECIAL CONTROL ORDERS

1. A local planning authority who propose—

(a) to designate an area of special control; or
(b) to modify an area of special control order,

shall make an area of special control order designating the area or indicating the modifications by reference to an annexed map.

2. If an area of special control order contains any descriptive matter relating to the area or

the modifications in question, that descriptive matter shall prevail, in the case of any discrepancy with the map, unless the order provides to the contrary.

3. As soon as may be after the making of an area of special control order, the authority shall submit it to the Secretary of State for approval, together with—

(a) two certified copies of the order;

(b) a full statement of their reasons for making it;

(c) in the case of an order modifying an existing order, unless the boundaries of the existing area of special control are indicated on the map annexed to the order, a plan showing both these boundaries and the proposed modifications; and

(d) any additional certified copy of any of the material in subparagraphs (a) to (c) above, which the Secretary of State requires.

4. The authority shall forthwith publish in the London Gazette, and in two successive weeks in at least one newspaper circulating in the locality, a notice in prescribed Form 1.

5. If any objection is made to an order, in the manner and within the time provided for in the prescribed form, the Secretary of State—

(a) may offer all interested parties an opportunity to make representations to him in writing about any such objection before such date as he may specify;

(b) may, and at the request of any interested party shall, either provide for a local inquiry to be held or afford to the parties an opportunity of a hearing before a person appointed by him.

6. After considering any representations or objections duly made and not withdrawn and, where applicable, the report of any person holding an inquiry or hearing, the Secretary of State may, subject to paragraph 7 below, approve the order with or without modifications.

7. If the Secretary of State proposes to make a modification for the inclusion of additional land in an order, he shall—

(a) publish notice of his intention to do so;

(b) afford an opportunity for the making of objections to, or representations about, the proposed modification; and

(c) if he considers it expedient, provide for a further inquiry or hearing to be held.

8. As soon as may be after the order has been approved, the local planning authority shall publish in the London Gazette, and in two successive weeks in at least one newspaper circulating in the locality, a notice of its approval in prescribed Form 2.

9. An area of special control order shall come into force on the date on which the notice of its approval is published in the London Gazette.

10. Where a local planning authority propose to make an order revoking an area of special control order, a map showing the existing area shall be annexed to the order, and the procedure prescribed in paragraphs 2 to 9 of this Schedule in relation to an order modifying an existing order shall be followed, subject to the modification that the prescribed forms of notice under paragraphs 4 and 8 respectively are prescribed Forms 3 and 4.

11. Any reference in this Part of this Schedule to a prescribed form is to the form bearing that number in Part II of this Schedule or a form substantially to the like effect. **[809]**

NOTES

Commencement: 6 April 1992.

PART II

FORMS OF NOTICE

FORM 1

NOTICE OF AN AREA OF SPECIAL CONTROL ORDER

Town and Country Planning Act 1990

1 Town and Country Planning (Control of Advertisements) Regulations 1992

We, the *(insert name of Council)* give notice that we have submitted an area of special control order, made under regulation 18 of the Town and Country Planning (Control of Advertisements) Regulations 1992, to the Secretary of State *for the Environment/for Wales for approval under Schedule 5 to the Regulations.

2. *The order designates the area of land described in the Schedule hereto and shown on the map accompanying the order.

Or

*The order modifies the (*insert name of relevant order*) by *adding/removing the area of land described in the Schedule hereto and shown on the map accompanying the order.

3. A copy of the order and of the statement of the reasons for making it have been deposited at and will be available for inspection free of charge between the hours of

4. The order is about to be considered by the Secretary of State. Any objection to it must be made in writing, stating the grounds of objection, and sent to the *Department of the Environment/Welsh Office at   before (*insert a date at least 28 days from the date of first publication of the local advertisement*).

Signed ....

On behalf of ....

Date ....

*Delete whichever is inappropriate

SCHEDULE

(insert description of land)

FORM 2

NOTICE OF APPROVAL OF AN AREA OF SPECIAL CONTROL ORDER

Town and Country Planning Act 1990

1 Town and Country Planning (Control of Advertisements) Regulations 1992

We, the (*insert name of Council*) give notice that the Secretary of State *for the Environment/for Wales has approved *with modifications the (*insert name of order*) for the purposes of Schedule 5 to the Town and Country Planning (Control of Advertisements) Regulations 1992.

2. The order *designates as an area of special control the land described in the Schedule hereto/modifies the (*insert name of relevant order*) by adding/removing the land described in the Schedule hereto.

3. The order comes into force on (*insert date of publication in London Gazette*).

4. A copy of the order as approved has been deposited at   and will be available for inspection free of charge between the hours of   .

IMPORTANT

Regulation 19 of the 1992 Regulations contains important provisions about—

The advertisements permitted in an area of special control.

The circumstances in which existing advertisements must be removed after this order comes into force.

Signed ....

On behalf of ....

Date ....

*Delete whichever is inappropriate

SCHEDULE

(insert description of land)

FORM 3

NOTICE OF REVOCATION OF AN AREA OF SPECIAL CONTROL ORDER

Town and Country Planning Act 1990

1 Town and Country Planning (Control of Advertisements) Regulations 1992

We, the *(insert name of Council)* give notice that we have submitted an order revoking the *(insert name of relevant order)* made under regulation 18 of the Town and Country Planning (Control of Advertisements) Regulations 1992 to the Secretary of State *for the Environment/ for Wales for approval under Schedule 5 to the Regulations.

2. A copy of the revocation order and of the statement of the reasons for making it have been deposited at   and will be available for inspection free of charge between the hours of   .

3. The revocation order is about to be considered by the Secretary of State. Any objection to it must be made in writing, stating the grounds of objection, and sent to the *Department of the Environment/Welsh Office at   before *(insert a date at least 28 days after the first publication of the local advertisement)*.

Signed ....

On behalf of ....

Date ....

*Delete whichever is inappropriate

FORM 4

NOTICE OF APPROVAL OF AN ORDER REVOKING AN AREA OF SPECIAL CONTROL ORDER

Town and Country Planning Act 1990

1 Town and Country Planning (Control of Advertisements) Regulations 1992

We, the *(insert name of Council)* give notice that the Secretary of State *for the Environment/for Wales has approved an order revoking the *(insert name of order revoked)* for the purposes of Schedule 5 to the Town and Country Planning (Control of Advertisements) Regulations 1992.

2. The revocation order comes into force on (insert date of publication in London Gazette).

3. A copy of the revocation order as approved has been deposited at and will be available for inspection free of charge between the hours of   .

Signed ....

On behalf of ....

Date ....

*Delete whichever is inappropriate
[810]

NOTES
Commencement: 6 April 1992.

TOWN AND COUNTRY PLANNING GENERAL REGULATIONS 1992
(SI 1992/1492)

NOTES
Made: 24 June 1992
Authority: Town and Country Planning Act 1990, ss 99(2), 107(1), 114(2), 115(2), 137(2), 144(2), 150(1), 151(1), 161(2), 162(1), 178(3), (5), 186(3), 209(3), 219(3), 250(3), 255, 316, 329(2), 333(1), 336(1)

1. Citation, commencement and interpretation

(1) These Regulations may be cited as the Town and Country Planning General Regulations 1992 and shall come into force on 17th July 1992.

(2) In these Regulations—

"the 1990 Act" means the Town and Country Planning Act 1990: and
"planning permission", except in regulations 7 to 9, includes any consent of
a local planning authority required under a development order.   **[811]**

NOTES
Commencement: 17 July 1992.

Land of interested planning authorities and development by them

2. Application of provisions of the 1990 Act

(1) Subject to paragraph (2), in relation to—

(a) land of an interested planning authority other than—

(i) land any part of which is within a National Park and which is land of a planning authority which is a non-metropolitan district council, and

(ii) land in respect of which an urban development corporation is a local planning authority and which is vested in another local planning authority, and

(b) development of any land by an interested planning authority or such authority jointly with any person other than development (whether or not jointly with any person)—

(i) by an interested planning authority which is a non-metropolitan district council of land any part of which is in a National Park, and

(ii) another local planning authority of land in respect of which an urban development corporation is a local planning authority,

the provisions of Parts III, VII and VIII of the 1990 Act, other than sections 76, 90(2), (5) and 223, shall apply subject to regulations 3 to 11 below.

(2) In the case of land falling within paragraph (1)(a)(i) the provisions of Part VIII of the 1990 Act apply subject to regulation 11.   **[812]**

NOTES
Commencement: 17 July 1992.

3. Applications for planning permission

Subject to regulation 4, an application for planning permission by an interested planning authority to develop any land of that authority, or for development of any land by an interested planning authority or by an interested planning authority jointly with any other person, shall be determined by the authority concerned, unless the application is referred to the Secretary of State under section 77 of the 1990 Act for determination by him. **[813]**

NOTES
Commencement: 17 July 1992.

4.—(1) Regulation 3 does not apply in the case of an application for planning permission to develop land of an interested planning authority where—

    (a) the authority do not intend to develop the land themselves or jointly with any person, and

    (b) if it were not such land the application would fall to be determined by another body.

(2) In the case of an application to which paragraph (1) applies the application shall be determined by that other body unless the application is referred to the Secretary of State under section 77 of the 1990 Act for determination by him. **[814]**

NOTES
Commencement: 17 July 1992.

5. Modifications and exceptions to Part III of the 1990 Act

(1) In the case of applications for planning permission for development to which regulation 3 applies—

    (a) sections 70A, 78 and 79 shall not apply;

    (b) sections 94 and 95 shall not apply except to the extent that they apply to a completion notice served under section 96 by the Secretary of State; and

    (c) the provisions of Part III of the 1990 Act listed in the first column of Schedule 1 to these Regulations shall have effect subject to the modifications in the second column of that Schedule.

(2) If an application for planning permission for development to which regulation 3 applies is referred to the Secretary of State under section 77 of the 1990 Act for determination by him that section shall have effect subject to the modification that, in subsection (5), for the words "if either the applicant or the local planning authority wish, give each of them an opportunity" substitute the words "if the interested planning authority wish, give them the opportunity". **[815]**

NOTES
Commencement: 17 July 1992.

6. In Part III of the 1990 Act any reference to "local planning authority", in relation to development to which regulation 3 applies, is a reference to the interested planning authority concerned, and references to "the authority" (except in section 71(3)) shall be construed accordingly. **[816]**

NOTES
Commencement: 17 July 1992.

7. Publicity

(1) Any provision made by virtue of section 65 or 71 of the 1990 Act by a development order shall apply to applications for planning permission for development to which regulation 3 applies subject to the modifications prescribed in paragraph (2).

(2) Any reference in such a development order to "local planning authority" is a reference to the interested planning authority concerned, and references to "the authority" shall be construed accordingly.	**[817]**

NOTES
Commencement: 17 July 1992.

8. Consultation

An urban development corporation in Greater London shall, before determining an application for planning permission falling within regulation 3, consult the council of the London borough for the area in which the land which is the subject of the application, or any part of it, is situated.	**[818]**

NOTES
Commencement: 17 July 1992.

9. Effect of planning permission

Any grant of planning permission by an interested planning authority for development [of any land by that interested planning authority] shall enure only for the benefit of the applicant interested planning authority, except in the case of development of any land by an interested planning authority jointly with any other person where that person is specified in the application for planning permission as a joint developer, in which case the permission shall enure for the benefit of the applicant interested planning authority and that other person.	**[819]**

NOTES
Commencement: 17 July 1992.
Amended by SI 1992/1982, reg 2.

10. Arrangements for discharge of functions

Notwithstanding anything in section 101 of the Local Government Act 1972 (arrangements for the discharge of functions by local authorities) no application for planning permission for development to which regulation 3 applies may be determined—

(a) by a committee or sub-committee of the interested planning authority concerned if that committee or sub-committee is responsible (wholly or partly) for the management of any land or buildings to which the application relates; or

(b) by an officer of the interested planning authority concerned if his responsibilities include any aspect of the management of any land or buildings to which the application relates.	**[820]**

NOTES
Commencement: 17 July 1992.

11. Other consents

Where an interested planning authority are seeking a consent of a local planning authority under Part III, VII or VIII of the 1990 Act other than planning permission to develop land or a consent under section 90(2) and that authority are themselves the local planning authority by whom such consent would be given, they shall make an application for such consent to the Secretary of State.	**[821]**

NOTES
Commencement: 17 July 1992.

General

12. Claims for compensation and purchase notices

(1) A claim for compensation made to a local planning authority under section 107 (including section 107 as applied by section 108), 114, 115, 144, 186 or 250 of the 1990 Act, or a purchase notice served on the council of a district or London borough under section 137 of that Act, shall be in writing and shall be served on that authority or council by delivering it at the offices of the authority or council, or by sending it by pre-paid post.

(2) The time within which any such claim or notice as is mentioned in paragraph (1) is served shall be 12 months from the date of the decision in respect of which the claim or notice is made or given, or such longer period as the Secretary of State may at any time in any particular case allow. **[822]**

NOTES
Commencement: 17 July 1992.

13. Marking of certain notices and documents

The manner in which any notice or document referred to in subsection (2) of section 329 of the 1990 Act shall be marked in order that it shall be taken to be duly served under paragraph (b) of that subsection shall be by inscribing clearly and legibly upon the notice or document, and upon the envelope containing it, the words "Important - This Communication affects your Property". **[823]**

NOTES
Commencement: 17 July 1992.

14. Application of the Public Health Act 1936 to certain notices

(1) The provisions of sections 276, 289 and 294 of the Public Health Act 1936 ("the 1936 Act") shall apply in relation to steps required to be taken by an enforcement notice, to requirements of a notice under section 207(1) of the 1990 Act, and to steps required to be taken by a notice under section 215 of that Act, as if—

    (a) references to a local authority were references to a local planning authority;
    (b) references (in whatever form) to the execution of works under the 1936 Act were references—

        (i) in the case of an enforcement notice or a notice under section 215 of the 1990 Act, to the taking of steps required to be taken by the notice; and
        (ii) in the case of a notice under section 207(1) of the 1990 Act, to the planting of trees of specified sizes and species;

    (c) references in section 289 of the 1936 Act to the occupier were references to a person having an interest in the premises other than the owner; and
    (d) the reference in section 294 of the 1936 Act to "expenses under this Act" were a reference to expenses incurred in the taking of steps or the planting of trees, as the case may be.

(2) The expenses recoverable by a local planning authority under section 178(1) of the 1990 Act are, until recovered, a charge that is binding on successive owners of the land to which the enforcement notice relates and the charge shall take effect as from the date of the completion by the local planning authority of the steps required to be taken by the enforcement notice. **[824]**

NOTES
Commencement: 17 July 1992.

15. Concurrent procedure for acquisition of land and extinguishment of rights of way

(1) Where—

    (a) under section 226 of the 1990 Act a compulsory purchase order for the acquisition of any land has been made by a local authority to whom that section applies and submitted to the Secretary of State in accordance with the provisions of the Acquisition of Land Act 1981, or

    (b) any land has been acquired by a local authority under section 227 of the 1990 Act,

the following provisions of this regulation shall have effect to secure that proceedings required to be taken for the purposes of orders under section 251 of the 1990 Act may be taken concurrently with any proceedings required to be taken for the purposes of the acquisition of the land over which the right of way is to be extinguished or for the purposes of the acquisition of any other land for the purpose of providing an alternative right of way.

(2) The Secretary of State may on or after such submission or acquisition as is mentioned in paragraph (1) publish in accordance with the provisions of section 252(1) of the 1990 Act notice of an order he proposes to make under section 251 of that Act relating to the extinguishment of any such right of way.

(3) On or after the publication of any such notice, the Secretary of State may prepare in draft, or a local highway authority may make, a compulsory purchase order under section 254(1)(b) of the 1990 Act for the acquisition of land for providing an alternative right of way.

(4) Subject to paragraph (5) any other proceedings required to be taken in connection with the making of an order under section 251 of the 1990 Act may be taken concurrently with the proceedings required to be taken in connection with such an order as is mentioned in paragraph (1)(a) and any other proceedings for the making or confirmation of such a compulsory purchase order as is referred to in paragraph (3) may be taken concurrently with either or both of the said proceedings.

(5) Until the land over which the right of way subsists has been acquired by the local authority—

    (i) no order under section 251 of the 1990 Act shall be made, and

    (ii) no such compulsory purchase order as is referred to in paragraph (3) shall be made by the Secretary of State or confirmed.   **[825]**

NOTES
Commencement: 17 July 1992.

16. Notices and counter-notices relating to planning blight

The forms set out in Schedule 2 to these Regulations or forms substantially to the like effect are the prescribed forms for blight notices and counter-notices for the purposes of sections 150(I), 151(1), 161(2) and 162(1) of the 1990 Act.   **[826]**

NOTES
Commencement: 17 July 1992.

17. Advertisement and notice of unopposed order revoking or modifying planning permission

(1) A local planning authority shall advertise the fact that an order has been made to which section 99(2) of the 1990 Act applies by publishing an advertisement in the form set out in Part 1 of Schedule 3 to these Regulations or a form substantially to the like effect in a newspaper circulating in the locality.

(2) The notice a local planning authority is required to serve under section 99(3) of the 1990 Act shall be in the form contained in Part 2 of Schedule 3 to these Regulations or a form substantially to the like effect. **[827]**

NOTES
　　Commencement: 17 July 1992.

18. Revocations

The regulations listed in the first column of Schedule 4 to these Regulations are hereby revoked to the extent specified in the third column of that Schedule. **[828]**

NOTES
　　Commencement: 17 July 1992.

SCHEDULE 1

Regulation 5

Provision of the 1990 Act	Modification
Section 62	In paragraph (b) omit the words ''or by directions given by the local planning authority under them''
Section 93	In subsection (2) omit paragraph (b) and the word ''or'' immediately preceding it. Omit subsection (3).
Section 95	In subsection (3) for the words ''him and the local planning authority'' substitute the words ''that person''.
Section 96	Omit subsection (3).
Section 98	In subsection (4) for the words ''both to him and the local planning authority'' substitute the words ''to that person''.
Section 100	Omit subsections (3) to (6).
Section 103	In subsection (5) for the words ''both to him and the local planning authority'' substitute the words ''to that person''.
Section 104	Omit subsections (3) to (7).
Schedule 5	Omit paragraph 1(6)(b).

[829]

NOTES
　　Commencement: 17 July 1992.

SCHEDULE 2

Regulation 16

TOWN AND COUNTRY PLANNING ACT 1990

Blight Notice

To *(insert name of the appropriate authority)*

At *(insert address of the appropriate authority)*

I/We ....of ....*(give full name(s)
and address(es) of claimant(s))*

HEREBY GIVE YOU NOTICE under section 150(1) [and by virtue of section 158] *(delete
unless this notice relates to an agricultural unit and a claim and requirement under section
158(2) of the Act are to be included)* of the Town and Country Planning Act 1990 ("the Act")
as follows:—

1. I am/We are entitled to the interest described in Schedule 1 *(Schedule 1 should contain
a description of the interest of the claimant, a list of any mortgages to which that interest is
subject with the names and addresses of the mortgagees, and a list of any other incumbrances
affecting the interest)* to this Notice in the property described in Schedule 2 *(the boundaries
of the property should normally be clearly marked on a plan annexed to the Blight Notice)* to
this Notice.

2. The whole/Part of *(use "Part" instead of "The whole" if only some of the land is
blighted land)* that property is blighted land within paragraph(s) *(insert relevant paragraph
number(s))* of Schedule 13 to the Act.

3. My/Our interest in that property qualifies for protection under Chapter II in Part VI of
the Act because

[EITHER]

the property is [part of] *(delete unless the interest is in only part of the hereditament or unit)*
a hereditament whose annual value does not exceed the amount prescribed for the purposes of
section 149(3)(a) of the Act and I am an owner-occupier/we are owner-occupiers of that
hereditament.

[OR]

the property is [part of] *(delete unless the interest is in only part of the hereditament or unit)*
a hereditament and I am a resident owner-occupier/we are resident owner-occupiers of that
hereditament.

[OR]

the property is [part of] *(delete unless the interest is in only part of the hereditament or unit)*
an agricultural unit and I am an owner-occupier/we are owner-occupiers of that unit.

4. (1) *[EITHER]* I/We have made reasonable endeavours to sell my/our interest in that
property, and details of those attempts are set out in [Schedule 3 to/the letter accompanying]
(delete as appropriate) this Notice. *[OR]* The powers of compulsory acquisition relevant for
the purposes of paragraph 21/22 of Schedule 13 to the Act remain exercisable *(the second
alternative may be used only if paragraph 2 of this notice refers to paragraph 21 or 22 of
Schedule 13 to the Act)*.

(2) In consequence of the fact that [part of] *(delete unless only part of the property is
blighted land)* the hereditament/agricultural unit was, or was likely to be, comprised in
blighted land, I/we have been unable to sell my/our interest except at a price substantially
lower than that for which it might reasonably have been expected to sell if no part of the
hereditament/unit were, or were likely to be, comprised in blighted land.

5. The [part of the] *(delete unless the interest is in only part of the hereditament or unit)*
agricultural unit in which my/our interest subsists contains land which is not blighted land as
well as land which is, and the land which is not blighted land is not reasonably capable of
being farmed, either by itself or with other relevant land, as a separate agricultural unit *(use
this paragraph (and the reference to section 158 at the top of the notice) only to make a claim
under section 158(2))*.

6. I/We therefore require you to purchase my/our interest in

[EITHER]

the property described in Schedule 2 to this Notice *(use if the property is a hereditament, or is an agricultural unit and paragraph 5 has been included)*.

[OR]

so much of the property described in Schedule 2 to this Notice as is blighted land *(use if the property is an agricultural unit but paragraph 5 has been deleted)*.

SCHEDULE 1

The Interest to which this Blight Notice Relates

SCHEDULE 2

The Property to which this Blight Notice Relates

SCHEDULE 3

Details of Attempts to Sell the Interest to which the Blight Notice Relates

Dated ....

Signed ....

[Solicitor/Surveyor/Land Agent, of ....

on behalf of ....] *(if this notice is signed by an agent insert here full name and address of agent or firm, and name(s) of claimant(s))*

TOWN AND COUNTRY PLANNING ACT 1990

Personal Representative's Blight Notice

To *(insert name of the appropriate authority)*

At *(insert address of the appropriate authority)*

I/We ....of ....*(give full name(s) and address(es) of claimant(s))*

HEREBY GIVE YOU NOTICE under section 161(2) [and by virtue of section 158] *(delete unless this notice relates to an agricultural unit and a claim and requirement under section 158(2) of the Act are to be included)* of the Town and Country Planning Act 1990 (''the Act'') as follows:—

1. I am/We are the personal representative(s) of a person (''the deceased'') who at the time of his/her death was entitled to the interest described in Schedule 1 *(Schedule 1 should contain a description of the interest of the deceased, a list of any mortgages to which that interest is subject with the names and addresses of the mortgagees, and a list of any other incumbrances affecting the interest)* to this Notice in the property described in Schedule 2 *(the boundaries of the property should normally be clearly marked on a plan annexed to the Blight Notice)* to this Notice.

2. One or more individuals are, to the exclusion of any body corporate, beneficially entitled to the deceased's interest in that property.

3. The whole/Part of *(use ''Part'' instead of ''The whole'' if only some of the land was blighted land)* that property was blighted land within paragraph(s) *(insert relevant paragraph number(s))* of Schedule 13 to the Act on the date of death of the deceased.

4. The deceased's interest in that property qualifies for protection under Chapter II in Part VI of the Act because on the date of death of the deceased

[EITHER]

the property was [part of] *(delete unless the interest is in only part of the hereditament or unit)* a hereditament whose annual value did not exceed the amount prescribed for the purposes of section 149(3)(a) of the Act and he/she was an owner-occupier of that hereditament.

[OR]

the property was [part of] *(delete unless the interest is in only part of the hereditament or unit)* a hereditament and he/she was a resident owner-occupier of that hereditament.

[OR]

the property was [part of] *(delete unless the interest is in only part of the hereditament or unit)* an agricultural unit and he/she was an owner-occupier of that unit.

5. (1) *[EITHER]* I/We have made reasonable endeavours to sell his/her interest in that property, and details of those attempts are set out in [Schedule 3 to/the letter accompanying] *(delete as appropriate)* this Notice. *[OR]* The powers of compulsory acquisition relevant for the purposes of paragraph 21/22 of Schedule 13 to the Act remain exercisable *(the second alternative may be used only if paragraph 3 of this notice refers to paragraph 21 or 22 of Schedule 13 to the Act)*.

(2) In consequence of the fact that [part of] *(delete unless only part of the property was blighted land)* the hereditament/agricultural unit was, or was likely to be, comprised in blighted land, I/we have been unable to sell the deceased's interest except at a price substantially lower than that for which it might reasonably have been expected to sell if no part of the hereditament/unit were, or were likely to be, comprised in blighted land.

6. The [part of the] *(delete unless the interest is in only part of the hereditament or unit)* agricultural unit in which the deceased's interest subsists contains land which is not blighted land as well as land which is, and the land which is not blighted land is not reasonably capable of being farmed, either by itself or with other relevant land, as a separate agricultural unit *(use this paragraph (and the reference to section 158 at the top of the notice) only to make a claim under section 158(2))*.

7. I/We therefore require you to purchase the deceased's interest in

[EITHER]

the property described in Schedule 2 to this Notice *(use if the property is a hereditament, or is an agricultural unit and paragraph 6 has been included)*.

[OR]

so much of the property described in Schedule 2 to this Notice as is blighted land *(use if the property is an agricultural unit but paragraph 5 has been deleted)*.

SCHEDULE 1
The Interest to which this Blight Notice Relates

SCHEDULE 2
The Property to which this Blight Notice Relates

SCHEDULE 3
Details of Attempts to Sell the Interest to which the Blight Notice Relates

Dated ....

Signed ....
....

[Solicitor/Surveyor/Land Agent, of ....

on behalf of ....] *(if this notice is signed by an agent insert here full name and address of agent or firm, and name(s) of claimant(s))*

TOWN AND COUNTRY PLANNING ACT 1990

Mortgagee's Blight Notice

To *(insert name of the appropriate authority)*

At *(insert address of the appropriate authority)*

I/We ....of ....*(give full name(s) and address(es) of claimant(s))*

HEREBY GIVE YOU NOTICE under section 162(1) [and by virtue of section 158] *(delete unless this notice relates to an agricultural unit and a claim and requirement under section 158(2) of the Act are to be included)* of the Town and Country Planning Act 1990 ("the Act") as follows:—

1. I am/We are entitled as mortgagee(s) by virtue of a power which has become exercisable, to sell the interest described in Schedule 1 *(Schedule 1 should contain a description of the interest which the claimant has power to sell, and a list of any other incumbrances to which (to the knowledge or belief of the claimant) that interest is subject, with the names and addresses of the mortgagees(* to this Notice in the property described in Schedule 2 *(the boundaries of the property should normally be clearly marked on a plan annexed to the Blight Notice)* to this Notice, giving immediate vacant possession of the land.

2. The whole/Part of *(use "Part" instead of "The whole" if only some of the land was blighted land)* that property is blighted land within paragraph(s) *(insert relevant paragraph number(s))* of Schedule 13 to the Act.

3. The said interest in that property qualifies for protection under Chapter II in Part VI of the Act because

[EITHER]

that property is [part of] *(delete unless the interest is in only part of the hereditament or unit)* a hereditament whose annual value does not exceed the amount prescribed for the purposes of section 149(3)(a) of the Act and the person entitled (otherwise than as mortgagee) to the interest [is an owner-occupier of that hereditament] [was an owner-occupier of that hereditament on and [part of] *(use "Part" instead of "The whole" if only some of the land was blighted land)* that property was blighted land on that date] *(the second alternative may only be used if the claimant was the relevant owner-occupier on the date inserted, being a date not more than six months before the service of this notice)*.

[OR]

that property is [part of] *(delete unless the interest is in only part of the hereditament or unit)* a hereditament and the person entitled (otherwise than as mortgagee) to the interest [is a resident owner-occupier of that hereditament] [was a resident owner-occupier of that hereditament on and [part of] *(use "Part" instead of "The whole" if only some of the land was blighted land)* that property was blighted land on that date] (the second alternative may only be used if the claimant was the relevant owner-occupier on the date inserted, being a date not more than six months before the service of this notice).

[OR]

that property is [part of] *(delete unless the interest is in only part of the hereditament or unit)* an agricultural unit and the person entitled (otherwise than as mortgagee) to the interest [is an owner-occupier of that agricultural unit] [was an owner-occupier of that unit on .. , and [part of] *(use "Part" instead of "The whole" if only some of the land was blighted land)* that property was blighted land on that date] *(the second alternative may only be used if the claimant was the relevant owner-occupier on the date inserted, being a date not more than six months before the service of this notice)*.

4. (1) *[EITHER]* I/We have made reasonable endeavours to sell the said interest in that property, and details of those attempts are set out in [Schedule 3 to/the letter accompanying] *(delete as appropriate)* this Notice. *[OR]* The powers of compulsory acquisition relevant for the purposes of paragraph 21/22 of Schedule 13 to the Act remain exercisable *(the second alternative may be used only if paragraph 2 of this notice refers to paragraph 21 or 22 of Schedule 13 to the Act).*

(2) In consequence of the fact that [part of] *(delete unless only part of the property was blighted land)* the hereditament/agricultural unit was, or was likely to be, comprised in blighted land, I/we have been unable to sell the interest except at a price substantially lower than that for which it might reasonably have been expected to sell if no part of the hereditament/ unit were, or were likely to be, comprised in blighted land.

5. The [part of the] *(delete unless the interest is in only part of the hereditament or unit)* agricultural unit in which the interest subsists contains land which is not blighted land as well as land which is, and the land which is not blighted land is not reasonably capable of being farmed, either by itself or with other relevant land, as a separate agricultural unit *(use this paragraph (and the reference to section 158 at the top of the notice) only to make a claim under section 158(2)).*

[EITHER]

6. I/We therefore require you to purchase the said interest *(use if the property is a hereditament, or is an agricultural unit and paragraph 5 has been included).*

[OR]

7. I/We therefore require you to purchase the said interest so far as it subsists in property which is described in Schedule 2 to this Notice and which is blighted land *(use if the property is an agricultural unit but paragraph 5 has been deleted).*

SCHEDULE 1

The Interest to which this Blight Notice Relates

SCHEDULE 2

The Property to which this Blight Notice Relates

SCHEDULE 3

Details of Attempts to Sell the Interest to which the Blight Notice Relates

Dated ....

Signed ....
....

[Solicitor/Surveyor/Land Agent, of ....

on behalf of ....] *(if this notice is signed by an agent insert here full name and address of agent or firm, and name(s) of claimant(s))*

TOWN AND COUNTRY PLANNING ACT 1990

Counter-Notice objecting to Blight Notice

To *(insert name(s) of claimant(s) as on Blight Notice)*

of *(insert address(es) of claimant(s) as on Blight Notice)*

THE [   ] *(insert name of authority serving counter-notice)* HEREBY GIVE[S] YOU NOTICE under section 151(1) of the Town and Country Planning Act 1990 that they/he OBJECT(S) to the Blight Notice served by you/by *(insert name of claimant's agent, if Blight Notice was served by an agent)* on your behalf on *(insert date when Blight Notice was received by authority)* under section 150(1)/161(2)/162(1) [and by virtue of section 158] of that Act in respect of the property described in [the Blight Notice/as appropriate] as *(insert description of property as in Blight Notice, or (where appropriate) in document referred to in Blight Notice).*

[EITHER]

The ground on which objection is taken is, under section 151(4)( ) *(insert letter of relevant paragraph of section 151(4))*/159(1) *(only applicable if Blight Notice was served by virtue of section 158)*/161(5) *(only applicable if Blight Notice was served under section 161(2))*/162(5) *(only applicable if Blight Notice was served under section 162(1))* of the said Act, that [   ] *(complete as appropriate).*

[OR]

The grounds on which objection is taken are—

(1) under section 151(4)( ) *(insert letter of relevant paragraph of section 151(4); use a separate numbered paragraph in this form for each ground of objection under section 151(4))* of the said Act, that [   ] *(complete as appropriate)*;

(2) under section 159(1) *(only applicable if Blight Notice was served by virtue of section 158)* of the said Act, that [   ] *(complete as appropriate)*;

(3) under section 161(5)( ) *(only applicable if Blight Notice was served under section 161(2); insert letter of relevant paragraph of section 161(5) and use a separate paragraph in this form for each ground of objection under section 161(5))*/162(5)( ) *(only applicable if Blight Notice was served under section 162(1); insert letter of relevant paragraph of section 162(5) and use a separate paragraph in this form for each ground of objection under section 162(5))* of the said Act, that [   ] *(complete as appropriate).*

Dated ....

....

[NAME]

On behalf of *(insert name of authority serving counter-notice)*

NOTE TO CLAIMANT: If you do not accept this objection, you may require the objection to be referred to the Lands Tribunal, under the provisions of section 153 of the Town and Country Planning Act 1990. In that case you should notify the Registrar, The Lands Tribunal, 48/49 Chancery Lane, London WC2A IJR within 2 months of the date of service of this notice.   **[830]**

NOTES
Commencement: 17 July 1992.

SCHEDULE 3

PART 1

TOWN AND COUNTRY PLANNING ACT 1990

Advertisement under section 99(2) of the making of a revocation order or modification order

Planning permission for *(insert description of the development for which permission has been granted)* at *(insert site or locality of development)*

NOTICE IS HEREBY GIVEN THAT THE *(insert name of council)* Council have made an order under section 97 of the Town and Country Planning Act 1990 to [revoke the above planning permission] [to the following extent *(insert particulars of extent of revocation)*] [modify the above planning permission as follows *(insert particulars of modification)*]*.

The Council have been notified in writing by the owner and the occupier of the land [and by all other persons who in the Council's opinion will be affected by the order]* that they do not object to the order.

Any person who will be affected by the order and who wishes for an opportunity of appearing before, and being heard by, a person appointed by the [Secretary of State for the Environment] [Secretary of State for Wales]* must give notice in writing to that effect to the

[Regional Controller (Planning) at the appropriate Regional Office of the Department of the Environment] [Secretary, Legal Group, Welsh Office, Cathays Park, Cardiff CFI 3NQ]* not later than   19   *(insert a date not less than 28 days later than the date on which the relevant advertisement first appears)*.

If no such notice has been given by that date, the order will take effect, by virtue of the provisions of section 99(7) of the Town and Country Planning Act 1990, on   19 *(insert a date not less than 14 days later than the date to which above date) relates)* without being confirmed by the Secretary of State.

*Delete where inappropriate.   **[831]**

NOTES
  Commencement: 17 July 1992.

PART 2

TOWN AND COUNTRY PLANNING ACT 1990

Notice under section 99(3) of the making of a revocation order or modification order

Planning permission for *(insert description of the development for which permission has been granted)* at *(insert site or locality of development)*TAKE NOTICE THAT THE *(insert name of council)* Council have made an order under section 97 of the Town and Country Planning Act 1990 to [revoke the above planning permission] [to the following extent *(insert particulars of extent of revocation)*] [modify the above planning permission as follows *(insert particulars of modification)*]*.

The Council have been notified in writing by the owner and the occupier of the land [and by all other persons who in the Council's opinion will be affected by the order]* that they do not object to the order.

If you will be affected by the order and wish for an opportunity of appearing before, and being heard by, a person appointed by the [Secretary of State for the Environment] [Secretary of State for Wales]* you should give notice in writing to that effect to the [Regional Controller (Planning) at the appropriate Regional Office of the Department of the Environment] [Secretary, Legal Group, Welsh Office, Cathays Park, Cardiff CFI 3NO]* not later than 19   *(insert a date not less than 28 days later than the date on which the relevant advertisement first appears)*.

If no such notice has been given by that date, the order will take effect, by virtue of the provisions of section 99(7) of the Town and Country Planning Act 1990, on   19 *(insert a date not less than 14 days later than the date to which note (f) relates)* without being confirmed by the Secretary of State.

* Delete where inappropriate.   **[832]**

NOTES
  Commencement: 17 July 1992.

SCHEDULE 4

Regulations revoked	References	Extent of revocation
The Town and Country Planning General Regulations 1976.	S.I. 1976/1419.	The whole Regulations.
The Town and Country Planning General (Amendment) Regulations 1981.	S.I. 1981/558.	The whole Regulations.
The Town and Country Planning (Local Government Reorganisation) (Miscellaneous Amendments) Regulations 1986.	S.I. 1986/443.	Paragraphs 1 to 4 of Schedule 1.

Regulations revoked	References	Extent of revocation
The Town and Country Planning (Enforcement Notices and Appeals) Regulations 1991.	S.I. 1991/2804.	Regulation 10(1).

[833]

NOTES
    Commencement: 17 July 1992.

TOWN AND COUNTRY PLANNING (SPECIAL ENFORCEMENT NOTICES) REGULATIONS 1992
(SI 1992/1562)

NOTES
    Made: 29 June 1992
    Authority: Town and Country Planning Act 1990, ss 295(6), 333(1)

1. Citation and commencement

These Regulations may be cited as the Town and Country Planning (Special Enforcement Notices) Regulations 1992, and shall come into force on 27th July 1992.   **[834]**

NOTES
    Commencement: 27 July 1992.

2. Special enforcement notices

The provisions of the Town and Country Planning Act 1990 specified in the Schedule to these Regulations shall apply to special enforcement notices and to appeals against such notices under section 295(3) of the Town and Country Planning Act 1990 as if the references in those provisions to an enforcement notice were references to a special enforcement notice and subject to the further modifications specified in that Schedule.   **[835]**

NOTES
    Commencement: 27 July 1992.

3. Revocation

The Town and Country Planning (Special Enforcement Notices) Regulations 1984 are hereby revoked.   **[836]**

NOTES
    Commencement: 27 July 1992.

SCHEDULE

Provisions of the Town and Country Planning Act 1990 applied	Modifications
Section 173(10)	in subsection (10)— (a) for "section 172", substitute "section 295(1)"; and (b) for "section 174" substitute "section 295(3)".
Section 173A	In subsection (1)(b), for "section 173(9)" substitute "section 294(6) and (7)".
Section 175(5) and (7)	None.
Section 179	In subsections (1) and (2), for "owner" substitute "occupier" in each place that it occurs. Omit subsections (4) and (5). In subsection (6), omit "or (5)".
Section 180(1) and (3)	In subsection (1), omit"; or (b) a breach of condition notice". In subsection (3), omit "or breach of condition notice".
Section 181	In subsection (2), omit", to the extent that it is in contravention of Part III". In subsection (3), omit all the words afier "were removed or altered". Omit subsection (4).
Section 183	In subsection (6), for "have an interest in" substitute "be occupying".
Section 184	In subsection (8), for "section 172" substitute "section 295(1)".
Section 186	In subsection (1), for paragraphs (a) to (c) substitute— "(a) the special enforcement notice is quashed; (b) the special enforcement notice is varied so that any activity the carrying out of which is prohibited by the stop notice ceases to be a relevant activity; (c) the special enforcement notice is withdrawn by the local planning authority;".
Section 187	None.
Section 188	None.
Section 285(1) and (2)	In subsection (1), for "Part VII" substitute "section 295(3)". In subsection (2)— (a) for paragraph (a) substitute— "(a) has occupied the land since before the special enforcement notice was issued under section 294(3);"; and (b) in paragraph (b), for "that Part" substitute "section 295(1)".
Section 289	In subsection (1), for "Part VII" substitute "section 295(3)".
Section 322	None.
Section 322A	None.

[837]

NOTES
Commencement: 27 July 1992.

TOWN AND COUNTRY PLANNING (ENFORCEMENT)
(INQUIRIES PROCEDURE) RULES 1992
(1992/1903)

NOTES
Made: 29 July 1992
Authority: Tribunals and Inquiries Act 1971, s 11; now have effect under Tribunals and Inquiries Act 1992, s 9

1. Citation and commencement

These Rules may be cited as the Town and Country Planning (Enforcement) (Inquiries Procedure) Rules 1992 and shall come into force on 1st September 1992.

[838]

NOTES
Commencement: 1 September 1992.

2. Interpretation

In these Rules, unless the context otherwise requires—

"assessor" means a person appointed by the Secretary of State to sit with an inspector at an inquiry or re-opened inquiry to advise the inspector on such matters arising as the Secretary of State may specify;

"certificate of lawful use or development" means a certificate under section 191 or 192 of the Planning Act;

"development order" has the meaning given in section 59 of the Planning Act; '-document" includes a photograph map or plan;

"enforcement appeal" means an appeal against an enforcement notice; 'enforcement notice" means a notice under section 172 of the Planning Act or under section 38 of the Listed Buildings Act;

"inquiry" means a local inquiry in relation to which these Rules apply; "inspector" means—

(a) in relation to a transferred appeal, the person appointed by the Secretary of State to determine the appeal;

(b) in relation to a non-transferred~appeal, the person appointed by the Secretary of State to hold the relevant inquiry or re-opened inquiry;

"land" means the land or building to which an inquiry relates;

"Listed Buildings Act" means the Planning (Listed Buildings and Conservation Areas) Act 1990;

"local planning authority" means—

(a) in relation to an enforcement appeal, the authority who issued the relevant enforcement notice;

(b) in relation to an appeal against the refusal or non-determination of an application for a certificate of lawful use or development, the authority to whom the application was made;

"non-transferred appeal" means an appeal which falls to be determined by the Secretary of State, including an appeal which falls to be so determined by virtue of a direction under paragraph 3(1) of Schedule 6 to the Planning Act or paragraph 3(1) of Schedule 3 to the Listed Buildings Act;

"Planning Act" means the Town and Country Planning Act 1990;

"pre-inquiry meeting" means a meeting held before an inquiry to consider what may be done with a view to securing that the inquiry is conducted efficiently and expeditiously, and where two or more such meetings are held references to the conclusion of a preinquiry meeting are references to the conclusion of the final meeting;

"relevant date" means the date of the Secretary of State's written notice to the appellant and the local planning authority of his intention to cause an inquiry to be held, and "relevant notice" means that notice;

"statement of case" means, and is comprised of, a written statement which contains full particulars of the case which a person proposes to put forward at an inquiry, and a list of any documents which that person intends to refer to or put in evidence;

"transferred appeal" means an appeal which falls to be determined by a person appointed by the Secretary of State under Schedule 6 to the Planning Act or Schedule 3 to the Listed Buildings Act.   **[839]**

NOTES
Commencement: 1 September 1992.

3. Application of Rules

These Rules apply in relation to any local inquiry held in England or Wales for the purposes of an appeal made on or after 1st September 1992 under—

(a) section 174 of the Planning Act (appeal against enforcement notice);

(b) section 195 of the Planning Act (appeal against refusal or non-determination of an application for a certificate of lawful use or development);

(c) section 39 of the Listed Buildings Act (appeal against listed building enforcement notice) or under that section as applied by virtue of section 74(3) of that Act (appeal against conservation area enforcement notice),

but do not apply to any local inquiry by reason of the application of any provision mentioned in this rule by or under any other enactment.   **[840]**

NOTES
Commencement: 1 September 1992.

4. Preliminary information to be supplied by local planning authority—enforcement appeal

In the case of an enforcement appeal, the local planning authority shall, on receipt of a relevant notice, forthwith inform the appellant in writing of the name and address of any person on whom a copy of the enforcement notice has been served.   **[841]**

NOTES
Commencement: 1 September 1992.

5. Notification of identity of inspector

(1) The Secretary of State shall, subject to paragraph (2), notify the name of the inspector to every person entitled to appear at the inquiry.

(2) Where the Secretary of State appoints another inspector instead of the person previously appointed and it is not practicable to notify the new appointment before the inquiry is held, the inspector holding the inquiry shall, at its commencement, announce his name and the fact of his appointment.   **[842]**

NOTES
Commencement: 1 September 1992.

6. Pre-inquiry meeting

(1) An inspector may hold a pre-inquiry meeting if he thinks it desirable.

(2) The inspector shall arrange for not less than 2 weeks written notice of a meeting he proposes to hold under paragraph (1) to be given to the local planning authority, the appellant, any person known at the date of the notice to be entitled to appear at the inquiry and any other person whose presence at the meeting appears to him to be desirable.

(3) The inspector shall preside at the meeting and shall determine the matters to be discussed and the procedure to be followed, and he may require any person present at the meeting who, in his opinion, is behaving in a disruptive manner, to leave and may refuse to permit that person to return to or attend any further meeting, or may permit him to return or attend only on such conditions as he may specify.

[843]

NOTES
Commencement: 1 September 1992.

7. Statement of relevant matters

In the case of a non-transferred appeal, the Secretary of State may, and in the case of a transferred appeal, the inspector may, before an inquiry is held for the purpose of the appeal, serve on the local planning authority, the appellant, any person required to serve a statement of case pursuant to rule 8(4) and, in the case of an enforcement appeal, any person on whom a copy of the enforcement notice has been served, a statement of the matters about which he particularly wishes to be informed for the purposes of his consideration of the appeal. **[844]**

NOTES
Commencement: 1 September 1992.

8. Service of statements of case etc

(1) The local planning authority shall—

    (a) where the date fixed for the holding of the inquiry is less than 18 weeks after the relevant date, at least 6 weeks before the date fixed for the holding of the inquiry; or

    (b) in any other case, not later than 12 weeks after the relevant date,

serve a statement of case on the Secretary of State, the appellant and, in the case of an enforcement appeal, any person on whom a copy of the enforcement notice has been served.

(2) The appellant shall—

    (a) where the date fixed for the holding of the inquiry is less than 18 weeks after the relevant date, at least 3 weeks before the date fixed for the holding of the inquiry; or

    (b) in any other case, not later than 15 weeks after the relevant date,

serve a statement of case on the Secretary of State, the local planning authority and, in the case of an enforcement appeal, any person on whom a copy of the enforcement notice has been served.

(3) The local planning authority and the appellant may each require the other to

send to them a copy of any document, or of the relevant part of any document, referred to in the list of documents comprised in that party's statement of case; and any such document, or relevant part, shall be sent as soon as practicable to the party who required it.

(4) The Secretary of State may in writing require any other person who has notified him of an intention or a wish to appear at an inquiry to serve a statement of case, within such period as he may specify, on him, the local planning authority, the appellant and, in the case of an enforcement appeal, on any person on whom a copy of the enforcement notice has been served.

(5) The Secretary of State shall supply any person from whom he requires a statement of case in accordance with paragraph (4) with a copy of the local planning authority's and the appellant's statement of case and shall inform that person of the name and address of every person on whom his statement of case is required to be served.

(6) The Secretary of State or an inspector may require any person who has served a statement of case in accordance with this rule to provide such further information about the matters contained in the statement as he may specify; and a person so required shall provide the Secretary of State or, as the case may be, the inspector, with that information in writing and shall, at the same time, send a copy of that information to any other person on whom the statement of case has been served.

(7) Any person other than the appellant who serves a statement of case on the local planning authority shall serve with it a copy of any document, or of the relevant part of any document, referred to in the list comprised in that statement unless a copy of the document or part of the document in question, is already available for inspection pursuant to paragraph (8).

(8) The local planning authority shall afford to any person who so requests a reasonable opportunity to inspect and, where practicable, take copies of—

(a) any statement of case or other document which, or a copy of which, has been served on them in accordance with this rule; and

(b) the authority's statement of case, together with a copy of any document, or of the relevant part of any document, referred to in the list comprised in that statement or otherwise served by them pursuant to this rule,

and the authority shall specify in the statement served in accordance with paragraph (1) the time and place at which the opportunity will be afforded.   **[845]**

NOTES

Commencement: 1 September 1992.

9. Inquiry time-table

(1) An inspector may arrange a time-table for the proceedings at, or at part of, an inquiry and may at any time vary the time-table.

(2) An inspector may specify in a time-table arranged pursuant to this rule a date by which any proof of evidence and summary required by rule 14(1) to be sent to him shall be so sent.   **[846]**

NOTES

Commencement: 1 September 1992.

10. Notification of appointment of assessor

Where the Secretary of State appoints an assessor he shall notify every person entitled to appear at the inquiry of the name of the assessor and of the matters on which he is to advise the inspector.   **[847]**

NOTES
    Commencement: 1 September 1992.

11. Date and notification of inquiry

(1) The date fixed by the Secretary of State for the holding of an inquiry shall be, unless he considers such a date impracticable, not later than 24 weeks after the relevant date.

(2) Where the Secretary of State considers it impracticable to fix a date in accordance with paragraph (1), the date fixed shall be the earliest date after the end of the relevant period mentioned in that paragraph which he considers to be practicable.

(3) Unless the Secretary of State agrees a lesser period of notice with the appellant and the local planning authority, he shall give not less than 4 weeks written notice of the date, time and place fixed by him for the holding of an inquiry to every person entitled to appear at the inquiry.

(4) The Secretary of State may vary the date fixed for the holding of an inquiry, whether or not the date as varied is within the relevant period mentioned in paragraph (1); and paragraph (3) shall apply to a variation of a date as it applied to the date originally fixed.

(5) The Secretary of State may vary the time or place for the holding of an inquiry and shall give such notice of any such variation as appears to him to be reasonable.

(6) The Secretary of State may require the local planning authority to take one or more of the following steps—

    (a) not less than 2 weeks before the date fixed for the holding of an inquiry, to publish a notice of the inquiry in one or more newspapers circulating in the locality in which the land is situated;

    (b) to serve a notice of the inquiry on such persons or classes of persons as he may specify, within such period as he may specify;

    (c) to post a notice of the inquiry in a conspicuous place near to the land, within such period as he may specify.

(7) Where the land is under the control of the appellant he shall, if so required by the Secretary of State, affix a notice of the inquiry firmly to the land or to some object on or near the land, in such manner as to be readily visible to and legible by members of the public; and he shall not remove the notice, or cause or permit it to be removed, for such period before the inquiry as the Secretary of State may specify.

(8) Every notice published, served or posted pursuant to paragraph (6), or affixed pursuant to paragraph (7), shall contain—

    (a) a clear statement of the date, time and place of the inquiry and of the powers enabling the Secretary of State or inspector to determine the appeal in question;

    (b) a written description of the land sufficient to identify approximately its location; and

    (c) a brief description of the subject matter of the appeal.   **[848]**

NOTES

Commencement: 1 September 1992.

12. Appearances at inquiry

(1) The persons entitled to appear at an inquiry are—

    (a) the appellant;

    (b) the local planning authority;

    (c) any of the following bodies if the land is situated in their area and they are not the local planning authority—

        (i) a county or district council;

        (ii) a National Park Committee within the meaning of paragraph 5 of Schedule 17 to the Local Government Act 1972;

        (iii) a joint planning board constituted under section 2(1) of the Planning Act or a joint planning board or special planning board reconstituted under Part I of Schedule 17 to the Local Government Act 1972;

        (iv) an urban development corporation established under section 135 of the Local Government, Planning and Land Act 1980;

        (v) an enterprise zone authority designated under Schedule 32 to the Local Government, Planning and Land Act 1980;

        (vi) the Broads Authority, within the meaning of the Norfolk and Suffolk Broads Act 1988;

        (vii) a housing action trust specified in an order made under section 67(1) of the Housing Act 1988;

    (d) where the land is in an area designated as a new town, the development corporation for the new town or the Commission for the New Towns as its successor;

    (e) in the case of an enforcement appeal, any person on whom a copy of the enforcement notice has been served;

    (f) in the case of an appeal under section 195 of the Planning Act, any person having an interest in the land;

    (g) where the inquiry relates to an enforcement notice under section 38 of the Listed Buildings Act concerning a building in Greater London and it is not otherwise entitled to appear, the Historic Buildings and Monuments Commission for England;

    (h) any other person who has served a statement of case in accordance with rule 8(4).

(2) Nothing in paragraph (1) shall prevent the inspector from permitting any other person to appear at an inquiry, and such permission shall not be unreasonably withheld.

(3) Any person entitled or permitted to appear may do so on his own behalf or be represented by counsel, solicitor or any other person.   **[849]**

NOTES

Commencement: 1 September 1992.

13. Representatives of government departments at inquiry

(1) Where the Secretary of State or any other Minister of the Crown or any government department has expressed in writing to the local planning authority a view on an appeal and the authority refer to that view in a statement prepared pursuant to rule 8(1), the appellant may, not later than 2 weeks before the date of an

inquiry, apply in writing to the Secretary of State for a representative of the Secretary of State or of the other Minister or department concerned to be made available at the inquiry.

(2) Where an application is made in accordance with paragraph (1), the Secretary of State shall make a representative available to attend the inquiry or, as the case may be, transmit the application to the other Minister or department concerned, who shall make a representative available to attend the inquiry.

(3) A person attending an inquiry as a representative in pursuance of this rule shall state the reasons for the expressed view and shall give evidence and be subject to cross-examination to the same extent as any other witness.

(4) Nothing in paragraph (3) shall require a representative of a Minister or government department to answer any question which, in the opinion of the inspector, is directed to the merits of government policy.   **[850]**

NOTES
   Commencement: 1 September 1992.

14. Proofs of evidence

(1) Where a person entitled to appear at an inquiry held for the purpose of an appeal under section 174 of the Planning Act proposes to give, or to call another person to give, evidence at the inquiry by reading a proof of evidence relating, in whole or in part, to the deemed application for planning permission under section 177(5) of that Act, he shall send a copy of the proof to the inspector together with, subject to paragraph (2), a written summary.

(2) No written summary shall be required where the proof of evidence proposed to be read contains no more than 1,500 words.

(3) The proof and any summary shall be sent to the inspector not later than—

    (a) 3 weeks before the date fixed for the holding of the inquiry; or
    (b) where a time-table has been arranged pursuant to rule 9 which specifies a
        date by which the proof and any summary shall be sent to he inspector,
        that date.

(4) Where the appellant or the local planning authority send a copy of a proof to an inspector in accordance with paragraph (1), with or without a summary, they shall at the same time send a copy of that proof and any summary to the other party and to any other person on whom a copy of the enforcement notice has been served; and where any other party so sends a copy of such documents he shall at the same time send a copy to the appellant and the local planning authority and to any other person on whom a copy of the enforcement notice has been served.

(5) Where a written summary is provided in accordance with paragraph (1), only that summary shall be read at the inquiry, unless the inspector permits or requires otherwise.

(6) Any person required by this rule to send a copy of a proof to any other person shall send with it a copy of the whole, or the relevant part, of any documents referred to in it, unless a copy of the document or part of the document in question is already available for inspection pursuant to rule 8(8).

(7) The local planning authority shall afford to any person who so requests a reasonable opportunity to inspect and, where practicable, take copies of any document sent to or by them in accordance with this rule.   **[851]**

NOTES
Commencement: 1 September 1992.

15. Procedure at inquiry

(1) Except as otherwise provided in these Rules, the inspector shall determine the procedure at an inquiry.

(2) Unless in any particular case the inspector with the consent of the appellant otherwise determines, the appellant shall begin and shall have the right of final reply; and the other persons entitled or permitted to appear shall be heard in such order as the inspector may determine.

(3) A person entitled to appear at an inquiry shall be entitled to call evidence and the local planning authority and the appellant shall be entitled to cross-examine persons giving evidence but, subject to the foregoing and paragraphs (4) and (5), the calling of evidence and the cross- examination of persons giving evidence shall otherwise be at the inspector's discretion.

(4) The inspector may refuse to permit—
    (a) the giving or production of evidence,
    (b) the cross-examination of persons giving evidence, or
    (c) the presentation of any other matter,
which he considers to be irrelevant or repetitious; but where he refuses to permit the giving of oral evidence, the person wishing to give the evidence may submit to him any evidence or other matter in writing before the close of the inquiry.

(5) Where a person gives evidence at an inquiry by reading a summary of his evidence in accordance with rule 14(5), the proof of evidence referred to in rule 14(1) shall, unless the person required to provide the summary notifies the inspector that he now wishes to rely on the contents of that summary only, be treated as tendered in evidence, and the person whose evidence the proof contains shall then be subject to cross-examination on it to the same extent as if it were evidence he had given orally.

(6) The inspector may direct that facilities shall be afforded to any person appearing at an inquiry to take or obtain copies of documentary evidence open to public inspection.

(7) The inspector may require any person appearing or present at an inquiry who, in his opinion, is behaving in a disruptive manner to leave and may refuse to permit that person to return, or may permit him to return only on such conditions as he may specify; but any such person may submit to him any evidence or other matter in writing before the close of the inquiry.

(8) The inspector may allow any person to alter or add to a statement of case served under rule 8 so far as may be necessary for the purposes of the inquiry; but he shall (if necessary by adjourning the inquiry) give every other person entitled to appear who is appearing at the inquiry an adequate opportunity of considering any fresh matter or document.

(9) The inspector may proceed with an inquiry in the absence of any person entitled to appear at it.

(10) The inspector may take into account any written representation or evidence or any other document received by him from any person before an inquiry opens or during the inquiry provided that he discloses it at the inquiry.

(11) The inspector may from time to time adjourn an inquiry and, if the date, time and place of the adjourned inquiry are announced at the inquiry before the adjournment, no further notice shall be required.   **[852]**

NOTES
Commencement: 1 September 1992.

16. Site inspections

(1) The inspector may make an unaccompanied inspection of the land before or during an inquiry without giving notice of his intention to the persons entitled to appear at the inquiry.

(2) The inspector may, during an inquiry or after its close, inspect the land in the company of the local planning authority, the appellant and, in the case of an enforcement appeal, any person on whom a copy of the enforcement notice was served; and he shall make such an inspection if so required by the local planning authority or the appellant before or during an inquiry.

(3) In all cases where the inspector intends to make an inspection of the kind referred to in paragraph (2) he shall announce during the inquiry the date and time at which he proposes to make it.

(4) The inspector shall not be bound to defer an inspection of the kind referred to in paragraph (2) where any person mentioned in that paragraph is not present at the time appointed. **[853]**

NOTES

Commencement: 1 September 1992.

17. Procedure after inquiry-non-transferred appeals

(1) This rule applies where an inquiry has been held for the purposes of a non-transferred appeal.

(2) After the close of the inquiry, the inspector shall make a report in writing to the Secretary of State, which shall include his findings of facts, his conclusions and his recommendations or his reasons for not making any recommendations.

(3) Where an assessor has been appointed, he may, after the close of the inquiry, make a report in writing to the inspector in respect of the matters on which he was appointed to advise.

(4) Where an assessor makes a report in accordance with paragraph (3), the inspector shall append it to his own report and shall state in his own report how far he agrees or disagrees with the assessor's report and, where he disagrees with the assessor, his reasons for that disagreement.

(5) If, after the close of the inquiry, the Secretary of State—

    (a) differs from the inspector on any matter of fact mentioned in, or appearing to him to be material to, a conclusion reached by the inspector, or

    (b) takes into consideration any new evidence or new matter of fact (not being a matter of government policy),

and is for that reason disposed to disagree with a recommendation made by the inspector, he shall not come to a decision which is at variance with that recommendation without first notifying the persons entitled to appear at the inquiry who appeared at it of his disagreement and the reasons for it' and affording to them an opportunity of making written representations to him within 3 weeks of the date of the notification, or (if the Secretary of State has taken into consideration any new evidence or new matter of fact, not being a matter of government policy) of asking within that period for the re-opening of the inquiry.

(6) The Secretary of State may, as he thinks fit, cause an inquiry to be re-opened, and he shall do so if asked by the local planning authority or the appellant in the circumstances and within the period mentioned in paragraph (5); and where an inquiry is re-opened (whether by the same or a different inspector)—

(a) the Secretary of State shall send to the persons entitled to appear at the inquiry who appeared at it a written statement of the matters with respect to which further evidence is invited; and

(b) paragraphs (3) to (8) of rule 11 shall apply as if the references to an inquiry were references to a re-opened inquiry. **[854]**

NOTES
Commencement: 1 September 1992.

18. Procedure after inquiry-transferred appeals

(1) This rule applies where an inquiry has been held for the purposes of a transferred appeal.

(2) Where an assessor has been appointed, he may, after the close of the inquiry, make a report in writing to the inspector in respect of the matters on which he was appointed to advise, and where he does so the inspector shall state in his notification of his decision pursuant to rule 20 that such a report was made.

(3) If, after the close of the inquiry, an inspector proposes to take into consideration any new evidence or any new matter of fact (not being a matter of government policy) which was not raised in the inquiry and which he considers to be material to his decision, he shall not come to a decision without first—

(a) notifying the persons entitled to appear at the inquiry who appeared at it of the matter in question; and

(b) affording to them an opportunity of making written representations to him with respect to it within 3 weeks of the date of the notification or of asking within that period for the re-opening of the inquiry.

(4) An inspector may, as he thinks fit, cause an inquiry to be re-opened, and he shall do so if asked by the local planning authority or the appellant in the circumstances and within the period mentioned in paragraph (3); and where an inquiry is re-opened—

(a) the inspector shall send to the persons entitled to appear at the inquiry who appeared at it a written statement of the matters with respect to which further evidence is invited; and

(b) paragraphs (3) to (8) of rule 11 shall apply as if the references to an inquiry were references to a re-opened inquiry. **[855]**

NOTES
Commencement: 1 September 1992.

19. Notification of decision-non-transferred appeals

(1) This rule applies where an inquiry has been held for the purposes of a non-transferred appeal.

(2) The Secretary of State shall notify his decision on the appeal, and his reasons for it, in writing to all persons entitled to appear at the inquiry who did appear, and to any other person who, having appeared at the inquiry, has asked to be notified of the decision.

(3) Where a copy of the inspector's report is not sent with the notification of the decision, the notification shall be accompanied by a statement of his findings of fact, his conclusions and of any recommendations made by him; and if a person entitled to be notified of the decision has not received a copy of that report, he shall be supplied with a copy of it on written application made to the Secretary of State within 4 weeks of the date of the decision.

(4) In this rule ''report'' includes any assessor's report appended to the inspector's report but does not include any other documents so appended; but any person who has received a copy of the report may apply to the Secretary of State in writing, within 6 weeks of the date of the Secretary of State's decision, for an opportunity of inspecting any such documents and the Secretary of State shall afford him that opportunity. **[856]**

NOTES
    Commencement: 1 September 1992.

20. Notification of decision-transferred appeals

(1) This rule applies where an inquiry has been held for the purposes of a transferred appeal.

(2) The inspector shall notify his decision on the appeal, and his reasons for it, in writing to all persons entitled to appear at the inquiry who did appear, and to any other person who, having appeared at the inquiry, has asked to be notified of the decision.

(3) Any person entitled to be notified of the inspector's decision under paragraph (2) may apply to the Secretary of State in writing, within 6 weeks of the date of the decision, for an opportunity of inspecting any documents listed in the notification and any report made by an assessor and the Secretary of State shall afford him that opportunity. **[857]**

NOTES
    Commencement: 1 September 1992.

21. Procedure following remitting of appeal

Where a decision of the Secretary of State or an inspector on an appeal in respect of which an inquiry has been held is remitted by any court for rehearing and determination, the Secretary of State—

    (a) shall send to the persons entitled to appear at the inquiry who appeared at it a written statement of the matters with respect to which further representations are invited for the purpose of the further consideration of the appeal;

    (b) shall afford to those persons the opportunity of making, within 3 weeks of the date of the written statement, written representations to him in respect of those matters or of asking for the re-opening of the inquiry; and

    (c) may, as he thinks fit, cause the inquiry to be re-opened, and if he does so paragraphs (3) to (8) of rule 11 shall apply as if the references to an inquiry were references to a re-opened inquiry. **[858]**

NOTES
    Commencement: 1 September 1992.

22. Allowing further time

The Secretary of State may at any time in any particular case allow further time for the taking of any step which is required or enabled to be taken by virtue of these Rules, and references in these Rules to a day by which, or period within which, any step is required or enabled to be taken shall be construed accordingly. **[859]**

NOTES
    Commencement: 1 September 1992.

23. Inspector acting in place of Secretary of State-transferred appeals

In the case of a transferred appeal, an inspector may in place of the Secretary of State take such steps as the Secretary of State is required or enabled to take under or by virtue of rule 8(4) and (5), rule 11, rule 13 and rule 22. **[860]**

NOTES
Commencement: 1 September 1992.

24. Service of notices by post

Notices or documents required or authorised to be served or sent under these Rules may be sent by post. **[861]**

NOTES
Commencement: 1 September 1992.

25. Revocations and savings

(1) Subject to paragraph (2), the Town and Country Planning (Enforcement) (Inquiries Procedure) Rules 1981 ("the 1981 Rules") and rule 2(3) of, and Schedule 3 to, the Town and Country Planning (Various Inquiries) (Procedure) (Amendment) Rules 1986 are hereby revoked.

(2) Subject to paragraph (3), the 1981 Rules shall continue to apply to any local inquiry held for the purposes of—

(a) an enforcement appeal made before 1st September 1992;
(b) an application or appeal to which section 196(1) of the Planning Act, as originally enacted, refers (established use certificates).

(3) In the application of the 1981 Rules by virtue of paragraph (2)—

(a) the reference to rule 2(1)(d) in rule 3, 6(1)(b) and 6(4) of the 1981 Rules shall be treated as a reference to rule 2(1)(e) of those Rules; and
(b) the reference to rule 2(1)(a), (b) or (c) in rule 6(1)(a) of the 1981 Rules shall be treated as including a reference to rule 2(1)(d) of those Rules.

[862]

NOTES
Commencement: 1 September 1992.

TOWN AND COUNTRY PLANNING (INQUIRIES PROCEDURE) RULES 1992
(SI 1992/2038)

NOTES
Made: 24 August 1992
Authority: Tribunals and Inquiries Act 1971, s 11; now have effect under Tribunals and Inquiries Act 1992, s 9

1. Citation and Commencement

These Rules may be cited as the Town and Country Planning (Inquiries Procedure) Rules 1992 and shall come into force on 30th September 1992. **[863]**

NOTES
Commencement: 30 September 1992.

2. Interpretation

In these Rules, unless the context otherwise requires—

"applicant", in the case of an appeal, means the appellant;

"assessor" means a person appointed by the Secretary of State to sit with an inspector at an inquiry or re-opened inquiry to advise the inspector on such matters arising as the Secretary of State may specify;

"the Commission" means the Historic Buildings and Monuments Commission for England;

"conservation area consent" has the meaning given in section 74(1) of the Listed Buildings Act;

"development order" has the meaning given in section 59 of the Planning Act; "document" includes a photograph, map or plan;

"inquiry" means a local inquiry in relation to which these Rules apply; "inspector" means a person appointed by the Secretary of State to hold an inquiry or a re-opened inquiry;

"land" means the land, tree or building to which an inquiry relates; "the Listed Buildings Act" means the Planning (Listed Buildings and Conservation Areas) Act 1990;

"listed building consent" has the meaning given in section 8(7) of the Listed Buildings Act;

"local planning authority" means—

(i) in relation to a referred application, the body who would otherwise have dealt with the application;

(ii) in relation to an appeal, the body who were responsible for dealing with the application occasioning the appeal;

"outline statement" means a written statement of the principal submissions which a person proposes to put forward at an inquiry;

"the Planning Act" means the Town and Country Planning Act 1990;

"pre-inquiry meeting" means a meeting held before an inquiry to consider what may be done with a view to securing that the inquiry is conducted efficiently and expeditiously, and where two or more such meetings are held references to the conclusion of a pre-inquiry meeting are references to the conclusion of the final meeting;

"referred application" means an application of any description mentioned in rule 3(1) which is referred to the Secretary of State for determination;

"relevant date" means the date of the Secretary of State's written notice to the applicant and the local planning authority of his intention to cause an inquiry to be held, and "relevant notice" means that notice;

"the 1988 Rules" means the Town and Country Planning (Inquiries Procedure) Rules 1988;

"statement of case" means, and is comprised of, a written statement which contains full particulars of the case which a person proposes to put forward at an inquiry, and a list of any documents which that person intends to refer to or put in evidence;

"statutory party" means—

(a) a person mentioned in paragraph (1)(b)(i) of article 22A of the Town and Country Planning General Development Order 1988 whose representations the Secretary of State is required by paragraph (3) of that article to take into account in determining the referred application or appeal to which an inquiry relates; and, in the case of an appeal, such a person whose representations the local planning authority were required by paragraph (1) of that article to take into account in determining the application occasioning the appeal; and

(b) a person whose representations the Secretary of State is required by paragraphs (3)(b) and (5) of regulation 6 of the Planning (Listed Buildings and Conservation Areas) Regulations 1990 to take into account in determining the referred application or appeal to which an inquiry relates; and, in the case of an appeal, a person whose representations the local planning authority were required by paragraph (3)(b) of that regulation to take into account in determining the application occasioning the appeal.

"tree preservation order" has the meaning given in section 198 of the Planning Act. **[864]**

NOTES
Commencement: 30 September 1992.

3. Application of Rules

(1) These Rules apply in relation to any local inquiry caused by the Secretary of State to be held in England or Wales before he determines—

(a) an application in relation to planning permission referred to him under section 77, or an appeal to him under section 78, of the Planning Act;

(b) an application for consent referred to him under a tree preservation order or an appeal to him under such an order, with the exceptions that rule 4(1) shall not apply and the references to a statutory party shall be omitted;

(c) an application for listed building consent referred to him under section 12, or for variation or discharge of conditions referred to him under that section as applied by section 19, or an appeal to him under section 20, of the Listed Buildings Act,

(d) an application for conservation area consent referred to him under section 12 (including an application to which that section is applied by section 19), or an appeal to him under section 20, of the Listed Buildings Act as those sections are applied by virtue of section 74(3) of that Act,but do not apply to any local inquiry by reason of the application of any provision mentioned in this paragraph by any other enactment.

(2) Where these Rules apply in relation to an appeal which at some time fell to be disposed of in accordance with the Town and Country Planning Appeals (Determination by Inspectors) (Inquiries Procedure) Rules 1992 or Rules superseded by those Rules, any step taken or thing done under those Rules which could have been done under any corresponding provision of these Rules shall have effect as if it had been taken or done under that corresponding provision. **[865]**

NOTES
Commencement: 30 September 1992.

4. Preliminary information to be supplied by local planning authority

(1) The local planning authority shall, on receipt of a notice from the Secretary of State of his intention to cause an inquiry to be held ("the relevant notice"), forthwith inform him and the applicant in writing of the name and address of any statutory party who has made representations to them; and the Secretary of State shall as soon as practicable thereafter inform the applicant and the local planning authority in writing of the name and address of any statutory party who has made representations to him.

(2) This paragraph applies where—

(a) the Secretary of State has given to the local planning authority a direction restricting the grant of planning permission for which application was made; or

(b) in a case relating to listed building consent, the Commission has given a direction to the local planning authority pursuant to section 14(2) of the Listed Buildings Act as to how the application is to be determined; or

(c) the Secretary of State or any other Minister of the Crown or any government department, or any body falling within rule 11(1)(c), has expressed in writing to the local planning authority the view that the application should not be granted either wholly or in part, or should be granted only subject to conditions, or, in the case of an application for consent under a tree preservation order, should be granted together with a direction requiring replanting; or

(d) any authority or person consulted in pursuance of a development order has made representations to the local planning authority about the application.

(3) Where paragraph (2) applies, the local planning authority shall forthwith after the date of the relevant notice ("the relevant date") inform the person or body concerned of the inquiry and, unless they have already done so, that person or body shall thereupon give the local planning authority a written statement of the reasons for making the direction, expressing the view or making the representations, as the case may be. **[866]**

NOTES
Commencement: 30 September 1992.

5. Procedure where Secretary of State causes pre-inquiry meeting to be held

(1) The Secretary of State may cause a pre-inquiry meeting to be held if it appears to him desirable and where he does so the following paragraphs apply.

(2) The Secretary of State shall serve with the relevant notice a notification of his intention to cause a meeting to be held and a statement of the matters about which he particularly wishes to be informed for the purposes of his consideration of the application or appeal in question; and where another Minister of the Crown or a government department has expressed in writing to the Secretary of State a view which is mentioned in rule 4(2)(c), the Secretary of State shall set this out in his statement and shall supply a copy of the statement to the Minister or government department concerned.

(3) The local planning authority shall cause to be published in a newspaper circulating in the locality in which the land is situated a notice of the Secretary of State's intention to cause a meeting to be held and of the statement served in accordance with paragraph (2).

(4) The applicant and the local planning authority shall, not later than 8 weeks after the relevant date, each serve an outline statement on the other and on the Secretary of State.

(5) Where rule 4(2) applies, the local planning authority shall—

(a) include in their outline statement the terms of—

(i) any direction given together with a statement of the reasons therefor; and

(ii) any view expressed or representation made on which they intend to rely in their submissions at the inquiry; and

(b) within the period mentioned in paragraph (4), supply a copy of their statement to the person or body concerned.

(6) The Secretary of State may in writing require any other person who has notified him of an intention or a wish to appear at the inquiry to serve, within 4 weeks of being so required, an outline statement on him, the applicant and the local planning authority.

(7) The meeting (or, where there is more than one, the first meeting) shall be held not later than 16 weeks after the relevant date.

(8) The Secretary of State shall give not less than 3 weeks written notice of the meeting to the applicant, the local planning authority, any person known at the date of the notice to be entitled to appear at the inquiry and any other person whose presence at the meeting seems to him to be desirable; and he may require the local planning authority to take, in relation to notification of the meeting, one or more of the steps which he may under rule 10(6) require them to take in relation to notification of the inquiry.

(9) The inspector shall preside at the meeting and shall determine the matters to be discussed and the procedure to be followed, and he may require any person present at the meeting who in his opinion, is behaving in a disruptive manner to leave and may refuse to permit that person to return or to attend any further meeting, or may permit him to return or attend only on such conditions as he may specify.

(10) Where a pre-inquiry meeting has been held pursuant to paragraph (1), the inspector may hold a further meeting. He shall arrange for such notice to be given of a further meeting as appears to him necessary; and paragraph (9) shall apply to such a meeting. **[867]**

NOTES

Commencement: 30 September 1992.

6. Service of statements of case etc.

(1) Subject to paragraph (4), the local planning authority shall, not later than—

    (a) 6 weeks after the relevant date, or
    (b) where a pre-inquiry meeting is held pursuant to rule 5, 4 weeks after the conclusion of that meeting,

serve a statement of case on the Secretary of State, the applicant and any statutory party.

(2) Where rule 4(2) applies, the local planning authority shall, unless they have already done so in an outline statement, include in their statement of case the matters mentioned in rule 5(5)(a) and shall supply a copy of the statement to the person or body concerned.

(3) Subject to paragraph (4), the applicant shall, not later than—

    (a) in the case of a referred application where no pre-inquiry meeting is held pursuant to rule 5, 6 weeks after the relevant date, or
    (b) in the case of an appeal where no such meeting is held, 9 weeks after the relevant date, or
    (c) in any case where a pre-inquiry meeting is held pursuant to rule 5, 4 weeks after the conclusion of that meeting,

serve a statement of case on the Secretary of State, the local planning authority and any statutory party.

(4) The statement of case mentioned in paragraph (1) or, as the case may be, paragraph (3) shall be served no later than the day which is 4 weeks before the date fixed for the holding of the inquiry, where that day falls within whichever of the periods mentioned in either of those paragraphs is applicable to the case.

(5) The applicant and the local planning authority may each require the other to send to them a copy of any document, or of the relevant part of any document, referred to in the list of documents comprised in that party's statement of case; and any such document, or relevant part, shall be sent as soon as practicable to the party who required it.

(6) The Secretary of State may in writing require any other person who has notified him of an intention or a wish to appear at an inquiry to serve a statement of case, within 4 weeks of being so required, on the applicant, the local planning authority, the Secretary of State and any (or any other) statutory party.

(7) The Secretary of State shall supply any person from whom he requires a statement of case in accordance with paragraph (6) with a copy of the applicant's and the local planning authority's statement of case and shall inform that person of the name and address of every person on whom his statement of case is required to be served.

(8) The Secretary of State or an inspector may require any person who has served a statement of case in accordance with this rule to provide such further information about the matters contained in the statement as he may specify; and a person so required shall provide the Secretary of State, or as the case may be, the inspector, with that information in writing and shall, at the same time, send a copy to any other person on whom the statement of case has been served.

(9) Any person other than the applicant who serves a statement of case on the local planning authority shall serve with it a copy of any document, or of the relevant part of any document, referred to in the list comprised in that statement, unless a copy of the document or part of the document in question is already available for inspection pursuant to paragraph (11).

(10) Unless he has already done so, the Secretary of State shall in the case of a referred application, and may in the case of an appeal, not later than 12 weeks from the relevant date serve a written statement of the matters referred to in rule 5(2) on the applicant, the local planning authority, any statutory party and any person from whom he has required a statement of case.

(11) The local planning authority shall afford to any person who so requests a reasonable opportunity to inspect and, where practicable, take copies of any statement of case or other document which, or a copy of which, has been served on them in accordance with this rule, and of their statement of case together with a copy of any document, or of the relevant part of any document, referred to in the list comprised in that statement or otherwise served by them pursuant to this rule; and shall specify in their statement of case the time and place at which the opportunity will be afforded.   [868]

NOTES
   Commencement: 30 September 1992.

7. Further power of inspector to hold pre-inquiry meetings

(1) Where no pre-inquiry meeting is held pursuant to rule 5, an inspector may hold one if he thinks it desirable.

(2) An inspector shall arrange for not less than 2 weeks written notice of a

meeting he proposes to hold under paragraph (1) to be given to the applicant, the local planning authority, any person known at the date of the notice to be entitled to appear at the inquiry and any other person whose presence at the meeting appears to him to be desirable.

(3) Rule 5(9) shall apply to a meeting held under this rule.   **[869]**

NOTES
   Commencement: 30 September 1992.

8. Inquiry time-table

(1) Where a pre-inquiry meeting is held pursuant to rule 5 an inspector shall, and in any other case may, arrange a time-table for the proceedings at, or at part of, an inquiry and may at any time vary the time-table.

(2) An inspector may specify in a time-table arranged pursuant to this rule a date by which any proof of evidence and summary required by rule 13(1) to be sent to him shall be so sent.   **[870]**

NOTES
   Commencement: 30 September 1992.

9. Notification of appointment of assessor

Where the Secretary of State appoints an assessor, he shall notify every person entitled to appear at the inquiry of the name of the assessor and of the matters on which he is to advise the inspector.   **[871]**

NOTES
   Commencement: 30 September 1992.

10. Date and notification of inquiry

(1) The date fixed by the Secretary of State for the holding of an inquiry shall be, unless he considers such a date impracticable, not later than—

   (a) 22 weeks after the relevant date; or
   (b) in a case where a pre-inquiry meeting is held pursuant to rule 5, 8 weeks after the conclusion of that meeting.

(2) Where the Secretary of State considers it impracticable to fix a date in accordance with paragraph (1), the date fixed shall be the earliest date after the end of the relevant period mentioned in that paragraph which he considers to be practicable.

(3) Unless the Secretary of State agrees a lesser period of notice with the applicant and the local planning authority, he shall give not less than 4 weeks written notice of the date, time and place fixed by him for the holding of an inquiry to every person entitled to appear at the inquiry.

(4) The Secretary of State may vary the date fixed for the holding of an inquiry, whether or not the date as varied is within the relevant period mentioned in paragraph (1); and paragraph (3) shall apply to a variation of a date as it applied to the date originally fixed.

(5) The Secretary of State may vary the time or place for the holding of an inquiry and shall give such notice of any such variation as appears to him to be reasonable.

(6) The Secretary of State may require the local planning authority to take one or more of the following steps—

(a) not less than 2 weeks before the date fixed for the holding of an inquiry, to publish a notice of the inquiry in one or more newspapers circulating in the locality in which the land is situated;

(b) to serve a notice of the inquiry on such persons or classes of persons as he may specify, within such period as he may specify;

(c) to post a notice of the inquiry in a conspicuous place near to the land, within such period as he may specify.

(7) Where the land is under the control of the applicant he shall, if so required by the Secretary of State, affix a notice of the inquiry firmly to the land or to some object on or near the land, in such manner as to be readily visible to and legible by members of the public; and he shall not remove the notice, or cause or permit it to be removed, for such period before the inquiry as the Secretary of State may specify.

(8) Every notice of inquiry published, served or posted pursuant to pararaph (6), or affixed pursuant to paragraph (7), shall contain—

(a) a clear statement of the date, time and place of the inquiry and of the powers enabling the Secretary of State to determine the application or appeal in question;

(b) a written description of the land sufficient to identify approximately its location; and

(c) a brief description of the subject matter of the application or appeal. **[872]**

NOTES
    Commencement: 30 September 1992.

11. Appearances at inquiry

(1) The persons entitled to appear at an inquiry are—

(a) the applicant;

(b) the local planning authority;

(c) any of the following bodies if the land is situated in their area and they are not the local planning authority—

   (i) a county or district council;

   (ii) a National Park Committee within the meaning of paragraph 5 of Schedule 17 to the Local Government Act 1972(a);

   (iii) a joint planning board constituted under section 2(1) of the Planning Act or a joint planning board or special planning board reconstituted under Part I of Schedule 17 to the Local Government Act 1972;

   (iv) an urban development corporation established under section 135 of the Local Government, Planning and Land Act 1980(a);

   (v) an enterprise zone authority designated under Schedule 32 to the Local Government, Planning and Land Act 1980;

   (vi) the Broads Authority, within the meaning of the Norfolk and Suffolk Broads Act 1988(b);

   (vii) a housing action trust specified in an order made under section 67(1) of the Housing Act 1988(c);

(d) where the land is in an area designated as a new town, the development corporation for the new town or the Commission for the New Towns as its successor;

(e) a statutory party;

(f) the council of the parish or community in which the land is situated, if that council made representations to the local planning authority in respect of the application in pursuance of a provision of a development order;

(g) where the application was required to be notified to the Commission under section 14 of the Listed Buildings Act, the Commission;

(h) any other person who has served a statement of case in accordance with rule 6(6) or who has served an outline statement in accordance with rule 5(6).

(2) Nothing in paragraph (1) shall prevent the inspector from permitting any other person to appear at an inquiry, and such permission shall not be unreasonably withheld.

(3) Any person entitled or permitted to appear may do so on his own behalf or be represented by counsel, solicitor or any other person.   **[873]**

NOTES
Commencement: 30 September 1992.

12. Representatives of government departments and other authorities at inquiry

(1) Where—

(a) the Secretary of State or the Commission has given a direction such as is described in rule 4(2)(a) or (b); or

(b) the Secretary of State or any other Minister of the Crown or any government department, or any body falling within rule 11(1)(c), has expressed a view such as is described in rule 4(2)(c) and the local planning authority have included the terms of the expression of view in a statement served in accordance with rule 5(4) or 6(1); or

(c) another Minister of the Crown or any government department has expressed a view such as is described in rule 4(2)(c) and the Secretary of State has included its terms in a statement served in accordance with rule 5(2) or 6(10),

the applicant may, not later than 2 weeks before the date of an inquiry, apply in writing to the Secretary of State for a representative of the Secretary of State or of the other Minister, department or body concerned to be made available at the inquiry.

(2) Where an application is made in accordance with paragraph (1), the Secretary of State shall make a representative available to attend the inquiry or, as the case may be, transmit the application to the other Minister, department or body concerned, who shall make a representative available to attend the inquiry.

(3) A person attending an inquiry as a representative in pursuance of this rule shall state the reasons for the direction or expressed view and shall give evidence and be subject to cross-examination to the same extent as any other witness.

(4) Nothing in paragraph (3) shall require a representative of a Minister or a government department to answer any question which in the opinion of the inspector is directed to the merits of government policy.   **[874]**

NOTES
Commencement: 30 September 1992.

13. Proofs of evidence

(1) A person entitled to appear at an inquiry who proposes to give, or to call another person to give, evidence at the inquiry by reading a proof of evidence shall send a

copy of the proof to the inspector together with, subject to paragraph (2), a written summary.

(2) No written summary shall be required where the proof of evidence proposed to be read contains no more than 1500 words.

(3) The proof and any summary shall be sent to the inspector not later than—

(a) 3 weeks before the date fixed for the holding of the inquiry, or
(b) where a time-table has been arranged pursuant to rule 8 which specifies a date by which the proof and any summary shall be sent to the inspector, that date.

(4) Where the applicant or the local planning authority send a copy of a proof to an inspector in accordance with paragraph (1), with or without a summary, they shall at the same time send a copy of that proof and any summary to the other party, and to any statutory party; and where any other party so sends a copy of such documents he shall at the same time send a copy to the applicant, the local planning authority and any (or any other) statutory party.

(5) Where a written summary is provided in accordance with paragraph (1), only that summary shall be read at the inquiry, unless the inspector permits or requires otherwise.

(6) Any person required by this rule to send a copy of a proof to any other person shall send with it a copy of the whole, or the relevant part, of any document referred to in it, unless a copy of the document or part of the document in question is already available for inspection pursuant to rule 6(11).

(7) The local planning authority shall afford to any person who so requests a reasonable opportunity to inspect and, where practicable, take copies of any document sent to or by them in accordance with this rule.   **[875]**

NOTES
Commencement: 30 September 1992.

14. Procedure at inquiry

(1) Except as otherwise provided in these Rules, the inspector shall determine the procedure at an inquiry.

(2) Unless in any particular case the inspector with the consent of the applicant otherwise determines, the applicant shall begin and shall have the right of final reply; and the other persons entitled or permitted to appear shall be heard in such order as the inspector may determine.

(3) A person entitled to appear at an inquiry shall be entitled to call evidence and the applicant, the local planning authority and a statutory party shall be entitled to cross- examine persons giving evidence, but, subject to the foregoing and paragraphs (4) and (5), the calling of evidence and the cross-examination of persons giving evidence shall otherwise be at the inspector's discretion.

(4) The inspector may refuse to permit—

(a) the giving or production of evidence,
(b) the cross-examination of persons giving evidence, or
(c) the presentation of any other matter,

which he considers to be irrelevant or repetitious; but where he refuses to permit the giving of oral evidence, the person wishing to give the evidence may submit to him any evidence or other matter in writing before the close of the inquiry.

(5) Where a person gives evidence at an inquiry by reading a summary of his evidence in accordance with rule 13(5), the proof of evidence referred to in rule 13(1) shall, unless the person required to provide the summary notifies the inspector that he now wishes to rely on the contents of that summary only, be treated as tendered in evidence, and the person whose evidence the proof contains shall then be subject to cross-examination on it to the same extent as if it were evidence he had given orally.

(6) The inspector may direct that facilities shall be afforded to any person appearing at an inquiry to take or obtain copies of documentary evidence open to public inspection.

(7) The inspector may require any person appearing or present at an inquiry who, in his opinion, is behaving in a disruptive manner to leave and may refuse to permit that person to return, or may permit him to return only on such conditions as he may specify; but any such person may submit to him any evidence or other matter in writing before the close of the inquiry.

(8) The inspector may allow any person to alter or add to a statement of case served under rule 6 so far as may be necessary for the purposes of the inquiry; but he shall (if necessary by adjourning the inquiry) give every other person entitled to appear who is appearing at the inquiry an adequate opportunity of considering any fresh matter or document.

(9) The inspector may proceed with an inquiry in the absence of any person entitled to appear at it.

(10) The inspector may take into account any written representation or evidence or any other document received by him from any person before an inquiry opens or during the inquiry provided that he discloses it at the inquiry.

(11) The inspector may from time to time adjourn an inquiry and, if the date, time and place of the adjourned inquiry are announced at the inquiry before the adjournment, no further notice shall be required. **[876]**

NOTES
Commencement: 30 September 1992.

15. Site inspections

(1) The inspector may make an unaccompanied inspection of the land before or during an inquiry without giving notice of his intention to the persons entitled to appear at the inquiry.

(2) The inspector may, during an inquiry or after its close, inspect the land in the company of the applicant, the local planning authority and any statutory party; and he shall make such an inspection if so requested by the applicant or the local planning authority before or during an inquiry.

(3) In all cases where the inspector intends to make an inspection of the kind referred to in paragraph (2) he shall announce during the inquiry the date and time at which he proposes to make it.

(4) The inspector shall not be bound to defer an inspection of the kind referred to in paragraph (2) where any person mentioned in that paragraph is not present at the time appointed. **[877]**

NOTES
Commencement: 30 September 1992.

16. Procedure after inquiry

(1) After the close of an inquiry, the inspector shall make a report in writing to the Secretary of State which shall include his conclusions and his recommendations or his reasons for not making any recommendations.

(2) Where an assessor has been appointed, he may, after the close of the inquiry, make a report in writing to the inspector in respect of the matters on which he was appointed to advise.

(3) Where an assessor makes a report in accordance with paragraph (2), the inspector shall append it to his own report and shall state in his own report how far he agrees or disagrees with the assessor's report and, where he disagrees with the assessor, his reasons for that disagreement.

(4) If, after the close of an inquiry, the Secretary of State—

   (a) differs from the inspector on any matter of fact mentioned in, or appearing to him to be material to, a conclusion reached by the inspector, or
   (b) takes into consideration any new evidence or new matter of fact (not being a matter of government policy),

and is for that reason disposed to disagree with a recommendation made by the inspector, he shall not come to a decision which is at variance with that recommendation without first notifying the persons entitled to appear at the inquiry who appeared at it of his disagreement and the reasons for it; and affording to them an opportunity of making written representations to him within 3 weeks of the date of the notification, or (if the Secretary of State has taken into consideration any new evidence or new matter of fact, not being a matter of government policy) of asking within that period for the re-opening of the inquiry.

(5) The Secretary of State may, as he thinks fit, cause an inquiry to be re-opened, and he shall do so if asked by the applicant or the local planning authority in the circumstances and within the period mentioned in paragraph (4); and where an inquiry is re-opened (whether by the same or a different inspector)—

   (a) the Secretary of State shall send to the persons entitled to appear at the inquiry who appeared at it a written statement of the matters with respect to which further evidence is invited; and
   (b) paragraphs (3) to (8) of rule 10 shall apply as if the references to an inquiry were references to a re-opened inquiry.   **[878]**

NOTES

Commencement: 30 September 1992.

17. Notification of decision

(1) The Secretary of State shall notify his decision on an application or appeal, and his reasons for it, in writing to all persons entitled to appear at the inquiry who did appear, and to any other person who, having appeared at the inquiry, has asked to be notified of the decision.

(2) Where a copy of the inspector's report is not sent with the notification of the decision, the notification shall be accompanied by a statement of his conclusions and of any recommendations made by him; and if a person entitled to be notified of the decision has not received a copy of that report, he shall be supplied with a copy of it on written application made to the Secretary of State within 4 weeks of the date of the decision.

(3) In this rule "report" includes any assessor's report appended to the

inspector's report but does not include any other documents so appended; but any person who has received a copy of the report may apply to the Secretary of State in writing, within 6 weeks of the date of the Secretary of State's decision, for an opportunity of inspecting any such documents and the Secretary of State shall afford him that opportunity. **[879]**

18. Procedure following quashing of decision

Where a decision of the Secretary of State on an application or appeal in respect of which an inquiry has been held is quashed in proceedings before any court, the Secretary of State—

    (a) shall send to the persons entitled to appear at the inquiry who appeared at it a written statement of the matters with respect to which further representations are invited for the purposes of his further consideration of the application or appeal; and

    (b) shall afford to those persons the opportunity of making, within 3 weeks of the date of the written statement, written representations to him in respect of those matters or of asking for the re-opening of the inquiry; and

    (c) may, as he thinks fit, cause the inquiry to be reopened (whether by the same or a different inspector) and if he does so paragraphs (3) to (8) of rule 10 shall apply as if the references to an inquiry were references to a re-opened inquiry. **[880]**

19. Allowing further time

The Secretary of State may at any time in any particular case allow further time for the taking of any step which is required or enabled to be taken by virtue of these Rules, and references in these Rules to a day by which, or a period within which, any step is required or enabled to be taken shall be construed accordingly. **[881]**

20. Service of notices by post

Notices or documents required or authorised to be served or sent under these Rules may be sent by post. **[882]**

21. Revocation, savings and transitional

(1) Subject to paragraph (2), the Town and Country Planning (Inquiries Procedure) Rules 1988 are hereby revoked, except rule 21 of those Rules so far as it makes provision for the continued application of the Town and Country Planning (Inquiries Procedure) Rules 1974.

(2) Any application or appeal to which the 1988 Rules applied which has not been determined on the date when these Rules come into force ("the commencement date") shall be continued under these Rules, but—

(a) rules 13 and 14(5) of the 1988 Rules shall continue to apply, and rules 8(2), 13 and 14(5) of these Rules shall not apply, in a case where at the commencement date—

    (i) an inquiry has been opened but not closed; or

    (ii) a date has been fixed for the holding of an inquiry which is less than 6 weeks after the commencement date; and

(b) persons who were section 29(3) parties under the 1988 Rules shall be treated as statutory parties. **[883]**

NOTES
Commencement: 30 September 1992.

TOWN AND COUNTRY PLANNING APPEALS (DETERMINATION BY INSPECTORS) (INQUIRIES PROCEDURE) RULES 1992
(SI 1992/2039)

NOTES
Made: 24 August 1992
Authority: Tribunals and Inquiries Act 1971, s 11; now have effect under Tribunals and Inquiries Act 1992, s 9

1. Citation and commencement

These Rules may be cited as the Town and Country Planning Appeals (Determination by Inspectors) (Inquiries Procedure) Rules 1992 and shall come into force on 30th September 1992. **[884]**

NOTES
Commencement: 30 September 1992.

2. Interpretation

In these Rules, unless the context otherwise requires—

    "assessor" means a person appointed by the Secretary of State to sit with an inspector at an inquiry or re-opened inquiry to advise the inspector on such matters arising as the Secretary of State may specify;

    "the Commission" means the Historic Buildings and Monuments Commission for England;

    "conservation area consent" has the meaning given in section 74(1) of the Listed Buildings Act;

    "development order" has the meaning given in section 59 of the Planning Act;

    "document" includes a photograph, map or plan;

    "inquiry" means a local inquiry in relation to which these Rules apply;

    "inspector" means a person appointed by the Secretary of State under Schedule 6 to the Planning Act or, as the case may be, Schedule 3 to the Listed Buildings Act to determine an appeal;

    "land" means the land or building to which an inquiry relates; "the Listed Buildings Act" means the Planning (Listed Buildings and Conservation Areas) Act 1990;

    "listed building consent" has the meaning given in section 8(7) of the Listed Buildings Act;

"local planning authority" means the body who were responsible for dealing
with the application occasioning the appeal;

"the Planning Act" means the Town and Country Planning Act 1990;

"pre-inquiry meeting" means a meeting held before an inquiry to consider
what may be done with a view to securing that the inquiry is conducted
efficiently and expeditiously;

"relevant date" means the date of the written notice informing the appellant
and the local planning authority that an inquiry is to be held, and "relevant
notice" means that notice;

"the 1988 Rules" means the Town and Country Planning Appeals
(Determination by inspectors) (inquiries Procedure) Rules 1988;

"statement of case" means, and is comprised of, a written statement which
contains full particulars of the case which a person proposes to put forward
at an inquiry, and a list of any documents which that person intends to
refer to or put in evidence.

"statutory party" means—

(a) a person mentioned in paragraph (1)(b)(i) of article 22A of the Town
and Country Planning General Development Order 1988 whose
representations the inspector is required by paragraph (3) of that
article to take into account in determining the appeal to which an
inquiry relates, and such a person whose representations the local
planning authority were required by paragraph (1) of that article to
take into account in determining the application occasioning the
appeal; and

(b) a person whose representations the inspector is required by paragraphs
(3)(b) and (5) of regulation 6 of the Planning (Listed Buildings and
Conversation Areas) Regulations 1990 to take into account in
determining the appeal to which an inquiry relates, and a person
whose representations the local planning authority were required by
paragraph (3)(b) of that regulation to take into account in determining
the application occasioning the appeal.   **[885]**

NOTES

Commencement: 30 September 1992.

3. Application of Rules

(1) These Rules apply in relation to any local inquiry held in England or Wales by
an inspector before he determines—

(a) an appeal to the Secretary of State in relation to planning permission under
section 78 of the Planning Act;

(b) an appeal to the Secretary of State in relation to listed building consent
under section 20 of the Listed Buildings Act, or in relation to conservation
area consent under that section as applied by virtue of section 74(3) of that
Act,

but do not apply to any local inquiry by reason of the application of any provision
mentioned in this paragraph by any other enactment.

(2) Where these Rules apply in relation to an appeal which at some time fell to
be disposed of in accordance with the Town and Country Planning (inquiries
Procedure) Rules 1992 or Rules superseded by those Rules, any step taken or thing
done under those Rules which could have been done under any corresponding
provision of these Rules shall have effect as if it had been taken or done under that
corresponding provision.   **[886]**

NOTES
Commencement: 30 September 1992.

4. Preliminary information to be supplied by local planning authority

(1) The local planning authority shall, on receipt of a notice informing them that an inquiry is to be held ("the relevant notice"), forthwith inform the Secretary of State and the appellant in writing of the name and address of any statutory party who has made representations to them; and the Secretary of State shall as soon as practicable thereafter inform the appellant and the local planning authority of the name and address of any statutory party who has made representations to him.

(2) This paragraph applies where—

    (a) the Secretary of State has given to the local planning authority a direction restricting the grant of planning permission for which application was made; or

    (b) in a case relating to listed building consent, the Commission has given a direction to the local planning authority pursuant to section 14(2) of the Listed Buildings Act as to how the application is to be determined; or

    (c) the Secretary of State or any other Minister of the Crown or any government department, or any body falling within rule 11(1)(c), has expressed in writing to the local planning authority the view that the application should not be granted either wholly or in part, or should be granted only subject to conditions; or

    (d) any authority or person consulted in pursuance of a development order has made representations to the local planning authority about the application.

(3) Where paragraph (2) applies the local planning authority shall forthwith after the date of the relevant notice ("the relevant date") inform the person or body concerned of the inquiry and, unless they have already done so, that person or body shall thereupon give the local planning authority a written statement of the reasons for making the direction, expressing the view or making the representations, as the case may be.   **[887]**

NOTES
Commencement: 30 September 1992.

5. Notification of identity of inspector

(1) Subject to paragraph (2), the Secretary of State shall notify the name of the inspector to every person entitled to appear at the inquiry.

(2) Where the Secretary of State appoints another inspector instead of the person previously appointed and it is not practicable to notify the new appointment before the inquiry is held, the inspector holding the inquiry shall, at its commencement, announce his name and the fact of his appointment.   **[888]**

NOTES
Commencement: 30 September 1992.

6. Service of statements of case etc.

(1) Subject to paragraph (4), the local planning authority shall, not later than 6 weeks after the relevant date, serve a statement of case on the Secretary of State, the appellant and any statutory party.

(2) Where rule 4(2) applies the local planning authority shall—

(a) include in their statement of case the terms of—

  (i) any direction given together with a statement of the reasons therefore; and

  (ii) any view expressed or representation made on which they intend to rely in their submissions at the inquiry; and

(b) within the period mentioned in paragraph (1) supply a copy of their statement to the person or body concerned.

(3) Subject to paragraph (4), the appellant shall, not later than 9 weeks after the relevant date, serve a statement of case on the Secretary of State, the local planning authority and any statutory party.

(4) The statement of case mentioned in paragraph (1) or, as the case may be, paragraph (3) shall be served no later than the day which is 4 weeks before the date fixed for the holding of the inquiry, where that day falls within the period mentioned in whichever of those paragraphs is applicable to the case.

(5) The appellant and the local planning authority may each require the other to send them a copy of any document, or of the relevant part of any document, referred to in the list of documents comprised in that party's statement of case; and any such document, or relevant part, shall be sent as soon as practicable to the party who required it.

(6) The Secretary of State may in writing require any other person who has notified him of an intention or a wish to appear at an inquiry to serve a statement of case, within 4 weeks of being so required, on the appellant, the local planning authority, the Secretary of State and any (or any other) statutory party.

(7) The Secretary of State shall supply any person from whom he requires a statement of case in accordance with paragraph (6) with a copy of the appellant's and the local planning authority's statement of case and shall inform that person of the name and address of every person on whom his statement of case is required to be served.

(8) The Secretary of State may require any person who has served a statement of case in accordance with this rule to provide such further information about the matters contained in the statement as he may specify; and a person so required shall provide the Secretary of State with that information in writing and shall, at the same time, send a copy to any other person on whom the statement of case has been served.

(9) Any person other than the appellant who serves a statement of case on the local planning authority shall serve with it a copy of any document, or of the relevant part of any document, referred to in the list comprised in that statement, unless a copy of the document or part of the document in question is already available for inspection pursuant to paragraph (11).

(10) The Secretary of State shall transmit any statement of case served on him in accordance with this rule to the inspector.

(11) The local planning authority shall afford to any person who so requests a reasonable opportunity to inspect and, where practicable, take copies of any statement of case or other document which, or a copy of which, has been served on them in accordance with this rule, and of their statement of case together with a copy of any document, or of the relevant part of any document, referred to in the list comprised in that statement or otherwise served by them pursuant to this rule; and shall specify

in their statement of case the time and place at which the opportunity will be afforded. **[889]**

NOTES
Commencement: 30 September 1992.

7. Statements of matters and pre-inquiry meetings

(1) An inspector may, not later than 12 weeks after the relevant date, cause to be served on the appellant, the local planning authority and any statutory party a written statement of the matters about which he particularly wishes to be informed for the purposes of his consideration of the appeal.

(2) An inspector may hold a pre-inquiry meeting where he considers it desirable and shall arrange for not less than 2 weeks written notice of it to be given to the appellant, the local planning authority, any statutory party, any other person known to be entitled to appear at the inquiry and any other person whose presence at the meeting appears to him to be desirable.

(3) The inspector shall preside at the pre-inquiry meeting and shall determine the matters to be discussed and the procedure to be followed, and he may require any person present at the meeting who, in his opinion, is behaving in a disruptive manner to leave and may refuse to permit that person to return or to attend any further meeting, or may permit him to return or attend only on such conditions as he may specify. **[890]**

NOTES
Commencement: 30 September 1992.

8. Inquiry time-table

(1) An inspector may at any time arrange a time-table for the proceedings at, or at part of, an inquiry and may at any time vary the time-table.

(2) An inspector may specify in a time-table arranged pursuant to this rule a date by which any proof of evidence and summary required by rule 14(1) to be sent to him shall be so sent. **[891]**

NOTES
Commencement: 30 September 1992.

9. Notification of appointment of assessor

Where the Secretary of State appoints an assessor, he shall notify every person entitled to appear at the inquiry of the name of the assessor and of the matters on which he is to advise the inspector. **[892]**

NOTES
Commencement: 30 September 1992.

10. Date and notification of inquiry

(1) The date fixed by the Secretary of State for the holding of an inquiry shall be, unless he considers such a date impracticable, not later than 20 weeks after the relevant date: and where he considers it impracticable to fix a date in accordance with the preceding provisions of this paragraph, the date fixed shall be the earliest date after the end of the period mentioned which he considers to be practicable.

(2) Unless the Secretary of State agrees a lesser period of notice with the appellant and the local planning authority, he shall give not less than 4 weeks written

notice of the date, time and place for the holding of an inquiry to every person entitled to appear at the inquiry.

(3) The Secretary of State may vary the date fixed for the holding of an inquiry, whether or not the date as varied is within the period of 20 weeks mentioned in paragraph (1); and paragraph (2) shall apply to the variation of a date as it applied to the date originally fixed.

(4) The Secretary of State may vary the time or place for the holding of an inquiry and shall give such notice of any such variation as appears to him to be reasonable.

(5) The Secretary of State may require the local planning authority to take one or more of the following steps—

   (a) not less than 2 weeks before the date fixed for the holding of an inquiry, to publish a notice of the inquiry in one or more newspapers circulating in the locality in which the land is situated;
   (b) to serve a notice of the inquiry on such persons or classes of persons as he may specify, within such period as he may specify;
   (c) to post a notice of the inquiry in a conspicuous place near to the land, within such period as he may specify.

(6) Where the land is under the control of the appellant he shall, if so required by the Secretary of State, affix a notice of the inquiry firmly to the land or to some object on or near the land, in such manner as to be readily visible to and legible by members of the public; and he shall not remove the notice, or cause or permit it to be removed, for such period before the inquiry as the Secretary of State may specify.

(7) Every notice of inquiry published, served or posted pursuant to paragraph (5), or affixed pursuant to paragraph (6), shall contain—

   (a) a clear statement of the date, time and place of the inquiry and of the powers enabling the inspector to determine the appeal in question;
   (b) a written description of the land sufficient to identify approximately its location; and
   (c) a brief description of the subject matter of the appeal.   **[893]**

NOTES

Commencement: 30 September 1992.

11. Appearances at inquiry

(1) The persons entitled to appear at an inquiry are—

   (a) the appellant;
   (b) the local planning authority;
   (c) any of the following bodies if the land is situated in their area and they are not the local planning authority—

      (i) a county or district council;
      (ii) a National Park Committee within the meaning of paragraph 5 of Schedule 17 to the Local Government Act 1972;
      (iii) a joint planning board constituted under section 2(1) of the Planning Act or a joint planning board or special planning board reconstituted under Part I of Schedule 17 to the Local Government Act 1972;
      (iv) an urban development corporation established under section 135 of the Local Government, Planning and Land Act 1980;
      (v) an enterprise zone authority designated under Schedule 32 to the Local Government, Planning and Land Act 1980;

      (vi) the Broads Authority, within the meaning of the Norfolk and Suffolk Broads Act 1988;

     (vii) a housing action trust specified in an order made under section 67(1) of the Housing Act 1988;

  (d) where the land is in an area designated as a new town, the development corporation for the new town or the Commission for the New Towns as its successor;

  (e) a statutory party;

  (f) the council of the parish or community in which the land is situated, if that council made representations to the local planning authority in respect of the application in pursuance of a provision of a development order;

  (g) where the application was required to be notified to the Commission under section 14 of the Listed Buildings Act, the Commission;

  (h) any other person who has served a statement of case in accordance with rule 6(6).

(2) Nothing in paragraph (1) shall prevent the inspector from permitting any other person to appear at an inquiry, and such permission shall not be unreasonably withheld.

(3) Any person entitled or permitted to appear may do so on his own behalf or be represented by counsel, solicitor or any other person. **[894]**

NOTES

Commencement: 30 September 1992.

12. Representatives of government departments and other authorities at inquiry

(1) Where—

  (a) the Secretary of State or the Commission has given a direction such as is described in rule 4(2)(a) or (b); or

  (b) the Secretary of State or any other Minister of the Crown or any government department, or any body falling within rule 1 1(1)(c), has expressed a view such as is described in rule 4(2)(c) and the local planning authority have included its terms in a statement served in accordance with rule 6(1),

the appellant may, not later than 2 weeks before the date of an inquiry, apply in writing to the Secretary of State for a representative of the Secretary of State or of the other Minister, department or body concerned to be made available at the inquiry.

(2) Where an application is made in accordance with paragraph (1), the Secretary of State shall make a representative available to attend the inquiry or, as the case may be, transmit the application to the other Minister, department or body concerned who shall make a representative available to attend the inquiry.

(3) A person attending an inquiry as a representative in pursuance of this rule shall state the reasons for the direction or expressed view and shall give evidence and be subject to cross-examination to the same extent as any other witness.

(4) Nothing in paragraph (3) shall require a representative of a Minister or a government department to answer any question which in the opinion of the inspector is directed to the merits of government policy. **[895]**

NOTES

Commencement: 30 September 1992.

13. Inspector may act in place of Secretary of State

An inspector may in place of the Secretary of State take such steps as the Secretary of State is required or enabled to take under or by virtue of rule 6(6) to (8), rule 10, rule 12(1) or (2) or rule 20; and where an inspector requires further information pursuant to rule 6(8), that information shall be sent to him.   **[896]**

NOTES
Commencement: 30 September 1992.

14. Proofs of evidence

(1) A person entitled to appear at an inquiry who proposes to give, or to call another person to give, evidence at the inquiry by reading a proof of evidence shall send a copy of the proof to the inspector together with, subject to paragraph (2), a written summary.

(2) No written summary shall be required where the proof of evidence proposed to be read contains no more than 1500 words.

(3) The proof and any summary shall be sent to the inspector not later than—
    (a) 3 weeks before the date fixed for the holding of the inquiry, or
    (b) where a time-table has been arranged pursuant to rule 8 which specifies a date by which the proof and any summary shall be sent to the inspector, that date.

(4) Where the appellant or the local planning authority send a copy of a proof to an inspector in accordance with paragraph (1), with or without a summary, they shall at the same time send a copy of that proof and any summary to the other party, and to any statutory party; and where any other party so sends a copy of such documents he shall at the same time send a copy to the appellant, the local planning authority and any (or any other) statutory party.

(5) Where a written summary is provided in accordance with paragraph (1), only that summary shall be read at the inquiry, unless the inspector permits or requires otherwise.

(6) Any person required by this rule to send a copy of a proof to any other person shall send with it a copy of the whole, or the relevant part, of any document referred to in it, unless a copy of the document or part of the document in question is already available for inspection pursuant to rule 6(11).

(7) The local planning authority shall afford to any person who so requests a reasonable opportunity to inspect and, where practicable, take copies of any document sent to or by them in accordance with this rule.   **[897]**

NOTES
Commencement: 30 September 1992.

15. Procedure at inquiry

(1) Except as otherwise provided in these Rules, the inspector shall determine the procedure at an inquiry.

(2) Unless in any particular case the inspector with the consent of the appellant otherwise determines, the appellant shall begin and shall have the right of final reply; and the other persons entitled or permitted to appear shall be heard in such order as the inspector may determine.

(3) A person entitled to appear at an inquiry shall be entitled to call evidence

and the appellant, the local planning authority and any statutory party shall be entitled to cross- examine persons giving evidence, but, subject to the foregoing and paragraphs (4) and (5), the calling of evidence and the cross-examination of persons giving evidence shall otherwise be at the inspector's discretion.

(4) The inspector may refuse to permit—

    (a) the giving or production of evidence,

    (b) the cross-examination of persons giving evidence, or

    (c) the presentation of any other matter,

which he considers to be irrelevant or repetitious; but where he refuses to permit the giving of oral evidence, the person wishing to give the evidence may submit to him any evidence or other matter in writing before the close of the inquiry.

(5) Where a person gives evidence at an inquiry by reading a summary of his evidence in accordance with rule 14(5), the proof of evidence referred to in rule 14(1) shall, unless the person required to provide the summary notifies the inspector that he now wishes to rely on the contents of the summary alone, be treated as tendered in evidence, and the person whose evidence the proof contains shall then be subject to cross-examination on it to the same extent as if it were evidence he had given orally.

(6) The inspector may direct that facilities shall be afforded to any person appearing at an inquiry to take or obtain copies of documentary evidence open to public inspection.

(7) The inspector may require any person appearing or present at an inquiry who, in his opinion, is behaving in a disruptive manner to leave and may refuse to permit that person to return, or may permit him to return only on such conditions as he may specify; but any such person may submit to him any evidence or other matter in writing before the close of the inquiry.

(8) The inspector may allow any person to alter or add to a statement of case served under rule 6 so far as may be necessary for the purposes of the inquiry; but he shall (if necessary by adjourning the inquiry) give every other person entitled to appear who is appearing at the inquiry an adequate opportunity of considering any fresh matter or document.

(9) The inspector may proceed with an inquiry in the absence of any person entitled to appear at it.

(10) The inspector may take into account any written representation or evidence or any other document received by him from any person before an inquiry opens or during the inquiry provided that he discloses it at the inquiry.

(11) The inspector may from time to time adjourn an inquiry and, if the date, time and place of the adjourned inquiry are announced before the adjournment, no further notice shall be required. **[898]**

NOTES
  Commencement: 30 September 1992.

16. Site inspections

(1) The inspector may make an unaccompanied inspection of the land before or during an inquiry without giving notice of his intention to the persons entitled to appear at the inquiry.

(2) The inspector may, during an inquiry or after its close, inspect the land in the company of the appellant, the local planning authority and any statutory party; and

he shall make such an inspection if so requested by the appellant or the local planning authority before or during an inquiry.

(3) in all cases where the inspector intends to make an inspection of the kind referred to in paragraph (2) he shall announce during the inquiry the date and time at which he proposes to make it.

(4) The inspector shall not be bound to defer an inspection of the kind referred to in paragraph (2) where any person mentioned in that paragraph is not present at the time appointed. **[899]**

NOTES
Commencement: 30 September 1992.

17. Procedure after inquiry

(1) Where an assessor has been appointed, he may, after the close of the inquiry, make a report in writing to the inspector in respect of the matters on which he was appointed to advise, and where he does so the inspector shall state in his notification of his decision pursuant to rule 18 that such a report was made.

(2) if, after the close of an inquiry, an inspector proposes to take into consideration any new evidence or any new matter of fact (not being a matter of government policy) which was not raised at the inquiry and which he considers to be material to his decision, he shall not come to a decision without first—

(a) notifying the persons entitled to appear at the inquiry who appeared at it of the matter in question; and

(b) affording to them an opportunity of making written representations to him with respect to it within 3 weeks of the date of the notification or of asking within that period for the re-opening of the inquiry.

(3) An inspector may, as he thinks fit, cause an inquiry to be re-opened, and he shall do so if asked by the appellant or the local planning authority in the circumstances and within the period mentioned in paragraph (2); and where an inquiry is re-opened—

(a) the inspector shall send to the persons entitled to appear at the inquiry who appeared at it a written statement of the matters with respect to which further evidence is invited; and

(b) paragraphs (2) to (7) of rule 10 shall apply as if the references to an inquiry were references to a re-opened inquiry. **[900]**

NOTES
Commencement: 30 September 1992.

18. Notification of decision

(1) An inspector shall notify his decision on an appeal, and his reasons for it, in writing to all persons entitled to appear at the inquiry who did appear, and to any other person who, having appeared at the inquiry, has asked to be notified of the decision.

(2) Any person entitled to be notified of the inspector's decision under paragraph (1) may apply to the Secretary of State in writing, within 6 weeks of the date of the decision, for an opportunity of inspecting any documents listed in the notification

and any report made by an assessor and the Secretary of State shall afford him that opportunity. **[901]**

NOTES
Commencement: 30 September 1992.

19. Procedure following quashing of decision

Where a decision of an inspector on an appeal in respect of which an inquiry has been held is quashed in proceedings before any court, the Secretary of State—

(a) shall send to the persons entitled to appear at the inquiry who appeared at it a written statement of the matters with respect to which further representations are invited for the purposes of the further consideration of the appeal; and

(b) shall afford to those persons the opportunity of making, within 3 weeks of the date of the written statement, written representations to him in respect of those matters or of asking for the re-opening of the inquiry; and

(c) may, as he thinks fit, direct that the inquiry be re-opened, and if he does so paragraphs (2) to (7) of rule 10 shall apply as if the references to an inquiry were references to a re-opened inquiry. **[902]**

NOTES
Commencement: 30 September 1992.

20. Allowing further time

The Secretary of State may at any time in any particular case allow further time for the taking of any step which is required or enabled to be taken by virtue of these Rules, and references in these Rules to a day by which, or a period within which, any step is required or enabled to be taken shall be construed accordingly. **[903]**

NOTES
Commencement: 30 September 1992.

21. Service of notices by post

Notices or documents required or authorised to be served or sent under these Rules may be sent by post. **[904]**

NOTES
Commencement: 30 September 1992.

22. Revocation, savings and transitional

(1) Subject to paragraph (2), the Town and Country Planning Appeals (Determination by Inspectors) (Inquiries Procedure) Rules 1988 are hereby revoked.

(2) Any appeal to which the 1988 Rules applied which has not been determined on the date when these Rules come into force ("the commencement date") shall be continued under these Rules, but—

(a) rules 14 and 15(5) of the 1988 Rules shall continue to apply, and rules 8(2), 14 and 15(5) of these Rules shall not apply, in a case where at the commencement date—

(i) an inquiry has been opened but not closed; or

(ii) a date has been fixed for the holding of an inquiry which is less than 6 weeks after the commencement date; and

(b) persons who were section 29(3) parties under the 1988 Rules shall be
treated as statutory parties. **[905]**

TOWN AND COUNTRY PLANNING (MODIFICATION AND DISCHARGE OF PLANNING OBLIGATIONS) REGULATIONS 1992
(SI 1992/2832)

NOTES
Made: 9 November 1992.
Authority: Town and Country Planning Act 1990, ss 106A(7), (9), 106B(3), (4), (7), 299A(4), 333(1), Sch 6, para 1(1).

1. Citation, commencement and interpretation

(1) These Regulations may be cited as the Town and Country Planning (Modification
and Discharge of Planning Obligations) Regulations 1992 and shall come into force
on 10th December 1992.

(2) In these Regulations, "the 1990 Act" means the Town and Country Planning
Act 1990. **[906]**

NOTES
Commencement: 10 December 1992.

2. Application

These Regulations apply to applications under section 106A of the 1990 Act and
appeals under section 106B of the 1990 Act made in respect of the modification or
discharge of planning obligations entered into under section 106 or section 299A of
the 1990 Act. **[907]**

NOTES
Commencement: 10 December 1992.
1990 Act: Town and Country Planning Act 1990.

3. Applications for the modification or discharge of planning obligations

(1) An application for the modification or discharge of a planning obligation shall
be made on a form provided by the local planning authority, which shall require the
following information—

    (a) the name and address of the applicant;
    (b) the address or location of the land to which the application relates and the
        nature of the applicant's interest in that land;
    (c) sufficient information to enable the authority to identify the planning
        obligation which the applicant wishes to have modified or discharged;
    (d) the applicant's reasons for applying for the modification or discharge of
        that obligation; and

(e) such other information as the authority consider necessary to enable them to determine the application.

(2) An application for the modification or discharge of a planning obligation shall include—

(a) the information required by the application form;
(b) a map identifying the land to which the obligation relates; and
(c) such other information as the applicant considers relevant to the determination of the application.   **[908]**

NOTES
Commencement: 10 December 1992.

4. Notification of applications by applicant

(1) An applicant for the modification or discharge of a planning obligation shall give notice of the application to any person (other than the applicant) against whom, on the day 21 days before the date of the application, the planning obligation is enforceable and whose name and address is known to the applicant.

(2) In order to comply with paragraph (1), the applicant shall take reasonable steps to ascertain the name and address of every such person.

(3) Where the names and addresses of all such persons are not known to the applicant after he has taken reasonable steps to ascertain that information, he shall, during the 21 day period immediately preceding the application, publish notice of the application in a local newspaper circulating in the locality of the land to which the application relates.

(4) The notice required to be served or published by this regulation shall be in the form set out in Part 1 of the Schedule and shall invite representations on the application to be made to the local planning authority within 21 days of the date on which the notice is served or published, as the case may be.

(5) An application for the modification or discharge of a planning obligation shall be accompanied by a certificate, in the appropriate form set out in Part 2 of the Schedule, certifying that the requirements in the preceding provisions of this regulation have been satisfied.   **[909]**

NOTES
Commencement: 10 December 1992.

5. Publicity for applications by local planning authority

(1) When a local planning authority receive an application for the modification or discharge of a planning obligation they shall publicise the application by—

(a) posting notice of the application on or near the land to which the planning obligation relates for not less than 21 days; or
(b) serving notice of the application on the owners and occupiers of land adjoining that land; or
(c) publishing notice of the application in a local newspaper circulating in the locality in which that land is situated.

(2) The notice posted, served, or published in accordance with paragraph (1) shall be in the form set out in Part 3 of the Schedule and shall invite representations on the application to be made to the local planning authority within 21 days of the date on which the notice is posted or served, or within 14 days of the date on which the notice is published, as the case may be.

(3) The local planning authority shall make a copy of the application and the relevant part of the instrument by which the planning obligation was entered into available for inspection during the period allowed for making representations pursuant to paragraph (2).

(4) In paragraph (1)(b) "owner" in relation to any land means any person who—

(a) is the estate owner in respect of the fee simple; or
(b) is entitled to a tenancy granted or extended for a term of years certain of which not less than seven years remain unexpired.   **[910]**

NOTES
Commencement: 10 December 1992.

6. Determination of applications by local planning authority

(1) A local planning authority shall not determine an application for the modification or discharge of a planning obligation before the expiry of the period or periods provided for making representations in accordance with regulations 4(4) and 5(2).

(2) Subject to paragraph (1), a local planning authority shall give the applicant written notice of their decision within—

(a) 8 weeks from the date on which the application is received; or
(b) except where the applicant has already given notice of appeal to the Secretary of State, such extended period as may be agreed upon in writing by the applicant and the authority.

(3) When a local planning authority determine that a planning obligation shall continue to have effect without modification, the notice of that decision shall—

(a) state, clearly and precisely, the authority's full reasons for their decision; and
(b) include a statement to the effect that the applicant may appeal to the Secretary of State against the decision within 6 months of the date of the notice or within such longer period as the Secretary of State may, at any time, allow.   **[911]**

NOTES
Commencement: 10 December 1992.

7. Appeals to the Secretary of State

(1) An appeal under section 106B of the 1990 Act shall be made with 6 months of—

(a) the date of the notice of the decision giving rise to the appeal; or
(b) in the case of an appeal under section 106B(1)(a) (non-determination), the expiry of the period specified in regulation 6(2),

or within such longer period as the Secretary of State may, at any time, allow.

(2) An appeal under section 106B shall—

(a) be made on a form obtained from the Secretary of State;
(b) include the information specified in the form; and
(c) be accompanied by a copy of—

(i) the application made to the local planning authority which has occasioned the appeal;
(ii) the certificate which accompanied the application in accordance with regulation 4(5);

      (iii) the instrument by which the planning obligation which is the subject of the application was entered into;

      (iv) any correspondence with the authority relating to the application; and

      (v) the notice of decision, if any.

    (3) An appellant shall send a copy of the completed notice of appeal form to the local planning authority at the same time as the appeal is made to the Secretary of State. **[912]**

NOTES

Commencement: 10 December 1992.

1990 Act: Town and Country Planning Act 1990.

8. Determination of appeals by appointed persons

Appeals under section 106B of the Town and Country Planning Act 1990 are prescribed for the purposes of paragraph 1(1) of Schedule 6 to that Act as a class of appeals which are to be determined by a person appointed by the Secretary of State for the purpose instead of by the Secretary of State. **[913]**

NOTES

Commencement: 10 December 1992.

SCHEDULE
PRESCRIBED NOTICES AND CERTIFICATES

PART 1

Regulation 4(5)

NOTICE OF AN APPLICATION TO MODIFY OR DISCHARGE A PLANNING OBLIGATION UNDER SECTION 106A OF THE TOWN AND COUNTRY PLANNING ACT 1990

(Notice to be given by applicant)

I give notice that (a)
is applying to the (b)
to modify/discharge (delete as appropriate) the planning obligation described below

Planning Obligation

Obligation: (c)
Land to which obligation relates: (d)
Date on which obligation was entered into: (e)

Any person against whom the planning obligation is enforceable who wishes to make representations about this application should write to the Council at (f) by (g). (Members of the public will be invited to make representations when the application has been submitted to the Council).

Signed ....

On behalf of (delete as appropriate) ....

Date ....

NOTES

Insert—

    (a) name of the applicant

    (b) name of the local planning authority to whom the application will be made

    (c) brief description of the planning obligation which the applicant wishes to have modified or discharged

    (d) address or location of the land

    (e) relevant date

  (f) address of the local planning authority

  (g) date giving a period of 21 days beginning with the date of service or publication of the notice, as the case may be.   **[914]**

NOTES

   Commencement: 10 December 1992.

PART 2

Regulation 4(5)

CERTIFICATE OF COMPLIANCE WITH THE NOTIFICATION REQUIREMENTS IN REGULATION 4

Certificate A

   I certify that on the day 21 days before the date of the accompanying application the planning obligation to which the application relates was enforceable against nobody other than the applicant.

                         Signed ....

On behalf of (delete where inappropriate) ....

                            Date ....

Certificate B

   I certify that the applicant has given notice to everyone else against whom, on the day 21 days before the date of the accompanying application, the planning obligation to which the application relates was enforceable, as listed below.

Person on whom notice was   *Address at which notice was*   *Date on which notice was*
served   *served*   *served*

                         Signed ....

On behalf of (delete where inappropriate) ....

                            Date ....

Certificate C

   I certify that:

     —the applicant cannot issue a Certificate A or B in respect of the accompanying application;

     —the applicant has given notice to the persons listed below, being persons against whom, on the day 21 days before the date of the application, the planning obligation to which the application relates was enforceable (delete where inappropriate)

Person on whom notice was   *Address at which notice was*   *Date on which notice was*
served   *served*   *served*

     —The applicant has taken reasonable steps to ascertain the name and address of every person against whom, on the day 21 days before the date of the application, the planning obligation to which the application relates was enforceable and who has not been given notice of the application but has been unable to do so. These steps were as follows—(a)

     —Notice of the application, as attached to this certificate, has been published in the (b) on (c).

                         Signed ....

On behalf of (delete where inappropriate) ....

                            Date ....

NOTES

   Insert—

     (a) description of steps taken

(b) name of local newspaper in which the notice was published
(c) date of publication. **[915]**

NOTES
Commencement: 10 December 1992.

PART 3

Regulation 5(2)

NOTICE OF AN APPLICATION TO MODIFY OR DISCHARGE A PLANNING OBLIGATION UNDER
SECTION 106A OF THE TOWN AND COUNTRY PLANNING ACT 1990

(Publicity by the local planning authority)

Take notice that (a) .... has applied to (b) to modify/discharge (delete as appropriate) the planning obligation described below.

Planning Obligation

Obligation (c)
Land to which obligation relates: (d)
Date on which the obligation was entered into: (e)

Members of the public may inspect copies of the application and the relevant part of the instrument creating the obligation at (f) during all reasonable hours until (g).

Anyone who wishes to make representations about the application should write to the Council at (h) by (g)

Signed ....

On behalf of (delete as appropriate) ....

Date ....

NOTES

Insert—

    (a) name of applicant
    (b) name of local planning authority
    (c) brief description of the planning obligation which the applicant wishes to have modified or discharged
    (d) address or location of the land
    (e) relevant date
    (f) address at which the documents may be inspected
    (g) date giving a period of 21 days beginning with the date on which the notice is posted, published or served, as the case may be
    (h) address of local planning authority. **[916]**

NOTES
Commencement: 10 December 1992.

ANCIENT MONUMENTS (CLASS CONSENTS) ORDER 1994
(SI 1994/1381)

NOTES
Made: 19 May 1994.
Authority: Ancient Monuments and Archaeological Areas Act 1979, ss 2, 3, 60.

1. Citation, commencement, interpretation and extent

(1) This Order may be cited as the Ancient Monuments (Class Consents) Order 1994 and shall come into force on 14th June 1994.

(2) In this Order, unless the context otherwise requires—

"the Act" means the Ancient Monuments and Archaeological Areas Act 1979;

"carried out lawfully" means carried out in accordance with the terms of a consent granted by order under section 3 of the Act, or which would have been so carried out if during the period in question the monument had been a scheduled monument;

"the Commission" means the Historic Buildings and Monuments Commission for England;

"consent" means scheduled monument consent;

"domestic gardening works" includes works carried out in the non-commercial cultivation of allotments;

"horticultural works" includes domestic gardening works; and

"ploughed land" means land on which ploughing has been carried out lawfully within the period of six years immediately preceding the works in question.

(3) This Order applies to England and Wales.   **[917]**

NOTES
Commencement: 14 June 1994.

2. Scheduled monument consent granted by this Order

(1) Subject to the provisions of this article, consent is hereby granted under section 3 of the Act for the execution of works of any class or description specified as permitted works in the Schedule to this Order.

(2) The consent granted is subject to any condition specified in the said Schedule in relation to works of a particular class or description.

(3) Nothing in this article shall operate so as to grant consent contrary to any limitation or condition specified in a consent granted under Part I of the Act otherwise than by this Order.   **[918]**

NOTES
Commencement: 14 June 1994.
The Act: Ancient Monuments and Archaeological Areas Act 1979.

3. Revocation and saving

(1) Subject to the provisions of this article, the Ancient Monuments (Class Consents) Order 1981 ("the 1981 Order") and the Ancient Monuments (Class Consents) (Amendment) Order 1984 ("the 1984 Order") are hereby revoked.

(2) The 1981 Order and the 1984 Order shall continue to be effective in respect of works commenced before this Order comes into force and any limitation or condition specified in this Order shall be disregarded in the application of article 2(3) of the 1981 Order.   **[919]**

NOTES
Commencement: 14 June 1994.

SCHEDULE

Article 2(1), (2)

CLASSES OR DESCRIPTIONS OF WORKS FOR THE EXECUTION OF WHICH
SCHEDULED MONUMENT CONSENT IS GRANTED BY ARTICLE 2 OF THIS
ORDER

CLASS 1. AGRICULTURAL, HORTICULTURAL AND FORESTRY WORKS

Permitted works:

Agricultural, horticultural and forestry works of the same kind as those previously carried out lawfully in the same location and on the same spot within that location within the period of six years immediately preceding the date on which the works commence; but excluding works falling into one or more of the following categories—

Works not permitted:

(a) in the case of ploughed land, any works likely to disturb the soil of any part of that land below the depth at which ploughing of that part has previously been carried out lawfully;

(b) in the case of land other than ploughed land, any works likely to disturb the soil below the depth of 300 millimetres;

(c) sub-soiling, drainage works, the planting or uprooting of trees, hedges or shrubs, the stripping of top soil, tipping operations, or the commercial cutting and removal of turf;

(d) the demolition, removal, extension, alteration or disturbance of any building, structure or work or of the remains thereof;

(e) the erection of any building or structure;

(f) in the case of works other than domestic gardening works, the laying of paths, hard-standings or foundations for buildings or the erection of fences or other barriers.

CLASS 2. WORKS BY [COAL MINING OPERATIONS]

Permitted works:

Works executed more than 10 metres below ground level [by any licensed operator (within the meaning of the Coal Industry Act 1994).]

CLASS 3. WORKS BY BRITISH WATERWAYS BOARD

Permitted works:

Works executed by the British Waterways Board, in relation to land owned or occupied by them, being works of repair or maintenance, not involving a material alteration to a scheduled monument, which are essential for the purpose of ensuring the functioning of a canal.

CLASS 4. WORKS FOR THE REPAIR OR MAINTENANCE OF MACHINERY

Permitted works:

Works for the repair or maintenance of machinery, being works which do not involve a material alteration to a scheduled monument.

CLASS 5. WORKS URGENTLY NECESSARY FOR SAFETY OR HEALTH

Permitted works:

Works which are urgently necessary in the interests of safety or health provided that:—

(a) the works are limited to the minimum measures immediately necessary; and

(b) notice in writing justifying in detail the need for the works is given to the Secretary of State as soon as reasonably practicable.

CLASS 6. WORKS BY THE COMMISSION

Permitted works: Works executed by the Commission.

CLASS 7. WORKS OF ARCHAEOLOGICAL EVALUATION

Permitted works: Works of archaeological evaluation carried out by or on behalf of a person who has applied for consent under section 2 of the Act being works carried out—

(a) in order to supply the Secretary of State with information required by him for the determination of that application;

(b) under the supervision of a person approved for that purpose in writing by the Secretary of State or the Commission; and

(c) in accordance with a written specification approved for that purpose by the Secretary of State or the Commission.

CLASS 8. WORKS CARRIED OUT UNDER CERTAIN AGREEMENTS CONCERNING ANCIENT MONUMENTS

Permitted works: Works for the maintenance or preservation of a scheduled monument or its amenities being works executed in accordance with the terms of a written agreement between the occupier of the monument and the Secretary of State or the Commission under section 17 of the Act.

CLASS 9. WORKS GRANT AIDED UNDER SECTION 24 OF THE ACT

Permitted works: Works for the preservation, maintenance or management of a scheduled monument being works executed in accordance with the terms of a written agreement under which the Secretary of State or the Commission defray, or contribute towards, the cost of those works pursuant to their powers under section 24 of the Act.

CLASS 10. WORKS UNDERTAKEN BY THE ROYAL COMMISSION ON THE HISTORICAL MONUMENTS OF ENGLAND OR THE ROYAL COMMISSION ON ANCIENT AND HISTORICAL MONUMENTS OF WALES

Permitted works: Works consisting of the placing of survey markers to a depth not exceeding 300 millimetres for the purpose of measured surveying of visible remains undertaken by the Royal Commission on the Historical Monuments of England or by the Royal Commission on Ancient and Historical Monuments of Wales.

[920]

NOTES

Commencement: 14 June 1994.

Class 2: in the heading and in column 2, words in square brackets substituted by SI 1994/2567, art 2, Schedule.

The Act: Ancient Monuments and Archaeological Areas Act 1979.

CONSERVATION (NATURAL HABITATS, &C) REGULATIONS 1994

(SI 1994/2716)

NOTES

Made: 20 October 1994.

Authority: European Communities Act 1972, s 2.

ARRANGEMENT OF REGULATIONS

PART I

INTRODUCTORY PROVISIONS

PART II

CONSERVATION OF NATURAL HABITATS AND HABITATS OF SPECIES

European sites

Register of European sites

Management agreements

Control of potentially damaging operations

Special nature conservation orders

PART I

INTRODUCTORY PROVISIONS

1. Citation and commencement

(1) These Regulations may be cited as the Conservation (Natural Habitats, &c) Regulations 1994.

(2) These Regulations shall come into force on the tenth day after that on which they are made.   **[921]**

NOTES

Commencement: 30 October 1994.

2. Interpretation and application

(1) In these Regulations—

"agriculture Minister" means the Minister of Agriculture, Fisheries and Food or the Secretary of State;

"competent authority" shall be construed in accordance with regulation 6;

"destroy", in relation to an egg, includes doing anything to the egg which is calculated to prevent it from hatching, and "destruction" shall be construed accordingly;

"enactment" includes a local enactment and an enactment contained in subordinate legislation within the meaning of the Interpretation Act 1978;

"European site" has the meaning given by regulation 10 and "European marine site" means a European site which consists of, or so far as it consists of, marine areas;

"functions" includes powers and duties;

"the Habitats Directive" has the meaning given by regulation 3(1);

"land" includes land covered by water and as respects Scotland includes salmon fishings;

"livestock" includes any animal which is kept—

(a) for the provision of food, skins or fur,

(b) for the purpose of its use in the carrying on of any agricultural activity, or

(c) for the provision or improvement of shooting or fishing;

"local planning authority" means—

(a) in England and Wales, except as otherwise provided, any authority having any function as a local planning authority or mineral planning authority under the Town and Country Planning Act 1990, and

(b) in Scotland, a planning authority within the meaning of section 172(1) of the Local Government (Scotland) Act 1973;

"management agreement" means an agreement entered into, or having effect as if entered into, under regulation 16;

"marine area" means any land covered (continuously or intermittently) by tidal waters or any part of the sea in or adjacent to Great Britain up to the seaward limit of territorial waters;

"Natura 2000" means the European network of special areas of conservation, and special protection areas under the Wild Birds Directive, provided for by Article 3(1) of the Habitats Directive;

"nature conservation body", and "appropriate nature conservation body" in relation to England, Wales or Scotland, have the meaning given by regulation 4;

"occupier", for the purposes of Part III (protection of species), includes, in relation to any land other than the foreshore, any person having any right of hunting, shooting, fishing or taking game or fish;

"planning authority", in Scotland, means a planning authority within the meaning of section 172(1) of the Local Government (Scotland) Act 1973;

"the register" means the register of European sites in Great Britain provided for by regulation 11;

"relevant authorities", in relation to marine areas and European marine sites, shall be construed in accordance with regulation 5;

"statutory undertaker" has the same meaning as in the National Parks and Access to the Countryside Act 1949;

"the Wild Birds Directive" means Council Directive 79/409/EEC on the conservation of wild birds.

(2) Unless the context otherwise requires, expressions used in these Regulations and in the Habitats Directive have the same meaning as in that Directive.

The following expressions, in particular, are defined in Article 1 of that Directive—

"priority natural habitat types" and "priority species";

"site" and "site of Community importance"; and

"special area of conservation".

(3) In these Regulations, unless otherwise indicated—

(a) any reference to a numbered regulation or Schedule is to the regulation or Schedule in these Regulations which bears that number, and

(b) any reference in a regulation or Schedule to a numbered paragraph is to the paragraph of that regulation or Schedule which bears that number.

(4) Subject to regulation 68 (which provides for Part IV to be construed as one with the Town and Country Planning Act 1990), these Regulations apply to the Isles of Scilly as if the Isles were a county and the Council of the Isles were a county council.

(5) For the purposes of these Regulations the territorial waters of the United Kingdom adjacent to Great Britain shall be treated as part of Great Britain and

references to England, Wales and Scotland shall be construed as including the adjacent territorial waters.

For the purposes of this paragraph—

(a) territorial waters include any waters landward of the baselines from which the breadth of the territorial sea is measured; and

(b) any question as to whether territorial waters are to be treated as adjacent to England, Wales or Scotland shall be determined by the Secretary of State or, for any purpose in relation to which the Minister of Agriculture, Fisheries and Food has responsibility, by the Secretary of State and that Minister acting jointly. [922]

NOTES
Commencement: 30 October 1994.

3. Implementation of Directive

(1) These Regulations make provision for the purpose of implementing, for Great Britain, Council Directive 92/43/EEC on the conservation of natural habitats and of wild fauna and flora (referred to in these Regulations as "the Habitats Directive").

(2) The Secretary of State, the Minister of Agriculture, Fisheries and Food and the nature conservation bodies shall exercise their functions under the enactments relating to nature conservation so as to secure compliance with the requirements of the Habitats Directive.

Those enactments include—

Part III of the National Parks and Access to the Countryside Act 1949,
section 49A of the Countryside (Scotland) Act 1967 (management agreements),
section 15 of the Countryside Act 1968 (areas of special scientific interest),
Part I and sections 28 to 38 of the Wildlife and Countryside Act 1981,
sections 131 to 134 of the Environmental Protection Act 1990,
sections 2, 3, 5, 6, 7 and 11 of the Natural Heritage (Scotland) Act 1991, and
these Regulations.

(3) In relation to marine areas any competent authority having functions relevant to marine conservation shall exercise those functions so as to secure compliance with the requirements of the Habitats Directive.

This applies, in particular, to functions under the following enactments—

the Sea Fisheries Acts within the meaning of section 1 of the Sea Fisheries (Wildlife Conservation) Act 1992,
the Dockyard Ports Regulation Act 1865,
section 2(2) of the Military Lands Act 1900 (provisions as to use of sea, tidal water or shore),
the Harbours Act 1964,
Part II of the Control of Pollution Act 1974,
sections 36 and 37 of the Wildlife and Countryside Act 1981 (marine nature reserves),
sections 120 to 122 of the Civic Government (Scotland) Act 1982 (control of the seashore, adjacent waters and inland waters),
the Water Resources Act 1991,
the Land Drainage Act 1991, and
these Regulations.

(4) Without prejudice to the preceding provisions, every competent authority in

the exercise of any of their functions, shall have regard to the requirements of the Habitats Directive so far as they may be affected by the exercise of those functions.

[923]

NOTES
Commencement: 30 October 1994.

4. Nature conservation bodies

In these Regulations "nature conservation body" means the Nature Conservancy Council for England, the Countryside Council for Wales or Scottish Natural Heritage; and references to "the appropriate nature conservation body", in relation to England, Wales or Scotland, shall be construed accordingly. **[924]**

NOTES
Commencement: 30 October 1994.

5. Relevant authorities in relation to marine areas and European marine sites

For the purposes of these Regulations the relevant authorities, in relation to a marine area or European marine site, are such of the following as have functions in relation to land or waters within or adjacent to that area or site—

    (a) a nature conservation body;
    (b) a county council, district council, London borough council or, in Scotland, a regional, islands or district council;
    (c) the National Rivers Authority, a water undertaker or sewerage undertaker, or an internal drainage board;
    (d) a navigation authority within the meaning of the Water Resources Act 1991;
    (e) a harbour authority within the meaning of the Harbours Act 1964;
    (f) a lighthouse authority;
    (g) a river purification board or a district salmon fishery board;
    (h) a local fisheries committee constituted under the Sea Fisheries Regulation Act 1966 or any authority exercising the powers of such a committee.

[925]

NOTES
Commencement: 30 October 1994.

6. Competent authorities generally

(1) For the purposes of these Regulations the expression "competent authority" includes any Minister, government department, public or statutory undertaker, public body of any description or person holding a public office.

The expression also includes any person exercising any function of a competent authority in the United Kingdom.

    (2) In paragraph (1)—
    (a) "public body" includes any local authority, joint board or joint committee; and
    (b) "public office" means—
        (a) an office under Her Majesty,
        (b) an office created or continued in existence by a public general Act of Parliament, or
        (c) an office the remuneration in respect of which is paid out of money provided by Parliament.

    (3) In paragraph (2)(a)—

"local authority"—

  (a) in relation to England, means a county council, district council or
      London borough council, the Common Council of the City of
      London, the sub- treasurer of the Inner Temple, the under treasurer
      of the Middle Temple or a parish council,

  (b) in relation to Wales, means a county council, district council or
      community council, and

  (c) in relation to Scotland, means a regional, islands or district council;

"joint board" and "joint committee" in relation to England and Wales
mean—

  (a) a joint or special planning board constituted for a National Park by
      order under paragraph 1 or 3 of Schedule 17 to the Local Government
      Act 1972, or a joint planning board within the meaning of section 2
      of the Town and Country Planning Act 1990, and

  (b) a joint committee appointed under section 102(1)(b) of the Local
      Government Act 1972,

and in relation to Scotland have the same meaning as in the Local Government
(Scotland) Act 1973.   **[926]**

NOTES

Commencement: 30 October 1994.

PART II

CONSERVATION OF NATURAL HABITATS AND HABITATS OF SPECIES

European sites

7. Selection of sites eligible for identification as of Community importance

(1) On the basis of the criteria set out in Annex III (Stage 1) to the Habitats Directive,
and relevant scientific information, the Secretary of State shall propose a list of sites
indicating with respect to each site—

  (a) which natural habitat types in Annex I to the Directive the site hosts, and

  (b) which species in Annex II to the Directive that are native to Great Britain
      the site hosts.

(2) For animal species ranging over wide areas these sites shall correspond to
the places within the natural range of such species which present the physical or
biological factors essential to their life and reproduction.

For aquatic species which range over wide areas, such sites shall be proposed only
where there is a clearly identifiable area representing the physical and biological
factors essential to their life and reproduction.

(3) Where appropriate the Secretary of State may propose modification of the
list in the light of the results of the surveillance referred to in Article 11 of the
Habitats Directive.

(4) The list shall be transmitted to the Commission on or before 5th June 1995,
together with information on each site including—

  (a) a map of the site,

  (b) its name, location and extent, and

  (c) the data resulting from application of the criteria specified in Annex III
      (Stage 1),

provided in a format established by the Commission.   **[927]**

NOTES
Commencement: 30 October 1994.

8. Adoption of list of sites: designation of special areas of conservation

(1) Once a site of Community importance in Great Britain has been adopted in accordance with the procedure laid down in paragraph 2 of Article 4 of the Habitats Directive, the Secretary of State shall designate that site as a special area of conservation as soon as possible and within six years at most.

(2) The Secretary of State shall establish priorities for the designation of sites in the light of—

(a) the importance of the sites for the maintenance or restoration at a favourable conservation status of—

(i) a natural habitat type in Annex I to the Habitats Directive, or
(ii) a species in Annex II to the Directive,

and for the coherence of Natura 2000; and

(b) the threats of degradation or destruction to which those sites are exposed.
[928]

NOTES
Commencement: 30 October 1994.

9. Consultation as to inclusion of site omitted from the list

If consultation is initiated by the Commission in accordance with Article 5(1) of the Habitats Directive with respect to a site in Great Britain hosting a priority natural habitat type or priority species and—

(a) the Secretary of State agrees that the site should be added to the list transmitted in accordance with regulation 7, or
(b) the Council, acting on a proposal from the Commission in pursuance of paragraph 2 of Article 5 of the Habitats Directive, so decides,

the site shall be treated as added to the list as from the date of that agreement or decision.   **[929]**

NOTES
Commencement: 30 October 1994.

10. Meaning of "European site" in these Regulations

(1) In these Regulations a "European site" means—

(a) a special area of conservation,
(b) a site of Community importance which has been placed on the list referred to in the third sub-paragraph of Article 4(2) of the Habitats Directive,
(c) a site hosting a priority natural habitat type or priority species in respect of which consultation has been initiated under Article 5(1) of the Habitats Directive, during the consultation period or pending a decision of the Council under Article 5(3), or
(d) an area classified pursuant to Article 4(1) or (2) of the Wild Birds Directive.

(2) Sites which are European sites by virtue only of paragraph (1)(c) are not within regulations 20(1) and (2), 24 and 48 (which relate to the approval of certain plans and projects); but this is without prejudice to their protection under other provisions of these Regulations.   **[930]**

NOTES
Commencement: 30 October 1994.

Register of European sites

11. Duty to compile and maintain register of European sites

(1) The Secretary of State shall compile and maintain, in such form as he thinks fit, a register of European sites in Great Britain.

(2) He shall include in the register—

    (a) special areas of conservation, as soon as they are designated by him;

    (b) sites of Community importance as soon as they are placed on the list referred to in the third sub-paragraph of Article 4(2) of the Habitats Directive, until they are designated as special areas of conservation;

    (c) any site hosting a priority natural habitat type or priority species in respect of which consultation is initiated under Article 5(1) of the Habitats Directive, during the consultation period or pending a Council decision under Article 5(3); and

    (d) areas classified by him pursuant to Article 4(1) or (2) of the Wild Birds Directive, as soon as they are so classified or, if they have been classified before the commencement of these Regulations, as soon as practicable after commencement.

(3) He may, if appropriate, amend the entry in the register relating to a European site.

(4) He shall remove the relevant entry—

    (a) if a special area of conservation is declassified by the Commission under Article 9 of the Habitats Directive; or

    (b) if a site otherwise ceases to fall within any of the categories listed in paragraph (2) above.

(5) He shall keep a copy of the register available for public inspection at all reasonable hours and free of charge. **[931]**

NOTES
Commencement: 30 October 1994.

12. Notification to appropriate nature conservation body

(1) The Secretary of State shall notify the appropriate nature conservation body as soon as may be after including a site in the register, amending an entry in the register or removing an entry from the register.

(2) Notification of the inclusion of a site in the register shall be accompanied by a copy of the register entry.

(3) Notification of the amendment of an entry in the register shall be accompanied by a copy of the amended entry.

(4) Each nature conservation body shall keep copies of the register entries relating to European sites in their area available for public inspection at all reasonable hours and free of charge. **[932]**

NOTES
Commencement: 30 October 1994.

13. Notice to landowners, relevant authorities, &c

(1) As soon as practicable after a nature conservation body receive notification under regulation 12 they shall give notice to—

    (a) every owner or occupier of land within the site,

    (b) every local planning authority in whose area the site, or any part of it, is situated, and

    (c) such other persons or bodies as the Secretary of State may direct.

(2) Notice of the inclusion of a site in the register, or of the amendment of an entry in the register, shall be accompanied by a copy of so much of the relevant register entry as relates to land owned or occupied by or, as the case may be, to land within the area of, the person or authority to whom the notice is given.

(3) The Secretary of State may give directions as to the form and content of notices to be given under this regulation. **[933]**

NOTES
Commencement: 30 October 1994.

14. Local registration: England and Wales

An entry in the register relating to a European site in England and Wales is a local land charge. **[934]**

NOTES
Commencement: 30 October 1994.

15. Local registers: Scotland

(1) A planning authority in Scotland shall keep available at their principal office for free public inspection a register of all the European sites of which they have been given notice under regulation 13(1)(b).

(2) A planning authority in Scotland may keep available at any other of their offices for free public inspection such part of the register referred to in paragraph (1) as appears to them to relate to that part of their area in which such office is situated.

(3) A planning authority shall supply to any person, on payment of such reasonable fee as they may determine, a copy, certified by the proper officer of the authority to be a true copy, of any entry in the register kept by them under paragraph (1). **[935]**

NOTES
Commencement: 30 October 1994.

Management agreements

16. Management agreements

(1) The appropriate nature conservation body may enter into an agreement (a "management agreement") with every owner, lessee and occupier of land forming part of a European site, or land adjacent to such a site, for the management, conservation, restoration or protection of the site, or any part of it.

(2) A management agreement may impose such restrictions as may be expedient for the purposes of the agreement on the exercise of rights over the land by the persons who can be bound by the agreement.

(3) A management agreement—

(a) may provide for the management of the land in such manner, the carrying out thereon of such work and the doing thereon of such other things as may be expedient for the purposes of the agreement;

(b) may provide for any of the matters mentioned in sub-paragraph (a) being carried out, or for the costs thereof being defrayed, either by the said owner or other persons or by the appropriate nature conservation body, or partly in one way and partly in another;

(c) may contain such other provisions as to the making of payments by the appropriate nature conservation body, and in particular for the payment by them of compensation for the effect of the restrictions mentioned in paragraph (2), as may be specified in the agreement.

(4) Where land in England and Wales is subject to a management agreement, the appropriate nature conservation body shall, as respects the enforcement of the agreement against persons other than the original contracting party, have the like rights as if—

(a) they had at all material times been the absolute owners in possession of ascertained land adjacent to the land subject to the agreement and capable of being benefited by the agreement, and

(b) the management agreement had been expressed to be for the benefit of that adjacent land;

and section 84 of the Law of Property Act 1925 (which enables the Lands Tribunal to discharge or modify restrictive covenants) shall not apply to the agreement.

(5) A management agreement affecting land in Scotland may be registered either—

(a) in a case where the land affected by the agreement is registered in that register, in the Land Register of Scotland, or

(b) in any other case, in the General Register of Sasines;

and, on being so recorded, it shall be enforceable at the instance of the appropriate nature conservation body against any person having an interest in the land and against any person deriving title from him:

Provided that a management agreement shall not be so enforceable against a third party who has *bona fide* onerously acquired right (whether completed by infeftment or not) to his interest in the land prior to the agreement being recorded as aforesaid, or against any person deriving title from such third party.   **[936]**

NOTES

  Commencement: 30 October 1994.

17. Continuation in force of existing agreement, &c

(1) Any agreement previously entered into under—

(a) section 16 of the National Parks and Access to the Countryside Act 1949 (nature reserves),

(b) section 15 of the Countryside Act 1968 (areas of special scientific interest), or

(c) section 49A of the Countryside (Scotland) Act 1967 (management agreements),

in relation to land which on or after the commencement of these Regulations becomes land within a European site, or adjacent to such a site, shall have effect as if entered into under regulation 16 above.

Regulation 32(1)(b) (power of compulsory acquisition in case of breach of agreement) shall apply accordingly.

(2) Any other thing done or deemed to have been done under any provision of Part III or VI of the National Parks and Access to the Countryside Act 1949, or under section 49A of the Countryside (Scotland) Act 1967, in respect of any land prior to that land becoming land within a European site, or adjacent to such a site, shall continue to have effect as if done under the corresponding provision of these Regulations.

For the purposes of this paragraph Part III of the 1949 Act shall be deemed to include section 15 of the Countryside Act 1968 and anything done or deemed to be done under that section and to which this paragraph applies shall have effect as if done or deemed to be done under section 16 of the 1949 Act.

(3) Any reference in an outlying enactment to a nature reserve within the meaning of section 15 of the National Parks and Access to the Countryside Act 1949 shall be construed as including a European site.

For this purpose an "outlying enactment" means an enactment not contained in, or in an instrument made under, the National Parks and Access to the Countryside Act 1949 or the Wildlife and Countryside Act 1981.   [937]

NOTES
  Commencement: 30 October 1994.

Control of potentially damaging operations

18. Notification of potentially damaging operations

(1) Any notification in force in relation to a European site under section 28 of the Wildlife and Countryside Act 1981 (areas of special scientific interest) specifying—

   (a) the flora, fauna, or geological or physiographical features by reason of which the land is of special interest, and
   (b) any operations appearing to the appropriate nature conservation body to be likely to damage that flora or fauna or those features,

shall have effect for the purposes of these Regulations.

(2) The appropriate nature conservation body may, for the purpose of securing compliance with the requirements of the Habitats Directive, at any time amend the notification with respect to any of the matters mentioned in paragraph (1)(a) or (b).

(3) Notice of any amendment shall be given—

   (a) to every owner and occupier of land within the site who in the opinion of the appropriate nature conservation body may be affected by the amendment, and
   (b) to the local planning authority;

and the amendment shall come into force in relation to an owner or occupier upon such notice being given to him.

(4) The provisions of—

   (a) section 28(11) of the Wildlife and Countryside Act 1981 (notification to be local land charge in England and Wales), and
   (b) section 28(12) to (12B) of that Act (local registration of notification in Scotland),

apply, with the necessary modifications, in relation to an amendment of a notification under this regulation as in relation to the original notification.   [938]

NOTES
  Commencement: 30 October 1994.

19. Restriction on carrying out operations specified in notification

(1) The owner or occupier of any land within a European site shall not carry out, or cause or permit to be carried out, on that land any operation specified in a notification in force in relation to the site under regulation 18, unless—

    (a) one of them has given the appropriate nature conservation body written notice of a proposal to carry out the operation, specifying its nature and the land on which it is proposed to carry it out, and

    (b) one of the conditions specified in paragraph (2) is fulfilled.

(2) Those conditions are—

    (a) that the operation is carried out with the written consent of the appropriate nature conservation body;

    (b) that the operation is carried out in accordance with the terms of a management agreement;

    (c) that four months have expired from the giving of the notice under paragraph (1)(a).

(3) A person who, without reasonable excuse, contravenes paragraph (1) commits an offence and is liable on summary conviction to a fine not exceeding level 4 on the standard scale.

(4) For the purposes of paragraph (3) it is a reasonable excuse for a person to carry out an operation—

    (a) that the operation was an emergency operation particulars of which (including details of the emergency) were notified to the appropriate nature conservation body as soon as practicable after the commencement of the operation; or

    (b) that the operation was authorised by a planning permission granted on an application under Part III of the Town and Country Planning Act 1990 or Part III of the Town and Country Planning (Scotland) Act 1972.

(5) The appropriate nature conservation body has power to enforce this regulation; but nothing in this paragraph shall be construed as authorising the institution of proceedings in Scotland for an offence.

(6) Proceedings in England and Wales for an offence under this regulation shall not, without the consent of the Director of Public Prosecutions, be taken by a person other than the appropriate nature conservation body.   **[939]**

NOTES

    Commencement: 30 October 1994.

20. Supplementary provisions as to consents

(1) Where it appears to the appropriate nature conservation body that an application for consent under regulation 19(2)(a) relates to an operation which is or forms part of a plan or project which—

    (a) is not directly connected with or necessary to the management of the site, and

    (b) is likely to have a significant effect on the site (either alone or in combination with other plans or projects),

they shall make an appropriate assessment of the implications for the site in view of that site's conservation objectives.

(2) In the light of the conclusions of the assessment, they may give consent for

the operation only after having ascertained that the plan or project will not adversely affect the integrity of the site.

(3) The above provisions do not apply in relation to a site which is a European site by reason only of regulation 10(1)(c) (site protected in accordance with Article 5(4)).

(4) Where in any case, whether in pursuance of this regulation or otherwise, the appropriate nature conservation body have not given consent for an operation, but they consider that there is a risk that the operation may nevertheless be carried out, they shall notify the Secretary of State.

(5) They shall take such steps as are requisite to secure that any such notification is given at least one month before the expiry of the period mentioned in regulation 19(2)(c) (period after which operation may be carried out in absence of consent).

[940]

NOTES
Commencement: 30 October 1994.

21. Provision as to existing notices and consents

(1) Any notice or consent previously given under section 28(5)(a) or (6)(a) of the Wildlife and Countryside Act 1981 in relation to land which on or after the commencement of these Regulations becomes land within a European site shall have effect, subject as follows, as if given under regulation 19(1)(a) or (2)(a) above.

(2) The appropriate nature conservation body shall review any such consent as regards its compatibility with the conservation objectives of the site, and may modify or withdraw it.

(3) Notice of any such modification or withdrawal of consent shall be given to every owner and occupier of land within the site who in the opinion of the appropriate nature conservation body may be affected by it; and the modification or withdrawal shall come into force in relation to an owner or occupier upon such notice being given to him.

(4) The modification or withdrawal of a consent shall not affect anything done in reliance on the consent before the modification or withdrawal takes effect.

(5) Where or to the extent that an operation ceases to be covered by a consent by reason of the consent being modified or withdrawn, the period after which in accordance with regulation 19(2)(c) the operation may be carried out in the absence of consent shall be four months from the giving of notice of the modification or withdrawal under paragraph (3) above.

(6) Regulation 20(4) and (5) (provisions as to notification of Secretary of State) apply in such a case, with the following modifications—

   (a) for the reference to consent not having been given substitute a reference to consent being modified or withdrawn;
   (b) for the reference to the period specified in regulation 19(2)(c) substitute a reference to the period specified in paragraph (5) above.   [941]

NOTES
Commencement: 30 October 1994.

Special nature conservation orders

22. Power to make special nature conservation order

(1) The Secretary of State may, after consultation with the appropriate nature conservation body, make in respect of any land within a European site an order (a "special nature conservation order") specifying operations which appear to him to be likely to destroy or damage the flora, fauna, or geological or physiographical features by reason of which the land is a European site.

(2) A special nature conservation order may be amended or revoked by a further order.

(3) Schedule 1 has effect with respect to the making, confirmation and coming into operation of special nature conservation orders and amending or revoking orders.

(4) A special nature conservation order in relation to land in England and Wales is a local land charge.

(5) A special nature conservation order in relation to land in Scotland shall be registered either—

    (a) in a case where the land affected by the order is registered in that Register, in the Land Register of Scotland; or

    (b) in any other case, in the appropriate Division of the General Register of Sasines.

(6) A report submitted by a nature conservation body to the Secretary of State under paragraph 20 of Schedule 6 to the Environmental Protection Act 1990 or section 10(2) of the Natural Heritage (Scotland) Act 1991 shall set out particulars of any land in their area as respects which a special nature conservation order has come into operation during the year to which the report relates.   **[942]**

NOTES

Commencement: 30 October 1994.

23. Restriction on carrying out operations specified in order

(1) No person shall carry out on any land within a European site in respect of which a special nature conservation order is in force any operation specified in the order, unless the operation is carried out, or caused or permitted to be carried out, by the owner or occupier of the land and—

    (a) one of them has, after the making of the order, given the appropriate nature conservation body written notice of a proposal to carry out the operation, specifying its nature and the land on which it is proposed to carry it out, and

    (b) one of the conditions specified in paragraph (2) is fulfilled.

(2) Those conditions are—

    (a) that the operation is carried out with the written consent of the appropriate nature conservation body;

    (b) that the operation is carried out in accordance with the terms of a management agreement.

(3) A person who, without reasonable excuse, contravenes paragraph (1) commits an offence and is liable—

    (a) on summary conviction, to a fine not exceeding the statutory maximum;

(b) on conviction on indictment, to a fine.

(4) For the purposes of paragraph (3) it is a reasonable excuse for a person to carry out an operation—

(a) that the operation was an emergency operation particulars of which (including details of the emergency) were notified to the appropriate nature conservation body as soon as practicable after the commencement of the operation; or

(b) that the operation was authorised by a planning permission granted on an application under Part III of the Town and Country Planning Act 1990 or Part III of the Town and Country Planning (Scotland) Act 1972.   **[943]**

NOTES
Commencement: 30 October 1994.

24. Supplementary provisions as to consents

(1) Where it appears to the appropriate nature conservation body that an application for consent under regulation 23(2)(a) relates to an operation which is or forms part of a plan or project which—

(a) is not directly connected with or necessary to the management of the site, and

(b) is likely to have a significant effect on the site (either alone or in combination with other plans or projects),

they shall make an appropriate assessment of the implications for the site in view of that site's conservation objectives.

(2) In the light of the conclusions of the assessment, they may give consent for the operation only after having ascertained that the plan or project will not adversely affect the integrity of the site.

(3) Where the appropriate nature conservation body refuse consent in accordance with paragraph (2) they shall give reasons for their decision.

(4) The owner or occupier of the land in question may—

(a) within two months of receiving notice of the refusal of consent, or

(b) if no notice of a decision is received by him within three months of an application for consent being made,

by notice in writing to the appropriate nature conservation body require them to refer the matter forthwith to the Secretary of State.

(5) If on the matter being referred to the Secretary of State he is satisfied that, there being no alternative solutions, the plan or project must be carried out for imperative reasons of overriding public interest (which, subject to paragraph (6), may be of a social or economic nature), he may direct the appropriate nature conservation body to give consent to the operation.

(6) Where the site concerned hosts a priority natural habitat type or a priority species, the reasons referred to in paragraph (5) must be either—

(a) reasons relating to human health, public safety or beneficial consequences of primary importance to the environment, or

(b) other reasons which in the opinion of the European Commission are imperative reasons of overriding public interest.

(7) Where the Secretary of State directs the appropriate nature conservation body to give consent under this regulation, he shall secure that such compensatory

measures are taken as are necessary to ensure that the overall coherence of Natura 2000 is protected.

(8) This regulation does not apply in relation to a site which is a European site by reason only of regulation 10(1)(c) (site protected in accordance with Article 5(4)). **[944]**

NOTES

Commencement: 30 October 1994.

25. Compensation for effect of order

(1) Where a special nature conservation order is made, the appropriate nature conservation body shall pay compensation to any person having at the time of the making of the order an interest in land comprised in an agricultural unit comprising land to which the order relates who, on a claim made to the appropriate nature conservation body within the time and in the manner prescribed by regulations, shows that the value of his interest is less than it would have been if the order had not been made.

(2) For this purpose an "agricultural unit" means land which is occupied as a unit for agricultural purposes, including any dwelling-house or other building occupied by the same person for the purpose of farming the land.

(3) No claim for compensation shall be made under this regulation in respect of an order unless the Secretary of State has given notice under paragraph 6(1) or (2) of Schedule 1 of his decision in respect of the order. **[945]**

NOTES

Commencement: 30 October 1994.

26. Restoration where order contravened

(1) Where a person is convicted of an offence under regulation 23, the court by which he is convicted may, in addition to dealing with him in any other way, make an order requiring him to carry out, within such period as may be specified in the order, such operations for the purpose of restoring the land to its former condition as may be so specified.

(2) An order under this regulation made on conviction on indictment shall be treated for the purposes of section 30 of the Criminal Appeal Act 1968 (effect of appeals on orders for the restitution of property) as an order for the restitution of property.

(3) In the case of an order under this regulation made by a magistrates' court the period specified in the order shall not begin to run—

(a) in any case until the expiration of the period for the time being prescribed by law for the giving of notice of appeal against a decision of a magistrates' court;

(b) where notice of appeal is given within the period so prescribed, until determination of the appeal.

(4) At any time before an order under this regulation has been complied with or fully complied with, the court by which it was made may, on the application of the person against whom it was made, discharge or vary the order if it appears to the court that a change in circumstances has made compliance or full compliance with the order impracticable or unnecessary.

(5) If a person fails without reasonable excuse to comply with an order under this regulation, he commits an offence and is liable on summary conviction to a fine

not exceeding level 5 on the standard scale; and if the failure continues after conviction, he may be proceeded against for a further offence from time to time until the order is complied with.

(6) If, within the period specified in an order under this regulation, any operations specified in the order have not been carried out, the appropriate nature conservation body may enter the land and carry out those operations and recover from the person against whom the order was made any expenses reasonably incurred by them in doing so.

(7) In the application of this regulation to Scotland—

(a) paragraphs (2) and (3) shall not apply, and
(b) for the purposes of any appeal or review, an order under this regulation is a sentence.   **[946]**

NOTES
Commencement: 30 October 1994.

27. Continuation in force of existing orders, &c

(1) Where an order is in force under section 29 of the Wildlife and Countryside Act 1981 (special protection for certain areas of special scientific interest) in relation to land which on or after the commencement of these Regulations becomes land within a European site, the order shall have effect as if made under regulation 22 above.

(2) Any notice previously given under section 29(4)(a) (notice by owner or occupier of proposal to carry out operation) shall have effect as if given under regulation 23(1)(a) and, if the appropriate nature conservation body have neither given nor refused consent, shall be dealt with under these Regulations.

(3) Any consent previously given under section 29(5)(a) shall be reviewed by the appropriate nature conservation body as regards its compatibility with the conservation objectives of the site, and may be modified or withdrawn.

(4) Notice of any such modification or withdrawal of consent shall be given to every owner and occupier of land within the site who in the opinion of the appropriate nature conservation body may be affected by it; and the modification or withdrawal shall come into force in relation to an owner or occupier upon such notice being given to him.

(5) The modification or withdrawal of a consent shall not affect anything done in reliance on the consent before the modification or withdrawal takes effect.

(6) Section 29(5)(c), (6) and (7) shall cease to apply and the carrying out, or continuation, of any operation on land within a European site which is not otherwise authorised in accordance with these Regulations shall be subject to the prohibition in regulation 23(1).   **[947]**

NOTES
Commencement: 30 October 1994.

Byelaws

28. Power to make byelaws

(1) The appropriate nature conservation body may make byelaws for the protection of a European site under section 20 of the National Parks and Access to the Countryside Act 1949 (byelaws for protection of nature reserves).

(2) Without prejudice to the generality of paragraph (1), byelaws under that section as it applies by virtue of this regulation may make provision of any of the following kinds.

(3) They may—

(a) provide for prohibiting or restricting the entry into, or movement within, the site of persons, vehicles, boats and animals;

(b) prohibit or restrict the killing, taking, molesting or disturbance of living creatures of any description in the site, the taking, destruction or disturbance of eggs of any such creature, the taking of, or interference with, vegetation of any description in the site, or the doing of anything in the site which will interfere with the soil or damage any object in the site;

(c) contain provisions prohibiting the depositing of rubbish and the leaving of litter in the site;

(d) prohibit or restrict, or provide for prohibiting or restricting, the lighting of fires in the site or the doing of anything likely to cause a fire in the site.

(4) They may prohibit or restrict any activity referred to in paragraph (3) within such area surrounding or adjoining the site as appears to the appropriate nature conservation body requisite for the protection of the site.

(5) They may provide for the issue, on such terms and subject to such conditions as may be specified in the byelaws, of permits authorising—

(a) entry into the site or any such surrounding or adjoining area as is mentioned in paragraph (4), or

(b) the doing of anything within the site, or any such surrounding or adjoining area,

where such entry, or doing that thing, would otherwise be unlawful under the byelaws.

(6) They may be made so as to relate either to the whole or to any part of the site, or of any such surrounding or adjoining area as is mentioned in paragraph (4), and may make different provision for different parts thereof.

(7) This regulation does not apply in relation to a European marine site (but see regulation 36).   **[948]**

NOTES
Commencement: 30 October 1994.

29. Byelaws: limitation on effect

Byelaws under section 20 of the National Parks and Access to the Countryside Act 1949 as it applies by virtue of regulation 28 shall not interfere with—

(a) the exercise by any person of a right vested in him as owner, lessee or occupier of land in the European site, or in any such surrounding or adjoining area as is mentioned in paragraph (4) of that regulation;

(b) the exercise of any public right of way;

(c) the exercise of any functions of statutory undertakers;

(d) the exercise of any functions of an internal drainage board, a district salmon fishery board or the Commissioners appointed under the Tweed Fisheries Act 1969; or

(e) the running of a telecommunications code system or the exercise of any right conferred by or in accordance with the telecommunications code on the operator of any such system.   **[949]**

NOTES
Commencement: 30 October 1994.

30. Compensation for effect of byelaws

Where the exercise of any right vested in a person, whether by reason of his being entitled to any interest in land or by virtue of a licence or agreement, is prevented or hindered by the coming into operation of byelaws under section 20 of the National Parks and Access to the Countryside Act 1949 as it applies by virtue of regulation 28, he shall be entitled to receive from the appropriate nature conservation body compensation in respect thereof.   **[950]**

NOTES
Commencement: 30 October 1994.

31. Continuation in force of existing byelaws

Any byelaws in force under section 20 of the National Parks and Access to the Countryside Act 1949 in relation to land which on or after the commencement of these Regulations becomes land within a European site, or adjacent to such a site, shall have effect as if made under the said section 20 as it applies by virtue of regulation 28 and shall be construed as if originally so made.   **[951]**

NOTES
Commencement: 30 October 1994.

Powers of compulsory acquisition

32. Powers of compulsory acquisition

(1) Where the appropriate nature conservation body are satisfied—

(a) that they are unable, as respects any interest in land within a European site, to conclude a management agreement on terms appearing to them to be reasonable, or

(b) where they have entered into a management agreement as respects such an interest, that a breach of the agreement has occurred which prevents or impairs the satisfactory management of the European site,

they may acquire that interest compulsorily.

(2) Such a breach as is mentioned in paragraph (1)(b) shall not be treated as having occurred by virtue of any act or omission capable of remedy unless there has been default in remedying it within a reasonable time after notice given by the appropriate nature conservation body requiring the remedying thereof.

(3) Any dispute arising whether there has been such a breach of a management agreement shall be determined—

(a) in the case of land in England and Wales, by an arbitrator appointed by the Lord Chancellor;

(b) in the case of land in Scotland, by an arbiter appointed by the Lord President of the Court of Session.   **[952]**

NOTES
Commencement: 30 October 1994.

Special provisions as to European marine sites

33. Marking of site and advice by nature conservation bodies

(1) The appropriate nature conservation body may install markers indicating the existence and extent of a European marine site.

This power is exercisable subject to the obtaining of any necessary consent under section 34 of the Coast Protection Act 1949 (restriction of works detrimental to navigation).

(2) As soon as possible after a site becomes a European marine site, the appropriate nature conservation body shall advise other relevant authorities as to—

    (a) the conservation objectives for that site, and

    (b) any operations which may cause deterioration of natural habitats or the habitats of species, or disturbance of species, for which the site has been designated.   **[953]**

NOTES

    Commencement: 30 October 1994.

34. Management scheme for European marine site

(1) The relevant authorities, or any of them, may establish for a European marine site a management scheme under which their functions (including any power to make byelaws) shall be exercised so as to secure in relation to that site compliance with the requirements of the Habitats Directive.

(2) Only one management scheme may be made for each European marine site.

(3) A management scheme may be amended from time to time.

(4) As soon as a management scheme has been established, or is amended, a copy of it shall be sent by the relevant authority or authorities concerned to the appropriate nature conservation body.   **[954]**

NOTES

    Commencement: 30 October 1994.

35. Direction to establish or amend management scheme

(1) The relevant Minister may give directions to the relevant authorities, or any of them, as to the establishment of a management scheme for a European marine site.

(2) Directions may, in particular—

    (a) require conservation measures specified in the direction to be included in the scheme;

    (b) appoint one of the relevant authorities to co-ordinate the establishment of the scheme;

    (c) set time limits within which any steps are to be taken;

    (d) provide that the approval of the Minister is required before the scheme is established; and

    (e) require any relevant authority to supply to the Minister such information concerning the establishment of the scheme as may be specified in the direction.

(3) The relevant Minister may give directions to the relevant authorities, or any of them, as to the amendment of a management scheme for a European marine site, either generally or in any particular respect.

(4) Any direction under this regulation shall be in writing and may be varied or revoked by a further direction.

(5) In this regulation "the relevant Minister" means, in relation to a site in England, the Secretary of State and the Minister of Agriculture, Fisheries and Food acting jointly and in any other case the Secretary of State.   **[955]**

NOTES
Commencement: 30 October 1994.

36. Byelaws for protection of European marine site

(1) The appropriate nature conservation body may make byelaws for the protection of a European marine site under section 37 of the Wildlife and Countryside Act 1981 (byelaws for protection of marine nature reserves).

(2) The provisions of subsections (2) to (11) of that section apply in relation to byelaws made by virtue of this regulation with the substitution for the references to marine nature reserves of references to European marine sites.

(3) Nothing in byelaws made by virtue of this regulation shall interfere with the exercise of any functions of a relevant authority, any functions conferred by or under an enactment (whenever passed) or any right of any person (whenever vested). **[956]**

NOTES
Commencement: 30 October 1994.

Miscellaneous

37. Nature conservation policy in planning contexts

(1) For the purposes of the planning enactments mentioned below, policies in respect of the conservation of the natural beauty and amenity of the land shall be taken to include policies encouraging the management of features of the landscape which are of major importance for wild flora and fauna.

Such features are those which, by virtue of their linear and continuous structure (such as rivers with their banks or the traditional systems of marking field boundaries) or their function as stepping stones (such as ponds or small woods), are essential for the migration, dispersal and genetic exchange of wild species.

(2) The enactments referred to in paragraph (1) are—

  (a) in the Town and Country Planning Act 1990, section 12(3A) (unitary development plans), section 31(3) (structure plans) and section 36(3) (local plans);
  (b) in the Town and Country Planning (Scotland) Act 1972, section 5(3)(a) (structure plans) and section 9(3)(a) (local plans).   **[957]**

NOTES
Commencement: 30 October 1994.

PART III

PROTECTION OF SPECIES

Protection of animals

38. European protected species of animals

The species of animals listed in Annex IV(a) to the Habitats Directive whose natural range includes any area in Great Britain are listed in Schedule 2 to these Regulations.

References in these Regulations to a "European protected species" of animal are to any of those species.   [958]

NOTES
Commencement: 30 October 1994.

39. Protection of wild animals of European protected species

(1) It is an offence—

- (a) deliberately to capture or kill a wild animal of a European protected species;
- (b) deliberately to disturb any such animal;
- (c) deliberately to take or destroy the eggs of such an animal; or
- (d) to damage or destroy a breeding site or resting place of such an animal.

(2) It is an offence to keep, transport, sell or exchange, or offer for sale or exchange, any live or dead wild animal of a European protected species, or any part of, or anything derived from, such an animal.

(3) Paragraphs (1) and (2) apply to all stages of the life of the animals to which they apply.

(4) A person shall not be guilty of an offence under paragraph (2) if he shows—

- (a) that the animal had not been taken or killed, or had been lawfully taken or killed, or
- (b) that the animal or other thing in question had been lawfully sold (whether to him or any other person).

For this purpose "lawfully" means without any contravention of these Regulations or Part I of the Wildlife and Countryside Act 1981.

(5) In any proceedings for an offence under this regulation, the animal in question shall be presumed to have been a wild animal unless the contrary is shown.

(6) A person guilty of an offence under this regulation is liable on summary conviction to a fine not exceeding level 5 on the standard scale.   [959]

NOTES
Commencement: 30 October 1994.

40. Exceptions from regulation 39

(1) Nothing in regulation 39 shall make unlawful—

- (a) anything done in pursuance of a requirement by the agriculture Minister under section 98 of the Agriculture Act 1947 or section 39 of the Agriculture (Scotland) Act 1948 (prevention of damage by pests); or
- (b) anything done under, or in pursuance of an order made under, the Animal Health Act 1981.

(2) Nothing in regulation 39(1)(b) or (d) shall make unlawful anything done within a dwelling-house.

(3) Notwithstanding anything in regulation 39, a person shall not be guilty of an offence by reason of—

- (a) the taking of a wild animal of a European protected species if he shows that the animal had been disabled otherwise than by his unlawful act and was taken solely for the purpose of tending it and releasing it when no longer disabled;

(b) the killing of such an animal if he shows that the animal has been so seriously disabled otherwise than by his unlawful act that there was no reasonable chance of its recovering; or

(c) any act made unlawful by that regulation if he shows that the act was the incidental result of a lawful operation and could not reasonably have been avoided.

(4) A person shall not be entitled to rely on the defence provided by paragraph (2) or (3)(c) as respects anything done in relation to a bat otherwise than in the living area of a dwelling-house unless he had notified the appropriate nature conservation body of the proposed action or operation and allowed them a reasonable time to advise him as to whether it should be carried out and, if so, the method to be used.

(5) Notwithstanding anything in regulation 39 a person—

(a) being the owner or occupier, or any person authorised by the owner or occupier, of the land on which the action authorised is taken, or

(b) authorised by the local authority for the area within which the action authorised is taken,

shall not be guilty of an offence by reason of the killing or disturbing of an animal of a European protected species if he shows that his action was necessary for the purpose of preventing serious damage to livestock, foodstuffs, crops, vegetables, fruit, growing timber or any other form of property or fisheries.

(6) A person may not rely on the defence provided by paragraph (5) as respects action taken at any time if it had become apparent before that time that the action would prove necessary for the purpose mentioned in that paragraph and either—

(a) a licence under regulation 44 authorising that action had not been applied for as soon as reasonably practicable after that fact had become apparent, or

(b) an application for such a licence had been determined.

(7) In paragraph (5) "local authority" means—

(a) in relation to England and Wales, a county, district or London borough council and includes the Common Council of the City of London, and

(b) in Scotland, a regional, islands or district council.   **[960]**

NOTES
Commencement: 30 October 1994.

41. Prohibition of certain methods of taking or killing wild animals

(1) This regulation applies in relation to the taking or killing of a wild animal—

(a) of any of the species listed in Schedule 3 to these Regulations (which shows the species listed in Annex V(a) to the Habitats Directive, and to which Article 15 applies, whose natural range includes any area of Great Britain), or

(b) of a European protected species, where the taking or killing of such animals is permitted in accordance with these Regulations.

(2) It is an offence to use for the purpose of taking or killing any such wild animal—

(a) any of the means listed in paragraph (3) or (4) below, or

(b) any form of taking or killing from the modes of transport listed in paragraph (5) below.

(3) The prohibited means of taking or killing of mammals are—

(a) blind or mutilated animals used as live decoys;
(b) tape recorders;
(c) electrical and electronic devices capable of killing or stunning;
(d) artificial light sources;
(e) mirrors and other dazzling devices;
(f) devices for illuminating targets;
(g) sighting devices for night shooting comprising an electronic image magnifier or image converter;
(h) explosives;
(i) nets which are non-selective according to their principle or their conditions of use;
(j) traps which are non-selective according to their principle or their conditions of use;
(k) crossbows;
(l) poisons and poisoned or anaesthetic bait;
(m) gassing or smoking out;
(n) semi-automatic or automatic weapons with a magazine capable of holding more than two rounds of ammunition.

(4) The prohibited means of taking or killing fish are—

(a) poison;
(b) explosives.

(5) The prohibited modes of transport are—

(a) aircraft;
(b) moving motor vehicles.

(6) A person guilty of an offence under this regulation is liable on summary conviction to a fine not exceeding level 5 on the standard scale.   **[961]**

NOTES
   Commencement: 30 October 1994.

Protection of plants

42. European protected species of plants

The species of plants listed in Annex IV(b) to the Habitats Directive whose natural range includes any area in Great Britain are listed in Schedule 4 to these Regulations.

References in these Regulations to a "European protected species" of plant are to any of those species.   **[962]**

NOTES
   Commencement: 30 October 1994.

43. Protection of wild plants of European protected species

(1) It is an offence deliberately to pick, collect, cut, uproot or destroy a wild plant of a European protected species.

(2) It is an offence to keep, transport, sell or exchange, or offer for sale or exchange, any live or dead wild plant of a European protected species, or any part of, or anything derived from, such a plant.

(3) Paragraphs (1) and (2) apply to all stages of the biological cycle of the plants to which they apply.

(4) A person shall not be guilty of an offence under paragraph (1), by reason of

any act made unlawful by that paragraph if he shows that the act was an incidental result of a lawful operation and could not reasonably have been avoided.

(5) A person shall not be guilty of an offence under paragraph (2) if he shows that the plant or other thing in question had been lawfully sold (whether to him or any other person).

For this purpose "lawfully" means without any contravention of these Regulations or Part I of the Wildlife and Countryside Act 1981.

(6) In any proceedings for an offence under this regulation, the plant in question shall be presumed to have been a wild plant unless the contrary is shown.

(7) A person guilty of an offence under this section is liable on summary conviction to a fine not exceeding level 4 on the standard scale.   **[963]**

NOTES
  Commencement: 30 October 1994.

Power to grant licences

44. Grant of licences for certain purposes

(1) Regulations 39, 41 and 43 do not apply to anything done for any of the following purposes under and in accordance with the terms of a licence granted by the appropriate authority.

(2) The purposes referred to in paragraph (1) are—
  (a) scientific or educational purposes;
  (b) ringing or marking, or examining any ring or mark on, wild animals;
  (c) conserving wild animals or wild plants or introducing them to particular areas;
  (d) protecting any zoological or botanical collection;
  (e) preserving public health or public safety or other imperative reasons of overriding public interest including those of a social or economic nature and beneficial consequences of primary importance for the environment;
  (f) preventing the spread of disease; or
  (g) preventing serious damage to livestock, foodstuffs for livestock, crops, vegetables, fruit, growing timber or any other form of property or to fisheries.

(3) The appropriate authority shall not grant a licence under this regulation unless they are satisfied—
  (a) that there is no satisfactory alternative, and
  (b) that the action authorised will not be detrimental to the maintenance of the population of the species concerned at a favourable conservation status in their natural range.

(4) For the purposes of this regulation "the appropriate authority" means—
  (a) in the case of a licence under any of sub-paragraphs (a) to (d) of paragraph (2), the appropriate nature conservation body; and
  (b) in the case of a licence under any of sub-paragraphs (e) to (g) of that paragraph, the agriculture Minister.

(5) The agriculture Minister shall from time to time consult with the nature conservation bodies as to the exercise of his functions under this regulation; and he shall not grant a licence of any description unless he has been advised by the appropriate nature conservation body as to the circumstances in which, in their opinion, licences of that description should be granted.   **[964]**

NOTES
Commencement: 30 October 1994.

45. Licences: supplementary provisions

(1) A licence under regulation 44—

    (a) may be, to any degree, general or specific;

    (b) may be granted either to persons of a class or to a particular person; and

    (c) may be subject to compliance with any specified conditions.

(2) For the purposes of a licence under regulation 44 the definition of a class of persons may be framed by reference to any circumstances whatever including, in particular, their being authorised by any other person.

(3) A licence under regulation 44 may be modified or revoked at any time by the appropriate authority; but otherwise shall be valid for the period stated in the licence.

(4) A licence under regulation 44 which authorises any person to kill wild animals shall specify the area within which and the methods by which the wild animals may be killed and shall not be granted for a period of more than two years.

(5) It shall be a defence in proceedings for an offence under section 8(b) of the Protection of Animals Act 1911 or section 7(b) of the Protection of Animals (Scotland) Act 1912 (which restrict the placing on land of poison and poisonous substances) to show that—

    (a) the act alleged to constitute the offence was done under and in accordance with the terms of a licence under regulation 44, and

    (b) any conditions specified in the licence were complied with.

(6) The appropriate authority may charge for a licence under regulation 44 such reasonable sum (if any) as they may determine.   **[965]**

NOTES
Commencement: 30 October 1994.

46. False statements made for obtaining licence

(1) A person commits an offence who, for the purposes of obtaining, whether for himself or another, the grant of a licence under regulation 44—

    (a) makes a statement or representation, or furnishes a document or information, which he knows to be false in a material particular, or

    (b) recklessly makes a statement or representation, or furnishes a document or information, which is false in a material particular.

(2) A person guilty of an offence under this regulation is liable on summary conviction to a fine not exceeding level 4 on the standard scale.   **[966]**

NOTES
Commencement: 30 October 1994.

PART IV

ADAPTATION OF PLANNING AND OTHER CONTROLS

Introductory

47. Application of provisions of this Part

(1) The requirements of—

(a) regulations 48 and 49 (requirement to consider effect on European sites), and

(b) regulations 50 and 51 (requirement to review certain existing decisions and consents, &c),

apply, subject to and in accordance with the provisions of regulations 54 to 85, in relation to the matters specified in those provisions.

(2) Supplementary provision is made by—

(a) regulation 52 (co-ordination where more than one competent authority involved), and

(b) regulation 53 (compensatory measures where plan or project is agreed to notwithstanding a negative assessment of the implications for a European site). **[967]**

NOTES
Commencement: 30 October 1994.

General provisions for protection of European sites

48. Assessment of implications for European site

(1) A competent authority, before deciding to undertake, or give any consent, permission or other authorisation for, a plan or project which—

(a) is likely to have a significant effect on a European site in Great Britain (either alone or in combination with other plans or projects), and

(b) is not directly connected with or necessary to the management of the site,

shall make an appropriate assessment of the implications for the site in view of that site's conservation objectives.

(2) A person applying for any such consent, permission or other authorisation shall provide such information as the competent authority may reasonably require for the purposes of the assessment.

(3) The competent authority shall for the purposes of the assessment consult the appropriate nature conservation body and have regard to any representations made by that body within such reasonable time as the authority may specify.

(4) They shall also, if they consider it appropriate, take the opinion of the general public; and if they do so, they shall take such steps for that purpose as they consider appropriate.

(5) In the light of the conclusions of the assessment, and subject to regulation 49, the authority shall agree to the plan or project only after having ascertained that it will not adversely affect the integrity of the European site.

(6) In considering whether a plan or project will adversely affect the integrity of the site, the authority shall have regard to the manner in which it is proposed to be carried out or to any conditions or restrictions subject to which they propose that the consent, permission or other authorisation should be given.

(7) This regulation does not apply in relation to a site which is a European site by reason only of regulation 10(1)(c) (site protected in accordance with Article 5(4)). **[968]**

NOTES
Commencement: 30 October 1994.

49. Considerations of overriding public interest

(1) If they are satisfied that, there being no alternative solutions, the plan or project must be carried out for imperative reasons of overriding public interest (which, subject to paragraph (2), may be of a social or economic nature), the competent authority may agree to the plan or project notwithstanding a negative assessment of the implications for the site.

(2) Where the site concerned hosts a priority natural habitat type or a priority species, the reasons referred to in paragraph (1) must be either—

(a) reasons relating to human health, public safety or beneficial consequences of primary importance to the environment, or

(b) other reasons which in the opinion of the European Commission are imperative reasons of overriding public interest.

(3) Where a competent authority other than the Secretary of State desire to obtain the opinion of the European Commission as to whether reasons are to be considered imperative reasons of overriding public interest, they shall submit a written request to the Secretary of State—

(a) identifying the matter on which an opinion is sought, and

(b) accompanied by any documents or information which may be required.

(4) The Secretary of State may thereupon, if he thinks fit, seek the opinion of the Commission; and if he does so, he shall upon receiving the Commission's opinion transmit it to the authority.

(5) Where an authority other than the Secretary of State propose to agree to a plan or project under this regulation notwithstanding a negative assessment of the implications for a European site, they shall notify the Secretary of State.

Having notified the Secretary of State, they shall not agree to the plan or project before the end of the period of 21 days beginning with the day notified to them by the Secretary of State as that on which their notification was received by him, unless the Secretary of State notifies them that they may do so.

(6) In any such case the Secretary of State may give directions to the authority prohibiting them from agreeing to the plan or project, either indefinitely or during such period as may be specified in the direction.

This power is without prejudice to any other power of the Secretary of State in relation to the decision in question. **[969]**

NOTES
Commencement: 30 October 1994.

50. Review of existing decisions and consents, &c

(1) Where before the date on which a site becomes a European site or, if later, the commencement of these Regulations, a competent authority have decided to undertake, or have given any consent, permission or other authorisation for, a plan or project to which regulation 48(1) would apply if it were to be reconsidered as of that date, the authority shall as soon as reasonably practicable, review their decision or, as the case may be, the consent, permission or other authorisation, and shall affirm, modify or revoke it.

(2) They shall for that purpose make an appropriate assessment of the implications for the site in view of that site's conservation objectives; and the provisions of regulation 48(2) to (4) shall apply, with the appropriate modifications, in relation to such a review.

(3) Subject to the following provisions of this Part, any review required by this regulation shall be carried out under existing statutory procedures where such procedures exist, and if none exist the Secretary of State may give directions as to the procedure to be followed.

(4) Nothing in this regulation shall affect anything done in pursuance of the decision, or the consent, permission or other authorisation, before the date mentioned in paragraph (1). **[970]**

NOTES
Commencement: 30 October 1994.

51. Consideration on review

(1) The following provisions apply where a decision, or a consent, permission or other authorisation, falls to be reviewed under regulation 50.

(2) Subject as follows, the provisions of regulation 48(5) and (6) and regulation 49 shall apply, with the appropriate modifications, in relation to the decision on the review.

(3) The decision, or the consent, permission or other authorisation, may be affirmed if it appears to the authority reviewing it that other action taken or to be taken by them, or by another authority, will secure that the plan or project does not adversely affect the integrity of the site.

Where that object may be attained in a number of ways, the authority or authorities concerned shall seek to secure that the action taken is the least onerous to those affected.

(4) The Secretary of State may issue guidance to authorities for the purposes of paragraph (3) as to the manner of determining which of different ways should be adopted for securing that the plan or project does not have any such effect, and in particular—

(a) the order of application of different controls, and
(b) the extent to which account should be taken of the possible exercise of other powers;

and the authorities concerned shall have regard to any guidance so issued in discharging their functions under that paragraph.

(5) Any modification or revocation effected in pursuance of this regulation shall be carried out under existing statutory procedures where such procedures exist.

If none exist, the Secretary of State may give directions as to the procedure to be followed. **[971]**

NOTES
Commencement: 30 October 1994.

52. Co-ordination where more than one competent authority involved

(1) The following provisions apply where a plan or project—

(a) is undertaken by more than one competent authority,
(b) requires the consent, permission or other authorisation of more than one competent authority, or
(c) is undertaken by one or more competent authorities and requires the consent, permission or other authorisation of one or more other competent authorities.

(2) Nothing in regulation 48(1) or 50(2) requires a competent authority to assess

any implications of a plan or project which would be more appropriately assessed under that provision by another competent authority.

(3) The Secretary of State may issue guidance to authorities for the purposes of regulations 48 to 51 as to the circumstances in which an authority may or should adopt the reasoning or conclusions of another competent authority as to whether a plan or project—

  (a) is likely to have a significant effect on a European site, or
  (b) will adversely affect the integrity of a European site;

and the authorities involved shall have regard to any guidance so issued in discharging their functions under those regulations.

(4) In determining whether a plan or project should be agreed to under regulation 49(1) (considerations of overriding public interest) a competent authority other than the Secretary of State shall seek and have regard to the views of the other competent authority or authorities involved.   **[972]**

NOTES

Commencement: 30 October 1994.

53. Compensatory measures

Where in accordance with regulation 49 (considerations of overriding public interest)—

  (a) a plan or project is agreed to, notwithstanding a negative assessment of the implications for a European site, or
  (b) a decision, or a consent, permission or other authorisation, is affirmed on review, notwithstanding such an assessment,

the Secretary of State shall secure that any necessary compensatory measures are taken to ensure that the overall coherence of Natura 2000 is protected.   **[973]**

NOTES

Commencement: 30 October 1994.

Planning

54. Grant of planning permission

(1) Regulations 48 and 49 (requirement to consider effect on European site) apply, in England and Wales, in relation to—

  (a) granting planning permission on an application under Part III of the Town and Country Planning Act 1990;
  (b) granting planning permission, or upholding a decision of the local planning authority to grant planning permission (whether or not subject to the same conditions and limitations as those imposed by the local planning authority), on determining an appeal under section 78 of that Act in respect of such an application;
  (c) granting planning permission under—

     (i) section 141(2)(a) of that Act (action by Secretary of State in relation to purchase notice),
     (ii) section 177(1)(a) of that Act (powers of Secretary of State on appeal against enforcement notice), or
     (iii) section 196(5) of that Act as originally enacted (powers of Secretary of State on reference or appeal as to established use certificate);

(d) directing under section 90(1), (2) or (2A) of that Act (development with government authorisation), or under section 5(1) of the Pipe-lines Act 1962, that planning permission shall be deemed to be granted;

(e) making—

(i) an order under section 102 of that Act (order requiring discontinuance of use or removal of buildings or works), including an order made under that section by virtue of section 104 (powers of Secretary of State), which grants planning permission, or

(ii) an order under paragraph 1 of Schedule 9 to that Act (order requiring discontinuance of mineral working), including an order made under that paragraph by virtue of paragraph 11 of that Schedule (default powers of Secretary of State), which grants planning permission,

or confirming any such order under section 103 of that Act;

(f) directing under—

(i) section 141(3) of that Act (action by Secretary of State in relation to purchase notice), or

(ii) section 35(5) of the Planning (Listed Buildings and Conservation Areas) Act 1990 (action by Secretary of State in relation to listed building purchase notice),

that if an application is made for planning permission it shall be granted.

(2) Regulations 48 and 49 (requirement to consider effect on European site) apply, in Scotland, in relation to—

(a) granting planning permission on an application under Part III of the Town and Country Planning (Scotland) Act 1972;

(b) granting planning permission, or upholding a decision of the planning authority to grant planning permission (whether or not subject to the same conditions and limitations as those imposed by the local planning authority), on determining an appeal under section 33 (appeals) of that Act in respect of such an application;

(c) granting planning permission under—

(i) section 172(2) of that Act (action by Secretary of State in relation to purchase notice),

(ii) section 85(5) of that Act (powers of Secretary of State on appeal against enforcement notice), or

(iii) section 91(3) of that Act as originally enacted (powers of Secretary of State on reference or appeal as to established use certificate);

(d) directing under section 37(1) (development with government authorisation) of that Act, or under section 5(1) of the Pipe-lines Act 1962 or paragraph 7 of Schedule 8 to the Electricity Act 1989, that planning permission shall be deemed to be granted;

(e) making an order under section 49 of that Act (order requiring discontinuance of use or removal of buildings or works), including an order made under that section by virtue of section 260 (default powers of Secretary of State), which grants planning permission, or confirming any such order;

(f) directing under—

(i) section 172(3) of that Act (powers of Secretary of State in relation to purchase notice), or

(ii) paragraph 2(6) of Schedule 17 to that Act (powers of Secretary of State in relation to listed building purchase notice),

that if an application is made for planning permission it shall be granted.

(3) Where regulations 48 and 49 apply, the competent authority may, if they consider that any adverse effects of the plan or project on the integrity of a European site would be avoided if the planning permission were subject to conditions or limitations, grant planning permission or, as the case may be, take action which results in planning permission being granted or deemed to be granted subject to those conditions or limitations.

(4) Where regulations 48 and 49 apply, outline planning permission shall not be granted unless the competent authority are satisfied (whether by reason of the conditions and limitations to which the outline planning permission is to be made subject, or otherwise) that no development likely adversely to affect the integrity of a European site could be carried out under the permission, whether before or after obtaining approval of any reserved matters.

In this paragraph "outline planning permission" and "reserved matters" have the same meaning as in section 92 of the Town and Country Planning Act 1990 or section 39 of the Town and Country Planning (Scotland) Act 1972. **[974]**

NOTES
Commencement: 30 October 1994.

55. Planning permission: duty to review

(1) Subject to the following provisions of this regulation, regulations 50 and 51 (requirement to review certain decisions and consents, &c) apply to any planning permission or deemed planning permission, unless—

    (a) the development to which it related has been completed, or

    (b) it was granted subject to a condition as to the time within which the development to which it related was to be begun and that time has expired without the development having been begun, or

    (c) it was granted for a limited period and that period has expired.

(2) Regulations 50 and 51 do not apply to planning permission granted or deemed to have been granted—

    (a) by a development order (but see regulations 60 to 64 below);

    (b) by virtue of the adoption of a simplified planning zone scheme or of alterations to such a scheme (but see regulation 65 below);

    (c) by virtue of the taking effect of an order designating an enterprise zone under Schedule 32 to the Local Government, Planning and Land Act 1980, or by virtue of the approval of a modified enterprise zone scheme (but see regulation 66 below).

(3) Planning permission deemed to be granted by virtue of—

    (a) a direction under section 90(1) of the Town and Country Planning Act 1990 or section 37(1) of the Town and Country Planning (Scotland) Act 1972 in respect of development for which an authorisation has been granted under section 1 or 3 of the Pipe-lines Act 1962,

    (b) a direction under section 5(1) of the Pipe-lines Act 1962,

    (c) a direction under section 90(1) of the Town and Country Planning Act 1990 or section 37(1) of the Town and Country Planning (Scotland) Act 1972 in respect of development for which a consent has been given under section 36 or 37 of the Electricity Act 1989,

    (d) a direction under section 90(2) of the Town and Country Planning Act 1990 or paragraph 7 of Schedule 8 to the Electricity Act 1989, or

(e) a direction under section 90(2A) of the Town and Country Planning Act
1990 (which relates to development in pursuance of an order under section
1 or 3 of the Transport and Works Act 1992),

shall be reviewed in accordance with the following provisions of this Part in
conjunction with the review of the underlying authorisation, consent or order.

(4) In the case of planning permission deemed to have been granted in any other
case by a direction under section 90(1) of the Town and Country Planning Act 1990
or section 37(1) of the Town and Country Planning (Scotland) Act 1972, the local
planning authority shall—

(a) identify any such permission which they consider falls to be reviewed
under regulations 50 and 51, and

(b) refer the matter to the government department which made the direction;

and the department shall, if it agrees that the planning permission does fall to be so
reviewed, thereupon review the direction in accordance with those regulations.

(5) Save as otherwise expressly provided, regulations 50 and 51 do not apply to
planning permission granted or deemed to be granted by a public general Act of
Parliament.

(6) Subject to paragraphs (3) and (4), where planning permission granted by the
Secretary of State falls to be reviewed under regulations 50 and 51—

(a) it shall be reviewed by the local planning authority, and

(b) the power conferred by section 97 of the Town and Country Planning Act
1990 or section 42 of the Town and Country Planning (Scotland) Act 1972
(revocation or modification of planning permission) shall be exercisable
by that authority as in relation to planning permission granted on an
application under Part III of that Act.

In a non-metropolitan county in England and Wales the function of reviewing any
such planning permission shall be exercised by the district planning authority unless
it relates to a county matter (within the meaning of Schedule 1 to the Town and
Country Planning Act 1990) in which case it shall be exercised by the county
planning authority.   **[975]**

NOTES
Commencement: 30 October 1994.

56. Planning permission: consideration on review

(1) In reviewing any planning permission or deemed planning permission in
pursuance of regulations 50 and 51, the competent authority shall, in England and
Wales—

(a) consider whether any adverse effects could be overcome by planning
obligations under section 106 of the Town and Country Planning Act 1990
being entered into, and

(b) if they consider that those effects could be so overcome, invite those
concerned to enter into such obligations;

and so far as the adverse effects are not thus overcome the authority shall make such
order under section 97 of that Act (power to revoke or modify planning permission),
or under section 102 of or paragraph 1 of Schedule 9 to that Act (order requiring
discontinuance of use, &c), as may be required.

(2) In reviewing any planning permission or deemed planning permission in
pursuance of regulations 50 and 51, the competent authority shall, in Scotland—

(a) consider whether any adverse effects could be overcome by an agreement under section 50 (agreements regulating development or use of land) of the Town and Country Planning (Scotland) Act 1972 being entered into, and

(b) if they consider that those effects could be so overcome, invite those concerned to enter into such an agreement;

and so far as the adverse effects are not thus overcome, the authority shall make such order under section 42 of that Act (power to revoke or modify planning permission), or under section 49 of that Act (orders requiring discontinuance of use, &c) as may be required.

(3) Where the authority ascertain that the carrying out or, as the case may be, the continuation of the development would adversely affect the integrity of a European site, they nevertheless need not proceed under regulations 50 and 51 if and so long as they consider that there is no likelihood of the development being carried out or continued. **[976]**

NOTES
Commencement: 30 October 1994.

57. Effect of orders made on review: England and Wales

(1) An order under section 97 of the Town and Country Planning Act 1990 (power to revoke or modify planning permission) made pursuant to regulation 55 shall take effect upon service of the notices required by section 98(2) of that Act or, where there is more than one such notice and those notices are served at different times, upon the service of the last such notice to be served.

(2) Where the Secretary of State determines not to confirm such an order, the order shall cease to have effect from the time of that determination, and the permission revoked or modified by the order shall thereafter have effect as if the order had never been made, and—

(a) any period specified in the permission for the taking of any action, being a period which had not expired prior to the date upon which the order took effect under paragraph (1) above, shall be extended by a period equal to that during which the order had effect; and

(b) there shall be substituted for any date specified in the permission as being a date by which any action should be taken, not being a date falling prior to the date upon which the order took effect under paragraph (1) above, such date as post-dates the specified date by a period equal to that during which the order had effect.

(3) An order under section 102 of, or under paragraph 1 of Schedule 9 to, the Town and Country Planning Act 1990 (order requiring discontinuance of use, &c) made pursuant to regulation 55 shall insofar as it requires the discontinuance of a use of land or imposes conditions upon the continuance of a use of land, take effect upon service of the notices required by section 103(3) or, where there is more than one such notice and those notices are served at different times, upon service of the last such notice to be served.

(4) Where the Secretary of State determines not to confirm any such order, the order shall cease to have effect from the time of that determination and the use which by the order was discontinued or upon whose continuance conditions were imposed—

(a) may thereafter be continued as if the order had never been made, and

(b) shall be treated for the purposes of the Town and Country Planning Act 1990 as if it had continued without interruption or modification throughout the period during which the order had effect.

(5) An order under section 97 of that Act (power to revoke or modify planning permission) made in pursuance of regulation 55 shall not affect so much of the development authorised by the permission as was carried out prior to the order taking effect.

(6) An order under section 102 of, or under paragraph 1 of Schedule 9 to, that Act (order requiring discontinuance of use, &c) made in pursuance of regulation 55 shall not affect anything done prior to the site becoming a European site or, if later, the commencement of these Regulations.   **[977]**

NOTES
Commencement: 30 October 1994.

58. Effect of orders made on review: Scotland

(1) An order under section 42 of the Town and Country Planning (Scotland) Act 1972 (power to revoke or modify planning permission) made pursuant to regulation 55 shall take effect upon service of the notices required by subsection (3) of that section or, where there is more than one such notice and those notices are served at different times, upon the service of the last such notice to be served.

(2) Where the Secretary of State determines not to confirm such an order, the order shall cease to have effect from the time of that determination, and the permission revoked or modified by the order shall thereafter have effect as if the order had never been made, and—

(a) any period specified in the permission for the taking of any action, being a period which had not expired prior to the date upon which the order took effect under paragraph (1) above, shall be extended by a period equal to that during which the order had effect; and

(b) there shall be substituted for any date specified in the permission as being a date by which any action should be taken, not being a date falling prior to that date upon which the order took effect under paragraph (1) above, such date as post-dates the specified date by a period equal to that during which the order had effect.

(3) An order under section 49 of the Town and Country Planning (Scotland) Act 1972 (order requiring discontinuance of use, &c) made pursuant to regulation 55 shall, insofar as it requires the discontinuance of a use of land or imposes conditions upon the continuance of a use of land, take effect upon service of the notices required by subsection (5) of that section or, where there is more than one such notice and those notices are served at different times, upon service of the last such notice to be served.

(4) Where the Secretary of State determines not to confirm any such order, the order shall cease to have effect from the time of that determination and the use which by the order was discontinued or upon whose continuance conditions were imposed—

(a) may thereafter be continued as if the order had never been made, and

(b) shall be treated for the purposes of the Town and Country Planning (Scotland) Act 1972 as if it had continued without interruption throughout the period during which the order had effect.

(5) An order under section 42 of that Act (power to modify or revoke planning permission) made in pursuance of regulation 55 shall not affect so much of the

development authorised by the permission as was carried out prior to the site becoming a European site or, if later, the commencement of these Regulations.

(6) An order under section 49 of that Act (order requiring discontinuance of use, &c) made in pursuance of regulation 55 above shall not affect any use made of the land prior to the site becoming a European site or, if later, the commencement of these Regulations.   **[978]**

NOTES
Commencement: 30 October 1994.

59. Planning permission: supplementary provisions as to compensation

(1) Where the Secretary of State determines not to confirm—

  (a) an order under section 97 of the Town and Country Planning Act 1990 (revocation or modification of planning permission) which has taken effect under regulation 57(1), or

  (b) an order under section 42 of the Town and Country Planning (Scotland) Act 1972 (revocation or modification of planning permission) which has taken effect under regulation 58(1),

any claim for compensation under section 107 of the Act of 1990 or section 153 of the Act of 1972 shall be limited to any loss or damage directly attributable to the permission being suspended or temporarily modified for the duration of the period between the order so taking effect and the Secretary of State determining not to confirm the order.

(2) Where the Secretary of State determines not to confirm—

  (a) an order under section 102 of the Town and Country Planning Act 1990 (order requiring discontinuance of use, &c) which has taken effect under regulation 57(3) above, or

  (b) an order under section 49 of the Town and Country Planning (Scotland) Act 1972 (order requiring discontinuance of use, &c) which has taken effect under regulation 58(3) above,

any claim for compensation under section 115 of the Act of 1990 or section 159 of the Act of 1972 shall be limited to any loss or damage directly attributable to any right to continue a use of the land being, by virtue of the order, suspended or subject to conditions for the duration of the period between the order so taking effect and the Secretary of State determining not to confirm the order.

(3) Where compensation is payable in respect of—

  (a) an order under section 97 of the Town and Country Planning Act 1990, or

  (b) any order mentioned in section 115(1) of that Act (compensation in respect of orders under s 102, &c), or to which that section applies by virtue of section 115(5),

and the order has been made pursuant to regulation 50, the question as to the amount of the compensation shall be referred, by the authority liable to pay the compensation, to and be determined by the Lands Tribunal unless and to the extent that in any particular case the Secretary of State has indicated in writing that such a reference and determination may be dispensed with.

(4) Where compensation is payable in respect of—

  (a) an order under section 42 of the Town and Country Planning (Scotland) Act 1972 (revocation or modification of planning permission), or

  (b) any order mentioned in section 153(1) of that Act (compensation in respect of orders under s 49), and the order has been made pursuant to regulation 50, the question as to the amount of the compensation shall be referred, by the authority liable to pay the compensation, to and be determined by the Lands Tribunal for Scotland unless and to the extent that in any particular case the Secretary of State has indicated in writing that such a reference and determination may be dispensed with.   **[979]**

NOTES
Commencement: 30 October 1994.

60. General development orders

(1) It shall be a condition of any planning permission granted by a general development order, whether made before or after the commencement of these Regulations, that development which—

    (a) is likely to have a significant effect on a European site in Great Britain (either alone or in combination with other plans or projects), and

    (b) is not directly connected with or necessary to the management of the site,

shall not be begun until the developer has received written notification of the approval of the local planning authority under regulation 62.

(2) It shall be a condition of any planning permission granted by a general development order made before the commencement of these Regulations that development which—

    (a) is likely to have a significant effect on a European site in Great Britain (either alone or in combination with other plans or projects), and

    (b) is not directly connected with or necessary to the management of the site,

and which was begun but not completed before the commencement of these Regulations, shall not be continued until the developer has received written notification of the approval of the local planning authority under regulation 62.

(3) Nothing in this regulation shall affect anything done before the commencement of these Regulations.   **[980]**

NOTES
Commencement: 30 October 1994.

61. General development orders: opinion of appropriate nature conservation body

(1) Where it is intended to carry out development in reliance on the permission granted by a general development order, application may be made in writing to the appropriate nature conservation body for their opinion whether the development is likely to have such an effect as is mentioned in regulation 60(1)(a) or (2)(a).

The application shall give details of the development which is intended to be carried out.

(2) On receiving such an application, the appropriate nature conservation body shall consider whether the development is likely to have such an effect.

(3) Where they consider that they have sufficient information to conclude that the development will, or will not, have such an effect, they shall in writing notify the applicant and the local planning authority of their opinion.

(4) If they consider that they have insufficient information to reach either of those conclusions, they shall notify the applicant in writing indicating in what respects they consider the information insufficient; and the applicant may supply

further information with a view to enabling them to reach a decision on the application.

(5) The opinion of the appropriate nature conservation body, notified in accordance with paragraph (3), that the development is not likely to have such an effect as is mentioned in regulation 60(1)(a) or (2)(a) shall be conclusive of that question for the purpose of reliance on the planning permission granted by a general development order.   **[981]**

NOTES
Commencement: 30 October 1994.

62. General development orders: approval of local planning authority

(1) Where it is intended to carry out development in reliance upon the permission granted by a general development order, application may be made in writing to the local planning authority for their approval.

(2) The application shall—
   (a) give details of the development which is intended to be carried out; and
   (b) be accompanied by—
        (i) a copy of any relevant notification by the appropriate nature conservation body under regulation 61, and
        (ii) any fee required to be paid.

(3) For the purposes of their consideration of the application the local planning authority shall assume that the development is likely to have such an effect as is mentioned in regulation 60(1)(a) or (2)(a).

(4) The authority shall send a copy of the application to the appropriate nature conservation body and shall take account of any representations made by them.

(5) If in their representations the appropriate nature conservation body state their opinion that the development is not likely to have such an effect as is mentioned in regulation 60(1)(a) or (2)(a), the local planning authority shall send a copy of the representations to the applicant; and the sending of that copy shall have the same effect as a notification by the appropriate nature conservation body of its opinion under regulation 61(3).

(6) In any other case the local planning authority shall, taking account of any representations made by the appropriate nature conservation body, make an appropriate assessment of the implications of the development for the European site in view of that site's conservation objectives.

In the light of the conclusions of the assessment the authority shall approve the development only after having ascertained that it will not adversely affect the integrity of the site.   **[982]**

NOTES
Commencement: 30 October 1994.

63. General development orders: supplementary

(1) The local planning authority for the purposes of regulations 60 to 62 shall be the authority to whom an application for approval under regulation 62 would fall to be made if it were an application for planning permission.

(2) The fee payable in connection with an application for such approval is—
   (a) £25 in the case of applications made before 3rd January 1995, and

(b) £30 in the case of applications made on or after that date.

(3) Approval required by regulation 60 shall be treated—

(a) for the purposes of the provisions of the Town and Country Planning Act 1990, or the Town and Country Planning (Scotland) Act 1972, relating to appeals, as approval required by a condition imposed on a grant of planning permission; and

(b) for the purposes of the provisions of any general development order relating to the time within which notice of a decision should be made, as approval required by a condition attached to a grant of planning permission.   **[983]**

NOTES
Commencement: 30 October 1994.

64. Special development orders

(1) A special development order made after the commencement of these Regulations may not grant planning permission for development which—

(a) is likely to have a significant effect on a European site in Great Britain (either alone or in combination with other plans or projects), and

(b) is not directly connected with or necessary to the management of the site;

and any such order made before the commencement of these Regulations shall, on and after that date, cease to have effect to grant such permission, whether or not the development authorised by the permission has been begun.

(2) Nothing in this regulation shall affect anything done before the commencement of these Regulations.   **[984]**

NOTES
Commencement: 30 October 1994.

65. Simplified planning zones

The adoption or approval of a simplified planning zone scheme after the commencement of these Regulations shall not have effect to grant planning permission for development which—

(a) is likely to have a significant effect on a European site in Great Britain (either alone or in combination with other plans or projects), and

(b) is not directly connected with or necessary to the management of the site;

and every simplified planning zone scheme already in force shall cease to have effect to grant such permission, whether or not the development authorised by the permission has been begun.   **[985]**

NOTES
Commencement: 30 October 1994.

66. Enterprise zones

An order designating an enterprise zone, or the approval of a modified scheme, if made or given after the commencement of these Regulations, shall not have effect to grant planning permission for development which—

(a) is likely to have a significant effect on a European site in Great Britain (either alone or in combination with other plans or projects), and

(b) is not directly connected with or necessary to the management of the site;

and where the order or approval was made or given before that date, the permission granted by virtue of the taking effect of the order or the modifications shall, from that date, cease to have effect to grant planning permission or such development, whether or not the development authorised by the permission has been begun. **[986]**

NOTES
Commencement: 30 October 1994.

67. Simplified planning zones and enterprise zones: supplementary provisions as to compensation

(1) Where in England and Wales—

 (a) planning permission is withdrawn by regulation 65 or 66, and
 (b) development authorised by the permission had been begun but not completed before the commencement of these Regulations, and
 (c) on an application made under Part III of the Town and Country Planning Act 1990 before the end of the period of 12 months beginning with the date of commencement of these Regulations, planning permission for the development is refused or is granted subject to conditions other than those imposed by the scheme,

section 107(1)(a) of that Act (compensation in respect of abortive expenditure) shall apply as if the permission granted by the scheme had been granted by the local planning authority under Part III of that Act and had been revoked or modified by an order under section 97 of that Act.

 (2) Where in Scotland—

 (a) planning permission is withdrawn by regulation 65 or 66, and
 (b) development authorised by the permission had been begun but not completed before the commencement of these Regulations, and
 (c) on an application made under Part III of the Town and Country Planning (Scotland) Act 1972 before the end of the period of 12 months beginning with the date of commencement of these Regulations, planning permission for the development is refused or is granted subject to conditions other than those imposed by the scheme,

section 153(1)(a) of that Act (compensation in respect of abortive expenditure) shall apply as if the permission granted by the scheme had been granted by the local planning authority under Part III of that Act and had been revoked or modified by an order under section 42 of that Act.

 (3) Paragraphs (1) and (2) above do not apply in relation to planning permission for the development of operational land by statutory undertakers.   **[987]**

NOTES
Commencement: 30 October 1994.

68. Construction as one with planning legislation

Regulations 54 to 67 shall be construed as one—

 (a) in England and Wales, with the Town and Country Planning Act 1990; and
 (b) in Scotland, with the Town and Country Planning (Scotland) Act 1972.
                             [988]

NOTES
Commencement: 30 October 1994.

Highways and roads

69. Construction or improvement of highways or roads

(1) Regulations 48 and 49 (requirement to consider effect on European site) apply in relation to any plan or project—

(a) by the Secretary of State—

    (i) to construct a new highway or to improve, within the meaning of the Highways Act 1980, an existing highway, or

    (ii) to construct a new road or to improve, within the meaning of the Roads (Scotland) Act 1984, an existing road; or

(b) by a local highway authority or local roads authority, to carry out within the boundaries of a road any works required for the improvement of the road.

(2) Regulations 50 and 51 (requirement to review certain decisions and consents, &c) apply to any such plan or project as is mentioned in paragraph (1) unless the works have been completed before the site became a European site or, if later, the commencement of these Regulations. **[989]**

NOTES
Commencement: 30 October 1994.

70. Cycle tracks and other ancillary works

As from the commencement of these Regulations, section 3(10) of the Cycle Tracks Act 1984 and section 152(4) of the Roads (Scotland) Act 1984 shall cease to have effect to deem planning permission to be granted for development which—

(a) is likely to have a significant effect on a European site in Great Britain (either alone or in combination with other plans or projects), and

(b) is not directly connected with or necessary to the management of the site,

whether or not the development authorised by the permission has been begun. **[990]**

NOTES
Commencement: 30 October 1994.

Electricity

71. Consents under Electricity Act 1989: application of general requirements

(1) Regulations 48 and 49 (requirement to consider effect on European site) apply in relation to the granting of—

(a) consent under section 36 of the Electricity Act 1989 to construct, extend or operate a generating station, or

(b) consent under section 37 of that Act to install an electric line above ground.

(2) Where in such a case the Secretary of State considers that any adverse effects of the plan or project on the integrity of a European site would be avoided if the consent were subject to conditions, he may grant consent subject to those conditions.

(3) Regulations 50 and 51 (requirement to review existing decisions and consents, &c) apply to such a consent as is mentioned in paragraph (1) unless—

(a) the works to which the consent relates have been completed before the site became a European site or, if later, the commencement of these Regulations, or

(b) the consent was granted subject to a condition as to the time within which the works to which it relates were to be begun and that time has expired without them having been begun, or

(c) it was granted for a limited period and that period has expired.

Where the consent is for, or includes, the operation of a generating station, the works shall be treated as completed when, in reliance on the consent, the generating station is first operated.

(4) Where on the review of such a consent the Secretary of State considers that any adverse effects on the integrity of a European site of the carrying out or, as the case may be, the continuation of the plan or project would be avoided by a variation of the consent, he may vary the consent accordingly.

(5) In conjunction with the review of any such consent the Secretary of State shall review any direction deeming planning permission to be granted for the plan or project and may vary or revoke it.   **[991]**

NOTES

Commencement: 30 October 1994.

72. Consents under the Electricity Act 1989: procedure on review

(1) Where the Secretary of State decides in pursuance of regulation 71 to revoke or vary a consent under the Electricity Act 1989, or a direction deeming planning permission to be granted, he shall serve notice on—

(a) the person to whom the consent was granted or, as the case may be, in whose favour the direction was made,

(b) in the case of a consent under section 36 of the Electricity Act 1989, any other person proposing to operate the generating station in question, and

(c) any other person who in his opinion will be affected by the revocation or variation,

informing them of the decision and specifying a period of not less than 28 days within which any person on whom the notice is served may make representations to him.

(2) The Secretary of State shall also serve notice on—

(a) the relevant planning authority within the meaning of paragraph 2(6) of Schedule 8 to the Electricity Act 1989, and

(b) the appropriate nature conservation body,

informing them of the decision and inviting their representations within the specified period.

(3) The Secretary of State shall consider whether to proceed with the revocation or variation, and shall have regard to any representations made to him in accordance with paragraph (1) or (2).

(4) If within the specified period a person on whom notice was served under paragraph (1), or the relevant planning authority, so requires, the Secretary of State shall before deciding whether to proceed with the revocation or variation give—

(a) to them, and

(b) to any other person on whom notice under paragraph (1) or (2) was required to be served, an opportunity of appearing before, and being heard by, a person appointed by the Secretary of State for the purpose.   **[992]**

NOTES
Commencement: 30 October 1994.

73. Consents under Electricity Act 1989: effect of review

(1) The revocation or variation pursuant to regulation 71 of a consent under section 36 or 37 of the Electricity Act 1989, or a direction deeming planning permission to be granted, shall take effect upon service of the notices required by regulation 72(1) or, where there is more than one such notice and those notices are served at different times, from the date on which the last of them was served.

(2) Where the Secretary of State decides not to proceed with the revocation or variation, the consent or direction shall have effect again from the time of that decision, and shall thereafter have effect as if—

(a) any period specified in the consent or direction for the taking of any action, being a period which had not expired prior to the date mentioned in paragraph (1), were extended by a period equal to that during which the revocation or variation had effect; and

(b) there were substituted for any date specified in the consent or direction as being a date by which any action should be taken, not being a date falling prior to that date mentioned in paragraph (1), such date as post-dates the specified date by a period equal to that during which the revocation or variation had effect.

(3) The revocation or variation pursuant to regulation 71 of a consent under section 36 or 37 of the Electricity Act 1989, or a direction deeming planning permission to be granted, shall not affect anything done under the consent or direction prior to the revocation or variation taking effect.   **[993]**

NOTES
Commencement: 30 October 1994.

74. Consents under Electricity Act 1989: compensation for revocation or variation

(1) Where a direction deeming planning permission to be granted is revoked or varied pursuant to regulation 71, that permission shall be treated—

(a) for the purposes of Part IV of the Town and Country Planning Act 1990 (compensation) as having been revoked or modified by order under section 97 of that Act, or

(b) for the purposes of Part VIII of the Town and Country Planning (Scotland) Act 1972 (compensation) as having been revoked or modified by order under section 42 of that Act.

(2) Where a consent under section 36 or 37 of the Electricity Act 1989 is revoked or varied pursuant to regulation 71, Part IV of the Town and Country Planning Act 1990 or Part VIII of the Town and Country Planning (Scotland) Act 1972 (compensation) shall apply as if—

(a) the consent had been planning permission granted on an application under that Act and had been revoked or modified by order under section 97 of the 1990 Act or section 42 of the 1972 Act; and

(b) each of those Parts provided that the Secretary of State was the person liable to pay any compensation provided for by that Part.

This paragraph shall not have effect to confer any right to compensation for any expenditure, loss or damage for which compensation is payable by virtue of paragraph (1) above.

(3) Where the Secretary of State decides not to proceed with the revocation or variation of a consent under section 36 or 37 of the Electricity Act 1989, or a direction deeming planning permission to be granted, any claim for compensation by virtue of this regulation shall be limited to any loss or damage directly attributable to the consent or direction ceasing to have effect or being varied for the duration of the period between the revocation or variation taking effect under regulation 73(1) and the Secretary of State deciding not to proceed with it.

(4) Where compensation is payable by virtue of this regulation, the question as to the amount of the compensation shall be referred to and determined by the Lands Tribunal, or the Lands Tribunal for Scotland, unless and to the extent that in any particular case the Secretary of State has indicated in writing that such a reference and determination may be dispensed with.   **[994]**

NOTES

Commencement: 30 October 1994.

Pipe-lines

75. Authorisations under the Pipe-lines Act 1962: application of general requirements

(1) Regulations 48 and 49 (requirement to consider effect on European site) apply in relation to the granting of a pipe-line construction or diversion authorisation under the Pipe-lines Act 1962.

(2) Where in such a case the Secretary of State considers that any adverse effects of the plan or project on the integrity of a European site would be avoided by granting an authorisation for the execution of works for the placing of the proposed pipe-line or, as the case may be, the portion of the pipe-line to be diverted, along a modified route, he may, subject to the provisions of Schedule 1 to the Pipe-lines Act 1962, grant such an authorisation.

(3) Regulations 50 and 51 (requirement to review existing decisions and consents, &c) apply to a pipe-line construction or diversion authorisation under the Pipe-lines Act 1962 unless—

    (a) the works to which the authorisation relates have been completed before the site became a European site or, if later, the commencement of these Regulations, or

    (b) the authorisation was granted subject to a condition as to the time within which the works to which it relates were to be begun and that time has expired without them having been begun, or

    (c) it was granted for a limited period and that period has expired.

(4) Where on the review of such an authorisation the Secretary of State considers that any adverse effects on the integrity of a European site of the carrying out or, as the case may be, the continuation of the plan or project would be avoided by a variation of the authorisation, he may vary it accordingly.

(5) In conjunction with the review of any such authorisation the Secretary of State shall review any direction deeming planning permission to be granted for the plan or project and may vary or revoke it.   **[995]**

NOTES

Commencement: 30 October 1994.

76. Authorisations under the Pipe-lines Act 1962: procedure on review

(1) Where the Secretary of State decides in pursuance of regulation 75 to revoke or vary an authorisation under the Pipe-lines Act 1962, or a direction deeming planning permission to be granted, he shall serve notice on—

(a) the person to whom the authorisation was granted or, as the case may be, in whose favour the direction was made, and

(b) any other person who in his opinion will be affected by the revocation or variation,

informing them of the decision and specifying a period of not less than 28 days within which any person on whom the notice is served may make representations to him.

(2) The Secretary of State shall also serve notice on—

(a) the local planning authority, and

(b) the appropriate nature conservation body,

informing them of the decision and inviting their representations within the specified period.

(3) The Secretary of State shall consider whether to proceed with the revocation or variation, and shall have regard to any representations made to him in accordance with paragraph (1) or (2).

(4) If within the specified period a person on whom notice was served under paragraph (1), or the local planning authority, so requires, the Secretary of State shall before deciding whether to proceed with the revocation or variation give—

(a) to them, and

(b) to any other person on whom notice under paragraph (1) or (2) was required to be served,

an opportunity of appearing before, and being heard by, a person appointed by the Secretary of State for the purpose. **[996]**

NOTES
  Commencement: 30 October 1994.

77. Authorisations under the Pipe-lines Act 1962: effect of review

(1) The revocation or variation pursuant to regulation 75 of an authorisation under the Pipe-lines Act 1962, or of a direction deeming planning permission to be granted, shall take effect upon service of the notices required by regulation 76(1) or, where there is more than one such notice and those notices are served at different times, upon the service of the last such notice to be served.

(2) Where the Secretary of State decides not to proceed with the revocation or variation, the authorisation or direction shall have effect again from the time of that decision, and shall thereafter have effect as if—

(a) any period specified in the authorisation or direction for the taking of any action, being a period which had not expired prior to the date mentioned in paragraph (1), were extended by a period equal to that during which the revocation or variation had effect; and

(b) there were substituted for any date specified in the authorisation or direction as being a date by which any action should be taken, not being a date falling prior to that date mentioned in paragraph (1), such date as post-dates the specified date by a period equal to that during which the revocation or variation had effect.

(3) The revocation or variation pursuant to regulation 75 of an authorisation under the Pipe-lines Act 1962, or a direction deeming planning permission to be granted, shall not affect anything done under the authorisation or direction prior to the revocation or variation taking effect. **[997]**

NOTES
Commencement: 30 October 1994.

78. Authorisations under the Pipe-lines Act 1962: compensation for revocation or variation

(1) Where a direction deeming planning permission to be granted is revoked or varied pursuant to regulation 75, that permission shall be treated—

  (a) for the purposes of Part IV of the Town and Country Planning Act 1990 (compensation) as having been revoked or modified by order under section 97 of that Act, or

  (b) for the purposes of Part VIII of the Town and Country Planning (Scotland) Act 1972 (compensation) as having been revoked or modified by order under section 42 of that Act.

(2) Where an authorisation under the Pipe-lines Act 1962 is revoked or varied pursuant to regulation 75, Part IV of the Town and Country Planning Act 1990 or Part VIII of the Town and Country Planning (Scotland) Act 1972 (compensation) shall apply as if—

  (a) the authorisation had been planning permission granted on an application under that Act and had been revoked or modified by order under section 97 of the 1990 Act or section 42 of the 1972 Act; and

  (b) each of those Parts provided that the Secretary of State was the person liable to pay any compensation provided for by that Part.

This paragraph shall not have effect to confer any right to compensation for any expenditure, loss or damage for which compensation is payable by virtue of paragraph (1) above.

(3) Where the Secretary of State decides not to proceed with the revocation or variation of an authorisation under the Pipe-lines Act 1962, or a direction deeming planning permission to be granted, any claim for compensation by virtue of this regulation shall be limited to any loss or damage directly attributable to the authorisation or direction ceasing to have effect or being varied for the duration of the period between the revocation or variation taking effect under regulation 77(1) and the Secretary of State deciding not to proceed with it.

(4) Where compensation is payable by virtue of this regulation, the question as to the amount of the compensation shall be referred to and determined by the Lands Tribunal, or the Lands Tribunal for Scotland, unless and to the extent that in any particular case the Secretary of State has indicated in writing that such a reference and determination may be dispensed with. **[998]**

NOTES
Commencement: 30 October 1994.

Transport and works

79. Orders under the Transport and Works Act 1992: application of general requirements

(1) Regulations 48 and 49 (requirement to consider effect on European site) apply in relation to the making of an order under section 1 or 3 of the Transport and Works Act 1992.

(2) Where in such a case the Secretary of State considers that any adverse effects of the plan or project on the integrity of a European site would be avoided by making modifications to the proposals, he may make an order subject to those modifications.

(3) Regulations 50 and 51 (requirement to review existing decisions and consents, &c) apply to an order under section 1 or 3 of the Transport and Works Act 1992 unless the works to which the order relates have been completed before the site became a European site.

(4) Where on the review of such an order the Secretary of State considers that any adverse effects on the integrity of a European site of the carrying out or, as the case may be, the continuation of the plan or project would be avoided by a variation of the order, he may vary it accordingly.

(5) In conjunction with the review of any such order the Secretary of State shall review any direction deeming planning permission to be granted for the plan or project and may vary or revoke it.   **[999]**

NOTES
    Commencement: 30 October 1994.

80. Orders under the Transport and Works Act 1992: procedure on review

(1) Where the Secretary of State decides in pursuance of regulation 79 to revoke or vary an order under the Transport and Works Act 1992, or a direction deeming planning permission to be granted, he shall serve notice on—

    (a) the person (if any) on whose application the order was made or, as the case may be, in whose favour the direction was made, and

    (b) any other person who in his opinion will be affected by the revocation or variation,

informing them of the decision and specifying a period of not less than 28 days within which any person on whom the notice is served may make representations to him.

(2) The Secretary of State shall also serve notice on—

    (a) the local planning authority, and

    (b) the appropriate nature conservation body,

informing them of the decision and inviting their representations within the specified period.

(3) The Secretary of State shall consider whether to proceed with the revocation or variation, and shall have regard to any representations made to him in accordance with paragraph (1) or (2).

(4) If within the specified period a person on whom notice was served under paragraph (1), or the local planning authority, so requires, the Secretary of State shall before deciding whether to proceed with the revocation or variation of the order or direction give—

    (a) to them,

    (b) to any other person on whom notice under paragraph (1) or (2) was required to be served,

an opportunity of appearing before, and being heard by, a person appointed by the Secretary of State for the purpose.   **[1000]**

NOTES
    Commencement: 30 October 1994.

81. Orders under the Transport and Works Act 1992: effect of review

(1) The revocation or variation pursuant to regulation 79 of an order under the Transport and Works Act 1992, or of a direction deeming planning permission to be granted, shall take effect upon service of the notices required by regulation 80(1) or,

where there is more than one such notice and those notices are served at different times, upon the service of the last such notice to be served.

(2) Where the Secretary of State decides not to proceed with the revocation or variation, the order or direction shall have effect again from the time of that decision, and shall thereafter have effect as if—

(a) any period specified in the order or direction for the taking of any action, being a period which had not expired prior to the date mentioned in paragraph (1), were extended by a period equal to that during which the revocation or variation had effect; and

(b) there were substituted for any date specified in the order or direction as being a date by which any action should be taken, not being a date falling prior to that date mentioned in paragraph (1), such date as post-dates the specified date by a period equal to that during which the revocation or variation had effect.

(3) The revocation or variation pursuant to regulation 79 of an order under section 1 or 3 of the Transport and Works Act 1992, or of a direction deeming planning permission to be granted, shall not affect anything done under the order or direction prior to the revocation or variation taking effect.   **[1001]**

NOTES

Commencement: 30 October 1994.

82. Orders under the Transport and Works Act 1992: compensation for revocation or variation

(1) Where a direction deeming planning permission to be granted is revoked or varied pursuant to regulation 79, that permission shall be treated for the purposes of Part IV of the Town and Country Planning Act 1990 (compensation) as having been revoked or modified by order under section 97 of that Act.

(2) Where an order under section 1 or 3 of the Transport and Works Act 1992 is revoked or varied pursuant to regulation 79, Part IV of the Town and Country Planning Act 1990 shall apply as if—

(a) the order had been planning permission granted on an application under that Act and had been revoked or modified by order under section 97 of that Act; and

(b) that Part provided that the Secretary of State was the person liable to pay any compensation provided for by that Part.

This paragraph shall not have effect to confer any right to compensation for any expenditure, loss or damage for which compensation is payable by virtue of paragraph (1) above.

(3) Where the Secretary of State decides not to proceed with the revocation or variation of an order under section 1 or 3 of the Transport and Works Act 1992, or a direction deeming planning permission to be granted, any claim for compensation by virtue of this regulation shall be limited to any loss or damage directly attributable to the order or direction ceasing to have effect or being varied for the duration of the period between the revocation or variation taking effect under regulation 81(1) and the Secretary of State deciding not to proceed with it.

(4) Where compensation is payable by virtue of this regulation, the question as to the amount of the compensation shall be referred to and determined by the Lands

Tribunal unless and to the extent that in any particular case the Secretary of State has indicated in writing that such a reference and determination may be dispensed with.

[1002]

NOTES
Commencement: 30 October 1994.

Environmental controls

83. Authorisations under Part I of the Environmental Protection Act 1990

(1) Regulations 48 and 49 (requirement to consider effect on European site) apply in relation to the granting of an authorisation under Part I of the Environmental Protection Act 1990 (integrated pollution control and local authority air pollution control).

(2) Where in such a case the competent authority consider that any adverse effects of the plan or project on the integrity of a European site would be avoided if the authorisation were subject to conditions, they may grant an authorisation, or cause an authorisation to be granted, subject to those conditions.

(3) Regulations 50 and 51 (requirement to review existing decisions and consents, &c) apply to any such authorisation as is mentioned in paragraph (1).

(4) Where on the review of such an authorisation the competent authority consider that any adverse effects on the integrity of a European site of the carrying out or, as the case may be, the continuation of activities authorised by it would be avoided by a variation of the authorisation, they may vary it, or cause it to be varied, accordingly.

(5) Where any question arises as to agreeing to a plan or project, or affirming an authorisation on review, under regulation 49 (considerations of overriding public interest), the competent authority shall refer the matter to the Secretary of State who shall determine the matter in accordance with that regulation and give directions to the authority accordingly.

[1003]

NOTES
Commencement: 30 October 1994.

84. Licences under Part II of the Environmental Protection Act 1990

(1) Regulations 48 and 49 (requirement to consider effect on European site) apply in relation to—

    (a) the granting of a waste management licence under Part II of the Environmental Protection Act 1990,

    (b) the passing of a resolution under section 54 of that Act (provisions as to land occupied by disposal authorities themselves), and

    (c) the granting of a disposal licence under Part I of the Control of Pollution Act 1974 and the passing of a resolution under section 11 of that Act.

(2) Where in such a case the competent authority consider that any adverse effects of the plan or project on the integrity of a European site would be avoided by making any licence subject to conditions, they may grant a licence, or cause a licence to be granted, or, as the case may be, pass a resolution, subject to those conditions.

(3) Regulations 50 and 51 (requirement to review existing decisions and consents, &c) apply to any such licence or resolution as is mentioned in paragraph (1).

(4) Where on the review of such a licence or resolution the competent authority

consider that any adverse effects on the integrity of a European site of the carrying out or, as the case may be, the continuation of the activities authorised by it would be avoided by a variation of the licence or resolution, they may vary it, or cause it to be varied, accordingly.   **[1004]**

NOTES
Commencement: 30 October 1994.

85. Discharge consents under water pollution legislation

(1) Regulations 48 and 49 (requirement to consider effect on European site) apply in relation to the giving of consent under—

    (a) Chapter II of Part III to the Water Resources Act 1991 (control of pollution of water resources), or

    (b) Part II of the Control of Pollution Act 1974 (which makes corresponding provision for Scotland).

(2) Where in such a case the competent authority consider that any adverse effects of the plan or project on the integrity of a European site would be avoided by making any consent subject to conditions, they may give consent, or cause it to be given, subject to those conditions.

(3) Regulations 50 and 51 (requirement to review existing decisions and consents, &c) apply to any such consent as is mentioned in paragraph (1).

(4) Where on the review of such a consent the competent authority consider that any adverse effects on the integrity of a European site of the carrying out or, as the case may be, the continuation of the activities authorised by it would be avoided by a variation of the consent, they may vary it, or cause it to be varied, accordingly.

                                                           [1005]

NOTES
Commencement: 30 October 1994.

PART V

SUPPLEMENTARY PROVISIONS

Supplementary provisions as to management agreements

86. Powers of limited owners, &c to enter into management agreements

(1) In the case of settled land in England and Wales—

    (a) the tenant for life may enter into a management agreement relating to the land, or any part of it, either for consideration or gratuitously;

    (b) the Settled Land Act 1925 shall apply as if the power conferred by sub-paragraph (a) had been conferred by that Act; and

    (c) for the purposes of section 72 of that Act (which relates to the mode of giving effect to a disposition by a tenant for life and to the operation thereof), and of any other relevant statutory provision, entering into a management agreement shall be treated as a disposition.

The above provisions of this paragraph shall be construed as one with the Settled Land Act 1925.

(2) Section 28 of the Law of Property Act 1925 (which confers the powers of a tenant for life on trustees for sale) shall apply as if the power of a tenant for life under paragraph (1)(a) above had been conferred by the Settled Land Act 1925.

(3) A university or college to which the Universities and College Estates Act 1925 applies may enter into a management agreement relating to any land belonging to it in England and Wales either for consideration or gratuitously.

That Act shall apply as if the power conferred by this paragraph had been conferred by that Act.

(4) In the case of glebe land or other land belonging to an ecclesiastical benefice—

(a) the incumbent of the benefice, and
(b) in the case of land which is part of the endowment of any other ecclesiastical corporation, the corporation,

may with the consent of the Church Commissioners enter into a management agreement either for consideration or gratuitously.

The Ecclesiastical Leasing Acts shall apply as if the power conferred by this paragraph had been conferred by those Acts, except that the consent of the patron of an ecclesiastical benefice shall not be requisite.

(5) In the case of any land in Scotland, any person being—

(a) the liferenter, or
(b) the heir of entail,

in possession of the land shall have power to enter into a management agreement relating to the land or any part of it.

(6) The Trusts (Scotland) Act 1921 shall have effect as if among the powers conferred on trustees by section 4 of that Act (which relates to the general powers of trustees) there were included a power to enter into management agreements relating to the trust estate or any part of it. **[1006]**

NOTES
Commencement: 30 October 1994.

Supplementary provisions as to potentially damaging operations

87. Carrying out of operation after expiry of period

(1) If before the expiry of the period of four months referred to in regulation 19(2)(c) the relevant person agrees in writing with the appropriate nature conservation body that, subject as follows, the condition specified in that provision shall not apply in relation to the operation in question, then, subject as follows, regulation 19(2) shall as from the date of the agreement have effect in relation to the operation (as regards both the owner or the occupier of the land in question) as if sub-paragraph (c) were omitted.

(2) If after such an agreement has been made the relevant person (whether a party to the agreement or not) gives written notice to the appropriate nature conservation body that he wishes to terminate the agreement, then as from the giving of the notice regulation 19(2) shall have effect in relation to the operation in question (as regards both the owner and the occupier of the land in question) as if paragraph (c) specified the condition that one month, or any longer period specified in the notice, has expired from the giving of the notice under this paragraph.

(3) In paragraphs (1) and (2) above "the relevant person"—

(a) in a case where the notice under regulation 19(1)(a) was given by the owner of the land in question, means the owner of that land;
(b) in a case where that notice was given by the occupier of that land, means the occupier of that land. **[1007]**

NOTES
Commencement: 30 October 1994.

88. Duties of agriculture Ministers with respect to European sites

(1) Where an application for a farm capital grant is made as respects expenditure incurred or to be incurred for the purpose of activities on land within a European site, the Minister responsible for determining the application—

(a) shall, so far as may be consistent with the purposes of the grant provisions, so exercise his functions thereunder as to further the conservation of the flora, fauna, or geological or physiographical features by reason of which the land is a European site; and

(b) where the appropriate nature conservation body have objected to the making of the grant on the ground that the activities in question have destroyed or damaged or will destroy or damage that flora or fauna or those features, shall not make the grant except after considering the objection and, in the case of land in England, after consulting with the Secretary of State.

(2) Where in consequence of an objection by the appropriate nature conservation body, an application for a grant as respects expenditure to be incurred is refused on the ground that the activities in question will have such an effect as is mentioned in paragraph (1)(b), the appropriate nature conservation body shall, within three months of their receiving notice of the Minister's decision, offer to enter into, in the terms of a draft submitted to the applicant, a management agreement—

(a) imposing restrictions as respects those activities, and

(b) providing for the making by them of payments to the applicant.

(3) In this regulation—

"farm capital grant" means—

(a) a grant under a scheme made under section 29 of the Agriculture Act 1970, or

(b) a grant under regulations made under section 2(2) of the European Communities Act 1972 to a person carrying on an agricultural business within the meaning of those regulations in respect of expenditure incurred or to be incurred for the purposes of or in connection with that business, being expenditure of a capital nature or incurred in connection with expenditure of a capital nature; and

"grant provisions" means—

(i) in the case of such a grant as is mentioned in paragraph (a) above, the scheme under which the grant is made and section 29 of the Agriculture Act 1970, and

(ii) in the case of such a grant as is mentioned in paragraph (b) above, the regulations under which the grant is made and the Community instrument in pursuance of which the regulations were made. **[1008]**

NOTES
Commencement: 30 October 1994.

89. Payments under certain agreements offered by authorities

(1) This regulation applies where the appropriate nature conservation body offers to enter into a management agreement providing for the making of payments by them to—

(a) a person who has given notice under regulation 19(1)(a) or 23(1)(a), or

(b) a person whose application for a farm capital grant within the meaning of regulation 88 has been refused in consequence of an objection by that body.

(2) Subject to paragraph (3), the said payments shall be of such amounts as may be determined by the offeror in accordance with guidance given—

(a) in England, by the Minister of Agriculture, Fisheries and Food and the Secretary of State, or

(b) in Wales or Scotland, by the Secretary of State.

(3) If the offeree so requires within one month of receiving the offer, the determination of those amounts shall be referred to an arbitrator to be appointed, in default of agreement, by the Secretary of State.

(4) Where the amounts determined by the arbitrator exceed those determined by the offeror, the offeror shall—

(a) amend the offer so as to give effect to the arbitrator's determination, or

(b) except in the case of an offer made to a person whose application for a farm capital grant has been refused in consequence of an objection by the offeror, withdraw the offer.

(5) In the application of this regulation in Scotland references to an arbitrator shall be construed as references to an arbiter.   **[1009]**

NOTES
Commencement: 30 October 1994.

90. Powers of entry

(1) A person authorised in writing by the appropriate nature conservation body may, at any reasonable time and (if required to do so) upon producing evidence that he is so authorised, enter any land—

(a) to ascertain whether a special nature conservation order should be made in relation to that land, or if an offence under regulation 23 is being, or has been, committed on that land; or

(b) to ascertain the amount of any compensation payable under regulation 25 in respect of an interest in that land.

But nothing in this paragraph shall authorise any person to enter a dwelling.

(2) A person shall not demand admission as of right to any land which is occupied unless either—

(a) 24 hours' notice of the intended entry has been given to the occupier, or

(b) the purpose of the entry is to ascertain if an offence under regulation 23 is being, or has been, committed on that land.

(3) A person who intentionally obstructs a person in the exercise of his powers under this regulation commits an offence and is liable on summary conviction to a fine not exceeding level 3 on the standard scale.   **[1010]**

NOTES
Commencement: 30 October 1994.

91. Compensation: amount and assessment

(1) The following provisions have effect as to compensation under regulation 25(1) (effect of special nature conservation order: decrease in value of agricultural unit).

(2) The amount of the compensation shall be the difference between the value of the interest in question and what it would have been had the order not been made.

(3) For this purpose—

    (a) an interest in land shall be valued as at the time when the order is made; and

    (b) where a person, by reason of his having more than one interest in land, makes more than one claim in respect of the same order, his various interests shall be valued together.

(4) Section 10 of the Land Compensation Act 1973 (mortgages, trusts for sale and settlements) or section 10 of the Land Compensation (Scotland) Act 1973 apply in relation to compensation under regulation 25(1) as in relation to compensation under Part I of that Act.

(5) For the purposes of assessing compensation under regulation 25(1), the rules set out in section 5 of the Land Compensation Act 1961 or section 12 of the Land Compensation (Scotland) Act 1963 have effect, so far as applicable and subject to any necessary modifications, as they have effect for the purpose of assessing compensation for the compulsory acquisition of an interest in land. **[1011]**

NOTES
Commencement: 30 October 1994.

92. Compensation: other supplementary provisions

(1) The following provisions have effect in relation to compensation under regulation 25 (compensation for effect of special nature conservation order).

(2) The compensation shall carry interest, at the rate for the time being prescribed under section 32 of the Land Compensation Act 1961 or section 40 of the Land Compensation (Scotland) Act 1963, from the date of the claim until payment.

(3) Except in so far as may be provided by regulations, any question of disputed compensation shall be referred to and determined by the Lands Tribunal or the Lands Tribunal for Scotland.

(4) In relation to the determination of any such question, the provisions of sections 2 and 4 of the Land Compensation Act 1961 or sections 9 and 11 of the Land Compensation (Scotland) Act 1963 (procedure and costs) shall apply, subject to any necessary modifications and to the provisions of any regulations. **[1012]**

NOTES
Commencement: 30 October 1994.

93. Compensation: procedural provisions

(1) The power to make regulations under section 30 of the Wildlife and Countryside Act 1981 (provisions as to compensation where order made under section 29 of that Act) shall be exercisable so as to make provision for the purposes of these Regulations corresponding to those for which provision may be made under that section.

(2) The references in regulation 25 to matters being prescribed by regulations, and in regulation 92(3) and (4) to matters being provided by regulations, are to their being so prescribed or provided.

(3) Any regulations in force under section 30 on the commencement of these Regulations shall have effect for the purposes of these Regulations as if made under that section as applied by this regulation. **[1013]**

NOTES
Commencement: 30 October 1994.

Supplementary provisions as to byelaws

94. Procedure for making byelaws, penalties, &c

(1) Sections 236 to 238 of the Local Government Act 1972 or sections 201 to 204 of the Local Government (Scotland) Act 1973 (procedure, &c for byelaws; offences against byelaws; evidence of byelaws) apply to all byelaws made under section 20 of the National Parks and Access to the Countryside Act 1949 as it applies by virtue of regulation 28 as if the appropriate nature conservation body were a local authority within the meaning of that Act.

(2) In relation to byelaws so made the confirming authority for the purposes of the said section 236 or section 201 shall be the Secretary of State.

(3) The appropriate nature conservation body shall have power to enforce byelaws made by them:

Provided that nothing in this paragraph shall be construed as authorising the institution of proceedings in Scotland for an offence. **[1014]**

NOTES
Commencement: 30 October 1994.

95. Powers of entry

(1) For the purpose of surveying land, or of estimating its value, in connection with any claim for compensation payable under regulation 30 in respect of that or any other land, an officer of the Valuation Office or person duly authorised in writing by the authority from whom the compensation is claimed may enter upon the land.

(2) A person authorised under this regulation to enter upon any land shall, if so required, produce evidence of his authority before entering.

(3) A person shall not under this regulation demand admission as of right to any land which is occupied unless at least 14 days' notice in writing of the intended entry has been given to the occupier.

(4) A person who intentionally obstructs a person in the exercise of his powers under this regulation commits an offence and is liable on summary conviction to a fine not exceeding level 3 on the standard scale. **[1015]**

NOTES
Commencement: 30 October 1994.

96. Compensation: England and Wales

(1) The following provisions have effect as to compensation under regulation 30 (compensation for effect of byelaws) in respect of land in England and Wales.

(2) Any dispute arising on a claim for any such compensation shall be determined by the Lands Tribunal.

(3) For the purposes of any such reference to the Lands Tribunal, section 4 of the Land Compensation Act 1961 (which relates to costs) has effect with the substitution for references to the acquiring authority of references to the authority from whom the compensation in question is claimed.

(4) Rules (2) to (4) of the Rules set out in section 5 of that Act (which provides rules for valuation of a compulsory acquisition) apply to the calculation of any such compensation, in so far as it is calculated by reference to the depreciation of the value of an interest in land.

(5) In the case of an interest in land subject to a mortgage—

  (a) any such compensation in respect of the depreciation of that interest shall be calculated as if the interest were not subject to the mortgage;

  (b) a claim or application for the payment of any such compensation may be made by any person who when the byelaws giving rise to the compensation were made was the mortgagee of the interest, or by any person claiming under such a person, but without prejudice to the making of a claim or application by any other person;

  (c) a mortgagee shall not be entitled to any such compensation in respect of his interest as such; and

  (d) any compensation payable in respect of the interest subject to the mortgage shall be paid to the mortgagee or, where there is more than one mortgagee, to the first mortgagee, and shall in either case be applied by him as if it were proceeds of sale.   **[1016]**

NOTES
Commencement: 30 October 1994.

97. Compensation: Scotland

(1) The following provisions have effect as to compensation under regulation 30 (compensation for effect of byelaws) in respect of land in Scotland.

(2) Any dispute arising on a claim for any such compensation shall be determined by the Lands Tribunal for Scotland.

(3) For the purposes of any such reference to the Lands Tribunal for Scotland section 8 of the Land Compensation (Scotland) Act 1963 (which relates to expenses) has effect with the substitution for references to the acquiring authority, of references to the authority from whom the compensation in question is claimed.

(4) Rules (2) to (4) of the Rules set out in section 12 of that Act (which provides rules for valuation on a compulsory acquisition) apply to the calculation of any such compensation, in so far as it is calculated by reference to the depreciation of the value of an interest in land.

(5) In the case of an interest in land subject to a heritable security—

  (a) any such compensation in respect of the depreciation of that interest shall be calculated as if the interest were not subject to the heritable security;

  (b) a claim or application for the payment of any such compensation may be made by any person who when the byelaws giving rise to the compensation were made was the creditor in a heritable security of the interest, or by any person claiming under such a person, but without prejudice to the making of a claim or application by any other person;

(c) a creditor in a heritable security shall not be entitled to any such compensation in respect of his interest as such; and

(d) any compensation payable in respect of the interest subject to the heritable security shall be paid to the creditor or, where there is more than one creditor in a heritable security, to the creditor whose heritable security has priority over any other heritable securities secured on the land, and shall in either case be applied by him as if it were proceeds of sale.   **[1017]**

NOTES
Commencement: 30 October 1994.

Supplementary provisions as to compulsory acquisition

98. Supplementary provisions as to acquisition of land

(1) The powers of compulsory acquisition conferred on the appropriate nature conservation body by regulation 32 are exercisable in any particular case on their being authorised so to do by the Secretary of State.

(2) In that regulation and in this regulation "land" includes any interest in land.

For this purpose "interest", in relation to land, includes any estate in land and any right over land, whether the right is exercisable by virtue of the ownership of an interest in land or by virtue of a licence or agreement, and in particular includes sporting rights.

(3) The Acquisition of Land Act 1981 applies in relation to any acquisition under these Regulations of land in England and Wales, and the Compulsory Purchase Act 1965 applies with any necessary modifications in relation to the acquisition of any interest in land in England and Wales.

(4) In relation to the compulsory acquisition of land in Scotland, the Acquisition of Land (Authorisation Procedure) (Scotland) Act 1947 shall apply as if these Regulations had been in force immediately before the commencement of that Act and as if in paragraph (a) of subsection (1) of section 1 thereof, in Part I of the First Schedule thereto and in the Second Schedule thereto references to a local authority included Scottish Natural Heritage:

Provided that section 2 of the said Act (which confers temporary powers for the speedy acquisition of land in urgent cases) shall not apply to any such compulsory acquisition as is mentioned in this paragraph.

The provisions of the Lands Clauses Acts incorporated with these Regulations by virtue of paragraph 1 of the Second Schedule to the Acquisition of Land (Authorisation Procedure) (Scotland) Act 1947, as applied by this paragraph, shall apply with the necessary modifications in relation to the compulsory acquisition of any interest in land, being an interest not falling within the definition of "lands" contained in the Lands Clauses Acts.   **[1018]**

NOTES
Commencement: 30 October 1994.

99. Powers of entry

(1) For the purpose of surveying land in connection with the acquisition thereof or of any interest therein, whether by agreement or compulsorily, in the exercise of any power conferred by these Regulations, a person duly authorised in writing by the authority having power so to acquire the land or interest may enter upon the land.

(2) A person authorised under this regulation to enter upon any land shall, if so required, produce evidence of his authority before entering.

(3) A person shall not under this regulation demand admission as of right to any land which is occupied unless at least 14 days' notice in writing of the intended entry has been given to the occupier.

(4) A person who intentionally obstructs a person in the exercise of his powers under this regulation commits an offence and is liable on summary conviction to a fine not exceeding level 3 on the standard scale.   **[1019]**

NOTES

Commencement: 30 October 1994.

Supplementary provisions as to protection of species

100. Attempts and possession of means of committing offence

(1) A person who attempts to commit an offence under Part III of these Regulations is guilty of an offence and punishable in like manner as for that offence.

(2) A person who, for the purposes of committing an offence under Part III of these Regulations, has in his possession anything capable of being used for committing the offence is guilty of an offence and punishable in like manner as for that offence.

(3) References below to an offence under Part III include an offence under this regulation.   **[1020]**

NOTES

Commencement: 30 October 1994.

101. Enforcement

(1) If a constable suspects with reasonable cause that any person is committing or has committed an offence under Part III of these Regulations, the constable may without warrant—

(a) stop and search that person if the constable suspects with reasonable cause that evidence of the commission of the offence is to be found on that person;

(b) search or examine any thing which that person may then be using or have in his possession if the constable suspects with reasonable cause that evidence of the commission of the offence is to be found on that thing;

(c) seize and detain for the purposes of proceedings under that Part any thing which may be evidence of the commission of the offence or may be liable to be forfeited under regulation 103.

(2) If a constable suspects with reasonable cause that any person is committing an offence under Part III of these Regulations, he may, for the purposes of exercising the powers conferred by paragraph (1) or arresting a person in accordance with section 25 of the Police and Criminal Evidence Act 1984 for such an offence, enter any land other than a dwelling-house.

(3) If a justice of the peace is satisfied by information on oath that there are reasonable grounds for suspecting that an offence under regulation 39, 41 or 43 has been committed and that evidence of the offence may be found on any premises, he may grant a warrant to any constable (with or without other persons) to enter upon and search those premises for the purpose of obtaining that evidence.

In the application of this paragraph to Scotland, the reference to a justice of the peace includes a sheriff.   **[1021]**

NOTES
Commencement: 30 October 1994.

102. Proceedings for offences: venue, time limits

(1) An offence under Part III of these Regulations shall, for the purposes of conferring jurisdiction, be deemed to have been committed in any place where the offender is found or to which he is first brought after the commission of the offence.

(2) Summary proceedings for—

(a) any offence under regulation 39(1) involving the taking or killing of a wild animal, and

(b) any offence under regulation 43(1),

may be brought within a period of six months from the date on which evidence sufficient in the opinion of the prosecutor to warrant the proceedings came to his knowledge.

But no such proceedings shall be brought by virtue of this paragraph more than two years after the commission of the offence.

(3) For the purposes of paragraph (2) a certificate signed by or on behalf of the prosecutor and stating the date on which such evidence as aforesaid came to his knowledge shall be conclusive evidence of that fact; and a certificate stating that matter and purporting to be so signed shall be deemed to be so signed unless the contrary is proved. **[1022]**

NOTES
Commencement: 30 October 1994.

103. Power of court to order forfeiture

(1) The court by which a person is convicted of an offence under Part III of these Regulations—

(a) shall order the forfeiture of any animal, plant or other thing in respect of which the offence was committed; and

(b) may order the forfeiture of any vehicle, animal, weapon or other thing which was used to commit the offence.

(2) In paragraph (1)(b) "vehicle" includes aircraft, hovercraft and boat. **[1023]**

NOTES
Commencement: 30 October 1994.

104. Saving for other protective provisions

Nothing in these Regulations shall be construed as excluding the application of the provisions of Part I of the Wildlife and Countryside Act 1981 (protection of wildlife) in relation to animals or plants also protected under Part III of these Regulations.

[1024]

NOTES
Commencement: 30 October 1994.

General supplementary provisions

105. Powers of drainage authorities

(1) Where the appropriate nature conservation body or any other person enter into an agreement with a drainage authority for the doing by that authority of any work

on land in a European site, no limitation imposed by law on the capacity of the drainage authority by virtue of its constitution shall operate so as to prevent the authority carrying out the agreement.

(2) In paragraph (1) "drainage authority" means the National Rivers Authority or an internal drainage board.   **[1025]**

NOTES
Commencement: 30 October 1994.

106. Offences by bodies corporate, &c

(1) Where an offence under these Regulations committed by a body corporate is proved to have been committed with the consent or connivance of, or to be attributable to any neglect on the part of, a director, manager, secretary or other similar officer of the body corporate, or a person purporting to act in any such capacity, he as well as the body corporate is guilty of the offence and liable to be proceeded against and punished accordingly.

For this purpose "director", in relation to a body corporate whose affairs are managed by its members, means any member of the body.

(2) Where an offence under these Regulations committed by a Scottish partnership is proved to have been committed with the consent or connivance of, or to be attributable to neglect on the part of, a partner, he (as well as the partnership) is guilty of the offence and liable to be proceeded against and punished accordingly.

[1026]

NOTES
Commencement: 30 October 1994.

107. Local inquiries

(1) The Secretary of State may cause a local inquiry to be held for the purposes of the exercise of any of his functions under these Regulations.

(2) The provisions of section 250(2) to (5) of the Local Government Act 1972 or section 210(4) to (8) of the Local Government (Scotland) Act 1973 (local inquiries: evidence and costs) apply in relation to an inquiry held under this regulation.   **[1027]**

NOTES
Commencement: 30 October 1994.

108. Service of notices

(1) Section 329 of the Town and Country Planning Act 1990 or section 269 of the Town and Country Planning (Scotland) Act 1972 (service of notices) apply to notices and other documents required or authorised to be served under these Regulations.

(2) Paragraph (1) does not apply to the service of any notice required or authorised to be served under the Acquisition of Land Act 1981 or the Acquisition of Land (Authorisation Procedure) (Scotland) Act 1947, as applied by these Regulations.   **[1028]**

NOTES
Commencement: 30 October 1994.

SCHEDULE 1

Regulation 22(3)

PROCEDURE IN CONNECTION WITH ORDERS UNDER REGULATION 22

Coming into operation

1.—(1) An original order or a restrictive amending order takes effect on its being made.

(2) The Secretary of State shall consider every such order, and the order shall cease to have effect nine months after it is made unless he has previously given notice under paragraph 6 that he has considered it and does not propose to amend or revoke it, or has revoked it.

(3) Subject to paragraphs 3(1) and 4(4), a revoking order, or an amending order which is not restrictive, does not take effect until confirmed by the Secretary of State.

(4) An amending or revoking order requiring confirmation shall stand revoked if the Secretary of State gives notice under paragraph 6 below that it is not to be confirmed.

Publicity for orders

2.—(1) The Secretary of State shall, where an order has been made, give notice setting out the order (or describing its general effect) and stating that it has taken effect or, as the case may be, that it has been made and requires confirmation.

(2) The notice shall—

(a) name a place in the area in which the land to which the order relates is situated where a copy of the order may be inspected free of charge at all reasonable hours; and

(b) specify the time (not being less than 28 days from the date of the first publication of the notice) within which, and the manner in which, representations or objections with respect to the order may be made.

(3) The notice shall be given—

(a) by publication in the Gazette and also at least one local newspaper circulating in the area in which the land to which the order relates is situated;

(b) by serving a iike notice—

(i) on every owner and occupier of that land (subject to sub-paragraph (4) below); and

(ii) on the local planning authority within whose area the land is situated.

(4) The Secretary of State may, in any particular case, direct that it shall not be necessary to comply with sub-paragraph (3)(b)(i); but if he so directs in the case of any land, then in addition to publication the notice shall be addressed to "The owners and any occupiers" of the land (describing it) and a copy or copies of the notice shall be affixed to some conspicuous object or objects on the land.

Unopposed orders

3.—(1) Where an order has taken effect immediately and no representations or objections are duly made in respect of it or any so made are withdrawn, the Secretary of State shall, as soon as practicable after considering the order, decide either to take no action on it or to make an order amending or revoking it.

An amending or revoking order under this sub-paragraph takes effect immediately and does not require confirmation nor shall any representation or objection with respect to it be entertained.

(2) Where an order requiring confirmation is made and no representations or objections are duly made in respect of it, or any so made are withdrawn, the Secretary of State may confirm the order (with or without modification).

Opposed orders

4.—(1) If any representation or objection duly made with respect to an order is not withdrawn, then, as soon as practicable in the case of an order having immediate effect and before confirming an order requiring confirmation, the Secretary of State shall either—

(a) cause a local inquiry to be held; or
(b) afford any person by whom a representation or objection has been duly made and not withdrawn an opportunity of being heard by a person appointed by the Secretary of State for the purpose.

(2) On considering any representations or objections duly made and the report of any person appointed to hold the inquiry or to hear representations or objections, the Secretary of State—

(a) if the order has already taken effect, shall decide either to take no action on the order, or to make an order amending or revoking it as he thinks appropriate in the light of the report, representations or objections; and
(b) if the order requires confirmation, may confirm it (with or without modifications).

(3) The provisions of section 250(2) to (5) of the Local Government Act 1972 or section 210(4) to (8) of the Local Government (Scotland) Act 1973 (local inquiries: evidence and costs) apply in relation to an inquiry held under this paragraph.

(4) An amending or revoking order made by virtue of sub-paragraph (2) above takes effect immediately and does not require confirmation nor shall any representation or objection with respect to it be entertained.

Restriction on power to amend orders or confirm them with modifications

5. The Secretary of State shall not by virtue of paragraphs 3(1) or 4(2) amend an order which has taken effect, or confirm any other order with modifications, so as to extend the area to which the order applies.

Notice of final decision on order

6.—(1) The Secretary of State shall as soon as practicable after making an order by virtue of paragraphs 3(1) or 4(2) give notice—

(a) setting out the order (or describing its effect) and stating that it has taken effect; and
(b) naming a place in the area in which the land to which the order relates is situated where a copy of the order may be inspected free of charge at all reasonable hours.

(2) The Secretary of State shall give notice of any of the following decisions of his as soon as practicable after making the decision—

(a) a decision under paragraph 3(1) or 4(2) to take no action on an order which has already taken effect;
(b) a decision to confirm or not to confirm an order requiring confirmation under this Schedule.

(3) A notice under this paragraph of a decision to confirm an order shall—

(a) set out the order as confirmed (or describe its general effect) and state the day on which the order took effect; and
(b) name a place in the area in which the land to which the order relates is situated where a copy of the order as confirmed may be inspected free of charge at all reasonable hours.

(4) Notice under this paragraph shall be given by publishing it in accordance with paragraph 2(3) and serving a copy of it on any person on whom a notice was required to be served under paragraph 2(3) or (4).

Proceedings for questioning validity of orders

7.—(1) This paragraph applies to any order which has taken effect and as to which the Secretary of State has given notice under paragraph 6 of a decision of his to take no action or to amend the order in accordance with paragraph 4; and in this paragraph ''the relevant notice'' means that notice.

(2) If any person is aggrieved by an order to which this paragraph applies and desires to question its validity on the ground that it is not within the powers of regulation 22, or that any of the requirements of this Schedule have not been complied with in relation to it, he may within six weeks from the date of the relevant notice make an application to the court under this paragraph.

(3) On any such application the court may, if satisfied that the order is not within those powers or that the interests of the applicant have been substantially prejudiced by a failure to comply with any of those requirements—

(a) in England and Wales, quash the order, or any provision of the order, either generally or in so far as it affects the interests of the applicant; or

(b) in Scotland, make such declarator as seems to the court to be appropriate.

(4) Except as provided by this paragraph, the validity of an order shall not be questioned in any legal proceedings whatsoever.

(5) In this paragraph "the court" means the High Court in relation to England and Wales and the Court of Session in relation to Scotland.

Interpretation

8. In this Schedule—

"amending order" and "revoking order" mean an order which amends or, as the case may be, revokes a previous order;

"the Gazette" means—

(a) if the order relates in whole or in part to land in England and Wales, the London Gazette; and

(b) if the order relates in whole or in part to land in Scotland, the Edinburgh Gazette;

"order" means an order under regulation 22;

"original order" means an order other than an amending or revoking order; and

"restrictive amending order" means an amending order which extends the area to which a previous order applies.   **[1029]**

NOTES

Commencement: 30 October 1994.

SCHEDULE 2

Regulation 38

EUROPEAN PROTECTED SPECIES OF ANIMALS

Common name	Scientific name
Bats, Horseshoe (all species)	Rhinolophidae
Bats, Typical (all species)	Vespertilionidae
Butterfly, Large Blue	Maculinea arion
Cat, Wild	Felis silvestris
Dolphins, porpoises and whales (all species)	Cetacea
Dormouse	Muscardinus avellanarius
Lizard, Sand	Lacerta agilis
Newt, Great Crested (or Warty)	Triturus cristatus
Otter, Common	Lutra lutra
Snake, Smooth	Coronella austriaca
Sturgeon	Acipenser sturio
Toad, Natterjack	Bufo calamita
Turtles, Marine	Caretta caretta
	Chelonia mydas
	Lepidochelys kempii
	Eretmochelys imbricata
	Dermochelys coriacea

NOTE. The common name or names given in the first column of this Schedule are included by way of guidance only; in the event of any dispute or proceedings, the common name or names shall not be taken into account. **[1030]**

NOTES
Commencement: 30 October 1994.

SCHEDULE 3
Regulation 41(1)(a)

ANIMALS WHICH MAY NOT BE TAKEN OR KILLED IN CERTAIN WAYS

Common name	Scientific name
Barbel	Barbus barbus
Grayling	Thymallus thymallus
Hare, Mountain	Lepus timidus
Lamprey, River	Lampetra fluviatilis
Marten, Pine	Martes martes
Polecat	Mustela putorius (otherwise known as Putorius putorius)
Salmon, Atlantic	Salmo salar (only in fresh water)
Seal, Bearded	Erignathus barbatus
Seal, Common	Phoca vitulina
Seal, Grey	Halichoerus grypus
Seal, Harp	Phoca groenlandica (otherwise known as Pagophilus groenlandicus)
Seal, Hooded	Cystophora cristata
Seal, Ringed	Phoca hispida (otherwise known as Pusa hispida)
Shad, Allis	Alosa alosa
Shad, Twaite	Alosa fallax
Vendace	Coregonus albula
Whitefish	Coregonus lavaretus

NOTE. The common name or names given in the first column of this Schedule are included by way of guidance only; in the event of any dispute or proceedings, the common name or names shall not be taken into account. **[1031]**

NOTES
Commencement: 30 October 1994.

SCHEDULE 4
Regulation 42

EUROPEAN PROTECTED SPECIES OF PLANTS

Common name	Scientific name
Dock, Shore	Rumex rupestris
Fern, Killarney	Trichomanes speciosum
Gentian, Early	Gentianella anglica
Lady's-slipper	Cypripedium calceolus
Marshwort, Creeping	Apium repens
Naiad, slender	Najas flexilis
Orchid, Fen	Liparis loeselii
Plantain, Floating-leaved water	Luronium natans
Saxifrage, Yellow Marsh	Saxifraga hirculus

NOTE. The common name or names given in the first column of this Schedule are included by way of guidance only; in the event of any dispute or proceedings, the common name or names shall not be taken into account. **[1032]**

NOTES
Commencement: 30 October 1994.

TOWN AND COUNTRY PLANNING (ENVIRONMENTAL ASSESSMENT AND PERMITTED DEVELOPMENT) REGULATIONS 1995
(SI 1995/417)

NOTES
Made: 22 February 1995.
Authority: European Communities Act 1972, s 2.

1. Citation and commencement

These Regulations may be cited as the Town and Country Planning (Environmental Assessment and Permitted Development) Regulations 1995 and shall come into force on 3rd June 1995. **[1033]**

NOTES
Commencement: 3 June 1995.

2. Interpretation

In these Regulations, unless the context otherwise requires—

"prospective developer" means a person, other than a relevant planning authority or a person who intends to undertake development with such an authority (whether or not with any other person), who is minded to undertake development which appears to him to be relevant development;

"relevant development" means development of any description specified in Schedule 2 to the Town and Country Planning (General Permitted Development) Order 1995 other than development of any description specified in article 3(12) of that Order;

"relevant planning authority" means the body by whom, assuming no direction were given under section 77 of the Town and Country Planning Act 1990, an application for planning permission in respect of the development concerned would be determined;

"Schedule 1" means Schedule 1 to the Town and Country Planning (Assessment of Environmental Effects) Regulations 1988; and

"Schedule 2" means Schedule 2 to those Regulations. **[1034]**

NOTES
Commencement: 3 June 1995.

3. Opinion as to need for environmental statement

(1) A prospective developer may apply to the relevant planning authority for their opinion as to whether the relevant development specified in the application is within a description mentioned in Schedule 1 or Schedule 2, and, if so, within which description, and if within a description mentioned in Schedule 2, whether it would be likely to have significant effects on the environment by virtue of factors such as its nature, size or location.

(2) An application under paragraph (1) shall be accompanied by—

(a) a plan sufficient to identify the land;

    (b) a brief description of the nature and purpose of the development and of its possible effects on the environment;

    (c) such other information or representations as the prospective developer may wish to provide or make.

(3) An authority which receives an application under paragraph (1) shall, if they consider that they have not been provided with sufficient information to give an opinion on the questions raised, notify the prospective developer of the particular points on which they require further information; and the information so requested shall be provided within such reasonable period as may be specified in the notice or such longer period as may be agreed in writing between the authority and the prospective developer.

(4) The authority shall give to the prospective developer written notice of their opinion within the period of 3 weeks beginning with the date of receipt of the application or such longer period as may be agreed in writing with the prospective developer; and if it is their opinion that the relevant development is—

    (a) within a description mentioned in Schedule 1, or

    (b) within a description mentioned in Schedule 2 and likely to have significant effects on the environment,

they shall provide with the opinion a written statement of their reasons for being of that opinion.   **[1035]**

NOTES
    Commencement: 3 June 1995.
    Schedules 1, 2: Town and Country Planning (Assessment of Environmental Effects) Regulations 1988, SI 1988/1199, Schs 1, 2 at **[657]**, **[658]**.

4. Directions by the Secretary of State

(1) Where an authority—

    (a) give an opinion in the terms mentioned in regulation 3(4)(a) or (b); or

    (b) fail to give an opinion within the period specified or agreed (as the case may be) for the purposes of regulation 3(4),

the prospective developer may apply to the Secretary of State, in accordance with the following provisions of this regulation, for his direction on the matter.

(2) An application under this regulation shall be accompanied by—

    (a) a copy of the application under regulation 3(1) and of the documents which accompanied it;

    (b) a copy of the notice (if any) given by the authority under regulation 3(3) and of the information (if any) supplied in response to that notice;

    (c) a copy of the authority's opinion (if any) and of the statement of reasons which accompanied it; and

    (d) such additional information or representations as the prospective developer may wish to provide or make.

(3) The prospective developer shall send to the relevant planning authority, at such time as he applies to the Secretary of State, a copy of the application under this regulation and of any additional information or representations made in accordance with paragraph (2)(d).

(4) If the Secretary of State considers that the information provided in accordance with paragraph (2) is insufficient to enable him to give a direction, he shall notify the prospective developer and the relevant planning authority of the matters in respect of which he requires further information; and the information so requested shall be

provided by the prospective developer within such reasonable period as may be specified in the notice or such longer period as may be agreed in writing between the prospective developer and the Secretary of State.

(5) The Secretary of State shall issue a direction within the period of three weeks beginning with the date of receipt of the application or such longer period as he may reasonably require.

(6) The Secretary of State shall send a copy of his direction to the prospective developer and to the relevant planning authority; and where he concludes that the development is—

    (a) within a description mentioned in Schedule 1; or
    (b) within a description mentioned in Schedule 2 and likely to have significant environmental effects,

he shall send with the copy of the direction a written statement of the reasons for his conclusion. **[1036]**

NOTES
    Commencement: 3 June 1995.
    Schedules 1, 2: Town and Country Planning (Assessment of Environmental Effects) Regulations 1988, SI 1988/1199, Schs 1, 2 at **[657]**, **[658]**.

5. Proposed development in which a relevant planning authority has an interest

(1) For the purposes of this regulation, ''developer'' means—

    (a) a relevant planning authority who are minded to undertake development (whether alone or with another or others) which appears to them to be relevant development; or
    (b) a person who is minded to undertake development with a relevant planning authority (whether or not with any other person) which appears to him to be relevant development.

(2) A developer may apply in writing to the Secretary of State for an opinion as to whether the development is within a description mentioned in Schedule 1 or Schedule 2, and, if so, within which description, and if within a description mentioned in Schedule 2, whether it would be likely to have significant effects on the environment by virtue of factors such as its nature, size or location.

(3) An application under paragraph (2) shall be accompanied by—

    (a) a plan sufficient to identify the land;
    (b) a brief description of the nature and purpose of the relevant development and of its possible effects on the environment;
    (c) such other information or representations as the developer may wish to provide or make.

(4) If the Secretary of State considers that the information provided in accordance with paragraph (3) is insufficient to enable him to give an opinion, he shall notify the developer and, where that person is not the relevant planning authority, that authority, of the matters in respect of which he requires further information; and the information so requested shall be provided by the developer within such reasonable period as may be specified in the notice or such longer period as may be agreed in writing between the developer and the Secretary of State.

(5) The Secretary of State shall give to the developer written notice of his opinion within the period of 3 weeks beginning with the date of receipt of the

application or such longer period as he may reasonably require; and if it is his opinion that the relevant development is—

(a) within a description mentioned in Schedule 1, or
(b) within a description mentioned in Schedule 2 and likely to have significant effects on the environment,

he shall provide with the opinion a written statement of his reasons for being of that opinion.

(6) Where the developer is not the relevant planning authority, the Secretary of State shall send to that authority a copy of the opinion and of the statement of reasons (if any) given in accordance with paragraph (5).   **[1037]**

NOTES
Commencement: 3 June 1995.
Schedules 1, 2: Town and Country Planning (Assessment of Environmental Effects) Regulations 1988, SI 1988/1199, Schs 1, 2 at **[657]**, **[658]**.

6. Public inspection of opinions and directions

(1) The relevant planning authority shall make available for public inspection at all reasonable hours at the place where the appropriate register (or relevant section of that register) is kept a copy of—

(a) every opinion given by the authority under regulation 3;
(b) the accompanying statement of reasons (if any);
(c) the application to which the opinion relates;
(d) the documents which accompanied the application;
(e) every direction or opinion received by the authority under regulation 4 or 5; and
(f) the statement of reasons (if any) accompanying each such direction or opinion,

and those copies shall remain so available for a period of two years or until particulars of the opinion or direction are entered in Part I of the register in accordance with paragraph (2), whichever is the sooner.

(2) Where particulars of an application for planning permission are entered in Part I of the appropriate register, the local planning authority shall take steps to secure that that Part also contains such particulars of—

(a) any opinion given under regulation 3; and
(b) any direction or opinion given under regulation 4 or 5,

as are relevant to the development which is the subject of the application.

(3) In this regulation, "appropriate register" means the register kept pursuant to section 69 of the Town and Country Planning Act 1990 on which particulars of an application for planning permission for the development concerned are required to be entered.   **[1038]**

NOTES
Commencement: 3 June 1995.

TOWN AND COUNTRY PLANNING (GENERAL PERMITTED DEVELOPMENT) ORDER 1995
(SI 1995/418)

NOTES
Made: 22 February 1995.
Authority: Town and Country Planning Act 1990, ss 59, 60, 61, 74, 333(7), and the Coal Industry Act 1994, s 54.

ARRANGEMENT OF ARTICLES

1. Citation, commencement and interpretation

(1) This Order may be cited as the Town and Country Planning (General Permitted Development) Order 1995 and shall come into force on 3rd June 1995.

(2) In this Order, unless the context otherwise requires—

"the Act" means the Town and Country Planning Act 1990;

"the 1960 Act" means the Caravan Sites and Control of Development Act 1960;

"aerodrome" means an aerodrome as defined in article 106 of the Air Navigation Order 1989 (interpretation) which is—

    (a) licensed under that Order,

    (b) a Government aerodrome,

    (c) one at which the manufacture, repair or maintenance of aircraft is carried out by a person carrying on business as a manufacturer or repairer of aircraft,

    (d) one used by aircraft engaged in the public transport of passengers or cargo or in aerial work, or

    (e) one identified to the Civil Aviation Authority before 1st March 1986 for inclusion in the UK Aerodrome Index,

and, for the purposes of this definition, the terms "aerial work", "Government aerodrome" and "public transport" have the meanings given in article 106;

"aqueduct" does not include an underground conduit;

"area of outstanding natural beauty" means an area designated as such by an order made by the Countryside Commission, as respects England, or the Countryside Council for Wales, as respects Wales, under section 87 of the National Parks and Access to the Countryside Act 1949 (designation of areas of outstanding natural beauty) as confirmed by the Secretary of State;

"building"—

    (a) includes any structure or erection and, except in Parts 24, 25 and 33, and Class A of Part 31, of Schedule 2, includes any part of a building, as defined in this article; and

    (b) does not include plant or machinery and, in Schedule 2, except in Class B of Part 31 and Part 33, does not include any gate, fence, wall or other means of enclosure;

"caravan" has the same meaning as for the purposes of Part I of the 1960 Act (caravan sites);

"caravan site" means land on which a caravan is stationed for the purpose of human habitation and land which is used in conjunction with land on which a caravan is so stationed;

"classified road" means a highway or proposed highway which—

    (a) is a classified road or a principal road by virtue of section 12(1) of the Highways Act 1980 (general provision as to principal and classified roads); or

    (b) is classified by the Secretary of State for the purposes of any enactment by virtue of section 12(3) of that Act;

"cubic content" means the cubic content of a structure or building measured externally;

"dwellinghouse" does not include a building containing one or more flats, or a flat contained within such a building;

"erection", in relation to buildings as defined in this article, includes extension, alteration, or re-erection;

"existing", in relation to any building or any plant or machinery or any use, means (except in the definition of "original") existing immediately before the carrying out, in relation to that building, plant, machinery or use, of development described in this Order;

"flat" means a separate and self-contained set of premises constructed or adapted for use for the purpose of a dwelling and forming part of a building from some other part of which it is divided horizontally;

"floor space" means the total floor space in a building or buildings;

"industrial process" means a process for or incidental to any of the following purposes—

   (a) the making of any article or part of any article (including a ship or vessel, or a film, video or sound recording);

   (b) the altering, repairing, maintaining, ornamenting, finishing, cleaning, washing, packing, canning, adapting for sale, breaking up or demolition of any article; or

   (c) the getting, dressing or treatment of minerals in the course of any trade or business other than agriculture, and other than a process carried out on land used as a mine or adjacent to and occupied together with a mine;

"land drainage" has the same meaning as in section 116 of the Land Drainage Act 1976 (interpretation);

"listed building" has the same meaning as in section 1 of the Planning (Listed Buildings and Conservation Areas) Act 1990 (listing of buildings of special architectural or historic interest);

"by local advertisement" means by publication of the notice in at least one newspaper circulating in the locality in which the area or, as the case may be, the whole or relevant part of the conservation area to which the direction relates is situated;

"machinery" includes any structure or erection in the nature of machinery;

"microwave" means that part of the radio spectrum above 1,000 MHz;

"microwave antenna" means a satellite antenna or a terrestrial microwave antenna;

"mine" means any site on which mining operations are carried out;

"mining operations" means the winning and working of minerals in, on or under land, whether by surface or underground working;

"notifiable pipe-line" means a pipe-line, as defined in section 65 of the Pipe-lines Act 1962 (meaning of pipe-line), which contains or is intended to contain a hazardous substance, as defined in regulation 2(1) of the Notification Regulations (interpretation), except—

   (a) a pipe-line the construction of which has been authorised under section 1 of the Pipe-lines Act 1962 (cross-country pipe-lines not to be constructed without the Minister's authority); or

   (b) a pipe-line which contains or is intended to contain no hazardous substance other than—

      (i) a flammable gas (as specified in item 1 of Part II of Schedule 1 to the Notification Regulations (classes of hazardous substances not specifically named in Part I)) at a pressure of less than 8 bars absolute; or

    (ii) a liquid or mixture of liquids, as specified in item 4 of Part II of that Schedule;

"Notification Regulations" means the Notification of Installations Handling Hazardous Substances Regulations 1982;

"original" means, in relation to a building existing on 1st July 1948, as existing on that date and, in relation to a building built on or after 1st July 1948, as so built;

"plant" includes any structure or erection in the nature of plant;

"private way" means a highway not maintainable at the public expense and any other way other than a highway;

"proposed highway" has the same meaning as in section 329 of the Highways Act 1980 (further provision as to interpretation);

"public service vehicle" means a public service vehicle within the meaning of section 1 of the Public Passenger Vehicles Act 1981 (definition of public service vehicles) or a tramcar or trolley vehicle within the meaning of section 192(1) of the Road Traffic Act 1988 (general interpretation);

"satellite antenna" means apparatus designed for transmitting microwave radio energy to satellites or receiving it from them, and includes any mountings or brackets attached to such apparatus;

"scheduled monument" has the same meaning as in section 1(11) of the Ancient Monuments and Archaeological Areas Act 1979 (schedule of monuments);

"by site display" means by the posting of the notice by firm affixture to some object, sited and displayed in such a way as to be easily visible and legible by members of the public;

"site of archaeological interest" means land which is included in the schedule of monuments compiled by the Secretary of State under section 1 of the Ancient Monuments and Archaeological Areas Act 1979 (schedule of monuments), or is within an area of land which is designated as an area of archaeological importance under section 33 of that Act (designation of areas of archaeological importance), or which is within a site registered in any record adopted by resolution by a county council and known as the County Sites and Monuments Record;

"site of special scientific interest" means land to which section 28(1) of the Wildlife and Countryside Act 1981 (areas of special scientific interest) applies;

"statutory undertaker" includes, in addition to any person mentioned in section 262(1) of the Act (meaning of statutory undertakers), the Post Office, the Civil Aviation Authority, the National Rivers Authority, any water undertaker, any public gas supplier, and any licence holder within the meaning of section 64(1) of the Electricity Act 1989 (interpretation etc of Part I);

"terrestrial microwave antenna" means apparatus designed for transmitting or receiving terrestrial microwave radio energy between two fixed points;

"trunk road" means a highway or proposed highway which is a trunk road by virtue of section 10(1) or 19 of the Highways Act 1980 (general provisions as to trunk roads, and certain special roads and other highways to become trunk roads) or any other enactment or any instrument made under any enactment;

"the Use Classes Order" means the Town and Country Planning (Use Classes) Order 1987.

(3) Unless the context otherwise requires, any reference in this Order to the height of a building or of plant or machinery shall be construed as a reference to its height when measured from ground level; and for the purposes of this paragraph

"ground level" means the level of the surface of the ground immediately adjacent to the building or plant or machinery in question or, where the level of the surface of the ground on which it is situated or is to be situated is not uniform, the level of the highest part of the surface of the ground adjacent to it.

(4) The land referred to elsewhere in this Order as article 1(4) land is the land described in Part 1 of Schedule 1 to this Order (land in listed counties).

(5) The land referred to elsewhere in this Order as article 1(5) land is the land described in Part 2 of Schedule 1 to this Order (National Parks, areas of outstanding natural beauty and conservation areas etc).

(6) The land referred to elsewhere in this Order as article 1(6) land is the land described in Part 3 of Schedule 1 to this Order (National Parks and adjoining land and the Broads). **[1039]**

NOTES
Commencement: 3 June 1995.

2. Application

(1) This Order applies to all land in England and Wales, but where land is the subject of a special development order, whether made before or after the commencement of this Order, this Order shall apply to that land only to such extent and subject to such modifications as may be specified in the special development order.

(2) Nothing in this Order shall apply to any permission which is deemed to be granted under section 222 of the Act (planning permission not needed for advertisements complying with regulations). **[1040]**

NOTES
Commencement: 3 June 1995.

3. Permitted development

(1) Subject to the provisions of this Order and regulations 60 to 63 of the Conservation (Natural Habitats, &c) Regulations 1994 (general development orders), planning permission is hereby granted for the classes of development described as permitted development in Schedule 2.

(2) Any permission granted by paragraph (1) is subject to any relevant exception, limitation or condition specified in Schedule 2.

(3) References in the following provisions of this Order to permission granted by Schedule 2 or by any Part, Class or paragraph of that Schedule are references to the permission granted by this article in relation to development described in that Schedule or that provision of that Schedule.

(4) Nothing in this Order permits development contrary to any condition imposed by any planning permission granted or deemed to be granted under Part III of the Act otherwise than by this Order.

(5) The permission granted by Schedule 2 shall not apply if—

    (a) in the case of permission granted in connection with an existing building, the building operations involved in the construction of that building are unlawful;

    (b) in the case of permission granted in connection with an existing use, that use is unlawful.

(6) The permission granted by Schedule 2 shall not, except in relation to development permitted by Parts 9, 11, 13 or 30, authorise any development which requires or involves the formation, laying out or material widening of a means of access to an existing highway which is a trunk road or classified road, or creates an obstruction to the view of persons using any highway used by vehicular traffic, so as to be likely to cause danger to such persons.

(7) Any development falling within Part 11 of Schedule 2 authorised by an Act or order subject to the grant of any consent or approval shall not be treated for the purposes of this Order as authorised unless and until that consent or approval is obtained, except where the Act was passed or the order made after 1st July 1948 and it contains provision to the contrary.

(8) Schedule 2 does not grant permission for the laying or construction of a notifiable pipe-line, except in the case of the laying or construction of a notifiable pipe-line by a public gas supplier in accordance with Class F of Part 17 of that Schedule.

(9) Except as provided in Part 31, Schedule 2 does not permit any development which requires or involves the demolition of a building, but in this paragraph "building" does not include part of a building.

(10) Subject to paragraph (12), development is not permitted by this Order if an application for planning permission for that development would be a Schedule 1 application or a Schedule 2 application within the meaning of the Town and Country Planning (Assessment of Environmental Effects) Regulations 1988 ("the Environmental Assessment Regulations") (descriptions of development).

(11) Where—

    (a) the local planning authority have given an opinion under regulation 3 of the Town and Country Planning (Environmental Assessment and Permitted Development) Regulations 1995 ("the Permitted Development Regulations") (opinion as to need for environmental statement) that an application for particular development would be a Schedule 1 application or a Schedule 2 application within the meaning of the Environmental Assessment Regulations and the Secretary of State has issued no direction to the contrary under regulation 4 of the Permitted Development Regulations (directions by the Secretary of State); or

    (b) the Secretary of State has given an opinion under regulation 5 of the Permitted Development Regulations (proposed development in which a relevant planning authority has an interest) that an application for particular development would be a Schedule 1 application or a Schedule 2 application within the meaning of the Environmental Assessment Regulations,

the development to which that opinion relates shall be treated, for the purposes of paragraph (10), as development which is not permitted by this Order.

(12) Paragraph (10) does not apply to—

    (a) development which comprises or forms part of a project serving national defence purposes;

    (b) development which consists of the carrying out by a drainage body within the meaning of the Land Drainage Act 1991 of improvement works within the meaning of the Land Drainage Improvement Works (Assessment of Environmental Effects) Regulations 1988;

    (c) development which consists of the installation of an electric line (within the meaning of Part I of the Electricity Act 1989 (electricity supply)) which replaces an existing line (as defined in regulation 2 of the Overhead

Lines (Exemption) Regulations 1990 (interpretation)) and in respect of which consent under section 37 of that Act (consent required for overhead lines) is not required by virtue of regulation 3(1)(e) of those Regulations (exemptions from section 37(1) of the Electricity Act 1989): provided that, in the circumstances mentioned in paragraph (1)(a) or (b) of regulation 5 of those Regulations (further restrictions on the exemptions contained in regulation 3), the determination for the purposes of that regulation that there is not likely to be a significant adverse effect on the environment shall have been made otherwise than as mentioned in paragraph (2) of that regulation;

(d) development for which permission is granted by Part 7, Class D of Part 8, Part 11, Class B of Part 12, Class F(a) of Part 17, Class A or Class B of Part 20 or Class B of Part 21 of Schedule 2;

(e) development for which permission is granted by Class C or Class D of Part 20, Class A of Part 21 or Class B of Part 22 of Schedule 2 where the land in, on or under which the development is to be carried out is—

(i) in the case of Class C or Class D of Part 20, on the same authorised site,

(ii) in the case of Class A of Part 21, on the same premises or, as the case may be, the same ancillary mining land,

(iii) in the case of Class B of Part 22, on the same land or, as the case may be, on land adjoining that land,

as that in, on or under which development of any description permitted by the same Class has been carried out before 3rd June 1995;

(f) the completion of any development begun before 3rd June 1995. **[1041]**

NOTES
Commencement: 3 June 1995.

4. Directions restricting permitted development

(1) If the Secretary of State or the appropriate local planning authority is satisfied that it is expedient that development described in any Part, Class or paragraph in Schedule 2, other than Class B of Part 22 or Class B of Part 23, should not be carried out unless permission is granted for it on an application, he or they may give a direction under this paragraph that the permission granted by article 3 shall not apply to—

(a) all or any development of the Part, Class or paragraph in question in an area specified in the direction; or

(b) any particular development, falling within that Part, Class or paragraph, which is specified in the direction,

and the direction shall specify that it is made under this paragraph.

(2) If the appropriate local planning authority is satisfied that it is expedient that any particular development described in paragraph (5) below should not be carried out within the whole or any part of a conservation area unless permission is granted for it on an application, they may give a direction under this paragraph that the permission granted by article 3 shall not apply to all or any particular development of the Class in question within the whole or any part of the conservation area, and the direction shall specify the development and conservation area or part of that area to which it relates and that it is made under this paragraph.

(3) A direction under paragraph (1) or (2) shall not affect the carrying out of—

(a) development permitted by Part 11 authorised by an Act passed after 1st July 1948 or by an order requiring the approval of both Houses of Parliament approved after that date;

(b) any development in an emergency; or

(c) any development mentioned in Part 24, unless the direction specifically so provides.

(4) A direction given or having effect as if given under this article shall not, unless the direction so provides, affect the carrying out by a statutory undertaker of the following descriptions of development—

(a) the maintenance of bridges, buildings and railway stations;

(b) the alteration and maintenance of railway track, and the provision and maintenance of track equipment, including signal boxes, signalling apparatus and other appliances and works required in connection with the movement of traffic by rail;

(c) the maintenance of docks, harbours, quays, wharves, canals and towing paths;

(d) the provision and maintenance of mechanical apparatus or appliances (including signalling equipment) required for the purposes of shipping or in connection with the embarking, disembarking, loading, discharging or transport of passengers, livestock or goods at a dock, quay, harbour, bank, wharf or basin;

(e) any development required in connection with the improvement, maintenance or repair of watercourses or drainage works;

(f) the maintenance of buildings, runways, taxiways or aprons at an aerodrome;

(g) the provision, alteration and maintenance of equipment, apparatus and works at an aerodrome, required in connection with the movement of traffic by air (other than buildings, the construction, erection, reconstruction or alteration of which is permitted by Class A of Part 18 of Schedule 2).

(5) The development referred to in paragraph (2) is development described in—

(a) Class A of Part 1 of Schedule 2, consisting of the enlargement, improvement or other alteration of a dwellinghouse, where any part of the enlargement, improvement or alteration would front a relevant location;

(b) Class C of Part 1 of that Schedule, where the alteration would be to a roof slope which fronts a relevant location;

(c) Class D of Part 1 of that Schedule, where the external door in question fronts a relevant location;

(d) Class E of Part 1 of that Schedule, where the building or enclosure, swimming or other pool to be provided would front a relevant location, or where the part of the building or enclosure maintained, improved or altered would front a relevant location;

(e) Class F of Part 1 of that Schedule, where the hard surface would front a relevant location;

(f) Class H of Part 1 of that Schedule, where the part of the building or other structure on which the satellite antenna is to be installed, altered or replaced fronts a relevant location;

(g) Part 1 of that Schedule, consisting of the erection, alteration or removal of a chimney on a dwellinghouse or on a building within the curtilage of a dwellinghouse;

(h) Class A of Part 2 of that Schedule, where the gate, fence, wall or other means of enclosure would be within the curtilage of a dwellinghouse and would front a relevant location;

(i) Class C of Part 2 of that Schedule, consisting of the painting of the exterior of any part, which fronts a relevant location, of—

    (i) a dwellinghouse; or

    (ii) any building or enclosure within the curtilage of a dwellinghouse;

  (j) Class B of Part 31 of that Schedule, where the gate, fence, wall or other means of enclosure is within the curtilage of a dwellinghouse and fronts a relevant location.

(6) In this article and in articles 5 and 6—

"appropriate local planning authority" means—

  (a) in relation to a conservation area in a non-metropolitan county, the county planning authority or the district planning authority; and

  (b) in relation to any other area, the local planning authority whose function it would be to determine an application for planning permission for the development to which the direction relates or is proposed to relate;

"relevant location" means a highway, waterway or open space. **[1042]**

NOTES
  Commencement: 3 June 1995.

5. Approval of Secretary of State for article 4(1) directions

(1) Except in the cases specified in paragraphs (3) and (4), a direction by a local planning authority under article 4(1) requires the approval of the Secretary of State, who may approve the direction with or without modifications.

(2) On making a direction under article 4(1) or submitting such a direction to the Secretary of State for approval—

  (a) a county planning authority shall give notice of it to any district planning authority in whose district the area to which the direction relates is situated; and

  (b) except in metropolitan districts, a district planning authority shall give notice of it to the county planning authority, if any.

(3) Unless it affects the carrying out of development by a statutory undertaker as provided by article 4(4), the approval of the Secretary of State is not required for a direction which relates to—

  (a) a listed building;

  (b) a building which is notified to the authority by the Secretary of State as a building of architectural or historic interest; or

  (c) development within the curtilage of a listed building,

and does not relate to land of any other description.

(4) Subject to paragraph (6), the approval of the Secretary of State is not required for a direction made under article 4(1) relating only to development permitted by any of Parts 1 to 4 or Part 31 of Schedule 2, if the relevant authority consider the development would be prejudicial to the proper planning of their area or constitute a threat to the amenities of their area.

(5) A direction not requiring the Secretary of State's approval by virtue of paragraph (4) shall, unless disallowed or approved by the Secretary of State, expire at the end of six months from the date on which it was made.

(6) Paragraph (4) does not apply to a second or subsequent direction relating to the same development or to development of the same Class or any of the same Classes, in the same area or any part of that area as that to which the first direction relates or related.

(7) The local planning authority shall send a copy of any direction made by them to which paragraph (4) applies to the Secretary of State not later than the date on which notice of that direction is given in accordance with paragraph (10) or (12).

(8) The Secretary of State may give notice to the local planning authority that he has disallowed any such direction and the direction shall then cease to have effect.

(9) The local planning authority shall as soon as reasonably practicable give notice that a direction has been disallowed in the same manner as notice of the direction was given.

(10) Subject to paragraph (12), notice of any direction made under article 4(1) shall be served by the appropriate local planning authority on the owner and occupier of every part of the land within the area to which the direction relates as soon as practicable after the direction has been made or, where the direction is required to be approved by the Secretary of State, as soon as practicable after it has been so approved; and a direction shall come into force in respect of any part of the land within the area to which the direction relates on the date on which notice is so served on the occupier of that part, or, if there is no occupier, on the owner.

(11) If a direction to which paragraph (4) applies is approved by the Secretary of State within the period of six months referred to in paragraph (5), then (unless paragraph (12) applies) the authority who made the direction shall, as soon as practicable, serve notice of that approval on the owner and occupier of every part of the land within the area to which the direction relates; and where the Secretary of State has approved the direction with modifications the notice shall indicate the effect of the modifications.

(12) Where in the case of a direction under article 4(1)(a) an authority consider that individual service in accordance with paragraph (10) or (11) is impracticable for the reasons set out in paragraph (14) they shall publish a notice of the direction, or of the approval, by local advertisement.

(13) A notice published pursuant to paragraph (12) shall contain a statement of the effect of the direction and of any modification made to it by the Secretary of State, and shall name a place or places where a copy of the direction, and of a map defining the area to which it relates, may be seen at all reasonable hours.

(14) The reasons referred to in paragraph (12) are that the number of owners and occupiers within the area to which the direction relates makes individual service impracticable, or that it is difficult to identify or locate one or more of them.

(15) Where notice of a direction has been published in accordance with paragraph (12), the direction shall come into force on the date on which the notice is first published.

(16) A local planning authority may, by making a subsequent direction and without the approval of the Secretary of State, cancel any direction made by them under article 4(1), and the Secretary of State may make a direction cancelling any direction under article 4(1) made by the local planning authority.

(17) Paragraphs (10) and (12) to (15) shall apply to any direction made under paragraph (16).　　　　　　　　　　　　　　　　　　　　　　　**[1043]**

NOTES

Commencement: 3 June 1995.

6. Notice and confirmation of article 4(2) directions

(1) Notice of any direction made under article 4(2) shall, as soon as practicable after the direction has been made, be given by the appropriate local planning authority—

(a) by local advertisement; and

(b) subject to paragraphs (4) and (5), by serving the notice on the owner and occupier of every dwellinghouse within the whole or the relevant part of the conservation area to which the direction relates.

(2) The notice referred to in paragraph (1) shall—

(a) include a description of the development and the conservation area or part of that area to which the direction relates, and a statement of the effect of the direction;

(b) specify that the direction is made under article 4(2) of this Order;

(c) name a place where a copy of the direction, and a copy of the map defining the conservation area or part of that area to which it relates, may be seen at all reasonable hours; and

(d) specify a period of at least 21 days, stating the date on which that period begins, within which any representations concerning the direction may be made to the local planning authority.

(3) The direction shall come into force in respect of any part of the land within the conservation area or part of that area to which it relates—

(a) on the date on which the notice is served on the occupier of that part of the land or, if there is no occupier, on the owner; or

(b) if paragraph (4) or (5) applies, on the date on which the notice is first published in accordance with paragraph (1)(a).

(4) The local planning authority need not serve notice on an owner or occupier in accordance with paragraph (1)(b) where they consider that individual service on that owner or occupier is impracticable because it is difficult to identify or locate him.

(5) The local planning authority need not serve any notice in accordance with paragraph (1)(b) where they consider that the number of owners or occupiers within the conservation area or part of that area to which the direction relates makes individual service impracticable.

(6) On making a direction under article 4(2)—

(a) a county planning authority shall give notice of it to any district planning authority in whose district the conservation area or part of that area to which the direction relates is situated; and

(b) except in metropolitan districts, a district planning authority shall give notice of it to the county planning authority, if any.

(7) A direction under article 4(2) shall expire at the end of six months from the date on which it was made unless confirmed by the appropriate local planning authority in accordance with paragraphs (8) and (9) before the end of that six month period.

(8) In deciding whether to confirm a direction made under article 4(2), the local planning authority shall take into account any representations received during the period specified in the notice referred to in paragraph (2)(d).

(9) The local planning authority shall not confirm the direction until a period of at least 28 days has elapsed following the latest date on which any notice relating to the direction was served or published.

(10) The appropriate local planning authority shall as soon as practicable give notice that a direction has been confirmed in the same manner as in paragraphs (1)(a) and (b) above.   **[1044]**

NOTES

Commencement: 3 June 1995.

7. Directions restricting permitted development under Class B of Part 22 or Class B of Part 23

(1) If, on receipt of a notification from any person that he proposes to carry out development within Class B of Part 22 or Class B of Part 23 of Schedule 2, a mineral planning authority are satisfied as mentioned in paragraph (2) below, they may, within a period of 21 days beginning with the receipt of the notification, direct that the permission granted by article 3 of this Order shall not apply to the development, or to such part of the development as is specified in the direction.

(2) The mineral planning authority may make a direction under this article if they are satisfied that it is expedient that the development, or any part of it, should not be carried out unless permission for it is granted on an application because—

   (a) the land on which the development is to be carried out is within—

      (i) a National Park,
     (ii) an area of outstanding natural beauty,
    (iii) a site of archaeological interest, and the operation to be carried out is not one described in the Schedule to the Areas of Archaeological Importance (Notification of Operations) (Exemption) Order 1984 (exempt operations),
    (iv) a site of special scientific interest, or
     (v) the Broads;

   (b) the development, either taken by itself or taken in conjunction with other development which is already being carried out in the area or in respect of which notification has been given in pursuance of the provisions of Class B of Part 22 or Class B of Part 23, would cause serious detriment to the amenity of the area in which it is to be carried out or would adversely affect the setting of a building shown as Grade I in the list of buildings of special architectural or historic interest compiled by the Secretary of State under section 1 of the Planning (Listed Buildings and Conservation Areas) Act 1990 (listing of buildings of special architectural or historic interest);

   (c) the development would constitute a serious nuisance to the inhabitants of a nearby residential building, hospital or school; or

   (d) the development would endanger aircraft using a nearby aerodrome.

(3) A direction made under this article shall contain a statement as to the day on which (if it is not disallowed under paragraph (5) below) it will come into force, which shall be 29 days from the date on which notice of it is sent to the Secretary of State in accordance with paragraph (4) below.

(4) As soon as is reasonably practicable a copy of a direction under this article shall be sent by the mineral planning authority to the Secretary of State and to the person who gave notice of the proposal to carry out development.

(5) The Secretary of State may, at any time within a period of 28 days beginning with the date on which the direction is made, disallow the direction; and immediately upon receipt of notice in writing from the Secretary of State that he has disallowed the direction, the mineral planning authority shall give notice in writing to the person

who gave notice of the proposal that he is authorised to proceed with the development. **[1045]**

NOTES
Commencement: 3 June 1995.

8. Directions

Any power conferred by this Order to give a direction includes power to cancel or vary the direction by a subsequent direction. **[1046]**

NOTES
Commencement: 3 June 1995.

9. Revocations

The statutory instruments specified in column 1 of Schedule 3 are hereby revoked to the extent specified in column 3. **[1047]**

NOTES
Commencement: 3 June 1995.

Article 1

SCHEDULE 1

PART 1

ARTICLE 1(4) LAND

Land within the following counties—

Cleveland, Cornwall, Cumbria, Devon, Durham, Dyfed, Greater Manchester, Gwynedd, Humberside, Lancashire, Merseyside, Northumberland, North Yorkshire, South Yorkshire, Tyne and Wear, West Glamorgan, West Yorkshire. **[1048]**

NOTES
Commencement: 3 June 1995.

PART 2

ARTICLE 1(5) LAND

Land within—
  (a) a National Park;
  (b) an area of outstanding natural beauty;
  (c) an area designated as a conservation area under section 69 of the Planning (Listed Buildings and Conservation Areas) Act 1990 (designation of conservation areas);
  (d) an area specified by the Secretary of State and the Minister of Agriculture, Fisheries and Food for the purposes of section 41(3) of the Wildlife and Countryside Act 1981 (enhancement and protection of the natural beauty and amenity of the countryside);
  (e) the Broads. **[1049]**

NOTES
Commencement: 3 June 1995.

PART 3

ARTICLE 1(6) LAND

Land within a National Park or within the following areas—

(a) In England, the Broads or land outside the boundaries of a National Park, which is within the parishes listed below—

in the district of Allerdale—

Blindcrake, Bothel and Threapland, Bridekirk, Brigham, Broughton, Broughton Moor, Camerton, Crosscanonby, Dean, Dearham, Gilcrux, Great Clifton, Greysouthen, Little Clifton, Loweswater, Oughterside and Allerby, Papcastle, Plumbland, Seaton, Winscales;

in the borough of Copeland—

Arlecdon and Frizington, Cleator Moor, Distington, Drigg and Carleton, Egremont, Gosforth, Haile, Irton with Santon, Lamplugh, Lowca, Lowside Quarter, Millom, Millom Without, Moresby, Parton, Ponsonby, St Bees, St Bridget's Beckermet, St John's Beckermet, Seascale, Weddicar;

in the district of Eden—

Ainstable, Asby, Bandleyside, Bolton, Brough, Brough Sowerby, Brougham, Castle Sowerby, Catterlen, Clifton, Cliburn, Crackenthorpe, Crosby Garrett, Crosby Ravensworth, Culgaith, Dacre, Dufton, Glassonby, Great Salkeld, Great Strickland, Greystoke, Hartley, Hesket, Hillbeck, Hunsonby, Hutton, Kaber, Kings Meaburn, Kirkby Stephen, Kirby Thore, Kirkoswald, Langwathby, Lazonby, Little Strickland, Long Marton, Lowther, Mallerstang, Milburn, Morland, Mungrisdale, Murton, Musgrave, Nateby, Newbiggin, Newby, Orton, Ousby, Ravenstonedale, Shap, Skelton, Sleagill, Sockbridge and Tirril, Soulby, Stainmore, Tebay, Temple Sowerby, Thrimby, Waitby, Warcop, Wharton, Winton, Yanwath and Eamont Bridge;

in the borough of High Peak—

Chapel-en-le-Frith, Charlesworth, Chinley Buxworth and Brownside, Chisworth, Green Fairfield, Hartington Upper Quarter, Hayfield, King Sterndale, Tintwistle, Wormhill;

in the district of South Lakeland—

Aldingham, Angerton, Arnside, Barbon, Beetham, Blawith and Subberthwaite, Broughton West, Burton, Casterton, Docker, Egton-with-Newland, Fawcett Forest, Firbank, Grayrigg, Helsington, Heversham, Hincaster, Holme, Hutton Roof, Killington, Kirkby Ireleth, Kirkby Lonsdale, Lambrigg, Levens, Lower Allithwaite, Lower Holker, Lowick, Lupton, Mansergh, Mansriggs, Middleton, Milnthorpe, Natland, New Hutton, Old Hutton and Holmescales, Osmotherley, Pennington, Preston Patrick, Preston Richard, Scalthwaiterigg, Sedgwick, Skelsmergh, Stainton, Strickland Ketel, Strickland Roger, Urswick, Whinfell, Whitwell and Selside;

in the district of West Derbyshire—

Aldwark, Birchover, Stanton; and

(b) In Wales, land outside the boundaries of a National Park which is—

(i) within the communities listed below—

in the borough of Aberconwy—

Caerhun, Dolgarrog;

in the borough of Arfon—

Betws Garmon, Bontnewydd, Llanberis, Llanddeiniolen, Llandwrog, Llanllyfni, Llanwnda, Waunfawr;

in the district of Meirionnydd—

Arthog, Corris, Llanfrothen, Penrhyndeudraeth; or

(ii) within the specified parts of the communities listed below—

in the borough of Aberconwy, those parts of the following communities which were on 31st March 1974 within the former rural district of Nant Conway—

Conwy, Henryd, Llanddoged and Maenan, Llanrwst, Llansanffraid Glan Conwy;

in the borough of Arfon, those parts of the following communities which were on 31st March 1974 within the former rural district of Gwyrfai—

Caernarfon, Llandygai, Llanrug, Pentir, Y Felinheli;

in the district of Dwyfor, that part of the community of Porthmadog which was on 31st March 1974 within the former rural district of Deudraeth and those parts of the following communities which were on that date within the former rural district of Gwyrfai—

Clynnog, Dolbenmaen, Llanaelhaearn;

in the district of Glyndwr, those parts of the following communities which were on 31st March 1974 within the former rural district of Penllyn—

Llandrillo, Llangwm;

in the district of Meirionnydd, those parts of the following communities which were on 31st March 1974 within the former rural district of Deudraeth—

Ffestiniog, Talsarnau;

and those parts of the following communities which were on that date within the former rural district of Dolgellau—

Barmouth, Mawddwy;

and that part of the community of Llandderfel which was on that date within the former rural district of Penllyn.   **[1050]**

NOTES

Commencement: 3 June 1995.

SCHEDULE 2

Article 3

PART 1

DEVELOPMENT WITHIN THE CURTILAGE OF A DWELLINGHOUSE

Class A

Permitted development	**A The enlargement, improvement or other alteration of a dwellinghouse.**
Development not permitted	A.1 Development is not permitted by Class A if—

    (a) the cubic content of the resulting building would exceed the cubic content of the original dwellinghouse—

        (i) in the case of a terrace house or in the case of a dwellinghouse on article 1(5) land, by more than 50 cubic metres or 10%, whichever is the greater,

        (ii) in any other case, by more than 70 cubic metres or 15%, whichever is the greater,

        (iii) in any case, by more than 115 cubic metres;

    (b) the part of the building enlarged, improved or altered would exceed in height the highest part of the roof of the original dwellinghouse;

    (c) the part of the building enlarged, improved or altered would be nearer to any highway which bounds the curtilage of the dwellinghouse than—

        (i) the part of the original dwellinghouse nearest to that highway, or

        (ii) any point 20 metres from that highway,

    whichever is nearer to the highway;

    (d) in the case of development other than the insertion, enlargement, improvement or other alteration of a window in an existing wall of a dwellinghouse, the part of the building enlarged, improved or altered would be within 2 metres of the boundary of the curtilage of the dwellinghouse and would exceed 4 metres in height;

(e) the total area of ground covered by buildings within the curtilage (other than the original dwellinghouse) would exceed 50% of the total area of the curtilage (excluding the ground area of the original dwellinghouse);

(f) it would consist of or include the installation, alteration or replacement of a satellite antenna;

(g) it would consist of or include the erection of a building within the curtilage of a listed building; or

(h) it would consist of or include an alteration to any part of the roof.

A.2 In the case of a dwellinghouse on any article 1(5) land, development is not permitted by Class A if it would consist of or include the cladding of any part of the exterior with stone, artificial stone, timber, plastic or tiles.

Interpretation of Class A

A.3 For the purposes of Class A—

(a) the erection within the curtilage of a dwellinghouse of any building with a cubic content greater than 10 cubic metres shall be treated as the enlargement of the dwellinghouse for all purposes (including calculating cubic content) where—
  (i) the dwellinghouse is on article 1(5) land, or
  (ii) in any other case, any part of that building would be within 5 metres of any part of the dwellinghouse;

(b) where any part of the dwellinghouse would be within 5 metres of an existing building within the same curtilage, that building shall be treated as forming part of the resulting building for the purpose of calculating the cubic content.

Class B

Permitted development

B The enlargement of a dwellinghouse consisting of an addition or alteration to its roof.

Development not permitted

B.1 Development is not permitted by Class B if—

(a) any part of the dwellinghouse would, as a result of the works, exceed the height of the highest part of the existing roof;

(b) any part of the dwellinghouse would, as a result of the works, extend beyond the plane of any existing roof slope which fronts any highway;

(c) it would increase the cubic content of the dwellinghouse by more than 40 cubic metres, in the case of a terrace house, or 50 cubic metres in any other case;

(d) the cubic content of the resulting building would exceed the cubic content of the original dwellinghouse—
  (i) in the case of a terrace house by more than 50 cubic metres or 10%, whichever is the greater,
  (ii) in any other case, by more than 70 cubic metres or 15%, whichever is the greater, or
  (iii) in any case, by more than 115 cubic metres; or

(e) the dwellinghouse is on article 1(5) land.

Class C

Permitted development

C Any other alteration to the roof of a dwellinghouse.

Development not permitted

C.1 Development is not permitted by Class C if it would result in a material alteration to the shape of the dwellinghouse.

Class D

Permitted development

D The erection or construction of a porch outside any external door of a dwellinghouse.

Development not permitted

D.1 Development is not permitted by Class D if—

(a) the ground area (measured externally) of the structure would exceed 3 square metres;

(b) any part of the structure would be more than 3 metres above ground level; or

(c) any part of the structure would be within 2 metres of any boundary of the curtilage of the dwellinghouse with a highway.

Class E
Permitted development

E The provision within the curtilage of a dwellinghouse of any building or enclosure, swimming or other pool required for a purpose incidental to the enjoyment of the dwellinghouse as such, or the maintenance, improvement or other alteration of such a building or enclosure.

Development not permitted

E.1 Development is not permitted by Class E if—

(a) it relates to a dwelling or a satellite antenna;

(b) any part of the building or enclosure to be constructed or provided would be nearer to any highway which bounds the curtilage than—

(i) the part of the original dwellinghouse nearest to that highway, or

(ii) any point 20 metres from that highway,

whichever is nearer to the highway;

(c) where the building to be constructed or provided would have a cubic content greater than 10 cubic metres, any part of it would be within 5 metres of any part of the dwellinghouse;

(d) the height of that building or enclosure would exceed—

(i) 4 metres, in the case of a building with a ridged roof; or

(ii) 3 metres, in any other case;

(e) the total area of ground covered by buildings or enclosures within the curtilage (other than the original dwellinghouse) would exceed 50% of the total area of the curtilage (excluding the ground area of the original dwellinghouse); or

(f) in the case of any article 1(5) land or land within the curtilage of a listed building, it would consist of the provision, alteration or improvement of a building with a cubic content greater than 10 cubic metres.

Interpretation of Class E

E.2 For the purposes of Class E—

"purpose incidental to the enjoyment of the dwellinghouse as such" includes the keeping of poultry, bees, pet animals, birds or other livestock for the domestic needs or personal enjoyment of the occupants of the dwellinghouse.

Class F
Permitted development

F The provision within the curtilage of a dwellinghouse of a hard surface for any purpose incidental to the enjoyment of the dwellinghouse as such.

Class G
Permitted development

G The erection or provision within the curtilage of a dwellinghouse of a container for the storage of oil for domestic heating.

Development not permitted

G.1 Development is not permitted by Class G if—

(a) the capacity of the container would exceed 3,500 litres;

(b) any part of the container would be more than 3 metres above ground level; or

(c) any part of the container would be nearer to any highway which bounds the curtilage than—

(i) the part of the original building nearest to that highway, or

(ii) any point 20 metres from that highway,

whichever is nearer to the highway.

Class H
Permitted development

H The installation, alteration or replacement of a satellite antenna on a dwellinghouse or within the curtilage of a dwellinghouse.

Development not permitted	H.1 Development is not permitted by Class H if—

(a) the size of the antenna (excluding any projecting feed element, reinforcing rim, mountings and brackets) when measured in any dimension would exceed—
    (i) 45 centimetres in the case of an antenna to be installed on a chimney;
    (ii) 90 centimetres in the case of an antenna to be installed on or within the curtilage of a dwellinghouse on article 1(4) land other than on a chimney;
    (iii) 70 centimetres in any other case;
(b) the highest part of an antenna to be installed on a roof or a chimney would, when installed, exceed in height—
    (i) in the case of an antenna to be installed on a roof, the highest part of the roof;
    (ii) in the case of an antenna to be installed on a chimney, the highest part of the chimney;
(c) there is any other satellite antenna on the dwellinghouse or within its curtilage;
(d) in the case of article 1(5) land, it would consist of the installation of an antenna—
    (i) on a chimney;
    (ii) on a building which exceeds 15 metres in height;
    (iii) on a wall or roof slope which fronts a waterway in the Broads or a highway elsewhere.

Conditions	H.2 Development is permitted by Class H subject to the following conditions—

(a) an antenna installed on a building shall, so far as practicable, be sited so as to minimise its effect on the external appearance of the building;
(b) an antenna no longer needed for the reception or transmission of microwave radio energy shall be removed as soon as reasonably practicable.

Interpretation of Part 1	I For the purposes of Part 1—

"resulting building" means the dwellinghouse as enlarged, improved or altered, taking into account any enlargement, improvement or alteration to the original dwellinghouse, whether permitted by this Part or not; and
"terrace house" means a dwellinghouse situated in a row of three or more dwellinghouses used or designed for use as single dwellings, where—
(a) it shares a party wall with, or has a main wall adjoining the main wall of, the dwellinghouse on either side; or
(b) if it is at the end of a row, it shares a party wall with or has a main wall adjoining the main wall of a dwellinghouse which fulfils the requirements of sub-paragraph (a) above.

[1051]

NOTES
    Commencement: 3 June 1995.

PART 2

MINOR OPERATIONS

Class A Permitted development	**A The erection, construction, maintenance, improvement or alteration of a gate, fence, wall or other means of enclosure.**

Development not
permitted

A.1 Development is not permitted by Class A if—
- (a) the height of any gate, fence, wall or means of enclosure erected or constructed adjacent to a highway used by vehicular traffic would, after the carrying out of the development, exceed one metre above ground level;
- (b) the height of any other gate, fence, wall or means of enclosure erected or constructed would exceed two metres above ground level;
- (c) the height of any gate, fence, wall or other means of enclosure maintained, improved or altered would, as a result of the development, exceed its former height or the height referred to in sub-paragraph (a) or (b) as the height appropriate to it if erected or constructed, whichever is the greater; or
- (d) it would involve development within the curtilage of, or to a gate, fence, wall or other means of enclosure surrounding, a listed building.

Class B

Permitted
development

B The formation, laying out and construction of a means of access to a highway which is not a trunk road or a classified road, where that access is required in connection with development permitted by any Class in this Schedule (other than by Class A of this Part).

Class C

Permitted
development

C The painting of the exterior of any building or work.

Development not
permitted

C.1 Development is not permitted by Class C where the painting is for the purpose of advertisement, announcement or direction.

Interpretation of
Class C

C.2 In Class C, "painting" includes any application of colour.

[1052]

NOTES
Commencement: 3 June 1995.

PART 3

CHANGES OF USE

Class A

Permitted
development

A Development consisting of a change of the use of a building to a use falling within Class A1 (shops) of the Schedule to the Use Classes Order from a use falling within Class A3 (food and drink) of that Schedule or from a use for the sale, or display for sale, of motor vehicles.

Class B

Permitted
development

B Development consisting of a change of the use of a building—
- **(a) to a use for any purpose falling within Class B1 (business) of the Schedule to the Use Classes Order from any use falling within Class B2 (general industrial) or B8 (storage and distribution) of that Schedule;**
- **(b) to a use for any purpose falling within Class B8 (storage and distribution) of that Schedule from any use falling within Class B1 (business) or B2 (general industrial).**

Development not
permitted

B.1 Development is not permitted by Class B where the change is to or from a use falling within Class B8 of that Schedule, if the change of use relates to more than 235 square metres of floor space in the building.

Class C
Permitted
development

C Development consisting of a change of use to a use falling within Class A2 (financial and professional services) of the Schedule to the Use Classes Order from a use falling within Class A3 (food and drink) of that Schedule.

Class D
Permitted
development

D Development consisting of a change of use of any premises with a display window at ground floor level to a use falling within Class A1 (shops) of the Schedule to the Use Classes Order from a use falling within Class A2 (financial and professional services) of that Schedule.

Class E
Permitted
development

E Development consisting of a change of the use of a building or other land from a use permitted by planning permission granted on an application, to another use which that permission would have specifically authorised when it was granted.

Development not
permitted

E.1 Development is not permitted by Class E if—
- (a) the application for planning permission referred to was made before the 5th December 1988;
- (b) it would be carried out more than 10 years after the grant of planning permission; or
- (c) it would result in the breach of any condition, limitation or specification contained in that planning permission in relation to the use in question.

Class F
Permitted
development

F Development consisting of a change of the use of a building—
- (a) to a mixed use for any purpose within Class A1 (shops) of the Schedule to the Use Classes Order and as a single flat, from a use for any purpose within Class A1 of that Schedule;
- (b) to a mixed use for any purpose within Class A2 (financial and professional services) of the Schedule to the Use Classes Order and as a single flat, from a use for any purpose within Class A2 of that Schedule;
- (c) where that building has a display window at ground floor level, to a mixed use for any purpose within Class A1 (shops) of the Schedule to the Use Classes Order and as a single flat, from a use for any purpose within Class A2 (financial and professional services) of that Schedule.

Conditions

F.1 Development permitted by Class F is subject to the following conditions—
- (a) some or all of the parts of the building used for any purposes within Class A1 or Class A2, as the case may be, of the Schedule to the Use Classes Order shall be situated on a floor below the part of the building used as a single flat;
- (b) where the development consists of a change of use of any building with a display window at ground floor level, the ground floor shall not be used in whole or in part as the single flat;
- (c) the single flat shall not be used otherwise than as a dwelling (whether or not as a sole or main residence)—
  - (i) by a single person or by people living together as a family, or
  - (ii) by not more than six residents living together as a single household (including a household where care is provided for residents).

Interpretation of
Class F

F.2 For the purposes of Class F—

"care" means personal care for people in need of such care by
reason of old age, disablement, past or present dependence on
alcohol or drugs or past or present mental disorder.

Class G
Permitted
development

G Development consisting of a change of the use of a building—

    **(a) to a use for any purpose within Class A1 (shops) of the
Schedule to the Use Classes Order from a mixed use for
any purpose within Class A1 of that Schedule and as a
single flat;**

    **(b) to a use for any purpose within Class A2 (financial and
professional services) of the Schedule to the Use Classes
Order from a mixed use for any purpose within Class A2
of that Schedule and as a single flat;**

    **(c) where that building has a display window at ground floor
level, to a use for any purpose within Class A1 (shops) of
the Schedule to the Use Classes Order from a mixed use
for any purpose within Class A2 (financial and professional
services) of that Schedule and as a single flat.**

Development not
permitted

G.1 Development is not permitted by Class G unless the part of the
building used as a single flat was immediately prior to being so used
used for any purpose within Class A1 or Class A2 of the Schedule to
the Use Classes Order.

[1053]

NOTES
    Commencement: 3 June 1995.

PART 4

TEMPORARY BUILDINGS AND USES

Class A
Permitted
development

**A The provision on land of buildings, moveable structures,
works, plant or machinery required temporarily in connection
with and for the duration of operations being or to be carried
out on, in, under or over that land or on land adjoining that land.**

Development not
permitted

A.1 Development is not permitted by Class A if—
    (a) the operations referred to are mining operations, or
    (b) planning permission is required for those operations but is not
granted or deemed to be granted.

Conditions

A.2 Development is permitted by Class A subject to the conditions
that, when the operations have been carried out—
    (a) any building, structure, works, plant or machinery permitted
by Class A shall be removed, and
    (b) any adjoining land on which development permitted by Class
A has been carried out shall, as soon as reasonably practicable,
be reinstated to its condition before that development was
carried out.

Class B
Permitted
development

**B The use of any land for any purpose for not more than 28 days
in total in any calendar year, of which not more than 14 days in
total may be for the purposes referred to in paragraph B.2, and
the provision on the land of any moveable structure for the
purposes of the permitted use.**

Development not
permitted

B.1 Development is not permitted by Class B if—
    (a) the land in question is a building or is within the curtilage of a
building,
    (b) the use of the land is for a caravan site,

(c) the land is, or is within, a site of special scientific interest and the use of the land is for—

    (i) a purpose referred to in paragraph B.2(b) or other motor sports;

    (ii) clay pigeon shooting; or

    (iii) any war game,

or

(d) the use of the land is for the display of an advertisement.

Interpretation of Class B

B.2 The purposes mentioned in Class B above are—

(a) the holding of a market;

(b) motor car and motorcycle racing including trials of speed, and practising for these activities.

B.3 In Class B, "war game" means an enacted, mock or imaginary battle conducted with weapons which are designed not to injure (including smoke bombs, or guns or grenades which fire or spray paint or are otherwise used to mark other participants), but excludes military activities or training exercises organised by or with the authority of the Secretary of State for Defence.

[1054]

NOTES

    Commencement: 3 June 1995.

PART 5

CARAVAN SITES

Class A
Permitted development

A The use of land, other than a building, as a caravan site in the circumstances referred to in paragraph A.2.

Condition

A.1 Development is permitted by Class A subject to the condition that the use shall be discontinued when the circumstances specified in paragraph A.2 cease to exist, and all caravans on the site shall be removed as soon as reasonably practicable.

Interpretation of Class A

A.2 The circumstances mentioned in Class A are those specified in paragraphs 2 to 10 of Schedule 1 to the 1960 Act (cases where a caravan site licence is not required), but in relation to those mentioned in paragraph 10 do not include use for winter quarters.

Class B
Permitted development

B Development required by the conditions of a site licence for the time being in force under the 1960 Act.

[1055]

NOTES

    Commencement: 3 June 1995.

PART 6

AGRICULTURAL BUILDINGS AND OPERATIONS

Class A   Development on units of 5 hectares or more
Permitted development

A The carrying out on agricultural land comprised in an agricultural unit of 5 hectares or more in area of—

    (a) works for the erection, extension or alteration of a building;
    or
    (b) any excavation or engineering operations,
which are reasonably necessary for the purposes of agriculture within that unit.

Development not
permitted

A.1 Development is not permitted by Class A if—

    (a) the development would be carried out on a separate parcel of land forming part of the unit which is less than 1 hectare in area;

    (b) it would consist of, or include, the erection, extension or alteration of a dwelling;

    (c) it would involve the provision of a building, structure or works not designed for agricultural purposes;

    (d) the ground area which would be covered by—

        (i) any works or structure (other than a fence) for accommodating livestock or any plant or machinery arising from engineering operations; or

        (ii) any building erected or extended or altered by virtue of Class A,

    would exceed 465 square metres, calculated as described in paragraph D.2 below;

    (e) the height of any part of any building, structure or works within 3 kilometres of the perimeter of an aerodrome would exceed 3 metres;

    (f) the height of any part of any building, structure or works not within 3 kilometres of the perimeter of an aerodrome would exceed 12 metres;

    (g) any part of the development would be within 25 metres of a metalled part of a trunk road or classified road;

    (h) it would consist of, or include, the erection or construction of, or the carrying out of any works to, a building, structure or an excavation used or to be used for the accommodation of livestock or for the storage of slurry or sewage sludge where the building, structure or excavation is, or would be, within 400 metres of the curtilage of a protected building; or

    (i) it would involve excavations or engineering operations on or over article 1(6) land which are connected with fish farming.

Conditions

A.2(1) Development is permitted by Class A subject to the following conditions—

    (a) where development is carried out within 400 metres of the curtilage of a protected building, any building, structure, excavation or works resulting from the development shall not be used for the accommodation of livestock except in the circumstances described in paragraph D.3 below or for the storage of slurry or sewage sludge;

    (b) where the development involves—

        (i) the extraction of any mineral from the land (including removal from any disused railway embankment); or

        (ii) the removal of any mineral from a mineral-working deposit,

    the mineral shall not be moved off the unit;

    (c) waste materials shall not be brought on to the land from elsewhere for deposit except for use in works described in Class A(a) or in the provision of a hard surface and any materials so brought shall be incorporated forthwith into the building or works in question.

(2) Subject to paragraph (3), development consisting of—

    (a) the erection, extension or alteration of a building;

    (b) the formation or alteration of a private way;

    (c) the carrying out of excavations or the deposit of waste material (where the relevant area, as defined in paragraph D.4 below, exceeds 0.5 hectare); or

    (d) the placing or assembly of a tank in any waters,

is permitted by Class A subject to the following conditions—

        (i) the developer shall, before beginning the development, apply to the local planning authority for a determination as to whether the prior approval of the authority will be required to the siting, design and external appearance of the building, the siting and means of construction of the private way, the siting of the excavation or deposit or the siting and appearance of the tank, as the case may be;

(ii) the application shall be accompanied by a written description of the proposed development and of the materials to be used and a plan indicating the site together with any fee required to be paid;

(iii) the development shall not be begun before the occurrence of one of the following—

(aa) the receipt by the applicant from the local planning authority of a written notice of their determination that such prior approval is not required;

(bb) where the local planning authority give the applicant notice within 28 days following the date of receiving his application of their determination that such prior approval is required, the giving of such approval; or

(cc) the expiry of 28 days following the date on which the application was received by the local planning authority without the local planning authority making any determination as to whether such approval is required or notifying the applicant of their determination;

(iv) (aa) where the local planning authority give the applicant notice that such prior approval is required the applicant shall display a site notice by site display on or near the land on which the proposed development is to be carried out, leaving the notice in position for not less than 21 days in the period of 28 days from the date on which the local planning authority gave the notice to the applicant;

(bb) where the site notice is, without any fault or intention of the applicant, removed, obscured or defaced before the period of 21 days referred to in sub-paragraph (aa) has elapsed, he shall be treated as having complied with the requirements of that sub-paragraph if he has taken reasonable steps for protection of the notice and, if need be, its replacement;

(v) the development shall, except to the extent that the local planning authority otherwise agree in writing, be carried out—

(aa) where prior approval is required, in accordance with the details approved;

(bb) where prior approval is not required, in accordance with the details submitted with the application; and

(vi) the development shall be carried out—

(aa) where approval has been given by the local planning authority, within a period of five years from the date on which approval was given;

(bb) in any other case, within a period of five years from the date on which the local planning authority were given the information referred to in sub-paragraph (d)(ii).

(3) The conditions in paragraph (2) do not apply to the extension or alteration of a building if the building is not on article 1(6) land except in the case of a significant extension or a significant alteration.

(4) Development consisting of the significant extension or the significant alteration of a building may only be carried out once by virtue of Class A(a).

Class B   Development on units of less than 5 hectares

Permitted development	**B The carrying out on agricultural land comprised in an agricultural unit of not less than 0.4 but less than 5 hectares in area of development consisting of—**

  (a) the extension or alteration of an agricultural building;
  (b) the installation of additional or replacement plant or machinery;
  (c) the provision, rearrangement or replacement of a sewer, main, pipe, cable or other apparatus;
  (d) the provision, rearrangement or replacement of a private way;
  (e) the provision of a hard surface;
  (f) the deposit of waste; or
  (g) the carrying out of any of the following operations in connection with fish farming, namely, repairing ponds and raceways; the installation of grading machinery, aeration equipment or flow meters and any associated channel; the dredging of ponds; and the replacement of tanks and nets,

where the development is reasonably necessary for the purposes of agriculture within the unit.

Development not permitted

B.1 Development is not permitted by Class B if—

  (a) the development would be carried out on a separate parcel of land forming part of the unit which is less than 0.4 hectare in area;
  (b) the external appearance of the premises would be materially affected;
  (c) any part of the development would be within 25 metres of a metalled part of a trunk road or classified road;
  (d) it would consist of, or involve, the carrying out of any works to a building or structure used or to be used for the accommodation of livestock or the storage of slurry or sewage sludge where the building or structure is within 400 metres of the curtilage of a protected building; or
  (e) it would relate to fish farming and would involve the placing or assembly of a tank on land or in any waters or the construction of a pond in which fish may be kept or an increase (otherwise than by the removal of silt) in the size of any tank or pond in which fish may be kept.

B.2 Development is not permitted by Class B(a) if—

  (a) the height of any building would be increased;
  (b) the cubic content of the original building would be increased by more than 10%;
  (c) any part of any new building would be more than 30 metres from the original building;
  (d) the development would involve the extension, alteration or provision of a dwelling;
  (e) any part of the development would be carried out within 5 metres of any boundary of the unit; or
  (f) the ground area of any building extended by virtue of Class B(a) would exceed 465 square metres.

B.3 Development is not permitted by Class B(b) if—

  (a) the height of any additional plant or machinery within 3 kilometres of the perimeter of an aerodrome would exceed 3 metres;
  (b) the height of any additional plant or machinery not within 3 kilometres of the perimeter of an aerodrome would exceed 12 metres;
  (c) the height of any replacement plant or machinery would exceed that of the plant or machinery being replaced; or

(d) the area to be covered by the development would exceed 465 square metres calculated as described in paragraph D.2 below.

B.4 Development is not permitted by Class B(e) if the area to be covered by the development would exceed 465 square metres calculated as described in paragraph D.2 below.

Conditions

B.5 Development permitted by Class B and carried out within 400 metres of the curtilage of a protected building is subject to the condition that any building which is extended or altered, or any works resulting from the development, shall not be used for the accommodation of livestock except in the circumstances described in paragraph D.3 below or for the storage of slurry or sewage sludge.

B.6 Development consisting of the extension or alteration of a building situated on article 1(6) land or the provision, rearrangement or replacement of a private way on such land is permitted subject to—

(a) the condition that the developer shall, before beginning the development, apply to the local planning authority for a determination as to whether the prior approval of the authority will be required to the siting, design and external appearance of the building as extended or altered or the siting and means of construction of the private way; and

(b) the conditions set out in paragraphs A.2(2)(ii) to (vi) above.

B.7 Development is permitted by Class B(f) subject to the following conditions—

(a) that waste materials are not brought on to the land from elsewhere for deposit unless they are for use in works described in Class B(a), (d) or (e) and are incorporated forthwith into the building or works in question; and

(b) that the height of the surface of the land will not be materially increased by the deposit.

Class C   Mineral working for agricultural purposes

Permitted development

C   The winning and working on land held or occupied with land used for the purposes of agriculture of any minerals reasonably necessary for agricultural purposes within the agricultural unit of which it forms part.

Development not permitted

C.1 Development is not permitted by Class C if any excavation would be made within 25 metres of a metalled part of a trunk road or classified road.

Condition

C.2 Development is permitted by Class C subject to the condition that no mineral extracted during the course of the operation shall be moved to any place outside the land from which it was extracted, except to land which is held or occupied with that land and is used for the purposes of agriculture.

Interpretation of Part 6

D.1 For the purposes of Part 6—

"agricultural land" means land which, before development permitted by this Part is carried out, is land in use for agriculture and which is so used for the purposes of a trade or business, and excludes any dwellinghouse or garden;

"agricultural unit" means agricultural land which is occupied as a unit for the purposes of agriculture, including—

(a) any dwelling or other building on that land occupied for the purpose of farming the land by the person who occupies the unit, or

(b) any dwelling on that land occupied by a farmworker;

"building" does not include anything resulting from engineering operations;

"fish farming" means the breeding, rearing or keeping of fish or shellfish (which includes any kind of crustacean and mollusc);

"livestock" includes fish or shellfish which are farmed;

''protected building'' means any permanent building which is normally occupied by people or would be so occupied, if it were in use for purposes for which it is apt; but does not include—

    (i) a building within the agricultural unit; or

    (ii) a dwelling or other building on another agricultural unit which is used for or in connection with agriculture;

''significant extension'' and ''significant alteration'' mean any extension or alteration of the building where the cubic content of the original building would be exceeded by more than 10% or the height of the building as extended or altered would exceed the height of the original building;

''slurry'' means animal faeces and urine (whether or not water has been added for handling); and

''tank'' includes any cage and any other structure for use in fish farming.

D.2 For the purposes of Part 6—

    (a) an area calculated as described in this paragraph comprises the ground area which would be covered by the proposed development, together with the ground area of any building (other than a dwelling), or any structure, works, plant, machinery, ponds or tanks within the same unit which are being provided or have been provided within the preceding two years and any part of which would be within 90 metres of the proposed development;

    (b) 400 metres is to be measured along the ground.

D.3 The circumstances referred to in paragraphs A.2(1)(a) and B.5 are—

    (a) that no other suitable building or structure, 400 metres or more from the curtilage of a protected building, is available to accommodate the livestock; and

    (b) (i) that the need to accommodate the livestock arises from—

        (aa) quarantine requirements; or

        (bb) an emergency due to another building or structure in which the livestock could otherwise be accommodated being unavailable because it has been damaged or destroyed by fire, flood or storm; or

      (ii) in the case of animals normally kept out of doors, they require temporary accommodation in a building or other structure—

        (aa) because they are sick or giving birth or newly born; or

        (bb) to provide shelter against extreme weather conditions.

D.4 For the purposes of paragraph A.2(2)(c), the relevant area is the area of the proposed excavation or the area on which it is proposed to deposit waste together with the aggregate of the areas of all other excavations within the unit which have not been filled and of all other parts of the unit on or under which waste has been deposited and has not been removed.

D.5 In paragraph A.2(2)(iv), ''site notice'' means a notice containing—

    (a) the name of the applicant,

    (b) the address or location of the proposed development,

    (c) a description of the proposed development and of the materials to be used,

    (d) a statement that the prior approval of the authority will be required to the siting, design and external appearance of the building, the siting and means of construction of the private way, the siting of the excavation or deposit or the siting and appearance of the tank, as the case may be,

(e) the name and address of the local planning authority,

and which is signed and dated by or on behalf of the applicant.

D.6 For the purposes of Class B—

   (a) the erection of any additional building within the curtilage of another building is to be treated as the extension of that building and the additional building is not to be treated as an original building;

   (b) where two or more original buildings are within the same curtilage and are used for the same undertaking they are to be treated as a single original building in making any measurement in connection with the extension or alteration of either of them.

D.7 In Class C, "the purposes of agriculture" includes fertilising land used for the purposes of agriculture and the maintenance, improvement or alteration of any buildings, structures or works occupied or used for such purposes on land so used.

[1056]

NOTES

Commencement: 3 June 1995.

PART 7

FORESTRY BUILDINGS AND OPERATIONS

Class A
Permitted
development

A The carrying out on land used for the purposes of forestry, including afforestation, of development reasonably necessary for those purposes consisting of—

   (a) works for the erection, extension or alteration of a building;

   (b) the formation, alteration or maintenance of private ways;

   (c) operations on that land, or on land held or occupied with that land, to obtain the materials required for the formation, alteration or maintenance of such ways;

   (d) other operations (not including engineering or mining operations).

Development not
permitted

A.1 Development is not permitted by Class A if—

   (a) it would consist of or include the provision or alteration of a dwelling;

   (b) the height of any building or works within 3 kilometres of the perimeter of an aerodrome would exceed 3 metres in height; or

   (c) any part of the development would be within 25 metres of the metalled portion of a trunk road or classified road.

A.2(1) Subject to paragraph (3), development consisting of the erection of a building or the extension or alteration of a building or the formation or alteration of a private way is permitted by Class A subject to the following conditions—

   (a) the developer shall, before beginning the development, apply to the local planning authority for a determination as to whether the prior approval of the authority will be required to the siting, design and external appearance of the building or, as the case may be, the siting and means of construction of the private way;

   (b) the application shall be accompanied by a written description of the proposed development, the materials to be used and a plan indicating the site together with any fee required to be paid;

   (c) the development shall not be begun before the occurrence of one of the following—

      (i) the receipt by the applicant from the local planning authority of a written notice of their determination that such prior approval is not required;

      (ii) where the local planning authority give the applicant notice within 28 days following the date of receiving his application of their determination that such prior approval is required, the giving of such approval;

      (iii) the expiry of 28 days following the date on which the application was received by the local planning authority without the local planning authority making any determination as to whether such approval is required or notifying the applicant of their determination;

(d) (i) where the local planning authority give the applicant notice that such prior approval is required the applicant shall display a site notice by site display on or near the land on which the proposed development is to be carried out, leaving the notice in position for not less than 21 days in the period of 28 days from the date on which the local planning authority gave the notice to the applicant;

      (ii) where the site notice is, without any fault or intention of the applicant, removed, obscured or defaced before the period of 21 days referred to in sub-paragraph (i) has elapsed, he shall be treated as having complied with the requirements of that sub-paragraph if he has taken reasonable steps for protection of the notice and, if need be, its replacement;

(e) the development shall, except to the extent that the local planning authority otherwise agree in writing, be carried out—

      (i) where prior approval is required, in accordance with the details approved;

      (ii) where prior approval is not required, in accordance with the details submitted with the application;

(f) the development shall be carried out—

      (i) where approval has been given by the local planning authority, within a period of five years from the date on which approval was given,

      (ii) in any other case, within a period of five years from the date on which the local planning authority were given the information referred to in sub-paragraph (b).

(2) In the case of development consisting of the significant extension or the significant alteration of the building such development may be carried out only once.

(3) Paragraph (1) does not preclude the extension or alteration of a building if the building is not on article 1(6) land except in the case of a significant extension or a significant alteration.

Interpretation of Class A

A.3 For the purposes of Class A—

"significant extension" and "significant alteration" mean any extension or alteration of the building where the cubic content of the original building would be exceeded by more than 10% or the height of the building as extended or altered would exceed the height of the original building; and

"site notice" means a notice containing—

    (a) the name of the applicant,

    (b) the address or location of the proposed development,

    (c) a description of the proposed development and of the materials to be used,

    (d) a statement that the prior approval of the authority will be required to the siting, design and external appearance of the building or, as the case may be, the siting and means of construction of the private way,

(e) the name and address of the local planning authority,

and which is signed and dated by or on behalf of the applicant.

[1057]

NOTES

Commencement: 3 June 1995.

PART 8

INDUSTRIAL AND WAREHOUSE DEVELOPMENT

Class A
Permitted
development

A The extension or alteration of an industrial building or a warehouse.

Development not
permitted

A.1 Development is not permitted by Class A if—
  (a) the building as extended or altered is to be used for purposes other than those of the undertaking concerned;
  (b) the building is to be used for a purpose other than—
    (i) in the case of an industrial building, the carrying out of an industrial process or the provision of employee facilities;
    (ii) in the case of a warehouse, storage or distribution or the provision of employee facilities;
  (c) the height of the building as extended or altered would exceed the height of the original building;
  (d) the cubic content of the original building would be exceeded by more than—
    (i) 10%, in respect of development on any article 1(5) land, or
    (ii) 25%, in any other case;
  (e) the floor space of the original building would be exceeded by more than—
    (i) 500 square metres in respect of development on any article 1(5) land, or
    (ii) 1,000 square metres in any other case;
  (f) the external appearance of the premises of the undertaking concerned would be materially affected;
  (g) any part of the development would be carried out within 5 metres of any boundary of the curtilage of the premises; or
  (h) the development would lead to a reduction in the space available for the parking or turning of vehicles.

Conditions

A.2 Development is permitted by Class A subject to the conditions that any building extended or altered—
  (a) shall only be used—
    (i) in the case of an industrial building, for the carrying out of an industrial process for the purposes of the undertaking or the provision of employee facilities;
    (ii) in the case of a warehouse, for storage or distribution for the purposes of the undertaking or the provision of employee facilities;
  (b) shall not be used to provide employee facilities between 7.00 pm and 6.30 am for employees other than those present at the premises of the undertaking for the purpose of their employment;
  (c) shall not be used to provide employee facilities if a notifiable quantity of a hazardous substance is present at the premises of the undertaking.

Interpretation of
Class A

A.3 For the purposes of Class A—

(a) the erection of any additional building within the curtilage of another building (whether by virtue of Class A or otherwise) and used in connection with it is to be treated as the extension of that building, and the additional building is not to be treated as an original building;

(b) where two or more original buildings are within the same curtilage and are used for the same undertaking, they are to be treated as a single original building in making any measurement;

(c) "employee facilities" means social, care or recreational facilities provided for employees of the undertaking, including creche facilities provided for the children of such employees.

Class B
Permitted development

B Development carried out on industrial land for the purposes of an industrial process consisting of—
(a) the installation of additional or replacement plant or machinery,
(b) the provision, rearrangement or replacement of a sewer, main, pipe, cable or other apparatus, or
(c) the provision, rearrangement or replacement of a private way, private railway, siding or conveyor.

Development not permitted

B.1 Development described in Class B(a) is not permitted if—
(a) it would materially affect the external appearance of the premises of the undertaking concerned, or
(b) any plant or machinery would exceed a height of 15 metres above ground level or the height of anything replaced, whichever is the greater.

Interpretation of Class B

B.2 In Class B, "industrial land" means land used for the carrying out of an industrial process, including land used for the purposes of an industrial undertaking as a dock, harbour or quay, but does not include land in or adjacent to and occupied together with a mine.

Class C
Permitted development

C The provision of a hard surface within the curtilage of an industrial building or warehouse to be used for the purpose of the undertaking concerned.

Class D
Permitted development

D The deposit of waste material resulting from an industrial process on any land comprised in a site which was used for that purpose on 1st July 1948 whether or not the superficial area or the height of the deposit is extended as a result.

Development not permitted

D.1 Development is not permitted by Class D if—
(a) the waste material is or includes material resulting from the winning and working of minerals, or
(b) the use on 1st July 1948 was for the deposit of material resulting from the winning and working of minerals.

Interpretation of Part 8

E For the purposes of Part 8, in Classes A and C—
"industrial building" means a building used for the carrying out of an industrial process and includes a building used for the carrying out of such a process on land used as a dock, harbour or quay for the purposes of an industrial undertaking but does not include a building on land in or adjacent to and occupied together with a mine; and
"warehouse" means a building used for any purpose within Class B8 (storage or distribution) of the Schedule to the Use Classes Order but does not include a building on land in or adjacent to and occupied together with a mine.

NOTES
    Commencement: 3 June 1995.

PART 9

REPAIRS TO UNADOPTED STREETS AND PRIVATE WAYS

Class A

Permitted
development

A The carrying out on land within the boundaries of an unadopted street or private way of works required for the maintenance or improvement of the street or way.

Interpretation of
Class A

A.1 For the purposes of Class A—
    "unadopted street" means a street not being a highway maintainable at the public expense within the meaning of the Highways Act 1980.

[1059]

NOTES
    Commencement: 3 June 1995.

PART 10

REPAIRS TO SERVICES

Class A

Permitted
development

The carrying out of any works for the purposes of inspecting, repairing or renewing any sewer, main, pipe, cable or other apparatus, including breaking open any land for that purpose.
[1060]

NOTES
    Commencement: 3 June 1995.

PART 11

DEVELOPMENT UNDER LOCAL OR PRIVATE ACTS OR ORDERS

Class A

Permitted
development

A Development authorised by—
    (a) a local or private Act of Parliament,
    (b) an order approved by both Houses of Parliament, or
    (c) an order under section 14 or 16 of the Harbours Act 1964 (orders for securing harbour efficiency etc, and orders conferring powers for improvement, construction etc of harbours)
which designates specifically the nature of the development authorised and the land upon which it may be carried out.

Condition

A.1 Development is not permitted by Class A if it consists of or includes—
    (a) the erection, construction, alteration or extension of any building, bridge, aqueduct, pier or dam, or
    (b) the formation, laying out or alteration of a means of access to any highway used by vehicular traffic,
unless the prior approval of the appropriate authority to the detailed plans and specifications is first obtained.

Prior approvals

A.2 The prior approval referred to in paragraph A.1 is not to be refused by the appropriate authority nor are conditions to be imposed unless they are satisfied that—
    (a) the development (other than the provision of or works carried out to a dam) ought to be and could reasonably be carried out elsewhere on the land; or

(b) the design or external appearance of any building, bridge, aqueduct, pier or dam would injure the amenity of the neighbourhood and is reasonably capable of modification to avoid such injury.

Interpretation of Class A

A.3 In Class A, "appropriate authority" means—
  (a) in Greater London or a metropolitan county, the local planning authority,
  (b) in a National Park, outside a metropolitan county, the county planning authority,
  (c) in any other case, the district planning authority.

[1061]

NOTES
Commencement: 3 June 1995.

PART 12

DEVELOPMENT BY LOCAL AUTHORITIES

Class A
Permitted development

A The erection or construction and the maintenance, improvement or other alteration by a local authority or by an urban development corporation of—
  (a) any small ancillary building, works or equipment on land belonging to or maintained by them required for the purposes of any function exercised by them on that land otherwise than as statutory undertakers;
  (b) lamp standards, information kiosks, passenger shelters, public shelters and seats, telephone boxes, fire alarms, public drinking fountains, horse troughs, refuse bins or baskets, barriers for the control of people waiting to enter public service vehicles, and similar structures or works required in connection with the operation of any public service administered by them.

Interpretation of Class A

A.1 For the purposes of Class A—
  "urban development corporation" has the same meaning as in Part XVI of the Local Government, Planning and Land Act 1980 (urban development).

A.2 The reference in Class A to any small ancillary building, works or equipment is a reference to any ancillary building, works or equipment not exceeding 4 metres in height or 200 cubic metres in capacity.

Class B
Permitted development

B The deposit by a local authority of waste material on any land comprised in a site which was used for that purpose on 1st July 1948 whether or not the superficial area or the height of the deposit is extended as a result.

Development not permitted

B.1 Development is not permitted by Class B if the waste material is or includes material resulting from the winning and working of minerals.

Interpretation of Part 12

C For the purposes of Part 12—
  "local authority" includes a parish or community council.

[1062]

NOTES
Commencement: 3 June 1995.

PART 13

DEVELOPMENT BY LOCAL HIGHWAY AUTHORITIES

Class A
Permitted
development

A The carrying out by a local highway authority on land outside but adjoining the boundary of an existing highway of works required for or incidental to the maintenance or improvement of the highway.

[1063]

NOTES
Commencement: 3 June 1995.

PART 14

DEVELOPMENT BY DRAINAGE AUTHORITIES

Class A
Permitted
development

A Development by a drainage body in, on or under any watercourse or land drainage works and required in connection with the improvement, maintenance or repair of that watercourse or those works.

Interpretation of
Class A

A.1 For the purposes of Class A—
    "drainage body" has the same meaning as in section 72(1) of the Land Drainage Act 1991 (interpretation) other than the National Rivers Authority.

[1064]

NOTES
Commencement: 3 June 1995.

PART 15

DEVELOPMENT BY THE NATIONAL RIVERS AUTHORITY

Class A
Permitted
development

A Development by the National Rivers Authority, for the purposes of their functions, consisting of—

(a) development not above ground level required in connection with conserving, redistributing or augmenting water resources,

(b) development in, on or under any watercourse or land drainage works and required in connection with the improvement, maintenance or repair of that watercourse or those works,

(c) the provision of a building, plant, machinery or apparatus in, on, over or under land for the purpose of survey or investigation,

(d) the maintenance, improvement or repair of works for measuring the flow in any watercourse or channel,

(e) any works authorised by or required in connection with an order made under section 73 of the Water Resources Act 1991 (power to make ordinary and emergency drought orders),

(f) any other development in, on, over or under their operational land, other than the provision of a building but including the extension or alteration of a building.

Development not
permitted

A.1 Development is not permitted by Class A if—
    (a) in the case of any Class A(a) development, it would include the construction of a reservoir,

      (b) in the case of any Class A(f) development, it would consist of
or include the extension or alteration of a building so that—
         (i) its design or external appearance would be materially
affected,
         (ii) the height of the original building would be exceeded, or
the cubic content of the original building would be
exceeded by more than 25%, or
         (iii) the floor space of the original building would be exceeded
by more than 1,000 square metres,

or

      (c) in the case of any Class A(f) development, it would consist of
the installation or erection of any plant or machinery exceeding
15 metres in height or the height of anything it replaces,
whichever is the greater.

Condition   A.2 Development is permitted by Class A(c) subject to the condition
that, on completion of the survey or investigation, or at the expiration
of six months from the commencement of the development concerned,
whichever is the sooner, all such operations shall cease and all such
buildings, plant, machinery and apparatus shall be removed and the
land restored as soon as reasonably practicable to its former condition
(or to any other condition which may be agreed with the local
planning authority).

[1065]

NOTES
    Commencement: 3 June 1995.

PART 16

DEVELOPMENT BY OR ON BEHALF OF SEWERAGE UNDERTAKERS

Class A
Permitted
development

**A Development by or on behalf of a sewerage undertaker
consisting of—**
      **(a) development not above ground level required in connection
with the provision, improvement, maintenance or repair
of a sewer, outfall pipe, sludge main or associated
apparatus;**
      **(b) the provision of a building, plant, machinery or apparatus
in, on, over or under land for the purpose of survey or
investigation;**
      **(c) the maintenance, improvement or repair of works for
measuring the flow in any watercourse or channel;**
      **(d) any works authorised by or required in connection with
an order made under section 73 of the Water Resources
Act 1991 (power to make ordinary and emergency drought
orders);**
      **(e) any other development in, on, over or under their
operational land, other than the provision of a building
but including the extension or alteration of a building.**

Development not
permitted

A.1 Development is not permitted by Class A(e) if—
      (a) it would consist of or include the extension or alteration of a
building so that—
         (i) its design or external appearance would be materially
affected;
         (ii) the height of the original building would be exceeded, or
the cubic content of the original building would be
exceeded, by more than 25%; or
         (iii) the floor space of the original building would be exceeded
by more than 1,000 square metres;

or

(b) it would consist of the installation or erection of any plant or machinery exceeding 15 metres in height or the height of anything it replaces, whichever is the greater.

Condition

A.2 Development is permitted by Class A(b) subject to the condition that, on completion of the survey or investigation, or at the expiration of 6 months from the commencement of the development concerned, whichever is the sooner, all such operations shall cease and all such buildings, plant, machinery and apparatus shall be removed and the land restored as soon as reasonably practicable to its former condition (or to any other condition which may be agreed with the local planning authority).

Interpretation of Class A

A.3 For the purposes of Class A—
"associated apparatus", in relation to any sewer, main or pipe, means pumps, machinery or apparatus associated with the relevant sewer, main or pipe;
"sludge main" means a pipe or system of pipes (together with any pumps or other machinery or apparatus associated with it) for the conveyance of the residue of water or sewage treated in a water or sewage treatment works as the case may be, including final effluent or the products of the dewatering or incineration of such residue, or partly for any of those purposes and partly for the conveyance of trade effluent or its residue.

[1066]

NOTES
Commencement: 3 June 1995.

PART 17
DEVELOPMENT BY STATUTORY UNDERTAKERS

Class A   Railway or light railway undertakings

Permitted development

A Development by railway undertakers on their operational land, required in connection with the movement of traffic by rail.

Development not permitted

A.1 Development is not permitted by Class A if it consists of or includes—
  (a) the construction of a railway,
  (b) the construction or erection of a hotel, railway station or bridge, or
  (c) the construction or erection otherwise than wholly within a railway station of—
    (i) an office, residential or educational building, or a building used for an industrial process, or
    (ii) a car park, shop, restaurant, garage, petrol filling station or other building or structure provided under transport legislation.

Interpretation of Class A

A.2 For the purposes of Class A, references to the construction or erection of any building or structure include references to the reconstruction or alteration of a building or structure where its design or external appearance would be materially affected.

Class B   Dock, pier, harbour, water transport, canal or inland navigation undertakings

Permitted development

B Development on operational land by statutory undertakers or their lessees in respect of dock, pier, harbour, water transport, or canal or inland navigation undertakings, required—
  (a) for the purposes of shipping, or

(b) **in connection with the embarking, disembarking, loading, discharging or transport of passengers, livestock or goods at a dock, pier or harbour, or with the movement of traffic by canal or inland navigation or by any railway forming part of the undertaking.**

Development not permitted

B.1 Development is not permitted by Class B if it consists of or includes—
(a) the construction or erection of a hotel, or of a bridge or other building not required in connection with the handling of traffic,
(b) the construction or erection otherwise than wholly within the limits of a dock, pier or harbour of—
    (i) an educational building, or
    (ii) a car park, shop, restaurant, garage, petrol filling station or other building provided under transport legislation.

Interpretation of Class B

B.2 For the purposes of Class B, references to the construction or erection of any building or structure include references to the reconstruction or alteration of a building or structure where its design or external appearance would be materially affected, and the reference to operational land includes land designated by an order made under section 14 or 16 of the Harbours Act 1964 (orders for securing harbour efficiency etc, and orders conferring powers for improvement, construction etc of harbours), and which has come into force, whether or not the order was subject to the provisions of the Statutory Orders (Special Procedure) Act 1945.

Class C Works to inland waterways

Permitted development

C The improvement, maintenance or repair of an inland waterway (other than a commercial waterway or cruising waterway) to which section 104 of the Transport Act 1968 (classification of the Board's waterways) applies, and the repair or maintenance of a culvert, weir, lock, aqueduct, sluice, reservoir, let-off valve or other work used in connection with the control and operation of such a waterway.

Class D Dredgings

Permitted development

D The use of any land by statutory undertakers in respect of dock, pier, harbour, water transport, canal or inland navigation undertakings for the spreading of any dredged material.

Class E Water or hydraulic power undertakings

Permitted development

E Development for the purposes of their undertaking by statutory undertakers for the supply of water or hydraulic power consisting of—
(a) **development not above ground level required in connection with the supply of water or for conserving, redistributing or augmenting water resources, or for the conveyance of water treatment sludge,**
(b) **development in, on or under any watercourse and required in connection with the improvement or maintenance of that watercourse,**
(c) **the provision of a building, plant, machinery or apparatus in, on, over or under land for the purpose of survey or investigation,**
(d) **the maintenance, improvement or repair of works for measuring the flow in any watercourse or channel,**
(e) **the installation in a water distribution system of a booster station, valve house, meter or switch-gear house,**
(f) **any works authorised by or required in connection with an order made under section 73 of the Water Resources Act 1991 (power to make ordinary and emergency drought orders),**

(g) any other development in, on, over or under operational land other than the provision of a building but including the extension or alteration of a building.

Development not permitted

E.1 Development is not permitted by Class E if—
- (a) in the case of any Class E(a) development, it would include the construction of a reservoir,
- (b) in the case of any Class E(e) development involving the installation of a station or house exceeding 29 cubic metres in capacity, that installation is carried out at or above ground level or under a highway used by vehicular traffic,
- (c) in the case of any Class E(g) development, it would consist of or include the extension or alteration of a building so that—
  - (i) its design or external appearance would be materially affected;
  - (ii) the height of the original building would be exceeded, or the cubic content of the original building would be exceeded by more than 25%, or
  - (iii) the floor space of the original building would be exceeded by more than 1,000 square metres, or
- (d) in the case of any Class E(g) development, it would consist of the installation or erection of any plant or machinery exceeding 15 metres in height or the height of anything it replaces, whichever is the greater.

Condition

E.2 Development is permitted by Class E(c) subject to the condition that, on completion of the survey or investigation, or at the expiration of six months from the commencement of the development, whichever is the sooner, all such operations shall cease and all such buildings, plant, machinery and apparatus shall be removed and the land restored as soon as reasonably practicable to its former condition (or to any other condition which may be agreed with the local planning authority).

Class F   Gas suppliers

Permitted development

F Development by a public gas supplier required for the purposes of its undertaking consisting of—
- **(a) the laying underground of mains, pipes or other apparatus;**
- **(b) the installation in a gas distribution system of apparatus for measuring, recording, controlling or varying the pressure, flow or volume of gas, and structures for housing such apparatus;**
- **(c) the construction in any storage area or protective area specified in an order made under section 4 of the Gas Act 1965 (storage authorisation orders), of boreholes, and the erection or construction in any such area of any plant or machinery required in connection with the construction of such boreholes;**
- **(d) the placing and storage on land of pipes and other apparatus to be included in a main or pipe which is being or is about to be laid or constructed in pursuance of planning permission granted or deemed to be granted under Part III of the Act (control over development);**
- **(e) the erection on operational land of the public gas supplier of a building solely for the protection of plant or machinery;**
- **(f) any other development carried out in, on, over or under the operational land of the public gas supplier.**

Development not permitted

F.1 Development is not permitted by Class F if—
- (a) in the case of any Class F(b) development involving the installation of a structure for housing apparatus exceeding 29 cubic metres in capacity, that installation would be carried out at or above ground level, or under a highway used by vehicular traffic,

(b) in the case of any Class F(c) development—
　(i) the borehole is shown in an order approved by the Secretary of State for Trade and Industry for the purpose of section 4(6) of the Gas Act 1965; or
　(ii) any plant or machinery would exceed 6 metres in height, or
(c) in the case of any Class F(e) development, the building would exceed 15 metres in height, or
(d) in the case of any Class F(f) development—
　(i) it would consist of or include the erection of a building, or the reconstruction or alteration of a building where its design or external appearance would be materially affected;
　(ii) it would involve the installation of plant or machinery exceeding 15 metres in height, or capable without the carrying out of additional works of being extended to a height exceeding 15 metres; or
　(iii) it would consist of or include the replacement of any plant or machinery, by plant or machinery exceeding 15 metres in height or exceeding the height of the plant or machinery replaced, whichever is the greater.

Conditions

F.2 Development is permitted by Class F subject to the following conditions—
(a) in the case of any Class F(a) development, not less than eight weeks before the beginning of operations to lay a notifiable pipe-line, the public gas supplier shall give notice in writing to the local planning authority of its intention to carry out that development, identifying the land under which the pipe-line is to be laid,
(b) in the case of any Class F(d) development, on completion of the laying or construction of the main or pipe, or at the expiry of a period of nine months from the beginning of the development, whichever is the sooner, any pipes or other apparatus still stored on the land shall be removed and the land restored as soon as reasonably practicable to its condition before the development took place (or to any other condition which may be agreed with the local planning authority),
(c) in the case of any Class F(e) development, approval of the details of the design and external appearance of the building shall be obtained, before the development is begun, from—
　(i) in Greater London or a metropolitan county, the local planning authority,
　(ii) in a National Park, outside a metropolitan county, the county planning authority,
　(iii) in any other case, the district planning authority.

Class G   Electricity undertakings

Permitted
development

G Development by statutory undertakers for the generation, transmission or supply of electricity for the purposes of their undertaking consisting of—
(a) the installation or replacement in, on, over or under land of an electric line and the construction of shafts and tunnels and the installation or replacement of feeder or service pillars or transforming or switching stations or chambers reasonably necessary in connection with an electric line;
(b) the installation or replacement of any telecommunications line which connects any part of an electric line to any electrical plant or building, and the installation or replacement of any support for any such line;

(c) **the sinking of boreholes to ascertain the nature of the subsoil and the installation of any plant or machinery reasonably necessary in connection with such boreholes;**
(d) **the extension or alteration of buildings on operational land;**
(e) **the erection on operational land of the undertaking or a building solely for the protection of plant or machinery;**
(f) **any other development carried out in, on, over or under the operational land of the undertaking.**

Development not permitted

G.1 Development is not permitted by Class G if—
   (a) in the case of any Class G(a) development—
      (i) it would consist of or include the installation or replacement of an electric line to which section 37(1) of the Electricity Act 1989 (consent required for overhead lines) applies; or
      (ii) it would consist of or include the installation or replacement at or above ground level or under a highway used by vehicular traffic, of a chamber for housing apparatus and the chamber would exceed 29 cubic metres in capacity;
   (b) in the case of any Class G(b) development—
      (i) the development would take place in a National Park, an area of outstanding natural beauty, or a site of special scientific interest;
      (ii) the height of any support would exceed 15 metres; or
      (iii) the telecommunications line would exceed 1,000 metres in length;
   (c) in the case of any Class G(d) development—
      (i) the height of the original building would be exceeded;
      (ii) the cubic content of the original building would be exceeded by more than 25% or, in the case of any building on article 1(5) land, by more than 10%, or
      (iii) the floor space of the original building would be exceeded by more than 1,000 square metres or, in the case of any building on article 1(5) land, by more than 500 square metres;
   (d) in the case of any Class G(e) development, the building would exceed 15 metres in height, or
   (e) in the case of any Class G(f) development, it would consist of or include—
      (i) the erection of a building, or the reconstruction or alteration of a building where its design or external appearance would be materially affected, or
      (ii) the installation or erection by way of addition or replacement of any plant or machinery exceeding 15 metres in height or the height of any plant or machinery replaced, whichever is the greater.

Conditions

G.2 Development is permitted by Class G subject to the following conditions—
   (a) in the case of any Class G(a) development consisting of or including the replacement of an existing electric line, compliance with any conditions contained in a planning permission relating to the height, design or position of the existing electric line which are capable of being applied to the replacement line;

(b) in the case of any Class G(a) development consisting of or including the installation of a temporary electric line providing a diversion for an existing electric line, on the ending of the diversion or at the end of a period of six months from the completion of the installation (whichever is the sooner) the temporary electric line shall be removed and the land on which any operations have been carried out to install that line shall be restored as soon as reasonably practicable to its condition before the installation took place;

(c) in the case of any Class G(c) development, on the completion of that development, or at the end of a period of six months from the beginning of that development (whichever is the sooner) any plant or machinery installed shall be removed and the land shall be restored as soon as reasonably practicable to its condition before the development took place;

(d) in the case of any Class G(e) development, approval of details of the design and external appearance of the buildings shall be obtained, before development is begun, from—

(i) in Greater London or a metropolitan county, the local planning authority,

(ii) in a National Park, outside a metropolitan county, the county planning authority,

(iii) in any other case, the district planning authority.

Interpretation of Class G

G.3 For the purposes of Class G(a), "electric line" has the meaning assigned to that term by section 64(1) of the Electricity Act 1989 (interpretation etc of Part 1).

G.4 For the purposes of Class G(b), "electrical plant" has the meaning assigned to that term by the said section 64(1) and "telecommunications line" means a wire or cable (including its casing or coating) which forms part of a telecommunication apparatus within the meaning assigned to that term by paragraph 1 of Schedule 2 to the Telecommunications Act 1984 (the telecommunications code).

G.5 For the purposes of Class G(d), (e) and (f), the land of the holder of a licence under section 6(2) of the Electricity Act 1989 (licences authorising supply etc) shall be treated as operational land if it would be operational land within section 263 of the Act (meaning of "operational land") if such licence holders were statutory undertakers for the purpose of that section.

Class H   Tramway or road transport undertakings

Permitted development

H Development required for the purposes of the carrying on of any tramway or road transport undertaking consisting of—

(a) **the installation of posts, overhead wires, underground cables, feeder pillars or transformer boxes in, on, over or adjacent to a highway for the purpose of supplying current to public service vehicles;**

(b) **the installation of tramway tracks, and conduits, drains and pipes in connection with such tracks for the working of tramways;**

(c) **the installation of telephone cables and apparatus, huts, stop posts and signs required in connection with the operation of public service vehicles;**

(d) **the erection or construction and the maintenance, improvement or other alteration of passenger shelters and barriers for the control of people waiting to enter public service vehicles;**

(e) **any other development on operational land of the undertaking.**

Development not permitted	H.1 Development is not permitted by Class H if it would consist of—

    (a) in the case of any Class H(a) development, the installation of a structure exceeding 17 cubic metres in capacity,

    (b) in the case of any Class H(e) development—

        (i) the erection of a building or the reconstruction or alteration of a building where its design or external appearance would be materially affected,

        (ii) the installation or erection by way of addition or replacement of any plant or machinery which would exceed 15 metres in height or the height of any plant or machinery it replaces, whichever is the greater,

        (iii) development, not wholly within a bus or tramway station, in pursuance of powers contained in transport legislation.

Class I   Lighthouse undertakings

Permitted development	**I Development required for the purposes of the functions of a general or local lighthouse authority under the Merchant Shipping Act 1894 and any other statutory provision made with respect to a local lighthouse authority, or in the exercise by a local lighthouse authority of rights, powers or duties acquired by usage prior to the 1894 Act.**
Development not permitted	I.1 Development is not permitted by Class I if it consists of or includes the erection of offices, or the reconstruction or alteration of offices where their design or external appearance would be materially affected.

Class J   Post Office

Permitted development	**J Development required for the purposes of the Post Office consisting of—**

    (a) the installation of posting boxes or self-service machines,

    (b) any other development carried out in, on, over or under the operational land of the undertaking.

Development not permitted	J.1 Development is not permitted by Class J if—

    (a) it would consist of or include the erection of a building, or the reconstruction or alteration of a building where its design or external appearance would be materially affected, or

    (b) it would consist of or include the installation or erection by way of addition or replacement of any plant or machinery which would exceed 15 metres in height or the height of any existing plant or machinery, whichever is the greater.

Interpretation of Part 17	K For the purposes of Part 17— "transport legislation" means section 14(1)(d) of the Transport Act 1962 (supplemental provisions relating to the Boards' powers) or section 10(1)(x) of the Transport Act 1968 (general powers of Passenger Transport Executive).

[1067]

NOTES
  Commencement: 3 June 1995.

PART 18

AVIATION DEVELOPMENT

Class A   Development at an airport

Permitted development	**A The carrying out on operational land by a relevant airport operator or its agent of development (including the erection or alteration of an operational building) in connection with the provision of services and facilities at a relevant airport.**

Development not
permitted

A.1 Development is not permitted by Class A if it would consist of
or include—
  (a) the construction or extension of a runway;
  (b) the construction of a passenger terminal the floor space of
      which would exceed 500 square metres;
  (c) the extension or alteration of a passenger terminal, where the
      floor space of the building as existing at 5th December 1988
      or, if built after that date, of the building as built, would be
      exceeded by more than 15%;
  (d) the erection of a building other than an operational building;
  (e) the alteration or reconstruction of a building other than an
      operational building, where its design or external appearance
      would be materially affected.

Condition

A.2 Development is permitted by Class A subject to the condition
that the relevant airport operator consults the local planning authority
before carrying out any development, unless that development falls
within the description in paragraph A.4.

Interpretation of
Class A

A.3 For the purposes of paragraph A.1, floor space shall be calculated
by external measurement and without taking account of the floor
space in any pier or satellite.

A.4 Development falls within this paragraph if—
  (a) it is urgently required for the efficient running of the airport,
      and
  (b) it consists of the carrying out of works, or the erection or
      construction of a structure or of an ancillary building, or the
      placing on land of equipment, and the works, structure,
      building, or equipment do not exceed 4 metres in height or
      200 cubic metres in capacity.

Class B   Air navigation development at an airport

**Permitted
development**

**B   The carrying out on operational land within the perimeter of
a relevant airport by a relevant airport operator or its agent of
development in connection with—**
  (a) the provision of air traffic control services,
  (b) the navigation of aircraft using the airport, or
  **(c) the monitoring of the movement of aircraft using the
      airport.**

Class C   Air navigation development near an airport

**Permitted
development**

**C   The carrying out on operational land outside but within 8
kilometres of the perimeter of a relevant airport, by a relevant
airport operator or its agent, of development in connection
with—**
  (a) the provision of air traffic control services,
  (b) the navigation of aircraft using the airport, or
  **(c) the monitoring of the movement of aircraft using the
      airport.**

Development not
permitted

C.1 Development is not permitted by Class C if—
  (a) any building erected would be used for a purpose other than
      housing equipment used in connection with the provision of
      air traffic control services, with assisting the navigation of
      aircraft, or with monitoring the movement of aircraft using the
      airport;
  (b) any building erected would exceed a height of 4 metres;
  (c) it would consist of the installation or erection of any radar or
      radio mast, antenna or other apparatus which would exceed
      15 metres in height, or, where an existing mast, antenna or
      apparatus is replaced, the height of that mast, antenna or
      apparatus, if greater.

Class D Development by Civil Aviation Authority within an airport

Permitted
development
: D The carrying out by the Civil Aviation Authority or its agents, within the perimeter of an airport at which the Authority provides air traffic control services, of development in connection with—
(a) the provision of air traffic control services,
(b) the navigation of aircraft using the airport, or
(c) the monitoring of the movement of aircraft using the airport.

Class E Development by the civil aviation authority for air traffic control and navigation

Permitted
development
: E The carrying out on operational land of the Civil Aviation Authority by the Authority or its agents of development in connection with—
(a) the provision of air traffic control services,
(b) the navigation of aircraft, or
(c) monitoring the movement of aircraft.

Development not
permitted
: E.1 Development is not permitted by Class E if—
(a) any building erected would be used for a purpose other than housing equipment used in connection with the provision of air traffic control services, assisting the navigation of aircraft or monitoring the movement of aircraft;
(b) any building erected would exceed a height of 4 metres; or
(c) it would consist of the installation or erection of any radar or radio mast, antenna or other apparatus which would exceed 15 metres in height, or, where an existing mast, antenna or apparatus is replaced, the height of that mast, antenna or apparatus, if greater.

Class F Development by the Civil Aviation Authority in an emergency

Permitted
development
: F The use of land by or on behalf of the Civil Aviation Authority in an emergency to station moveable apparatus replacing unserviceable apparatus.

Condition
: F.1 Development is permitted by Class F subject to the condition that on or before the expiry of a period of six months beginning with the date on which the use began, the use shall cease, and any apparatus shall be removed, and the land shall be restored to its condition before the development took place, or to any other condition as may be agreed in writing between the local planning authority and the developer.

Class G Development by the Civil Aviation Authority for air traffic control etc

Permitted
development
: G The use of land by or on behalf of the Civil Aviation Authority to provide services and facilities in connection with—
(a) the provision of air traffic control services,
(b) the navigation of aircraft, or
(c) the monitoring of aircraft,
and the erection or placing of moveable structures on the land for the purpose of that use.

Condition
: G.1 Development is permitted by Class G subject to the condition that, on or before the expiry of the period of six months beginning with the date on which the use began, the use shall cease, and any structure shall be removed, and the land shall be restored to its condition before the development took place, or to any other condition as may be agreed in writing between the local planning authority and the developer.

Class H Development by the Civil Aviation Authority for surveys etc

Permitted
development
: H The use of land by or on behalf of the Civil Aviation Authority for the stationing and operation of apparatus in connection with the carrying out of surveys or investigations.

Condition   H.1 Development is permitted by Class H subject to the condition
                         that on or before the expiry of the period of six months beginning
                         with the date on which the use began, the use shall cease, and any
                         apparatus shall be removed, and the land shall be restored to its
                         condition before the development took place, or to any other
                         condition as may be agreed in writing between the local planning
                         authority and the developer.

Class I   Use of airport buildings managed by relevant airport operators
Permitted   **I The use of buildings within the perimeter of an airport**
development   **managed by a relevant airport operator for purposes connected**
                         with air transport services or other flying activities at that
                         airport.

Interpretation of   J For the purposes of Part 18—
Part 18   "operational building" means a building, other than a hotel,
                         required in connection with the movement or maintenance of
                         aircraft, or with the embarking, disembarking, loading, discharge
                         or transport of passengers, livestock or goods at a relevant airport;
                         "relevant airport" means an airport to which Part V of the Airports
                         Act 1986 (status of certain airports as statutory undertakers etc)
                         applies; and
                         "relevant airport operator" means a relevant airport operator
                         within the meaning of section 57 of the Airports Act 1986 (scope
                         of Part V).

                                                                                    [1068]

NOTES
    Commencement: 3 June 1995.

PART 19

DEVELOPMENT ANCILLARY TO MINING OPERATIONS

Class A
Permitted   **A The carrying out of operations for the erection, extension,**
development   **installation, rearrangement, replacement, repair or other altera-**
                         tion of any—
                         (a) plant or machinery,
                         (b) buildings,
                         (c) private ways or private railways or sidings, or
                         (d) sewers, mains, pipes, cables or other similar apparatus,
                         on land used as a mine.

Development not   A.1 Development is not permitted by Class A—
permitted   (a) in relation to land at an underground mine—
                                (i) on land which is not an approved site; or
                                (ii) on land to which the description in paragraph D.1(b)
                                     applies, unless a plan of that land was deposited with the
                                     mineral planning authority before 5th June 1989;
                            (b) if the principal purpose of the development would be any
                                purpose other than—
                                (i) purposes in connection with the winning and working of
                                    minerals at that mine or of minerals brought to the surface
                                    at that mine; or
                                (ii) the treatment, storage or removal from the mine of such
                                     minerals or waste materials derived from them;
                            (c) if the external appearance of the mine would be materially
                                affected;
                            (d) if the height of any building, plant or machinery which is not
                                in an excavation would exceed—
                                (i) 15 metres above ground level; or

(ii) the height of the building, plant or machinery, if any, which is being rearranged, replaced or repaired or otherwise altered,

whichever is the greater;

(e) if the height of any building, plant or machinery in an excavation would exceed—
  (i) 15 metres above the excavated ground level; or
  (ii) 15 metres above the lowest point of the unexcavated ground immediately adjacent to the excavation; or
  (iii) the height of the building, plant or machinery, if any, which is being rearranged, replaced or repaired or otherwise altered,

whichever is the greatest;

(f) if any building erected (other than a replacement building) would have a floor space exceeding 1,000 square metres; or

(g) if the cubic content of any replaced, extended or altered building would exceed by more than 25% the cubic content of the building replaced, extended or altered or the floor space would exceed by more than 1,000 square metres the floor space of that building.

Condition   A.2 Development is permitted by Class A subject to the condition that before the end of the period of 24 months from the date when the mining operations have permanently ceased, or any longer period which the mineral planning authority agree in writing—

(a) all buildings, plant and machinery permitted by Class A shall be removed from the land unless the mineral planning authority have otherwise agreed in writing; and

(b) the land shall be restored, so far as is practicable, to its condition before the development took place, or restored to such condition as may have been agreed in writing between the mineral planning authority and the developer.

Class B
Permitted   **B The carrying out, on land used as a mine or on ancillary**
development   **mining land, with the prior approval of the mineral planning**
authority, of operations for the erection, installation, extension,
rearrangement, replacement, repair or other alteration of any—
  (a) plant or machinery,
  (b) buildings, or
  (c) structures or erections.

Development not   B.1 Development is not permitted by Class B—
permitted   (a) in relation to land at an underground mine—
  (i) on land which is not an approved site; or
  (ii) on land to which the description in paragraph D.1(b) applies, unless a plan of that land was deposited with the mineral planning authority before 5th June 1989;

or

(b) if the principal purpose of the development would be any purpose other than—
  (i) purposes in connection with the operation of the mine,
  (ii) the treatment, preparation for sale, consumption or utilization of minerals won or brought to the surface at that mine, or
  (iii) the storage or removal from the mine of such minerals, their products or waste materials derived from them.

B.2 The prior approval referred to in Class B shall not be refused or granted subject to conditions unless the authority are satisfied that it is expedient to do so because—

(a) the proposed development would injure the amenity of the neighbourhood and modifications can reasonably be made or conditions reasonably imposed in order to avoid or reduce that injury, or

(b) the proposed development ought to be, and could reasonably be, sited elsewhere.

Condition

B.3 Development is permitted by Class B subject to the condition that before the end of the period of 24 months from the date when the mining operations have permanently ceased, or any longer period which the mineral planning authority agree in writing—

(a) all buildings, plant, machinery, structures and erections permitted by Class B shall be removed from the land unless the mineral planning authority have otherwise agreed in writing; and

(b) the land shall be restored, so far as is practicable, to its condition before the development took place or restored to such condition as may have been agreed in writing between the mineral planning authority and the developer.

Class C

Permitted development

C The carrying out with the prior approval of the mineral planning authority of development required for the maintenance or safety of a mine or a disused mine or for the purposes of ensuring the safety of the surface of the land at or adjacent to a mine or a disused mine.

Development not permitted

C.1 Development is not permitted by Class C if it is carried out by the Coal Authority or any licensed operator within the meaning of section 65 of the Coal Industry Act 1994 (interpretation).

Prior approvals

C.2(1) The prior approval of the mineral planning authority to development permitted by Class C is not required if—

(a) the external appearance of the mine or disused mine at or adjacent to which the development is to be carried out would not be materially affected;

(b) no building, plant, machinery, structure or erection—

(i) would exceed a height of 15 metres above ground level, or

(ii) where any building, plant, machinery, structure or erection is rearranged, replaced or repaired, would exceed a height of 15 metres above ground level or the height of what was rearranged, replaced or repaired, whichever is the greater,

and

(c) the development consists of the extension, alteration or replacement of an existing building, within the limits set out in paragraph (3).

(2) The approval referred to in Class C shall not be refused or granted subject to conditions unless the authority are satisfied that it is expedient to do so because—

(a) the proposed development would injure the amenity of the neighbourhood and modifications could reasonably be made or conditions reasonably imposed in order to avoid or reduce that injury, or

(b) the proposed development ought to be, and could reasonably be, sited elsewhere.

(3) The limits referred to in paragraph C.2(1)(c) are—

(a) that the cubic content of the building as extended, altered or replaced does not exceed that of the existing building by more than 25%, and

(b) that the floor space of the building as extended, altered or replaced does not exceed that of the existing building by more than 1,000 square metres.

Interpretation of
Part 19

D.1 An area of land is an approved site for the purposes of Part 19
if—

   (a) it is identified in a grant of planning permission or any
instrument by virtue of which planning permission is deemed
to be granted, as land which may be used for development
described in this Part; or

   (b) in any other case, it is land immediately adjoining an active
access to an underground mine which, on 5th December 1988,
was in use for the purposes of that mine, in connection with
the purposes described in paragraph A.1(b)(i) or (ii) or
paragraph B.1(b)(i) to (iii) above.

D.2 For the purposes of Part 19—

"active access" means a surface access to underground workings
which is in normal and regular use for the transportation of
minerals, materials, spoil or men;

"ancillary mining land" means land adjacent to and occupied
together with a mine at which the winning and working of minerals
is carried out in pursuance of planning permission granted or
deemed to be granted under Part III of the Act (control over
development);

"minerals" does not include any coal other than coal won or
worked during the course of operations which are carried on
exclusively for the purpose of exploring for coal or confined to the
digging or carrying away of coal that it is necessary to dig or carry
away in the course of activities carried on for purposes which do
not include the getting of coal or any product of coal;

"the prior approval of the mineral planning authority" means
prior written approval of that authority of detailed proposals for
the siting, design and external appearance of the building, plant or
machinery proposed to be erected, installed, extended or altered;

"underground mine" is a mine at which minerals are worked
principally by underground methods.

[1069]

NOTES
   Commencement: 3 June 1995.

PART 20

COAL MINING DEVELOPMENT BY THE COAL AUTHORITY AND LICENSED OPERATORS

Class A
  Permitted
  development

**A Development by a licensee of the Coal Authority, in a mine
started before 1st July 1948, consisting of—**

   **(a) the winning and working underground of coal or coal-
related minerals in a designated seam area; or**

   **(b) the carrying out of development underground which is
required in order to gain access to and work coal or coal-
related minerals in a designated seam area.**

Conditions

A.1 Development is permitted by Class A subject to the following
conditions—

   (a) subject to sub-paragraph (b)—

     (i) except in a case where there is an approved restoration
scheme or mining operations have permanently ceased,
the developer shall, before 31st December 1995 or before
any later date which the mineral planning authority may
agree in writing, apply to the mineral planning authority
for approval of a restoration scheme;

(ii) where there is an approved restoration scheme, reinstatement, restoration and aftercare shall be carried out in accordance with that scheme;

(iii) if an approved restoration scheme does not specify the periods within which reinstatement, restoration or aftercare should be carried out, it shall be subject to conditions that—

    (aa) reinstatement or restoration, if any, shall be carried out before the end of the period of 24 months from either the date when the mining operations have permanently ceased or the date when any application for approval of a restoration scheme under sub-paragraph (a)(i) has been finally determined, whichever is later, and

    (bb) aftercare, if any, in respect of any part of a site, shall be carried out throughout the period of five years from either the date when any reinstatement or restoration in respect of that part is completed or the date when any application for approval of a restoration scheme under sub-paragraph (a)(i) has been finally determined, whichever is later;

(iv) where there is no approved restoration scheme—

    (aa) all buildings, plant, machinery, structures and erections used at any time for or in connection with any previous coal-mining operations at that mine shall be removed from any land which is an authorised site unless the mineral planning authority have otherwise agreed in writing, and

    (bb) that land shall, so far as practicable, be restored to its condition before any previous coal-mining operations at that mine took place or to such condition as may have been agreed in writing between the mineral planning authority and the developer,

before the end of the period specified in sub-paragraph (v);

(v) the period referred to in sub-paragraph (iv) is—

    (aa) the period of 24 months from the date when the mining operations have permanently ceased or, if an application for approval of a restoration scheme has been made under sub-paragraph (a)(i) before that date, 24 months from the date when that application has been finally determined, whichever is later, or

    (bb) any longer period which the mineral planning authority have agreed in writing;

(vi) for the purposes of sub-paragraph (a), an application for approval of a restoration scheme has been finally determined when the following conditions have been met—

    (aa) any proceedings on the application, including any proceeding on or in consequence of an application under section 288 of the Act (proceedings for questioning the validity of certain orders, decisions and directions), have been determined, and

    (bb) any time for appealing under section 78 (right to appeal against planning decisions and failure to take such decisions), or applying or further applying under section 288, of the Act (where there is a right to do so) has expired;

(b) sub-paragraph (a) shall not apply to land in respect of which there is an extant planning permission which—

(i) has been granted on an application under Part III of the Act, and

(ii) has been implemented.

<table>
<tr><td>Interpretation of Class A</td><td>A.2 For the purposes of Class A—</td></tr>
</table>

A.2 For the purposes of Class A—

"a licensee of the Coal Authority" means any person who is for the time being authorised by a licence under Part II of the Coal Industry Act 1994 to carry on coal-mining operations to which section 25 of that Act (coal-mining operations to be licensed) applies;

"approved restoration scheme" means a restoration scheme which is approved when an application made under paragraph A.1(a)(i) is finally determined, as approved (with or without conditions), or as subsequently varied with the written approval of the mineral planning authority (with or without conditions);

"coal-related minerals" means minerals other than coal which are, or may be, won and worked by coal-mining operations;

"designated seam area" means land identified, in accordance with paragraph (a) of the definition of "seam plan", in a seam plan which was deposited with the mineral planning authority before 30th September 1993;

"previous coal-mining operations" has the same meaning as in section 54(3) of the Coal Industry Act 1994 (obligations to restore land affected by coal-mining operations) and references in Class A to the use of anything in connection with any such operations shall include references to its use for or in connection with activities carried on in association with, or for purposes connected with, the carrying on of those operations;

"restoration scheme" means a scheme which makes provision for the reinstatement, restoration or aftercare (or a combination of these) of any land which is an authorised site and has been used at any time for or in connection with any previous coal-mining operations at that mine; and

"seam plan" means a plan or plans on a scale of not less than 1 to 25,000 showing—

(a) land comprising the maximum extent of the coal seam or seams that could have been worked from shafts or drifts existing at a mine at 13th November 1992, without further development on an authorised site other than development permitted by Class B of Part 20 of Schedule 2 to the Town and Country Planning General Development Order 1988, as originally enacted;

(b) any active access used in connection with the land referred to in paragraph (a) of this definition;

(c) the National Grid lines and reference numbers shown on Ordnance Survey maps;

(d) a typical stratigraphic column showing the approximate depths of the coal seam referred to in paragraph (a) of this definition.

Class B
Permitted development

B Development by a licensee of the British Coal Corporation, in a mine started before 1st July 1948, consisting of—

(a) the winning and working underground of coal or coal-related minerals in a designated seam area; or

(b) the carrying out of development underground which is required in order to gain access to and work coal or coal-related minerals in a designated seam area.

Interpretation of Class B

B.1 For the purposes of Class B—

"designated seam area" has the same meaning as in paragraph A.2 above;

"coal-related minerals" means minerals other than coal which can only be economically worked in association with the working of coal or which can only be economically brought to the surface by the use of a mine of coal; and

"a licensee of the British Coal Corporation" means any person who is for the time being authorised by virtue of section 25(3) of the Coal Industry Act 1994 (coal-mining operations to be licensed) to carry on coal-mining operations to which section 25 of that Act applies.

Class C

Permitted development

C Any development required for the purposes of a mine which is carried out on an authorised site at that mine by a licensed operator, in connection with coal-mining operations.

Development not permitted

C.1 Development is not permitted by Class C if—
  (a) the external appearance of the mine would be materially affected;
  (b) any building, plant or machinery, structure or erection or any deposit of minerals or waste—
    (i) would exceed a height of 15 metres above ground level, or
    (ii) where a building, plant or machinery would be rearranged, replaced or repaired, the resulting development would exceed a height of 15 metres above ground level or the height of what was rearranged, replaced or repaired, whichever is the greater;
  (c) any building erected (other than a replacement building) would have a floor space exceeding 1,000 square metres;
  (d) the cubic content of any replaced, extended or altered building would exceed by more than 25% the cubic content of the building replaced, extended or altered or the floor space would exceed by more than 1,000 square metres, the floor space of that building;
  (e) it would be for the purpose of creating a new surface access to underground workings or of improving an existing access (which is not an active access) to underground workings; or
  (f) it would be carried out on land to which the description in paragraph F.2(1)(b) applies, and a plan of that land had not been deposited with the mineral planning authority before 5th June 1989.

Conditions

C.2 Development is permitted by Class C subject to the condition that before the end of the period of 24 months from the date when the mining operations have permanently ceased, or any longer period which the mineral planning authority agree in writing—
  (a) all buildings, plant, machinery, structures and erections and deposits of minerals or waste permitted by Class C shall be removed from the land unless the mineral planning authority have otherwise agreed in writing; and
  (b) the land shall, so far as is practicable, be restored to its condition before the development took place or to such condition as may have been agreed in writing between the mineral planning authority and the developer.

Class D

Permitted development

D Any development required for the purposes of a mine which is carried out on an authorised site at that mine by a licensed operator in connection with coal-mining operations and with the prior approval of the mineral planning authority.

Development not permitted

D.1 Development is not permitted by Class D if—

(a) it would be for the purpose of creating a new surface access or improving an existing access (which is not an active access) to underground workings; or

(b) it would be carried out on land to which the description in paragraph F.2(1)(b) applies, and a plan of that land had not been deposited with the mineral planning authority before 5th June 1989.

Condition

D.2 Development is permitted by Class D subject to the condition that before the end of the period of 24 months from the date when the mining operations have permanently ceased, or any longer period which the mineral planning authority agree in writing—

(a) all buildings, plant, machinery, structures and erections and deposits of minerals or waste permitted by Class D shall be removed from the land, unless the mineral planning authority have otherwise agreed in writing; and

(b) the land shall, so far as is practicable, be restored to its condition before the development took place or to such condition as may have been agreed in writing between the mineral planning authority and the developer.

Interpretation of
Class D

D.3 The prior approval referred to in Class D shall not be refused or granted subject to conditions unless the authority are satisfied that it is expedient to do so because—

(a) the proposed development would injure the amenity of the neighbourhood and modifications could reasonably be made or conditions reasonably imposed in order to avoid or reduce that injury, or

(b) the proposed development ought to be, and could reasonably be, sited elsewhere.

Class E

**Permitted
development**

E The carrying out by the Coal Authority or a licensed operator, with the prior approval of the mineral planning authority, of development required for the maintenance or safety of a mine or a disused mine or for the purposes of ensuring the safety of the surface of the land at or adjacent to a mine or a disused mine.

Prior approvals

E.1(1) The prior approval of the mineral planning authority to development permitted by Class E is not required if—

(a) the external appearance of the mine or disused mine at or adjacent to which the development is to be carried out would not be materially affected;

(b) no building, plant or machinery, structure or erection—

(i) would exceed a height of 15 metres above ground level, or

(ii) where any building, plant, machinery, structure or erection is rearranged, replaced or repaired, would exceed a height of 15 metres above ground level or the height of what was rearranged, replaced or repaired, whichever is the greater,

and

(c) the development consists of the extension, alteration or replacement of an existing building, within the limits set out in paragraph (3).

(2) The approval referred to in Class E shall not be refused or granted subject to conditions unless the authority are satisfied that it is expedient to do so because—

(a) the proposed development would injure the amenity of the neighbourhood and modifications could reasonably be made or conditions reasonably imposed in order to avoid or reduce that injury, or

(b) the proposed development ought to be, and could reasonably be, sited elsewhere.

(3) The limits referred to in paragraph E.1(1)(c) are—

(a) that the cubic content of the building as extended, altered or replaced does not exceed that of the existing building by more than 25%, and

(b) that the floor space of the building as extended, altered or replaced does not exceed that of the existing building by more than 1,000 square metres.

Interpretation of Part 20

F.1 For the purposes of Part 20—

"active access" means a surface access to underground workings which is in normal and regular use for the transportation of coal, materials, spoil or men;

"coal-mining operations" has the same meaning as in section 65 of the Coal Industry Act 1994 (interpretation) and references to any development or use in connection with coal-mining operations shall include references to development or use for or in connection with activities carried on in association with, or for purposes connected with, the carrying on of those operations;

"licensed operator" has the same meaning as in section 65 of the Coal Industry Act 1994;

"normal and regular use" means use other than intermittent visits to inspect and maintain the fabric of the mine or any plant or machinery; and

"prior approval of the mineral planning authority" means prior written approval of that authority of detailed proposals for the siting, design and external appearance of the proposed building, plant or machinery, structure or erection as erected, installed, extended or altered.

F.2(1) Subject to sub-paragraph (2), land is an authorised site for the purposes of Part 20 if—

(a) it is identified in a grant of planning permission or any instrument by virtue of which planning permission is deemed to be granted as land which may be used for development described in this Part; or

(b) in any other case, it is land immediately adjoining an active access which, on 5th December 1988, was in use for the purposes of that mine in connection with coal-mining operations.

(2) For the purposes of sub-paragraph (1), land is not to be regarded as in use in connection with coal-mining operations if—

(a) it is used for the permanent deposit of waste derived from the winning and working of minerals; or

(b) there is on, over or under it a railway, conveyor, aerial ropeway, roadway, overhead power line or pipe-line which is not itself surrounded by other land used for those purposes.

[1070]

NOTES
Commencement: 3 June 1995.

PART 21

WASTE TIPPING AT A MINE

Class A
Permitted development

A The deposit, on premises used as a mine or on ancillary mining land already used for the purpose, of waste derived from the winning and working of minerals at that mine or from minerals brought to the surface at that mine, or from the treatment or the preparation for sale, consumption or utilization of minerals from the mine.

Development not permitted	A.1 Development is not permitted by Class A if—

    (a) in the case of waste deposited in an excavation, waste would be deposited at a height above the level of the land adjoining the excavation, unless that is provided for in a waste management scheme or a relevant scheme;

    (b) in any other case, the superficial area or height of the deposit (measured as at 21st October 1988) would be increased by more than 10%, unless such an increase is provided for in a waste management scheme or in a relevant scheme.

Conditions	A.2 Development is permitted by Class A subject to the following conditions—

    (a) except in a case where a relevant scheme or a waste management scheme has already been approved by the mineral planning authority, the developer shall, if the mineral planning authority so require, within three months or such longer period as the authority may specify, submit a waste management scheme for that authority's approval;

    (b) where a waste management scheme or a relevant scheme has been approved, the depositing of waste and all other activities in relation to that deposit shall be carried out in accordance with the scheme as approved.

Interpretation of Class A	A.3 For the purposes of Class A—

"ancillary mining land" means land adjacent to and occupied together with a mine at which the winning and working of minerals is carried out in pursuance of planning permission granted or deemed to be granted under Part III of the Act (control over development); and

"waste management scheme" means a scheme required by the mineral planning authority to be submitted for their approval in accordance with the condition in paragraph A.2(a) which makes provision for—

    (a) the manner in which the depositing of waste (other than waste deposited on a site for use for filling any mineral excavation in the mine or on ancillary mining land in order to comply with the terms of any planning permission granted on an application or deemed to be granted under Part III of the Act) is to be carried out after the date of the approval of that scheme;

    (b) where appropriate, the stripping and storage of the subsoil and topsoil;

    (c) the restoration and aftercare of the site.

Class B

Permitted development	**B** The deposit on land comprised in a site used for the deposit of waste materials or refuse on 1st July 1948 of waste resulting from coal-mining operations.

Development not permitted	B.1 Development is not permitted by Class B unless it is in accordance with a relevant scheme approved by the mineral planning authority before 5th December 1988.

Interpretation of Class B	B.2 For the purposes of Class B—

"coal-mining operations" has the same meaning as in section 65 of the Coal Industry Act 1994 (interpretation).

Interpretation of
Part 21

C For the purposes of Part 21—
"relevant scheme" means a scheme, other than a waste management scheme, requiring approval by the mineral planning authority
in accordance with a condition or limitation on any planning
permission granted or deemed to be granted under Part III of the
Act (control over development), for making provision for the
manner in which the deposit of waste is to be carried out and for
the carrying out of other activities in relation to that deposit.

[1071]

NOTES
Commencement: 3 June 1995.

PART 22

MINERAL EXPLORATION

Class A
Permitted
development

A Development on any land during a period not exceeding 28
consecutive days consisting of—
   (a) **the drilling of boreholes;**
   (b) **the carrying out of seismic surveys; or**
   (c) **the making of other excavations,**
for the purpose of mineral exploration, and the provision or
assembly on that land or adjoining land of any structure required
in connection with any of those operations.

Development not
permitted

A.1 Development is not permitted by Class A if—
   (a) it consists of the drilling of boreholes for petroleum explora-
      tion;
   (b) any operation would be carried out within 50 metres of any
      part of an occupied residential building or a building occupied
      as a hospital or school;
   (c) any operation would be carried out within a National Park, an
      area of outstanding natural beauty, a site of archaeological
      interest or a site of special scientific interest;
   (d) any explosive charge of more than 1 kilogram would be used;
   (e) any excavation referred to in paragraph A(c) would exceed 10
      metres in depth or 12 square metres in surface area;
   (f) in the case described in paragraph A(c) more than 10
      excavations would, as a result, be made within any area of 1
      hectare within the land during any period of 24 months; or
   (g) any structure assembled or provided would exceed 12 metres
      in height, or, where the structure would be within 3 kilometres
      of the perimeter of an aerodrome, 3 metres in height.

Conditions

A.2 Development is permitted by Class A subject to the following
conditions—
   (a) no operations shall be carried out between 6.00 pm and 7.00
      am;
   (b) no trees on the land shall be removed, felled, lopped or topped
      and no other thing shall be done on the land likely to harm or
      damage any trees, unless the mineral planning authority have
      so agreed in writing;
   (c) before any excavation (other than a borehole) is made, any
      topsoil and any subsoil shall be separately removed from the
      land to be excavated and stored separately from other excavated
      material and from each other;
   (d) within a period of 28 days from the cessation of operations
      unless the mineral planning authority have agreed otherwise
      in writing—

(i) any structure permitted by Class A and any waste material arising from other development so permitted shall be removed from the land,
(ii) any borehole shall be adequately sealed,
(iii) any other excavation shall be filled with material from the site,
(iv) the surface of the land on which any operations have been carried out shall be levelled and any topsoil replaced as the uppermost layer, and
(v) the land shall, so far as is practicable, be restored to its condition before the development took place, including the carrying out of any necessary seeding and replanting.

Class B
Permitted
development

B Development on any land consisting of—
(a) the drilling of boreholes;
(b) the carrying out of seismic surveys; or
(c) the making of other excavations,
for the purposes of mineral exploration, and the provision or assembly on that land or on adjoining land of any structure required in connection with any of those operations.

Development not
permitted

B.1 Development is not permitted by Class B if—
(a) it consists of the drilling of boreholes for petroleum exploration;
(b) the developer has not previously notified the mineral planning authority in writing of his intention to carry out the development (specifying the nature and location of the development);
(c) the relevant period has not elapsed;
(d) any explosive charge of more than 2 kilograms would be used;
(e) any excavation referred to in paragraph B(c) would exceed 10 metres in depth or 12 square metres in surface area; or
(f) any structure assembled or provided would exceed 12 metres in height.

Conditions

B.2 Development is permitted by Class B subject to the following conditions—
(a) the development shall be carried out in accordance with the details in the notification referred to in paragraph B.1(b), unless the mineral planning authority have otherwise agreed in writing;
(b) no trees on the land shall be removed, felled, lopped or topped and no other thing shall be done on the land likely to harm or damage any trees, unless specified in detail in the notification referred to in paragraph B.1(b) or the mineral planning authority have otherwise agreed in writing;
(c) before any excavation other than a borehole is made, any topsoil and any subsoil shall be separately removed from the land to be excavated and stored separately from other excavated material and from each other;
(d) within a period of 28 days from operations ceasing, unless the mineral planning authority have agreed otherwise in writing—
(i) any structure permitted by Class B and any waste material arising from other development so permitted shall be removed from the land,
(ii) any borehole shall be adequately sealed,
(iii) any other excavation shall be filled with material from the site,
(iv) the surface of the land shall be levelled and any topsoil replaced as the uppermost layer, and

     (v) the land shall, so far as is practicable, be restored to its condition before the development took place, including the carrying out of any necessary seeding and replanting, and

  (e) the development shall cease no later than a date six months after the elapse of the relevant period, unless the mineral planning authority have otherwise agreed in writing.

Interpretation of Class B

B.3 For the purposes of Class B—
"relevant period" means the period elapsing—
  (a) where a direction is not issued under article 7, 28 days after the notification referred to in paragraph B.1(b) or, if earlier, on the date on which the mineral planning authority notify the developer in writing that they will not issue such a direction, or
  (b) where a direction is issued under article 7, 28 days from the date on which notice of that decision is sent to the Secretary of State, or, if earlier, the date on which the mineral planning authority notify the developer that the Secretary of State has disallowed the direction.

Interpretation of Part 22

C For the purposes of Part 22—
"mineral exploration" means ascertaining the presence, extent or quality of any deposit of a mineral with a view to exploiting that mineral; and
"structure" includes a building, plant or machinery.

[1072]

NOTES
  Commencement: 3 June 1995.

PART 23
REMOVAL OF MATERIAL FROM MINERAL-WORKING DEPOSITS

Class A
Permitted development

A The removal of material of any description from a stockpile.

Class B
Permitted development

B The removal of material of any description from a mineral-working deposit other than a stockpile.

Development not permitted

B.1 Development is not permitted by Class B if—
  (a) the developer has not previously notified the mineral planning authority in writing of his intention to carry out the development and supplied them with the appropriate details;
  (b) the deposit covers a ground area exceeding 2 hectares, unless the deposit contains no mineral or other material which was deposited on the land more than 5 years before the development; or
  (c) the deposit derives from the carrying out of any operations permitted under Part 6 of this Schedule or any Class in a previous development order which it replaces.

Conditions

B.2 Development is permitted by Class B subject to the following conditions—
  (a) it shall be carried out in accordance with the details given in the notice sent to the mineral planning authority referred to in paragraph B.1(a) above, unless that authority have agreed otherwise in writing;

(b) if the mineral planning authority so require, the developer shall within a period of three months from the date of the requirement (or such other longer period as that authority may provide) submit to them for approval a scheme providing for the restoration and aftercare of the site;

(c) where such a scheme is required, the site shall be restored and aftercare shall be carried out in accordance with the provisions of the approved scheme;

(d) development shall not be commenced until the relevant period has elapsed.

Interpretation of Class B

B.3 For the purposes of Class B—

"appropriate details" means the nature of the development, the exact location of the mineral-working deposit from which the material would be removed, the proposed means of vehicular access to the site at which the development is to be carried out, and the earliest date at which any mineral presently contained in the deposit was deposited on the land; and

"relevant period" means the period elapsing—

(a) where a direction is not issued under article 7, 28 days after the notification referred to in paragraph B.1(a) or, if earlier, on the date on which the mineral planning authority notify the developer in writing that they will not issue such a direction; or

(b) where a direction is issued under article 7, 28 days from the date on which notice of that direction is sent to the Secretary of State, or, if earlier, the date on which the mineral planning authority notify the developer that the Secretary of State has disallowed the direction.

Interpretation of Part 23

C For the purposes of Part 23—

"stockpile" means a mineral-working deposit consisting primarily of minerals which have been deposited for the purposes of their processing or sale.

[1073]

NOTES
    Commencement: 3 June 1995.

PART 24

DEVELOPMENT BY TELECOMMUNICATIONS CODE SYSTEM OPERATORS

Class A
Permitted development

A Development by or on behalf of a telecommunications code system operator for the purpose of the operator's telecommunication system in, on, over or under land controlled by that operator or in accordance with his licence, consisting of—

(a) the installation, alteration or replacement of any telecommunication apparatus,

(b) the use of land in an emergency for a period not exceeding six months to station and operate moveable telecommunication apparatus required for the replacement of unserviceable telecommunication apparatus, including the provision of moveable structures on the land for the purposes of that use, or

(c) development ancillary to radio equipment housing.

Development not permitted

A.1 Development is not permitted by Class A(a) if—

(a) in the case of the installation of apparatus (other than on a building or other structure) the apparatus, excluding any antenna, would exceed a height of 15 metres above ground level;

(b) in the case of the alteration or replacement of apparatus already installed (other than on a building or other structure), the apparatus, excluding any antenna, would when altered or replaced exceed the height of the existing apparatus or a height of 15 metres above ground level, whichever is the greater;

(c) in the case of the installation, alteration or replacement of apparatus on a building or other structure, the height of the apparatus (taken by itself) would exceed—

    (i) 15 metres, where it is installed, or is to be installed, on a building or other structure which is 30 metres or more in height; or

    (ii) 10 metres in any other case;

(d) in the case of the installation, alteration or replacement of apparatus on a building or other structure, the highest part of the apparatus when installed, altered or replaced would exceed the height of the highest part of the building or structure by more than—

    (i) 10 metres, in the case of a building or structure which is 30 metres or more in height;

    (ii) 8 metres, in the case of a building or structure which is more than 15 metres but less than 30 metres in height;

    (iii) 6 metres in any other case;

(e) in the case of the installation, alteration or replacement of any apparatus other than—

    (i) a mast,

    (ii) an antenna,

    (iii) a public call box,

    (iv) any apparatus which does not project above the level of the surface of the ground, or

    (v) radio equipment housing,

the ground or base area of the structure would exceed 1.5 square metres;

(f) in the case of the installation, alteration or replacement of an antenna on a building or structure (other than a mast) which is less than 15 metres in height; on a mast located on such a building or structure; or, where the antenna is to be located below a height of 15 metres above ground level, on a building or structure (other than a mast) which is 15 metres or more in height—

    (i) the antenna is to be located on a wall or roof slope facing a highway which is within 20 metres of the building or structure on which the antenna is to be located;

    (ii) in the case of dish antennas, the size of any dish would exceed 0.9 metres or the aggregate size of all of the dishes would exceed 1.5 metres, when measured in any dimension;

    (iii) in the case of antennas other than dish antennas, the development would result in the presence on the building or structure of more than two antenna systems; or

    (iv) the building or structure is a listed building or a scheduled monument;

(g) in the case of the installation, alteration or replacement of an antenna on a building or structure (other than a mast) which is 15 metres or more in height, or on a mast located on such a building or structure, where the antenna is located at a height of 15 metres or above, measured from ground level—

    (i) in the case of dish antennas, the size of any dish would exceed 1.3 metres or the aggregate size of all of the dishes would exceed 3.5 metres, when measured in any dimension;

    (ii) in the case of antenna systems other than dish antennas, the development would result in the presence on the building or structure of more than three antenna systems; or

  (iii) the building or structure is a listed building or a scheduled monument;

(h) in the case of development of any article 1(5) land, it would consist of—

   (i) the installation or alteration of an antenna or of any apparatus which includes or is intended for the support of such an antenna; or

  (ii) the replacement of such an antenna or such apparatus by an antenna or apparatus which differs from that which is being replaced,

    unless the development is carried out in an emergency;

(i) it would consist of the installation, alteration or replacement of system apparatus within the meaning of section 8(6) of the Road Traffic (Driver Licensing and Information Systems) Act 1989 (definitions of driver information systems etc);

(j) in the case of the installation of a mast, on a building or structure which is less than 15 metres in height, such a mast would be within 20 metres of a highway;

(k) in the case of the installation, alteration or replacement of radio equipment housing—

   (i) the development is not ancillary to the use of any other telecommunication apparatus;

  (ii) it would exceed 90 cubic metres or, if located on the roof of a building, it would exceed 30 cubic metres;

  (iii) on any article 1(5) land, it would exceed 2 cubic metres, unless the development is carried out in an emergency; or

(l) it would consist of the installation, alteration or replacement of any telecommunication apparatus on, or within the curtilage of, a dwellinghouse.

Conditions   A.2(1) Class A(a) and Class A(c) development is permitted subject to the condition that any antenna or supporting apparatus, radio equipment housing or development ancillary to radio equipment housing constructed, installed, altered or replaced on a building in accordance with that permission shall, so far as is practicable, be sited so as to minimise its effect on the external appearance of the building.

(2) Class A(a) and Class A(c) development is permitted subject to the condition that any apparatus or structure provided in accordance with that permission shall be removed from the land, building or structure on which it is situated—

(a) if such development was carried out on any article 1(5) land in an emergency, at the expiry of the relevant period, or

(b) in any other case, as soon as reasonably practicable after it is no longer required for telecommunication purposes,

and such land, building or structure shall be restored to its condition before the development took place, or to any other condition as may be agreed in writing between the local planning authority and the developer.

(3) Class A(b) development is permitted subject to the condition that any apparatus or structure provided in accordance with that permission shall at the expiry of the relevant period be removed from the land and the land restored to its condition before the development took place.

(4) Class A development on—

(a) article 1(5) land (unless carried out in an emergency), or

(b) any other land and consisting of the construction, installation, alteration or replacement of a mast or a public call box, or of radio equipment housing with a volume in excess of 2 cubic metres, or of development ancillary to radio equipment housing,

is permitted subject to the following conditions—

(i) where the proposed development consists of the installation of a mast within 3 kilometres of the perimeter of an aerodrome, the developer shall notify the Civil Aviation Authority or the Secretary of State for Defence, as appropriate, of the proposal, before making the application required by sub-paragraph (ii);

(ii) before beginning the development, the developer shall apply to the local planning authority for a determination as to whether the prior approval of the authority will be required to the siting and appearance of the development;

(iii) the application shall be accompanied—

    (aa) by a written description of the proposed development and a plan indicating its proposed location together with any fee required to be paid; and

    (bb) where sub-paragraph (i) applies, by evidence that the Civil Aviation Authority or the Secretary of State for Defence, as the case may be, has been notified of the proposal;

(iv) the development shall not be begun before the occurrence of one of the following—

    (aa) the receipt by the applicant from the local planning authority of a written notice of their determination that such prior approval is not required;

    (bb) where the local planning authority gives the applicant notice that such prior approval is required, the giving of such approval to the applicant within 28 days following the date on which they received his application; or

    (cc) the expiry of 28 days following the date on which the local planning authority received the application, without the local planning authority making any determination as to whether such approval is required, notifying the applicant of their determination, or giving or refusing approval to the siting or appearance of the development;

(v) the development shall, except to the extent that the local planning authority otherwise agree in writing, be carried out—

    (aa) where prior approval has been given as mentioned in sub-paragraph (iv)(bb), in accordance with the details approved;

    (bb) in any other case, in accordance with the details submitted with the application; and

(vi) the development shall be begun—

    (aa) where prior approval has been given as mentioned in sub-paragraph (iv)(bb), not later than the expiration of five years beginning with the date on which approval was given;

    (bb) in any other case, not later than the expiration of five years beginning with the date on which the local planning authority were given the information referred to in sub-paragraph (iii).

(5) In a case of emergency, development on any article 1(5) land is permitted by Class A subject to the condition that the operator shall

give written notice to the local planning authority of such development as soon as possible after the emergency begins.

Interpretation of
Class A

A.3 For the purposes of Class A—

"antenna system" means a set of antennas installed on a building or structure and operated by a single telecommunications code system operator in accordance with his licence;

"development ancillary to radio equipment housing" means the construction, installation, alteration or replacement of structures, equipment or means of access which are ancillary to and reasonably required for the purposes of radio equipment housing;

"development in accordance with a licence" means development carried out by an operator in pursuance of a right conferred on that operator under the telecommunications code, and in accordance with any conditions, relating to the application of that code imposed by the terms of his licence;

"land controlled by an operator" means land occupied by the operator in right of a freehold interest or a leasehold interest under a lease granted for a term of not less than 10 years;

"mast" means a radio mast or a radio tower;

"relevant period" means a period which expires—

(i) six months from the commencement of the construction, installation, alteration or replacement of any apparatus or structure permitted by Class A(a) or Class A(c) or from the commencement of the use permitted by Class A(b), as the case may be, or

(ii) when the need for such apparatus, structure or use ceases,

whichever occurs first;

"telecommunication apparatus" means any apparatus falling within the definition of that term in paragraph 1 of Schedule 2 to the Telecommunications Act 1984 ("the 1984 Act") (the telecommunications code), and includes radio equipment housing;

"the telecommunications code" means the code contained in Schedule 2 to the 1984 Act;

"telecommunications code system operator" means a person who has been granted a licence under section 7 of the 1984 Act (power to license systems) which applies the telecommunications code to him in pursuance of section 10 of that Act (the telecommunications code); and

"telecommunication system" has the meaning assigned to that term by section 4(1) of the 1984 Act (meaning of "telecommunication system" and related expressions).

[1074]

NOTES

Commencement: 3 June 1995.

PART 25

OTHER TELECOMMUNICATIONS DEVELOPMENT

Class A
Permitted
development

A The installation, alteration or replacement on any building or other structure of a height of 15 metres or more of a microwave antenna and any structure intended for the support of a microwave antenna.

Development not
permitted

A.1 Development is not permitted by Class A if—

(a) the building is a dwellinghouse or the building or other structure is within the curtilage of a dwellinghouse;

(b) it would consist of development of a kind described in paragraph A of Part 24;

(c) the development would result in the presence on the building or structure of more than two microwave antennas;

(d) in the case of a satellite antenna, the size of the antenna, including its supporting structure but excluding any projecting feed element, would exceed 90 centimetres;

(e) in the case of a terrestrial microwave antenna—

　(i) the size of the antenna, when measured in any dimension but excluding any projecting feed element, would exceed 1.3 metres; and

　(ii) the highest part of the antenna or its supporting structure would be more than 3 metres higher than the highest part of the building or structure on which it is installed or is to be installed;

(f) it is on article 1(5) land; or

(g) it would consist of the installation, alteration or replacement of system apparatus within the meaning of section 8(6) of the Road Traffic (Driver Licensing and Information Systems) Act 1989 (definitions of driver information systems etc).

Conditions　　A.2 Development is permitted by Class A subject to the following conditions—

(a) the antenna shall, so far as is practicable, be sited so as to minimise its effect on the external appearance of the building or structure on which it is installed;

(b) an antenna no longer needed for the reception or transmission of microwave radio energy shall be removed from the building or structure as soon as reasonably practicable.

Class B
Permitted　　**B The installation, alteration or replacement on any building or**
development　　**other structure of a height of less than 15 metres of a satellite**
　　　　　　　antenna.

Development not　　B.1 Development is not permitted by Class B if—
permitted

(a) the building is a dwellinghouse or the building or other structure is within the curtilage of a dwellinghouse;

(b) it would consist of development of a kind described in paragraph A of Part 24;

(c) it would consist of the installation, alteration or replacement of system apparatus within the meaning of section 8(6) of the Road Traffic (Driver Licensing and Information Systems) Act 1989 (definitions of driver information systems etc);

(d) the size of the antenna (excluding any projecting feed element, reinforcing rim, mountings or brackets) when measured in any dimension would exceed—

　(i) 90 centimetres in the case of an antenna to be installed on a building or structure on article 1(4) land;

　(ii) 70 centimetres in any other case;

(e) the highest part of an antenna to be installed on a roof would, when installed, exceed in height the highest part of the roof;

(f) there is any other satellite antenna on the building or other structure on which the antenna is to be installed;

(g) it would consist of the installation of an antenna on a chimney;

(h) it would consist of the installation of an antenna on a wall or roof slope which fronts a waterway in the Broads, or a highway elsewhere.

Condition　　B.2 Development is permitted by Class B subject to the following conditions—

(a) the antenna shall, so far as practicable, be sited so as to minimise its effect on the external appearance of the building or structure on which it is installed;

(b) an antenna no longer needed for the reception or transmission of microwave radio energy shall be removed from the building or structure as soon as reasonably practicable.

[1075]

NOTES
Commencement: 3 June 1995.

PART 26

DEVELOPMENT BY THE HISTORIC BUILDINGS AND MONUMENTS COMMISSION FOR ENGLAND

Class A

Permitted development	**A Development by or on behalf of the Historic Buildings and Monuments Commission for England, consisting of—**

    (a) the maintenance, repair or restoration of any building or monument;

    (b) the erection of screens, fences or covers designed or intended to protect or safeguard any building or monument; or

    (c) the carrying out of works to stabilise ground conditions by any cliff, watercourse or the coastline;

where such works are required for the purposes of securing the preservation of any building or monument.

Development not permitted

A.1 Development is not permitted by Class A(a) if the works involve the extension of the building or monument.

Condition

A.2 Except for development also falling within Class A(a), Class A(b) development is permitted subject to the condition that any structure erected in accordance with that permission shall be removed at the expiry of a period of six months (or such longer period as the local planning authority may agree in writing) from the date on which work to erect the structure was begun.

Interpretation of Class A

A.3 For the purposes of Class A—
"building or monument" means any building or monument in the guardianship of the Historic Buildings and Monuments Commission for England or owned, controlled or managed by them.

[1076]

NOTES
Commencement: 3 June 1995.

PART 27

USE BY MEMBERS OF CERTAIN RECREATIONAL ORGANISATIONS

Class A

Permitted development

A The use of land by members of a recreational organisation for the purposes of recreation or instruction, and the erection or placing of tents on the land for the purposes of the use.

Development not permitted

A.1 Development is not permitted by Class A if the land is a building or is within the curtilage of a dwellinghouse.

Interpretation of Class A

A.2 For the purposes of Class A—
"recreational organisation" means an organisation holding a certificate of exemption under section 269 of the Public Health Act 1936 (power of local authority to control use of moveable dwellings).

[1077]

NOTES
Commencement: 3 June 1995.

PART 28

DEVELOPMENT AT AMUSEMENT PARKS

Class A
Permitted
development

A Development on land used as an amusement park consisting of—

(a) **the erection of booths or stalls or the installation of plant or machinery to be used for or in connection with the entertainment of the public within the amusement park; or**

(b) **the extension, alteration or replacement of any existing booths or stalls, plant or machinery so used.**

Development not
permitted

A.1 Development is not permitted by Class A if—
(a) the plant or machinery would—
    (i) if the land or pier is within 3 kilometres of the perimeter of an aerodrome, exceed a height of 25 metres or the height of the highest existing structure (whichever is the lesser), or
    (ii) in any other case, exceed a height of 25 metres;
(b) in the case of an extension to an existing building or structure, that building or structure would as a result exceed 5 metres above ground level or the height of the roof of the existing building or structure, whichever is the greater, or
(c) in any other case, the height of the building or structure erected, extended, altered or replaced would exceed 5 metres above ground level.

Interpretation of
Class A

A.2 For the purposes of Class A—
"amusement park" means an enclosed area of open land, or any part of a seaside pier, which is principally used (other than by way of a temporary use) as a funfair or otherwise for the purposes of providing public entertainment by means of mechanical amusements and side-shows; but, where part only of an enclosed area is commonly so used as a funfair or for such public entertainment, only the part so used shall be regarded as an amusement park; and "booths or stalls" includes buildings or structures similar to booths or stalls.

[1078]

NOTES
    Commencement: 3 June 1995.

PART 29

DRIVER INFORMATION SYSTEMS

Class A
Permitted
development

A The installation, alteration or replacement of system apparatus by or on behalf of a driver information system operator.

Development not
permitted

A.1 Development is not permitted by Class A if—
(a) in the case of the installation, alteration or replacement of system apparatus other than on a building or other structure—
    (i) the ground or base area of the system apparatus would exceed 1.5 square metres; or
    (ii) the system apparatus would exceed a height of 15 metres above ground level;
(b) in the case of the installation, alteration or replacement of system apparatus on a building or other structure—
    (i) the highest part of the apparatus when installed, altered, or replaced would exceed in height the highest part of the building or structure by more than 3 metres; or

         (ii) the development would result in the presence on the building or structure of more than two microwave antennas.

Conditions   A.2 Development is permitted by Class A subject to the following conditions—

       (a) any system apparatus shall, so far as practicable, be sited so as to minimise its effect on the external appearance of any building or other structure on which it is installed;

       (b) any system apparatus which is no longer needed for a driver information system shall be removed as soon as reasonably practicable.

Interpretation of A.3 For the purposes of Class A—
Class A

       "driver information system operator" means a person granted an operator's licence under section 10 of the Road Traffic (Driver Licensing and Information Systems) Act 1989 (operators' licences); and

       "system apparatus" has the meaning assigned to that term by section 8(6) of that Act (definitions of driver information systems etc).

                           [1079]

NOTES
 Commencement: 3 June 1995.

PART 30
TOLL ROAD FACILITIES

Class A
Permitted   **A** **Development consisting of—**
development   **(a)** **the setting up and the maintenance, improvement or other alteration of facilities for the collection of tolls;**

       (b) **the provision of a hard surface to be used for the parking of vehicles in connection with the use of such facilities.**

Development not A.1 Development is not permitted by Class A if—
permitted

       (a) it is not located within 100 metres (measured along the ground) of the boundary of a toll road;

       (b) the height of any building or structure would exceed—

         (i) 7.5 metres excluding any rooftop structure; or

        (ii) 10 metres including any rooftop structure;

       (c) the aggregate area of the floor space at or above ground level of any building or group of buildings within a toll collection area, excluding the floor space of any toll collection booth, would exceed 1,500 square metres.

Conditions   A.2 In the case of any article 1(5) land, development is permitted by Class A subject to the following conditions—

       (a) the developer shall, before beginning the development, apply to the local planning authority for a determination as to whether the prior approval of the authority will be required to the siting, design and external appearance of the facilities for the collection of tolls;

       (b) the application shall be accompanied by a written description, together with plans and elevations, of the proposed development and any fee required to be paid;

       (c) the development shall not be begun before the occurrence of one of the following—

         (i) the receipt by the applicant from the local planning authority of a written notice of their determination that such prior approval is not required;

(ii) where the local planning authority give the applicant notice within 28 days following the date of receiving his application of their determination that such prior approval is required, the giving of such approval; or

(iii) the expiry of 28 days following the date on which the application was received by the local planning authority without the local planning authority making any determination as to whether such approval is required or notifying the applicant of their determination;

(d) the development shall, except to the extent that the local planning authority otherwise agree in writing, be carried out—

(i) where prior approval is required, in accordance with the details approved;

(ii) where prior approval is not required, in accordance with the details submitted with the application;

and

(e) the development shall be carried out—

(i) where approval has been given by the local planning authority, within a period of five years from the date on which the approval was given;

(ii) in any other case, within a period of five years from the date on which the local planning authority were given the information referred to in sub-paragraph (b).

Interpretation of
Class A

A.3 For the purposes of Class A—

"facilities for the collection of tolls" means such buildings, structures, or other facilities as are reasonably required for the purpose of or in connection with the collection of tolls in pursuance of a toll order;

"ground level" means the level of the surface of the ground immediately adjacent to the building or group of buildings in question or, where the level of the surface of the ground on which it is situated or is to be situated is not uniform, the level of the highest part of the surface of the ground adjacent to it;

"rooftop structure" means any apparatus or structure which is reasonably required to be located on and attached to the roof, being an apparatus or structure which is—

(a) so located for the provision of heating, ventilation, air conditioning, water, gas or electricity;

(b) lift machinery; or

(c) reasonably required for safety purposes;

"toll" means a toll which may be charged pursuant to a toll order;

"toll collection area" means an area of land where tolls are collected in pursuance of a toll order, and includes any facilities for the collection of tolls;

"toll collection booth" means any building or structure designed or adapted for the purpose of collecting tolls in pursuance of a toll order;

"toll order" has the same meaning as in Part I of the New Roads and Street Works Act 1991 (new roads in England and Wales); and

"toll road" means a road which is the subject of a toll order.

[1080]

NOTES
  Commencement: 3 June 1995.

PART 31

DEMOLITION OF BUILDINGS

Class A
**Permitted
development**

A Any building operation consisting of the demolition of a building.

Development not
permitted

A.1 Development is not permitted by Class A where—
(a) the building has been rendered unsafe or otherwise uninhabit-
able by the action or inaction of any person having an interest
in the land on which the building stands; and
(b) it is practicable to secure safety or health by works of repair
or works for affording temporary support.

Conditions

A.2 Development is permitted by Class A subject to the following
conditions—
(a) where demolition is urgently necessary in the interests of
safety or health and the measures immediately necessary in
such interests are the demolition of the building the developer
shall, as soon as reasonably practicable, give the local planning
authority a written justification of the demolition;
(b) where the demolition does not fall within sub-paragraph (a)
and is not excluded demolition—
(i) the developer shall, before beginning the development,
apply to the local planning authority for a determination
as to whether the prior approval of the authority will be
required to the method of demolition and any proposed
restoration of the site;
(ii) the application shall be accompanied by a written
description of the proposed development, a statement that
a notice has been posted in accordance with sub-paragraph
(iii) and any fee required to be paid;
(iii) subject to sub-paragraph (iv), the applicant shall display
a site notice by site display on or near the land on which
the building to be demolished is sited and shall leave the
notice in place for not less than 21 days in the period of
28 days beginning with the date on which the application
was submitted to the local planning authority;
(iv) where the site notice is, without any fault or intention of
the applicant, removed, obscured or defaced before the
period of 21 days referred to in sub-paragraph (iii) has
elapsed, he shall be treated as having complied with the
requirements of that sub-paragraph if he has taken
reasonable steps for protection of the notice and, if need
be, its replacement;
(v) the development shall not be begun before the occurrence
of one of the following—
(aa) the receipt by the applicant from the local planning
authority of a written notice of their determination
that such prior approval is not required;
(bb) where the local planning authority give the applicant
notice within 28 days following the date of receiving
his application of their determination that such prior
approval is required, the giving of such approval; or
(cc) the expiry of 28 days following the date on which
the application was received by the local planning
authority without the local planning authority
making any determination as to whether such
approval is required or notifying the applicant of
their determination;
(vi) the development shall, except to the extent that the local
planning authority otherwise agree in writing, be carried
out—
(aa) where prior approval is required, in accordance with
the details approved;
(bb) where prior approval is not required, in accordance
with the details submitted with the application;

and
(vii) the development shall be carried out—
    (aa) where approval has been given by the local planning authority, within a period of five years from the date on which approval was given;
    (bb) in any other case, within a period of five years from the date on which the local planning authority were given the information referred to in sub-paragraph (ii).

Interpretation of
Class A

A.3 For the purposes of Class A—
"excluded demolition" means demolition—
(a) on land which is the subject of a planning permission, for the redevelopment of the land, granted on an application or deemed to be granted under Part III of the Act (control over development),
(b) required or permitted to be carried out by or under any enactment, or
(c) required to be carried out by virtue of a relevant obligation;
"relevant obligation" means—
(a) an obligation arising under an agreement made under section 106 of the Act, as originally enacted (agreements regulating development or use of land);
(b) a planning obligation entered into under section 106 of the Act, as substituted by section 12 of the Planning and Compensation Act 1991 (planning obligations), or under section 299A of the Act (Crown planning obligations);
(c) an obligation arising under or under an agreement made under any provision corresponding to section 106 of the Act, as originally enacted or as substituted by the Planning and Compensation Act 1991, or to section 299A of the Act; and
"site notice" means a notice containing—
(a) the name of the applicant,
(b) a description, including the address, of the building or buildings which it is proposed be demolished,
(c) a statement that the applicant has applied to the local planning authority for a determination as to whether the prior approval of the authority will be required to the method of demolition and any proposed restoration of the site,
(d) the date on which the applicant proposes to carry out the demolition, and
(e) the name and address of the local planning authority,
and which is signed and dated by or on behalf of the applicant.

Class B
Permitted
development

B Any building operation consisting of the demolition of the whole or any part of any gate, fence, wall or other means of enclosure.

[1081]

NOTES
Commencement: 3 June 1995.

PART 32

SCHOOLS, COLLEGES, UNIVERSITIES AND HOSPITALS

Class A
Permitted
development

A The erection on the site of any school, college, university or hospital of any building required for use as part of, or for a purpose incidental to the use of, the school, college, university or hospital as such, as the case may be.

Development not   A.1 Development is not permitted by Class A—
permitted   (a) unless—
                                  (i) in the case of school, college or university buildings, the
                                      predominant use of the existing buildings on the site is
                                      for the provision of education, or
                                  (ii) in the case of hospital buildings, the predominant use of
                                       the existing buildings on the site is for the provision of
                                       any medical or health services;
                              (b) where the cumulative total floor space of any buildings erected
                                  on a particular site (other than the original school, college,
                                  university or hospital buildings) would exceed 10% of the
                                  total floor space of the original school, college, university or
                                  hospital buildings on that site;
                              (c) where the cumulative total cubic content of buildings erected
                                  on a particular site (other than the original school, college,
                                  university or hospital buildings) would exceed 250 cubic
                                  metres;
                              (d) where any part of a building erected would be within 20
                                  metres of the boundary of the site;
                              (e) where, as a result of the development, any land, used as a
                                  playing field immediately before the development took place,
                                  could no longer be so used.

Condition   A.2 Development is permitted by Class A subject to the condition
                         that, in the case of any article 1(5) land, any materials used shall be
                         of a similar appearance to those used for the original school, college,
                         university or hospital buildings.

Interpretation of   A.3 For the purposes of Class A—
Class A   "cumulative total floor space" or "cumulative total cubic
                         content", as the case may be, of buildings erected, includes the
                         total floor space or total cubic content of any existing buildings
                         previously erected at any time under Class A; and
                             "original school, college, university or hospital buildings" means
                         any school, college, university or hospital buildings, as the case
                         may be, other than any buildings erected at any time under Class
                         A.

                                                                                        [1082]

NOTES
   Commencement: 3 June 1995.

PART 33

CLOSED CIRCUIT TELEVISION CAMERAS

Class A
Permitted   **A The installation, alteration or replacement on a building of a**
development   **closed circuit television camera to be used for security purposes.**

Development not   A.1 Development is not permitted by Class A if—
permitted   (a) the building on which the camera would be installed, altered
                                  or replaced is a listed building or a scheduled monument;
                              (b) the dimensions of the camera including its housing exceed 75
                                  centimetres by 25 centimetres by 25 centimetres;
                              (c) any part of the camera would, when installed, altered or
                                  replaced, be less than 250 centimetres above ground level;
                              (d) any part of the camera would, when installed, altered or
                                  replaced, protrude from the surface of the building by more
                                  than one metre when measured from the surface of the
                                  building;

(e) any part of the camera would, when installed, altered or replaced, be in contact with the surface of the building at a point which is more than one metre from any other point of contact;

(f) any part of the camera would be less than 10 metres from any part of another camera installed on a building;

(g) the development would result in the presence of more than four cameras on the same side of the building; or

(h) the development would result in the presence of more than 16 cameras on the building.

Conditions
A.2 Development is permitted by Class A subject to the following conditions—

(a) the camera shall, so far as practicable, be sited so as to minimise its effect on the external appearance of the building on which it is situated;

(b) the camera shall be removed as soon as reasonably practicable after it is no longer required for security purposes.

Interpretation of Class A
A.3 For the purposes of Class A—

"camera", except in paragraph A.1(b), includes its housing, pan and tilt mechanism, infra red illuminator, receiver, mountings and brackets; and

"ground level" means the level of the surface of the ground immediately adjacent to the building or, where the level of the surface of the ground is not uniform, the level of the highest part of the surface of the ground adjacent to it.

[1083]

NOTES

Commencement: 3 June 1995.

SCHEDULE 3

Article 9

STATUTORY INSTRUMENTS REVOKED

1 Title of Instrument	2 Reference	3 Extent of Revocation
The Town and Country Planning General Development Order 1988	SI 1988/1813	Paragraphs (3), (5) (6) and (7) of article 1 and articles 3, 4, 5 and 6 and Schedules 1 and 2
The Town and Country Planning General Development (Amendment) Order 1989	SI 1989/603	Paragraphs (2) to (8) of article 2
The Town and Country Planning General Development (Amendment) (No 2) Order 1989	SI 1989/1590	Paragraphs (3) and (4) of article 2
The Town and Country Planning General Development (Amendment) Order 1990	SI 1990/457	The whole Order to the extent not already revoked
The Town and Country Planning General Development (Amendment) (No 2) Order 1990	SI 1990/2032	The whole Order
The Town and Country Planning General Development (Amendment) Order 1991	SI 1991/1536	The whole Order to the extent not already revoked
The Town and Country Planning General Development (Amendment) (No 2) Order 1991	SI 1991/2268	The whole Order to the extent not already revoked

1 *Title of Instrument*	2 *Reference*	3 *Extent of Revocation*
The Town and Country Planning General Development (Amendment) (No 3) Order 1991	SI 1991/2805	Articles 8, 9 and 10 and the Schedule
The Town and Country Planning General Development (Amendment) Order 1992	SI 1992/609	The whole Order
The Town and Country Planning General Development (Amendment) (No 2) Order 1992	SI 1992/658	Article 3
The Town and Country Planning General Development (Amendment) (No 3) Order 1992	SI 1992/1280	The whole Order
The Town and Country Planning General Development (Amendment) (No 4) Order 1992	SI 1992/1493	Articles 8, 9 and 12(2)
The Town and Country Planning General Development (Amendment) (No 5) Order 1992	SI 1992/1563	Paragraph 2 of the Schedule
The Town and Country Planning General Development (Amendment) (No 6) Order 1992	SI 1992/2450	Articles 2, 3, 4 and 6
The Town and Country Planning General Development (Amendment) Order 1994	SI 1994/678	Article 4
The Town and Country Planning General Development (Amendment) (No 2) Order 1994	SI 1994/2595	Articles 4, 5 and 6 and paragraph (3) of article 7
The Town and Country Planning General Development (Amendment) Order 1995	SI 1995/298	The whole Order except article 3(1)

[1084]

NOTES
    Commencement: 3 June 1995.

TOWN AND COUNTRY PLANNING (GENERAL DEVELOPMENT PROCEDURE) ORDER 1995
(SI 1995/419)

NOTES
    Made: 22 February 1995.
    Authority: Town and Country Planning Act 1990, ss 59, 61(1), 65, 69, 71, 73(3), 74, 77(4), 78, 79(4), 188, 193, 196(4), 333(7), Sch 1, paras 5, 6, 7(6), 8(6).

ARRANGEMENT OF ARTICLES

1. Citation, commencement and interpretation

(1) This Order may be cited as the Town and Country Planning (General Development Procedure) Order 1995 and shall come into force on 3rd June 1995.

(2) In this Order, unless the context otherwise requires—

"the Act" means the Town and Country Planning Act 1990;

"building" includes any structure or erection, and any part of a building, as defined in this article, but does not include plant or machinery or any structure in the nature of plant or machinery;

"dwellinghouse" does not include a building containing one or more flats, or a flat contained within such a building;

"environmental information" and "environmental statement" have the same meanings respectively as in regulation 2 of the Town and Country Planning (Assessment of Environmental Effects) Regulations 1988 (interpretation);

"erection", in relation to buildings as defined in this article, includes extension, alteration, or re-erection;

"flat" means a separate and self-contained set of premises constructed or adapted for use for the purpose of a dwelling and forming part of a building from some other part of which it is divided horizontally;

"floor space" means the total floor space in a building or buildings;

"landscaping" means the treatment of land (other than buildings) being the site or part of the site in respect of which an outline planning permission is granted, for the purpose of enhancing or protecting the amenities of the site and the area in which it is situated and includes screening by fences, walls or other means, the planting of trees, hedges, shrubs or grass, the formation of banks, terraces or other earthworks, the laying out of gardens or courts, and the provision of other amenity features;

"by local advertisement" means by publication of the notice in a newspaper circulating in the locality in which the land to which the application relates is situated;

"mining operations" means the winning and working of minerals in, on or under land, whether by surface or underground working;

"outline planning permission" means a planning permission for the erection of a building, which is granted subject to a condition requiring the subsequent approval of the local planning authority with respect to one or more reserved matters;

"proposed highway" has the same meaning as in section 329 of the Highways Act 1980 (further provision as to interpretation);

"1988 Regulations" means the Town and Country Planning (Applications) Regulations 1988;

"reserved matters" in relation to an outline planning permission, or an application for such permission, means any of the following matters in respect of which details have not been given in the application, namely—

    (a) siting,
    (b) design,
    (c) external appearance,
    (d) means of access,
    (e) the landscaping of the site;

"by site display" means by the posting of the notice by firm affixture to some object, sited and displayed in such a way as to be easily visible and legible by members of the public;

"special road" means a highway or proposed highway which is a special road in accordance with section 16 of the Highways Act 1980 (general provisions as to special roads);

"trunk road" means a highway or proposed highway which is a trunk road by virtue of sections 10(1) or 19 of the Highways Act 1980 (general provisions as to trunk roads, and certain special roads and other highways to become trunk roads) or any other enactment or any instrument made under any enactment. **[1085]**

NOTES
Commencement: 3 June 1995.

2. Application

(1) This Order applies to all land in England and Wales, but where land is the subject of a special development order, whether made before or after the commencement of this Order, this Order shall apply to that land only to such extent and subject to such modifications as may be specified in the special development order.

(2) Nothing in this Order shall apply to any permission which is deemed to be granted under section 222 of the Act (planning permission not needed for advertisements complying with regulations). **[1086]**

NOTES
Commencement: 3 June 1995.

3. Applications for outline planning permission

(1) Where an application is made to the local planning authority for outline planning permission, the authority may grant permission subject to a condition specifying reserved matters for the authority's subsequent approval.

(2) Where the authority who are to determine an application for outline planning permission are of the opinion that, in the circumstances of the case, the application ought not to be considered separately from all or any of the reserved matters, they shall within the period of one month beginning with the receipt of the application notify the applicant that they are unable to determine it unless further details are submitted, specifying the further details they require.   **[1087]**

NOTES
Commencement: 3 June 1995.

4. Applications for approval of reserved matters

An application for approval of reserved matters—

   (a) shall be made in writing to the local planning authority and shall give sufficient information to enable the authority to identify the outline planning permission in respect of which it is made;

   (b) shall include such particulars, and be accompanied by such plans and drawings, as are necessary to deal with the matters reserved in the outline planning permission; and

   (c) except where the authority indicate that a lesser number is required, shall be accompanied by three copies of the application and the plans and drawings submitted with it.   **[1088]**

NOTES
Commencement: 3 June 1995.

4A. Applications in respect of Crown land

See SI 1995/1139, reg 2, Sch at **[1134]**.

5. General provisions relating to applications

(1) Any application made under regulation 3 of the 1988 Regulations (applications for planning permission) or article 4 above, shall be made—

   (a) where the application relates to land in Greater London or a metropolitan county, to the local planning authority;

   (b) where the application relates to land in neither Greater London nor a metropolitan county and—

      (i) that land is in a National Park, or

      (ii) the application relates to a county matter,

   to the county planning authority;

   (c) in any other case, to the district planning authority.

(2) When the local planning authority with whom an application has to be lodged receive—

   (a) in the case of an application made under paragraph (1) of regulation 3 of the 1988 Regulations, the form of application required by that paragraph, together with the certificate or other documents required by article 7;

   (b) in the case of an application made under regulation 3(3) of the 1988 Regulations, sufficient information to enable the authority to identify the previous grant of planning permission, together with the certificate or other documents required by article 7;

   (c) in the case of an application made under article 4 above, the documents and information required by that article, and the fee, if any, required to be paid in respect of the application, the authority shall as soon as is reasonably practicable, send to the applicant an acknowledgement of the application in the terms (or substantially in the terms) set out in Part 1 of Schedule 1 hereto.

(3) Where an application is made to a county planning authority in accordance with paragraph (1), that authority shall, as soon as practicable, send a copy of the application and of any accompanying plans and drawings to the district planning authority, if any.

(4) Where, after sending an acknowledgement as required by paragraph (2) of this article, the local planning authority consider that the application is invalid by reason of a failure to comply with the requirements of regulation 3 of the 1988 Regulations or article 4 above or any other statutory requirement, they shall as soon as reasonably practicable notify the applicant that his application is invalid.

(5) In this article, "county matter" has the meaning given to that expression in paragraph 1(1) of Schedule 1 to the Act (local planning authorities — distribution of functions). **[1089]**

NOTES
Commencement: 3 June 1995.

6. Notice of applications for planning permission

(1) Subject to paragraph (2), an applicant for planning permission shall give requisite notice of the application to any person (other than the applicant) who on the prescribed date is an owner of the land to which the application relates, or a tenant,—

    (a) by serving the notice on every such person whose name and address is known to him; and

    (b) where he has taken reasonable steps to ascertain the names and addresses of every such person, but has been unable to do so, by local advertisement after the prescribed date.

(2) In the case of an application for planning permission for development consisting of the winning and working of minerals by underground operations, instead of giving notice in the manner provided for by paragraph (1), the applicant shall give requisite notice of the application to any person (other than the applicant) who on the prescribed date is an owner of any of the land to which the application relates, or a tenant,—

    (a) by serving the notice on every such person whom the applicant knows to be such a person and whose name and address is known to him;

    (b) by local advertisement after the prescribed date; and

    (c) by site display in at least one place in every parish or community within which there is situated any part of the land to which the application relates, leaving the notice in position for not less than seven days in the period of 21 days immediately preceding the making of the application to the local planning authority.

(3) The notice required by paragraph (2)(c) shall (in addition to any other matters required to be contained in it) name a place within the area of the local planning authority to whom the application is made where a copy of the application for planning permission, and of all plans and other documents submitted with it, will be open to inspection by the public at all reasonable hours during such period as may be specified in the notice.

(4) Where the notice is, without any fault or intention of the applicant, removed,

obscured or defaced before the period of seven days referred to in paragraph (2)(c) has elapsed, he shall be treated as having complied with the requirements of that paragraph if he has taken reasonable steps for protection of the notice and, if need be, its replacement.

(5)

(a) The date prescribed for the purposes of section 65(2) of the Act (notice etc of applications for planning permission), and the ''prescribed date'' for the purposes of this article, is the day 21 days before the date of the application;

(b) The applications prescribed for the purposes of paragraph (c) of the definition of ''owner'' in section 65(8) of the Act are minerals applications, and the minerals prescribed for the purposes of that paragraph are any minerals other than oil, gas, coal, gold or silver.

(6) In this article—

''minerals applications'' mean applications for planning permission for development consisting of the winning and working of minerals;

''requisite notice'' means notice in the appropriate form set out in Part 1 of Schedule 2 to this Order or in a form substantially to the like effect; and

''tenant'' means the tenant of an agricultural holding any part of which is comprised in the land to which an application relates. **[1090]**

NOTES
    Commencement: 3 June 1995.
    Modification: see SI 1995/1139, reg 2, Sch at **[1134]**.

7. Certificates in relation to notice of applications for planning permission

(1) Where an application for planning permission is made, the applicant shall certify, in the appropriate form prescribed in Part 2 of Schedule 2 to this Order or in a form substantially to the like effect, that the requirements of article 6 have been satisfied.

(2) If an applicant has cause to rely on paragraph (4) of article 6, the certificate must state the relevant circumstances. **[1091]**

NOTES
    Commencement: 3 June 1995.

8. Publicity for applications for planning permission

(1) An application for planning permission shall be publicised by the local planning authority to which the application is made in the manner prescribed by this article.

(2) In the case of an application for planning permission for development which—

(a) is the subject of an E.A. Schedule 1 or E.A. Schedule 2 application accompanied by an environmental statement;

(b) does not accord with the provisions of the development plan in force in the area in which the land to which the application relates is situated; or

(c) would affect a right of way to which Part III of the Wildlife and Countryside Act 1981 (public rights of way) applies,

the application shall be publicised in the manner specified in paragraph (3).

(3) An application falling within paragraph (2) (''a paragraph (2) application'') shall be publicised by giving requisite notice—

(a) by site display in at least one place on or near the land to which the application relates for not less than 21 days, and

(b) by local advertisement.

(4) In the case of an application for planning permission which is not a paragraph (2) application, if the development proposed is major development the application shall be publicised by giving requisite notice—

(a) (i) by site display in at least one place on or near the land to which the application relates for not less than 21 days, or

(ii) by serving the notice on any adjoining owner or occupier,

and

(b) by local advertisement.

(5) In a case to which neither paragraph (2) nor paragraph (4) applies, the application shall be publicised by giving requisite notice—

(a) by site display in at least one place on or near the land to which the application relates for not less than 21 days, or

(b) by serving the notice on any adjoining owner or occupier.

(6) Where the notice is, without any fault or intention of the local planning authority, removed, obscured or defaced before the period of 21 days referred to in paragraph (3)(a), (4)(a)(i) or (5)(a) has elapsed, the authority shall be treated as having complied with the requirements of the relevant paragraph if they have taken reasonable steps for protection of the notice and, if need be, its replacement.

(7) In this article—

"adjoining owner or occupier" means any owner or occupier of any land adjoining the land to which the application relates;

"E.A. Schedule 1 application" and "E.A. Schedule 2 application" have the same meanings as "Schedule 1 application" and "Schedule 2 application" respectively in regulation 2 of the Town and Country Planning (Assessment of Environmental Effects) Regulations 1988 (interpretation);

"major development" means development involving any one or more of the following—

(a) the winning and working of minerals or the use of land for mineral-working deposits;

(b) waste development;

(c) the provision of dwellinghouses where—

(i) the number of dwellinghouses to be provided is 10 or more; or

(ii) the development is to be carried out on a site having an area of 0.5 hectare or more and it is not known whether the development falls within paragraph (c)(i);

(d) the provision of a building or buildings where the floor space to be created by the development is 1,000 square metres or more; or

(e) development carried out on a site having an area of 1 hectare or more;

"requisite notice" means notice in the appropriate form set out in Schedule 3 to this Order or in a form substantially to the like effect;

"waste development" means any operational development designed to be used wholly or mainly for the purpose of, or a material change of use to, treating, storing, processing or disposing of refuse or waste materials.

[1092]

NOTES
Commencement: 3 June 1995.

9. Applications for planning permission referred to the Secretary of State and appeals to the Secretary of State

(1) Articles 6 and 7 apply to any appeal to the Secretary of State under section 78 of the Act (right to appeal against planning decisions and failure to take such decisions) as they apply to applications for planning permission.

(2) Subject to paragraph (3), if the local planning authority have failed to satisfy the requirements of article 8 in respect of an application for planning permission at the time the application is referred to the Secretary of State under section 77 of the Act (reference of applications to Secretary of State), or any appeal to the Secretary of State is made under section 78 of the Act, article 8 shall continue to apply, as if such referral or appeal to the Secretary of State had not been made.

(3) Where paragraph (2) applies, when the local planning authority have satisfied the requirements of article 8, they shall inform the Secretary of State that they have done so. **[1093]**

NOTES
Commencement: 3 June 1995.

10. Consultations before the grant of permission

(1) Before granting planning permission for development which, in their opinion, falls within a category set out in the table below, a local planning authority shall consult the authority or person mentioned in relation to that category, except where—

    (i) the local planning authority are the authority so mentioned;
    (ii) the local planning authority are required to consult the authority so mentioned under articles 11 or 12; or
    (iii) the authority or person so mentioned has advised the local planning authority that they do not wish to be consulted.

TABLE

Para	Description of Development	Consultee
(a)	Development likely to affect land in Greater London or in a metropolitan county	The local planning authority concerned
(b)	Development likely to affect land in a non-metropolitan county, other than land in a National Park	The district planning authority concerned
(c)	Development likely to affect land in a National Park	The county planning authority concerned
(d)	Development within an area which has been notified to the local planning authority by the Health and Safety Executive for the purpose of this provision because of the presence within the vicinity of toxic, highly reactive, explosive or inflammable substances and which involves the provision of—	The Health and Safety Executive

    (i) residential accommodation;
    (ii) more than 250 square metres of retail floor space;
    (iii) more than 500 square metres of office floor space; or
    (iv) more than 750 square metres of floor space to be used for an industrial process,

Para	*Description of Development*	*Consultee*
	or which is otherwise likely to result in a material increase in the number of persons working within or visiting the notified area	
(e)	Development likely to result in a material increase in the volume or a material change in the character of traffic—	
	(i) entering or leaving a trunk road; or	In England, the Secretary of State for Transport and, in Wales, the Secretary of State for Wales
	(ii) using a level crossing over a railway	The operator of the network which includes or consists of the railway in question, and in England, the Secretary of State for Transport and, in Wales, the Secretary of State for Wales
(f)	Development likely to result in a material increase in the volume or a material change in the character of traffic entering or leaving a classified road or proposed highway	The local highway authority concerned
(g)	Development likely to prejudice the improvement or construction of a classified road or proposed highway	The local highway authority concerned
(h)	Development involving—	
	(i) the formation, laying out or alteration of any means of access to a highway (other than a trunk road); or	The local highway authority concerned
	(ii) the construction of a highway or private means of access to premises affording access to a road in relation to which a toll order is in force	The local highway authority concerned, and in the case of a road subject to a concession, the concessionaire
(i)	Development which consists of or includes the laying out or construction of a new street	The local highway authority
(j)	Development which involves the provision of a building or pipe-line in an area of coal working notified by the Coal Authority to the local planning authority	The Coal Authority
(k)	Development involving or including mining operations	The National Rivers Authority
(l)	Development within three kilometres of Windsor Castle, Windsor Great Park, or Windsor Home Park, or within 800 metres of any other royal palace or park, which might affect the amenities (including security) of that palace or park	The Secretary of State for National Heritage

Para	Description of Development	Consultee
(m)	Development of land in Greater London involving the demolition, in whole or part, or the material alteration of a listed building	The Historic Buildings and Monuments Commission for England
(n)	Development likely to affect the site of a scheduled monument	In England, the Historic Buildings and Monuments Commission for England, and, in Wales, the Secretary of State for Wales
(o)	Development likely to affect any garden or park of special historic interest which is registered in accordance with section 8C of the Historic Buildings and Ancient Monuments Act 1953 (register of gardens) and which is classified as Grade I or Grade II*.	The Historic Buildings and Monuments Commission for England
(p)	Development involving the carrying out of works or operations in the bed of or on the banks of a river or stream	The National Rivers Authority
(q)	Development for the purpose of refining or storing mineral oils and their derivatives	The National Rivers Authority
(r)	Development involving the use of land for the deposit of refuse or waste	The National Rivers Authority
(s)	Development relating to the retention, treatment or disposal of sewage, trade-waste, slurry or sludge (other than the laying of sewers, the construction of pumphouses in a line of sewers, the construction of septic tanks and cesspools serving single dwellinghouses or single caravans or single buildings in which not more than ten people will normally reside, work or congregate, and works ancillary thereto)	The National Rivers Authority
(t)	Development relating to the use of land as a cemetery	The National Rivers Authority
(u)	Development—	The Council which gave, or is to be regarded as having given, the notice
	(i) in or likely to affect a site of special scientific interest of which notification has been given, or has effect as if given, to the local planning authority by the Nature Conservancy Council for England or the Countryside Council for Wales, in accordance with section 28 of the Wildlife and Countryside Act 1981 (areas of special scientific interest); or	
	(ii) within an area which has been notified to the local planning authority by the Nature Conservancy Council for England or the Countryside Council for Wales, and which is within two kilometres of a site of special scientific interest of which notification has been given or has effect as if given as aforesaid	
(v)	Development involving any land on which there is a theatre	The Theatres Trust

Para	*Description of Development*	*Consultee*

(w)	Development which is not for agricultural purposes and is not in accordance with the provisions of a development plan and involves—
	
	    (i) the loss of not less than 20 hectares of grades 1, 2 or 3a agricultural land which is for the time being used (or was last used) for agricultural purposes; or
	    (ii) the loss of less than 20 hectares of grades 1, 2 or 3a agricultural land which is for the time being used (or was last used) for agricultural purposes, in circumstances in which the development is likely to lead to a further loss of agricultural land amounting cumulatively to 20 hectares or more
		In England, the Minister of Agriculture, Fisheries and Food and, in Wales, the Secretary of State for Wales

(x)	Development within 250 metres of land which—
	    (i) is or has, at any time in the 30 years before the relevant application, been used for the deposit of refuse or waste; and
	    (ii) has been notified to the local planning authority by the waste regulation authority for the purposes of this provision
		The waste regulation authority concerned

(y)	Development for the purposes of fish farming	The National Rivers Authority

(2) In the above table—

    (a) in paragraph (d)(iv), ''industrial process'' means a process for or incidental to any of the following purposes—

        (i) the making of any article or part of any article (including a ship or vessel, or a film, video or sound recording);

        (ii) the altering, repairing, maintaining, ornamenting, finishing, cleaning, washing, packing, canning, adapting for sale, breaking up or demolition of any article; or

        (iii) the getting, dressing or treatment of minerals in the course of any trade or business other than agriculture, and other than a process carried out on land used as a mine or adjacent to and occupied together with a mine (and in this sub-paragraph, ''mine'' means any site on which mining operations are carried out);

    (b) in paragraph (e)(ii), ''network'' and ''operator'' have the same meaning as in Part I of the Railways Act 1993 (the provision of railway services);

    (c) in paragraphs (f) and (g), ''classified road'' means a highway or proposed highway which—

        (i) is a classified road or a principal road by virtue of section 12(1) of the Highways Act 1980 (general provision as to principal and classified roads); or

        (ii) is classified for the purposes of any enactment by the Secretary of State by virtue of section 12(3) of that Act;

    (d) in paragraph (h), ''concessionaire'', ''road subject to a concession'' and ''toll order'' have the same meaning as in Part I of the New Roads and Street Works Act 1991 (new roads in England and Wales);

    (e) in paragraph (i), ''street'' has the same meaning as in section 48(1) of the New Roads and Street Works Act 1991 (streets, street works and undertakers), and "new street" includes a continuation of an existing street;

(f) in paragraph (m), "listed building" has the same meaning as in section 1 of the Planning (Listed Buildings and Conservation Areas) Act 1990 (listing of buildings of special architectural or historic interest);

(g) in paragraph (n), "scheduled monument" has the same meaning as in section 1(11) of the Ancient Monuments and Archaeological Areas Act 1979 (schedule of monuments);

(h) in paragraph (s), "slurry" means animal faeces and urine (whether or not water has been added for handling), and "caravan" has the same meaning as for the purposes of Part I of the Caravan Sites and Control of Development Act 1960 (caravan sites);

(i) in paragraph (u), "site of special scientific interest" means land to which section 28(1) of the Wildlife and Countryside Act 1981 (areas of special scientific interest) applies;

(j) in paragraph (v), "theatre" has the same meaning as in section 5 of the Theatres Trust Act 1976 (interpretation); and

(k) in paragraph (x), "waste regulation authority" has the same meaning as in section 30(1) of the Environmental Protection Act 1990 (authorities for purposes of Part II).

(3) The Secretary of State may give directions to a local planning authority requiring that authority to consult any person or body named in the directions, in any case or class of case specified in the directions.

(4) Where, by or under this article, a local planning authority are required to consult any person or body ("the consultee") before granting planning permission—

(a) they shall, unless an applicant has served a copy of an application for planning permission on the consultee, give notice of the application to the consultee; and

(b) they shall not determine the application until at least 14 days after the date on which notice is given under paragraph (a) or, if earlier, 14 days after the date of service of a copy of the application on the consultee by the applicant.

(5) The local planning authority shall, in determining the application, take into account any representations received from a consultee. **[1094]**

NOTES
Commencement: 3 June 1995.

11. Consultation with county planning authority

Where a district planning authority are required by paragraph 7 of Schedule 1 to the Act (local planning authorities — distribution of functions) to consult the county planning authority before determining an application for planning permission, they shall not determine the application until the expiry of at least 14 days after the date of the notice given to the county planning authority in accordance with sub-paragraph (6)(b) of that paragraph. **[1095]**

NOTES
Commencement: 3 June 1995.

12. Applications relating to county matters

(1) A county planning authority shall, before determining—

(a) an application for planning permission under Part III of the Act (control over development);

(b) an application for a certificate of lawful use or development under section 191 or 192 of the Act (certificates of lawfulness of existing or proposed use or development); or

(c) an application for approval of reserved matters,

give the district planning authority, if any, for the area in which the relevant land lies a period of at least 14 days, from the date of receipt of the application by the district authority, within which to make recommendations about the manner in which the application shall be determined; and shall take any such recommendations into account.

(2) A county planning authority shall—

(a) on determining an application of a kind mentioned in paragraph (1), as soon as reasonably practicable notify the district planning authority, if any, of the terms of their decision; or

(b) if any such application is referred to the Secretary of State, inform the district planning authority, if any, of the date when it was so referred and, when notified to them, of the terms of the decision.   **[1096]**

NOTES

Commencement: 3 June 1995.

13. Notice to parish and community councils

(1) Where the council of a parish or community are given information in relation to an application pursuant to paragraph 8(1) of Schedule 1 to the Act (local planning authorities — distribution of functions), they shall, as soon as practicable, notify the local planning authority who are determining the application whether they propose to make any representations about the manner in which the application should be determined, and shall make any representations to that authority within 14 days of the notification to them of the application.

(2) A local planning authority shall not determine any application in respect of which a parish or community are required to be given information before—

(a) the council of the parish or community inform them that they do not propose to make any representations;

(b) representations are made by that council; or

(c) the period of 14 days mentioned in paragraph (1) has elapsed,

whichever shall first occur; and in determining the application the authority shall take into account any representations received from the council of the parish or community.

(3) The district planning authority (or, in a metropolitan county, the local planning authority) shall notify the council of the parish or community of the terms of the decision on any such application or, where the application is referred to the Secretary of State, of the date when it was so referred and, when notified to them, of the terms of his decision.   **[1097]**

NOTES

Commencement: 3 June 1995.

14. Directions by the Secretary of State

(1) The Secretary of State may give directions restricting the grant of permission by a local planning authority, either indefinitely or during such a period as may be

specified in the directions, in respect of any development or in respect of development of any class so specified.

(2) The Secretary of State may give directions—

(a) that particular proposed development of a description set out in Schedule 1 or Schedule 2 to the Town and Country Planning (Assessment of Environmental Effects) Regulations 1988 (descriptions of development) is exempted from the application of those Regulations, in accordance with Article 2(3) of Council Directive 85/337/EEC;

(b) as to whether particular proposed development is or is not development in respect of which those Regulations require the consideration of environmental information (as defined in those Regulations) before planning permission can be granted; or

(c) that development of any class described in the direction is development in respect of which those Regulations require the consideration of such information before such permission can be granted.

(3) A local planning authority shall deal with applications for planning permission for development to which a direction given under this article applies in such manner as to give effect to the direction. **[1098]**

NOTES
Commencement: 3 June 1995.

15. Special provisions as to permission for development affecting certain existing and proposed highways

(1) Where an application is made to a local planning authority for planning permission for development which consists of or includes—

(a) the formation, laying out or alteration of any access to or from any part of a trunk road which is either a special road or, if not a special road, a road subject to a speed limit exceeding 40 miles per hour; or

(b) any development of land within 67 metres (or such other distance as may be specified in a direction given by the Secretary of State under this article) from the middle of—

(i) any highway (other than a trunk road) which the Secretary of State has provided, or is authorised to provide, in pursuance of an order under Part II of the Highways Act 1980 (trunk roads, classified roads, metropolitan roads, special roads) and which has not for the time being been transferred to any other highway authority;

(ii) any highway which he proposes to improve under Part V of that Act (improvement of highways) and in respect of which notice has been given to the local planning authority;

(iii) any highway to which he proposes to carry out improvements in pursuance of an order under Part II of that Act; or

(iv) any highway which he proposes to construct, the route of which is shown on the development plan or in respect of which he has given notice in writing to the relevant local planning authority together with maps or plans sufficient to identify the route of the highway,

the local planning authority shall notify the Secretary of State by sending him a copy of the application and any accompanying plans and drawings.

(2) An application referred to in paragraph (1) above shall not be determined unless—

(a) the local planning authority receive a direction given under article 14 of this Order (and in accordance with the terms of that direction);

(b) they receive notification by or on behalf of the Secretary of State that he does not propose to give any such direction in respect of the development to which the application relates; or

(c) a period of 28 days (or such longer period as may be agreed in writing between the local planning authority and the Secretary of State) from the date when notification was given to the Secretary of State has elapsed without receipt of such a direction.

(3) The Secretary of State may, in respect of any case or any class or description of cases, give a direction specifying a different distance for the purposes of paragraph 1(b) above.   **[1099]**

NOTES

Commencement: 3 June 1995.

16. Notification of mineral applications

(1) Where notice has been given for the purposes of this article to a mineral planning authority as respects land which is in their area and specified in the notice—

(a) by the Coal Authority that the land contains coal;

(b) by the Secretary of State for Trade and Industry that it contains gas or oil; or

(c) by the Crown Estates Commissioners that it contains silver or gold,

the mineral planning authority shall not determine any application for planning permission to win and work any mineral on that land, without first notifying the body or person who gave the notice that an application has been made.

(2) In this article, "coal" means coal other than that—

(a) won or worked during the course of operations which are carried on exclusively for the purpose of exploring for coal; or

(b) which it is necessary to dig or carry away in the course of activities carried on for purposes which do not include the getting of coal or any product of coal.   **[1100]**

NOTES

Commencement: 3 June 1995.

17. Development not in accordance with the development plan

A local planning authority may in such cases and subject to such conditions as may be prescribed by directions given by the Secretary of State under this Order grant permission for development which does not accord with the provisions of the development plan in force in the area in which the land to which the application relates is situated.   **[1101]**

NOTES

Commencement: 3 June 1995.

18. Notice of reference of applications to the Secretary of State

On referring any application to the Secretary of State under section 77 of the Act (reference of applications to Secretary of State) pursuant to a direction in that behalf, a local planning authority shall serve on the applicant a notice—

(a) setting out the terms of the direction and any reasons given by the Secretary of State for issuing it;

(b) stating that the application has been referred to the Secretary of State; and

(c) containing a statement that the Secretary of State will, if the applicant so desires, afford to him an opportunity of appearing before and being heard by a person appointed by the Secretary of State for the purpose, and that the decision of the Secretary of State on the application will be final.

[1102]

NOTES
Commencement: 3 June 1995.

19. Representations to be taken into account

(1) A local planning authority shall, in determining an application for planning permission, take into account any representations made, where any notice of the application has been—

(a) given by site display under article 6 or 8, within 21 days beginning with the date when the notice was first displayed by site display;

(b) served on—

(i) an owner of the land or a tenant of an agricultural holding under article 6, or

(ii) an adjoining owner or occupier under article 8,

within 21 days beginning with the date when the notice was served on that person, provided that the representations are made by any person who satisfies them that he is such an owner, tenant or occupier; or

(c) given by local advertisement under article 6 or 8, within 14 days beginning with the date on which the notice was published,

and the representations and periods in this article are representations and periods prescribed for the purposes of section 71(2)(a) of the Act (consultations in connection with determinations under section 70).

(2) A local planning authority shall give notice of their decision to every person who has made representations which they were required to take into account in accordance with paragraph (1)(b)(i), and such notice is notice prescribed for the purposes of section 71(2)(b) of the Act.

(3) Paragraphs (1) and (2) of this article apply to applications referred to the Secretary of State under section 77 of the Act (reference of applications to Secretary of State) and paragraphs (1)(b) and (2) apply to appeals to the Secretary of State made under section 78 of the Act (right to appeal against planning decisions and failure to take such decisions), as if the references to—

(a) a local planning authority were to the Secretary of State, and

(b) determining an application for planning permission were to determining such application or appeal, as the case may be. **[1103]**

NOTES
Commencement: 3 June 1995.

20. Time periods for decision

(1) Subject to paragraph (5), where a valid application under article 4 or regulation 3 of the 1988 Regulations (applications for planning permission) has been received by a local planning authority, they shall within the period specified in paragraph (2) give the applicant notice of their decision or determination or notice that the application has been referred to the Secretary of State.

(2) The period specified in this paragraph is—

    (a) a period of eight weeks beginning with the date when the application was received by a local planning authority;

    (b) except where the applicant has already given notice of appeal to the Secretary of State, such extended period as may be agreed in writing between the applicant and the local planning authority by whom the application falls to be determined; or

    (c) where a fee due in respect of an application has been paid by a cheque which is subsequently dishonoured, the appropriate period specified in (a) or (b) above calculated without regard to any time between the date when the authority sent the applicant written notice of the dishonouring of the cheque and the date when the authority are satisfied that they have received the full amount of the fee.

(3) For the purposes of this article, the date when the application was received shall be taken to be the date when each of the following events has occurred—

    (a) the application form or application in writing has been lodged with the authority mentioned in article 5(1);

    (b) any certificate or documents required by the Act or this Order has been lodged with that authority; and

    (c) any fee required to be paid in respect of the application has been paid to that authority and, for this purpose, lodging a cheque for the amount of a fee is to be taken as payment.

(4) A local planning authority shall provide such information about applications made under article 4 or regulation 3 of the 1988 Regulations (including information as to the manner in which any such application has been dealt with) as the Secretary of State may by direction require; and any such direction may include provision as to the persons to be informed and the manner in which the information is to be provided.

(5) Subject to paragraph (6), a local planning authority shall not determine an application for planning permission, where any notice of the application has been—

    (a) given by site display under article 6 or 8, before the end of the period of 21 days beginning with the date when the notice was first displayed by site display;

    (b) served on—

        (i) an owner of the land or a tenant of an agricultural holding under article 6, or

        (ii) an adjoining owner or occupier under article 8,

    before the end of the period of 21 days beginning with the date when the notice was served on that person;

    (c) given by local advertisement under article 6 or 8, before the end of the period of 14 days beginning with the date on which the notice was published,

and the periods in this paragraph are periods prescribed for the purposes of section 71(1) of the Act (consultations in connection with determinations under section 70).

(6) Where, under paragraph (5), more than one of the prescribed periods applies, the local planning authority shall not determine the application before the end of the later or latest of such periods.   **[1104]**

NOTES

Commencement: 3 June 1995.

21. Applications made under planning condition

Where an application has been made to a local planning authority for any consent, agreement or approval required by a condition or limitation attached to a grant of planning permission (other than an application for approval of reserved matters or an application for approval under Part 24 of Schedule 2 to the Town and Country Planning (General Permitted Development) Order 1995 (development by telecommunications code system operators)) the authority shall give notice to the applicant of their decision on the application within a period of eight weeks from the date when the application was received by the authority, or such longer period as may be agreed by the applicant and the authority in writing. **[1105]**

NOTES
Commencement: 3 June 1995.

22. Written notice of decision or determination relating to a planning application

(1) When the local planning authority give notice of a decision or determination on an application for planning permission or for approval of reserved matters, and a permission or approval is granted subject to conditions or the application is refused, the notice shall—

    (a) state clearly and precisely their full reasons for the refusal or for any condition imposed; and

    (b) where the Secretary of State has given a direction restricting the grant of permission for the development for which application is made or where he or a Government Department has expressed the view that the permission should not be granted (either wholly or in part) or should be granted subject to conditions, give details of the direction or of the view expressed,

and shall be accompanied by a notification in the terms (or substantially in the terms) set out in Part 2 of Schedule 1 to this Order.

(2) Where—

    (a) the applicant for planning permission has submitted an environmental statement; and

    (b) the local planning authority have decided (having taken environmental information into consideration) to grant permission (whether unconditionally or subject to conditions),

the notice given to the applicant in accordance with article 20(1) shall include a statement that environmental information has been taken into consideration by the authority. **[1106]**

NOTES
Commencement: 3 June 1995.

23. Appeals

(1) An applicant who wishes to appeal to the Secretary of State under section 78 of the Act (right to appeal against planning decisions and failure to take such decisions) shall give notice of appeal to the Secretary of State by—

    (a) serving on him, within the time limit specified in paragraph (2), a form obtained from him, together with such of the documents specified in paragraph (3) as are relevant to the appeal; and

(b) serving on the local planning authority a copy of the form mentioned in paragraph (a), as soon as reasonably practicable, together with a copy of any relevant documents mentioned in paragraph (3)(e).

(2) The time limit mentioned in paragraph (1) is six months from—

(a) the date of the notice of the decision or determination giving rise to the appeal;

(b) the expiry of the period specified in article 20 or, as the case may be, article 21; or

(c) in a case in which the authority have served a notice on the applicant in accordance with article 3(2) that they require further information, and he has not provided the information, the date of service of that notice,

or such longer period as the Secretary of State may, at any time, allow.

(3) The documents mentioned in paragraph (1) are—

(a) the application made to the local planning authority which has occasioned the appeal;

(b) all plans, drawings and documents sent to the authority in connection with the application;

(c) all correspondence with the authority relating to the application;

(d) any certificate provided to the authority under article 7;

(e) any other plans, documents or drawings relating to the application which were not sent to the authority;

(f) the notice of the decision or determination, if any;

(g) if the appeal relates to an application for approval of certain matters in accordance with a condition on a planning permission, the application for that permission, the plans submitted with that application and the planning permission granted. **[1107]**

NOTES

Commencement: 3 June 1995.

24. Certificate of lawful use or development

(1) An application for a certificate under section 191(1) or 192(1) of the Act (certificates of lawfulness of existing or proposed use or development) shall be in writing and shall, in addition to specifying the land and describing the use, operations or other matter in question in accordance with those sections, include the following information—

(a) the paragraph of section 191(1) or, as the case may be, section 192(1), under which the application is made;

(b) in the case of an application under section 191(1), the date on which the use, operations or other matter began or, in the case of operations carried out without planning permission, the date on which the operations were substantially completed;

(c) in the case of an application under section 191(1)(a), the name of any use class specified in an order under section 55(2)(f) of the Act (meaning of "development") which the applicant considers applicable to the use existing at the date of the application;

(d) in the case of an application under section 191(1)(c), sufficient details of the planning permission to enable it to be identified;

(e) in the case of an application under section 192(1)(a), the use of the land at the date of the application (or, when the land is not in use at that date, the purpose for which it was last used) and the name of any use class specified in an order under section 55(2)(f) of the Act which the applicant considers applicable to the proposed use;

  (f) the applicant's reasons, if any, for regarding the use, operations or other matter described in the application as lawful; and

  (g) such other information as the applicant considers to be relevant to the application.

(2) An application to which paragraph (1) applies shall be accompanied by—

  (a) a plan identifying the land to which the application relates;

  (b) such evidence verifying the information included in the application as the applicant can provide; and

  (c) a statement setting out the applicant's interest in the land, the name and address of any other person known to the applicant to have an interest in the land and whether any such other person has been notified of the application.

(3) Where such an application specifies two or more uses, operations or other matters, the plan which accompanies the application shall indicate to which part of the land each such use, operation or matter relates.

(4) Articles 5(1) and 20(4) shall apply to an application for a certificate to which paragraph (1) applies as they apply to an application for planning permission.

(5) When the local planning authority receive an application to which paragraph (1) applies and any fee required to be paid in respect of the application, they shall, as soon as reasonably practicable, send to the applicant an acknowledgement of the application in the terms (or substantially in the terms) set out in Part 1 of Schedule 1.

(6) Where, after sending an acknowledgement as required by paragraph (5), the local planning authority consider that the application is invalid by reason of the failure to comply with the preceding paragraphs of this article or any other statutory requirement, they shall, as soon as practicable, notify the applicant that his application is invalid.

(7) The local planning authority may by notice in writing require the applicant to provide such further information as may be specified to enable them to deal with the application.

(8) The local planning authority shall give the applicant written notice of their decision within a period of eight weeks beginning with the date of receipt by the authority of the application and any fee required to be paid in respect of the application or, except where the applicant has already given notice of appeal to the Secretary of State, within such extended period as may be agreed upon in writing between the applicant and the authority.

(9) For the purpose of calculating the appropriate period specified in paragraph (8), where any fee required has been paid by a cheque which is subsequently dishonoured, the time between the date when the authority send the applicant written notice of the dishonouring of the cheque and the date when the authority receive the full amount of the fee shall not be taken into account.

(10) Where an application is refused, in whole or in part (including a case in which the authority modify the description of the use, operations or other matter in the application or substitute an alternative description for that description), the notice of decision shall state clearly and precisely the authority's full reasons for their decision and shall include a statement to the effect that if the applicant is aggrieved

by the decision he may appeal to the Secretary of State under section 195 of the Act (appeals against refusal or failure to give decision on application).

(11) A certificate under section 191 or 192 of the Act shall be in the form set out in Schedule 4, or in a form substantially to the like effect.

(12) Where a local planning authority propose to revoke a certificate issued under section 191 or 192 of the Act in accordance with section 193(7) of the Act (certificates under sections 191 and 192: supplementary provisions), they shall, before they revoke the certificate, give notice of that proposal to—

    (a)　the owner of the land affected;

    (b)　the occupier of the land affected;

    (c)　any other person who will in their opinion be affected by the revocation; and

    (d)　in the case of a certificate issued by the Secretary of State under section 195 of the Act, the Secretary of State.

(13) A notice issued under paragraph (12) shall invite the person on whom the notice is served to make representations on the proposal to the authority within 14 days of service of the notice and the authority shall not revoke the certificate until all such periods allowed for making representations have expired.

(14) An authority shall give written notice of any revocation under section 193(7) of the Act to every person on whom notice of the proposed revocation was served under paragraph (12).　　　　　　　　　　　　　　　　　　　　**[1108]**

NOTES
    Commencement: 3 June 1995.
    Modification: see SI 1995/1139, reg 2, Sch at **[1134]**.

25. Register of applications

(1) In this article and in article 26, ''the local planning register authority'' means—

    (a)　in Greater London or a metropolitan county, the local planning authority (and references to the area of the local planning register authority are, in this case, to the area of the local planning authority);

    (b)　in relation to land in a National Park (except in a metropolitan county), the county planning authority (and references to the area of the local planning register authority are, in this case, to the area of the county planning authority within a National Park);

    (c)　in relation to any other land, the district planning authority (and references to the area of the local planning register authority are, in this case, to the area of the district planning authority, other than any part of their area falling within a National Park).

(2) Each local planning register authority shall keep, in two parts, a register of every application for planning permission relating to their area.

(3) Part I of the register shall contain a copy of each such application, and a copy of any application for approval of reserved matters made in respect of an outline planning permission granted on such an application, made or sent to the local planning register authority and not finally disposed of, together with any accompanying plans and drawings.

(4) Part II of the register shall contain, in respect of every application for planning permission relating to the local planning register authority's area—

    (a)　a copy (which may be photographic) of the application and of plans and drawings submitted in relation thereto;

(b) particulars of any direction given under the Act or this Order in respect of the application;

(c) the decision, if any, of the local planning authority in respect of the application, including details of any conditions subject to which permission was granted, the date of such decision and the name of the local planning authority;

(d) the reference number, the date and effect of any decision of the Secretary of State in respect of the application, whether on appeal or on a reference under section 77 of the Act (reference of applications to Secretary of State);

(e) the date of any subsequent approval (whether approval of reserved matters or any other approval required) given in relation to the application.

(5) Where, on any appeal to the Secretary of State under section 174 of the Act (appeal against enforcement notices), the appellant is deemed to have made an application for planning permission and the Secretary of State has granted permission, the local planning register authority shall, on receipt of notification of the Secretary of State's decision, enter into Part II of the register referred to in paragraph (2) particulars of the development concerned, the land on which it was carried out, and the date and effect of the Secretary of State's decision.

(6) The register kept by the local planning register authority shall also contain the following information in respect of every application for a certificate under section 191 or 192 of the Act (certificates of lawfulness of existing or proposed use or development) relating to the authority's area—

(a) the name and address of the applicant;

(b) the date of the application;

(c) the address or location of the land to which the application relates;

(d) the description of the use, operations or other matter included in the application;

(e) the decision, if any, of the local planning authority in respect of the application and the date of such decision; and

(f) the reference number, date and effect of any decision of the Secretary of State on an appeal in respect of the application.

(7) The register shall contain the following information about simplified planning zone schemes in the area of the authority—

(a) brief particulars of any action taken by the authority or the Secretary of State in accordance with section 83 of or Schedule 7 to the Act (making of simplified planning zone schemes etc) to establish or approve any simplified planning zone scheme, including the date of adoption or approval, the date on which the scheme or alteration becomes operative and the date on which it ceases to be operative;

(b) a copy of any simplified planning zone scheme, or alteration to an existing scheme, including any diagrams, illustrations, descriptive matter or any other prescribed material which has been made available for inspection under Schedule 7 to the Act;

(c) an index map showing the boundary of any operative or proposed simplified planning zone schemes, including alterations to existing schemes where appropriate, together with a reference to the entries in the register under sub-paragraph (a) and (b) above.

(8) To enable any person to trace any entry in the register, every register shall include an index together with a separate index of applications for development involving mining operations or the creation of mineral working deposits.

(9) Every entry in the register shall be made within 14 days of the receipt of an application, or of the giving or making of the relevant direction, decision or approval as the case may be.

(10) The register shall either be kept at the principal office of the local planning register authority or that part of the register which relates to land in part of that authority's area shall be kept at a place within or convenient to that part.

(11) For the purposes of paragraph (3) of this article, an application shall not be treated as finally disposed of unless—

(a) it has been decided by the authority (or the appropriate period allowed under article 20(2) of this Order has expired without their giving a decision) and the period of six months specified in article 23 of this Order has expired without any appeal having been made to the Secretary of State;

(b) if it has been referred to the Secretary of State under section 77 of the Act (reference of applications to Secretary of State) or an appeal has been made to the Secretary of State under section 78 of the Act (right to appeal against planning decisions and failure to take such decisions), the Secretary of State has issued his decision and the period of six weeks specified in section 288 of the Act (proceedings for questioning the validity of certain orders, decisions and directions) has expired without any application having been made to the High Court under that section;

(c) an application has been made to the High Court under section 288 of the Act and the matter has been finally determined, either by final dismissal of the application by a court or by the quashing of the Secretary of State's decision and the issue of a fresh decision (without a further application under the said section 288); or

(d) it has been withdrawn before being decided by the authority or the Secretary of State, as the case may be, or an appeal has been withdrawn before the Secretary of State has issued his decision. **[1109]**

NOTES
Commencement: 3 June 1995.

26. Register of enforcement and stop notices

(1) Subject to paragraph (2) of this article, the register under section 188 of the Act (register of enforcement and stop notices) shall contain the following information with respect to every enforcement notice issued in relation to land in the area of the authority maintaining the register—

(a) the address of the land to which the notice relates or a plan by reference to which its situation can be ascertained;

(b) the name of the issuing authority;

(c) the date of issue of the notice;

(d) the date of service of copies of the notice;

(e) a statement or summary of the breach of planning control alleged and the requirements of the notice, including the period within which any required steps are to be taken;

(f) the date specified in the notice as the date on which it is to take effect;

(g) information on any postponement of the date specified as the date on which the notice will take effect by reason of section 175(4) of the Act (appeals: supplementary provisions) and the date of the final determination or withdrawal of any appeal;

(h) the date of service and, if applicable, of withdrawal of any stop notice referring to the enforcement notice, together with a statement or summary of the activity prohibited by any such stop notice;

(i) the date, if any, on which the local planning authority are satisfied that steps required by the notice for a purpose mentioned in section 173(4)(b) of the Act (remedying any injury to amenity) have been taken.

(2) That register shall also contain the following information with respect to every breach of condition notice served in relation to land in the area of the authority maintaining the register—

(a) the address of the land to which the notice relates or a plan by reference to which its situation can be ascertained;

(b) the name of the serving authority;

(c) the date of service of the notice;

(d) details of the relevant planning permission sufficient to enable it to be identified;

(e) a statement or summary of the condition which has not been complied with and the requirements of the notice, including the period allowed for compliance.

(3) All entries relating to an enforcement notice, stop notice or breach of condition notice shall be removed from the register if—

(a) in the case of an enforcement notice or stop notice, the relevant enforcement notice is quashed by the Secretary of State;

(b) in the case of a breach of condition notice, the notice is quashed by a court;

(c) in any case, the relevant notice is withdrawn.

(4) Every register shall include an index for enabling a person to trace any entry in the register by reference to the address of the land to which the notice relates.

(5) Where a county planning authority issue an enforcement notice or serve a stop notice or a breach of condition notice, they shall supply the information specified in paragraph (1) or (2) of this article, as the case may be, in relation to the notice to the district planning authority in whose area the land to which the notice relates is situated and shall inform that authority if the notice is withdrawn or the relevant enforcement notice or breach of condition notice is quashed.

(6) The information prescribed in paragraphs (1) and (2) of this article shall be entered in the register as soon as practicable and in any event within 14 days of the occurrence to which it relates, and information shall be so supplied under paragraph (5) that entries may be made within the said period of 14 days.

(7) The register shall either be kept at the principal office of the local planning register authority or that part of the register which relates to land in part of that authority's area shall be kept at a place within or convenient to that part.   **[1110]**

NOTES
Commencement: 3 June 1995.

27. Directions

Any power conferred by this Order to give a direction includes power to cancel or vary the direction by a subsequent direction.   **[1111]**

NOTES
Commencement: 3 June 1995.

28. Revocations, transitionals and savings

(1) Subject to paragraphs (2) to (5) of this article, the statutory instruments specified in Schedule 5 are revoked to the extent not already revoked.

(2) Where an area of coal working has been notified to the local planning authority for the purposes of paragraph (i) of the table in article 18 of the Town and Country Planning General Development Order 1988 (consultations before the grant of permission) before the date of the coming into force of this Order, such notification shall be treated as if it had been made for the purposes of paragraph (j) of the table in article 10 of this Order by the Coal Authority on or after that date; and, in relation to a particular application for planning permission made before 31st October 1994, the local planning authority are not required to consult the Coal Authority if they have already consulted the British Coal Corporation.

(3) Any notice given for the purposes of article 13 of the Town and Country Planning General Development Order 1988 (notification of mineral applications) before the date of the coming into force of this Order, shall be treated as if it had been given for the purposes of article 16 of this Order by the Coal Authority on or after that date; and, in relation to a particular application for planning permission made before 31st October 1994, the mineral planning authority are not required to notify the Coal Authority, before determining the application, if they have already notified the British Coal Corporation that that application has been made.

(4) The relevant provisions of the Town and Country Planning General Development Order 1988, in the form in which they were in force immediately before 27th July 1992, shall continue to apply with respect to applications made under section 64 of the Act (applications to determine whether planning permission required) before 27th July 1992.

(5) The relevant provisions of the Town and Country Planning General Development Order 1988, in the form in which they were in force immediately before 27th July 1992, shall continue to apply with respect to applications for established use certificates made under section 192 of the Act (applications for established use certificates), as originally enacted, before 27th July 1992.   **[1112]**

NOTES
Commencement: 3 June 1995.

SCHEDULES
SCHEDULE 1 Articles 5, 22 and 24

PART 1

TOWN AND COUNTRY PLANNING ACT 1990

Letter to be sent by a local planning authority when they receive an application for planning permission or for a certificate of lawful use or development.

Thank you for your application dated ....

which I received on ....

I am still examining your application form and the accompanying plans and documents to see whether they comply with the law.*

If I find that your application is invalid because it does not comply with the statutory requirements then I shall write to you again as soon as I can.*

If, by (*insert date at end of period of eight weeks beginning with the date when the application was*

received) ....

- you have not been told that your application is invalid; or

*• you have not been told that your fee cheque has been dishonoured; or

- you have not been given a decision in writing; or

- you have not agreed in writing to extend the period in which the decision may be given,

then you can appeal to the Secretary of State for the Environment/Wales* under section 78/ section 195* of the Town and Country Planning Act 1990. You should appeal within six months and you must use a form which you can get from the Planning Inspectorate at Tollgate House, Houlton Street, Bristol BS2 9DJ/Cathays Park, Cardiff CF1 3NQ*. This does not apply if your application has already been referred to the Secretary of State for the Environment/Wales*.

*delete where inappropriate **[1113]**

PART 2

TOWN AND COUNTRY PLANNING ACT 1990

Notification to be sent to an applicant when a local planning authority refuse planning permission or grant it subject to conditions *(To be endorsed on notices of decision)*

Appeals to the Secretary of State

- If you are aggrieved by the decision of your local planning authority to refuse permission for the proposed development or to grant it subject to conditions, then you can appeal to the Secretary of State for the Environment/Wales* under section 78 of the Town and Country Planning Act 1990.

- If you want to appeal, then you must do so within six months of the date of this notice, using a form which you can get from the Planning Inspectorate at Tollgate House, Houlton Street, Bristol BS2 9DJ/Cathays Park, Cardiff CF1 3NQ*.

- The Secretary of State can allow a longer period for giving notice of an appeal, but he will not normally be prepared to use this power unless there are special circumstances which excuse the delay in giving notice of appeal.

- The Secretary of State need not consider an appeal if it seems to him that the local planning authority could not have granted planning permission for the proposed development or could not have granted it without the conditions they imposed, having regard to the statutory requirements, to the provisions of any development order and to any directions given under a development order.

- In practice, the Secretary of State does not refuse to consider appeals solely because the local planning authority based their decision on a direction given by him.

Purchase Notices

- If either the local planning authority or the Secretary of State for the Environment/Wales* refuses permission to develop land or grants it subject to conditions, the owner may claim that he can neither put the land to a reasonably beneficial use in its existing state nor render the land capable of a reasonably beneficial use by the carrying out of any development which has been or would be permitted.

- In these circumstances, the owner may serve a purchase notice on the Council (District Council, London Borough Council or Common Council of the City of London) in whose area the land is situated. This notice will require the Council to purchase his interest in the land in accordance with the provisions of Part VI of the Town and Country Planning Act 1990.

*delete where inappropriate   **[1114]**

SCHEDULE 2   Articles 6, 7 and 9

PART 1

Town and Country Planning (General Development Procedure) Order 1995

NOTICE UNDER ARTICLE 6 OF APPLICATION FOR PLANNING PERMISSION

(to be published in a newspaper or to be served on an owner* or a tenant**)

Proposed development at *(a)* ....

I give notice that *(b)* ....

is applying to the *(c)* .... Council

for planning permission to *(d)* ....

Any owner* of the land or tenant** who wishes to make representations about this application

should write to the Council at *(e)* ....

by *(f)* ....

*   "owner" means a person having a freehold interest or a leasehold interest the unexpired term of which is not less than seven years, or, in the case of development consisting of the winning or working of minerals, a person entitled to an interest in a mineral in the land (other than oil, gas, coal, gold or silver).

**   "tenant" means a tenant of an agricultural holding any part of which is comprised in the land.

Signed ....

†On behalf of ....

Date ....

Statement of owners' rights

     The grant of planning permission does not affect owners' rights to retain or dispose of their property, unless there is some provision to the contrary in an agreement or in a lease.

Statement of agricultural tenants' rights

     The grant of planning permission for non-agricultural development may affect agricultural tenants' security of tenure.

†delete where inappropriate

Insert:
- *(a)* address or location of the proposed development
- *(b)* applicant's name
- *(c)* name of Council
- *(d)* description of the proposed development
- *(e)* address of the Council
- *(f)* date giving a period of 21 days beginning with the date of service, or 14 days beginning with the date of publication, of the notice (as the case may be)   **[1115]**

Town and Country Planning (General Development Procedure) Order 1995

NOTICE UNDER ARTICLE 6 OF APPLICATION FOR PLANNING PERMISSION

(to be posted in the case of an application for planning permission for development consisting of the winning and working of minerals by underground operations (in addition to the service or publication of any other requisite notices in this Schedule))

Proposed development at *(a)* ....

I give notice that *(b)* ....

is applying to the *(c)* .... Council

for planning permission to *(d)* ....

Members of the public may inspect copies of:

- the application

- the plans

- and other documents submitted with it

at *(e)* .... during

all reasonable hours until *(f)* ....

Anyone who wishes to make representations about this application should write to the Council

at *(g)* ....

.... by *(f)* ....

                   Signed ....

                   †On behalf of ....

                   Date ....

†Delete where inappropriate

Insert:
(a) address or location of the proposed development
(b) applicant's name
(c) name of Council
(d) description of the proposed development
(e) address at which the application may be inspected (the applicant is responsible for making the application available for inspection within the area of the local planning authority)
(f) date giving a period of 21 days, beginning with the date when the notice is posted
(g) address of Council   **[1116]**

Town and Country Planning (General Development Procedure) Order 1995

NOTICE UNDER ARTICLES 6 AND 9(1) OF APPEAL

(to be published in a newspaper or to be served on an owner* or a tenant**)

Proposed development at *(a)* ....

I give notice that *(b)* ....

having applied to the *(c)* .... Council

to *(d)* ....

is appealing to the Secretary of State for the Environment/Secretary of State for Wales†

against the decision of the Council†

on the failure of the Council to give notice of a decision†

Any owner* of the land or tenant** who wishes to make representations about this appeal should write to the Secretary of State for the Environment/Wales† at the Department of the Environment at Tollgate House, Houlton Street, Bristol BS2 9DJ/Welsh Office at Planning Division, Cathays Park, Cardiff CF1 3NQ†, by *(e)* ....

*   "owner" means a person having a freehold interest or a leasehold interest the unexpired term of which is not less than seven years, or, in the case of development consisting of the winning or working of minerals, a person entitled to an interest in a mineral in the land (other than oil, gas, coal, gold or silver).

** "tenant" means a tenant of an agricultural holding any part of which is comprised in the land.

Signed ....

†On behalf of ....

Date ....

Statement of owners' rights

The grant of planning permission does not affect owners' rights to retain or dispose of their property, unless there is some provision to the contrary in an agreement or in a lease.

Statement of agricultural tenants' rights

The grant of planning permission for non-agricultural development may affect agricultural tenants' security of tenure.

†delete where inappropriate

Insert:
(a) address or location of the proposed development
(b) applicant's name
(c) name of Council
(d) description of the proposed development
(e) date giving a period of 21 days beginning with the date of service, or 14 days beginning with the date of publication, of the notice (as the case may be) **[1117]**

Town and Country Planning (General Development Procedure) Order 1995

NOTICE UNDER ARTICLES 6 AND 9(1) OF APPEAL

(to be posted in the case of an application for planning permission for development consisting of the winning and working of minerals by underground operations (in addition to the service or publication of any other requisite notices in this Schedule))

Proposed development at *(a)* ....

I give notice that *(b)* ....

having applied to the *(c)* .... Council

to *(d)* ....

is appealing to the Secretary of State for the Environment/Secretary of State for Wales*

     against the decision of the Council*

     on the failure of the Council to give notice of a decision*

Members of the public may inspect copies of:

• the application

• the plans

• and other documents submitted with it

at *(e)* .... during

all reasonable hours until *(f)* ....

Anyone who wishes to make representations about this appeal should write to the Secretary of State for the Environment/Wales* at the Department of the Environment at Tollgate House, Houlton Street, Bristol BS2 9DJ/Welsh Office at Planning Division, Cathays Park, Cardiff CF1 3NQ* by *(f)* ....

....

                            Signed ....

                     *On behalf of ....

                           Date ....

*delete where inappropriate

Insert:
  (a) address or location of the proposed development
  (b) applicant's name
  (c) name of Council
  (d) description of the proposed development
  (e) address of Council
  (f) date giving a period of 21 days, beginning with the date when the notice is posted

[1118]

PART 2

Town and Country Planning (General Development Procedure) Order 1995

CERTIFICATE UNDER ARTICLE 7

Certificate A*(a)*

I certify that:

on the day 21 days before the date of the accompanying application/appeal* nobody, except the applicant/appellant*, was the owner*(b)* of any part of the land to which the application/appeal* relates.

Signed ....

*On behalf of ....

Date ....

*delete where inappropriate

(a) This Certificate is for use with applications and appeals for planning permission (articles 7 and 9(1) of the Order). One of Certificates A, B, C or D (or the appropriate certificate in the case of certain minerals applications) must be completed, together with the Agricultural Holdings Certificate.

(b) "owner" means a person having a freehold interest or a leasehold interest the unexpired term of which is not less than seven years, or, in the case of development consisting of the winning and working of minerals, a person entitled to an interest in a mineral in the land (other than oil, gas, coal, gold or silver). **[1119]**

Town and Country Planning (General Development Procedure) Order 1995

CERTIFICATE UNDER ARTICLE 7

Certificate B*(a)*

I certify that:

I have/The applicant has/The appellant has* given the requisite notice to everyone else who, on the day 21 days before the date of the accompanying application/appeal*, was the owner*(b)* of any part of the land to which the application/appeal* relates, as listed below.

Owner's *(b)* name	Address at which notice was served	Date on which notice was served

Signed ....

*On behalf of ....

Date ....

*delete where inappropriate

(a) This Certificate is for use with applications and appeals for planning permission (articles 7 and 9(1) of the Order). One of Certificates A, B, C or D (or the appropriate certificate in the case of certain minerals applications) must be completed, together with the Agricultural Holdings Certificate.

(b) "owner" means a person having a freehold interest or a leasehold interest the unexpired term of which is not less than seven years, or, in the case of development consisting of the winning and working of minerals, a person entitled to an interest in a mineral in the land (other than oil, gas, coal, gold or silver).   **[1120]**

Town and Country Planning (General Development Procedure) Order 1995

CERTIFICATE UNDER ARTICLE 7

Certificate C*(a)*

I certify that:

- I/The applicant/The appellant* cannot issue a Certificate A or B in respect of the accompanying application/appeal*.

- I have/The applicant has/The appellant has* given the requisite notice to the persons specified below, being persons who on the day 21 days before the date of the application/ appeal*, were owners*(b)* of any part of the land to which the application/appeal* relates.

Owner's*(b)* name	Address at which notice was served	Date on which notice was served

- I have/The applicant has/The appellant has* taken all reasonable steps open to me/him/ her* to find out the names and addresses of the other owners*(b)* of the land, or of a part of it, but have/has* been unable to do so. These steps were as follows:

  (c) ....

  ....

- Notice of the application/appeal*, as attached to this Certificate, has been published in

  the*(d)* ....

  ....

  on*(e)* ....

Signed ....

*On behalf of ....

Date ....

*delete where inappropriate

(a) This Certificate is for use with applications and appeals for planning permission (articles 7 and 9(1) of the Order). One of Certificates A, B, C or D (or the appropriate certificate in the case of certain minerals applications) must be completed, together with the Agricultural Holdings Certificate.

(b) "owner" means a person having a freehold interest or a leasehold interest the unexpired term of which is not less than seven years, or, in the case of development consisting of the winning and working of minerals, a person entitled to an interest in a mineral in the land (other than oil, gas, coal, gold or silver).

Insert:
(c) description of steps taken
(d) name of newspaper circulating in the area where the land is situated
(e) date of publication (which must be not earlier than the day 21 days before the date of the application or appeal) **[1121]**

Town and Country Planning (General Development Procedure) Order 1995

CERTIFICATE UNDER ARTICLE 7

Certificate D*(a)*

I certify that:

- I/The applicant/The appellant* cannot issue a Certificate A in respect of the accompanying application/appeal*.

- I/The applicant/The appellant* have/has* taken all reasonable steps open to me/him/her* to find out the names and addresses of everyone else who, on the day 21 days before the date of the application/appeal*, was the owner*(b)* of any part of the land to which the application/appeal* relates, but have/has* been unable to do so. These steps were as follows:

  (c) ....

  ....

- Notice of the application/appeal*, as attached to this certificate, has been published in the

  (d) ....

  ....

  on *(e)* ....

                                Signed ....

                            *On behalf of ....

                                  Date ....

---

*delete where inappropriate

(a) This Certificate is for use with applications and appeals for planning permission (articles 7 and 9(1) of the Order). One of Certificates A, B, C or D (or the appropriate certificate in the case of certain minerals applications) must be completed, together with the Agricultural Holdings Certificate.

(b) "owner" means a person having a freehold interest or a leasehold interest the unexpired term of which is not less than seven years, or, in the case of development consisting of the winning and working of minerals, a person entitled to an interest in a mineral in the land (other than oil, gas, coal, gold or silver).

Insert:

(c) description of steps taken

(d) name of newspaper circulating in the area where the land is situated

(e) date of publication (which must be not earlier than the day 21 days before the date of the application or appeal)   **[1122]**

Town and Country Planning (General Development Procedure) Order 1995

CERTIFICATE UNDER ARTICLE 7

Agricultural Holdings Certificate *(a)*

Whichever is appropriate of the following alternatives must form part of Certificates A, B, C or D. If the applicant is the sole agricultural tenant he or she must delete the first alternative and insert "not applicable" as the information required by the second alternative.

• None of the land to which the application/appeal relates is, or is part of, an agricultural holding.

or

• I have/The applicant has/The appellant has given the requisite notice to every person other than my/him/her* self who, on the day 21 days before the date of the application/ appeal*, was a tenant of an agricultural holding on all or part of the land to which the application/appeal* relates, as follows:

Tenant's name	Address at which notice was served	Date on which notice was served

Signed ....

*On behalf of ....

Date ....

*delete where inappropriate

(a) This Certificate is for use with applications and appeals for planning permission (articles 7 and 9(1) of the Order). One of Certificates A, B, C or D (or the appropriate certificate in the case of certain minerals applications) must be completed together with the Agricultural Holdings Certificate. **[1123]**

Town and Country Planning (General Development Procedure) Order 1995

CERTIFICATE UNDER ARTICLE 7

(for use with applications and appeals for planning permission for development consisting of the winning and working of minerals by underground operations)

I certify that:

•   I have/The applicant has/The appellant has given the requisite notice to the persons specified below being persons who, on the day 21 days before the date of the accompanying application/appeal, were owners *(a)* of any part of the land to which the application/appeal* relates.

Owner's *(a)* name	Address at which notice was served	Date on which notice was served

•   There is no person (other than me/the applicant/the appellant*) who, on the day 21 days before the date of the accompanying application/appeal*, was the owner *(a)* of any part of the land to which this application/appeal* relates, whom I/the applicant/the appellant* know/s* to be such a person and whose name and address is known to me/the applicant/the appellant* but to whom I have/the applicant/the appellant has* not given the requisite notice.

•   I have/The applicant/The appellant has* posted the requisite notice, sited and displayed in such a way as to be easily visible and legible by members of the public, in at least one place in every parish or community within which there is situated any part of the land to which the accompanying application/appeal* relates, as listed below.

Parish/Community	Location of notice	Date posted

•   Save as specified below* this/these* notice/s* was/were* left in position for not less than seven days in the period of 21 days immediately preceding the making of the application/appeal*.

•   The following notice/s was/were*, however, left in position for less than seven days in the period of not more than 21 days immediately preceding the making of the application/appeal*.

Parish/Community	Location of notice	Date posted

This happened because it/they* was/were* removed/obscured/defaced* before seven days had passed during the period of 21 days mentioned above. This was not my/the applicant's/the appellant's* fault or intent.

I/The applicant/The appellant* took the following steps to protect and replace the notice:

(b) ....

....

•   Notice of the application/appeal*, as attached to this certificate, has been published in the

(c) ....

....

on *(d)* ....

Agricultural Holdings Certificate

Whichever is appropriate of the following alternatives must form part of this certificate. If the applicant is the sole agricultural tenant he or she must delete the first alternative and insert "not applicable" as the information required by the second alternative.

• None of the land to which the application/appeal relates is, or is part of, an agricultural holding.

or

• I have/The applicant has/The appellant has given the requisite notice to every person other than my/him/her* self who, on the day 21 days before the date of the application/appeal*, was a tenant of an agricultural holding on all or part of the land to which the application/appeal* relates, as follows:

Tenant's name	Address at which notice was served	Date on which notice was served

Signed ....

*On behalf of ....

Date ....

*delete where inappropriate

(a) "owner" means a person having a freehold interest or a leasehold interest the unexpired term of which is not less than seven years or a person entitled to an interest in a mineral in the land (other than oil, gas, coal, gold or silver).

Insert:
(b) description of steps taken
(c) name of newspaper circulating in the area where the land is situated
(d) date of publication (which must be not earlier than the day 21 days before the date of the application or appeal) **[1124]**

SCHEDULE 3   Article 8

NOTICE OF APPLICATION FOR PLANNING PERMISSION

Town and Country Planning (General Development Procedure) Order 1995

NOTICE UNDER ARTICLE 8

(to be published in a newspaper, displayed on or near the site, or served on owners and/or occupiers of adjoining land)

Proposed development at *(a)* ....

I give notice that *(b)* ....

is applying to the *(c)* .... Council

for planning permission to *(d)* ....

The proposed development does not accord with the provisions of the development plan in force in the area in which the land to which the application relates is situated*

Members of the public may inspect copies of:

- the application

- the plans

- and other documents submitted with it

at *(e)* .... during

all reasonable hours until *(f)* ....

Anyone who wishes to make representations about this application should write to the Council

at *(g)* ....

.... by *(f)* ....

Signed ....

....
(Council's authorised officer)

On behalf of .... Council

Date ....

*delete where inappropriate

Insert:
- *(a)* address or location of the proposed development
- *(b)* applicant's name
- *(c)* name of Council
- *(d)* description of the proposed development
- *(e)* address at which the application may be inspected
- *(f)* date giving a period of 21 days, beginning with the date when the notice is first displayed on or near the site or served on an owner and/or occupier of adjoining land, or a period of 14 days, beginning with the date when the notice is published in a newspaper (as the case may be)
- *(g)* address of Council   **[1125]**

NOTICE OF APPLICATION FOR PLANNING PERMISSION

Town and Country Planning (General Development Procedure) Order 1995

NOTICE UNDER ARTICLE 8 OF APPLICATION FOR PLANNING PERMISSION ACCOMPANIED BY AN ENVIRONMENTAL STATEMENT

(to be published in a newspaper and displayed on or near the site)

Proposed development at *(a)* ....

I give notice that *(b)* ....

is applying to the *(c)* .... Council

for planning permission to *(d)* ....

and that the application is accompanied by an environmental statement

The proposed development does not accord with the provisions of the development plan in force in the area in which the land to which the application relates is situated*

Members of the public may inspect copies of:

● the application

● the plans

● the environmental statement

● and other documents submitted with the application

at *(e)* .... during

all reasonable hours until *(f)* ....

Members of the public may obtain copies of the environmental statement from *(g)* ....

....

so long as stocks last, at a charge of *(h)* ....

Anyone who wishes to make representations about this application should write to the Council

at *(i)* ....

.... by *(f)* ....

Signed ....

....

(Council's authorised officer)

On behalf of .... Council

Date ....

*delete where inappropriate

Insert:
(a) address or location of the proposed development
(b) applicant's name
(c) name of Council
(d) description of the proposed development
(e) address at which the application may be inspected
(f) date giving a period of 21 days, beginning with the date when the notice is first displayed on or near the site, or a period of 14 days, beginning with the date when the notice is published in a newspaper (as the case may be)
(g) address from where copies of the environmental statement may be obtained (whether or not the same as *(e)*)
(h) amount of charge, if any
(i) address of Council

[1126]

SCHEDULE 4

Article 24

TOWN AND COUNTRY PLANNING ACT 1990: SECTIONS 191 AND 192 (as amended by section 10 of the Planning and Compensation Act 1991)

TOWN AND COUNTRY PLANNING (GENERAL DEVELOPMENT PROCEDURE) ORDER 1995: ARTICLE 24

CERTIFICATE OF LAWFUL USE OR DEVELOPMENT

The *(a)* .... Council hereby certify that on *(b)* .... the use*/operations*/matter* described in the First Schedule to this certificate in respect of the land specified in the Second Schedule to this certificate and edged*/hatched*/coloured* *(c)* .... on the plan attached to this certificate, was*/were*/would have been* lawful within the meaning of section 191 of the Town and Country Planning Act 1990 (as amended), for the following reason(s):

....

....

....

....

Signed .... (Council's authorised officer)

On behalf of *(a)* .... Council

Date ....

First Schedule
(d)

Second Schedule
(e)

Notes

1   This certificate is issued solely for the purpose of section 191*/192* of the Town and Country Planning Act 1990 (as amended).

2   It certifies that the use*/operations*/matter* specified in the First Schedule taking place on the land described in the Second Schedule was*/were*/would have been* lawful, on the specified date and, thus, was not*/were not*/would not have been* liable to enforcement action under section 172 of the 1990 Act on that date.

3   This certificate applies only to the extent of the use*/operations*/matter* described in the First Schedule and to the land specified in the Second Schedule and identified on the attached plan. Any use*/operations*/matter* which is*/are* materially different from that*/those* described or which relate/s* to other land may render the owner or occupier liable to enforcement action.

*4   The effect of the certificate is also qualified by the proviso in section 192(4) of the 1990 Act, as amended, which states that the lawfulness of a described use or operation is only conclusively presumed where there has been no material change, before the use is instituted or the operations begun, in any of the matters relevant to determining such lawfulness.

*delete where inappropriate

Insert:
(a) name of Council
(b) date of application to the Council
(c) colour used on the plan
(d) full description of use, operations or other matter, if necessary, by reference to details in the application or submitted plans, including a reference to the use class, if any, specified in an order under section 55(2)(f) of the 1990 Act, within which the certificated use falls
(e) address or location of the site

[1127]

SCHEDULE 5

STATUTORY INSTRUMENTS REVOKED

1 *Title of Instrument*	2 *Reference*
The Town and Country Planning General Development Order 1988	S.I. 1988/1813
The Town and Country Planning General Development (Amendment) Order 1989	S.I. 1989/603
The Town and Country Planning General Development (Amendment) (No. 2) Order 1989	S.I. 1989/1590
The Town and Country Planning General Development (Amendment) (No. 3) Order 1991	S.I. 1991/2805
The Town and Country Planning General Development (Amendment) (No. 2) Order 1992	S.I. 1992/658
The Town and Country Planning General Development (Amendment) (No. 4) Order 1992	S.I. 1992/1493
The Town and Country Planning General Development (Amendment) (No. 5) Order 1992	S.I. 1992/1563
The Town and Country Planning General Development (Amendment) (No. 6) Order 1992	S.I. 1992/2450
The Town and Country Planning General Development (Amendment) Order 1994	S.I. 1994/678
The Town and Country Planning General Development (Amendment) (No. 2) Order 1994	S.I. 1994/2595
The Town and Country Planning General Development (Amendment) Order 1995	S.I. 1995/298

TOWN AND COUNTRY PLANNING (CROWN LAND APPLICATIONS) REGULATIONS 1995
(SI 1995/1139)

NOTES
   Made: 22 April 1995.
   Authority: Town and Country Planning Act 1990, ss 299(5), 333(1).

1. Citation, commencement and interpretation

(1) These Regulations may be cited as the Town and Country Planning (Crown Land Applications) Regulations 1995 and shall come into force on 3rd June 1995.

   (2) In these Regulations—

   "the Act" means the Town and Country Planning Act 1990; and
   "the Order" means the Town and Country Planning (General Development Procedure) Order 1995.   **[1130]**

NOTES
   Commencement: 3 June 1995.

2. Applications in respect of Crown land

The Act and Order shall, in their application, by virtue of section 299(2) of the Act, to the making and determination of applications in respect of Crown land for planning permission or for a certificate under section 192 of the Act, have effect subject to the modifications specified in the Schedule to these Regulations.   **[1131]**

NOTES
   Commencement: 3 June 1995.

3. Notice of disposals of interests in Crown land

The appropriate authority shall, as soon as practicable after disposing of, or disposing of any interest in, any Crown land in respect of which planning permission has been granted or a certificate has been issued under section 192(2) of the Act on an application made by virtue of section 299(2) of the Act, give notice of the disposal in writing to the local planning authority to whom the application was made. **[1132]**

NOTES
   Commencement: 3 June 1995.

4. Revocation of Regulations

The Town and Country Planning (Crown Land Applications) Regulations 1992 are hereby revoked.   **[1133]**

SCHEDULE

Regulation 2

MODIFICATIONS OF THE ACT AND THE ORDER
The Act

1. In section 72(1)(a) of the Act, for "any land under the control of the applicant (whether or not it is land in respect of which the application was made," substitute "the land in respect of which the application was made".

The Order

2. Before article 5 (general provisions relating to applications) of the Order insert—

"Applications in respect of Crown land

4A. An application for planning permission made by virtue of section 299(2) of the Act shall be accompanied by—

(a) a statement that the application is made, by virtue of section 299(2) of the Act, in respect of Crown land; and

(b) where the application is made by a person authorised in writing by the appropriate authority, a copy of that authorisation.".

3. In article 6 (notice of applications for planning permission) of the Order, after paragraph (6), insert—

"(7) For the purposes of this article and the certificates required by article 7, where an application for planning permission is made by virtue of section 299(2) of the Act, the applicant shall be treated as an owner of the land and no account shall be taken of any Crown interest or Duchy interest in the land or in any mineral in the land.".

4. In article 24 (certificate of lawful use or development) of the Order, after paragraph (2), insert—

"(2A) Where, by virtue of section 299(2) of the Act, an application for a certificate under section 192(1) of the Act is made in respect of Crown land, it shall, in addition to the documents required by paragraph (2), be accompanied by—

(a) a statement that the application is made, by virtue of section 299(2) of the Act, in respect of Crown land; and

(b) where the application is made by a person authorised in writing by the appropriate authority, a copy of that authorisation.". **[1134]**

NOTES

Commencement: 3 June 1995.

INDEX

BLIGHT NOTICE—*cont.*
claimant, [157]
whole hereditament, right to sell, [173]
compulsory acquisition following, [164]
constructive notice to treat, no withdrawal of, [174]
counter-notice, [158], [830]
further, [159]
intention to acquire, disclaiming, [162]
forms, [830]
land affected by provisions, [156], [363]
Lands Tribunal, reference of objection to, [160]
mortgagee's, [169], [830]
new town, orders in, [172]
objection to, [158], [159]
money advanced for purchase, [314]
owner-occupier, meaning, [175]
partnership, provisions applying to, [171]
personal representative's, [168], [830]
power to serve, [157]
qualifying interest, [156]
scope of provisions, [156]
simultaneous, [170]
urban development area, land within, [172]
valid, effect of, [161]
whole agricultural unit, requiring purchaser of, [165]–[167]
withdrawal of, [163]

BREACH OF CONDITION NOTICE
service of, [194A]

BRIDLEWAY
maintenance of, [559SS]
National Park, in, [597K]
order on, [266], [364], [365]

BRITISH RAILWAYS BOARD
transport systems, application or objection to orders for, [559Q]

BRITISH WATEREWAYS BOARD
transport systems, application or objection to orders for, [559Q]

BROADS AUTHORITY
Broads, planning authority for, [12]

BUILDING
advertisement in, [802]
advertisement on, [62]
alteration or removal, local planning authority ordering, [107]
easements, etc, power to override, [244]
ecclesiastical, works on, [428]
features of special architectural or historic interest, preservation of, [369]
listed. *See* LISTED BUILDING
meaning, [343]
not intended to be listed, certificate of, [374]
preservation notice. *See* BUILDING PRESERVATION NOTICE
rebuilding and alterations, condition applicable to, [360]
unlisted, in conservation area, demolition of, [675], [676]
use of, planning permission specifying, [82]

BUILDING OPERATIONS
meaning, [62]

BUILDING PRESERVATION NOTICE
compensation for, [397], [398]

BUILDING PRESERVATION NOTICE—*cont.*
lapse, provisions applicable on, [464]
service of, [371]
urgent cases, in [372]

BUILDING PRESERVATION ORDER
buildings formerly subject to, [369], [463]

BURIAL GROUND
use and development of, [246], [247]

C

CARAVAN SITE
control of land for, xvii
permitted development, [1055]
site licence, issue of, [78]

CERTIFICATE OF LAWFUL USE OR DEVELOPMENT
appeals, [202], [203]
application for, [199], [200]
contents of, [1108]
contents of, [198]
established use certificates, effect of, [523]
form of, [1108], [1127]
issue of, [198]
offences, [201]
revocation of, [200]
Secretary of State, references to, [203]

CERTIFICATE OF LAWFULNESS OF PROPOSED USE OR DEVELOPMENT
appeals, [202], [203]
application for, [199], [200]
contents of, [199]
issue of, [199]
offences, [201]
revocation of, [200]
Secretary of State, references to, [203]

CLOSED-CIRCUIT TELEVISION
development, [1082]

COAL AUTHORITY
development by, [1070]

COLLEGES
development, [1082]

COMMON
appropriation of land, [236]
disposal of, [240]
use and development of, [248]

COMPENSATION
advertising, in respect of, [788], [791]
building, alteration or removal of, [122]
building preservation notice, loss or damage following, [397], [398]
claim, determination of, [125]–[143]
compulsory acquisition, for. *See* COMPULSORY ACQUISITION
depreciation, for, [124]
apportionment, [116]
registration of, [117]
development order, withdrawal of, [115]
discontinuing use of land, for, [122]
government department, recovery of expenses of, [318]
hazardous substance consent, revocation or modification of, [482], [485]
interest on, [537], [553]